GW01606508

THE CERAMIC ART OF GREAT BRITAIN

THE

CERAMIC ART

OF

GREAT BRITAIN

BY

LLEWELLYNN JEWITT, F.S.A.

VICE-PRESIDENT OF THE DERBYSHIRE ARCHÆOLOGICAL AND NATURAL HISTORY SOCIETY;
HON. AND ACTUAL MEMBER OF THE RUSSIAN IMPERIAL ARCHÆOLOGICAL COMMISSION, AND STATISTICAL COMMITTEE, PSKOV;
HON. MEMBER OF THE ESSEX ARCHÆOLOGICAL SOCIETY AND OF THE MANX SOCIETY, ETC.;
COR. MEMBER OF THE ROYAL HISTORICAL SOCIETY;
COR. MEMBER OF THE NUMISMATIC AND ANTIQUARIAN SOCIETY OF PHILADELPHIA
ETC. ETC. ETC.

ILLUSTRATED WITH NEARLY TWO THOUSAND ENGRAVINGS

NEW EDITION, REVISED

NEW ORCHARD EDITIONS

First published 1985 by
NEW ORCHARD EDITIONS LTD
ROBERT ROGERS HOUSE
NEW ORCHARD
POOLE, DORSET BH15 1LU

ISBN 1 85079 033 7
Copyright © 1985 New Orchard Editions Ltd

All rights reserved. No part of this book may be reproduced or transmitted in any form or by any means, electronic or mechanical, including photocopying, recording or any information storage and retrieval system, without permission in writing from the Publisher.

Printed in Portugal by Printer Portuguesa

INTRODUCTION TO THE SECOND EDITION.

IT having been suggested by the Publishers that a new edition, slightly abridged, printed in smaller type, and compressed into one goodly volume in place of the two of the first edition, so as to sell at a somewhat less price, would not only be advisable commercially, but would be a great and decided convenience to the public, I have gladly fallen in with their views. The whole work has therefore been carefully gone through in every part, and while its bulk has been here and there considerably reduced by altogether omitting some portions and condensing others, the alterations have, I hope, been so made that its value has not in any material degree been impaired, while the revision it has undergone and the emendations made will add much to its value. So far as time would allow, and the exigencies of the American and home requirements permit, the notices of existing works have been brought down to the present day. In all cases where replies have been vouchsafed to my inquiries as to changes of proprietorship or in the classes and character of the goods produced, these points have been carefully noted, and every available means that so short a time would allow have been taken to insure that scrupulous accuracy which alone gives value to a work, and which I have ever striven to secure.

With the exception of the coloured and other plates (which it was found necessary to omit), the whole of the engravings used in the first edition have been retained, and some few altogether new illustrations have been added. Means have thus, as in every other way, been taken to render the work in its present form as useful and reliable as may be.

As mine was the first and is still the only work devoted exclusively to the Ceramic Art in Great Britain, I have an intense desire that it should continue to occupy and fully maintain the position and ground it has so far taken up, and the present condensed and revised edition will, I hope and trust, extend and enhance its value and usefulness as a book of reference upon one of the most beautiful, all-important, interesting, and useful branches of native Art-industry.

In the first edition I attempted—all too feebly, I fear—to express my thanks to all who had in any way assisted me in my inquiries, and I desire now not only to repeat but to emphasize those thanks, and to express my deep obligation to all who have in any way "given a helping hand" over my labours. To my good friends Mr. W. H. Goss and Mr. Harvey Adams, to whom I am deeply indebted for much time bestowed and much trouble ungrudgingly taken in revising much of the matter relating to the Staffordshire Pottery district, I beg to tender grateful thanks, as I do also to those manufacturers who have fully responded to my invitation to supply me with the necessary data, etc., concerning their works and productions. In view of future editions I ask that manufacturers throughout the kingdom will from time to time communicate with me regarding any changes in their works or in the classes and varieties of wares and goods to which their energies, time, and art-producing skill may be devoted.

LLEWELLYNN JEWITT.

THE HOLLIES,
DUFFIELD, DERBYSHIRE,
October 22, 1883.

TO

MANUFACTURERS AND COLLECTORS

ON BOTH SIDES THE BROAD ATLANTIC,

AND TO EVERY ONE, ALL THE WORLD OVER, WHO HAS

A LOVE FOR,

OR IS IN ANY WAY ENGAGED OR TAKES AN INTEREST IN,

ANY BRANCH OF

THE BEAUTIFUL ART OF THE POTTER,

TO WHOSE HISTORY THIS VOLUME IS DEVOTED,

I Dedicate

THIS EDITION OF MY

"CERAMIC ART OF GREAT BRITAIN."

LLEWELLYNN JEWITT.

THE HOLLIES, DUFFIELD, DERBY
October 22, 1883.

INTRODUCTION TO THE FIRST EDITION.

IN issuing my present work I have two distinct personal duties to perform, and I hasten, in these few brief lines of introduction, to discharge them, First, I earnestly desire to ask indulgence from my readers for any shortcomings which may be apparent in its contents; and next, I desire emphatically to express my thanks to all who have in any way, or even to the smallest extent, assisted me in my labours. The preparation of the work has extended over a considerable period of time, and I have had many difficulties to contend with that are, and must necessarily be, wholly unknown to any but myself—hard literary digging to get at facts and to verify dates, that is not understood, and would scarce be believed in, by the reader who turns to my pages—and hence errors of omission and of commission may have, nay, doubtless have, crept in, and may in some places, to a greater or less extent, have marred the accuracy of the page whereon they have occurred. I can honestly say I have left nothing undone, no source untried, and no trouble untaken to secure perfect accuracy in all I have written, and yet I am painfully aware that shortcomings may, and doubtless will, be laid to my charge; for these, wherever they occur, I ask, and indeed claim indulgence. I believe in *work*, in hard unceasing labour, in patient and painstaking research, in untiring searchings, and in diligent collection and arrangement of facts—to make time and labour and money subservient to the end in view, rather than that the end in view, and the time and labour and money expended, should bend and bow and ultimately break before *time*. Thus it is that my "Ceramic Art" has been so long in progress, and thus it is that many changes have occurred during the time it has been passing through the press which it has been manifestly impossible to chronicle.

I have the proud satisfaction, however, of knowing that my work is the only one of its kind yet attempted, and I feel a confident hope that it will fill a gap that has long wanted filling, and will be found alike useful to the manufacturer, the china collector, and the general reader.

When, some twenty years ago, at the instance of my dear friend Mr. S. C. Hall, I began my series of papers in *The Art Journal* upon the various famous earthenware and porcelain works of the kingdom, but little had been done in that direction, and the information I got together from time to time had to be procured from original sources, by prolonged visits to the places themselves, and by numberless applications to all sorts of people from whom even scraps of reliable matter could be obtained. Books on the subject were not many, and the information they contained on English Ceramics was meagre in the extreme. Since then numerous workers have sprung up, and their published volumes—many of them sumptuous and truly valuable works—attest strongly to the interest and pains they have taken in the subject. To all these, whoever they may be, the world owes a debt of gratitude for devoting their time and their talents to so important a branch of study. To each of them I tender my own thanks for having devoted themselves to the elucidation of one of my favourite pursuits, and for having given to the world the result of their labours. No work has, however, until now been entirely devoted to the one subject of British Ceramics, and I feel therefore that in presenting my present volumes to the public I am only carrying out the plan I at first laid down, and am not even in the slightest degree encroaching on the province of any other writer.

I think I may safely say there is scarcely a manufacturer—even if there be one at all—in the length and breadth of the kingdom with whom I have not frequently communicated in the progress of this work. Except in some few solitary instances I have received the information I have sought, and my inquiries have met with the most cordial and ready response.

To all those who have thus assisted me with information or otherwise, and especially to my friend Mr. Goss, who has greatly assisted me over the onerous task of some of the Staffordshire potteries, I offer my warmest thanks; and to those few others, who from inattention, shortsightedness, or other cause, have not responded to my inquiries, I would express my sorrow if, through that inattention on their part, I have been unable to give as full particulars regarding their potteries as I could have wished. To thank by name those who have assisted me with information would require a long list indeed; I therefore tender my acknowledgments to all in the one emphatic good old English expression—"*Thank you!*"

LLEWELLYNN JEWITT.

WINSTER HALL, DERBYSHIRE,
November, 1877.

CONTENTS.

CERAMIC ART IN GREAT BRITAIN.

CHAPTER I.

THE History of the Ceramic Art in our own country is one of intense interest and of paramount importance. I open my present work with this assertion, and before its close I hope I shall have proved its truth.

It is a subject which may be treated in more ways than one. It may be considered technically, *i.e.* with regard to manipulation, to the mixing of bodies and glazes, and the practical parts of the potter's art; or historically, so as to treat of the introduction and progress of the art in this country, its gradual extension and improvement, the chief seats of its operations, and the characteristics of the productions of each age and place. To neither of these do I purpose confining myself; but to the latter I shall, here and there, mix up just sufficient of the former to render it more intelligible and useful. The main ingredients of the "body"—to use a potter's term—of my work will be history, description, and biography, with just sufficient technicology to temper it and give it its proper tenacity and consistency. For the facts relating to the earliest examples of that art, from which I shall deduce my narrative, I rely upon actual researches into grave-mounds and otherwise, undertaken by myself or by others; and for the rest—those relating to the art in mediæval and later times—upon constant inquirings and searchings and readings carried on, with this special end in view, during the course of many years.

It is impossible to show when the potter's art was first invented or when it was first brought into use in this island; but that it was practised here in the very earliest days of its being inhabited by its savage population can be abundantly proved. To this prehistoric period, then, I shall first direct attention; and then endeavour to trace the history of the art down from the Celtic to the Romano-British period; from the time of the Romans to the Anglo-Saxons and Normans; and so gradually downwards through mediæval to modern times, giving, under each separate seat of the more modern manufacture, historical notices of the works and their founders, and descriptive particulars of the more characteristic of their productions.

The practice of the fictile art in England dates back, as I have already said, to a very remote period—that of its Celtic or ancient British population, by whom there is abundant evidence it was much esteemed. It is pleasant to know, and to be able indisputably to prove, that in pottery, as in nothing else, an unbroken chain connecting us in our present high state of civilisation with our remote barbarian forefathers of the Stone Age, exists. The weapons and other implements of imperishable stone and flint have, long ages ago, died out, and any possible connection between them and the weapons or tools of our own day has died with them; but the vessels of simple clay have an abiding-place with us which has lasted without a

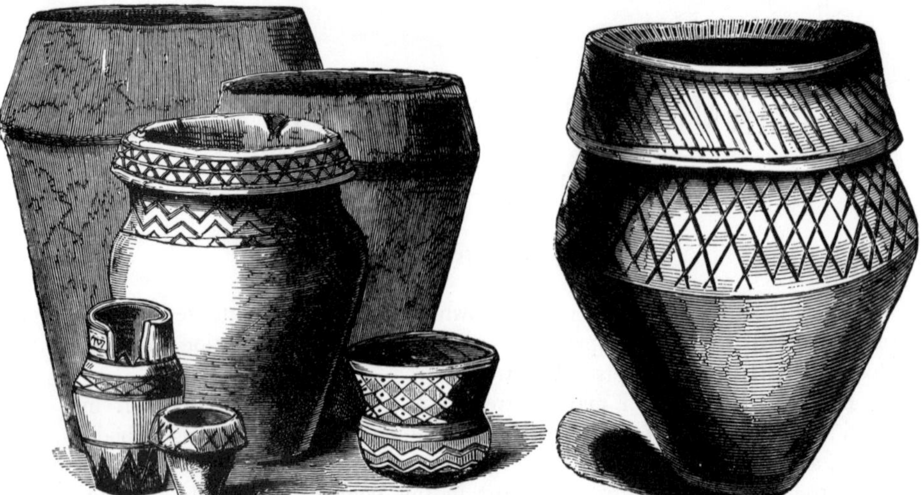

Fig. 1.—Celtic Pottery in the Norwich Museum.

Fig. 2.—Monsal Dale.

break until now, and will yet last for ever. Hitherto the course of the potter's art has been one of constant and gradual improvement; but its capabilities for further

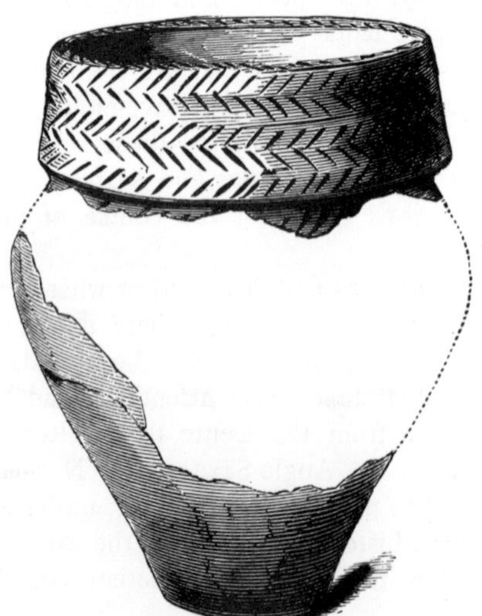

Fig. 3.—Cleatham.

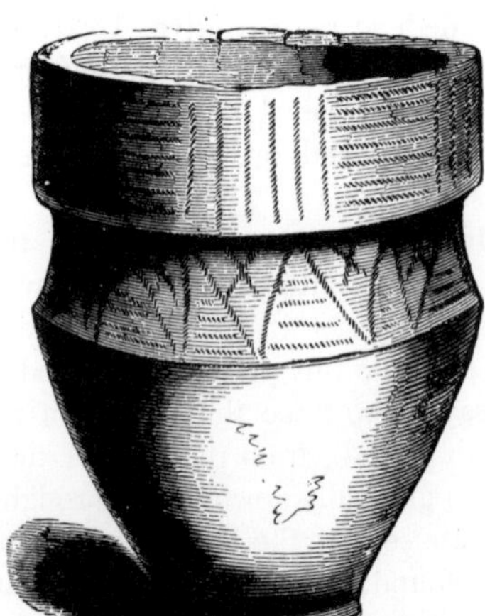

Fig. 4.—Ballidon Moor.

development are almost unbounded, and another generation will witness advances of which we can now but dimly dream.

Among the ancient Britons, vessels of clay were formed for sepulchral and other uses, and it is entirely to their grave-mounds that we are indebted for the examples which have survived to our time, and by constant comparison of the "finds" of one locality with the discoveries of another, that a proper estimate of their character has been, or can be, drawn.

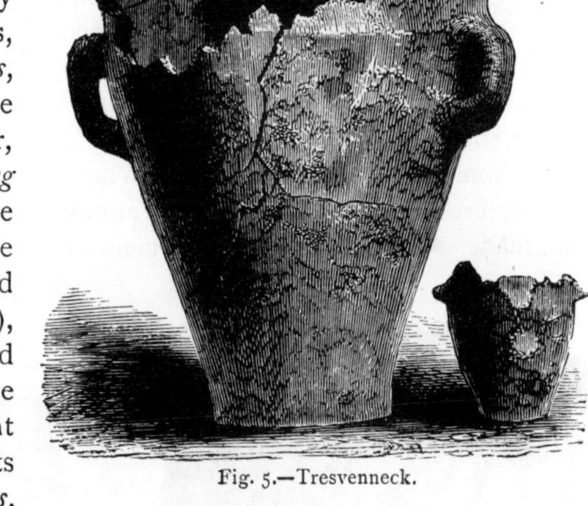

Fig. 5.—Tresvenneck.

The pottery of this period may be safely arranged in four classes, viz.—1. *Sepulchral* or *Cinerary Urns*, which have been made for and have contained, or been inverted over, calcined human bones; 2. *Drinking Cups*, which, in a similar manner, are supposed to have contained some liquid to be placed with the dead body; 3. *Food Vessels* (so called), which are supposed to have contained an offering of food, and which are more usually found with unburnt bodies than along with interments by cremation; 4. *Immolation Urns*, which are very small vessels, found only with burnt bones (and usually also containing them), placed in the mouths of, or close by, the larger cinerary urns. These latter I believe to have been simply small urns intended to receive the ashes of the infant, perhaps sacrificed at the death of its mother, so as to admit of being placed within the larger urn containing the ashes of the parent: I venture, therefore, to name them "Immolation Urns," instead of their old name of "Incense Cups."

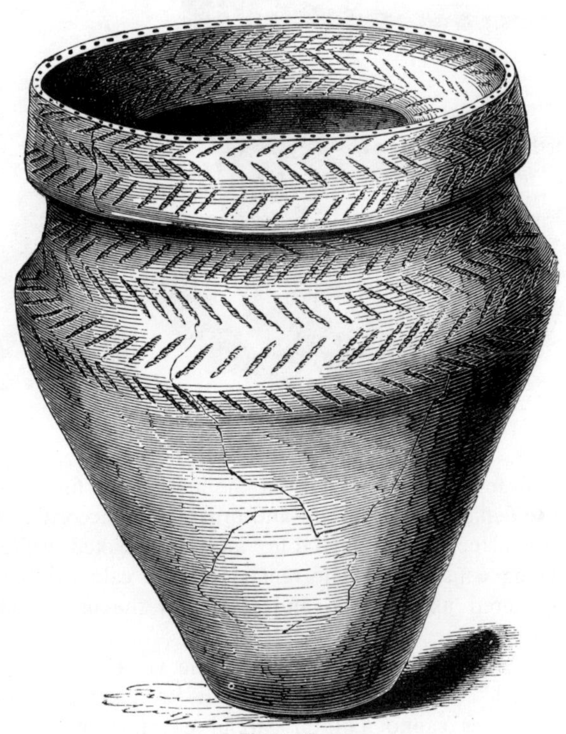

Fig. 6.—Trentham.

No notice of the pottery of this period is to be found in ancient writers, if we except the allusion of Strabo (Lib. III. c. 5, § ii.), who says that one of the commodities with which the Phœnicians traded to the Cassiterides was earthenware. But in connection with this it is necessary to state that no example of pottery which can possibly be traced to Phœnician origin has as yet been found in any of the hundreds of barrows which have been opened.

The pottery exhibits considerable difference, both in clay, in size, and in ornamentation. Those examples presumed to be the oldest are of coarse clay mixed with small pebbles and sand; the later ones of a somewhat less clumsy form, and perhaps a finer mixture of clays. They are entirely wrought by hand without the assistance of the wheel, and are mostly very thick and clumsy. They are very imperfectly fired, having probably been baked on the funeral pyre.

In the examination of barrows of this period it not unfrequently happens that the spot where the funeral pyre has been lit can very clearly be perceived. In these instances the ground beneath is generally found to be burned to some considerable depth; sometimes, indeed, it is burned to a fine red colour, and approaches in texture somewhat to that of brick.. Where it was intended that the remains should be placed in an urn for interment, it appears, from careful examinations which have been made, that the urn being formed of clay—most probably, judging from the

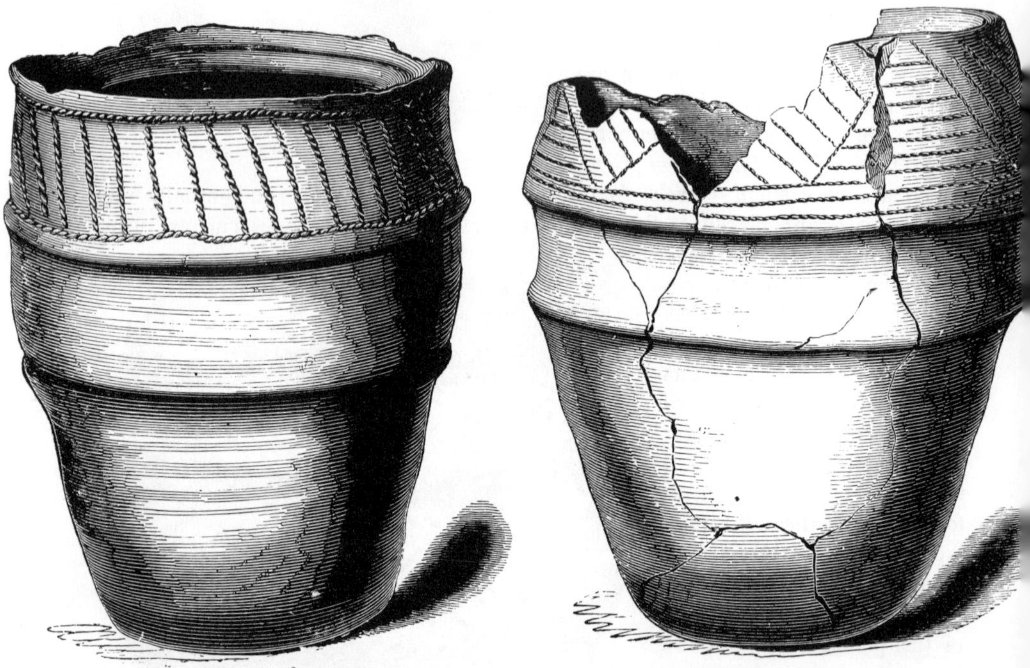

Fig. 7.—Darley Dale. Fig. 8.—Darley Dale.

delicacy of touch, and from the impress of fingers which occasionally remains, by the females of the tribe—and ornamented according to the taste of the manipulator, was placed in the funeral fire and there baked, while the body of the deceased was being consumed. The remains of the calcined bones, the flints, &c., were then gathered up together, and placed in the urn; over which the mound was next raised.

From their imperfect firing, the vessels of this period are usually called "sun-baked" or "sun-dried;" but this is a grave error, as any one conversant with examples cannot fail, on careful examination, to see. If the vessels were "sun-baked" only, their burial in the earth—in the tumuli wherein, some two thousand years ago, they were deposited, and where they have all that time remained—would soon soften them, and they would, ages ago, have returned to their old clayey consistency. As it is, the urns have remained of their original form, and although, from imperfect baking, they are sometimes found partially softened, they still retain their form, and soon regain their original hardness. They bear abundant evidence of the action of fire, and are, indeed, sometimes sufficiently burned for the clay to have attained a red colour—a result which no "sun-baking" could produce. They are mostly of an earthy brown colour outside, and almost black in fracture, and many of the cinerary urns bear internal and unmistakable evidence of having been filled with the burnt bones and ashes of the deceased, while those ashes were of a glowing and intense heat. The urns were, there is reason to believe, fashioned, when death occurred, by the females of the tribe, from clay found nearest to the spot, and baked on or by the funeral pyre. In some instances,

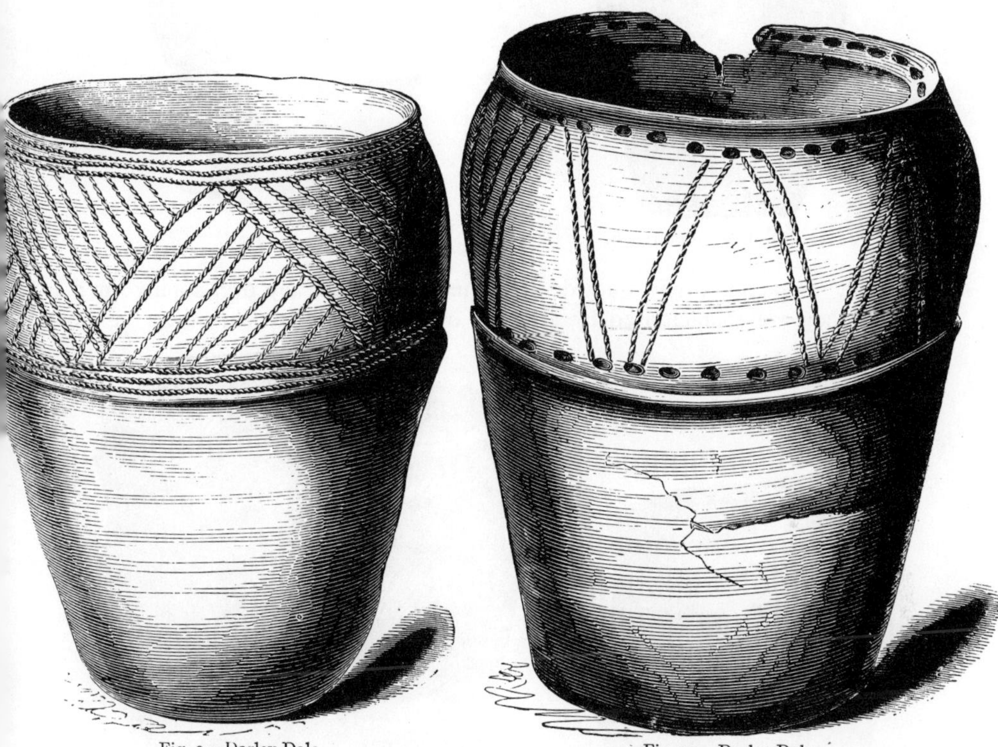

Fig. 9.—Darley Dale. Fig. 10.—Darley Dale.

however, it is probable that even the cinerary urns were burned in a separate fire, as were the "drinking-cups," which are usually fired to a much harder degree. No kiln, or anything approaching to one, however, could of course have been used.

The *Cinerary* or *Sepulchral Urns* vary very considerably in size, in form, in ornamentation, and in material—the latter, naturally, depending on the locality where the urns were made; and, as a general rule, they differ also in the different tribes. Those which are supposed to be the most ancient, from the fact of their frequently containing flint instruments along with the calcined bones, are of larger size, ranging from nine or ten, to sixteen or eighteen inches in height. Those which are considered to belong to a somewhat later period, when cremation had again become general, are of a smaller size, and of a somewhat finer texture. With them objects of flint are rarely found, but articles of bronze are occasionally dis-

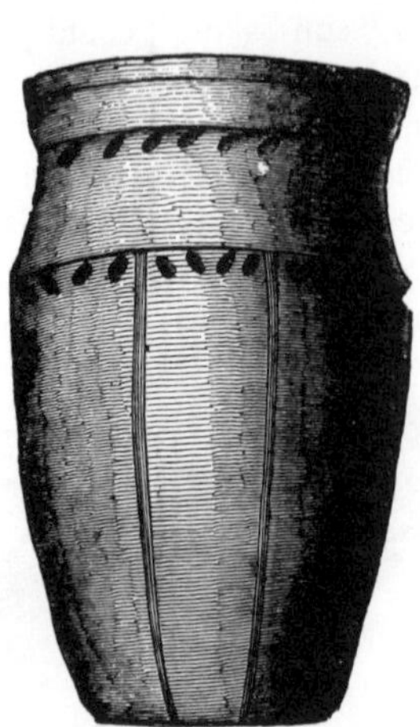

Fig. 11.—Launceston Heath.

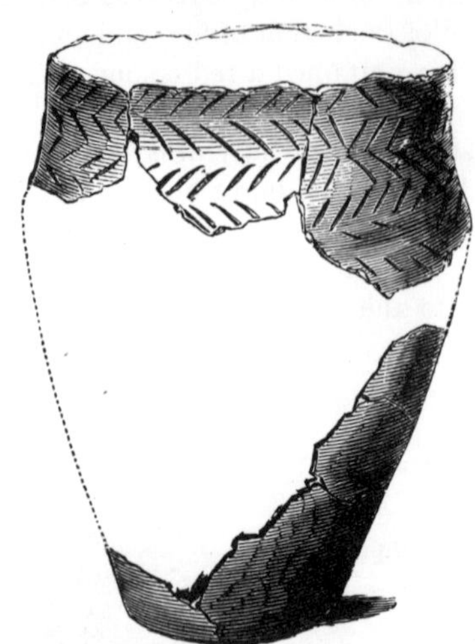

Fig. 12.—Cleatham.

covered. Sometimes they are wide at the mouth, without any overlapping rim; at others they are characterised by a deeply overlapping lip or rim; others are more

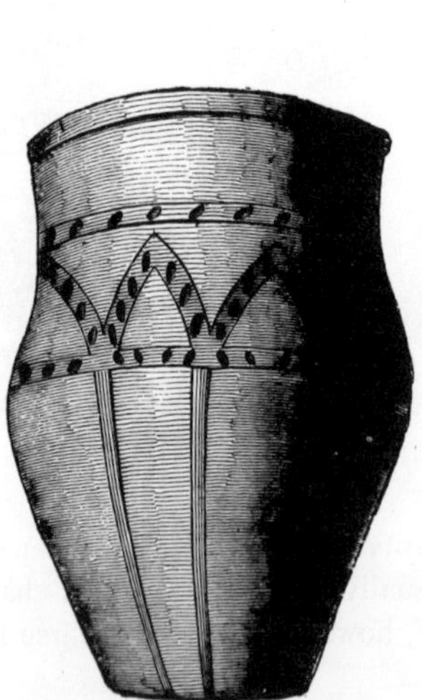

Fig. 13.—Launceston Heath.

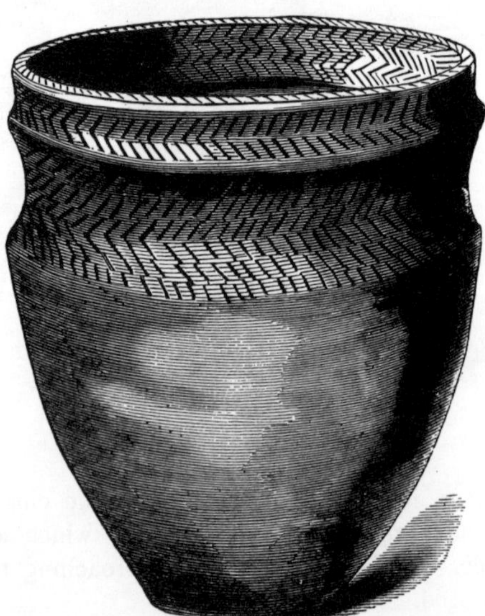

Fig. 14.—Stone.

of "flower-pot" form, with encircling raised bands, while others again are contracted inwardly at the mouth by curved rims. Some also have loops at the sides. The ornamentation is produced chiefly by incised lines, or punctures, or by lines, &c., produced by indenting into the soft clay a twisted thong (Fig. 37). Encircling and zigzag lines of various forms, reticulated and lozenge-formed patterns, and rows of indentations, are the usual decorations; but occasionally, as at West Kennet and Launceston Heath, clearly-defined patterns are produced by the finger or thumb nail.

The more usual of the forms will be best understood by the engraved examples, selected from the proceeds of many barrow openings in different parts of the kingdom.

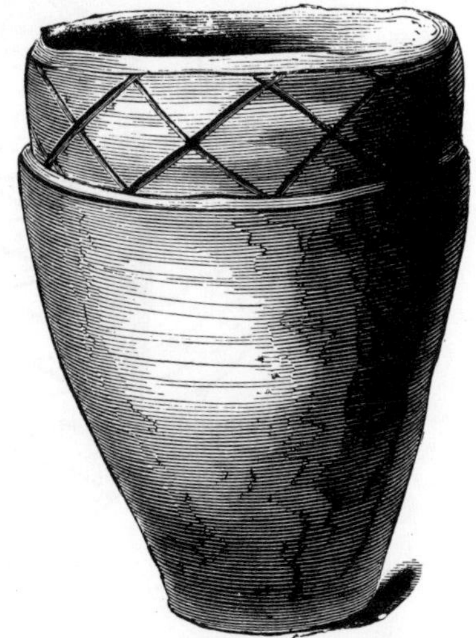

Fig. 15.—Cleatham.

The four urns (Figs. 2, 3, 4, and 6) are characteristic examples of the variety with the broad or deep overlapping border or rim. The first of these has the pattern incised in the soft clay, that on the rim being in diagonal lines, and the central portion reticulated. The second has the herring-bone or chevron ornament around its rim, and the third example is ornamented with horizontal and vertical lines alternately on its rim, and zigzagged, filled in with horizontal and crossed, lines on the central part. The lines in this are all produced by indenting a twisted thong into the clay in a soft state. Fig. 16 has its ornamentation indented with twisted thongs in "herring-bone" pattern both on the outside and inside the rim and around the central part. Fig. 8 has a central band as well as overhanging lip. Figs. 11 and 13, from Dorsetshire barrows, are of different form, the ornamentation

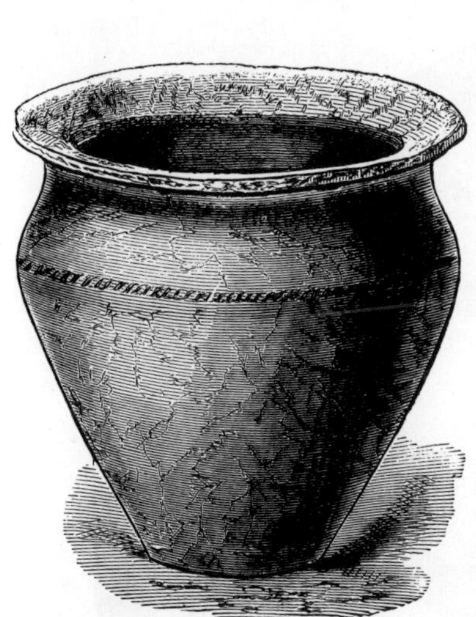

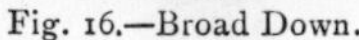

Fig. 16.—Broad Down.

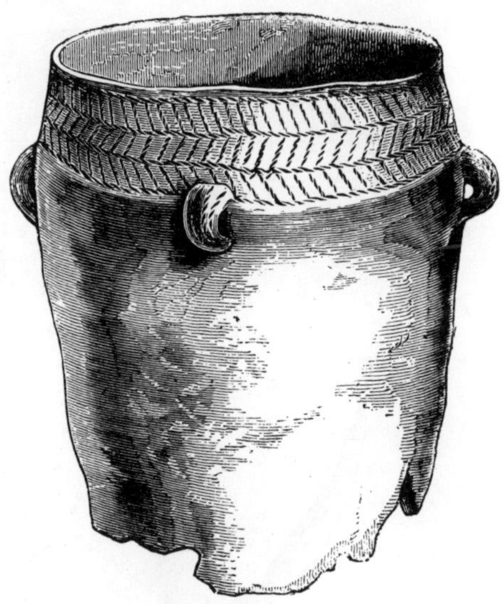

Fig. 17.—Tredenny.

consisting of incised lines and impressed thumbmarks, &c. The remaining engravings also give excellent examples of other forms and varieties of these sepulchral vessels. Figs. 9 and 10 have the upper part curved, and almost approaching to cup shape, and Fig. 7 has raised bands; in Fig. 14 the upper parts

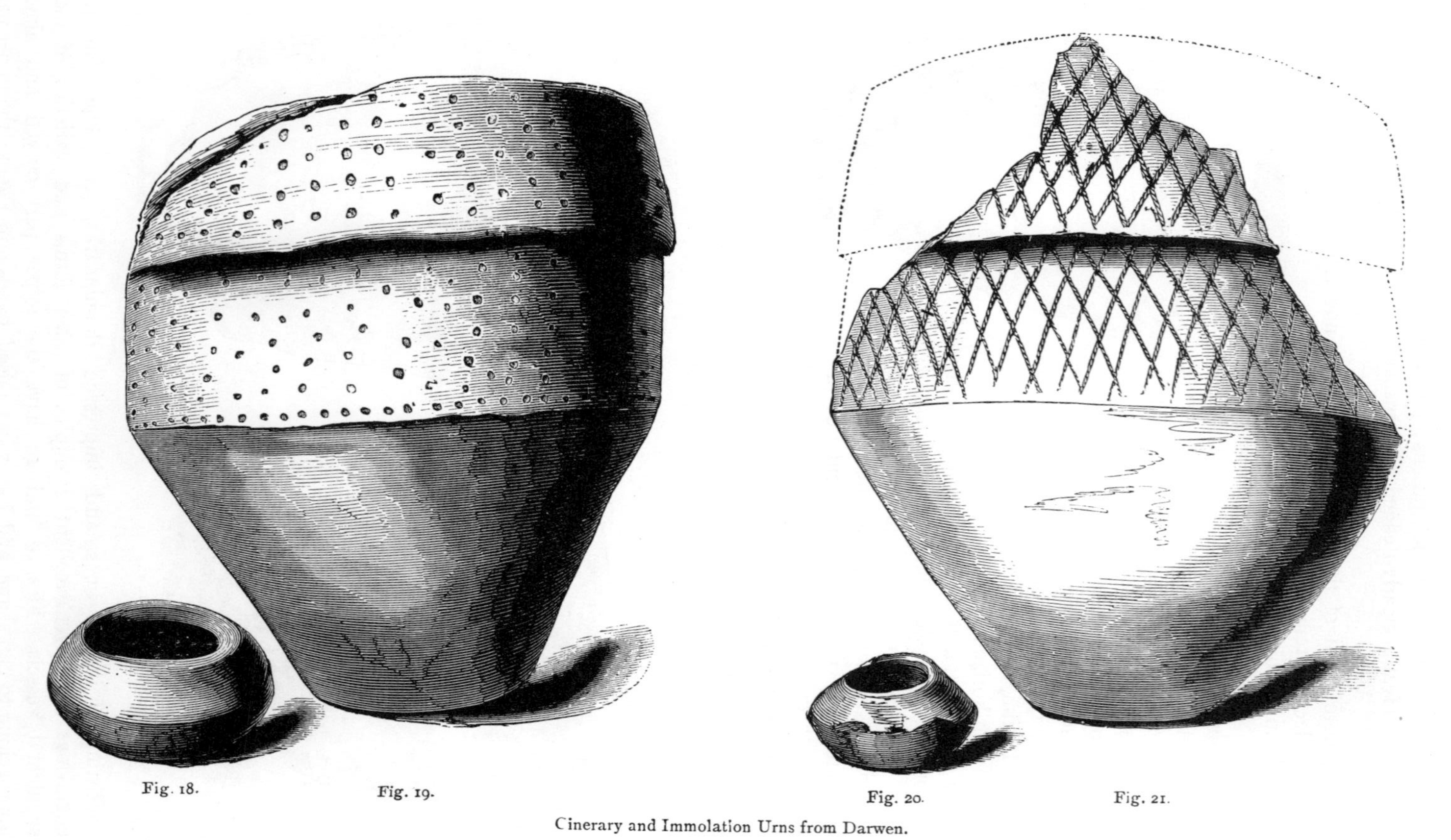

Fig. 18. Fig. 19. Fig. 20. Fig. 21.

Cinerary and Immolation Urns from Darwen.

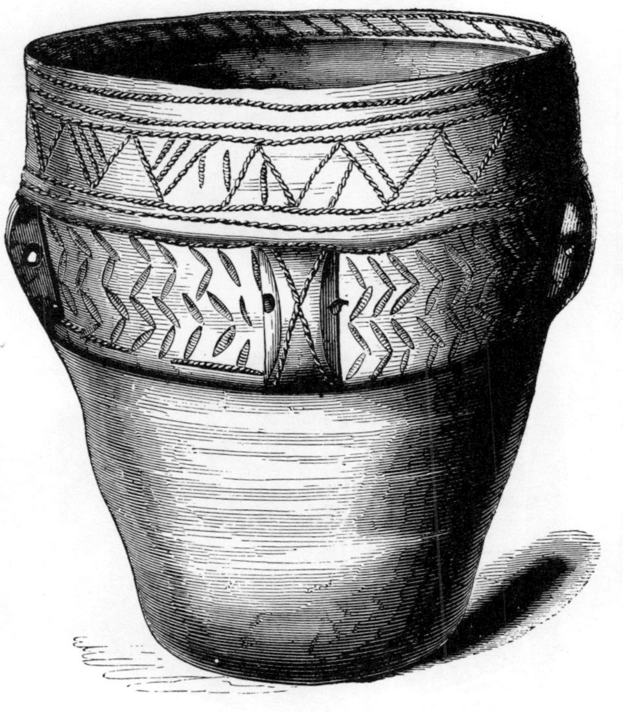
Fig. 22.—Darley Dale.

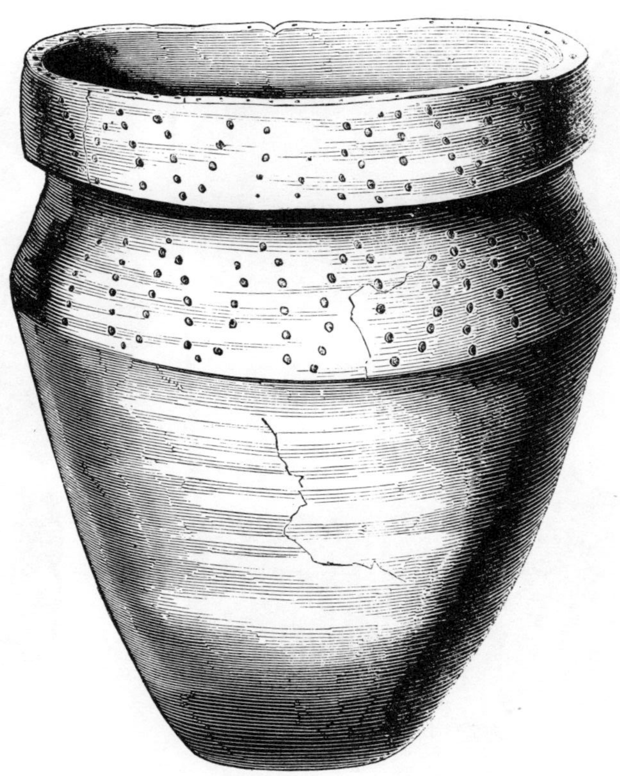
Fig 23.—Calais Wold.

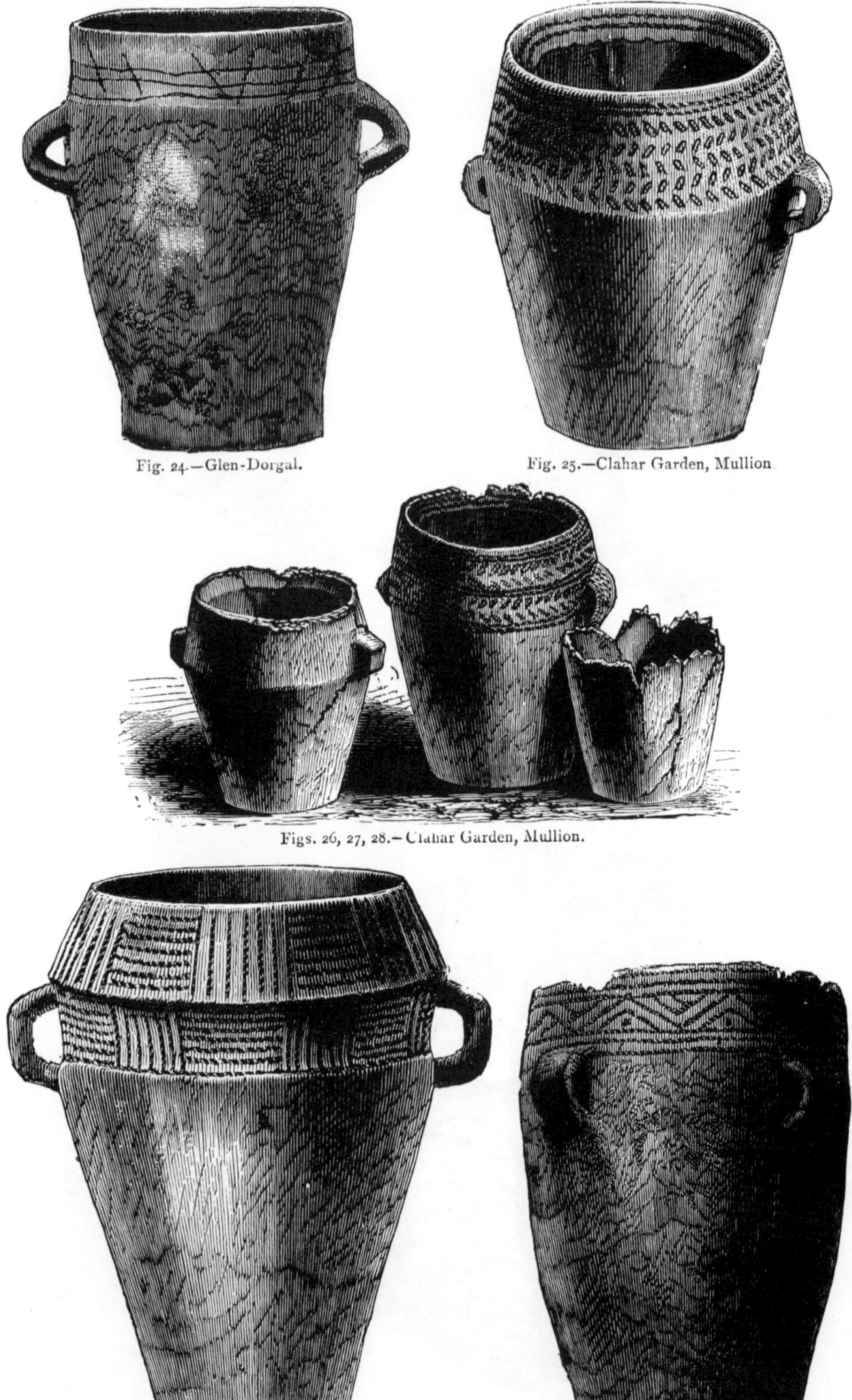

Fig. 24.—Glen-Dorgal.

Fig. 25.—Clahar Garden, Mullion.

Figs. 26, 27, 28.—Clahar Garden, Mullion.

Fig. 29.—Denzell.

Fig. 30.—Gerrans.

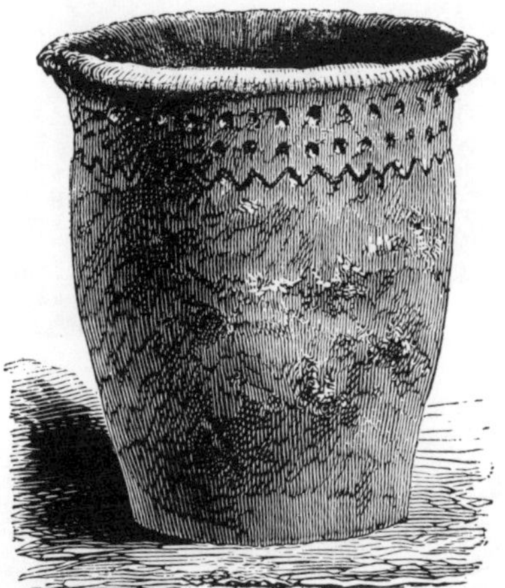

Fig. 31.—Place, near Fowey.

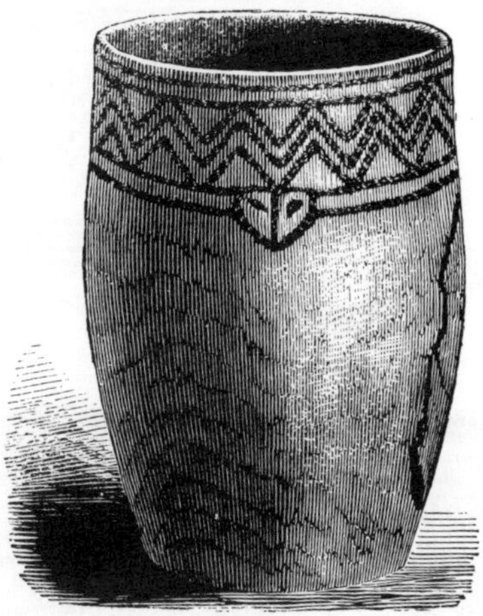

Fig. 32.—Lanlawren.

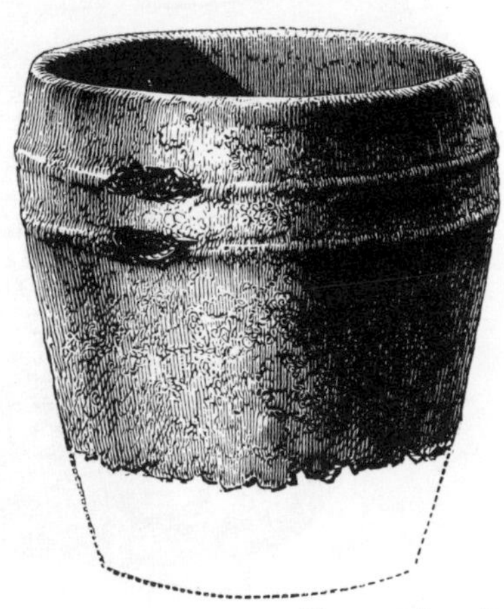

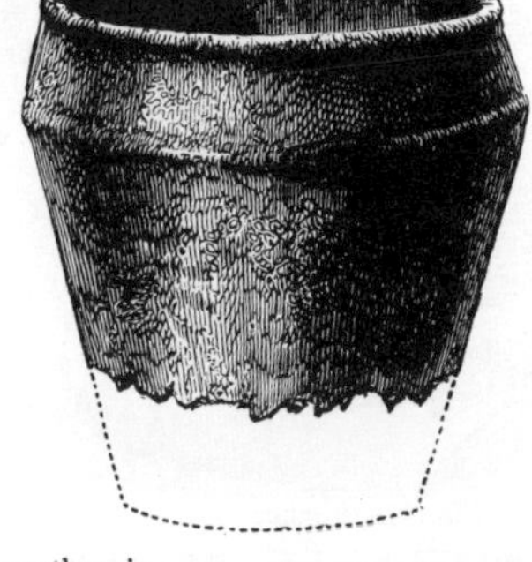

Figs. 33 and 34.—Bosporthennis.

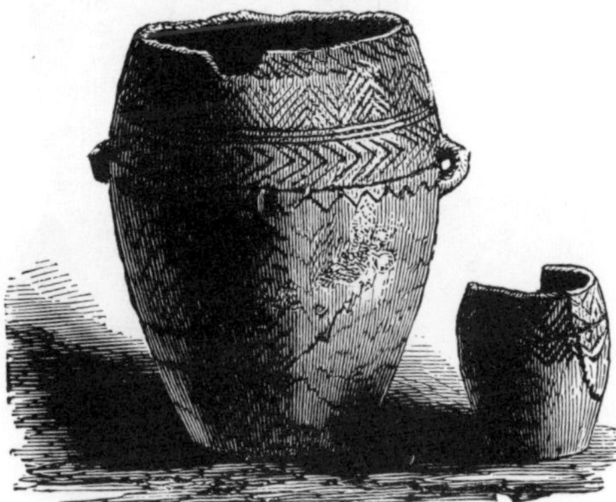

Fig. 35.—Trevello.

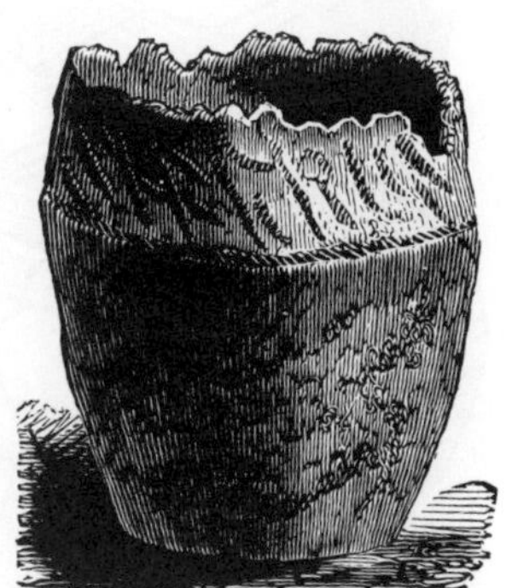

Fig. 36.—Boscawen-Un.

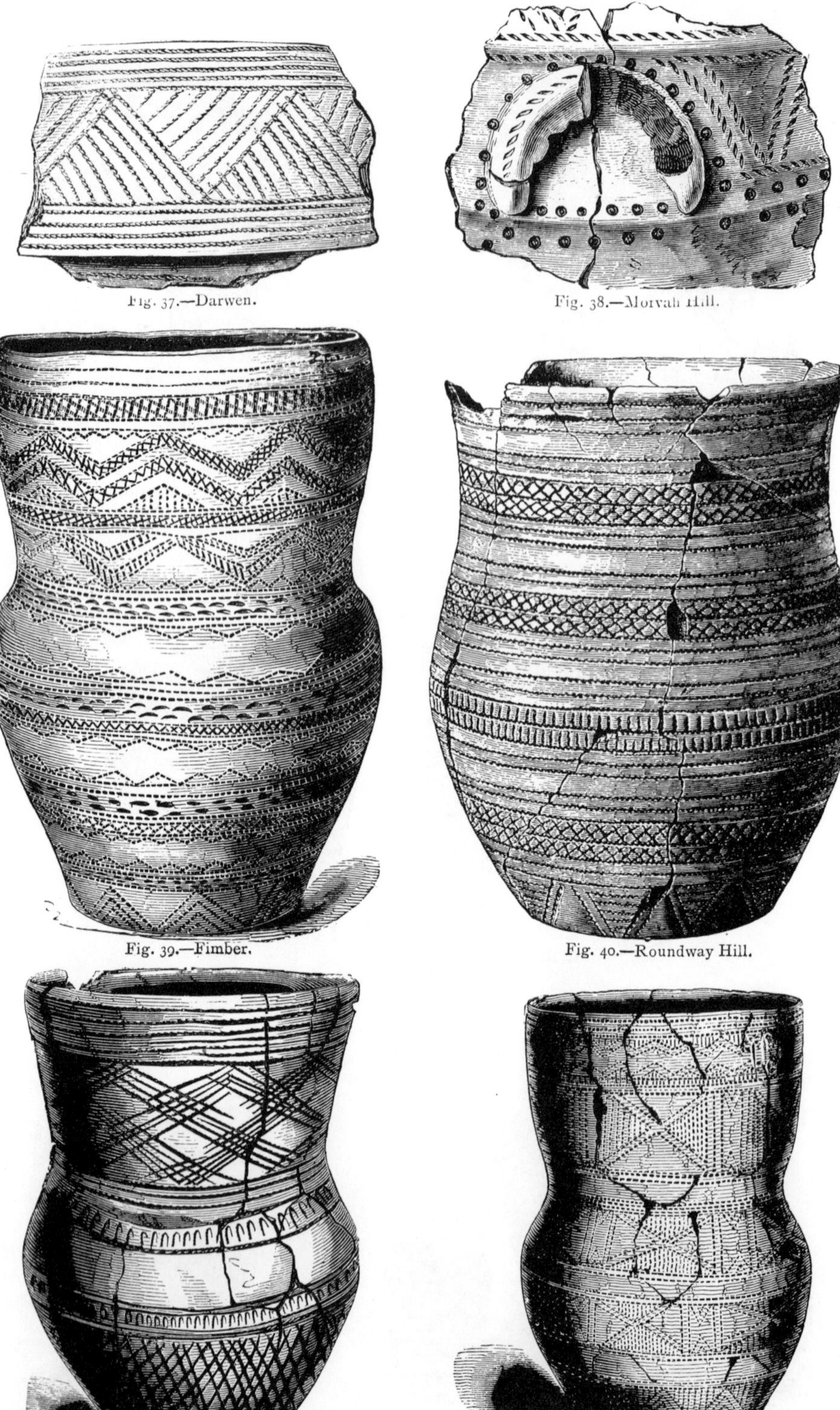

Fig. 37.—Darwen.

Fig. 38.—Morvah Hill.

Fig. 39.—Fimber.

Fig. 40.—Roundway Hill.

Fig. 41.—Monsal Dale.

Fig. 42.—Green Low.

are hollowed out; and in Fig. 15 the upper part is marked with lozenges. Figs. 19 and 23 are ornamented with indented dots produced by pressing the end of a stick

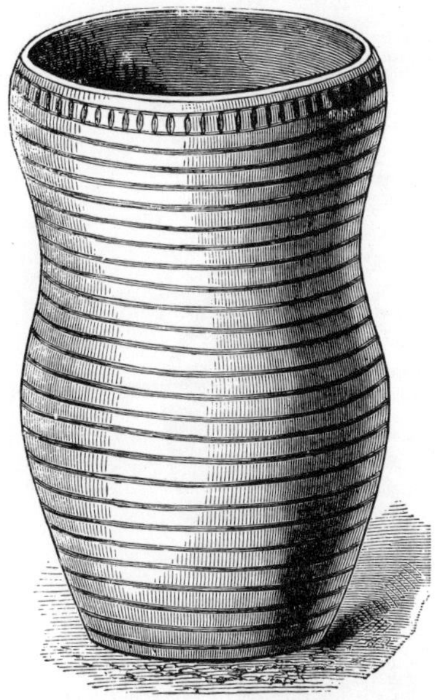

Fig. 43.—Broad Down.

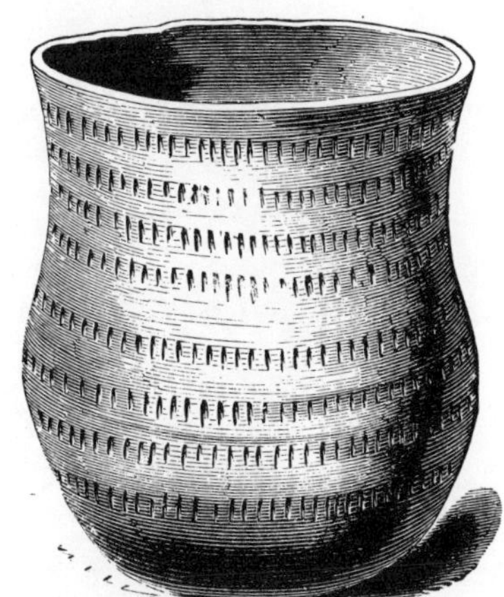

Fig. 44.—Gospel Hillock.

or other substance into the soft clay. Fig. 23 has these dots in zigzag lines. Fig. 21 has the reticulated lines produced by indentations from twisted thongs. Fig. 22

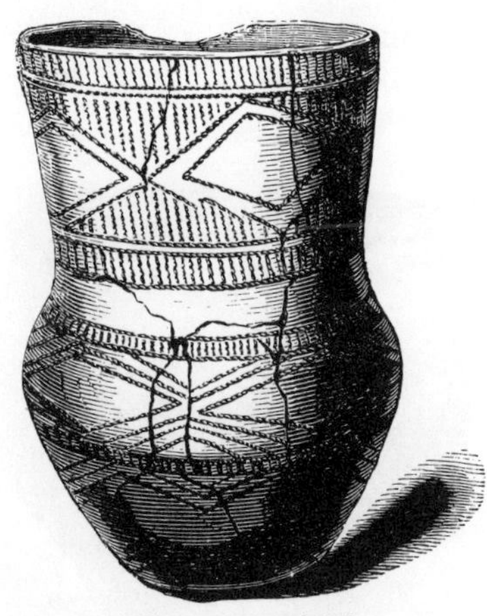

Fig. 45.—Monsal Dale.

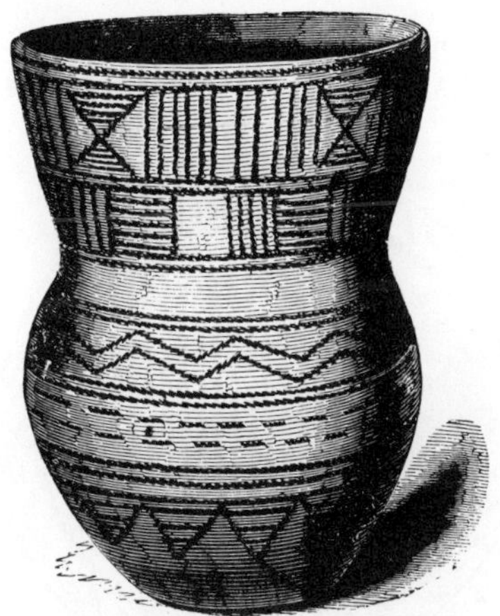

Fig. 46.—Grindlow.

is a remarkably fine example. Around its upper portion are encircling lines, between which is the usual zigzag ornament. Around the central band, too, are encircling lines, between which are a series of vertical zigzag lines. The whole of the ornamentation has been produced by twisted thongs; some, however, being of tighter twist than others. Inside, the rim is ornamented by encircling and diagonal lines.

It has on its central band four projecting handles or loops, which are pierced. Nine

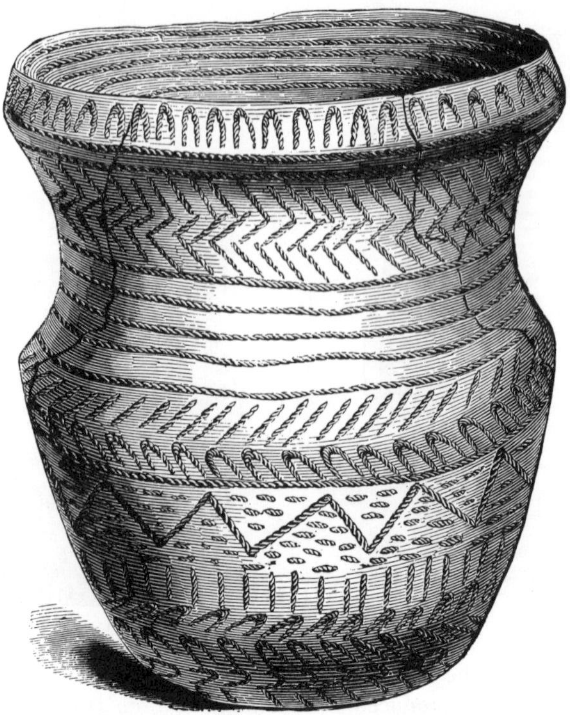

Fig. 47.—Elk Low.

other looped examples, from Cornwall, are shown on Figs. 5, 17, 24, 25, 26, 27, 29, 30, and 35; along with other examples from the same county. Figs. 18 and 20 are

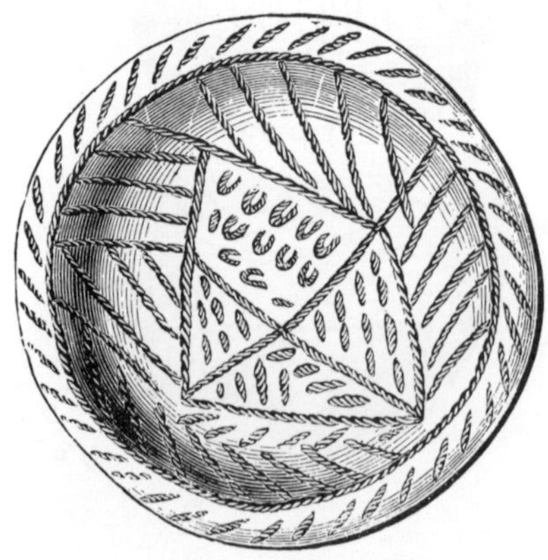

Fig. 48.—Elk Low.

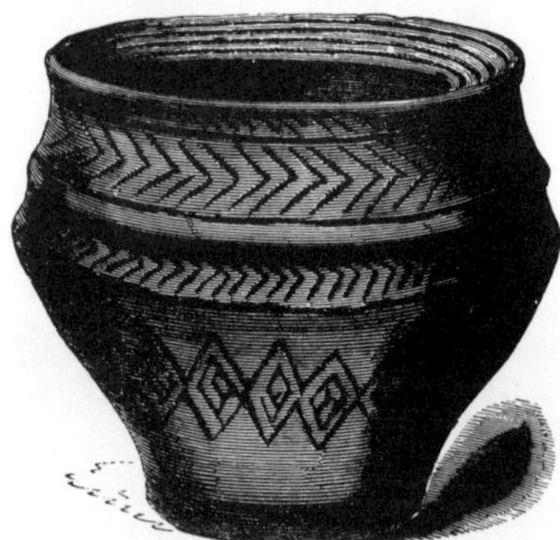

Fig. 49.—Hitter Hill.

two "Immolation Urns," found along with, or in, Figs. 19 and 21. Fig. 38 shows a kind of ear or handle on the side of another vessel.

The *Drinking Cups* are usually of tall form, globular in the lower half, contracted in the middle, and expanding at the mouth. In ornamentation they are more elaborate than the cinerary urns, many of them, in fact, being covered over their entire surface with impressed or incised patterns, frequently of considerable delicacy in manipulation, and always of a finer and higher quality than those of the other

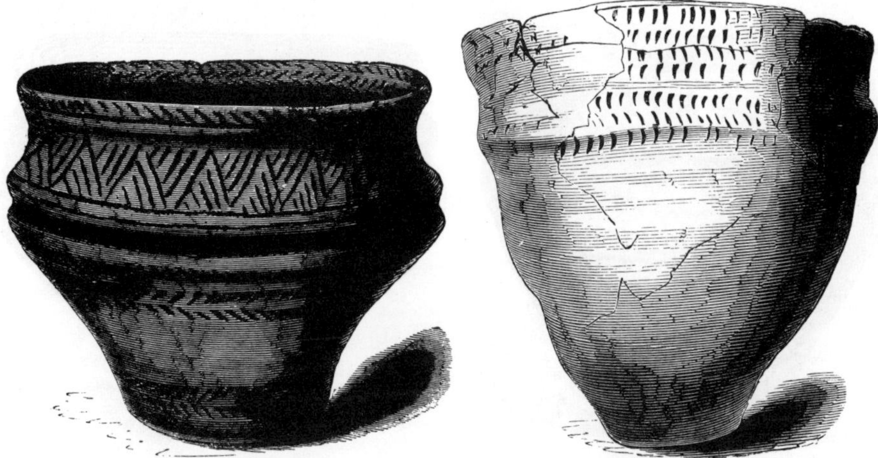

Fig. 50.—Hitter Hill.

Fig. 51.—Trentham.

descriptions of pottery, Figs. 39 to 48 will show some of the varieties both of form and style of decoration. Instances have been known in which a kind of incrustation has been very perceptible on the inner surface, thus showing that their use as vessels for holding liquor is certain; the incrustation being produced by the

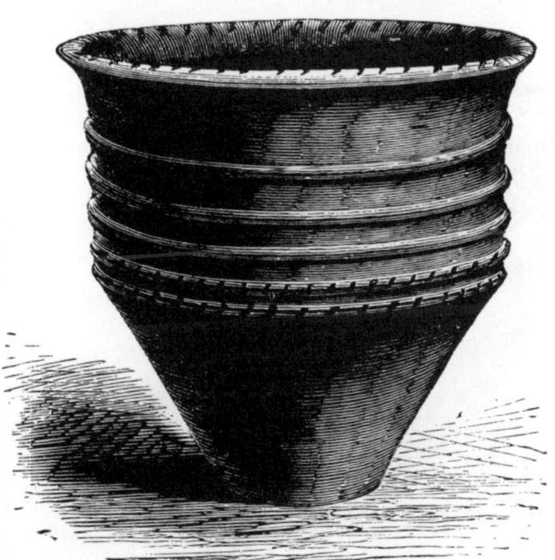

Fig. 52.—Penquite.

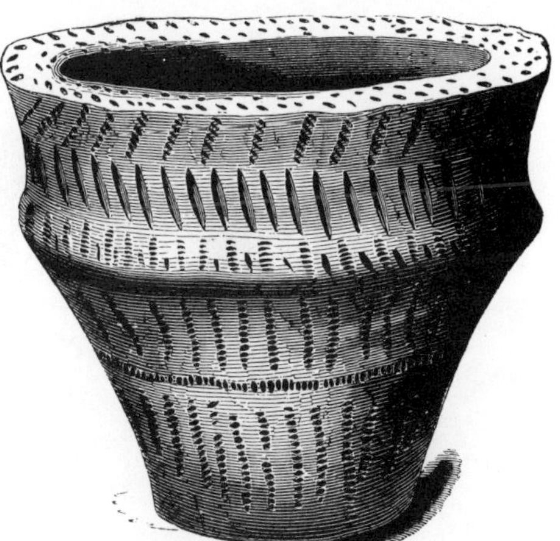

Fig. 53.—Fimber.

gradual drying up of the liquid with which they had been filled when placed with the dead body.

Fig. 47, which, however, may perhaps be a food vessel, has the unusual feature of being ornamented on the bottom quite as elaborately as around its sides. The bottom is shown on Fig. 48. The whole of the ornamentation has been produced by the indentation of twisted thongs into the pliant clay.

Fig. 39, from Fimber, is richly and elaborately ornamented over its entire surface with the most delicate indentations, and is (with Fig. 42) one of the best and most perfect of known examples. When found it stood close to the shoulders

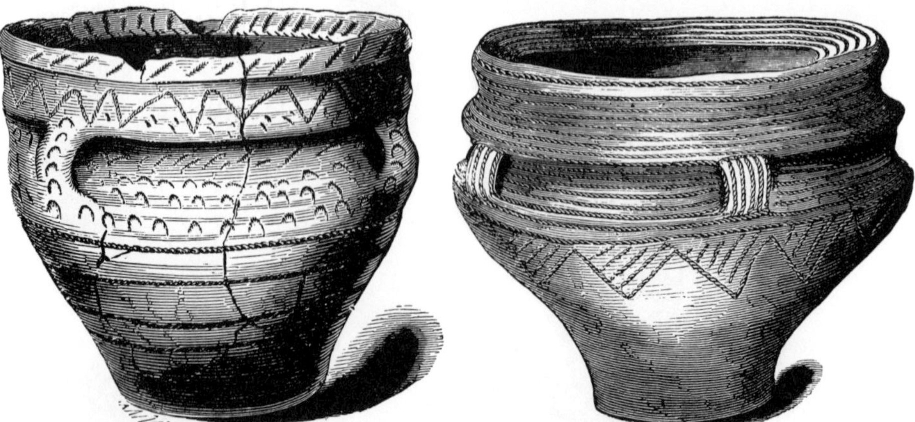

Fig. 54.—Hay Top, Monsal Dale. Fig. 55.—Fimber.

of the skeleton of a strong-boned, middle-aged man, which lay on the right side. Fig. 42 is equally as elaborate in ornamentation, and as good in form. Like the former, it is ornamented by thong indentations. Fig. 41 is of the same general shape, but not so elaborate in design; the greater portion of the ornamentation consisting of reticulated and lozenge patterns. Fig. 45 is also a remarkably good example, and is about equal in point of ornament with Fig. 46. Fig. 40 is of very

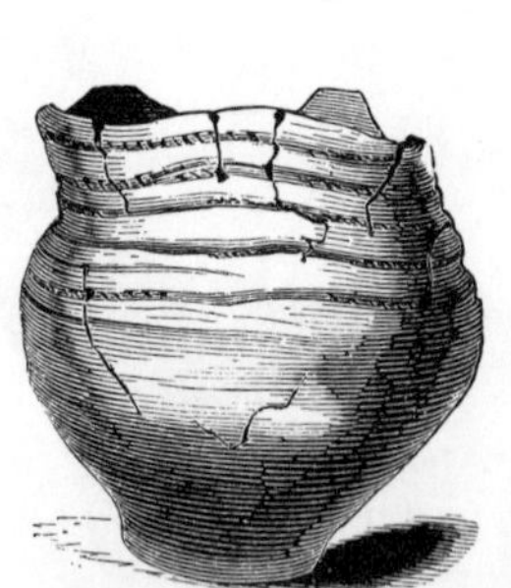

Fig. 56.—Trentham.

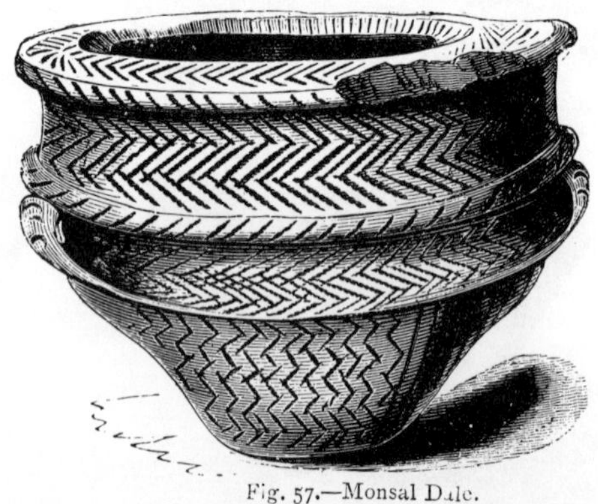

Fig. 57.—Monsal Dale.

different form, as are also Figs. 43 and 44. The ornamentation on the first of these is produced in the usual way, and on the second, by simple indentations. Other forms of drinking-cups are met with, but these are the most usual.

The *Food Vessels*—small urns, so called because they were probably intended to contain an offering of food—are of various forms and sizes, and are, in point of decoration, more or less elaborate. They are usually small at the bottom, and gradually swell out until they become, frequently, wider at the mouth than they are

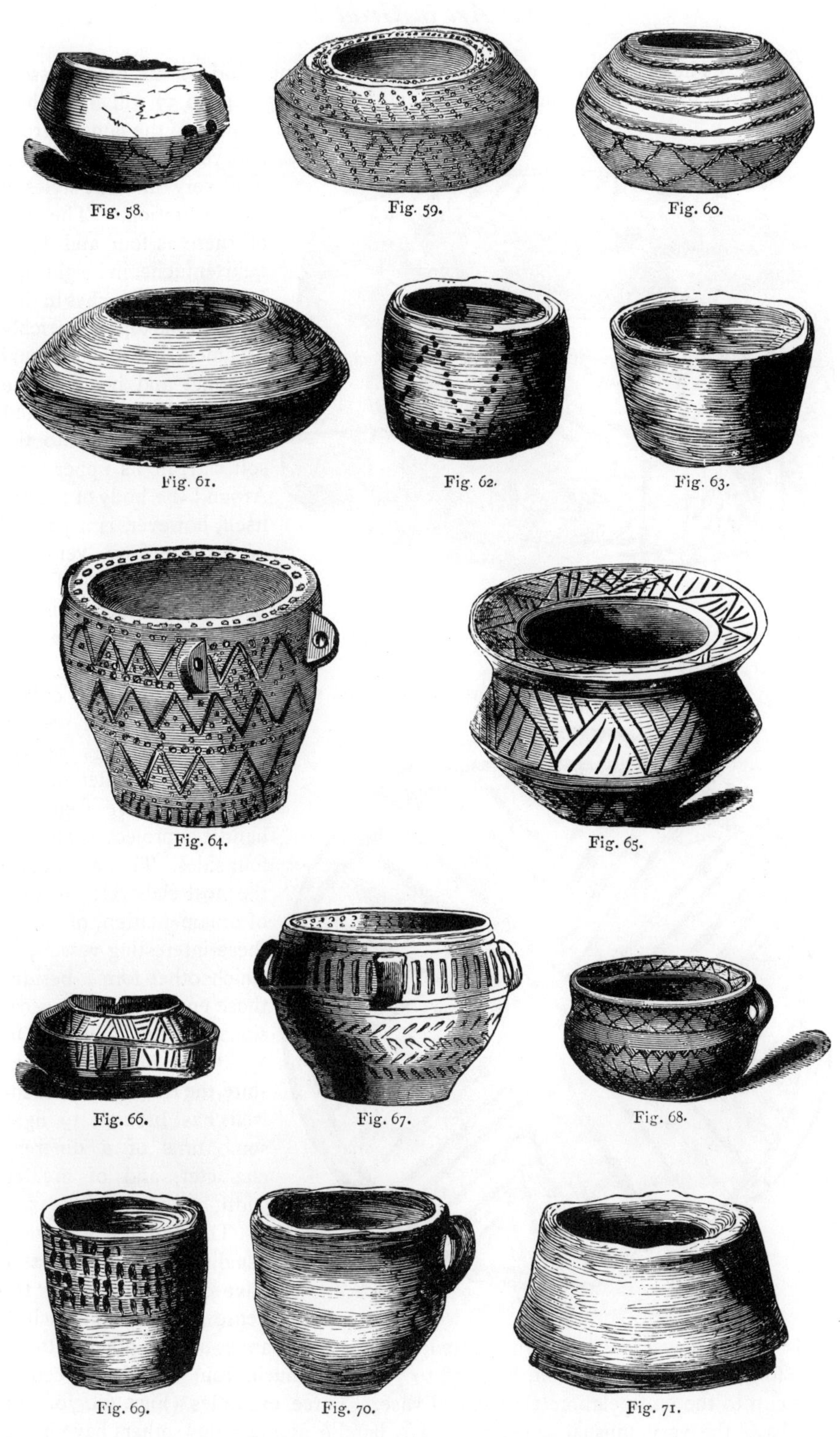
Fig. 58. Fig. 59. Fig. 60.
Fig. 61. Fig. 62. Fig. 63.
Fig. 64. Fig. 65.
Fig. 66. Fig. 67. Fig. 68.
Fig. 69. Fig. 70. Fig. 71.

in height. They are formed of clay of much the same kind as the other vessels, and are fired to about the same degree of hardness. Figs. 49 to 57 will show their general form and style of decoration. Figs. 49 and 50 were found in the same barrow, and yet, as will be seen, exhibit very different styles of ornamentation. The first of these is four and three quarter inches in height, and five and a half inches in diameter at the top. It is richly ornamented with the usual diagonal and herring-bone lines, formed by twisted thongs impressed into the soft clay, in its upper part. Around the body of the urn itself, however, is a pattern of lozenge form, very unusual on vessels of this period. The second is five and a quarter inches in height, and six and a quarter inches in diameter at the top. It is very richly ornamented.

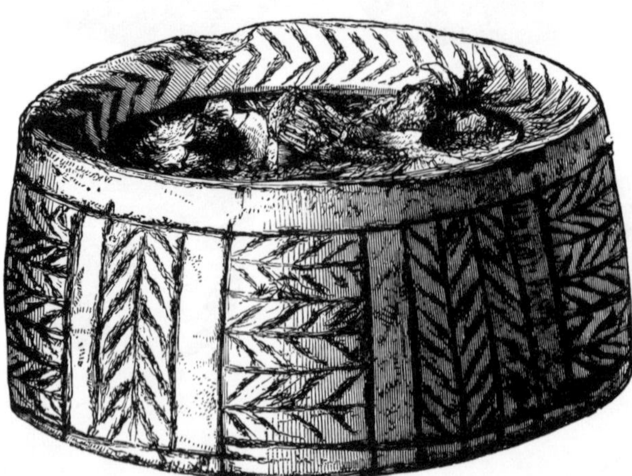

Fig. 72.—Broad Down.

Fig. 53 has the pattern rudely indented over its whole surface. Fig. 51 is coarse and rude, and the pattern very simple. Figs. 54, 55, and 57 are of different character, and have a kind of handle or projecting stud on four sides. They are among the most elaborate, in point of ornamentation, of any of these interesting vessels, of which other forms besides those engraved have occasionally been found. On Wykeham Moor, in Yorkshire, the Rev. Canon Greenwell has brought to light some urns of a different character, and of greater width at the mouth.

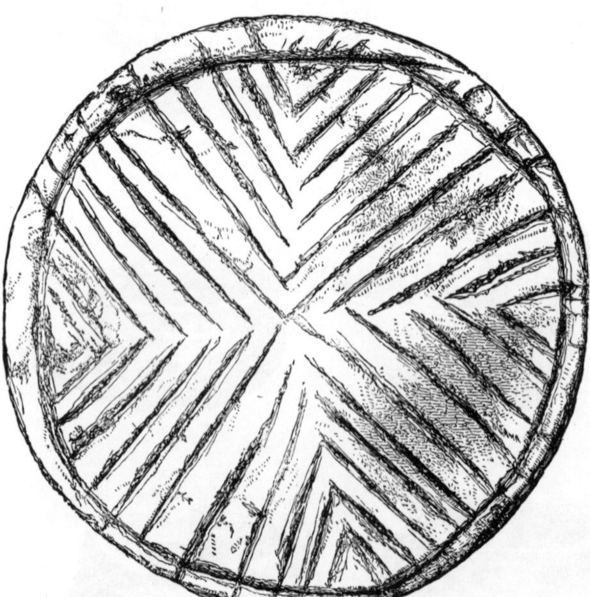

Fig. 73.—Broad Down.

The diminutive vessels, usually called (though, as I have said, erroneously) "Incense Cups," but which I call "*Immolation Urns*," are ornamented in the same manner as the other pottery. The form, as will be seen from Figs. 58 to 75, varies much, from a plain salt-cellar-like cup to the more elaborately rimmed vase. Three examples (Figs. 68, 70, and 75) have the very unusual appendage of a handle at one side; others have holes in their sides, as if for suspension, and I suspect this has been the case in the urn containing the ashes of the mother. Fig. 67 has four handles.

Holes for, as supposed, suspension, are shown in Figs. 58, 72, and 74; these have each two of these small perforations in the side. Others, as in Figs. 64 and 67, have perforated loops at their sides. Fig. 65 is of unusual form, having a broad rim round its mouth; it is elaborately ornamented. Figs. 5, 18 and 20 are shown with the urns with which they were found.

Other forms of these interesting little vessels, which generally range from an inch and a half to three inches in height, occur. They will be best understood

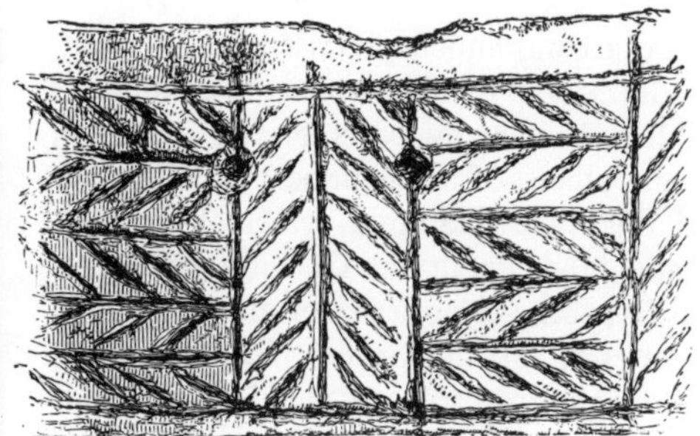

Fig. 74.—Broad Down.

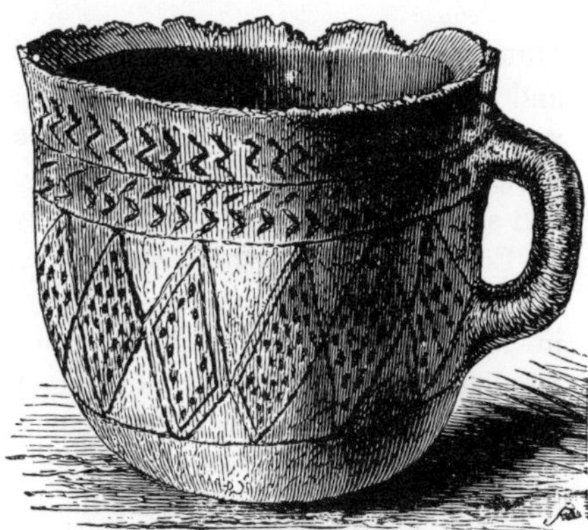

Fig. 75.—Denzell.

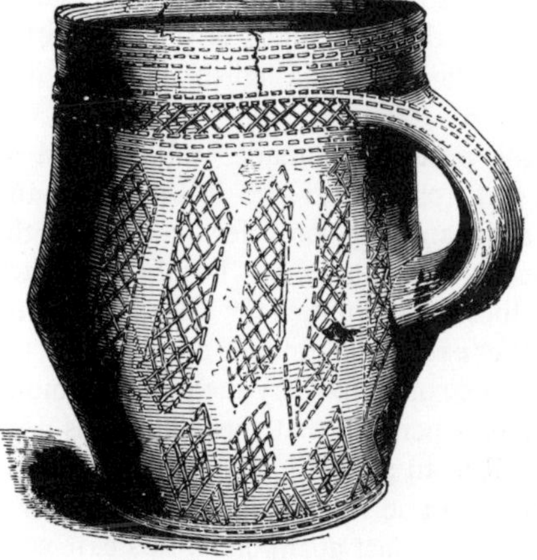

Fig. 76.—Pickering.

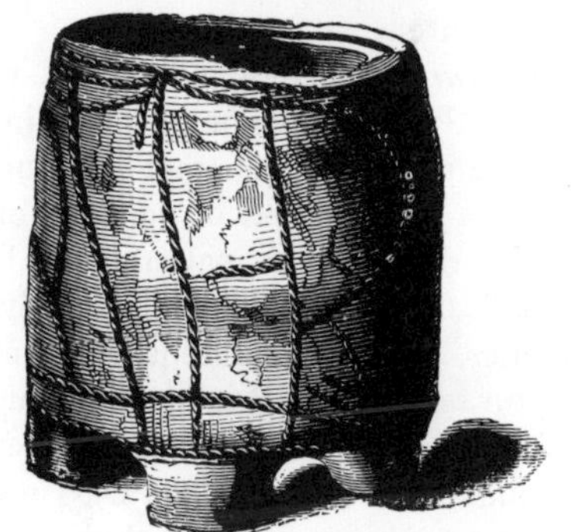

Fig. 77.—Pickering.

from the engravings. One of these (Fig. 72), for the purpose of showing its pattern more carefully, is engraved of its FULL SIZE. It is a remarkable example, and has its bottom ornamented as well as its sides and rim, which are shown on Figs. 73 and 74. When found it was filled with burnt bones, probably of an infant. On one side were two perforations.

Among the unusual forms of Celtic pottery may be named the curious examples (Figs. 76 and 77), one of which is a kind of drinking-mug with a handle, and the other is supported on feet. Fig. 76, and another of somewhat similar kind in the Ely Museum, are the only two known examples of this form of vessel, and they will be seen to be very richly ornamented. Fig. 76 is in the Bateman collection, as is also Fig. 77. It is one of the class of vessels hitherto called incense-cups, and is, I believe, unique—no other example on feet having come under my notice.

CHAPTER II.

DURING the Romano-British period the fictile art was much practised in England, and not only was a large variety of wares produced, but an almost endless number of vessels were made. Pot works were established in many parts of the kingdom, some of which grew to large dimensions, while others of a less important character and size still made wares of extremely good quality. The three principal potteries in England at this period were those on the Medway, in the Upchurch marshes, extending towards Sheerness, in Kent; the Durobrivian potteries on the river Nen, in Northamptonshire; and the Salopian potteries on the Severn, in Shropshire. Smaller pot works, however, being scattered over various parts of the kingdom.

With the well-known "Samian Ware," the finest and most beautiful of the pottery of the Romans which is found in this country, I have, of course, nothing to do in my present work; for, although found so frequently and so abundantly in England, it was not manufactured here, and therefore does not come within its scope. I proceed, therefore, to speak of the various English seats of the manufacture.

Upchurch Ware.—The district wherein this pottery was made and is found so abundantly, is of five or six miles in length, and from one to two in breadth; and over the whole of this tract of country, at a distance of some few feet below the surface, a regular layer of remains of Roman fictile art occurs. To Mr. C. Roach Smith is due the principal credit of bringing these under notice: "There can be no doubt," says Mr. Wright, "not only from the extent of ground covered by the potteries, but from the frequent occurrence of the sort of pottery made here, among Roman remains in Britain belonging to different periods, that these potteries were in full activity during the whole extent of the Roman period. The site of the kilns was moved as the clay was used up, and at the same time the refuse pottery was thrown on the ground behind them, so that, when at last abandoned, this extensive site presented a surface of ground covered almost entirely by a bed of refuse pottery." Here, then, the Roman *figuli* exercised their art more extensively than anywhere else in England, and continued its practice for a long series of years. In those days the ground would of course be firm and dry. Since then, as is usually the case in so long a number of years, the soil has accumulated to the thickness of about three feet—the inroads which the Medway is constantly making upon it forming the creeks, and continually disclosing the remains left by the potters.

The ware made at Upchurch must have been in considerable repute, for it is found in Roman localities in most parts of the kingdom. On Roman sites in France and Germany and in Flanders, &c., wares of a precisely similar kind are found, and show that it is probable they were simultaneously made at different places. The prevailing colour of the ware is a bluish or greyish black, with a smooth and rather shining surface. A good deal, however, is of a dark drab colour,

The black colour has been produced by the process of "firing" in "smother kilns"—a process well known to potters. The forms of the vessels, as well as the sizes, vary to a surprising extent, but they are all remarkable for the gracefulness and elegance of their outline, and, in many instances for the simplicity and effective character of the patterns with which they are decorated. The decorations consist chiefly of circles or semicircles; lines, vertical or otherwise; bands, and numbers of

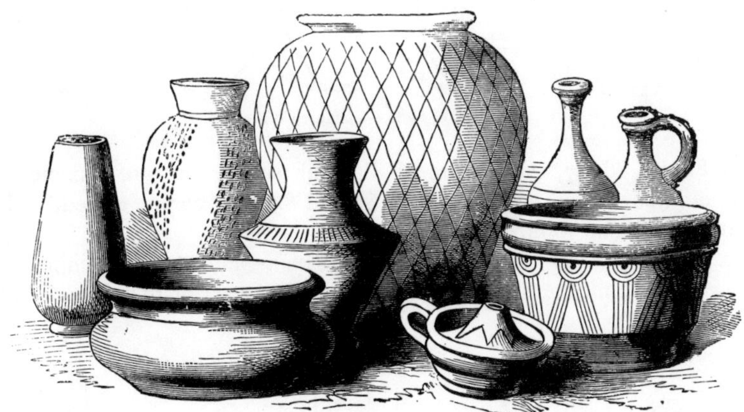

Fig. 78.—Group of Upchurch Ware.

raised dots arranged in a variety of ways. The clay used is fine, and the vessels are light and thin, and remarkably well "potted."

The instruments used in the ornamentation of this pottery appear to have been of a very rude description, and were, as it seems, chiefly mere sticks, some sharpened to a point, and others with a transverse section cut into notches. The former were used in tracing the lines already described; the latter had the section formed into a square or rhomboid, the surface of which was cut into parallel lines crossing each other so as to form a dotted figure, and this was stamped on the surface of the

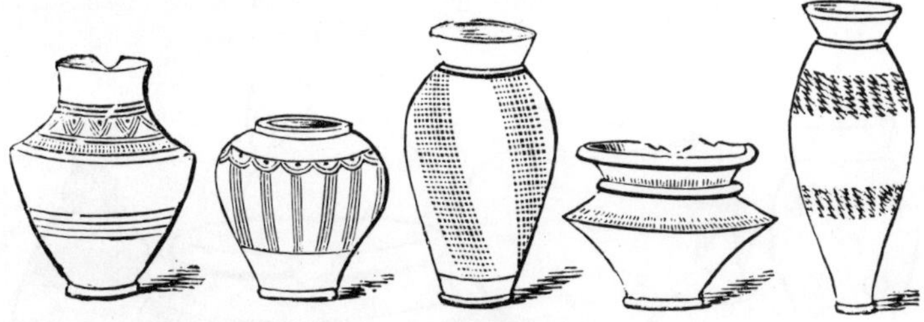

Figs. 79 to 83.—Upchurch Ware.

pottery in various combinations and arrangements. Sometimes these dots are arranged so as to form bands; and in others simply "patch" ornaments. Other vessels were covered with reticulation, the lines being simply scratched into the surface of the clay; and others have bands of serrated lines.

The forms of some of the vessels from the Upchurch works will be seen on Fig. 78, and a series of other characteristic examples are given on Figs. 79 to 95.

One example (Fig. 80) is ornamented with half-circles traced on the clay as with compasses, from which run downwards rows of incised lines. On Fig. 78 is an example of much the same character of ornamentation although different in form.

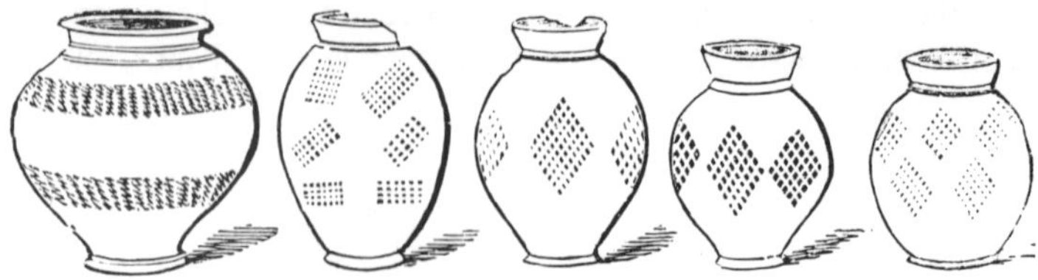

Figs. 84 to 88.—Upchurch Ware.

Figs. 81, 85, 86, 87, and 88 are of different shape, and are ornamented with raised dots in bands and patches; while 83 and 84 are "engine turned." They are of remarkably elegant form.

Figs. 91, 92, 93, and 95 are more bottle shaped—in fact, approaching somewhat to the form of the mediæval bellarmine. Many varieties of this general form have

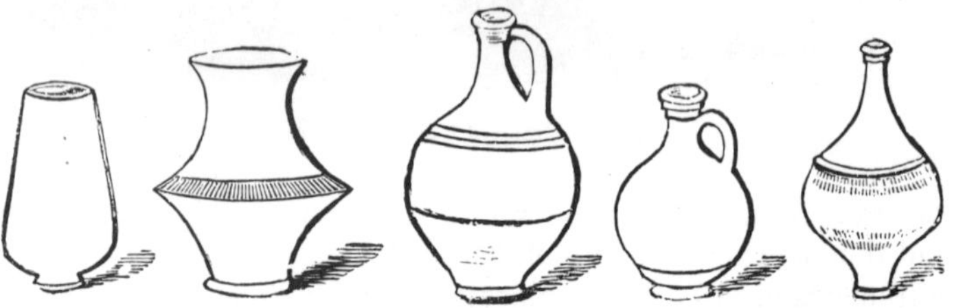

Figs. 89 to 93.—Upchurch Ware.

been found in the marshes and elsewhere. Fig. 89 is particularly simple and elegant in shape, as are also several shown in the groups on this and the preceding pages. Among these is an example of another variety of ornamentation common to the Upchurch ware. It is formed by diagonal intersecting lines, and in form is much

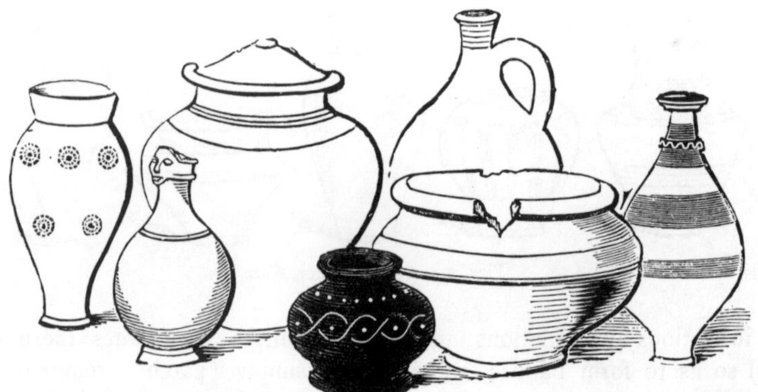

Fig. 94.—Upchurch Ware.

the same as the ordinary kind of Roman cinerary urns. In the group, Fig. 94, are some examples of Upchurch and other wares.

Castor Ware, or Durobrivian Ware, as it is variously called, is the production of the extensive Romano-British potteries on the river Nen, in Northamptonshire and Huntingdonshire; near Castor and Chesterton, in those counties respectively. In this locality, as the names of Chesterton and Castor undeniably prove to have been the case, an important settlement of the Romans was made, and excavations have

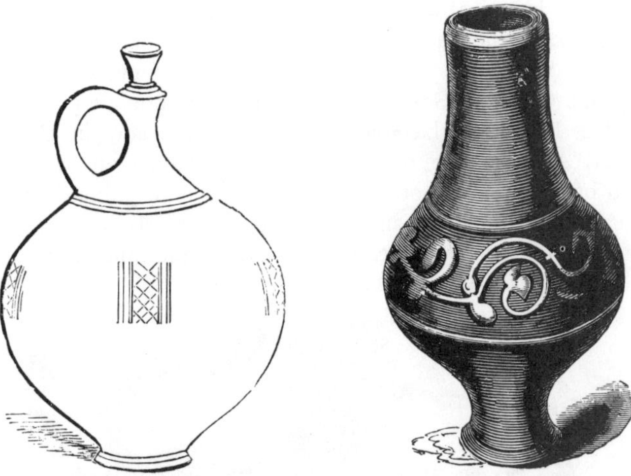

Fig 95.—Upchurch Ware. Fig. 96.—Castor Ware.

brought to light the remains of a considerable town, and in connection with it, of a settlement of potters with the remains of their works extending over a district many miles in extent.

The great interest attaching to this locality is in the fact that this was not the first, but the first well-ascertained discovery of a Roman pot-manufactory in this kingdom, and that at this spot the first kilns of that period have been uncovered, and the processes adopted by the Roman *figuli* brought to light.

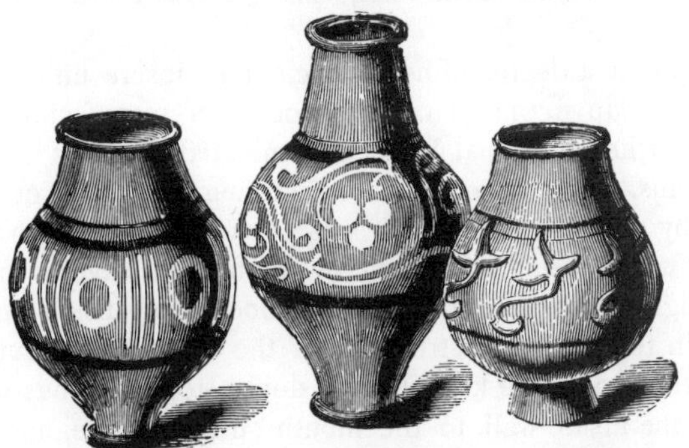

Figs. 97, 98, 99.—Castor Ware.

The situation of the potteries was well chosen for carrying on an extensive trade with distant parts of the kingdom, and from researches which were made, the late Mr. Artis, to whom the discovery is due, computed that probably two thousand people had been employed in the fabrication of fictile vessels. It is on the line of one of the most important of the Roman roads—the Ermyn street—and close to the navigable river Nen; and that the products of the manufactory were supplied to places throughout the kingdom is abundantly testified by the remains which are almost invariably found in course of excavations wherever Roman occupation is known. Mr. Artis unfortunately, although he published, in 1828, a fine folio volume of plates of the more remarkable of the objects he discovered, never issued the descriptive and historical text which was intended to accompany it. The great bulk of the information he had gleaned he had not committed to paper, and consequently it died with him. Mr. Artis, however, communicated some valuable particulars to Mr. C. Roach Smith, and these have been made public by him in the "Journal of the British Archæological Association" and in the "Collectanea Antiqua." Mr. Artis in one of these says that during an examination of the pigments used by the Roman potters of Castor and its neighbourhood, he was "led to the conclusion that the blue and slate-coloured vessels met with here in such abundance were coloured by suffocating the fire of the kiln at the time when its

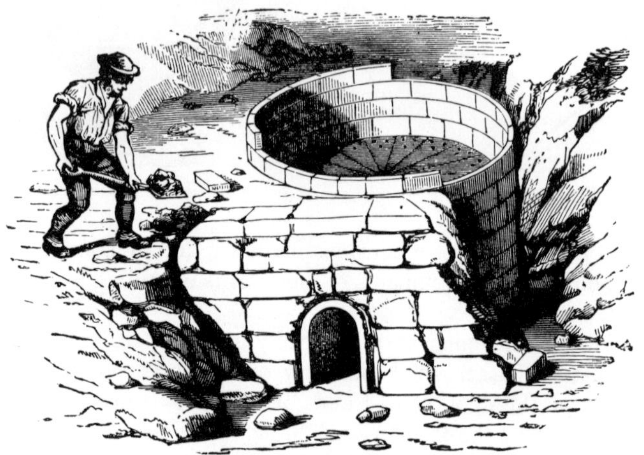

Fig. 100.—Potter's Kiln, Normangate Field, Castor.

contents had acquired a degree of heat sufficient to insure uniformity of colour. I had so firmly made up my mind on the process of manufacturing and firing this peculiar kind of earthenware, that I had denominated the kilns in which it had been fired 'smother kilns.' The mode of manufacturing the bricks of which these kilns are made is worthy of notice. The clay was previously mixed with about one-third of rye in the chaff, which being consumed by the fire, left cavities in the room of the grains. This might have been intended to modify expansion and contraction, as well as to assist in the gradual distribution of the colouring vapour. The mouth of the furnace and the top of the kiln were no doubt stopped: thus we find every part of the kiln, from the inside wall to the mouth on the outside, and every part of the clay wrappers of the domes penetrated with the colouring exhalation."

The researches further proved that the colour could not be attributed to any metallic oxide (although it must be confessed that in many instances the surface has a strongly-developed metallic appearance) either in the clay itself or applied externally, and this conclusion is confirmed by the appearance of the clay wrappers of the dome of the kilns; and it may be added, the colour is so fugitive that it is expelled entirely, by submitting the pottery to an open fire. During the examination of the Upchurch pottery, Mr. Artis remarked that he thought a coarse kind of sedge had been used in the manufactory. His practical eye alone guided him to this conclusion, for he had never visited the site, and was quite unaware that below the strata of broken vessels, a layer of sedge peat is in several places visible. The same kind of arrangement probably obtained pretty generally with the Roman potters.

The kilns for firing the Castor ware, discovered by Mr. Artis, are among the most interesting of all the remains of Roman arts which have been brought to light. The kilns which were removed in the course of the investigations were "all constituted on the same principle: a circular hole was dug from three to four feet deep, and four in diameter, and walled round to the height of two feet. A furnace, one-third of the kiln in length, communicated with the side. In the centre of the circle, so formed, was an oval pedestal, the height of the sides, with the end pointing to the mouth of the furnace. Upon this pedestal and side walls the floor of the kiln rests.

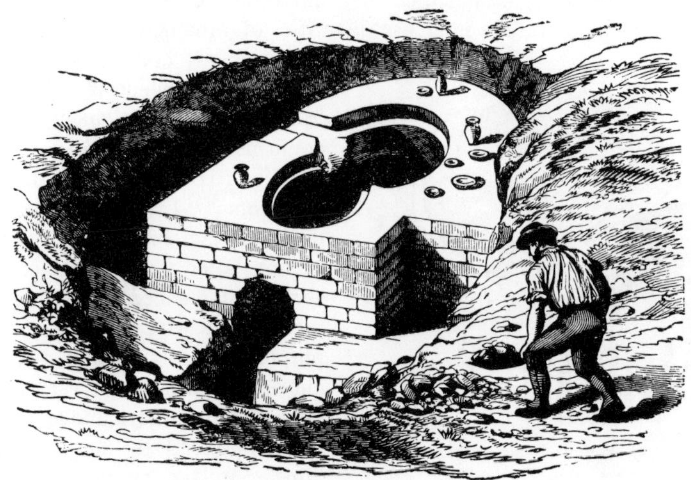

Fig. 101.—Potter's Kiln, Normangate Field, Castor.

It was formed of perforated angular bricks, meeting at one point in the centre; the furnace was arched with bricks, moulded for the purpose; the side of the kiln was constructed with curved bricks set edgeways (see Fig. 100) in a thick slip (the same material made into a thin mortar) to the height of two feet. The process of packing the vessels and securing uniform heat in firing the ware was the same in the two different kinds of kilns—namely, that before described, called 'smother kiln,' and that for various other kinds of pottery. They were first carefully loose-packed with the articles to be fired, up to the height of the side walls. The circumference of the bulk was then gradually diminished, and finished in the shape of a dome. As this arrangement progressed, an attendant seems to have followed the packer, and thinly covered a layer of pots with coarse hay or grass. He then took some thin clay, the size of his hand, and laid it flat over the grass upon the vessels: he then placed more grass on the edge of the clay just laid on—then more clay—and so on until he had completed the circle. By this time the packer would have raised another tier of pots, the plasterer following as before, hanging the grass over the top edge of the last layer of plasters, until he had reached the top, in which a small aperture was left, and the clay nipped round the edge; another coating would then be laid on as before described. Directly after, gravel or loam was thrown up against the side wall where the clay wrappers were commenced—probably to secure the bricks and the clay coating. The kiln was then fired with wood. In consequence of the care taken to place grass between the edges of the wrappers, they could be unpacked in the same size pieces as when laid on in a plastic state; and thus the danger in breaking the coat to obtain the contents of the kiln could be obviated. In the course of my excavations I discovered a curiously-constructed furnace, of which I have never before or since met an example. Over it had been placed two circular vessels; the next above the furnace was a third less than the other, which would hold about eight gallons; the fire passed partly under both of them, the smoke escaping by a smoothly-plastered flue, from seven to eight inches wide. The vessels were suspended by the rims fitting into a circular groove or rabbet, formed for the purpose. They contained pottery, both perfect and fragmentary. It is probable they had covers, and I am inclined to think were used for glazing peculiar kinds of the immense quantities of ornamented ware made in this district. Its contiguity to one of the workshops in which the glaze (oxide of iron) and other pigments were found confirms this opinion."

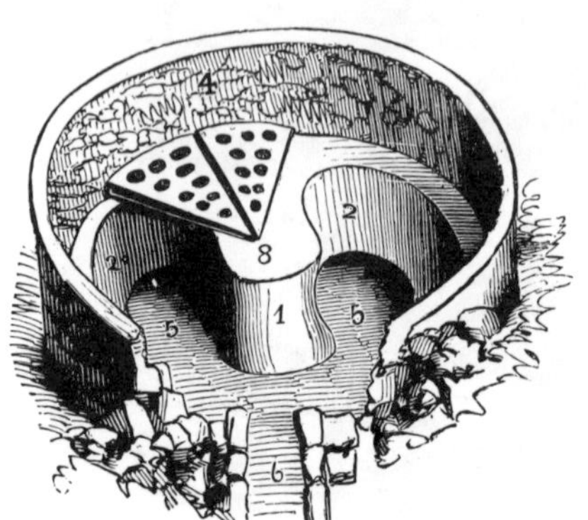

Fig. 102.—Potter's Kiln, Castor.

Fig. 102 is a kiln of a different construction. "In it, instead of modelling or moulding bricks for the kiln, the potters, after forming a tolerably round shaft, commenced plastering it three inches thick with clay, prepared for that purpose, leaving a flange twenty inches above the furnace floor to receive the floor of the kiln; a mode of construction unnoticed by me before in these kilns. In the centre was placed an oval pedestal, for the double purpose of dividing the fire and of giving support to the centre of the floor. To attach the pedestal to the back of the kiln, and to shut out the cold air which would lodge in the angle formed by the pedestal being so placed, the angle was filled with coarse materials, which were stopped up with clay, so as to draw the flame more towards the centre, and induce a union with the flame and heat entering the front part of the kiln. The more usual plan with the potters of this district in packing their kilns was, when the contents had reached the surface of the earth, to form a dome by covering the urns and vases lightly with dry grass, sedge, or the like, and plastering it over with patches of prepared clay, divided by strewing a small quantity of hay between each portion to facilitate removal. In place of this usual process, in this kiln bricks were used of an oblong shape, four inches by two and a half inches, wedge-shaped at one end, with a sufficient curve to traverse the circumference when set edgeways, with the wedge ends lapped over each other. The sides would be thus raised for three or four courses or more, as circumstances might require, and probably be afterwards backed up with loose earth. These bricks were modelled and kneaded with chaff and grain." The numbers indicate as follows:—1, front of the pedestal supporting the

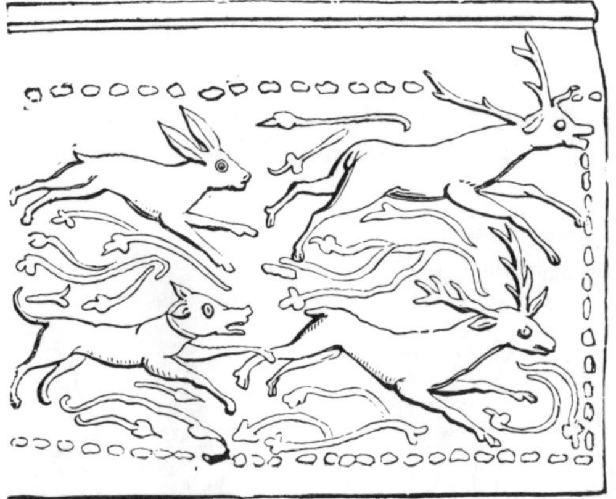
Fig. 103.

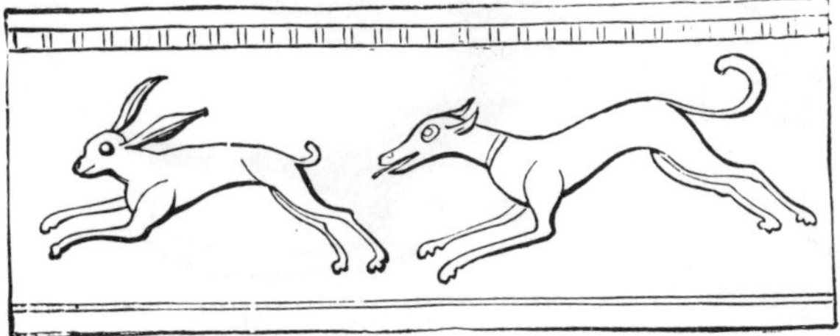
Fig. 104.

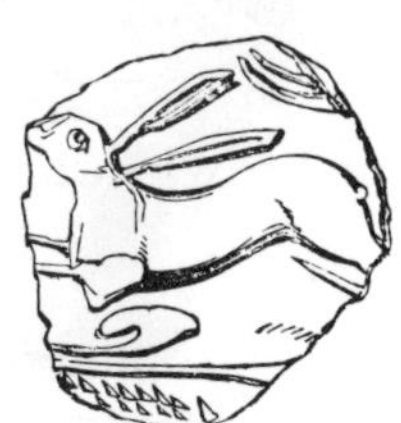
Fig. 105.

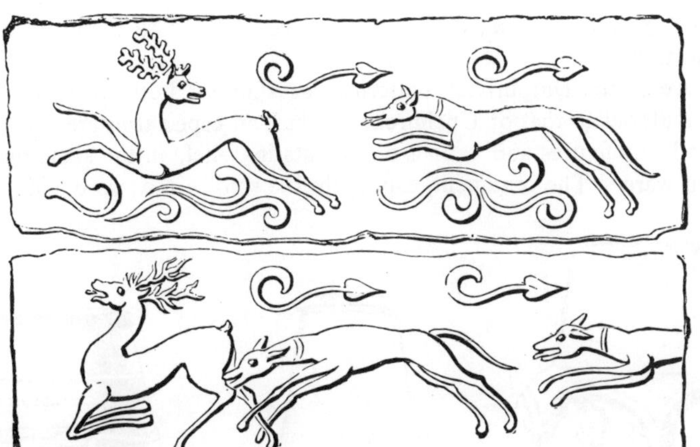
Figs. 106 and 107.

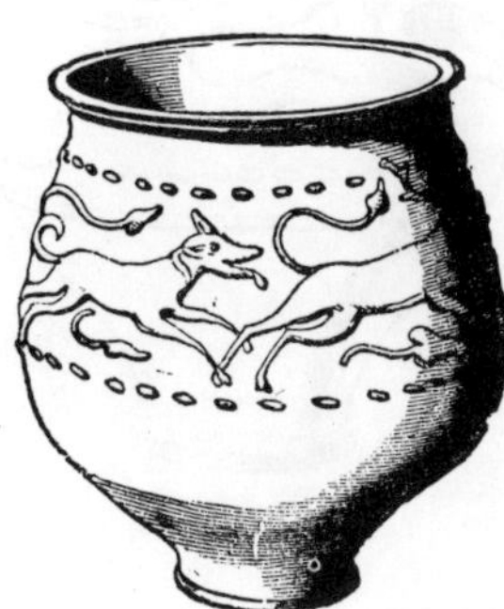
Fig. 108.

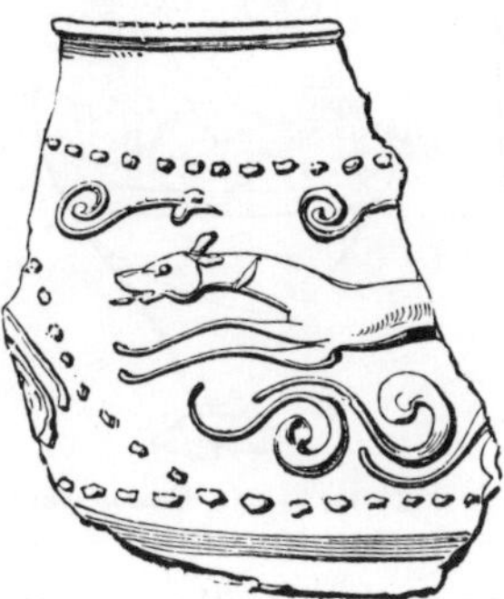
Fig. 109.

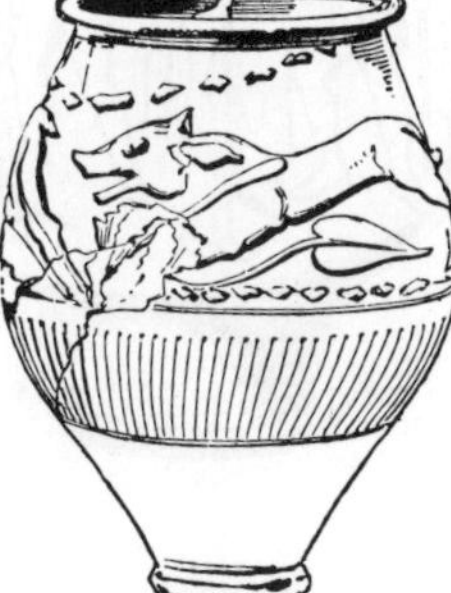
Fig. 110.

Representations of Field Sports on Castor Ware.

floor of the kiln; 2 2, slopes, probably intended to produce a more uniform heat; 3 3, part of the kiln floor; 4, bricks, before used; 5, area of the furnace; 6, mouth

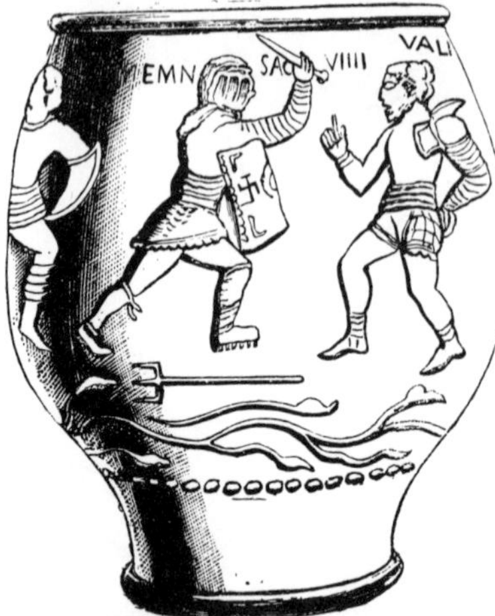

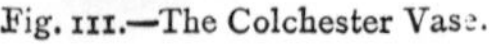

Fig. 111.—The Colchester Vase.

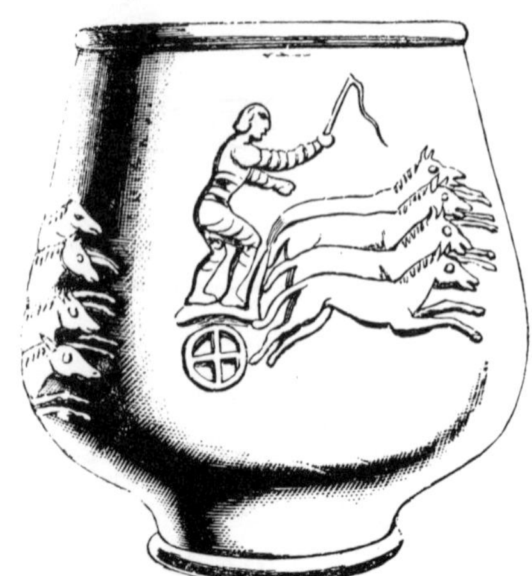

Fig. 112.—Castor Ware.

of furnace; 7, wall of kiln; 8, top of the pedestal. The mouth of the furnace, No. 6, was arched over.

The ware of the Durobrivian potteries was superior both in style of art and in form and material to that of Upchurch, and has an especial interest over it in the fact that it bears figures and various ornaments in relief, in the same manner as on the Samian ware. The ornament, especially the scrolls, &c., were laid on "in slip."

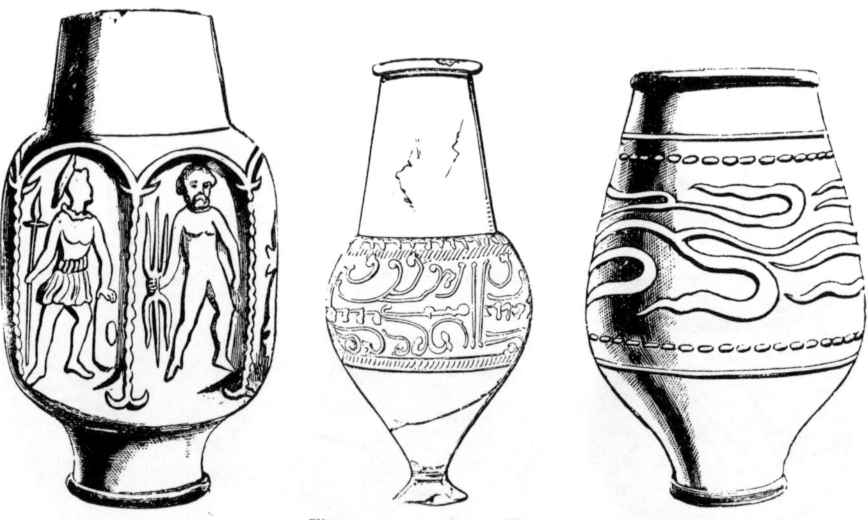

Figs. 113 to 115.—Castor Ware.

The vessel, after having been thrown on the wheel, would be allowed to become somewhat firm, but only sufficiently so for the purpose of the lathe. In the indented

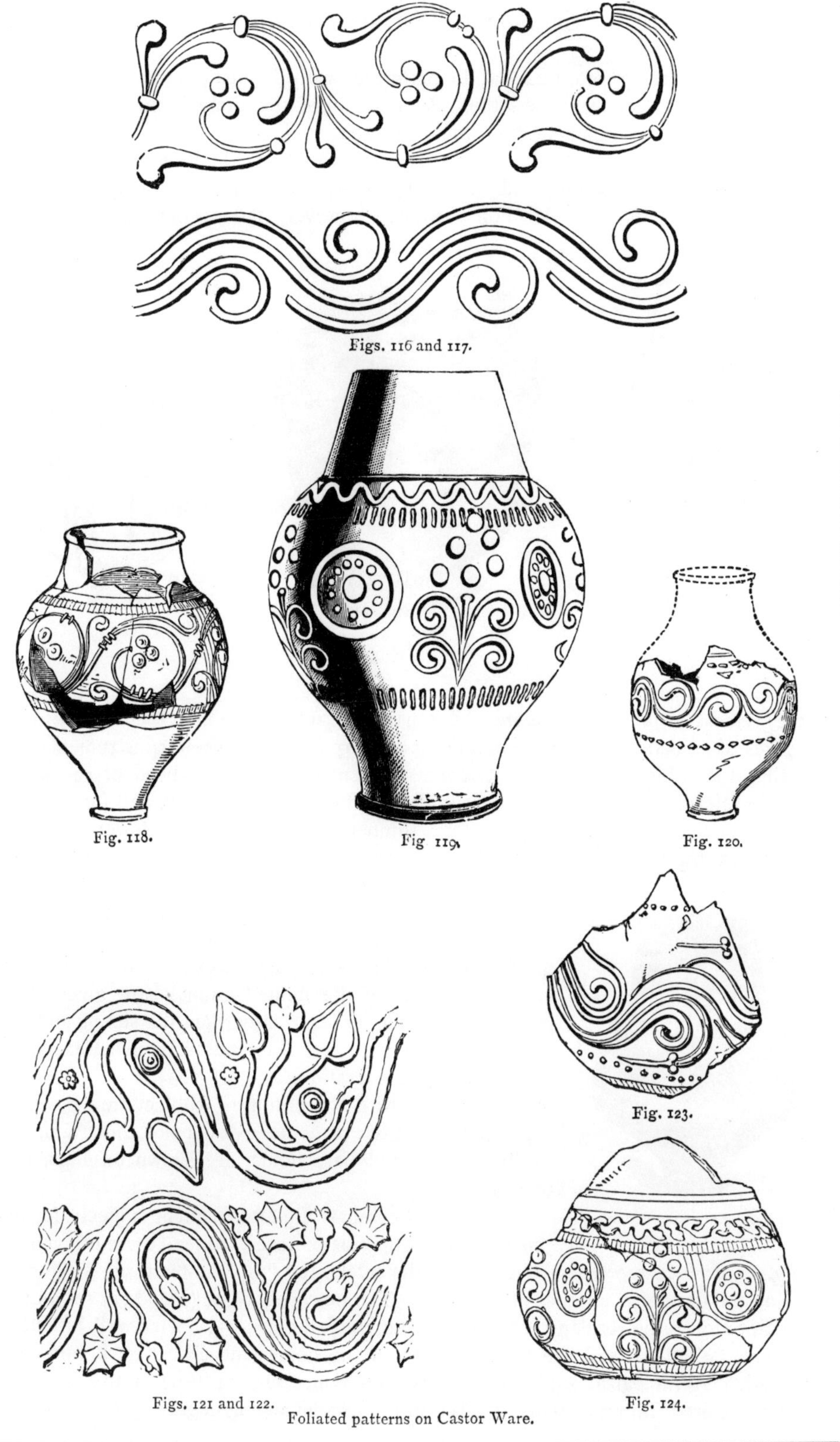

Figs. 116 and 117.

Fig. 118.

Fig 119.

Fig. 120.

Fig. 123.

Figs. 121 and 122.

Fig. 124.

Foliated patterns on Castor Ware.

ware, the indenting would have to be performed with the vessel in as pliable a state as it could be taken from the lathe. A thick slip of the same body would then be procured, and the ornamentation would proceed.

"The vessels—on which are displayed a variety of hunting subjects, representations of fishes, scrolls, and human figures—were all glazed," Mr. Artis says, "after the figures were laid on; where, however, the decorations are white,

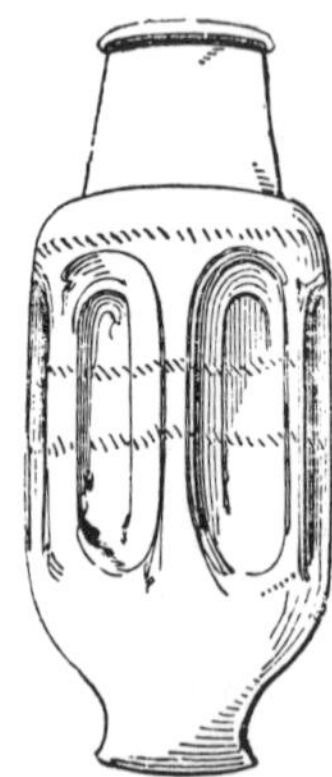

Fig. 125.

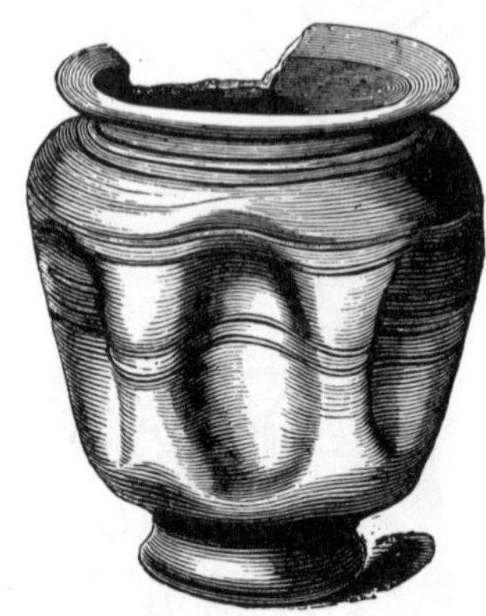

Fig. 126.

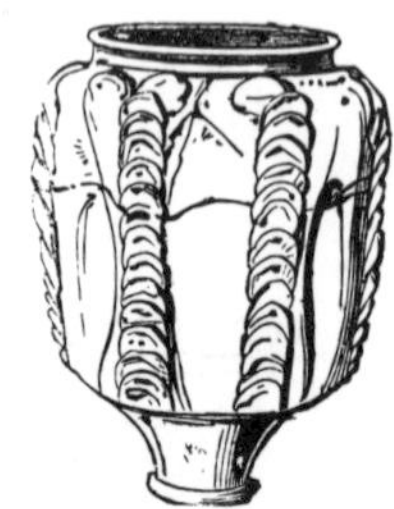

Fig. 127.

Castor Ware.

the vessels were glazed before the ornaments were added. Ornamenting with figures of animals was effected by means of sharp and blunt skewer instruments and a slip of suitable consistency. These instruments seem to have been of two kinds —one thick enough to carry sufficient slip for the nose, neck, body, and front thigh; the other of a more delicate kind, for a thinner slip, for the tongue, lower jaws, eye, fore and hind legs, and tail. There seems to have been no retouching, after the slip trailed from the instrument. Field sports seem to have been favourite subjects with our Romano-British artists. The representations of deer and hare hunts are good and spirited; the courage and energy of the hounds and the distress of the hunted animals are given with great skill and fidelity, especially when the simple and off-handed process by which they must have been executed is taken into consideration.

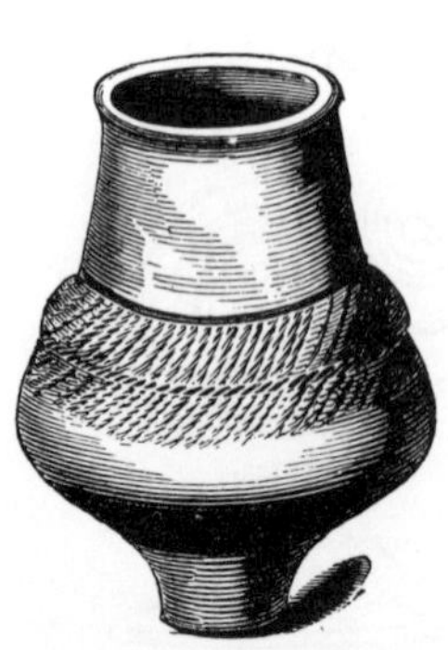

Fig. 128.—Engine-turned Ware.

Two vessels with these hunting subjects are given in Figs. 108 and 110; and other designs of this character, exhibiting stag and hare hunts, are shown on Figs. 103 to 109.

Gladiatorial combats are also frequent subjects for representation on the Castor vases. One of these is given on Fig. 111, which represents one side of the celebrated "Colchester vase;" Fig. 103 being the design of another of its sides. The next engraving (Fig. 112) shows the chariot race in the Roman racecourse or stadium—the quadriga being well, although rudely, fashioned, and the position both of the horses and charioteer boldly conceived. Mythological subjects were also common. One of these, of the indented form, restored from fragments, is given in the accompanying engraving (Fig. 113).

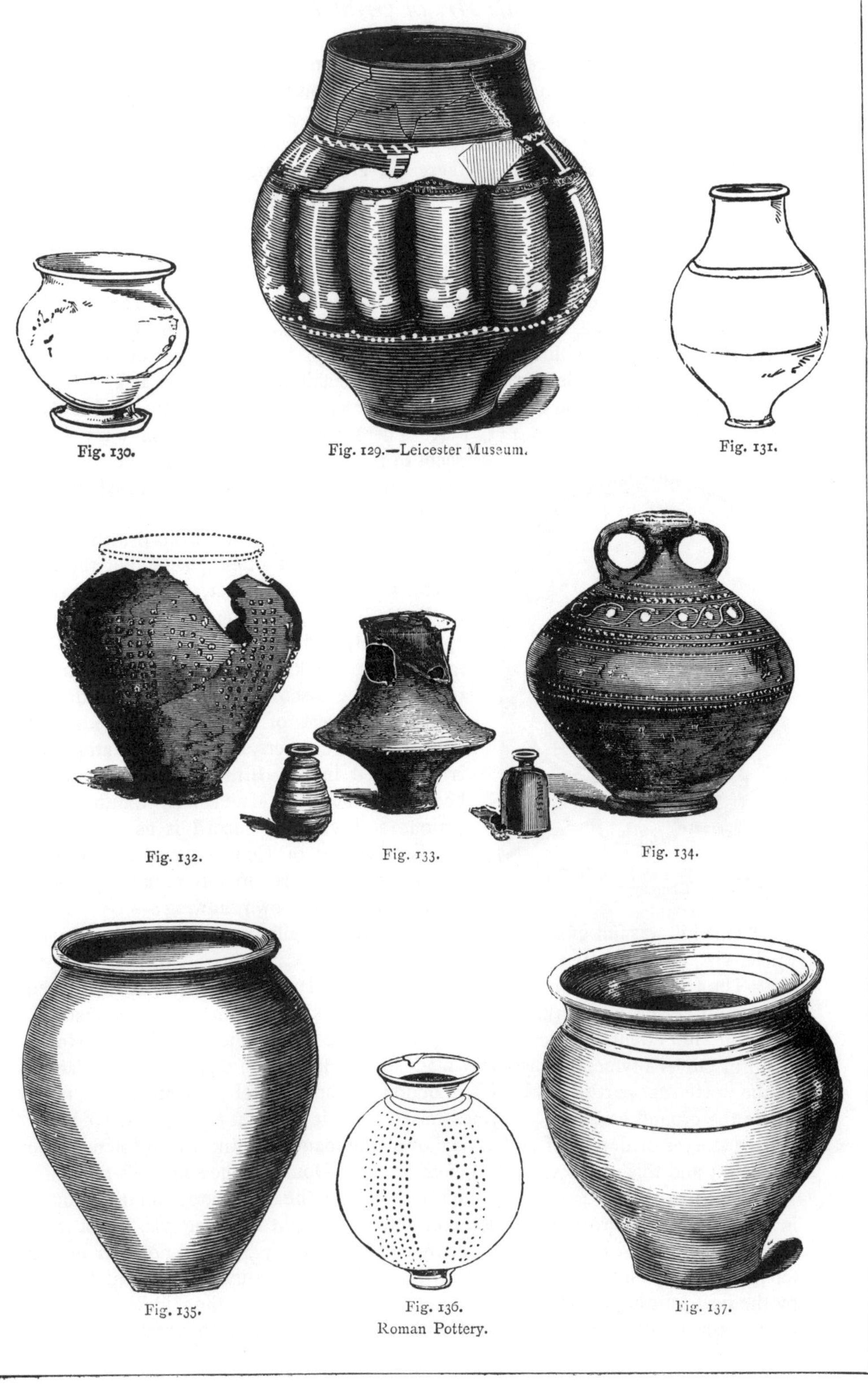

Fig. 130. Fig. 129.—Leicester Museum. Fig. 131.

Fig. 132. Fig. 133. Fig. 134.

Fig. 135. Fig. 136. Fig. 137.

Roman Pottery.

Another and equally pleasing variety of ornamentation, and one peculiar, it may be said, to the Durobrivian potteries, is that whereon the pattern consists of scrolls and flowers in white slip on the dark bluish black ground. The effect of these simple patterns, which are generally graceful and always elegantly formed, is remarkably pleasing. Examples of these are given on Figs. 114 to 124, which will serve to show the general style of this kind of decoration. Figs. 125 to 128 are admirable examples of the indented form of vessel. Many other shapes and varieties of Castor ware might be adduced, but the illustrations I have given will be sufficient to give a clear insight into their general characteristics.

One of the most curious and interesting urns of this ware (Fig. 129) was dug up in Leicester in 1869, and is preserved in the museum of that town. It is of a fine rich deep colour, with the pattern in white slip, and has borne an inscription, also in slip, the only letters of which now remaining are M E I I VI. In the same museum, among other varieties of Romano-British ware, are the beautiful vessels shown on Figs. 132, 133, 134. There are also fragments of ware which seem to point at pottery which I believe, at one period of Roman occupation, existed in the neighbourhood of Leicester.

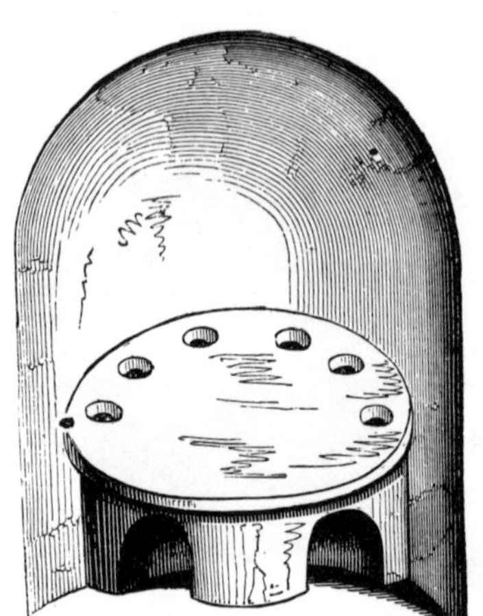

Fig. 138.—Potter's Kiln, St. Paul's Churchyard.

Potters' kilns of the Romano-British period have been found in other places, but those at Castor are the most perfect, and in every way the best. Indeed, the others may be said, more appropriately perhaps, to be indications of kilns rather than the kilns themselves. A curious record of the discovery of a kiln in London, at the north-west of St. Paul's Cathedral, in 1677, by John Conyers, a collector of antiquities, is preserved in the British Museum, and has been published by Mr. Roach Smith. This curious and valuable record is as follows, in the handwriting of Conyers, and the accompanying engraving is carefully reduced (see Fig. 138) from Conyers' own drawing:—

"This kill was full of the coarser sorts of potts or cullings, so that few were saved whole, viz., lamps, bottles, urnes, dishes.

"The forme of a kill in which the olde Romans' lamps, urnes, and other earthen pottes and vessels was burnt, and some left in the kill; and that within a unstired, loamy ground about 26 foot deep near about the place where the Market House stood in Oliver's tyme, the discovery made anno 1677 at the digging the foundacion of the north-east part of St. Paull's, London, among gravel pitts and loam pitts, where the ground had been at tymes raised over it 3 or 4 tymes, and so many 8 foote storyes or depths of coffins lay over the loamy kill, the lowest coffins made of chalk; and this supposed to be before or about Domitian the emperor's tyme.

"Of these (kilns) 4 severall have been made in the sandy loam on the ground in the fashion of a cross foundacion and only this height standing, viz. 5 foot from topp to bottom and better; and as many feet in breadth; and had no other matter for its form and building but the outward loame as it naturally lays, crusted hardish by the heat burning the loame redd like brick. The floor in the middle supported by and cut out of loame, and helped with old-fashioned Roman tyles shards, but very few, and such as I have seen used for repositorys for urns in the fashion of like ovens, and they plastered within with a reddish mortar or tarris; but here was no mortar, but only the sandy loam for cement."

"observed and thus described

"by Jo[N] CONYERS, Apothecary."

From the drawings which accompany the descriptions, the Romano-British origin of the examples found actually in the kiln is placed beyond doubt. Most of them are precisely the same types as hundreds of fragments which have been found all over London, and are the common table and culinary ware of the period. Some bear a very striking resemblance to the vessels from the Upchurch pottery. Amongst them is a mortarium. Most of the vessels are plain, but some are ornamented with rows of dots, &c., and others with a reticulated pattern. The forms are elegant and simple.

In another part of his MS. Conyers describes other kinds of pottery found during the excavations. "Now these pottsherds," he writes, "are some glass and some potts like broken urns, which were curiously laid on the outside with like thorne pricks of rose trees and in the manner of raised work: this upon potts of murry collour, and here and there grey houndes and stags and hares all in raised work: other of these cinamon collour urne fashion and were as gilded with gold but vaded: some of strange fashioned juggs the sides bent in so as to be six squares, and these raised work upon them and curiously pinched as curious raisers of paist may imitate: some like black earth for pudding panns; one the outside indented and crossed quincunx fashion. Now many of these potts of the finer kind are lite and thinn and these workes raised or indented were instead of collours: yet I find they had some odd collours, not blew, in those ymes, and a way of glazing different to what now; and here takes notice that the redd earth before mencioned bore away the belle."

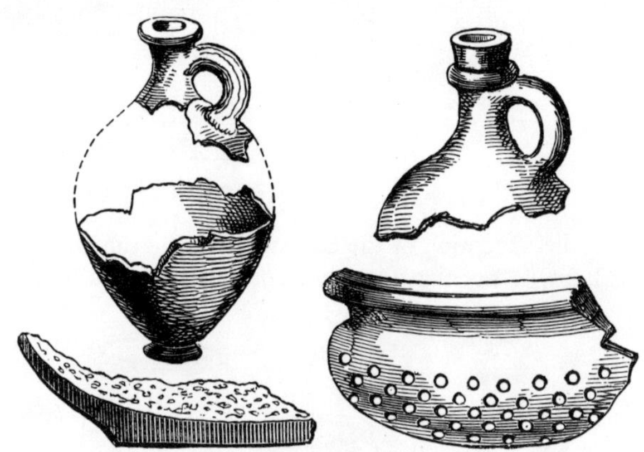

Fig. 139.—Salopian Ware.

Remains of potteries of this period have also been discovered in Norfolk (between Brixton and Brampton); at Botham in Lincolnshire; in Somersetshire; at Worcester; at Marlborough; at Sibson; at various places in Yorkshire; in Shropshire; in Oxfordshire; in Dorsetshire; in the New Forest, Hampshire; at Colchester, in Essex; at Wilderspool, near Warrington; and in many other parts of the kingdom. Of some of these I shall now proceed briefly to speak.

To the Shropshire potteries—those of the clays of the Severn valley, probably at Broseley,—a vast number of varieties of vessels are to be traced; and it is, as I shall show in a later chapter, interesting to know that the same bed of clay which at the present day produces articles of daily use, produced fifteen hundred years ago the vessels for the table, &c., of the inhabitants of the then great neighbouring city of Uriconium. In the excavations which have been undertaken on the site of this ruined city immense quantities of fragments of pottery have been found, and,

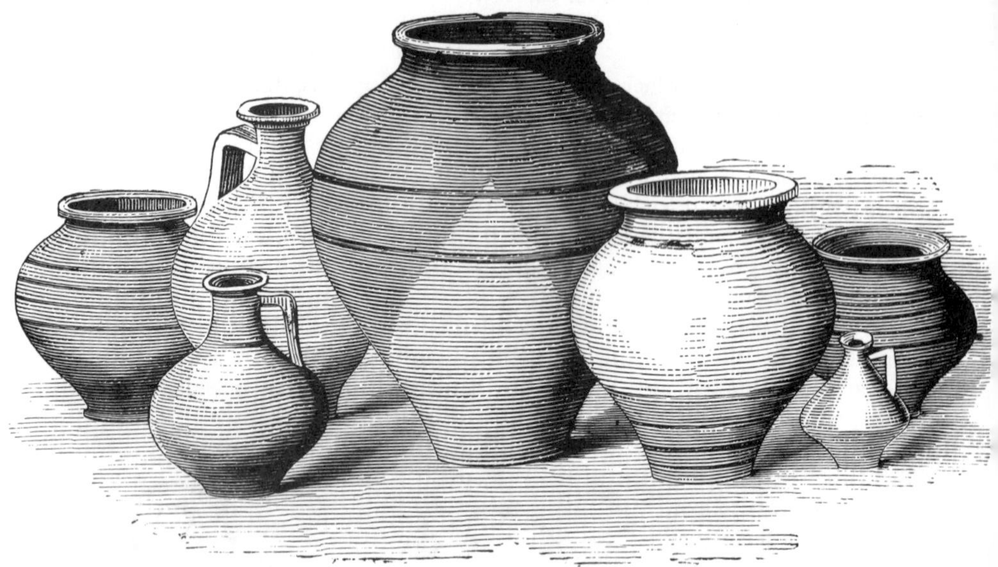

Fig. 140.—Pottery from Uriconium.

with the exception of the Samian ware and the Durobrivian ware, it is not too much, perhaps, to say that the whole, or nearly so, has been made in the Severn valley. Of

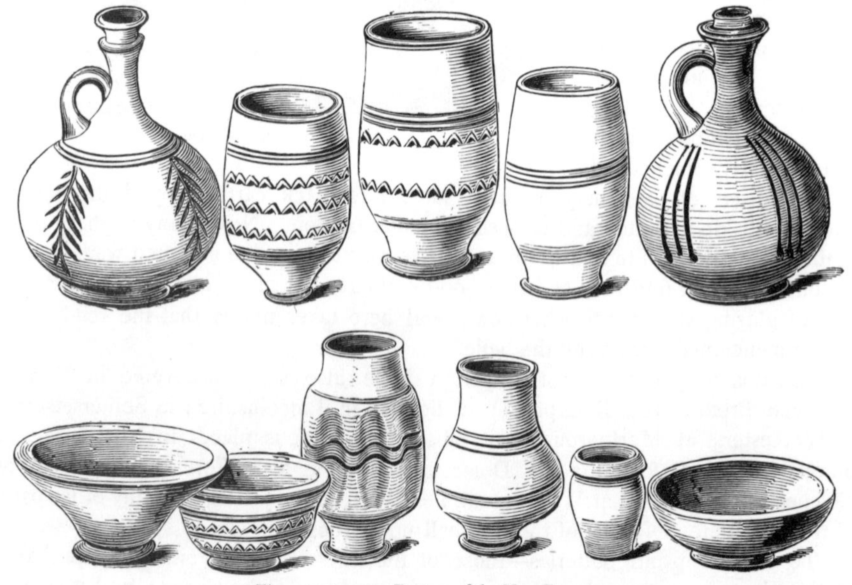

Figs. 141 to 151.—Pottery of the New Forest.

these wares, two sorts especially are found in considerable abundance; the one white, the other of a rather light red colour. The white, which is made of what is commonly called Broseley clay, and is rather coarse in texture, consists chiefly of rather handsomely-shaped jugs or bellarmine-shaped vessels, of different sizes, the general shape of which somewhat resembles Fig. 96; of Mortaria; and of bowls of different shapes and sizes, which are often *painted* with stripes of red and yellow. The other variety, the red Romano-Salopian ware, is also made from one of the clays of the Severn Valley, but is of finer texture, and consists principally of jugs not dissimilar to those in the white ware, except in a very different form of mouth and of bowl-shaped colanders.

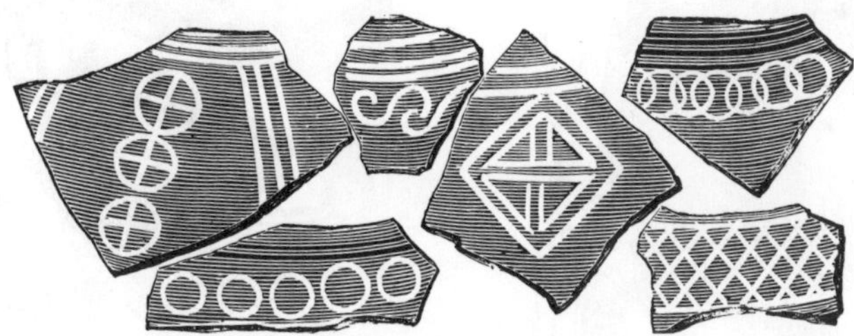

Figs. 152 to 157.—Pottery of the New Forest.

Two examples of Romano-Salopian ware—the first of the white, and the second of the red variety—are given on Fig. 139, and on Fig. 140 is represented a group of vessels of this make, from the cemetery at Uriconium.

The potteries of the New Forest in Hampshire, for a lucid account of which we are indebted to Mr. J. R. Wise, were of great extent, and, as is proved by the researches which have been made on their sites, of considerable importance. The potteries were noticed in 1853 by the Rev. J. P. Bartlett, who prepared an account of his researches for the Society of Antiquaries, and since that period both that gentleman and Mr. Wise continued their explorations with great success. The

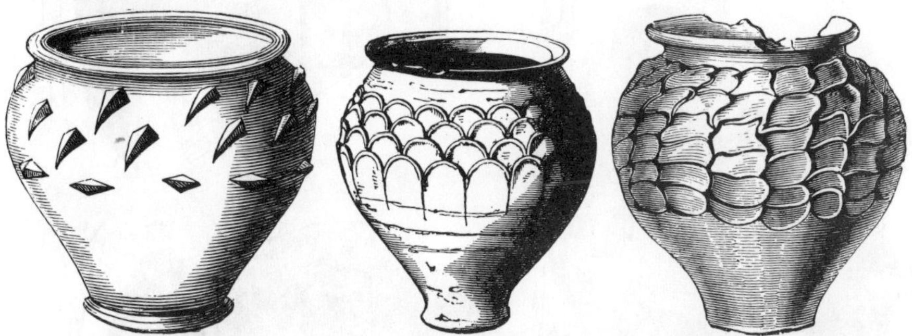

Fig. 158.—Derby Museum. Fig. 159.—Jermyn Street Museum. Fig. 160.—York Museum.

names of the localities where these ancient potteries exist—*Crockle* (crock kiln or crock hill) and *Panshard*—are highly suggestive. During the excavations kilns were found in a perfect state. The kiln at Crockle was circular, and measured six yards in circumference, its shape being well defined by small hand-formed masses of red brick-earth. The floor, about two feet below the natural surface of the ground, was paved with a layer of sand-stones, some of them cut into a circular shape so as to fit the kiln, the upper surfaces being tooled, whilst the under remained in their original state. At the potteries at Audenwood no kilns were discovered; but at

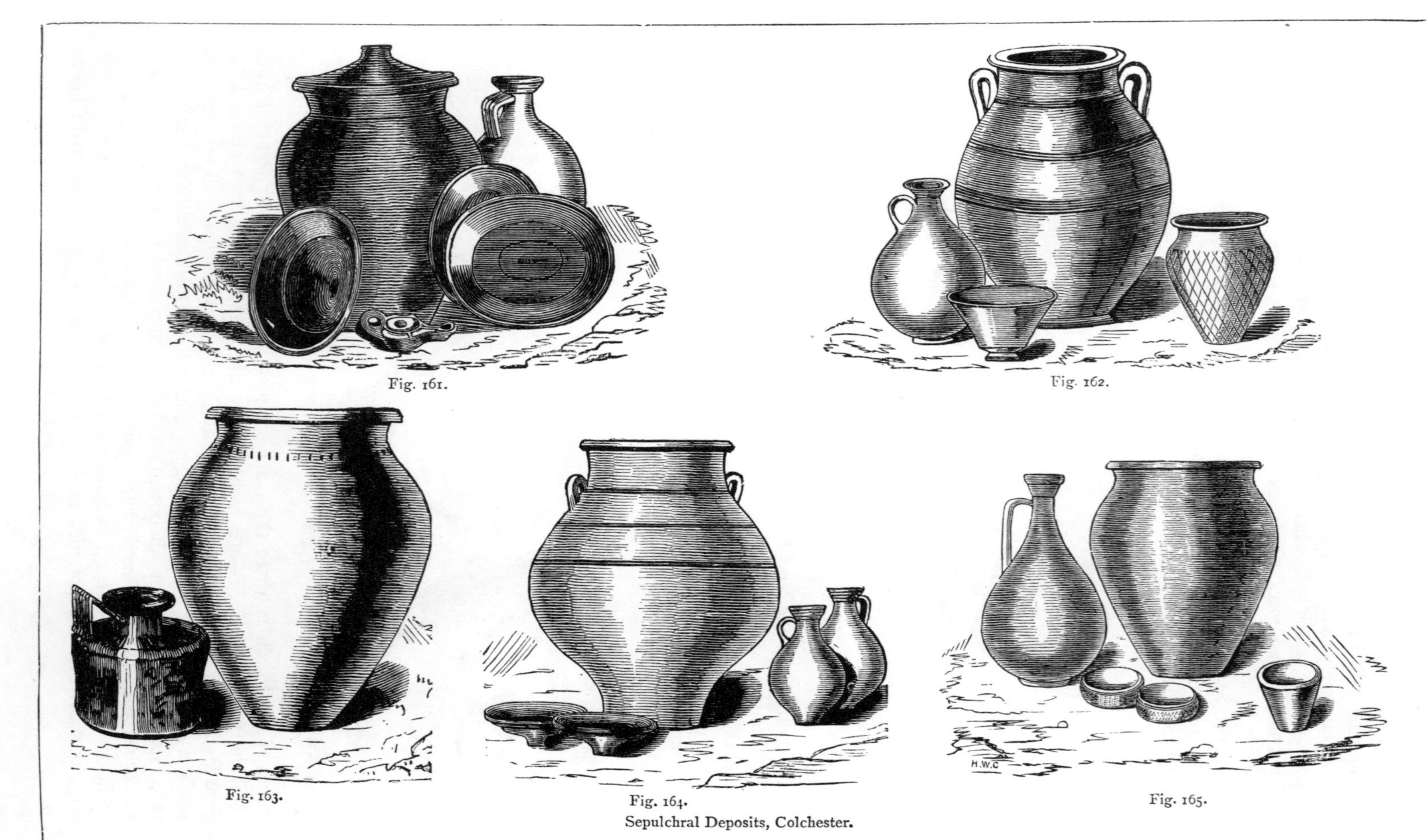

Fig. 161.

Fig. 162.

Fig. 163.

Fig. 164.

Fig. 165.

Sepulchral Deposits, Colchester.

Sloden, where the works cover several acres, "two large mounds marking the sites of kilns" are remaining, along with the sites of potters' huts, &c. At Island Thor more kilns and innumerable fragments of vessels of various kinds were discovered. In *Pitt's Enclosure*, besides mounds opened by Mr. Bartlett, Mr. Wise discovered in one mound five kilns, ranged in a semicircle, and paved with irregular masses of sandstone. They were close together, separated only by mounds of the natural soil. Besides fragments of various vessels, "two distinct heaps of white and fawn-coloured clay and red earth, placed ready for mixing, and a third of the two worked together, fit for the immediate use of the potter," were found with these kilns.

Some of the more usual and more striking forms of the vessels from New Forest potteries are grouped together on Figs. 141 to 151. A selection of patterns from the wares are grouped on Figs. 152 to 157, some of which will be seen to bear a close resemblance to those of the Castor ware.

Of the potter's kiln, &c., found near Colchester, where probably some ware in imitation of the fine red Samian was produced, a notice will be found in "Collectanea Antiqua." In the Yorkshire potteries—for there can be little doubt that at

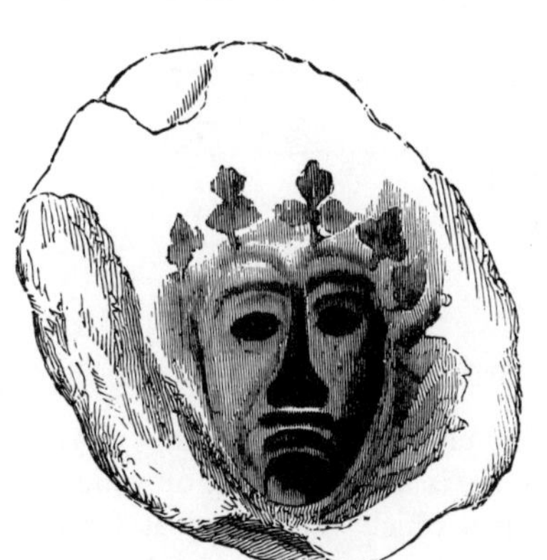

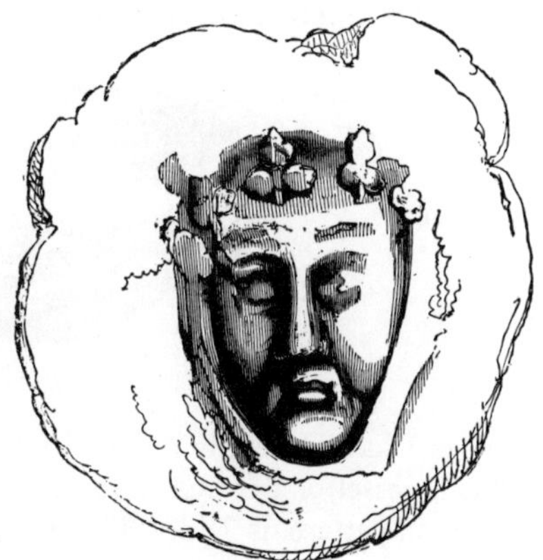

Figs. 166 and 167.—Potter's Mould, Headington.

Potters Newton, at York, and at other places pot works existed in these early times —the curious vessels ornamented with what are usually called "frill patterns" were made, as also other slip and scaled patterns, as on Figs. 158, 159, and 160.

At Headington, Oxfordshire, I had the good fortune myself to discover in 1849, along with the remains of a villa and other buildings traces of a kiln and of many other interesting features, of which I published an account in the "Journal of the British Archæological Association." The fragments of pottery found on this site were extremely varied, and attended with some very unusual facts. One of the most curious and interesting matters was the discovery of a clay mould bearing a beautifully-formed female head (a bacchante) with a wreath of vine leaves encircling her brow, for the forming of heads on Romano-British pottery. Fig. 166 shows this mould, and Fig. 167 gives the impression taken from it. The face has a remarkably pleasing expression, and is beautifully formed. The mould is a rough lump of red clay, and has been broken on its sides.

The pottery, with but one or two exceptions, was in fragments; from these the engravings here given have been carefully restored. One very remarkable feature was the immense assemblage—a cartload at least—of fragments of mortaria. In form and material they differed considerably from those found in other localities. Some were of a fine buff-coloured clay, others of a lead colour, as produced by the smother kiln, and all well studded with broken quartz. In size they varied from

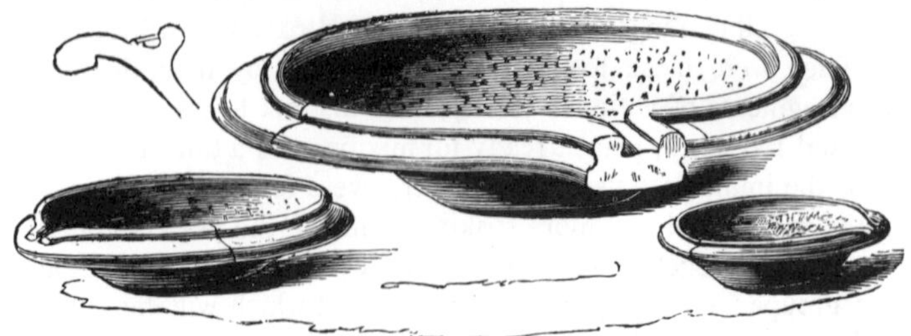

Figs. 168 to 170.—Mortaria, from Headington.

seven and a half inches to nearly two feet in diameter. The larger one on Fig. 168 was one foot nine inches in diameter, while the smaller one is only seven and a half inches. The sections of the rims of the Headington mortaria are dissimilar to

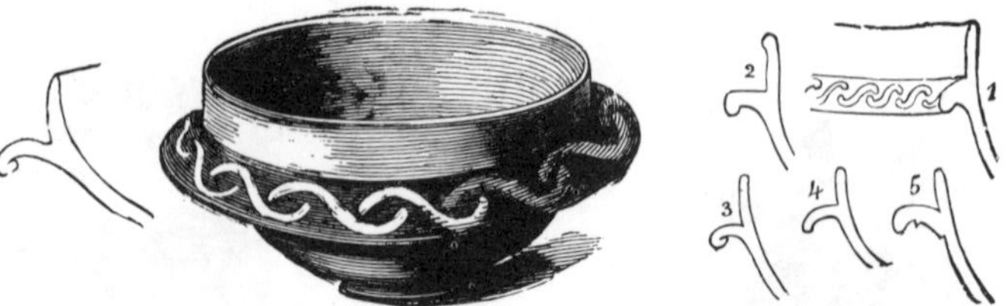

Fig. 171.—From Headington.

others, as I have carefully pointed out in the communication mentioned. Fig. 171 exhibits a vessel of fine red ware, the rim of which is painted black, on which the white scroll-pattern is laid. The sections of rims which accompany it for com-

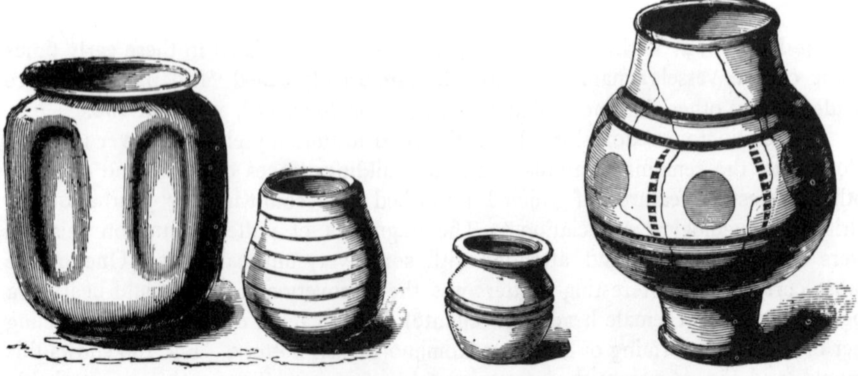

Figs. 172 to 175.—From Headington.

parison sake are, besides its own rim,—1, red with white pattern; 2, a fine red ware; 3, a fine ware, with a metallic surface; and 4 and 5, imported Samian. Fig. 175 is of chocolate colour, and is ornamented with an indented pattern of lines of squares, alternating with flat circles. Fig. 172 is of blue-gray colour, of fine and close and

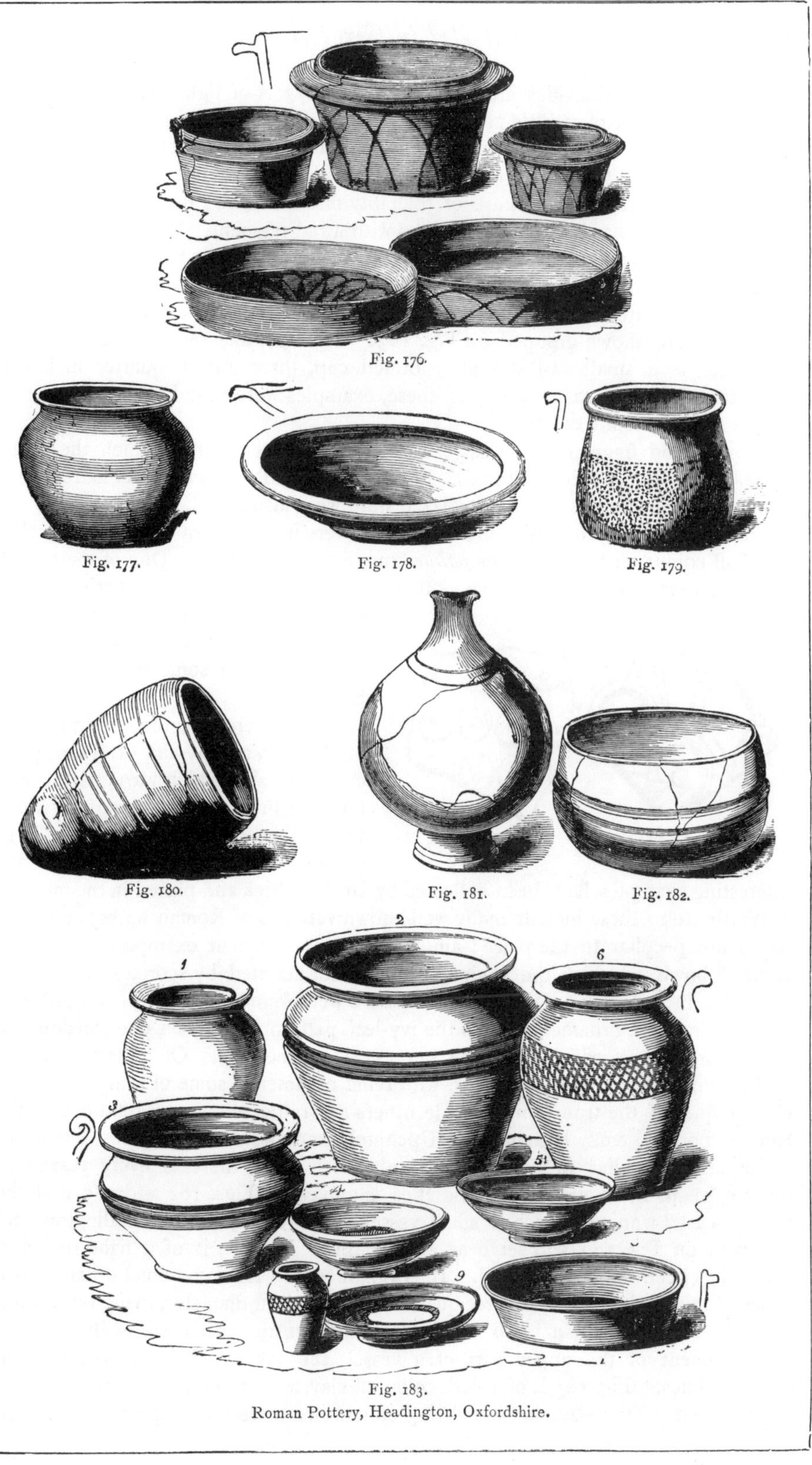

Fig. 176.

Fig. 177. Fig. 178. Fig. 179.

Fig. 180. Fig. 181. Fig. 182.

Fig. 183.

Roman Pottery, Headington, Oxfordshire.

very hard texture; the sides are indented. Fig. 173 is of light buff colour. The curious assemblage of vessels grouped on Fig. 176 are formed of a fine black clay mixed with sand. They are beautifully formed, and many of them are ornamented with surface lines traced on the clay without incision or indentation. The two examples (Figs. 181 and 182) are of tolerably fine red ware; the taller one (which has had a handle) has been surface-coated with a red pigment. Fig. 178 is of coarse red ware, and, as will be seen, is much the same in form as our modern soup-plates. Fragments of vessels of the form of Fig. 180 were very numerous. They were of coarse, buff-coloured ware. Other examples found during the excavations which I carried on are shown grouped on Fig. 183. Fig. 179, like the rest, restored from fragments, is a small and delicately-formed cup, three and a quarter inches in diameter, of "rough-cast" ware; of these, examples were found, some of red, and others of a chocolate colour.

Some good fragments of Castor ware were discovered, from which the group (Figs. 97 to 99) has been restored. Fig. 174 is a small cup of buff-coloured ware. Several small fragments of a green glazed ware were also found.

Among the most curious of the discoveries were fragments of vessels of fine clay, of a buff colour, with the patterns *painted* in red on their surface. One of these bears the rude representation of a cock; others have waved and scrolled patterns; and others again, lines, dots, circles, &c. Many other varieties of wares were also found, as were some few fragments of Samian.

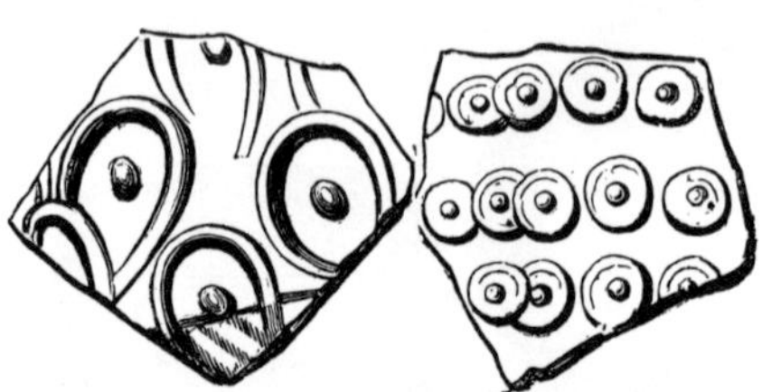

Figs. 184 and 185.—From Wilderspool

At Wilderspool, the presumed site of *Condate*, an outskirt of Warrington, evidence exists which warrants the supposition that pottery of various kinds was there made by the Romans. A large quantity of fragments, including many interesting examples, have been collected by Dr. Kendrick and placed in the museum at Warrington; these include many well-known varieties of Roman wares, and some which are peculiar to the place; among these are excellent examples of "engine-turned" bowls, in which the engine-turning is surmounted by scoriated ornament; these are in red clay. Of Durobrivian ware were found portions of a bowl with overhanging rim, ornamented with the ivy-leaf pattern in slip; on one portion is a potter's mark, PAT, which has been impressed on the side. Of imitation, or English, Samian, are several fragments, with relief ornaments, some of which are pretty close copies of the true Samian, while others are rather clumsy adaptations of the Samian borders, &c. Examples of Upchurch ware were also found. The wares which seem peculiar to Wilderspool, and which were, there is every reason to believe, made there, are the two varieties engraved on Figs. 184 and 185, and the "rough-cast" ware, of which a small vessel found by myself at Headington, and engraved on Fig. 179, will serve as an example. Fig. 184 is of a light red clay, which has been surface-coloured. It is ornamented with a mammal ornament—a series of raised circles, about three-quarters of an inch in diameter, dying off in their lower half, and having a knob or nipple in the centre. This has evidently been the ornament of the upper part of a vessel, the lower being engine-turned in diagonal lines. Fig. 185 is of a dark-coloured clay, with a similar kind of ornament, but of much smaller size, the discs being only rather more than a quarter of an inch in diameter. The "rough-cast" ware, as this variety (Fig. 179) has been appropriately named by Dr. Kendrick, is a fine kind of red-ware, the vessels in which, after having been "thrown," have, while in their soft, moist state, been powdered all over with small bits of dry clay, and then dipped in thin slip before firing—the roughness having previously been carefully removed from the rims and other parts which were intended to be left plain. Dr. Kendrick claims this to be hitherto "unnoticed, and therefore undescribed;" but here he is in error, for in 1850, in the "Journal of the British Archæological Association," I described a similar ware—the only fragment then known—which I discovered at Headington (Fig. 179), that example being, perhaps, a little finer and of better quality than the present Wilderspool specimens.

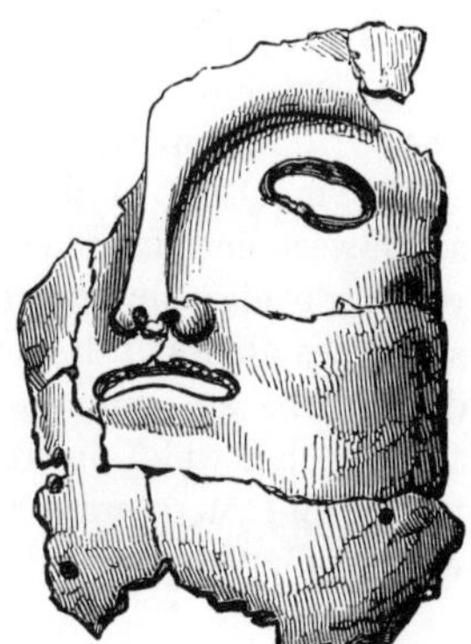

Fig. 186.—Mask, Wilderspool.

Among the most special objects found at Wilders pool are two tetinæ, a tragic mask, and a triplet vase. Of the mask, engraved on Fig. 186, Dr. Kendrick says: "Although it is sadly mutilated, an earthenware mask or visor for the human face is certainly the most rare and curious of the Roman antiquities discovered at Wilderspool. As such it has been described and figured in the seventeenth volume of the "Journal of the Archæological Association." In the British Museum is a single specimen of the comic mask, such as we often see represented on Greek and Roman sculptures or intaglio seals; there is also another mask, with the mouth closed, for the silent actor. The Wilderspool mask appears to be an equally solitary example of the tragic mask, although Pollux, an ancient writer, enumerates twenty-five typical or standing masks of tragedy—six for old men, seven for young men, nine for females, and three for slaves."

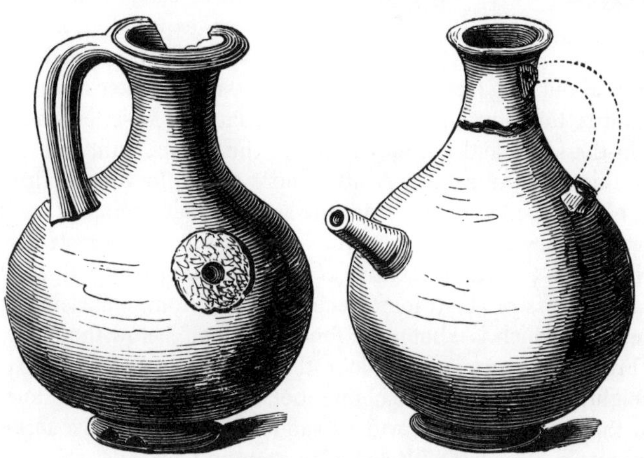

Figs. 187 and 188.—Tetinæ, Wilderspool.

The tetinæ, or feeding-bottles, are engraved on Figs. 187 and 188; they have tubular spouts at the side, and, when used, they were no doubt furnished with soft nipples or teats for the tender mouth of the infant. When found the mouth of each was covered by a fragment of pottery, and, from their upright position and contents, there can be no doubt that they contained the ashes of one or more children. It is also curious to remark that one handle was suited for the right hand of the nurse, and the other for the left, as if to compel a change of posture for the infant.

The triple, or triune vase, restored on Fig. 189, is an excellent specimen, the connecting bands being hollow tubes, so that when the liquor was placed in one, it rose to the same height in each. Many other objects of great interest were found at Wilderspool, and have been carefully described by Dr. Kendrick and illustrated by his daughter.

At Ashdon, in Essex, a potter's kiln was discovered by the Hon. R. C. Neville in 1852. It was of square form, being, as nearly as could be measured, eighteen feet square, inclusive of the outer walls. The furnace appeared to have been at the south-west end, immediately communicating with the central and largest flue; in it was a considerable quantity of charcoal and black ashes. This flue was two feet six inches across at the entrance and two feet in width along the entire length, which divided the structure into two equal portions. From it eight lateral flues (each seven inches wide) diverged opposite each other on either side. It was closed by the north-eastern wall, which was carefully constructed of Roman tiles, which, as well as the flanged tiles in other parts, had evidently been used in some former building. Many fragments of tiles and pottery were strewed about, but no perfect vessel was found.

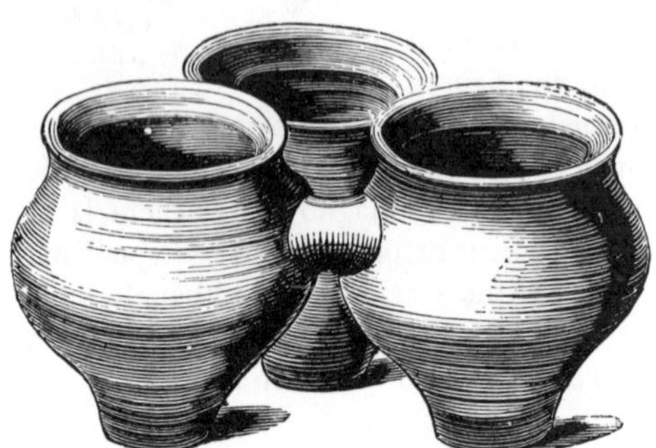

Fig. 189.—Wilderspool.

A kiln was discovered in 1868 at Winterton, near Brigg, on a site about half a mile from the Roman road, and not far from where a tesselated pavement had been previously discovered. By the falling of a portion of the side of a pit where sand was being dug, there was exposed a rudely constructed kiln or oven, made by sinking a circular cavity about six feet deep and six feet in diameter at the top, becoming narrower towards the bottom, so as to be in fact an inverted cone. The lower half of it is in the sand, and the upper half in the surface soil, and in a thin bed of clay between this and the sand. A little more than a foot in depth of the bottom of the pit had been filled with soil from the surface, quite compact, as if it had been mixed with water and well rammed down. On the top of this rested the oven itself, formed by lining the pit with a mixture of coarse mud or clay with small stones and pebbles, to a thickness of about four inches at the bottom, increasing upward to ten inches at the brim, which is about one foot and a half below the present surface of the field. From the centre of the floor thus made rises a pillar of one foot nine inches in height, and widening from one foot diameter at the bottom to one foot ten inches at the top, which pillar widens suddenly so as to form a sort of mushroom head, continuous in structure with the clay or mud floor and walls just described. Two shallow grooves run all round the inside of the oven, a little above the top of the pillar, and broken pieces of blue Roman pottery are laid across from the pillar to the side of the basin so as to cover in a sort of circular flue. Over these has been spread a thin coat of clay similar to the rest of the lining, so that the upper storey, so to speak, is a shallow pit, about three and a half feet diameter and one foot and a half deep. A large quantity of black ashes, and of fragments of Roman pottery,

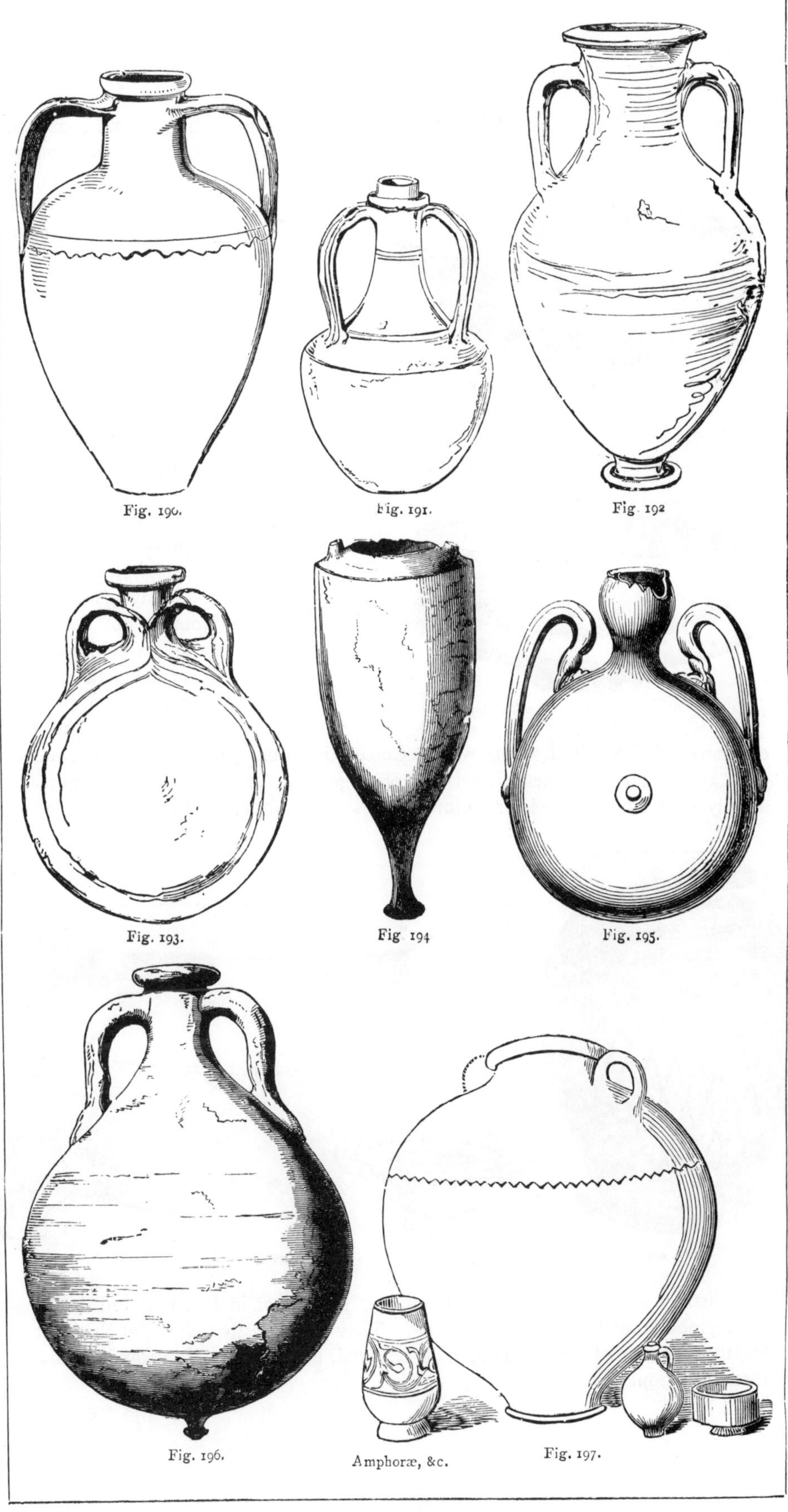

Fig. 190. Fig. 191. Fig. 192

Fig. 193. Fig. 194 Fig. 195.

Fig. 196. Fig. 197.

Amphoræ, &c.

was found in and around the kiln. An account of this discovery, with an engraving of the kiln, appeared in vol. ix. of "The Reliquary." Another, in the same county, was discovered near Ancaster; and in Somersetshire a kiln has been uncovered.

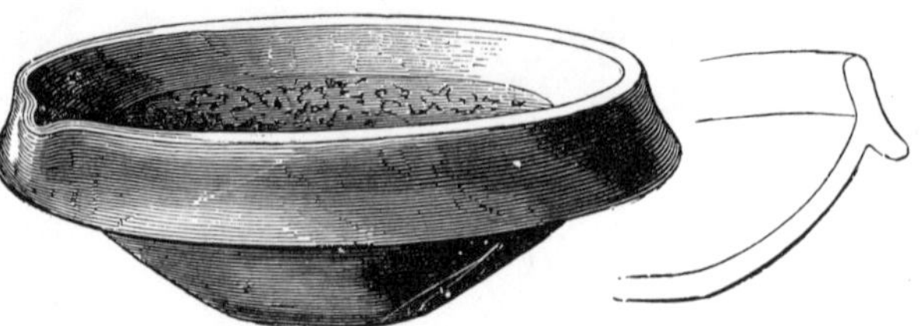
Fig. 198.—Chesterfield.

Many potteries besides those whose productions have been here spoken of might be described; but as their productions were the usual classes of domestic or sepulchral vessels, or flue and other tiles, it is not perhaps necessary to enumerate them. I will therefore proceed to speak of some of the vessels not already particularised in this chapter.

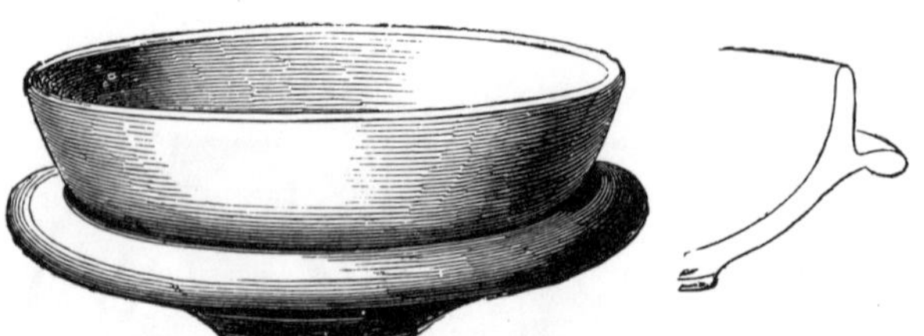
Fig. 199.—Chesterfield.

Amphoræ were undoubtedly made in the Roman pot works of Britain; evidences of their manufacture having been observed in various localities. The most extensive of these indications was at Colchester, from which place the example (Fig. 194) is taken. These vessels are of large dimensions, strongly formed, and usually of a buff, or reddish-yellow colour. The forms of these vessels are of

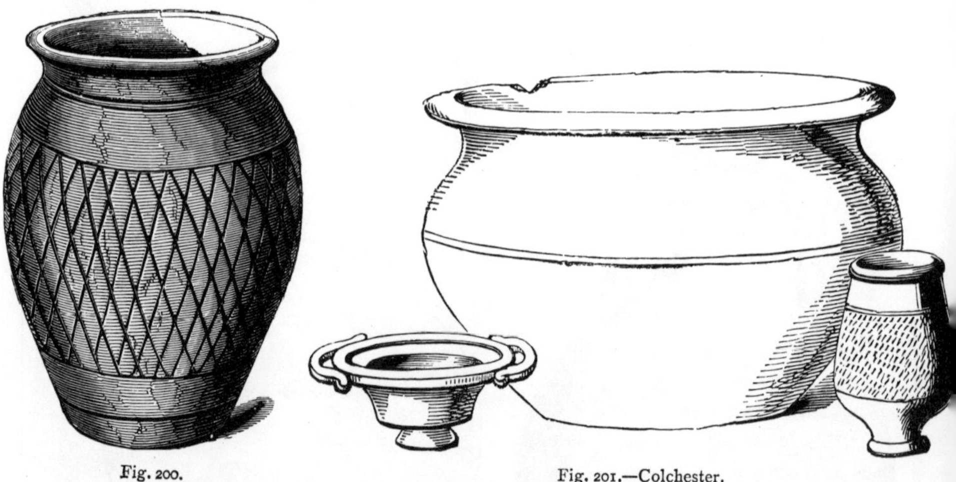
Fig. 200. Fig. 201.—Colchester.

two distinct kinds—the one being tall and slender, as in Fig. 194, and the other more globular, as in Figs. 196 and 197. They were mostly pointed at the bottom, for the purpose of fixing them, it is believed, in the earth, or in stands made for their reception.

Mortaria, of which three examples have been given (Figs. 168 to 170), formed another extensive class of domestic vessels. Their use appears to have been the pounding and beating up, for culinary purposes, of vegetables and other articles. Some of the examples which have been found bear unmistakable signs of long and hard use. Their inner surface was studded, while the clay was soft, either with small fragments of quartz or with scoriæ of iron, so as to promote trituration. The example (Fig. 198) is of somewhat different character, having more upright, and somewhat higher, sides than usual. It has been much used.

Another of the more usual of the domestic vessels, of Romano-British manufacture, is the very convenient kind of basin (Fig. 199), which will be seen to be of the same general shape as Fig. 171. The form of this basin is infinitely better, more elegant, and more convenient than those in use among us at the present day. The central flanged rim is a very secure and handy arrangement for holding. This example, and the mortarium (Fig. 198) were found together—in fact inverted one into the other—in the churchyard at Chesterfield, in Derbyshire. Many other varieties of domestic vessels were also extensively made, but to these it is not necessary farther to refer.

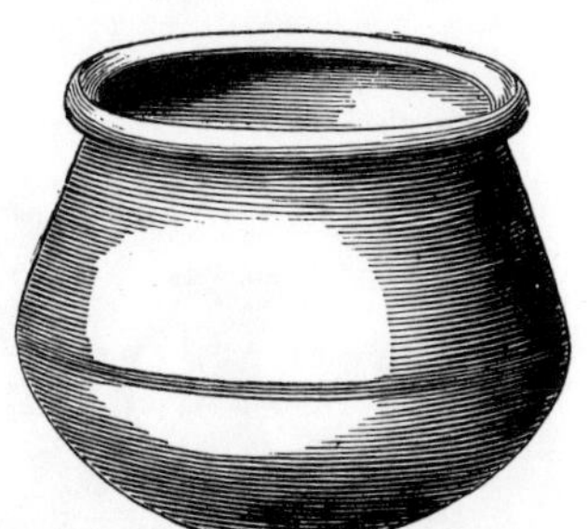

Fig. 202.—Little Chester.

The sepulchral urns of Romano-British manufacture are of extremely varied form and ornamentation. Figs. 78, 135, 137, 140, 161 to 165, and 183, will serve as examples of some of the varieties. The most usual forms, however, are perhaps, Figs. 200 to 205. They are of various kinds of clays, and were generally plain, or but slightly ornamented.

Other good examples of sepulchral urns of various kinds, and of different shapes, will be seen on the three groups of pottery, &c., found at Cirencester, shown on Figs. 203, 204, and 205. On the same engravings will be seen many other characteristic examples of Roman Ceramic Art, as well as some metallic remains.

Building-tiles, flue-tiles, and drain-tiles were a branch of manufacture which was carried on to a considerable extent in various parts of the country, and, no doubt, generally in the immediate neighbourhood of the buildings where they were used. The building-tiles which are to be seen in the remains of the period, as in the Jewry Wall at Leicester, engraved on Fig. 206, where occasionally they form "herring-bone" masonry, are usually from about seven to ten inches square, and about an inch and a half in thickness. They are frequently marked with letters, and with feet of animals which have passed over them (Figs. 207 and 209). The flue-tiles are of various dimensions. They are usually of an oblong square form, hollow throughout, with a lateral opening in one side for the heated air to pass through (see Fig. 214). Others have two channels through the entire length, and are without side openings. They are much ornamented with incised patterns, and occasionally are stamped with letters. Some, too, have figures of dogs, stags, &c. They were used for various purposes. Another example is shown lying down in the centre of the group of tiles on Fig. 210. In this group, the tall example, represented standing upright, will be sufficient to show the form and excellence of construction of the drain-tiles—the small end of each being made to fit with an elbow-joint into the thick end of the next. In the same group are some open-flanged drain-tiles. An inscribed flange-tile is shown on Fig. 217.

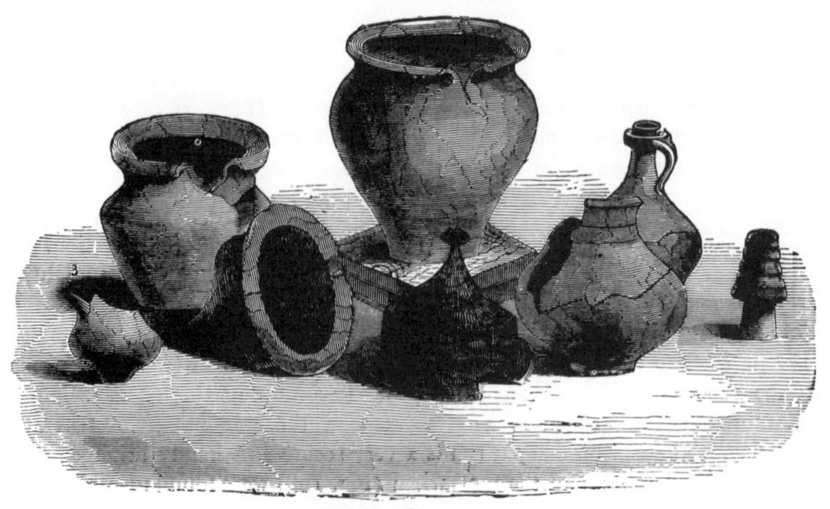

Fig. 203.—Cirencester.

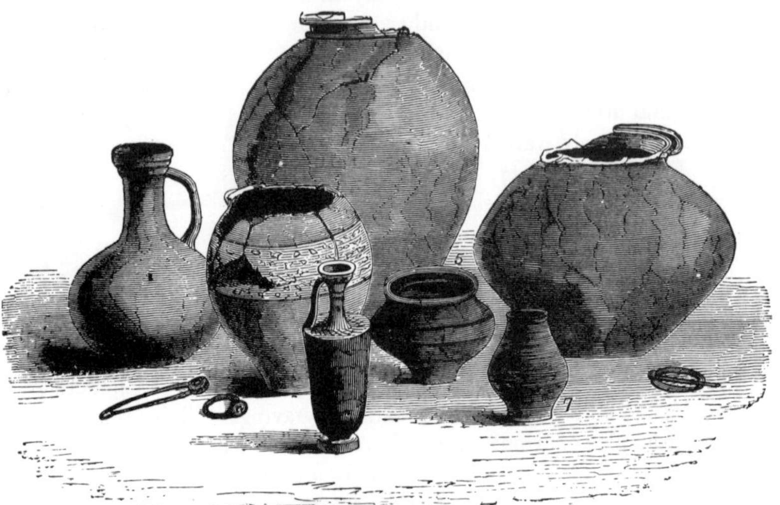

Fig 204.—Cirencester.

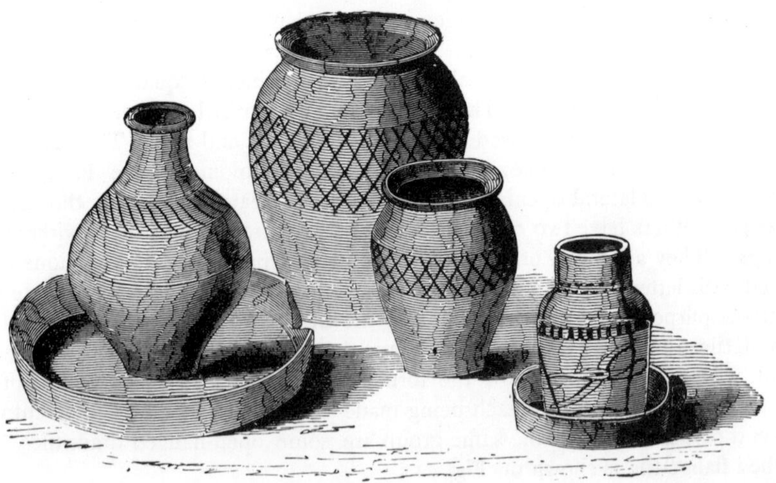

Fig. 205.—Cirencester.

The roofing-tiles were much more calculated to resist the wind and rain than those of later invention. They had flanged sides, which fitted close to each other and were covered at the joint by a small semicircular tile, like a draining or ridge-tile, imbedded in mortar and resting on the two roofing-tiles, as a draining-tile rests on its sole. This arrangement is shown on Fig. 211, which represents some roofing-tiles found at Walesby. Of the ridge-tiles, of semicircular form, to cover the joints, two good examples (Figs. 212 and 215), from Headington, are here given.

It may be added that, on tiles of one kind or other, the name of the legions and cohorts quartered in particular localities where they were made, are frequently found impressed. The soldiers were brick-makers and masons, and made the tiles and built the houses, &c., at the places where they were stationed. Tile-stamps thus become important aids to history.

It is curious to add that some of the tiles which have been found tell a silent

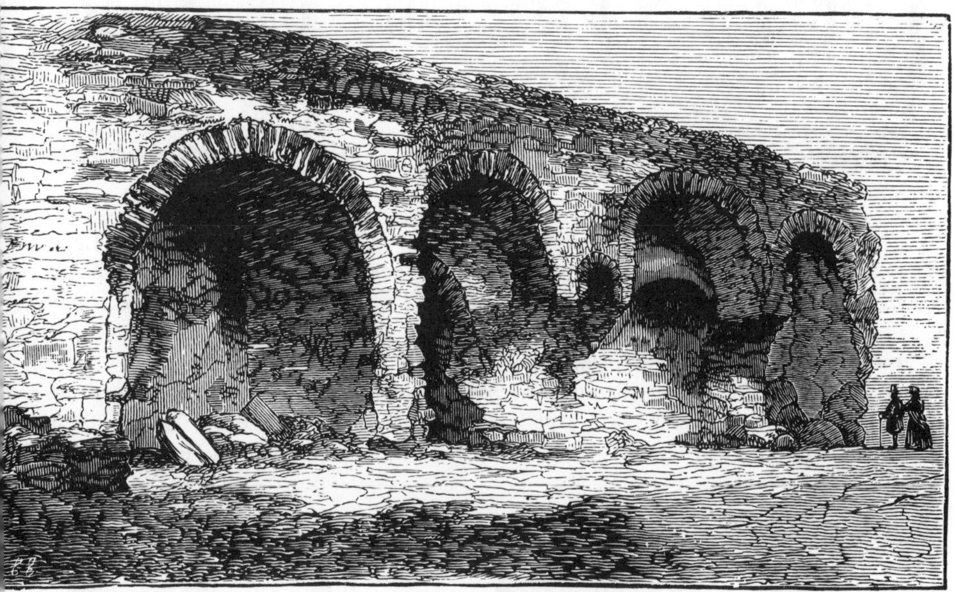

Fig. 206.—The Jewry Wall, Leicester.

tale, which they were never intended to carry, of the dress or hand or foot of the maker, which have become accidentally impressed upon their surface while in a soft state, and are afterwards rendered imperishable by firing in the kiln. One example of this kind of accidental ornamentation (Fig. 207), which exhibits the impress of a man's feet, or, rather, shoes thickly studded with nails,—like the "hob-nailed" boots of our own day,—will suffice as an illustration.

One extraordinary and highly interesting use of tiles among the Roman inhabitants of Britain was that of forming them into tombs. A large tile was laid flat on the ground; two others of the same length were placed upright, one at each side, to form the sides; two shorter ones were placed upright as ends; and another tile formed the cover (Fig. 216). Thus a fictile cist, or chest, was formed, and in this was deposited the sepulchral urn containing the ashes of the departed, with its accompanying group of smaller vessels. Cists of this kind are found frequently in the Roman cemeteries at Colchester. "The practice of enclosing or covering the sepulchral deposits with tiles appears to have been so general, that the word *tegula*, a tile, was often used to signify a tomb."

It appears from Ovid that it was the custom for the relatives to place garlands, fruit, and salt on the tile which covered the sepulchral deposit.

At York, graves, or rather tombs, formed of a number of roof-tiles, have been found. Fig. 218 represents one of these curious tombs. It was formed of ten roof-tiles, four of which were placed on either side and one at each end, and four ridge-

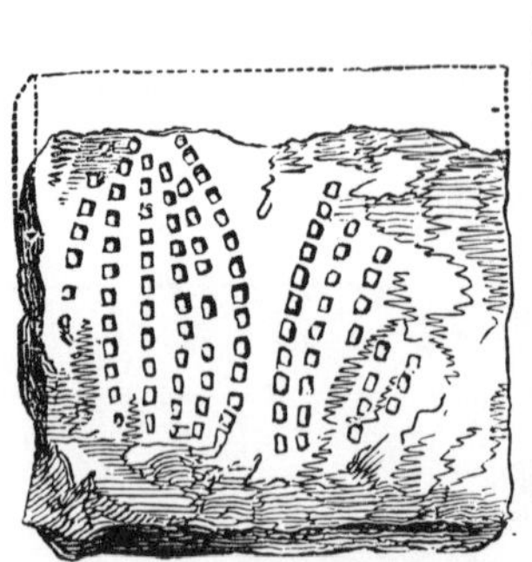

Fig. 207.

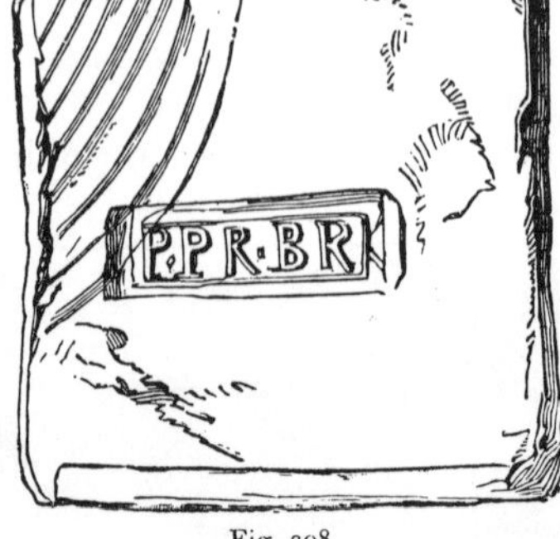

Fig. 208.

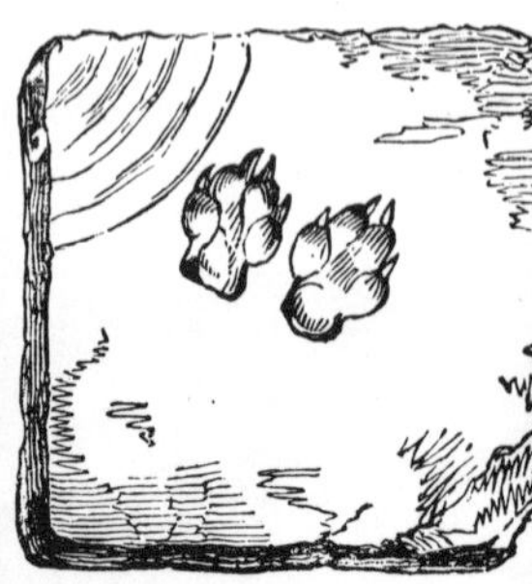

Fig. 209.

tiles arranged along the top. Each tile bore the impressed stamp of the VI. Legion (Leg. VI., *Legio sexta victrix*—the sixth legion victorious). In these tile-tombs urns had in one instance been placed; in another (the one engraved) were the remains of the funeral fire, with the ashes of the dead. Clay coffins have also occasionally been found. One of these, from Aldborough, is shown on Fig. 219.

Lamps were undoubtedly made in various parts of this kingdom, and were more or less ornamented; some bear excellently-executed figures and other devices. Many appear to have been made at Colchester, and are spoken of by Mr. Roach Smith in

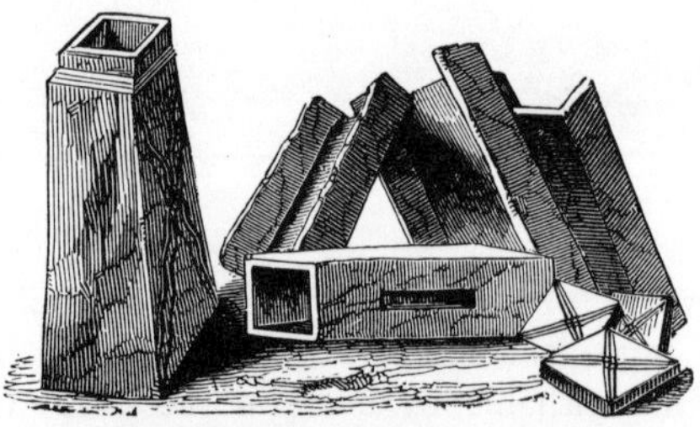

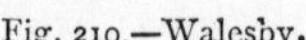

Fig. 210.—Walesby.

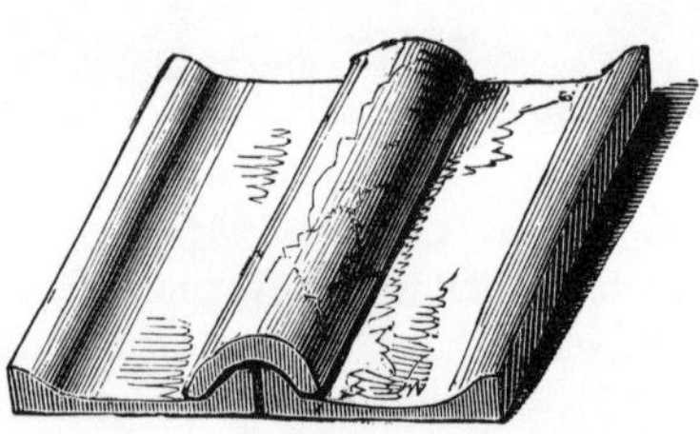

Fig. 211.—Walesby.

his "Collectanea Antiqua." The pot works at this place appear to have been on the Lexden Road, where a kiln and many other remains have been brought to light.

Penates and other figures, or statuettes, were also made in this country; and these, again, it is pretty certain, were made in considerable numbers at Colchester, as were also lachrymatories, unguentaria, &c.

Coin moulds, for the manufacture of spurious Roman coins, were also made of clay, and the arrangement was very simple but effective. The clay, being properly tempered and prepared, was formed into small round tablets of uniform size and

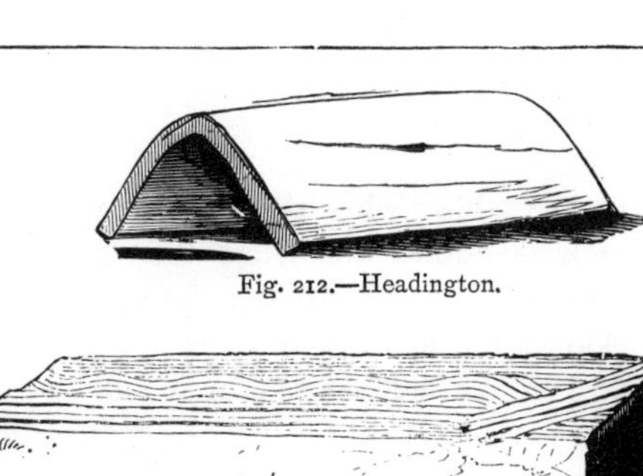

Fig. 212.—Headington.

Fig. 213.—London.

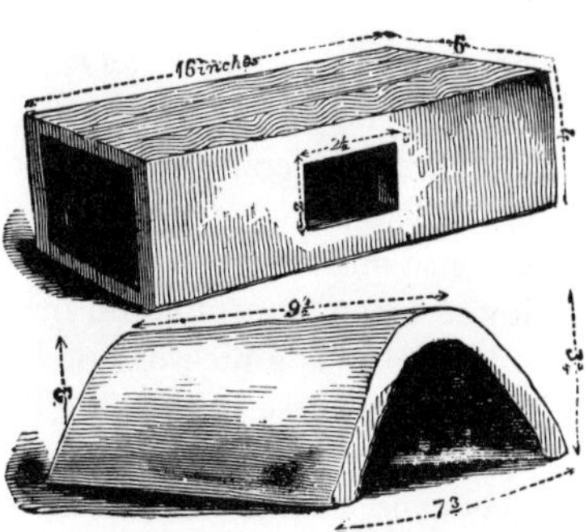

Figs. 214 and 215.—Headington.

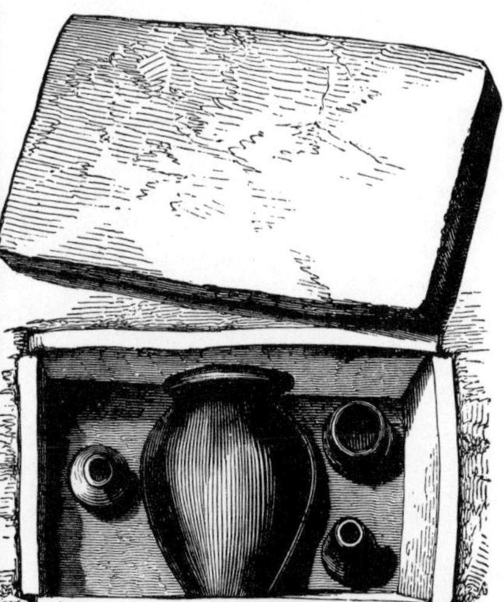

Fig. 216.—Tile Cist, Colchester.

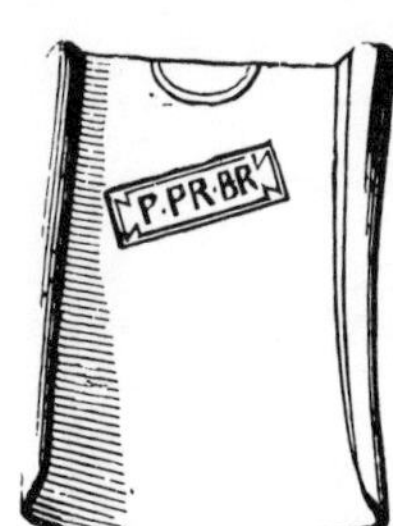

Fig. 217.

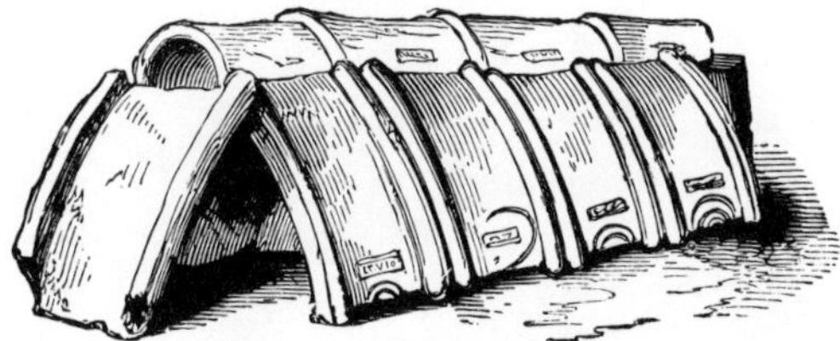

Fig. 218.—Tile Tomb, York.

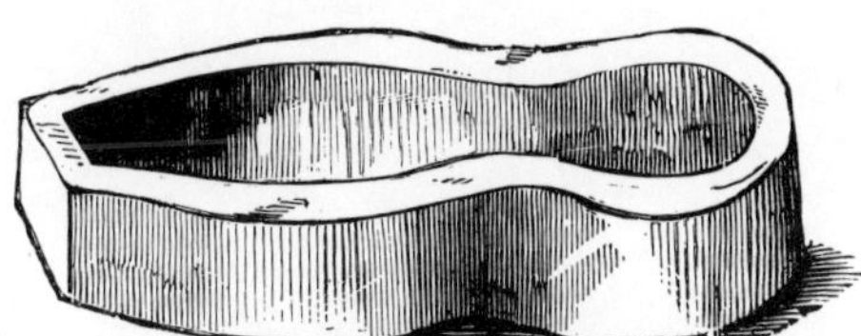

Fig. 219.—Clay Coffin, Aldborough.

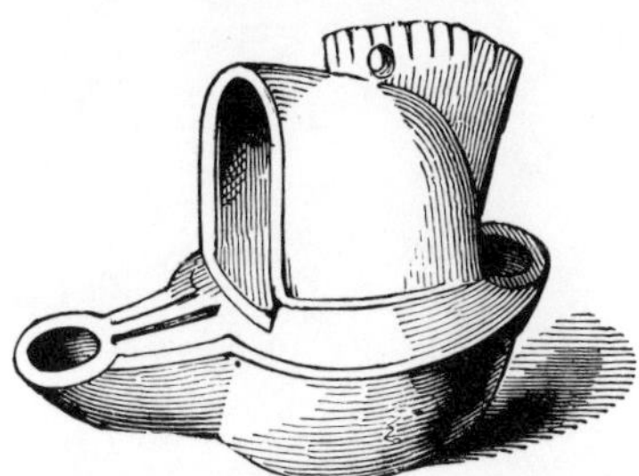

Fig. 220.—Colchester.

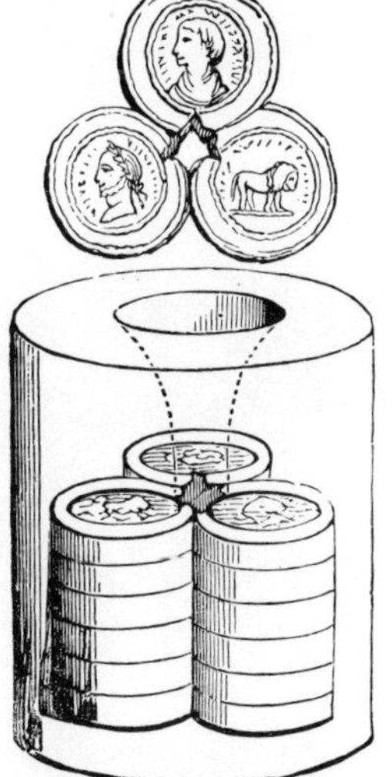

Fig. 221.—Coin Mould.

thickness. A coin was then pressed between two tablets while the clay was soft, so as to leave a perfect impression, and these impressions, which had thus become obverse and reverse moulds, were arranged together in little piles; the upper and lower being impressed on one side only. Down the sides of each of these little piles or heaps a nick or notch was then cut, so as to admit the molten metal. Two or three of these heaps were then, as shown in the engraving (Fig. 221), placed side by side with the notches joined together, and these were then surrounded by a clay cone with a hole at the top, into which the metal was poured, and ran down through the notches, and so into the moulds. Impressions were thus taken the exact counterpart of the original coin from which the moulds had been taken.

CHAPTER III.

FOR examples of the Ceramic Art of the Anglo-Saxon period we are mainly indebted to the cemeteries and burial-grounds of that people. The art during this period, as far as this country is concerned, was but little practised, except, as in the Celtic period, for the manufacture of sepulchral urns of one kind or other. Still, it is pretty certain that many of the vessels found in the barrows were made for the purposes of life, and used for those of death when urns were wanted. In the preceding era the population of this country—the Romano-Britons—were essentially a pot-producing people, and they established, as will have been seen, extensive manufactories in various parts of the kingdom, and made and supplied vessels for every conceivable use and purpose. When the Saxons took possession of the country, and gradually extended themselves over its length and breadth, they found the Roman towns, as well as the stations and detached dwellings—nay, they found every part of the island—well and, indeed, profusely stocked with crockery of every kind, from the finest Samian cup and bowl down to the coarsest mortarium and amphora, in such profusion, and in such variety, as well as of such elegance, use, and beauty, as they had not previously known. Fighting their way here, and settling there, they utilised the crockery which so abundantly lay ready to their hands, and, as there can be no doubt the Roman potters continued their works long after the advent of the Saxons, they used these Roman vessels for all purposes, and thus did not, except in the case of their burial urns, and ordinary domestic vessels, resembling in a somewhat striking manner some modern utensils, leave the impress of what little taste or skill they had upon the productions of the fictile art. The cinerary urns are, therefore, almost the only productions of the Saxon potter which are known. These, like those of the Celtic period, were, there can be no doubt, usually made in pretty close proximity to their place of burial, and, consequently, were formed of the clays of the district. They assumed a peculiar character, and are entirely dissimilar to those of either of the preceding periods.

Of the forms of other vessels of the Anglo-Saxons—for there is no doubt that coarse domestic utensils were to some extent made—a tolerable idea may be gained from the illuminated MSS. of the time. Some few, but very few, examples have also been brought to light, which may with tolerable certainty be assigned to this period.

The engravings (Figs. 222 to 227) showing a few of the forms taken from the illuminated MSS. of this and the succeeding period, are interesting examples. Some of these will be seen to owe their origin—as, for instance, Fig. 226—to Roman design, while others are equally as clearly Franco-Gaulish in character. The Anglo-Saxons were not, like their Roman forerunners, an artistic race. They could not draw the form of the human figure correctly, nor, indeed, that of animals; but their delineations of jugs and pitchers are proved by existing examples to be

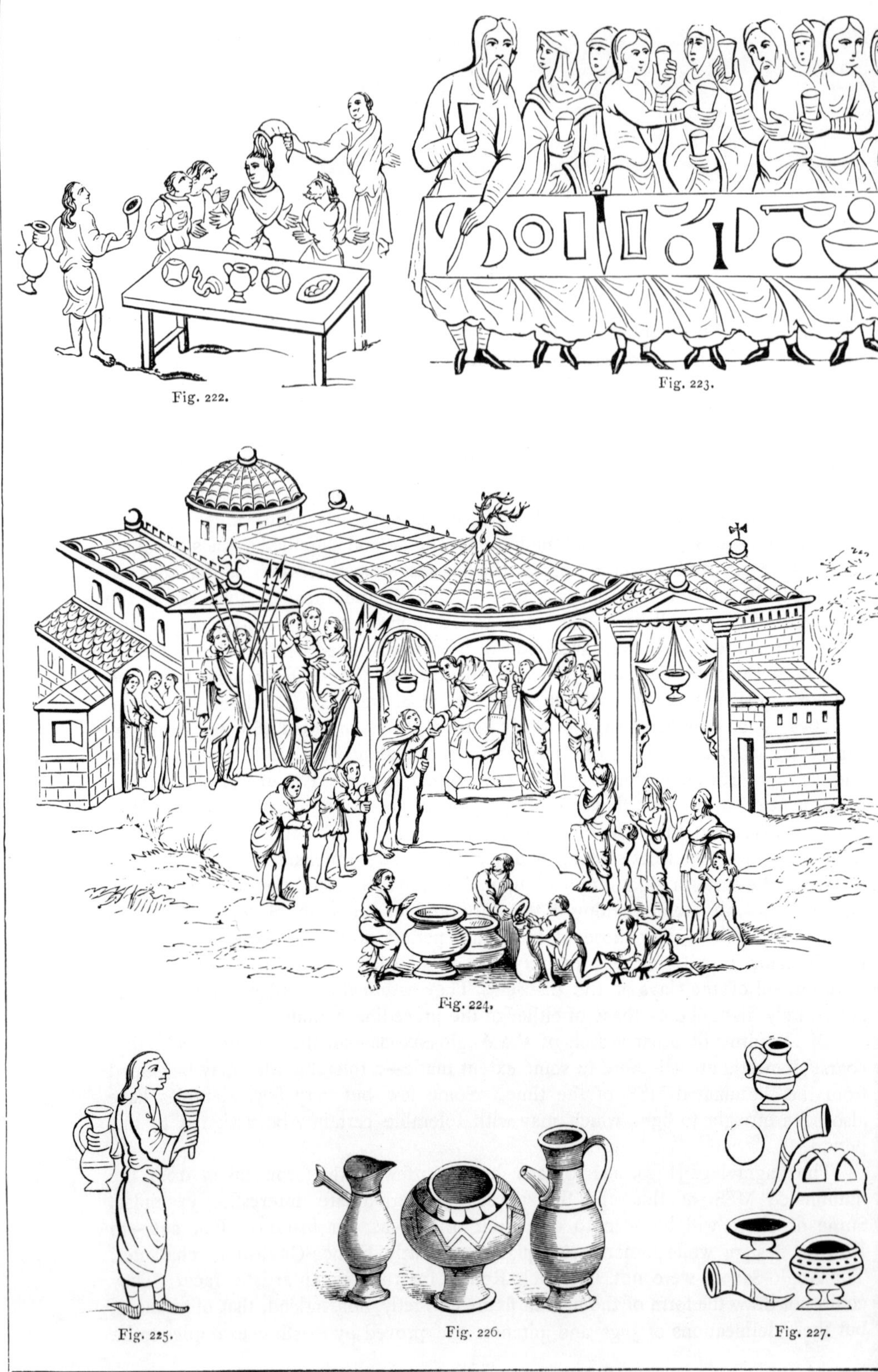

Fig. 222.

Fig. 223.

Fig. 224.

Fig. 225.

Fig. 226.

Fig. 227.

pretty accurate. Their mind, as a rule, was coarse and unpoetic as their own beer, while that of the Roman was bright and sparkling as his own champagne.

The scene depicted on Fig. 224 exhibits some well-formed vessels in the foreground, while the dinner scene on Fig. 222 shows other varieties.

For culinary purposes the Anglo-Saxons appear to have had an aversion to clay, hence their bowls were principally of metal or wood—generally of ash, and their drinking-vessels were of horn or glass. These glasses were made rounded or pointed at the bottom; thus they must have been filled while held, and could not without spilling have been set down till emptied. From these the name of "tumblers" takes its origin. For a drinking-cup and wine-pitcher, see our cut, Fig. 225, and for two of these "tumblers," see Figs. 228 and 231. One form of

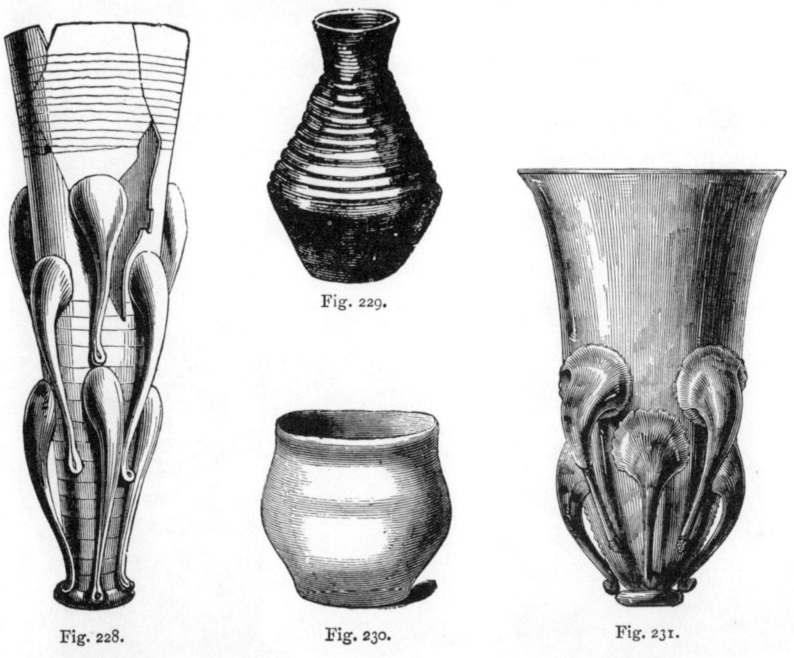

Fig. 228. Fig. 229. Fig. 230. Fig. 231.

vessel, made of coarse buff-coloured clay, is here shown (Fig. 229); and another of simple form is shown on Fig. 230.

The pottery of the Anglo-Saxon grave-mounds and cemeteries consists, unlike that of the preceding periods, almost exclusively of cinerary urns, and these have as has been already stated on a previous page, been made near the place of sepulture; and, as a natural consequence, of the clays found in the neighbourhood. This is proved, incontestably, in the case of the urns found at King's Newton, where the bed of clay still exists, and has very recently been used for common pottery purposes.

The shape of the cinerary urns is somewhat peculiar, and partakes of the Frankish form, which may be called degraded Roman. Instead of being wide at the mouth, like the Celtic urns, they are more or less contracted, and have a kind of neck instead of the overhanging lip or rim which is so eminently characteristic of the pottery of that period. Some, however, are tolerably wide at the mouth; but these are usually low and shallow. The cinerary urns were formed by hand, not

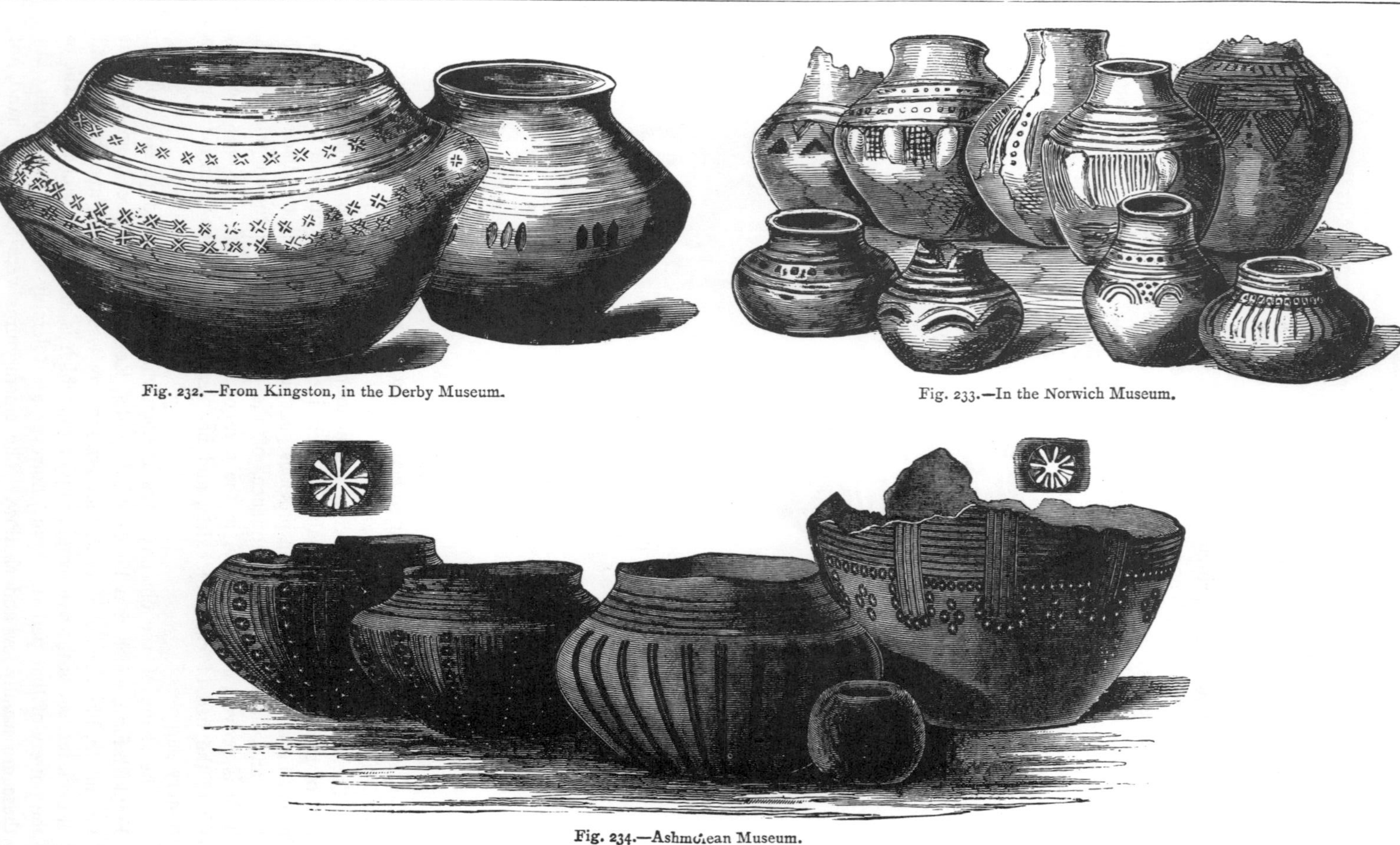

Fig. 232.—From Kingston, in the Derby Museum.

Fig. 233.—In the Norwich Museum.

Fig. 234.—Ashmolean Museum.

on the wheel, although on some other vessels evidence of wheel-turning is apparent. This is another proof that these sepulchral urns were made on the spot where wanted. They are as a rule, perhaps, more firmly fired than those of the Celtic period. They are usually of a dark-coloured clay, sometimes nearly black, at other times of a dark brown, and occasionally of a slate, or greenish tint, produced by surface-colouring.

Their general form will be best understood by reference to the engravings, Figs. 232 to 244. One of these will be seen to have projecting knobs or bosses, which have been formed by simply pressing out the pliant clay from the inside with the hand. In other examples these raised bosses take the form of ribs gradually swelling out from the bottom, till, at the top, they expand into semi-egg-shaped protuberances. The ornamentation on the urns from these cemeteries usually consists of encircling incised lines in bands or otherwise, and vertical or zigzag lines arranged in a variety of ways, and, not unfrequently, the knobs or protuberances of which I have just spoken. Sometimes, also, they present evident attempts at imitation of the Roman egg-and-tongue ornament. The marked features of the pottery of this period is the frequency of small punctured or impressed ornaments, which

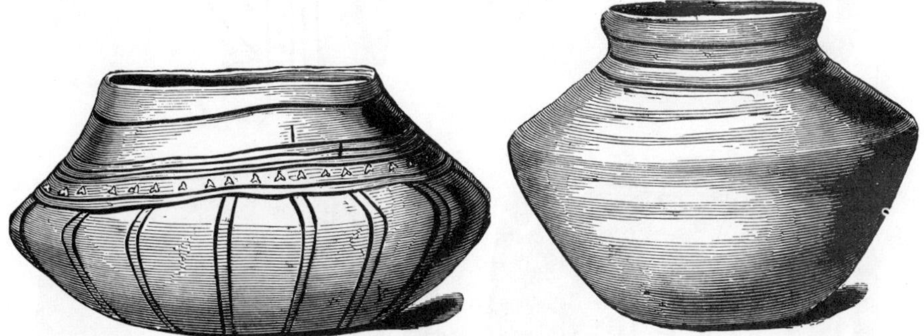

Figs. 235 and 236.—King's Newton.

are introduced along with the lines or bands with very good effect. These ornaments were evidently produced by the end of a stick cut and notched across in different directions, so as to produce crosses and other patterns. In some districts, especially in the East Angles, these vessels are ornamented with simple patterns painted upon their surface in white; but, so far as my knowledge goes, no example of this kind of decoration has been found in the Mercian cemeteries.

The sepulchral vases found in the district of the Middle Angles vary but slightly in form from the East-Anglian burial urns. An example is given in Fig. 246, from Chestersovers, in Warwickshire, where it was found with an iron sword, a spear-head, and other articles of Anglo-Saxon character.

It has become an established fact that the varied remains of the tribes, all of Teutonic descent, who settled on the borders of the Roman empire along the whole extent of the country from Great Britain to Switzerland, present the same character and bear a close resemblance. A few figures here given will illustrate this resemblance. Figs. 248 and 251 are two Alemannic urns from the cemetery of Selzen. It will be seen that they resemble in form the East Anglian urns, and the same ornamentation is also found among our general Anglo-Saxon pottery. These urns are described as being usually made of the clay of the neighbourhood, in most cases turned on a lathe, but many of them imperfectly baked. They are found in graves

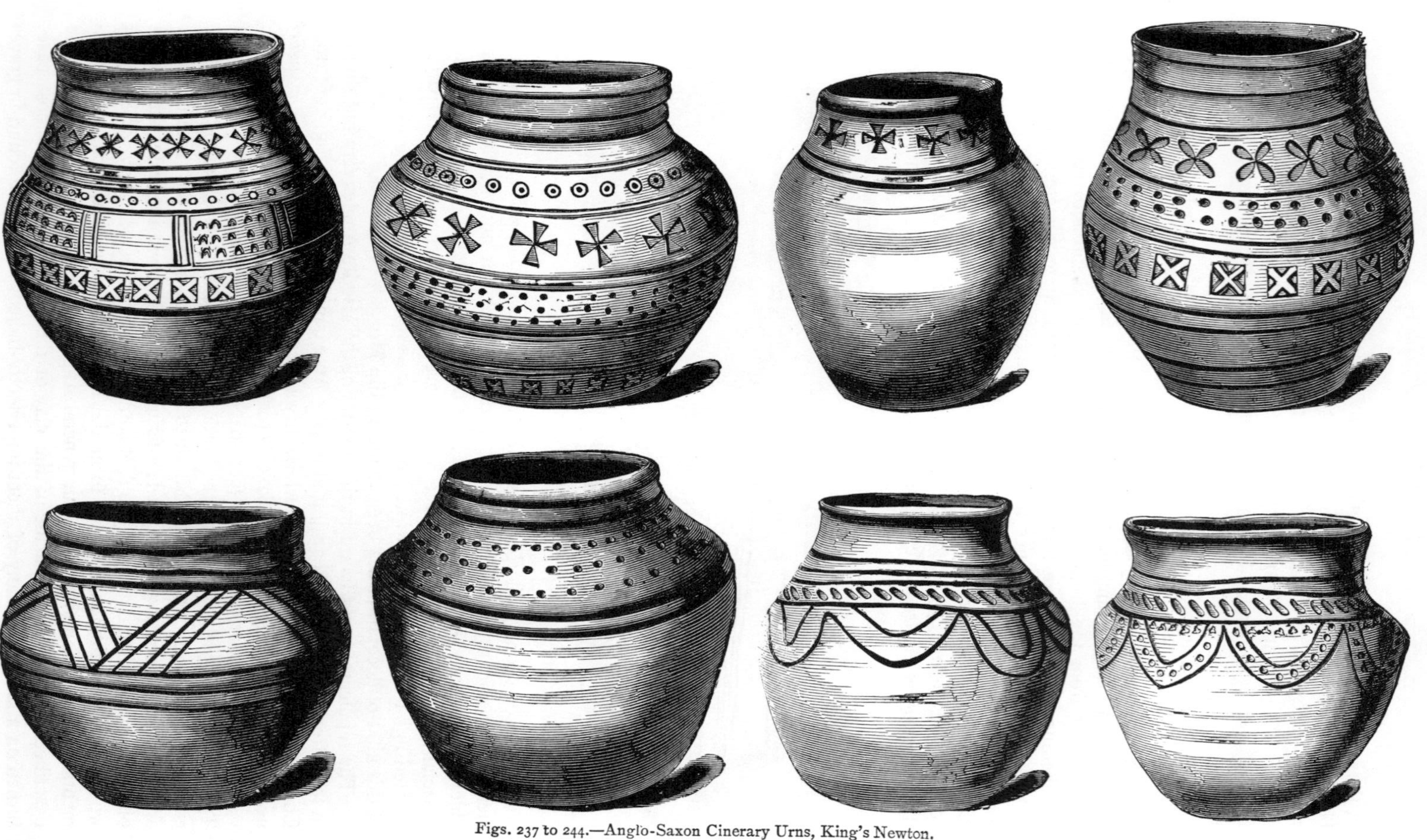

Figs. 237 to 244.—Anglo-Saxon Cinerary Urns, King's Newton.

where the body had not undergone cremation, and were used for containing articles of a miscellaneous description. Fig. 252 is a slate-coloured urn, procured at Cologne,

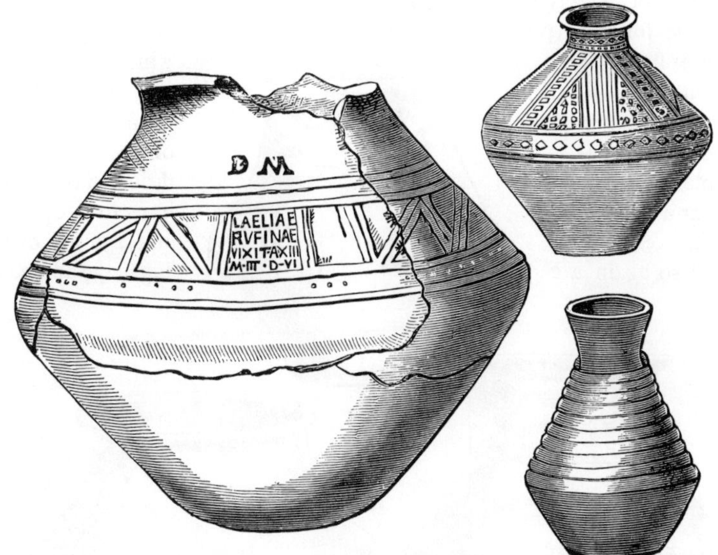

Figs. 245 to 247.—Mayer Museum.

and is ornamented with circular stamps. Figs. 249 and 251 are Frankish urns, obtained by the Abbé Cochet from Londinières, in Normandy, and show at a glance

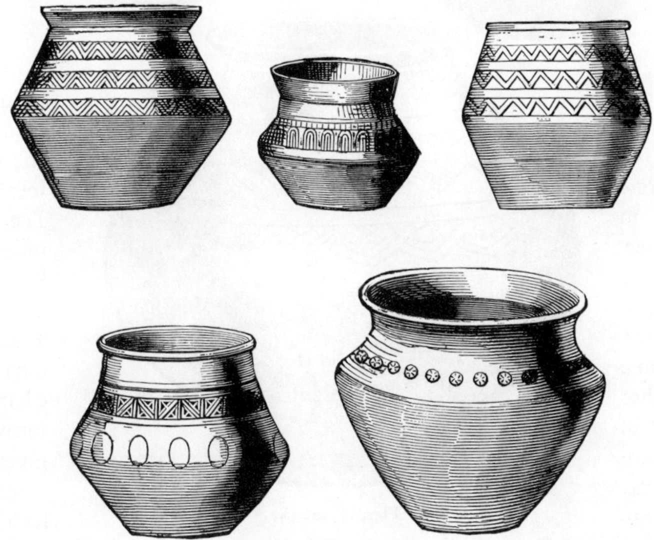

Figs. 248 to 252.

the identity of the Frankish pottery with the Germanic as well as with the Anglo-Saxon. The third of these is surrounded with a row of the well-known bosses, which are equally characteristic of the three divisions of this Teutonic pottery—Anglo-Saxon, Frankish, and Alemannic. Above these bosses is an ornament identical with that of the East Anglian urn with the sepulchral inscription. Figs. 253 to 256 are urns from the Swiss Lacustrine habitations, for comparison of form.

The series of engravings (Figs. 232 to 244) will show the general and more characteristic forms of purely Anglo-Saxon cinerary urns. Figs. 232 and 235 are of the low or flat variety, which is of not unfrequent occurrence. Figs. 234 and 236 are also of a not uncommon form, while 240 is more uncommon. Fig. 241 is of excellent form and is very simple in ornamentation, having only encircling and diagonal lines to decorate its surface. Figs. 243, 244, and 239 are of different shape, and so again are Figs. 237 and 240, which are almost unique in form and in ornamentation. Most of these examples are from one locality, King's Newton, in Derbyshire, within a few miles of the capital of the kingdom of Mercia. The others (Fig. 232) are from Kingston, in the same neighbourhood. Other characteristic examples of form and decoration are given on Figs. 233 and 234. These are from the Ashmolean Museum at Oxford, and from the Norwich Museum, and exhibit excellent specimens of forms and decoration from those districts.

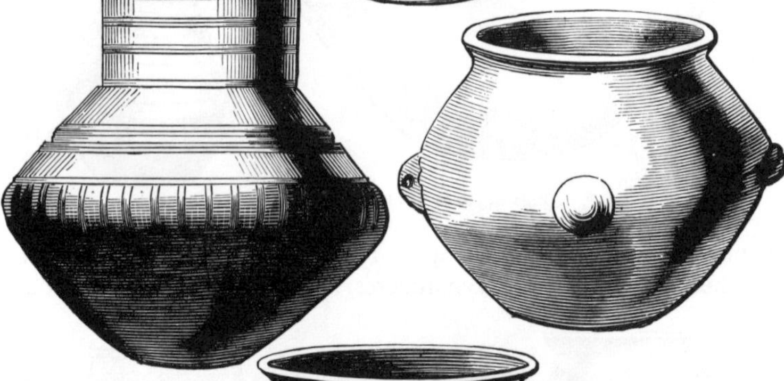

Figs. 253 to 256.

The ornamentation on Anglo-Saxon cinerary urns consists usually of encircling lines, in bands or otherwise; in vertical or zigzag lines, arranged in a variety of ways; of impressed or punctured ornament; and of knobs or protuberances.

Sometimes also, as in a Bedfordshire urn, they present evident attempts at imitation of the Roman egg-and-tongue ornament. In some districts small ornaments are painted on the surface and a white pigment. The marked feature of the pottery of this period is the frequency of the small punctured or impressed ornaments to which I have alluded, which are introduced along with the lines or bands with very

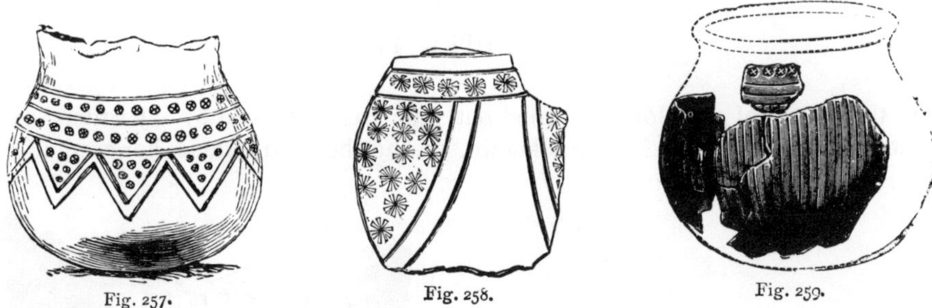

Fig. 257. Fig. 258. Fig. 259.

good effect. These ornaments were evidently usually produced by the end of a stick, cut and notched across in different directions, so as to produce crosses and other patterns. In other instances these impressed ornaments have been produced by twisted slips of metal, &c.

In the woodcut (Figs. 260 and 261) I have endeavoured to show two of the

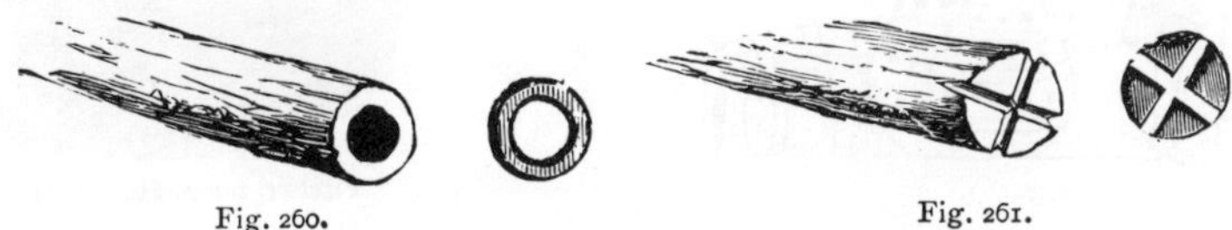

Fig. 260. Fig. 261.

notched-stick "punches," such as I have reason to believe were used for pressing into the soft clay, and also the impressed patterns produced by them.

The quatrefoils (or as they may almost be called, crosses patée) on some of the urns I have engraved, particularly on Figs. 237, 238, and 239, are very unusual, as are also those in the lower bands of Figs. 237 and 240, and in the upper band of the latter example.

Other modes of ornamenting are shown on Fig. 234.

CHAPTER IV.

Of the pottery of the Norman period but little has been said by any writers, and that simply because but little was known. I had the good fortune, however, a few

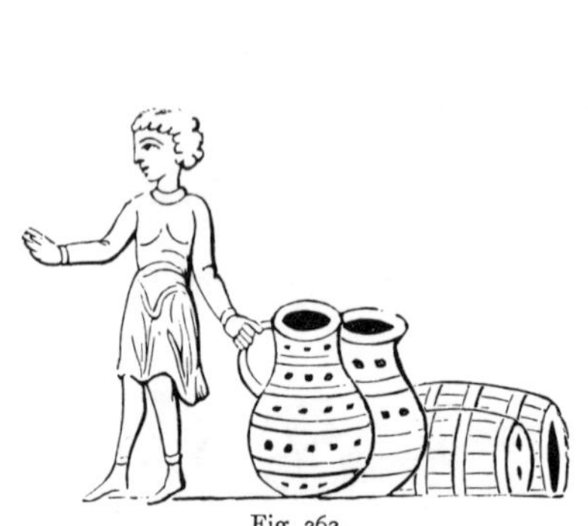

Fig. 262.

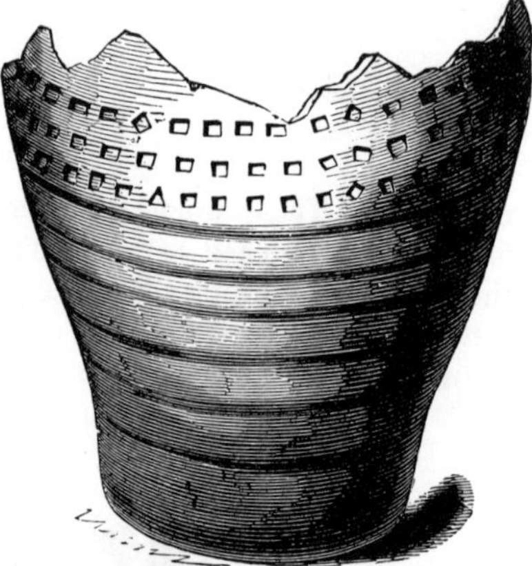

Pitcher, temp. Henry III.

years back, to discover the remains of a kiln of that period, in and around the remains of which were many vessels—" wasters " as they would be technically called

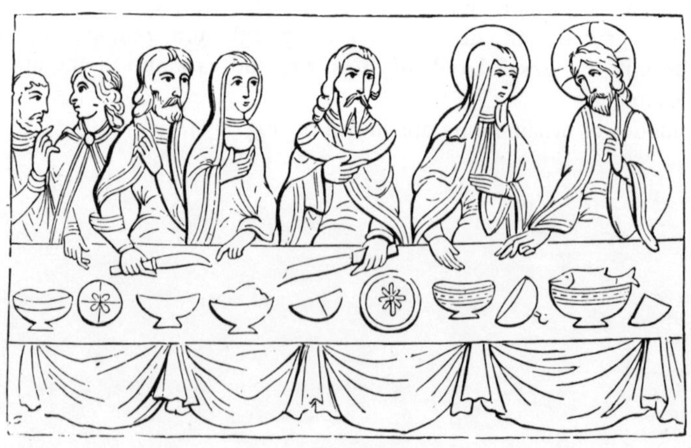

Fig. 263.

—of various kinds. This discovery was all the more interesting and valuable, as being the only instance of the finding of a kiln either of the Anglo-Saxon or Norman periods, and it has enabled me to identify and appropriate to this age vessels from other localities. To these I shall presently refer.

The pottery of this period consisted chiefly of pitchers, dishes, bowls, or basins, and what we should now term porringers or pipkins; the bowls or basins and dishes being used for drinking purposes as well as for placing cooked meats in; the

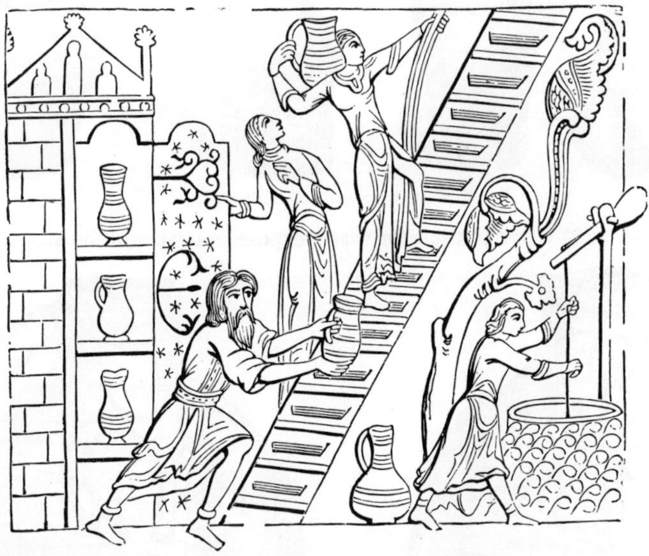

Fig. 264.

pitchers for holding and carrying ale, mead, water, and other liquors to the table, and the porringers both for eating and for cooking with. The uses of these vessels, as well as their general forms, are gathered from the illuminated MSS. of the time which have come down to us. The annexed engraving (Fig. 264), from a twelfth-century MS., shows the pitchers, the water or wine vessels—both in their locker and being carried up to the feast by attendants, one of whom is drawing water from

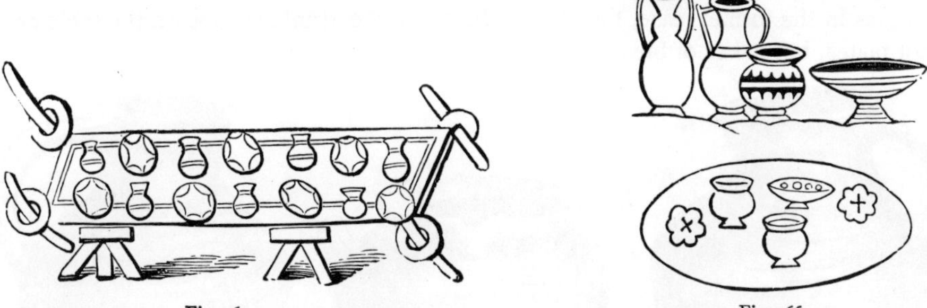

Fig. 265. Fig. 266.

a draw-well in the yard. Fig. 263 shows, on a table set out for dinner, the bowls or basins for the food and for drinking from, one of which holds a fish. The plate-like articles, it should be mentioned, are bread which was made in cakes, and variously ornamented with the knife. The other engravings (Figs. 262 and 266) are excellent representations of pitchers and wine vessels, drinking-cups and bowls, and other characteristic vessels. The next Fig. (265) gives the form of the drinking-cups excellently well, and enables one to determine that the small vessel

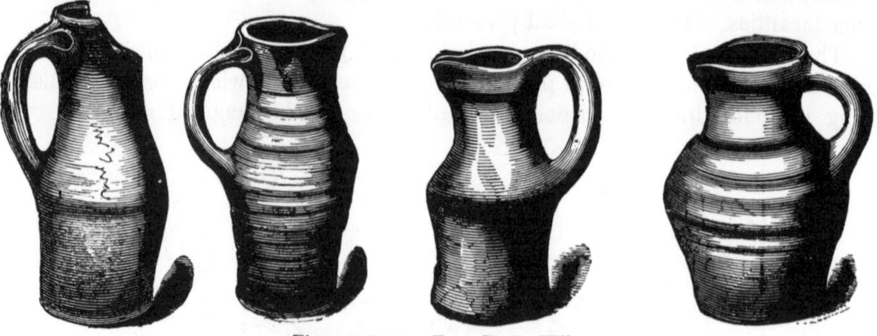

Figs. 267 to 270.—From Burley Hill.

engraved (Fig. 246) was one used for that purpose. It should be stated, however,

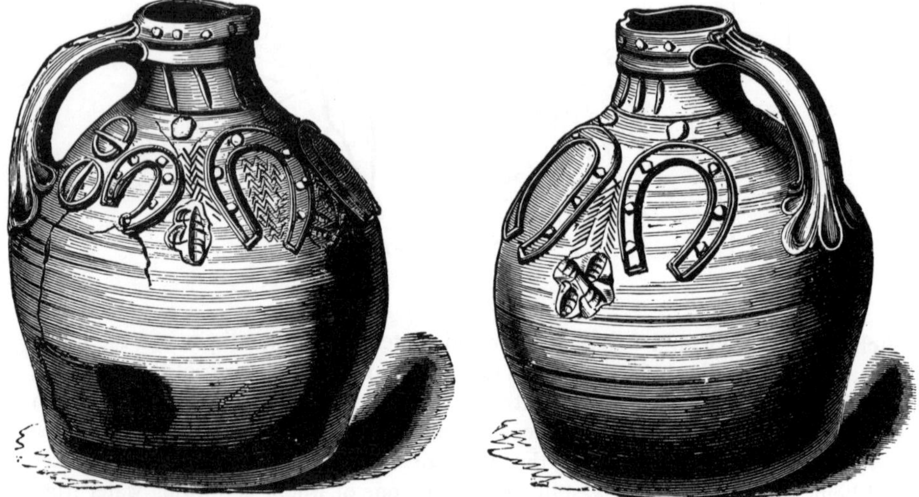

Figs. 271 and 272.—From Burley Hill.

that, as in the former case, the objects between the drinking-cups on the table are not plates, but cakes of bread.

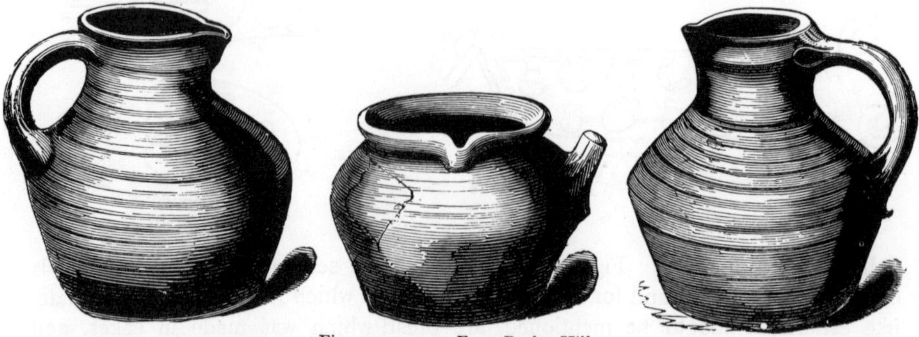

Figs. 273 to 275.—From Burley Hill.

The clay of which Norman pottery is formed is usually of a coarse kind, and the vessels bear evidence in many instances of the wheel having been used. In colour they are sometimes of a reddish brown, at others of a tolerably good red, while at others again they are nearly black; and many of the pitchers, &c., are either wholly or partially covered with a green or other glaze. Many are quite devoid of ornament, but others have the ends of the handles formed into foliage, &c., by the pressure of the finger. Some, however, are rather highly decorated. . Figs. 267 to 270 show four small-sized jugs, ranging from four and a half to seven inches in height, two of which are devoid of ornament, and the other two have their handles foliated. Figs. 273 and 275 show pitchers of a larger growth, of the same clumsy, coarse kind of clay, and ornamented in the same primitive manner. They are about nine inches in height, and are green glazed.

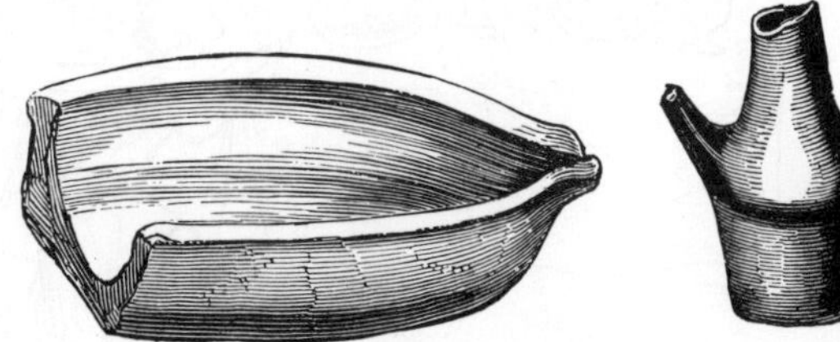

Figs. 276 and 277.—From Burley Hill.

Figs. 271 and 272 represent the two sides of a remarkably fine pitcher, which (as well as Figs. 267 to 279) was discovered by myself in the kiln to which reference has been made. It is sixteen inches in height, and is, perhaps, the finest and most interesting fictile remain of the Norman period in existence. It bears, as will be seen, five horseshoes and two buckles, all of which were badges of the Ferrars family (Norman Earls of Derby), who were lords of the soil where, and at the time when, these vessels were made. The decorations are all laid on in "slip" of a finer kind of clay than that of which the body is composed, and the pitcher is glazed. Herring-bone pattern is incised in the body of the pitcher itself.

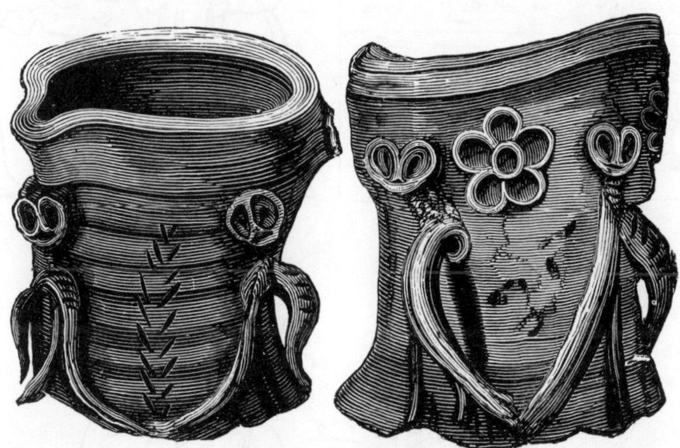

Figs. 278 and 279.—From Burley Hill.

While speaking of this pitcher it may not be out of place to allude to a ludicrous mistake made in Miss Meteyard's "Life of Wedgwood." On page 38, vol. i., of that work, Miss Meteyard has copied my own woodcut which appeared some little time before, both in the "Reliquary" and in my own "Life of Wedgwood; but her artist having made his tracing from my woodcut has *reversed* it in his copy, and thus made it worse than useless.

Fig. 274 represents a "porringer" or pipkin from the same place. It is of red

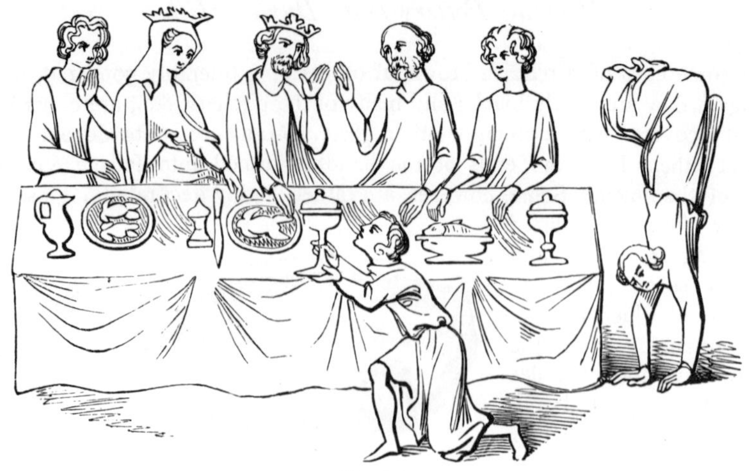

Fig. 280.

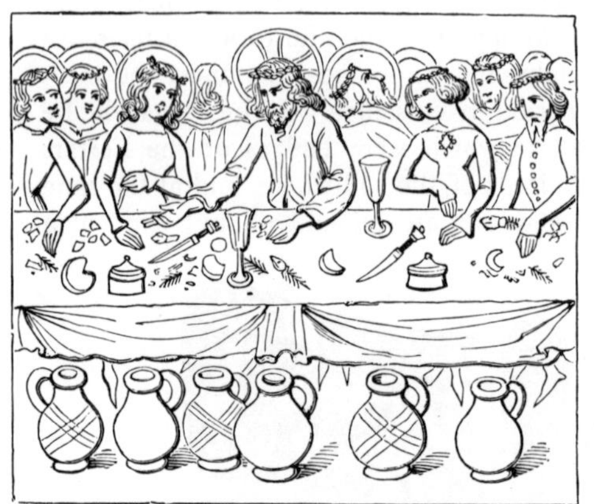

Fig. 281.

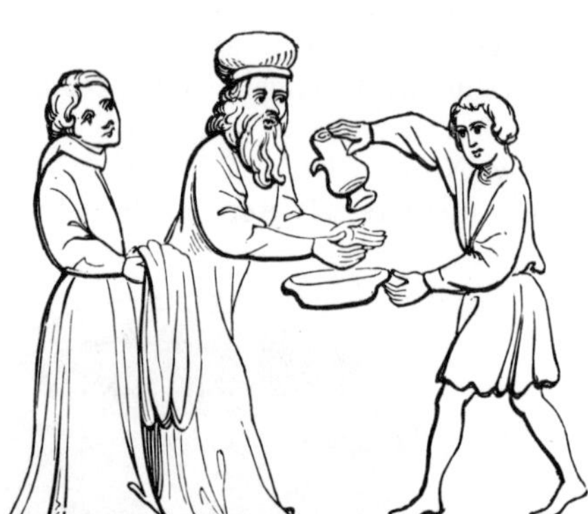

Fig. 282.

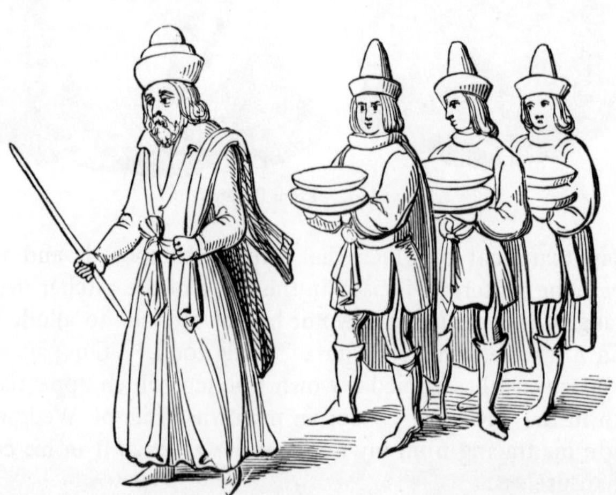

Fig. 283.

clay; but others were found of a dark clay, and partly glazed. A kind of clumsy dish and a bottle-shaped vessel with a side handle are shown on the next engravings (Figs. 276 and 277).

Fragments of a number of large pitchers, highly decorated with flowers, bosses, &c., in slip, and incised patterns, were also found. Among the more interesting

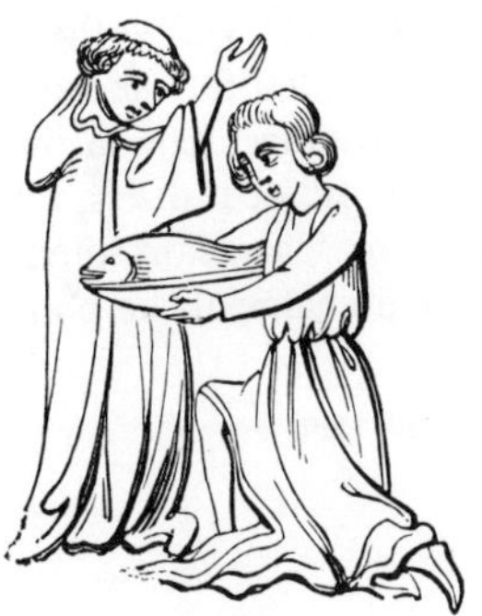

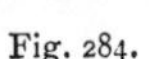

Fig. 284.

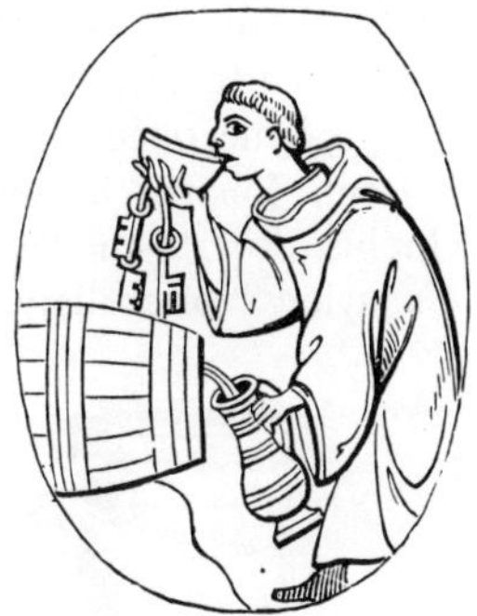

Fig. 285.

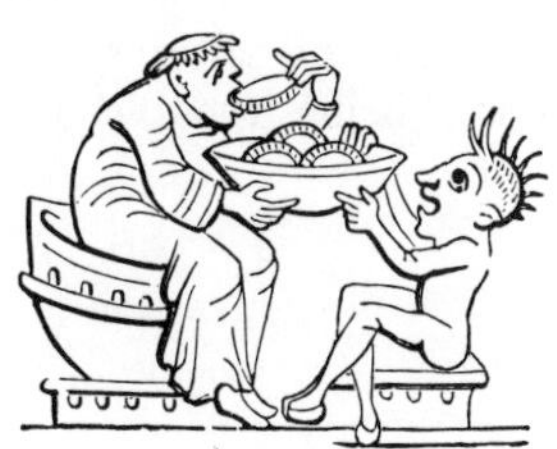

Fig. 286.

of these were some bearing round the neck rude attempts at faces and arms. Two of these are shown on Figs. 278 and 279.

The domestic vessels of a somewhat later date appear, in many instances, to retain the same general form, but in others present new shapes. Fortunately, we can again fall back upon the illuminated MSS. for forms of these vessels, and can compare them with actual examples.

Thus on Fig. 284 we have a dish of the fourteenth, and in Fig. 283 those of the fifteenth century; while in the others we have drinking-cups, bowls, three-legged

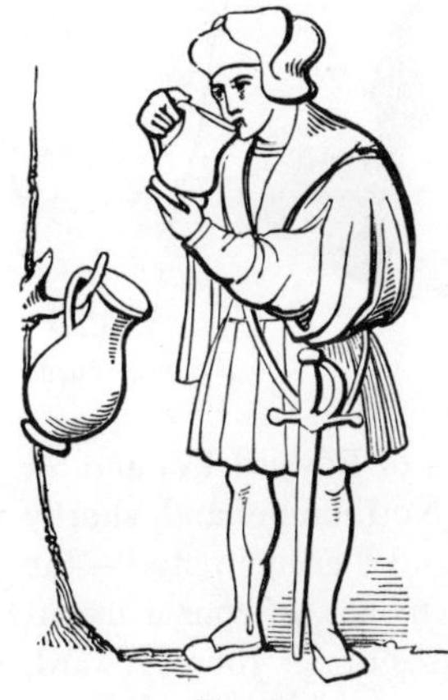

Fig. 287.

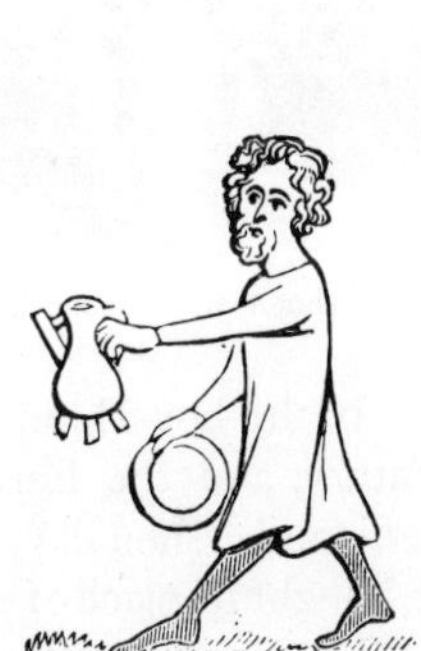

Fig. 288.

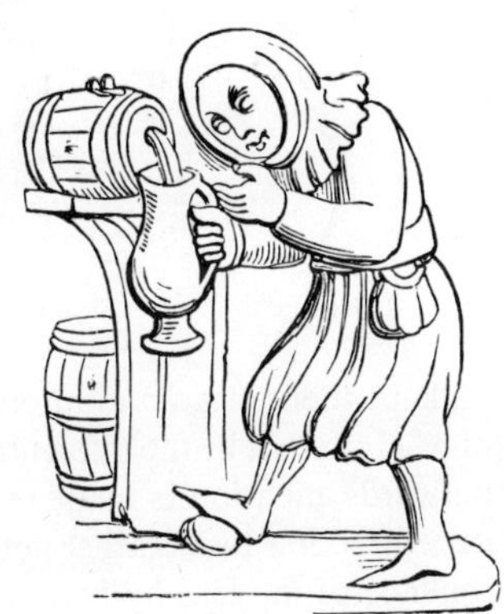

Fig. 289.

vessels with spouts, &c. Fig. 282 gives us a wash-hand basin and jug—an attendant holding the basin in one hand and jug in the other while the guest washes his hands, a female standing by with the towel. In Fig. 281 we have a remarkably fine assemblage of pitchers of the fourteenth century, some of which appear to be ornamented with cross bands; while in Fig. 280 (the daughter of Herodias dancing before

Herod) we have dishes, jugs, and bowls. Some of the vessels in these illuminations, it must be borne in mind, may be of metal, but the form is still of the same value and importance. Some excellent figures of mediæval jugs are also given in the next engravings, one of which (Fig. 287) likewise shows a drinking-mug.

One of the earliest written notices of crockery we have is the oft-quoted entry in the account of payments by the executors of Queen Eleanor, wife of Edward I. "Item, Juliana la potere pro ccc picheriis die anniversarii Reginæ viij*s.* vj*d.*"—these three hundred pitchers being probably earthenware vessels "provided for the feast given to the poor on the anniversary of the queen's death." Another item in the same accounts is also curious: "Item, Johanni le squeler pro M[le] et D discis, tot platelles, tot salseriis, et cccc chiphis, xlij*s.*"—the "squeler," or "sargeant-squylloure," being "pourveyour of the squylery," or scullery, who had charge of the pots,

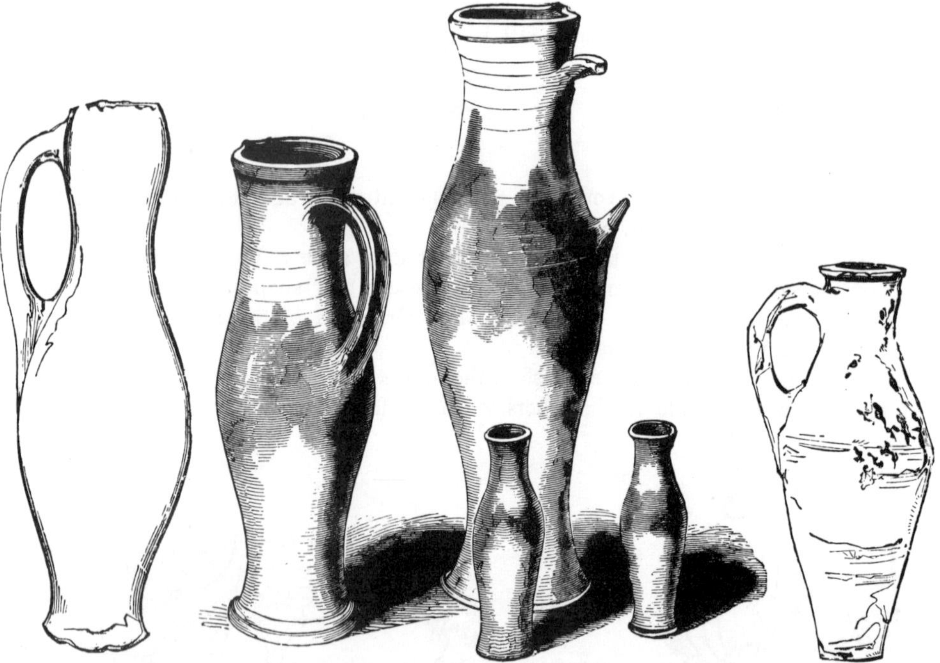

Fig. 290.—London. Figs. 291 to 294.—Ashmolean Museum, Oxford. Fig. 295.—London.

and kept them clean and in order. In the household books of Edward IV. and Sir John Howard, in the fifteenth century, and the Earl of Northumberland, shortly afterwards, mention is made of "earth and asshen cuppes" and "erthyn potts"—the latter directing that leather pots be bought in place of earthen ones, of course in consequence of the loss by breakage. The entry in the expenses of Sir John Howard, in 1466, referred to, shows somewhat curiously the cost of "potes" in those days:— "Watekin bocher of Stoke delyvered of my mony to on of the poteres of Horkesley iv[s.] vi[d.] to pay hemselfe and his felawes for xi dosen potes," which would be about $4\frac{3}{4}$*d.* per dozen for them.

The vessels made in England in mediæval times principally consisted of pitchers and jugs, cups or bowls, bottles and dishes; the term "pottes" being applied to the drinking cups then in general use. From them and their successors the "ale pots," of which I shall yet speak, the still common term of a *pot* of ale has gradually come down to us. One shape of these drinking vessels is shown in the two smaller vessels, Figs. 293 and 294, the larger ones being excellent examples of the jugs in use along with them. These were dug up in Oxford, in 1838, and are preserved in the Ashmolean Museum. Other good examples of jugs, in the Jermyn Street Museum, are shown on Figs. 290 and 295. These are all plain, but are glazed.

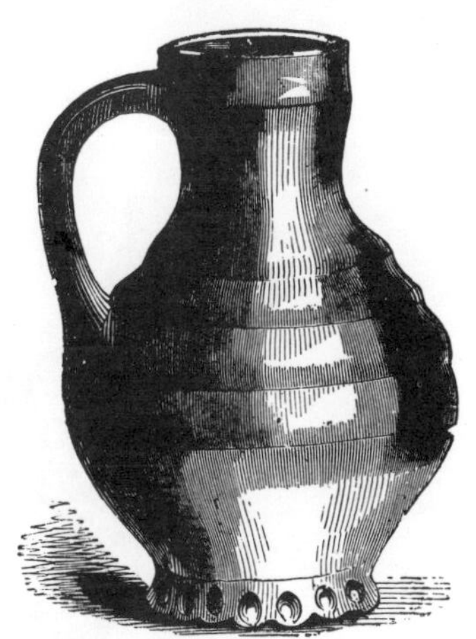

Fig. 296.

The larger jugs, or pitchers, are frequently ornamented with heads, foliage, or other devices, in somewhat high relief. Many of these are very curious. They were made in different parts of the country, of the common clays of the locality, and decorated according to the taste and skill of the maker.

Jugs or vessels for liquor were occasionally, from a very early period, made in form of mounted knights. Indeed, from the occurrence of grotesque heads and portions of figures on the Norman vessels which I had the good fortune to exhume a few years back, it is probable these grotesque vessels may, in some instances, trace from that date. A very interesting example (Fig. 297) was found at Lewes in 1846. It is in the form of a mounted knight. The workmanship is very rude, but there are certain details, such as the long pointed toes and pryck spurs, from which its probable date is assigned to the time of Henry II. Its length is ten and a half inches, and its full height, when perfect, would be thirteen or fourteen inches. The material is coarse clay, the upper parts green glazed. There can be no doubt it was intended to contain liquor, and the handle, which passes from the back of the knight to the tail of the horse, was evidently intended for pouring out the contents; whilst a circular aperture at the lower end of the handle afforded the means of filling the vessel. There is no evidence to show where this was made.

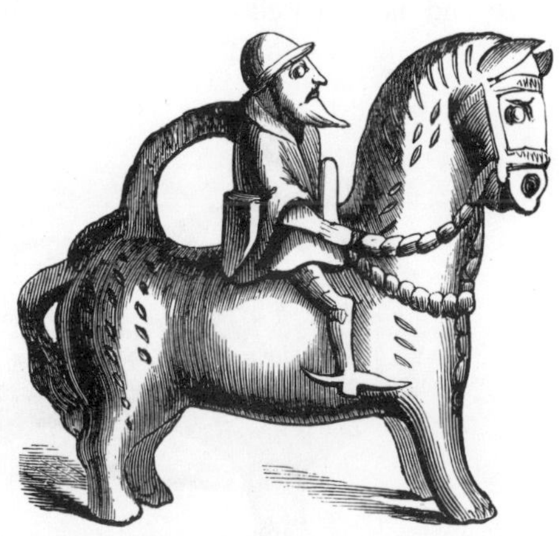

Fig. 297.—Lewes.

Another curious example (Fig. 298), preserved in the Salisbury Museum, was found at Mere, in Wiltshire, and is believed to belong to the latter half of the twelfth century. The costume and accoutrements of this figure (which is a knight on horseback, armed with shield, &c.) correspond almost precisely to that of the effigy of King Richard I. on his great seal. The impressed circles are probably intended to represent chain mail.

Another vessel, of analogous character, preserved in the Scarborough Museum, is engraved on Fig. 299. It is in the form of an animal with a twisted horn, but its handle and other parts are imperfect. It is covered with a green glaze, and was, there cannot be the shadow of a doubt, made at Scarborough, where, as I shall show, the remains of a potter's kiln was found in 1854, but has not, as yet, been named in any work on pottery.

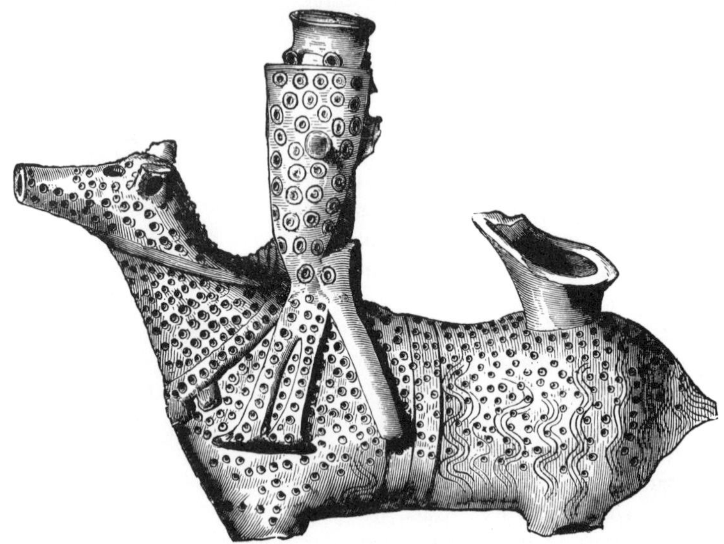

Fig. 298.—Salisbury Museum.

A jug, which would almost appear to have been the origin of the bellarmine, to be hereafter described, was communicated by Mr. Kirwan to the *Journal of the British Archæological Association,* where it is engraved. It is covered with green glaze, and bears a well and powerfully moulded head, with the flowing hair and

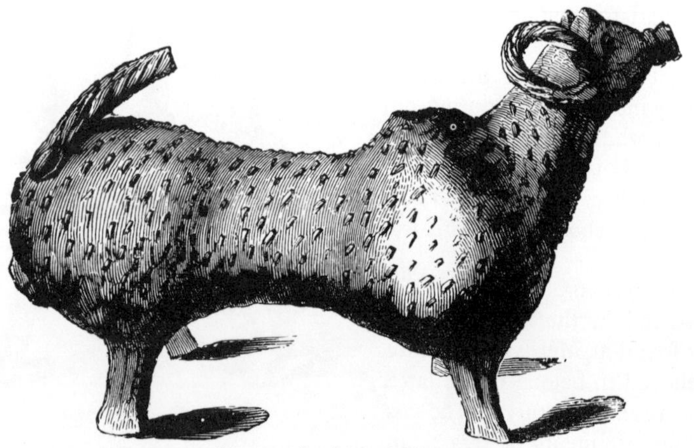

Fig. 299.—Scarborough Museum.

beard so characteristic of the time of Edward I., II., and III. To this period some clay moulds for the forming of faces upon mediæval pottery, found at Lincoln by Mr. Arthur Trollope, may be assigned; they are engraved by Marryatt, and will be referred to later on in this volume. It will be seen, too, on comparison of this jug with the fragments of Norman pottery on another page, that it is the same kind of general idea, somewhat amplified, but carried out in the taste of the day.

The costrils, or pilgrims' bottles as they are commonly called, *i.e.* bottles for liquor to be carried and hung on the person, were much made in the Middle Ages, and although usually plain, were, nevertheless, sometimes rather highly decorated.

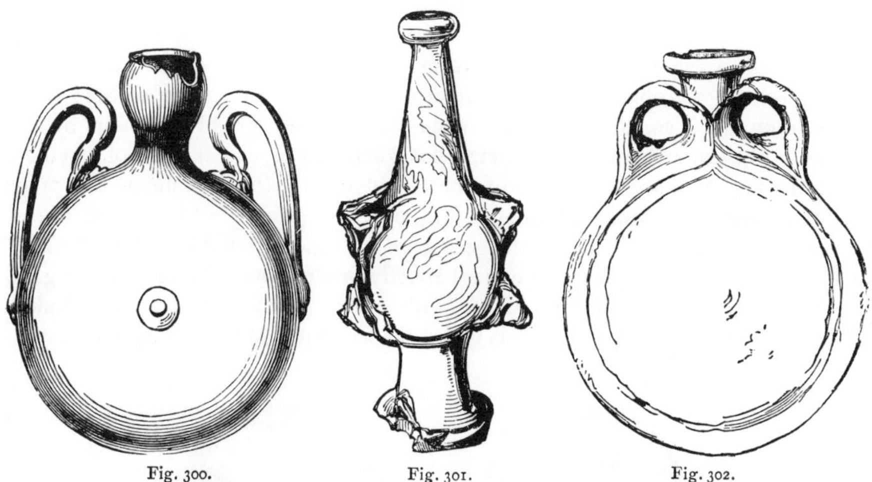

Fig. 300. Fig. 301. Fig. 302.

Fig. 300 is the shape mostly known as a pilgrim's bottle, and will be seen to vary but little from the flattened globular amphora of Roman times (Fig. 303). Sometimes they had four loops instead of handles, so that the strap could pass through the four loops and make the carrying safer. To this class a remarkably fine example in the Roach Smith collection in the British Museum belongs. On one

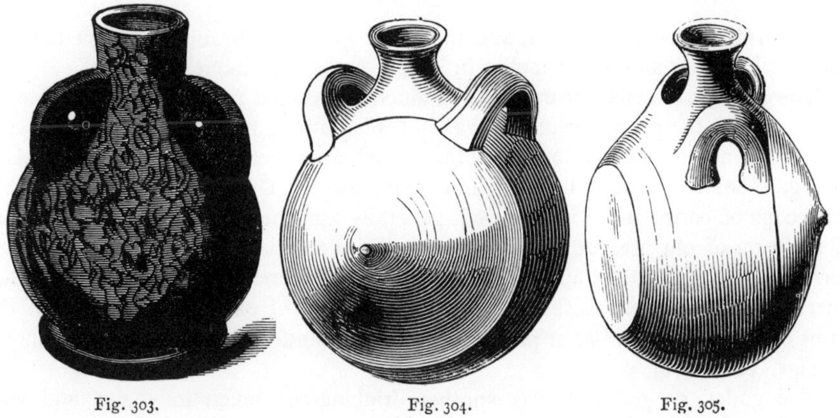

Fig. 303. Fig. 304. Fig. 305.

side are the royal arms of Henry VIII. within a rose and garter, and with supporters and crown, with the legend DNE SALVVM FAC REGEM REGINAM ET REGNVM (God keep safe the King, Queen, and kingdom): on the other side are four medallions: one contains the sacred monogram, I.H.S.; two others have radiating patterns; and the fourth a heart, with love-knot of flowers and the word LEAL.

Fig. 303 shows another example, somewhat of the form of Figs. 300 and 302; but in this case it is globular, or gourd-shaped, and not flattened on the sides, and the handles for the loops are simply flat pieces of clay pierced for suspension. This interesting example, which is of Tickenhall make, belongs to Sir J. H. Crewe, Bart., and is mottled with green all over its surface. Another excellent form of mediæval "pilgrim's bottle" was found at Collingbourne Ducis by the Rev. W. C. Lukis, F.S.A. It is of barrel shape, and has handles and mouth at the top, and, at the bottom, a stand. In front is a face surrounded by oak-leaves, within a circle of foliage, all in relief, and above this is an aperture. Other vessels partaking of the barrel-shape and mammiform character are also met with: some of their forms will be seen on Figs. 304 to 307. When carried, they would be slung by the handles in the same manner as others; but when not in use, instead of having a base, as in Fig. 303, one end is seen to be flattened for it to stand upon; the other end is in form of a woman's breast—this, of course, in allusion to the use of the vessel, from the mouth of which the person who used it would drink or "suck" the liquor it contained. A much more perfectly formed mammiform bottle I give, from a beautiful drawing furnished me, with others, by the late Mr. F. C. Lukis, F.S.A., on Figs. 304 and 305. It is gourd-shaped, with one side flattened to pre-

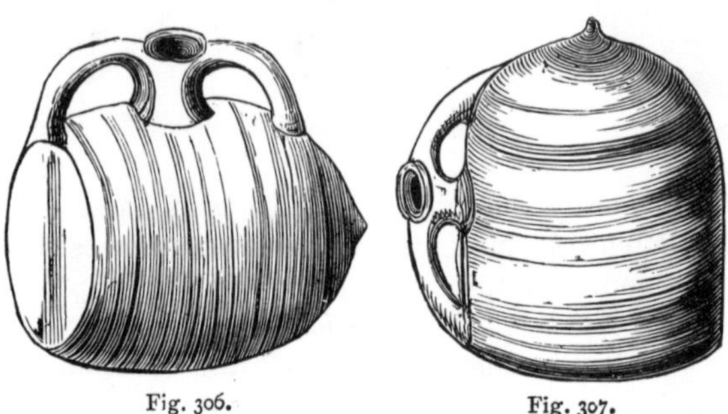

Fig. 306. Fig. 307.

vent its rolling when set down, and the other side is a beautifully formed female breast. It is four and a half inches in height, and holds about half a pint.

The cruskin, or cruse, or cruske, was much in use, and made of somewhat varied form. It was the precursor of the tyg, and was nothing more than a drinking-cup. References are frequently found to this vessel, as a "crusekyn de terre," and as having, in some instances, been mounted with silver. Usually, however, they were plain cups of earthenware or of wood, generally ash, the latter partaking somewhat of the form of our present basin. I am inclined to think, too, that the pipkin, or porringer, was also called a cruske or cruskin. The term is still in use in Ireland, where a "cruisken of whiskey" is a common form of expression. Some of the forms of the "cruisken" as at present in use in Ireland—made of wood—are shown on Figs. 308 to 311.

The godet, or goddard, was another drinking-cup much in vogue, and was, evidently, a kind of large cup or bowl, in which spiced liquor was mixed and drunk by "gossips" and friends. Some of these bowls will be spoken of later. Besides these, various other names for drinking-vessels were more or less in use.

In the sixteenth and seventeenth centuries the potter's art was principally confined to the manufacture of common domestic vessels—large coarse dishes, cruiskeens, tygs, pitchers, bowls, cups, candlesticks, pans, butter-pots, and other articles being among the number. Many things, not made in England, were imported from Holland and other countries, and came into general use. They were, however, soon copied by our own workmen and made to a large extent. Among the principal of the imported vessels were bellarmines, or grey beards; and ale-pots. In the reign of Queen Elizabeth, one William Simpson proposed to manufacture, "in some decayed town within this realm," these ale-pots, which had till that time been solely imported from Cologne by Garnet Tynes, by which he promised that "manie a hundred poore men may be sett at worke." As a preliminary to this, he petitioned the queen to grant him sole licence to bring them into the realm, but there is no record to show whether his petition was granted or not.

In 1570, according to Stow, Jasper Andries and Jacob Janson, potters, who had settled in Norwich in 1567, "removed to London. They set forth in a petition to Queen Elizabeth that they were the first that brought in and exercised the said science in this realm, and were at great charges before they could find materials in this realm. They beseeched her, in recompense of their great cost and charges, that she would grant them house room in or without the liberties of London, by the water side." In 1626 a patent was granted to Thomas Rous, *alias* Rius, and

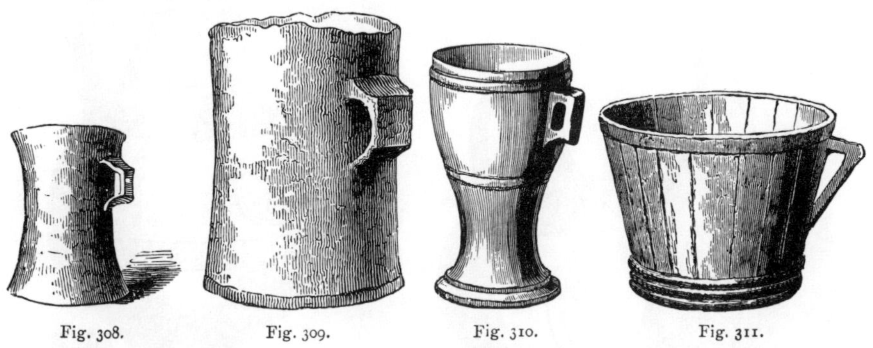

Fig. 308. Fig. 309. Fig. 310. Fig. 311.

Abraham Cullen, of London, for the manufacture of "Stone Potts, Stone Juggs, and Stone Bottells."

In 1635 a patent was granted to "David Ramsey, Esquier, one of the groomes of our pryvie chamber, Michael Arnold, and John Ayliffe, of the citty of Westminster, Brewers," for a new method of heating boilers by means of sea coal, which "invencion is alsoe very usefull for the Dryeinge of Bricke, all manner of Tyles, and all such sortes of Tyles as cannot be made in this kingdome but in the Heat of Sumer; and alsoe that they have found out the Arte and Skill of Makeinge and Dyeinge of all sortes of Panne Tyles, Stone Juggs, Bottles of all sizes, Earthen Wicker Bottles; Meltinge Pottes for Gouldsmythes, and other Earthen Comodityes within this our Realme, which nowe are made by Straungers in Forraigne Partes; and that in the makinge of the same Earthen Comodityes as aforesaid, the saide David Ramsey, Michaell Arnold, and John Ayliffe shall have employment for many of our poore Subjects, whoe thereby shalbee sett on worke, and bee competently mainteyned, and will alsoe sell them cheaper than they are now sould." This patent was for fourteen years, the parties being bound to pay one-fourth part of their profit yearly into the exchequer.

The stone-ware was usually called "Cologne ware," from Cologne, from whence it was first imported; and by this name that made in our own country continued to be in great measure known. It will be well here, therefore, to speak of the ale-pots and bellarmines of that kind of ware.

The *Bellarmine*, or *Grey Beard*, or *Long Beard*, as it was commonly called, was a stone-ware pot of bottle form, mostly with a handle at the back and ornament on the front. The neck is narrow, and the lower part, or "belly," as it is technically called, very wide and protuberant. They were in very general use at the "ale-houses" to serve ale in to customers, and were of different sizes—the *gallonier* containing a gallon; the *pottle pot*, two quarts; the *pot*, a quart; and the *little pot*, a pint. These jugs were derisively named after Cardinal Bellarmine, who died in 1621. The cardinal having, by his determined and bigoted opposition to the Reformed religion, made himself obnoxious in the Low Countries, became naturally an object of derision and contempt with the Protestants, who, among other modes of showing their detestation of the man, seized on the potter's art to exhibit his short stature, his hard features, and his rotund figure, to become the jest of the ale-house and the byword

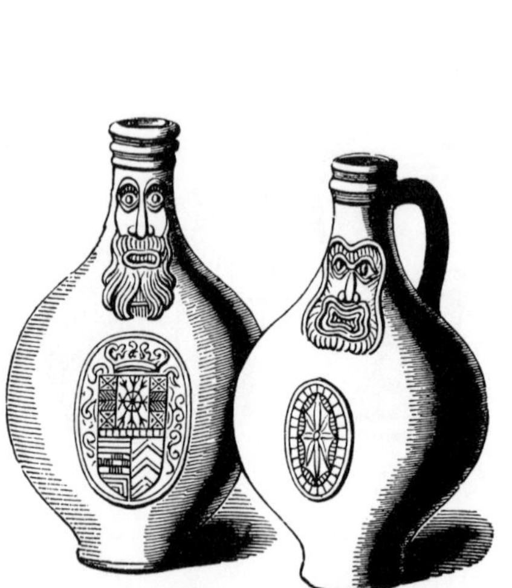
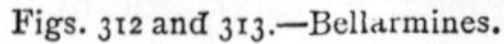

Figs. 312 and 313.—Bellarmines.

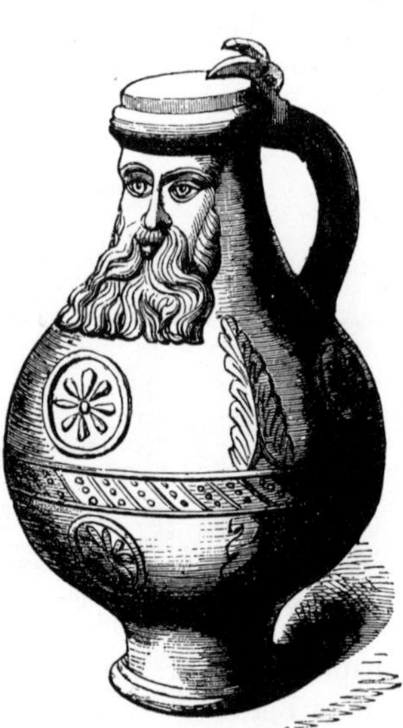

Fig. 314.—Bellarmine.

of the people. Allusions to the bellarmines are very common in the productions of the English writers of the period.

The ale-pots being formed with the corpulent proportions and the "hard-mouthed visage" of the cardinal, became a popular and biting burlesque upon him. From them, too, from the face upon the ale *mug* or ale pot, the vulgar name of "mug" for the human face is probably derived. The engravings, Figs. 312 to 314, show three bellarmines; the first two are "foreign" make, but the latter is English; and a strong general resemblance will be seen to the pitchers before engraved. Another English bellarmine is engraved under the head of "Fulham."

The ordinary "ale-pots," or "little pots,"—the pint jugs,—were, like the bellarmines, at first imported into this country, but they were afterwards made to a considerable extent in various parts of the kingdom. They were made of a light-coloured clay, and took the name of "stone-ware," from their hardness and colour. They were turned on the wheel, the necks being usually covered with deep encircling lines; and the ornaments consisted of foliage, flowers, scrolls, circles, &c., scratched, or incised, into the soft clay with a sharp point, and then washed in with blue colour. In some instances a pattern was impressed, from a mould, on the front, as in the manner of the bellarmines. They are generally very thick, and must have been extremely durable. One example is engraved (Fig. 315).

Salt-glazing appears to have been introduced about 1680, and it gradually superseded the lead-glazing which till that time was in regular use. The account given of this discovery is, that "at Mr. Joseph Yates', Stanley, near Bagnall, five miles east of Burslem, in Staffordshire, the servant was preparing, in an earthen vessel, a salt-ley for curing pork, and during her temporary absence the liquid boiled over, and the sides of the pot were quickly red hot from intense heat; yet, when cold, were covered with an excellent glaze. The fact was detailed to Mr. Palmer, potter, of Bagnall, who availed himself of the occurrence, and told other potters. At the small manufactories in Holden Lane (Adams's), Green Head, and Brownhill's (Wedgwood's), salt-glazed ware was soon afterwards made." "The ovens employed for the purpose being used only once weekly, and the ware being cheap, were large in diameter, and very high, to contain a sufficient quantity to be baked each time to cover all contingent expenses. They were constructed with a scaffold round them, on which the firemen could stand, while casting in the salt through holes made in the upper part of the cylinder, above the bags or inner vertical flues; and the saggers were made of completely refractory materials, with holes in their sides, for the vapourised salt to circulate freely among all the vessels in the oven to affect their surfaces." The ware thus glazed, and made from the common clay, with a mixture of fine sand from Mole Cop, was called "Crouch ware," and in this all the ordinary articles of domestic use, including jugs, cups, dishes, &c., were made. At this time, it is stated, there were only twenty-two ovens in Burslem and its neighbourhood. "The employment of salt in glazing Crouch ware was a long time practised before the introduction of white clay and flint. The vast volumes of smoke and vapours from the ovens entering the atmosphere produced that dense white cloud which, from about eight o'clock till twelve on the Saturday morning (the time of 'firing up,' as it is called), so completely enveloped the whole interior of the town as to cause persons often to run against each other, travellers to mistake the road; and strangers have mentioned it as extremely disagreeable, and not unlike the smoke of Etna or Vesuvius."

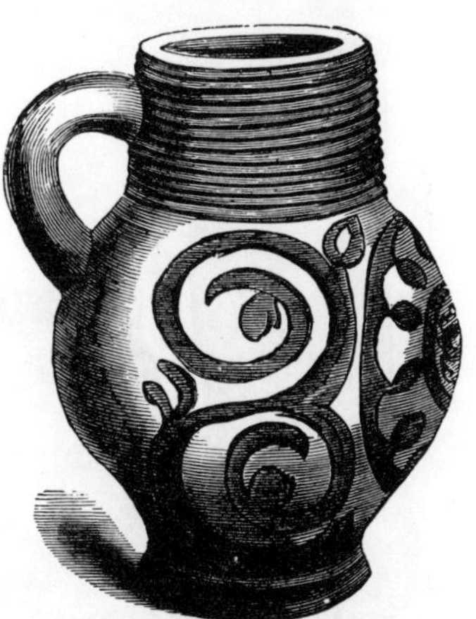

Fig. 315.—Ale Pot.

In 1685 a white stone-ware was made at Shelton by Thomas Miles, and at the same time and place a brown stone-ware was also made. These would be the same as the ale-pots and bellarmines were made of.

In 1686, Dr. Plot thus spoke of the butter-pots then made:—"The Butter they buy by the *Pot* of a long cylendrical form, made at *Burslem*, in this county, of a certain size, so as not to weigh above six pounds at most, and yet to contain at least 14 pounds of Butter, according to an Act of Parliament made about 14 or 16 years agoe, for regulateing the abuses of this trade in the make of Pots, and false packing of the Butter."

These butter-pots (Fig. 316), tall cylindrieal vessels, of coarse clay, are now of great rarity, but specimens may be seen in the Hanley Museum and in the Museum of Practical Geology. It is worthy of remark that even yet Irish or Dutch butter, which is generally imported in casks, and known as "tub butter," is, in the potteries, usually called "pot butter."

Of the state of the Staffordshire potteries at the latter half of the seventeenth century, Dr. Plot gives a most interesting and valuable account, in which he shows not only what clays and sand, &c., were then used, and where got, but also speaks of the glazes, and describes the modes of the manufacture of some of the vessels. Thus :—"When the potter has wrought the clay either into hollow or flat ware, they set it abroad to dry in faire weather, but by the fire in foule, turning them as they see occasion, which they call *whaving*. When they are dry they *stouk* them, *i.e.* put ears and handles to such vessels as require them. These also being dry, they *slip* or *paint* them, with their severall sorts of slip, according as they designe their work; when the first slip is dry, laying on the others at their leisure, the *orange slip* makeing

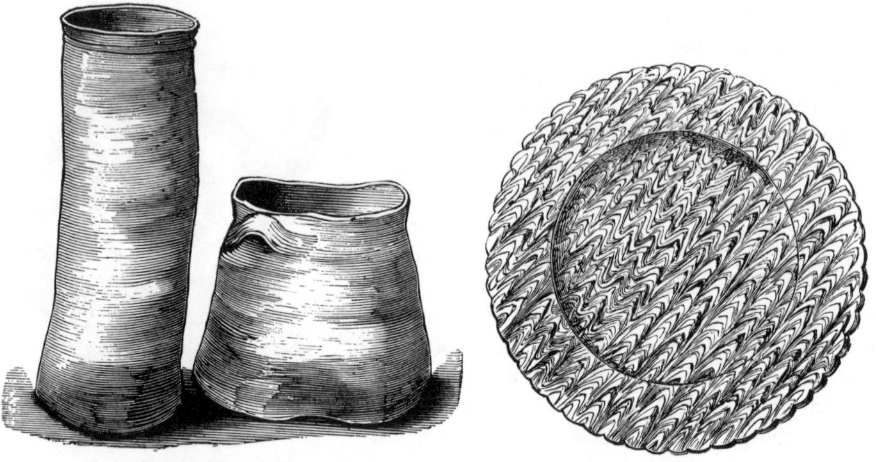

Fig. 316.—Butter Pots.

Fig. 317.

the ground, and the *white* and *red* the paint; which two colours they break with a *wire brush*, much after the manner they doe when they *marble* paper, and then *cloud* them with a *pencil* when they are pretty dry. After the vessels are painted they *lead* them with that sort of *Lead Ore* they call *Smithum*, which is the smallest *ore* of all, beaten into dust, finely sifted, and strewed upon them; which gives them the *gloss*, but not the colour; all the colours being chiefly given by the variety of slips, except the *motley colour*, which is procured by blending the *Lead* with *Manganese*, by the workmen call'd *Magnus*. But when they have a mind to shew the utmost of their skill in giving their wares a fairer gloss than ordinary, they lead them then with lead calcined into powder, which they also sift fine and strew upon them as before, which not only gives them a higher gloss, but goes much further too in their work than the lead ore would have done."

A round dish of this "combed ware," or marbled or mottled ware, is shown on Fig. 317. Some of the examples I have seen are exceedingly delicate and minute in their patterns; others, as the engraving, have been "combed" with a coarse comb or wire brush. The lead for glazing was procured from the Derbyshire lead mines—the ore being powdered, or "punned," and dusted on to the soft clay vessel before firing.

Previous to this, in 1671, John Dwight took out a patent, in the petition for which he stated that "he had discovered the Mistery of Transparent Earthen Ware, comonly knowne by the Names of Porcelaine or China and Persian Ware, as alsoe the Misterie of the Stone Ware vulgarly called Cologne Ware; and that he designed to introduce a Manufacture of the said Wares into our Kingdome of Englande, where they have not hitherto been wrought or made." This was the origin of the famous Fulham works, an account of which will be given in another part of this volume.

In 1676 John Ariens Van Hamme, "in pursuance of the incouragement he hath received from our Ambassadour at the Hague, is come over to settle in this our kingdome with his family, to exercise his 'Art of makeing Tiles and Porcelaine and other Earthen Wares, after the way practised in Holland,' which hath not beene practised in this our kingdome," took out a patent for fourteen years for the sole practice of his art. The "tiles" named in his patent would, of course, be the "Dutch Tiles," as they were always called, and which were used for the lining of rooms, the decoration of fire-places, and for various other purposes. They were

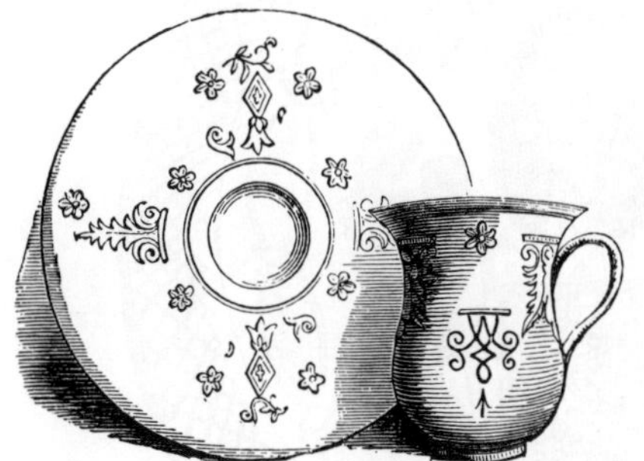

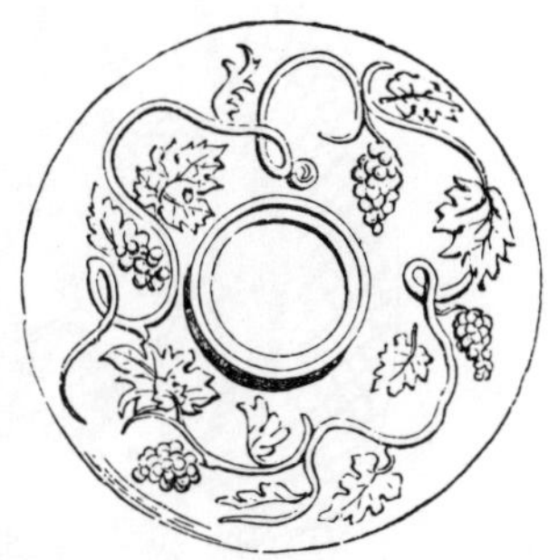

Figs. 318 and 319.—Elers Ware.

about four inches square, made of a common kind of clay, and faced, as all delf ware was, with a fine white slip. On this was painted a pattern—a group of figures, the illustration of some sacred or profane story, foliage, birds, or other devices, in blue colour, and then glazed and fired. On one of these tiles is represented a lady letting her lover down from her chamber into the street below, by a rope which she holds in her hand, and others have various devices. The manufacture of these tiles was carried on largely in England, and further notices will be given under the head of Liverpool, &c.

In 1684 John Dwight, having represented "that by his owne industry and at his owne proper costes and charges hee hath invented and sett vp at Fulham, in our County of Middlx, 'Severall New Manufactures of Earthenwares, called by the names of White Gorges, Marbled Porcellane Vessels, Statues, and Figures, and Fine Stone Gorges and Vessells never before made in England or elsewhere; and alsoe discovered the Mistery of Transparent Porcellane, and Opacous, Redd, and Dark-coloured Porcellane or China and Persian Wares, and the Mistery of the Cologne or Stone Wares, and is endeavouring to settle manufactures of all the said wares within this our kingdome of England," had another patent for fourteen years granted to him. To Dwight, therefore, it will be seen by these patents, the credit of being the first inventor and maker of porcelain in England belongs. His name is thus one entitled to lasting honour as the pioneer of one of the best, most beautiful, and most flourishing arts practised in our kingdom.

In 1688 the brothers Eler or Elers, traditionally believed to have been potters from Holland, are said to have come over with William, Prince of Orange (William III.), to England at the time of the "Glorious Revolution," and, two years later, to have settled at Bradwell and Dimsdale, not far from Burslem, in Staffordshire, where they erected kilns and commenced the making of a fine red ware (probably the kind spoken of by Dwight), in imitation of foreign red porcelain, from a vein of clay which, by some means, they had discovered existed at this spot. Here they produced remarkably fine and good red ware, of compact and hard texture, good colour, and of very characteristic and excellent designs.

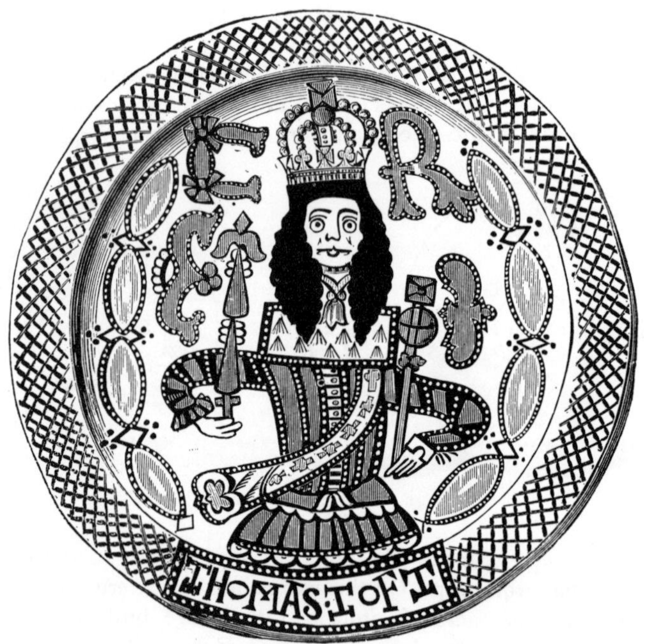

Fig. 320.

They were men of much skill and taste, and their productions so closely resemble those of Japan as to be occasionally taken for them. An example, from the Museum of Practical Geology, is shown on p. 75. The Elers, besides the red ware, also produced an exceedingly good Egyptian black, by a mixture of manganese with the clay; and this was the precursor and origin of the fine black bodies of Josiah Wedgwood and others. "Their extreme precaution," says Shaw, "to keep secret their processes, and jealousy lest they might be accidentally witnessed by any purchasers of their wares—making them at Bradwell, and conveying them over the fields to Dimsdale, there to be sold, being only two fields distant from the turnpike road, and having some means of communication (believed to be earthenware pipes, like those for water) laid in the ground between the two contiguous farmhouses, to intimate the approach of persons supposed to be intruders—caused them to experience considerable and constant annoyance. In vain did they adopt measures for self-protection in regard to their manipulations, by employing an idiot to turn the thrower's wheel, and the most ignorant and stupid workmen to perform the laborious operations, and by locking up these persons while at work, and strictly examining each prior to quitting the manufactory at night—all their most important processes were however developed, and publicly stated for general benefit. Mortified at the failure of all their precaution, disgusted at the prying inquisitiveness of their Burslem neighbours, and fully aware that they were too far distant from the principal market for their productions—even had not other kinds of porcelain been announced, which probably would diminish their sales — about 1710 they discontinued their Staffordshire manufactory, and removed to Lambeth or Chelsea (where is at this day a branch of the family), and connected the interests of their new manufactory with those of a glass manufacture, established in 1676 by Venetians, under the auspices of the Duke of Buckingham. Others, however, have stated that their removal was consequent on misunderstanding and persecution

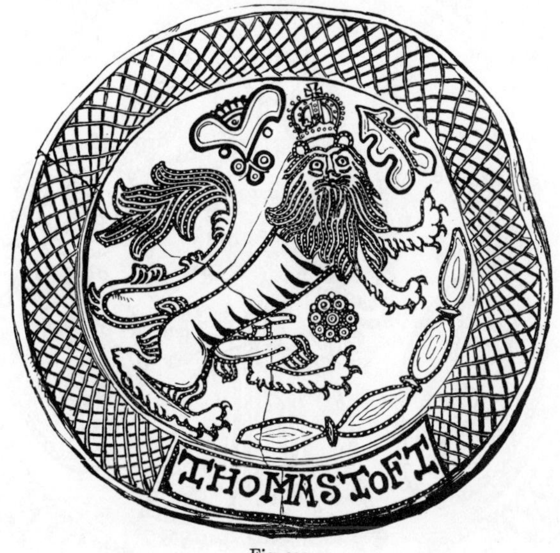

Fig. 321.

because their oven cast forth such tremendous volumes of smoke and flame, during the time of glazing, as were terrific to the inhabitants of Burslem, and caused all its (astonishing number of *eight*) master potters to hurry in dismay to Bradwell."

The two potters who had wormed out the secret of the Elers were named Astbury and Twyford, and they are said each to have commenced business on his own account at Shelton, and to have made "RED," "CROUCH," and "WHITE STONE" wares from native clays, using salt glaze for some of the vessels, and lead ore for others. It is interesting to add that the oven erected and used by the Elers was in existence as late as the beginning of the present century, and that the place, in an old account-book in my possession, is called "the Eller field."

About the period when Dwight was taking out his patent, Thomas Toft and Ralph Toft were making, in Staffordshire, some large domestic dishes, which, from some of them bearing their names, put on in large letters, are universally known to collectors as "Toft Dishes." Under this name, however, it is well to state many dishes and other vessels pass which never were, or could have been, made by them, and I warn collectors against too easily pinning their faith to a belief that their examples are genuine "Tofts" unless they bear the name. The style was common to all makers of that date. Besides dishes, tygs of various forms, with one, two, three, or four handles; pitchers of various sizes, candlesticks, posset-pots, gossips' bowls, pans or pancheons, utensils for the chamber, and many other articles, were made of precisely the same coarse materials, and of exactly the same kind of decoration as the dishes.

The material of these pots is a coarse reddish or buff-coloured clay, and the ornaments are laid on in different coloured clays, and the whole is then glazed

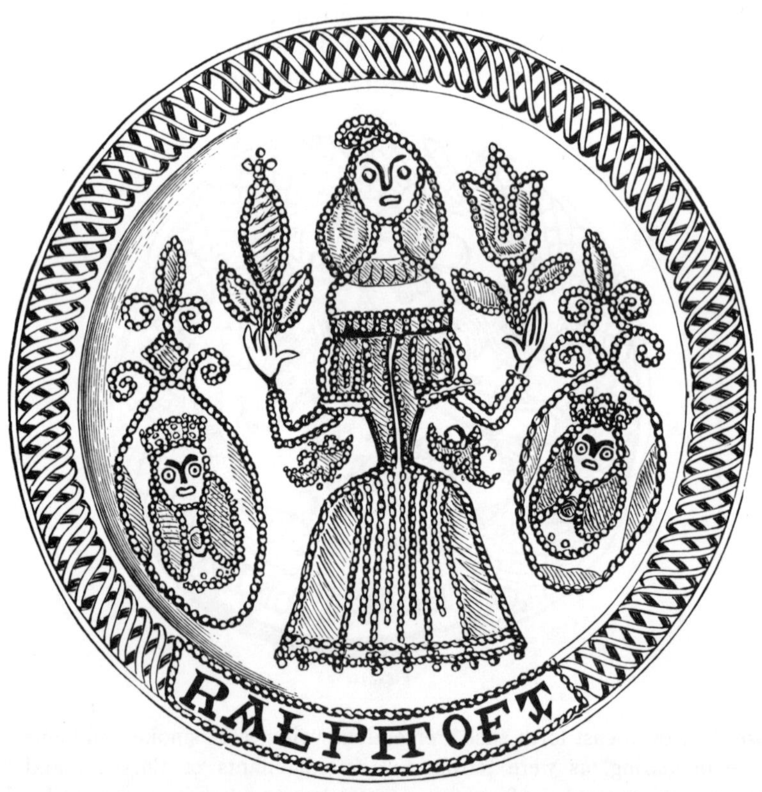

Fig. 322.

thickly over. One of these large dishes, now in the Museum of Practical Geology, is shown on Fig. 321. The body is of buff-coloured clay, with the ornaments laid on in relief in light and dark brown. The border is trellised, and in the centre is a lion rampant, crowned. On the rim beneath the lion is the name of the maker, THOMAS TOFT. In the same museum is a fragment of another similar dish, with a lion and unicorn. A very fine dish of a similar kind, and by the same maker, in the Bateman Museum, is engraved on Fig. 320. It is twenty-two inches in diameter, and bears a half-length crowned portrait of King Charles, with sceptre in each hand, and the initials C.R. Below the figure, on the rim, which, as usual, is trellised in red and black, is the name THOMAS TOFT. In the same museum

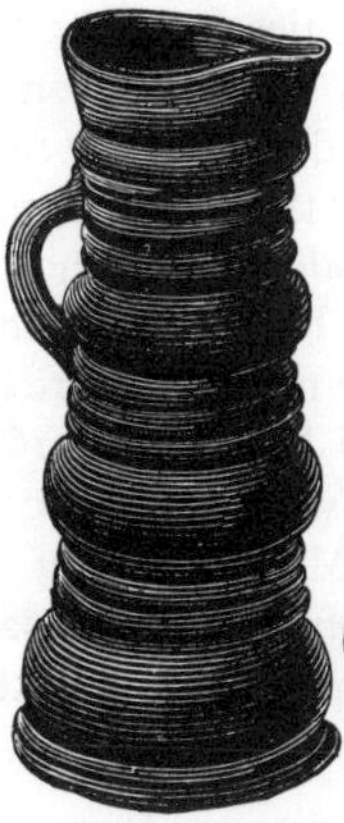

Fig. 323.

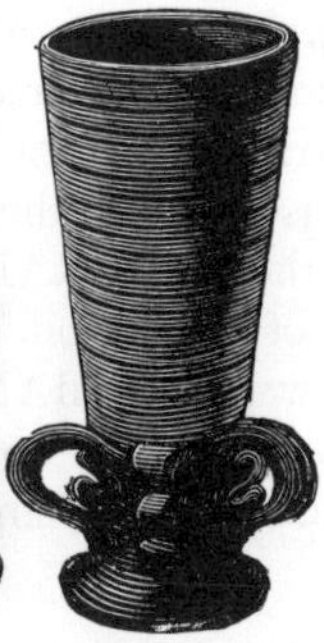

Fig. 323*a*

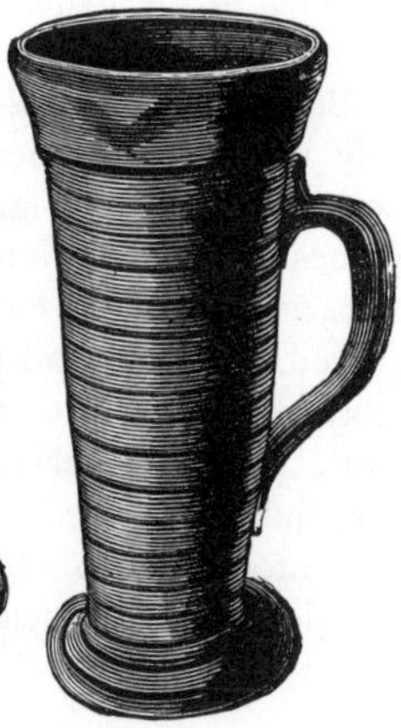

Fig. 324.

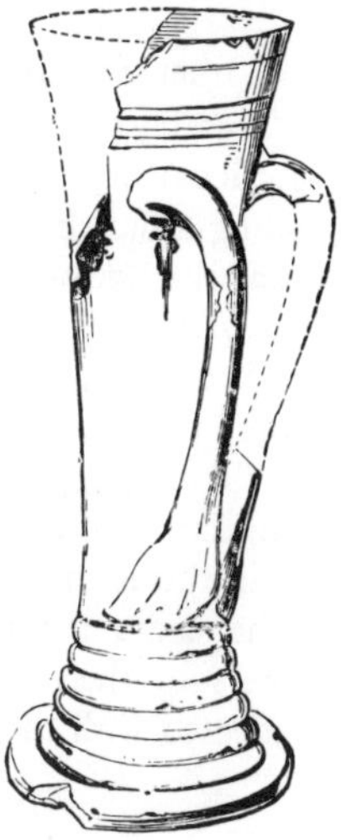

Fig. 325.

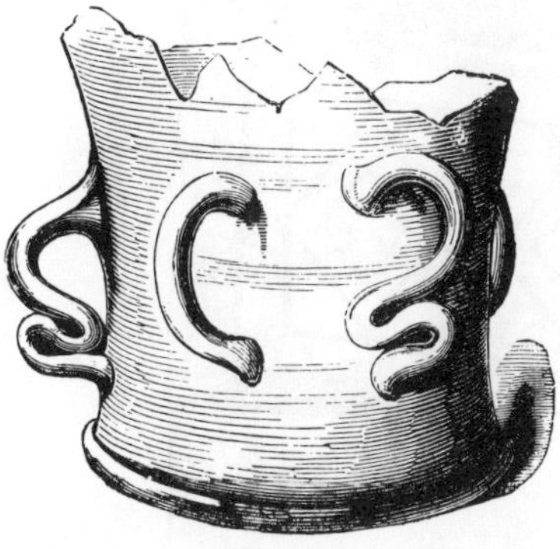

Fig. 326.

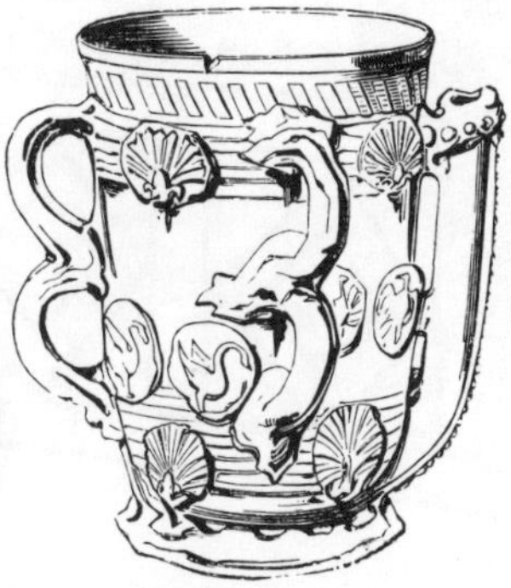

Fig. 327.

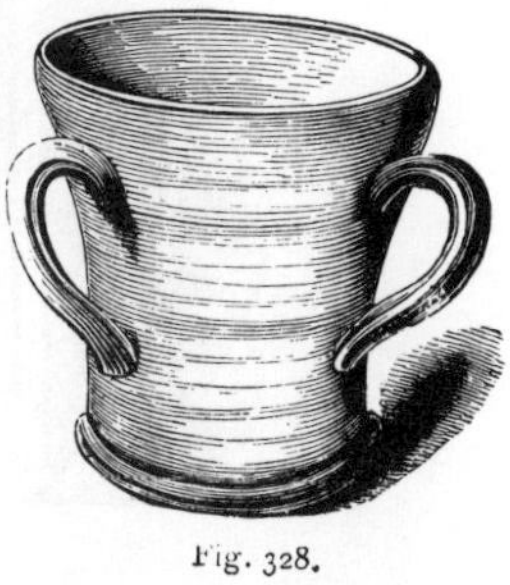

Fig. 328.

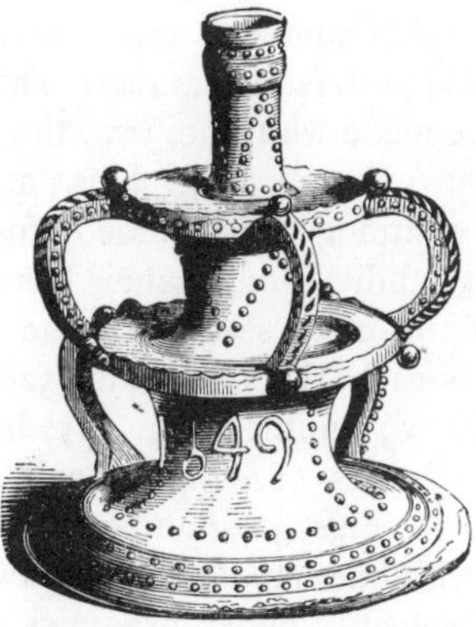

Fig. 329.—Candlestick, Jermyn Street.

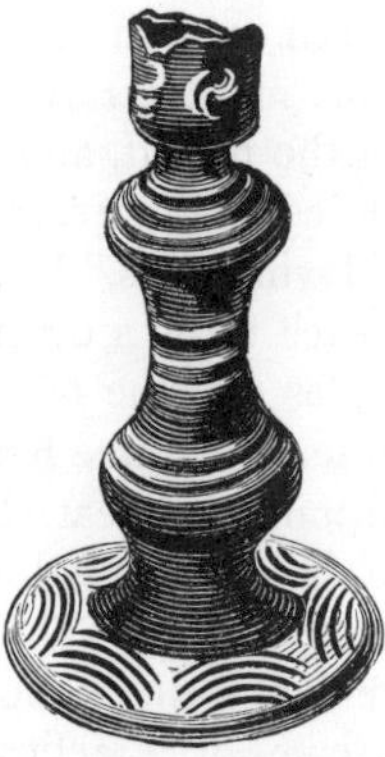

Fig. 330.—Candlestick.

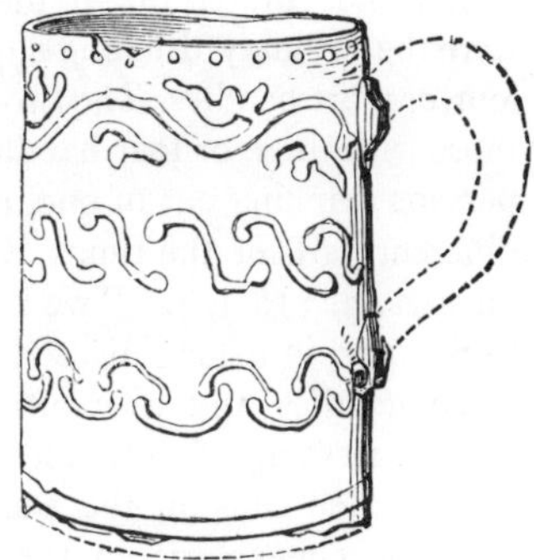

Fig. 331.—Mug.

is another remarkably fine dish, bearing two full-length figures in the costume of the Stuarts, the gentleman holding in his hand his hat and feather, and having "petticoat breeches," tied stockings, and high-heeled boots with ties, and the lady holding a bunch of flowers. Between the figures are the initials W. T., and on the rim at the bottom, in precisely the same manner as the Toft dishes, is the name WILLIAM : TALOR. Another Toft dish (Fig. 322), now in the possession of Mr. Bagshawe, is nineteen inches in diameter, and bears a female figure, and two heads in ovals, with foliage, &c., and the name RALPHOFT, or Ralph Toft, the H and T being apparently conjoined. The ground is buff, and the ornaments are laid on in dark and light brown clay. Another with the name RALPH TOFT, 1677, was in the Reynolds' collection. Another maker of this period, whose name occurs in the same manner as those just described, was WILLIAM SANS. Of the makers of these dishes, it is interesting to observe that Toft is an old name connected with the pottery district, and that members of the family are still potters

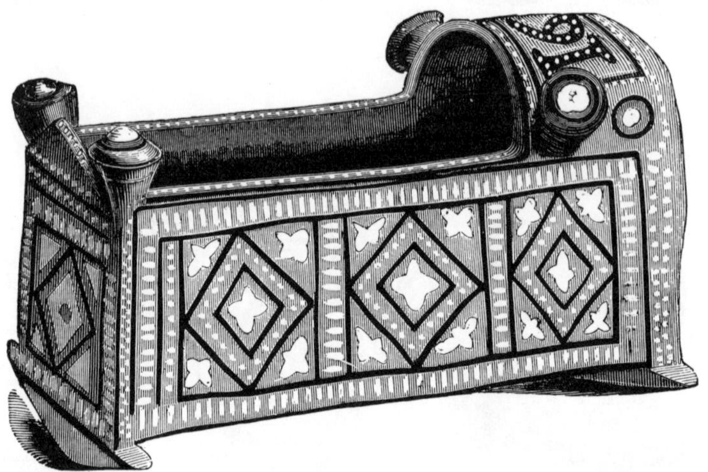

Fig. 332.—Earthenware Cradle.

in the neighbourhood. It is also an old Derbyshire name, being connected with Youlgreave and other places in that neighbouring county.

The "Tygs" appear to have been made in considerable numbers, and, indeed, to have constituted one of the staple manufactures of the potters of that day. They were the ordinary drinking-cups of the period, and were made with one, two, three, four, or more handles. The two-handled ones are said to have been "parting cups," and those with three or four handles "loving cups," being so arranged that three or four persons drinking out of one, and each using a different handle, brought their lips to different parts of the rim. Examples of some of the forms of these tygs are shown on Figs. 323 to 328. Two of these, with three handles each (Figs. 326 and 328), were found in a long-disused lead mine at Great Hucklow; another (Fig. 327) has three handles and a spout, and is ornamented with bosses of a lighter colour, bearing a swan, a flower, and a spread eagle. The fourth (Figs. 323*a* and 325) are two-handled cups, of the same general form as those with one handle. These two latter specimens are in the Museum of Practical Geology. Other examples of various forms are shown on the remaining engravings.

A curious candlestick, shown on Fig. 329, in the Museum of Practical Geology, is of much the same kind of ware as the tygs, and has its ornaments in white clay slip; it bears the date 1649, and the initials E. M. Another, in my own collection (Fig. 330), is made of precisely the same coarse kind of ware as the tygs; dark reddish brown, with ornaments in white slip—the slip at the base having been laid on in a broad band, and then scratched through to the dark clay. The mug, Fig. 331, is exactly the same kind of ware.

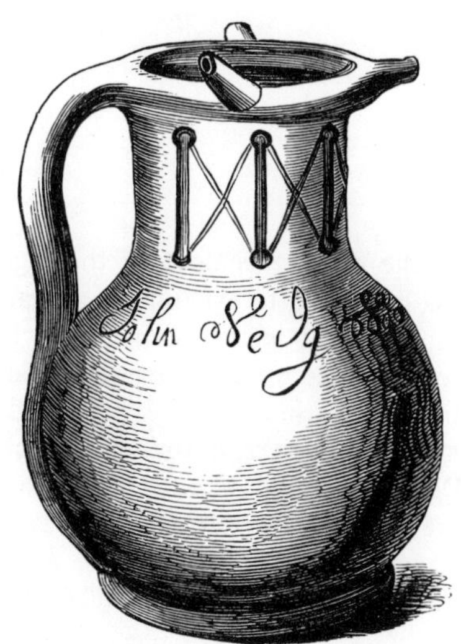

Fig. 333.—Puzzle Jug.

Another curious article of this same kind of ware, in the Bateman collection, is engraved on Fig. 332. It is a small earthenware cradle of excellent form, and elaborately ornamented; the ground is a rich reddish brown, the ornaments of buff and black. It bears the date on its top of 1693, and is 7¾ inches long, and 4¾ inches in height. To this period belongs the interesting puzzle-jug in the Museum of Practical Geology, shown on Fig. 333. It is of brown ware, and bears the name, incised in writing letters, of "John Wedgwood, 1691," and is the first and earliest example of the name of Wedgwood occurring on pottery.

It is very clear that brown ware of the same general character as the tygs and the Toft dishes, was made in very many parts of the country besides Staffordshire, and that much now by collectors appropriated to that county has no connection with it.

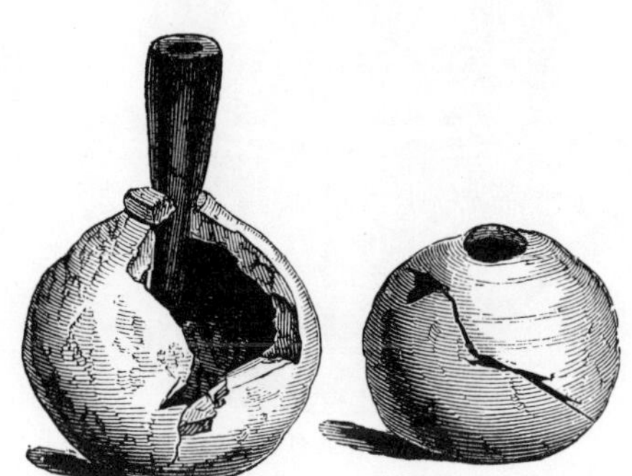

Figs. 334 and 335.—Hand Grenades.

A peculiar use for ceramics should here be noticed; it has not before been spoken of in any work upon pottery. I allude to hand-grenades, two of which, preserved in the Leicester Museum, are here engraved (Figs. 334 and 335). These were found in the Old Magazine, or Newarke, Gateway at Leicester. They are formed of red clay, and fired in the kiln in the usual manner, and they have fuse-plugs of wood fitted into the opening at the top.

CHAPTER V.

At the commencement of the eighteenth century, the Ceramic Art in this country was beginning to expand in a remarkable degree, and many important strides for its improvement were taken. The brown-ware dishes, tygs, and other vessels for domestic use were still made as before, and stoneware bottles, ale pots, and other articles continued to be produced; but, beyond these, some much finer kinds of earthenware were introduced, which gradually took their place. Among these were Delft ware and Crouch ware, to which I have referred, and the White ware (frequently, but erroneously, called "Elizabethan ware") which was probably introduced about this time. A good specimen of the slip-painted brown ware of this period, identical in character with the dishes, tygs, and cradle before

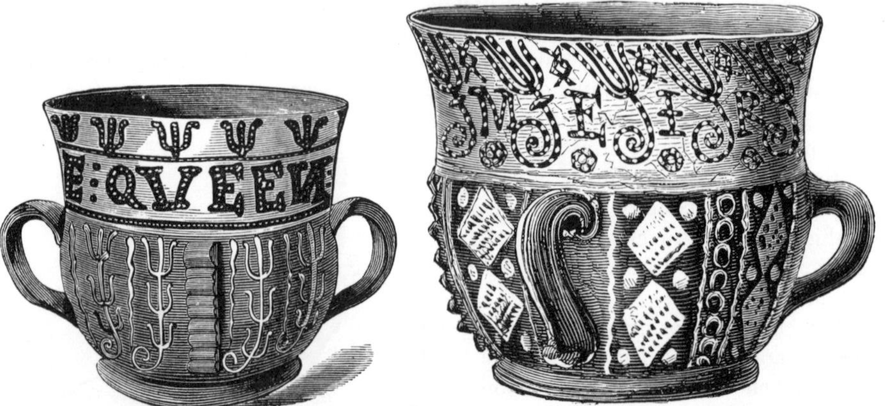

Fig. 336.—Posset Pot.

Fig. 337.

spoken of, is the posset pot, Fig. 336, which bears the words "GOD : SAVE : THE : QVEEN : 1711," and is of much the same character as the wassail or "gossips' bowl" bearing the name of "RICHARD MEIR," Fig. 337. The form of Fig. 336 is somewhat different from the usual later shape of posset pots, as will be shown on engravings which will follow. As posset and posset pots are local matters, a few words concerning them will here be interesting. Posset pots have been made and regularly used in Derbyshire and the neighbouring counties from an early period until the present time. "Posset" is an excellent mixture of hot ale, milk, sugar, spices, and sippets, or, perhaps, more correctly speaking, dice, of bread or oat-cake. In these counties, this beverage was formerly almost, if not quite, universal for supper on Christmas-eve; and the "posset pot" was thus used but once a year, and often became an heirloom in the family. A small silver coin and the wedding-ring of the mistress ofthe family were generally dropped into the posset when the guests were assembled, and those who partook of it took each a spoonful in turn as the "pot" was handed round. Whichever of the party fished up the coin was considered certain of good luck in the coming year, while an early and happy marriage was believed to be the enviable fate of the lucky individual who fished up the ring. Other posset pots will be found engraved in other parts of this volume, under the heads of Nottingham and Brampton.

It is clear that about this time the art of pot-making began to make rapid strides; for in the space of twenty-seven years—from 1722 to 1749—no less than nine separate patents were taken out, and were followed in rapid succession by others. In 1722, Richard Holt and Samuel London, gentlemen, took out a patent for "a certain new composicon or mixture (without any sort of clay) for making of white ware, which is formed and moulded in a method hitherto not known or practised, and far surpasses the finest of delf ware, or any other sort made in any part of Europe, and also by their new method of impression make the fabrick of earthenware of a more exquisite shape than the present method of turning could ever perform or arrive to, by which meanes our subjects will be able to excell all Europe, and not only employ a great many of our own poor, to the great benefit of trade and the manufactures of our kingdom, but also prevent the clandestine running of delf ware, &c., from foreign parts into Great Brittain;" granted "for the term of fourteen years." It does not say of what materials the composition is made, except that it is without any sort of clay, nor does it describe any method of impression.

In the same year, Thomas Billin, having "by many long, laborious, and chargeable experiments found out and invented a method for making the most refined earthenware, with help of clay and other materials found within this kingdom, which ever yet appeared in this part of Europe, of a nature and composicon, not only transparent, but so perfect in its kind, and of principles so firmly vnited, as (contrary to the nature of all other earthenwares) to resist almost any degree of heat, by which qualities it is more valuable, and of greater vse and ornament than all other kinds ever yet invented or practised in this kingdom, and capable of being wrought into vessels and ornaments for any vse; and for the working of the same invention he hath invented particular and proper engines and tools." No description is given of the mode of manufacture, or of the engines or tools mentioned in the title of the invention.

In 1724 Robert Redrich and Thomas Jones had a patent granted "for staining, veining, spotting, clouding, damasking, or otherwise imitating the various kinds of marble, porphyry, and other rich stones, and tortoiseshell," on earthenware, and other substances.

In 1726, and again in 1732, important patents were taken out by Thomas Benson for methods of grinding flints, &c. The first of these is described as "an engine or new method for the more expeditious working the said flint stone, whereby all the said hazards and inconveniences attending the same will effectually be prevented." It is stated that in the making of "white pots," flint stone is "the chief ingredient," and that the method hitherto used in preparing it "has been by pounding or breaking it dry, and afterwards sifting it through fine lawns, which has proved very destructive to mankind;" and this invention is to obviate it, and is as follows:—The flint stones are first wetted, then crushed as fine as sand by two large wheels, of the bigness and shape of mill-stones, of iron, and made to turn upon the edges by the power of a water-wheel. This material is afterwards conveyed into large circular iron pans, "in which there are large iron balls, which, by the power of the water-wheel above named, are swiftly driven round: in a short time the operation is concluded, and by turning a tap the material empties itself into casks."

In 1729 Samuel Bell took out a patent for fourteen years "for a new method not hitherto practiced within Great Brittain for making of a red marble stoneware with minerall earth, found within this kingdom, which being firmly vnited by fire will make it capable of receiving a gloss so beautiful as to imitate, if not to compare with rubie;" but no specification is given to show what the mineral earth was.

In 1733 (April 24th) Ralph Shawe, potter, of Burslem, who, like many other potters of the district, had long adopted the improvements of Mr. Astbury and others, took out a patent for employing "various sorts of mineral, earth, clay, and other earthy substances, which, being mixt and incorporated together, make up a fine body, of which a curious ware may be made, whose outside will be of a true chocolate colour, striped with white, and the inside white, much resembling the brown China ware, and glazed with salt." The *secret* was merely *washing* the inside, and forming broad lines on the outside of the articles with a very thick slip of flint and pipe-clay. "To keep his process more secluded and secret, he was accustomed to evaporate his mixed clays on a long trough, in a place locked up under cover, beneath which were flues, for the heat from fire applied on the outside. This also kept the clay free from any kind of dirt; and the idea is supposed to have been gained from the tile-makers' method of drying their tiles in stoves. A pair of flower-pots, excellent specimens of this person's manufacture, which had been received as a present from the maker by his wife's grandfather, were in the author's possession till very recently. Mr. Shawe became so litigious and overbearing, that many of the manufacturers were extremely uncomfortable, and prevented improving their productions. Not content with the success he experienced, and the prospect of speedily acquiring affluence, his excessive vanity and insatiable avarice incited to proceedings that terminated in his ruin. Unwilling to admit the customary practices of the business, and to brook any appearance of competition, he was constantly objecting to every trifling improvement as an infringement of his patent, and threatening his neighbours with suits in equity to protect his *sole* rights; till at length self-defence urged them to bear the expenses of a suit he had commenced against J. Mitchell, to try the validity of the patent, at Stafford, in 1736; and very aged persons, whose parents were present, give the general facts of the trial:—All the manufacturers being interested in the decision, those most respectable were in the court. Witnesses proved Astbury's invention and prior usage of the practice, and a special jury of great intelligence and wealth gave a verdict against Mr. Shawe. The learned judge, after nullifying the patent, thus addressed the audience—'Go home, potters, and make whatever kinds of pots you please.' The hall re-echoed with acclamations, and the strongest ebullitions of satisfaction from the potters, to the indescribable mortification of Mr. Shawe and his family, who afterwards went to France, where he carried forward his manufactory, whence some of his family returned to Burslem about 1750."

The kind of ware just described was sometimes known as "bitstone ware," from "bits" of stone being used to separate the pieces in the oven. This was, of course, prior to the use of "stilts," "triangles," or "cockspurs."

In 1744, Edward Heylyn, in the parish of Bow, in the county of Middlesex, merchant, and Thomas Frye, of the parish of West Ham, in the county of Essex, painter, took out a patent for "A New Method of Manufacturing a Certain Mate-

RIAL, WHEREBY A WARE MIGHT BE MADE OF THE SAME NATURE OR KIND, AND EQUAL TO, IF NOT EXCEEDING IN GOODNESS AND BEAUTY, CHINA OR PORCELAIN WARE IMPORTED FROM ABROAD; which Invention we, the Petitioners, apprehended would be of vast advantage to the kingdom, as it would not only save large sums of money that were yearly paid to the Chinese and Saxons, but also imploy large numbers of men, women, and children."

The description of the invention follows:—"The material is an earth, the produce of the Chirokee nation in America, called by the natives unaker, the propertys of which are as follows, videlicet, to be very fixed, strongly resisting fire and menstrua, is extremely white, tenacious, and glittering with mica. The manner of manufacturing the said material is as follows:—Take unaker, and by washing separate the sand and mica from it, which is of no use; take pott ash, fern ash, pearl ash, kelp, or any other vegetable lixiviall salt, one part of sands, flints, pebbles, or any other stones of the vitryfying kind; one other part of these two principles form a glass in the usual manner of making glass, which when formed reduce to an impalpable powder. Then mix to one part of this powder two parts of the washed unaker, let them be well worked together until intimately mixed for one sort of ware; but you may vary the proportions of the unaker and the glass; videlicet, for some parts of porcelain you may use one half unaker and the other half glass, and so in different proportions, till you come to four unaker and one glass; after which knead it well together, and throw it on the wheel, cast it into moulds, or imprint it into utensils, ornaments, &c.; those vessells, ornaments, &c., that are thrown, should be afterwards turned on a lathe and burnished, it will then be in a situation to be put into the kiln and burned with wood, care being taken not to discolour the ware, otherwise the process will be much hurt. This first burning is called biscuiting, which, if it comes out very white, is ready to be painted blue, with lapis lazuli, lapis armenis, or zapher, which must be highly calcined and ground very fine. It is then to be dipt into the following glaze:—Take unaker forty pounds, of the above glass ten pounds, mix and calcine them in a reverberatory; then reduce, and to each pound when reduced add two pounds of the above glass, which must be ground fine in water, and left of a proper thickness for the ware to take up a sufficient quantity. When the vessells, ornaments, &c., are dry, put them into the kiln in cases, burn them with a clean wood fire, and when the glaze runs true lett out the fire, and it is done, but must not be taken out of the kiln till it is thorough cold."

In this specification, and in another taken out in 1748 by Thomas Frye, we have important materials touching the Bow china works, under which head they will again be referred to. About this time, the Chelsea, Worcester, and Derby, and, a little later, the Plymouth, porcelain works were established. The year in which the later specification was enrolled, 1749, is memorable as the year when Josiah Wedgwood completed his term of apprenticeship, and when, consequently, he entered upon that course of work and life which have ever since had so brilliant and so marked an effect upon the potter's art in this country. At this time, too, there were in Staffordshire a number of very skilful potters, who were, even before Wedgwood's time, making rapid strides in the art.

The next patent taken out was in 1762, by "William White, of Fulham, in the county of Middlesex, potter," for making white crucibles or melting-pots of Stourbridge clay and Dorsetshire clay, calcined, mixed with Woolwich sand, and water, and trodden together, and burned. Two years later James Williamson and Joseph Spackman patented "a new method of turning ovals in pewter, English china, and all other earthenwares," on a lathe with movable chucks and sliding ring, of their inventing. In 1766, "the Count de Lauraguais, of London," having, "by his petition, humbly represented unto us, that by labour, study, travelling, and expence in trying experiments, he hath found out and invented 'a new method of making porcelain ware in all its different branches, viz.—to make the coarser species of china, the more beautiful of the Indies, and the finest of Japan, in a manner different from any that is made in our dominions, and he, having the materials tryed in Great Britain, has brought the same to so great perfection that the porcelain made therewith after his new method far excells any that has hitherto been made in Great Britain, the same not being fusible by fire, as all other china made there is,' " took out a patent for fourteen years, but no specification seems to have been enrolled.

During all this time the pottery district of Staffordshire was rapidly increasing, and important strides were being made by its manufacturers in the improvement of their art. In various parts of the country, too, old pot works continued their business in an improved state, and new ones sprang up in every direction. The history of the art, therefore, becomes that of the various works which I shall have to pass under review. The patents taken out from this period to the close of the century are some guide to this state of progress, but not much; for it is an undoubted fact, that many of the most important improvements and most reliable inventions were never patented at all, while others, which were the gradual result of daily practice, were not sufficiently "inventions" to entitle them to patent right.

In 1768 William Cookworthy, of Plymouth, took out a patent for his newly invented porcelain, which was renewed in 1775 to Richard Champion; and in 1769 Josiah Wedgwood took out his only patent, which was for decorative, not manufacturing, processes.

In 1782 James Crease patented some inventions in the making of sanitary vessels; and in the two following years "Joseph Cartledge, of Blackley, in the county of York, Doctor of Physic," enrolled his specification for "a method of glazing earthenware."

The next patent, in 1785, was by Thomas De-la-Mayne, for "making buttons of burnt earth or porcelain;" and the next, in 1786, by John Skidmore, for ornamenting various articles and "all sorts of china and earthenware with foil stones, Bristol stones, paste, and all sorts of pinched glass, lapped glass, and every other stone, glass, and composition used in or applicable to the jewellery trade," in ways therein described. In 1789 an improvement in the form and construction of "soup ladles, tureens, gravy spoons, ladles, and skimmers," was patented by John Baynes; and in 1790, Johanna Hempel patented newly invented filters. In 1796, James Keeling patented improvements in decorative and glazing processes; and in the same year, in conjunction with Valentine Close, an improved mode of constructing "ovens, kilns, and firing-places, so as to make and cause a very great saving of coals and fuel in and about the firing, hardening, and baking all manner of porcelain, china ware, and all manner of earthenwares, in every state wherein firing is needful and necessary."

In the same year, 1796, Ralph Wedgwood took out three separate patents. The first of these was for a "new-discovered and invented method of making earthenware, whereby the article of earthenware may be made at a less cost than hitherto, to the great advantage of the manufacturers thereof, and of the public." This consists "in casing over inferior compositions with compositions commonly used for making cream-coloured ware, white ware, or china." "Thick bats or laminæ" of the inferior are covered on each side with thin bats of the superior clay, and if the edges of the ware are required to be cased, they are surrounded "with a square piece commonly called a wad." Afterwards the "bats" are beat, pressed, or rolled out to the required dimensions, "as are proper for the wares to be made from the same." For moulding the wares single moulds may be used, but double are preferred, of wood, or "wood cased with plaster, or metal," or any material capable of standing much pressure. The press is such as is used for stamping buttons. The glazing is applied dry to the bats; if the edges of the ware, after moulding, are not properly covered with dry glaze, supply these parts "with wet glaze, by means of a pencil;" afterwards stove and burn the ware. The others were respectively for a new method of making glass from old earthenware, china, &c.; and for "a new-invented stove," "calculated principally for the use of manufacturers of earthenware and china." On the same day on which this patent was dated, one was also granted to John Pepper, for a new construction of kilns or ovens for the same purpose. In 1799 Messrs. William and John Turner patented "a new method or methods of manufacturing porcelain or earthenware, by the introduction of a material not heretofore used in the manufacturing of those articles;" the material being "Tabberner's Mine rock," "Little Mine rock," and "New rock," mixed with the growan, or Cornish stone, and flint.

This is the last patent connected with ceramics before the year 1800, and therefore brings us down to the commencement of the present century. From 1800 to 1861 no less than three hundred and twenty-two patents were taken out for improvements in the potter's art or in matters connected with that art. These will be briefly enumerated at the close of this work, and of many of them notices will be found incorporated in its body.

In the early part of this century, with the exception of the productions of a few houses, the state of the art was still at a low ebb; and although improvements were constantly being made, when the great world-struggle took place in 1851, we, as a nation, were found to be lamentably behind some other countries, not only in the beauty of form and decoration of our ceramic productions, but even in quality of body and glaze. Between the Exhibitions of 1851 and 1862 a marked improvement was effected, and this has gone on steadily extending itself, until now in this art Great Britain, without exception, stands foremost of all the nations.

I now proceed, in succeeding chapters, to speak of the various earthenware and porcelain works and seats of pottery manufacture of the kingdom.

CHAPTER VI.

Fulham.

In 1671, as I have already shown (page 75), John Dwight took out a patent for "the mistery of transparent earthenware, comonly knowne by the names of Porcelaine or China, and Persian Ware, as alsoe the Misterie of the Stone Ware vulgarly called Cologne Ware." Dwight appears to have been a man of considerable learning and ability. He graduated as M.A. at Christ Church, Oxford, and successively held the appointments of secretary to more than one Bishop of Chester. He seems to have long experimented upon clays and mineral products in the search after the body of which the oriental china was made, and at length to have brought those researches to a successful issue. An interesting notice of his inventions, discoveries, and productions, is given in Plot's "Oxfordshire," published six years after the granting of the patent.

Dwight having patented his discovery of "the mistery," in April, 1671, it is perfectly clear that that discovery was made before that time, and must have been the result of a long series of patient trials and experiments. Thus, I think, we may safely say that the actual discovery was made some time prior to 1671. In 1684 the patent expired, and a new one was granted, in June, for another term of fourteen years—this time the wares and articles being more specifically named, as "Severall New Manufactures of Earthenwares, called by the names of White Gorges, Marbled Porcellane Vessells, Statues, and Figures, and Fine Stone Gorges and Vessells, never before made in England or elsewhere; and alsoe discovered the Mistery of Transparent Porcellane, and Opacous, Redd, and Darke-coloured Porcellane or China and Persian Wares, and the Mistery of the Cologne or Stone Wares."

In 1694 Houghton thus, in his "Letters on Husbandry and Trade," wrote while speaking of the tobacco-pipe clays, "gotten at or nigh Pool, a post-town in Dorsetshire, and there dug in square pieces, of the bigness of about half a hundred-weight each; from thence 'tis brought to London, and sold in peaceable times at about eighteen shillings a ton, but now in this time of war is worth about three-and-twenty shillings." And again he says: "This sort of clay, as I hinted formerly, is used to clay sugar; and the best sort of mugs are made with it, and the ingenious Mr. *Daught* of *Fulham* tells me that 'tis the same earth *China-ware* is made of, and 'tis made, not by lying long in the earth, but in the fire; and if it were worth while, we may make as good *China* here as any is in the world. And so for this time, farewel Clay." Again, on "March 13, 1695," he thus writes: "Of *China-ware* I see but little imported in the year, 1694, I presume by reason of the war and our bad luck at sea. There came only from Spain certain, and from India certain twice. 'Tis a curious manufacture, and deserves to be encourag'd here, which without doubt money would do; and Mr. *Dowoit* at *Fulham* has done it, and can again in anything that is flat: but the difficulty is that if a hollow dish be made, it must be burnt so much that the heat of the fire will make the sides fall. He tells me that our clay will very well do it; the main skill is in managing the fire. By my consent, the man that would bring it to perfection should have for his encouragement one thousand pound from the publick, though I help'd to pay a tax towards it."

Although no specifications are preserved with Dwight's patents,* two extremely curious private pocket-books in his own handwriting were recently discovered, and throw considerable light on the history of the plastic art at this period. On one of the books is written, "All that is in this book was enterd since 9 ber 15 1695;" but the other contains many earlier entries, from 1691, among which are a number of curious recipes.

Dwight is stated to have buried, in a similar way to what there is proof to show he did his money, all his models, tools, moulds, &c., in some still-unknown secret hiding-place of his manufactory, that his descendants might not continue that branch of the trade which he had been the first to invent; and very securely he has, evidently, done this; for, whatever may be found in future alterations and excavations, it is certain that these have never yet been brought to light. Some years ago, however, after taking down some of the old buildings, which had become much dilapidated, the workmen, while digging foundations for the new workshops, &c., discovered a vaulted chamber or cellar which had been firmly walled up, and which, on being broken into, was found to contain a number of stoneware grey-beards or bellarmines and ale-pots, &c., undoubtedly of Dwight's manufacture. These were of the same form, precisely, as the old Cologne ones which they were intended to, and did, supersede in this country—and were those "fine stone gorges never before made in England"—and for which his patent was granted. One of these, presented to me by the present proprietor of the works, Mr. Bailey, I here engrave (Fig. 338).

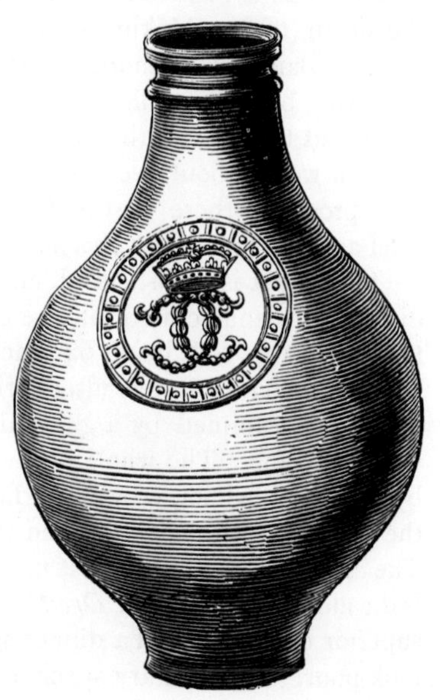

Fig. 338.

Nothing, at present, is known as to when the death of John Dwight took place, or who succeeded him. A Dr. Dwight died at Fulham in 1737, who, according to the *Gentleman's Magazine* of that year, was "author of several curious treatises on physic. He was the first that found out the secret to colour earthenware like china;" but this was not John Dwight, as supposed by some writers, but Samuel Dwight. As the death of this Samuel Dwight took place in 1737, or sixty-six years after the date of John Dwight's patent, the probability is that he was the son of John Dwight, and that his finding out the secret of colouring earthenware like china took place while engaged in his father's business. About this time it would appear (probably

* I perceive that Mr. Chaffers, in the 1870 edition of his work, says: "The discovery of the two patents granted to John Dwight . . . . . now published for the first time, in treating on this matter," &c.; but here he is in error. In 1863 Mr. Woodcroft printed abridgments of these very patents, and to these abridgments Mr. Chaffers is indebted for the knowledge he possessed of them. In 1864 I, too, gave notices of these patents, four years before the date of his publication.

after the death of Samuel Dwight) the business was carried on by a Margaret Dwight, in partnership with Thomas Warland, and these two—Margaret Dwight and Thomas Warland, of Fulham, potters—became bankrupt in 1746. This lady is said afterwards to have married a Mr. White, or Wight, who continued the works. In 1762 "William White, of Fulham, in the county of Middlesex, potter," took out a patent for the manufacture of "white crucibles or melting potts made of British materials, and never before made in England or elsewhere, and which I have lately sett up at Fulham aforsaid," and which were composed of "Stourbridge clay and Dorsetshire clay, calcined; mix them with Woolwich sand and water, to be trodden with the feet, and then burned." For these he had, in the previous year, obtained a premium from the Society of Arts. In 1795 the works were, according to Lysons, "carried on by Mr. White, a descendant in the female line of the first proprietor," and they were so continued until 1862, when, on the death of the then Mr. White, they passed into the hands of Messrs. Makintosh and Clements. Two years later, however, on the death of Mr. Makintosh, the works were sold to the present proprietor, Mr. C. I. C. Bailey, who shortly afterwards considerably enlarged and improved them; he having built a new factory and introduced improved machinery.

About the time of the sale in 1862, Mr. Baylis, of Priors Bank, obtained from the Fulham works about twenty-five curious and historically valuable specimens of the ware produced there by the Dwights, and kept in the family. Of these he sent a brief account to the *Art Journal* for October, 1862, in which he says:—

"The first is a dish, said, and with more than mere probability, to be one of a dinner set manufactured for the especial service of Charles II. It is of a round form and large size, being 64½ inches in circumference. The groundwork is a rich blue, approaching to the ultramarine; it is surrounded by a broad rim nearly four inches wide, formed by a graceful border of foliage and birds in white, and shaded with pale blue. The whole of the centre is occupied by the royal arms, surmounted by its kingly helmet, crown and lion crest. The arms themselves are encircled with the garter, on which is inscribed the well-known motto, '*Honi soi qui mal y pense.*' The arms and supporters rest upon a groundwork of foliage, in the middle of which is the motto, '*Dieu et mon Droit.*' The workmanship of this piece of crockery is of very superior character, and a dinner set of similar ware would make many a modern one look poor. The solitary specimen left of this once-magnificent royal dinner service *is believed to be by far the finest extant of this early English manufacture*, and includes five classical figures of brown ware, of admirable execution, testifying to the skill and taste of the Italian workmen: they consist of Saturn—at least we presume it is meant for him, as he is represented with a child in his arms, which he seems to be on the point of devouring, according to his agreement with his brother Titan. He has already got the child's hand in his mouth, and the bite of his teeth is by no means agreeable to his offspring, as is evident by the expression of pain on his countenance. The next figure is Jupiter, the third is Neptune, the fourth Mars, and the fifth either Adonis or Meleager, the emblem of the boar's head applying to either—the former being killed by a boar; the latter having killed the boar; and as the head is cut off, and lying at his feet, it is most probably Meleager, as he cut off the head of the beast and presented it to Atalanta. The grey ware consists of a bust of Charles II.; a bust of his queen, Catherine of Braganza; another of James II., and a companion one of his queen, Mary d'Este—all four of meritorious execution and excellent likenesses; a statuette of Flora; a likeness of one of the Dwight family, thirteen inches high; another of Adonis, same height; and a likeness of a lady; a portrait of one of the Dwights; a smaller pair of statuettes of a gentleman and lady of the court of Charles II., probably intended as likenesses; a curious figure, or rather bust, of one sleeping, or rather lying on a pillow, for it was a death likeness, and is inscribed 'Lydia Dwight, dyd March the 3rd, 1762;' a drinking cup, called Hogarth's cup—it is lettered 'Midnight Conversation,' and has on it a representation of Hogarth's picture in raised figures, and also four arms of the City companies. There are also four brown liqueur bottles, with white figures in relief, *temp.* Charles II., with his initial letter; and one or two specimens, such as a butter-boat and a couple of pickle saucers, of fine grey ware; but these appear of a somewhat different kind of manufacture, and may have been brought from Delft." It may be mentioned that this collection afterwards passed into the hands of Mr. C. W. Reynolds, and has since been dispersed by auction.

In the Jermyn Street Museum are some examples of this ware, and others may be found in various private collections. Among the latter may be named an historically interesting flip-can, belonging to "Robinson Crusoe," and carefully preserved by his family. It bears the incised inscription—"Alexander Selkirke. This is my one. When you take me on bord of ship, Pray fill me full with punch or flipp. Fulham." It is said to have been made for him in or about 1703.

The goods now made at these works are glazed and unglazed stoneware, brown ware, porous ware, terra-cotta, and china. In stoneware, or "Bristol ware," all the usual domestic vessels are made very extensively, as also are drain, sanitary, and chemical appliances of every description, including Field's syphon traps (of which they are sole makers), War Office pattern pipes, and others. Works of art of a high order, in stoneware, terra-cotta, china, and other bodies are also produced. For the stoneware department, M. Cazin, late Director of the School of Art at Tours, in France, was engaged to design figured and other fancy jugs, mugs, cannettes, &c. Some of these, with armorial bearings and other decorations in incised lines, or impressed, are good adaptations of the antique. A cannette, in my own possession, bearing the artist's name, "CAZIN, 1872, STUDY," is remarkably good, as is another example made expressly for me, which bears an admirably modelled armorial medallion, and other incised and relief ornaments, with the date, "1873," and artist's name, C. CAZIN, also incised. The coloured stone, or "sgraffito," ware equals in many respects that made at the later establishment at Lambeth, and is in much repute. In 1872 Mr. Bailey received a medal at the Dublin Exhibition for his stoneware and terra-cotta. He has also introduced a marked improvement in the construction of filters—the water passing downwards at the back, and then rising in zigzag direction by its own force to the tap at the top in front—thus the water has to travel a much further distance through the filtering matter (as shown by the arrows in the section) than by the old method, and having to be taken a far more circuitous course, it is brought more thoroughly in contact with the purifying medium. Terra-cotta stoves, of simple and effective construction, are also made at these works. In "Sunderland Ware"—*i.e.* brown ware, white inside—cream pots, starch pans, milk bowls, dishes, trays, and basins are largely manufactured. Chemical apparatus—receivers, retorts, evaporating dishes, condensing worms, filtering and other funnels, still heads, &c.,—are, as well as porous ware, a speciality in these works, and are of high repute. In terra-cotta, the Fulham Works produce vases, statues, architectural

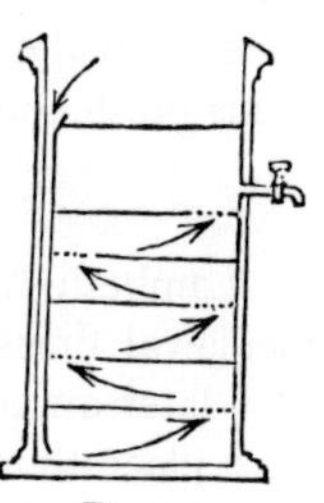
Fig. 339.

enrichments, chimney shafts, stoves, &c., of very good quality and of admirable design; Mr. R. W. Martin, sculptor, student of the Royal Academy and Government Schools of Art, having been engaged as modeller and designer, and giving to some of the productions the name of "Martin Ware." In colour the Fulham terra-cotta is a light pink and a rich red, and, when these are combined, a peculiar delicacy and finished effect is produced. The mark R. W. MARTIN *fecit* occurs on the productions of this artist.

The manufacture of china ware was, during the year 1873, very wisely and successfully added to this establishment, and, with the aid of the good workmen and artists who have been engaged, has done much to establish a fresh fame for Fulham. The art direction of this branch was placed by Mr. Bailey in the hands of Mr. E. Bennet, a well-known sculptor, while the china body flowers, &c., were undertaken by Mr. Hopkinson. I am the more particular in stating these arrangements as, being the beginning of a new manufacture, I am desirous of putting on record the circumstances of its commencement. The "body," it may be well to note, is made from Dwight's original recipe—the very body of which the first china ware made in England was produced—and therefore the "Fulham china" of to-day has an historical interest attached to it which is possessed by no other. It was a wise thought that induced Mr. Bailey to restore to Fulham the special manufacture which has rendered its name famous in the ceramic annals of this country; and it is to be hoped that the spirit he has shown will be amply compensated by a liberal patronage of his productions.

LAMBETH.

Lambeth has been a seat of pottery manufacture from an early period. In mediæval times the characteristic brown-ware pitchers, pans, tygs, &c., were made; and, later on, at this place was quite a colony of makers of Delft ware, who in turn gave place to stoneware manufacturers. China, too, appears to have been made at Lambeth from perhaps 1760, or thereabouts. It is recorded that in the middle of the seventeenth century the Delft-ware manufacture commenced; but it is not unlikely that Rous and Cullyn, some years earlier, here established themselves in the making of "stone potts, stone jugs, and stone bottels," for which they received a patent in 1626. It is conjectured, and with some probability, that one of the Delft-ware makers at this place was John Ariens Van Hamme, a Dutchman, who had come over from the Hague under the encouragement of our ambassador, who, as has already been shown (page 75), took out a patent in 1676 for the "Art of makeinge Tiles and Porcelane and other Earthen Wares, after the way practiced in Holland," and who, with his staff of workmen, probably formed the nucleus of what was afterwards a nest of potters, comprising, according to the "History of Lambeth," no less than twenty manufactories. In 1693 a trial took place in the Court of Exchequer concerning some parcels of potter's clay which had been seized by the Custom House officers, under the pretence that it was fuller's earth. In this trial five London potters, William Knight, Thomas Harper, Henry De Wilde, John Robins, and Moses Johnson, gave evidence in favour of the clay being potter's clay. One of these, William Knight, was undoubtedly the "William Knight of the parish of St. Buttolph Without, Aldgate, London, Pottmaker," concerning whom I give, from the original deed in my possession, some particulars under the head of "Aldgate;" some of the others were, I believe, of Lambeth.

The Delft ware made at Lambeth was of the ordinary kind, same as imported from Holland, and as that made in various English localities, and, being without mark, is not to be distinguished from others. Besides tiles, plates, jugs, mugs, dishes, &c., sack and other wine bottles, apothecaries' pill-slabs, wine-bin labels, &c., were made. Some of these pill-slabs are preserved in the Jermyn Street Museum, as are also some of the "sack-pots," both of which may most probably, as well as the apothecaries' jars, be ascribed to Lambeth. They are all of Delft ware, painted with blue, in the same manner as the tiles and other articles of this ware.

In 1820 there "were six or seven potters in Lambeth," says Mr. Goddard, "working some sixteen small kilns, of seven or eight feet in diameter, the produce of each kiln being under £20 worth of ware, the principal articles made being blacking bottles, ginger-beer bottles (very extensively made still), porter and cider bottles (not so largely made now), spruce-beer bottles (gone, with the beer, quite out of fashion), ink bottles (more used now than ever), oil bottles, pickle jars, hunting jugs, &c. A few chemical vessels were also turned out well from one kiln belonging to an eccentric individual, whose chief boast was to drink a gallon of beer a day, and do without rest on Sundays." In 1860: "In place of some sixteen kilns, turning out each under £20 per kiln, we have now about seventy, turning out each, perhaps, on an average £50. They consume upwards of 20,000 tons of coal, paying a corporation tax of say £2,100 per annum. The law requires this quantity to be burnt without smoke, and, after immense cost and labour, this difficulty may be called surmounted. Twenty-three thousand tons of clay are annually changed into useful articles, giving employment to more than eight hundred persons. The returns of the Lambeth potters cannot be estimated at less than £140,000."

High Street.—From about 1750 to 1770 the Delft-ware works were carried on by a Mr. Griffiths, who had, for those days, a large establishment. A curious reference to this manufactory occurs in the following extract from the *Monthly Magazine* for 1797. A man, at that time unknown, but who turned out to be James Doe, a potter, committed suicide by drowning, on the 14th of September in that year, at Sea Mill Docks, two and a half miles from Bristol, having remained "fasting and praying," without food or bedding, in the ruined building there from the 11th, waiting opportunity and determination to commit the rash act; and having, during the whole of that time, written a kind of diary of his feelings and intentions, his hopes and fears, on the walls of the old room he remained in. Mr. Joseph James interested himself much in the matter, and wrote an account of it for the *Monthly Magazine* in October, 1797.

In the possession of Mr. R. C. Ring is a mug painted by Doe—said to be his last work. It is signed "J. Doe, Sept. 1797;" and as he committed suicide on the 14th of that month, it would certainly be one of his last productions. Mr. Owen's assertion that he committed suicide through a fear that painting would injure the enameller's trade is amply shown to be without foundation.

Coades.—Coade's Artificial Stone Works, at Pedlar's Acre, King's Arms Stairs, Narrow Wall, Lambeth, opposite Whitehall Stairs or Ferry, were established about 1760 by Mrs. or the Misses Coade, under the name of "Coade's Lithodipyra, Terra-Cotta, or Artificial Stone Manufactory." This material was intended to take the place of carved stone for vases, statues, and architectural enrichments. In 1769 the two Misses Coade took into partnership their cousin, a Mr. Sealy (the nephew of Mr. Coade), and by these the works were carried on. In 1811 the firm was still "Coades & Sealy." At the death of Mr. Sealy, who survived the Misses Coade, a Mr. Croggan, who had for a long time been a clerk or manager attached to the business, became the proprietor of the works, which he continued for many years. He then disposed of the business to Messrs. Routledge, Greenwood, & Keene, who were succeeded by Messrs. Routledge & Lucas. These gentlemen, about 1840, dissolved partnership and sold off all their moulds, models, plant, &c., by auction.

The Coades are said to have come from Lyme Regis, in Dorsetshire, and probably it was for the purpose of turning their native clay to good account in London that induced them to establish this manufactory. Bacon, Flaxman, Banks, Rossi, and Panzetta, the sculptors, were employed to model for these works, and many of the old mansions and public buildings in London and in the country, as well as abroad—including the bas-relief in the pediment over the western portico of Greenwich Hospital, representing the death of Nelson, designed by Benjamin West, and modelled by Bacon and Panzetta; and the rood-screen of St. George's Chapel, Windsor; the statue of Britannia on the Nelson monument at Yarmouth, &c.—were executed at these works. The works principally produced at Coades were capitals of columns, statues, vases, bassi-relievi, monuments, coats-of-arms, keystones, angle rusticated blocks, balustrades, &c. They were of durable quality and excellent manufacture.

Another person employed at Coades was William John Coffee, who afterwards attained some celebrity as a modeller at the Derby China Works, and as a terra-cotta maker, for a short time, at Derby. I believe he was employed as a fire-man at Coades, and here, no doubt, being a clever fellow, picked up his knowledge of modelling and of mixing bodies.

The London Pottery is in High Street, Lambeth. It was established on a small scale in 1751, on a portion of old "Hereford House," the palace of one of the former bishops of Hereford, and has been carried on, without intermission, from that time to the present. In 1840 the manufactory came into the hands of Mr. James Stiff, the head of the present firm of "James Stiff & Sons." At that time the works consisted only of two small kilns, and covered an area of probably less than a quarter of an acre of ground, while at the present time it comprises fourteen kilns (some of them more than twenty feet in diameter) and covers no less than two acres. It has a very extensive frontage on the Albert Embankment, overlooking the river Thames, and by means of a private dock, with entrance under the Embankment, is enabled directly to carry on a very extensive export trade, and also to import the coals, clay, and other raw material used in the production of brown and white stoneware, terra-cotta, &c. Until 1860, when fresh buildings were erected, a Delft-ware sign-board existed in the front of this pottery.

The *five* principal kinds of pottery manufactured by Messrs. Stiff & Sons are: 1. Brown salt-glazed stoneware, in which the tubular socket drain-pipes, so extensively made here, are produced; telegraph insulators, battery jars (with which they supply the Post Office, Government of India, colonial telegraphs, railways, &c.); water-filters, jugs, bottles, jars, and all kinds of chemical apparatus are also made in this class of ware. 2. White stoneware, or "double-glazed" ware, or "Bristol ware," in which salt is not used, but the glazing is obtained by the application of a liquid glaze to the interior and exterior of each article before it is placed in the kiln. This ware, which is generally made with a rich yellow ochre on the upper parts of goods, while the lower part is of a creamy-white colour, has only been introduced into Lambeth about a quarter of a century, but has, to a considerable extent, superseded the old brown stoneware. 3. Buff and red terra-cotta, in which are made garden vases, pedestals, chimney-tops, window arches, string-courses,

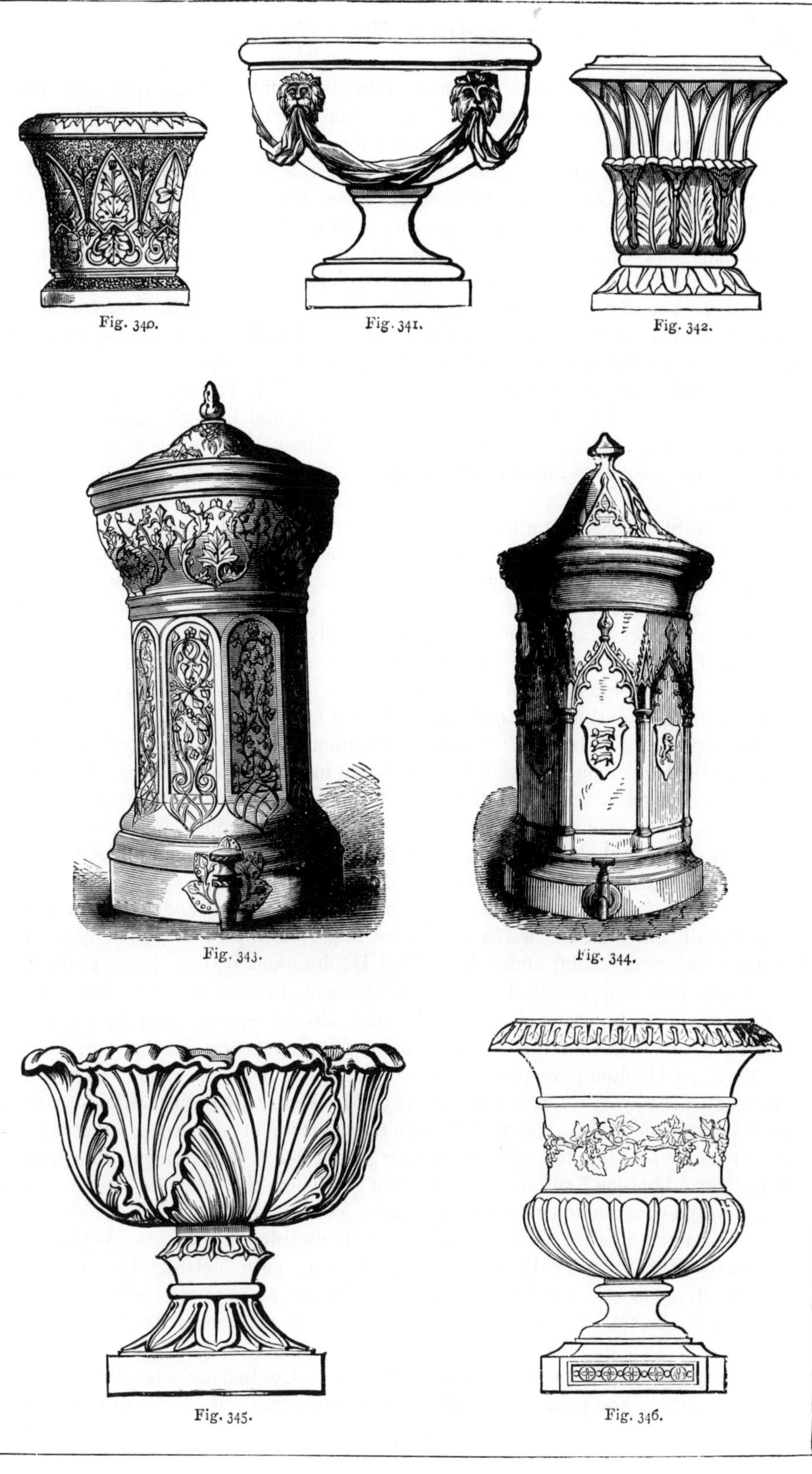

Fig. 340. Fig. 341. Fig. 342.

Fig. 343. Fig. 344.

Fig. 345. Fig. 346.

groups of figures, coats-of-arms, enormous statuary ten or twelve feet in length, lions, and every description of architectural decoration for buildings, &c. This terra-cotta, being thoroughly vitrified, is valuable for all purposes where durability is of importance; another great advantage being that, in it the choicest and most elaborate patterns, either raised or countersunk, can be obtained at little more than the cost of perfectly plain stone. 4. Porous ware, in which porous cells, plates, &c., of every shape and different degrees of porosity, are extensively made, and have been used by some of the first telegraphic engineers, philosophical instrument makers, &c., of the day. For these and electric and telegraph pottery Messrs. Stiff were awarded a prize medal at the Paris Electrical Exhibition. 5. Plumbago and fire-clay crucibles for every conceivable purpose, and of the very highest quality.

The quality of the stoneware or "Bristol ware" is remarkably good, being extremely hard, and covered with an excellent, clear, and firm glaze, not surpassed by any other house. The artistic execution of terra-cotta goods is of a high order of excellence; some of the ordinary designs are engraved on Figs. 340 to 342, and 345, 346.

Messrs. Stiff & Sons produce a large number of filters of excellent construction and of artistic design. Some of these have Gothic arches, with figures or armorial decorations, and others are decorated with elegant foliage; two of these are shown on Figs. 343 and 344. The filtering medium consists of alternate layers of charcoal, silica, and another purifying substance, all carefully cleansed, and so arranged as to retain full efficiency for eight or ten years without further cost or trouble. The "Popular" filter—intended for common use among all classes—purifies eight gallons of water per day, and is sold complete and fitted for a mere trifle.

The potteries of Messrs. Stiff & Sons are among the largest in London. They employ about two hundred hands; their annual import of raw material, clay, coals, &c., is about 15,000 tons; and they have business relations in almost all parts of the world. It is well to add that at this pottery antique jugs and water-jugs, of excellent design and clever manipulation, are made. The carriage and foot warmers, &c., are also extremely good in quality and design.

The Lambeth Pottery.—In 1818 Mr. John Doulton established stoneware works at Vauxhall, and soon afterwards was joined in partnership by Mr. John Watts, the business being carried on under the style of Doulton and Watts. Some years after the works were removed to High Street, Lambeth, to premises near those which had formerly been occupied by Mr. Griffiths, already spoken of. In 1858 Mr. Watts died, and from that time to the present the manufactory has been carried on by Mr. John Doulton in co-partnership with his sons, under the style of Doulton & Watts, and Henry Doulton & Co. In 1854 Mr. Henry Doulton took out a patent for "improvements in kilns used in the manufacture of stoneware, earthenware, and china." In 1859 he took out another patent for "improvements in earthenware jars and bottles," and in 1861 the same gentleman also patented his "improvements in the construction of vats and similar vessels for containing liquids." At the Exhibitions of 1851 and 1862 medals were awarded to this firm, as they were also at the Exhibitions at Paris, Hamburg, Oporto, New Zealand, Auxerre, Caen, and Amsterdam. At the International Exhibitions of 1871 and 1872 they also received the highest commendation, and also at those of Vienna, Philadelphia, and Paris.

The goods manufactured by Messrs. Doulton & Co. include chemical vessels of large size (up to 500 gallons) and all kinds of stoneware suitable for the laboratory and works of the manufacturing chemist, and articles of domestic use; terra-cotta for architectural and gardening purposes; sanitary ware of all kinds; plumbago and other crucibles, muffles, furnaces, &c.: and, in addition to Lambeth, they have fire-clay and tile works at Rowley-Regis, Smethwick, and St. Helens. The production of their stoneware and terra-cotta goods gives employment to about 600 men; and the consumption of coals is over 10,000 tons per annum.

In stoneware Messrs. Doulton produce every possible variety of household vessels, as well as force-pumps, retorts, receivers, condensing-worms, filtering-funnels, and every kind of chemical and manufacturing vessels and sanitary goods. Many of the salt-glazed stoneware productions are of extremely artistic character, and evince a purity of taste which is highly meritorious. Some of the jugs and

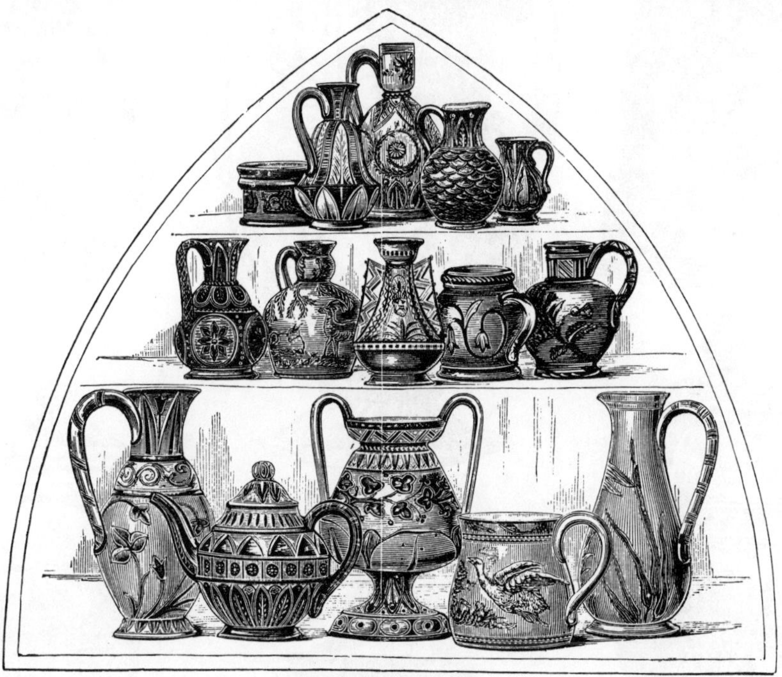

Fig. 347.—Doulton Ware.

tankards, from antique examples, both in brown, blue, claret, and fine white stoneware, are remarkably chaste and elegant, and remind one of the best periods of German and Flemish art. The forms are admirable, and the decorations, whether in repoussé or incised or other style, are well considered, and especially adapted to the material, the mode of production, and the use of the object.

In terra-cotta, Messrs. Doulton's works rank high, both for the beauty of their productions, the variety of designs they have introduced, and the durability and excellence of their material. In vases for gardens, &c.—the finest of which is their Amazon vase (Fig. 354) sent to the Exhibition of 1871—pedestals, fountains, garden-seats, flower-boxes and pendants, brackets, &c.—they produce a large number of exquisite patterns. In statuary and architectural decorations the productions consist of figures, busts, and medallions; keystones, arches, trusses, and string-courses; capitals, bases, and finials; rain-water heads, of marvellously bold and effective design; parapets and balustrades; panels of coloured stoneware and terra-cotta, modelled in very high relief, for out-door decoration; and everything requisite for the architect or the builder. Some of the highest achievements in art, as applied to original conceptions modelled in the most masterly manner in terra-cotta—the creations of George Tinworth—have been produced at these works, and have formed

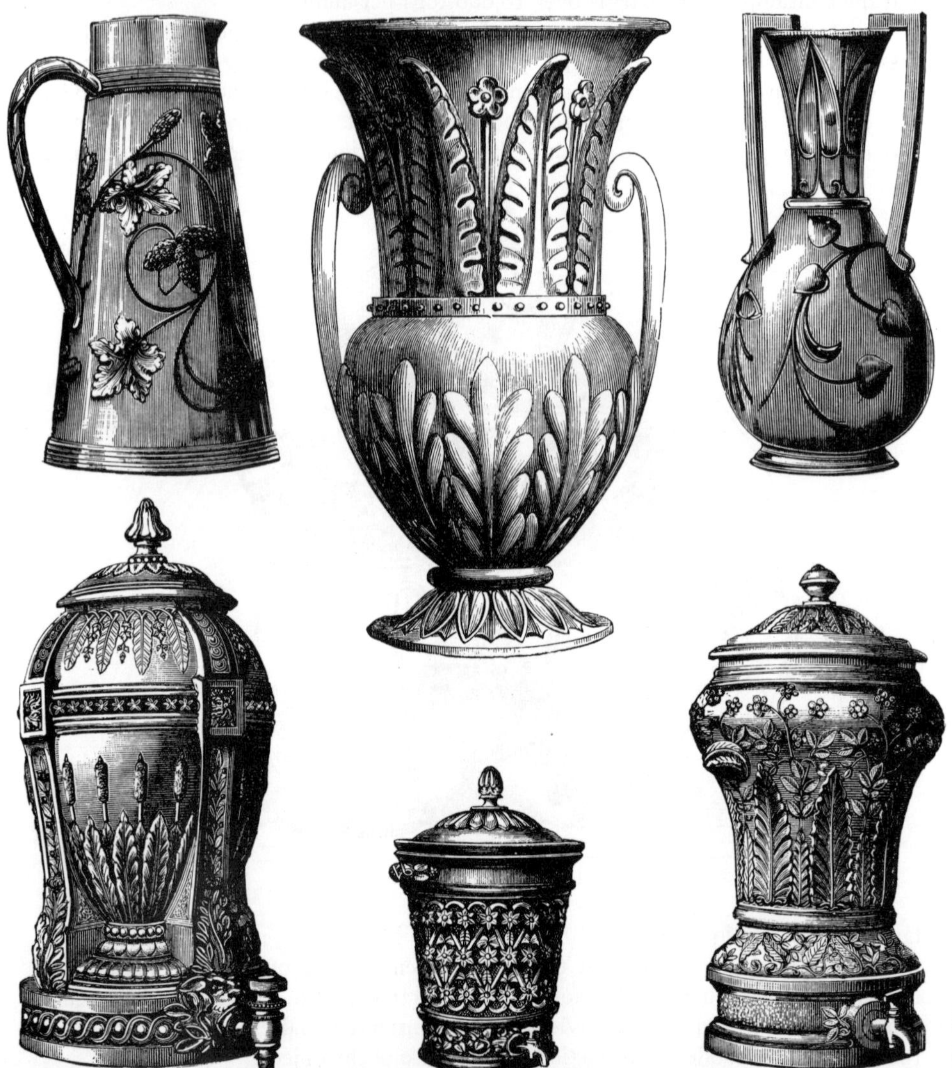

Figs. 348 to 353.—Doulton's Vases, Filters, &c.

a separate "Tinworth Exhibition" in 1883. Painting on pottery has also of late been introduced into this manufactory with very good results.

One especially noteworthy class of objects consists of claret cups, loving cups, jugs, flower vases, candlesticks, hunting jugs, pitchers, inkstands, and other vessels on which the ornament is principally executed in *sgraffimento*, or incised outline. This is sometimes effected as soon as the vessel leaves the wheel, but more generally after

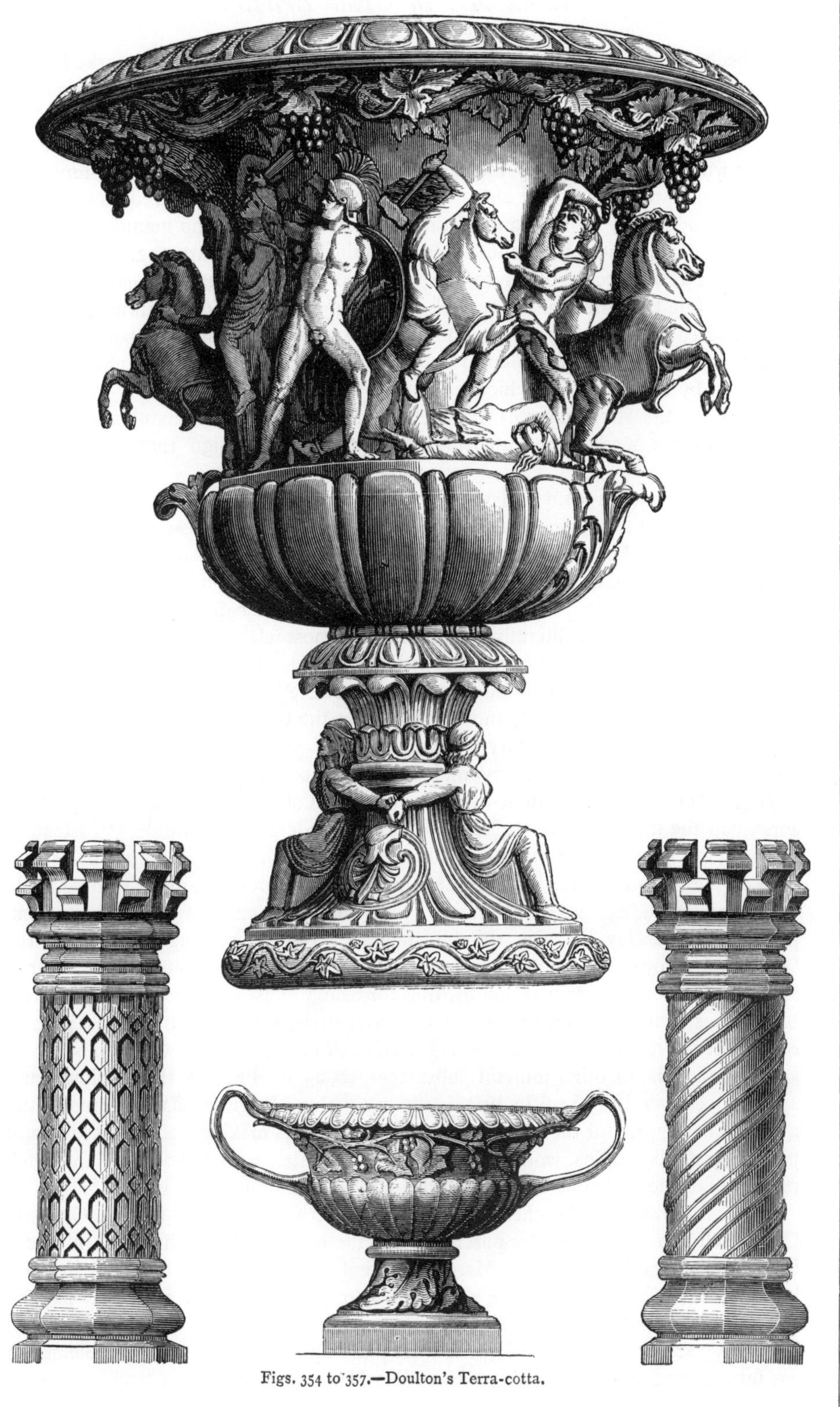

Figs. 354 to 357.—Doulton's Terra-cotta.

it has been allowed to dry to a consistency which will permit of its being worked upon. To the designs thus engraved in outline, especially to the leafage, colour is applied with an ordinary water-colour brush, and burnt in. This ware is called "Doulton ware," or "sgraffito ware," and no two pieces are formed alike. With regard to the body it will be sufficent to say that the great strength of stoneware in comparison with that of earthenware, and also its perfect cleanliness, have secured its adoption, whether produced by this or any of the other eminent firms who manufacture it, in all kinds of appliances in connection with drainage and sanitary engineering; and the perfect resistance it offers to the strongest acids proves the material to be admirably fitted for the manufacture of every kind of vessel and apparatus employed in trades depending in any degree on chemical operations. Another specialty is the *impasto* ware, in which the colour is applied to the raw clay, and is, moreover, so thickened by the vehicle by which it is incorporated that it models the form as well as paints it—the slight amount of relief obtained by the artist giving a surpassing richness to the work, and imparting a reality to the design that is eminently pleasing.

One of the more recent and certainly most striking and elegant achievements of Ceramic Art is the silicon ware, a body of such extreme hardness that, like Wedgwood's agate and Basaltes wares, it is, especially in the inlaid varieties, polished by the lapidary after leaving the kiln. In this ware vases of exquisite design and finish are delicately perforated, and the floral, arabesque, or other designs with which they are profusely covered, literally carved in the most elaborate manner and then worked up by the *pâte-sur-pâte* process with the richest, softest, and most harmonious effects. In the same silicon body are also produced graceful designs of foliage, hand-modelled in alto-relievo, and enamelled on the unglazed body of the ware.

Fore Street.—A manufactory of various kinds of pottery existed here in the beginning of the present century, and was carried on by Mr. Richard Waters, who in June, 1811, took out a patent for "a new method of manufacturing pottery ware." First, "in the fabrication of various articles of considerable magnitude," "instead of throwing or moulding them on a revolving table, the clay is made into sheets and then applied upon moulds and finished by beating or pressure, or by turning while in a revolving state;" second, forming "delf-ware pots and other articles by compression of the clay between suitable moulds;" third, "making or clouding the 'Welsh ware,' by using a number of pipes instead of one in distributing the colour;" fourth, "making earthenware jambs, tiles for facing houses, and for paving hearths, balustrades, balconies, and bricks vein-coloured, variegated either by the last process or by putting together masses differing from each other," and in the admixture of stony or metallic or other mineral substances, so as to differ in their colours and appearance when baked; fifth, by this process making "figures, statues, ornaments, armorial bearings, and the like;" sixth, by this process making "stone mortars and pestles, cisterns, coffins, worms for distillers' use, tiles, with a hook on the back instead of a knob, also with a higher edge and deeper return than usual."

Imperial Pottery.—Another pottery at Lambeth was that of Messrs. Green & Co., which in 1858 passed, by purchase, into the hands of Mr. John Cliff, by whom it was considerably enlarged. Mr. Cliff here brought into use his own "patent kiln for what is known as double glaze or Bristol glaze kiln, and a circular bag for the salt glaze and pipe kiln, since adopted generally." Here also Carr's "Disintegrant" was first proved and got to work; and here, under his own eye, Siemens's gas furnace was tried on pottery. Here also Mr. Cliff brought out, and into work,

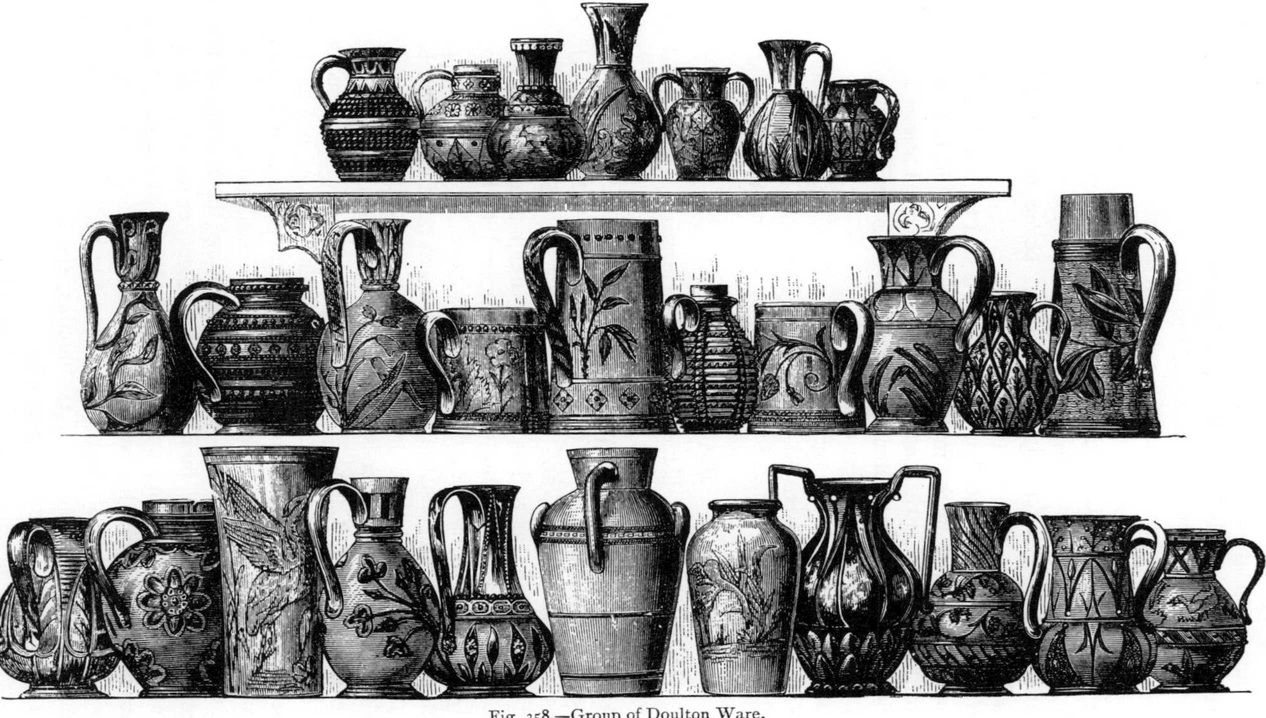

Fig. 358.—Group of Doulton Ware.

his patent wheel and patent lathe—two most important improvements in the potter's art, and said to be the most perfect and convenient machines extant. The works were closed in 1869, through the site being required by the Metropolitan Board of Works for improvements, and Mr. Cliff removed to Runcorn, in Cheshire. The works were originally established for the manufacture of common red ware; but after a time Mr. Green added a little salt-glazed ware; and then, as the double glazed gained favour, added it, and made it his principal business, giving up the red ware entirely. Later still, he manufactured drain pipes and a good deal of chemical stoneware; and, besides all the usual articles, filters were here extensively made for the celebrated George Robins, the auctioneer. The old works were many times much injured by fire—being nearly destroyed just before passing into Mr. Cliff's hands in 1858.

Crispe's China.—Crispe, of Bow Churchyard, is said to have had a manufactory of china ware at Lambeth in the middle of last century; and to him John Bacon, the sculptor, is stated to have been apprenticed in 1755. Little is known of this manufactory of Crispe's, but reference to him and to his connection with the china trade will be made in another part of this book.

Several other potteries—one carried on by Mr. Northen, who was an apprentice to Mr. White of Fulham—existed at Lambeth, but have been removed, like the "Imperial," by the improvements on the banks of the Thames.

BLACKFRIARS ROAD.

The terra-cotta works of Blanchard & Co., formerly carried on here, were established in 1839 by Mr. H. M. Blanchard, who served his apprenticeship with Coades & Sealy at Lambeth (see page 93). The productions consisted of vases, tazzas, statues, busts, groups of figures, brackets, pedestals, terminals, crosses, fountains, balustrades, trusses, and every species of architectural enrichment. In 1851, and again in 1862, as well as at the Paris Exhibition, the firm was awarded medals for terra-cotta goods, and they are considered to be among the best produced. Among the more successful of the works executed may be named the terra-cotta for the Brighton Aquarium; the permanent buildings, South Kensington Museum; the columns, &c., of the arcades in the Royal Horticultural Gardens; the Charing Cross and Cannon Street hotels and termini; the Grosvenor mansions; the Grand Hotel, Cairo; and the chastely beautiful and effective enrichments of the Wedgwood Institute, Burslem. Of this last, as one of the greatest achievements of Ceramic Art, as applied to external decoration of buildings, I give a series of engravings. The principal features of these designs are a series of twelve nearly square panels, in alto-relievo, representing the months of the year—each month being represented by a seated, recumbent, or stooping life-size figure, with the attribute of the season; and a series of oblong panels or plaques, representing, in similar relief, all the more striking details of the work of the potter, thus, very appropriately, illustrating the staple trade of the district in which the Wedgwood Institute is situated. Of the months, the four illustrations here given (Figs. 364 to 367) will convey a correct idea.

After continuing in Blackfriars Road for upwards of forty years, Messrs. Blanchard, in 1880, removed their works to Bishops Waltham, in Hampshire, where they now cover an extent of some twenty acres of ground, and possess some of the finest beds of clay in the kingdom. The productions are terra-cotta, as before, and roofing and blue ware paving tiles, and other goods.

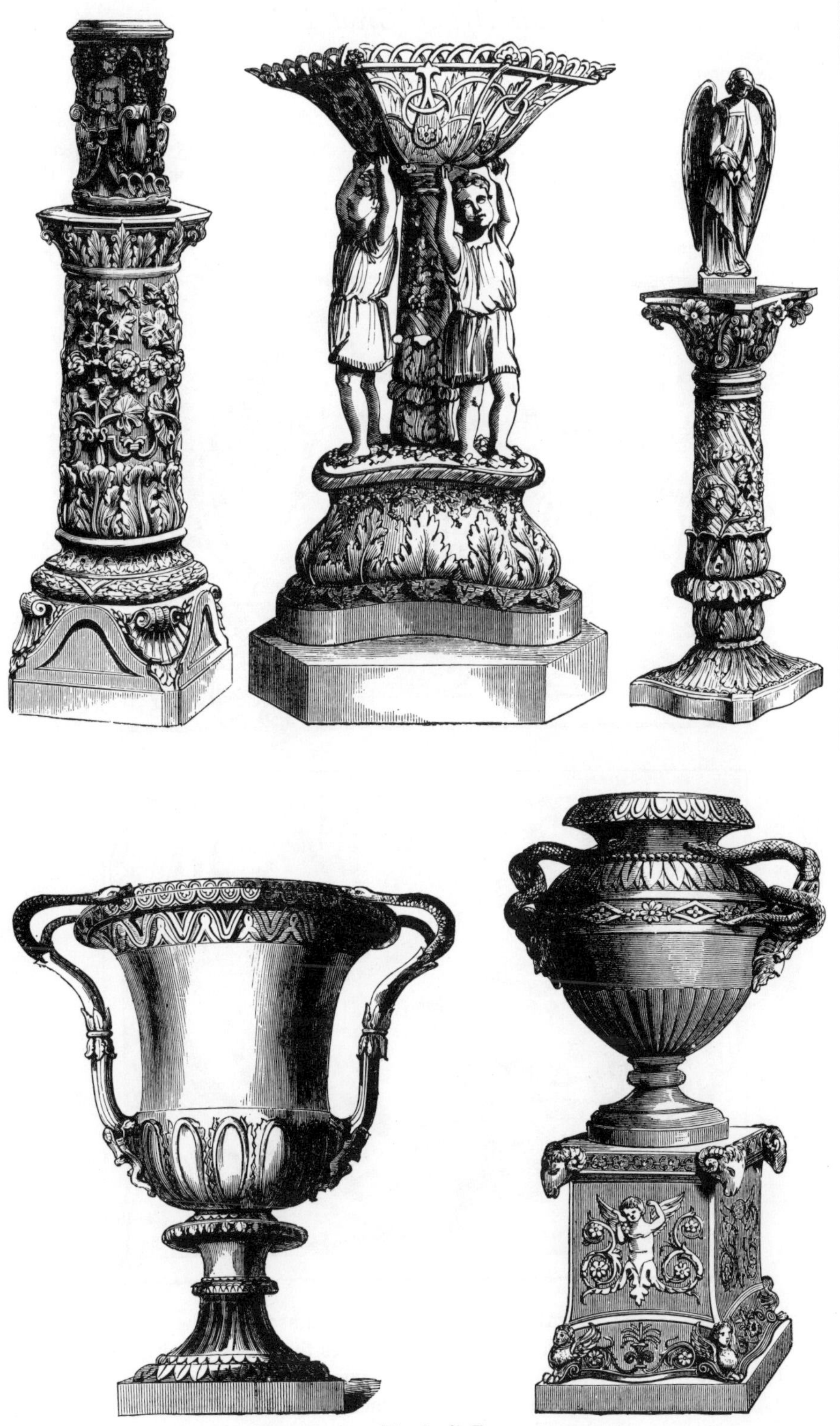

Figs. 359 to 363.—Blanchard's Terra-cotta, &c.

VAUXHALL.

Thomas Houghton, to whom I have in other parts of this work referred, in his "Husbandry and Trade Improved," writing on March 13, 1695-6, says, speaking of the imports during the year 1694, "of tea-pots there came but ten, and those from Holland. To our credit be it spoken, we have about Faux-Hall (as I have

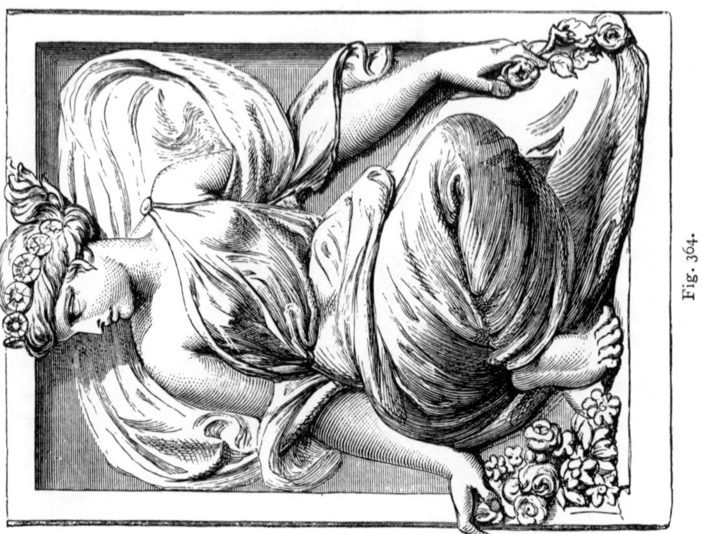

Fig. 364.

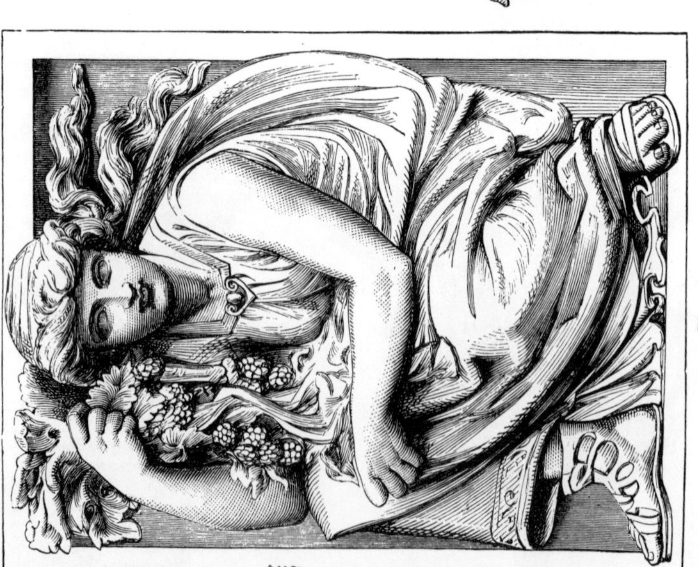

Fig. 365.

been informed) made a great many, and I cannot gainsay but they are as good as any come from abroad." In 1714 Thoresby writes that he "went by water to Fox-Hall and the Spring-gardens. After dinner we viewed the pottery and various apartments there. Was most pleased with that where they were painting divers colours, which yet appear more beautiful and of divers colours when baked." The Vauxhall

Pottery is said to have been situated close by Vauxhall Bridge, in High Street. The Delft-ware Pottery in Princess Street, Lambeth, is said to have belonged to the same works. The Vauxhall Pottery, which was for the production of stoneware similar to that at Lambeth, was carried on towards the close of last century by a Mr. Wagstaffe; and on his death, in or about 1803, it passed into the hands of his nephew,

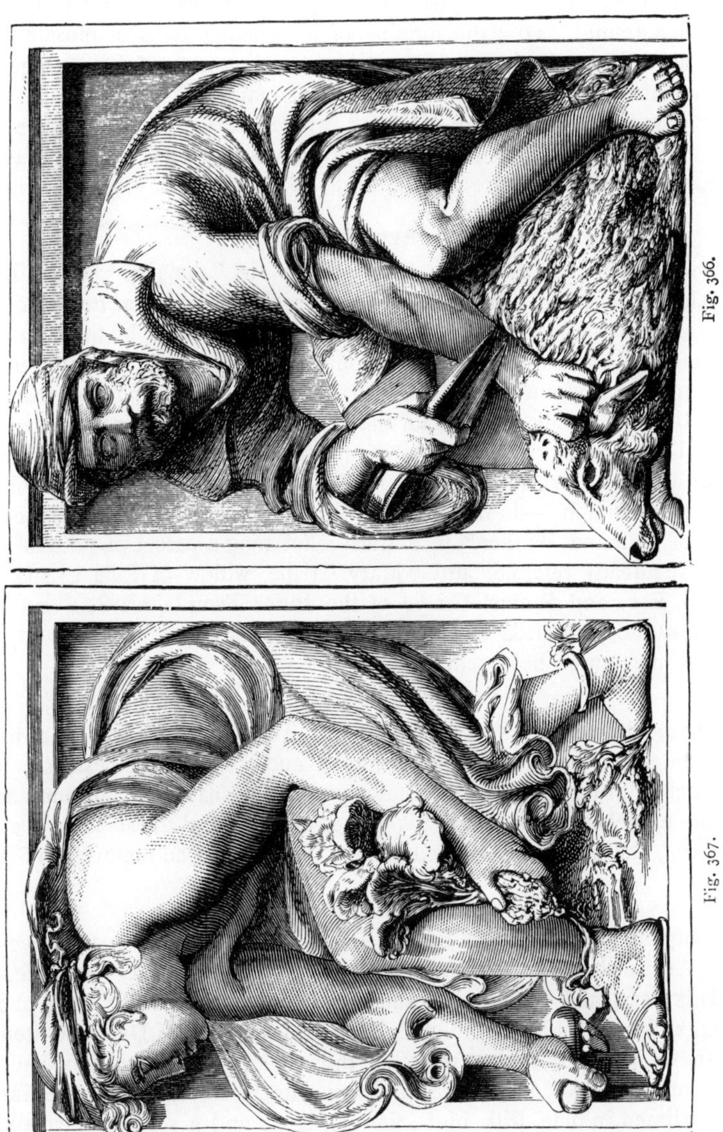

Fig. 366.

Fig. 367.

Mr. John Wisker, who carried it on until his decease in 1838, he having, in 1833, taken out a patent "for certain improvements in machinery or apparatus for grinding covers or stoppers for jars, bottles, and other vessels made of china, stone, or other earthenware," such as are described in the patent of Robert Burton Cooper, taken out in 1831. On the death of Mr. Wisker, the works were purchased of his executors by Mr. Alfred Singer, but have been discontinued and pulled down, and the site built over, for some years. At these works Mr. Singer, in conjunction with Mr. Henry Pether, manufactured small tiles, or tesseræ, for tesselated pavements. In 1839 they took out a patent "for certain improvements in the preparation and combination of earthenware or porcelain, for the purpose of mosaic or tesselated work," "by cutting clay or other plastic material into rectilinear figures, by means of intersecting wires stretched in a frame," and "the forming of ornamental slabs of mosaic work by cementing together small pieces of porcelain or earthenware, of various figures and colours, on slabs of slate, stone, or other suitable material."

There was another pottery at Vauxhall, where coarse red or brown ware was made, and where also, later on, a fine stoneware was produced. There was also a manufactory of white stoneware carried on, in 1811, by a Mr. Joseph Kishire.

Aldgate.

In 1690 William Knight was a "pott-maker" in "the parish of St. Buttolph without Aldgate, London," and made "white ware." In that year he had conveyed to him, by deed, some land and premises which were situated "by the river running from Merton Mill to Wandsworth, in the county of Surrey," and consisted in part of a mill "formerly used for a Fulling Mill and Brasill Mill and now and of late used for a Colour Mill for Grinding Colours for the Glazeing of White Ware" made by him.

The William Knight of this deed was the same whose name appears in 1693, along with Thomas Harper, Henry De Wilde, John Robins, and Moses Johnson—"all potters in London"—in the curious "Brief Account of the Evidence given on behalf of Edmund Warner" in a trial concerning a parcel of potters' clay, to which I have already referred, and "Mary Crispe, widow of Ellis Crispe, late of Wimbledon, Esq., and Samuel Crispe of the Inner Temple, his Son and Heire," were, there can be but little doubt, of the same family to which, later on, Crispe, the china manufacturer, belonged.

Mill-Wall.

Mr. Blasfield, afterwards of the Stamford Terra-cotta Works, who had previously been engaged in the plastic, scagliola, and cement business, commenced the manufacture of terra-cotta vases, statues, chimney-shafts, &c., turning to good account the models he had used in his former business and those he had acquired from Coades; these works he carried on until 1858, when he removed to Stamford.

Mortlake.

Delft-ware works appear to have been in existence here in the seventeenth century. At the close of the eighteenth they were taken by Mr. Wagstaffe, of the Vauxhall Pottery, and passed with them to his nephew, Mr. Wisker, about the year 1804, and were by him continued for the manufacture of Delft and stonewares until 1820 or 1821, when he removed the whole concern to Vauxhall. Two examples of Mortlake Delft-ware—a large punch bowl, twenty-one inches in diameter, painted in blue, with birds, flowers, &c.; and a set of twelve tiles, also painted in blue, with landscape, ruins, figures, &c., are in the South Kensington Museum. They were removed from the old factory.

Southwark.

Gravel Lane.—In the beginning of last century a pottery was carried on by Nathaniel Oade, connected with whom and whose business a shocking circumstance is detailed in the *Post Boy* of March 1st, 1718. In 1750 the roof of a pottery belonging to Mr. Oade was thrown down by an earthquake, and an account of the circumstance was sent to the Royal Society by William Jackson, a potter.

Isleworth.

The manufacture of porcelain at Isleworth was commenced by Joseph Shore in 1760, and was continued to be made about forty years. In 1795 Lysons says: "There is a china manufactory at Isleworth belonging to Messrs. Shore & Co." In 1800 it was discontinued, but the stock is said to have remained on the premises until 1830, when the works, having in the meantime been used for the manufacture of earthenware—principally "Welsh" or "streaked" ware,—were closed. A few years afterwards the manufactory was removed to Hounslow, and the site converted to other purposes. Joseph Shore is said to have come from the Worcester China Works, and his partner and principal painter, Richard Goulding, was his son-in-law, who was later on assisted by his son, William Goulding (a dated piece of his having the name as in the margin). I am inclined, however, to think that Joseph Shore must have originally belonged to the

Wm. Goulding,
June 20th 1770.
*

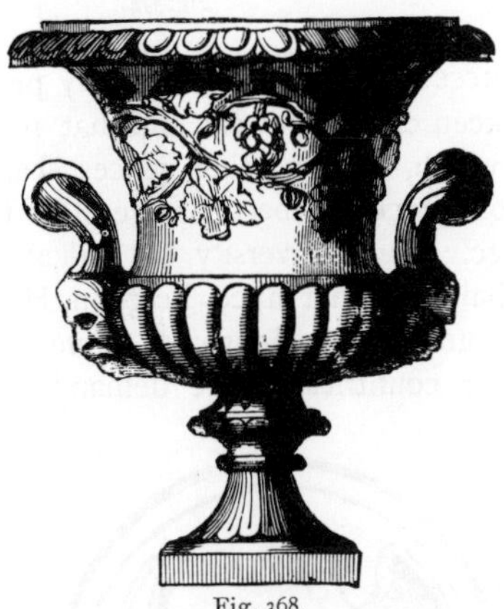

Fig. 368.

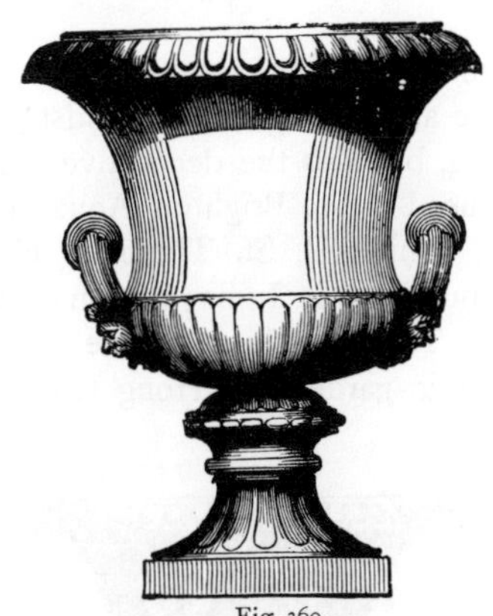

Fig. 369.

Derby China Works, as several of that name were connected with them. After Shore's death, the works were continued by the Gouldings. The works were at Railshead Creek, by the ferry side.

Stepney.

A manufacture of porcelain was carried on here in the middle of last century: for Jonas Hanway, writing in 1750-1, says, "It is with great satisfaction that I observe the manufactories of Bow, Chelsea, and Stepney have made such a considerable progress."

Greenwich.

In 1747 it appears there was a small manufactory of China here, but nothing is known of its history. In the *London Tradesman* of that year occurs this note:— "Of late we have made some attempts to make porcelain or china-ware, after the manner it is done in China and Dresden. There is a house at Greenwich, and another at Chelsea, where the undertakers have been for some time trying to imitate that beautiful manufacture."

Ransome's Patent Stone Works.—These works were established at Ipswich in 1844, and removed to this locality in January, 1866. Mr. Frederick Ransome, the inventor of the processes, a member of the well-known Ipswich family, was in early life connected with the Orwell Works firm of Ransomes and Sims. It was while there, and noticing a workman engaged in dressing a millstone, that he conceived the idea of producing artificial stone, capable of being moulded to any form, and to be a perfect imitation, both in appearance and substance, of the blocks taken from our best quarries. For ten years the difficulties he had to

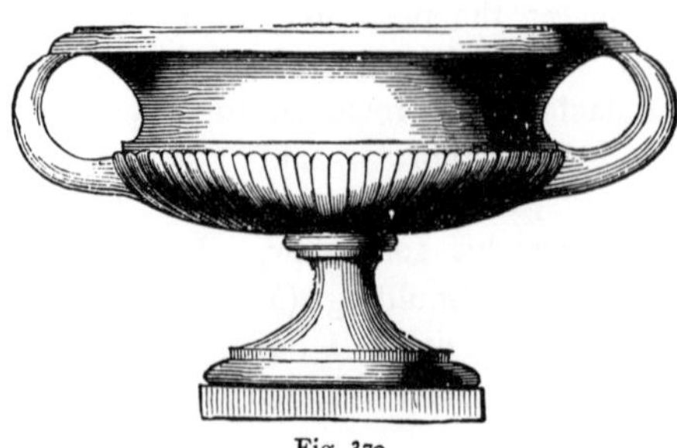

Fig. 370.

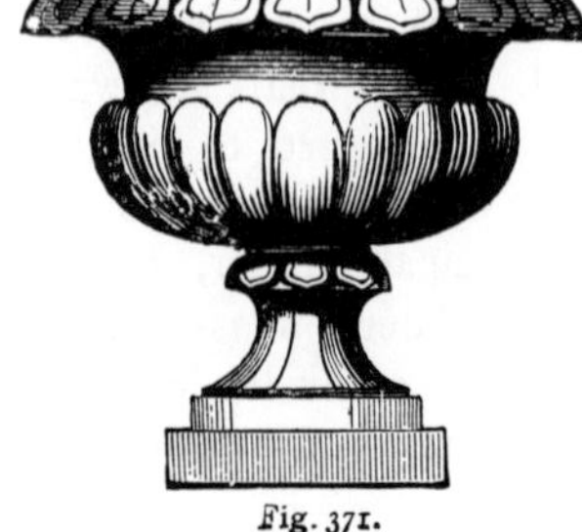

Fig. 371.

encounter were very great, but he at length succeeded in making not only perfectly equable and homogeneous grindstones, with keen cutting powers, and that need no dressing, but also the decorative stonework which, among other places, has been introduced in the Brighton Aquarium, London Docks, Albert Bridge, the Indian Court, Whitehall, St. Thomas's Hospital, &c.; the University of Calcutta and other buildings in India; and in ornamental buildings in France, Belgium, Holland, Egypt, Turkey, China (where a splendid fountain of Ransome stone adorns the public gardens at Hong Kong), and other countries. The demand for this

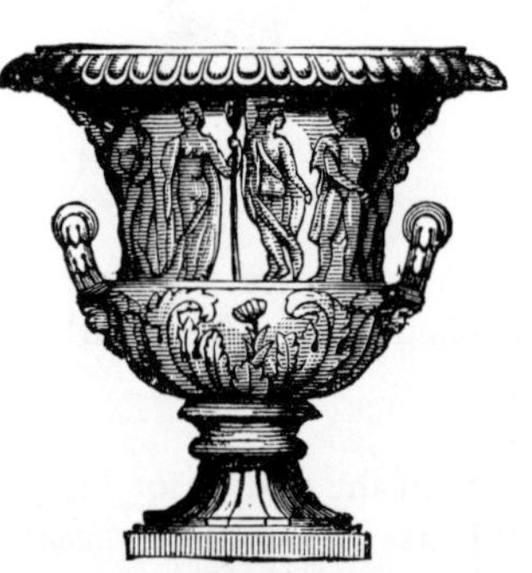

Fig. 372.

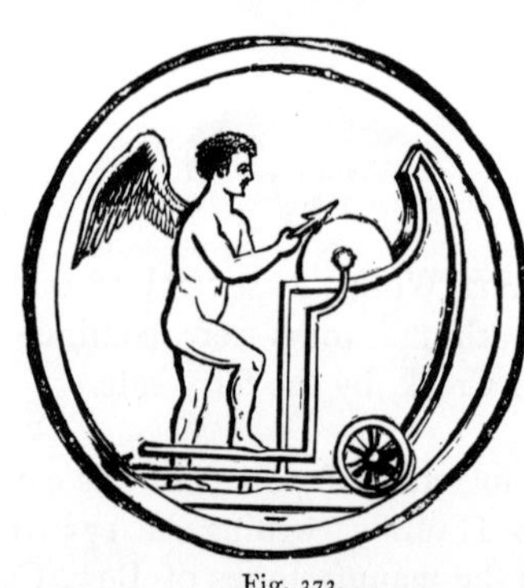

Fig. 373.

artificial stone becoming much extended, the inventions were in 1871 taken up by a company, and extensive works were erected at East Greenwich, to which the business was transferred. They are now carried on by A. H. Bateman and Co., Limited.

The material is, to all intents and purposes, a pure sandstone, whose silicious particles are bound together by a cement of silicate of lime—a mineral substance well known to be of the most indestructible nature; its composition, mechanically and chemically, is precisely that of the Craigleith and other best quality building-stones. It can be moulded to any form while in a plastic state, and can be worked with the chisel the same as any natural stone. The process of manufacture is based upon one of the most beautiful of chemical reactions; flints are dissolved by means of caustic alkali under high pressure, so as to form silicate of soda, a kind of water-glass. This viscous and tenacious substance is then rapidly mixed with a proportion of very fine and sharp silicious sand in a pug mill, so as to form a soft plastic mass, which can be moulded into any shape that is desired. The soft stone is next immersed in a bath of chloride of calcium solution, which is made to penetrate every pore by means of hydraulic or atmospheric pressure. Whenever this solution comes into contact with the silicate of soda the two liquids are mutually and instantaneously decomposed, the silica taking possession of the calcium and forming the hard, solid silicate of lime, and the soda uniting with the chlorine to form chloride of sodium in a small quantity. Instead, then, of the particles of sand being covered with a thin film of the liquid silicate of soda, they are covered and united together with a film of solid silicate of lime—one of the most indestructible substances known. The small quantity of soluble chloride of sodium, one of the results of decomposition, is then washed out of the stone by a douche of clean water, or by hydraulic pressure, its complete removal being ensured by chemical tests. The stone is then dried and is fit for use.

The productions of these works embrace vases of admirable design, fountains, tazzas (in these three departments some two hundred different designs are produced), terminals, flower-boxes, flower-pots, tree-pots, garden edgings, figures, busts, chimney-pieces, balustrades, chimney-shafts and tops, window-heads, and plinths, capitals, memorial crosses, grave-stones, &c. Filters, too, for reservoirs are made extensively, and have the reputation of being among the most effective. Pavement tiles of various colours, and also with inlaid patterns, are made; these were adopted on the Albert Bridge, at Chelsea, with good effect, and have given entire satisfaction, on account of their great hardness, strength, and non-liability to become slippery.

Another admirable and important element of Mr. Ransome's inventions is the applying of the silicate of lime to the preservation of stone. The sculpture on St. George's Hall, Liverpool, the Custom House at Greenock, Trinity College, Dublin, and many other public buildings, have been successfully treated with this solution, which hardens and renders the surface indestructible by time or weather.

The trade mark of the company, the only mark used in this manufactory, is a winged genius grinding an arrow, from an antique gem at Rome (Fig. 373).

Deptford.

In the seventeenth century a pottery existed here, where were manufactured melting-pots, "the best in the world, especially for founders." These were in great repute, and gradually superseded those imported from Holland, Germany and Denmark.

Merton (see "Aldgate").

Hounslow.

About 1830 the manufacture of earthenware (commenced by Joseph Shore and carried on after his death by his son and grandson Richard and William Goulding) at Isleworth was removed to Hounslow, but died out in the course of a year or two, and has not been renewed.

WANDSWORTH (see "Aldgate").

EWELL.

"*Nonsuch Pottery*."—A pottery existed here in the early part of last century, but about or soon after 1790, the bed of clay having been exhausted, it was discontinued. About 1800 the steward of the Nonsuch estates, on which the pottery was situated, gave permission for a new pottery to be established wherever the clay could be found; and soon afterwards the present "Nonsuch Pottery" was opened in Nonsuch Park. It was founded by Mr. William Richard Waghorn, who was joined in partnership by his son. This firm continued the works until 1851, when they were transferred to Mr. Swallow, who had until that time been their foreman. By him and his partner, Mr. Stone, the business was continued under the style of "Stone and Swallow," and by them a pottery—principally for the manufacture of fire-bricks—was established at Epsom. Mr. Swallow died in 1866 or 1867, and since then his partner, Mr. Stone, continued the works alone: they are known as the "Nonsuch Pottery," or as "Stone's Ewell and Epsom Potteries." The goods manufactured by Mr. W. Waghorn were "Italian tiling"—used very extensively in the buildings of the time and remarkable for their strength and durability; ornamental roof tiles; ridge tiles; "Nonsuch fire-bricks;" "Nonsuch fire-loam;" paving and other tiles; moulded bricks, &c., for Gothic buildings; ornamented chimney-pots; pipes; flower-pots and vases, &c.; and on their lists was a view of the old Nonsuch Palace, with an historical notice of the same. The mark was simply "Stone and Co."

CHEAM.

A pottery was worked here, about 1840, by Messrs. Waghorn, of the Ewell Pottery: but on their retiring, in 1851, was transferred to Mr. Baker, by whom it was worked until 1868, when he was succeeded by Messrs. Cowley and Aston. It was closed in 1869. In the same year another pottery was opened by Mr. Henry Clark, for the manufacture of ornamental and plain flower-pots, rustic fern-stands, vases, chimney-pots, drain-tiles, &c. They are of a bright red colour, and when a mark is used, it is simply "Henry Clark, Cheam Pottery."

CHISELHURST.

The West Kent Potteries were opened in 1820, before which time other works were in operation and carried on by the steward of Lord Sydney, the owner of the estate, for the manufacture of wares for the use of the estate. At Christmas, 1822, the works were taken by Mr. Pascall, who continued to carry them on until January, 1869, when he died in the ninety-second year of his age. Since then it was carried on by his sons, Messrs. Pascall Brothers, the present owners. The productions are the ordinary red-ware flower and root pots, sea-kale pots, and other horticultural ware; building and paving bricks and tiles; roofing and ridge tiles; drain, socket, and other pipes; chimney tops, &c. Messrs. Pascall are patentees of the famous West Kent flower-pots with loose bottoms, celebrated for their convenience for changing and examining the roots; and of the patent sea kale pots for growing sea-kale in hot-houses.

CHAPTER VII.

"CHELSEA buns," "Chelsea pensioners," and "Chelsea china" are surely three things, each one in itself sufficient to make a place famous, but when brought together, a three-fold fame must certainly attach to the locality which has given them a name. With the buns and the pensioners, however, I disclaim all connection in my present work, and shall devote my attention to the "china" only, of whose story the least is known.

It is better to state at the outset that the history of the Chelsea China works is very obscure. A little of the cloud of mist I have already removed, and I trust that in the course of future researches I may be able to almost entirely dispel it. At all events, every item of information is valuable, and in the following narrative a vast deal of new matter will be found, which will materially assist the collector in understanding the history of these, the most celebrated of any of the old china manufactories of the United Kingdom.

The south-western district of London, on both sides of the water, has for a long period, as we have already seen, been the seat of fictile manufactories of an extensive and important character. Fulham, Chelsea, Battersea, Vauxhall, Pedlar's Acre, Lambeth—all had their potteries at an early date, and all, probably, had their origin from one common source. What that first source was—*i.e.*, where the first pottery was founded—is, of course, difficult to say, but from it others sprung up, in different directions, until quite a nest of manufactories was located in the suburban districts. The artisans of the seventeenth century were chiefly Dutchmen; indeed, the manufacture was of that kind of ware known as "Delft-ware"—originally made in Holland, and introduced into England by workmen from thence. The importation of "Delft-ware" in this (seventeenth) century was considerable, and at that period the manufacture of a kind of porcelain is said to have been achieved at Delft.

I have shown on another page that large quantities of ware were imported into England from Holland in the seventeenth century, and that Dutch workmen of skill and enterprise were induced, from the prospect of a good home trade here, to settle in England. These workmen, it is not too much to believe, were acquainted with the art of manufacturing porcelain as produced in Delft, as well as the ordinary kind of ware made in their native country; and thus the knowledge was brought into our kingdom, and carried on, to some little extent, by those who settled here. The first maker of china, as I have shown in my account of the Fulham Works, was Mr. Dwight, and to him I am inclined to award the honour of being the father of the Chelsea China Works, about whose origin so little is known. The probability is that after Dwight had succeeded in making porcelain, and abandoned it, some other potter started the works at Chelsea, and with good result.

When first commenced the works at Chelsea were, of course, of a very small size, and were, it is said, principally confined to painting and finishing Oriental china, which was imported for that purpose. There is a tradition—but only tradition—that the origin of the Chelsea works took its rise from the fact of clay being brought as ballast in vessels from Chinese ports, which was found to be the veritable clay used by the Oriental potters. This clay is said to have been used both at Chelsea and at Bow, and to have enabled the workmen successfully to compete with their Eastern rivals. The tradition, however, goes on to recount that the Chinese, finding that the uses of this clay had been discovered, and perceiving that they were losing trade in consequence, wisely "stopped the supplies," and peremptorily refused to allow any more to leave their ports. The workmen were then driven to seek elsewhere for material, and soon found enough to use in our own country.

By whom the works were carried on in their early days is not recorded, but in the year 1745 the art had evidently attained a high Continental as well as home celebrity. In this year the French company, in their petition for the exclusive privilege of establishing a porcelain manufactory at Vincennes, urged the benefit which France might be expected to derive by having a manufactory of porcelain which should counteract the reputation of English and German make, and stop their importation into France. There is nothing to show that Chelsea, any more than Bow, was intended by this; but as ten years later, according to Rouquet, "that of Chelsea is the most considerable" of the three or four china manufactories in the neighbourhood of London, it is probable it was then one of the seats of manufacture of which France was jealous.

George II. gave the Chelsea establishment his countenance and earnest support, and did much to encourage its works, and to ensure its success. He procured for it workmen, models, and materials from the State of Saxony, and thus enabled the factory to produce works of such high merit as to successfully rival the productions of Sèvres and Dresden. This royal favour of course produced its results, in procuring the patronage of many of the leading men of the day. Thus, the Duke of Cumberland not only took it under his special care, but allowed a sum of money annually for its furtherance and support. In 1750 it belonged to M. Nicholas Spremont, or Sprimont, a foreigner of considerable taste and talent, who did much towards establishing its already acquired reputation. At this time the productions of the establishment must have been of a particularly high order. In Watkins's "Life of Queen Charlotte," it is stated that "there are several rooms in Buckingham Palace full of curiosities and valuable movables, but not ranged in proper order. Among other things I beheld with admiration a complete service of Chelsea china, rich and beautiful in fancy beyond expression. I really never saw any Dresden near so fine. Her Majesty made a present of this choice collection to the duke, her brother—a present worthy of so great a prince." Horace Walpole, too, in 1763, wrote, "I saw yesterday (March 3, 1763) a magnificent service of Chelsea china, which the king and queen are sending to the Duke of Mecklenberg. There are dishes and plates without number, an epergne, candlestick, salt-cellars, sauce-boats, tea and coffee equipages, &c. In short it is complete, and cost £1,200."

In the Lansdowne MSS. in the British Museum is a curious document relating to the Chelsea works, which, being particularly interesting, I here give in full. It is entitled "The case of the Undertaker of the Chelsea manufacture of Porcelain Ware."

"Many attempts towards this art have been made in Europe for a long course of years past: the success which has been met with at Dresden has revived these pursuits in many parts of Europe. The Empress Queen has a manufacture of her own. The French King has one, and has patronised and encouraged several; the King of Naples has one; the late Duke of Orleans was, at the time of his death, and had been for many years, engaged very earnestly in this pursuit, but none have come up to the pattern they have been endeavouring to imitate.

"Several attempts have likewise been made here; few have made any progress, and the chief endeavours at Bow have been towards making a more ordinary sort of ware for common uses. This undertaker, a silversmith by profession, from a casual acquaintance with a chymist who had some knowledge this way, was tempted to make a trial, which, upon the progress he made, he was encouraged to pursue with great labour and expense; and as the town and some of the best judges expressed their approbation of the essays he produced of his skill, he found means to engage some assistance.

"The manufacture was then put upon a more extensive footing, and he had the encouragement of the public to a very great degree, so that the last winter he sold to the value of more than £3,500, which is a great deal, considering the thing is new, and is of so great extent that it has been beyond the reach of his industry to produce such complete assortments as are required in a variety of ways. This has been a great spur to his industry, so that, notwithstanding some discouragements, the ground-plot of his manufacture has gone on still increasing.

"The discouragements, besides the immense difficulties in every step towards the improvement of the art, have been the introduction of immense quantities of Dresden porcelain.

"It was known that, as the laws stand, painted earthenware, other than that from India, is not enterable at the Custom House, otherwise than for private use, and of course becomes forfeit when offered to sale, as well as lace from France, or any other unenterable commodity; and though it was publicly sold in a great many shops, and that there were even very frequent public sales of it, it was hoped that what was exposed to sale was chiefly the stock in hand, and when that should be got off, this grievance would cease. It has, nevertheless, happened quite otherwise, for not only the importations continue, and considerable parcels are allowed to pass at the Custom House, as for private use, by which means the shops abound with new stock, and public sales are advertised at the very beginning of the winter, and in large quantities; but there is reason to believe, from the diminution in the price of the Dresden china, that this is done on purpose to crush the manufactory established here, which was a project threatened last year.

"It is apprehended that if recourse is had to the Custom House books, it will be found that considerable quantities have been entered there for private use, besides what may have been allowed to pass as Furniture to foreign ministers.

"This earthenware pays eightpence by the pound when entered for private use; but a figure of very little weight may be worth five pounds, so that the real value of what is sold here will be found to be considerable; and, indeed, it must be so, as this ware makes an important article in a number of great shops, besides the number of public sales during the course of a winter, and the other private ways there are of carrying it about.

"It may be a motive to let it be entered at the Custom House, that great names are made use of there; but it is to be regretted, that either these names are often made use of without authority, or that names are often given for very mean purposes; and as nobody is named, it may be said that a certain foreign minister's house has been, for a course of years, a warehouse for this commerce, and the large parcel, advertised for public sale on the seventh of next month, is come, or is to come from thence. Even the right of entering this ware at all is a doubtful point, and the affirmative is taken upon presumption, because the law says it shall not be entered for sale.

"The manufacture in England has been carried on so far by great labour, and at a large expense; it is in many points to the full as good as the Dresden, and the late Duke of Orleans told Colonel York that the metal or earth had been tried in his furnace, and was found to be the best made in Europe. It is now daily improving, and already employs at least one hundred hands, of which is a nursery of thirty lads, taken from the parishes and charity schools, and bred to designing and painting—arts very much wanted here, and which are of the greatest use in our silk and printed linen manufactures.

"Besides the advantage great honour accrues to the nation, from the progress made in so fine an art, without any of those aids by which it has been set on foot and supported abroad; nor has there even been any application for new laws or prohibitions in its favour, which has been a rule in every country upon the establishment of new manufactures.

"The execution of the laws which have all along been in force, and which can give no offence to anybody, it is apprehended will answer the purpose; all that is therefore requested is, that the Commissioners of the Customs may be cautioned with regard to the admission of this ware under the pretence of private use, and that the public sale of it may not be permitted any more than that of other prohibited goods. A few examples of seizures would put a stop to this, and which cannot be difficult, as all Dresden china has a sure mark to distinguish it by: but if this commerce is permitted to go on, the match between a crowned head and private people must be very unequal, and the possessors of the foreign manufactures will at any time, by the sacrifice of a few thousand pounds, have it in their power to ruin any undertaking of this kind here.

"This must be the case at present with the Chelsea manufacture, unless the administration will be pleased to interpose, and enjoin, in the proper place, a strict attention to the execution of the laws; for if, while the manufacture is filled with ware, these public sales of, and the several shops furnished with, what is prohibited, are to take off the ready money which should enable the manufacturer to go on, it must come to a stop, to the public detriment, and the ruin of the undertaker, as well as great loss to those who have engaged in his support."

Who the "undertaker" of the works here referred to was, is not stated in the document, which, according to Mr. Franks, bears internal evidence of having been written after 1752 and before 1759. Whether the Customs acceded to his views or not does not appear; but certain it is that, despite the abuse of import privilege enjoyed by cabinet ministers and others, he was, by his own showing, carrying on a very extensive business, selling £3,500 worth of goods in one winter, and employing more than a hundred hands, including a nursery of about thirty lads, who were learning the arts of potting and painting.

After much research I find that Mr. Spremont continued the works until 1768 or 1769, when he retired, principally through ill health, after having amassed a comfortable fortune; his ledgers dating from 1759 to 1768. During the time of his carrying on the establishment the works were very flourishing—indeed, it was said that "the china was in such repute as to be sold by auction; and as a set was purchased, as soon as baked, dealers were surrounding the doors for that purpose."

Mr. Spremont's managing man was Francis Thomas, of whom I shall have a few words to say presently. When Spremont retired from the concern, it was purchased by, or assigned over to, Mr. James Cox, who engaged Francis Thomas as overseer, at a salary of £100 a year, and this arrangement continued to the 6th of January, 1770, when Mr. Thomas died. Shortly afterwards the concern again, and for the last time, changed hands. Mr. Thomas was a man of good ability and of much practical skill, and to his energy in directing the works under Mr. Spremont much of their fame may be traced. He was buried in the south aisle of the parish church of Chelsea, where an inscription to his memory now remains. I possess a bill from Elizabeth, widow of Francis Thomas, which is interesting, as refuting the statements which have been made as to the position held by this gentleman.

The following announcements refer to the sales and proposed sales of the manufactory, and its models, plant, &c.

In 1764 it was announced that there would be a sale by auction, by Mr. Burnsall, "at the Chelsea porcelane manufactory. Every thing in general belonging to it, and all the remaining unfinished pieces, glazed and unglazed; some imperfect enamelled ditto of the useful and ornamental, all the materials, the valuable and extensive variety of fine models in wax, in brass, and in lead; all the plaster molds and others, the mills, kilns, and iron presses; together with all the fixtures of the different warehouses; likewise all the outbuildings, &c., &c. And as Mr. Sprimont, the sole possessor of this rare porcelain secret, is advised to go to the German spaw, all his genuine household furniture, &c., will be sold at the same time;" and that "soon after, when everything is sold belonging to the manufactory, &c., and the large warehouse cleared, there will be some most beautiful pieces of the truly inimitable Mazarin blue, crimson, and gold, that Mr. Sprimont has thought deserving finishing; that will be sold at Chelsea, as the whole remaining and the last produce of that once most magnificent porcelane manufactory."

Again, in April, 1799, it was announced, "There is to be sold at the Chelsea manufactory, by order of the proprietor (having recently left off making the same), every thing in general belonging to it, as all the plaster moulds, models in wax, lead and brass; kilns, mills, iron presses, and a large quantity of biscuit work, &c., &c., likewise all the buildings and many other articles;" and other announcements are also extant. In reference to one of these Josiah Wedgwood wrote to have inquiries made with a view to purchase. About this time Dr. Johnson was busying himself in experimentalising in compositions for the manufacture of porcelain, and was allowed to make use of the Chelsea works for that purpose, and after the close of the manufactory he visited the Derby China Works.

In 1769 Mr. William Duesbury, the proprietor of the famous Derby China Works, became the purchaser of the Chelsea works, and for many years carried on the two establishments conjointly. The Derby works had at that time attained to a high degree of excellence and of celebrity, and Mr. Duesbury (who became the purchaser, not only of the Chelsea works, but those of Bow, Giles's, Pedlar's Acre, &c.) was doing more trade than was done at any other establishment in the kingdom. He had opened an extensive connection with London, and was rapidly increasing his concern, both in that and other markets, and had become more than a successful rivaller of the excellence of the Chelsea wares.

I 2

The purchase of the Chelsea works was arranged on the 17th of August, 1769, and completed on the 5th of February, 1770, when a payment of £400, in part of the purchase money, was made. The original document, now in my possession, is highly interesting, and is as follows:—"Recd. London, 5th Feby., 1770, of Mr. Wm. Duesbury, four hundred pounds, in part of the purchase of the Chelsea Porcelain Manufactory and its apurtenances and lease thereof, which I promise to assign over to him on or before the 8th instant.—James Cox." Thus the Chelsea works, which had been taken to by Mr. Duesbury in August, 1769, and had been, indeed, carried on at his cost from about that period, finally passed into his hands on the 8th of February, 1770. The purchase included not only the "porcelain manufactory and its appurtenances and the lease thereof," but the stock of finished and unfinished goods then on the premises; and this gave rise to a long and tedious lawsuit, of which I shall have to speak hereafter. Mr. Duesbury also, it would appear, covenanted to pay all liabilities on the estate, and of course to receive all moneys due to it. At the foot of a bill from Mrs. Thomas to Mr. Cox, there is this very significant foot-note:—"Mr. Cox sold Mr. Duesbury the whole, who was to pay the above, and every other matter." Other bills, in my possession, including one from William Payne, the carpenter, for £19 15*s.* 5*d.*, for repairs done at the works for Mr. Cox, are endorsed as paid by Mr. Duesbury.

The lawsuit to which I have alluded was commenced the same year that the works finally passed into the hands of Mr. Duesbury, and was brought by that gentleman against Burnsall (I presume the auctioneer who conducted the sale on May 17th, 1769), to recover a quantity of goods said to have been unlawfully sold to him by Francis Thomas, and which in reality belonged to Duesbury, as a part of his purchase. The goods, which appear to have been made by Spremont, and of his own materials, were alleged by Thomas to have been sold to him by Spremont; but although the books of the concern were kept by Thomas himself, no entry of such sale and purchase was to be found. There were also cross actions. The action was first heard in Michaelmas Term, 1770, and lasted until Hilary Term, 1772. Evidence was given that the articles demanded of Burnsall were made of Mr. Spremont's materials, and at his manufactory; that Mr. Spremont never sold them to Thomas, and that they were found in rooms lately belonging to the factory, and were therefore included in Mr. Duesbury's purchase by the formal words. Mr. Spremont, whose health had been gradually failing, died while the action was going on, in June, 1771, and in the end the defendant Burnsall's counsel, representing to the court "Mrs. Thomas's situation in a madhouse, and four small children, and the attorney swearing that there was nothing else for to support them, the court would not let us keep the action at law any longer in court, so we must pay the costs." The action thus came to an end, and Burnsall immediately announced a sale of china, "in which are some capital pieces of Chelsea porcelain"—a part, doubtless, of the disputed goods.

Under Mr. Duesbury, the manager of the Chelsea works was Richard Barton (a modeller and general workman); and the "weekly bills" of wages and disbursements, now in my possession, as made out by him, are highly interesting and valuable, as showing the kind of articles then made at Chelsea, the names of the workmen and painters, and the amounts earned by each from week to week. These bills (some of which, with lists and prices, I printed in the larger edition of this work, to which I refer my readers) commence in March, 1770, and run over the next three or more years, a period, it must be borne in mind, *later* than that at which the works are generally said to have been discontinued. It must be remembered that, until my own account of the "Derby China Works" appeared in the columns of the *Art Journal*, in 1862, nothing had ever been known of the connection of Duesbury with the concern. The information I there gave of his purchase of the Chelsea factory was new; and upon what I then wrote every later account of the Chelsea works by whomsoever prepared has been founded. The works were till then generally believed to have been discontinued in 1765, but I have been enabled to show that they were not finally given up until 1784, when the kilns were taken down.

Mr. Duesbury continued working the manufactory at Chelsea, together with his large and important works at Derby, until the year 1784, when he pulled down the buildings, removed all that was useful to that place, and so totally put an end to the manufacture of "Chelsea china." The correspondence connected with this pulling down is in my own possession. In one of these letters mention is made of a "mould of the large figure of Britannia;" this was one of the finest figures produced at Chelsea or Derby, and is now of great rarity.

It has been said, and generally believed, that the excellence of the Derby works dates from the time when the Chelsea workmen and the Chelsea models were brought to it; but this is, undoubtedly, a great and a grave error. The truth is, the Derby works had risen to such extreme eminence, and had attained to so high a degree of excellence, as to more than rival Chelsea, which, in consequence, began to decline. The successful owner of the Derby establishment was thus enabled to purchase the Chelsea works, as he also did those of Bow, and to carry them on, as long as he considered advisable, conjointly. During this time he held periodical sales by Christie and Ansell, "at their Great Room, next Cumberland House, Pall Mall," and afterwards "by the candle," at his own warehouse, by Mr. William Hunter, of New Bond Street. The goods offered for sale were evidently the best that were produced, and many of them are of a most costly and magnificent character.

The manufactory was situated in Lawrence Street, Chelsea, at the corner of Justice Walk, and was held by Mr. Spremont—or, at all events, one house was—at the yearly rental of £24. Several of the adjoining houses are said to have been used as show and warerooms; but the whole of the premises have been, of course, rebuilt many years. In a pleasant gossiping conversation between Nollekens, the sculptor, and Betew, a friend of Hogarth, related in Smith's "Life of Nollekens," the following allusion to the works and its situation is made:—"The factory stood just below the bridge, upon the site of Lord Dartery's House. 'My father worked for them at one time,' said Nollekens. 'Yes,' replied Betew, 'and Sir James Thornhill designed for them. Mr. Walpole has at Strawberry Hill half-a-dozen china plates by Sir James, which he bought at Mr. Hogarth's sale. Paul Ferg painted for them. The cunning rogues produced very white and delicate ware, but then they had their clay from China, which when the Chinese found out, they would not let the captains have any more for ballast, and the consequence was that the whole concern failed.'"

It is much to be regretted that no view of the works is known to be in existence; and their absolute site is not, as far as I am aware, marked on any plan of the locality.

The body of the Chelsea china is very frequently uneven—*i.e.* it has often the appearance of being unequally mixed. One of its peculiarities is that it would bear no fresh exposure to the heat of the kiln, and consequently could not be re-painted and altered. The second application of heat would most probably end in the entire cracking and destruction of the piece. The body was not so compact as the Derby, and of very different general character from Worcester.

The earliest examples made at Chelsea I believe to have been the ordinary white with blue patterns, after the Delft and other makes; and in these early days no marks were used. The glaze, too, was somewhat thick and clumsy, and unevenly laid on. A little later, Oriental patterns were copied very successfully, both in blue and white and in mixed colours, and the potting became careful and less clumsy. Some early specimens of cups and saucers copied from Oriental patterns, which I have seen, are remarkably well potted, and bear a wonderfully close resemblance to the originals, both in body and in ornamentation. The best Oriental specimens which could be had were, however, used as models, as were also those of France and Germany; and very soon the articles produced at Chelsea most successfully rivalled the best productions of Dresden and Sèvres, both in modelling, potting, colouring, and glazing. The colours were remarkably fine and vivid; and as only the

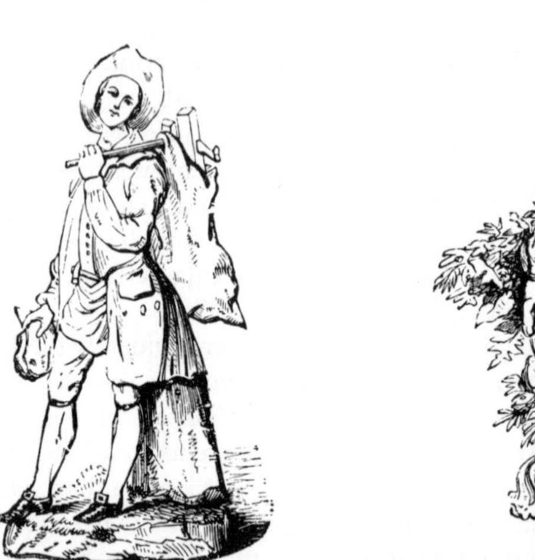

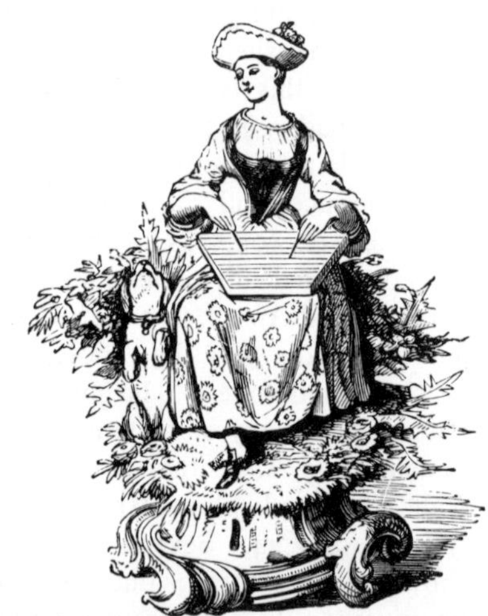

Figs. 374 and 375.—Figures in the Museum of Practical Geology.

best artists were employed as painters, the pieces produced were extremely choice and good. Many of the landscapes, of which Boreman (or Bowman) was for a long time the chief painter, are in most exquisite taste, both in colouring and choice of subject. The groups of figures, historical, mythological, or otherwise, are, too, remarkably fine, and evince a correct taste and a high degree of manipulation on the part of the artists employed. In modelling, Bacon, Nollekens, and many other of the most eminent men were employed, and the figures they produced were of the highest possible degree of beauty.

In flowers and insects, the Chelsea painters were particularly happy and successful, and they had a peculiar "knack" in "accidental arrangement" which produced a most pleasing effect. Thus, on a plate or dish, the little groups or single sprigs of flowers were often thrown on, as it were, "hap-hazard" along with butterflies, bees, lady-cows, flies, moths, and other insects, and thus produced a pleasing, because an apparently unstudied, effect. The raised flowers, arranged on vases and other ornamental pieces, are usually of extremely good character, and are well painted; and the birds and figures which are introduced along with them are also very nicely and carefully modelled.

Specimens of Chelsea china are to be found in most collections, both public and private, and, being much sought after, usually produce high prices when offered for sale.

At the sale of the late Queen Charlotte's collection, the Chelsea porcelain realised in many instances very exorbitant prices. At the Strawberry Hill sale a pair of cups of the famed claret colour, without saucers, enriched with figures of gold, sold for 25 guineas. Another pair, blue, with gold figures, sold for 17 guineas; and a similar pair, with groups of flowers on a ground of gold, made £11 6s. At the sale of the Angerstein collection a pair of bleu-de-roi vases, with paintings, were bought by Lord Kilmory for 100 guineas. Another pair, pink and gold ground, with paintings, and with open-work lips, realised 142 guineas. A single vase and cover, from Queen Charlotte's collection, sold for 106 guineas; and a pair of splendid globular vases and covers, with paintings of Bathsheba and Susanna, realised 203 guineas. On April 6, 1881, two pairs of vases 9 inches high, with white flowers in high relief over blue, and figures, after Boucher, sold for £504; and at the same sale a pair of vases, with small necks, having ruby grounds, realized £415. In June of the same year, a group of girl and boy, 15 inches high, belonging to Mr. Grunnell, was sold for £420. At the Hamilton sale, on July 17, 1882, a Chelsea vase and cover, oviform in shape and on plinth, realized £267; and on the preceding May 4th a pair of deep blue vases, the property of Lord Arbuthnot, fetched £215.

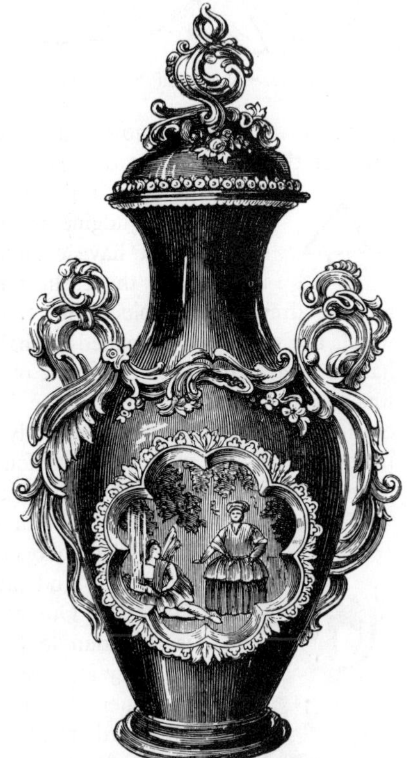

Fig. 376.—Vase formerly in the Foundling Hospital.

In the British Museum are some good examples of Chelsea porcelain, presented to that institution in 1763; and in the Museum of Practical Geology, in Jermyn Street, are also some excellent specimens, which can be examined by the collector. The Foundling Hospital, until recently, possessed a remarkably fine blue vase, richly gilt and painted, which was presented to that excellent institution in 1763, during the time the works were in the hands of Mr. Spremont, by Dr. Garnier. The vase, which has been broken, has passed by purchase into the hands of the Earl of Dudley, who, about the same time, became the purchaser, for the sum of £2,000, of the famous vase belonging to the late Earl of Chesterfield.

The earliest specimens of Chelsea ware have no mark, and can only be judged by the body, the general style of workmanship, and the glaze. But it is difficult correctly to appropriate many examples, especially those in which the *painting* alone was Chelsea work on foreign bodies. In many of the old examples the marks produced by the triangle or tripod are said to be indicative of the Chelsea works; but this is by no means to be relied on, as the same appearances are frequently found on the productions of other work.

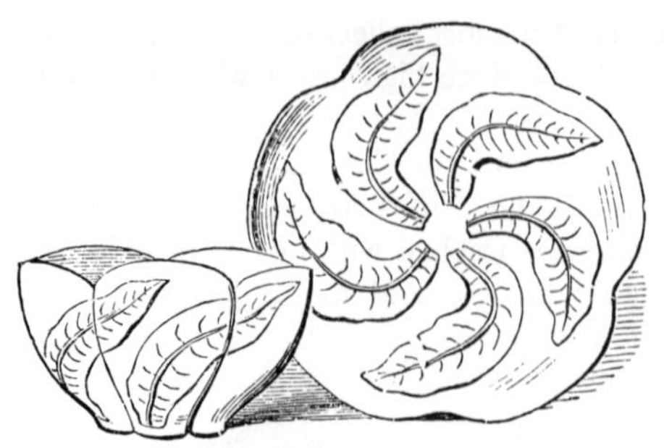

Fig. 377.—Museum of Practical Geology.

The general distinctive mark of Chelsea is an anchor—sometimes drawn with the pencil, at others raised from a hollow mould; and this is used either singly, two together, or in conjunction with one or more daggers. It is usually said that the *raised* anchor is the oldest mark; but this can scarcely be depended on, for instances are known where, on the same set, the raised anchor appears on some of the pieces, while the anchor drawn with the pencil occurs on others. This being the case, it is difficult to decide which is the oldest; but, judging from the workmanship of the specimens I have examined, I should feel inclined to say that the earliest mark was the simple plain anchor, drawn on the piece with the hair pencil, in the colour which the workman happened to have in use at the time. It has been asserted that the mark of the best kind of porcelain was an anchor in gold, and of the inferior an anchor in red. This is, however, erroneous: the quality of the body had nothing whatever to do with it, and I believe the golden anchor is never found on pieces except where gold is used in the ornamentation. The raised anchor appears on the cup and saucer.

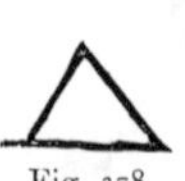

Fig. 378.

Chelsea
1745

Fig. 379.

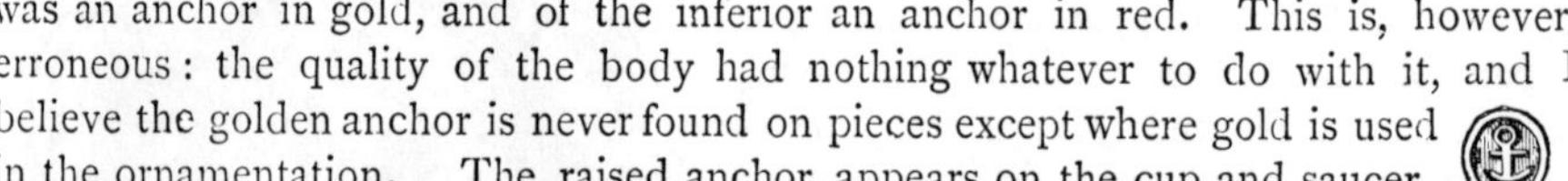

One of the most, if not the most, interesting marks connected with Chelsea occurs on a cream ewer formerly belonging to Dr. Wellesley, and afterwards to Mr. W. Russell, the Accountant-General. One of the marks usually ascribed to the Bow works is the triangle (Fig. 378); and in the Museum of Practical Geology is a cream ewer bearing this mark in the paste. This specimen was formerly in the Strawberry Hill collection, and afterwards in Mr. Bandinell's. The cream ewer which belonged to Mr. Russell is moulded in the same mould, and is, in fact identically the same as the one in the Museum, but has, in addition to the above mark, the word "Chelsea" and the date "1745" upon it. The mark and the words "Chelsea, 1745," are graved or scratched in the soft paste before firing, and, of course, under the glazing (Fig. 379). This mark is particularly interesting and curious, as being the earliest *dated* example of English porcelain known. This example, and the occurrence of the triangle with the name of Chelsea, was first noticed by me in my history of the Chelsea works in the *Art Journal* of 1863.

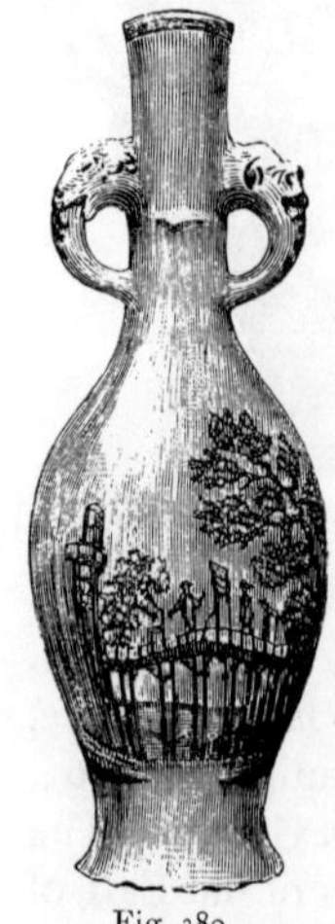

Fig. 380.

Fig. 380 is an engraving of an elegant little scent-bottle, formerly in my own collection, which bears the embossed anchor. The bottle has a continuous landscape running around it, which is beautifully pencilled, and is evidently of early work. The plain anchor, drawn in red ( ) I have copied from a leaf-shaped dessert dish of early workmanship. The dish is beautifully painted in small groups and sprigs of flowers, thrown indiscriminately on the surface, and intermixed with well-painted insects. The form of the anchor varied, as is natural to be supposed, according to the ibea of the workman, and it was occasionally drawn with the cable attached. Figs. 382 to 389 exhibit some of the varieties; they are drawn in different colours, red, blue, and brown, and in gold.

Fig. 381.

Two anchors, side by side, occasionally occur. Fig. 381 is from a small vase in the Museum of Practical Geology, Jermyn Street. The vase is of deep blue colour, with peacocks, and is painted in compartments and richly gilt. An anchor and a sword, or an anchor and two swords, are not unusual marks, and Fig. 391 is an elegant vase, with openwork rim, on which it occurs. The raised flowers are beautiful in their modelling, and the colouring is extremely

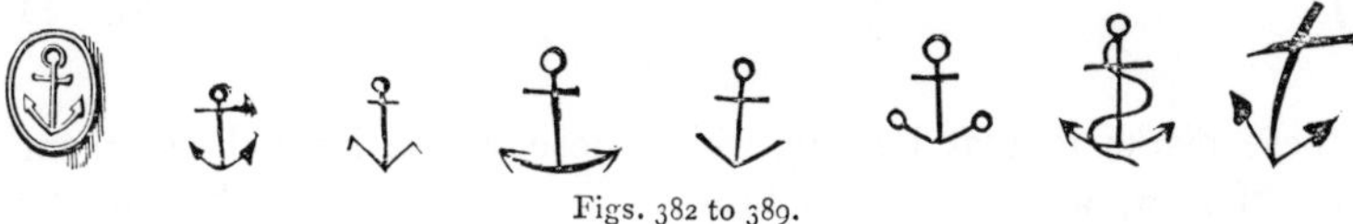

Figs. 382 to 389.

good. Between the flowers, leaves, &c., are painted on the vase, which is also decorated with butterflies, caterpillars, and other insects. On either side is a cherub's head, surrounded by raised flowers. The mark on this vase engraved

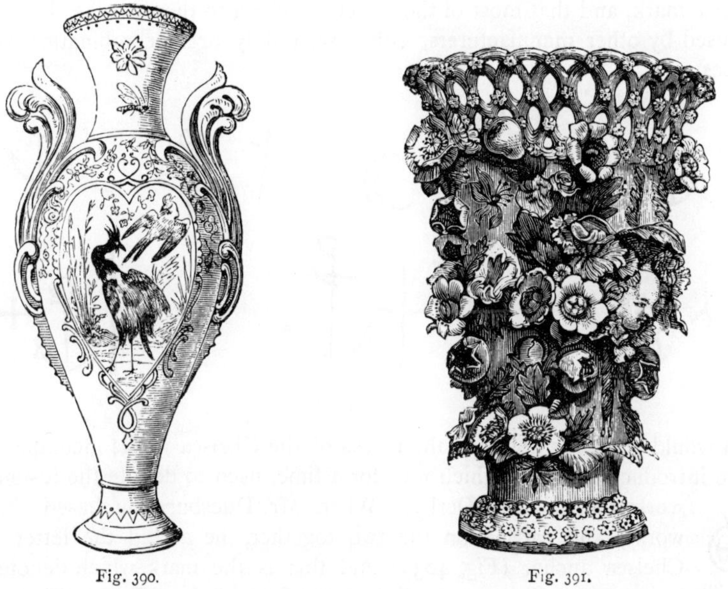

Fig. 390. Fig. 391.

(Fig. 392) is the usual anchor, preceded by a dagger, in red. It is worthy of remark that on the inside of the cover of the centre vase—a globular cover surmounted by a bird, and covered with raised flowers of similar character to those on the vase here given—the mark is reversed, the anchor preceding the dagger.

A singular mark (Fig. 394), communicated to me by Mr. Octavius Morgan, M.P., occurring on some small groups of figures belonging to Lady Mary Long, is an anchor, with cable, in red; on one side is an upright dagger, point upwards, in red; while on the other is a horizontal dagger, point outwards, in *blue*. This mark occurs on each piece. Another mark is the anchor with cable, and dagger sometimes on its right, and at others on its left side. It has been surmised that the cabled anchor and dagger, or sword, may be Bow; but there is no reason for supposing this to be the case, and I am inclined to believe they are really what I have named them—Chelsea. In reference to this remark I give the following marks, which were considered by Mrs. Palliser to belong to Bow; but of course there is no proof either way. Those collectors whose affections mainly centre in Chelsea ascribe pieces

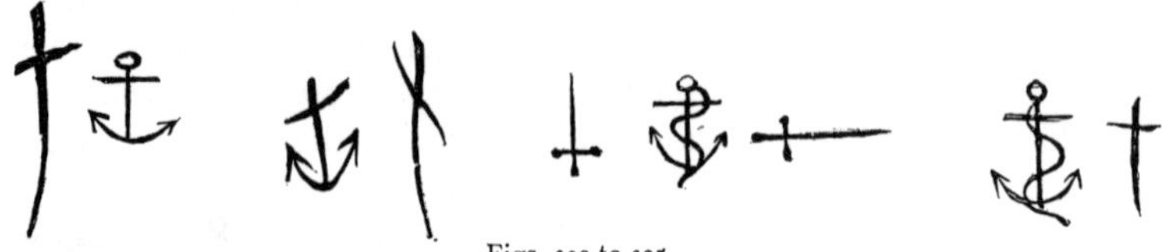

Figs. 392 to 395.

having these marks to that locality, while those whose loves direct them to the attractions of Bow, with equally as little hesitation pronounce them to belong to those works. It seems in fact to be, in the instance of these marks, that the collector has to act on the showman's advice—he "pays his money" for the rare piece of china and "takes his choice" whether he appropriates it to Chelsea or to Bow! I am disposed to think the anchor really is, as has always been considered, the true Chelsea mark, and that most of the varieties belong to those works, but that it was also used by other manufacturers, either separately or in combination with other devices.

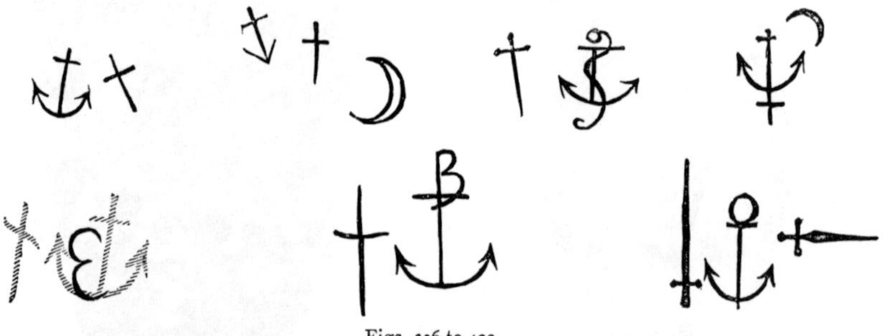

Figs. 396 to 402.

It would leave my notice of the marks of the Chelsea works incomplete, were I not to introduce the mark which was, for a time, used to denote the fusion of these works into those of Derby. When Mr. Duesbury purchased the Chelsea works, and carried on the two together, he added the letter D to the Chelsea anchor (Fig. 403): and this is the mark which denotes what is known to collectors as "Chelsea Derby" or "Derby Chelsea" ware, and which, being of comparative rarity, is eagerly sought after.

Fig. 403.

It may be well, perhaps, to notice a curious mark which I have described in my account of "Salopian china," for the purpose of suggesting that it *may* have been engraved for marking on porcelain made at Caughley, and intended to pass as "Chelsea Derby." This mark I reproduce. It occurs on a copper plate (for a mug), and represents a landscape—a river, with swans sailing, trees on either side, boat with fishermen, sailing boat, &c.; and in the background a bridge, a church with ruins to the left, and a tall, gabled building, over which are the words "Sutton Hall," to the right, above which are the words "English Hospitality." It is also well to hint that all china bearing the well-known red or golden anchor must not be taken to be Chelsea, for examples which are undoubtedly the production of other works are constantly occurring.

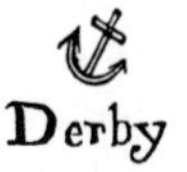

Derby

Fig. 404.

Second China Works.—Another small china manufactory was commenced, according to Lysons, at an old mansion by the water-side. This would probably be the works started by a party of workmen from Staffordshire, thus spoken of by Shaw:—"Carlos Simpson was born at Chelsea, to which place his father, Aaron Simpson, went in 1747 along with Thomas Lawton, slip maker; Samuel Parr, turner; Richard Meir, fireman; and John Astbury, painter, all of Hot Lane; Carlos Wedgwood, of the Stocks, a good thrower; Thomas Ward, and several others, from Burslem, to work at the Chelsea manufactory. They soon ascertained that they were the principal workmen, on whose exertions all the excellence of the porcelain must depend; they then resolved to commence business on their own account at Chelsea, and were in some degree successful; but at length, owing to some disagreement among themselves, they abandoned it and returned to Burslem." The fact may be as Shaw stated it, so far as regards the workmen going to Chelsea, for some reason leaving it again and commencing for themselves; but his remark as to their being "the principal workmen on whose exertions all the excellence of the porcelain must depend" is sheer nonsense, as at that time (1747) the Staffordshire workmen did not make porcelain at all.

Wedgwood's Chelsea Works.—In 1769 or 1770 Josiah Wedgwood established a branch of his manufactory at Chelsea. This was for the decoration of his vases by his "peculiar species of encaustic painting in various colours, in imitation of the ancient Etruscan and Roman earthenware." The reason for the founding of this branch was that it was judged better to have this peculiar style of ornamentation carried on near London, where suitable artists could easily be got together, and where the operations could be conducted under the personal superintendence of Mr. Bentley, who there resided, and for whom in 1769 a house was taken at Chelsea. The partnership between Wedgwood and Bentley had reference only to the *ornamented*, not to the *useful* ware; but both kinds were decorated at Chelsea, the two being kept separate in the accounts. The workmen at Chelsea were thus employed on both branches, the amounts paid them in wages being distinguished as on "Josiah Wedgwood's account" and as on "Wedgwood and Bentley's account."

How long the establishment at Chelsea was continued I do not know; but painting was done in London for Wedgwood to a late date. A letter, dated February, 27th, 1795—the month following Josiah Wedgwood's death—while speaking of painters and enamellers on porcelain, says, "I believe Wedgwood's men here do not get less than 26*s*. or 28*s*. per week," and the presumption is that these men might be employed at his Chelsea establishment.

Chelsea Pottery.—About 1774 a pottery was established in Upper Cheyne Row, Chelsea, for the manufacture of crucibles and melting-pots. It was begun by a person named Ruhl, or Ruelle, who was succeeded by his son-in-law, C. F. Hempel. It had the reputation of producing the best-made crucibles in this country. After the death of Mr. Hempel, his widow, Johanna Hempel, on the expiration of the lease, removed the works from Cheyne Row to the King's Road, where she not only made crucibles, but table services; being patronised by Queen Charlotte. In 1790 she took out a patent for "a certain composition made of earth and other materials, and the means of manufacturing the same into basins and other vessels, which, so manufactured, hath the power of filtering water and other liquids in a more cheap, easy, and convenient manner than water or other liquids could then be filtered." In 1797 Mrs. Hempel became bankrupt, and the plant and stock-in-trade, including table services, vases, crucibles, stoves, &c., and a carved sign of the Queen's Arms, were sold by auction. The manufactory was afterwards carried on by Messrs. Ludwig and Warner.

Near this pottery, in 1795, was a manufactory of artificial stone, carried on by a Mr. Triquet.

Bow.

Nothing is known definitely as to the date of the first establishment of this very important china manufactory situated at Stratford-le-Bow. It must, however, have been in existence some little time prior to 1744, for in that year it was carried on by "Edward Heylyn, in the parish of Bow, in the county of Middlesex, merchant," who, in conjunction with "Thomas Frye, of the parish of West Ham, in the county of Essex, painter," took out a patent for "a new method of manufacturing a certain material, whereby a ware might be made of the same nature or kind, and equal to, if not exceeding in goodness and beauty, china or porcelain ware imported from abroad." The patent, which was for fourteen years, bore date the 6th of December, 1744, and the specification was duly enrolled on the 5th of April, 1745. On the 17th of November, 1748, the same "Thomas Frye, of the parish of West Ham, in the county of Essex, painter," took out another patent, by which he "lawfully might make, use, exercise, and vend my new method of making a certain ware, which is not inferior in beauty and fineness, and is rather superior in strength, than the earthenware that is brought from the East Indies, and is commonly known by the name of China, Japan, or Porcelain ware." The specification was duly enrolled on the 17th of March, 1749, and is highly interesting.

There is nothing in these patents or specifications to show that the works at Bow were carried on by Heylin and Frye—the one being simply described as of the "parish of Bow, *merchant*" (not potter), and the other "of the parish of West Ham, *painter;*" nor has anything yet been found, to my knowledge, to prove that they were actual proprietors of the manufactory. Indeed, Frye is stated, in more than one work, to have been engaged to *superintend* the manufactory. He was an artist of considerable skill, who is said to have come to London in 1738, and soon afterwards to have painted a portrait of Frederick, Prince of Wales, for the Saddlers' Company. He was also a mezzotint engraver of considerable note. To his skill as an artist no doubt he was in the main indebted for the position he held at Bow; and here it would appear he remained some fifteen years, to the great injury of his health, and then returned to his previous occupation; he died in 1763. His daughters are stated to have assisted him in the painting of china at Bow.

In 1750 the works appear, from the original account-books in the possession of Lady Charlotte Schrieber, to have come into the hands of Messrs. Weatherby & Crowther, who, I may add, were potters at St. Catherine's, near the Tower. At this time the manufactory was evidently called "New Canton," by which name it continued to be known for some years. It was thus named because, as Thomas

Craft wrote in 1790, "the model of the building was taken from that at Canton in China." With reference to this name of "New Canton" a remarkably curious and very interesting example is in existence, and belongs to Mr. Binns, F.S.A. It is an inkstand of flat circular form, and is decorated in blue with flowers, &c. On the top it bears the words, "MADE AT NEW CANTON, 1750." In the centre of the well for the ink, and around it, are five pen-holes. It is shown on the accompanying engraving (Fig. 405). The date, 1750, would show that it was made in the year when the works first passed, as is supposed, into the hands of Crowther & Weatherby. Another similar inkstand, deposited in the Museum of Practical Geology by Mr. Brooks, is dated one year later, its inscription being, "MADE AT NEW CANTON, 1751."

On the 7th of February, 1753, the Bow manufactory opened a wholesale and retail warehouse in Cornhill, London; and in 1760, among the many clever artists employed was one Thomas Craft, who has left a most interesting souvenir of his connection with these works in the shape of a fine punch-bowl, measuring nearly nine inches in diameter, which is accompanied by the following note in his own handwriting:—"This Bowl was made at the Bow China Manufactory at Stratford-le-Bow, Essex, about the year 1760, and painted there by me, Thomas Craft: my cipher is in the bottom. It is painted in what we used to call the old Japan taste, a taste at that time much esteemed by the then Duke of Argyle; there is nearly two pennyweight of gold—about 15 shillings; I had it in hand, at different times, about three months; about two weeks' time wás bestowd upon it; it could not have been manufactured, &c., for less than £4. There is not its similitude. I took it in a box to Kentish Town, and had it burned there in Mr. Gyles's kiln, cost me 3s; it was cracked the first time of using it. Miss Nancy Sha, a daughter of the late Sir Patrick Blake, was christened with it. I never used it but in particular respect to my company, and I desire my legatee (as mentioned in my will) may do the same. Perhaps it may be thought I have said too much about this trifling toy; a reflection steals in upon my mind, that this said bowl may meet with the same fate that the manufactory where it was made has done, and like the famous cities of Troy, Carthage, &c., and similar to Shakespear's Cloud Cap't Towers, &c.

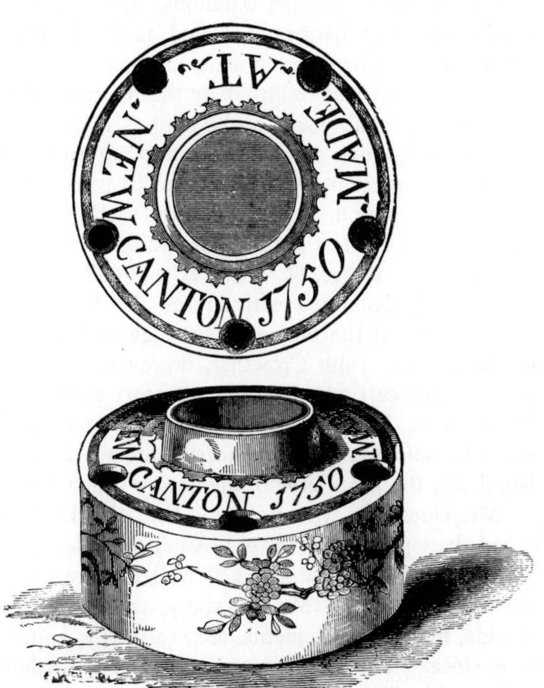

Fig. 405.—Inkstand in possession of Mr. R. W. Binns.

"The above manufactory was carried on many years under the firm of Messrs. Crowther and Weatherby, whose names were known almost over the world; they employed 300 persons; about 90 Painters (of whom I was one), and about 200 turners; throwers, &c., were employed under one roof. The model of the building was taken from that at Canton in China; the whole was heated by two stoves on the outside of the building, and conveyed through flues or pipes and warmed the whole, sometimes to an intense heat, unbarable in winter. It now wears a miserable aspect, being a manufactory for turpentine and small tenements, and like Shakespeare's baseless fabric, &c. Mr. Weatherby has been dead many years; Mr. Crowther is in Morden College, Blackheath, and I am the only Person of all those employed there who annually visit him. "T. CRAFT, 1790."

In October, 1762, the *London Chronicle* says, "Mr. Weatherby, one of the proprietors of the Bow china warehouse in Cornhill, died at his house on Tower Hill, on the 15th October, 1762;" and, in the following year, 1763, his partner, "John Crowther, of Cornhill, chinaman," was gazetted a bankrupt. This bankruptcy however (which was followed by that of "Benjamin Weatherby, of St. Catherine's, merchant," probably son of the above), appears only to have had reference to the London warehouse and business, and not to the manufactory at Bow. The stock was sold by auction, by order of the assignees of John Crowther, on March 12 and following days, and on May 19th and 30th, the two first at the Bow warehouse in Cornhill, and the last at the great exhibition room in Spring Gardens, and consisting, among other things, of "curious figures," "girandoles," "branches for chimney-pieces finely decorated with figures and flowers," "dishes," "compotiers," "beautiful desserts of the fine old partridge and wheatsheaf patterns," "knife and fork handles," &c. John Crowther, however, it seems, retained and still, in his own name alone, carried on the manufactory at Bow, and after a time opened a warehouse in St. Paul's Churchyard, which he continued to hold from 1770 to 1775, when he sold his entire concern—the works, moulds, tools, &c.—to Mr. William Duesbury, the proprietor of the Derby China Works.

Mr. Duesbury, who not only held the Derby China Works, but, as previously stated, had purchased those of Chelsea, Giles's, and one at Vauxhall, thus became proprietor of the Bow works as well, and was therefore the largest holder either in those or later days. Mr. Duesbury, as he did with those of Chelsea, removed the moulds, models, implements, &c., to Derby, and the Bow manufactory was brought to a close. The next year, 1777, John Crowther became an inmate of Morden College, Blackheath, being elected on the foundation on the 17th of March, and here he was still residing in 1790, "and," says Thomas Craft, "I am the only person of all those employed there (at Bow) who annually visit him." On the site of the works some small tenements and a turpentine manufactory soon sprang up, and their exact site was forgotten, having been later on converted into chemical works by Mr. Macmurdo, the calico printer. Afterwards a portion of the place was used as emery mills by Mr. Marshall, and, since then, as a manufactory of lucifer matches, vesta lights, &c., by Messrs. Bell and Black. In 1867, during some sewering operations at these works, a considerable number of fragments of Bow china—probably on the site of one of the old kilns—was discovered; an interesting account of which appeared in the *Art Journal* for 1869.

After some instructive details of the pieces found, it says, "that there were found a great variety of china biscuit knife-handles, some plain, others with rococo scrolls in relief, heightened with blue; two specimens are here given (Figs. 414 and 415). Some few pieces of an ornamental character are among the débris. The foot of a salt-cellar beautifully modelled in biscuit, formed of three shells, with smaller shells

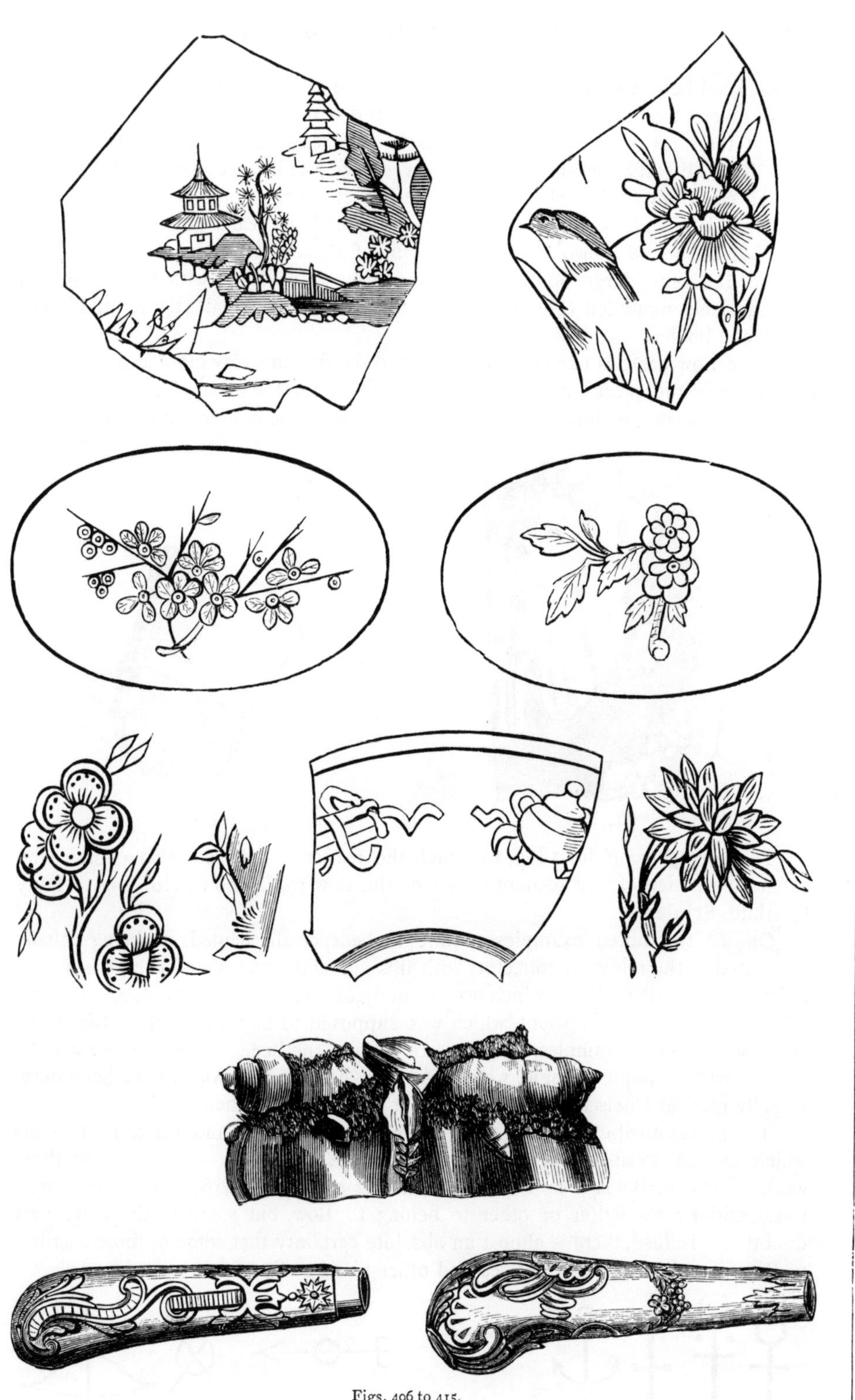

Figs. 406 to 415.

and seaweed between; the upper shell, to hold the salt, is wanting. A sketch of it is here given (Fig. 413). To these may be added the foot of a large centre ornament of the same character as the last, to hold sweetmeats, also modelled by hand in shells of all sorts, rock-work, coral, seaweed, &c., with three escalop shells: this has had one or more tiers above, but broken off at stem. Some natural shells were found which served as copies. There are two pug-dogs nearly perfect, with collars on which are roses. Two handles, in form of female heads, in high relief, for tureens and other large bowls (Fig. 416); and a man's head, with a high cap and feather, nicely modelled (Fig. 417); also the body of a female figure in biscuit, with laced bodice.

"The Bow paste is exceedingly hard, and the fracture very close and compact; consequently the pieces, as a rule, are very heavy for their size, but many of the cups and saucers are almost of egg-shell thickness. The colour is a milky white."

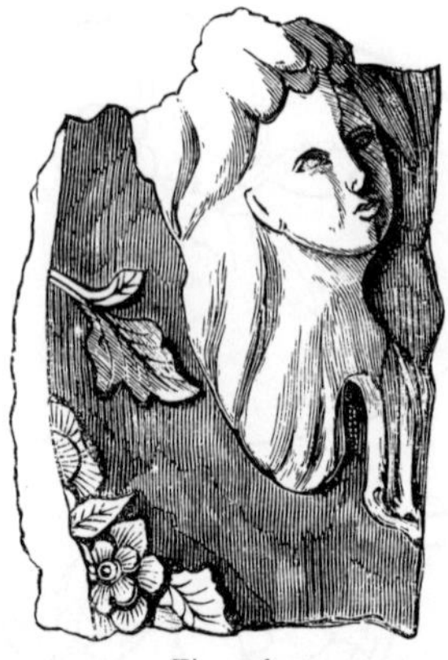

Fig. 416.

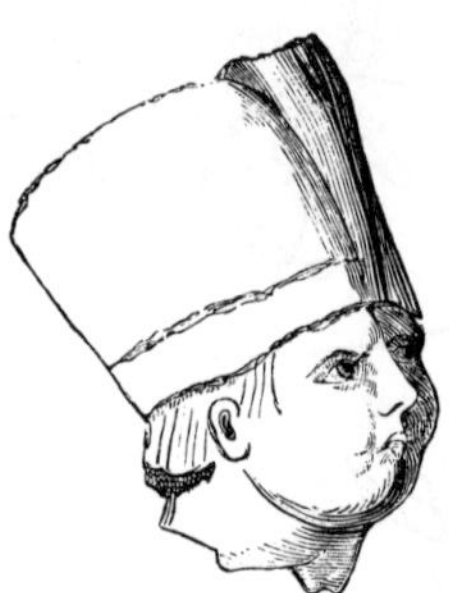

Fig. 417.

The *Art Journal* for 1869, to which the reader is referred, also contains an exhaustive notice of the account-books of the Bow works, now belonging to Lady Charlotte Schrieber.

One or two noted examples require to be specially named, as being usually associated in the minds of collectors with this manufactory. One of these is a well-known small goat milk-jug which was formerly always attributed to Bow. It bears a bee in relief under the spout, which was supposed to be allegorical of the initial B of Bow. Some examples, however, are without the bee. They are occasionally marked with a simple triangle, which, however, has been shown to have been occasionally used at Chelsea; and that the goat jugs were also there made.

The marks attributed to the Bow factory are numerous and varied; and some which are so ascribed have not, I believe, the slightest connection with those works. The marks here and on the following page (Figs. 418 to 450) are among those said by one writer or other to belong to Bow, but some of them are very doubtful. Indeed, there is almost an absolute certainty that some of those ascribed to Bow in reality belong o Chelsea and other places. Some are incised.

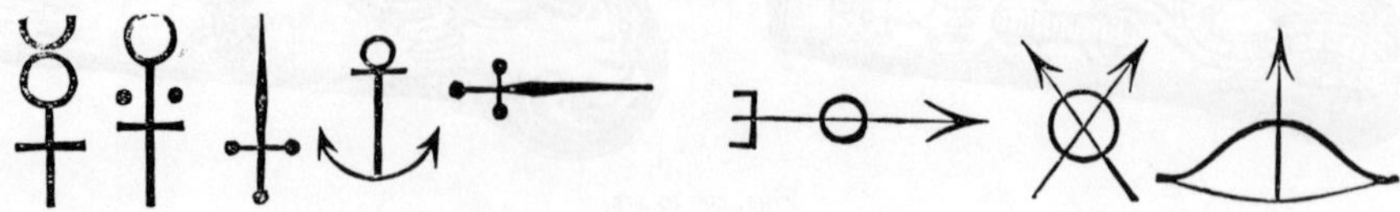

Figs. 418 to 425.—Marks attributed to Bow.

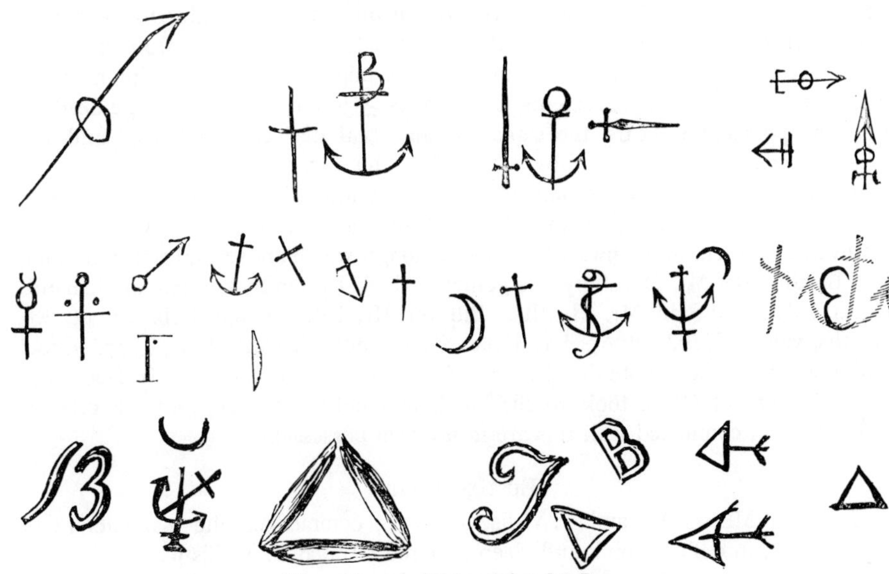

Figs. 426 to 450.—Marks attributed to Bow.

STRATFORD.

The *London Chronicle* of 1755 contains the following paragraph: "Yesterday four persons, well skilled in the making of British China, were engaged for Scotland, where a new porcelain manufacture is going to be established in the manner of that now carried on at Chelsea, Stratford, and Bow." From this it is evident that in 1755 a china manufactory, distinct from that at Bow, was carried on at this place. Nothing, however, is at present known as to its history.

KENTISH TOWN.

In the middle of last century John Giles had a small establishment and kiln at Kentish Town, where he finished and burned china, &c., procured in the white from other manufactories. He advertised "to procure and paint, for any person, Worcester porcelain to any or in any pattern;" and here vases and other articles, decorated by himself and by other artists and amateurs, were burned. An interesting reference to this kiln will be found in my account of the Bow China works on another page (125), where Thomas Craft, speaking of a bowl he had made, writing from memory in 1790, says, "about the year 1760:" "I took it in a box to Kentish Town, and had it burned there in Mr. Gyles's kiln, cost me 3*s*." In 1771 Giles took premises in Cockspur Street, as a sale-room, &c. On the 9th of July in that year the lease of these premises was granted from "George Stubbs, of the parish of St. Margaret, Westmr., in the county of Middx., Esq., to James Giles, of the parish of St. James, within the liberty of Westmr., in the said county of Middx., chinaman," of "all that messuage or tenement and premises, lately called or known by the name of the Gun Tavern, in the parish of St. Martin-in-the-Fields, in the same county of Middx., situate and being on the north side of a street called Cockspur Street, leading from Pall Mall to Charing Cross, and lately in the tenure or occupation of Susannah Cannon, deceased, together with all ways," &c. &c., for a term of 21 years, at an annual rental of £110. These premises were held from the Crown, on a longer lease, by Stubbs, so that this was a sub-letting to Giles, who had power to enter upon them on the above date, but to be free from rent until September 29th in consideration of any sums he might lay out in repairs, he covenanting to lay out in improvements and repairs £300, if requisite. The deed, in my own possession, bears the signature and seal of "Geo. Stubbs," and the attesting signatures of "G. Stubbs. Jos. Mead, his Clerk."

Giles appears to have become involved soon after this, and was assisted with loans and money and in other ways, by Duesbury, of the Derby china works. This is proved by papers in my own possession, amongst which are several notes of hand, as "Borrowed of Mr. Duesbury five guineas, which I promise to repay on demand. James Giles." "Paid Mr. Heath a Bill on Mr. Giles, dated Feb. 20, at two months, value £120." "April 1, James Giles's note due 4th June, 1777, £50." "May 29, Jas. Giles's note due July 12, £50," etc. etc. Ultimately Mr. Duesbury, on the failure of Giles, took to his stock and entire concern, and the original accounts, &c., connected with this are in my own possession.

Euston Road.

In 1860 Messrs. W. and T. Wills, sculptors, commenced the manufacture of works of art, in delicate pink and deep rich red terra-cotta, at this place, and produced vases, groups of figures, busts, &c., for drawing-room use. Their names are marked on each piece.

Oxford Street.

Mortlocks was established in 1746, by John Mortlock, and has been since continued through five generations, in direct line, of the same family. The old John Mortlock was London agent for the Rockingham works, one of whose specialities was the "Cadogan" teapot, formed on the model of an example of Indian green ware brought from abroad by the Marquess and Marchioness of Rockingham, or the Hon. Mrs. Cadogan. The first of these was made for the Marchioness; and when the Prince Regent visited Wentworth House, these teapots being in use, were much admired, the prince bringing one of them away with him. On the return of the prince to town, inquiries were made for them of John Mortlock, who seeing they would come into repute, ordered a large quantity, stipulating that MORTLOCK should be stamped upon them in place of ROCKINGHAM, and they thus passed as his own make. When the Nantgarw works were first started, Mr. Mortlock became a large purchaser as well as agent. Buying the ware in the white, he had it painted in London, by Webster, Randall, and other artists, and fired at the enamel kiln of Messrs. Robins and Randall, in Spa Fields. He was also agent to the Coalport and Swansea works.

Hoxton.

In 1693 there was "a famous brick-moulder at Hoxton." Some very interesting particulars are given by Houghton, in his "Husbandry and Trade Improved," 1693.

Hammersmith.

Houghton, in 1693, thus alludes to the brick works at this place: "Some can make fourteen or 15,000 in a day, some 18,000; but *Nicholas Gooding*, of *Hammersmith*, for a wager of 10*l.*, made in one day 22,000 bricks, upon which *Sir Nicholas Crisp* assisted him to set up, and he is now living at *Hammersmith*, and worth several thousand pounds. His master's name was *Gosling*, who had three men whom he often encouraged to wagers."

CHAPTER VIII.

WORCESTER—THE ROYAL PORCELAIN WORKS.

THERE are three things for which the "faithful city" of Worcester, so celebrated in history for its loyalty, is at the present day especially famous. These are its porcelain, its gloves, and its sauce. For who has not drunk out of "Worcester china," worn "Dent's gloves," or tasted "Lea and Perrins' Worcestershire sauce"? These three are things which are identified with its name wherever Worcester is heard, and, in the minds of some people, take precedence of its glorious cathedral, its tomb of King John, or its exquisitely beautiful shrine of Prince Arthur.

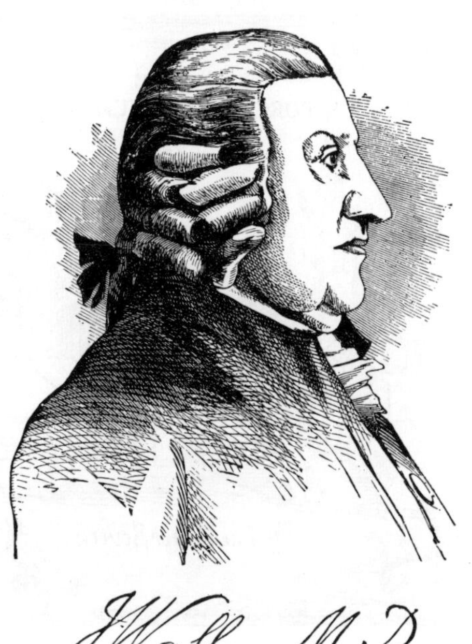

Fig. 451.—Portrait of Dr. Wall, from a drawing by S. Dance, R.A.

At a time when foreign china was much sought after, when Fulham, Chelsea, Bow, and Derby were gradually working their way into favour, and gaining ground on their foreign rivals in the estimation of people of taste, Worcester was quietly experimentalising in the same direction, and gradually paving the way for the establishment of those works which have since become so great a benefit to it, and so great an honour to the country. Exactly in the middle of the last century these experiments were carried on, and the works were soon afterwards established, and rapidly grew into note. So rapidly, indeed, did the ware made at this manufactory come into repute, that in the year following the opening of the works it was noticed in the *Gentleman's Magazine,* and in 1763 was alluded to in the "Annual Register."

The "faithful city" was indebted for the establishment of its pottery to the exertions and scientific researches of Dr. John Wall, a physician of that city. The learned doctor was born at Powick, a village in Worcestershire, in the year 1708. His father was a tradesman in Worcester, of which city he served the office of mayor in 1703; he was descended from a good family in Herefordshire. Dr. Wall was educated at the King's School, Worcester, and in 1726 entered Worcester College, Oxford, and nine years later became a fellow of Merton College. Having also studied at St. Thomas's Hospital, he took his degree in 1739, and commenced practice in Worcester. He married Catherine Sandys, cousin to the first Lord

Sandys. Besides being a clever practitioner and an excellent chemist, he was also an artist of noteworthy ability, many of his pictures being held in high repute. He also etched some remarkably clever plates, and designed the stained-glass windows at Hartlebury and Oriel College. He was also author of several medical works, was instrumental in bringing the Malvern waters into notice, and was one of the main supporters of the Worcestershire Infirmary.

Dr. Wall, who was a practical chemist, turned his attention to experimenting on materials which might be used for the manufacture of porcelain; and in 1751, about a year after the establishment of the works at Derby, and while those at Chelsea and Bow were being carried on, brought those experiments to a successful issue by the discovery of a body of surpassing excellence, and at once formed a company for its manufacture.

The "Worcester Porcelain Company," thus founded, in 1751, appears to have

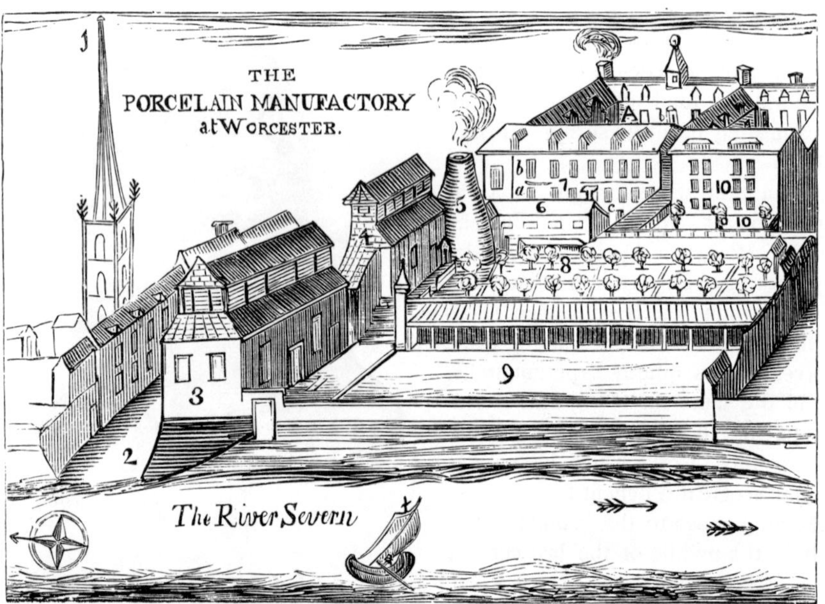

Fig. 452.

at first consisted of Dr. Wall, Richard Holdship, the Rev. Benj. Blayney, and Samuel Bradley. To these were subsequently added Rev. Samuel Pritchett, Wm. Oliver, David Henry (in place of Richard Holdship), Wm. Davis, John Salway, Germain Lavie, Rev. Thomas Vernon, Mary Blayney, Richard Cook, Henry Cook, and John Thorneloe. In 1772-4 the partners were Dr. Wall, the two William Davises, father and son, Rev. T. Vernon, Robert Hancock the engraver, and Richard Cook of London. In 1774 Hancock left the concern, and from 1776 to 1783 the two Davises and Vernon were the only proprietors. The company commenced operations in Warmstrey House, whose grounds run down to the banks of the Severn, and is now occupied by Messrs. Dent and Co. for the manufacture of gloves, and at first turned its attention to the production of imitations, both in form and colour, of Chinese porcelain. Thus the blue and white patterns so characteristic of Nankin ware were for a time almost exclusively followed. The brilliant colours of the Japanese were, however, soon attempted, and with complete success; and by the conventional arrangement of these colours in new patterns the Worcester potters were gradually led on to more elaborate productions.

The works must have risen rapidly in importance, for in 1752—only a year after the formation of the company—an engraving of the premises appeared in the *Gentleman's Magazine*; of that view the accompanying is a reduced fac-simile. The explanatory references are:—1. St. Andrew's. 2. Warmstrey Slip. 3. Biscuit kilns. 4. Glazing kilns. 5. Great kiln for segurs. 6. Pressing and modelling gallery. 7. Rooms for throwing, turning, and stove-drying the ware on the first floor, *a*, of the chamber floors. 8. The garden. 9. The yard for coals. 10. Mr. Evett's house and garden, landlord of the premises. *b*. The eight windows in two large chambers, in which the ware is placed on stallions, on the east and north, where are the painters' rooms. All the beginning of the process is carried on under the quadrangular building, ground floor, marked A; in its N.W. angle is the great rowl and ring; in the N.E. the horses turn the same, and the levigators near to the rowl. The next (on the ground floor) is the slip and treading-rooms; behind No. 4 is the glazing-room; behind 5 is the secret-room on the ground-floor. The engraving bears the initials "*J. D. delin.*" (probably John Davis, one of the partners) and "J. C. sculp." (probably J. Cave), and is accompanied by the following note:—"N.B. A sale of this manufacture will begin at the *Worcester* music-meeting on Sept. 20, with great variety of ware, and, 'tis said, at a moderate price." This was probably the first time the Worcester goods were brought into the public market. They were first vended by Samuel Bradley, one of the partners, at a shop opposite the Guildhall, in High Street, and afterwards in larger premises near the Cross.

The characteristic of the early ware was a peculiarly soft greenness of hue in the body, and by this, as well as the general style of ornamentation, and the marks, Worcester specimens may without difficulty be recognised. The first mark used I believe to have been a simple letter W., but the marks are so various in the early period of the manufacture that it is most difficult, indeed impossible, to arrange them chronologically. Like the D on the Derby porcelain, which might be either the initial of the founder of the works, *Duesbury*, or that of the town, *Derby*, the Worcester ware had a W., which might be the initial of *its* founder, *Wall*, or of the city, *Worcester*, itself. The different varieties of the letter W which have come under my notice are the following, and these may certainly all of them be ascribed

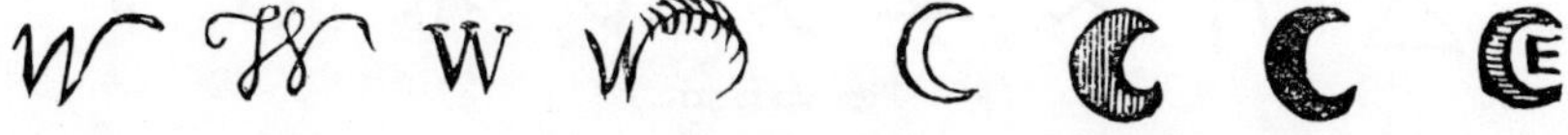

Figs. 453 to 460.

to an early period. Another distinctive mark of about the same time is the crescent, which is sometimes drawn in outline, sometimes filled in in lines, and sometimes of full blue colour. This mark is supposed to be taken, and perhaps with some probability, from the arms of the Warmstreys, which decorated the rooms used by the workmen. It is worthy of note here, that one of the marks of the Caughley or Coalport porcelain was also a crescent. As these works are said to have been established by Worcester workmen, the use of this mark may be attributed to them, and it may have had the double signification of a crescent and a C for *Caughley*.

As the Worcester aim was to copy, and emulate in design and material, the productions of China and Japan, so it appears to have been a study of the artists to copy, or to simulate, their marks; some of the more characteristic I here append.

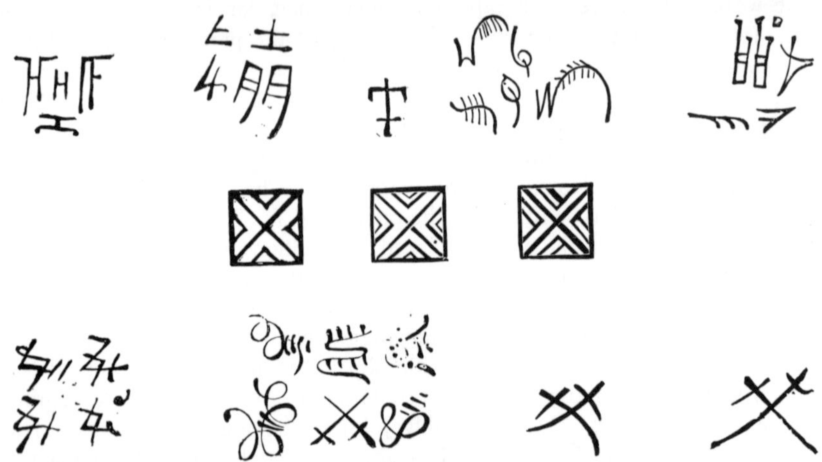

Figs. 461 to 481.

A considerable variety of other marks are known, but are probably merely the distinctive marks of the artists employed. It must be borne in mind that in other factories the "hands" were numbered, and, at Derby, each one was required to attach his number below the general mark of the establishment. At Worcester I am not aware that such a regulation existed; and thus, probably, each artist had his "mark" instead. A few examples of these I here give:—

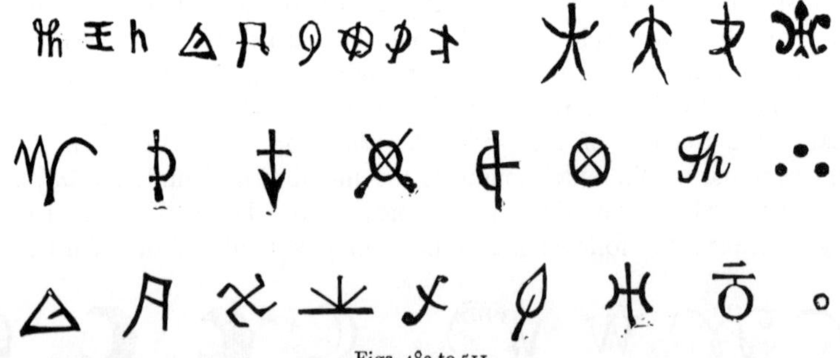

Figs. 482 to 511.

After a time the Dresden and Sèvres productions were studied and successfully followed at Worcester, the salmon-coloured ground and *bleu de roi* being excellently managed. Tea and dessert services, vases, &c., were produced in these styles, some of which are remarkable for the elegance of their painting and ornamentation. On many of these the Dresden mark was used, as here shown. In March, 1756, "The proprietors of the Worcester China Manufacture, for the better accommodation of merchants and traders," opened a warehouse at London House, Aldersgate Street, London.

Fig. 512.

A remarkable bowl, in the possession of Mrs. Barr, and bearing the date of the commencement of the works, is apparently made from a mould cast from a silver original.

In 1756, the important invention of printing on china, *i.e.* transferring printed impressions from engraved copper-plates on to the china body, is said to have been made in Worcester. At all events, it is an undoubted fact that, in 1757, the art in Worcester had arrived at such a state of perfection as to show that the belief in its being practised in the previous year is well founded. The invention of transfer

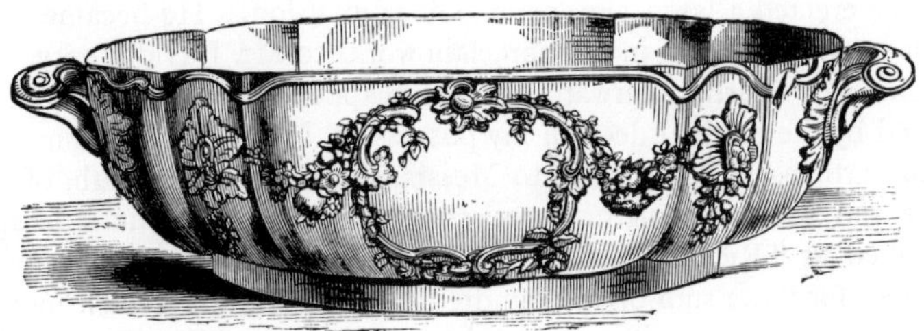

Fig. 513.

printing is claimed, and very plausibly, for Liverpool, and is said to have been made by Mr. John Sadler, who drew up papers, and procured affidavits, for obtaining a patent, in August, 1756; on the 27th of July in that year he and his partner, Guy Green, were sworn to have printed more than twelve hundred earthenware tiles in six hours. Whether the Worcester idea was taken from Liverpool, or whether both were taken from Battersea, or whether, as is not unfrequently the case, the invention originated in two minds about the same time, without one being at all connected with the other, it is not for me to determine; it is enough to say that *highly finished* printed goods were made at Worcester in 1757, as the dated example here engraved sufficiently proves. On this mug there appeared in the *Gentleman's Magazine* for December, 1757, a "Poem on seeing an arm'd bust of the King of Prussia curiously imprinted on a porcelain cup of the Worcester manufacture, with the emblems of his victories, inscribed to Mr. Josiah Holdship;" and a different version was printed in the *Worcester Journal* of January, 1758, with an "*extempore* on the compliment of imprinting the King of Prussia's Bust being ascribed to Mr. Josiah Holdship.

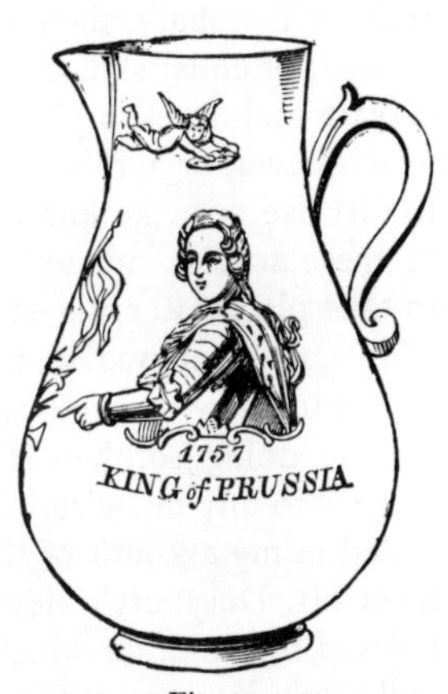

Fig. 514.

"Handcock, my friend, don't *grieve*, tho' Holdship has the praise,
'Tis yours to execute—'tis his to wear the bays."

From this it is clear that the credit of the invention was even then a vexed question in Worcester; some ascribing it to Holdship, and others to Hancock; and, no doubt, each of those individuals claiming it for himself. Robert Hancock was an engraver of some eminence in Worcester, and "was chief engraver to the Worcester Porcelain Company on its first establishment;" and it is also said he was in partnership with Dr. Wall. He died in 1817, aged eighty-seven. Valentine Green, the historian of Worcester, and a famous mezzotint engraver, who died in 1813, was a pupil of Robert Hancock's (by whom many of the plates in his "History of Worcester" are engraved), as was also James Ross, the line engraver. Hancock had, it is believed, previously to printing on porcelain at Worcester, produced some printed plaques at Battersea, specimens of which, with his name attached, are in existence. Richard Holdship, it will have been seen, was one of the original proprietors of the Worcester works, and became, in 1751, the lessee of the premises (Warmstrey House) in which the manufacturing operations were commenced. In 1759, he, conjointly with his brother, Josiah Holdship, purchased the property for £600, having previously purchased some houses to the south of the works, on whose site he erected a large and commodious mansion. He became bankrupt in 1761, having sold his shares in the porcelain works to Mr. David Henry, of London, for five shillings. Shortly afterwards Holdship appears to have left Worcester, and, as evidenced by the original deed in my possession, in 1764 bound himself by bond and various articles of agreement, to Messrs. Duesbury and Heath, of Derby, for the making and printing china or porcelain ware. In these "articles of agreement" he is described as "Richard Holdship, of the city of Worcester, china maker," and in it he agrees for "the sum of one hundred pounds of lawful British money," to be paid down, and for an annuity of thirty pounds a year, to be paid to him during life, to deliver to Messrs. Duesbury and Heath, in writing under his hand, "the process now pursued by him the said Richard Holdship, in the making of china or porcelain ware, agreeable to the proofs already made (by him) at the china manufactory of the said John Heath and William Duesbury, in Derby;" also, "during his life to supply and furnish" them "with a sufficient quantity of soapy rock used in the making of china or porcelain ware, at such a price as any other china manufacturers do, shall, or may at any time hereafter give for that commodity;" and "also that he, the said Richard Holdship, shall and will during his life print, or cause to be printed, all the china or porcelain ware which the said John Heath and William Duesbury, their heirs, &c., shall from time to time have occasion to be printed, of equal skill and workmanship, and upon as reasonable terms as the said (Heath and Duesbury) can have the same done for by any other person or persons whomsoever, or agreeable to the prices now given in." He also binds himself not to disclose or make known his process to any other persons during the continuance of these articles, nor to bequeath, sell, or communicate them to any persons, so as to take place after his death, unless the articles are cancelled during his lifetime. The agreement was to continue in force so long as Duesbury and Heath determined to carry on the business according to his process; and whenever they should decline doing so, then Holdship was to be at liberty to sell or communicate his process to any one else. At Derby, Holdship also printed stone-ware. As I have stated in my account of the Derby china works, the printed ware did not appear to meet Mr. Duesbury's views, or to be so advantageous as the higher class of goods painted by hand, for which he was famed, and thus there were constant complaints and recriminations passing between Holdship and his employers. From some of the documents I glean that his process was "for printing enamell and blew;" that he had an assistant named William Underwood; that he valued his press at £10 10s.; offered his "utensils and copper engraved plates at half prime cost;" that his "enamell collours, weight 151 lbs.," he valued at £35, including his process for making the same; and that he proposes to "yield his process for printing enamell and blew, for which he hath been offered several hundred pounds." How long the agreement continued I cannot say, but at all events, Holdship was still employed at Derby at the end of 1769.

Of much of the work of Robert Hancock, fortunately, there can be no possible doubt, for his name appears in full on some examples, and his initials—at least, initials believed to be his—on others. These will be seen in the accompanying engraving:—

R Hancock . fecit. RH RH . Worcester.

Figs. 515 to 517.

Two of these, it will be seen, are somewhat curious, having the Chelsea anchor attached to the name of Worcester. It is a problem worth solving whether this monogram of RH conjoined was that of Robert Hancock, and, if so, whether he had previously been connected with the Chelsea works; or whether the anchor was adopted as a mark by Richard Holdship in allusion to his name, *hold ship*, which, it must be admitted, would be a clever and very appropriate colophon. In Mr. Binns's possession is a watch-back of Battersea enamel, transfer printed, bearing the initials "R. H. f." (Fig. 518). Examples of his engravings, transferred on to *Chinese* porcelain, are also preserved, and are considered to be his trial pieces. The copper-plate itself from which these foreign china specimens as well as many of the choicest known examples of Worcester china have been printed, I had myself the good fortune to discover some years ago at Coalport. It bears the engraver's name —*R. Hancock fecit*. In the first edition of this work I, for the first time such a thing had been done, gave as an illustration impressions actually printed from this very plate engraved by Hancock a century ago, and on the same plate, another engraving by him, of a group of children playing at "Blind Man's Buff." In 1769 Hancock purchased from the mortgagees of Richard Holdship the buildings he had erected, and became a partner in the china works, in which he held a sixth share. The partnership, however, did not last long, and in 1774 he was "paid out," as appears by the following entry:— "Whereas certain controversies, differences, and disputes had arisen between the parties touching the said Robert Hancock's share of the said stock, it was agreed by indenture, dated October 31, 1774, in order to prevent all such disputes, to purchase from him his share in said stock for the sum of £900, being exactly one-sixth."

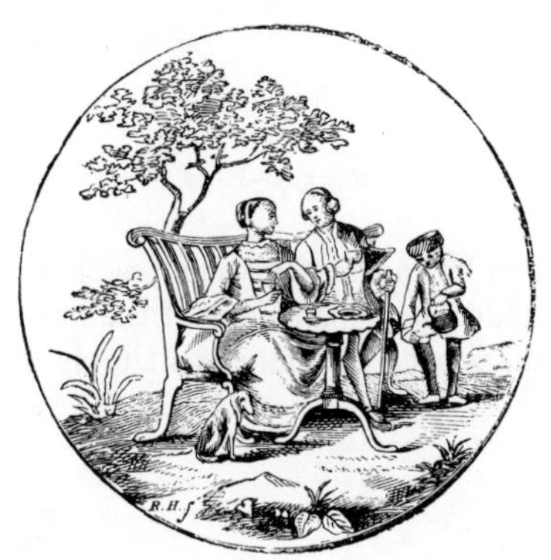

Fig. 518.

A few years before the Chelsea works passed into the hands of Duesbury of Derby, it appears that some of the workmen migrated to Worcester, and this circumstance gave a fresh impetus to the manufacture of porcelain in that city, and enabled the proprietors of the works to produce many exquisite articles after the Dresden and Sèvres schools of art. Some examples of this Chelsea style are shown grouped on Fig. 520. In 1776 Dr. Wall died, and was buried at the Abbey Church, Bath, in which city he had resided for some time for the benefit of his declining health.

In 1783, after having undergone many changes in proprietorship, the Worcester works were purchased by its London agent, Mr. T. Flight, a merchant of Bread Street and of Hackney, for his sons, Joseph and John, for the sum of £3,000, including premises, models, plant, and stock, and here he established them. These

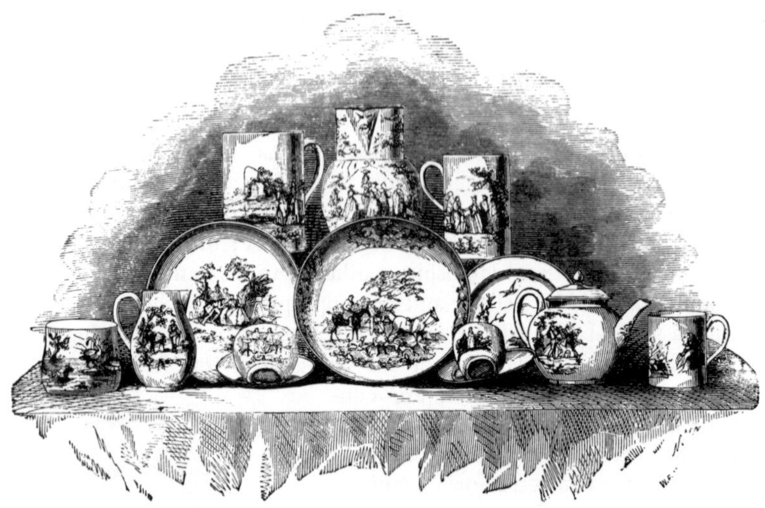

Fig. 519.—Early Worcester Transfer Printing, by Hancock, Holdship and others.

two brothers, who were jewellers, carried on both concerns at the same time, and under their management the works more than regained their former eminence. The mark used by them was simply the name in writing letters. Another mark of this

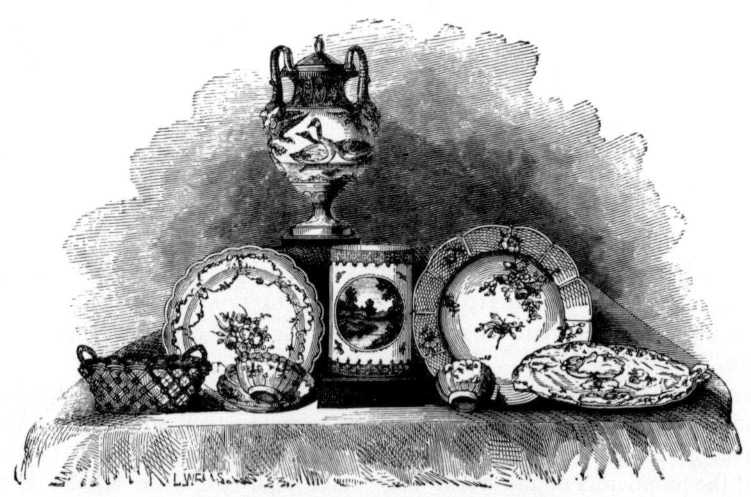

Fig. 520.—Worcester China in the Chelsea style.

period was the name *FLIGHTS*, in italic capitals, impressed on the ware, sometimes with the crescent painted in blue. In 1786 Joseph Flight, one of the partners, "jeweller and china manufacturer," advertised that he had taken Mr. Bradley's shop, 33, High Street. Shortly afterwards he removed to larger premises, No. 45, where he received the king and queen.

Flight

Fig. 521.

In 1788 the king, George III., with Queen Charlotte and the princesses, visited Worcester, and having gone through the porcelain works, and been much pleased with the beauty of the articles manufactured, his majesty desired that the word "royal" might be prefixed to the name, and recommended the proprietors to open a show-room in London. This suggestion was acted upon, and a warehouse opened in Coventry Street, which secured a large and very fashionable patronage for the ware. After the king's visit the crown was added to the marks, which at this time were the following. The subsequent changes in the prporietorship, consequent on deaths, were "Messrs. Flight and Barr"—Mr. Martin Barr, having joined the concern in 1793—"Barr, Flight, and Barr," and "Flight, Barr, and Barr" (Joseph Flight, Martin Barr, and Martin Barr, jun., and afterwards George Barr in place of the elder Martin). From 1829 till 1840 the

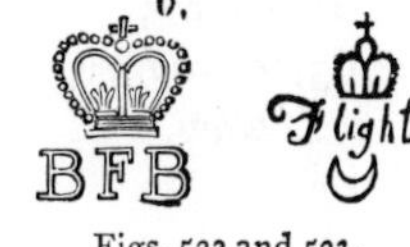

Figs. 522 and 523.

Flight & Barr.

BARR FLIGHT & BARR.
Royal Porcelain Works.
WORCESTER.
London-House.
No. 1 Coventry Street.

Flight & Barr
Worcester
Manufacturers to their
Majesties

Figs. 524 to 526.

firm was simply "Barr and Barr," the parties being Martin and George Barr. Some of the marks I here give. Others, which were *printed* marks, are—"*Flight, Barr, and Barr*"—B, the initial of Barr, scratched in the ware. "Barr, Flight, and Barr, Royal Porcelain Works, Worcester; London House, Flight and Barr, Coventry Street" (within an oval), "Manufacturers to their Majesties, Prince of Wales, and Royal Family; established 1751" (surrounding the oval); the whole surmounted by a crown and the Prince of Wales's feathers: "Flight, Barr, and Barr, Proprietors of the Royal Porcelain Works, Worcester, established 1761," in five lines; above are the royal arms, and beneath are the Prince of Wales's feathers, the whole within a circle; surrounding the circle is, "Manufacturers to their Majesties and the Prince Regent; London Warehouse, No. 1, Coventry Street."

In 1786, Robert Chamberlain, who was the first apprentice to the old Worcester Porcelain Company, and who had continued with the different proprietors up to that period, commenced business for himself in premises at Diglis—the same which are now carried on by the Royal Worcester Porcelain Company. Chamberlain was a painter, and on the first establishment of his business bought his porcelain from the Caughley works (Coalbrookdale) and painted it at Worcester. In a very short time, however, he made his own, and his works soon grew into public favour and eminence. His son was an excellent artist, and a portrait of the Princess Charlotte, which he painted, is said to have given the highest satisfaction to Prince Leopold and others. The mark adopted by Chamberlain was simply his name in writing, thus, *Chamberlains*, or *Chamberlains. Worcester*

Afterwards the following marks were used :—

Chamberlain's
Worcester,
& 63, *Piccadilly,*
London.

Chamberlain's
Regent China,
Worcester,
& 155,
New Bond Street,
London.

Chamberlain's
Worcester,
& 155,
New Bond Street,
London.
Royal Porcelain Manufactory.

CHAMBERLAINS.

CHAMBERLAIN & CO.,
WORCESTER,
155, NEW BOND STREET,
& NO. 1,
COVENTRY ST.,
LONDON.

Chamberlain & Co., Worcester.

CHAMBERLAIN & Co. WORCESTER

Figs. 527 to 536.

As a companion picture to that of Dr. Wall's works I give a view of those of Chamberlain's (Fig. 537), (afterwards Flight and Barr) copied from an engraving

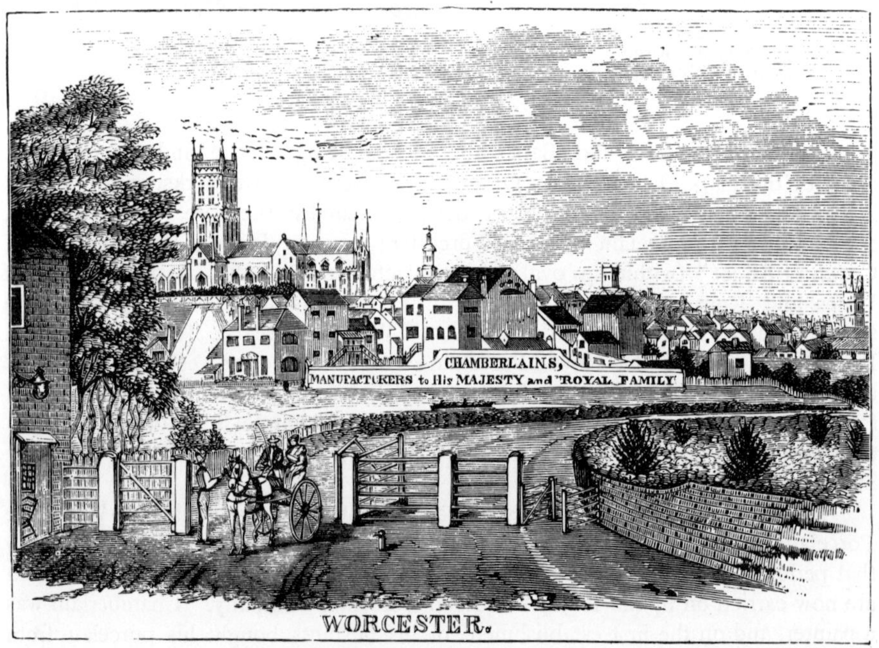

Fig. 537.—Chamberlain's Worcester Porcelain Works.

transferred to porcelain. The business was afterwards carried on successively by "Chamberlain and Sons" and "Chamberlain and Co." During the continuance of the two works it is believed that by far the greater part of the entire production of porcelain in the kingdom was made at Worcester; and certainly the books and the samples of various sets still remaining in the show-rooms bear evidence both of the high patronage and the extent of orders received, and of the beauty of workmanship to which the proprietary had attained. The successive changes were:—1786—1798, Robert Chamberlain, senior, Humphrey Chamberlain, and Richard Nash (sleeping partner); 1798—1804, Humphrey Chamberlain and Robert Chamberlain, junior; 1804—1811, the same, with G. E. Boulton as sleeping partner; 1811—1827, the same, without Boulton; 1828—1840, Walter Chamberlain and John

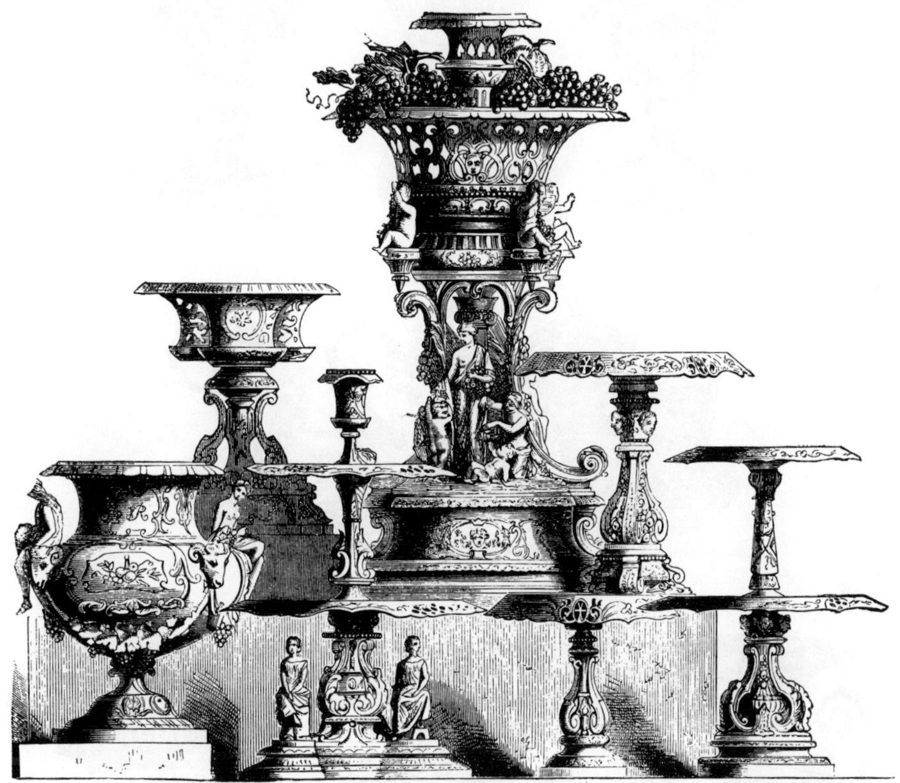

Fig. 538.

Lilly. The marks then used, from 1840 to 1850, being *Chamberlain & Co., Worcester*, in writing italics, and CHAMBERLAIN'S in capital letters.

The manufactories of "Flight, Barr, & Barr," and "Chamberlain & Co.," continued separate until 1840, when they amalgamated, and formed one joint-stock company. The plant and stock were removed from Warmstrey House to Chamberlain's premises, and the works were there carried on under the style of "Chamberlain & Co." From 1840 to 1847 the managing directors were Walter Chamberlain, John Lilly, Martin and George Barr, and Fleming St. John; from 1848 to 1850 the proprietors were Walter Chamberlain and John Lilly; in 1850, Walter Chamberlain and Edward Lilly. In 1850 Mr. W. H. Kerr joined the concern, which was for a short time carried on under the style of "Chamberlain, Lilly, & Kerr;" but on the

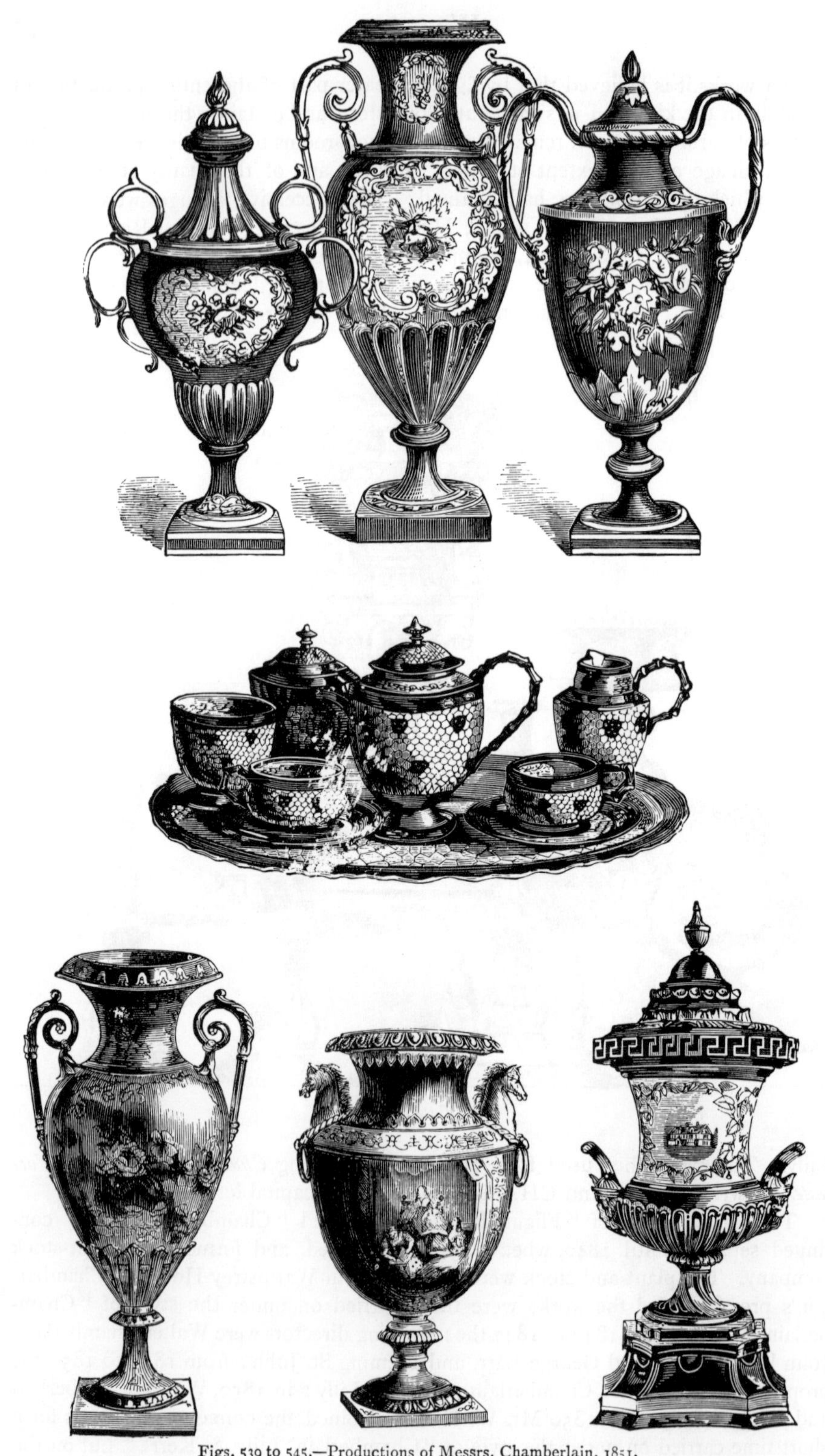

Figs. 539 to 545.—Productions of Messrs. Chamberlain, 1851.

1st of January, 1852, Chamberlain and Lilly retired, and Mr. R. W. Binns entering into partnership with Mr. Kerr, the firm was carried on under the style of "Kerr & Binns," and "W. H. Kerr & Co." In 1852 the works were considerably increased and rebuilt by Mr. Kerr, who, in 1862, retired from the concern, and it is now carried on by a company of shareholders, Mr. R. W. Binns, F.S.A., holding the position of "Art Director."

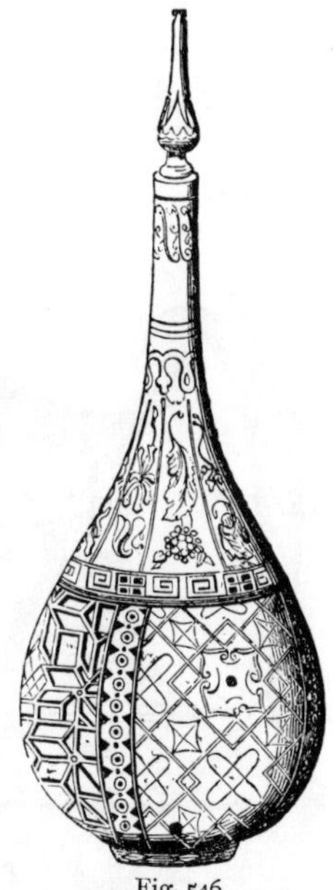

Fig. 546.

The productions of the Worcester works have been brought to a wondrous state of perfection, both as to body, glaze, form, and decoration. Certainly neither in ancient nor in modern specimens of ceramic art have such exquisitely beautiful works been produced as some of the enamels which, under the fostering hand of Mr. Binns, have been here made. The body, unlike the works of Limoges or the Sèvres imitations, is *pure porcelain*, not a coating of porcelain over sheets of metal; and the effect is produced by the partial transparency of the white laid on the blue ground, instead of by heightening. The tone is peculiarly soft and delicate, and the colours pure and intense. Examples are given on Figs. 547 to 553. The late Mr. Bott, an artist of the very highest eminence, was brought up by Mr. Binns specially for the production of these enamels, and through his early death examples have become very scarce, and realise high

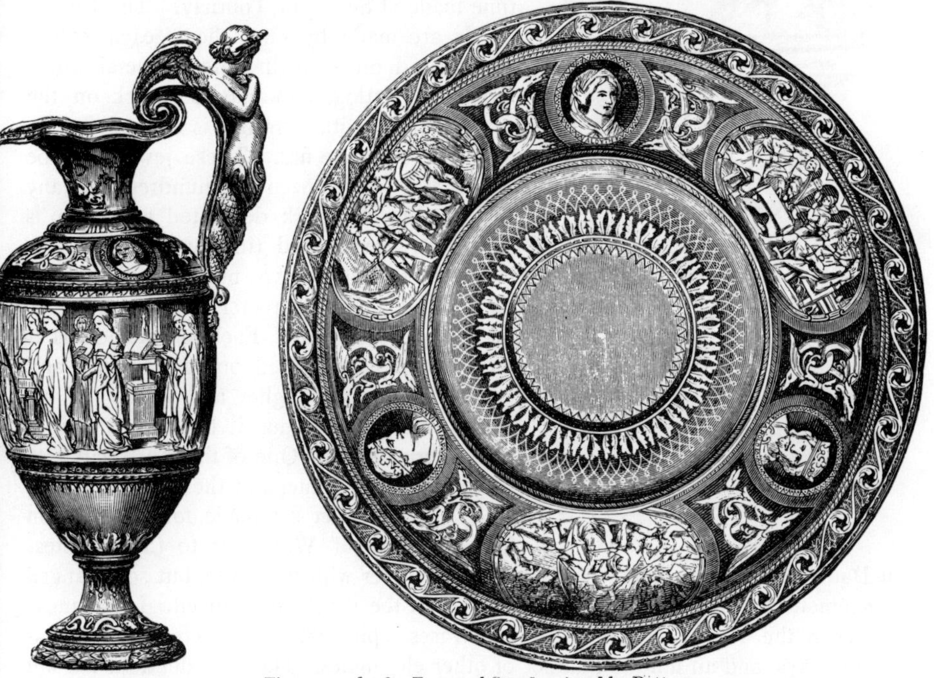

Figs. 547 and 548.—Ewer and Stand, painted by Bott.

prices. A pair of vases—still in the hands of the Worcester Company—are valued at 1,500, and an ewer and basin at 350, guineas, and the probability is that they will still increase rapidly in value. To Mr. Binns is due the introduction and carrying out of the Worcester enamels in the style of Limoges; the ivory porcelain, a soft-glaze body of an ivory tint; the Raphaelesque porcelain; jewelled porcelain, of a totally different and far higher character than that of Sèvres; and Japanese decoration on porcelain and pottery.

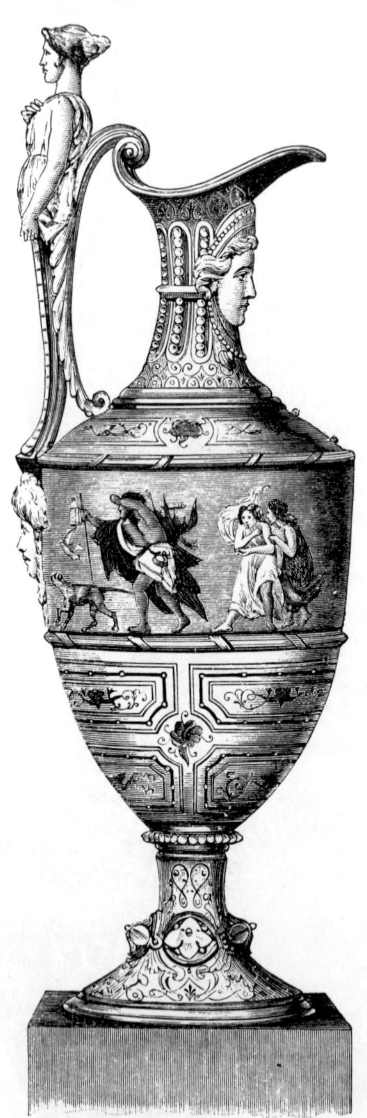

Fig. 549.

In parian, the Worcester works produce figures, busts, groups, and ornamental articles of a remarkably clean and pure body. Ivory porcelain—an improvement upon parian, and capable of greater development—is a speciality of these works, and was first introduced for the Exhibition of 1862. Besides being used for busts, figures, and ornamental pieces, in its simple state, when it has all the softness, beauty, and natural tint of ivory itself, it forms the basis of many of the ornamental decorations, especially the Raphaelesque ware, which is the colouring of the surface in relief in the style of the old Capo di Monte and Buen Retiro porcelain.

The jewelled porcelain, for which Worcester is famous, is totally different from that at any time made at Sèvres or Tournay. The French jewels are made by enamellers, each colour being fused on a small plate of metal which forms the setting, and may be stuck on the vase or plate with gum if it is not required to pass it through the fire. These jewels may be bought by the dozen or hundred in any variety; but the work decorated with them is essentially French, and tinselly. The English jewelling, though perhaps not so brilliant, is of higher and purer character, and more legitimate as a decoration. Each of the jewels is formed of colour melted on to the china, and occasionally raised higher and higher by repeated firings, and thus it becomes a part of the material itself. One of the most elaborate pieces of work produced at these works, in this style, is a déjeûner set made for presentation from the city of Worcester to the Countess of Dudley on her marriage; it is powdered all over with turquoise, but so arranged in geometric lines that only the different sizes of the jewels are noticed. In Japanese porcelain the Worcester works produce vases, spill-cases, jardinières, toilet ornaments, trays, and an infinite number of other elegancies. These productions are not servile imitations, but are Japanese art and art-characteristics adapted and rendered subservient to the highest aims of pure design of our own country. Mr. Binns, in

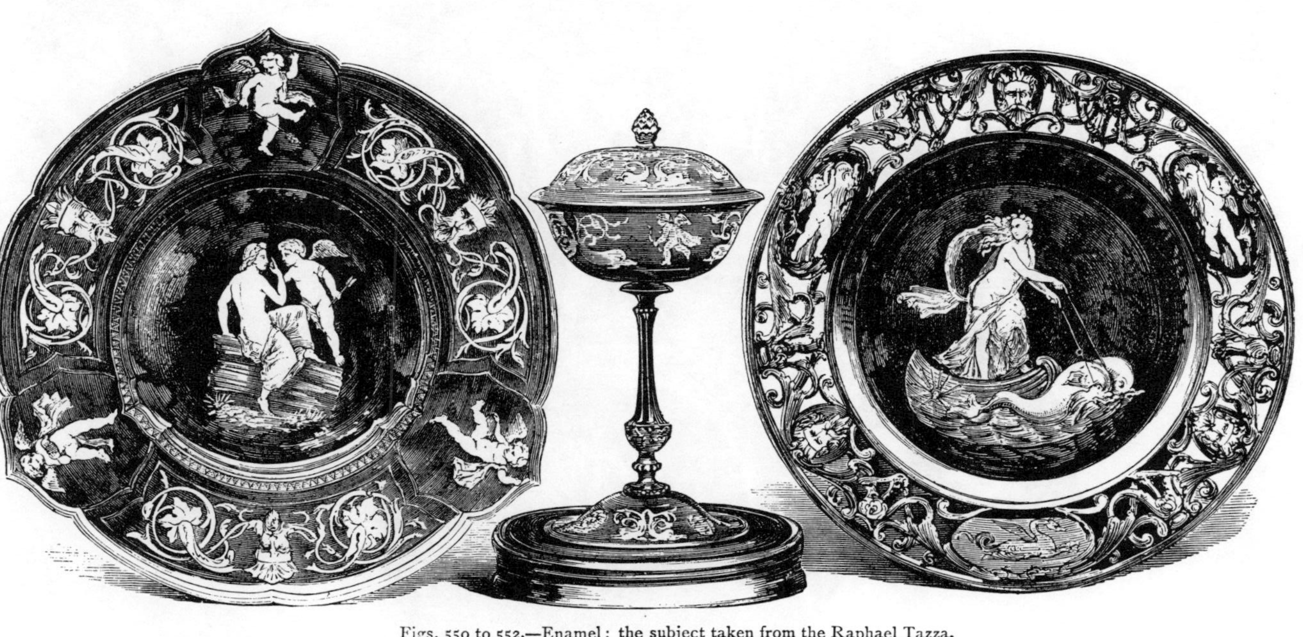

Figs. 550 to 552.—Enamel; the subject taken from the Raphael Tazza.

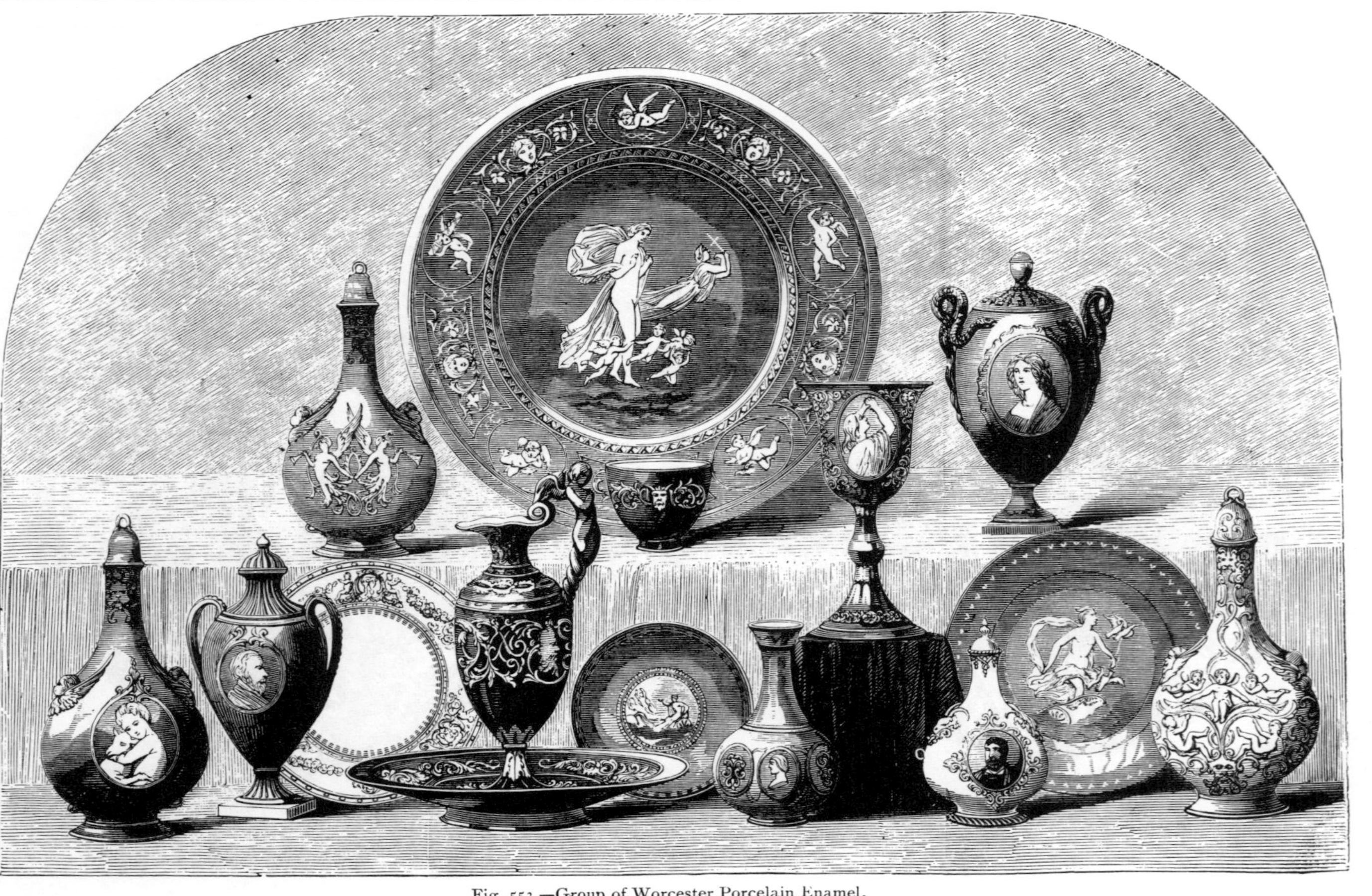

Fig. 553.—Group of Worcester Porcelain Enamel.

the introduction of this style, caught the very spirit of Japanese art, and so grafted it upon English productions that the one becomes a component part of the other. Among the more characteristic of the vases is a set on which the designs, in relief (modelled by Mr. Hadley), represent the processes of the potter's art as followed in the East; and these are so minutely painted and gilded (by Callowhill), that it requires a good lens to bring out their minute beauties.

In majolica the Worcester works produce dessert services, floral table decorations, shell-pieces, spill-cases, vases, &c. The body is finer and more compact than that frequently used by manufacturers, and the colouring faultless and in the purest taste. In the ordinary useful classes of goods these works produce every possible variety, from the simple gold and white to the most highly decorated tea, coffee, déjeûner, dinner, toilet, and other services, in large quantities.

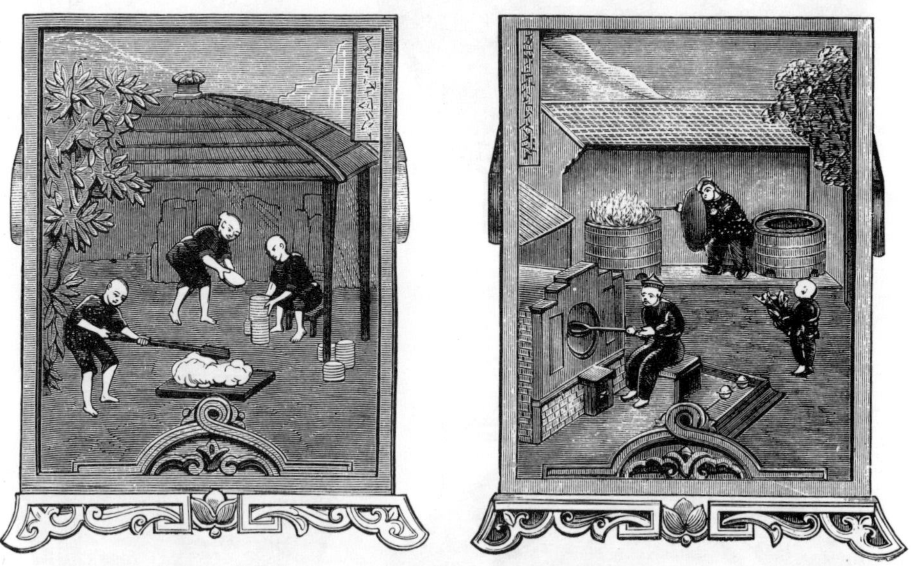

Figs. 554 and 555.—Worcester Japanese Ware.

It is a common belief that high art and commercial success cannot go hand in hand; that to make things *sell* you must sink *art;* or that, if you produce high art examples, you must give up all expectations of a remunerative trade. In this theory I do not believe. I hold it to be the mission of the manufacturer, in whatever branch he may be engaged, to produce such goods as shall tend to educate the public taste, and to lead it gradually upwards to a full appreciation of the beautiful. The manufacturer is quite as much a *teacher* as the writer or the artist, and he is frequently a much more effectual one. In pottery especially, where the wares of one kind or other are hourly in the hands of every person in the kingdom, it behoves the manufacturers to produce such perfect forms, and to introduce such ornamentation, even in the commonest and coarsest ware, as shall teach the eye, and induce a taste for whatever is beautiful and perfect and lovely in art. The mission of the manufacturer is to *create* a pure taste, not to perpetuate and pander to a vicious and barbarous one; and I believe, in the end, that those who do their best to elevate

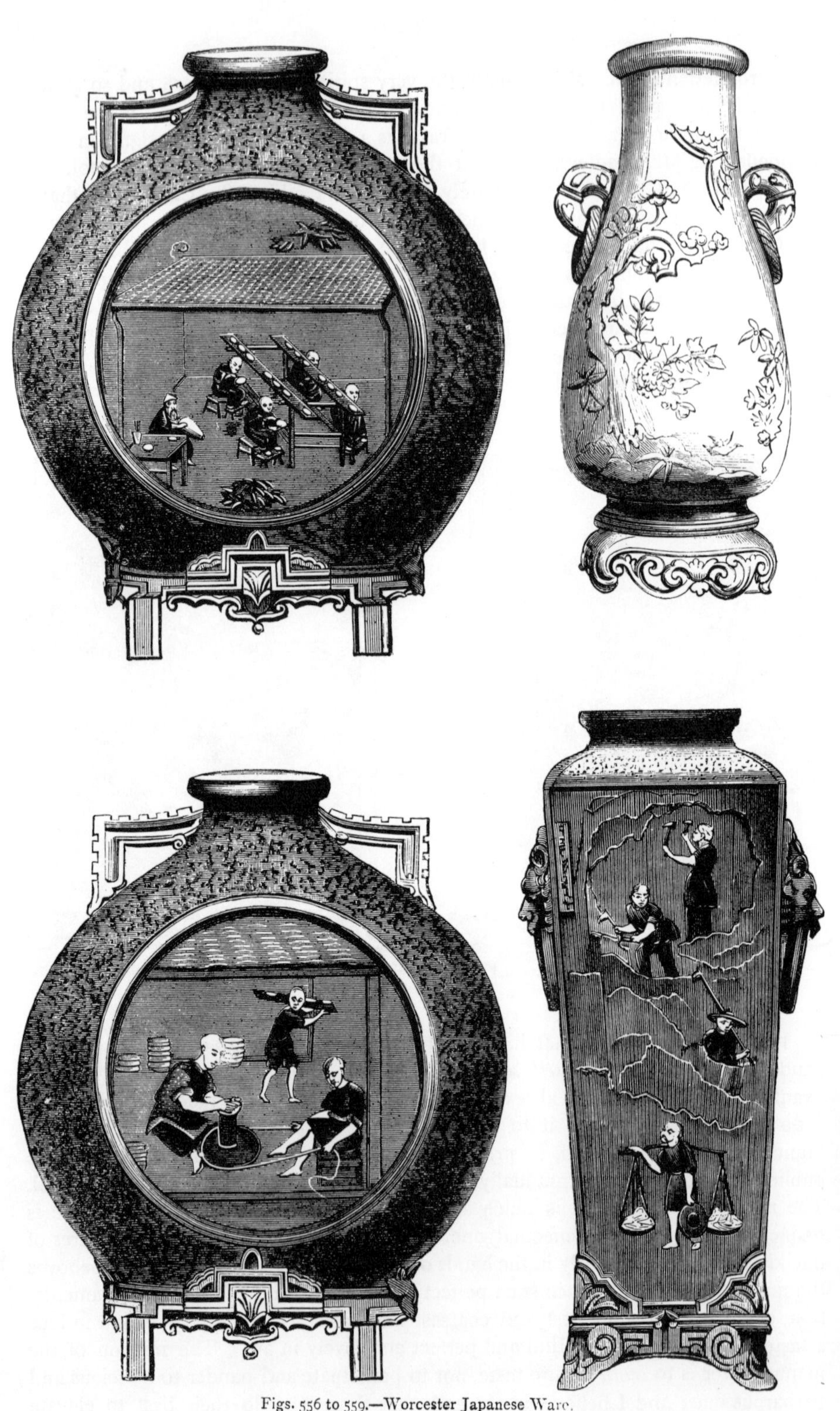

Figs. 556 to 559.—Worcester Japanese Ware.

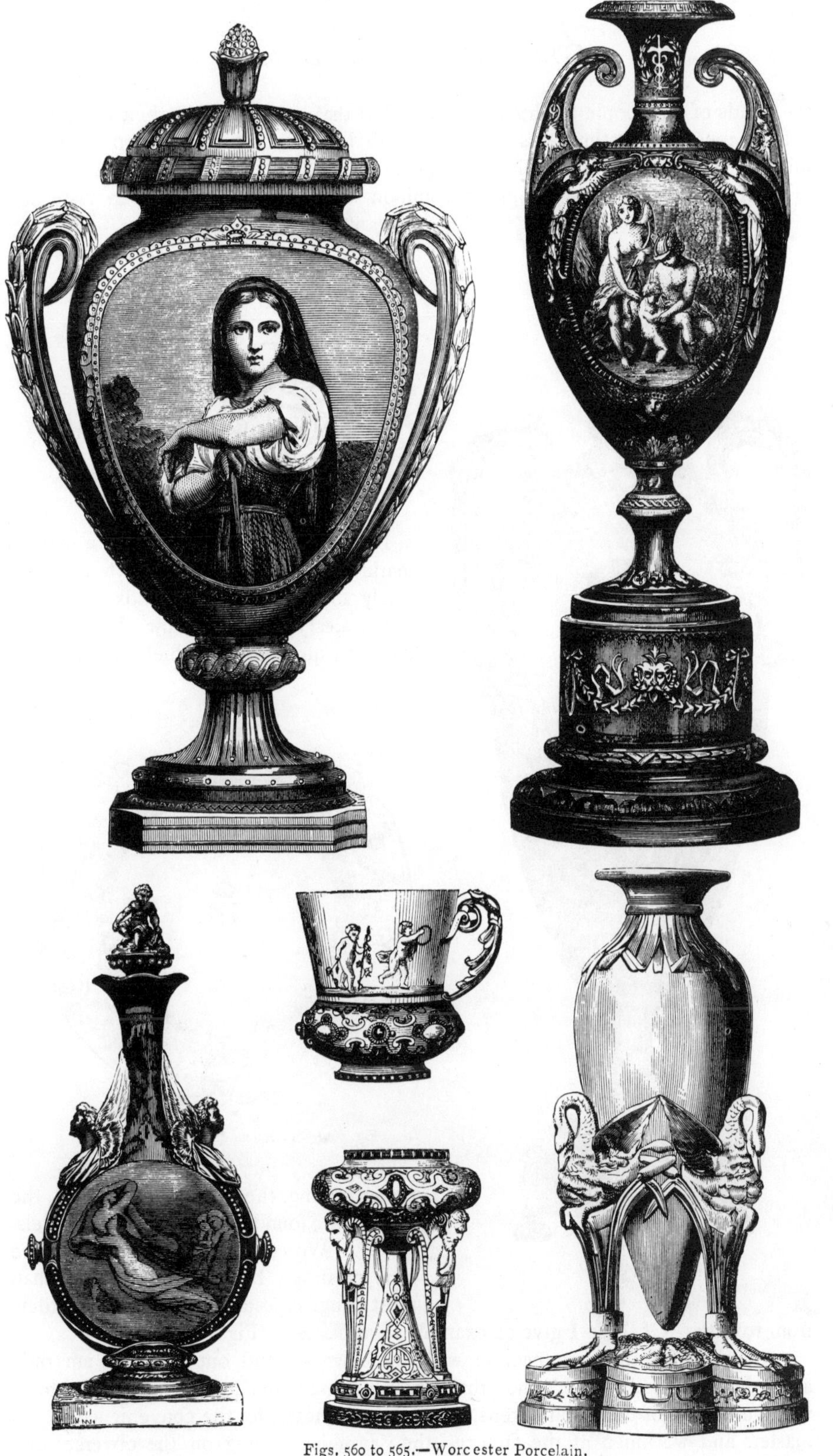

Figs. 560 to 565.—Worcester Porcelain.

the minds of the people by this means will find that, commercially, their endeavours will be most satisfactory—assuredly they will be the most pleasant to their own minds. The Worcester people seem to understand this thoroughly, and nothing, even of the most simple design or common use, which is not pure in taste and elegant issues from their works.

The marks of Messrs. Kerr & Binns were the following:—

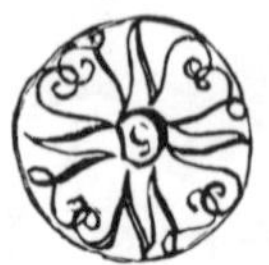

Figs. 567 and 568.

But they had also another, a special mark, designed by Digby Wyatt, and used solely for marking the goods made for her Majesty. In the mark (Fig. 568) in the third quarter of the shield, left white in the engraving, the initials of Mr. Bott, the painter, are found on his beautiful enamels.

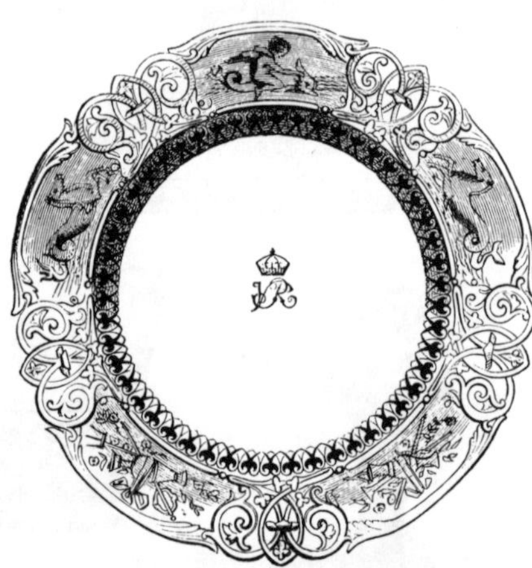

Fig. 569.—Service made for Queen Victoria.

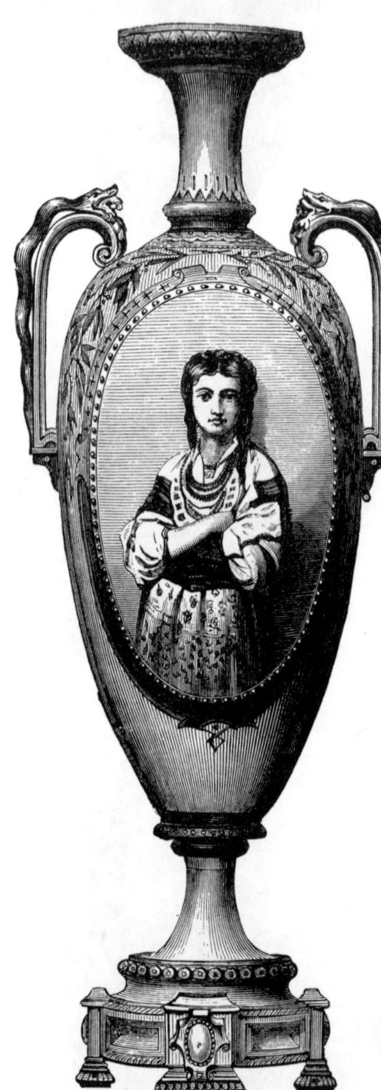

Fig. 565.

The Worcester works have, at one time or other, been favoured more than most English establishments with orders from royalty. Of these I give as examples five plates. (Figs. 569 to 573.)

A curious feature in connection with these works, and one which I am only aware has been followed by one other English china manufactory (that of Pinxton), was the issuing of porcelain tokens, or promissory notes, for the convenience of the masters and workmen at the factory—the "promise" being on the obverse, and

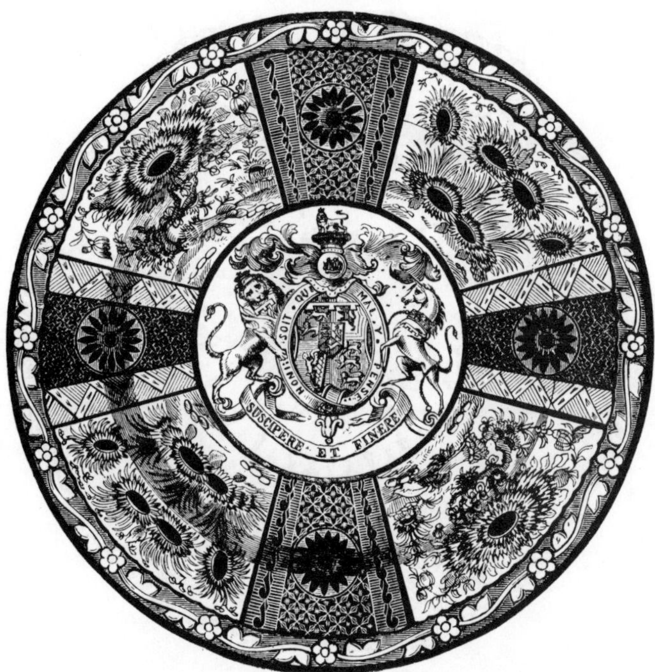

Fig. 570.—Breakfast Service made for the Duke of Cumberland in 1806.

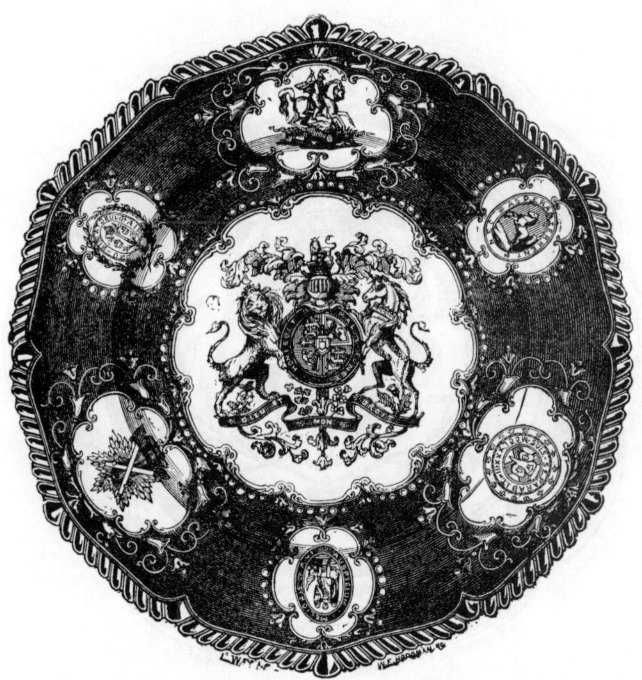

Fig. 571.—Service made for King William IV. in 1831.

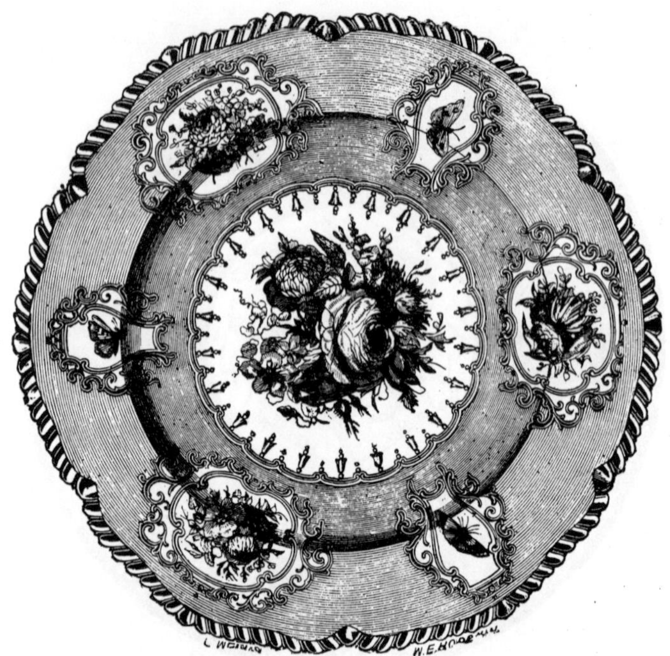

Fig. 572.—Service made for the Princess Charlotte on her marriage in 1816.

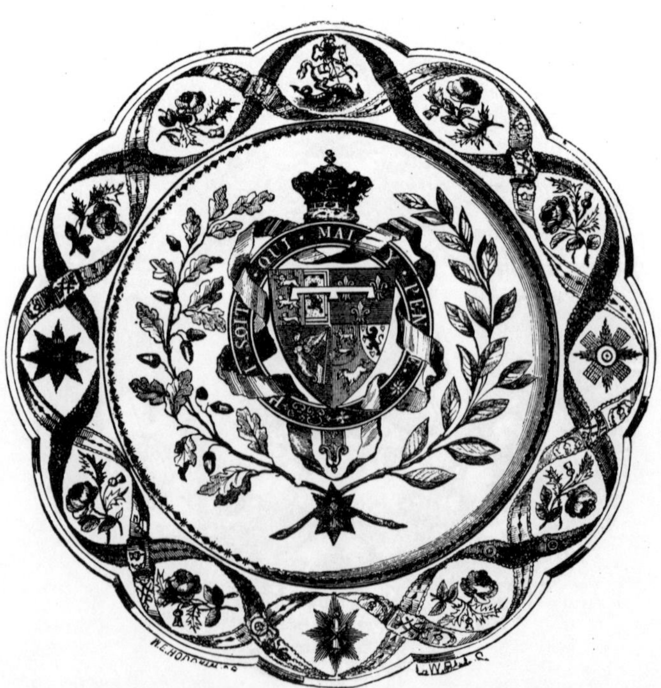

Fig. 573.—Service made on the occasion of the creation of the Duke of Clarence in 1789.

on the reverse the initials W P C of the Worcester Porcelain Company. They were issued for various amounts.

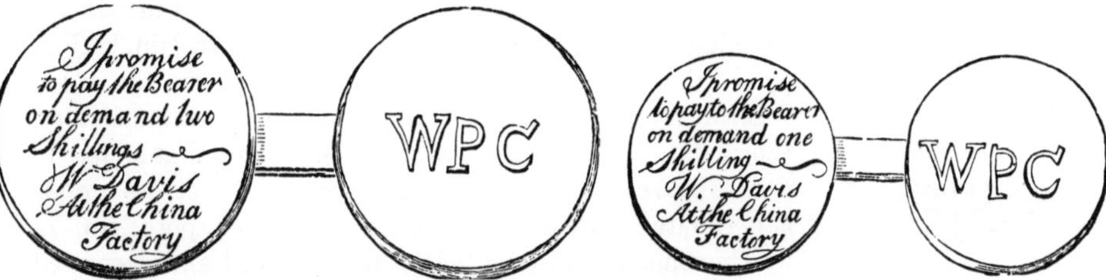

Figs. 574 and 575.—China Tokens.

Royal China Works.—The porcelain works of Messrs. Grainger and Co., in St. Martin's Street, were established in 1800 by Thomas Grainger, nephew to Mr. Chamberlain, to whom he served apprenticeship as a painter, and assisted in the general management of the works. When out of his time, Mr. Grainger started a manufactory on his own account, and took into partnership a Mr. Wood, a painter of considerable skill, whose productions are characterized by a peculiar mellowness of shade, and who excelled in "mezzotint drawing;" and the works were carried on under the firm of "Grainger and Wood." In 1812 Mr. Grainger took into partnership his brother-in-law, Mr. Lee, and the style was then changed to "Grainger and Lee." About two years before this time, the works, having been destroyed by fire, were rebuilt on the opposite side of the street, and since then have been considerably enlarged. After Mr. Lee retired from the business it was carried on by Mr. Grainger until his decease in 1839, when his son, George Grainger, succeeded him, and has since carried on the works, under the style of "G. Grainger and Co." Up to the year 1850 porcelain alone was made, but in that year Mr. Grainger invented a new body, which he named "*semi-porcelain,*" which was first made public at the Exhibition of 1851, where, from its peculiar qualities of durability, hardness, and freedom from cracking with heat, attracted considerable attention. The surface of the semi-porcelain bears every characteristic of the finest china, and, in colour, painting, and gilding, can be made quite equal to it; but it has the additional advantage of being so completely vitrified that the inside, in case of being chipped or broken, remains of its original whiteness. It is peculiarly adapted for dinner-

Grainger Lee
&co
Worcester.

Fig. 576.

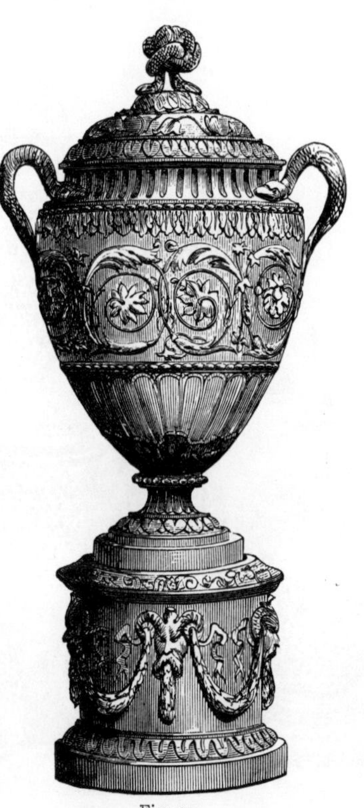
Fig. 577.

services through not flying or cracking with heat so readily as the ordinary china does, and because of its power of retaining heat for a much longer time. It is extensively exported to France, India, and America. Of this material, too, are made chemical vessels, batteries, insulators, &c. At the Exhibition of 1862 a medal was awarded for this "semi-" or "chemical porcelain." Fig. 578 is the usual mark of the firm; another has the words "Chemical Porcelain, Grainger and Co., Manufactory, Worcester." They also produce some admirable parian vases, figures, and ornaments. Another variety of goods is perforated parian; and another perforated porcelain, in which some exquisite articles are produced and decorated in the very highest style of art. The firm also stands high for the production of lace drapery.

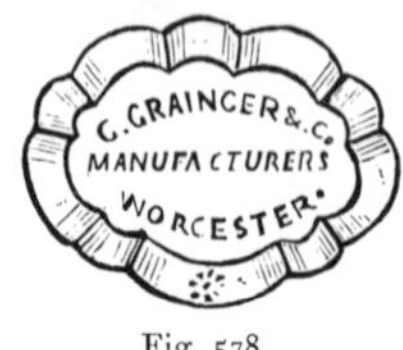

Fig. 578.

Another of the specialities is "Opalite," a fine and highly vitrified body, in which are produced embossed tiles for external decorations; and others are—decorations in coloured clays in imitation of Cloisonné enamels; imitations of marbles, agates, and other stones; and a process of *pâte-sur-pâte* floral decoration.

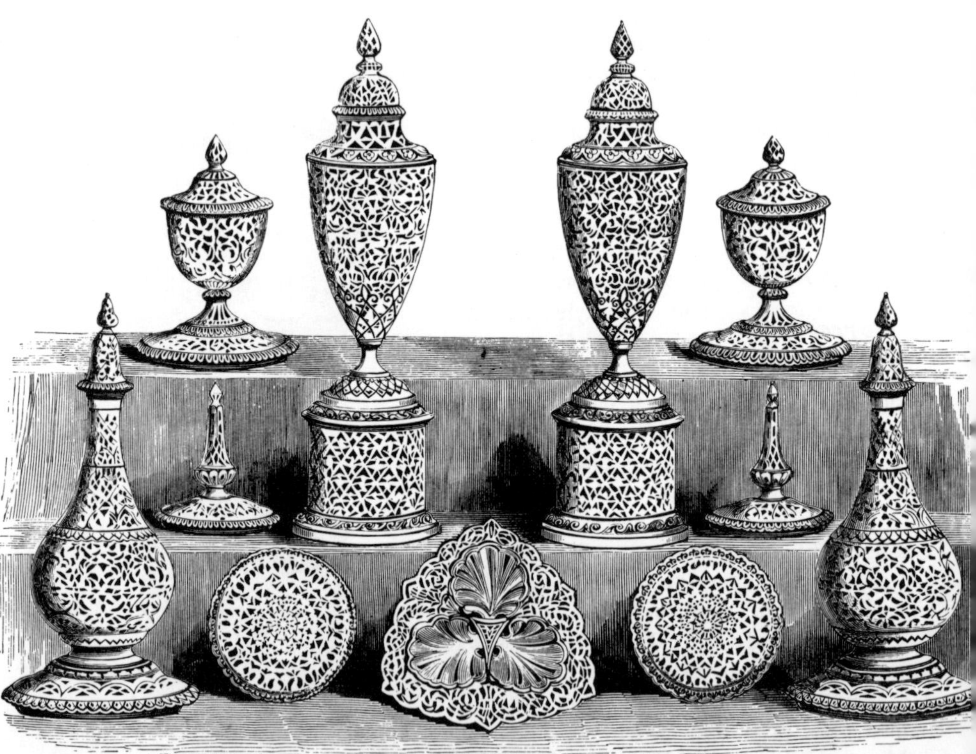

Fig. 579.—Perforated Parian Goods.

Mr. St. John's Encaustic Tile Works.—After the removal of Flight and Barr's works to the present site of the Royal porcelain manufactory, Mr. Barr for a time continued making encaustic paving tiles on the old premises. In this he was joined by Mr. Fleming St. John, one of the managing directors of the Royal porcelain

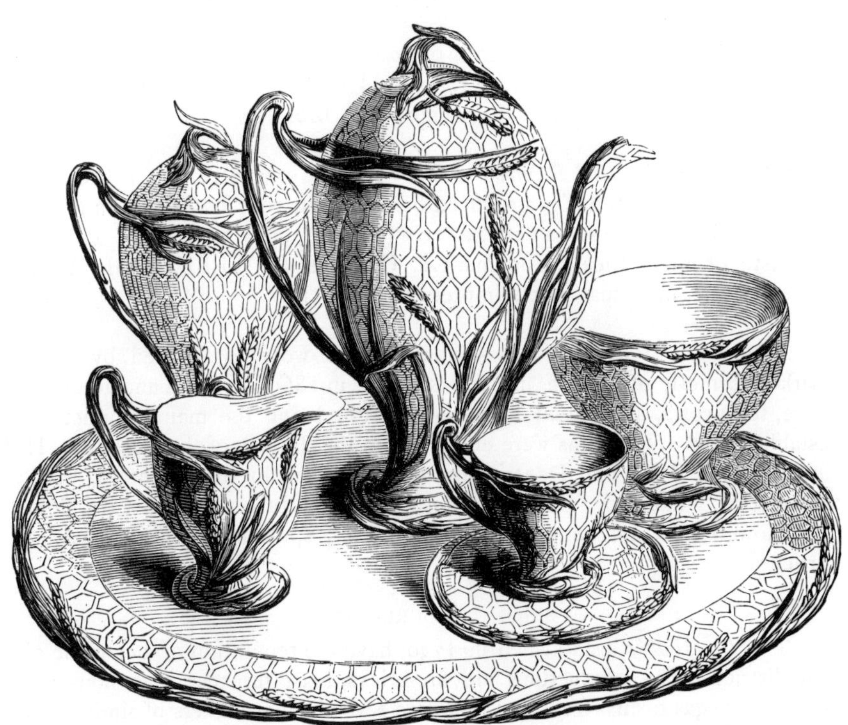

Fig. 580.—Honeycombed Coffee Service.

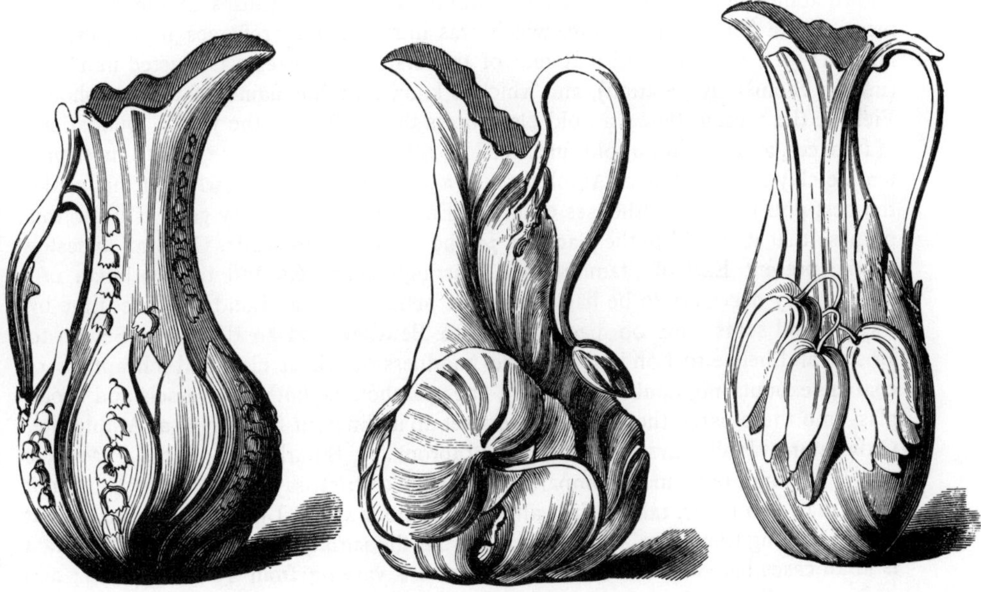

Figs. 581 to 583.—Toilet Services.

works, and some excellent patterns, of good colour and material, were produced. The tile works were, however, in 1850, sold to Messrs. Maw, who carried on the manufacture until 1852, when they removed to Broseley.

"*Worcester Tileries,*" *Rainbow Hill.*—These works were established in 1870 by Mr. H. C. Webb; the tiles produced being black, red, buff, grey, and chocolate geometrical tiles; the same with patterns in cream, fawn, blue, white, and green, and encaustic or inlaid tiles. The mark is HENRY C. WEBB, WORCESTER, in raised letters, in a small circle impressed in the clay.

St. George's Pottery Works.—These works were established by Mr. D. W. Barker, formerly of Frome, in Somersetshire, in 1869, for the manufacture of rustic ware, terra-cotta, and patent bricks—the latter being the main production of the establishment. The kilns were erected from the designs of the patentees, Hoffman and Licht, of Berlin and Dantzic, and the machinery by the patentees, Bradley and Craven, of Wakefield. The rustic terra-cotta comprises garden-seats, flower-pots, and flower-vases, mignonette and other boxes, spill-cases, and a variety of other articles.

STOURBRIDGE.

The *Lye Works*, established in 1750, have the reputation of being the oldest in the district. The productions are fire-bricks, blast furnaces, glass-house furnaces, gas retorts, gas ovens, &c.; and there are several other makers of similar wares.

I am indebted to Mr. G. K. Harrison, of the "Lye Works," for the following particulars:—"The earliest account I have been able to obtain respecting Stourbridge fire-clay shows that, in the year 1566, a lease was granted for the purpose of getting and digging Glasshouse pot-clay. It is probable at that time it had only recently been discovered, and that its peculiar properties and purity, with the well-known abundance of fuel in the neighbourhood, were the causes of the establishment of the glass manufacture, which was introduced by refugees from Lorraine about 1557. It is believed that one of the first glasshouses was erected in a field (near to Stourbridge Station), and which is known by the name of the Glasshouse Field at the present time; an old plan shows the position of the works, foundations of furnaces, and portion of old furnace." Dr. Plot, in 1686, wrote, "The most preferable clay of any is that of Amblecote, of a dark blewish colour, whereof they make the best pots for the glasshouses of any in England; nay, so very good is it for this purpose that it is sold in the place for 7*d.* the bushel, whereof Mr. Gray (an ancestor of the present Earl of Stamford and Warrington) has 6*d.* and the workman 1*d.*, and so very necessary to be had that it is sent as far as London, some time by waggon and some time on pack horses to Bewdley, and so down the Severn to Bristol, and hence to London." "The goodness of which clay and cheapness of coal hereabouts no doubt has drawn the glasshouses both for vessels and broad glass into these parts, there being divers set up in different forms here at Amblecote, Oldwynford, Hollowaysend, and Coburnbrook." Stourbridge clay (*properly so called*) is found only in a comparatively small district, say within a circle of not more than two miles, taking the valley of the Stour at the Lye as the centre, and at depths varying from 3 or 4, to 180 yards from the surface; its position in the strata is in all cases below the thick coal, at distances varying from 12 to 25 yards; and it is generally overlaid by a shaly, friable kind of coal, called "batts," from 12 to 24 inches thick. The thickness of the seam varies from 5 or 6 up to 40 inches. The quality is in some instances as hard as stone, having to be blasted with powder, and in others soft and easily workable. There is a great variation in its component parts, arising principally in the proportion of silica; a clay containing only about 50 per cent. of silica being very inferior, and contracting very much on exposure to intense heat.

The usual treatment of clay for glasshouse purposes is as follows. After having been carefully selected, it is broken into small pieces by women accustomed to its appearance, who throw on one side all pieces of discoloured and irregular clay; it is finely ground by heavy edge-runners, and mixed with a certain proportion of ground potsherds (old broken burnt pots), the proportion of which varies according to the purpose for which it is to be used; it is then mixed with water, and tempered with the foot, and allowed to lie not less than six or seven weeks, so as to acquire great tenacity before being made into pots. These pots are built up by hand gradually, great care being taken that the last layer of clay is not allowed to become hard or dry, or it will not unite properly; neglect in this respect causing the pot to give way in the furnace. The pots are dried very gradually, and are seldom fit for use under six to eight months. The ordinary clay is allowed to lie in large heaps, subjected to the action of the atmosphere, and is then used in the manufacture of gas-retorts, fire-bricks, &c. The quantity of bricks made annually in the district is about fifty millions.

CHAPTER IX.

In the midst of one of the most historically interesting districts of the kingdom—a district abounding in spots rendered famous in various ages by the events which have occurred within its boundaries, and full of associations as varied as they are interesting—within a few miles of Boscobel and Tong, and numberless other places possessing a sad interest as connected with the wanderings and the painful vicissitudes of King Charles II.—within a short distance of those two glorious monastic ruins, Buildwas Abbey and Wenlock Priory—not far from the "English Nineveh," Uriconium, and within easy distance of Shrewsbury and Ludlow—is a group of manufactories whose simple history is as interesting as that of many of these places.

Broseley, whose pipe manufactories two hundred and fifty years ago were as famed as they are now, and whose makers then got rid of their goods without advertising the emphatic words, "When you ask for a Broseley pipe, see that you get it!"—Jackfield, famed of old for its earthenware, and where it is still to some little extent made;—Caughley, formerly a successful rival of Worcester in the excellence of its porcelains;—Coalport, a rival of all other works at the present day;—Horsehay, with its discontinued pot works;—Benthall, where "yellow ware" works are in constant operation, and where the magnificent encaustic and enamelled tile and mosaic works of Messrs. Maw are situated;—Ironbridge, with its famous one-arch bridge, the first iron bridge erected in England, from which it takes its name, spanning the Severn;—Madeley, with its extensive iron furnaces;—Benthall Edge, with its limestone works;—Coalbrookdale, whose iron works are known throughout the world;—and a score of other busy hives of industry, are here gathered together, and demand careful attention. To the history of some of these I therefore devote this chapter.

Like those of Worcester and Derby, the Salopian manufactory of porcelain dates from the middle of last century; and, like them, has continued from its first introduction to the present time without interruption. Indeed, it may be said of the district that an almost—if not an entirely—unbroken historical chain may be traced from the Romano-British period down to the present day; for, as I have already shown, the same beds of clay which, fifteen hundred years ago, produced some of the fictile ware of the Roman occupiers of the soil, have been worked in the intermediate ages, and still produce, more largely than ever, domestic vessels for use by every class of the people of England. The same beds which supplied the magnificent city of Uriconium with jugs, mortaria, bowls, and colanders of white ware, still supply the neighbourhood with innumerable articles of daily use.

Caughley.

The Worcester porcelain works, as I have shown, were established in the year 1751; and the commencement of those in Shropshire must have been, if not coeval, at all events closely subsequent to that event. Indeed, the two works may be almost said to have sprung into existence at the same time. The site of the first Salopian china works was at Caughley, about a mile from the present manufactory (on the opposite or south side of the river), and were situated on the hill overlooking the valley of the Severn, as it flowed on to Bridgnorth. Here, it is said, a small pottery was begun by a Mr. Browne, of Caughley Hall, and after his death managed by a relative named Gallimore, to whom, in 1754, a lease was granted for 62 years. He does not appear to have been long connected with the works; for the only name, as proprietor, which I have at present been able to establish is that of Thomas Turner, who married Dorothy, daughter of Mr. Gallimore and niece to Mr. Browne, and carried on the manufactory.

Mr. Thomas Turner (son of Dr. Richard Turner, of Magdalen Hall, Oxford, rector of Cumberton, vicar of Elmly Castle and Norton, in 1754, and chaplain to the Countess of Wigtoun), was born in 1749, and is said to have been brought up as a silversmith at Worcester; but this is an error, as, for the purpose of obtaining the freedom of the city, he was, as a matter of legal form only, apprenticed to his father. It seems pretty certain that he was at an early period connected with the Worcester china works, and he was an excellent chemist, had thoroughly studied the various processes relating to porcelain manufacture, was a skilful draftsman, designer, and engraver; and was also a clever musician. He became a J. P. for Shropshire, was a freeman of Worcester, Wenlock, and Bridgnorth, and chairman of the Court of Equity for the three counties. In 1772, he succeeded his father-in-law, Mr. Gallimore, at the Caughley works (Mr. Gallimore having leased them from Mr. Browne in 1754), and carried them on until 1799, when he sold out and retired from business. He died at Caughley in 1809, aged sixty, and was buried in the family vault at Barrow, where, later, his daughter, Mrs. Smith, the mother of Hubert Smith, Esq., Town Clerk, Bridgnorth, was also buried. He had a partner named Shaw, with a warehouse in London, and had periodical sales by auction of their goods. In my own possession is a bill of this firm, dated January 24th, 1794, and headed, "Salopian China Warehouse. Bought of Turner and Shaw." The lots in this bill were bought "at public sale," and consisted of "jugs," "bakings," "china dishes," and other "sundry pieces;" the lots were "put up at half price" at the sale. In 1795 Mr. Turner's manager at Caughley was one Thomas Blase; and I have a letter of his, dated 20th February in that year, concerning a painter, named Withers, at that time employed there, but who had wrongfully left his employment at the Derby china works, where he was "Mr. Deusbury's articled servant." In 1776 the works had attained some repute, and an existing example bearing that date gives evidence of the excellence of the body. It is a mug, white, with blue and gold flowers, and bears the words "Francis Benbow, 1776," surmounted by an anchor; the Francis Benbow for whom it was made being a barge-owner. In the early years of the Caughley manufactory the ware was not many degrees removed from earthenware; but it gradually assumed a finer and more transparent character. Like the early Worcester examples, the patterns were principally confined to blue flowers, &c., on a white ground:

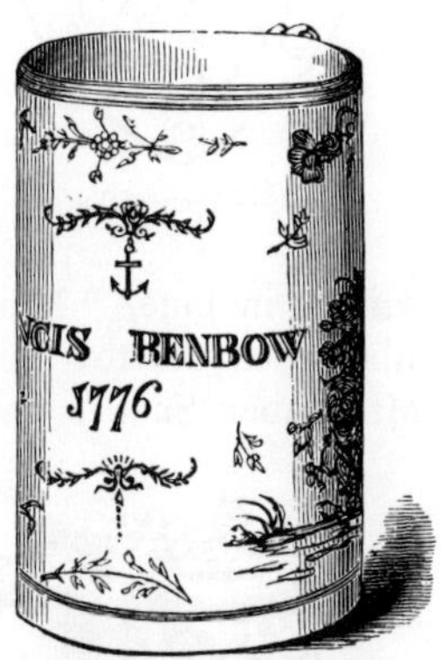

Fig. 584.

and in this style and colour the Caughley works excelled, in many respects, their competitors.

In 1772, as I have shown, Mr. Turner succeeded Mr. Gallimore, and set about enlarging the works. In 1775 we read, "The porcelain manufactory erected near Bridgnorth, in this county, is now quite completed, and the proprietors have received and completed orders to a very large amount. Lately we saw some of their productions, which in colour and fineness are truly elegant and beautiful, and have the bright and lively white of the so much extolled oriental." In 1780 he visited France, for the purpose of "picking up knowledge" on the porcelain manufactures of Paris, and on his return brought with him some skilled workmen, and at once entered with increased spirit into the manufacture.

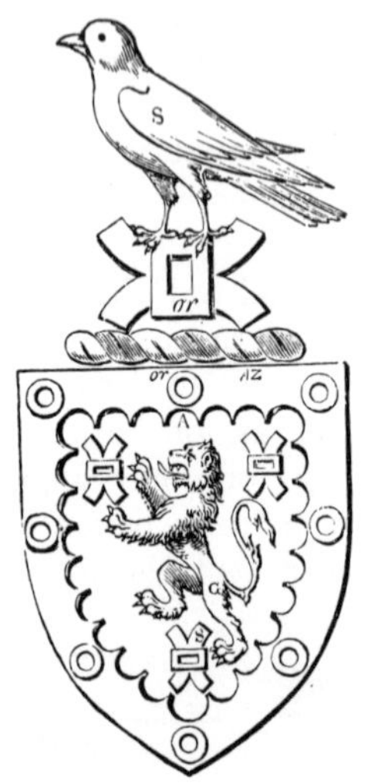
Fig. 585.—Arms of Turner.

In 1780 Mr. Turner introduced the making of the famous "Willow Pattern"—the first made in England—at Caughley, and about the same time the "Broseley Blue Dragon" pattern. The willow pattern is still commonly known in the trade as "Broseley pattern." An excellent example of dated Caughley ware is the puzzle-jug, Fig. 586. It is decorated with blue sprigs, and bears on its front the name of "John Geary Cleak of the old Church Brosley 1789." On the bottom is written in blue, "Matthew the v & 16," though one would fail to see any allusion in the text here referred to either to the vessel or to its purpose. In Mr. Hubert Smith's possession is a fine Caughley mug; white, with blue flowers of bold character, which bears the words, "Wm. Haslewood, 1791," and has the mark S on the bottom.

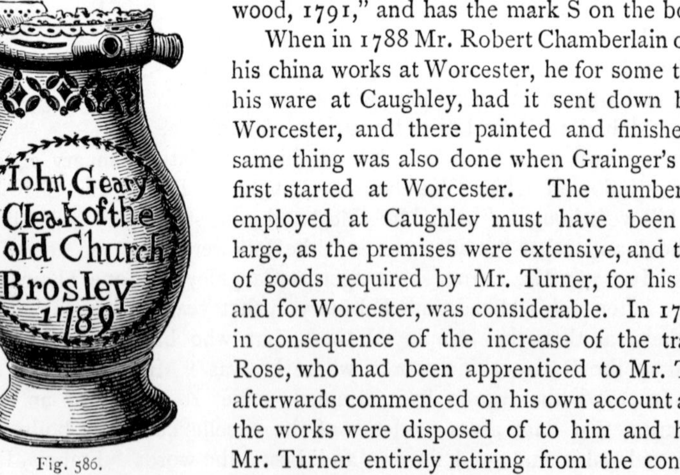

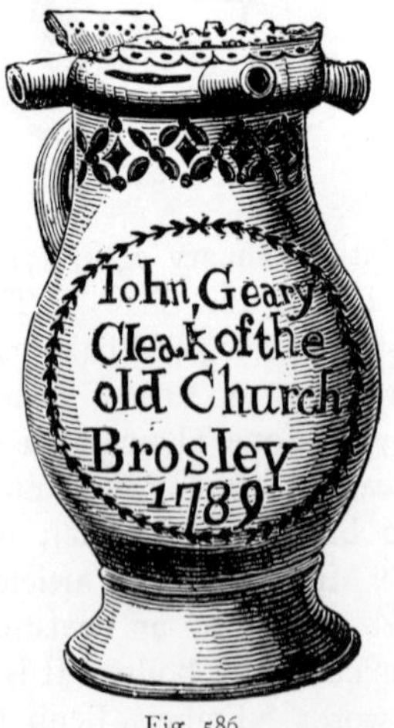

Fig. 586.

When in 1788 Mr. Robert Chamberlain commenced his china works at Worcester, he for some time bought his ware at Caughley, had it sent down by barge to Worcester, and there painted and finished it. The same thing was also done when Grainger's works were first started at Worcester. The number of hands employed at Caughley must have been somewhat large, as the premises were extensive, and the quantity of goods required by Mr. Turner, for his own trade and for Worcester, was considerable. In 1798 or 1799, in consequence of the increase of the trade of Mr. Rose, who had been apprenticed to Mr. Turner, and afterwards commenced on his own account at Coalport, the works were disposed of to him and his partner; Mr. Turner entirely retiring from the concern. The Caughley works were then carried on by Rose and Co., in conjunction with their own. The coal at Caughley beginning to work out, and the cost of carrying the unfinished ware from thence down the hill and across the water to Coalport was so great—the unfinished ware being carried on women's heads the whole distance—that Mr. Rose determined to remove the works to

Coalport, which he did at different times, gradually drafting off the workmen, until about 1814 or 1815, when they were finally removed, the kilns and rooms taken down, and the materials used for the enlargement of the works at Coalport. The last of the buildings, with the house, were not, however, destroyed until 1821, when the materials were brought to Coalport to build the present burnishing-shops and some workmen's cottages.

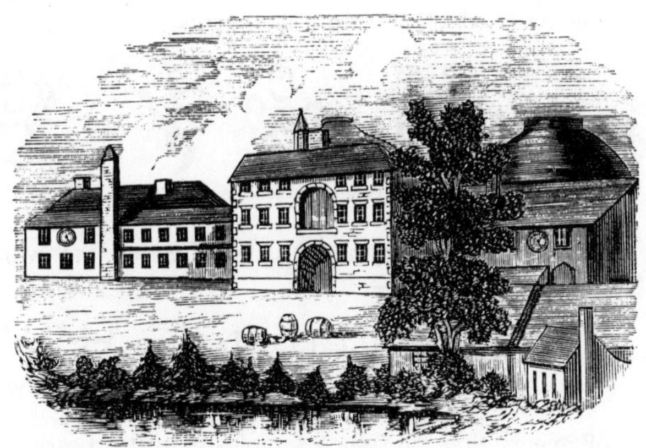

Fig. 587.—The Caughley China Works, taken down in 1815.

The marks used at Caughley and Coalport have been very few, but they are very important, and require careful attention at the hands of the collector. In my account of the Worcester works I have given several varieties of the *crescent* as a mark of that establishment, and have also stated that it was used at Caughley. I believe the first mark used at Caughley to have been the crescent alone, and that it was, as I have before stated, intended to have the signification of a C for Caughley, and that its connection with the Worcester works may, in a great measure, be traced to the fact of the goods on which it appears being printed, not at that city, but at Caughley. I have seen examples of this mark on undoubted Worcester body, and also on equally undoubted Caughley make, bearing precisely the same printed patterns. The following are some of the varieties of the crescent occurring on Caughley specimens, and show pretty clearly its transition from a common "half-moon" (I have often heard it called "half-moon china") to the finished and engraved C. Another mark said to have been used at Caughley, but of which I have met with no example, is the accompanying, which is very similar to the mark ascribed to the Leeds manufactory. Another distinctive mark of the Salopian works was the capital letter S, of which figs. 594 to 600 are varieties.

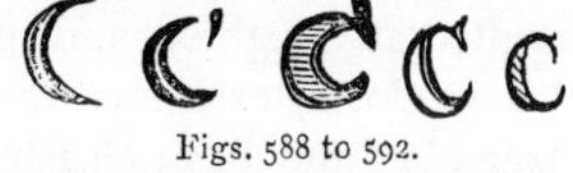

Figs. 588 to 592.

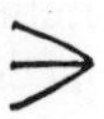

Fig. 593.

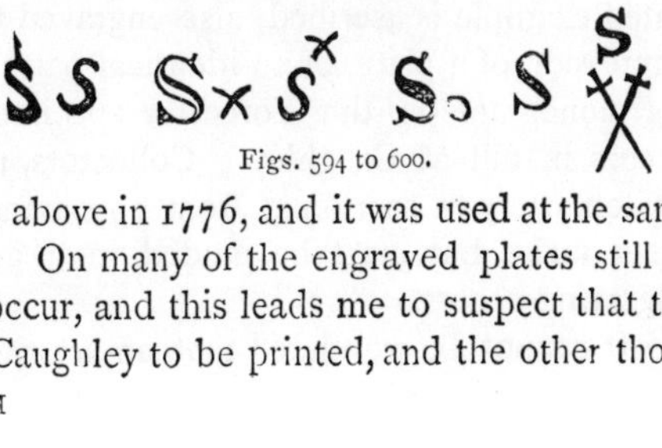

Figs. 594 to 600.

When the S was introduced it is difficult to say; but, at all events, it appears on the dated example alluded to above in 1776, and it was used at the same time as the C for a considerable period. On many of the engraved plates still in existence, indeed, both the C and the S occur, and this leads me to suspect that the one was used to mark the goods sent to Caughley to be printed, and the other those made and printed for their own market. I have seen precisely similar articles in pattern, bearing each of these letters. Occasionally the S and crossed daggers occur. Another circumstance is also worthy of note. On two mugs printed from the same engraved plate, which I have seen, the one bears the S, and the other the accompanying curious mark (Fig. 601), which is evidently of the same character as the examples of assimilated Chinese ones, which are occasionally ascribed to Worcester, but which are in reality, I believe, those of Caughley. Of these I give the following as examples; many of which are disguised figures.

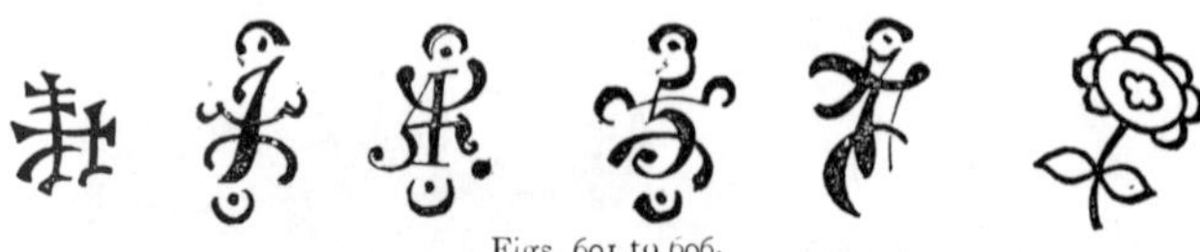

Figs. 601 to 606.

Following the C and S, two *impressed* marks, bearing the word "Salopian," were used. These are as follows:—

Salopian SALOPIAN

Figs. 607 and 608.

Figs. 609 and 610.—Workmen's Marks.

and it is worthy of remark that, on some examples of plates bearing this impressed mark, the blue printed S also appears; as, on others, does also the crescent.

The subject of *printing* upon porcelain, to which I have already alluded under "Worcester," is one so intimately and intricately connected with the Caughley and Coalport works, that it will be necessary to consider the period of its introduction at some length. I have already shown that transfer-printing was used on Worcester porcelain as early as 1757, and I have little doubt that quite as early, if not a few years before that period, it was practised at Caughley. Indeed, in the early years of the manufactory, the two works, Caughley and Worcester, seem to have been closely connected, and to have worked "in and in," if I may be allowed the use of so unscientific an expression, and I believe, with ample reason, that a great proportion of the printed goods bearing the Worcester mark were printed at Caughley. Indeed, it is known that the ware was sent up from Worcester by barge to be printed at Caughley, and returned, when finished, by the same mode of conveyance. I have closely examined the style of engraving and the patterns of a large number of examples, and I am clearly of opinion that they are the work of the same hands. I do not, by this, claim for Caughley the honour of *inventing* the art of transfer-printing on to porcelain; but I feel assured that that art must have been there practised at quite as early a period as the dated example of Worcester make; and I am led to this belief partly from the fact that the Robert Hancock, of whose beautiful productions I have before spoken, and to whom the engraving of the dated example is ascribed, also engraved for the Caughley works. And I have an impression of a plate, of an identical pattern with the famous tea group, which bears his monogram on the Worcester specimens, on which his name, *R. Hancock, fecit*, occurs in full at Caughley. Collectors, therefore, in a case of this kind, must not be too hasty in ascribing, from appearance *alone*, examples to either one or the other make, but must be guided, in a great measure, by the *body* on which the engraving occurs.

It cannot be wondered that an art, then such an important secret, should have been followed at Caughley,—a place so perfectly retired from the world, situated in the midst of woods and wilds, almost unapproachable to strangers, and with every facility for keeping the workmen away from all chance of imparting the secret to others,—in place of in Worcester, where secrecy would be almost impossible, and where the information would ooze out from the workmen, at the alehouse or elsewhere, and be greedily caught up by those interested in the process. At Caughley every possible precaution seems to have been taken to secure secrecy; and the workmen—the engravers and printers—were locked up and kept apart from every one else. Who the engravers were I cannot satisfactorily say. It is, however, certain, that Hancock engraved for the works; and it is said that Holdship, of whom I have before spoken, was also employed. Among the other engravers was a man named Dyas, who was apprenticed as an engraver at Caughley about the year 1768, and who continued at the works until his death, at the ripe age of eighty-two. It is also worthy of note that Mr. Minton, the father of Mr. Herbert Minton, was in his early days employed as an engraver at these works.

Amongst the painters apprenticed and employed at Caughley, were John Parker, Thomas Fennell, and Henry Boden, famous for their skill in flowers; and Muss, Silk, and others who excelled in landscapes and figures—some sepia landscapes being remarkable for their pure artistic treatment; while among the gilders were Rutland, Marsh, and Randall, who were considered proficients.

I have named above that Robert Hancock engraved for Caughley as well as for Worcester, or at all events that plates of his were printed from at the former place, possibly for the latter. His name appears on one of the plates thus:—*R Hancock fecit.* and other plates are evidently the work of his hand, though without name. I engraved a curious mark, the monogram RH, anchor, and name of Worcester, in the account of those works. This I reproduce on Fig. 611, and give another which occurs on a plate from Caughley, with the anchor and the word Derby, which I introduce for the purpose of comparison, and to suggest the probability that the place which produced the one with the word Derby (for whatever reason that may have been done), which was undoubtedly Caughley, also produced the one with the word Worcester. The engraved plate, with the anchor and Derby, represents a landscape—a river, with trees on either side, swans sailing in the foreground, behind them two fishermen in a boat drawing a net, beyond them a boat with sails, and in the background a bridge, and church with ruins to the left, and a tall gabled building on the right, over which are the words "Sutton Hall," whilst above the whole picture is "English Hospitality."

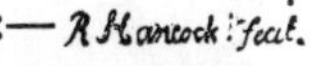

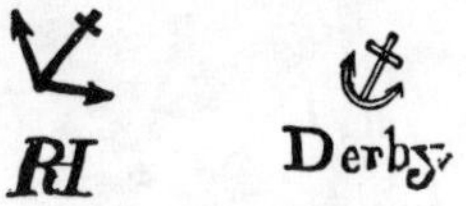

RH Derby

Figs. 611 and 612.

Coalport.

The Coalport works, at one time also known as "Coalbrook Dale," were founded by Mr. John Rose, to whom the ceramic art is indebted for many important improvements. He was the son of a farmer, and was apprenticed to Turner, of the Caughley China Works, by whom he was taken into the house, and taught the art in all its branches. Ultimately a difference arose between them, and Mr. Rose left Mr. Turner, and commenced a small business on his own account at Jackfield, from whence ere long he removed to the present site at Coalport (on the opposite bank of the Severn), which had previously been a small pottery belonging to a Mr. Young, a mercer of Shrewsbury. Mr. John Rose had not long established himself at Coalport, when other works were started on the opposite side of the canal, and only a few yards distant, by his brother, Thomas Rose, and partners, who commenced business under the style of "Anstice, Horton, and Rose." These works, however, did not continue long, but passed into the hands of Mr. John Rose and partners, who formed them into one establishment. In three or four years from their establishment the Coalport works had become so successful that the Caughley works of Mr. Turner were gradually beaten out of the market, and in 1799 he gave up the business and sold the concern to Messrs. Rose and Co., who thus became proprietors of all three works, to which soon afterwards considerable additions were made.

Although many changes in the proprietary have taken place, the commercial style of the firm has been, "John Rose and Company," the proprietary changes

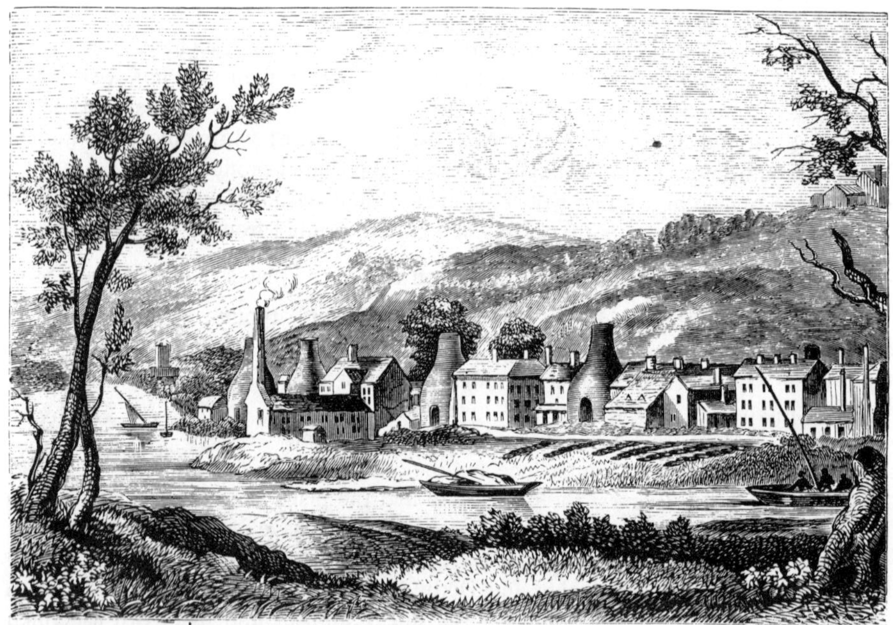

Fig. 613.—Coalport China Works at the beginning of the present century, from a painting by Muss.

having been:—"Rose and Blakeway;" "Rose, Blakeway, and Rose;" "Rose, Johnson, and Winter;" "Rose, Johnson, Clarke, and Winter;" "Rose, Winter, and Clarke;" "Rose, Clarke, and Maddison;" "Maddison, Pugh, Rose, and Rose;" "W. Pugh and W. F. Rose;" and "William Pugh;" and since his death the firm has still been known by its old style of "John Rose and Co." Mr. John Rose, who died in 1841, was succeeded by his nephew, Mr. W. F. Rose, of Rock House, Coalport, who retired from the firm in the autumn of 1862, and died in London in 1864, having in the meantime started some small works at Hanley, where he shortly afterwards failed, and unsuccessfully attempted to commence others in Derbyshire. He was a man of the most generous disposition and kindly nature, and his losses were a source of deep sorrow to myself and his other many friends. It will be seen from what I have said, that the Coalport

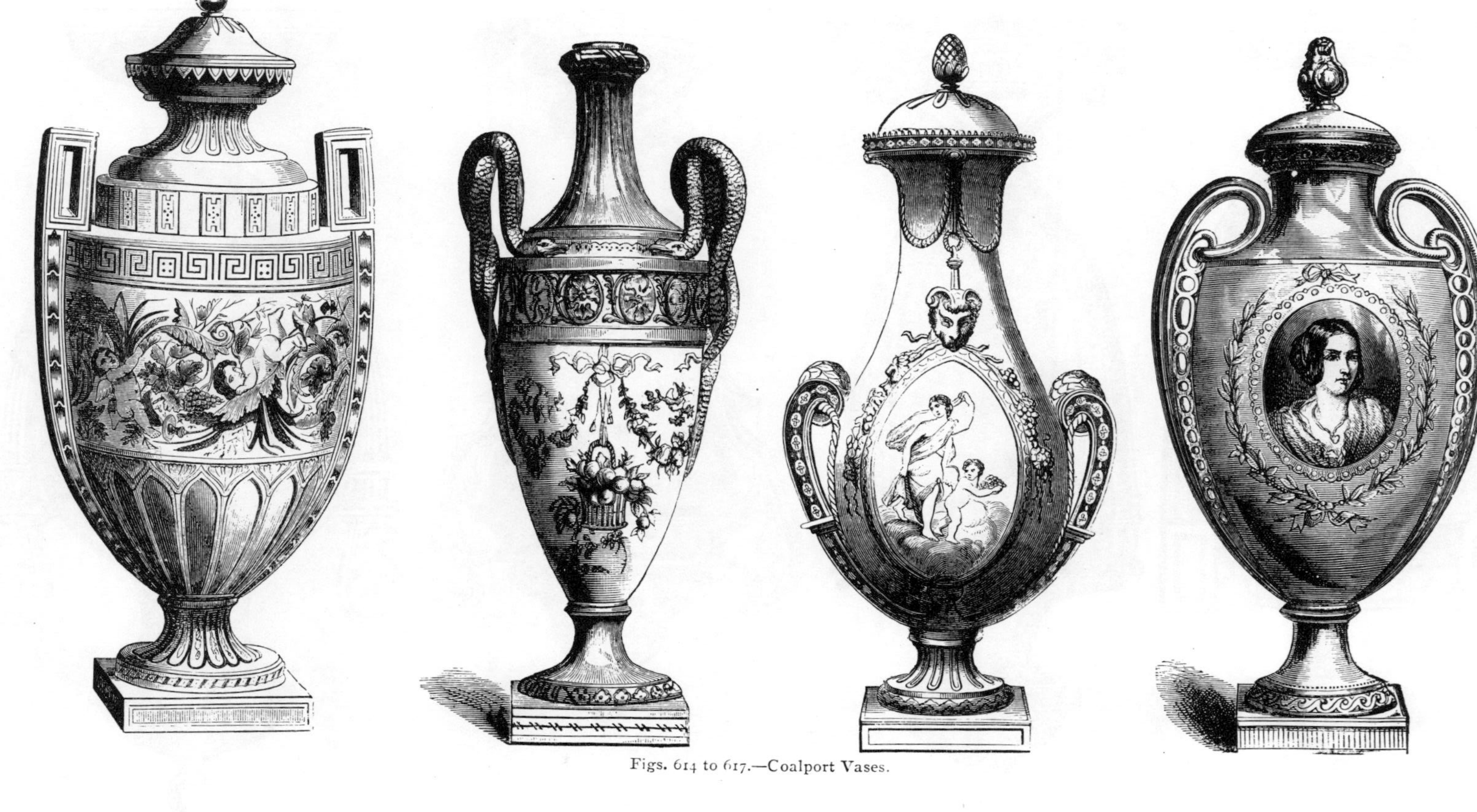

Figs. 614 to 617.—Coalport Vases.

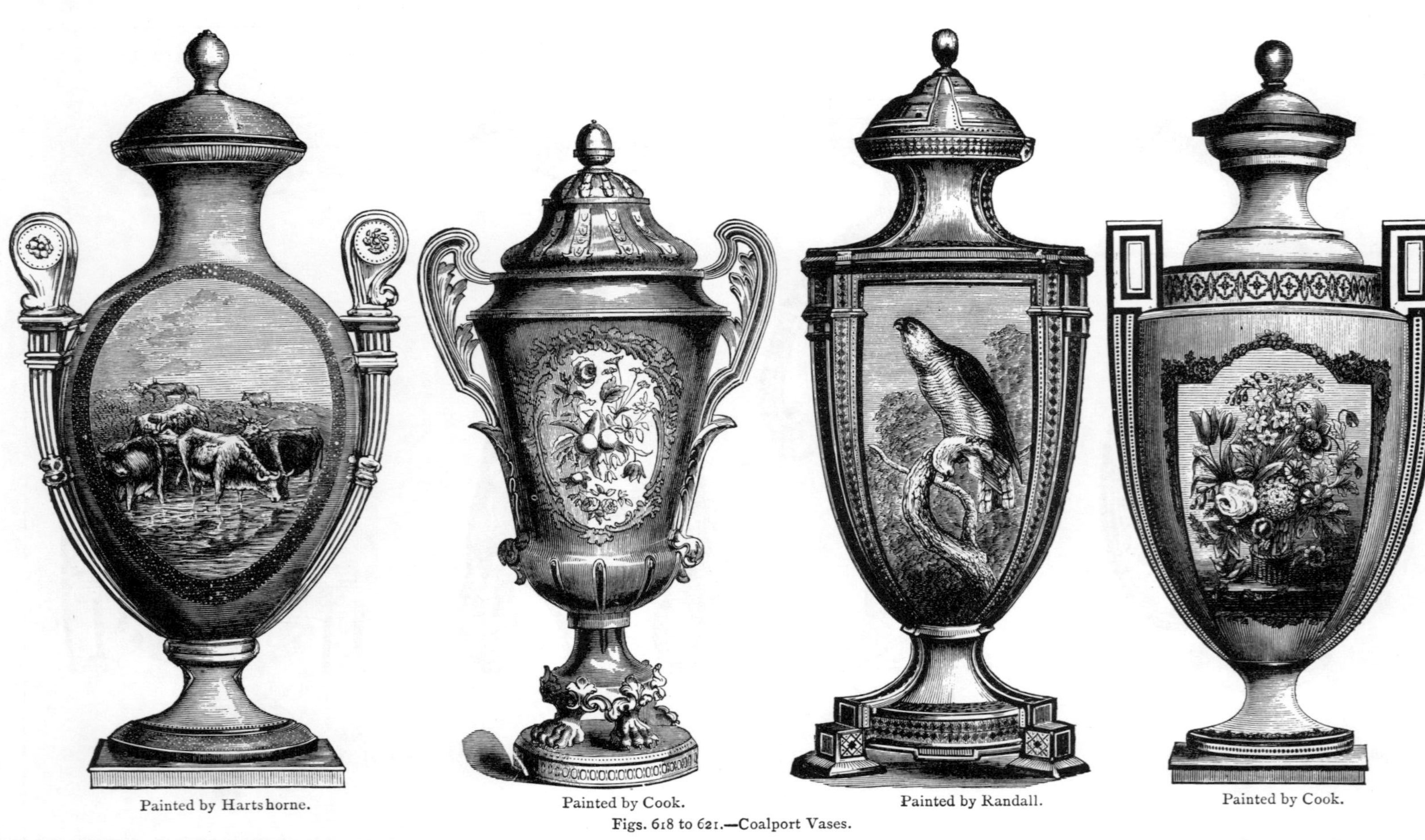

Painted by Hartshorne. Painted by Cook. Painted by Randall. Painted by Cook.

Figs. 618 to 621.—Coalport Vases.

works had already, before the commencement of the present century, absorbed those of Caughley, of Jackfield, and of the opposition establishment of Messrs. Anstice, Horton, and Rose. Some years later, the Swansea Porcelain Works, which had risen somewhat into repute, were discontinued, and the moulds, &c., bought by Mr. Rose, who removed them, along with the workmen, to Coalport, about the year 1820. Another famed manufactory, though small, that of Nantgarw, established by Billingsley, the famous flower painter, of Derby, and his son-in-law, Walker, also of Derby, in 1816 (under the assumed name of *Beeley* and Walker), and which produced, perhaps, the finest examples of porcelain with granulated

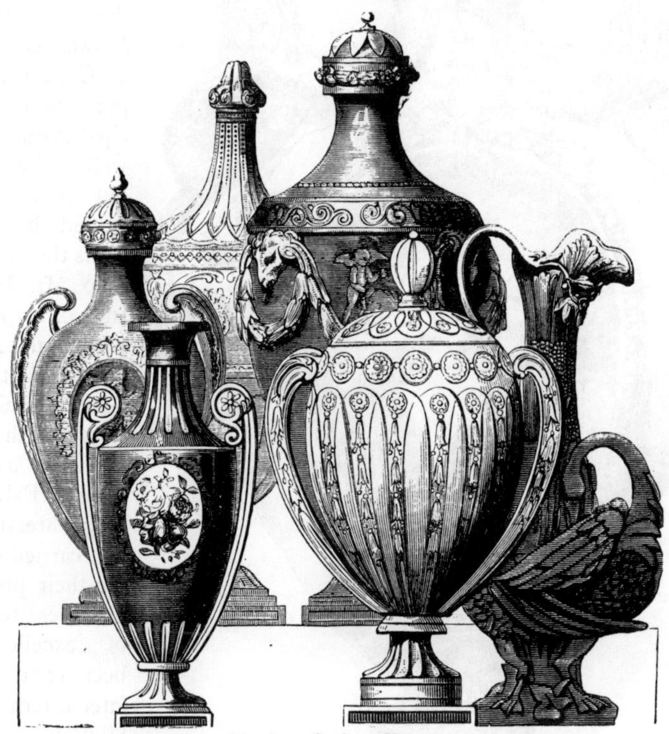

Fig. 622.—Coalport Vases.

fracture ever made, also soon afterwards was merged into the Coalport establishment. Billingsley and Walker, on discontinuing the works at Nantgarw, removed to Coalport, with all their moulds and processes, and continued employed there until Billingsley's death, which took place in 1828. Walker was a remarkably clever workman, and did much during the time of his continuance at Coalport to improve the art of china-making. He removed thence to America, where he established a pottery, which became very successful. The Nantgarw porcelain was very expensive to make, but was remarkably fine in its body and texture. The original recipes for this peculiar body are in the possession of Messrs. Rose & Co.; and it can be made at Coalport of as fine a quality as ever. I have carefully examined specimens made *at* Nantgarw with others made by Billingsley and Walker when they first came to Coalport, and these again with examples made by Messrs. Rose in 1860, and they appear all to be of equal excellence of body. It is, however,

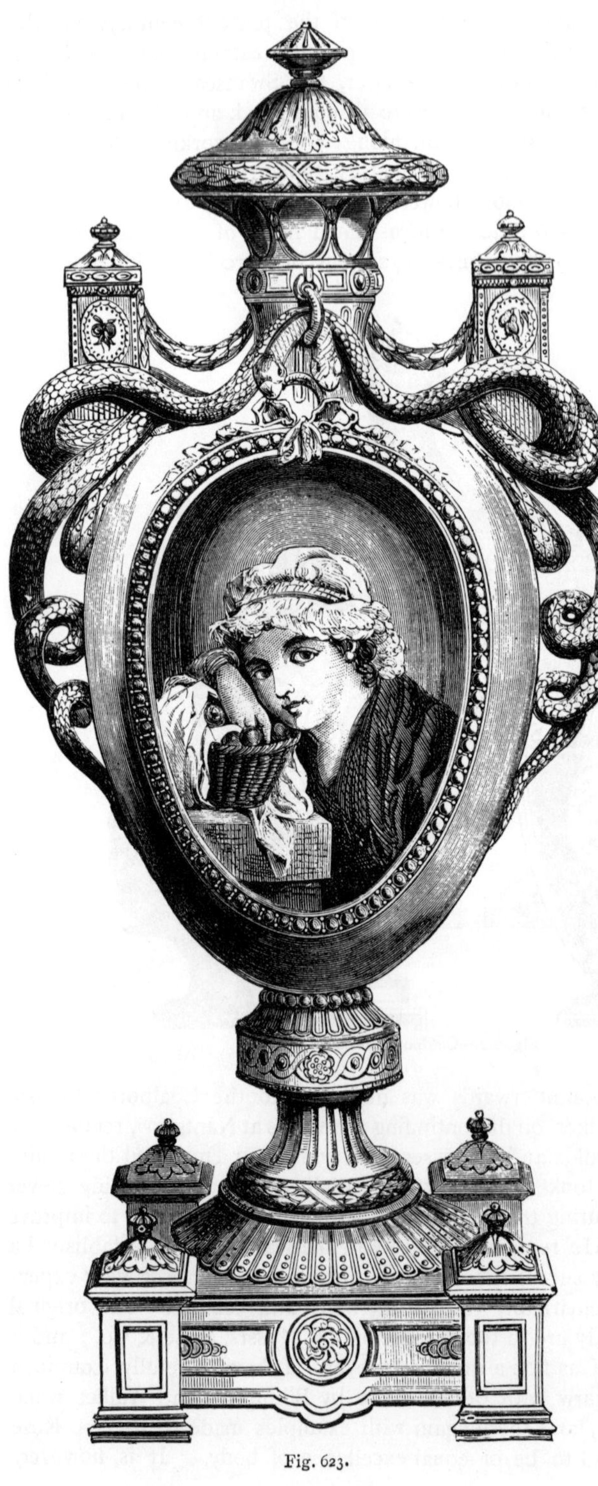

Fig. 623.

too expensive a process to be followed to any extent, and is never manufactured there now.

In 1820 Mr. John Rose received the gold medal of the Society of Arts for the best porcelain glaze produced without lead. It was competed for by Copelands, Davenports, and other principal manufacturers, as well as by Mr. Rose, but was honourably gained by him. It bears the inscription—"To Mr. John Rose, MDCCCXX., for his improved glaze for porcelain." Both at the Great Exhibition in 1851 and that of 1862, as well as at the French Exhibition in 1855, Messrs. Rose & Co. carried off medals for their productions; and these recognitions of excellence have been continued at the later International Exhibitions. The productions have, indeed, always taken a foremost rank among the best porcelain of the kingdom; many of the specialities of this firm being marvels of beauty; the colours pure and full, and of extreme richness. Sardinian green—a colour for the extreme depth and richness of which these works are celebrated — is introduced with remarkable effect both in services and otherwise. One of the finest pieces of this colour is a tripod wine goblet, with flowers in tablets, and raised and jewelled gold borders. A lighter shade of this fine green is introduced, with tablets of flowers and Westbourne birds, with great effect on two-handled goblets, &c. *Rose du Barry* has always been a speciality of the Coalport works, and a colour on the excellence of which its proprietors, especially the late clever and enlightened Mr. W. F. Rose, have always prided themselves. This is used as a ground in every conceivable variety of decoration, and when enriched with raised dead and burnished gold, and with the exquisite painting by which it is usually accompanied, has a remarkably rich and chaste effect. A new jardinière, with pierced key top and Sèvres fruit and flowers, is one of the prettiest examples of this colour, combined with raised gold and flowers, which has

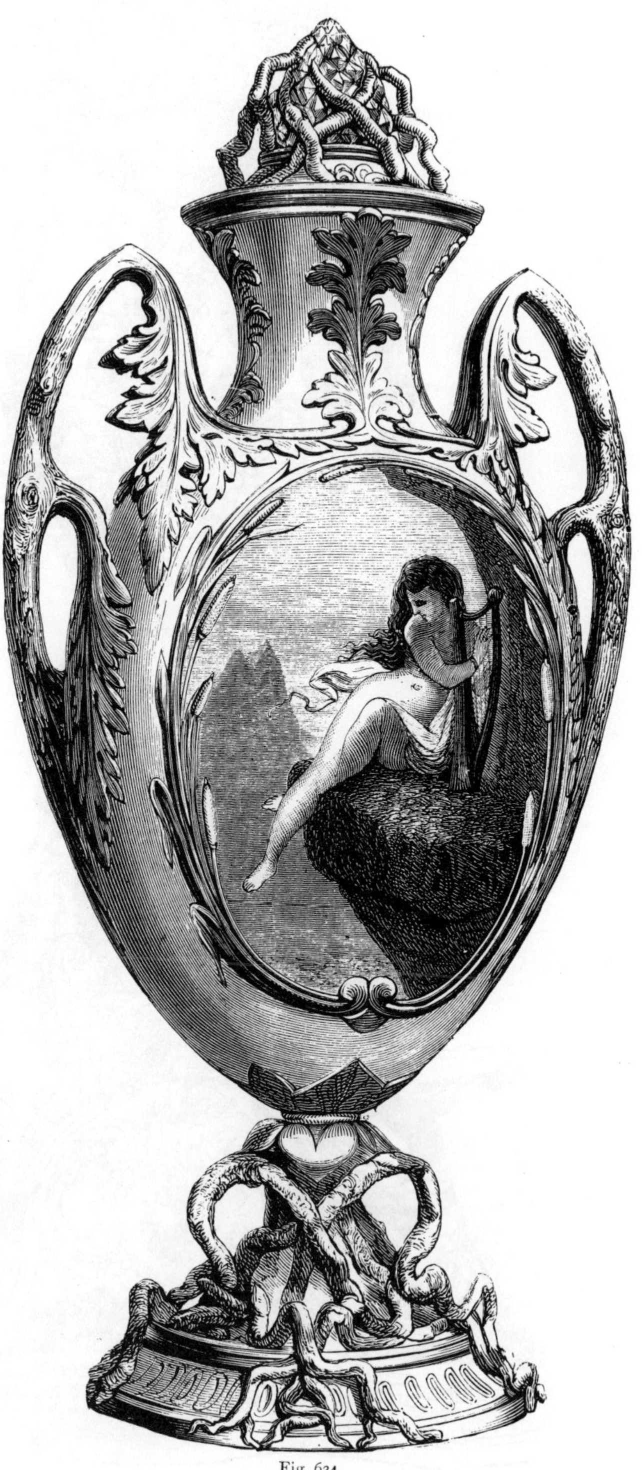

Fig. 624.

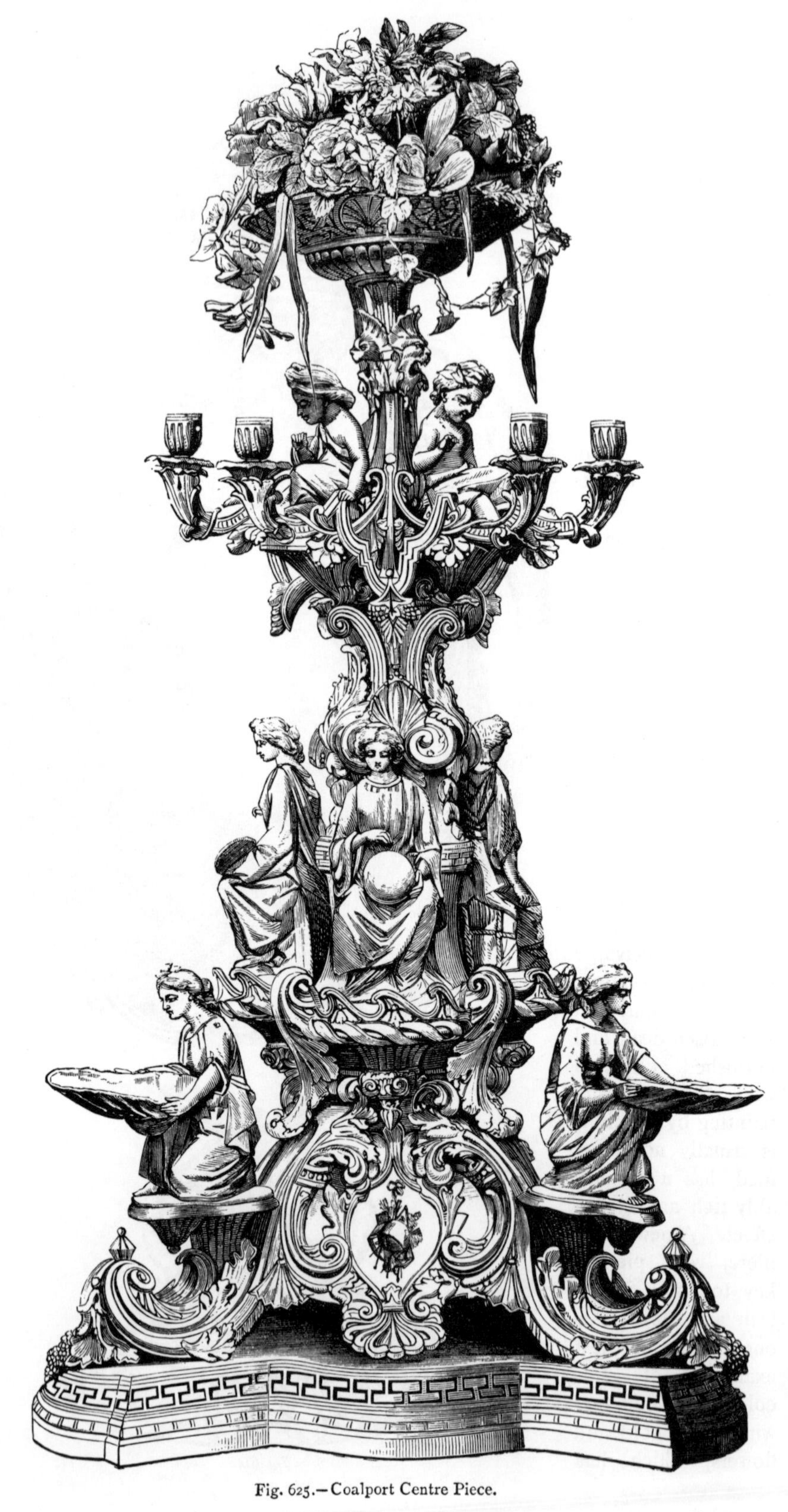

Fig. 625.—Coalport Centre Piece.

been produced. One of the finest and most massive pieces in this colour is a claret jug, with raised gold vine-leaves and grapes and other decorations, and splendidly painted on one side with the head of a bacchante and on the other a bunch of grapes. A pink, or light *Rose du Barry*, is also much used as a ground for pilgrims' bottles, vases, services, &c., where, for some kinds of decoration, it harmonizes better than the full colour would. A blue with a slightly purplish cast, which gives it an additional richness and fulness, has been introduced, and forms a splendid ground for Japanese decoration in vases, pilgrims' bottles, &c., in which style of now very fashionable decoration the Coalport artists excel. In these Japanese patterns some of the designs are unusually elaborate and intricate, and the workmanship is charac-

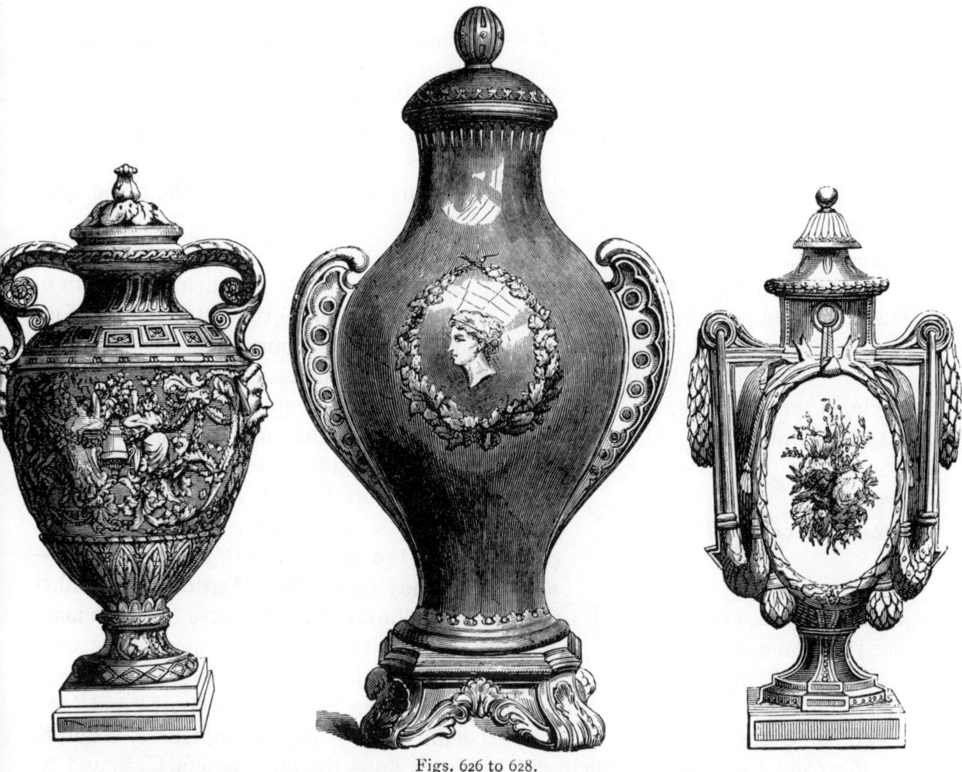

Figs. 626 to 628.

terized by extreme precision and regularity, while the gilding and colour, especially the deep reds and blues, are rich and full in the extreme. Some of the vases in this style vie with those of the native art of the Japanese, and are not excelled by any other house. The principal artists employed at that time at the works were Mr. Charles Palmere, Mr. Cooke, Mr. John Randall, Mr. Birbeck, Mr. A. Bowdler, Mr. J. Hartshorne, and Mr. Jabez Aston; and among those previously engaged here was Mr. R. F. Abraham, a student from Antwerp and Paris and a successful follower of the school of Etty. Modellers of a very high class in their respective branches are also employed, and the excellence of their work is apparent in all the higher class productions of this establishment.

The marks used by the Caughley works have already been fully described (pp.

161-163). After the removal of these works to Coalport, the same letters, both C and S, for many years were used. At Coalport, however, marks have been adopted,

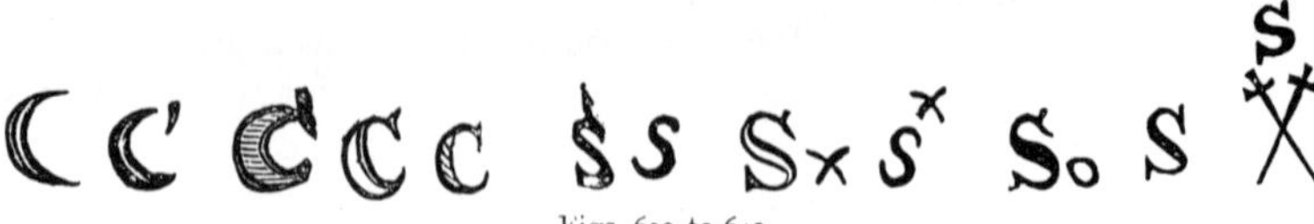

Figs. 629 to 640.

perhaps, more sparingly than at any other works; and the great bulk of the goods have been manufactured, from the first down to the present time, without any mark at all. On some examples of the early part of the present century, the written name of "Coalport," thus—*Coalport*—appears; but these are of very rare occurrence. Another mark, adopted somewhat later, though only used very sparingly, was simply the letters C D for Coalbrookdale, or the same two letters conjoined thus—CD; sometimes also Coalbrookdale appears in full, and at others the contraction "C Dale," in similar writing letters.

Another mark, of large size, adopted in 1820, is a circle in which is a wreath of laurel surrounding the words, "Coalport Improved Felt Spar Porcelain," in four lines across. Encircling the wreath are the words, "Patronised by the Society of Arts. The Gold Medal awarded May 30, 1820;" while beneath, and outside the circle, is the name "I. Rose and Co." This mark was adopted consequent on Mr. Rose obtaining the gold medal before alluded to. Other marks adopted by this firm, although but seldom used, are, first, a monogram of the letters C B D, for Coalbrookdale; second, the same monogram, surrounded by a garter bearing the name of "Daniell, London"—a firm for many years, like Mortlocks and other leading houses, connected with Coalport or Coalbrookdale, who have had that mark used for some especial orders; and third, the initials of the various manufactories which have from time to time been incorporated with, or merged into, the Coalport establishment. Thus the scroll—which at first sight looks like a short "and" (&) —will, on examination, be seen to be a combination of the writing letters, C and S, for *Coalport* and *Salopian*, enclosing within its bows the three letters, C, S, and N, denoting respectively *Caughley*, *Swansea*, and *Nantgarw*.

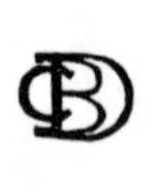

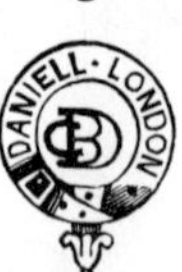

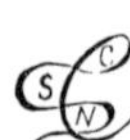

Having now passed through the history of these famed works, and shown their connection with others, both in manufacture and in printing, it only remains to say a few words on the varieties of goods for which the Salopian works have been famed, both in times past and at present. Foremost are the blue painted and printed wares copied from Chinese patterns, for which both it and the early Worcester works were remarkable. The first painted, as well as printed, wares were close imitations of the foreign; but groups of flowers of original design, &c. were also introduced, and designs *based*, perhaps, on foreign models were adopted. Groups of figures, in the characteristic costume of the period, were also executed with great taste and ability. Of the Chinese patterns, the two most famous—the well-known "willow pattern" (known generally among the trade as the "Broseley pattern")

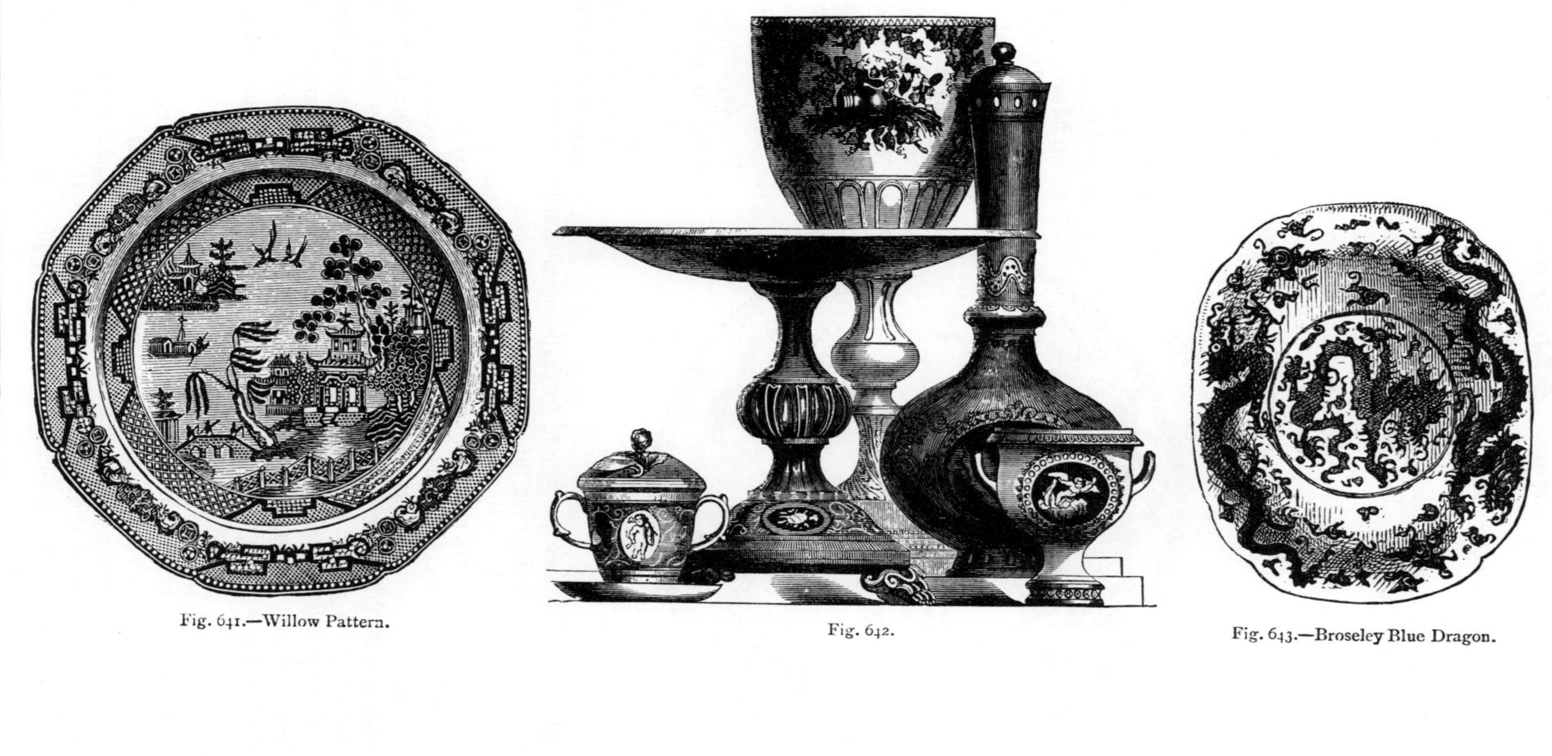

Fig. 641.—Willow Pattern.

Fig. 642.

Fig. 643.—Broseley Blue Dragon.

and the "blue dragon" (also known as the "Broseley blue dragon" or "Broseley blue Canton"), I have already said, owe their first introduction to the Caughley works; and this fact alone is sufficient to entitle them to more than ordinary notice. Of the willow pattern, which has undoubtedly been the most popular, and had the most extensive sale of any pattern ever introduced, the early examples, bearing the Caughley mark—the cups without handles, and ribbed and finished precisely like the foreign—are rare, and fetch high prices. A special form of jug, known technically as the "cabbage-leaf jug," was also first made at the Caughley works, and is rare. Later the "worm sprig" pattern, the "tournay sprig," and other equally successful patterns were here introduced from the Dresden, as were also the celebrated Dresden raised flowers and the "Berlin chain edge" pattern. About 1821 a peculiar marone-coloured ground, which is much sought after, was introduced at Coalport, by Walker, of Nantgarw, of whom I have before spoken; and at this time many marked improvements were made in the different processes of manufacture.

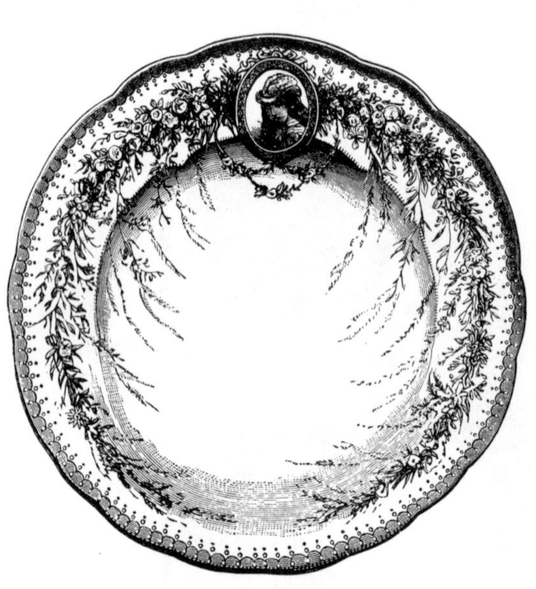

Fig. 644.

The copies, both in embossing, in body, in colour, and oiliness of the glaze, and in style of painting of birds and flowers, of the Dresden at this period were perfect, and as the Dresden mark was (perhaps injudiciously) introduced as well, were capable of deceiving even the most knowing connoisseur. It may be well to note that at this period an *impressed* anchor was sometimes used. This must not be taken to be anything more than a workman's mark. Very successful copies of the Sèvres and Chelsea have also been at one time or other produced, and on these the marks of those makers have been also copied. Collectors of "old Chelsea," especially of the famous green examples, must be careful, therefore, not to take everything for granted as belonging to that place on which the gold anchor is found.

The *egg-shell china* produced at Coalport is among the finest and purest which has come under my notice, from the fact that the body is *pure porcelain*, being composed of one stone and one clay alone, unmixed with bone or any other material.

Broseley.

Broseley is perhaps more universally known as a seat of the manufacture of tobacco-pipes than in any other way; for in this particular it has "held its own" against other localities for about three centuries, and seems still likely to do so for three centuries more, should the habit of smoking continue so long.

The names of the pipe-makers at Broseley, judging from the examples I have

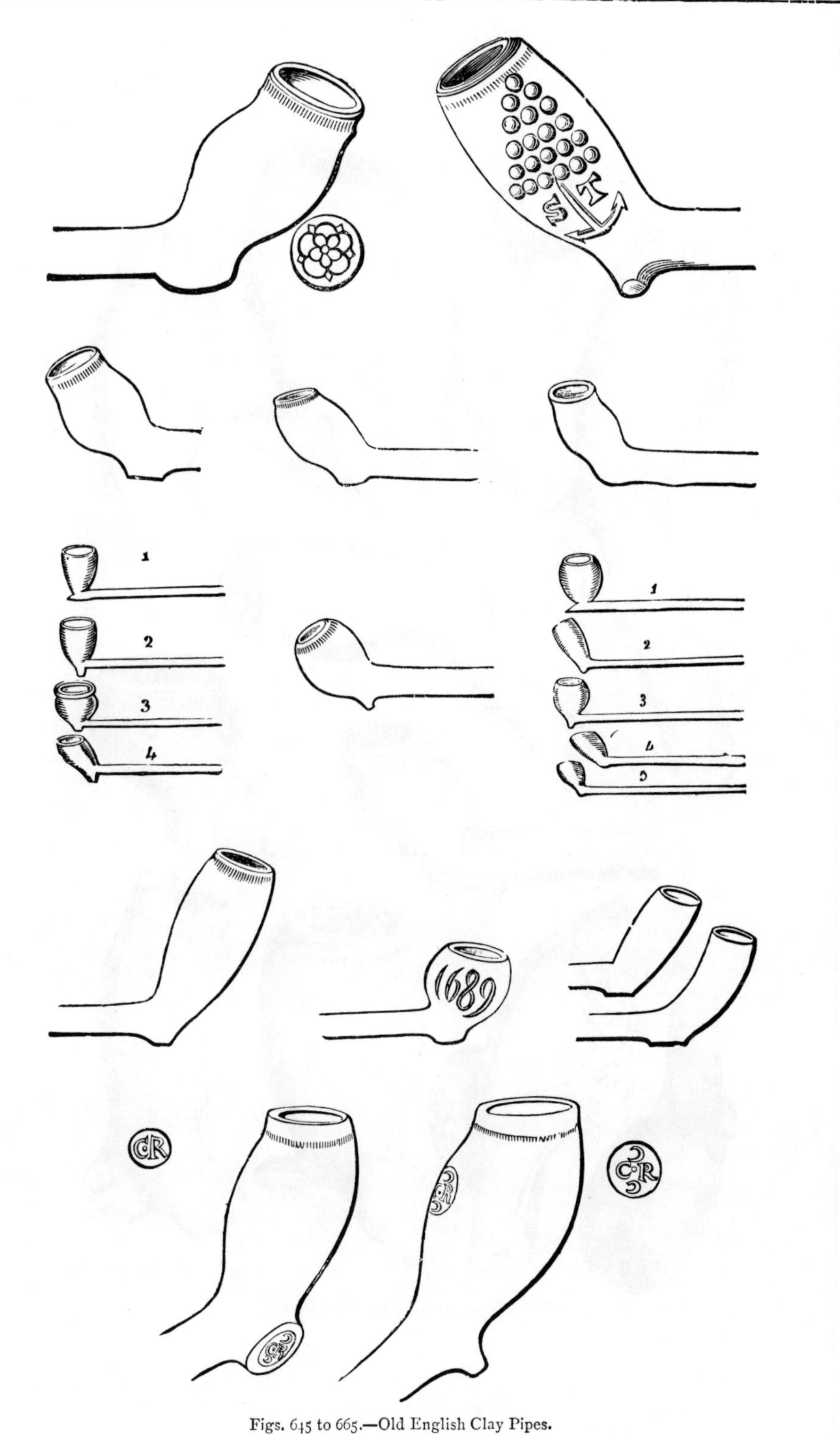

Figs. 645 to 665.—Old English Clay Pipes.

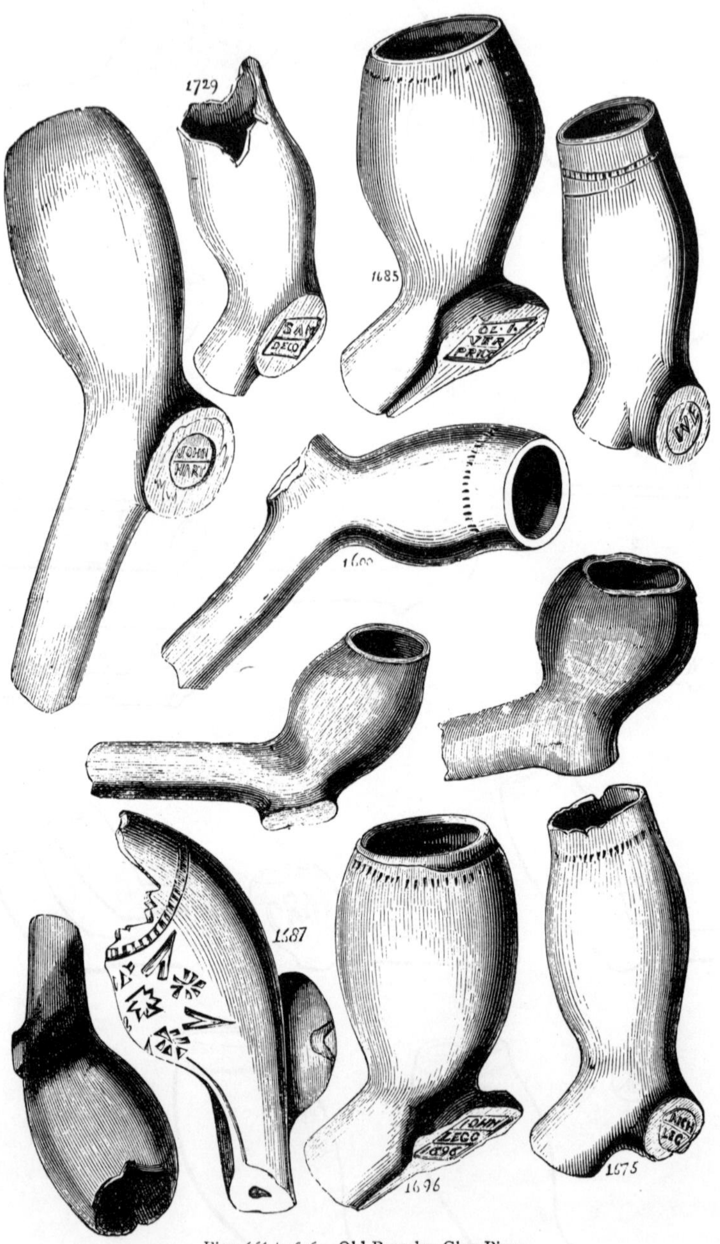

Figs. 666 to 676.—Old Broseley Clay Pipes.

seen, appear to commence first as follows:—Clarke in 1647, Roden in 1681, Legg 1575, Darbey 1700, Decon 1608, Evans 1615, Hughes 1641, Hartshorne 1620, James 1600, Jones 1590, Price 1608, Partridge 1718, Overton 1700, Smith 1709, Shaw 1630, Wilksone 1733, and Ward 1700. Other names (Brown, Bradley, Dry, Hart, Harper, Overley, and Roberts, for instance) occur as pipe-makers here in the olden time. More than a hundred years ago, the pipe-makers began to stamp their names and residences on the *stems* of the pipes instead of the spurs, the stems being, in many instances, 16 or 18 inches or more in length. They likewise made a small twist or bead mid-stem, at such a length from the bowl that, when held between the fingers at that spot, the pipe was balanced.

A pipe-maker, named Noah Roden, brought the long pipes to great perfection, and supplied most of the London clubs and coffee-houses of that day; he died about 1829, and his business was carried on by the late William Southorn, who improved the manufacture, and whose descendant is the maker of the patent "Real Broseleys."

About the middle of last century, and since, the Rodens were famous makers of pipes at Broseley, and to them is due the introduction of "churchwardens" and "London straws," and they were succeeded in the early part of this century by Mr. Southorn, father of the late Mr. Edwin Southorn. The works were established about 1830 by Noah Roden. In 1856 they passed into the hands of Mr. Southorn, who in 1860 introduced the process of transfer-printing upon pipes, the same as practised in other branches of ceramics. By this means the crests or armorial bearings, names, mottoes, or monograms of his patrons, trade marks or initials of firms, and signs and names of hotels and inns are produced, as are also other devices in colours. In 1868 he introduced steam-power into the manufactory, and was thus enabled to produce about 10,500 gross, or 1,500,000 pipes, in the course of a year. In 1851 Mr. Southorn received honourable mention as "superior tobacco-pipes" at the Exhibition in that year, and he also introduced the plan of dipping, or "tipping," his pipes at the mouthpiece with green or any other coloured glaze; and also the "patent Broseley Narghilé" in which the clay pipe is enclosed for a portion of its length in a glass tube, filled with water, which draws away the colouring matter and narcotic poison from the smoke before reaching the smoker's mouth. There are at the present time several pipe-makers in the locality.

COALBROOKDALE.

The terra cotta works belonging to the world-famed "Coalbrookdale Iron Company" were established in 1861. The beds of clay belonging to this company being peculiarly adapted for the finest and best kinds of terra cotta, they, in conjunction with others in the neighbourhood, undertook to prepare and send, for the Exhibition of 1862, examples of goods made from the various clays of the Shropshire coal fields. The result was the establishment of this branch of manufacture, which, so far as it was carried out, proved eminently successful. The colour of it was a peculiarly light buff of a soft and pleasing tint, and the quality of high order both for firmness, fineness, hardness, and durability. In it the company produced vases, tazzas, pedestals, brackets, pendants, flower-pots and boxes, chimney-pots, and every variety of architectural decoration. The manufacture is now entirely discontinued, the company confining itself to the making of roofing and ridge tiles, &c.

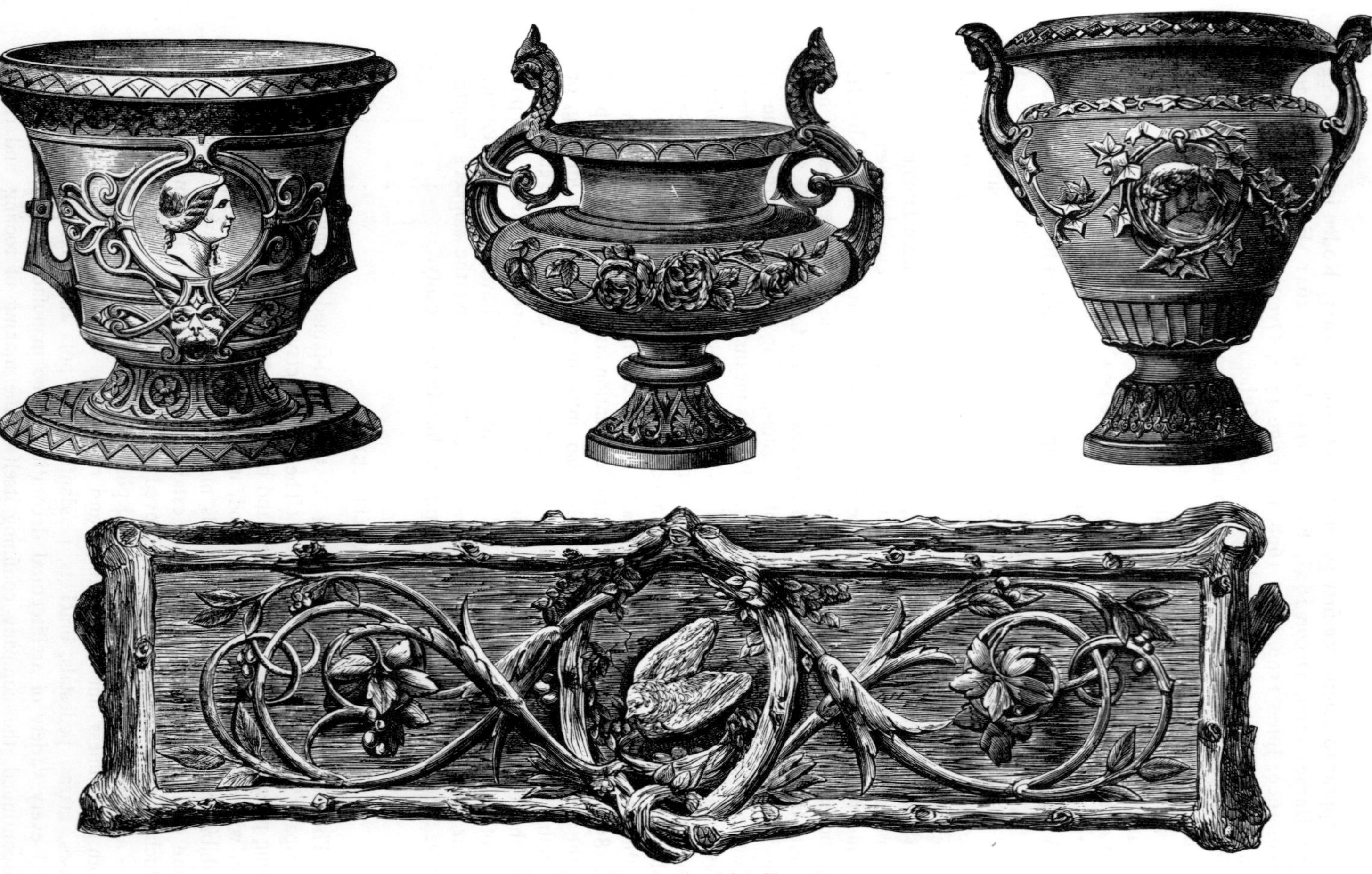

Figs. 677 to 680.—Coalbrookdale Terra Cotta.

Madeley.

A small manufactory of china was established and carried on for about a quarter of a century at Madeley, by Mr. Martin Randall, who served his apprenticeship at the Coalport works; his elder brothers, Edward and William Randall, having been apprenticed at Caughley. From Coalport Martin Randall went to the Derby China Works, where he remained for some time, and became the friend of two of their famed painters, Phillip Cleve and William Pegg. From Derby he removed to London, and entered into business with a Mr. Robins, at Islington. Upon a dissolution of partnership he came down to Madeley, and fixed himself in Park Place, where for a few years he confined himself to

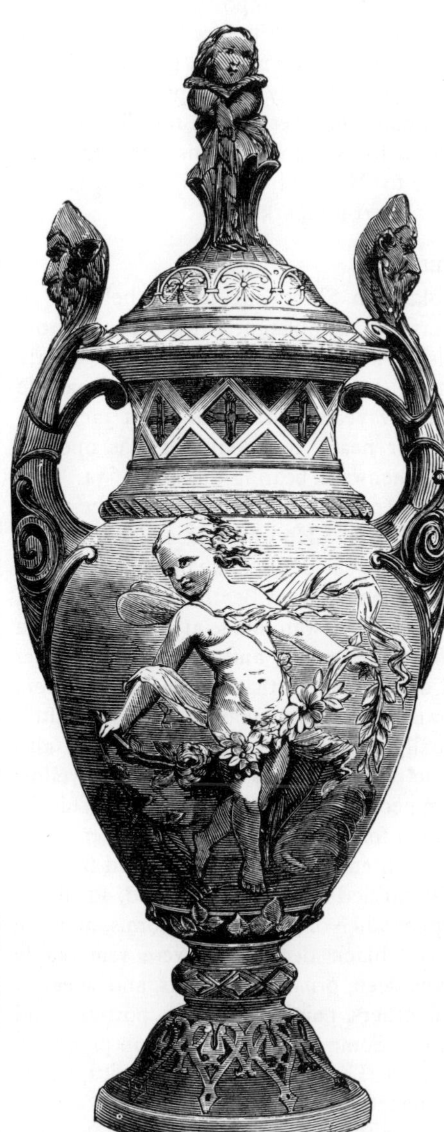

Fig. 681.—Coalbrookdale Terra Cotta.

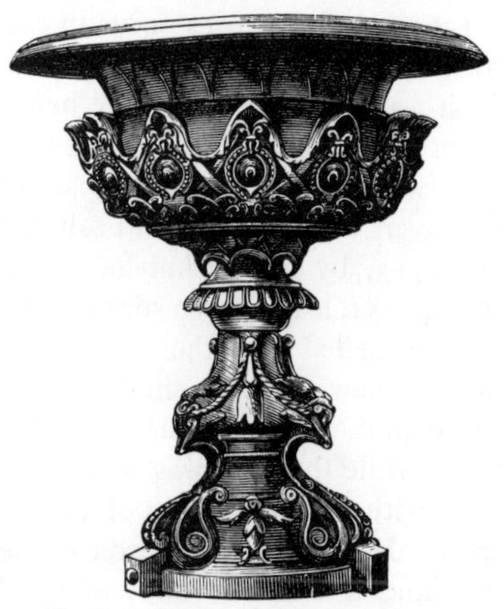

Fig. 682.—Coalbrookdale Terra Cotta.

redecorating Sèvres china, which was procured by agents; chiefly of Baldock and Garman, in Paris. White china was obtained where feasible; but when that could not be had, dessert, tea, and breakfast services, vases, wine coolers, jardinières, and other articles, ornamented simply with blue and gold lines, dots, or sprigs of flowers, were purchased; the latter of which were removed by fluoric acid, the glaze being so blended with the body that it gave back a new surface on being passed through the enamelling kiln; this he put up at a larger house to which he removed at the bottom of Madeley. His want of experience in the processes of making led to frequent errors and losses, the latter being the greater from his constant desire to produce a body which should equal Nantgarw and Sèvres. He at length succeeded, however, in producing the nearest approach to the old Sèvres of any at that time made in this kingdom. It had all the mellow transparency and richness, and the same capability of receiving the colours into the glaze, of that famous ware, and had this to such an extent that the most experienced connoisseurs found it impossible to distinguish between them, excepting by the mark, which no bribe would induce them to imitate. From Madeley, Mr. Randall removed his business to Shelton; and here it was that the late Mr. Herbert Minton was so struck with the beauty of his productions that he made overtures to him to join his firm, which, however, he did not do; and he soon afterwards retired from business, and went to live at Barlaston, near Trentham, where he died. Mr. Randall, who was uncle to Mr. John Randall, F.G.S., one of the celebrated painters of the Coalport works, used no mark.

Jackfield.

The Jackfield Pottery was one of the oldest in Shropshire, and is believed to have been worked for centuries. The potters had, at different times, probably from being expert hands, migrated into Staffordshire; and I am informed that, as early as 1560, several entries occur in the parish registers of Stoke-upon-Trent of people (potters, of course) as "*from Jackfield.*" A few years ago a coal-pit at Jackfield, which was known not to have been entered for nearly two centuries, was opened, and in it was found a small mug of brown earthenware, bearing the date 1634. The works were, probably not long after this period, carried on by a person of the name of Glover, who used the old salt glaze for his ware. He was succeeded, about the year 1713, by John Thursfield, son of John Thursfield of Stoke-upon-Trent, who died in 1751, leaving two sons—John, who built the works at Benthall; and Maurice, who succeeded his father at Jackfield. The kind of ware made at Jackfield was a white stoneware, very similar to the Staffordshire make, and on some examples flowers and other ornaments were incised and coloured, that is, the outlines were cut in while the clay was soft, and the flowers and other ornaments touched afterwards with colour. Tiles of the kind usually known as "Dutch tiles" were also made. In 1763 Mr. Simpson carried on the pottery at Jackfield, and made yellow ware, and a ware the body of which was pipeclay and glazed with salt. This he sent down the Severn to the Bristol Channel for export to America—a trade to which the American war of independence put an end. Maurice Thursfield made at Jackfield a very superior black ware, highly vitrified and glazed; indeed, so highly glazed was it that it had all the outward appearance of glass. The forms, and the potting of these articles, locally known as "black decanters," were remarkably good, and on some specimens which I have seen, ornaments, heads, and wreaths, &c., executed in gold and colour; and on others, paintings in oils, portraits and views, and raised ornaments, are introduced. Some good examples are preserved in the Museum of Practical Geology. Maurice Thursfield died in America, where he had, it appears, considerable business connections.

In these works Mr. Rose, in conjunction with a Mr. Blakeway, soon after the death of Maurice Thursfield, began making china. The works were not, however, carried on long, but were removed to Coalport, to some buildings which had formerly been a pottery belonging to a Mr. Young, as I have already stated.

In the early part of this century a pottery—spoken of in 1836 as the "new pottery"—was established here by Mr. John Myatt, for brown and yellow stonewares. Here, too, at the same time, near the Calcuts, extensive brick and tile-works were then and still are carried on.

Jackfield Encaustic Tiles.—Many years ago Mr. Peter Stephan (afterwards a modeller at Coalport), son of Stephan the potter, who was a Frenchman, and at one time at Derby and afterwards of Jackfield, where he had a small pottery, produced some strikingly good arabesque patterns in blue printing. His mark was an anchor with cable, impressed in the body of the ware; and also the crest of an anchor on an heraldic roll, with his name above (see Figs. 683 and 684), and printed in blue on the bottom of the ware. His pieces are of rare occurrence. He also made encaustic tiles. These were the first made in this district.

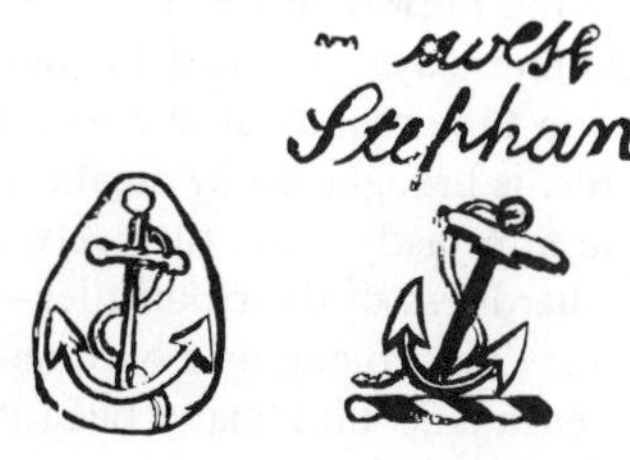

Figs. 683 and 684.

The Jackfield Works.—The site of the present works carried on by Craven, Dunnill, & Co., for the manufacture of Encaustic and Geometrical tiles, is that of the above old pottery in Jackfield, in which Hargreaves and Craven for several years made geometrical tiles by the clay-dust process, and encaustic tiles from

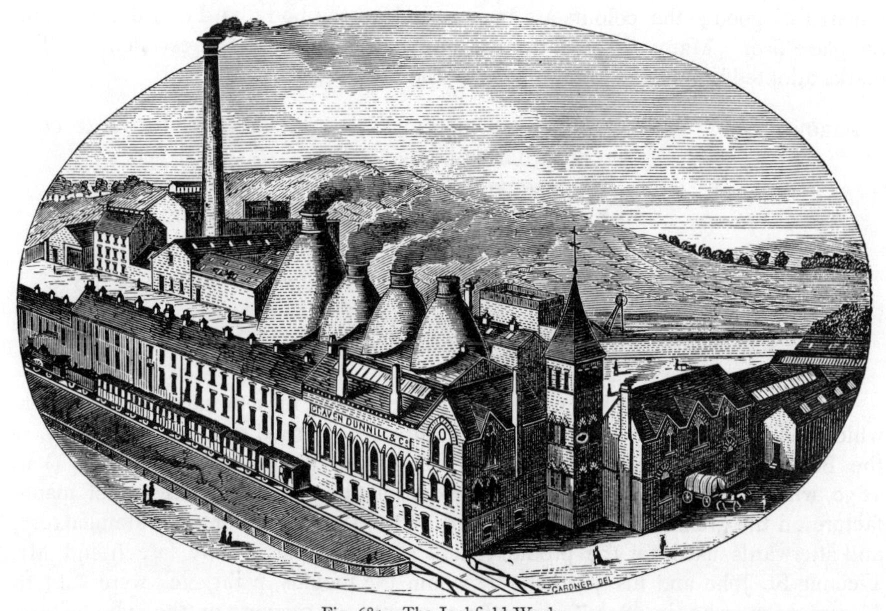

Fig. 685.—The Jackfield Works.

plastic clay; but the buildings being old and dilapidated, Mr. H. P. Dunnill formed a limited liability company, consisting of seven shareholders, for rebuilding and carrying on the concern. The old buildings were taken down, a considerable extent of land added to the premises, and on this land the present works were erected. They are fitted with machinery and arrangements specially adapted to the requirements of the trade, each department succeeding the other in perfect rotation;

so that the clay goes into the blunging-house at one point, from thence into the slip-kilns, mill-room, damping-houses, press-shops, encaustic rooms, drying-stove, seggar-house, firing and glaze-kilns, sorting-house, warehouses, packing-room, and finally, having in the various processes gone the circuit of the manufactory, passes into the railway lurries to be conveyed to various parts of the kingdom and abroad. The fine clays of Jackfield and Broseley are largely used in the manufacture, and within the grounds of the works there is a pit in which, from a depth of thirty-five yards, is brought up by steam-power a beautiful red clay, of very fine tone of colour. The firm justly pride themselves on the colour and quality of their plain tiles; and the hardness of their buff tiles—a point much desired by the trade—is very noticeable. The colour and hardness of body of their dove-tiles are also very apparent. In encaustic tiles many beautiful designs by Waterhouse, Goldie, Gibbs, Bentley, and other architects are produced. At the instance of one of the firm, Mr. A. H. Brown, M.P. for Wenlock, a noticeable arrangement has been made in the interest of the workpeople. Any profit made after ten per cent. paid to the proprietors is equally divided between them and the workpeople, and the latter have thus a direct interest to do their work in the best manner, so as to add to the reputation of the firm. Glazed tiles for hearths, of great variety and beauty of pattern, are made here, and also glazed wall-tiles in white, cream, celadon, and other tones. The company also produce majolica tiles of the richest class, with an endless variety of printed, painted, and art tiles for decorative purposes. The quality of the tiles is remarkably good; the colours are pure and clear, the body hard and durable, and the glaze firm. Many of the patterns are of extreme beauty and excellence. The marks adopted, impressed on the back of the tiles, are—

HARGREAVES
&
CRAVEN

HARGREAVES CRAVEN
DUNNILL & CO
JACKFIELD
N^{R} IRONBRIDGE SALOP

CRAVEN DUNNILL & CO
LIMITED
JACKFIELD
N^{R} IRONBRIDGE SALOP

HARGREAVES
CRAVEN DUNNILL & CO
JACKFIELD

CRAVEN
DUNNILL & CO
JACKFIELD
SALOP

CRAVEN
& CO

BENTHALL WORKS.—The manufactory of encaustic tiles, mosaics, and majolica, which has for more than a quarter of a century been carried on by Messrs. Maw, at the Benthall works, near Broseley, was initiated at Worcester (see page 154) in 1850, where Messrs. Maw commenced experimenting on the processes of manufacture on the premises formerly occupied by the Worcester Porcelain Manufactory, and afterwards used for the production of encaustic tiles by my late friend Mr. Fleming St. John and his partners, by whom the moulds, plant, &c., were sold to Messrs. Maw, who, in 1852, feeling the necessity for carrying on the manufacture, removed to these works, where another seven years was spent by them in a series of costly experiments upon the clays of the Shropshire coal-field, as well as the plastic materials found throughout the kingdom, many of which no one had before attempted to turn to economic account. The results of these experiments have been illustrated in an extensive series of specimens of the clays or plastic slates of Great Britain presented by Mr. Geo. Maw, F.S.A., to the Government Museum of Practical Geology, and printed in the supplement to the catalogue by Sir H. De La

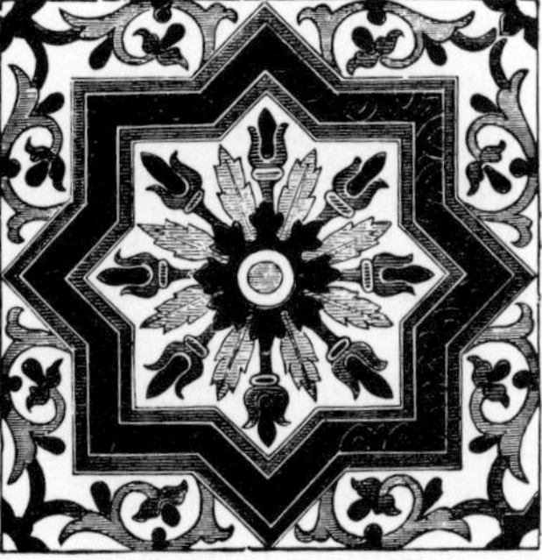
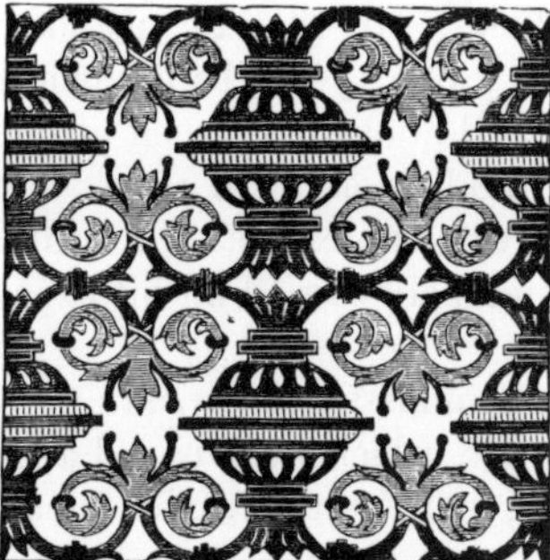
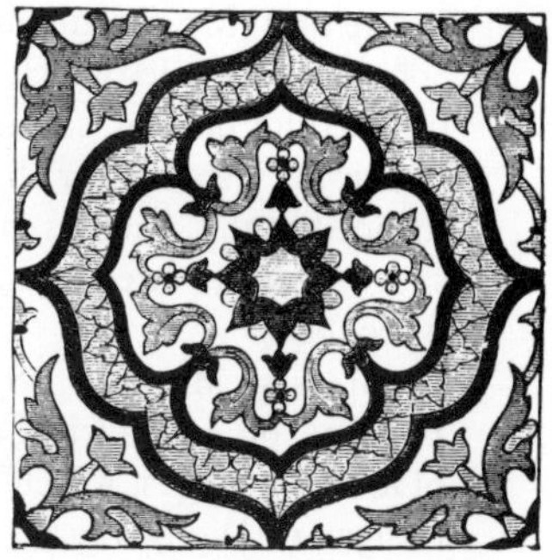
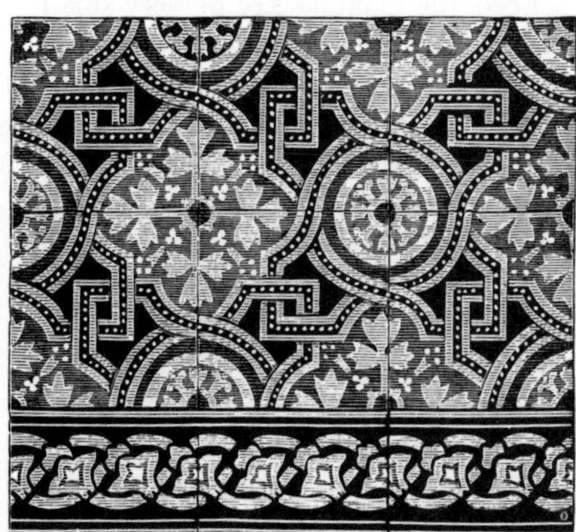
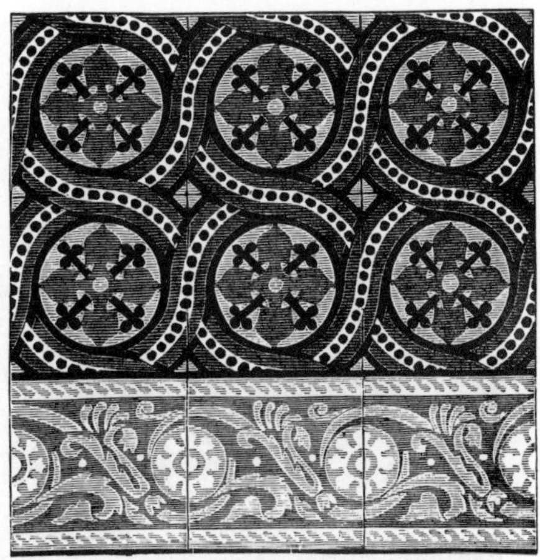

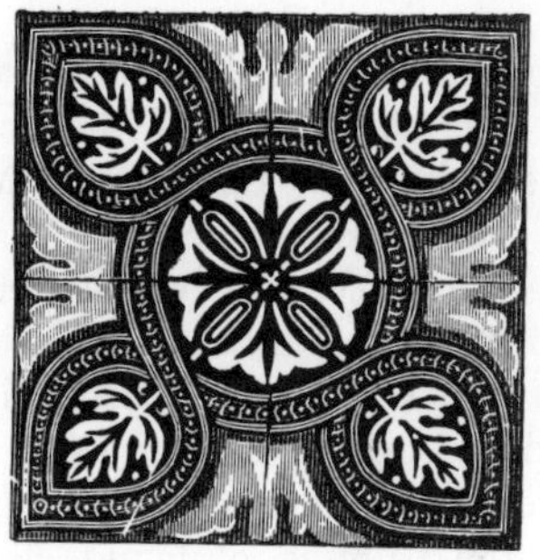
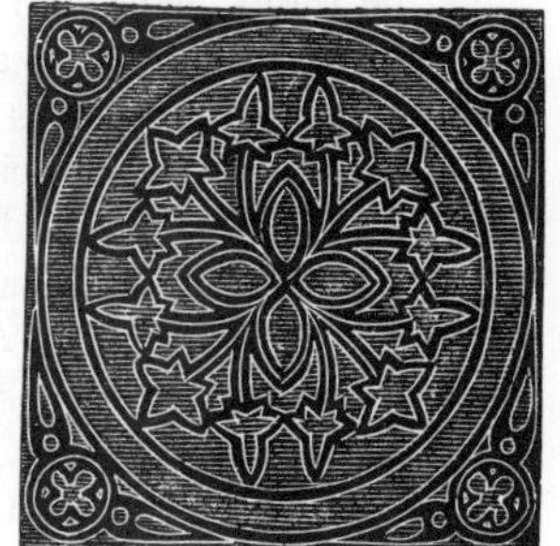

Figs. 686 to 693.—Examples of Messrs. Maw's Tiles.

Beche and Mr. Trenham Reeks. In 1857 the manufacture was commenced on a commercial scale, which for several years barely paid its expenses; but from that time to the present continual additions have been made to the works to meet the increasing demand for their productions. In 1871 supplementary works were commenced at the Tuckies, about two miles from the Benthall works, celebrated as the spot where the late Lord Dundonald carried on his experiments in the manufacture of coal-gas.

Messrs. Maw, in 1856, commissioned Mr. M. D. Wyatt to design a series of patterns of geometrical mosaic, which were issued as a small lithographed volume of fourteen pages, which was, in 1867, superseded by a larger volume, including the designs of Digby Wyatt, George Goldie, J. P. Seddon, George E. Street, J. Burgess, H. B. Garling, and others, as well as the reproduction of all the best obtainable examples of ancient tiles, geometrical and Roman mosaic, majolica, &c.

In 1851 Messrs. Maw began the manufacture of plain, geometrical, mosaic, and the ordinary encaustic tiles, but since 1857 there has been a continual grafting on of specialities, and the production of new colours. In 1861 they commenced the manufacture of very small tesseræ for the formation of pictorial mosaics, and produced for the Exhibition of 1862 their well-known mosaic of "*The Seasons*," (Fig. 695), from a design expressly made by Digby Wyatt. The production of coloured enamels for the surface decoration of majolica tiles next occupied their attention, and after years of experimenting, all the colours employed in the ancient tiles of Spain or Italy were successfully reproduced, as well as others which were unknown to the mediæval and Moorish manufacturers.

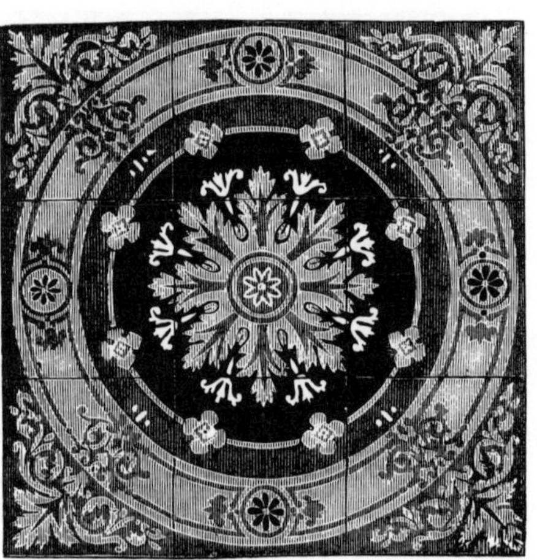

Fig. 694.

A stone chimney-piece, enriched with tiles executed for the International Exhibition of 1862, was their first attempt in the application of enamels and majolica in architectural work. Shortly afterwards the successful decoration of ceilings was carried out in the corridors of the India Office, and among other important works are the staircase executed for Sir D. Majoribanks, a portion of which was shown at the Exhibition of 1871, and the chimney-pieces for the board-room of the South Kensington Museum, and the Museum of Science and Art, at Edinburgh. Messrs. Maw were the first in this country to produce the transparent celeste, or turquoise blue, employed in ancient Chinese enamels, specimens of which were exhibited in the Paris Exhibition of 1867. Among the productions may be mentioned tesseræ for mosaic work, decorated with rich enamels; embossed tiles; "*sgrafito*," a ware the decoration of which is produced by the cutting away of superimposed layers of different coloured clays, after the fashion of cameo carving; "*slip-painting*," the production of a pattern by the painting of liquid clay on a ground of another colour, and the whole glazed over, after the first burning, with transparent coloured enamels; "*pâte sur pâte*," tiles in which the design in high relief is superimposed on a ground of a different colour; mixed coloured glasses and enamels for the decoration of pottery, by which the most subtle and brilliant effects are produced;

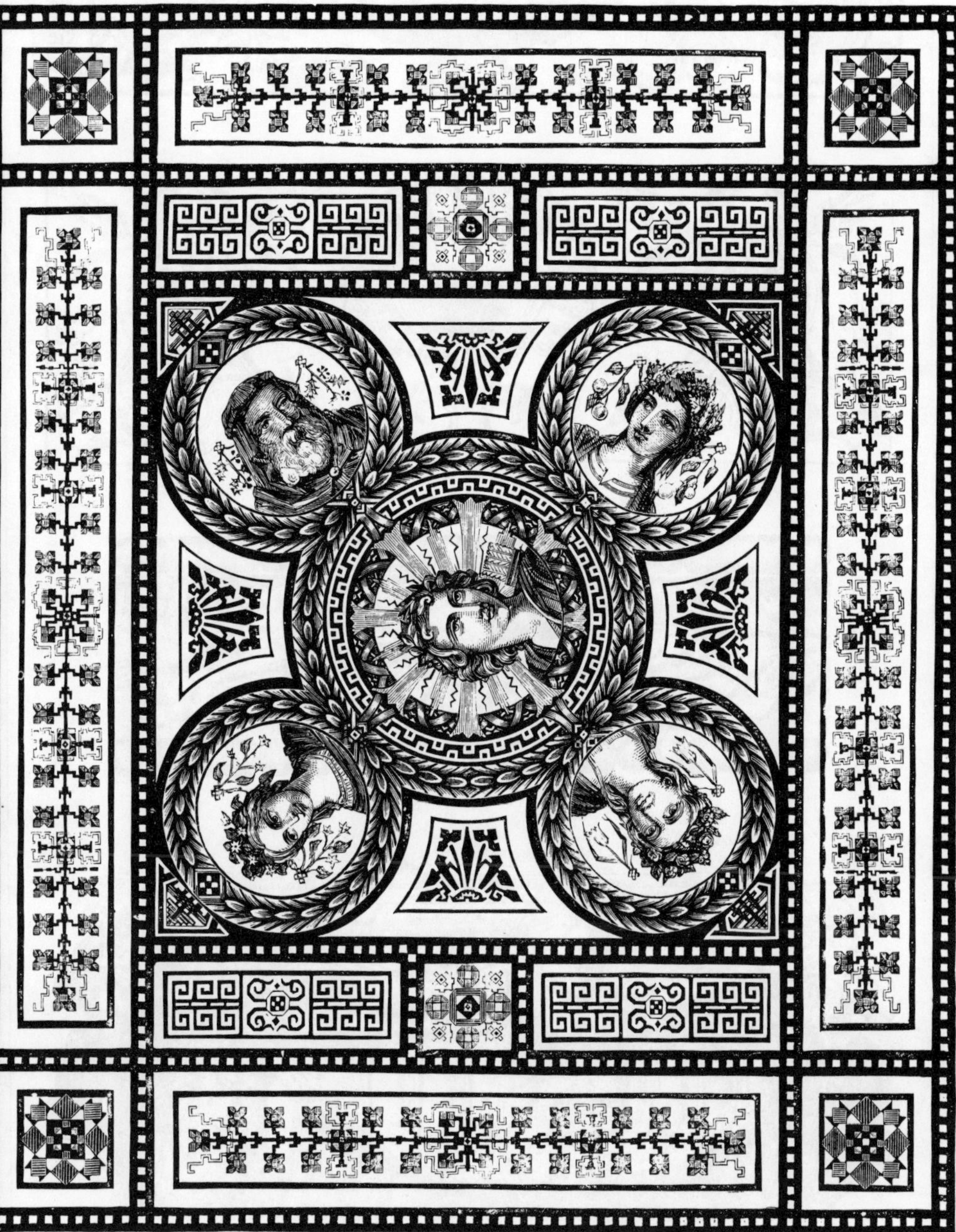

Fig. 695.—Maw's Mosaic Pavement of "*The Seasons.*"

and *terra cotta and Parian plant-markers,* on which the names of trees and shrubs are written in a permanent black enamel and burnt in.

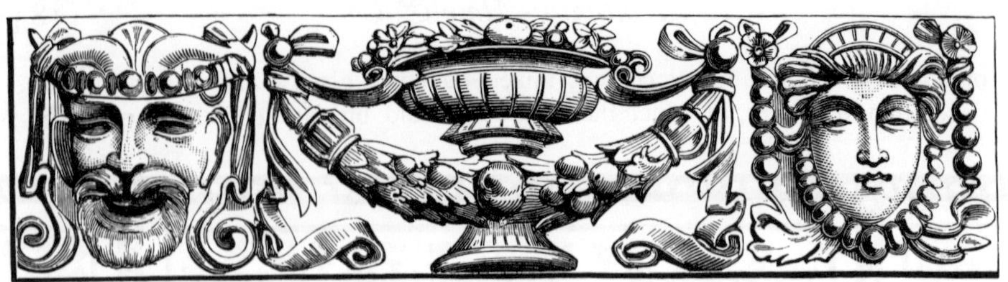

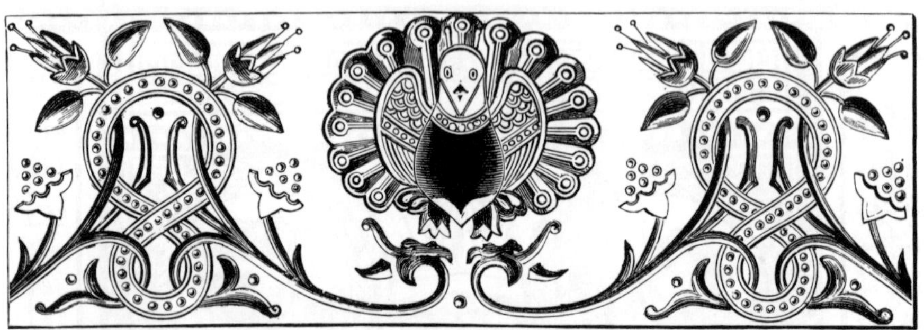

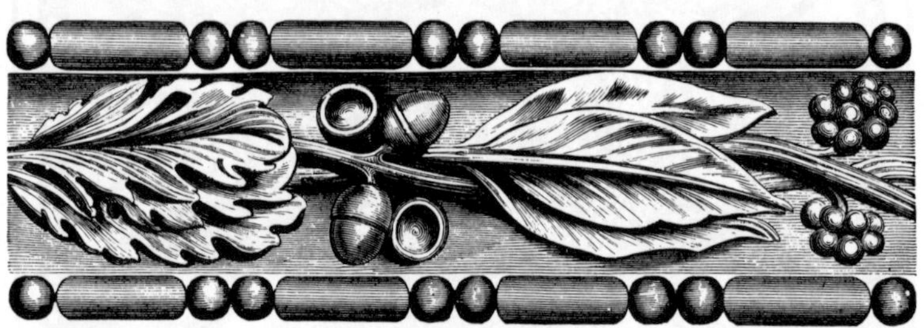

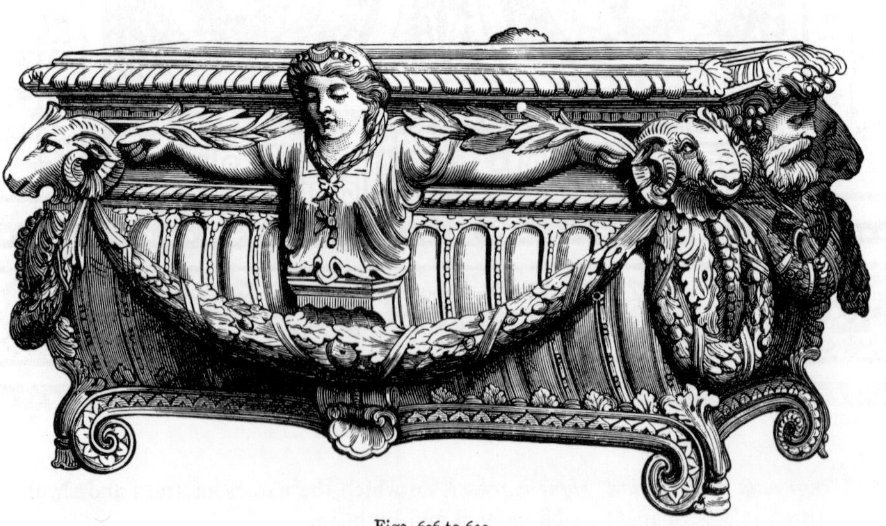

Figs. 696 to 699.

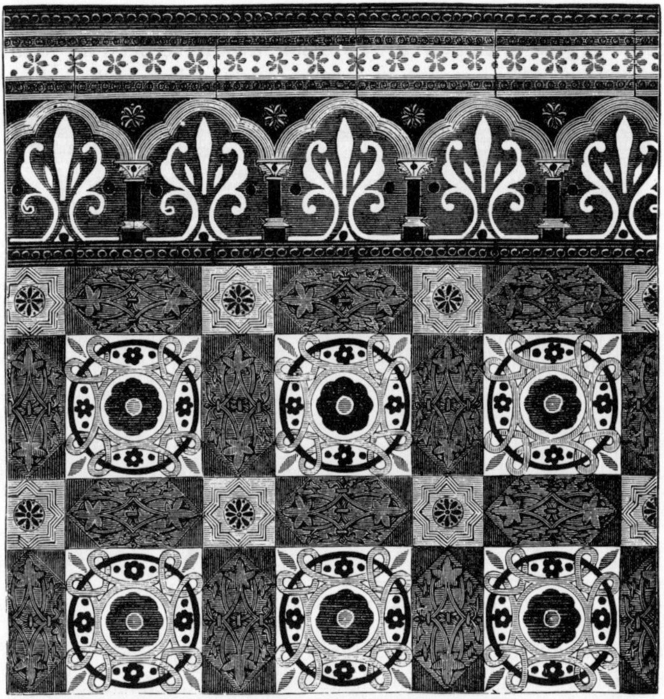

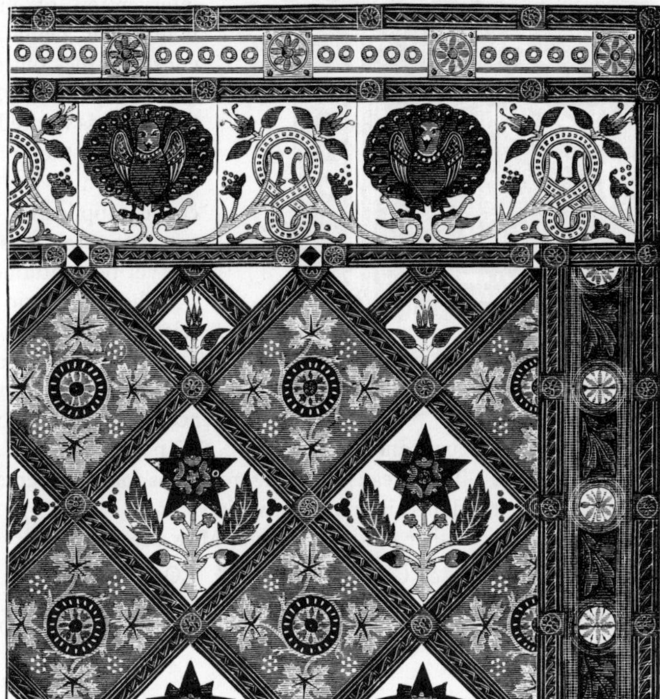

Figs. 700 and 701.—Examples of Maw's Tile Pavements.

The special processes employed by Messrs. Maw have been made the subject of a number of patents, among which may be mentioned their mill machinery, used in

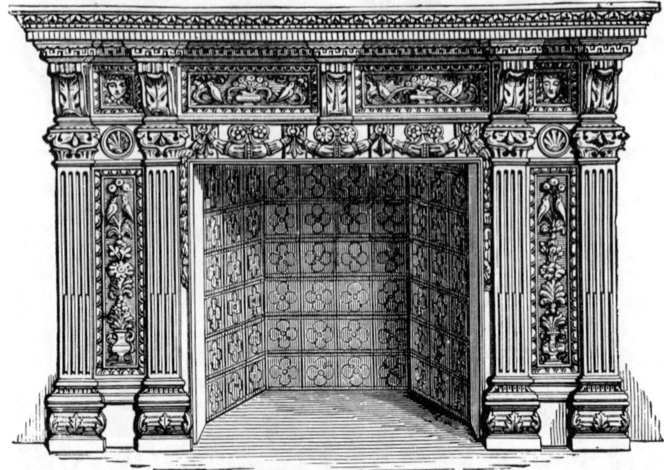

Fig. 702.—Maw's Majolica Chimney-piece.

the preparation of clay for the manufacture of tiles by Prosser's process ; the *steam blunger*, by which the rough clay is levigated, sifted, and refined ready for drying on the slip-kilns, without the intervention of manual labour ; the manufacture of encaustic tiles out of pulverised nearly dry clay, and their patent press worked by steam power for the pressing of tiles, which is the only successful application of steam power to screw presses which has yet been attained.

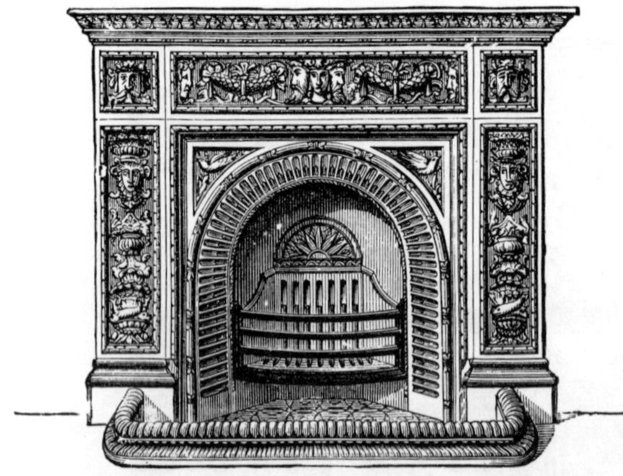

Fig. 703.—Maw's Majolica Chimney-piece.

The geometric and tesselated pavements produced by Messrs. Maw are made with the utmost mechanical accuracy, and of the finest quality, both in body, in colours, and in glaze, and the patterns are of exquisite beauty and endless variety. The encaustic, or figured, tiles for pavements, are also a great speciality, and are produced in immense variety.

The marks at one time or other used by Messrs. Maw are—

MAW & CO
BENTHALL
WORKS
BROSELEY
SALOP

MAW & CO
BROSELEY

MAW & CO
BENTHALL
BROSELEY

MAW & CO
BROSELEY
SALOP

MAW & CO

The newest, registered, mark is circular, and has MAW within the inner circle, surrounded by the words FLOREAT SALOPIA.

The enamelled hearth-pavements and wall-tiles are another great speciality of these works, and are of unsurpassable richness and beauty, as are also their majolica tiles and fireplace linings. These are produced in every possible variety, and are remarkable, not only for the richness and delicacy of the colours which are used, and for their purely artistic and masterly combination, but for the excellence of both body and glaze, and the scrupulous accuracy of forms for fitting together. The same remark applies to the embossed and indented tiles, and also to those which are partially pierced for open-work. They are all equally good, and bear evidence of that thorough appreciation of art which pervades all the productions of the Benthall works. The engravings (Figs. 702 and 703) show two of their majolica chimney-pieces. The first is of the finest majolica, with a fireplace lining of encaustic, or enamel, tiles, which would also be used for the hearth. The decorations are in high and bold relief, and being coloured with pure artistic taste, have a charming and very striking effect. It is 4 feet 8 inches in height, and 7 feet in width, and is, of course, furnished with a marble shelf at the top—which, however, is not shown in the illustration. The next shows another of these chimney-pieces entirely complete; it is, like the other, of majolica. The ornaments are in bold relief, set off with an excellent arrangement of groundwork and colour; the hearth is formed of encaustic, or enamelled, or mosaic tiles; and the fender is of majolica.

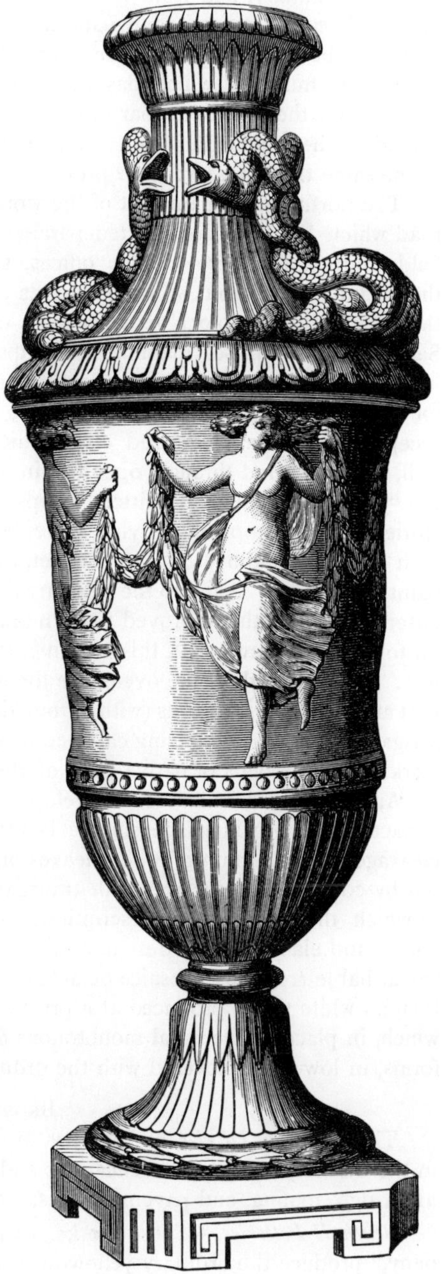

Fig. 704.

Another branch of ceramics—that of "Art Pottery"—has been added to Messrs. Maw's manufactory. This is the production in majolica of vases, tazzas, and other articles, more or less decorated with raised or surface ornamentation. They are of excellent design, the body light but compact, and the decorations of remarkably good and artistic character.

In 1882-3 Messrs. Maw entirely rebuilt their works on land purchased by them at the Tuckies, Jackfield, where they had for some years carried on an auxiliary branch. The river Severn forms the eastern and the Great Western Railway the western boundary, and from it a private siding communicates with every department. The site comprises five and a half acres of ground, which is laid out with buildings best adapted for their manufacture, and fitted with the most scientific machinery, much of which has been designed by themselves for the purpose of carrying out their own peculiar processes. Ample provision has also been made for extending the various departments, so as to provide for an increasing demand, and at the same time preserve their proper relation to each other.

The northern, or main part of the works has entrance gates opening on to a new road which has been constructed parallel with the railway from a point near Jackfield Church, and here are the offices, show-room, a part of the warehouses, and the packing-room, from which the goods are delivered direct on to the siding. On the eastern side the block extends for a distance of 500 feet along the banks of the Severn, and comprises manufacturing apartments, mess-rooms, and rooms for the use of the workpeople. On the south, in an apartment 98 by 43 feet, are the presses for the semi-dry moulding process; the whole being surrounded by a series of receptacles for the pulverized clays, which are brought direct from the grinding-mill, and delivered through openings in a corridor above. On the same side are the "sagger"-making and fitters' shops, &c.; and on the western side is a two-storied block, comprising drying stove, heated by exhaust steam from the engines, with warehouse above 230 by 21 feet, and various workshops for printing, hand-painting, &c. &c. Again, to the west, are the sorting, placing, and oven houses; which latter have both the improved "down-draught" and older up-draught systems, and on to a subway, level with this building, the coal is discharged direct from the railway. To the north of the ovens are the glazing and enamelling kilns. In another part are the fire-brick works (with automatic machinery), and rooms for refining clays, levigating colours, pulverizing calcined flints, &c.; while on the higher ground are the workings in the beds of native clays of the coal formation, used in the manufacture.

Amongst the more recent developments of the manufacture are the "natural surface" tiles, in which the surface is moulded from casts or electrotypes of rock cleavages, fossils, grain of wood, leaves of plants, &c. &c., the effect being brought out by covering the surfaces with transparent enamels. "Encaustic mosaic" tiles, in which the more costly descriptions of mosaic are imitated in every variety of colour and elaboration of design, and having actual cement joints, are almost undistinguishable from the mosaics of actual tesseræ which they also produce; "patent intaglio white tiles," produced at a price almost as low as the ordinary dairy tile, on which, in place of the usual monotonous flat surface, an endless variety of beautiful forms, in low relief, covered with the ordinary colourless glaze, are produced.

Broseley.

The *Broseley Tileries*, at Broseley, are said to be the oldest brick and tile works in the district, and produce encaustic and geometrical glazed and unglazed tiles; and ridge, roofing, and pavement tiles, sanitary pipes, &c.

Benthall Potteries.—These works, carried on by the "Benthall Pottery Company," produce the ordinary yellow and other common wares.

Coalmoor.

At Coalmoor, near Horsehay, a pottery of common coarse ware formerly existed. The hovels are still standing, but converted to other purposes.

CHAPTER X.

One of the names most intimately connected with the early history of the porcelain manufactures of this kingdom is that of William Cookworthy, to whom that art is indebted for the discovery of the two most important of its ingredients, the native kaolin and the petunse, and to whose successful experiments and labours its excellence was and is in a great measure to be attributed. At the time when he first made his experiments—although Dwight had patented his invention for making transparent porcelain, although Van Hamme and others had also secured their rights for similar purposes, although Chelsea and other places made their china (it is said) of Chinese materials, and although many experiments had been made on the nature and properties of the earths supposed to be employed for its manufacture—the art of china-making from *native* materials was unknown; and Cookworthy pursued his course of study unaided by the experience of others, and, though beset with difficulties at every turn, brought it to a perfectly successful and satisfactory issue. The history of these experiments, and the life of this man, are the *history* of the Plymouth works. The one is inseparable from the other. The history of the works is the story of the life of Cookworthy, and the story of that life is the origin, the success, and the close of those works. The narrative of William Cookworthy, then, must be the thread of my present history.

William Cookworthy was born at Kingsbridge, not many miles from Plymouth, on the 12th of April, 1705, his parents being William and Edith Cookworthy, who were Quakers. His father was a weaver, and died, leaving his family but ill provided for, in 1718. Thus young Cookworthy, at the age of thirteen, and with six younger brothers and sisters—for he was the eldest of the family of seven—was left fatherless. His mother entered upon her heavy task of providing for and maintaining her large family with true courage, and appears to have succeeded in working out a good position for them all. She betook herself to dressmaking, and as her little daughters grew old enough to handle the needle, they were taught to aid her, and thus she maintained them in comparative comfort. In the following spring, at the age of fourteen, young Cookworthy was apprenticed to a chemist in London, named Bevans; but his mother's means being too scanty to admit of his being sent to the metropolis in any other way, he was compelled to walk there on foot. This task, no light one at any time for a boy of fourteen, he successfully accomplished.

His apprenticeship he appears to have passed with extreme credit, and on its termination returned into Devonshire, not only with the good opinion, but with the co-operation of his late master, and commenced business in Nutt Street, Plymouth, as wholesale chemist and druggist, under the name of Bevans and Cookworthy. Here he gradually worked his way forward, and became one of the little knot of intelligent men who in those days met regularly together at each other's houses, of whom Cookworthy, Dr. Huxham, Dr. Mudge, and the elder Northcote were among the most celebrated. Here he brought his mother to live under his roof, and she became, by her excellent and charitable character, a general favourite among the leading people of the place, and was looked up to with great respect by the lower classes whom she benefited. In 1735 Cookworthy married a young Quaker lady of Somersetshire, named Berry. This lady, to whom he seems to have been most deeply attached, lived only ten years after their marriage, and left him with five little daughters; and Cookworthy remained a widower for the remaining thirty-five years of his life.

In 1745 his attention seems first to have been seriously directed to experimenting in the manufacture of porcelain—at all events, in this year the first allusion to the matter which is made in his papers occurs in a letter to his friend, "Richard Hingston, Surgeon, in Penryn," dated May 5th, 1745. "I had lately with me the person who hath discovered the china-earth. He had several samples of the china-ware of their making with him, which were, I think, equal to the Asiatic. 'Twas found in the back of Virginia, where he was in quest of mines; and having read Du Halde, discovered both the petunse and kaulin. 'Tis the latter earth, he says, is the essential thing towards the success of the manufacture. He is gone for a cargo of it, having bought the whole country of the Indians where it rises. They can import it for £13 per ton, and by that means afford their china as cheap as common stone ware. But they intend only to go about 30 per cent. under the company. The man is a Quaker by profession, but seems to be as thorough a Deist as I ever met with. He knows a good deal of mineral affairs, but not *funditùs*. I have at last hearkened to thy advice, and begun to commit to black and white what I know in chemistry—I mean so far as I have not been obliged to other folks. Having finished my observations on furnaces, I intend to continue it as I have leisure, as it may be of use after my death."

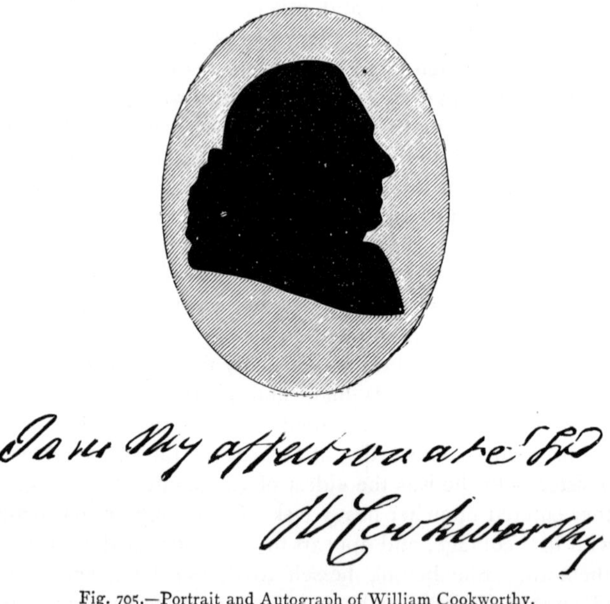

Fig. 705.—Portrait and Autograph of William Cookworthy.

At this time the business was still carried on under the style of "Bevans and Cookworthy." The death of his wife, which took place within a few months of the writing of this letter, entirely took away his attention from business, and his researches into china clays were thrown aside. He retired into seclusion at Looe, in Cornwall, where he remained for several months, and, on his return to business, took his brother Philip, who, it appears, had lately returned from abroad, into partnership, and carried it on, with him, under the style of "William Cookworthy & Co." This arrangement enabled Cookworthy to devote his time to the scientific part of the business, and to the prosecution of his researches, while his brother took the commercial management of the concern. Left thus more to the bent of his scientific inclinations, he pursued his inquiries relative to the manufacture of porcelain, and lost no opportunity of searching into and experimenting upon the properties of the different natural productions of Cornwall; and it is related of him that, in his journeys into that county, he has passed many nights sitting up with the managers of mines, obtaining information on matters connected with mines and their products. In the course of these visits he first became acquainted with the supposed wonderful properties of the "Divining Rod," or "Dowsing Rod," as it was called by the Cornish miners, in the discovery of ore of various kinds. His journeys into Cornwall, however, were productive of much more important results than the fabulous properties of the divining rod, for it was in these journeys that he succeeded in discovering, after much anxious inquiry and research, the materials for the manufacture of genuine porcelain. The information given him by the "Quaker" in 1745 had never been lost sight of, and he prosecuted inquiries wherever he went. After many searchings and experiments, he at length discovered the two materials, first in Tregonnin Hill, in Germo parish; next in the parish of St. Stephen's; and again at Boconnoc, the family seat of Thomas Pitt, Lord Camelford. There is a kind of traditionary belief that he first found the stone he was anxious to discover in the tower of St. Columb Church, which is built of stone from St. Stephen's, and which thus led him to the spot where it was to be procured. This discovery would probably be about 1754 or 1755, and he appears to have determined at once to carry out his intention of making porcelain, and to secure the material to himself. To this end he went to London to see the proprietors of the land, and to arrange for the royalty of the materials. In this he succeeded; and ultimately Lord Camelford joined him in the manufacture of china, and, as appears from a letter of that nobleman to Polwhele, the historian of Cornwall, the two expended about three thousand pounds in prosecuting the work.

The experiments on the Cornish materials having been perfectly successful, Cookworthy, who wrote a full and most interesting and valuable account of these and other properties (which I gave *in extenso* in the first edition), established himself as a china manufacturer at Plymouth. The works were at Coxside, at the extreme angle which juts into the water at Sutton Pool. Some parts of the buildings still exist, and are used as a shipwright's yard. They are still known by the name of the "China House," and it is really pleasant to find that a memory of these once celebrated works is yet retained on the spot where they were carried on. In these works Cookworthy prosecuted his new art with great success, and was soon enabled to enter the market with English-made hard-paste china, composed of native materials alone. The early examples are, as is natural to expect, very coarse, rough, and inferior, but they evidence, nevertheless, considerable skill in mixing, though not so much, perhaps, in firing. And they are also remarkable for their clumsiness, as well as for their bad colour, their uneven glazing, and their being almost invariably disfigured by fire cracks—if nowhere else, almost invariably at the bottom. On many of the pieces the colour (blue) on which the pattern was drawn, has "run" in the glazing, and thus disfigured the pieces. As examples of the early make of Plymouth, an inkstand belonging to Mrs. Lydia Prideaux, of Plymouth, is an excellent specimen. It was for many years the office inkstand of her father, who died in 1796, and was got by him from the son of a workman in the china factory. It is very clumsy in make, of coarse body, rough in the glaze, uneven in colour, and is, perhaps, one of the best and most characteristic existing specimens of the *early* make of Plymouth. It is circular, nearly five and a half inches in diameter; around

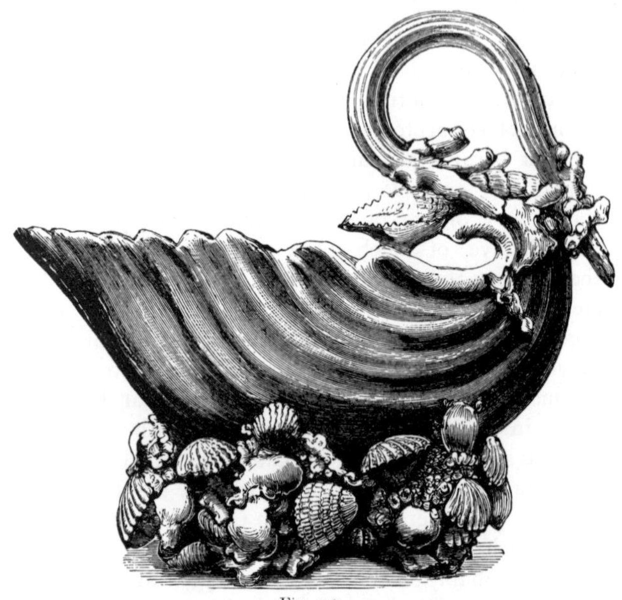

Fig. 706.

the top is a border in blue, and round the hollowed sides are octagonal spaces with Chinese figures and landscapes, connected together by a diapered band, all in blue. The inkstand bears the usual Plymouth mark on the bottom, in blue. Another early example worthy of note is a pounce-pot, formerly in the possession of the late

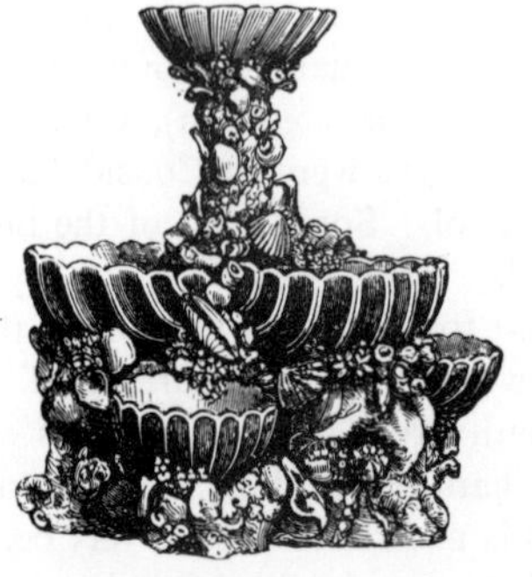

Fig. 707.

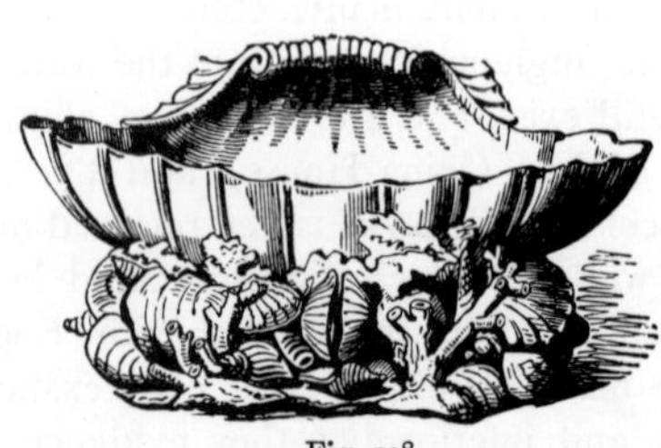

Fig. 708.

Mr. James, of Bristol. It is coarse in texture, rough on the surface, imperfect in the glaze, is painted with flowers in blue, and has the mark, also in blue, on the bottom.

As on the earliest productions of all the old china works, the decorations on the Plymouth examples are invariably blue; the blue at first being of a heavy, dull, blackish shade, but gradually improving, until, on some specimens which I have seen, it had attained a clear brilliance. Cookworthy, being a good chemist, paid considerable attention to the producing of a good blue, and was the first who succeeded in this country in manufacturing cobalt blue direct from the ore. Before this time the colour was prepared by grinding foreign imported zaffres with slab and muller; but after a series of experiments he succeeded in producing a fine and excellent blue from the cobalt ore, and prepared it by a better process. It is said that Cookworthy himself painted some of the earlier blue and white productions of his manufactory, and this is not at all improbable. Examples of the finer and more advanced class of blue and white are, like the earlier and more primitive attempts, scarce.

The white porcelain of Plymouth is one of its notable features, for in it some remarkably fine works exist in different collections. These mostly consist of salt-cellars, pickle-cups, and toilet-pieces, formed of shells and corals, beautifully, indeed exquisitely, modelled from nature. The shells and corals, and other marine objects which compose these pieces, are remarkably true to nature, and their arrangement in groups is very artistic and good. As a rule these pieces are not marked. Some of the forms of these shell groups are shown in the accompanying engravings. The accidental arrangement of the small shells, sea-weeds, and coral, are very characteristic of Plymouth manufacture, and evince a high degree of artistic excellence. The salt-cellars of this description, in the Museum of Practical Geology, are good examples, and useful for reference. In white, too, Cookworthy produced figures, birds, and animals, both singly and in groups, which bore no mark. Amongst the most successful and important productions of the Plymouth works, in white, are busts, of which one or two excellent examples are in existence. The finest of these, a large bust of King George II., was in possession of the late Dr. Cookworthy, of Plymouth, the great-nephew of the founder of the works; it is exquisitely modelled, evidences a very advanced state of Art, and shows great skill, both in body and in firing. Its height is seventeen, and its extreme width thirteen, inches. Dr. Cookworthy also possessed some remarkably fine allegorical figures, groups for candlesticks, &c., all, although unmarked, said to be authenticated as Plymouth manufacture. An elephant said to be probably of Plymouth manufacture is in the Museum of Practical Geology, as are also Figs. 708 and 713.

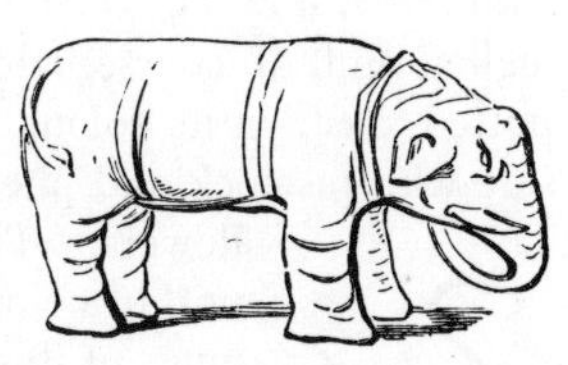

Fig. 709.

The prosecution of the new works having progressed satisfactorily, Cookworthy in 1768 took out a patent for the manufacture of "a kind of porcelain newly invented by me, composed of moor-stone or growan, and growan clay." The patent was dated the 17th of March, 1768, and contained the usual proviso that full specification should be lodged and enrolled within four months of that date. This specification, which was duly enrolled, I gave *in extenso* in my first edition.

It is natural to suppose that the finest and best goods of the Plymouth Works were produced in the six years which intervened between the enrolling of this specification and the removal of the Works to Bristol, previous to their sale to Champion. The progress of the manufactory had hitherto been great and satisfactory, but continuing at the same rate of improvement, the perfection to which the best productions arrived could only have been attained a very short time before its close.

Cookworthy determined to make his porcelain equal to that of Sèvres and Dresden, both in body, which he himself mixed, and in ornamentation, for which he procured the services of such artists as were available. To this end he engaged a Mons. Saqui, or Soqui, from Sèvres, who was a man of rare talent as a painter and enameller, and to whose hands, and those of Henry Bone, a native of Plymouth, who there is reason to suppose was apprenticed to Cookworthy, and afterwards became very celebrated, the best painted specimens may be ascribed. Besides these, several other artists were employed, but they were principally engaged in painting in blue, while Saqui and Bone painted the high-class birds and flowers. In a town like Plymouth, where Art has always found a home, and whose sons have so greatly distinguished themselves, it is not to be wondered that the paintings and decorations on china should assume a high character for design and treatment. In a neighbourhood which has the honour of having given birth to Sir Joshua Reynolds, to James Northcote, to Haydon, to Sir Charles Eastlake, to Opie, to William Cooke, and to a score others, it would be strange indeed if the Art part of the manufacture had not been prominently good, and had not produced artists, like Henry Bone, of more than local excellence.

The ware made at Plymouth consisted of dinner services, tea and coffee services, mugs and jugs, vases, trinket and toilet stands, busts, single figures and groups, animals, "Madonnas," and other figures after foreign models, candlesticks with birds, flowers, &c. The quart mug (Fig. 712) is an excellent example of the higher, and, of course, later, productions of Cookworthy's manufactory. It is well potted, clear in its colour and glaze, and exquisitely painted by Saqui on the one side with peacock and pheasant and landscapes, and on the other with a group of flowers. The peculiarity is, that it is marked with the usual sign, not in colour, but *incised* before glazing. (Fig. 710). Some good mugs of this form and style were shown in Phillips's case, illustrating the raw material and productions of the clay district, at the Exhibition of 1851; they were marked in red, and belonged to Mr. Pridham, of Plymouth. That Cookworthy endeavoured to procure good artists is evident by the following advertisement in 1770:—"China painters wanted, for the Plymouth new invented Patent Porcelain Manufactory.—A number of sober, ingenious artists, capable of painting in enamel or blue may hear of constant employ by sending their proposals to Thomas Frank, in Castle Street, Bristol."

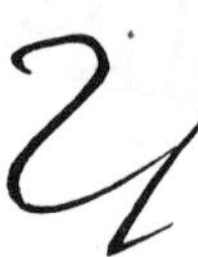

Fig. 710.

Among the busts and statuettes are an admirable bust of George II., after the statue by Ruysbranch, in Queen's Square, Bristol; Woodward, the actor; Mrs. Clive; a shepherd; and shepherdess, &c., which show that excellent modellers must have been employed.

Among the finest and evidently latest productions of the Plymouth Works, is a pair of splendid vases and covers, sixteen inches high, in the possession of Mr. Francis Fry, of Bristol. One of these (Fig. 714) is hexagonal, and enriched with festoons of beautifully-modelled raised flowers, and painted butterflies, leaves, and borders. These vases are of precisely the same general form as some unique examples of Bristol make, of which I shall speak under the heading of those works; and though they differ in ornament and detail, are evidently the production of the same artists. In Lord Mount Edgcumbe's possession, too, is a pair of vases of very similar character (but more nearly resembling Mr. Fry's specimens of Bristol), on which the Plymouth mark has at a later period, been added. In the Museum of Practical Geology are a pair of shell-salts (Fig. 708); a pair of figures, "Europe" and "Asia," and some other figures; some remarkably good mugs, jugs, and

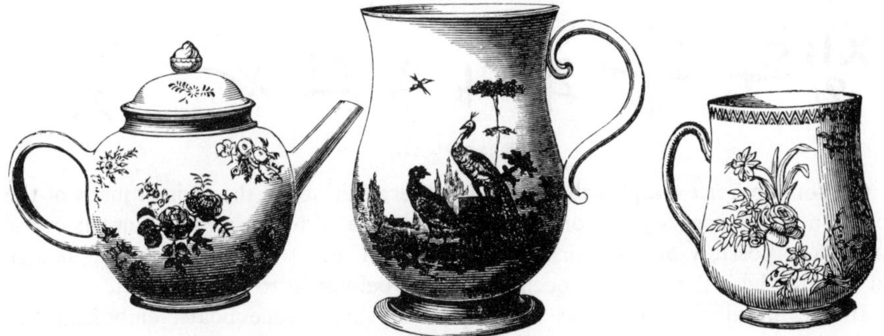

Figs. 711 to 713.—Plymouth Teapot and Mugs.

sauce boats; one or two cups and saucers; and other pieces, including two plates (Fig. 715), described as "in earthenware, with thick white enamel, painted," the one with flowers, and the other "in green, with flowers on the border and crest of the Parker family in the centre. Unmarked."

The mark of the Plymouth china is usually painted in red or blue on the bottom of the pieces. No mark has yet, however, come under my notice on the white examples. On the early blue and white the mark appears invariably to be in blue, and somewhat thick and clumsy in its drawing. On the later and more advanced goods it is more neatly drawn in red or blue. It varies a little in form, according to the different "hand" by which it was affixed. The mark is the chemical sign for tin or mercury, ♃, and was doubtless chosen by Cookworthy, the

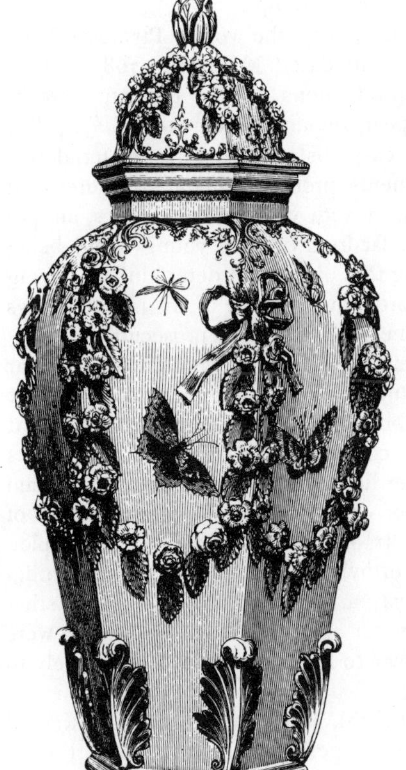

Fig. 714.

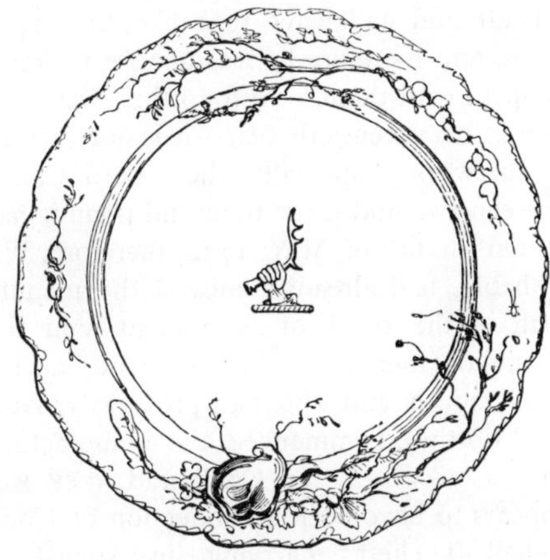

Fig. 715.

chemist, to denote that the materials from which it was made, and which he had discovered, were procured from the stanniferous district of Cornwall. The following are varieties of the mark selected from different specimens:—

Figs. 716 to 724.

On some other examples the sign with the addition of the Bristol mark of the cross beneath it occurs; and on others a number, as if to denote the number of the pattern (or possibly of the workman), occurs. These two marks, the simple sign and the sign with the number, occur on pieces belonging to the same set.

In Mr. Skardon's possession was a pair of small sauce boats, embossed and painted with birds and flowers in colours; they each bear the name, painted on the bottom, as here shown. In Dr. Ashford's possession is an example bearing a very similar mark, but in writing letters; and another curious example, formerly in the possession of Mr. C. W. Reynolds, bears the word "Plymouth," the arms of the borough, some illegible letters, and the date "March 14 1768 C F."

M^{r}
Wm Cookworthy's
Factory Plym^{o}
1770

M^{r}
W. Cookworthy's
Factory Plymouth
1770

However beautiful and satisfactory the productions of the Plymouth works might be as *china*, they were not, it would appear, remunerative *commercially*. The clay and the stone Cookworthy had within easy distance, but his material was difficult and expensive to make, his experiments produced frequent failures and losses, and therefore he was unable to keep pace with other manufactories, and to compete with them. Add to this that he was far from being a young man—being then in his seventieth year—it is not surprising that he should determine on giving up the works, especially when Lord Camelford, who was one of his partners, says between two and three thousand pounds had been sunk in their prosecution.

On the 6th of May, 1774, therefore, William Cookworthy (who, it would appear probable, had already removed the manufacture to Bristol), for considerations set forth in the deed of assignment, sold the business and patent-right to Richard Champion, merchant, of Bristol, who had been connected pecuniarily with the works at Plymouth, and who had previously, "under license from the patentee" (William Cookworthy), commenced the manufacture of china in Bristol, under the style of "W. Cookworthy & Co.," and they were transferred to that city. Champion appears to have been a connection of Cookworthy's—a cousin of the latter, Phillip Debell Tuckett, marrying, in August, 1774, a sister of the former (Esther Champion), about the time when the affairs for the transfer of the works were finally completed; and the arrangements appear to have been completed entirely to Cookworthy's satisfaction.

The works having been transferred to Bristol, were carried on by Richard Champion, who having incurred considerable expense without a proportionate return, petitioned in the same year for a further term of fourteen years patent-right to be extended to him, which was accordingly done by Act of Parliament passed in the session which commenced the 29th of November in the same year (1774). This Act and others will be found noticed in my account of the Bristol china works.

Thus ended, after the brief period of nineteen or twenty years from the first discovery of the material to its close, the manufacture of porcelain in Plymouth—a manufacture which was an honour to the locality, a credit to all concerned in it, and which has given it, and Cookworthy its founder, an imperishable name in the ceramic annals of this country.

Having passed through the history of the works, so far as space will allow, it only remains to turn back for a few minutes to the thread of the life of Cookworthy with which I started, and to follow it, so far as may be necessary, to its close.

During the time he was engaged on the manufacture of china-ware, his ever-active mind seems to have been busied with other things as well, and he appears to have been sought, and much esteemed, by the *savans* of the day. Smeaton, the builder of the Eddystone Lighthouse, was an inmate of his house while the lighthouse was in progress, and they were constant companions in examining the dovetailed blocks of stone as they were prepared on the Hoe for shipping; Wolcot—"Peter Pindar"—was a frequent visitor for days together at his house; Sir Joseph Banks, Captain Cook, and Dr. Solander, were his guests just before the famous "Voyage Round the World" and on their return, when their *protégé*, Omai the Otaheitan, was also his guest; Earl St. Vincent, then Captain Jervis, was his attached friend, and he was looked up to by all as a man of such large understanding, such varied and extensive knowledge, and such powers of intellectual conversation, that, as Lord St. Vincent is said often to have remarked, "whoever was in Mr. Cookworthy's company was always wiser and better for having been in it." He carried on considerable experiments to discover a method by which sea-water might be distilled for use on board ship. He was a disciple of Swedenborg, some of whose works he translated, and was also an accomplished astronomer, and an ardent disciple of "good old Izaac Walton." As a preacher among the Society of Friends he seems to have been most highly esteemed by the whole of that body. In 1780, Cookworthy, then seventy-five, died in the same house in Nutt Street, Plymouth, which he had occupied from the time of his first starting in life, and a touching "testimony" to his character was given by the "monthly meeting." He was interred with every mark of respect at Plymouth.

Plymouth Earthenware.—The manufacture of china-ware having ceased in Plymouth in 1774 this useful and elegant art was lost to the town. Some years later rough common brown and yellow earthenware was made here. In addition to these, manufactories of fine "Queen's Ware," and painted, printed, and enamelled ware, were established in 1810. In 1815 there were three separate manufactories in Plymouth. The proprietors of these various potteries were Mr. Fillis, Mr. Algar, and Mr. Hellyer, the latter of which being continued.

Plymouth Pottery Company.—Mr. William Alsop (who made coarse ware near the Gas Works) built a manufactory for fine earthenware of the ordinary commoner quality, but afterwards removed to Swansea, his works passing into the hands of Messrs. Bryant, Burnell, and James. Subsequently Mr. Alsop returned from Swansea and formed a Limited Liability Company for the carrying on of this concern, and produced large quantities of the common classes of pottery and printed goods. On the death of Mr. Alsop a Mr. Bishop, from the Staffordshire pottery district, took the management of the works, but the manufacture gradually died out, and about 1863 the plant was sold off and the place disposed of to the Gas Company.

The mark used by this company was the Queen's Arms, with the words "P.P. COY. L. (Plymouth Pottery Company Limited.) Stone China." The quality of the ware was of the commonest description of white earthenware, blue printed in various patterns.

Watcombe.

Watcombe Pottery.—The works at Watcombe, St. Mary Church, about two miles from Torquay, in Devonshire, established in 1869, owe their origin to the discovery, a few years ago, by G. T. Allen, Esq., of Watcombe House, of a bed of the finest plastic clay, of considerable extent and depth. This discovery was made while excavating behind his residence, and Mr. Allen, who is a gentleman of great learning and of refined taste, took immediate steps to have its qualities for ceramic purposes tested. A company was immediately afterwards formed for the getting and sale of the terra-cotta clay to various potters; but, after experiments had been made, and its unique beauty, when worked, discovered, it was wisely resolved to erect a pottery on the spot, and to convert the clay immediately from the pits into Art-manufactures and architectural enrichments. Shortly afterwards, the company were fortunate enough to secure the services of Mr. Charles Brock, of Hanley, in Staffordshire—a gentleman of the most enlightened taste, and of the most extensive practical knowledge—to become the manager and Art-director of the concern. Mr. Brock at once turned his attention to the development of the resources of the clay thus fortunately discovered; and having brought together a number of skilled workmen and work-women from the Staffordshire potteries, and procured the best possible models and modellers, soon produced Art-works which are quite unequalled in this country, in works of this character and material. At the present time about one hundred persons are employed at the Watcombe works, and there can be but little doubt that, as they are yet quite in their infancy, that number will be considerably increased as their resources become more developed. The Watcombe clay is remarkably fine, clean, and pure; and is eminently adapted for most decorative purposes. Many of the borders and pressed ornaments have almost the sharpness, as they have quite the general effect, of those made of jasper body; indeed, many of the productions bear a very strong and marked general resemblance, in appearance, to those of jasper ware; and they are superior in many respects to the much-vaunted terra cotta of France and Germany.

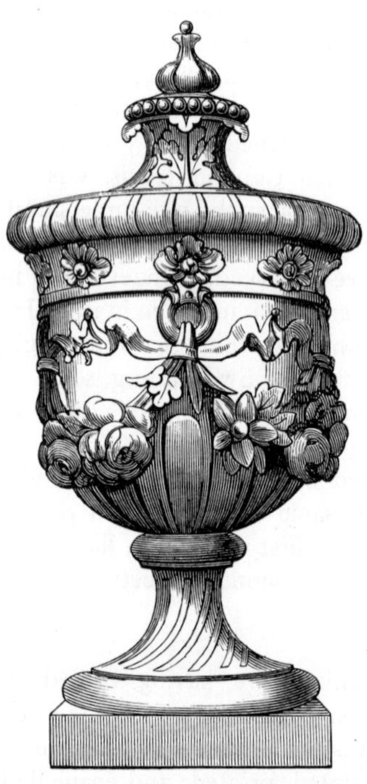

Fig. 725.

The Art-productions of the Watcombe pottery are extremely varied, and show how capable this local clay is of being turned to good account in a variety of ways. Among the more notable productions are statuettes and busts, for which the clay is peculiarly suitable. Of these, the figure of "The Disc Thrower" is one of the most successful, and among other statuettes is a sweetly pretty figure of a barefooted country girl. In some a charming effect is produced by leaving the figure itself of the natural red of the body, and introducing a lighter tinted clay for the drapery in which they are partly enveloped; this, again, being lighted up and relieved here and there with a slight touch of colour. Among the busts are a pair of Byron and Scott—two of the most popular subjects that could be produced—and of full life-size, being about two feet six inches in height, and two feet in width. In modelling, these busts are among the most easy, graceful, and life-like we have ever seen, either in marble, in parian, or in any other material, while as productions in warm-tinted terra-cotta they surpass anything yet produced. They are not only life-like portraits of these two great and widely-different types of men, as regards features and figure and pose, but they convey an actual reflex of the mind of each in the expression which the modeller has caught and perpetuated. The vases, which are made in endless variety, are characterized by extreme chasteness and elegance of outline, and by excellent taste in decoration, whether that decoration consists in festoons of handsome modelled flowers, in pressed work, in milling, in printing, or in painting. Many of them in form and in ornamentation, although of so different a body, bear comparison with the better specimens of Wedgewood-ware, and exhibit a purity of taste which is quite refreshing. For tea or déjeuné services, the insides of the tea-pots and cream-ewers are simply but judiciously glazed; while the cups are, as in some old oriental examples, lined with celeste, which colour is also occasionally introduced, with good taste, on the handles and mouldings. Brackets of charming design, candlesticks, jugs, medalions, tobacco-jars, spill-cases, flower-stands—and, indeed, all the articles produced—bear the same stamp of care and elegance. The turning is done with admirable precision; the moulding with a refreshing delicacy of finish; and the gilding and enamelling—only sparsely introduced, by the way, and then only as an accessory to the general design—executed with a pure taste and by a master mind. Besides these, it is necessary to mention that architectural decorations and enrichments, statues, garden and flower-vases, pedestals, and garden edgings, besides other articles, are made; the commoner strata of clay being remarkably well adapted, from its hardness and durability, for these purposes. Of the more recent departures in art matters are some that are especially noteworthy. These are vases, water-bottles, and other elegant articles formed of buff or other delicately tinted clay, and coated on the surface with a thin covering of other coloured clay. On these the pattern or design is literally carved, the outline being traced through the coating of darker clay, and the surface then entirely cut away down to the lighter body beneath. The pattern is thus left in more or less relief, of a darker tint than the body itself, upon which it appears. The effect of this process, which is entirely done by hand and the work of skilled artists, is charming in the extreme. Another high class of productions is the introduction of painting, in exquisite groups of flowers buds, &c., upon glazed vases of elegant form and of different coloured clays, the painting of which evinces a purity of taste and a delicacy and softness of finish that is

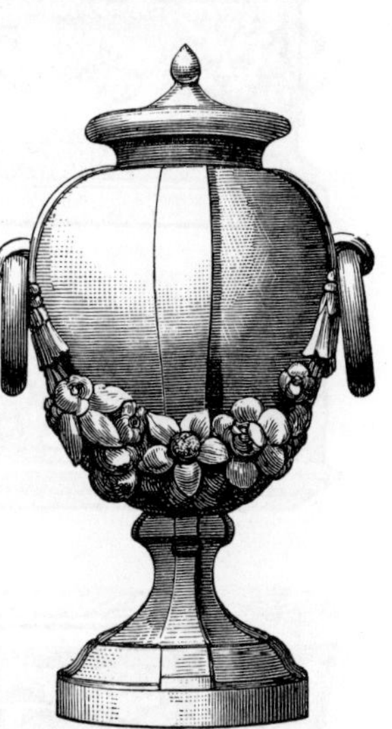

Fig. 726.

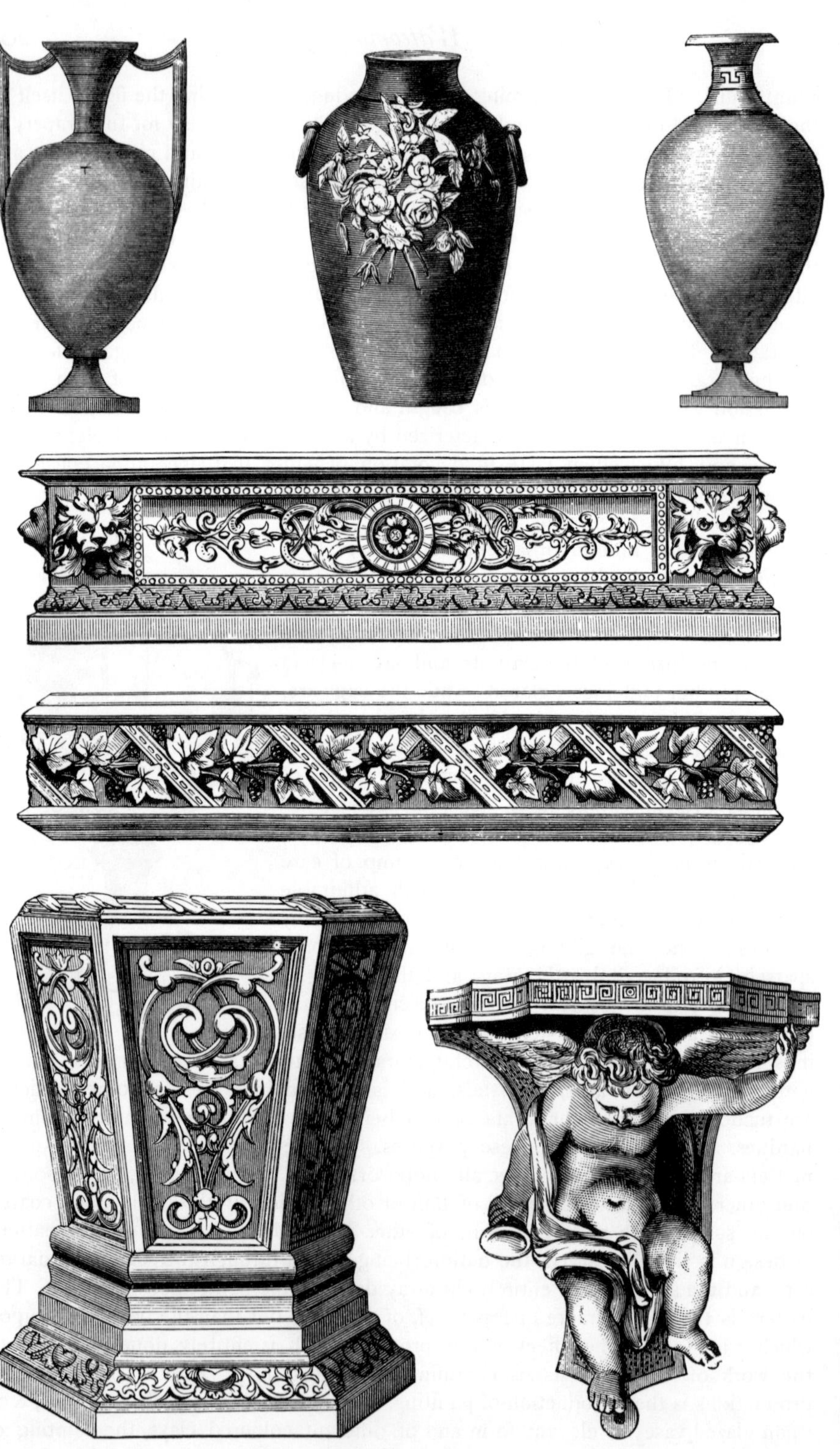

Figs. 527 to 733.—Watcombe Terra Cotta.

eminently refreshing. The introduction of enamel decoration upon the unglazed surface of others has also been accomplished with perfect success. Our engravings convey but a very poor idea of the beauty and elegance of form of the vases, &c., here produced; the purest taste characterizes the various articles. The works are carried on by a company, under the style of "The Watcombe Terra Cotta Clay Company," consisting of seven proprietors. They are situate about two miles from Torquay, on the Teignmouth Road, near to the picturesque rocks and downs of Watcombe. Large show-rooms have been erected, and everything done to make the Watcombe works attractive and useful. The marks used by the company are simply impressed in the body of the ware, or printed on its surface. The usual mark is simply the words "Watcombe, Torquay," or "Watcombe;" but another, and very picturesque mark has also been adopted—it is a woodpecker on a branch of a tree, with a distant landscape and ship on the sea, within a garter, on which are the words, WATCOMBE TORQUAY.

WATCOMBE,
TORQUAY.

Honiton.

A manufactory of common brown and red ware for ordinary domestic use—the common "cloam" of the country—existed here in the early part of the present century.

Exeter.

In *Felix Farley's Bristol Journal* of December 29th, 1764, is the following:—"We hear that a few gentlemen of fortune have undertaken to set up a new manufactory of china at Exeter." Probably rumour was all, for as yet I have found nothing to lead to the inference that the works were ever established.

Bovey Tracey.

The great source of Devonshire clay used in most of the potteries of the kingdom is the district near the estuary of the river Teign. This clay is known by various names—"Black clay," "Ball clay," "Devonshire clay," "Kingsteignton clay," or "Potter's clay:" and is sent off in immense quantities to the various seats of earthenware manufacture. Yet in the whole of this district where the clay is raised, and one would expect to find earthenware extensively made, only one pottery exists, and that one not on a large scale. Coal, which is such an important item in the manufacture of earthenware, is wanting in the district; and it is found more economical and advantageous to take the clay to the coal, than to bring the coal to the clay. Although no true coal is found in this district (that is, coal of the Carboniferous formation), a lignite is found on Bovey Heathfield. The beds of this lignite crop out in a line running east and west for about the length of half a mile in the vicinity of the present Bovey Tracey Pottery Works. In the middle of the last century these beds had been but little worked, and lignite could easily be obtained by open pits. In consequence of the sandy and soft nature of the beds which alternate with the lignite, it has been found impossible to work underground on the plan adopted in ordinary coal-mines. The raising of Bovey lignite has, therefore, been almost given up—all the coal near the surface having been worked out. The existence of a cheap fuel in the proximity of the potters' clay no doubt led to the establishment of potteries at Bovey Tracey. This lignite is a light bituminous coal which occurs in the Miocene formation, being the same geological formation in which the potter's clay is found. This lignite is highly gaseous, but only possesses about a third of the heat-giving power of average English coal. It is the same as the Norwegian "Surturbrand," and emits a disagreeable odour in burning. Large pieces of fir-trees are occasionally found perfect in it.

Indiho Pottery.—About 1772 a pottery was established at Indiho, or Indio, or Indeo, in the parish of Bovey Tracey, and continued to be worked until 1841, when it was superseded by the Bovey Pottery, which had been established a few years previously to that time. The Indiho Pottery was a small manufactory, and is supposed to have been commenced by one George Tufnell, and was afterwards in the hands of proprietors of the names of Inglett and Steer. About the beginning of the present century a really good earthenware was made at Indio; the printed ware was of a superior class, and some tea and coffee cups of a brown body with an interior enamelled with white slip and painted outside with small sprigs are characteristic and pretty.

Bovey Pottery.—The first pottery at Bovey Tracey was not on the site of the present pottery known under this name, but was carried on in some houses, which are parish property, near the modern railway station. The house is at present a carpenter's shop, and is at a corner just where the road turns off to the Bovey Heathfield. Tradition states that this pottery had mills to grind materials close to Bovey Bridge, and the remains of a mill and water-wheel existed on the left bank of the stream up to 1844. These works were carried on by a family of the name of Ellis; they were probably commenced in the earlier half of the eighteenth century and certainly were in work in 1755, and lasted for thirty years after that period. Nothing certain is known of the character of the ware of this first attempt at Bovey Tracey. Clay pipes are said to have been made, and jugs of a yellow body which are attributed to this period are to be found in houses in the neighbourhood.

In 1842 the Bovey Pottery was purchased by two Devonshire gentlemen, Captain Buller and Mr. J. Divett, who enlarged the works, and obtained the lignite from underground workings. The supply of this substance, however, proving insufficient for the increased requirements of the manufacture, ordinary coal was substituted in its stead; and, after the opening of a railway to the works, Somersetshire coal has been used to the entire exclusion of the lignite. The works are still carried on by Messrs. Buller and Divett, under the style of the "Bovey Tracey Pottery Company." In general character they are similar to those of the pottery district, and on the average five glost-ovens are fired each week. The quality of the ware is about equal to the ordinary and commoner classes of Staffordshire goods. It consists of all the ordinary services and articles in white, printed, and coloured wares, and is principally supplied to the home markets in the West of England, and to Mediterranean ports.

The Folly Pottery.—Another pottery in Bovey Tracey parish was the "Folly Pottery." This pottery may be looked upon as the origin of the present Bovey Tracey Pottery. No doubt the site was chosen for its proximity to the main outcrop of the lignite. Considerable uncertainty exists as to the date of this manufacture. It was probably commenced in the last years of the eighteenth or the first years of the nineteenth century by a man of the name of Mead. It was then for a considerable period contemporaneous with the Indio Pottery. The earthenware, however, seems hardly, at any time, to have equalled in quality that of the last-named pottery. In 1835 the works were carried on by Messrs. John and Thomas Honeychurch. It is thus described in an advertisement of sale :—"To be sold by public auction, as directed by the assignees of John and Thomas Honeychurch, bankrupts, at the Union Inn, Bovey Tracey, on the 2nd May, 1836, the Folly Pottery, situate in the parish of Bovey Tracey, in the county of Devon. This may be designated one of the largest and most complete potteries in the West of England, 14 miles from Exeter and 28 from Plymouth ; its situation being in the land of clay, from which nearly all the potteries in Staffordshire draw their supply, with coal-mine and railroad, &c." The advertisement, after giving particulars regarding the processes, &c., speaks of a glost-kiln, and a biscuit-kiln, capable of containing 1,600 saggers of ware ; flint kilns ; a quantity of Cornish clay and flints, copper-plates, moulds, &c. No purchaser was found until 1842, when the concern was bought by Captain Buller and Mr. J. Divett, and converted into the "Bovey Tracey Pottery Company," as last described.

BIDEFORD.

Pot works appear to have existed at Bideford ever since the fourteenth century, but nothing beyond the ordinary coarse earthenware has been produced. Nothing

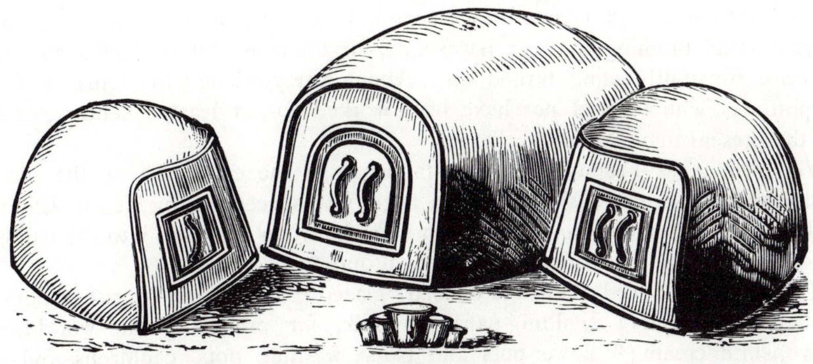

Fig. 734.—Earthenware Ovens.

is known as to the early history of these works, but fragments of ware of mediæval character have not unfrequently been dug up. An interesting relic, a chimney-pot, is in the possession of Mr. Crocker. It is of square form, and bears the name "Bideford," and the date "1668."

The Bideford Old Pottery, belonging to Mr. W. H. Crocker, has been in the possession of himself and his ancestors for more than a century, but of late years its productions, under the present proprietor, have received a marked improvement. The works were almost entirely rebuilt, and much extended, in 1870.

Ornamental goods are to some extent made, and consist of garden vases, edgings, jugs, and other articles. Flower-pots, sea-kale and rhubarb pots, chimney tops, &c., are also largely made.

The great speciality, however, of the productions are the fire-clay ovens, which are made in considerable numbers and of various sizes. They are of peculiar shape, and so constructed as to retain the heat for a considerable time. Their form may be said, in some measure, to approximate to the old *couvre-feu*, as will be seen by the engraving (Fig. 734). The bottom is flat, and the walls, which are of great strength and thickness, are arched, so that the heat is thrown upon the bread in every direction. In front is a loose fire-clay door made to fit with exactness; or, occasionally, a cast-iron door is fixed. These ovens are heated with gorse, or wood, and one bundle of either is said to be sufficient to thoroughly bake three pecks of dough. The ovens are, and for generations have been, in much repute in Devonshire and Cornwall, and in the Welsh districts, and the bread baked in them is said to have a sweeter and more wholesome flavour than when baked in ordinary ovens. They are ornamented in a primitive manner with impressed and incised lines, and the mark used is the proprietor's name.

W. H. CROCKER
BIDEFORD

North Devon Pottery.—This pottery was established in 1848 by a company formed for the purpose. The productions are confined to stone-ware pipes, and sanitary appliances of various kinds. The goods are made from the strong clay deposits of the northern side of Dartmoor—a clay of peculiar hardness and tenacity—and the articles are therefore what may be called "real vitrified stone ware," as distinguished from the pipes and sanitary goods made in other districts from fire-clay. The works are under the management of Mr. Henry Jones.

FREMINGTON.

The manufacture of coarse brown ware has evidently been carried on for many generations at Fremington, near Barnstaple, for fragments of mediæval and later wares are constantly being turned up. About fifty years ago the remains of five old potteries, which could not have been worked for, at least, a century, existed near the present manufactory.

The Pottery, at Fremington, was established in the early part of the present century by Mr. George Fishley, who, in 1839, was succeeded by his son Edmund Fishley, who continued it until his death in 1861, when it passed into the hands of his son, Mr. Edwin B. Fishley, the present proprietor.

The goods produced are of the ordinary glazed red ware, and consist principally of pitchers and jars; scalding-pans for milk, for producing the world-famed "Devonshire cream;" flower-pots and pans; washing pots, cauldrons, and ewe pans; baking dishes and bread pans; salting vessels and chimney pots, and many other articles. Some of the water pitchers bear the peculiar names of "Long Toms," "Thirty Tales," "Gullymouths," &c. Yellow-ware jugs and other domestic vessels are also made.

In ornamental wares some good designs in jars, beer jugs, and vases are produced. These are formed of a body of red clay, with figures and flowers in white clay. They are sometimes coloured, with good effect. The beer jugs, which are a speciality of the works, are generally white with drawings in red, of the same colour as the body.

The great speciality of the Fremington Pottery, like that of Bideford, is the manufacture of fire-clay ovens. These are made of various sizes for baking from one peck up to twelve. Their general form will be best understood from Fig. 734. The material of which they are composed is remarkably firm, hard, and compact, and retains the heat for a considerable time. These ovens, which are a peculiarity of the West of England and of some of the Welsh districts, are simply enclosed in raised brickwork, leaving the mouth open to the front. They are heated in the inside with wood or gorse, and are remarkable for the small quantity of fuel that is required—two pennyworth of wood being said to be amply sufficient to bake seven or eight shillings' worth of flour. The bread is stated to be of a peculiarly wholesome and sweet character. The mark used on the ovens, &c., is simply the proprietor's name impressed in the clay while moist. On the ornamental ware the name is written on the bottom of the ware.

E. B. FISHLEY,
FREMINGTON.

Aller.

The Aller Pottery, near Newton Abbot, was commenced for the manufacture of common brown ware in 1865, and three years later came into the hands of Messrs. John Phillips & Co., for the production of architectural pottery, consisting of tiles, sanitary and sewage ware, garden edgings, ornamental chimney pots, decorative bricks, flower vases, &c., the markets principally supplied being those of Devonshire, Somersetshire, and Cornwall. The mark is a horse's head, couped, with the Greek words ΦΙΛΕΩ ΙΠΠΟΝ, being a playful allusion to the name of the proprietor, "Phillips."

Pednandrea, Redruth.

Crucible Works.—These works at Pednandrea and at Fore Street, Redruth, were established about 1760 by John Juleff, and carried on by him until his decease, when he was succeeded by his son, John Juleff, by whom they were continued until 1875. In that year he died and the works passed into the hands of his two sons, "John and David Juleff," who are the only manufacturers of the original Cornish crucibles, and have the reputation of being the best for dry assaying and for standing intense heat. They are made to a large extent and sent to most parts of the world. The firm also make mufflers, scorifiers, special bricks and covers for assay furnaces, plumbago crucibles for tin assaying, plumbago brass melting pots, &c., of various shapes and sizes. Mr. Juleff received honourable mention for his goods at the 1861 Exhibition. The goods are usually marked with the name of the firm.

CHAPTER XI.

Bristol.

The first record of pot-making in Bristol appears to have been in the reign of Edward I., but it seems certain that vessels were made in the neighbourhood in Saxon and Norman times, as well as in the earlier Celtic and Romano-British periods. Mediæval earthenware vessels of different periods, and probably made in the locality, have now and then been found at Bristol, and during the reign of Elizabeth, there is no doubt, a manufactory of fictile vessels was in operation. "Six hundred years ago," says Mr. Owen, "the art of pottery was practised in Bristol, but in what form is beyond our speculation. The record, though authentic, is too terse to give more than the bare fact, and the imagination must be fertile indeed that can supply the details. The Governor of Bristol Castle under Edward I., in his accounts, preserved in the Pipe Roll for the twelfth year of that reign (1284), has an item—'*pro terra fodienda ad vasa fictilia facienda*'—which shows that this claim for high antiquity is well founded." Fragments of some curious pitchers and other mediæval domestic vessels are engraved by Mr. Owen, and appear to be of about the period alluded to.

The Delft Works.—At the close of the seventeenth century, Delft ware was made here, and continued to be produced until about the time when procelain began to be produced in this city. Many specimens of Bristol Deft ware have come under my notice, some of which are, fortunately, dated. The earliest dated example I have seen is a plate marked on the rim with the initials S · M · B, and the date 1703, thus—

B
S M.
1703

The ware is of a very nice quality, with a good glaze, and the blue of good colour. The next in chronological order, is a Delft high-heeled shoe, or choppine, dated on the sole thus—

M S
1722,

which is said to be of Bristol make and was in possession of the late Mr. James, of that city. Two of these Delft stands in the form of high-heeled shoes, marked M I 1705, formerly belonging to Queen Charlotte, were sold at the Bernal sale. Another example is a plate bearing on its rim

17 P 40.
R S

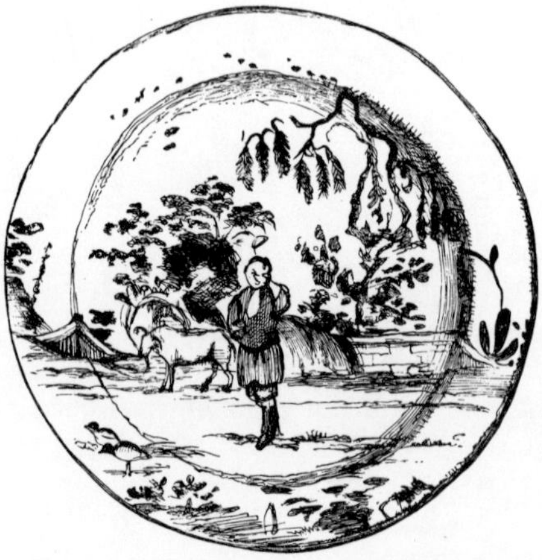

Fig. 735.—Edkins' Plate, belonging to Mr. Owen.

One of the latest dated examples is the plate Fig. 735, which formed part of a set belonging to a descendant of Edkins who painted it, and had remained in the family from the time of its manufacture until it came into my hands. It is a plate painted in a somewhat peculiar style, in blue, with a Chinese figure, trees, cattle, and birds, and having on its under side the date 1760, and the initials M · B · E, (Fig. 736) of Michael and Betty Edkins, of Bristol.

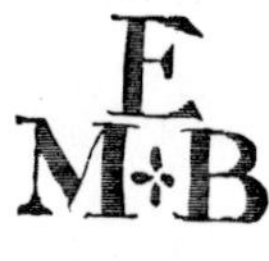

Fig. 736.

The Delft ware works were situated on "Redcliffe Backs," near Little and Longmans' glass works. The names of the first potters are not known, but in the early part of last century the works belonged to a Richard Frank, who employed, along with other workmen, a Thomas Patience, and a family of the name of Hope. Richard Frank, who had also works at Brislington, was the son of Thomas Frank, "gallipot maker," of Bristol, who was married in 1697; he, the "gallipot maker," is therefore the earliest recorded potter of this place. The goods produced at Richard Frank's manufactory—who, as well as his father, is described as a "gallipot maker" in 1734—9 and 1754—were principally plates, dishes, and "Dutch tiles" for fireplaces, dairies, &c. In the Museum of Practical Geology is a slab composed of twenty-four tiles, on which is painted in blue a view of St. Mary Redcliffe Church, Bristol. These were made by Richard Frank, about 1738—50, and the arms of Bishop Butler appear upon one of them. The tiles were all, of course, painted by hand, and we have it on the authority of Michael Edkins (painter of the plate, Fig. 735), that the brushes which he and the other workmen used were made by themselves from the hairs pulled from the nostrils and eyelids of cattle. Michael Edkins was, it appears, from Birmingham, where he was apprenticed to a house painter. His master dying before his term expired, he made his way to Bristol, where, becoming acquainted with Patience and Hope, he got employed at Frank's pottery, where he became a "pot painter," and continued in that employment till the Delft pottery declined, "when (in 1761) he became a coach and general painter and decorator, and quickly rose to eminence, was employed about most public works in the city, assisted in painting the bas-reliefs to the altar-piece of St. Mary Redcliffe, and also assisted Hogarth in fixing his celebrated pictures in that altar-piece." He was also a successful actor at the theatre. One branch of his business that he followed was "enamelling glass ware," which he did for Little and Longmans, and their successors, Vigor and Stevens, whose glass house adjoined the Delft pottery on Redcliffe Backs.

A plate bearing the words "Nugent only 1754," was in all probability made by Richard Frank, who was a supporter of Nugent at the general election of that year. Another plate, commemorating the same year's election for Tewkesbury, is supposed to be from the same works; it bears the words "Calvert and Martin For Tukesbury 1754 Sold by Webb." Among other dated examples of Bristol Delft are the following, which may be from Frank's pottery. A piece bearing the words "Ye 1st Septr 1761 Bowen · fecit;" a pair of plates made for a member of the family of Davis, with the

letters
D
T × H,
1716
and others with the following

H S × H 1751	U ✣ D 1760	ELIZABETH BARNESS 1738	IOHN SAUNDERS 1754

"Hannah Hopkins Born Sep 17 New Style 1752," occurs on a christening bowl in the Edkins collection.

A fine plate, painted by Bowen, engraved on Fig. 738, is in possession of Mr.

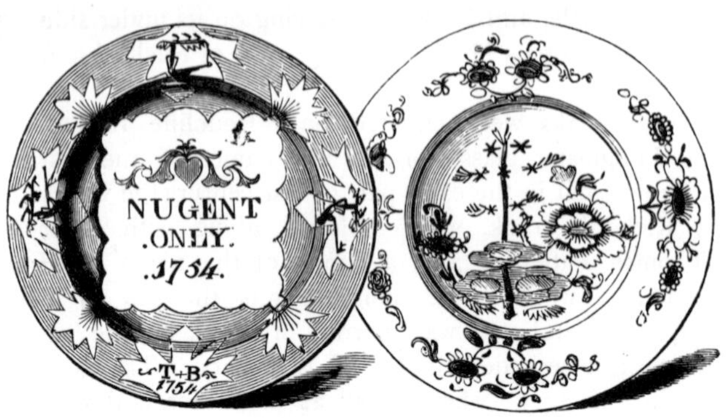

Fig. 737.—Bristol Election Plate, 1754.

Willet, of Brighton, who also possesses a grand tile picture, consisting of seventy-two tiles, painted with Hogarth's "March to Finchley." Mr. Fry has two clever tile pictures of nine tiles each, one representing a cat and the other a dog. On the collar of the latter are the words "*Bristol*, 1752." Richard Frank afterwards took his son Thomas into partnership, and in 1777 the works were removed to a manufactory in Water Lane, which, in 1775, had been carried on by James Alsop, a brown stone-ware potter. The following advertisement, of the year 1777, refers to this change: "Richard Frank and Son, Earthen and Stone Pot Works, are removed from Redcliffe Backs to Water Lane, where they continue the same business in all its branches."

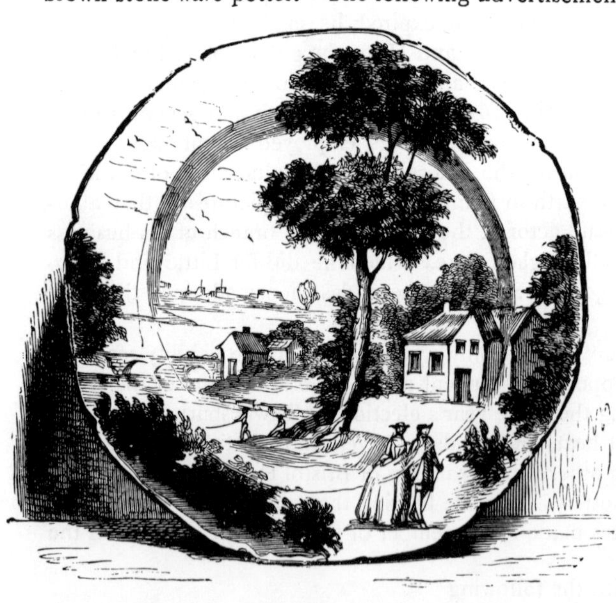

Fig. 738.

In 1784, Joseph Ring, rectifier and vinegar maker, who had married Elizabeth, daughter of Richard Frank (and was father of Sarah, the wife of Frederick Cookworthy, nephew of William Cookworthy), purchased the business of Frank and Son for £669 1s. 3½d.

Richard Frank died in 1785, aged about seventy-three, and was buried in the Quakers' ground at Redcliffe Pit. "Joseph Ring, successor to Richard Frank in the Pottery Business," in his address stated that he "continues the manufactory of the Bristol Stone Ware, and sells all other sorts of Queen's and other Ware wholesale and retail." This last branch of his business he cultivated considerably, and appears to have traded with most of the manufacturers of the day. In 1786 Mr. Ring determined upon manufacturing Queen's ware, and to that end engaged Anthony Hassel (or Hassells), a potter of Shelton, in Staffordshire, buying from him his stock and moulds, and removing them to Bristol. In 1788 he took two partners, Taylor and Carter, he bringing in a capital of £3,000, and they £1,500 jointly. "The Stock and Utensils in Trade at the Pot House in Water Lane, as per Inventory taken this day," January 9th, 1788, were sold by Mr. Ring to himself and partners, "under the firm of Ring and Taylor," for £2,038 1s. 10d. The manufacture of Delft ware then came to a close.

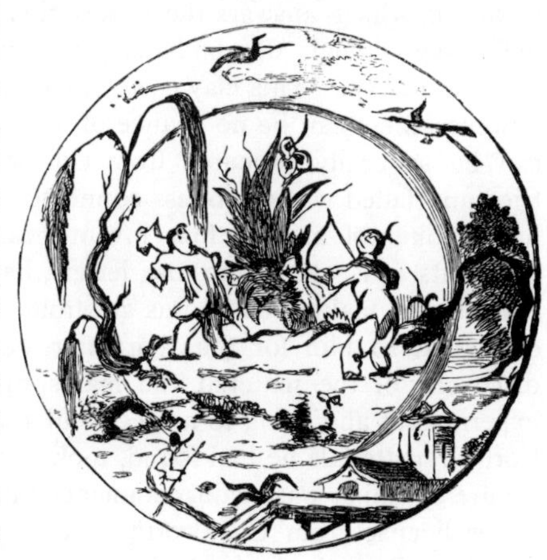

Fig. 739.

Another Delft ware potter was Joseph Flower, who, in 1775 lived at No. 2 on the Quay, and in 1777 removed to 3, Corn Street, where he put a sign-board, painted black, with "Flower, Potter," in gold letters, for the painting of which he paid Michael Edkins 10s. 6d. Flower's ware, says Mr. Owen, is thinner and neater in make than most British Delft; the glaze good, and the colour clear and brilliant in tone—indeed, in no respect inferior to Dutch. Fig. 739 is a plate belonging to a dinner service made by Joseph Flower, in the possession of his descendant Mr. J. Flower Fussel; the different pieces bear initials and dates varying from 1742 to 1750 (Fig. 740). In the same hands is a plate dated 1741-2, painted with a view of the river Avon and the old Hotwells House; and two dishes bearing the plan of a battle, and the words "The taking of Chagre in the West Indies by Admiral Vernon."

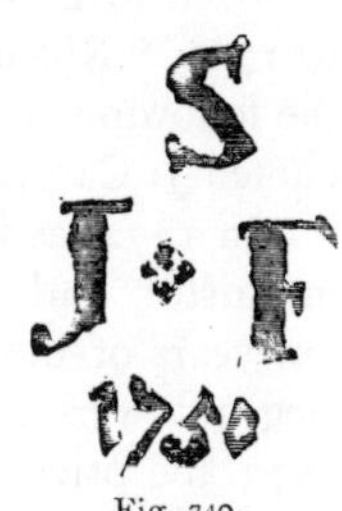

Fig. 740.

Bristol China.

The first mention of the making of china in Bristol occurs in a letter of Richard Champion, dated February 26, 1766. In July, 1765, a box of "porcelain earth" "from the internal part of the Cherokee nations, 400 miles from hence (Charles Town), on mountains scarcely accessible," was consigned to him, by his brother-in-law, to be forwarded to the Worcester china works to be used there in experiments. The letter of advice was dated Charles Town, 1765. At the same time another box of this earth was sent to Champion for the Earl of Hyndford, who desired Champion to open it and try experiments, or give it to Thomas Goldney "who is a very curious gentleman." In the letter of February 28th Champion, writing to Lloyd, by whom it was consigned, says Mr. Goldney has declined the clay. "I therefore," he adds, "had it tried at a manufactory set up here some time ago on the principle of the Chinese porcelain; but not being successful is given up." "The proprietors of the work in Bristol imagined they had discovered in Cornwall all the materials similar to the Chinese; but though they burnt the body part tolerably well, yet there were impurities in the glaze or stone, which were insurmountable even in the greatest fire they could give it, and which was equal to a glass-house heat." These works he had personally, in November, 1765, spoken of as "a new work just established," and says, "this new work is from a clay and stone discovered in Cornwall, which answers the description of the Chinese; but in burning there is a deficiency, though the body is perfectly white within but not without, which is always smoaky. This clay is very much like, but not quite so fine as the Cherokee; however there can be no chance of introducing the latter as a manufacture when it can be so easily procured from Cornwall." This "new work" which had been tried and failed was doubtless connected with Cookworthy of Plymouth. In 1764 he is spoken of as "the first inventor of the Bristol china works." Champion, at all events, it is clear from the letters, had nothing to do with it, and probably his first idea of making china was got from the fact of the box of porcelain earth being consigned to him for the Worcester works. In March, 1768, Cookworthy, the discoverer of the material, the mainspring in all those matters, and the first to try experiments and bring to a successful issue the manufacture of porcelain from the Cornish materials he had found, took out his patent. Soon after this the manufacture of china was again commenced in Bristol by Richard Champion, doubtless under license from Cookworthy. In 1771 a china manufactory, carried on by "William Cookworthy & Co.," appears to have been in operation in Castle Green —the "Co.," there can be no reasonable doubt, being Richard Champion and others. In May, 1774, William Cookworthy assigned his patent right, &c., to Champion, and the Plymouth manufactory, which had probably been previously removed to Bristol, was finally closed; in the rate-books the firm being, from 1773 to 1780, "Richard Champion & Co.," in 1781 "Richard Champion" only; and in the following year the premises are stated to have been occupied by a pipe-maker named J. Carey.

In 1772, as is proved by advertisements, the china works were in full operation in Bristol, and were carried on simultaneously with those of Plymouth in the last few years of those later works, and, as at Plymouth, "vases, jars, and beakers, very elegant," were produced, as well as the ordinary classes of useful goods. In June, 1773, the prices are advertised as "Complete Tea Sets in the Dresden taste highly ornamented £7 0s. 0d. to £12 12s. 0d. and upwards. Tea Sets, 43 pieces, of various prices as low as £2 2s. 0d. Cups and Saucers from 3s. 6d. to 5s. 6d. per half-dozen, and all other sorts of useful Ware proportionately cheap."

Whatever may have been the position of the manufactory at Bristol, and by whomever—whether "W. Cookworthy & Co.," "R. Champion & Co.," or "R. Champion" alone—it was carried on previous to that date, certain it is that in 1774 Cookworthy sold his patent right, &c., to Champion, closed his Plymouth works, and from that time forth ceased to have any connection with china making.

In 1774, then, "Richard Champion, of Bristol, merchant," became possessed of Cookworthy's patent. The deed of assignment of the patent rights, &c., from Cookworthy to Champion, is dated May 6th, 1774, and among other "considerations" it was covenanted that whatever the amount of value of the raw material (the Cornish clay and stone which Cookworthy had discovered and brought into use) Champion used in the course of a year, an equal amount of money should be paid to Cookworthy. For example, if, in the course of a year, Champion paid £1,000 for material in Cornwall, he would also have to pay another £1,000 to Cookworthy for the privilege of using it, thus doubling the price of the material from that at which Cookworthy had himself worked it; and it was also at first arranged that this royalty was to be perpetual, but it was afterwards restricted to ninety-nine years—the time of the lease for the raw materials. Having thus become the proprietor of the concern which had at one time been carried on jointly by Cookworthy, Lord Camelford, and himself (and probably others), Champion, on the 22nd of the following February, 1775, presented a petition to the House of Commons, praying for the term of patent right to be enlarged to himself for a further period of fourteen years. His petition was referred to a committee, which began its sittings on the 28th of April, and leave was given to bring in a Bill for enlarging the Letters Patent.

For examination by this committee Champion prepared and produced some remarkably fine specimens of china made at his works, and it is not too much to say that at this period his productions were of the highest rank. The result of his application was the ultimate passing of an Act of Parliament, by which the patent was, as prayed, enlarged. It was passed in 1775 (15 George III., cap. 52), and is entitled, "An Act for enlarging the term of Letters Patent granted by his present Majesty to William Cookworthy, of Plymouth, Chymist, for the sole use and exercise of a discovery of certain materials for making Porcelain, in order to enable Richard Champion, of Bristol, merchant (to whom the said Letters Patent have been assigned), to carry the said discovery into effectual execution for the benefit of the public."

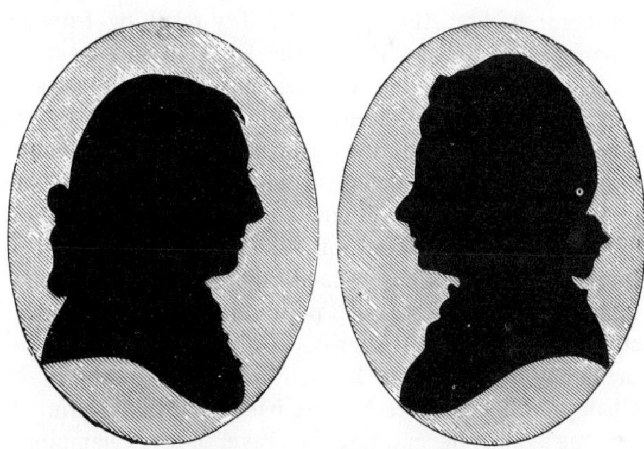

Figs. 741 and 742.—Portraits of Richard Champion and Judith his wife.

Between the time, however, of the committee's sitting and the passing of the Act, Josiah Wedgwood, whose name is always received with reverence by all who study the history of Ceramic Art, ostensibly as the spokesman of the Staffordshire potters, but really at first alone, opposed the grant, on the ground, among others, that the use of the natural productions of the soil ought to be the right of all, and that the restrictions would be detrimental to trade and injurious to the public. In Wedgwood's "memorial" against the petition of Champion, which he presented to Parliament, "Josiah Wedgwood on behalf of himself and the manufacturers of earthenware in Staffordshire," urges "that the manufacture of earthenware in that county has of late received many essential improvements, and is continually advancing to higher degrees of perfection; that the further improvement of the manufactory must depend upon the application and the *free use* of the various raw materials that are the natural products of this country; that the raw materials, now secured for a limited time to the petitioner (Champion) may, at the expiration of the patent assigned to him, be of great use to enable the potters throughout Great Britain to improve their manufactures into the finest porcelain, and thereby produce a branch of commerce of more national importance than any of this kind hitherto established;" that Mr. Champion "was not the inventor, but the *purchaser* only of the unexpired patent granted to another man, who does not appear to have any interest in this application; that the petitioner, therefore, *not being the original discoverer*, and having purchased the remaining term of the patent at a *proportionate price*, can have no right to expect a further extension of a monopoly injurious to the community at large, which neither the ingenious discover nor the purchaser, for want perhaps of skill and experience in this particular business, have been able, during the space of seven years already elapsed, to bring to any useful degree of perfection;" and that, if he has brought his discovery to perfection, as alleged, the unexpired term of seven years ought to be enough to enable him to reimburse himself. To this memorial of Josiah Wedgwood's, Champion presented a lengthy and at the same time honourable, dignified, and liberal-minded reply, in which he justly said, "When Mr. Champion presented a petition to the Honourable House of Commons, praying the aid of Parliament for a prolongation of the term granted by the patent for making porcelain, he built his hopes of success on two circumstances: the first, the apparent utility resulting from such a manufacture carried to a perfection equal to that of the Dresden and Asiatic. The second circumstance on which he grounded his expectation was the sense which he hoped the House would entertain of the justice of compensating, by some reasonable privilege, the great labour, expense, and risque which had been incurred, not only in the invention of the material and composition, but in the improvement of this important manufacture. He was also almost certain that no person whatsoever in this kingdom could, on a supposition of their being prejudiced in their rights in a similar property, have had any cause of complaint, or pretence to interfere with him, or to oppose the prayer of his petition. Mr. Champion, however, finds with some surprise that Mr. Wedgwood, who has never hitherto undertaken any similar manufacture, conceives himself likely to be injured by the indulgence which Mr. Champion has solicited. He has accordingly printed a memorial containing his reasons against the granting the prayer of Mr. Champion's petition, and is now actually gone in person into Staffordshire in order to solicit others to prefer a petition to Parliament against Mr. Champion's Bill. . . . Mr. Champion presented his petition on the 22nd day of February. The committee did not sit until the 28th of April, during which time Mr. Wedgwood neither made any public application against Mr. Champion, or gave him any sort of private information of intended opposition. Neither did any manufacturers in Staffordshire or elsewhere express any uneasiness or make any complaint of Mr. Champion's application. . . . Mr. Champion most cheerfully joins in the general praise which is given to Mr. Wedgwood for the many improvements which he has made in the Staffordshire earthenware, and the great pains and assiduity with which he has pursued them. He richly deserves the large fortune he has made from these improvements. But should he not be content with the rewards he has met with, and not have the avidity to grasp at a manufacture which another has been at as great pains as Mr. Wedgwood has employed in his own to establish?—a manufacture entirely original in this kingdom, and which all nations in Europe have been desirous to obtain. Mr. Wedgwood says the application and free use of the raw materials of this country will make a great improvement in the manufacture of Staffordshire earthenware. Mr. Champion has no objection to the use which the potters of Staffordshire may make of his or any other raw materials, provided earthenware only, as distinguished by that title, is made from it. He wants to interfere with no manufacture whatever, and is content to insert any clause to confine him to the invention which he possesses, and which he has improved.

He is contented that Mr. Wedgwood, and every manufacturer, should reap the fruit of their labour; all he asks is, such a protection for his own as the legislature in its wisdom shall think it merits. . . . If the various difficulties which have attended his work from its beginning could have been foreseen, this patent ought not to have been applied for at so early a period. The time in which profit was to be expected has necessarily been laid out in experiment. It was thought that when the principle was found the work was done; but the perfecting a chemical discovery into a merchantable commodity has been found a troublesome and a tedious work. It is therefore presumed that the legislature will distinguish between the over-sanguine hopes, in point of time, of an invention which, however, has at length succeeded, and those visionary projects which deceive for ever. Upon the whole, Mr. Champion humbly rests his pretensions to the protection of the legislature upon three grounds—that he has been almost from the beginning concerned in the work which has cost so much labour and expense; that he now allows the inventor a certain and increasing recompense, though the carrying that invention to an actual merchantable manufacture was entirely his own work; that the potteries of chinaware in most other countries in Europe have been at the charge of sovereign princes. It has been immediately so in France, Austria, Dresden, and Brandenburgh; in Italy they have been under the care of great noblemen. In this original work Mr. Champion claims the principal share of supporting, improving, and carrying into execution a manufacture so much admired in China and Japan, and now first attempted in Britain, in capacity of resisting the greatest heat, equal to the Asiatic and Dresden."

Wedgwood answered this "Reply" (which I have printed *in extenso* in my first edition) of Champion's by some not very ingenuous "Remarks," which he issued to the members of the legislature, wherein he reminds them that he "has all his life been concerned in the manufacture and improvement of various branches of pottery and porcelain; that he has long had an ambition to carry these manufactures to the highest pitch of perfection they will admit of; and that so far from having any personal interest in opposing Mr. Champion, it would evidently have been his interest to have accepted of some of the obliging proposals that have been made to him by Mr. Champion and his friends, and to have said nothing more upon the subject; but Mr. Wedgwood is so fully convinced of the great injury that would be done to the landed, manufacturing, and commercial interests of this nation by extending the term of Mr. Champion's monopoly of raw materials, of which there are immense quantities in the kingdom, and confining the use of them to one or a few hands, that he thought it a duty of moral obligation to take the sense of his neighbours upon this subject, and to give up to the manufactory at large all advantages he might have secured to himself. . . . . When Mr. Wedgwood discovered the art of making Queen's Ware, which employs ten times more people than all the china works in the kingdom, he did not ask for a patent for this important discovery. A patent would greatly have limited its public utility. Instead of one hundred manufactories of Queen's Ware there would have been one; and instead of an exportation to all quarters of the world, a few pretty things would have been made for the amusement of the people of fashion in England." Wedgwood continued his "remarks" by replying that Mr. Champion's offer of inserting a clause to allow the potters the free use of the raw material in all kinds of earthenware, restricting its use in porcelain only to himself, was a useless concession, because Champion had failed to define the difference between earthenware and porcelain, and had failed to impart the secret of his manufacture to the public, either by his specifications or otherwise. "How, then," he asked, "are the Staffordshire potters to use the growan stone and growan clay for the improvement of their finer stone and earthenwares, without producing such a manufacture as may in Westminster Hall be deemed porcelain?" He also said that, judging from Mr. Champion's own words, Cookworthy's patent "ought not to have been applied for at so early a period," it was evident that the "patent was taken out for a discovery of the art of making true porcelain before it *was* made; and if the discovery has been since made there can have been no specification of it; it has not been revealed to the public, it is in Mr. Champion's own possession, and being *unknown*, it is presumed the right to practise it cannot be confirmed or extended by Act of Parliament, which ought to have some clear ground to go upon." The patent, he says, has evidently been considered as a privilege to the patentee, "for the sole right of *making experiments* upon materials which many persons have thought would make good porcelain, and on which experiments have been prosecuted by several successive sets of operators many years before the date of the patent." He contended that it would have been an "egregious injury to the public" to continue the patent to one person who was no original discoverer, who was only just commencing the commonest and most useful part of his business with the aid of a foreign artificer, in the hope that a discovery might at some future time be made. He considered that if the raw materials were thrown open to all, "a variety of experienced hands would probably produce more advantage to the nation in a few years than they would ever do when confined to one manufactory, however skilful the director might be," and that the extension of the patent securing the monopoly "would be a precedent of the most dangerous nature, contrary to policy, and of general inconvenience," and therefore he "humbly hopes the legislature will not grant the prayer of Mr. Champion's petition,"—a hope which, however earnestly expressed, and however tenaciously followed, was eventually of no avail. To this opposition, however, is doubtless to be traced the ultimate abandonment of the patent, and the manufacture of the less difficult soft paste to so great an extent in Staffordshire.

The term of the original patent, it will be remembered, was for fourteen years, of which nearly eight years remained unexpired at the time when it was assigned over by Cookworthy to Champion. The extension petitioned for would thus have given Champion nearly twenty-two years' exclusive right to the raw materials, and it was this extended monopoly which aroused the watchfulness of Wedgwood, and made him determined to use his utmost efforts to prevent its being enacted. In this opposition—which was determined and energetic, and, it must be confessed, selfish and unjust, though only partially successful—Wedgwood, besides memorialising the legislature against granting the prayer of the petition, issued a number of "Reasons why the extension of the term of Mr. Cookworthy's patent, by authority of Parliament, would be injurious to many landowners, to the manufacturers of earthenware, and to the public," and also made out and presented a "Case of the manufacturers of earthenware in Staffordshire," setting forth the advantages that would be derived from throwing open the use of the raw materials, and the disadvantages which an extension of the monopoly would entail, not only on the manufacturers, but on the public at large.

These "Reasons" I was the first, in the *Art Journal,* to make public, and to that Journal (1863) and to my first edition I refer the reader for the full text of them and of the "Case."

Despite all the factious opposition that could possibly be brought to bear upon the matter—for it was factious in the extreme—by Wedgwood, as the representative of the potters, and by the members of parliament for the county of Stafford, and others who had been moved by the exertions of Wedgwood and his friends, the Bill passed the House of Commons, and was sent up to the Lords without amendment. The "Case," along with extracts from the Bill, with comments, was printed for circulation among the members of the Upper House, and their presentation produced more effect, it would seem, than the efforts in a similar direction had done in the Commons. The consequence was, that "Lord Gower and some other noble lords, having fully informed themselves of the facts upon which the merits of the case depended, and having considered the subject with a degree of attention proportioned to its importance, saw clearly the injurious nature of the Bill, and were determined to oppose it." This determination brought on a conference between the two noble lords who took the most active part for and against the Bill, and the result was the introduction of two clauses, the first making it imperative on Champion to enrol anew his specification of both body and glaze within the usual period of four months; the second, throwing open the use of the raw materials to potters for any purpose except the manufacture of porcelain, was as follows:—"Provided also, that nothing in this Act contained shall be construed to hinder or prevent any potter or potters, or any other person or persons, from making use of any such raw materials, or any mixture or mixtures thereof (except such mixture of raw materials, and in such proportions, as are described in the specification herein-before directed to be enrolled), anything in this Act to the contrary notwithstanding." The Act being obtained (specimens of his skill in making porcelain having been submitted to the Committee by Champion), the specification was duly enrolled on the 15th of September, 1775; it is as follows:—

"TO ALL TO WHOM THESE PRESENTS SHALL COME, I, RICHARD CHAMPION, of Bristol, Merchant, send greeting, and so forth.

"WHEREAS his present Majesty, King George the Third, in the eighth year of his reign, did grant his Royal Letters Patent to William Cookworthy, of Plymouth, chymist, for the sole use and exercise of 'A DISCOVERY OF CERTAIN MATERIALS FOR MAKING OF PORCELAIN,' which Letters Patent have been duly assigned to me the said Richard Champion; and whereas by a certain Act of Parliament (intitled an Act for enlarging the Term of Letters Patent granted by his present Majesty to William Cookworthy, of Plymouth, chymist, for the sole Use and Exercise of a Discovery of certain Materials for making Porcelain, in order to enable Richard Champion, of Bristol, Merchant—to whom the said Letters Patent have been assigned—to carry the said Discovery into execution for the Benefit of the Public), all and every the powers, liberties, rights, and advantages by the said Letters Patent granted to the said William Cookworthy are granted to me, the said Richard Champion, my executors, administrators, and assigns, during the remainder of the term of the said Letters Patent, and from the expiration thereof for a further term therein mentioned, provided I, the said Richard Champion, should cause to be inrolled in the High Court of Chancery, within four months after passing the said Act, a specification of the mixture of the raw materials of which my porcelain is composed, and likewise of the mixture and proportions of the raw materials which compose the glaze of the same, which specification was in the hands of the Lord High Chancellor of Great Britain:

"NOW KNOW YE THEREFORE, that I, the said Richard Champion, do hereby testify and declare that the specification hereinafter contained is the true and just specification of the mixture and proportions of the raw materials of which my porcelain is composed, and likewise of the mixture and proportions of the raw materials which compose the glaze of the same, and which, at the time of passing the beforementioned Act, was in the hands of the Lord High Chancellor of Great Britain (that is to say) :—

"The raw materials of the above porcelain are plastic clay, generally found mixed with mica and a coarse gravelly matter. It is known in the counties of Devon and Cornwall by the name of growan clay. The other raw material is a mixed micarious earth or stone called in the aforesaid counties moor-stone and growan. The gravel found in the growan clay is of the same nature, and is used for the same purpose in making the body of my porcelain as the moor-stone and growan. The mixture of these materials to make the body of the porcelain is according to the common potter's method, and has no peculiar art in it. The proportions are as follow :—The largest proportion of the stone or gravel aforesaid to the clay aforesaid is four parts of stone to one of clay. The largest proportion of clay to stone is sixteen parts of clay to one part of stone mixed together. I use these and every proportion intermediate, between the foregoing proportions of the stone to the clay and the clay to the stone, and all this variation I make without taking away from the ware the distinguishing appearance and properties of Dresden and Oriental porcelains, which is the appearance and are the properties of mine. The raw materials of which the glaze is composed are, the stone or gravel aforesaid, and the clay aforesaid, magnesia, nitre, lime, gypsum, fusible spar, arsenic, lead, and tin ashes.

"The proportions of our common glaze are as follows, together with every intermediate proportion, videlicet:—

Growan gravel	128 parts	The materials ground and mixed together with water.
Growan or moor-stone	112 ,,	
and I vary it from 96 to	144 ,,	
Magnesia	16 ,,	
and I vary it from 14 to	18 ,,	
Gypsum	3 ,,	
Lime	8 ,,	

"But I also use the following materials for glaze :—

Growan clay	128 parts	The materials ground and mixed together with water.
Growan or moor-stone	112 ,,	
and I vary it from 84 to	140 ,,	
Magnesia	20 ,,	
and I vary it from 16 to	24 ,,	
Lime	8 ,,	
and I vary it from 6 to	10 ,,	
Nitre	1 ,,	
and I vary it to	2 ,,	
Fusible spar	20 ,,	
Arsenic	20 ,,	
Lead and tin ashes	20 ,,	
and I vary it from 16 to	24 ,,	

"I have described truly and justly the raw materials, the mixture and proportions of them which are used in making my porcelain, which has the appearance and properties of Dresden or Oriental porcelain, and which porcelain may be distinguished from the frit or false porcelain, and from the pottery, or earthen or stone wares, as follows :—

"The frit or false porcelain will all melt into a vitreous substance, and lose their form and original appearance in a degree of heat which my porcelain, agreeing in all properties with Asiatic and Dresden, will not only bear, but which is necessary for its perfection. My porcelain may be distinguished from all other wares which are vulgarly called earthen or stone wares, which can sustain an equal degree of heat, by the grain, the colour of the grain, and by its semi-transparency; whereas the earthenwares, such as Staffordshire white and yellow earthenwares and all other earthenwares which sustain a strong heat without being fused, are found, when subjected to the most intense heat, to appear cellular or otherwise, easily by the eye to be distinguished from the true porcelain.

"In witness whereof, I, the said Richard Champion, have hereunto set my hand and seal this twelfth day of September, in the year of our Lord one thousand seven hundred and seventy-five, and in the fifteenth year of the reign of our Sovereign Lord, George the Third, by the grace of God, of Great Britain, France, and Ireland, King, Defender of the Faith, and so forth.

"RICH. (L. S.) CHAMPION.

"Sealed and delivered in the presence of us,

"HENRY SHERWOOD,

"Of Wood Street, London.

"ROBERT REYNOLDS,

"Of Coventry.

"AND BE IT REMEMBERED, that the twelfth day of September, in the year above written, the said Richard Champion came before our said Lord the King in his Chancery, and acknowledged the writing aforesaid, and all and everything therein contained and specified, as form above written. And also the writing aforesaid was stampt according to the tenor of the statute made in the sixth year of the reign of the King and Queen William and Mary of England, and so forth.

"Enrolled the fifteenth day of September, in the year above written."

The works of Richard Champion were in Castle Green, Bristol, and I was enabled, in 1863, assisted by the researches of Mr. Edkins, kindly undertaken at my request, to fix the exact locality both of the works and of Champion's residence. This he determined by the fortuitous circumstance of a Directory for the city of Bristol having been published—and for that one year only—in the year in which Champion obtained his Act of Parliament, 1775.

Armed with his new Act of Parliament, by which he was empowered to enjoy nearly twenty-two years' patent right, Champion spared no pains and no expense to make the productions of his works as good as possible. The commoner description of goods, the blue and white ware, he seems naturally to have considered to be the branch most likely to pay him, commercially, and this he at one time cultivated to a greater extent than any other. His acknowledged and advertised model was the Dresden, and his best efforts were turned in that direction; the patterns he adopted, being, in many cases, almost identical with those produced at Worcester and other places —which, of course, arose from the fact of the different works copying from the same models. In blue and white, Champion produced dinner, tea, and coffee services, toilet pieces, jugs, mugs, and all the varieties of goods usually made at that period. The blue is usually of good colour, and the painting quite equal to that of other manufactories. Some of these pieces are embossed, and of really excellent workmanship. A good deal of the blue and white ware was marked with the usual cross, but it appears more than probable that the greatest part passed out of the works unmarked.

Another characteristic class of goods made by Champion was the imitation of the most common Chinese patterns, examples of which are shown in Figs. 743—4. The saucer bears the usual mark of the cross, but many examples of this class are not marked at all, and pass as foreign pieces. In the same group is a cup of elegant form, but of different style. Transfer printing was not, it would appear, practised by Champion, but some examples, Mr. Owen informs me, are known, which, although made at Bristol, were evidently printed at Worcester.

The expenses attendant on Wedgwood's unwarrantable opposition in Parliament drained Champion's exchequer, and despite the energy of himself, the skill of his workmen, and the beauty of the ware produced at his manufactory, Richard Champion's hopes of permanently establishing an art in Bristol, which should not only be an honourable and useful, but a remunerative one, proved fallacious, and in little more than five years from his obtaining of the Act of Parliament, the works which he had laboured so hard to establish, and on which he had expended so much time, money, and skill, were lost to the city of Bristol, and removed for ever from its walls, but not, fortunately, until he had proved incontestably his ability to produce a genuine porcelain of the finest texture, and of the most artistic and finished style.

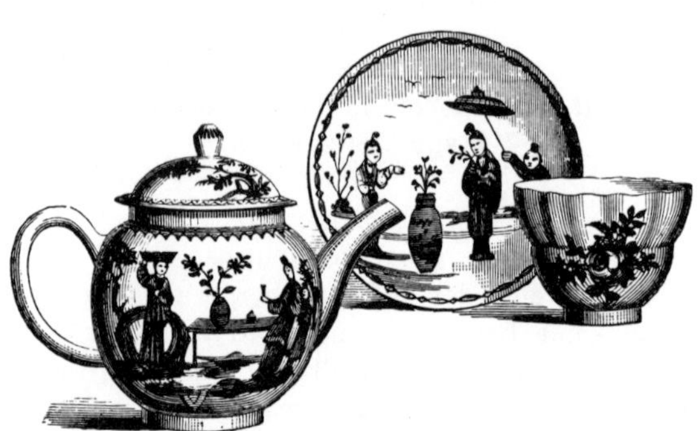

Figs. 743 to 745.—Champion's Imitations of the Chinese.

In 1778, Josiah Wedgwood, in a letter, dated August 24th in that year, says, "Poor Champion, you may have heard is quite demolished; it was never likely to be otherwise, as he had neither professional knowledge, sufficient capital, nor scarcely any real acquaintance with the materials he was working upon. I suppose we might buy some *growan stone* and *growan clay* now upon easy terms, for they have prepared a large quantity this last year." This curious letter, whose sympathy was certainly left-handed, did but little credit to Wedgwood—the man who of all others had worked hard to crush him, and had succeeded in so doing. His hope, now that Champion was "quite demolished," was that he might be able to gain his point and get the growan stone and clay on easy terms! It is lamentable to feel that a great name could sink so low. It does not appear, however, that Champion ever became bankrupt, or even appealed to his creditors.

In his Bristol works, although only his own name appears in the various documents to which I have alluded, Champion had friends who assisted pecuniarily in his undertaking. One of these friends was Joseph Fry, the grandfather of the present Mr. Francis Fry, F.S.A., of Bristol, whose name is as well known among biblists and connoisseurs in china for his fine collection of old bibles and choice porcelain as the firm to which he belongs is to the general public for the "Fry's Chocolate" which they manufacture to so large an extent. Mr. Joseph Fry, the friend of Champion, died in 1786, about nine years after the works had been closed on their removal into Staffordshire; and it appears that the only return he got for

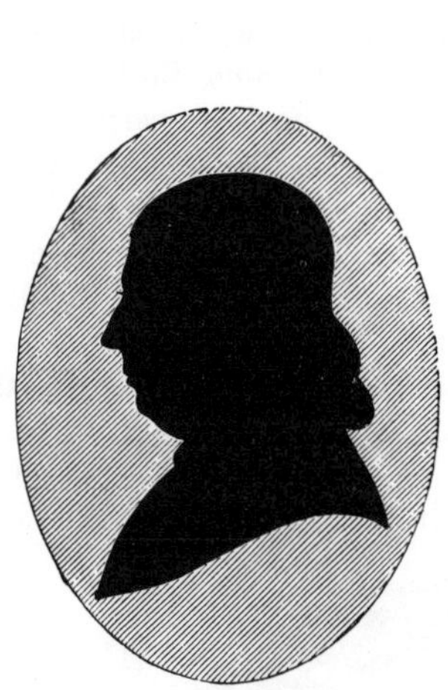

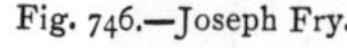

Fig. 746.—Joseph Fry.

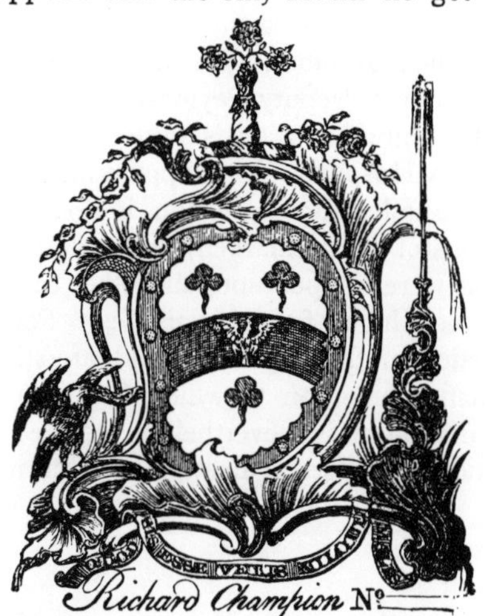

Fig. 747.—Book Plate, with arms of Champion.

the capital he had sunk in the concern, was the beautiful set of vases now in the possession of his grandson.

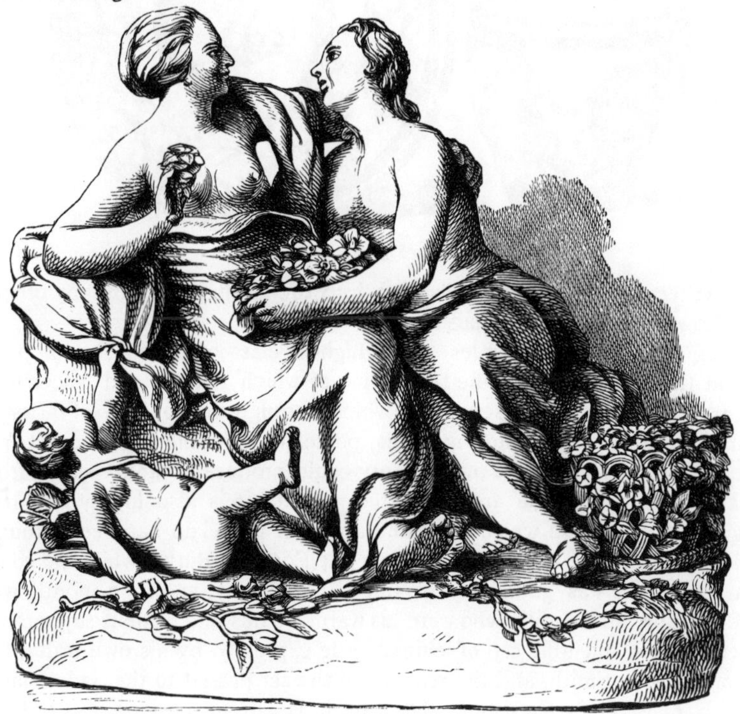

Fig. 748.—Venus and Adonis, belonging to Lady Charlotte Schreiber.

The patent right was sold by Champion, in 1781—not 1777, as stated by Shaw—to a company of Staffordshire potters, who continued the manufacture at New

Hall (which see for a continuation of this narrative) for some time, when the ordinary soft-paste china was allowed to supersede it. Champion himself with his family removed for a time into Staffordshire, fixing themselves at Newcastle-under-Lyne, in November, 1781, and there remained until April, 1782, when, having been appointed a Deputy Paymaster-General of the Forces, by Edmund Burke, he left Staffordshire "at a day's notice," and removed to London, having apartments at Chelsea Hospital. This appointment he only held till 1784. In October of that year he sailed for Charleston, in South Carolina, and there he died, in 1791.

Bristol china (marked), every description of which, owing to the short time the works were in operation, and other causes, is scarce, is particularly rare in the finer and more highly finished varieties. Fortunately, however, examples of these different varieties, of the very finest kind, are still preserved, and attest most strongly to the extreme perfection to which Champion succeeded in bringing his works. Much discrimination is, nevertheless, required in appropriating examples, and it is well to caution collectors against placing too much reliance on the sweeping way in which,

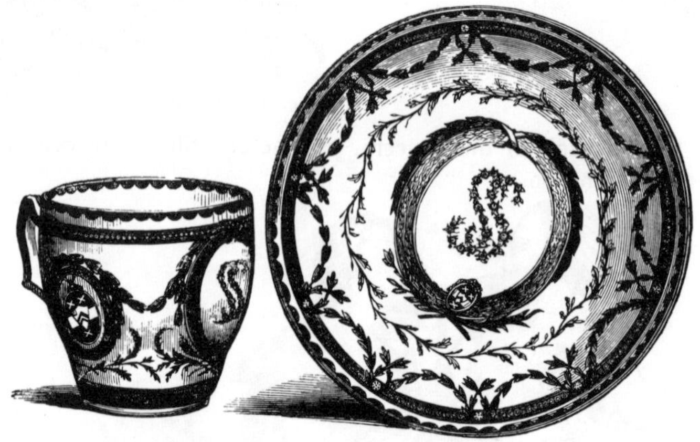

Fig. 749.

by some writers, all examples are hauled into the Bristol net; and by others into those of Lowestoft and others places.

One of the choicest examples of the highest class of art in Bristol porcelain existing at the present day, is the tea-service of which the cup and saucer Fig. 749 forms a part. This splendid service, of which, through the courtesy of Miss Smith, this cup and saucer passed into my hands, possesses a double interest, first from its being made "the best that the manufactory could produce;" and, second, from the historical associations which are connected with it; it is also highly important as showing the perfection to which the manufacture of porcelain had been brought by Champion in 1774—5. It seems that in 1774 Edmund Burke, while the contested election for Bristol was going on, remained in that city, and for a month was the guest of Mr. and Mrs. Smith, who were his warm friends and zealous supporters, and he presented this splendid set of china, made expressly, by his own order, by Mr. Champion, to Mrs. Smith, and the remains of the set passed to that lady's daughter, Miss Smith, of Berkeley Crescent. This set, it is fair to presume, was ordered by Burke while remaining in Bristol, or at all events about that time, which would be the very year in which the transfer of the Plymouth works to Champion of Bristol was completed. As a service of such exquisite beauty and such minute detail in painting would necessarily be a work of time, the absolute date of its completion may be set down to the beginning of the year 1775. The service is profusely and massively gilt in both dead and burnished gold, the wreaths of laurel, &c., being in green, which was Burke's electioneering colour. Each piece bears the monogram of Mrs. Smith, S S conjoined, formed of wreaths of roses in pink and gold, and also the arms of Smith, *sable*, a fesse between three saltiers *or;* on an escutcheon of pretence the arms of Pope, *or*, two chevronels and a canton *gules*, the latter charged with a mullet of the first; and the crest of Smith, a saltier *or*. The pieces of this service are marked with the usual cross. In the Museum of Practical Geology is a cup and saucer of the same form, presented by the Duchess of Northumberland, in which the festoons and borders are of similar character, but of very inferior workmanship to those just described. Another remarkably fine and, of course, unique service was brought under the hammer in 1871, and deserves more than a passing notice. This service had been made by Champion and presented by him and his wife to Mrs. Burke.

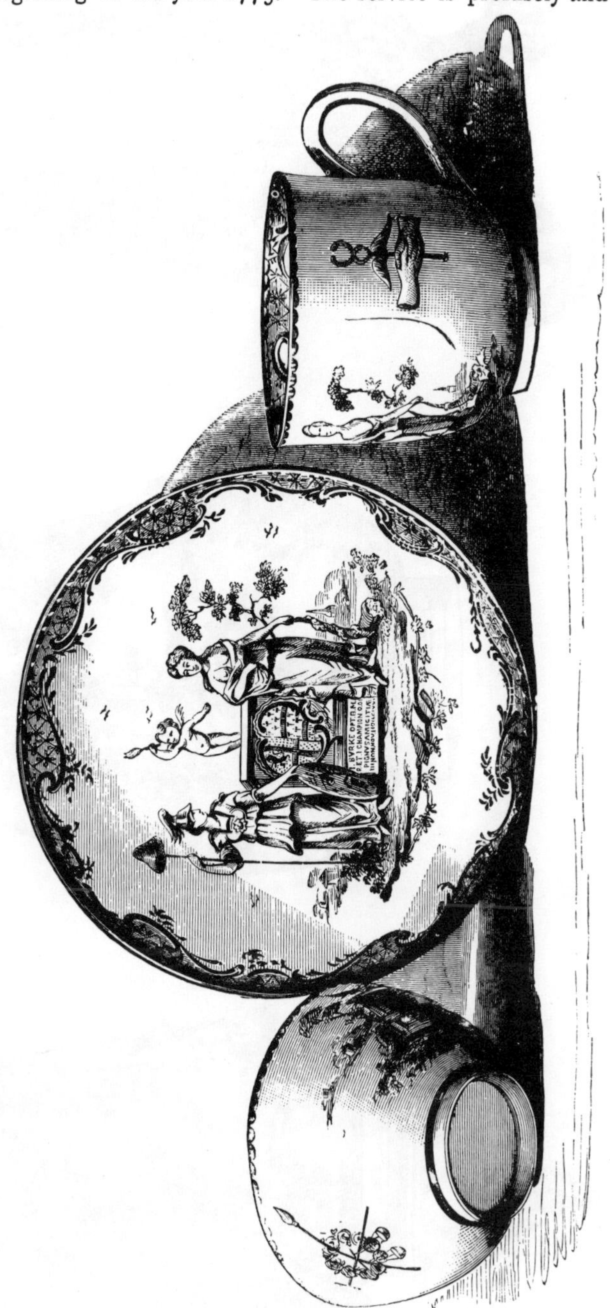

Fig. 750.—Part of the Service presented to Edmund Burke by Mr. and Mrs. Champion.

On the larger pieces were the arms of Burke impaling Nugent on a pedestal, supported, dexter, by a figure of Liberty; and, sinister, by a figure of Plenty. On the top of the pedestal is Cupid with a flaming torch, and at the base the

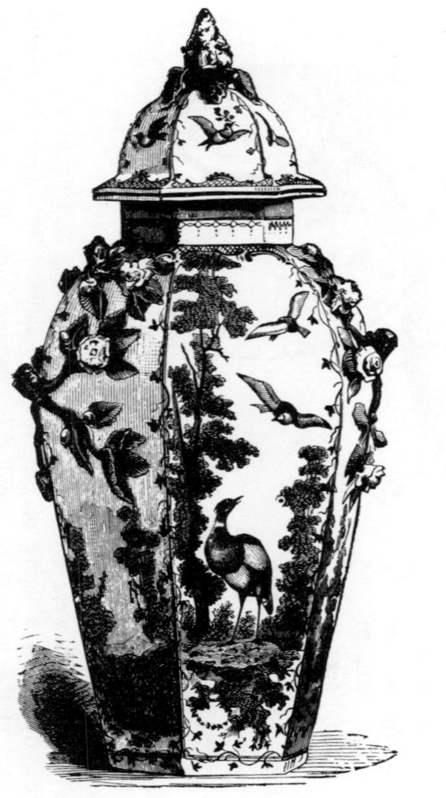
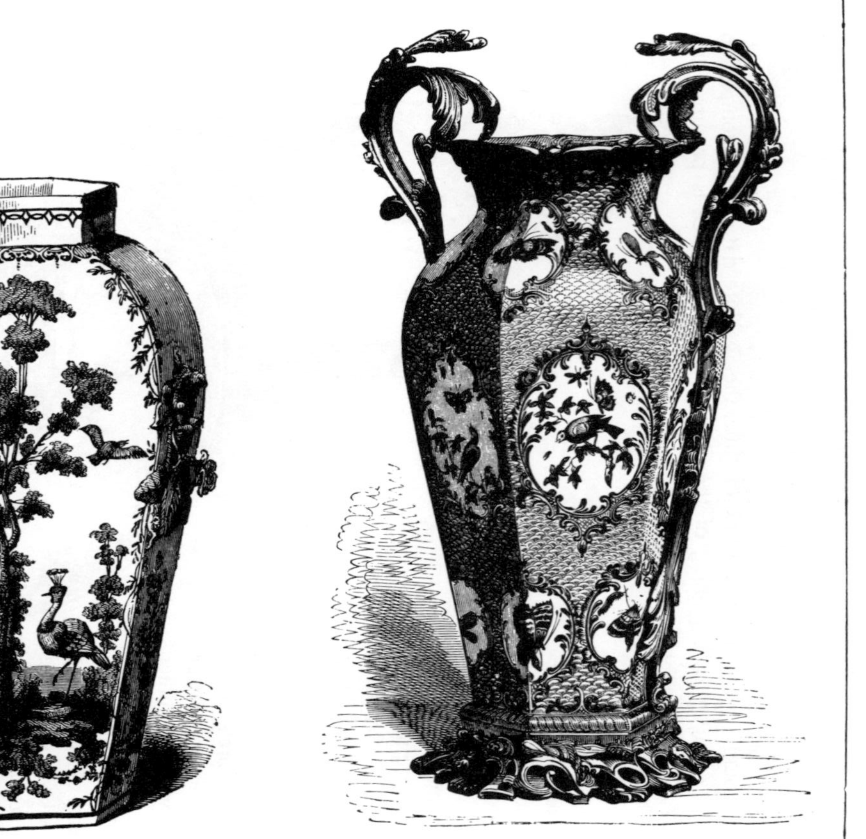

Figs. 751 to 753.—Bristol Vases, belonging to Mr. Fry, Mr. Nightingale, and Mr. Callender.

inscription, "I BVRKE, OPT. B. M. R. ET I. CHAMPION. D. D.D. PIGNVS. AMICITIÆ. III. NON. NOV. MDCCLXXIV." Other decorations also are introduced. Portions of this service (which it is a pity was ever dispersed) passed into the possession of Mr. Callender, Mr. Edkins, Mr. Fry, and others. I am indebted to Mr. Owen for permission to reproduce from his admirable volume the engraving of a portion of this service (Fig. 750), and for the use of several other woodcuts.

Amongst the finest known productions of the Bristol works are the series of splendid vases in the possession of Mr. Francis Fry, to which I alluded in my account of Plymouth china. One of these (Fig. 754), is 12¼ inches in height, and of hexangular form. The landscapes are exquisitely painted, and it has well-modelled female busts on two of its sides, from which hang festoons of raised coloured flowers. The other vases in Mr. Fry's possession, one of which has a perforated neck, though differing in form, style, and ornamentation, exhibit the same excellence and skill in workmanship and in decoration which are so remarkable on this specimen. That these vases were painted by the same artists as the highest class of Plymouth china is very apparent to those who are conversant with their works. The birds are clearly "of the same family," and the general style of decoration bears evident mark of coming from the same hands. They are *not marked*, and therefore a doubt very naturally arises as to whether they were made before the works were removed from Plymouth, and so brought as part of the "stock" to Bristol, or whether they were really made after their establishment in that city. They are, however, of a finer and higher quality than the marked Plymouth example, and therefore there can be no reasonable doubt that they are Champion's production. Vases are distinctly spoken of in the evidence of John Britain before the House of Commons in 1774. He said "that he has great experience in several China manufactories, and has made several Trials upon all those which had been manufactured in *England*, and finds that all of them, except that of *Bristol*, were destroyed in the same Fire that brings the Bristol to Perfection. And he produced to your Committee several Samples of the said kinds of China, which showed the effects upon china severally; and said, that they have not been able to bring the *Bristol* China to a marketable commodity, so as to furnish an Order, until within the last Six Months, but that sometimes they succeeded, and at other Times not, but that now they can execute any order. That they have lately made considerable improvements in the said Manufacture, and particularly are endeavouring to perfect the Blue, in which they have not as yet entirely succeeded, though they have now a Gentleman who has succeeded in a small Way, in which

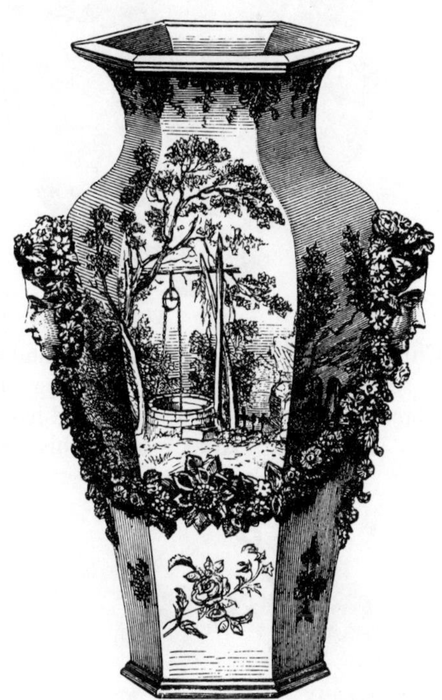

Fig. 754.—Bristol Vase, belonging to Mr. Francis Fry.

they have been at a considerable Expense; that the witness thinks the Manufacture is capable of further improvements; that they can afford it at a price equal to Foreign China of equal Goodness, and that they have made some Specimens equal to good *Dresden;* that he has not seen any *Dresden* ornamental China equal to the Vases produced to your Committee, nor any Thing in Biscuit equal to the Biscuit in those Vases, and other Ornaments; that the Gilding stands well; that the *Seve*

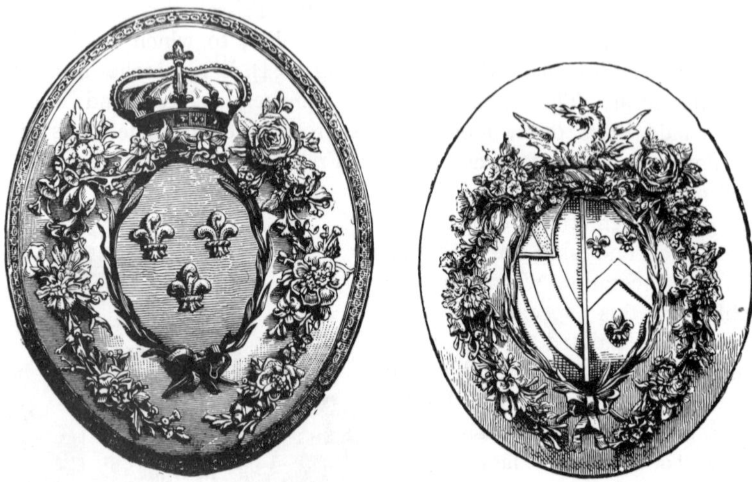

Figs. 755 and 756.—Bristol Bisque Plaques.

China differs from this; the Ornamental is more of a Cream colour, but the Glaze is so soft that it will not bear using; that he believed the enamel of the *Bristol* China is as hard as the *Dresden,* and harder than the Chinese," &c. Mr. Champion also spoke very markedly upon this improvement when he wrote these words; "Mr. Champion can assert, with truth, that his hazard and expense were many

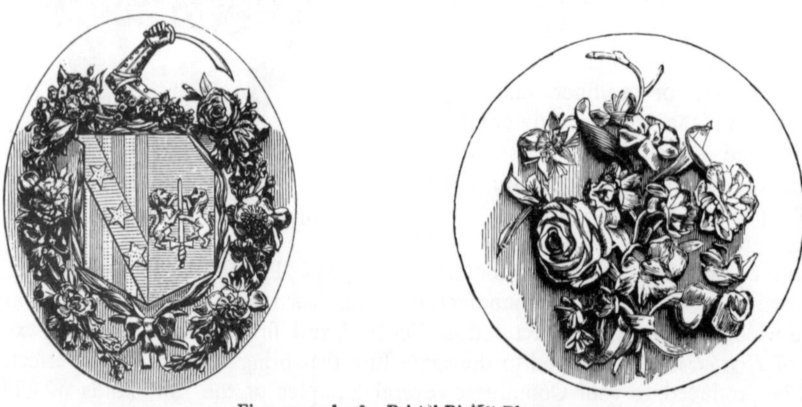

Figs. 757 and 758.—Bristol Bisque Plaques.

times greater than those of the original inventor. Mr. Champion mentions this without the least disparagement to the worthy gentleman, Mr. Cookworthy, who is his particular friend; he gives him all the merit which is due to so great a discovery; he deserves it for finding out the means of a manufacture, which will, in all probability, be a very great advantage to this country; but yet Mr. Champion claims the merit of supporting the work, and, when the inventor declined the undertaking himself, with his time, his labour, and his fortune, improved it from a very imperfect to an almost perfect manufacture; and he hopes, soon, with proper encouragement, to one altogether perfect."

The vases under notice fell to the lot of Mr. Fry's grandfather at the time of the close of the works, and have never been out of the possession of the family. They are therefore attested as coming from Champion's establishment. In Mr. Fry's possession is also a remarkably interesting "waster" vase of the same general form and character, which has apparently been spoiled by smoke in the kiln. This vase, I believe, was purchased by its present possessor from a family in Bristol, in whose possession it was stated to have been for seventy years. Other vases of great merit, all said to be Bristol, are in the possession of Mr. Edkins, Mr. Nightingale, and Mr. Walker.

Another notable and beautiful feature of the Bristol works was the production of plaques, bouquets of flowers, wreaths, and armorial bearings, in biscuit (Figs. 755 to 758.) One of these (Fig. 757), bears the arms and crest of the Eltons (who were connected with Bristol for the last two centuries as bankers, members of parliament, and mayors, and of which the present representative is Sir Arthur Hallam Elton, Bart.) impaling Tierney, surrounded by a wreath of exquisitely and delicately modelled leaves and flowers. Another in the possession of Miss Smith bears the arms of Smith, with escutcheon of Pope, also surrounded with a wreath of raised flowers of surpassing beauty. Another (Fig. 755), in Mr. Fry's collection, has the arms of France beautifully surrounded by a crowned wreath of elaborately modelled flowers—the crown, wreath, and border of which are of dead and burnished gold; and another bearing the arms of Harford impaling Lloyd (Fig. 756). In her Majesty's possession are two remarkably fine examples with medallion profiles of George III. and Queen Charlotte, presented to that queen by Champion himself in 1775, together with a pair of smaller flower plaques of exquisite finish and delicacy; and others exist in various collections.

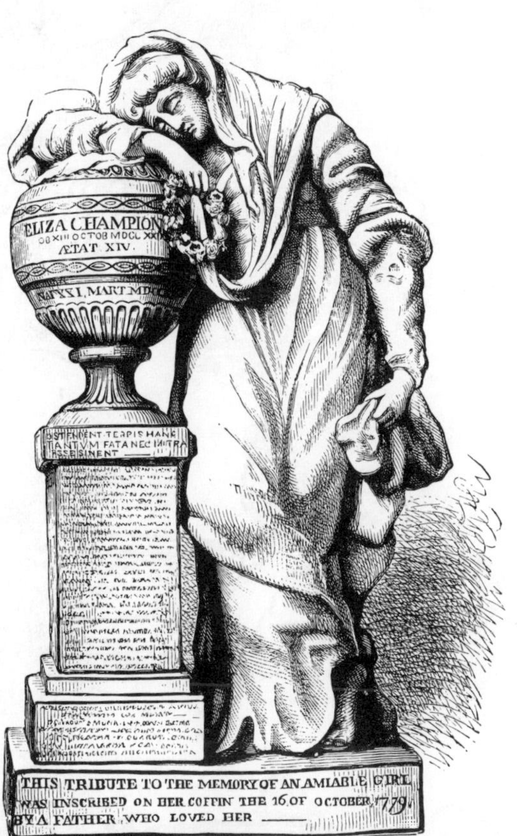

Fig. 759.—Champion's Memorial to his daughter Eliza, belonging to Mr. Desaussure, of South Carolina.

Figures were, to some extent, made at Bristol, and in Mr. James's possession were a pair—a man with a bird, and a woman with a barrel and a pig—bearing an incised cross on the bottom. Other figures are in the possession of Mr. Fry, Mr.

Edkins, Lady Charlotte Schreiber, and others. (See Figs. 759 to 770.) Among these are the "Four Elements" and "Four Seasons," which all bear, in the examples now remaining, the mark T o, which is probably the modeller's own mark, or contraction of his name. The most authentic and interesting figure is a memorial to Champion's daughter Eliza, who died Oct. 13, 1779, aged fourteen. The figure (Fig. 759), is a monumental statuette of a mourning female figure, leaning on an urn, holding in her right hand a votive wreath and her left closed on the drapery. The urn and pedestal bear a long and very touching inscription. This interesting relic stands thirteen inches in height; it is in the possession of Mr. J. M. Desaussure, of Camden, South Carolina, who married a granddaughter of Champion. Two admirable figures (Figs. 768 and 769) of a shepherd and milkmaid, marked with the To marks, are in the possession of Mr. Francis Fry, and a group, "Love subdued by Time," was in the Edkins collection (Fig. 770). Busts were also made; but as these and the examples made at Plymouth are not marked, and are made of the same body, and by the same workmen, it is manifestly impossible to correctly appropriate them.

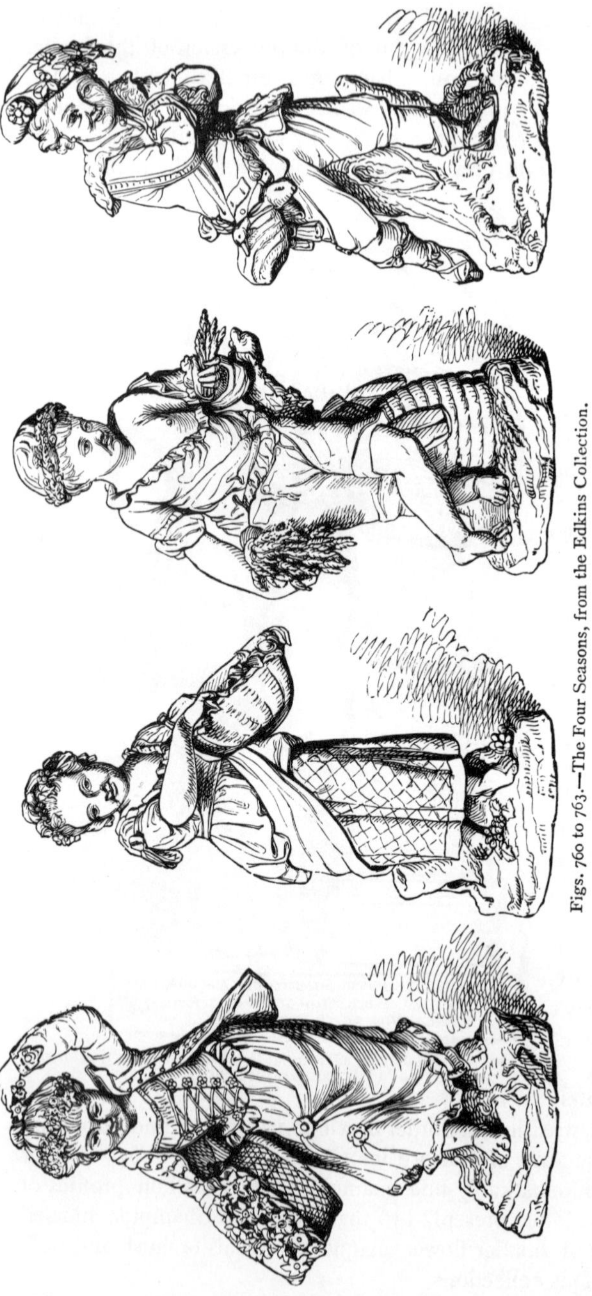

Figs. 760 to 763.—The Four Seasons, from the Edkins Collection.

A cup, part of the Harford service, bears in the bottom in the inside the +, the initials J H (of Joseph Harford), and the date 1774, and is the earliest known dated example of Bristol china. Another excellent dated example, bearing the repeated monogram W C on the inside, has on the bottom the +, 1776, and figure 1. The pounce-box (Fig. 772) bears the × and figure 3.

The mark which usually denotes Bristol porcelain is a plain saltire, or cross, in blue, neutral tint, or red, sometimes with the addition of figures or other marks, but more commonly by itself. The figures probably denoted the workman, not the pattern, as on the same sets different numbers appear, which would not be the case if the design was denoted. The following are varieties of the mark, the cross being sometimes in one colour, and the figure or character in another. One, it will be seen, bears, besides the saltire, the sign for a drachm (or perhaps figure 3), and another the Greek character epsilon (ε). These marks occur the one on a teapot, the other on a saucer lately in the possession of Mr. Norman. The letter B also sometimes occurs painted in the same manner as the cross, and also in combination with figures, &c. (Figs. 783 to 786.) Other marks have been ascribed to Bristol, but many of them, I believe, wrongly. In Mr. James's collection was a small fluted cream-boat, blue and white, with an unusual mark, the blue cross, above which is an embossed letter T, as shown on Fig. 789. The same mark occurs on a specimen in the Nightingale collection. Another mark variously ascribed

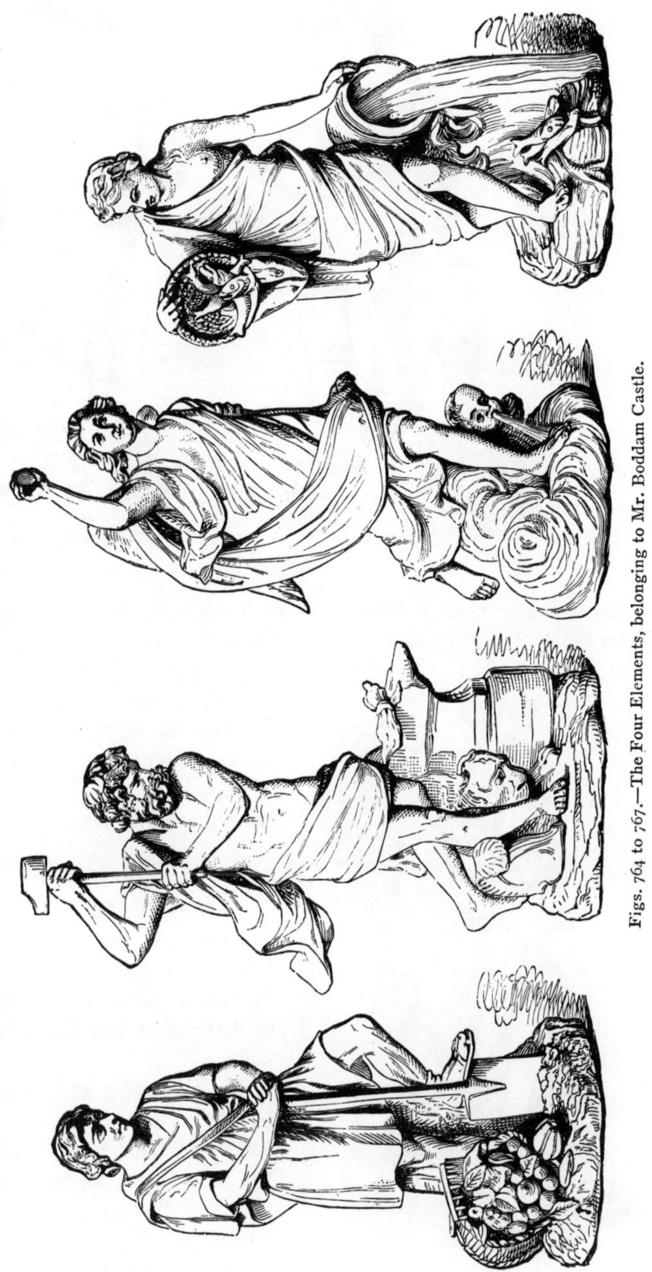

Figs. 764 to 767.—The Four Elements, belonging to Mr. Boddam Castle.

to Bristol and Bow is To (Fig. 790), and one very early trial piece in the Edkins collection bears the unique mark of the word Bristoll in relief. The Dresden mark of crossed daggers occasionally occurs in connection with the cross or the letter B; the latter marks being in some instance painted *over* the former, and in others close by (Figs. 791 to 796). Other marks said to be Bristol are shown on Figs. 799 and 800.

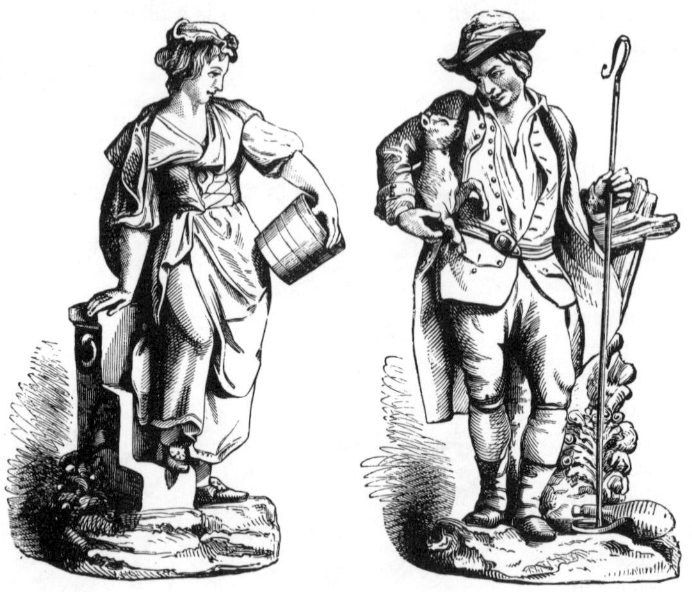

Figs. 768 and 769.—Belonging to Mr. Francis Fry, F.S.A.

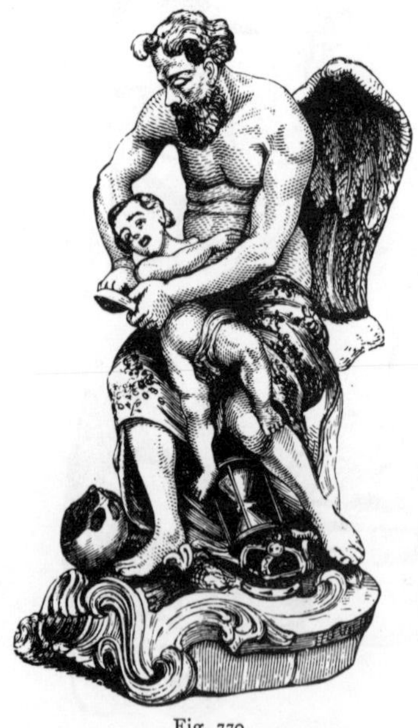

Fig. 770.

The ♃ mark of Plymouth and the + of Bristol are on one or two known pieces, found in combination thus (Fig. 798), from the Schreiber collection.

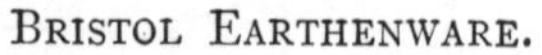

Bristol Earthenware.

Temple Backs.—In 1786 the pottery for fine earthenware was established at No. 9, Water Lane, Temple Street, called "Temple Back," by Joseph Ring, as I have shown in my notice of that potter and his delft-ware productions on page.

In December of the same year, as is shown by an invoice of goods, the following goodly variety of articles was made: "oval dishes," 10, 11, 12, 13, and 14 inches respectively; "table plates;" "soups;" "suppers;" "twifflers;" "tureens;" "quart jugs;" "pint jugs;" "sallad dishes;" "coffee-pots;" "sugar dishes with covers;" "coffee cups;" "bowles;" "coffee cups and saucers, paynted;" "table plates, paynted:" "twifflers paynted;" "quart mugs variagated;" and "pint mugs variagated."

On the 5th of April, 1788, "Mr. Joseph Ring, potter, in Temple Street was unfortunately killed by the falling in of a warehouse. He has left a widow and nine children to lament his loss." He was superintending some alterations at the time, when the roof fell in, and he was killed in the presence of his wife. The business was carried on as usual "by the widow of the late Joseph Ring, and late partners, under the firm of Ring, Taylor, and Carter."

Fig. 771.

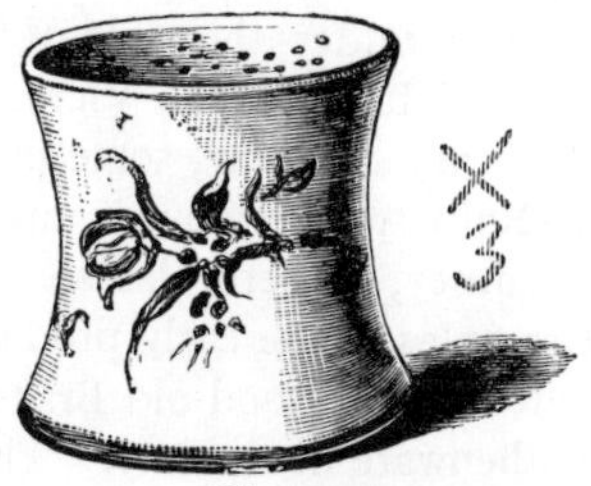
Fig. 772.

In 1797 these works are described as "a large pottery," so they must at that time have been very extensive. In that year a curious reference to "two gentlemen of the name of Ring," sons, no doubt, to Joseph Ring, occurs in the account of the death of James Doe, a potter who worked there under them, which I have given under the head of Lambeth (see page 137, *ante*). In 1813 a deed of partnership

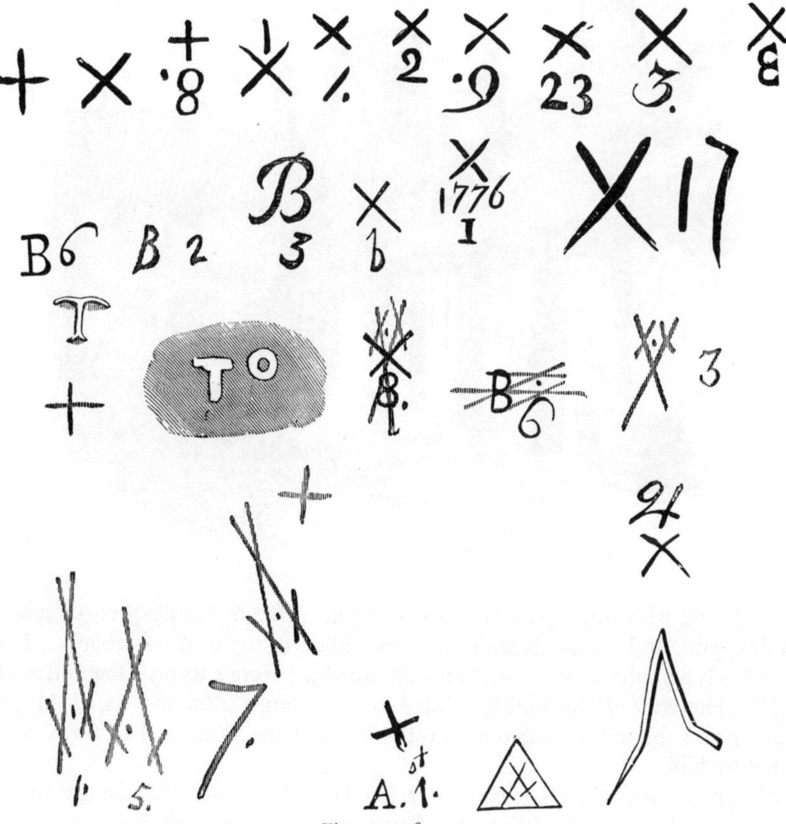
Figs. 773 to 800.

between Joseph Ring (son of the late owner), Henry Carter, and John D. Pountney was drawn up, but through the death of the first-named was not executed. The business was therefore carried on by Pountney and Carter, under the style of Elizabeth Ring & Co., until 1816, when Carter retired and was succeeded by Edward

Allies, the style being Pountney and Allies. Mr. Allies retired in 1835, and in the following year Mr. Gouldney entered into partnership and retired in 1850. Mr. Pountney died in 1852, and the works were continued by his widow until her death in 1872, under the style of "Pountney & Co.," when they were purchased by Mr. H. S. Cobden, of the Victoria Pottery, by whom they were extended. During Mr. Pountney's lifetime, some parian figures, &c., were made, and some examples, made by Raby, who removed into Staffordshire, were in the possession of the late Mrs. Pountney, as were also some excellent imitations of the Etruscan and other styles. Examples of the early productions of these works are scarce, and it is interesting to state that the good old Bristol mark of the cross was used on some of the pieces of earthenware here made. The mark is sometimes in blue, and sometimes impressed. A name well known in connection with these works is that of William Fifield (and

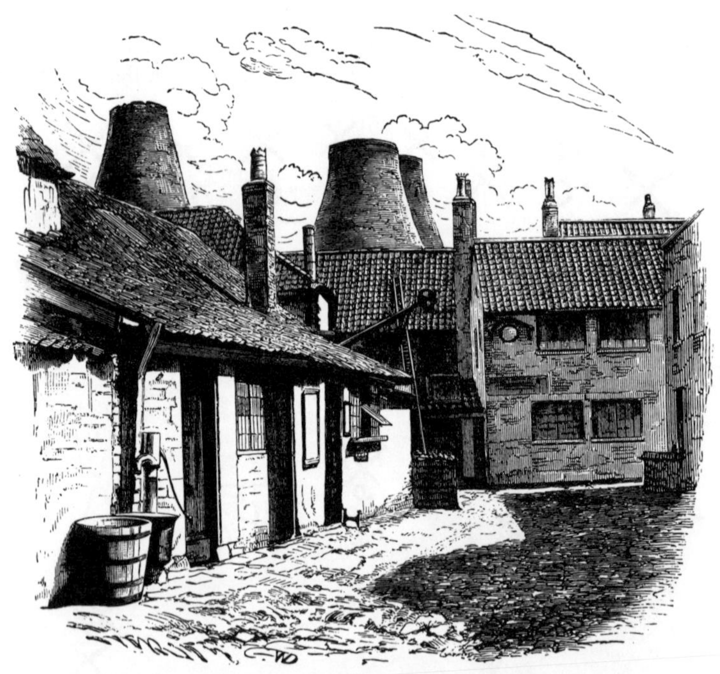

Fig. 801.—Bristol Pottery in 1869.

his son John), who was a painter of some merit. One of his plaques—a sportsman with dog, gun, and glass—is, with other examples, in my own possession. It bears on the back his initials, "W. F.," and the words, "Here's to my Dog and my Gun, 1855." The view of the works, painted on four large tiles, and dated May 15th, 1820, now on the wall of the office of the Water Lane Pottery (Fig. 802), was also painted by him.

The Temple and St. Thomas's Street Works.—The oldest stoneware pottery in Bristol, that of J. and C. Price and Brothers, in St. Thomas's Street and Temple Street, was established about 1735 or 1740, and continued by succeeding generations of the same family. The old "Salt Glaze" was used till 1842, when great improvements having been made through the experiments of Mr. Powell it was found practicable to *dip* the stoneware into liquid glaze in its green state, instead of first burning and then "smearing," as formerly practised. Messrs. Price, having adopted the new method, continued to improve their works, and built much larger kilns than usual in potteries of the kind. The superiority of "Bristol stoneware" over others became so well established, that, until recently, the metropolitan makers bought their glaze from that city. The stoneware goods are of the highest quality, and some excellent imitations of the antique, of very fine body, faultless glaze, and elegant form are produced. Among the useful goods are filters of simple but excellent construction and elegant form; feet and carriage warmers; barrels and churns; bread, cheese, and other pans; bottles, jugs, and every other kind of domestic vessel. Messrs. Price also make all the other usual varieties of stoneware goods.

Other stoneware potters besides those already named were, in former times, John Hope, in Temple Street; Thomas Patience, in the same district; James Alsop, first at 9, Water Lane, and afterwards at Temple Street, and others, as well as at Baptist Mills, Easton, and Westbury.

Temple Gate Pottery.—At Temple Gate a stoneware pottery was long ago established by Messrs. Powell. The goods are what are generally termed "Bristol

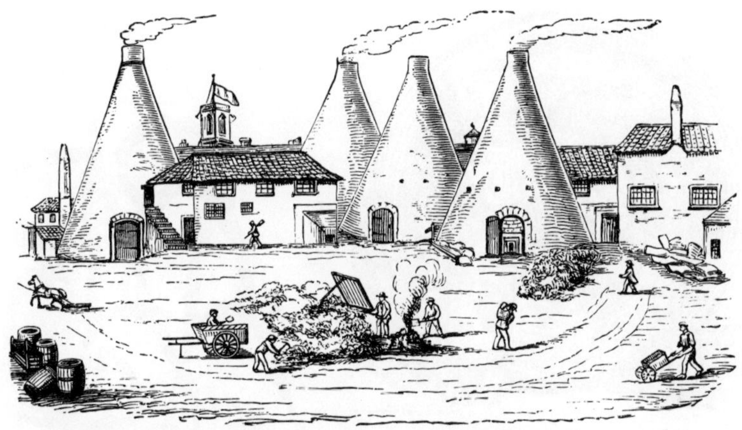

Fig. 802.—Pountney's Bristol Pottery.

ware" or "Improved stone," which was invented half a century ago by Mr. Powell. "Its peculiarity consists in its being coated with a glaze which is produced simultaneously with the ware itself, so that one firing only is needed." So great was Mr. Powell's success in his discovery, that "shortly after its introduction at the Temple Gate Pottery almost every other manufacturer of stoneware adopted it, and it has now, in a large measure, superseded the old salt-glazed ware." The goods made are bread-pans, filters, foot-warmers, bottles, jars, and other domestic vessels. Messrs. Powell have a registered arrangement for fitting, fastening, and keeping air-tight, by means of a three-pronged, or tripod, iron clamp furnished with an elastic washer, the lids of preserve and other jars—thus doing away with the necessity of any other covering. Vases and bottles of classic shape are occasionally made, as are also enormous jugs—one of which, capable of holding twenty-five gallons, has been exhibited by the firm.

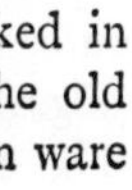

Fig. 803.

Wilder Street Pottery.—About 1820 a pottery on a small scale was worked in Wilder Street by a family named Macken, a descendant of the owner of the old pottery at St. Ann's, at Brislington, where flower-pots and other coarse brown ware was made. Macken afterwards went to America.

Salt Glaze.

It is said that the delft-ware potteries were preceded by a maker of salt-glazed stoneware—a German named Wrede, or Read—and a curious story is told in connection with him and the difficulty he had in establishing his works. It appears that the people being surprised at the glaze he produced on his ware, and at the secrecy he endeavoured to preserve regarding his pottery, and noticing the dense clouds of vapour which every now and then arose from his kiln (caused, of course, by the throwing in of the salt through the fire holes when the ware had arrived at a certain degree of heat), believed that he had called in supernatural aid, and that the fumes which ascended were caused by the visits of the devil. He was "mobbed" by the people, his place injured, and he was forced to fly the town.

Brislington.

About a century ago, I am informed, there was a pottery at St. Ann's, in this

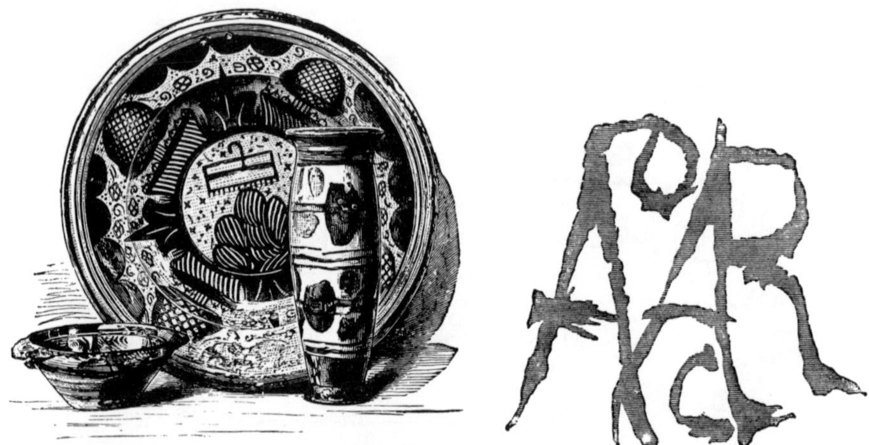

Figs. 804 and 805.—Brislington Ware.

parish, conducted by a family named Macken, one of which family had a pottery in Bristol. These works, probably the same as were carried on by Richard Frank, of Bristol, and his family, were closed in the latter part of last century; they have been converted into cottages. "They are situated at the bottom of St. Ann's Wood, between St. Ann's Vale and the river, on a line about half a mile beyond Netham Dam," and opposite to Crewshole. The older productions are described as "a drab-coloured ware with a plum-coloured glaze; the more modern were the same ware covered with a layer resembling porcelain; white, and apparently of felspar, this kind has almost invariably a rough blue pattern." The ware closely approaches, in general appearance and effect, the common descriptions of Turkish pottery. The patterns were produced, in coarse and rude designs, in a kind of copper or red lustre, on the plain buff clay ground. Some good examples of this ware, which is clumsy and coarse, but curious, are preserved in the Bristol Museum (Fig. 804). The dish is 14 inches in diameter; on its back is the rude monogram (Fig. 805) of Richard Frank, its maker.

CREWS-HOLE.

A small stoneware pottery—a wooden shed or two—was established here by a clever but somewhat peripatetic potter, Anthony Amatt, originally of Derby, who was one of the workmen employed by Richard Champion at the Bristol china works. He afterwards, I believe, had a small pottery at Temple Gate, which came into the hands of Mr. Powell when Mr. Amatt entered into his employ. Previous to this it is believed a small pottery for producing the same kind of ware as that of Brislington had existed at Crews-hole. In 1794-5 Amatt was living at Twerton, in Somersetshire, painting (as proved by bills in my possession) on earthenware and china for Mr. Egan, of Bath, brother-in-law of the second William Duesbury, of the Derby China Works. He was afterwards a stocking weaver.

WESTBURY.

The *Sugar House Pottery* at Westbury, which had been for many years carried on by George Hart, passed, on the 8th of December, 1775, into the hands of Stephen Fricker, potter and publican, who was host of the Fountain tavern in High Street, Bristol. Besides sugar bakers' moulds, which gave the name of "Sugar-house Pottery" to the works, the usual classes of brown ware articles were made.

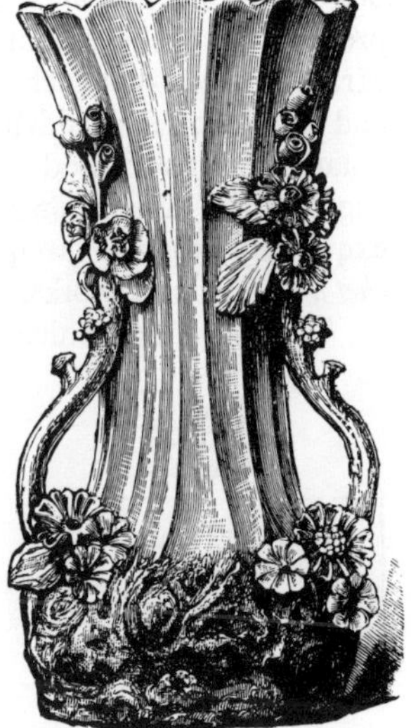

Fig. 806.

EASTON.

A small manufactory was established here for the manufacture of various articles by a process for using the magnesian limestone of the district in its body. Many very creditable and artistic articles were produced, but the affair proved a failure, and the works were closed. The spill case (Fig. 806) is said to have been made here.

WESTON-SUPER-MARE.

The *Royal Pottery* was established in 1836 by Mr. Charles Phillips as a brick and tile manufactory. In the following year glazed ware, for domestic vessels, was introduced, as was also, to a small extent, the manufacture of flower-pots, &c. In 1840 the production of glazed ware was discontinued; and, the clay of the locality being found to be admirably adapted for horticultural vessels, vases, statuary, &c., special attention was directed to them, and with such marked effect that, at the Great Exhibition of 1851, medals and certificates of merit were awarded for them. In 1870 Mr. Phillips retired from the business, which was purchased by Mr. John Matthews, by whom it has been very considerably extended; several new branches added; and a new and better taste infused into the art decorations. Notably among these introductions are rustic-work, baskets of artificial flowers, busts, vases, suspenders, &c. Flower-pots, of which from 20,000 to 30,000 are made weekly, and of all sizes, from 1¾ inches to 30 inches in diameter, are a staple production of the "Royal Pottery," and are supplied to H.M. gardens at Windsor Castle, H.M. Commissioners of Works at Kew, Hampton Court, the Parks, &c., the Royal

Horticultural Society, and to most of the principal gardens in this country, as well as being exported in large quantities to New Zealand, Port Natal, and Chili. They have the reputation of being the best, most compact, and most durable of any manufacture; and, although of such enormous size, are turned with marvellous precision, and fired without running or casting. Two specialites are the "Oxford Pot" with perforated rim for training pelargoniums, azaleas, roses, &c., without the aid of sticks, and the "Alpine-plant pot. The more notable ornamental productions are figure, shell, and other fountains, of various tiers in height; figures, groups of figures, statuettes and busts; eagles, lions, and other gigantic figures on artificial rocks and pedestals; flower and other brackets; vases and tazzas, pedestals and garden-seats; fern-stands and flower and fern-baskets decorated with wicker-work, fern-leaves, and other ornamentation; crocus pots; suspenders for flowers, orchid pots; window-boxes for flowers; arborettes for architectural decorations, &c. The general colour is a delicate red. The greatest achievement of Art in terra-cotta which has ever been gained is the production of baskets of flowers, each individual leaf or flower modelled from nature; and vases decorated in the same manner. Those who are acquainted with the exquisite beauty of the groups of porcelain bisque flowers produced at the old Bristol and Derby works, will scarcely be prepared to believe that they are successfully vied in the coarser material by Mr. Matthews; but such is the case. So true to nature are many of the flowers, and so delicately modelled in all their minutest details, that the most skilful botanist can scarce find in them a deviation from nature. The basket engraved on Fig. 807 is a fair specimen of the Matthews' reproduction of flowers; but the most exquisitely beautiful group yet produced is an example in my own possession—the *chef-d'œuvre* of the works.

The clay from which the various objects are made is the native clay of the place, and is got in the field in which the works are situated. The first six or eight feet in depth is fine plastic clay, from which the vases, statuary, busts, fern-stands, flower-baskets, and other finer goods are made. Below this are several feet in depth of blue clay, used for bricks, drain-pipes, &c., which lies in a bed of peat about fifteen inches in depth. Below this is a considerable depth of soft clay, from which ordinary bricks are made.

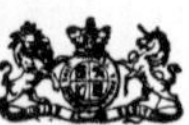

JOHN MATTHEWS,
LATE PHILLIPS,
ROYAL POTTERY,
WESTON-SUPER-MARE.

The mark is sometimes the Royal Arms alone, and at others the Royal Arms surmounting a tablet with the name. There are also other potteries, where coarse common ware is produced, in the same neighbourhood.

Poole, Dorset.

The Architectural Pottery Company's works were established in 1854 by Messrs. Thomas Sanders Ball, John Ridgway (china manufacturer, of Cauldon Place, Hanley), Thomas Richard Sanders, and Frederick George Sanders. In 1857, Mr. Ridgway retired, as did Mr. Ball in 1861, and the works were continued by T. R. and F. G. Sanders alone. The productions are patent coloured and glazed bricks and mouldings, semi-perforated and pressed; patent mosaic, tessellated, encaustic, vitreous, and other glazed wall tiles; embossed and perforated tiles; quarries and fire-clay goods, &c.—the clays used being Purbeck clay, Cornish china clay, and Fareham clay, while those for plain quarries are from the Canford estate.

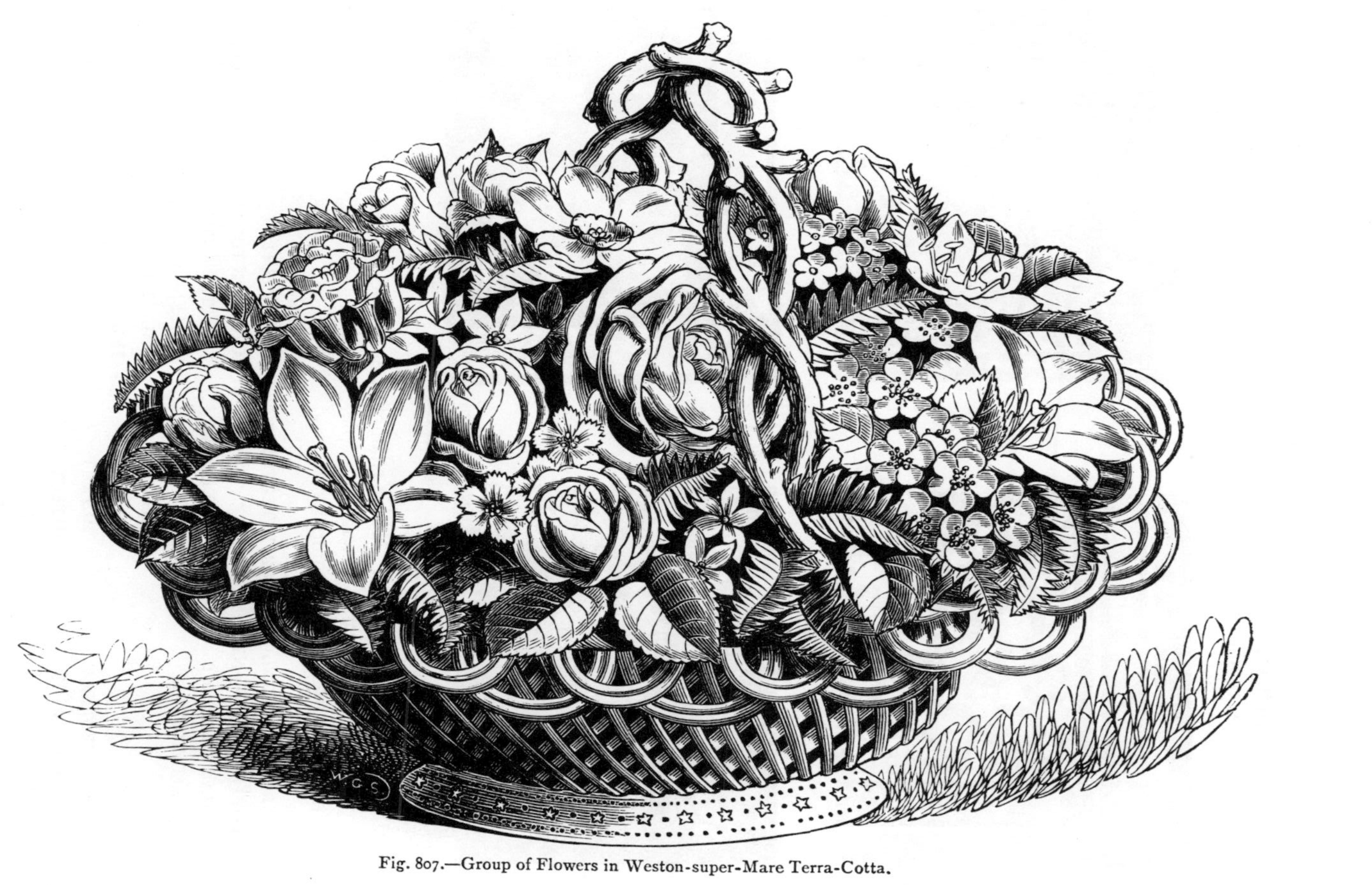

Fig. 807.—Group of Flowers in Weston-super-Mare Terra-Cotta.

The encaustic paving tiles are of good design, many being carefully copied from mediæval examples. A speciality of these works are the tessellated tiles, under Bale's patent process. These are literally formed of thin tesseræ of various colours, laid on and forming a part of the quarry itself. By this means all the richness and intricacy of the geometrical designs of tessellated pavements are produced, and at

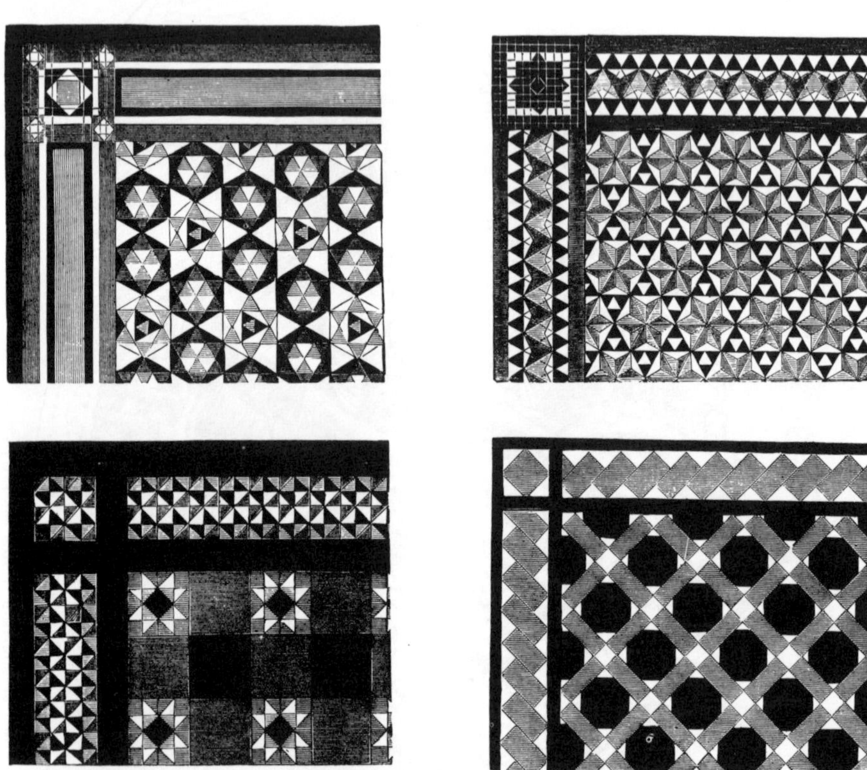

Figs. 808 to 811.

small trouble in laying down. Their character, as a rule, is better than the Italian tiles produced on the same general principle.

The marks used by the company are :—

<table>
<tr><td>ARCHITECTURAL
POTTERY COMPANY
POOLE DORSET
REGISTERED</td><td>ARCHITECTURAL
POTTERY CO.
POOLE DORSET
PATENT · INLAID
MOSAIC</td><td>PATENT
ARCHITECTURAL
POTTERY CO
POOLE,—DORSET
BALE'S PATENT
INLAID MOSAIC</td><td>A. P. CO.</td></tr>
<tr><td>ARCHITECTURAL
POTTERY CO
POOLE : DORSET</td><td>PATENT
ARCHITECTURAL
POTTERY . CO
POOLE · DORSET</td><td>A P · CO
POOLE
PATENT</td><td>A. P · CO
POOLE</td></tr>
</table>

Bourne Valley Pottery.—At this pottery, worked by Messrs. Standing and Marten, who have an establishment at Bourne Valley Wharf, Nine Elms, London, glazed stoneware sewage and sanitary pipes, on Creshes' patent, and terra-cotta vases, figures, chimney-tops, garden edgings, and architectural enrichments are made.

Branksea Pottery.—These potteries were built in 1855 by Col. Waugh for the manufacture of stoneware sanitary goods and terra-cotta; they have the advantage of a large bed of excellent clay close at hand.

Kinson.

The works at Kinson, near Poole, established in the middle of the present century, consisted of twelve kilns with boiler, engine-house, drying-sheds, stables, offices, &c. After a few years they were closed, and so remained until 1867, when the property was purchased by the present "Kinson Pottery Company," who commenced making stoneware drain-pipes. Shortly afterwards the company introduced the making of terra-cotta goods, in which they were very successful. The estate consists of about twenty-seven acres of freehold land, which is underlaid through its whole area with a thick compact bed of clay, in layers of various descriptions. It is (roughly speaking) of three qualities, about 40 feet thick, lying in nearly equal beds of each description.

The productions include all the usual sanitary goods, and other articles; and terra-cotta vases, rustic seats, brackets, garden edgings, chimney-pots, architectural enrichments, &c.

CHAPTER XII.

NOTTINGHAM.

THAT pottery and encaustic paving-tiles were made at Nottingham during mediæval times is abundantly proved by the discovery, in April, 1874 (when digging the foundations for the Methodist New Connection Chapel), of kilns and examples of tiles and domestic vessels.

The vessels seem to be of very much the same general character and period as those found at Burley Hill, described on pages 62 and 63. They consist principally of pitchers of almost identical form with those engraved on Figs. 266 to 269 and 272 and 274; the most remarkable one bearing a mask on either side.

In 1861 there appears, from a list of trades compiled in that year and given by Dering, to have been only one master-potter at Nottingham. In 1693 "glass-pots" —*i.e.* crucibles for glass makers—were made of Derbyshire crouch clay. This is thus alluded to by Houghton in that year, "*clay with flat or thin sand glittering with mica.* Crouch white clay, Derbyshire, of which the glass pots are made at Nottingham."

In the beginning of last century Mr. Charles Morley was a manufacturer of brown glazed earthenware in the lower part of Beck Street, on the way to St. Ann's Well. He amassed a considerable fortune by his pottery, and built the large house in Beck Lane, afterwards occupied by his son, Mr. C. L. Morley, and still later used as the School of Design. In 1737 Mr. Charles Morley, the potter, was one of the Sheriffs of Nottingham. One of his principal branches of manufacture was in brown ware ale-mugs, for the ale-houses of the district, and in pitchers, and other domestic utensils. In 1739, according to a list of trades in that year, there were two master potters in Nottingham.

Dering, who wrote his "Nottingamia vetus et nova" in 1751, says that at that time Nottingham sends down the river Trent "coals, lead, timber, corn, wool, and potter's ware." In 1772-4 it is stated, in a curious and scarce little work, "A Short Tour in the Midland Counties of England," that at Nottingham "the making of glass wares is laid aside, and that of pots become very trifling."

In 1815, Blackner in his history of Nottingham says, "there were likewise two potteries within the last thirty years," "but the clay was principally brought from a considerable distance, which added so much to the cost of the pots as to prevent the proprietors maintaining a competition with the Staffordshire dealers."

The names of "Mug-House Yard" and "Mug-House Lane" in Beck Street, take their origin from the old pot works of Mr. Morley, and show, incontestably, that those works, where "mugs" were the staple production, were known as the "Mug-house."

The greater part of the clay was brought from out of Derbyshire, but some is said also to have been procured from Hucknall Torkard.

The following names of Nottingham "pot makers" occur in a list of burgesses and freeholders, 1744: "John Ash, William Barns, John Clayton, Moses Colclough, John Coppock, Thomas Elnor, Thomas Glover, John Handley ('mug maker'), John Hazeley, Thomas Hough, William Lockett, Isaac Selby, Leonard Twells, Samuel Wyer and John Wyer, senior; and James and George Sefton, pipe makers." In 1780, "John Coppock, Isaac Dance, Thomas Hough, John Handley ('mug maker'). Isaac Selby, Thomas Wyer, Richard Reeves, William Barnes, Moses Coleclough, Leonard Twells, Richard Wyer, Thomas Glover, William Lockett, and Thomas Elnor; and John Clayton, 'pipe maker.'" In 1802, "Moses Colclough, John Key, John Reynolds, and Samuel Woodhouse."

The earliest known dated example of Nottingham ware is the remarkably fine posset-pot (Fig. 812), in the possession of the Rev. J. S. Doxey. It is of the general form, but fashioned with more than ordinary care and lightness, with a light brown lustrous glaze. It is of a very unusual mode of construction, the "belly" part having double sides, the outer of which is ornamented with foliage and flowers, the stalks incised and the flowers and leaves perforated. A tube commencing about an inch from the top runs down the exterior side as far as the top of the "belly," where it

Samuel Watkinson *Major*
& Sarah his Wife *& Majoress* } *of Nottingham.*
1 7 0 0

passes through and is continued to the bottom of the interior. This tube, whose mouth-piece is broken off, was so constructed that a draught of the posset could by suction be taken apart from the bread, spices, &c. On the front is inscribed in cursive characters as above, and on the other side are the royal arms of the period (William III.) with crest, supporters, garter, and motto. Though this cup is of the same general form as the posset-pot, and may have been used as such, it may also have been used on occasions of mayoral and other hospitality as a "loving-cup," or as some would prefer to call it, from its having only two handles, a "parting-cup." Samuel Watkinson, the owner of the posset-pot, or in whose honour it was made, was mayor of Nottingham in 1700, 1708, and 1715. In Mr. Briscoe's possession is a mug discovered during excavations in Victoria Street, close to the site of the Old Ship Inn, of "Gideon Giles" notoriety. Another mug belonging to Mr. Kidd (Figs. 813 and 814) has in front a full-blown rose on a stem, surmounted by a crown, and there are two other crowns, one on either side, a little lower down, between what are evidently intended for thistles; there is also a terminal rose at each end, and the remainder

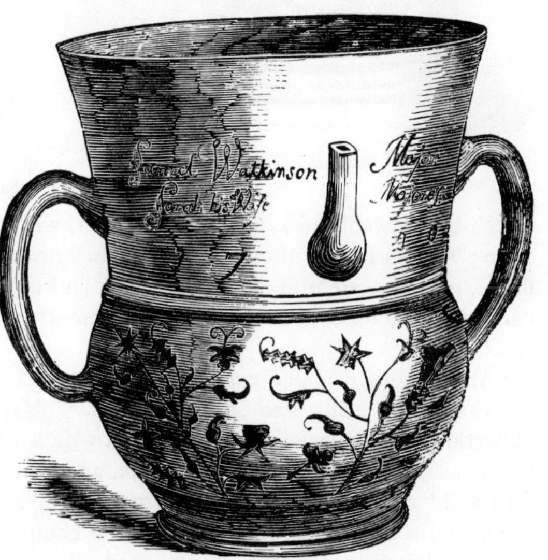

Fig. 812.—Posset-pot, Nottingham ware.

of the body is ornamented with their stems and foliage. At the back, by the handle, are the incised words, *John Johnson, Schoolmaster, Nottingham. Sept. ye* 3, 1762, and on the bottom, in the same kind of incised writing letters, is the maker's name, *Wm Lockett*, who is one of the makers included in the foregoing lists. The name stands thus in the 1774 list: "Lockett William, pot-maker, *New Buildings*" (in 1780 he was of *St. Ann's Street*), and he appears to have given a plumper for the Hon. William Howe, of Epperstone. In the same list is a Henry Lockett, saddler, Smithy Row, who voted in the same manner. In the same list the name of the schoolmaster for whom this special mug was made also occurs, but he voted for Lord Edward Bentinck, and Sir Charles Sedley, of Nutthall, Bart. The name stands thus: "Johnson John, school-master, *St. Mary's Church side.*"

A jug formerly belonging to Mr. Norman has the inscription, incised in writing letters, as follows: "*John Smith junr of Bassford near Nottingham* 1712."

In the Museum of Practical Geology is a "christening bowl," thirteen inches in diameter, bearing the incised words, in writing letters, "*Nouember* 20 1726;" a

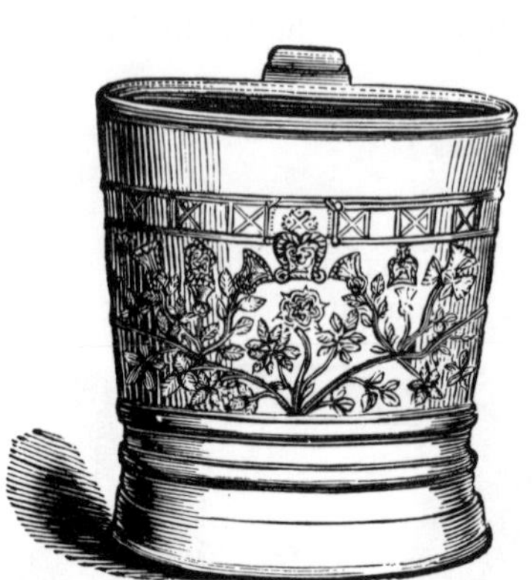

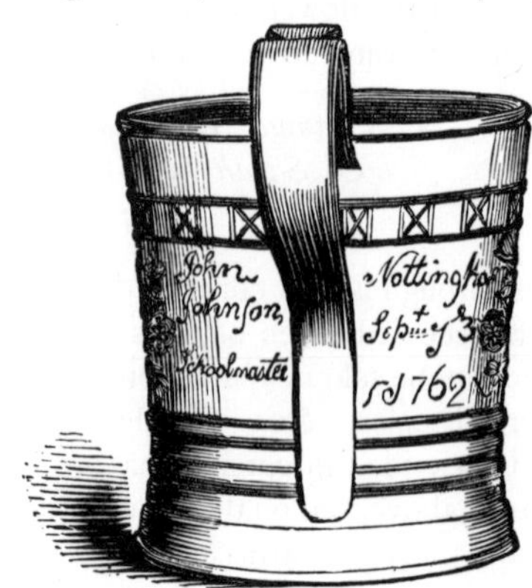

Figs. 813 and 814.—Nottingham ware.

punch-bowl, twenty-two inches in diameter, with the words "Old England for Ever, 1750;" and a highly interesting mug "in brown earthenware with glaze of metallic lustre, ornamented with stamped flowers laid on in relief, and incised inscription in cursive characters, round the rim, '*Made at Nottingham ye* 17*th Day of August A.D.* 1771.'"

Another good dated example, brought under my notice by Mr. Briscoe, bears the names of "*Thos. and Mary Brammer, May ye* 21 1753." In the Hawkins collection was a puzzle jug, ornamented with a vase of pinks and scrolls around the lower part, and bearing the date 1755, and initials, "G. B." In the same collection was "a tobacco-jar, in form of a bear, of bright lustrous glaze, his head being the cover, a collar round his neck, and a chain, to which is attached a large hollow perforated ball, containing stones, used as a rattle; on the ball is impressed the name 'Elizabeth Clark, Dec ye 25th 1769.'"

One of the favourite productions of the Nottingham "Mug-house" and its predecessors was drinking-jugs in form of a bear, which were also made at Brampton in the same kind of ware, and at Fulham and other places in other wares. A strikingly good example (Fig. 815) is in my own possession. It is 9½ inches in height, and formed of the usual hard brown glazed ware of this pottery. The whole, with the exception of the neck, is powdered with small fragments of dry clay (not "potsherds" as usually but erroneously stated) which have been sprinkled over its surface before firing and burnt in with it. This, it may be remarked, is the usual characteristic of these vessels wherever made. The one under notice has the eyes, outlines of the ears, teeth, and claws, laid on in white "slip." It, like many other "bears," is made to rest as in the engraving, or to stand upright when placed on its hams; the body contains the liquor, and the head lifts off to be used as a drinking-cup, holding it by the muzzle.

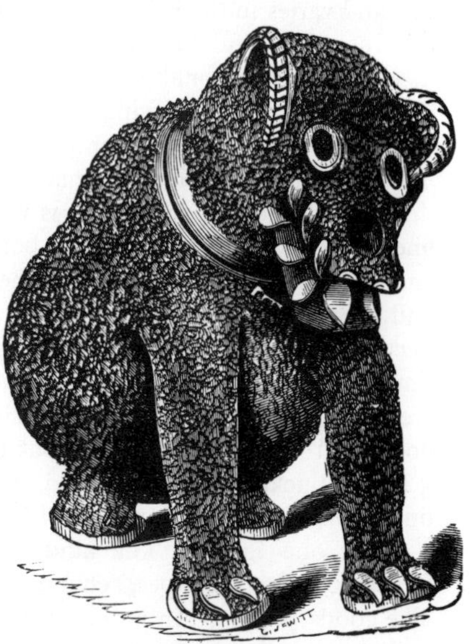

Fig. 815.—Nottingham ware.

Lowesby.

In 1835 Sir F. G. Fowke, Bart., commenced some Terra-Cotta Works at Lowesby, in Leicestershire, and produced vases of good character and of remarkably hard and fine body from the clays of the neighbourhood. He had previously, about 1833, made some garden-pots for his own use, and finding the clay good and tenacious, determined upon utilising it. In colour the terra-cotta was a full rich red, and in some cases the articles were decorated with Etruscan figures and ornaments in black enamel. Vases, ornamented flower-pots, butter-pots, and other articles of domestic use were produced, and these were mostly decorated with patters in black, or occasionally in colours, and gilt.

A shop for the sale of the Lowesby ware was opened in King William Street, London, under the management of a Mr. Purden. The ornamental vases, made of different sizes, were sent up to London as they came from the kiln, and many of the antique shapes were there painted and enamelled under Mr. Purden's superintendence. The manufacture was only continued for a few years, and then, not being found to answer, died out. The place is now used as a brick and tile works, and flower-pots are also made. The mark is a fleur-de-lis, beneath the name "LOWESBY" in a curved line (Fig. 816) Occasionally the name LOWESBY without the fleur-de-lis occurs. The arms of Sir Frederick G. Fowke, Bart., the founder of the works, are, *vert*, a fleur-de-lis, *argent*, and the seat is Lowesby Hall, so that the mark represented the armorial bearing of the family and the name of the estate.

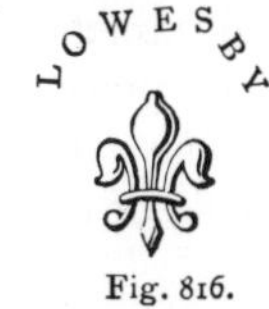

Fig. 816.

Coalville and Ibstock.

In 1859 the attention of Mr. George Smith (so well known for his exertions in improving the condition of the brick-yard children and those of the canal population) was drawn to the clays of the neighbourhood of Coalville and Whitwick, and he procured some for the purpose of experiments. The trials proving satisfactory, Mr. Smith entered into an arrangement with Mr. J. Whetstone and others under which terra-cotta works in connection with the Whitwick Colliery Company were established at Coalville and Ibstock. These are worked by the Midland Brick and Terra-Cotta Company, who produce three kinds, viz. red, white or light buff, and yellow or cream-colour. These varieties are thus described for me by Mr. Smith: "First, the red. This is made out of the surface clay, of a greyish tint, and varies in thickness from 4 to 30 feet, and does not shrink much in burning; it burns a beautiful bright red colour, and will stand the severest weather and keep its colour. Occasionally a little white scum may be seen on the surface: this is the result of making, drying, and burning too quickly; but this will disappear after it has been in use a winter or so. Second, the light buff or glypto terra-cotta. The clay out of which this is made underlies the red terra-cotta clay and varies in thickness from 6 to 20 feet; it is very hard and difficult to be ground to a proper fineness. This terra-cotta when burnt very much resembles Bath stone in colour, and may, if it be kept dry from the time it is burnt to the time it is used, be cut and carved with much ease, and it is very suitable for head-stones, &c. But this peculiar speciality disappears after it has been exposed to the weather for a little time, when it gets hard, and turns the edge of the tools. Third, the yellow or cream-coloured terra cotta. The clay is got out of the coal-pits in the neighbourhood, and lies at a depth of about 120 yards from the surface. It averages about 5 feet in thickness, and is a kind of clay between pot-clay and fire-clay. It is very fine, strong, free from iron, and will stand a great heat, but shrinks a deal in burning —about one-eighth. The kind of goods this clay is most suitable for are the following: Sewage-pipes, chimney-pots, vases, flower-boxes, tiles, and pottery. The goods produced in architectural enrichments are bases and capitals; cornices, corbels, and brackets; arch moulds, vaulting-ribs, and balustrades; diapers, finials and ridge-tiles, and other articles. Garden and conservatory as well as table vases."

Polesworth.

Terra-Cotta Works.—This manufactory of terra-cotta by the "Midland Brick and Terra Cotta Company" was established in 1875, under the directorship of Mr. J. Joiner, for many years principal manager at the Stamford Terra-Cotta Works. The productions consist of fountains; garden, conservatory, and other vases of various designs; architectural details and enrichments; chimney-tops, chimney-pieces, capitals and columns, crestings and finials, tomb-stones, monuments, memorial tablets and urns; moulded and plain bricks; roofing-tiles, garden-edgings, drain-pipes, and other useful goods. The terra-cotta is both red and buff, and is of fine hard and durable quality, and, with a clean, good surface, unites a pleasant shade of colour.

Market Bosworth.

Terra-Cotta Works, belonging to the "Midland" Company, were established here for the production of bricks, tiles, and ordinary terra-cotta goods.

Tamworth.

The *Terra-Cotta Works* at Tamworth, established by Gibbs and Canning in 1847, produce architectural, horticultural, and other useful and ornamental goods; Della Robbia ware, sanitary goods, tiles and bricks, &c. In terra-cotta, for architectural purposes, are trusses and cornices, bosses and pateræ, brackets and corbels, capitals and bases, balustrades and parapets, window and door-heads, terminals and finials, friezes, diaper work, and every other detail, of a quality for sharpness, hardness, and durability scarcely to be surpassed. Among ornamental goods are fountains, vases, tazzas, pedestals, garden-seats, brackets, suspenders, figures and groups, and every variety of articles for the lawn, the garden, or the conservatory. The "Della Robbia ware"—a fine terra-cotta beautifully and effectively enamelled in brilliant and flat colours on the surface—is produced in endless variety in plaques, &c., for ceilings and walls, where it takes the place of plaster or other surface-covering, garden and flower-vases, jardinières, mignonette-boxes, and other articles.

WILNECOTE.

The *Wilnecote Works*, near Tamworth, established in 1860 by Mr. George Skey, who purchased the coal-mines at this place, and in the course of sinking shafts discovered important and valuable beds of fire and other clays well adapted for pottery purposes. He determined at once to erect kilns and work-rooms, which

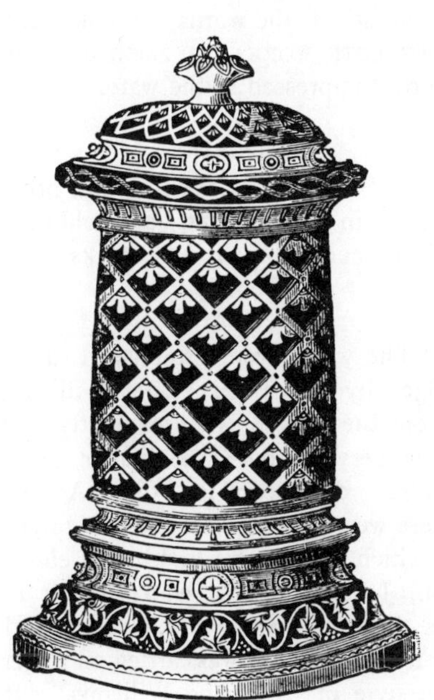

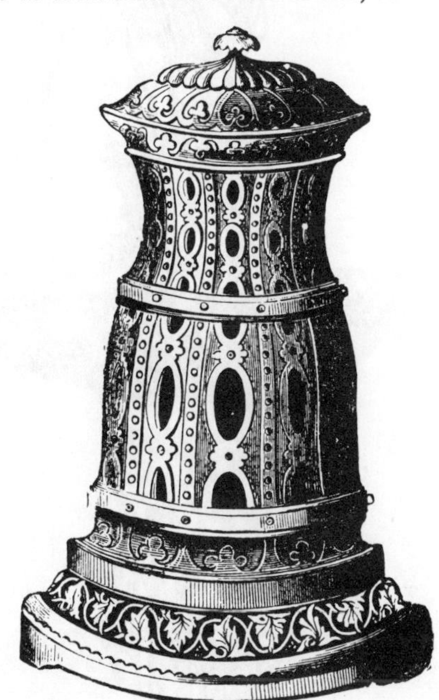

Figs. 817 and 818.—Terra-Cotta Gas-stoves.

he fitted up with suitable machinery, steam-presses, lathes, &c., and the manufactory was opened in 1862. The goods produced were so well received that the works had very shortly to be enlarged and fresh work-rooms and kilns erected. In 1864 Mr. Skey having found the concern grown to more than his own personal care could, single-handed, control, formed it into a limited liability company, with a capital of £60,000, under the style of the "Wilnecote Company, Limited," afterwards altered to "George Skey and Company, Limited." The goods produced are fountains, vases, tazzas, brackets, pedestals, suspenders, terminals, flower-vases, mignonette-boxes, fern-stands, garden-seats, balustrades, cornices, chimney-tops, and every description of architectural enrichment. Game-pie dishes and other domestic articles are also produced, as are vases, garden-seats, flower-pots, brackets, fern-stands, and a variety of other articles in "rustic ware," which is a fine buff-coloured terra-cotta, glazed with a rich brown glaze, and sometimes heightened with a green tinge, just sufficient to give it a pleasing effect. In stoneware, or

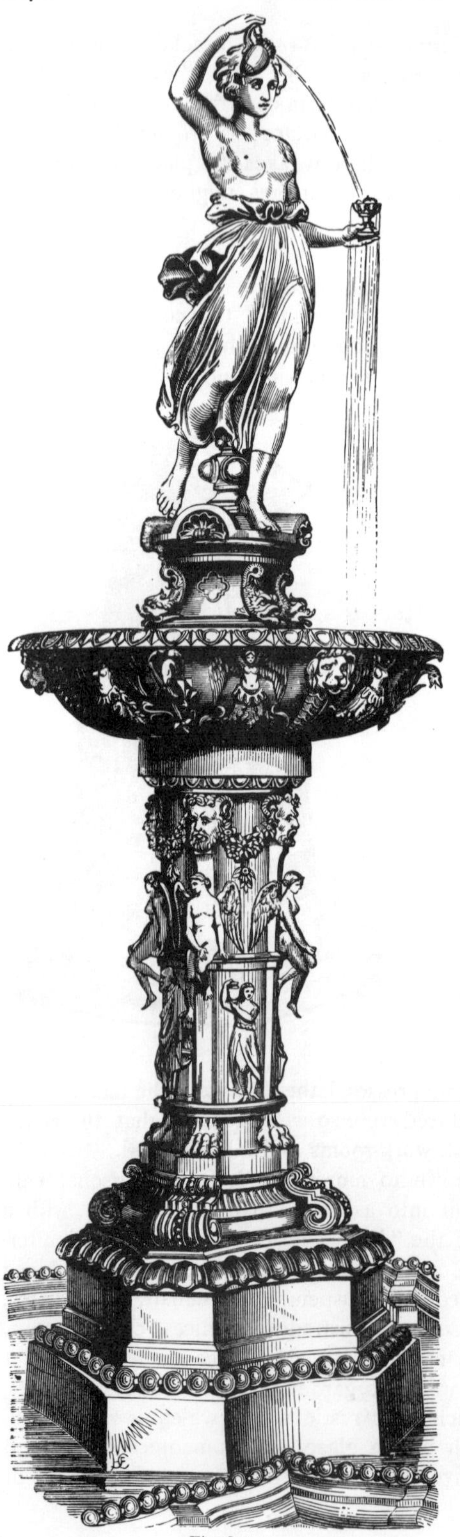

Fig. 819.

Bristol ware, and sanitary ware, all the usual and many additional articles are made; and ridge- and roofing-tiles, sewerage-pipes, garden-edgings, paving-tiles, and facing-bricks of various colours, are staple productions. Terra-cotta gas-stoves are extensively made and are of admirable construction. Some of the patterns are in high relief, and others, in addition to the relief, are perforated, and have a striking and pleasing effect. Two of these are shown on Figs. 817 and 818. The mark used is the words GEORGE SKEY WILNECOTE WORKS NR TAMWORTH, in an oval impressed in the ware.

COVENTRY.

At Stoke, near Coventry, and other places in the district, are old-established coarse brown ware works.

NUNEATON.

The works were established about 1830, by Mr. Peter Wager Williams, upon the site of what evidently had been very old pot-works, but of which no record appears to exist. At first there were two distinct manufactories, of which one was worked by his eldest son, John Williams, who sold it to his three brothers, Peter, Charles, and James, by whom it was carried on under the style of "Caroline Williams." It afterwards passed by purchase into the hands of Mr. J. Rawlins, and was taken by "Messrs. Broadbent and Stanley Brothers," by whom it was considerably extended. The other manufactory was carried on by Mr. Walter Handley, at whose death it passed to his son-in-law, Mr. David Wheway, at whose decease it was incorporated with the other, and carried on jointly by Broadbent and Stanley Brothers. In 1871 Mr. Broadbent retired from the concern. The goods included terra-cotta vases, chimney-pots, &c.; coloured paving-tiles for geometric designs; garden-edging, ornamental, ridging, and plain building and ornamental bricks; and sanitary and other pipes, &c. The marls from which the various goods are made, on the ground worked by this firm, comprise about twenty different measures of divers colours and qualities. The works occupy nearly ten acres of ground.

BROXBOURNE.

In 1843 Mr. Pulham succeeded in making terra-cotta of a good stone-colour and a rich pale red. Having done this, he began to produce various small objects for architectural purposes—bosses, angle-quoins, brackets, balustrades, small flower-pots, and vases—which remain at the present day as sharp and good as when they left the kiln. He also introduced what is termed granulated terra-cotta, having the appearance of stone.

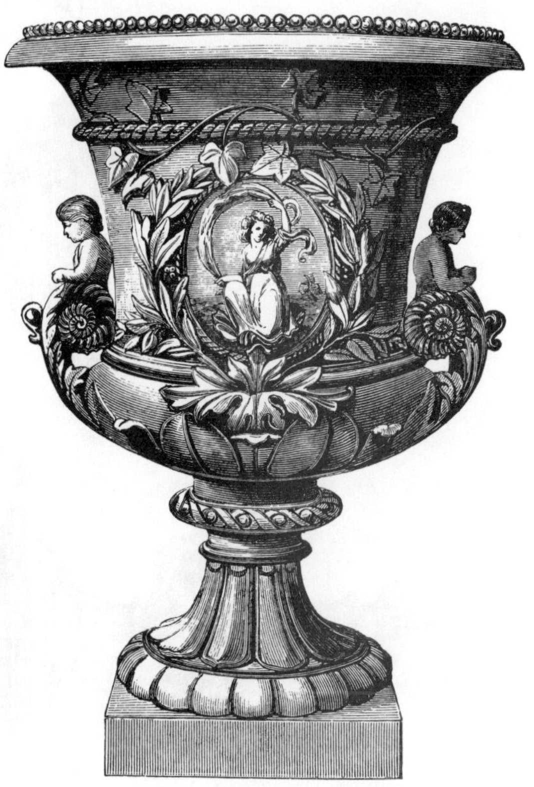

Fig. 820.

In 1871, besides other of his productions, Mr. Pulham exhibited a small fountain, which was at play during the whole time of the Exhibition; and also several new vases. The fountains (for which a prize medal was awarded) and principal exhibits were very favourably noticed. Some of these I give on Figs. 819 to 824. At the Paris Exhibition in 1867 fountains, vases, and architectural embellishments, amongst which may be named the Preston vase (a number of which were made for the People's Park, Preston), with medallions representing the staple commerce of the place; some rich columns, novel window-jambs and dressings; and notably among the rest was the Mulready monument, erected for the Science and Art Department, South Kensington, and at whose instigation it was sent to Paris. The design of this is a pedestal 15 ft. by 10 ft., round the sides of which are sketched in outline some of Mulready's principal pictures. This pedestal supports a large-sized effigy, 7 ft. long, on a raised bier, the whole of this bier and effigy being fired successfully, just as it left the sculptor's and modeller's hands, and which was highly commended and spoken of as quite a *chef-d'œuvre* in the terra-cotta art, and obtained the silver medal. It is now in Kensal Green Cemetery, where it was fixed on its return from Paris.

STAMFORD.

That pottery was in mediæval times made in Stamford was incontestably proved in the latter end of 1874 by the discovery of a kiln during the course of excavations

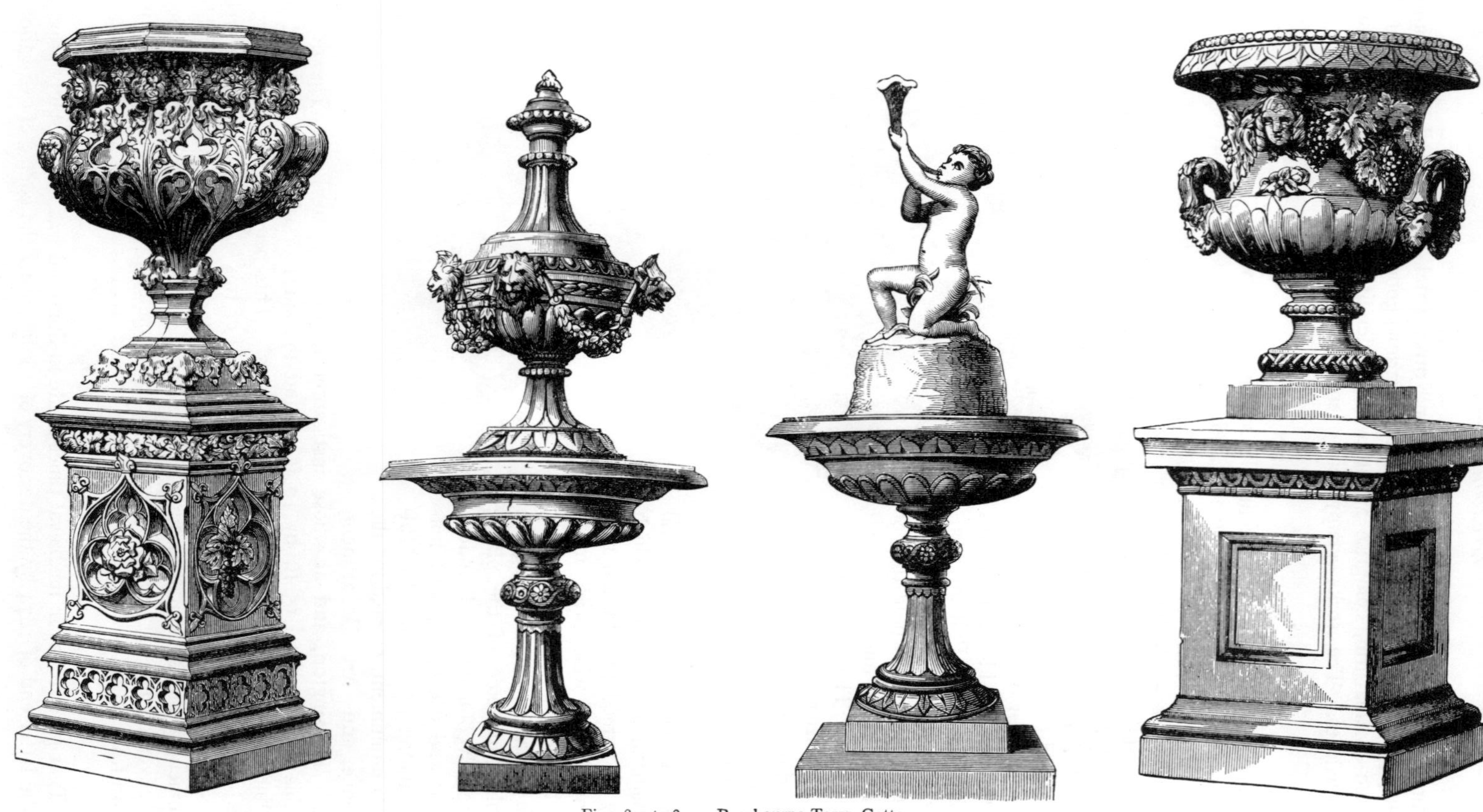

Figs. 821 to 824.—Broxbourne Terra-Cotta.

in the rear of a house occupied by the Rev. E. F. Gretton, but from that early time until 1858 pottery was not made there. In that year terra-cotta works were established by Mr. J. M. Blashfield. Previous to this time, Mr. Blashfield had been until 1851 engaged in Southwark Bridge Road, Albion Place, Blackfriars, and Millwall, in the Italian marble trade, and the manufacture of cements and scagliola, and the making and laying down of tesselated pavements, &c. In 1851 he commenced the manufacture of terra-cotta at Millwall, London, having previously purchased a number of moulds, models, &c., from Coades when that manufactory was closed. In 1858 Mr. Blashfield (whose name is intimately connected with the subject of encaustic paving-tiles, having been associated with the late Mr. Herbert Minton in their revival) removed his moulds, plant, &c., to Stamford, where a suitable clay was found to exist. In 1874 the works merged into a limited liability company, under the style of the "Stamford Terra-Cotta Company," which failed and was

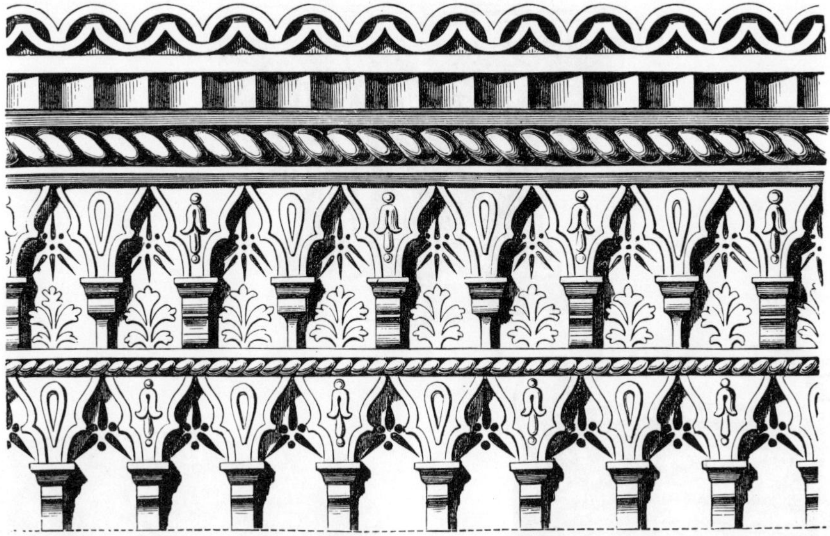

Fig. 825.

wound up in 1875, when the plant and stock were sold by auction, but afterwards to some extent revived.

The productions of this manufactory were terra-cotta as applied to every purpose, glazed or enamelled tiles and bricks for wall-facings, hard ordinary paving-tiles, enamelled architectural enrichments for internal use, and red and buff moulded bricks.

Among the public buildings which were enriched by the art-works of Mr. Blashfield's manufactory are the urns, antifixa, and pavements in the royal mausoleums, Windsor; vases and terminals, &c., at Buckingham Palace; vases, tazzas, borders, &c., at Kew and Hampton Court Gardens and Dairy Farm, Windsor; colossal statues, fountains, vases, &c., and roofs and other decorations, at the Crystal Palace; chimney-shafts, &c., Sandringham; vases and pedestals, Marlborough House; the entire red, buff, grey, and black terra-cotta details and enrichments for Dulwich College, Lady Alford's mansion, and many other places; and, indeed, for most of the public buildings and private mansions of this country and abroad. Of these,

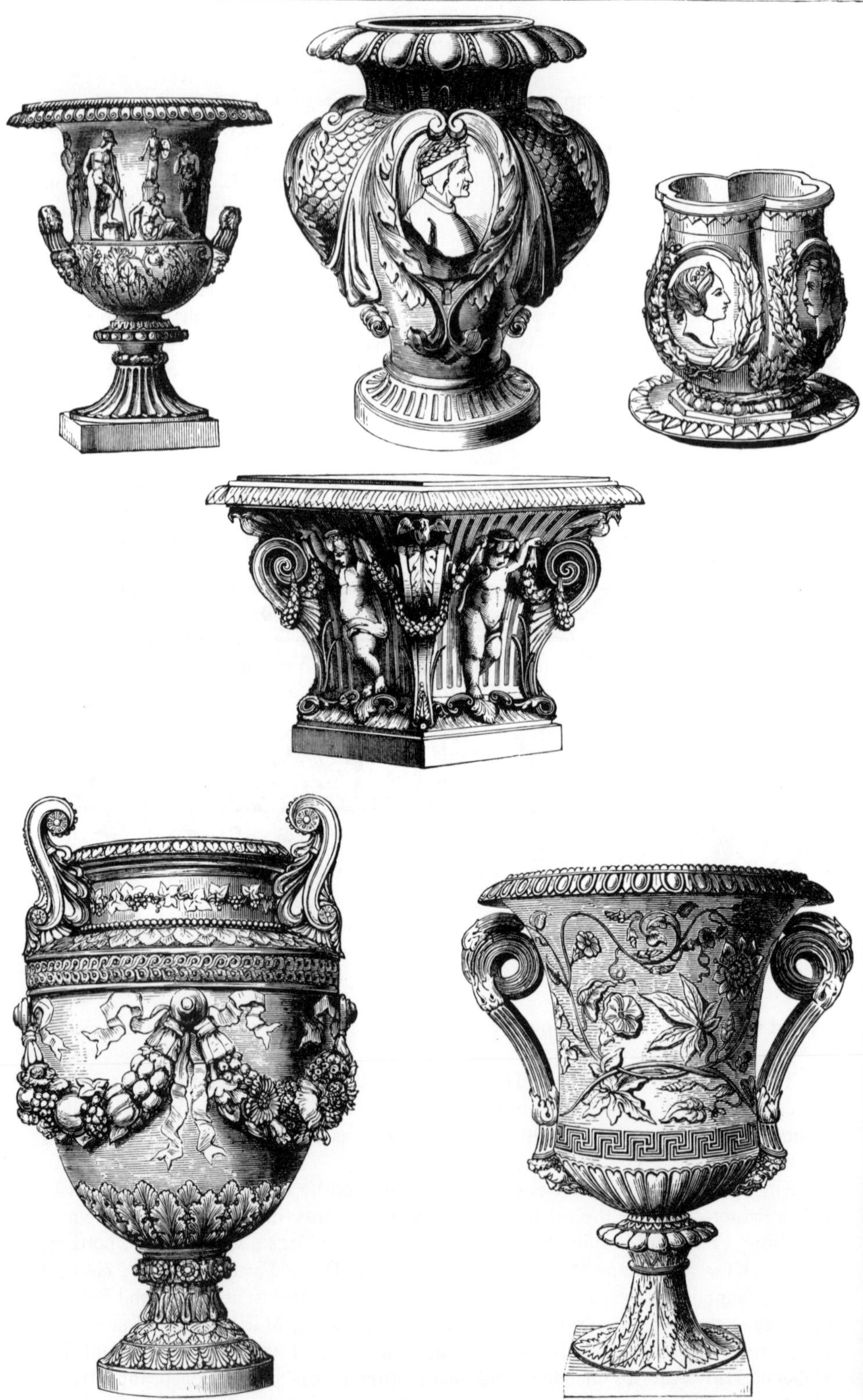

Figs. 826 to 831.—Blashfield's Stamford Terra-Cotta.

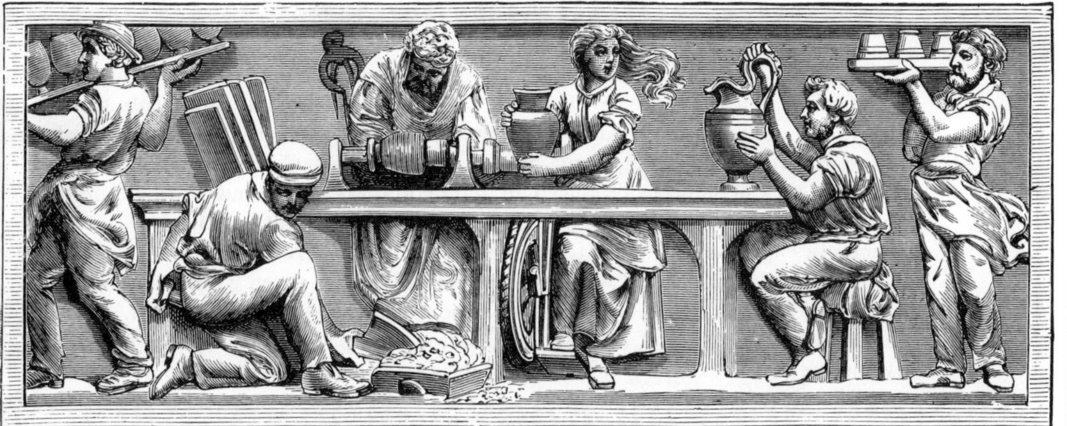

Fig. 832.—Blashfield's Terra-Cotta Frieze of the Plastic Art. "Turning."

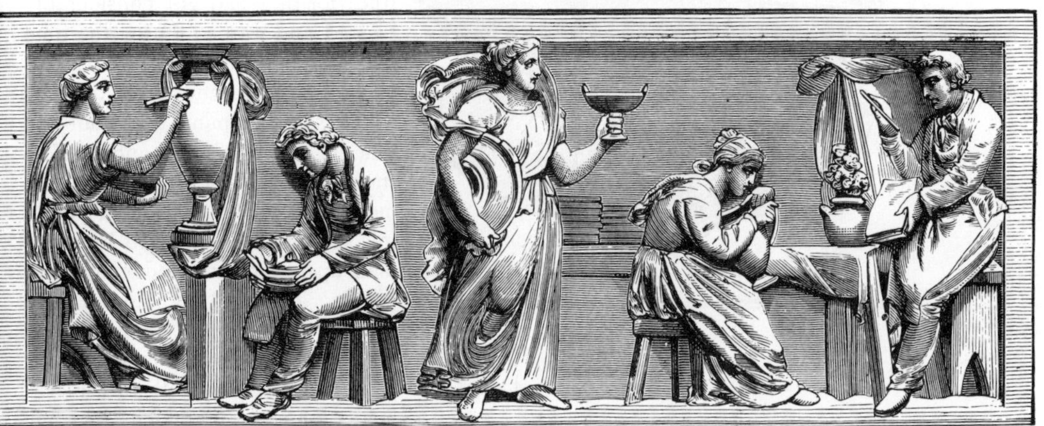

Fig. 833.—Blashfield's Terra-Cotta Frieze of the Plastic Art. "Painting."

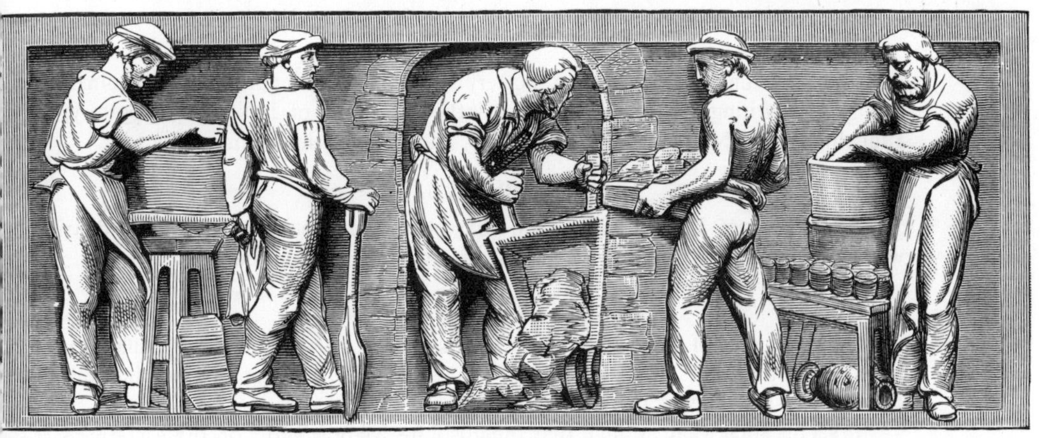

Fig. 834.—Blashfield's Terra-Cotta Frieze of the Plastic Art. "Firing.'

perhaps one of the most important, and which will ever remain a lasting monument of Stamford ceramic art, is the new Dulwich College, erected from designs by Mr. Charles Barry, and entirely composed of terra-cotta, no stone whatever being used, the value of the material alone being, in the gross, calculated at £28,000. One of the most striking series of subjects produced in terra-cotta was the manufacturing "process panels" on the exterior of the Wedgwood Memorial Institute at Burslem (three of which are engraved on Figs. 832 to 834), modelled by Mr. J. Morris. The history of these panels is a somewhat interesting feature as connected with Stamford terra-cotta works. The whole of the clay was there prepared by Mr. Blashfield. A large case, lined with plaster of Paris, was made for each panel; the clay was firmly and evenly pressed into it, and thus each of the twelve was transmitted to South Kensington. Mr. Morris wrought his modelling on the faces of these cases of clay, and they were returned to Stamford when ready for the later process to be accomplished. At Stamford they were cut up into suitable pieces for "firing;" made true (for they had got considerably twisted and warped during the time they were in the modeller's hands), carefully dried, and burned; the whole series coming out from the kiln in the admirable and perfect state in which they now stand, as monuments of Mr. Blashfield's ceramic skill, in the Wedgwood Institute. The operations in producing these panels occupied about twelve months in time, and their cost, of course, was something considerable. They were marked with Mr. Blashfield's name. Engravings of some of Mr. Blashfield's vases are given on Figs. 820 to 835. The marks used were the name, impressed, "J. M. BLASHFIELD," or "BLASHFIELD, STAMFORD," or "STAMFORD TERRA COTTA CO. LIMITED."

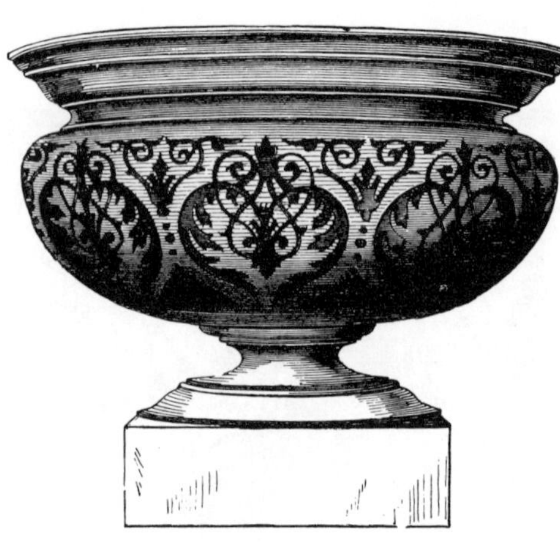

Fig. 835.

Bolingbroke.

In the seventeenth century a pottery existed at Bolingbroke, in Lincolnshire. Houghton, writing in 1693, speaks of "the blue clay of Bolingbroke pottery, in Lincolnshire." Nothing, however, is now known as to this manufactory.

Wisbech.

Terra-cotta of a remarkably good character, made from the clay of the district, was made here in 1859; but the works were not of long continuance.

Lowestoft and Gunton.

Here, on one of the easternmost points of the East Angles, a manufactory of fine porcelain existed in the latter half of last century, and genuine productions of those works are much sought for by collectors.

It seems somewhat strange that the absolute "land's end" on the eastern coast of England should have been chosen as the spot on which porcelain should be made, when the clay for the purpose had to be procured from the western "Land's End," Cornwall, and the coal from the extreme northern coast of Northumberland and Durham. It is not improbable, however, that the same cause which conduced to the establishment of the Chelsea works had much to do with the formation of those at Lowestoft. Certain it is that an extensive trade was in the early and middle part of last century carried on, as it is at the present day, with Holland; and certain it is, that at that time, as now, the town was the constant resort of Dutch fishermen and others; and as the *first* productions of the Ceramic Art in this neighbourhood appear, so far as I have been able to ascertain, to have been delft-ware, it is not too much to suppose that the first potters were from Holland, and made the ware from clay found in the neighbourhood. Specimens of this fine delft-ware, inscribed with names of people in the neighbourhood, and with dates, still exist, and attest pretty strongly to the correctness of this opinion.

According to Gillingwater, it appears that the first pottery was established at Gunton, near Lowestoft, in 1756; but I am inclined to think that pot-making had been carried on some years before this date. Marryat describes two plates, of coarse paste, with blue borders, which bear, respectively, the words—

QUINTON	QUINTON
BENJAMIN	MARY
YARMOUTH	YARMOUTH
1752.	1752.

which he considers may have been ante-dated; but the probability is that they are not, but that they were painted at Gunton or Lowestoft at the period whose date they bear. A remarkably fine blue and white delft plate, or dish, which belonged to the late Mr. James Mills, of Norwich, and traditionally said to be painted at Lowestoft, has a bold border of blue colour round the rim, and the centre bears a heart-shaped tablet (Fig. 836), with the words—*Robart & Ann Parrish in Norwich* 1756. Other examples have also come under my notice, and strengthen my opinion that they must have been made somewhat prior to 1756. It is a matter of extreme importance, and very noteworthy, that of the *dated* examples of wares known or recorded, those of 1752, 1756, 1759, and 1760 are not china but delft-ware; and that those from 1762 forward to 1789 are china. The inference is that the manufacture of delft-ware at Gunton or Lowestoft continued till about 1760, and that about that time the manufacture of porcelain was gradually making its way.

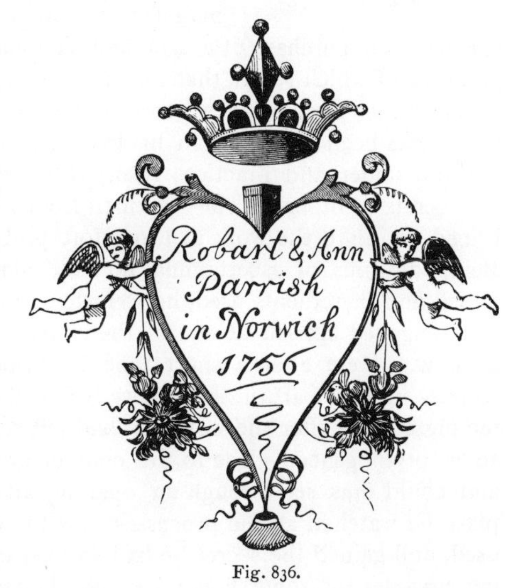

Fig. 836.

The proprietors of the porcelain works in 1757 are stated by Gillingwater to be Messrs. Walker, Brown, Aldred, and Rickman. By 1770 the manufacture had considerably advanced, and a warehouse for its sale was established in London:—

"Clark Durnford, Lowestoft China Warehouse, No. 4, Great St. Thomas the Apostle, Queen Street, Cheapside, London, where merchants and shopkeepers may be supplied with any quantity of the said ware at the usual prices. N.B. Allowance of Twenty per cent. for Ready Money."

The firm was carried on (as is proved by the address furnished to Mr. Duesbury, of the Derby China factory) under the style of "Robert Browne & Co."; the address is Mr. Robt. Browne & Co., China Manufactory, Lowestoft, Suffolk."

One of the partners of the early firm, and the manager of the works, was Mr. Robert Browne, who died in 1771, when the management fell to his son, also Robert Browne, who, being an excellent practical chemist, made great improvements in the ware. He was constantly experimenting on "bodies," and succeeded in bringing the art nearer to the Oriental original than had been at that time attained by any other individual. Of the first of these Robert Brownes an interesting relic remained in the possession of his great-grandson when I made my notes upon it. It is a small nine-sided inkstand, white, and has Chinese figures on seven of its sides, the other two being taken up with the initials "R. B., 1762," of Robert Browne, all in blue.

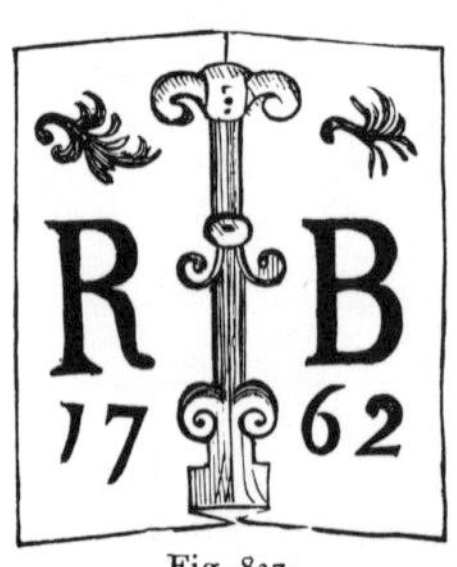

Fig. 837.

The manufacture of porcelain under the management of the second Robert Browne must have attained some great degree of excellence in 1775, for in that year I find a man named David Rhodes, who was apparently employed by his master, Josiah Wedgwood, to collect together for him examples of the productions of the different manufactories of this country, enters in his account of expenses the purchase of a Lowestoft slop-basin, for which he gave ninepence, the purchase of which shows that tea-services must, prior to that time, have been made.

A curious circumstance connected with the first Robert Browne, the memory of which has been preserved in his family, is worth relating, as showing the schemes and the underhand practices resorted to by manufacturers to worm out and steal the secrets of others. The workmen from London having been tampered with and bribed to injure the work at Lowestoft probably induced Mr. Browne to retaliate. Being desirous of ascertaining how the glaze was prepared, some of the colours mixed and ingredients used, he went to London, and, under the disguise of a workman, engaged himself at one of the china manufactories—of course either Chelsea or Bow. Here, after a short time, he bribed the warehouseman to lock him up secretly in that part of the factory where the principal was in the habit of mixing the ingredients after the workmen had left the premises. Browne was placed under an empty hogshead close to the counter or table on which the principal operated, and could thus see through an opening all that was going on. From his hiding-place he watched all the processes, saw the proportions of the different ingredients used, and gained the secret he had so long coveted. Having thus remained a willing prisoner for some hours, he was at last released when the principal left the place, and shortly afterwards returned to Lowestoft, after an absence of only two or three weeks, in full possession of the, till then, secret information possessed by the famed works of Chelsea or Bow.

It may be well to note that the Brownes, I am informed, were engaged in the staple trade of the place—that of the herring fishery—as well as in that of the manufacture of porcelain. The firm also were shipowners, and kept vessels constantly running "to the Isle of Wight for a peculiar sand, which, with pulverised glass and pipe-clay, formed principally the ingredients of the groundwork of the ware," and to Newcastle for coals.

Lowestoft is, fortunately, particularly rich in dated examples of its productions; but it is worthy of remark that the whole of these examples with names and dates which have come under my notice are *white and blue*; showing that, during the period through which these dates run, that was the character of the china made at these works, and that the finer body and the elaborate colouring which distinguish so much of the Lowestoft porcelain were of later date. The earliest dated example I have seen is the inkstand bearing the initials "R. B., 1762." Another was a bowl with the name "ABRM. MOORE, 1765;" and another, a basin, has "S. C., 1765," for Sarah Crisp. Next is a fine bowl, with a large group of Chinese figures—emperor, mandarins, &c.—painted in blue, and inscribed on the bottom with the name of an eccentric old maid, well known in the town, and whose gravestone lies in the churchyard:—"ELIZA[TH] BUCKLE 1768." This bowl and other pieces of a service (notably a basin and cream-jug, painted with shepherd and shepherdess) made for her, were painted by her nephew, Robert Allen, who, as a boy, was one of the first employed when the manufactory was established. The bowl when I saw it was in the possession of his aged daughter, Mrs. Johnson. This Robert Allen may well be classed amongst the "worthies" of Lowestoft. Working at the china manufactory from the first, he became foreman, and was entrusted with the mixing of the colours and the ingredients of the material itself, and remained so till the close of the factory in 1803. As a painter he appears to have been chiefly employed on blue; at all events the only authenticated specimens of his work which I have seen are of that colour. He also employed himself in staining glass, his principal work being the east window of the parish church, which he completed in 1819 (being then in his seventy-fourth year) and presented to the town. In acknowledgment of this service a silver cup, bearing a suitable inscription, was presented to him: "A token of respect to Mr. Robert Allen, from his fellow-townsmen at Lowestoft, for having, at the advanced age of seventy-four, gratuitously and elegantly ornamented the East Window of their Parish Church. Anno Dom. 1819." After the closing of the Lowestoft works, Allen, who dealt in china, &c., put up a small kiln at his own house, where he carried on operations on a limited scale, buying the unfinished ware from the Rockingham works and painting and finishing it himself for sale. Mr. Brameld, of the Rockingham works, who was an excellent painter on china, occasionally visited Lowestoft, and became attached to Allen, to whom he presented a set of five vases, beautifully painted from nature with flowers copied from specimens he had gathered on the Dene. He also presented him with a snuff-box, painted by himself.

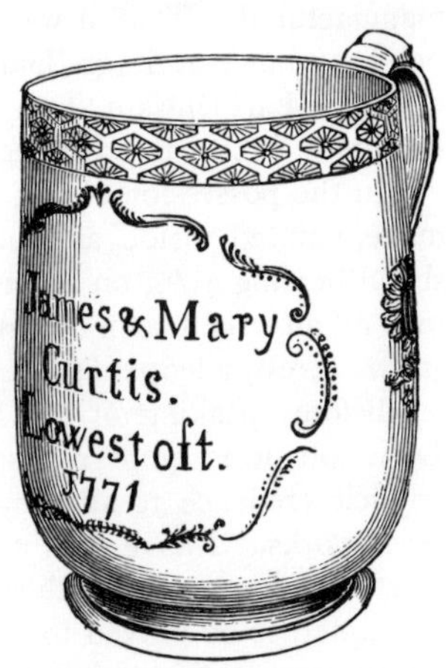

Fig. 838.

Other dated examples are a bowl, with the words, "EDWARD MORLEY 1768;" another, with "RICD. MASON JANY. 1TH 1771;" and a mug (Fig. 838), with the words "James and Mary Curtis, Lowestoft, 1771," painted by their son, Thomas Curtis, "porcelain-painter," who was, it is said, employed at Dresden, and became a "silent partner" in the Lowestoft works. Part of a set of china painted by him on Oriental body in 1775 as a wedding present for his son James is preserved in the family. Another example is a mug, inscribed "ROBT. HAWARD 1781." In Mr. Seago's collection is an inkstand marked *S. A. Sept.* 26 1782, being the initials of Samuel Aldred; and a later example has W / J S / 1784. The *latest* known dated specimen, in the possession of Mr. J. Williams, is a mug, painted in blue with borders and flowers, and on the front "G C LOWESTOFT 1789." The whole of the dated examples which I have described (with the exception of this last) and those of 1765 and 1782, I fully described in the *Art Journal* for 1863, and they have served, unacknowledged, as the foundation upon which Chaffers and every other later writer have built up their notices of Lowestoft. These will be sufficient to show the range of years over which the Lowestoft blue and white porcelain was manufactured. That it was made to the close of the works there is every probability; but that it gradually gave way to a finer and higher class of goods is certain. Earthenware, too, of a fine kind, of which I have seen some so-called examples, is said to have been made at Lowestoft.

In the possession of Mr. Andreas Cockayne is a pair of salt-cellars of Lowestoft make, painted inside and out with roses and other flowers, and on either side a shield bearing *gules*, on a bend, *argent*, three leopards' heads, caboshed, of the field; over all an escutcheon of pretence with the arms of Cockayne, *argent*, three cocks, *gules*. Crest, a leopard's head, caboshed, *gules*.

Before speaking of the later and higher class of goods made or painted at Lowestoft, it is quite necessary to put collectors on their guard against giving implicit credence to all they hear in the locality as to the kinds of ware made at these works. I have seen undoubted specimens of early Worcester, of Caughley, of Bristol, and of several other localities, gravely asserted to be Lowestoft, and even attempted to be proved to be such by the very marks they bear. As a proof of this I may just mention that it is said the company did a large trade with Turkey, and the ware prepared for that market "had on it no representation of man or beast (so as not to offend Mahometan law), and at the bottom of each piece the Crescent was painted!" It is perhaps unnecessary to say that the pieces marked with the "Turkish Crescent" are the ordinary blue and white with the Worcester and Caughley marks, and that some of the pieces are the well-known "cabbage-leaf" and other forms of those makes.

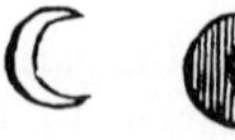

Figs. 839, 840.

The great characteristic of the latter more advanced porcelain made at Lowestoft is its extreme minuteness and intricacy of pattern and beauty of finish. Indeed the decorations on many of the specimens which I have examined are of a character far superior, both in design and in the exquisite and almost microscopic nicety of the pencilling and finish, to those mostly produced at other English manufactories. The borders are frequently very minute and elaborate, and the wreaths, festoons, or groups of flowers are equally delicate in their proportions.

Some of the productions of the Lowestoft works are apparently painted on Oriental body, but there are many good examples in existence which are of very fine quality where the body is of Lowestoft make. The collector will be able to distinguish immediately between the examples painted at Lowestoft on Oriental body and those which were potted and painted there. Punch-bowls and tea and coffee services appear to have been the staple productions of these works, and, fortunately, many of the former, and several almost complete sets of the latter, are remaining in the hands of families in the neighbourhood and in those of local collectors, who seem imbued with a laudable desire to keep alive the memory of what has been done for the Ceramic Art in their town. The bowls are usually of remarkably good form and highly ornamented. They are mostly painted at Lowestoft, on Oriental body. Some of these, though not dated, nevertheless give collateral evidence of the period at which they were made, and become, therefore, historically valuable; as do also, indeed, some of the services bearing the initials, heraldic bearings, and monograms of families in the neighbourhood. A punch-bowl in the possession of the town clerk of Lowestoft, which is elaborately ornamented inside and out, bears inside a well-painted representation of a fishing lugger at full sail, within a circle, beneath which is the name of the vessel, *The Judas*. This bowl was made for the boat *Judas*, and was filled with punch and drank to its success before each fishing voyage, and at carousals at their end. In the same collection is another beautiful bowl, bearing on either side, within ovals, and surrounded by ornamental scrolls, &c., portraits of the notorious John Wilkes, and another, with the words, "Wilkes and Liberty."

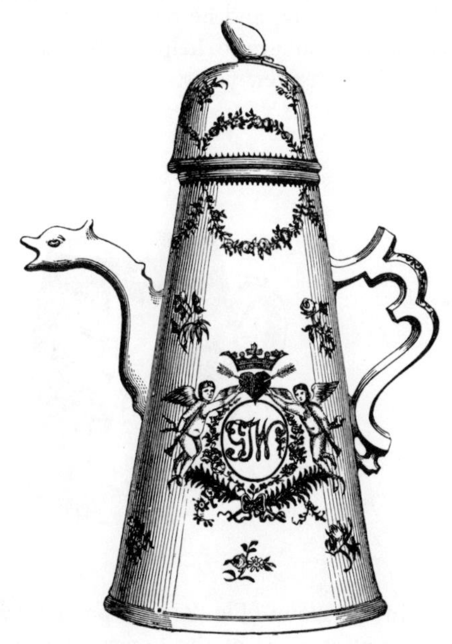

Fig. 841.

The coffee-pot (Fig. 841) formerly belonging to Mr. Norman is a good specimen of Lowestoft painting. It forms part of a service, evidently a marriage-service, originally made for Captain Walsh. The initials it bears are probably those of himself and his bride. They are enclosed in an oval within a wreath of roses and palm-branches, tied with a true lover's knot. On either side is a Cupid, who supports a human heart pierced with two arrows, and this is surmounted by a coronet. On reference to the delft plate just described and engraved (Robert and Ann Parrish), it will be seen how strongly the design of that early example of Lowestoft earthenware accords with this, perhaps one of the most highly finished of its productions in porcelain.

It is unnecessary to describe other services, although many of them are of the highest beauty. One tea service, with the crest (an owl) and the monogram of W. W. conjoined, is especially deserving of notice, however, as being one of the choicest examples of porcelain-painting of its kind which have come under my notice. This service, until lately intact, has unfortunately been dispersed, and portions of it passed into the collections of Sir Henry Tyrwhitt, Mr. Norman, Mr. Seago, and others.

It is worthy of remark that on much of the Lowestoft china the rose is plentifully introduced. The reason for this is probably twofold; first, the arms of the borough is the Tudor (or full-blown) rose, crowned with an open arched crown; and this may probably have been the principal incentive in giving the rose so constant and so prominent a place in the ornamentation of the china. Second, during the period of the great Revolution, a French refugee of the name of Rose, one of the cleverest of the French porcelain-painters, found his way to Lowestoft, and was engaged by the company. He became the principal, and by far the best, of the artists employed, and probably introduced the rose more generally, in allusion to his name, than would otherwise have been done. To him may probably be ascribed the finest and most minutely finished specimens of painting which the works produced, and it was his taste which gave that French character to the general style of ornamentation which is so discoverable on many of the services. It is well to remark that on some of the pieces painted by him he is said to have introduced a small rose under the handle as a special mark of his work. Like that of many another man of genius, the lot of this clever refugee artist was a sad one. He was an aged man when he came to Lowestoft, and he remained at the works till his eyesight failed him, and he became very poor. A subscription was entered into, and a couple of donkeys to help him to carry water in the town purchased, and thus he passed his last few years.

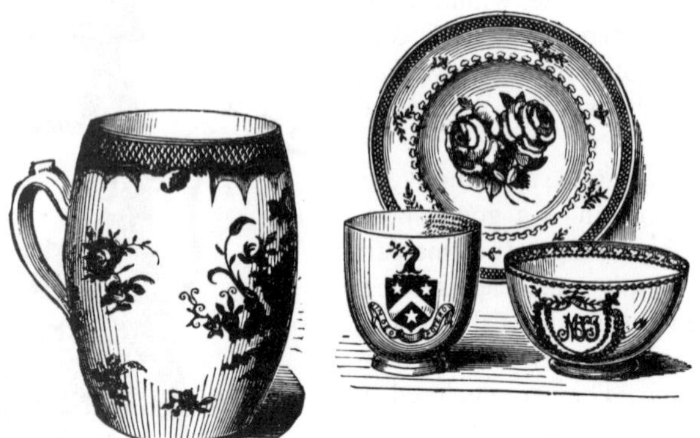

Fig. 842.

In the group (Fig. 842), I have shown some very characteristic examples of the higher class make of the Lowestoft works. The saucer is an excellent specimen of floral decoration, and shows better than many the rose which was so plentifully introduced in decoration. The painting, however, of these bolder groups of flowers is not so good as in the more minute ones—the artists, as I have before said, excelling in minute, careful, and elaborate pencilling rather than in breadth of style and colour. The coffee-cup is a simple but very good specimen of heraldic decoration. It is part of a set made for the celebrated writer, the Rev. Robert Potter, Prebendary of Norwich and Vicar of Lowestoft, and bears his arms : *or*, a chevron, *sable*, between three mullets, *gules*, pierced of the first ; with crest, and motto, " IN DEO POTERO." The tea-cup in the same group is a good example of the not unusual French style of ornamentation, in wreaths, monograms, and initials. The shield bears the initials " M. S. J.," and is surrounded by a wreath of flowers and surmounted by a crest (Fig. 843). The mug, of a form very unusual in Lowestoft specimens, is decorated with groups and sprays of flowers, among which the rose is predominant.

Transfer printing on china does not seem to have been practised to any extent at Lowestoft. One jug, however, which has been handed down from father to son in the family of the most active proprietor, is preserved, with a memorandum that the copper-plate from which it was printed was given to Mr. Browne by a Mr. Gamble, of Bungay, who, with his family, was in the habit of visiting Lowestoft. Probably the plate was given that the family might be supplied with ware printed from it. The design is a sportsman with dog and gun, and on the spout of the jug are the letters "S. A.," the initials of Samuel Aldred. I have seen a set of beakers, &c., printed in blue, which are said to have been bought at the factory, and to be attested as Lowestoft make.

The Lowestoft works did not excel in figures, which were usually simple in design, and of small size. They are usually single rustic figures, and possess no notable features; four examples, purchased at the factory just before its close, were in the possession of the late Lady Smith and are highly interesting as being well authenticated. Among the principal artists employed at the works were Rose, the refugee, of whom I have just spoken; Powles, a clever artist, whose name is well known as the draughtsman of the plates illustrating Gillingwater's "History of Lowestoft;" Allen, of whom I have spoken, who painted the east window of the parish church, and was the mixer of the colours at the factory; Redgate, who also was a good flower-painter; Curtis, of whom I have already spoken; Abel, John, and Joseph Bly; James, John, and Margaret Redgrave; and others named Stevenson, Balls, Mottershed, and Simpson. Besides these, several women were employed in painting and gilding.

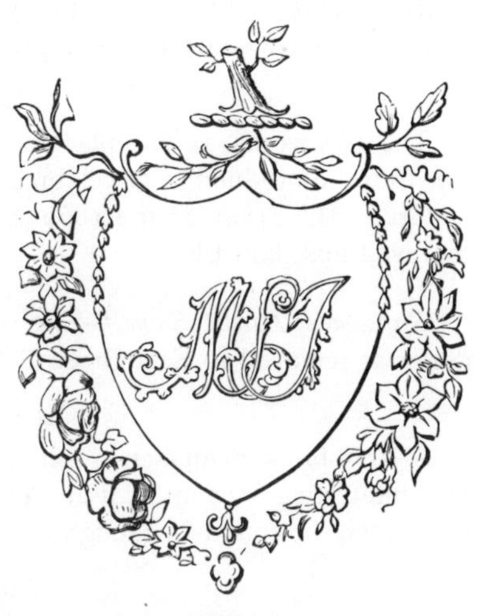

Fig. 843.

The works were brought to a close in the year 1803 or 1804, and the materials and finished goods were sold by auction. The causes which led to their discontinuance were many, but principally the losses sustained by the company, and the successful competition of the Staffordshire manufacturers. One great loss was caused by the failure of their London agents; another and more serious one by the destruction of a very large quantity of Lowestoft china in Holland, with which country an extensive trade was carried on, as thus stated:—"When Napoleon crossed the river during a hard frost and captured Holland, amongst the British property destroyed was a quantity of Lowestoft china at Rotterdam, in value several thousand pounds." The trade with Rotterdam was very large, and the ware was sent weekly in hogsheads by way of Yarmouth. These two losses, coming closely together, crippled the company; and the cost of manufacture, through having no coal nor any other requisite material in the neighbourhood, preventing them from producing ware so cheaply as could be done in Staffordshire and at Derby and Worcester, the works were closed, after the proprietors had realised considerable sums; and the town thus lost a branch of manufacture which was an honour to it, and which has given it a name in the annals of the Ceramic Art of this country.

And here, before proceeding further, let me again utter a word or two of caution to collectors against placing too implicit a reliance upon what has been written concerning Lowestoft china, and against taking for granted that all which is nowadays called Lowestoft china is really the production of that manufactory. If all that is ascribed to Lowestoft was ever made there, the works must have been about the most extensive, and—if all the varieties of wares that are now said to have been there produced were made, as is asserted, simultaneously—the most extraordinary on record. The great bulk of the specimens now unblushingly ascribed to Lowestoft I believe never were in that town, much less were ever made there.

The mill for grinding the materials for the manufactory "was in a ravine by the Warren House on Gunton Denes, where a fine stream of water constantly flows. This was dammed up, and when it had arrived at a certain height, was set to flow over a very large wheel (the largest of the kind at that time in the kingdom), for the purpose of grinding the materials for the china." The factory was situated in the town, on premises since occupied as a brewery, and the street is still called Factory Lane. It is worthy of note that no mark was used upon Lowestoft china. Marryat mentions a mark of three parallel straight blue lines; but this is evidently an error, as no such examples appear to be known.

Stowmarket.

The tile works at this place are of old establishment, and have always been noted for the production of celebrated "white bricks," spoken of in the seventeenth century. Mr. Fison, at the 1862 Exhibition, received honourable mention for his improved malt-kiln tile.

Ipswich.

Ransome's Patent Stone.—The manufacture was commenced in 1844, but in 1866 was removed to East Greenwich (which see).

Ebbisham, Surrey.

A large brick manufactory existed in the seventeenth century, and a long and most interesting account of it and of the clays, as well as all the processes of manufacture, will be found in Houghton's "Husbandry and Trade Improved," 1693.

Wrotham, Kent.

A pottery was in existence here, in the middle of the seventeenth century, but nothing is known as to its history. The ware was the usual coarse brown ware, of much the same character as the Toft dishes. An example, formerly belonging to Mr. C. W. Reynolds, decorated with an incised pattern, and bearing the date 1668, and the initials H. L. and I. A., is traditionally said to be of this make. In the British Museum is a large brown dish with the words E. W. E., WROTHAM, 1669, and in the Museum of Practical Geology is a two-handled posset-pot with raised ornaments and inscription laid on in yellow slip, before glazing, T. E., WROTHAM, 1703. Another good example, belonging to Mr. Baldwin, is a four-handled tyg ornamented with fleur-de-lis, &c., and bearing

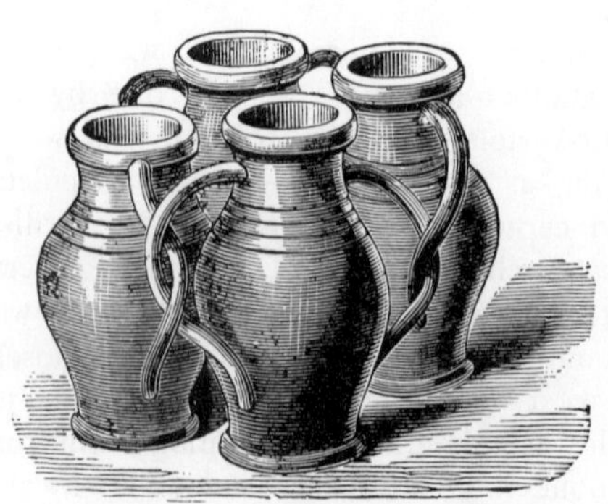

Fig. 844.

the words WROTHAM W R · S C R 1659. Another example, considered by Marryat to be Wrotham, is given on Fig. 844.

YARMOUTH.

Although the name " Absolon, Yarmouth," occurs on pieces of ware in different collections, it must not for one moment be taken for granted that the pottery was produced there. The Absolons were china and glass dealers in Yarmouth, and one of the family appears to have erected a kiln, called the Ovens, and there to have burnt-in the flowers and other designs which he employed himself in painting upon ware procured from other places. His plan appears to have been to buy the ordinary cream-coloured ware plates, &c., and paint upon them flowers in the manner of those of Swinton, Don, &c., and in the same manner to write their names on the back, and then to burn them in in his own "oven." Mr. Norman possessed some plates of Absolon's painting which bore on the back the usual mark of his name, pencilled on and burnt in, and the name " TURNER " impressed in the ware. These pieces, there can be no reasonable doubt, were made by John Turner, of Lane End. Mr. Chaffers says, that having the name of " Turner " stamped upon them "proves that they were actually made at Caughley, and decorated at Yarmouth; " but this carries its own condemnation on the face of it, for Turner of Caughley is not known to have stamped his *name* on his ware, and beyond this he did not produce cream ware at his works. There is reason to believe that Absolon bought his ware from Staffordshire and Leeds. He put his name in colour on the bottom of the pieces he decorated. (Fig. 845.)

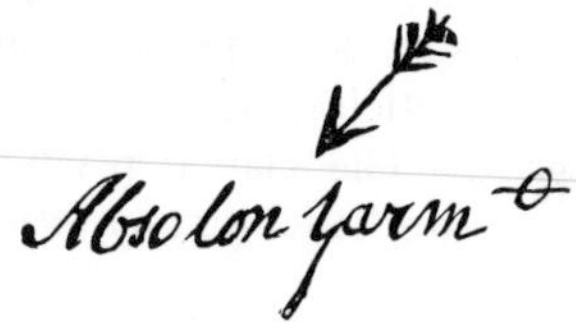

Fig. 845.

COSSEY.

The works at Cossey, near Norwich, were established about 1800, as a brick-yard, and so continued until about 1827, when Cossey, or Costessy Hall, the seat of its noble owner, Lord Stafford, was rebuilt, when they were enlarged, so as to enable a full supply for the purpose to be made. The foreman was Mr. Gunton, and under his care the manufacture of ornamental bricks for the new hall was tried, and with marked success. On this hall—one of the best of brick buildings, and one which may be looked upon as a gigantic example of Cossey ceramic art—are some remarkably fine Tudoresque chimney-shafts, as well as excellently designed and well-executed cusped window-heads, transoms, mullions, &c., and finials, door-jambs, cornices, panelling, and string-courses, all formed of moulded brick made at Cossey from native clays. After the completion of the hall the brick-works were closed for about four years, when Mr. Gunton succeeded in renting them in the hope of manufacturing decorated brick-work. They were afterwards carried on by his son, Mr. George Gunton.

CADBOROUGH.

The *Cadborough Pottery*, near Rye, in Sussex, was first built about 1807, and carried on by Mr. James Smith, and afterwards by his son, Jeremiah Smith. In 1840, the business passed into the hands of the late Mr. William Mitchell (who had had the management of it, under Mr. Smith, since 1827), who carried it on in his own name until 1859, when he took one of his sons, Mr. Frederick Mitchell, into partnership, and the firm became "Wm. Mitchell & Son," and so continued until 1869, when the partnership was dissolved, Mr. Mitchell, sen., continuing the Cadborough business for common earthenware, and his son, Mr. Frederick Mitchell, taking the fancy department, which was his own creation, to new premises, the Bellevue Pottery. In 1870, Mr. Mitchell, sen., died, and the business at Cadborough was then taken by Mr. Henry Mitchell. The goods produced are the ordinary common brown wares, glazed and unglazed, and consist of flower-pots, chimney-pots, pitchers, and crocks of various kinds; and all the usual domestic vessels, many of which are mottled or "splashed" under the glaze.

At Crowborough, Chailey, and Burgess Hill, brown ware is also made; that of Chailey being of somewhat curious character with impressed ornaments.

Rye.

The "*Bellevue Pottery*" in the Ferry Road, Rye, Sussex, was established in 1869, by the late Mr. Frederick Mitchell (son and partner of the late Mr. William Mitchell, of the Cadborough Pottery) for the manufacture of "Sussex Rustic Ware." This ware is of peculiar but highly pleasing character, and in it a large variety of fancy articles, flower-baskets, candlesticks, jugs, vases, pilgrims' bottles, &c., are made. The clay is peculiarly light, of tolerably close texture, and is capable of being worked into any form. The glaze, which is of equal richness with that of

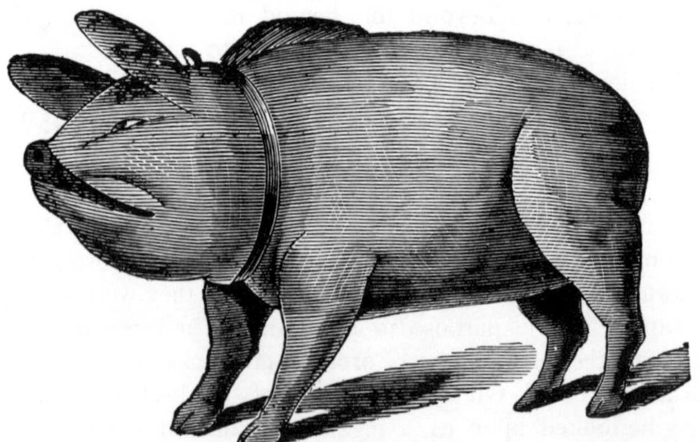

Fig. 846.—"Sussex Pig" Drinking Vessel.

"Rockingham" ware, is of exceedingly good quality, and it has a rich effect over the mottling or "splashing" which characterizes this ware. Some of the vessels are decorated with the leaf and head of the staple product of the county—the hop—or with other excellent copies of leaves and flowers, &c. The peculiarity of this "Sussex Rustic Ware" is its extreme lightness, and the richness of its mottling and glaze.

One article, worthy of especial notice, as made at these works (and formerly at Cadborough), is the "Sussex Pig" (Fig. 846). This is a drinking vessel of the same general character as the "bears," which will be found described under the heads of Brampton, Nottingham, &c. The body, when filled with ale, stands on end, on its tail, and the head lifts off to be used as a drinking-cup, precisely in the same manner as with the "bears." In Sussex these "pigs" are used at weddings, when each guest is invited to "drink a *hogshead* of beer to the health of the bride," and at other social and convivial meetings. On these occasions each person is expected to drink this cup—or "hog's-head"—full of liquor.

Gestingthorpe.

Pavement-tiles and other articles were, according to Houghton, 1693, made at Gestingthorpe, in Essex.

Holkham.

In 1849, the Earl of Leicester, anxious to turn the clays of his estate in Norfolk to good account, commenced the manufacture of red terra-cotta at Holkham, and produced some good Tudor chimney-tops and moulded bricks.

Nuneham Courtney.

Pot-works existed here in the beginning of the seventeenth century, and are spoken of by Plot, in 1677, as being "now deserted; nor, indeed, was there, as I ever heard of, anything extraordinary performed during the working these earths."

Marsh Balden.

The pottery at this place, existing in the beginning of the seventeenth century, is included in the above remark by Dr. Plot.

Horspath.

Tobacco-pipes were made here in the latter end of the seventeentn century.

Shotover.

At Shotover, in the parish of Headington, tobacco-pipes were made prior to 1677, at which time the "place was deserted."

CHAPTER XIII.

YORK.

"*Place's Ware.*"—Francis Place, who may be looked upon as one of the pioneers of modern pottery, commenced the manufacture of what, at the time, was considered "equal to true china ware," about 1665. But little, however, is known either of the manufactory, or of the ware he produced. Francis Place was, according to Walpole, a younger son of Mr. Rowland Place, of Dimsdale, in the county of Durham, and was placed as clerk to an attorney in London until 1665; "in which year going into a shop the officers came to shut up the house, on its having the Plague in it. This occasioned his leaving London," and having "discovered an earth for, and a method of making, Porcelain," he tells us "he put it in practice at the Manor house at York, of which manufacture he gave Thoresby a fine mug. His pottery cost him much money; he attempted it solely from a turn for experiments, but one Clifton took the hint from him, and made a fortune by it." Thoresby, who, in his "Ducatus Leodiensis" (1714), several times mentions Place and his wares, says, when speaking of the vein of white clay in the hundred of Wortley, "Here is a good vein of fine clay that will retain its whiteness after it is burnt (when others turn red), and therefore used for the making of tobacco-pipes, a manufacture but lately begun at Leeds," and, adds he, "having a specimen in this Museum made of English materials in the Manor house at York, by the very ingenious Mr Francis Place, who presented it to me with one of the outer covers purposely made to secure them from the violence of the fire in baking."

From the examples at present in existence—and there are only two or three known—it appears that the ware was simply a tolerably fine kind of earthenware, of a greyish colour streaked with black and brown; and this is the way in which Horace Walpole describes his specimen: "I have a coffee-cup of his ware; it is of grey earth, with streaks of black, and not superior to common earthenware." This example at the Strawberry Hill sale passed into the hands of Mr. Franks, who presented it to the Museum of Practical Geology. It is of thin glazed greyish ware, streaked with black and brown, and has a narrow rib or raised band running round it at about two-thirds of its height from the top. An old pasteboard label, probably in the handwriting of Horace Walpole, attached to the handle bears the words "Mr. Francis Place's china." Examples in the hands of some of the descendants of Mr. Place are of precisely the same character as the one just described. In the same hands is "a small portrait of Place, by himself, in which he has introduced one of his cups, the original of which his descendant possesses, and which is traditionally said to be one which he considered to be his masterpiece." Mr. Place, in 1712, visited Thoresby, and in 1728 he died, leaving a widow and an only child, a daughter, married to Wadham Wyndham, Esq.

York China Manufactory.—In 1838 Mr. Haigh Hirstwood, formerly of the

Rockingham china works, established a china manufactory in York, and by the succeeding spring had so far progressed that the following paragraph appeared in the York papers :—

"York China Manufactory.—Mr. Hirstwood, of Stonegate, is erecting a kiln, extensive warehouses, &c., in the Groves, for manufacturing, gilding, and burnishing china, which has not previously been attempted in this city."

The works were established in Lowther Street, Groves, and were continued until about 1850, when the concern was wound up. Mr. Haigh Hirstwood was born at Royd's Hall, near Huddersfield, in 1778, and learnt the art of china making and decorating under the Bramelds at the Rockingham works, as did also afterwards his sons and son-in-law. He continued at the Rockingham works upwards of forty years, leaving them only towards their close, when he removed to York and commenced business as a china-dealer. In 1839, as I have stated, he erected kilns, &c., at York, and commenced business in the decorating and finishing departments, buying his china in the white from Sampson Bridgwood & Co. of Longton, and from others. In this business he was assisted by his son-in-law, Mr. William Leyland, also from the Rockingham works, who became his managing partner. Disagreements having arisen, however, the business was broken up, Mr. Hirstwood remaining in York, where he died in 1854, and Mr. Leyland removing to London, when he took to painting and decorating lamps, where he died in 1853, leaving a widow (who soon afterwards died) and a family of two sons and four daughters, who are now of Lawrence, near Boston, Massachusetts, North America. Mr. Leyland, who was a painter, gilder, and enameller, understood all the practical details of the potter's art. Mr. Hirstwood was a painter of flowers, &c., and was considered the best fly-painter at the Rockingham works. In 1826 he copied, for use in the decoration of the Rockingham china, upwards of five hundred insects, at Wentworth House, which had been arranged by Lady Milton, the daughter-in-law of Earl Fitzwilliam. He and his sons Joseph and William (who were brought up at the Rockingham works) were engaged upon the *chef-d'œuvres* of that manufactory, the services for King William IV. and for the Duchess of Cumberland. He was succeeded in his business in Coney Street by his son, Mr. William Hirstwood, father of the present proprietor, but the manufactory has been entirely discontinued since 1850. The goods principally produced were dinner, tea, dessert, and other services, vases, figures, &c., and the style closely assimilated that of Rockingham china. No mark was used.

Layerthorpe Pottery.

This manufactory of coarse ware—flower-pots, chimney-pipes, bowls, socket-pipes, &c.—was established in 1846 by Mr. John Webster.

Osmotherley.

A pottery, discontinued many years back, existed at this place. Its productions were the ordinary brown ware, in which jugs, mugs, pitchers, tobacco-boxes, &c., were produced.

Hull.

There can be no doubt but that common earthenware was made at Hull, if not earlier, at all events in the middle of the seventeenth century ; but no record of such works has at present been brought to light. In June, 1875, however, some property at Sculcoates, formerly an outskirt of Hull, was brought to the hammer by Mr. Charles Johnson. It was in extent about one-third of an acre, and has always been known by the name "Pot-House Yard." Inquiries have resulted in ascertaining that this pottery at Sculcoates had not been worked in the memory of any one living. There are still remaining three cottages, probably two hundred years old, fronting into the ground. Part of the site has been occupied in recent years by Messrs. Stewart and Gregson, oil refiners. Very early in the eighteenth century pipe-making was carried on at Hull, and Gent, in 1735, records among the epitaphs in the churchyard one to "Thomas Cook, Pipe-maker, who died the 7th of February, 1720, aged 64." The first distinct information I have been able to gather regarding pot-works at this place is that in 1802 (eighteen years earlier than the first date given by Chaffers), by a deed, dated August 10 in that year, Thomas English, of Hull, merchant, sold a plot of land on what is called the Humber Bank, in a part of what was then the outskirts of the town, and known as "Myton." The piece of land consisted of 3,718 square yards, and was conveyed to James Smith and Jeremiah Smith. both of Hull, potters; Job Ridgway, of Shelton, Staffordshire, potter; and Josiah Hipwood, of Hull, blockmaker. That part of the town has for fifty years, to the writer's knowledge, been known as the "Pottery," a name doubtless derived from these works. The deed of partnership between these parties was dated 23rd November, 1802. From the fact of two of the parties, James Smith and Jeremiah Smith, being described as "of Hull, potters," while Job Ridgway was of "Shelton, Staffordshire, potter," the probability is that the Smiths were already in business there as pot-makers, and that Ridgway joined them for the purpose of increasing and improving their manufacture. The partnership, however, was but of short duration, for in 1804 Mr. Ridgway, being desirous of retiring, agreed to sell to the remaining partners all his *fourth* part of the lands, works, stock-in-trade, debts, &c., for the sum of £1,000. Hipwood left the concern in the same year, when a Mr. James Rose became a partner with the Smiths. In 1806 the proprietors assigned all their interest in the works to Messrs. Job and George Ridgway, who carried them on for some years. In 1826 they were succeeded by Mr. William Bell, who became the proprietor in that year, by deed of conveyance from the brothers Ridgway. By Mr. Bell the manufactory was very much extended, and the operations were carried on on a large scale, chiefly for export, the principal part of the trade being with Hamburg, where his brother, Mr. Edward Bell, was in business, and a large German and Dutch trade was done through his means. The works were closed in 1841, when the plant and stock were disposed of by auction.

At this sale Mr. Charles Johnson, of Hull, acted as auctioneer for Mr. Stamp, and I am informed by him that the copper-plates, the stock of which weighed about three hundredweight, and amongst which were some of the "willow pattern," "were sold to a pottery works at or near Rotherham," which I presume to be either the Swinton or the Don works.

The wares produced were cream-coloured, green-glazed, ordinary white, and blue printed wares; and in them the usual classes of useful goods, consisting of services of various kinds and miscellaneous articles, were made. One notable dinner-service was made to commemorate an exploit in connection with the noted pirate, Paul Jones, and was, it would appear, made for the owner, or family of the owner, of the "Crow Isle." Only one plate of this service is now known to be in existence, and this is preserved in the Hull Museum, to which it was presented by the late Mr. Charles Hassell, grandson to the late Francis Hall, Esq., of Hull, who was owner of the "Crow Isle," Baltic trader. In the centre is represented the "Crow Isle" successfully beating off Paul Jones, on its homeward voyage, when off the Yorkshire coast in 1779. Another example of the Belle Vue Pottery is a butter-pot in form of a cow, with moveable lid, in yellow ware. Mr. Johnson has also in his possession a portion of a remarkably fine green-glazed dessert-service, of very artistic design, in embossed leaves, with basket-work centres to the plates, which was bought at the Hull works from Mr. Bell in 1838. It has the impressed mark (Fig. 847), viz. two bells, surrounded by the words "BELLE VUE POTTERY, HULL;" but sometimes the bells alone appear, without the lettering. In the possession of the late Mr. Bagshawe were some of the later accounts of these works, from which a good idea of the extent to which the operations were carried on may be gleaned.

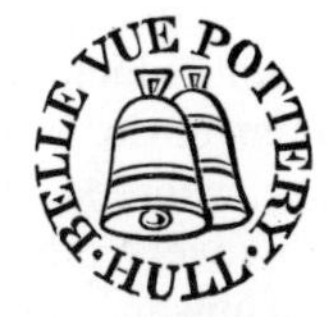

Fig. 847.

The works have been entirely discontinued since 1841, and the site included in the extensive engineering works of Messrs. C. D. Holmes & Co. In 1804 Mr. William Clowes (also from the Staffordshire pottery district), one of the founders of Primitive Methodism, worked at the Hull pottery. Mr. Clowes was born at Burslem in 1780; he "came from Nottingham to Hull to establish a missionary centre, on the 15th of January, 1819;" the day after his arrival "he informs us that he visited the Pottery by the Humber Bankside, where he had worked as a potter fifteen years before, but he found the working of the pottery had been discontinued;" *i.e.* I presume it was then in a transition state before being transferred to Mr. Bell by the brothers Ridgway.

In *Stepney Lane* is a small pottery for the manufacture of the common brown ware pancheons, flower-pots, &c.

LEEDS.

There is no doubt that pottery has been made at Leeds or in its immediate neighbourhood from the earliest times of our British history. Celtic and Romano-British relics have, from time to time, been found in the neighbourhood, which were, without doubt, made at the place; and the village of Potters Newton evidently takes its name from a colony of potters having settled there in early times. That it *was* so in days of yore is evidenced by the fact of the name appearing in deeds of the thirteenth century. In later times coarse brown earthenware was made at Leeds, as were also tobacco-pipes in the reign of Charles II. These were made from clays found at Wortley—the same bed of clay which was worked for the old Leeds pottery, and is still used for making yellow ware and saggars. Ralph Thoresby, in his "Ducatus Leodiensis," 1714, speaking of Wortley Hundred, says: "Here is a good vein of fine clay, that will retain its whiteness after it is burnt (when others turn red), and therefore used for the making of tobacco-pipes, a manufacture but lately begun at Leeds." Probably to the existence of this bed of fine clay is to be attributed the founding of the pot-works at Leeds, of the date of whose first establishment nothing definite is known. It is, however, certain that they were in existence about the middle of last century, and that they were then producing wares of no ordinary degree of excellence. Before this time a kind of delft-ware was, to a small extent, made, and I have seen some very creditable copies of Oriental patterns, with salt glaze, also produced at these works. The delft-ware was succeeded by the manufacture of that fine cream-coloured earthenware which made the works so famous, and enabled them in that particular branch to compete successfully with Wedgwood and other makers. As early as 1770 considerable progress had been made in the ornamental productions, and I have seen remarkably good dated examples of open and embossed basket-work ware of 1777 and 1779.

The first proprietors of whom there appears to be any record were two brothers named Green, in 1760; and it is believed their earliest productions were in black ware, in which the firm afterwards excelled. It was next carried on by Humble, Green, & Co. "Mr. Wilson has found the draft of an agreement, dated November 11, 1775, whereby 'Joshua Green, of Middleton, gent., John Green, of Hunslet, potter, with divers others, under the firm of Humble, Green, & Co.,' agree with Messrs. Hutchinson and Evers to erect and maintain in repair at their mill a water-wheel, with all necessary machinery for grinding flints. For thirteen years the wheel was to be used exclusively by the Greens, who were to supply burnt flints and to pay 10s. for every 100 pecks of well-ground and levigated flints, the workmen's wages being first deducted." In 1783 the firm was Hartley, Greens, & Company, and they had so far advanced in their work and were so firmly established and well known by that year as to justify them in issuing a book of "designs" of some of the articles they were then producing. A copy of this rare volume, in my own possession, contains all three of the lists—English, French, and German. The English title is "Designs of sundry Articles of Queen's or Cream-colour'd Earthen-Ware, manufactured by Hartley, Greens, & Co., at Leeds-Pottery: with A Great Variety of other Articles. The same Enamel'd, Printed or Ornamented with Gold to any Pattern; also with Coats of Arms, Cyphers, Landscapes, &c., &c. Leeds, 1783." This catalogue, with some variations, continued to be issued till a much later period. A copy presented by myself in 1865 to the Jermyn Street Museum supplies the plates missing in the former copy. It has no title-page, but is printed on paper bearing a water-mark of 1814. The words "Leeds Pottery" are engraved on each plate of the book. The plates, forty-four in number, are very effectively engraved on copper, and exhibit a wonderful, and certainly exquisite, variety of designs for almost all articles in use, both plain, ornamented, perforated, and basket-work, including services, vases, candlesticks, flower-stands, inkstands, baskets, spoons, &c., &c. The partners at this time (1783-4) composing the firm of Hartley, Greens, & Co. were William Hartley, Joshua Green, John Green, Henry Ackroyd, John Barwick, Samuel Wainwright, Thomas Wainwright, George Hanson, and Saville Green. The business was, it appears, divided into six shares, of which William Hartley, Joshua and John Green, and Henry Ackroyd, had each one; John Barwick and the two Wainwrights half of one each; and George Hanson and Saville Green a quarter share each, the latter acting as "book-keeper" to the firm. The proprietors were extremely systematic and particular in their mode of keeping accounts and in their dealings with each other. They held regular meetings, and appointed independent and disinterested persons as valuers in each department; for instance, one to value the stock of finished goods in the ware-rooms, another the unfinished ware, another the copper plates, another the buildings, others the moulds and models, the windmill, the horses, the waggons and carts, the raw materials, the woodwork, and every imaginable thing. The reports of these various valuers, whose names and awards for many years I have carefully examined, were submitted to a meeting of the partners, when a balance was struck, to which the names of each one were attached.

In 1785, and again in 1786, fresh editions of the catalogue and book of plates were issued, without change either in the number of articles enumerated or in their variety or form. The works at this time had been considerably increased in size, and the wares made were exported in large quantities to Germany, Holland, France, Spain, and Russia. So great had the concern become five years later (1791), that the yearly balance then struck amounted to over £51,500; and it is worth recording that in that year the value of the copper plates from which the transfer-printing was effected was £204, while at the present time they represent about £1,000. These copper plates consisted of teapot borders, landscapes, Nankin borders, and others. The general stock in this year (1791) was valued at about £6,000, and the windmill at about £1,200. The house of the partners, entered as "Hartley, Green, & Co.'s House," was at Thorpe Arch, near Tadcaster and Wetherby. At Thorpe Arch, too, were the grinding-mills. These mills were ten miles from the works at Leeds, and a team of four horses was kept constantly at work carrying the ground flint and stone. They, with the men who worked them, stayed six days, going and coming, between the two places, and then six at Thorpe Arch, alternately. The raw material was taken from Leeds to the mills at Thorpe Arch, when the horses who had brought it worked the mill to grind it, and returned with it, when prepared, to Leeds for use. This continued until 1814, when the windmill on the Leeds premises, which had been used as a corn-mill, was converted into a flint-mill, and an engine, made by the builders of the first successful locomotive, Fenton, Murray, & Co., put up. This mill is still used for the same purpose.

In 1794 another edition of the catalogue and pattern-book was issued. It was precisely the same in contents as the previous editions, both in the plates and letter-press; and contained the catalogue, or list, in English, French, and German. Fresh designs appear to have been continually added, and, the connections of the company increasing, a translation of the catalogue into the Spanish language was in a few years issued. Instead of 152 general articles, as enumerated in the previous editions, 221 appear in this; and instead of 32 in tea-ware, 48 appear. In 1814, too, another edition was issued, a copy of which is in my own possession; it contains 71 plates of patterns, exhibiting 221 general articles, and 48 patterns of tea, coffee, and chocolate services. In this edition the whole of the plates, both those from the other copies and those newly engraved, have the words "Leeds Pottery" engraved upon them.

In 1796, as named in Hutchins' "History of Dorset," much of the Poole clay in that county was sent "to Selby for the use of the Leeds potteries."

In 1800 Ebenezer Green and E. Parsons joined the concern, the firm at this time consisting of William Hartley, Joshua Green, John Green, Ebenezer Green, E. Parsons, Mrs. Ackroyd and her daughter Mary (widow and daughter of Henry Ackroyd, deceased), John Barwick, Thomas Wainwright, George Hanson, Saville Green, and Samuel Wainwright. On the death of Mr. Hartley the business was still carried on as Hartley, Greens, & Co., and a Mr. Ruperti, a Russian, became, I believe, a partner in the firm. The trade at this time was principally with Russia, Norway, Spain, and Portugal, and hence, I presume, Mr. Ruperti's connection with it. The agent in Russia at one time was Mr. Barwick, and afterwards his nephew, Mr. Jubb. Among other changes in the proprietary, the Rev. W. Parsons, who married Miss Ackroyd, became a partner; and for a time the style of the firm was changed from "Hartley, Greens, & Co.," to "Greens, Hartley, & Co." These repeated changes and the unpleasantness and disputes that arose in consequence appear to have been detrimental to the concern, which was ultimately thrown into Chancery, and a large portion of the stock sold off. Some idea of the extent of the business done about this time may be formed from the fact, which I have gathered from a personal reference to the accounts, that the annual sales amounted, in round numbers, to about £30,000; that about £8,000 was paid in wages.

In 1825, by an advantageous arrangement effected through the good offices of his friend Mr. Hardy, the then Recorder of Leeds, I am informed the affair was got out of Chancery, and passed, by purchase, into the hands of Mr. Samuel Wainwright, one of the partners, who carried it on in the name of "Samuel Wainwright and Company," and engaged as confidential cashier Stephen Chappell, who up to that time was employed as a book-keeper in one of the Leeds cloth manufactories. At Wainwright's death (of cholera) in 1832, the trustees carried on the business under the style of the "Leeds Pottery Company," with Stephen Chappell, until 1840, when the trustees transferred the whole concern to Chappell, who took it at his own valuation. Shortly after his brother James became a partner in the concern, the firm consisting of "Stephen and James Chappell," until 1847, when they became bankrupt. The pottery was then carried on for about three years, for the benefit of the creditors, by the assignees, under the management of Mr. Richard Britton, who had for some time held a confidential position with Mr. Chappell. In 1850 the concern passed, by purchase, into the hands of Mr. Samuel Warburton and Mr. Britton, and was by them carried on under the style of "Warburton and Britton," until 1863, when, on the death of Mr. Warburton, Mr. Richard Britton became sole proprietor. On July 1st, 1872, he was joined in partnership by his two eldest sons, John Broadbent Britton and Alfred Britton, the firm consequently becoming "Richard Britton & Sons."

The Leeds Pot Works, occupying an area of considerably more than seven acres of ground, are situated in Jack Lane, and are intersected for a considerable portion of their length by the Brandling's Railway, and are also crossed in a cutting by the main line of the Midland Railway. Closely adjoining them is the Leathley Lane Pottery.

The wares manufactured at different periods at these interesting works consist of the coarse brown earthenwares, made on its first establishment; delft-ware, produced only in small quantities, and for a short period; hard and highly vitrified stone-ware, with a strong salt glaze; cream-coloured, or Queen's ware; Egyptian black ware; Rockingham ware; white earthenware; yellow ware, &c., &c. The great speciality of the works was the perforated "Queen's or cream-coloured earthenware," for which they became universally famed, and successfully competed with Wedgwood. It is this kind of ware which among collectors has acquired the name of "Leeds Ware." In colour the old Leeds ware—*i.e.* the cream-coloured earthenware—is of a particularly clear rich tint, usually rather deeper in tone than Wedgwood's Queen's ware, and of a slightly yellowish cast. The body is particularly fine and hard, and the glaze of extremely good quality. This glaze was produced with arsenic, and its use was so deleterious to the workmen that they usually became hopelessly crippled after four or five years' exposure to its effects.

The perforated pieces, as well as those of open basket-work, exhibit an unusual degree of skill and an elaborateness of design that is quite unequalled. The chestnut basket and stand (Fig. 848), of the finest and most elaborate description, is faultless in form and in moulding. The upper part of the cover and the lower portion of the bowl are fluted, and the handles, which are double twisted, terminate in flowers and foliage. Both bowl and cover are elaborately perforated; and here it may be well to note, for the information of collectors, that the perforations of this description were produced by punches, by which the soft clay was pierced by hand. I name this more particularly because I have heard an opinion expressed, by those not conversant with the matter, that this description of open-work was produced in the mould. The fact of each of the perforations being produced separately by the hands of the workman adds materially to the interest attached to the piece, and to its value. The wholesale price of this piece (eleven inches in diameter), the pattern

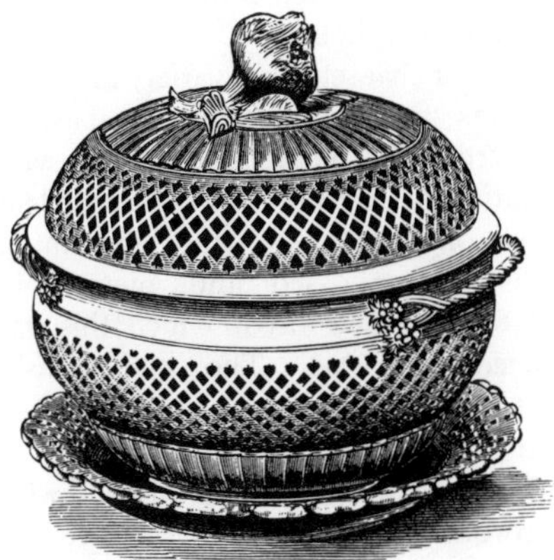

Fig. 848.—Leeds Ware Chestnut Tureen.

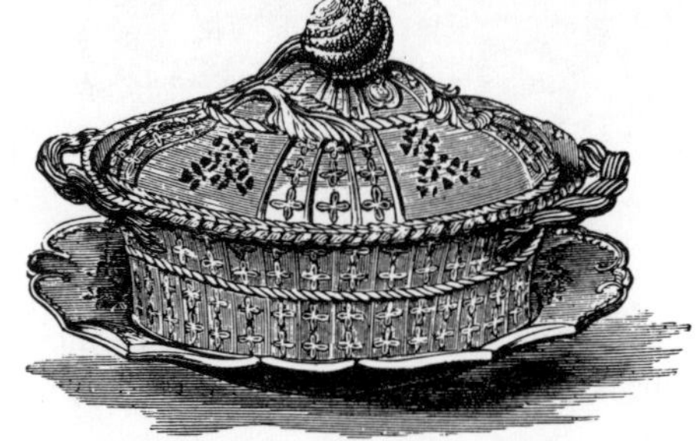

Fig. 849.—Leeds Ware Butter Stand.

for which was probably produced about 1782-83, was, in 1794, 8*s.* 6*d.*—a price which collectors at the present time would gladly multiply by ten.

The butter-tub and stand (Fig. 849), which belonged to the late Mr. Manning, is well covered with embossed work, and has both cover and stand perforated. Fig. 851 is one of the "pierced fruit baskets" for which these works were famous, and Fig. 850 an asparagus shell.

The next variety is that of twig baskets, of which Fig. 852 is a good and

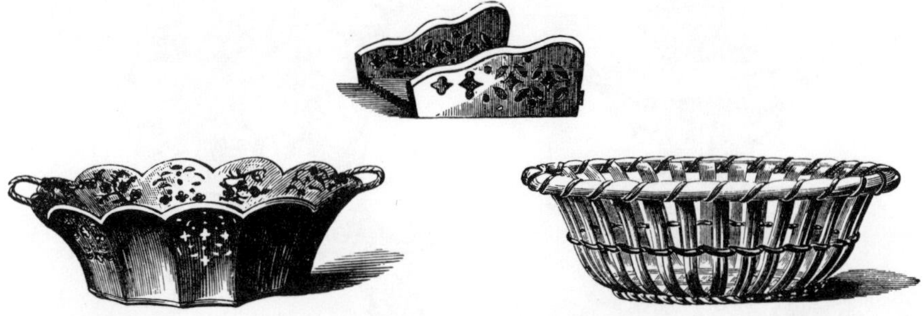

Figs. 850 to 852.—Leeds Ware.

characteristic example. In these pieces, which were produced in different varieties of wicker work, the "twigs," or "withies," are really composed of clay in long or short "strips," as occasion required, and then twisted and formed into shape. The process was one which required considerable care and nicety in manipulation, and was well calculated to exhibit the skill of the workman. Baskets of this kind were made by various makers, as well as at Leeds, and all on much the same model, so that without an intimate knowledge of the body and glaze of the Leeds ware, it is difficult to distinguish them from others. One of these baskets on its oval stand or dish (the wholesale price in 1794 ranging from 1*s.* 4*d.* to 3*s.* 6*d.*, according to size) is engraved in the book of patterns of which I have spoken, and those who are able to refer to that extremelv scarce work, "Wedgwood's Engraved Pattern Book" (18 plates, 4to), will there find one engraved on Plate 13, Fig. 851. The same baskets were produced at Castleford and Don, and by Staffordshire houses.

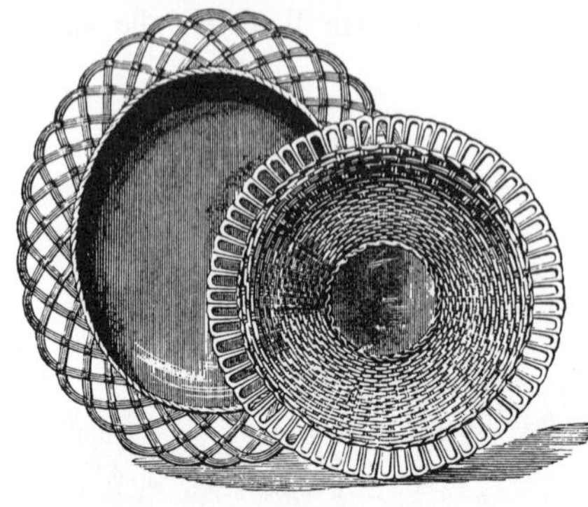

Fig. 853.

Another characteristic variety of Leeds ware, was the combination in basket-work, &c., of embossed patterns with perforations. Of these I give an excellent example on Fig. 853, in which the rim of the dish is embossed and pierced in basket-work. The way in which this was produced was this. The plate, dish, basket, or other piece, was formed in the mould so that the pattern stood out in relief above the parts intended to be incised. These were then cut out by hand with a penknife, leaving the pattern entirely in openwork. The dish here engraved is

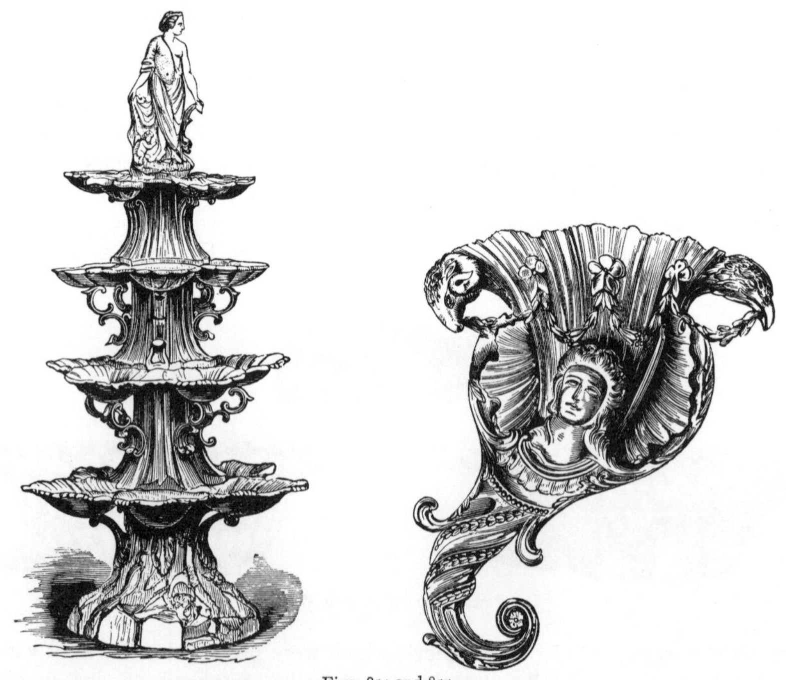

Figs. 854 and 855.

one of the simplest kind, but is an extremely early specimen, having probably been made about 1779, and is therefore a good illustration of this class of work. It is marked in small capital letters LEEDS POTTERY.

In this same ware—the Queen's or cream-coloured earthenware—the Leeds works produced services of various kinds, as well as the usual vessels for domestic use, and works of Art in the shape of vases, candelabra, centres, &c. &c. Of these decorative pieces Figs. 854 to 856 will show collectors to what degree of perfection in design these almost forgotten works had arrived. The first is a magnificent centre, or "grand platt menage," of four tiers, and composed of five separate pieces. The base is rock, and each tier is composed of shells supported on elegant brackets, and the whole is surmounted by a female figure.

The next is a *jardinière* of cornucopia form, with a head of Flora, crowned with flowers, in front, and festoons above held by a ram's and an eagle's head; and the third exhibits a "grand platt menage," similar to one engraved in the "Book of Patterns," except that the engraved design has a base for cruets added. Around the centre of the base is a series of rams' heads with large bent horns, hooked at the end, and the foliage beneath the pine-apple at the top is also deeply bent downwards, with the point of each leaf hooked up at the end. On these—the horns and leaves—it was intended to hang small earthenware wickerwork baskets, and on the engravings to which I have alluded these are all shown *in situ*. In Mr. Hailstone's collection is a precisely similar piece (with the addition of a circular base), which is of Wedgwood's Queen's ware, and marked WEDGWOOD in the usual manner. This shows that the design was common to both manufactories, and the natural inference is that Hartley, Greens, & Co., in this instance, as in others, copied and reproduced Wedgwood's designs; while in other cases it is equally possible Wedgwood copied from them. It is curious, in going through the Leeds pattern-books of 1783, and downwards to 1814, Wedgwood's of 1815, and the "Don," to note the similarity of the designs, some of which are so nearly identical as to appear almost to have been produced from the same moulds.

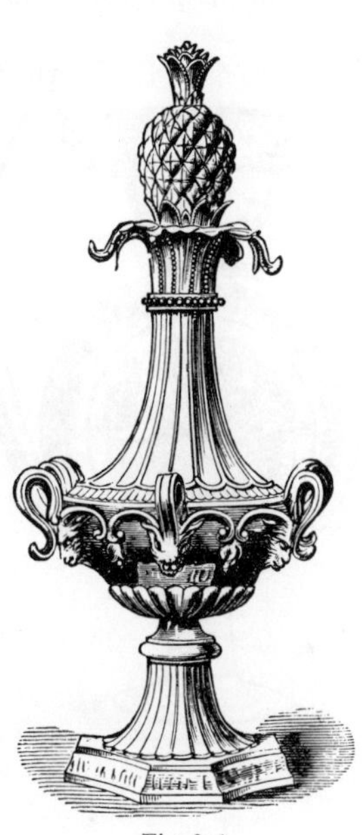
Fig. 856.

Many of the vases, scent jars, cockle pots, and *potpourri* produced at Leeds were of elaborate design and large size, and decorated with raised figures, medallions, flowers, festoons, shells, &c., and with perforated work. They were also frequently painted, or enamelled, in various colours, blue, green, and red being the prevailing ones. One "cockle pot," 22 inches in height, standing on four feet, has a square stand, highly decorated with shells, &c., in relief, and with perforations. At each corner is a raised seated figure. From the centre rises the stem, supporting a solid globe, on which rests the bowl, supported by mermaids. The bowl is decorated with festoons of shells, flowers, and sea-weeds in high relief. The cover is also ornamented with raised groups of shells and sea-weed, and is perforated in an elaborate and somewhat intricate pattern. It is surmounted by a spirited figure of Neptune with his trident and horses.

Candlesticks were made in great variety, and were highly decorated. Some were in the form of vases, and in this variety vases were produced in the same manner as Wedgwood's jasper ware, with reversible tops, so as to serve either as ornaments only, or as candlesticks. Others have dolphins; others again Corinthian and other pillars; others have massive bases perforated and embossed, while the candlestick itself rose from griffins; and others again are vases with branches for two or more candles springing out from their tops. Single figures and groups of figures were also produced, principally in the plain cream-coloured ware, but sometimes painted. It is also said that some minute works of Art, small cameos, were made at Leeds. In Mr. Hailstone's possession is a fountain of large size, with dolphin spout, shell terminations, and mermaids and shells for handles.

In tea, coffee, and chocolate services, a large variety of patterns were produced, both plain, engined, fluted, pierced, and otherwise decorated. Many of these are of similar form to Wedgwood's, to whom their manipulation would, indeed, have been no discredit. The great peculiarity of the tea and coffee pots, &c., is their double twisted handles, with flowers and leaves for terminations. Many of these are extremely beautiful, both in design and in execution. These services were made either in plain cream-colour, or painted with borders and sprigs of flowers in various colours. The chocolate cups are usually two-handled, or without handles. The stands are, in many instances, highly ornamented with perforations, or take the form of melon or other leaves, and have ornamental sockets for the cups attached. Tea-kettles and milk-pails with covers were also made.

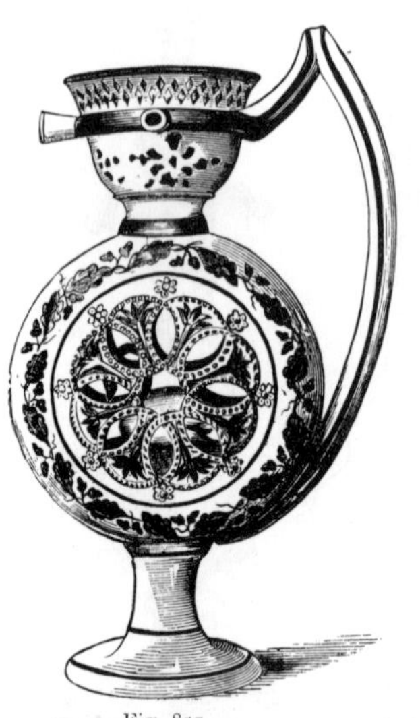

Fig. 857.

In the early part of the present century, white earthenware was made at these works. It was a fine, hard, compact body, and had, like the cream-coloured, a remarkably good glaze. In this ware, services, especially dinner and tea, were produced, and were decorated with transfer printing, painting, lustre, and tinsel. "Tinselling," it must be understood, is the peculiar process by which a part of the pattern is made to assume a metallic appearance by being washed here and there over the transfer or drawing. An excellent example of the white earthenware is the puzzle jug in the possession of Mr. Alfred Britton (Fig. 857). It is of elaborate design. The upper part ornamented with "punched" perforations, and the centre open throughout, having an open flower on either side, between which is a swan. The jug is painted with borders and sprigs of flowers, and has the impressed mark of LEEDS POTTERY. In Mr. Hailstone's possession is a large jug, having on one side a spirited engraving of "the Vicar and Moses" in black transfer printing, and coloured, and on the other side the old ballad of "the Vicar and Moses," engraved in two columns, and surrounded by a border. In front of the jug, pendent from the spout, is painted the arms of the borough of Leeds, the golden fleece, commonly called the "tup in trouble." On each side of this are the initials J. B. and S. B., and beneath are the words—"Success to Leeds Manufactory." Transfer printing was introduced at Leeds, probably about 1780, but this is very uncertain. In the title-page of the "Book of Patterns in 1783," it is said, "the same enamel'd, *Printed* or Ornamented with Gold to any pattern; also with Coats of Arms, Cyphers, Landscapes, &c.;" and in 1791, the copper plates then in use were valued at £204. The patterns were principally willow pattern, Nankin pattern, borders, groups of flowers, landscapes, and ruins. I may mention that several of the original pattern-books of drawings of the articles themselves, and of borders and other decorations of the early Leeds productions, are in my own possession.

Lustre, both gold and silver, was used occasionally in the decorations at Leeds, and excellent examples of "lustre ware" were also produced. About the year 1800, black ware was introduced at Leeds. This was of the same character as the Egyptian black, then so largely made in Staffordshire by Wedgwood, by Mayer, by Neale, and others. The body is extremely compact, firm, and hard, but had a more decided bluish cast than is usual in other makes. In this ware, tea and coffee pots, the latter both with spouts and with snips, cream ewers, and other articles were made. I believe there are but few collectors cognizant of the fact that this Egyptian black ware was made at Leeds at all; but I have been fortunate enough, by careful examination, to ascertain, that up to 1812–13, probably from ninety to a hundred distinct patterns and sizes of teapots alone were produced in black at these works. This is an interesting fact to note, and is one which will call attention for the first time to this particular branch of Leeds manufacture. The patterns of the teapots were very varied, both in form, in style of ornamentation, and in size. In form, were round, oval, octagonal, and other shapes, including some of twelve sides. In ornamentation some were engine-turned in a variety of patterns, while others were chequered or fluted. Others again were formed in moulds elaborately ornamented in relief with flowers, fruits, borders, festoons, &c. &c.; while others still had groups of figures, trophies, and medallions in relief on their sides. The "knobs" of the lids were seated figures, lions, swans, flowers, &c. &c. The lids were made of every variety, both inward and outward fitting, sliding, and attached with hinges. In speaking of engine-turning, it may be well to note that "engined" mugs, jugs, &c., were made at these works as early as 1782, if not at an earlier date.

The marks used at Leeds are not numerous, and are easily distinguished. Collectors, however, need to be told that very few indeed of the productions of this manufactory were marked. The great bulk of the pottery, whether in Queen's ware or otherwise, was made for foreign markets—Russia, Holland, Spain, Germany, Portugal, France, &c.—and as a rule the goods were sent off unmarked. It is worthy of note, too, that the finest examples of Leeds make, both in the perforated and other varieties, now known, have been recovered from the Continent. The marks, so far as I have been able to ascertain, which were used at the Leeds works, are the following—

LEEDS · POTTERY *

in large capitals, with a terminal asterisk impressed. (This mark occurs on a large-sized "Melon Terine" same as the one engraved in the pattern-book of 1783, figure 68, plate 16.)

LEEDS * POTTERY

in small capital letters.

HARTLEY GREENS & CO.
LEEDS * POTTERY

Fig. 858.

in small capital letters.

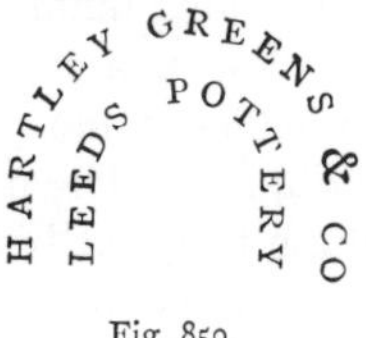

Fig. 859.

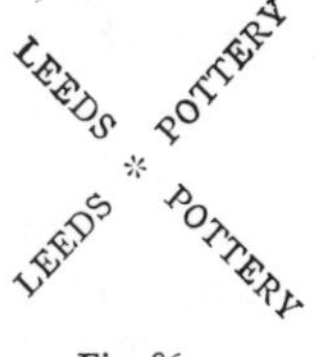

Fig. 860.

in small capital letters, in two curved or horseshoe lines. In the Museum of Practical Geology one example is marked with the impressed Leeds mark twice in form of a saltire (Fig. 860).

The marks, "*on china*," usually ascribed to Leeds are the following:—but there is no proof that any such were ever used at the works. They have been said to be the initials of Charles Green, but there does not ever appear to have been a *Charles* Green connected with the Leeds works; and *china* was certainly never made there.

C G or C. G. W.

The Leeds Pottery at the present time produces the ordinary descriptions of earthenware for domestic use, consisting of dinner, tea and coffee, toilet and other services, jugs and mugs, screw jugs, bowls and basins, and all the other usual articles mainly for the London market, which takes nearly one-half of the whole productions of the works. White earthenware, same as the ordinary Staffordshire ware, is produced in the usual styles, and pearl white is also manufactured in toilet ware, and tea, and breakfast services, &c., as well as for bottoms for washing-machines, and for patented machines for cloth manufacturers. Rockingham ware, tea and coffee pots and other articles are also made, as are also Egyptian black glazed wares and yellow earthenware, which is made from native clays procured from Wortley. The marks used at the present day are, an old English letter 𝔏 within a gothic quatrefoil in a circle, impressed in the body of the ware; or the name of the pattern within an ornamental circle, and below it, the initials of the firm, "R. B. & S.," printed on the surface.

Leathley Lane Pottery.

This was established in the early part of the present century, by, I believe, a Mr. North, for the manufacture of black ware, but afterwards used for ordinary white earthenware. From Mr. North the works passed into the hands of a Mr. Hepworth, who made the ordinary brown salt-glazed ware. It was next worked by Mr. Dawson, one of the trustees of the Leeds pottery, who took into partnership Mr. Chappell, and it was carried on by Dawson and Chappell, afterwards by Chappell alone, and then, till 1851, by Shackleton, Taylor, & Co., and next by Taylor & Gibson and Gibson & Co. The premises are small, and produce white ware of the commonest kind, yellow ware made from the Wortley clays, and Rockingham ware.

Castleford.

Castleford, which lies about 12 miles from Leeds, is, in great measure, supported by its glass-houses, its chemical works, and its potteries, where common brown ware, pancheons, and other vessels were made from an early period. The Castleford Pottery was established, towards the close of the last century, by David Dunderdale, for the manufacture of the finer kinds of earthenware, more especially Queen's or cream-coloured ware, which was then being made so largely at Leeds and other places, as well as in Staffordshire. He took into partnership a Mr. Plowes, and in 1803 the firm of D. Dunderdale & Co. (which was not of long duration), as stamped on the goods, consisted of these two persons. Mr. Plowes, after the dissolution, removed to Ferrybridge, where he joined the proprietors of the pot-works there, and Mr. Dunderdale continued the Castleford Works alone. The next partner was Mr. T. E. Upton, a relative of Dunderdale's, and these two shortly afterwards took into partnership John Bramley (or Bramler) and Thomas Russell, an hotel proprietor at Harrogate—Dunderdale owning one-half of the concern, Russell a fourth, and Upton and Bramley an eighth each.

In 1820 the manufactory was closed, and in 1821 a part of the works was taken by some of the workmen—George Asquith, William and Daniel Byford, Richard Gill, James Sharp, and David Hingham. They were succeeded by Taylor, Harrison, & Co., Harrison having been an apprentice of David Dunderdale's; and the place was for several years carried on by the latter and the son of the former, under the style of Taylor and Harrison, who gave up the manufacture of earthenware, and continued it for stoneware alone.

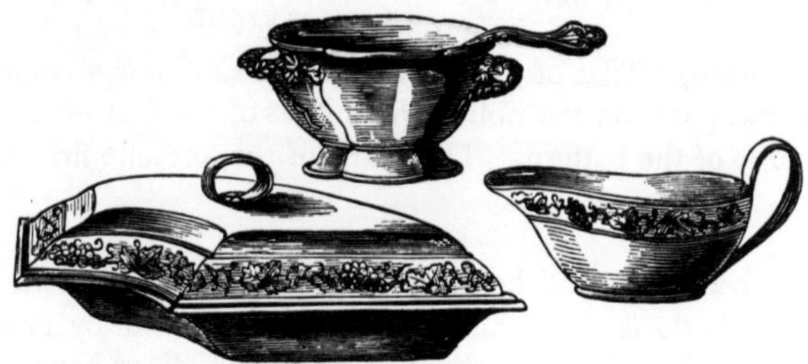

Figs. 861 to 863.

In 1825, the old works were again opened by Asquith, Wood, & Co., who were joined in partnership by Thomas Nicholson, who had served his apprenticeship with Hartley, Greens, & Co., of the Leeds Pottery, and carried on the business as "Asquith, Wood, and Nicholson," and afterwards as "Wood and Nicholson." In 1854 Mr. Nicholson took into partnership Thomas Hartley, the style being "Thomas Nicholson & Co." Later on, Mr. Nicholson having retired from the concern, it was carried on by Thomas Hartley alone, and afterwards with partners, under the old name of "Nicholson & Co." In 1871 Mr. Hartley died, after which the Castleford Pottery was carried on by his co-partners, Hugh McDowell Clokie and John Masterman, under the style of "Clokie and Masterman."

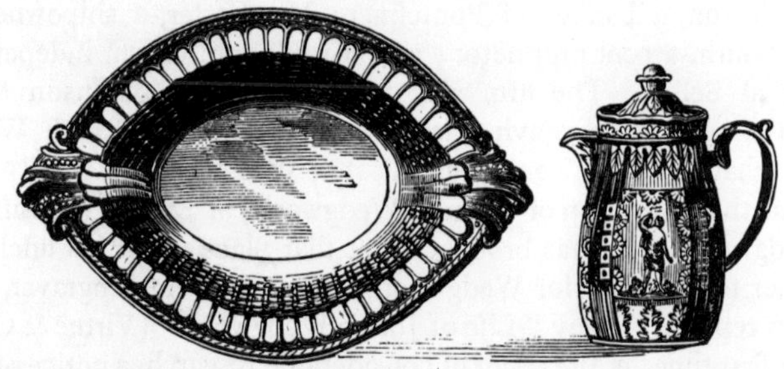

Figs. 864 and 865.

The staple production in Dunderdale's time was the "Queen's" or "cream-coloured ware," which in appearance assimilated closely to the cream ware made at the Herculaneum Works, and was not so fine or so perfect in glaze as that made at Leeds. In this ware dinner, dessert, and other services, as well as open-work baskets, vases, candlesticks, and a large variety of other articles, were made, both plain and painted, or enamelled, and decorated with transfer printing. Fig. 862 is one of a set of four central covered dishes painted in sepia with a border of vine-leaves, grapes, and tendrils, of precisely the same design as appears on examples of

Wedgwood's make, and of Herculaneum, and other places. This set of dishes, when placed together for use, forms a circle of twenty-two inches in diameter. The sauce-boat (Fig. 863) is a part of the same service. In what would now be called Parian, the Castleford Works in their early days produced some good and effective pieces. One of these, a hot-milk jug with its cover (Fig. 865), is decorated with borders, and groups of figures in relief. Examples are in the Museum of Practical Geology. Black or Egyptian ware of fine quality was also made, as was also fine white earthenware of remarkably hard and compact body. The marks used at these old works are— D D & Co* CASTLEFORD or D·D & Co CASTLEFORD POTTERY impressed in the ware. That of "T. Nicholson & Co." was a circular garter, surmounted by a crown, and on the ribbon the initials of the firm—"T. N. & Co."; in the centre the name of the pattern. The mark of the present firm is their initials within a border.

The *Eagle Pottery* was established in 1854 by a company of workmen, under the style of "John Roberts & Co.," and afterwards continued by Pratt & Co., who sold it to Mr. H. McDowall, since whose death the buildings have been converted into a glass bottle manufactory.

PONTEFRACT.

Thoresby records that Francis Place, of the Manor House at York, spent much money upon his manufacture of "fine muggs," and that he attempted it solely from a turn for experiments; but one Clifton, of Pontefract, took the hint from him, and made a fortune by it. The works of Mr. Clifton would probably be the forerunners of those of Ferrybridge.

The FERRYBRIDGE POTTERY, by Knottingley, is only a short distance from that famous seat of the growth of liquorice, Pontefract, whose "Pomfret cakes" are so well known. They were established in 1792 by William Tomlinson, who had for partners Mr. Seaton, a banker of Pontefract; Mr. Foster, a shipowner, of Selby; Mr. Timothy Smith, a coal proprietor; and Mr. Thompson, an independent gentleman, residing at Selby. The firm was styled "William Tomlinson & Co.," until 1796, when the proprietors having taken into partnership Ralph Wedgwood, of Burslem, was changed to "Tomlinson, Foster, Wedgwood, & Co." This Ralph Wedgwood was the eldest son of Thomas Wedgwood, of Etruria (cousin and partner of Josiah Wedgwood), and was brought up at that place under his uncle and father. He was brother to John Taylor Wedgwood, the eminent line engraver, whose works are so justly in repute. In my "Life of Josiah Wedgwood" (Virtue & Co., London), I gave, for the first time, as the result of considerable research, a notice of this remarkable man, Ralph Wedgwood, and of his inventions, and of his family and connections, and to this I refer my readers. He had carried on business as a potter, under the style of "Wedgwood & Co.," at the Hill Works, Burslem, and while there prepared and presented to Queen Charlotte some fine examples of his manufacture, on the occasion of the restoration of health to the king. His partnership with Tomlinson & Co., of Ferrybridge, was not of long duration. His partners being dissatisfied at the large amount of breakage caused by his experiments and peculiar mode of firing, the partnership was dissolved, and he retired from the concern, having succeeded in getting a thousand pounds awarded to him as his share of the business.

After the dissolution, which took place about 1800 or 1801, the style of "Tomlinson & Co." was resumed, and so continued until 1834, when it changed to "Tomlinson, Plowes, & Co.;" Mr. Plowes, of the Castleford Works, having joined the proprietary. In 1804, the name of the manufactory, which, up to that period, had been called the *Knottingley Pottery*, was changed to that of the *Ferrybridge Pottery*.

Mr. Tomlinson was succeeded by his son Edward Tomlinson, who continued the works under the firm of Edward Tomlinson & Co., until 1826, when he retired from the concern. A part of the premises were then worked by Wigglesworth and Ingham, and afterwards the whole place was again taken by Reed, Taylor, and Kelsall, and after the retirement of Kelsall by James Reed and Benjamin Taylor. Mr. Reed, who was father of the late Mr. John Reed, of the "Mexborough Pottery," was a man of great practical skill; and in his time many improvements in the ware were made, and the manufacture of china introduced. He, in conjunction with his partner, took the Mexborough Pottery, and carried on the two establishments conjointly. Ultimately Mr. Reed gave up the Ferrybridge works, and confined himself to those at Mexborough, while Mr. Taylor carried on the Ferrybridge works alone.

After Mr. Taylor gave up the works Mr. Lewis Woolf entered upon them as tenant for a few years, and in 1856 became the purchaser. In 1857, the "Australian Pottery," closely adjoining, and, indeed, connected with the "Ferrybridge Pottery," was built by the sons of Mr. Lewis Woolf, and is still in full work; the proprietors of the joint works, "The Ferrybridge and Australian Potteries," being Lewis, Sidney, and Henry Woolf, who trade under the style of "Lewis Woolf and Sons."

The wares principally made were cream and cane coloured ware; green glazed ware, in which dessert services and other articles were made, and which were of a lighter colour than what Wedgwood produced; Egyptian black ware, of the usual quality; and fine white earthenware, in which was produced all the usual kinds of goods in enamelling, blue printing, painting, &c.

In the time of Reed and Taylor china of a very fine quality was made, but the manufacture was not of long duration. Tea and coffee services, dessert services, scent bottles, and a variety of articles, were made of this body, and were remarkably good in form and in style of decoration. Examples of Ferrybridge china are now of extreme rarity.

Cameos, medallions, and other ornamental articles in the time of Ralph Wedgwood's connection with the works, were made in imitation of those of Josiah Wedgwood, to which they were, however, very inferior both in body and finish.

The marks used at the Ferrybridge Pottery have been but few. So far as my knowledge goes, those which will be of interest to the collector are the following—TOMLINSON & CO. impressed upon the bottom of the ware; WEDGWOOD & CO. impressed on cameos, made during the time of Ralph Wedgwood's connection with the works; FERRYBRIDGE, also impressed, and one variety of which mark is peculiar from having the letter D reversed thus, FERRYBRIᗡGE

P

Another is a shield, with the words—OPAQUE GRANITE CHINA in three lines, supported by a lion and unicorn and surmounted by a crown. The present mark is the lion and unicorn with the shield and crown, and the words, "Ferrybridge and Australian Potteries."

SWINTON—ROCKINGHAM CHINA.

When pot-making was first practised in Swinton and its districts, it is, of course, impossible to say, but I believe that as early as the beginning of last century (if not much earlier) a hard brown ware, of much the same quality as that made at Nottingham and Chesterfield, was produced on Swinton Common, where clays useful for various purposes were abundantly found. In 1745 Mr. Edward Butler, seeing the advantage offered by the locality through its clays, which consisted of a "common yellow clay used for the purposes of making bricks, tiles, and coarse earthenware; a finer white clay for making pottery of a better quality; an excellent clay for making fire-bricks; and also a white clay usually called pipe-clay;" established a tile-yard and pot-works for common earthenware, on a part of the estate of the Marquis of Rockingham, which lay closely contiguous to Swinton Common, where these clays existed. The memory of this old potter, the founder of the works which afterwards became so famous as the "Royal Rockingham China Works," is, it is pleasant to record, at the present day preserved in the name of a field near the now ruined factory called "Butler's Park." Butler at these works produced the ordinary classes of goods then in use, but principally the hard brown ware to which I have just alluded. An interesting example of this period was in the possession of the late Dr. Brameld,

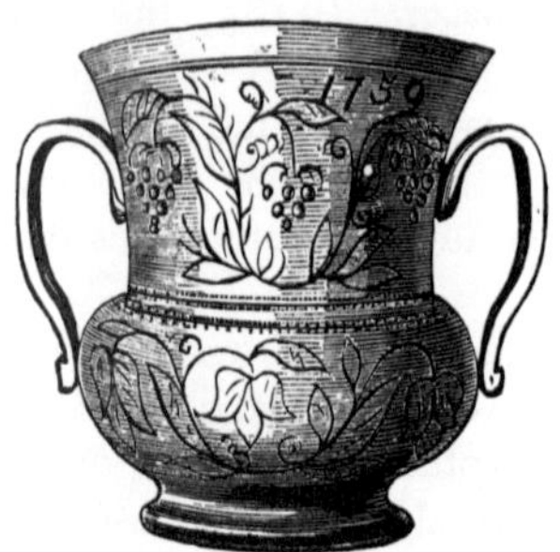

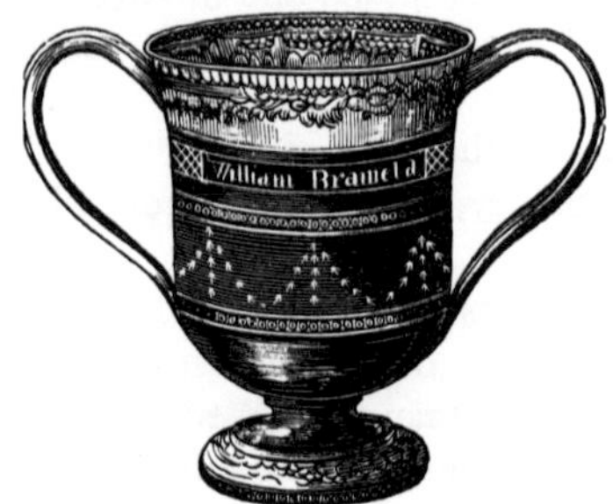

Figs. 866 and 867.

and is engraved on Fig. 866. It is a "posset-pot" of the useful form of those which, at that period, were in such general use in Derbyshire and Yorkshire; it bears the date of 1759. This interesting example has a fragment of a label, written at "Swinton Pottery," which authenticates it as having been made by, or for, John Brameld.

In 1765 the works were taken by William Malpass, who held another small pot-work at Kilnhurst, in the same neighbourhood, and he continued them for some years. With him were associated in partnership, I believe, John Brameld, and subsequently his son, William Brameld, of whom I shall have more to say presently. Mr. Malpass continued to manufacture the same varieties of ware as his predecessor, and held the works, or rather was a partner in them, at all events as late as 1786.

In 1778 Mr. Thomas Bingley became a principal proprietor of the Swinton works, and had for partners, among others, John and William Brameld, and a person named Sharpe. Mr. Bingley was a member of a family of that name which had been resident at Swinton for more than four hundred years, and is now worthily represented in the person of Mr. Thomas Bingley, who still resides there. The firm at this time was carried on under the style of Thomas Bingley & Co., and, being thriving, indeed opulent, people, the works were greatly enlarged, and conducted with much spirit. An extensive trade was at this time carried on, and besides the ordinary brown and yellow wares, blue and white dinner, tea, coffee, and other services were made, as also a white earthenware of remarkably fine and compact body, and other wares of good quality.

An interesting example of this period is a two-handled drinking-cup (Fig. 867), with the name of one of the proprietors, "William Brameld, 1788." It is of fine white earthenware with a bluish coloured glaze, some parts ornamented with blue transfer printing, and the rest of the vessel black, with the name, date, and ornaments in gold. The printed borders are much the same as those around "willow-pattern" plates, and from this it may be inferred that the "willow pattern" was at that period produced at Swinton. From about 1787 to 1800, the firm, consequent on some of the Greens of the "Leeds Pottery" having become partners, traded under the style of "Greens, Bingley, & Co.," and Mr. John Green became acting manager of the Swinton works, and afterwards, I am informed, founded the "Don Pottery."

The partnership with John Green was carried on in the style of "Greens, Bingley, & Co., Swinton Pottery;" and the same price-lists which were printed at Leeds, with the Leeds pottery heading, had that heading cut off, and that of "Greens, Bingley, & Co., Swinton Pottery," written in its place. Later on large fresh price-lists were printed. They were headed "Greens, Hartley, & Co., Swinton Pottery, make, sell, and export wholesale all sorts of Earthenware, Cream Coloured or Queens, Nankeen Blue, Tortoise Shell, Fine Egyptian Black, Brown China, &c. &c. All the above sorts enameled, printed, or ornamented with gold or silver." On the fly-leaf was a printed circular, dated "Swinton Pottery, 1st February, 1796," announcing an advance in prices and a revised system of counting. The Leeds patterns were evidently, to some extent, adopted at Swinton; and I possess some original drawings and designs on which the numbers for each of those works are given. For instance, in teapots, Leeds No. 149 was Swinton No. 68; Leeds 133 was Swinton No. 69; 218 was 70; and 252 was 71, and so on.

Late in the last century, about the time of which I am now writing, a peculiar kind of ware was first made at these works, and took the name of "Brown China," and afterwards that which it has ever since maintained where attempted to be made, of "Rockingham Ware." This ware, which is of a fine reddish-brown, or chocolate colour, is one of the smoothest and most beautiful ever produced. The body is of fine hard and compact white earthenware, and the brown glaze, by which the peculiar shaded and streaky effect of this class of goods was produced, is as fine as it is possible to conceive, and required to be "dipped" and passed through the firing process no fewer than three times before it arrived at perfection. In this ware, tea, coffee, and chocolate services, jugs, drinking-cups, &c., were produced, and continued to be made to the close of the works in 1842. Since that time "Rockingham ware"—in every instance falling far short of the original in beauty and in excellence—has been made by almost every manufacturer in the kingdom, and has always, especially for tea and coffee pots, met a ready and extensive sale. One special article produced in this ware was the curious coffee-pot, formed on purely scientific principles, which is usually known to collectors as the "Cadogan pot," Fig. 868, already alluded to. It was constructed with a small opening in the bottom to admit the coffee, but none at the top, and no lid. From the hole in the bottom a tube, slightly spiral, was made to pass up inside the vessel to within half an inch of the top, so that after filling, on the "pot" being turned over into its proper position for table use, the coffee was kept in without chance of spilling or escape.

In 1796, the firm was, as before, "Greens, Bingley, & Co.;" and from a list of prices and goods now in my possession, it appears that a large variety were produced. Among the articles in cream ware enumerated, are all the separate items for services in Paris, Bath, concave, royal, queen's, feather, and shell-edge patterns, which were produced "printed or enamelled with coats-of-arms, crests, cyphers, landscapes, &c.; also blue printed Nankeen patterns;" dishes, covers, compotiers, tureens, plates, butter-tubs, baking-dishes, nappies, glass trays, fruit plates, fruit baskets pierced and plain, tea-trays, garden-pots and stands, shaving-basins, salts, castors, cruets, egg-cups, spoons plain and pierced, ice-cellars, candlesticks, ink-stands, wafer and sand boxes, fountain inkstands, bidets, &c., furnished castors, tureen ladles, chocolate stands, quintal flower horns, radish dishes, crosses with holy-water cup, ice pails, broad mugs, bowls, ewers, basins, &c., milk ewers, tea and coffee pots, tea canisters, chocolate cups and saucers, &c. &c.

In 1806, the firm of "Greens, Bingley, & Co." was dissolved. At this time, as appears from a memorandum of resolutions, passed at a meeting held on January 22nd, 1806, preparatory to the dissolution, that the partners (present) were—"William Hartley for himself and others (this was William Hartley, principal proprietor in the Leeds Pottery), Ebenezer Green for himself and others (this was another of the partners in the Leeds Pottery), George Hanson, Thomas Bingley, John Brameld, and William Brameld." At this dissolution, the concern fell into the hands of John and William Brameld, who, with partners, continued the works as "Brameld & Co." until their death. The old price-lists, which I have already named, continued to be used, but had the words "Greens, Bingley" erased with the pen, and "Brameld" substituted, so that the heading commenced "Brameld & Co., Swinton Pottery." They were later on joined in partnership by younger branches of the family, who eventually became proprietors of the manufactory. By John and William Brameld, by whom additional buildings were erected, cream-coloured ware was made very extensively, and a remarkably fine white earthenware—"chalk-body," as it was technically called—was successfully produced, but, owing to its costliness through loss in firing, was made only to a small extent, and is now of great rarity.

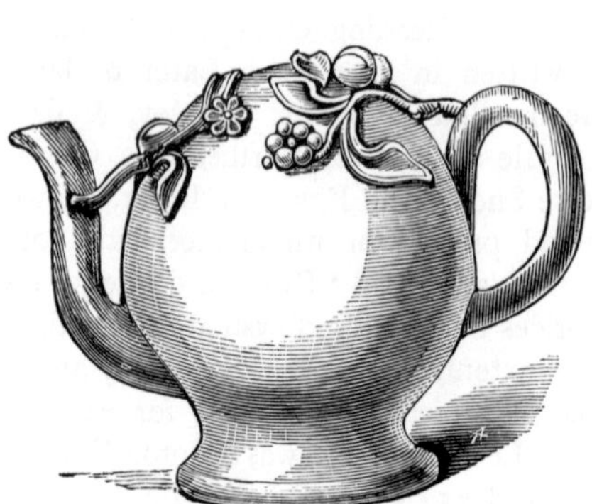

Fig. 868.—Cadogan Pot.

About 1813, the sons, Thomas Brameld, George Frederick Brameld, and John Wager Brameld, succeeded to the concern of the old proprietors, and to them the great after-success of the works was due. They considerably enlarged the manufactory, made many improvements in the wares, and erected a flint mill on the premises. Thomas Brameld, the eldest of the partners, a man of exquisite taste, laboured hard to raise the character of the productions of the Swinton Works to a high standard of excellence, and he succeeded to an eminent degree. In 1820 he turned his attention to the production of china ware, and made many experiments in bodies and glazes. Having expended large sums of money in the prosecution of this his favourite project, and in making Art-advances in his manufactory, the firm became, as is too frequently the case with those who study the beautiful instead of the strictly commercial in the management of their works, slightly embarrassed, which was increased by the great losses sustained through the war. In 1825, a year of great commercial difficulties, the firm succumbed to the embarrassments that had affected them, and at a meeting held at Rotherham, Mr. Thomas Brameld produced some remarkable examples of his china ware, the result of long and patient labour on his part, and these being highly approved by all who were present, and appearing likely to succeed, Earl Fitzwilliam, the owner of the property at Swinton, in the most laudable and kindly manner, agreed to assist in the prosecution of the work by the advance of capital, and by taking an active part in the scheme.

This being done, Mr. Brameld set himself to his task with renewed spirit, and with a determination to make his porcelain at least equal to any which could then be produced, and in this he certainly succeeded. The works were altered and enlarged ; modellers and painters, the most skilful that could be procured, were employed ; and every means taken to ensure that success, artistically and manipulatively, which quickly followed. In this ware, dinner, dessert, breakfast, and tea services, vases, groups of figures and flowers, and numberless articles, both of utility and ornament, were produced, and were all characterized by pure taste, and an excellence of design and workmanship which told much for the skill and judgment of the mind that governed the whole of the manufactory.

Mr. George Frederick Brameld, the second of the partners, devoted himself to the strictly commercial part of the business on the Continent. He for some time resided at St. Petersburg, a large trade with Russia being carried on by the firm.

Mr. John Wager Brameld, like his brother, was a man of pure taste. He was an excellent artist, and some exquisite paintings on porcelain by him have come under my notice. He was a clever painter of flowers and of figures, and landscapes. In flowers Mr. Brameld went to Nature herself, collecting specimens wherever he went, and reproducing their beauties on the choice wares of the works. At Lowestoft, I remember seeing a set of three vases painted in flowers, which, it is said, Mr. Brameld gathered on the Dene, at that place, on one of his visits, and which vases he presented to the father of their owner. In the same hands is an elegant snuff-box, bearing an exquisite painting of "The Politician," with groups of flowers, and bearing the words, "Brameld, Rockingham Works, near Rotherham," "The Politician, J. W. Brameld." This being a signed piece of John Wager Brameld's, is particularly interesting. Mr. Brameld's time was chiefly devoted, however, to travelling for the firm in the United Kingdom, and to the management of the London house, so that his artistic productions did not make a feature in the goods generally made at the works. Mr. Thomas Brameld, who resided at Swinton House, Swinton, died in 1850; Mr. John Wager Brameld, in 1851; and Mr. George Frederick Brameld, in 1853.

Earthenware of various kinds—"Brown China," or "Rockingham ware," green glazed ware, biscuit figures and ornaments, hard fine white stoneware, cream-coloured ware, and other varieties of goods were also still made ; and the works, which, at this time—the time when china began regularly to be made (1826)—with the assistance of the Earl Fitzwilliam, assumed the name of the "ROCKINGHAM

WORKS," began to use the crest of the Fitzwilliam family as the mark of the firm. In 1826 (November 17), Messrs. Brameld & Co. secured the services of "Mr. John Cresswell, painter on china," and articles of agreement (in my own possession) were drawn up by which Cresswell engaged himself to them for five years at 7s. 6d. a day for the first three years; 9s. 3d. a day for the fourth year; and 10s. 6d. a day for the fifth year. In 1830 the firm received orders for services from the Duchess of Cumberland, the Duke of Sussex, and others of the Royal family. In the same year they purchased from Mr. George Green his interest in the Kilnhurst Pottery, and in 1840 were in negotiation for the purchase from Mr. Dillwyn of the Glamorgan Pottery at Swansea, which purchase, however, was not made.

In 1830, the Rockingham Works received an order for a splendid dessert service for King William IV., which was executed in the highest style of the art, and gave intense satisfaction. The original sketches for this service are in my own possession, and are named "Original Designs for His Majesty's Dessert, 12th Nov., 1830, per J. W. B." (John Wager Brameld). They are pen-and-ink sketches by himself. At this time the works assumed the name of "Royal Rockingham Works," and the proprietors called themselves China Manufacturers and Potters to the King, Queen, and Royal Family. In 1838, the manufacture of china and earthenware bed-posts, cornices, &c.—a somewhat novel feature in the art—was added to the other productions of the Rockingham Works. In that year a patent (which, with others, I printed in full in my first edition) was taken out in the name of William Dale for "certain improvements in constructing columns, pillars, bed-posts, and other such-like articles;" "consisting of several ornamental pieces or compound parts of china or earthenware," "united, strengthened and supported by a shaft or rod passing through the whole length of the same, and furnished with screw nuts or other description of fastenings, and collars," &c. These bed-posts and other similar things were made at the Rockingham Works, though never to any extent. They are now of very great rarity, but examples are in my own possession. The body is white, the prevailing colour being *Rose-du-Barry*, with yellow flowers, &c. Another of these interesting examples is white with an effective chintz pattern in colours: while others have small groups and sprigs of flowers, the outline in transfer printing, and filled in with colour. In my own possession, too, are several of the original drawings of designs for beds, window cornices, lamps, candelabra, tables, &c., which are remarkable for their elegance and beauty. An elegant work-table of this description of ware, of simple but very effective design and excellent workmanship, is in the possession of Mr. Wilson of Sheffield. It is 2 feet 6 inches high, and 1 foot 6 inches in diameter at the top. Among the designs to which I have alluded is one representing a small and remarkably elegant table of somewhat similar but much more ornate character, on which is a fish-globe stand of corresponding design.

Although the Rockingham Works were eminently successful in an artistic point of view, they were not so commercially, and in 1842 were closed, after involving not only their noble owner, but the absolute proprietors, in a loss of very many thousands of pounds. Only sixteen years had elapsed since the introduction of the china manufacture to the works, but those had been sixteen years of beauty, and of artistic and manipulative success. No man better understood his art than Mr. Thomas Brameld, no man laboured harder and more disinterestedly in the ennobling of that art than he did, and few men, either before his time or since, succeeded in accomplishing greater or more honourable things. He and his brother looked to Art instead of commerce, and the result was embarrassment and loss.

At the close of the works, in 1842, the stock, &c., was sold off and dispersed, and the manufactory was discontinued. A small portion of the building was, however, taken by an old and experienced workman, Isaac Baguley (formerly employed at the famous Derby China Works), who was one of Brameld's best painters and gilders. Here he commenced business in a small way on his own account, and so continued until his death. Mr. Baguley did not manufacture the wares himself, but purchased what he required in the biscuit and white state, from other makers, and then painted, gilt, and otherwise ornamented them for sale. At his death, his son, Alfred Baguley, succeeded him, and, for a few years, carried on this decorative branch of the business at the old premises. Mr. Baguley decorated with commendable taste earthenware and porcelain, and produced some extremely good and effective designs in modelling, and clever patterns in decoration. One of his specialities was the old Rockingham ware, which he produced of a far purer and better quality than any other house. To this branch he paid particular attention, and produced the Rockingham chocolate or brown glaze on a china body. In this "Rockingham china," breakfast and tea services, tea and coffee pots of the good old designs, drinking-horns, jugs, &c., were made, and, being gilt in the same manner as the old Rockingham ware, have a remarkably pleasing appearance, while in touch they are all that can be desired. He also made the famous old "Bishopthorpe" and "Wentworth" jugs. His mark was the same as that of the old works —the crest of Earl Fitzwilliam (Fig. 880) with the name—

Baguley
Rockingham Works.

Fig. 869.

In 1852, a small portion of the works was tenanted by some earthenware manufacturers, who traded as "P. Hobson & Son," but their occupation was of only short duration, and since then the whole place has been closed.

The "brown china" or "Rockingham ware" services made at these works, though not all marked, usually bore the impressed words "ROCKINGHAM," "BRAMELD," or "BRAMELD & Co.," or the name of "MORTLOCK."

In fine hard "white stoneware," and in fine cane-coloured ware, jugs of remarkably good design were made, and were decorated with groups in relief in the same manner, indeed strongly resembling, both in body and in design, those of Turner, which are so well known to collectors. Some noteworthy jugs have their handles formed of the leg and tail of a horse. In "green-glazed earthenware," dessert services, flower vases, garden seats, and all the usual varieties of articles were made. The green, as a rule, was a somewhat lighter colour and not so good in quality as Wedgwood's. The pieces were generally marked with the usual impressed mark. In fine "earthenware," services of every kind were produced, both white, blue-printed, painted, and gilt. The glaze on the earlier pieces, it should be remarked, is of a decided blue tint, and somewhat inferior in quality. Some of the dessert-services produced in the early part of the present century are particularly interesting. On each piece is painted some flower as large as life, and coloured true to nature in every particular. The name of the plant represented is in each case pencilled at the back of the piece. The plants represented on the two examples (Fig. 870) are respectively marked as "*Althea Frutex*" and "*Virgilia helioides.*"

In the late Dr. Brameld's possession was a service of this same kind, in which the flowers were beautifully painted by Collinson, the best flower-painter at the Swinton Works, and they were made between the years 1810-15. The ware is particularly light, and has a remarkably pleasant feel in handling. I have been somewhat particular in speaking of this variety of goods, because similar services were produced far more extensively at the Don Works, at Swansea, and at other places.

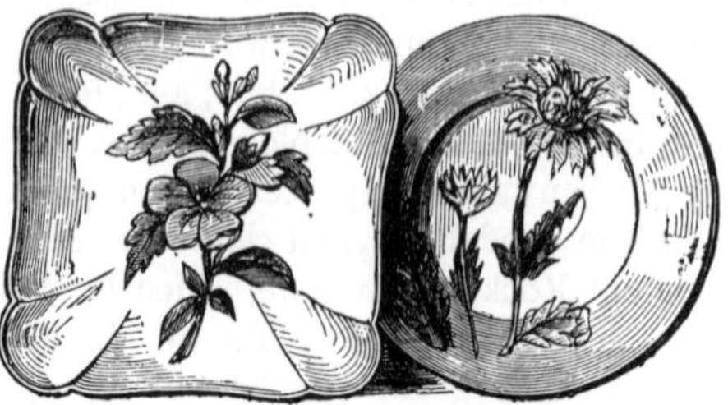

Fig. 870.

Of works of Art, in earthenware, the Swinton Pottery produced many vases and other objects of a high degree of excellence, both in design, manipulation, and in decoration, and were, indeed, far in advance of most of their competitors. Fig. 871 represents one of a pair of remarkably fine *pot-pourris*, which were "thrown" at the

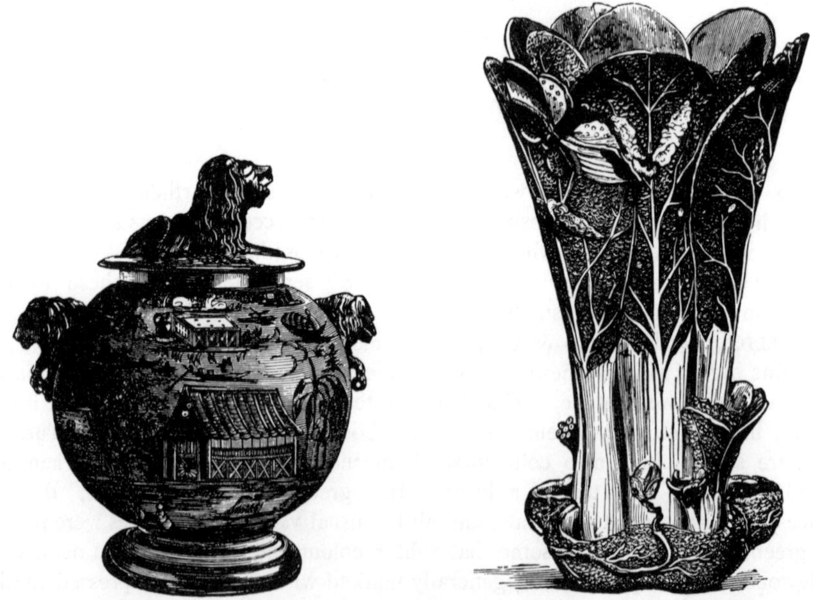

Figs. 871 and 872.

Swinton Works by Mr. Thomas Brameld the year he was out of his apprenticeship, in 1805, and were, till his death, in the possession of his son, Dr. Brameld. They are 18 inches high, and have lions' heads for handles, while on the top of the lid is a lion couchant, the family crest, gilt. The jars are beautifully painted in Chinese subjects. The next engraving shows one of the specialities of the Swinton pottery, a "lotus vase," from an example in the late Mr. Manning's possession. It is formed of leaves, &c., and has butterflies, &c., raised, as if resting upon the leaves. The whole is carefully enamelled, and altogether forms a flower vase of surpassing beauty. It is pleasant to add that at the close of the Rockingham Works, the moulds for the production of these "lotus vases," as well as others, including the model of the keep of Conisborough Castle, which, by the way, was another of the specialities of the Swinton Works, passed into the hands of the late Mr. John Reed, of the "Mexborough Pottery," by whose successors they continue to be made, both in the fine old green-glazed style and enamelled.

In "Queen's ware," or "cream-coloured ware," services were formerly made at Swinton. It was of a very similar quality to that made at Leeds and at Castleford, and, being unmarked, is generally ascribed to one or other of those works. In Dr. Brameld's possession was a teapot of this material (Fig. 873), which is said to have been made in the latter part of last century by his grandfather. It bears the name and date, "Amelia Hallam, 1773." In the late Mr. Reed's possession was a double-handled drinking-cup, with the name, "IOHN ALSEBROOK, 1795."

That this kind of ware was not made extensively at Swinton until after the dissolution of partnership with Hartley, Greens, & Co., is perhaps to be easily accounted for in the fact that these proprietors of the Leeds Pottery, where it was manufactured so extensively and so well, being also partners here, the cream ware would be made principally at Leeds, while at the Swinton Works was produced what had not been made at the other place. From the time the works fell entirely into the hands of the Bramelds, however, this kind of ware became the staple production of the manufactory, and an immense trade was carried on in it in the Baltic and elsewhere. Not being marked, it probably often passes for Leeds ware in the eyes of collectors. In this material beautiful openwork baskets, and many other elegant articles, were made.

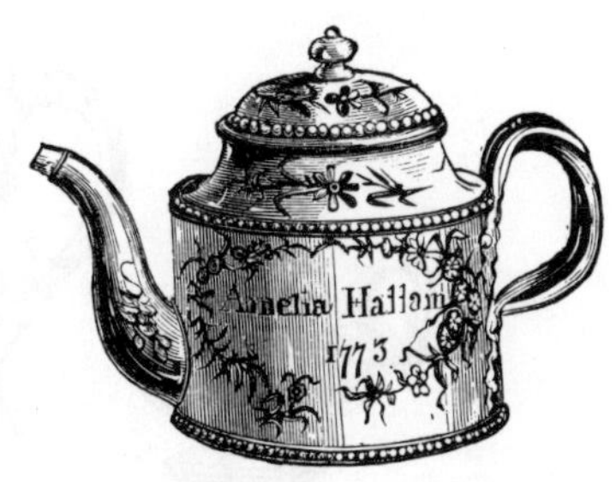

Fig. 873.

Transfer printing was introduced at Swinton, at all events as early as 1788, and was continued to the close of the works. In the later years, some extremely tasteful groups of flowers, butterflies, &c., were engraved and transferred in outline, and then painted in the usual manner. In dinner, tea, toilet, and other services, the designs were extremely good, and one of them, the Don Quixote pattern, became very popular. Engine-turned tea and coffee pots, plates, &c., were also manufactured, and in manipulation were equal to any produced in ordinary earthenware. Groups of flowers, figures, trophies, borders, &c., in relief, were also introduced. In "china" the earliest examples are two trial pieces by Mr. Thomas Brameld, which I saw in the possession of his son, the late Dr. Brameld. These are a pair of small leaves, the body of which is of good quality, painted of a salmon colour with gold veins, and probably date from 1820–22. In 1826 china ware began to be made largely, and from that time (in this year it will be remembered the works changed their name from "Swinton" to "Rockingham") to 1842 was one series of successes in all but profit. Tea, coffee, dinner, dessert, toilet, and other services were made in every variety of style, from the ordinary blue printed, or white with raised blue ornaments, to the most elaborately painted and gilt varieties. Vases, and numberless ornamental articles for the drawing-room and the toilet, were also made, and were generally distinguished by good taste in design and skill in decoration. To show how Art was, by the taste of the Bramelds, made subservient to the production of things of every-day use, I give, in Figs. 874 to 876, three examples which were in the late Mr. Manning's possession.

In vases, some of the finest which had ever been produced were made at these works. At Wentworth House, the seat of Earl Fitzwilliam, among other fine examples of Swinton Art, is one of surpassing beauty. It stands 3 feet 9 inches in height, and is 3 feet 1 inch in circumference. The base, of tripod form, has a blue ground, with flowers in compartments, and is massively gilt. From it rises the vase, supported on three lions' paws in white and gold. From between the feet on each side spring branches of oak, solidly gilt, which entwine their leaves around the paws, and form an elegant border to each of the large painted subjects on the sides. The neck of the vase is in honeycomb open-work, with raised bees upon it; and the handles are of massive coral in white and gold. On each of the three sides of the vase is a large subject from Don Quixote, exquisitely painted in enamel colours. The cover has a blue ground, on which are flowers and trophies in tablets, surrounded by oak-leaves and acorns in gold. It is surmounted by a large and

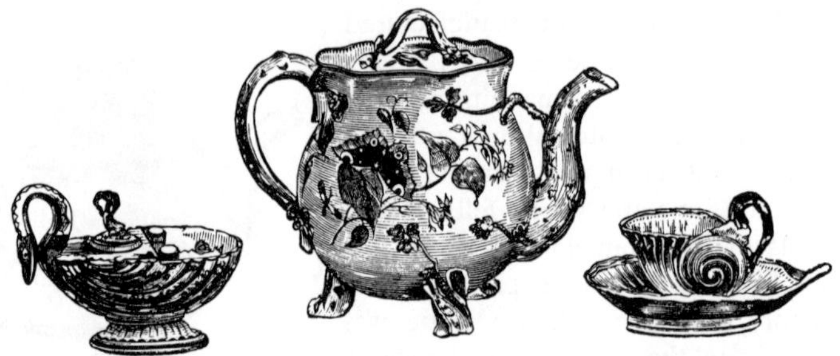

Figs. 874 to 876.

powerfully-modelled rhinoceros, gilt. The under side of the cover, quite out of sight except when lifted off the vase, is painted in a series of small landscapes, alternating with subjects taken from Bewick's celebrated tail-pieces. Inside the cover is the mark of the crest, and the words "Rockingham Works, Brameld," and the date 1826. This splendid vase was painted by John Wager Brameld. At Wentworth House, too, the Earl and Countess Fitzwilliam have, along with a large number of choice examples of Chelsea, Chelsea-Derby, and other rare makes of China (which I have examined), several other notable pieces of Rockingham china. Among these are a set of three "Canova-shape" vases, painted with groups of flowers; a dessert-service of white and gold "sea-weed" pattern, each piece bearing the crest and the date 1838; three of the pattern-plates submitted to William IV. in competition for the royal service; a number of example-plates of different designs; a breakfast service painted in flowers, each flower named; an elegant tray with raised flowers and a view of Arundel Castle; a pair of "monkey" beakers nineteen inches high; and a pair of fine biscuit scent bottles, sixteen inches high, decorated with exquisite raised flowers.

In the possession of the late Dr. Brameld, who had, among other things, a remarkably beautiful ice-pail and other pieces of note, was the fine vase engraved in Fig. 877, which is known as the "Dragon Vase," and occasionally by the not very euphonious name of the "Infernal Vase." It is 3 feet 4½ inches in height, and has dragons for handles, and also a dragon on the top of the cover. Another of these "Dragon" vases belonged to Mr. Henry Barker. In the late Mr. Bagshawe's collection were three landscape vases, green and gold, with swan handles; Mr. Reed had pieces bearing views of Newstead Abbey, &c.; and in Mr. Hobson's possession are vases with views of Chatsworth and other places.

The *chef-d'œuvre* of the Rockingham China Works was, however, the gorgeous dessert service made for William IV., which is now preserved with the most scrupulous care at Buckingham Palace, and is, we are credibly informed, justly prized by Her Majesty as among her more precious ceramic treasures. This service, which cost no less a sum than £5,000, consists of one hundred and forty-four plates and fifty-six large pieces, and is one of the finest produced in this or any other country. The plates have raised oak borders in dead and burnished gold running over a raised laced pattern, also in gold, and the centres are splendidly painted with the royal arms, &c. The comports, which were all designed by Mr. Thomas Brameld, are emblematical of the use to which each piece has to be put. For instance, the comports for biscuit are supported by ears of wheat; the fruit pieces have central open-work baskets of fruit; the ice pails are supported by holly berries and leaves; and in each case the landscapes are also in unison with the uses of the pieces, which are of exquisite design, and have also oak-leaf and lace decorations, so massively gilt in dead and burnished gold as to have the appearance of *ormolu* laid on the porcelain, and each piece is decorated with views of different seats, the sketches for which were taken expressly for the purpose, and by groups of figures, &c. In Dr. Brameld's possession were some portions of the comports, and the specimen plate which was submitted to, and approved by, the king, &c.; and in Mrs. Barker's hands was one of the comports (with views of "Langthwait Bridge," and "Kentmore Hall," and a group of bird-catchers), which for its extreme beauty and rarity is an almost priceless treasure. She also possessed a cup and saucer of the breakfast service prepared for Her Majesty. In Mrs. Reed's possession is an unique example, being one of the specimen plates submitted for royal approval in a competition with the principal china manufacturers of the kingdom for the royal order. In this competition, twelve plates of different patterns were specially prepared and submitted by the Rockingham Works. Of these plates, the examples in Mr. Reed's, Dr. Brameld's, the Earl Fitzwilliam's, Mr. Hobson's, and other hands, form a part. In the centre are the royal arms, and the rim is decorated with oak-leaves and acorns. Another unique pattern-plate belonged to Dr. Brameld, and is of the most delicate and exquisitely beautiful character. In the centre are the royal arms, and on the rim are three compartments, two of which contain groups of flowers, and the third a view, while between these the "garter" is repeated. The cost at which in the estimate it was calculated these plates could be produced was twelve guineas each.

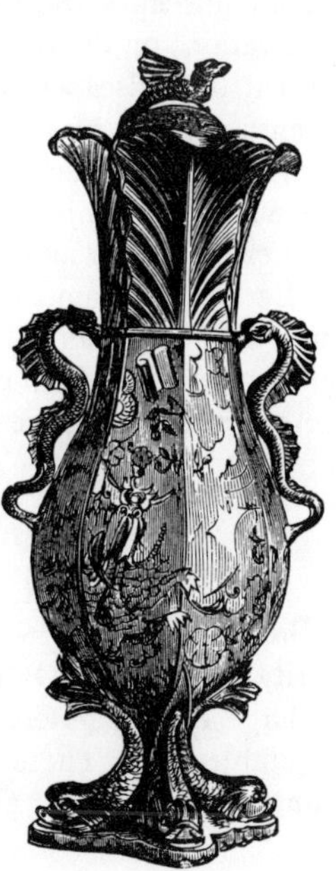

Fig. 877.

The dessert service made for William IV. was first used on the occasion of the coronation of our beloved Queen, and has only, I am informed, been used on very special state occasions from that time to the present. Although so large a sum of money was paid for it, the cost of its production was so great that the actual outlay was, I am told by those who are in the best position to know, considerably more than was charged. The royal service had some little to do with the embarassments that caused the final stoppage of the works.

In "biscuit," figures, busts, and groups, as well as vases, of which splendid examples belonged to Earl Fitzwilliam, were produced. Among other specimens that have come under my notice are a Swiss boy and girl, a fine bust of Earl Fitzwilliam, Chantrey's Sleeping Child, Chantrey's full-length statue of Lady Russell, &c.

Among the artists employed at the Rockingham works were Collinson, who painted flowers; Llandig, who was a charming fruit and flower painter; Bailey, who was the principal butterfly painter, and who also painted landscapes and crests; Speight (father and son), the latter of whom painted many of the finest subjects, both landscapes and figures, on the royal service, and who also painted the heraldic decorations on the same; Brentnall, who was a clever flower painter; Cordon, who executed landscapes and figures; Tilbury, who painted landscapes and figures; Mansfield, who was the principal embosser and chaser in gold; Aston, who was clever as a modeller of flowers; and Cowen, who was an artist of much repute, and for many years enjoyed the patronage of the Fitzwilliam family. William Eley, too, was employed as modeller, and executed some admirable works, including the bust of Earl Fitzwilliam. No marks were used on the early productions of these works, and they are, therefore, only to be ascertained by a knowledge of the body, the glaze, and the style of ornamentation used. The following are the marks which have come under my notice:—

Rockingham

Fig. 878.

This incised mark, the earliest used by these works, occurs on one of the famous "Brown China" high-shaped teapots of which I have spoken. It is a mark of great rarity.

ROCKINGHAM

ROCKINGHAM

in large capital letters, impressed into the body of the ware. The same in small capital letters. These occur on early examples of "Rockingham ware," &c. The name MORTLOCK also occurs on examples of this ware.

BRAMELD ✠ ✠

in capital letters, impressed. This occurs on green glazed ware, &c.

BRAMELD & CO' or BRAMELD * *

also in small capital letters, impressed.

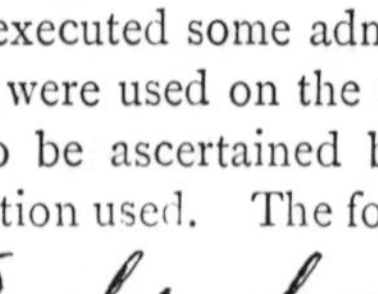

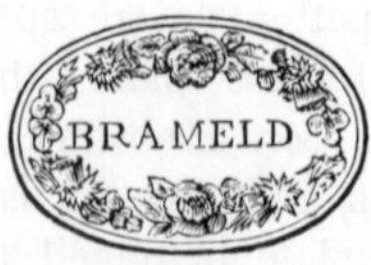

Fig. 879.

An embossed mark, in an oval, stuck on the ware, from which it generally differs in colour, being usually in blue.

ROYAL
ROCKINGHAM
WORKS
BRAMELD

in small capitals, in four lines, impressed. This mark occurs in biscuit figures, &c.

This mark (Fig. 880) is the crest of the Earl Fitzwilliam, and was adopted in

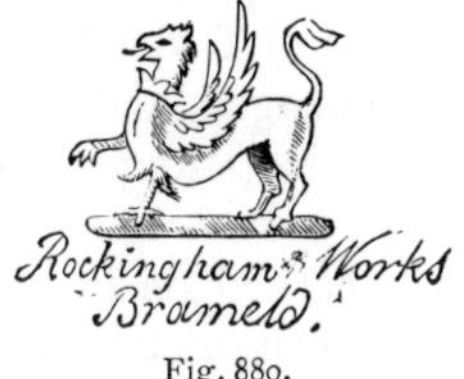

Fig. 880.

1825-6 on the commencement of the manufacture of china, under the assistance of that nobleman, who was owner of the works. It is usually printed in *red*.

Rockingham Works
(Same crest.)
Brameld

(Same crest.)
Rockingham Works
Brameld
Manufacturers to the King

(Same crest.)
Royal Rockingham Works
Brameld

in writing letters. The first of these marks occurs, with the date 1826, on the Rhinoceros Vase at Wentworth House. The others are also in writing letters in purple.

(Same crest.)
ROYAL ROCKINGHAM
BRAMELD

(Same crest.)
ROYAL ROCKINGHAM WORKS
BRAMELD

in capital letters. Sometimes in gold.

(Same crest.)
Rockingham Works.
Brameld
Manufacturer to the King
Queen and Royal Family.

surrounded by a wreath of roses, &c. Printed in purple. Good examples of Rockingham china are in the Jermyn Street Museum.

MEXBOROUGH.

The Rock Pottery or *Mexbro' Pottery* is situate at Mexborough, a rising town near Swinton, with stations on the South Yorkshire and Midland lines of railway. The works, at first very small, were, I believe, established for the manufacture of brown and yellow wares, and for common red garden-pots, by a person named Beevers, who, with a partner named Ford—trading as Beevers and Ford—carried on the business for some years. The workrooms at this time were built close up to the rock, which, indeed, formed the back wall of the manufactory; and from this circumstance the place was called the "Rock Pottery," a name by which it is still occasionally known. The goods at this time, and subsequently, during the proprietorship of Ford, Simpson, and Beevers, were made entirely from native clays, and were confined to "cane" or "yellow ware" dishes, jugs, &c., for household use, garden and root pots of red ware, and pitchers, &c., of a brown ware. The works next passed into the hands of Reed and Taylor, who also owned the works at Ferrybridge, and by whom they were enlarged, and the manufacture of finer kinds of earthenware introduced. In 1839 the pottery passed into the hands of Mr. James Reed, who, in 1849, was succeeded by his son, Mr. John Reed, who continued it until his decease. It was then carried on by his executors under the management of the late Mr. C. Bullock. During the time of Mr. Reed's proprietorship and that of his father considerable alterations and additions were made to the works, and new kilns erected; the character of the productions was also much improved, and several new varieties of wares were introduced. In 1873 Messrs. Sydney Woolf & Co., the owners of the "Australian Pottery," at Ferrybridge, became the purchasers of this manufactory, and carried it on conjointly with their other works at Ferrybridge, under the management of Mr. Bowman Heald. By Messrs. Woolf & Co. the works have been considerably extended, and several new varieties of shapes and patterns introduced. The goods are—in ordinary white earthenware—all the most marketable varieties of painted, printed, enamelled, and gilt dinner, toilet and other services; in Rockingham ware all the usual kinds of vessels; in "terra-cotta" Mr. Reed manufactured large-sized flower-vases for gardens and other decorative purposes; pendant flower-vases for conservatories, entrance-halls, &c.; root-pots of tasteful design, butter-coolers, &c., &c. In green glazed earthenware, dessert services, in which the plates, centres, comports, &c., are embossed with leaves, flowers, and other patterns, are made, many of them from the original moulds of the Swinton Works, which passed by purchase to the Mexborough pottery; and others of equally elegant design from moulds expressly belonging to Mexborough. In this ware garden seats, both plain and foliated, of the same designs as those produced in the old days of the Rockingham Works, and also root-pots and flower-vases, are made. Of these the "lotus vase" (Fig. 872) is, I believe, made only at the Mexborough Pottery, as is also the model of the keep of Conisborough Castle already alluded to. The mark used by Mr. Reed was simply * REED * in large capitals, impressed in the ware.

Mexborough Old Pottery.—At Mexborough was formerly another pot-work, known as the "Mexborough Old Pottery." This was established at the end of the last century by Messrs. Sowter and Bromley, who held the works until 1804, when they came into the possession of Mr. Peter Barker. Peter Barker was the son of Joseph Barker, who came out of Staffordshire as manager of the Swinton Pottery. He became partner with Mr. Wainwright at the pot-works at Rawmarsh (afterwards Hawley's), and ultimately took to the works at Mexborough. These were continued by the brothers Peter and Jesse Barker, who were succeeded by Mr. Samuel Barker, the son of the latter, until 1834, when they acquired the Don Pottery. By Mr. Samuel Barker they were continued until 1844. The Mexborough Old Pottery was then discontinued, and is now converted into ironworks for the manufacture of wheels for locomotives. At these works the commoner descriptions of earthenware, including blue printing, were produced.

Rawmarsh.

In the latter part of last century a pottery was carried on here by Mr. Peter Barker and his partner, under the style of "Barker and Wainwright." He afterwards joined his brother Jesse at the Mexborough Old Pottery.

Rotherham.

North Field Pottery.—This pottery was established in 1851 by Joseph Lee, a working potter, who had previously carried on a small manufactory (now disused) in the town of Rotherham. In 1855 it was purchased by Mr. George Hawley, of Rawmarsh, who on his death was succeeded by his sons, the late Mr. William Hawley, father of the present proprietors, Mr. Matthew Hawley and his two brothers. The firm was for a time carried on as "W. and G. Hawley," and then "Hawley Brothers." The goods manufactured are the commoner descriptions of earthenware; and a large trade is carried on in furniture-polish bottles and articles of a similar class.

Holmes Pottery.—These works were built on part of the Holmes Hall Estate—the kitchen-garden, in fact—formerly belonging to the Walker family, who owned the large ironworks there, where at one time the notorious Tom Payne worked, The pottery was at first extremely small, but has gradually extended itself until it is now of considerable extent. It was first worked by Earnshaw and Greaves, who were succeeded by Dickinson and Jackson, next by Thomas Jarvis. and later still by John Jackson & Co., the present owners. The goods produced are the commoner class of white and blue printed earthenware. Some years ago an attempt at china manufacture was made here, but was abandoned.

The Don Pottery.

The Don Pottery, closely adjoining the canal at Swinton, on which it has a wharf, was established in a very small way about 1790, and considerably increased in 1800 by John Green, of Newhill. He was one of the Greens of Leeds, of the same family as the proprietors of the Leeds Pottery, and a proprietor in the Swinton Pottery, who, about 1800, purchased a plot of land at Swinton, and, with the aid of partners, set about the erection of the present works. At this time a person named Newton, father to the more than octogenarian from whom, some years ago, I picked up many scraps of the information I record, had an enamel kiln at the back of his house at Swinton, where he used to burn such wares as he decorated. To this man for the first twelve months Green, of the Don Pottery, brought his pattern pieces to be fired, as he prepared them. In 1807 other members of the family united with John Green, who also had partners named Clarke, the firm trading as "Greens, Clarke, & Co." In 1831 Mr. Green was proprietor of the Don Pottery. In 1834 the Don Pottery passed by purchase to Mr. Samuel Barker, of the Mexborough Old Pottery, which latter works he closed in 1844, and confined his operations entirely to the Don manufactory. In 1851 the firm became "Samuel Barker and Son," under which style it continued until 1882, when the surviving proprietor, Mr. Edward Barker, retired from the business, which he transferred in November of that year to his successors, Messrs. E. T. Smith, J. Adamson, J. Wilkinson, and C. Scorah, who continue it under the old style of "Samuel Barker and Son."

Of the ordinary fine earthenware made soon after the opening of the works, some specimens, whose actual date can be satisfactorily ascertained, have come under my notice, and show to what perfection in body and glaze, in manipulation, and in decoration, the manufacture had already arrived. The most remarkable of these early specimens is a jug, commonly called the "Jumper Jug," which is of great rarity. On either side is the figure of a very uncouth, coarse, and slovenly-looking man, in red coat, pink waistcoat, striped green and white under waistcoat, orange neckerchief, orange breeches above which his shirt is seen, top-boots, and spurs. In his hand he holds his hat, orange, with red ribands, on which is a card bearing the words "Milton for ever." Beneath the spout, on a scroll, is the following curious verse:—

> "The Figure there is no mistaking,
> It is the famous Man for—*breaking*.
> Oh, that instead of Horse and Mare,
> He had but broken Crockery-ware,
> Each grateful Potter in a bumper
> Might drink the health of
> Orange Jumper."

This man, who was known all the country round as "Orange Jumper," was a very eccentric character, and a great mover in the political "stirs" of his county. He was a horsebreaker at Wentworth, and many extraordinary stories are remembered in connection with him. One of these, as connected with the story of this jug, is worth repeating. In the great Yorkshire election of 1807—the most costly and the most strongly contested election on record—when the candidates who were so mercilessly pitted against each other were Lord Milton, Wilberforce, and Lascelles, "Orange Jumper" was employed to carry dispatches regularly backwards and forwards from York to Wentworth House, the seat of Earl Fitzwilliam, the father of Lord Milton, who eventually won the election, and was returned as the colleague of Wilberforce. Orange was the Fitzwilliam colour, and blue that of Lascelles (son of the Earl of Harewood), his opponent; and on one occasion "Jumper" was seen entering York decked out as usual in orange, but riding on an ass gaily decorated with bright blue ribands. On being jeered at for this apparent inconsistency in wearing both colours, he replied that *he* wore the right colour, orange, and that his ass was only like other asses, for they were all donkeys that wore blue! The election was gained by the party he espoused, and in commemoration these jugs, with his portrait and verse, were made. They are marked "Don Pottery," pencilled in red on the bottom.

An engraved pattern-book was issued by the firm, in the same style and of the same size as that of Hartley, Greens, & Co., of the Leeds Pottery. A careful comparison of the two books reveals the fact that whereas in the latest edition of that of Leeds 269 patterns are engraved, in that of the Don Pottery 292 are given. It also reveals the important fact that many of the Don patterns are identical with those of Leeds, the engraver of the former having evidently traced from those of the latter (Leeds) in preparing his plates. Many of the remaining patterns are slightly altered from Leeds, while others do not appear in the book of those works at all. In this pattern-book Figs. 1 to 8 are covered tureens; 10 to 12 are leaves; 13 to 18, covered vegetable dishes; 19 to 23, sauce-tureens with covers, stands, and ladles; 24, a two-handled drinking-cup; 26 to 30, butter-boats; 31 to 49, dishes and plates, &c.; 50 to 69, fruit-bowls, side dishes, &c.; 70 to 76, perforated, open-work, and embossed baskets and stands, some of which have covers, and are precisely of the same kind as those of the Leeds works; 77, a perforated chestnut tureen, like that of the Leeds works; 78, also perforated and embossed; 79 to 83, perforated dishes and plates; 84 to 91, covered sugar-bowls, &c.; 111 is a melon bowl of the same kind as those made at Leeds; 113 to 116 are egg-cups and stands; 118 to 130, cruets, &c.; 131, an asparagus-holder, like the Leeds; 139 to 145, mugs and jugs;

146, a toast-rack; 147, an invalid's feeding-cup; 148 to 159, dishes, tureens, &c.; 160 and 161, vegetable trays in compartments; 163 to 176, ice pails and domestic vessels; 177 to 183, inkstands; 184, 185, flower-pots; 186 to 202, toilet services and shaving-basins; 201 is a *scaphium;* 206 is a quintal flower-horn; 207, a pastile-burner; and then come candlesticks, egg-cups, flower-vases, flower-stands, vases, crosses with cup for holy water, &c. Another series of plates, the figures numbered from 1 to 54 and from A to K, are devoted to tea equipages, consisting of a remarkable and very striking variety of tea-pots, coffee-pots, milk-jugs, sugar-bowls, cake-trays, tea-canisters, basins or bowls, tea, coffee, and chocolate cups and saucers, &c., &c. On each plate throughout the series the name "*Don Pottery*" is engraved in a scroll.

Open-work baskets, tureens, &c., twig baskets, in which the "withies" were of precisely the same form as those of Leeds and Wedgwood, &c., perforated plates, dishes, tureens, spoons, ladles, and other articles, ice-pails, salt-cellars, flower-vases, cruets and stands, inkstands, seals, bird-fountains, smelling-bottles, and, indeed, every variety of articles, as well as services of all descriptions, and ornamental vases of several designs, were made in these wares, and such as were adapted for the

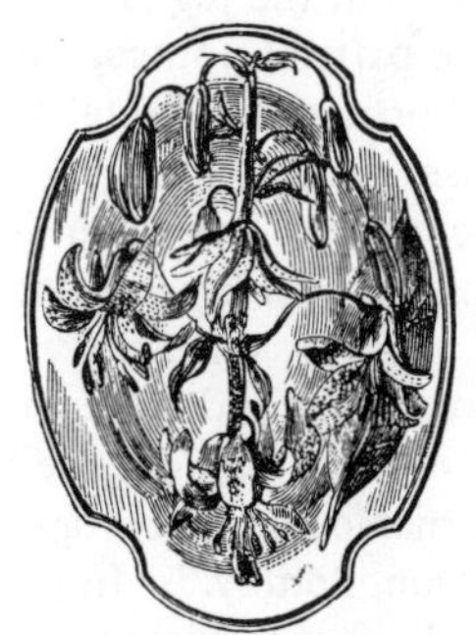

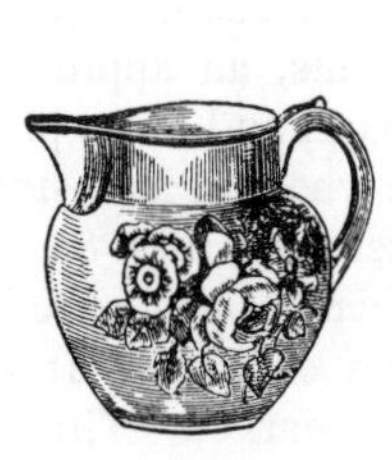

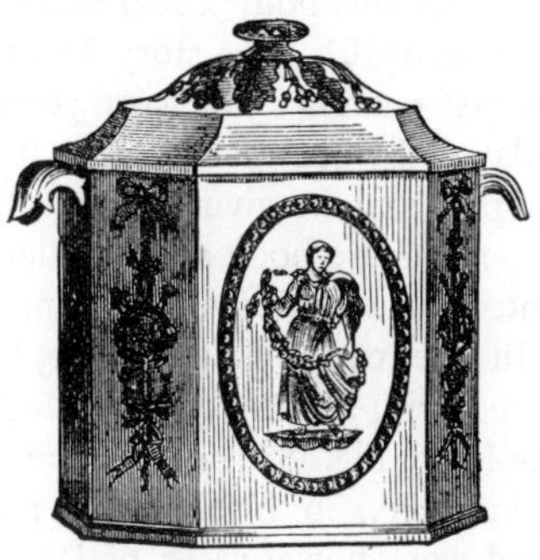

Figs. 881 to 883.

colour were made in green glazed ware. Of tea-pots, many patterns, with raised groups, trophies, &c., and others for loose metal "kettle-handles," are also engraved.

In the cream-coloured ware, and also in the fine white earthenware, excellent dessert and other services were made, and were painted with flowers, &c., with a truth to nature which has seldom been equalled. In my own collection were also some remarkable plates of small size of fine earthenware. In these the underside of the plate is left white, while the whole of the rest is tinted of a deep buff. The edge, and a line on the inner side of the rim, is black, and in the centre of each plate is a landscape, which has all the beauty and effect of a well-executed Indian ink drawing.

About 1810-12, *china* of an excellent quality was, to a very small extent indeed, made at the Don Pottery, and examples of this are of extreme rarity. In Mr. Manning's possession was a coffee-mug marked "Don Pottery" in red. This interesting specimen is the only marked one which has come under my notice. Two other specimens of this very rare china ware are Figs. 881 and 882. The first is a jug to which a curious story is attached. The china body of which it was made was mixed by Godfrey Speight and Ward Booth, both of whom were originally from Staffordshire; the latter, it is said, was brought from that county "with a whole regiment of hands" to work at the new Don Pottery, of which he became the manager. The jug was painted by his son, Taylor Booth, who was brought up with Enoch Wood, of Burslem, and afterwards was at the old Derby China Works, and given to Speight, from whose aged son's hands it passed into my own. It is beautifully painted with groups of flowers on either side, and a sprig of jasmine beneath the spout, and has a broad gold line round the top. The curious part of the story connected with this jug is that in the body of which it is composed, by one of those strange and unaccountable freaks to which potters as well as other people are liable, are two of the fingers of a noted malefactor, Spencer Broughton, who was gibbeted on Attercliffe Common at the close of the last century. It appears that a party of the Don and Swinton potters, who had been to Sheffield for a carousal, and had stayed there till the small hours of the morning, were, when sober, returning over the moor, when, on passing the gibbet on which the gaunt skeleton of the malefactor still hung, as it had for years, in chains, one of them, saying, "Let's ha' a rap at him," picked up a stone and threw it, knocking off the bones of two of the fingers. These were picked up and carefully carried home as trophies of the exploit; and some time afterwards, when trials in the manufacture of china were being made, they were brought out, calcined, and mixed with some of the body. Of this body a seal was made, "with a gibbet on it," and the jug (Fig. 882) just described. This story I had from the lips of one of the party of potters, a man then fast nearing "fourscore years and ten" in age. The horrible and brutal taste displayed by the potters has, it must be admitted, its use in authenticating the example, and in giving it, at all events, an approximate date. The other is a comport of fine body and excellent glaze, and has a plant of the tiger-lily exquisitely painted of natural size occupying the whole of its inside.

In fine, cane-coloured ware, tea-services, jugs, &c., were made, and were ornamented with figures, borders, and other designs in relief. Of this kind of ware the sugar-box (Fig. 883) will serve as an example. It is ornamented with figures, trophies, &c., in black relief, and is marked "Green's Don Pottery." In green glazed ware flower-vases of large size, root-pots, dessert and other services; in red ware, scent jars of bold and good design, large-sized mignonette vases, and many other articles; and in "Egyptian black," teapots, cream-ewers, jugs. &c., were made. The "brown china" spoken of in the list of goods was the "Rockingham Ware," which was attempted to be made at the Don Pottery, and is still made of the common marketable quality. A considerable trade was and is carried on with Russia, France, and Belgium, and South America, as well as to South Africa, East Indies, Ceylon, &c., to which markets the greater part of the goods produced were consigned.

At the "Don Pottery" at the present day are produced all the usual varieties of ordinary earthenware to a large extent, the works giving employment to between two and three hundred hands. In toilet services many excellent patterns are produced, both enamelled, gilt, and lustred, as the dinner, tea, dessert, and other services, and all the usual varieties of goods for home and foreign consumption.

The marks adopted by these works have been but few, and these only very occasionally used. They are, so far as I have been able to ascertain, as follows:— "Don Pottery" pencilled in red on the bottom of the vessel, or "DON POTTERY" impressed on the bottom of the pieces.

GREEN
DON POTTERY.

also impressed.

The first of these (Fig. 884) was impressed, the second (Fig. 885) was printed and transferred on the ware. It was the first mark used by Samuel Barker, and was adopted by him on purchasing the Don Pottery on its discontinuance by the Greens.

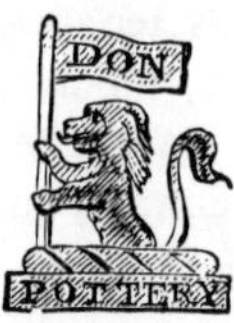

Fig. 884.

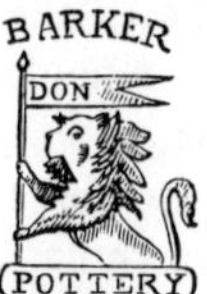

Fig. 885.

The first of these marks (Fig. 886), also in transfer printing, an eagle displayed rising from out a ducal coronet, was adopted by the firm when it became Samuel Barker & Son, at which time the old mark was discontinued. The eagle displayed

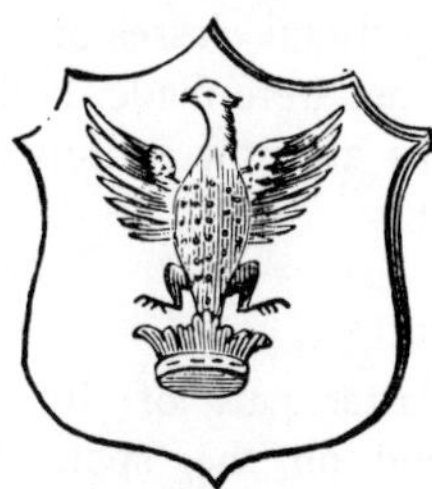
Fig. 886.

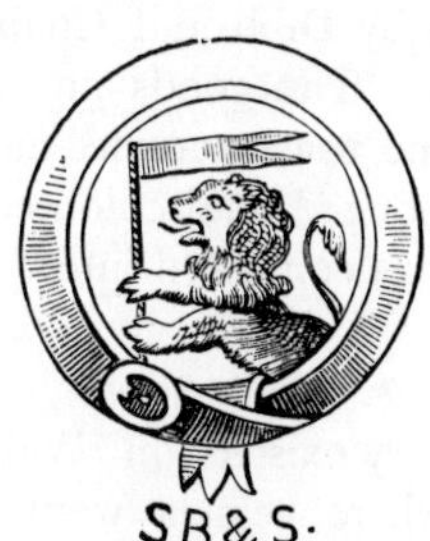

Fig. 887.

is not now used, the firm having adopted the old mark of the demi-lion rampant holding in his paws the pennon, and enclosed within a garter, beneath which are the initials of the firm, "S. B. & S." (Fig. 887). On the ribbon of the garter is usually given the name of the pottery, as, for instance, YORK.

DENABY.

The Denaby Pottery, established for the manufacture of fire-bricks, &c., was, about 1864, taken by Mr. John Wardle (from Messrs. Alcocks, of Burslem), who was joined in partnership by Mr. W. Wilkinson, under the style of "Wilkinson and Wardle," for the production of all the ordinary classes of printed earthenware, pearl body, and cream ware, &c. In these all the more popular and favourite patterns were produced from entirely new copper plates, and dinner, tea, coffee, toilet, and other services, and other articles of really good and effective design, were produced. Yellow or cane-coloured ware was also made, as well as tiles for external decorative purposes, from clay found at Conisborough, where branch works were established. The mark adopted by the firm was the Staffordshire knot, with the words "Wilkinson and Wardle, Denaby Potteries." These works, after an existence of a few years only, were closed in 1869 or 1870, and the buildings converted into bone and glue works.

KILNHURST.

At Kilnhurst, a place which one would naturally say took its name from potworks, is a manufactory of earthenware, known as the "Kilnhurst Old Pottery."

Established about the middle of last century, on the estate of the Shore family, it was held at the beginning of this century by a potter named Hawley, who had also a pottery at Rawmarsh, and who was suceeeded by George Green (one of the family of the Greens at Leeds), from whom, in 1832, it was purchased by Brameld & Co. (subject to Mr. Shore, the owner, accepting them as tenants), at a valuation, Green retaining the manufactured goods, copper-plates, moulds, &c. In 1839 it came into the hands of Twigg Brothers, and is carried on by the surviving partner, John Twigg, who produces the usual varieties of earthenware, and has made some unsuccessful trials in china.

Wath-upon-Dearne.

The "Newhill Pottery" was established about 1822 by Joseph Twigg (who up to that time had the management of the Swinton Old Pottery), by whom, in partnership with his sons John, Benjamin, and Joseph Twigg, it was carried on until about 1866, when it passed into the hands of Binney and Matthews, who were succeeded by Dibb and Coulter. In 1872 the works were sold to Bedford and Richmond. The goods produced were the ordinary useful classes of earthenware, in which the usual services and articles of everyday use were made, both in white, printed, sponged, and coloured varieties. The works are now entirely closed, and the buildings converted into cottages.

Wakefield.

A pottery existed on Wakefield Moor in the latter part of the seventeenth century, where vessels were made from clay found on the spot. This clay Houghton, in 1693, calls "The potters' pale yellow clay of Wakefield Moor."

Potovens.

The village of Potovens lies about two miles from Wakefield, and, as its name implies, takes its origin from some old potteries established at this place, Ralph Thoresby in his Diary (1702) says, under date of March 16th: "From Wakefield then by Allerthorpe (Alverthorpe) and Silkhouse to the Pott-Ovens (Little London, in the dialect of the poor people), where I stayed a little to observe not only the manner of their forming their earthenware—which brought to mind the words of the prophet, 'As clay in the hands of the potter, so are we in the Lord's'—but to observe the manner of building the furnaces, their size and materials, which are small, and upon the surface of the ground, confirming me in my former apprehensions that those remains at Hawcaster-rigg (Philosoph. Trans. No. 222) are really the ruins of a Roman pottery." These works were carried on about the time, or in the time, when Thoresby wrote, by one Caleb Glover. In his will, dated 29th of January, 1728, recorded in the Rolls Office, February 6th, 1729, this Caleb Glover "of Pott-Ovens, pott-maker," bequeaths to his wife all his chattels excepting his "working tools and oven house," and to his son Daniel Glover he leaves all his "working tools belonging to the trade of a potmaker, and the pot oven." He was succeeded at his death, in 1728-9, by this son Daniel Glover, who continued the works. No manufactory of the kind now exists at this place, and the name of the village itself is somewhat ambiguous, far it is occasionally known as Wrenthorp.

Yearsley.

The earliest, and, indeed, only potters of whom anything is known at this place, are members of the Wedgwood family, as recounted in my "Life of Josiah Wedgwood" (p. 583), where these works were first brought into notice. One branch of the Wedgwoods of Staffordshire settled at Yearsley, in the Yorkshire Wolds at an early date, and commenced pot-making, which was carried on successfully for some generations. In 1682 John Wedgwood, of Yearsley, was "buried in woollen," as were also in 1692 William Wedgwood, and in 1690 Isabell, who was wife of one of these. John, the son of this John Wedgwood, who died in 1737, was, I believe, the John Wedgwood whose name, with the date 1691, appears on the puzzle jug, Fig. 888, in the Museum of Practical Geology. It is of brown ware body, coated with green lead glaze, and has round the body the name "John Wedg Wood 1691," incised in writing letters.

The ware made by the Yorkshire Wedgwoods was the common hard brown ware made from the clays of the district, and consisted mainly of pitchers, pancheons, porringers, and other vessels of homely kind. So well known were the Wedgwoods of this district, that one member of the family was immortalised in an old Yorkshire ballad thus :—

"At Yearsley there are pancheons made
By Willie Wedgwood, that young blade."

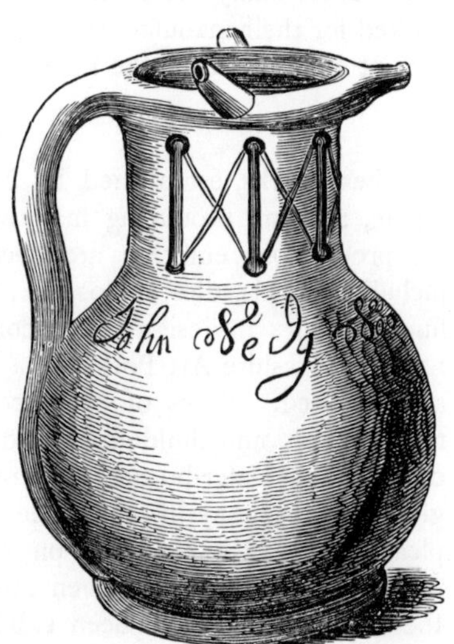
Fig. 888.

"Pancheons" are thick coarse earthenware pans, made of various sizes, and used for setting away milk in, and for washing purposes. They are made in several localities, and, besides being sold by earthenware dealers, are hawked about the country by men who make their living in no other way. Several fragments of brown pottery have at one time or other been dug up at Yearsley, and, among the rest, a brown earthenware oven, green glaze, semicircular, open at top, with a hollowed ledge round the inner side about half way, and a flat bottom, having two handles at the sides, and between them a crinkled ornament, bearing some letters and the date 1712.

WORTLEY.

These works were established in 1795 by Mr. John Cliff, father of the head of the firm of "Joseph Cliff and Son," for the manufacture of fire-bricks, for which the clay of the locality was considered highly valuable. In 1820 the manufacture of clay retorts was commenced and continued until 1830, when it died out, but was revived about 1850, the retorts being considered to be both better and cheaper than those in iron. About 1847 the manufacture of drain-pipes was added, and these were, and are, made at the rate of several miles per week ; blast-furnace lumps being also largely made. In 1866 terra-cotta was added to the other productions, and about the same time white and coloured glazed bricks were made, and form one of the staple trades of the works, as do plumbago crucibles, the manufacture of which was introduced in 1869. In terra-cotta, vases, tazzas, and pedestals ; figures and brackets ; capitals, trusses, keystones, terminals, and other architectural ornaments ; flower-boxes, baskets, and suspenders ; chimney-shafts, and many other articles, are made and are of artistic character. In stoneware, sanitary goods of every description; troughs, mangers, and sinks; enamelled retorts for gas, and chemical goods, &c., are made. Fire and other bricks and tiles are also made, as are garden edgings, and fire-backs, for which a patent was obtained by the firm, who were awarded a medal in 1862 and at the Paris Exhibition of 1867.

HEALEY.

A mediæval pottery existed here, in the parish of Masham, in the North Riding of Yorkshire. Its site was on the spot where Healey church now stands, the ground bearing the name of "Potters Field. When the church was erected in 1848 considerable quantities of "wasters" and fragments of pottery were dug up by the workmen.

COLSTERDALE.

A pottery of similar character existed at this place on a spot called "Potter's-Pit." Here many vessels have been found, as well as the clay pits which had been worked for their manufacture. The place was, according to some old maps, a very ancient enclosure from the moor.

BURMANTOFTS.

These works, established by Messrs. Wilcock & Co., have sprung rapidly into repute, and are producing many works of a high order of merit. In terra-cotta the productions embrace architectural details and enrichments of every kind, including panels, tiles, dados, etc., in immense variety and of the most masterly and finished styles in design and decoration. In pottery, which Messrs. Wilcock & Co. name "Yorkshire Art-Pottery," a large number of articles more or less decorative are produced. Vases of every conceivable variety and of a large range of sizes, flower-stands and holders, pot-pourris, rose-leaf bowls, dessert services, comports, cake-stands, water-bottles, and other articles, are produced, and the coloured glazes are, in many instances, clear and effective, and the flown varieties extremely pleasing. The introduction on some pieces of sgraffito and of stipple decoration under the rich glaze has been attended with satisfactory results, as—judging from the drawings that have been submitted—also has the adoption of hand-modelled flowers, foliage, and examples of animal life. The faience tiles, panels, and other productions of the firm are of a high standard of excellence.

CHAPTER XIV.

THE following brief account of the earthenware works of Newcastle-upon-Tyne and its district, drawn up by Mr. C. T. Maling, one of the manufacturers, may serve as an introduction to this chapter. "The manufacture of white earthenware was introduced into this district by Mr. Warburton, at Carr's Hill Pottery, near Gateshead, about 1730 or 1740. Those works were very successfully carried on for seventy years, when they gradually declined, and in 1817 were closed. A small portion of the building is still used as a brown ware pottery. The next manufactory was built by Mr. Byers, at Newbottle, in the county of Durham, about 1755, where brown and white earthenware still continue to be made. In 1762, Messrs. Christopher Thompson and John Maling erected works at North Hilton, in the county of Durham; their successor, Mr. Robert Maling, in 1817 transferred his operations to the Tyne, where his descendants still continue the manufacture. St. Anthony's, Stepney Bank, and Ouseburn Old Potteries were commenced about the year 1780 or 1790. Messrs. A. Scott & Co. and Messrs. Samuel Moor & Co. erected potteries at Southwick, near Sunderland, the former in the year 1789, the latter in 1803. The pottery carried on by Messrs. John Dawson & Co., at South Hylton, was built by them in 1800. The works of Messrs. John Carr & Sons, at North Shields, were erected in 1814. Messrs. Thomas Fell & Co. built St. Peter's Pottery in 1817. The establishment of Messrs. Skinner & Co., Stockton-on-Tees, dates from 1824. There are now (1863) about twenty-five potteries in this district, of which, on the Tyne, six manufacture white and printed wares; four white, printed, and brown wares; and three brown ware only. . . . . . On the Wear there are two potteries manufacturing white and printed wares; two white, printed, and brown wares; and two brown ware only. . . . . . On the Tees there are four potteries manufacturing white and printed wares. . . . . . Two at Norton manufacture brown wares. . . . . The potteries in this district, being situated upon navigable rivers, have great advantages over their inland competitors, Staffordshire and Yorkshire." The description of goods manufactured is that used by the middle and working classes, no first-class goods being made. The principal markets, in addition to the local trade, are the Danish, Norwegian, German, Mediterranean, and London, for exportation to the colonies.

The potteries of the Tyne are:—

NEWCASTLE-UPON-TYNE.

Warburton Pottery was established about 1730, on Pandon Dean, Newcastle-on-Tyne. Coarse ware was, I believe, its only product. It was removed between 1740 and 1750 to Carr's Hill, Gateshead (which see).

Newcastle Pottery, or *Forth Banks Pottery*, commenced about 1800, by Addison and Falconer, from whom it passed into the occupation of Redhead, Wilson, and Co., and afterwards Wallace and Co.

STEPNEY BANK.

The *Stepney Bank Pottery*, established about 1780 or 1790, was in 1801 occupied by Messrs. Head and Dalton; in 1816 by Messrs. Dryden, Coxon, and Basket; in 1822 by Messrs. Davies, Coxon, and Wilson; in 1833 by Messrs. Dalton and Burn, who were succeeded by Mr. G. R. Turnbull, by whom the character of the ware was considerably improved. About 1872 the works passed into the hands of Mr. John Wood.

OUSEBURN.

Ouseburn Bridge Pottery was commenced in 1817 by Mr. Robert Maling (see North Hylton Pottery), who manufactured white and printed ware chiefly for the Dutch market. He was succeeded, in 1853, by his son, C. T. Maling, who in 1859 built Ford Pottery, and discontinued his old works. They were reopened under the name of the Albion Pottery by Bell Brothers about 1863, next by Atkinson and Galloway, and lastly by Mr. W. Morris, and were finally closed in 1872.

Ford Pottery, built in 1859 by Mr. Christopher T. Maling (son of Mr. Robert Maling, who in 1817 had removed the Hylton pottery to Newcastle) for manufacturing by machinery marmalade, jam, and extract-of-beef pots. These are of a very fine and compact white body, with an excellent glaze made from borax without any lead; and it is said that at least 95 per cent. of these pots used by wholesale manufacturers in Great Britain are made at this establishment. The pots being entirely made by machinery are necessarily much more uniform in size and weight and thickness than those made by any other process. The mark is simply the name MALING or MALING impressed in the clay, with, sometimes, the initial of the house for whom they are made, as MALING K for "Keiller," and so on.

Ouseburn Pottery was built about the same date as Stepney Bank Pottery, by Mr. Yellowley, who was succeeded by T. and J. Thompson, then by Mr. I. Maling; it was finally closed about 1864. White, printed, and brown ware were its productions.

Another "Ouseburn Pottery" was established at the latter end of last or the early part of the present century by Mr. Ralph Charlton, who carried on the business on a small scale for the manufacture of brown ware. On his death he was succeeded by his son, John Charlton, who after a few years was succeeded by Mr. George Gray, who was followed by Morrow and Parke, and Mr. Rogers, who extended the buildings. It was next worked, until 1860, by Mr. William Blakey, when it passed into the hands of Robert Martin and Co.

Another "Ouseburn Pottery," established some years ago, passed in 1860 into the hands of Mr. John Hedley Walker, its productions being flower-pots, chimney-pots, and horticultural vessels of various kinds, as well as the lead-pots and lead-dishes which are so extensively used in the lead-works of the district.

The *Low Pottery*, identical with the Ouseburn Pottery, now discontinued, was carried on by Thompson Brothers, for the manufacture of white and Sunderland wares.

South Shore Pottery.—Now discontinued.

The Phœnix Pottery, built by John Dryden & Co. about 1821, at first produced brown ware, and afterwards white and printed ware. About 1844 it passed into the hands of Isaac Bell & Co., and was afterwards carried on successively by Carr

& Patton (who at same time had North Shields Pottery); Mr. John Patton; and Cook Brothers, who discontinued manufacturing earthenware in 1860, and converted the premises into a chemical factory.

Mr. John Charlton had also a small manufactory in the Ouseburn.

St. Peter's Pottery, established in 1817 by Thomas Fell and Thomas Bell, was carried on, under the style of "Thomas Fell & Co.," until 1869, when it became a limited liability company. The productions are the ordinary classes of common earthenware, in white, printed, and sponged varieties. The mark was formerly an anchor with the letter *F* ⚓ (for "Fell") on one side, and the workman's mark or number on the other, impressed in the body of the ware. Later on this mark was discontinued, and the name FELL substituted, and later FELL & Co.

St. Anthony's Pottery.—This is one of the oldest potteries for fine ware on the Tyne, being established about 1780, but nothing is known as to its earlier history. In 1803 or 1804 it passed into the hands of a Mr. Sewell, in whose family it was continued under the styles of "Sewell & Donkin," and "Sewell & Co.," the principal productions being cream-coloured, painted, and blue-printed goods (the cream-coloured ware, to *imitate Wedgwood's* table ware, being made in considerable quantities for Holland and other Continental markets); "biscuit painted, printed very dark engraved patterns, also stamping with *glue*, and printing on the glaze from wood engravings, also with *glue*, the first that was done in this way; gold and silver lustre, &c." In 1882 the works were reopened by Mr. Lloyd. The fact of printing on pottery from *wood* engravings, being practised at these works is highly interesting, as I have been enabled to ascertain that engravings by Bewick were thus brought into use; specimens are, however, very rare. In the Museum of Practical Geology are examples of St. Anthony's ware; they bear the mark SEWELL. SEWELL & DONKIN. SEWELLS & DONKIN. or SEWELLS & CO.

GATESHEAD.

The *Carr's Hill Pottery* was the first manufactory for white ware in the north of England. Painted, enamelled, and brown ware was also made. It was established about 1750 by a Mr. Warburton, who removed to this place from Newcastle (see Warburton Pottery), and was successfully carried on by him and his successors until 1817, when it was closed. A part of the premises was afterwards carried on by Messrs. Kendall and Walker, and later still by Messrs. Isaac Fell & Co.

SHERIFF HILL.

Sheriff Hill Pottery.—These works are carried on by Mr. George Patterson, as the successor of the firm of Jackson and Patterson. His chief productions are white ware, which he supplies largely to the Norwegian markets.

Messrs. Lewins and Parsons are also stated to have had a pottery here for the manufacture of the commoner kinds of earthenware.

Tyne Main Pottery, on the opposite side of the river to St. Peter's, was built by Messrs. R. Davies & Co. in the year 1833, and carried on by them, manufacturing white, printed, and lustre ware, chiefly for the Norwegian market. It was closed in 1851. Mr. R. C. Wilson, the managing partner, then commenced manufacturing at Seaham Harbour.

There was also a pottery at Heworth Shore, carried on by Patterson, Fordy, & Co. It was closed about 1835.

There was also a pottery at Jarrow for a few years, which manufactured brown ware only.

North Shields.

The *Low Light Pottery* was established in 1814 by Mr. Nicholas Bird, and afterwards passed from him, in or about 1829, to Messrs. Cornfoot, Colville, & Co. The firm was afterwards changed to Cornfoot, Patton, & Co., and on the withdrawal of Mr. Cornfoot and the addition of Mr. John Carr the style was changed to that of "Carr and Patton." Next the firm was "John Carr & Co.," and when the concern became the property of the first of these partners, the late Mr. John Carr, he and his sons carried it on under the style of "John Carr and Sons." Originally brown and black wares of the usual common kinds were made, in addition to the ordinary earthenware, but in 1856 these were discontinued, and the ordinary white earthenware in cream-coloured, printed, painted, and lustred varieties substituted. These goods are exported principally to the Mediterranean ports, and to Alexandria for transport to Cairo, and by the Red Sea to Bombay, &c. The mark—which, however, has been but seldom used—is a stag's head.

South Shields.

The *Tyne* or *Shields Pottery* was established about 1830 by a Mr. Robertson, from whom, about 1845, it passed into the hands of Mr. John Armstrong, by whom the works were considerably enlarged. In 1871 the concern was purchased by Messrs. Isaac Fell and George Shields Young, by whom it was carried on under the style of "Isaac Fell & Co." The goods manufactured are "Sunderland" and "brown" wares, of which large quantities are shipped for the Continent, as well as supplied to the London, Scottish, and other home markets.

The potteries of the Wear are:—

North Hylton.

A pottery was established here in 1762 by Christopher Thompson and John Maling, for the manufacture of the ordinary brown and white earthenware for the home trade and for France. The first printed ware made in the north of England was manufactured at these works, which were also celebrated for their enamel and lustre wares. In 1817 Mr. Robert Maling removed the works from Hylton to the neighbourhood of Newcastle-on-Tyne, where he manufactured principally for the Dutch markets. They were afterwards carried on by Dixon, Austin, Phillips, & Co., who at the same time carried on the Sunderland Pottery. In the Mayer Museum is a large jug of this lustre ware. It is of creamy-white earthenware, very light, ornamented with purple lustre in wavy lines, &c. On one side is an engraved and coloured view of the iron bridge over the river Wear, and underneath it, in three small ovals, with borders, &c., are the inscriptions:—"A South-East View of the Iron Bridge over the Wear, near Sunderland. Foundation-stone laid by R. Burdon, Esq., September 24th, 1795. Opened August 9th, 1796. Nil Desperandum. Auspice Deo." "Cast Iron, 214 tons; Wrought do., 40." "Height, 100 feet; Span, 256." "J. Phillips, Hylton Pottery." Many other curious examples, having engravings, verses, &c., are in various collections.

South Hylton or *Ford Pottery*, erected by John Dawson & Co. in 1800, was carried on by that firm until 1864, when, on the death of the last of the family, Mr. Charles Dawson, they were closed and converted into bottle houses; these were destroyed by fire. The flint-mill was taken by Mr. Ball, of the Deptford Pottery. The mark was simply the name "DAWSON" impressed in the ware. A part of the premises were, several years afterwards, used as a brown-ware manufactory, and later still by Messrs. Isaac Fell & Co.

SOUTHWICK.

The *Southwick Pottery* was built in 1788 by Mr. Anthony Scott, who had, previously to that time, carried on a small pot-work at Newbottle, and it is still the property of one of his descendants, Mr. Anthony Scott, and is carried on by that family, under the style of "Scott Brothers & Co." At these large works the usual classes of white, coloured, and brown earthenware are produced for foreign markets.

The *Wear Pottery*, founded by Brunton & Co. in 1803, and soon after carried on by Samuel Moore & Co., passed, about 1861, into the hands of Mr. R. T. Wilkinson, who carried it on under the style of "Samuel Moore & Co." The works closed in 1882. The goods manufactured were the ordinary descriptions of white, sponged, and printed earthenware, and brown ware.

The *High Southwick Pottery*, for Sunderland ware, is carried on by Mr. Thomas Snowball.

Deptford Pottery.—These works were established at Diamond Hall, in 1857, by Mr. Wm. Ball for the manufacture of flower-pots, in which he effected many important improvements, one of the principal of which is the "making them hollow-footed, or with concave bottoms, with apertures for drainage and air, and kept free from the attacks of worms. This gives them a superiority over most, and has gained an extensive patronage." In 1863 the manufacture of "Sunderland ware" was introduced, and is carried on very largely for the London and Scottish markets. At these works, too, suspenders, highly decorated, and other flower-vases, seed-boxes, &c., are extensively made.

MONKWEARMOUTH.

The *Sheepfold Pottery*, for Sunderland ware, is carried on by Messrs. T. J. Rickaby & Co.

The *Sunderland Pottery*, or the *Garrison Pottery*, also established by Mr. Phillips, and carried on by Dixon, Austin, Phillips, & Co., produced white and Queen's ware, in all the usual variety of articles. Sponged, printed, painted, and lustred earthenware were also produced. The works are now discontinued. The marks were

PHILLIPS & CO.

Phillips & Co.

PHILLIPS & CO.
SUNDERLAND, 1813

PHILLIPS & CO.
SUNDERLAND POTTERY.

In the Mayer collection is a well-painted quart mug, with allegorical group of the arts, with the name "W. DIXON, 1811," pencilled on the bottom. Among other examples in the Jermyn Street Museum is a printed coloured and lustred jug, bearing on one side the common view of the bridge over the Wear, and on the other the Farmers' Arms, while in front are the words—"Forget me not," within a wreath. It bears the name DIXON AUSTIN & CO., SUNDERLAND. Figures were also produced, and marked examples may be seen in the same museum. The name occurs in various ways beyond those just given. Thus, among others, are "*W. Dixon*," "*Dixon & Co.*," "*Dixon & Co., Sunderland Pottery*,"

DIXON AUSTIN & CO
Sunderland Pottery

DIXON & CO
Sunderland Pottery.
X

DIXON & CO
SUNDERLAND

Seaham Harbour.

A brown-ware manufactory was built here about the year 1836 by Captain Plowright, of Lynn, and in 1838 it was altered into a white and printed ware manufactory by a number of workmen from Messrs. Dawson & Co., of Hylton. It was closed about 1841, re-opened in 1851 by Mr. R. C. Wilson, and finally closed in 1852.

Newbottle.

These works were founded about 1755 by Mr. Byers, and he manufactured both brown and white wares. They passed into the hands of Mr. Anthony Scott, who carried them on until 1788 (see "Southwick"). They are now discontinued. A pottery for the manufacture of common brown ware and flower-pots, &c., was also carried on by Messrs. Broderick, but is now discontinued.

Bishop Auckland.

New Moor Pottery, at Evenwood, carried on by Mr. George Snowdon for the manufacture of brown ware.

The potteries of the Tees are :—

Stockton-on-Tees.

Stafford Pottery.—Several earthenware manufactories have been carried on at this place. The largest, called the "Stafford Pottery," at South Stockton, or Thornaby, was established for brown ware, in 1825, by Mr. William Smith, a builder of Stockton, who shortly afterwards added general earthenware to its productions. To this end he engaged and ultimately took into partnership Mr. John Whalley, a Staffordshire potter of considerable skill. The firm commenced under the style of "William Smith & Co." in January, 1826. In 1829 a further partnership was entered into with William and George Skinner, sons of Mr. Skinner, banker, of Stockton, and continued for some years, when George Skinner having purchased the interest of his brother, and of Mr. Smith, changed the style to that of "George Skinner & Co." By Mr. Skinner and Mr. Whalley it was thus carried on for some years, when the latter retired, and the management devolved upon Mr. Ambrose Walker, who, shortly after the death of Mr. Skinner in April, 1870, succeeded to the business, and carried it on in connection with the executors of Mr. Skinner under the style of "Skinner and Walker." It is now continued as "Ambrose Walker & Co." The goods manufactured were principally "Queen's ware;" a fine white earthenware; and a fine brown ware, which were shipped in large quantities for Belgium, Holland, and some parts of Germany. I am informed that the firm at one time established a branch pottery at Genappes, near Mons, in Belgium, sending workmen from Stockton; and that the manufactory there was carried on under the style of "Capperman & Co." The marks used are :—

W. S. & CO. QUEEN'S WARE. STOCKTON.	S. & W. QUEEN'S WARE. STOCKTON.

or STOCKTON impressed in the body.

In 1848 the firm consisted of William Smith, John Whalley, George Skinner, and Henry Cowap, and in that year an injunction was granted restraining them from using, as they had illegally done, the name of "WEDGEWOOD & Co." or "WEDGEWOOD," stamped or otherwise marked on goods produced by them.

In 1845, Messrs. George Skinner and John Whalley took out a patent for "certain improvements in the manufacture of earthenware pastes and vitreous bodies, and also a new composition and material for the same, with certain new modes of combination thereof, which improvements, compositions, and combinations are applicable to the manufacture of earthenware pastes, vitreous bodies, slabs, tiles, and pavement, and various other useful and ornamental purposes, and is especially adapted for grave indicators, hydrant indicators, etc., as it is impervious to all weather and unaffected by change of atmosphere." This consists in "combining chalk or carbonate of lime in union with silica, flint, or silex." In the specification seven compositions are given, five of which are for ware and the other two for glaze. The compositions for ware are various "combinations of the above substances, and they contain besides some or all of the following substances, namely, Cornwall stone, china clay, ball clay, felspar, helspar, or sulphate of barytes." The wares may be tinted with the oxides generally used. Nos. 1 and 2 compositions do not require glazing; Nos. 3, 4, and 5 can be glazed with glazes which either do or do not contain lead. In this patent two glazes without lead are claimed. One of these is made of felspar and chalk, and the other of chalk, silica, flint, or silex, Cornwall stone, china clay, ball clay, and felspar, mixed in certain proportions.

North Shore Pottery.

The "*North Shore Pottery*" was established about 1840, by Mr. James Smith, afterwards of Danby Grange, near Yarm, in Yorkshire, and was carried on by his nephew, Mr. William Smith, Jun. (son of the William Smith to whom I have alluded as the founder of the "Stafford Pottery"), under the style of "William Smith, Jun., and Co." Subsequently it was carried on as "G. F. Smith and Co." and "G. and W. Smith." The classes of goods made at this pottery were both in white and cream-coloured wares, the principal markets for which were, besides the home trade, Holland, Germany, and Denmark. Large quantities of wares are also exported to Constantinople and other Mediterranean markets. In white earthenware, and printed and coloured goods, dinner, tea, toilet, and other services; bread, cheese, and other trays of good design; mugs, jugs, basins, and all the usual varieties of domestic vessels are made. The "sponge patterns" for foreign markets are extensively used, and green-glazed ware in flower-pots, &c., is also made. The impressed mark is "W. S., Stockton," and the printed marks, besides an ornamental border and the name of the pattern, being the initials W. S.

Other potteries are or have been Messrs. Ainsworth's, at North Stockton, for white and printed wares; Mr. Harwood, "The Norton Pottery," at Norton, for Sunderland and yellow wares; "Clarence Pottery Company" for Sunderland and brown ware; and Mr. John Harwood for brown ware; at Hartlepool, Mr. William Smith.

Middlesborough-on-Tees.

The Middlesborough Pottery was established in 1831, and was the first public works established in that place. From 1831 to 1844 the firm traded as "The Middlesborough Pottery Company;" from that time until 1852 as "The Middlesborough Earthenware Company;" and from then to the present time as "Isaac Wilson & Co." The works, with wharf, occupy an area of about 9,702 square yards. The goods produced are the ordinary "opaque china," cream-coloured ware, and lustre enamelled ware in dinner, tea, and toilet services, and all the general classes of domestic vessels, enamelled flower-pots, bread-trays, &c. Some of these are of very good quality, and the printed services are equal to the more ordinary Staffordshire goods. The printed marks indicating the pattern have, in addition to the name of the pattern, the initials of the firm, as "M. P. Co." for "Middlesborough Pottery Company;" and "I. W. & Co." for "Isaac Wilson & Co."

LINTHORPE.

These works, which are of recent establishment, and whose productions, from the smallest and simplest objects up to the larger and more pronounced achievements, are characterised by a purity of art-treatment not found elsewhere, are situated on the outskirts of the important town of Middlesborough-on-Tees, the chief seat of the Cleveland iron manufacture—the long and lofty range of the Cleveland hills, from which the ore is obtained, rising up as a distant background and forming a striking contrast to the flat and low-lying level of the general prospect. Originally a brick-yard, known as the "Sun Brick Works," it was conjectured that the extensive beds of fine clay upon which they were erected were capable of being utilised for much higher purposes, and their owner, Mr. John Harrison, having put himself in communication with others, entered upon a series of experiments, caused trial-pieces to be made, and became so fully impressed with the capabilities of his raw material, that he wisely determined upon entering on the manufacture of high-class pottery, and to give to it a distinctive character that should at once assert itself and take up a position in ceramics unknown to, and untried for by, other manufacturers. In this he was so eminently successful that "Linthorpe" mottling, flowing, and blending of colours and glazes has become sufficient of a speciality to form of itself a distinctive feature in decoration of plastic ware.

At the first starting of the works, in 1879, Mr. Harrison called in the services of Dr. Dresser, who supplied numbers of the forms and designs for pieces then and afterwards produced, and his name was, for a time, impressed in the body of the ware. Future collectors will, from this hint, know that pieces bearing the stamp "Chr. Dresser," date back to the first three or four years of the history of these works. Of late the works, untrammelled by the former conventionalities, and casting off the rigid severity of angular outlines on the one hand and grotesque combinations and distortions on the other, have entered on another, newer, and far more graceful and effective phase of art, with the result that the Linthorpe ware now takes its stand among the very highest productions of any locality, and in some of its main features is, indeed, unique.

In the "Linthorpe Ware" proper—*i.e.* the peculiar ware for which it first gained so enviable a notoriety, and which is still the secret and speciality of the works—vases ranging in size from the tiny little stand for a single flower up to those of gigantic growth, of as many feet as the others are inches in height; rose-petal and other bowls, with or without covers, and, in many cases, elaborately perforated; flower-stands, holders, and suspenders; plaques, tazzas, and card-trays; ewers, beakers, and jugs innumerable; rose-water and other bottles; and, indeed, every variety of ornamental articles that can be required, are made, as are also breakfast, tea, dessert, and toilet services, and other domestic vessels; the breakfast services, especially those of the beautifully blended, or flown sage-green, having a charming effect on the table and being especially "nice" to the touch in use. The peculiarity of this ware lies, of course, in the marvellous and never-ending variety and effect of the "Linthorpe glaze," and the peculiar mode of treatment adopted in the preparation and arrangement of the colours. No two pieces ever made can, by any possibility, be alike. The general colour will be the same in any number of pieces of a service, the form will be strictly identical, and the whole will harmonize together; but the accidental pattern (so to speak) which the peculiar glaze assumes in the firing varies in its minute details in such an endless, and, at the same time, lovely variety, as only nature herself could produce. No art can so arrange the material that two pieces shall be identical in every part. It can arrange the colours and apportion the treatment so as to form a strong family likeness in any number of pieces, but in each the features will and must vary. The gradation of tones, and the gradual blending and merging of one colour into another; the soft mossy or tufa-like appearance of some, and the close resemblance to harder materials in the richness, glow, and fulness of colour of this, and the subdued and æsthetic tints of those, are all equally pleasing to the eye. Nothing harsh or incongruous is indeed possible under the present system of ornamentation and glazing. In this same general style tiles for fireplaces and wall decoration are also made, and have a remarkably pleasing effect.

In other branches of decorative art, though totally distinct from the Linthorpe speciality of flowing glazes, these works are equally successful. Whether in underglaze painting, in sgraffito, or in the perhaps more beautiful process of pâte-sur-pâte, the vases produced by Mr. Harrison are all characterised by a strict adherence to the highest and truest principles of art. By the latter process a rich and pleasing effect of highly glazed floral decoration upon the dead or semi-dead natural surface is produced, and the vases become art treasures of rare beauty and value. Another variety of ornamentation introduced very effectively at these works is that of flowers, foliage, &c., very fairly modelled by hand in full natural relief, as in the Tunisian ware. These are marked by masterly and powerful treatment, as is also a "dragon vase" of considerable merit. Among the latest achievements is a ewer, three feet in height, elaborately decorated in relief, which, with a large number of other examples, is to form a portion of Mr. Harrison's exhibit at the Calcutta Exhibition.

The works at Linthorpe employ from eighty to a hundred hands, and are arranged with a marked attention to the comfort—in abundance of room, light, air, and ventilation—of all employed; the ladies' painting-room, presided over by a trained lady artist, and in which many are engaged in the various processes of decorating, being a model which most of our manufactories, and, indeed, Schools of Art, might with advantage follow. The marks used are simply the word LINTHORPE, or the same word across the outline of a flat urn, "Number One" pattern of the work, impressed in the body of the ware.

Wolviston Pottery, now discontinued, formerly produced yellow ware.

Coxhoe Pottery, also discontinued, produced Sunderland ware.

Alnwick.

There were formerly pot-works here; but no trace of them is now left, save the name of the street, "Potter Gate," where they existed. The former name of this street was, in 1567, "Barresdale Street," but potters having there located themselves, it became gradually changed. Another old street in this town now known as "Clay-port," was formerly called "Clay-peth," *peth* being a provincialism for a steep road, and *clay* the nature of the soil; probably it was this clay that the Alnwick potters turned to good account.

CHAPTER XV.

LIVERPOOL.

It would, perhaps, scarcely be expected that in such a busy, bustling, and gigantic place of enterprise and commercial activity as Liverpool—in the midst of shipping of every description, and surrounded by the most enormous and busy undertakings of one kind or other—we should successfully look for the full and perfect accomplishment of so quiet, so unostentatious, so peaceful, and so delicate an art as that of the potter. But thus it is; and Liverpool, which counts its docks by tens, its wharves and stores by hundreds, its shipping by thousands, and its wealth by millions—which can boast of its far more than half-a-million inhabitants, its overground and underground railways, and every appliance which skill and enterprise can give or trade and commerce possibly require—which has projected the accomplishment of some of the most wonderful and gigantic schemes the world ever knew, and has carried them out in that spirit of commendable and boundless energy that invariably characterises all its undertakings—has not been behindhand with its more inland and more modest neighbours in the manufacture of delicate porcelain, and of pottery of the most fragile nature. It is more than probable that in mediæval times the coarse ware of the period—the pitchers, porringers, dishes, &c.—was made on the banks of the Mersey. The first mention of pottery, however, occurs in 1674, when the following items appear in the list of town dues :—"For every cart-load of muggs (shipped) into foreign ports, 6*d.* For every cart-load of muggs along the coasts, 4*d.* For every crate of cupps or pipes into foreign ports, 2*d.* For every crate of cupps or pipes along the coast, 1*d.*"

Shaw's Delft Ware Works.—The earliest pot-works of which there is any reliable information appears to have been that of Alderman Shaw, situate at Shaw's Brow, which afterwards became a complete nest of pot-works belonging to different individuals. At these works was most probably made the earliest-known dated example of Liverpool delft ware, a large flat oblong-square plaque, preserved in the Mayer Museum (Fig. 889). It is 2 feet 7 inches in length, by 1 foot 8 inches in depth, and is composed of the ordinary buff-coloured clay, smeared, like what are usually called "Dutch tiles," on the face with a fine white clay, on which the design is drawn in blue, and then glazed. The plaque represents the village of Great Crosby as seen from the river Mersey, and bears the name and date, "A west prospect of Great Crosby, 1716," on a ribbon at the top. In the foreground is the river Mersey, with ships and brigs, and a sloop and a schooner. The large ship in the centre of the picture has a boat attached to her stern, and another boat containing two men is seen rowing towards her, while on the water around them are a number of gulls and other sea-birds. On the sandy banks of the river are several figures, consisting of a woman with a basket on her arm, apparently looking across the river; another woman, also with a basket on her arm, walking with a long stick; a man also walking with a stick; a gentleman on horseback; and a man driving an ass before him. Beyond these figures rise the sandbanks, covered with long grass and heather, in which is a rabbit warren. The warren-keeper's house is shown, as are also numbers of rabbits. Beyond this again, in the open space, are a number of figures: men are seen galloping on horseback; women are carrying baskets; men are walking about, some with dogs, others without; and the intermediate space is pretty well studded with cattle, rabbits, and birds; a milkmaid milking one of the cows. Behind this, again, the ground is divided by hedgerows into fields, in which are cattle, people walking to and fro, and a milkmaid carrying a milkpail on her head. In the background is the village of Great Crosby including the school-house and numerous other buildings, with long rows of trees, palings, gates, and other objects incidental to the scene, and to the left of the spectator is Crosby windmill, still standing.

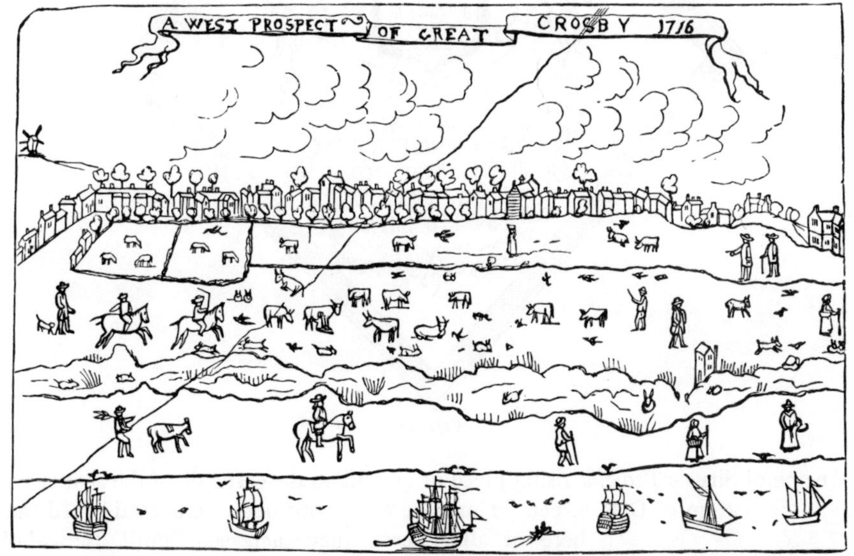

Fig. 889.

Another curious plaque (Fig. 890) is affixed to tne wall over one of the seats of old Crosby Church, and bears the arms of the Merchant Taylors' Company, and the inscription—"THIS SEAT WAS ERECTED BY JOHN HARRISON AND HENRY HARRISON, OF LEVERPOOLE, 1722," who are said to have been natives of Crosby, the grammar-school of which village they erected and endowed, after having made large fortunes as merchants in London, the trust being held by the Company of Merchant Taylors. Another of these curious plaques, or slabs, Mr. Mayer says, was attached to the front of a house at Newton-cum-Larten; is was circular, and bore the arms of Johnson and Anton impaled, with the date 1753. Mr. Johnson, who was afterwards Mayor of Liverpool, and formed St. James's Walk, married Miss Anton, an heiress, and built the house where the slab was affixed. Another dated example is a mug in the Mayer Museum, and bears on its front the initials and date

P
I · R
1728

There were, it appears, two potters, at least, of the name of Shaw—Samuel Shaw, who died in October, 1775, and Thomas Shaw who, I believe, was his son. The works were, as I have stated, at a place which, from that circumstance, took

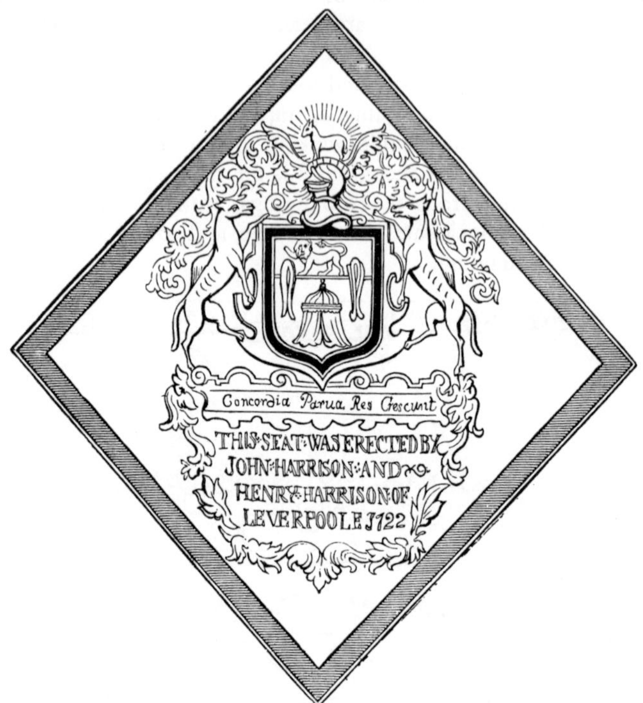

Fig. 890.

the name of Shaw's Brow, a rising piece of ground on the east side of the rivulet that ran at the bottom of Dale Street. Here the early pot-works were established, and here in after years they increased, until the whole "Brow" became one mass of potter's banks, with houses for the workmen on both sides of the street; and so numerous where they that, according to the census taken in 1790, there were as many as 74 houses, occupied by 437 persons, the whole of whom were connected with the potteries. At these works, Richard Chaffers, to whom credit is due for the advances he made in the manufacture of porcelain, was apprenticed to Shaw, and on the Brow he established his own manufactory.

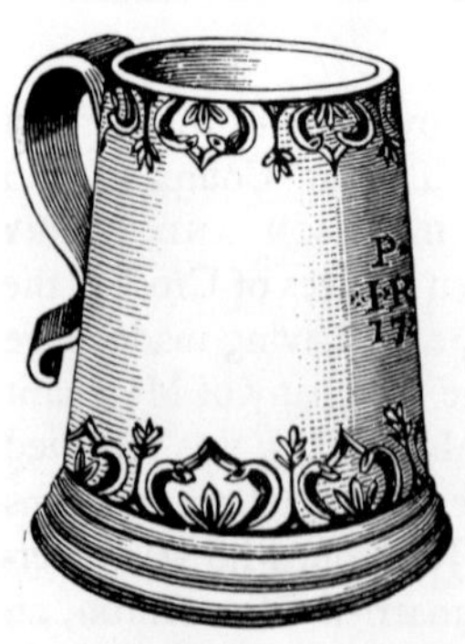

Fig. 891.

Among the examples in the Mayer Museum, is the blue-painted Delft-ware punch-bowl (Fig. 892), 17½ inches in diameter, "made for Captain Metcalfe, who commanded the *Golden Lion*, which was the first vessel that sailed out of Liverpool on the whale fishery and Greenland trade, and was presented to him on his return from his second voyage, by his employers, who were a company composed of the principal merchants of Liverpool, in the year 1753; some char-pots, decorated with fishes (Fig. 893); and two mugs (Figs. 894 and 895), of the same body and glaze as the plaques already described. The larger one bears the initials and date T. F. 1757, of Thomas Fazackerley, to whom it was presented by its maker, a workman at

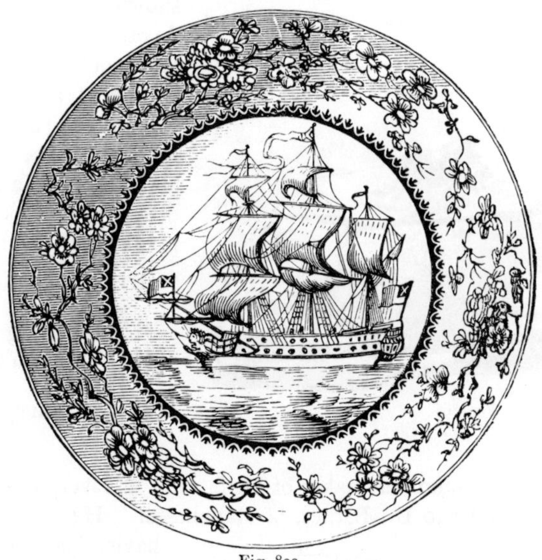

Fig. 892.

Shaw's pottery. In 1758 Mr. Fazackerley having married, his friend made the smaller of the two mugs, a pint one, on which he placed the initials of the lady, Catherine Fazackerley, and the date C. F. 1758 within an oval on its front. Fig. 896 is one of a pair of butter-pots in form of cows; they are excellently modelled, and painted in flowers, evidently by the same artist as the Fazackerley mugs, in yellow, blue, and green. Fragments of figures were, I believe, found in excavating on the site of Shaw's pottery. Another dated example is a Delft ware bowl, painted on the outside with birds, butterflies and flowers, and on the inside a man-of-war, and the words, "Success to the *Monmouth*, 1760."

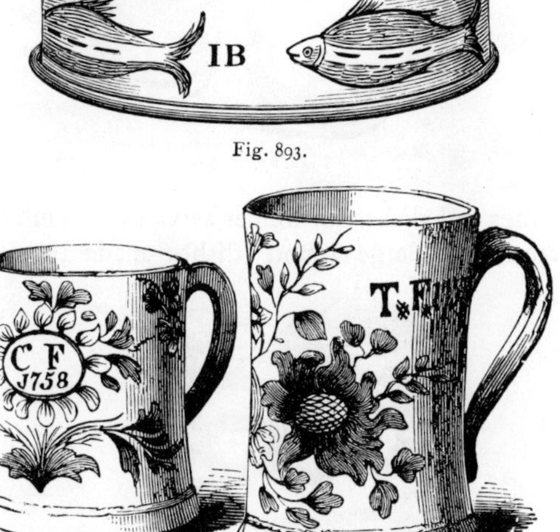

Fig. 893.

Figs. 894 and 895.

An interesting matter in connection with the Delft ware works at Shaw's Brow is the fact of a number of broken vessels being discovered on its site during excavations for building the Liverpool Free Library and Museum, in 1857. On that occasion an old slip-vat was found containing clay, which might probably have been prepared as early as 1680. The clay was of the common coarse kind, the same as the general body of Delft ware. Of this clay so discovered Mr. Mayer had a vase thrown and fired. Some of the exhumed Delft cups, &c., are shown on Figs. 897 to 902. Another example said to be Liverpool Delft ware (Fig. 903), is one of a pair of flower-vases, elaborately painted in blue, and marked on the bottom. D W A; and another is a puzzle jug (Fig. 904), which bears the appropriate verse painted in blue—

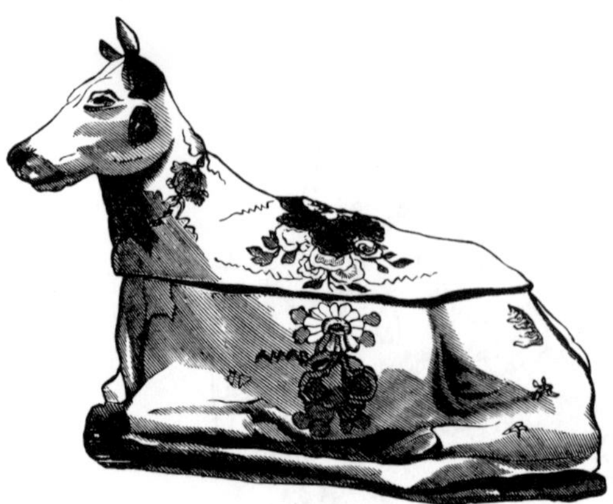

Fig. 896.

"Here, Gentlemen, come try yr skill,
I'll hold a wager, if you will,
That you Don't Drink this liqr all
Without you spill or lett some Fall."

Zachariah Barnes—another maker of Delft ware in Liverpool—was a native of Warrington, and brother to Dr. Barnes, of Manchester. He was born in 1743, and having learnt the "art, mystery, and occupation," of throwing, &c., commenced business as a potter in the old Haymarket, at the left-hand side in going to Byrom Street. He is said to have first made china, but afterwards turned his attention to Delft ware, and soon became proficient in the art. The principal varieties of goods made by him were jars and pots for druggists; large dishes, octagonal plates and dishes for dinner services; "Dutch tiles;" labels for liquors; char-pots, &c. The large round dishes made by Barnes were chiefly sent into Wales,

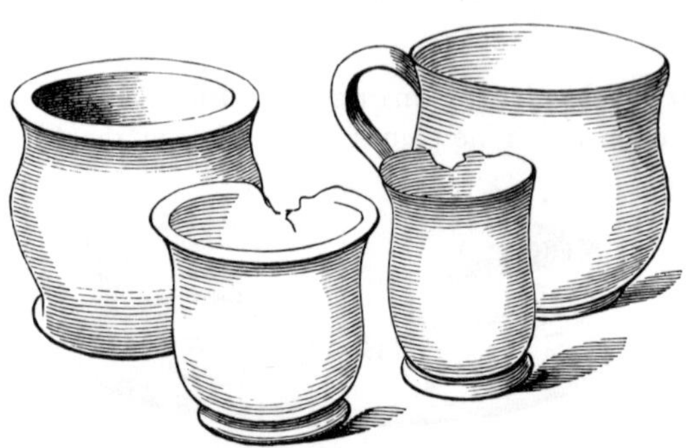

Figs. 897 to 900.

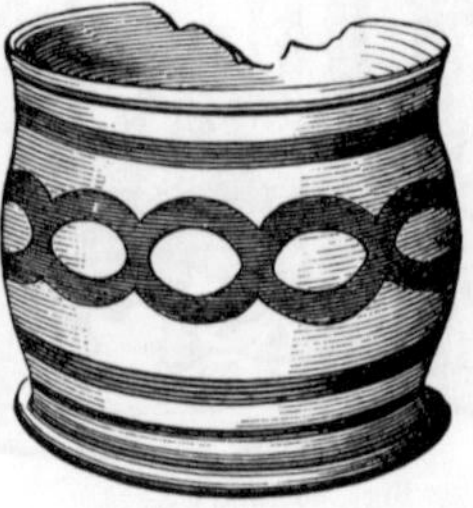

Fig. 901.

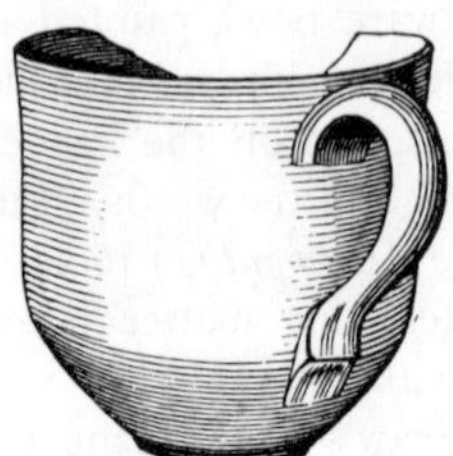

Fig. 902.

where the simple habits of their forefathers remained unchanged among the people long after their alteration in England; and the master of the house and his guests dipped their spoons into the mess and helped themselves from the dish placed in the middle of the table. Quantities of this ware were sent to the

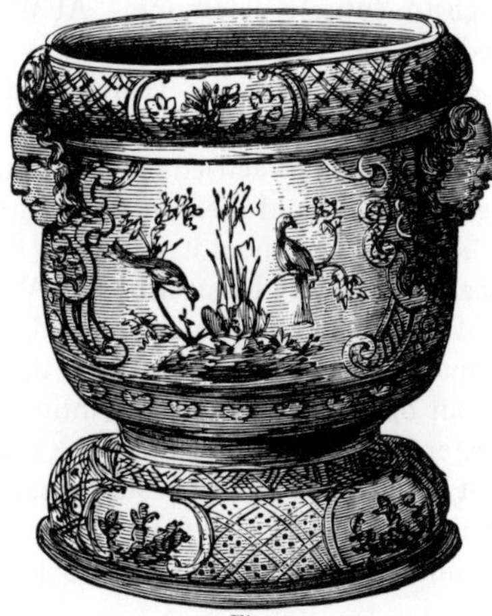

Fig. 903.

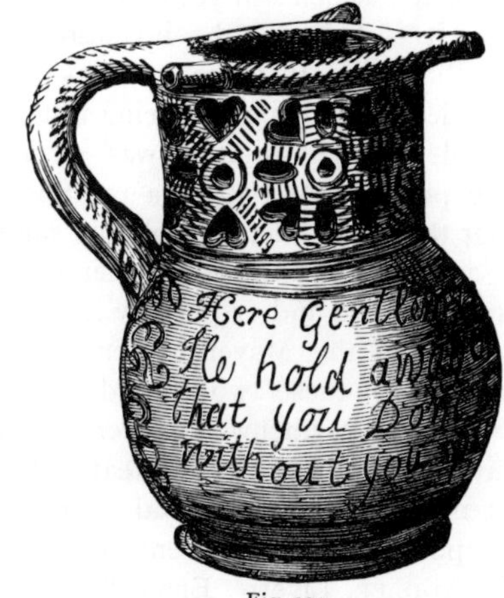

Fig. 904.

great border fairs, held at Chester, whither the inhabitants of the more remote and inaccessable parts of the mountain districts of Wales assembled to buy their stores for the year. Barnes's principal *forte* lay in the manufacture of square tiles, commonly known as Dutch tiles, both painted on blue, and printed by Sadler and Green. He also made large quantities of pots for potting char, which were sent to the lakes. The ovens were fired with turf brought from the bogs at Kirkley, and on the night of firing, the men were always allowed potatoes to roast at the kiln fires, and a certain quantity of ale to drink. The labels for different kinds of liquors to which I have alluded were of various sizes, the one engraved (Fig. 905) being 5½ inches long. Examples in the Mayer Museum are respectively lettered for "Rum," "Cyder," "Tent," "Brandy," "Lisbon," "Peppermint," "Wormwood," "Aniseed," "Geneva," "Claret," "Spruce," "Perry," "Orange," "Burgundy," "Port," "Rasin," and other liquors. A *plaque* of Liverpool Delft (Fig. 906), painted in two or three colours, is in the possession of Mr. Rathbone.

WORMWOOD

Fig. 905.

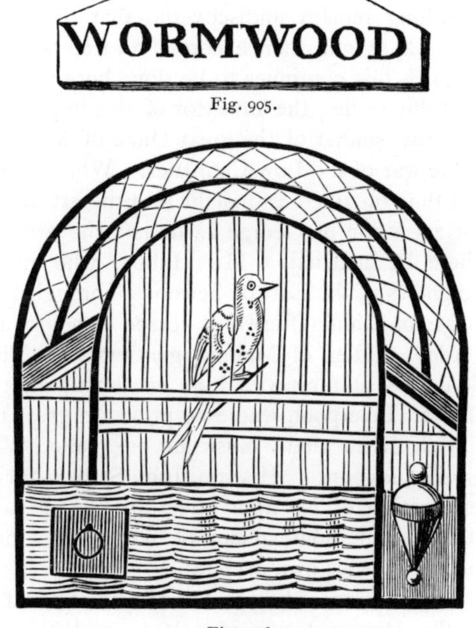

Fig. 906.

Sadler and Green.—The tiles to which I have alluded bring me to a very interesting part of the subject of this chapter. I mean the introduction of *printing* on earthenware, an invention which has been attributed to, and claimed by, several places, and which will yet require further research to entirely determine. At Worcester it is believed the invention was applied in the year 1756, and it is an undoubted fact that the art was practised there in the following year, a dated example of the year 1757 being in the Museum of Practical Geology, London. At Caughley transfer-printing was, as I have already shown, practised at about the same period. At Battersea printing on enamels was, it would seem, carried on at about the same date, or probably somewhat earlier. At Liverpool it is certain that the art was known at an earlier period than can with safety be ascribed to Worcester. A fine and exquisitely sharp specimen of transfer-printing on enamel, dated 1756, is in the Mayer Museum. It is curious that these two earliest dated exemplars of these two candidates for the honour of the invention of printing on enamels and earthenware, Liverpool and Worcester, should be portraits of the same individual—Frederick the Great of Prussia. But so it is. The Worcester example is a mug, bearing the royal portrait with trophies, &c., and the date 1757; the Liverpool one, an oval enamel (and a much finer work of art), with the name "J. SADDLER, Liverp[l]. Enam."

The art is said to have been invented by this John Sadler, of Liverpool, in 1752. In "Moss's Liverpool Guide," published in 1790, it is stated:—"Copper-plate printing upon china and earthenware originated here in 1752, and remained some time a secret with the inventors, Messrs. Sadler and Green, the latter of whom still continues the business in Harrington Street. It appeared unaccountable how uneven surfaces could receive impressions from copper-plates. It could not, however, long remain undiscovered that the impression from the plate is first taken upon paper, and thence communicated to the ware after it is glazed. The manner in which this continues to be done here remains still unrivalled in perfection."

John Sadler, the inventor of this important art, was the son of Adam Sadler, a favourite soldier of the great Duke of Marlborough, and was out with that general in the war of the Low Countries. While there, he lodged in the house of a printer, and thus obtained an insight into the art of printing. On returning to England, on the accession of George I., he left the army in disgust and retired to Ulverstone, where he married a Miss Bibby, who numbered among her acquaintance the daughters of the Earl of Sefton. Through the influence of these ladies he removed to Melling, and afterwards leased a house at Aintree. In this lease he is styled "Adam Sadler, of Melling, gentleman." The taste he had acquired in the Low Countries abiding with him, he shortly afterwards, however, removed to the New Market, Liverpool, where he printed a great number of books—among which, being himself an excellent musician, one called "The Muses' Delight" was with him an especial favourite. His son, John Sadler, having learned the art of engraving, on the termination of his apprenticeship bought a house from his father in Harrington Street for the nominal sum of five shillings, and in that house, in 1748, commenced business on his own account.

He was, according to Mr. Mayer, the first person who applied the art of printing to the ornamentation of pottery, and the story of his discovery is thus told:—Sadler had been in the habit of giving waste and spoiled impressions from his engraved plates to little children, and these they frequently stuck upon pieces of broken pot from the pot-works at Shaw's Brow, for their own amusement, and for building dolls' houses. This gave him the idea of decorating pottery with printed pictures, and, keeping the idea secret, he made many experiments, and ultimately explained his views to Guy Green, who had then recently succeeded Adam Sadler in his business; and the two having "laid their heads together," conducted joint experiments and ultimately entered into partnership, with a determination to take out a patent, which, however, under the advice of friends, was not done. The art was first of all turned to good account in the decoration of "Dutch tiles," as they are usually called, and in some affidavits in the possession of Mr. Mayer, they make oath that on Tuesday, the 27th day of July [1756] they, "without the aid or assistance of any other person or persons, did within the space of six hours, to wit, between the hours of nine in the morning and three in the afternoon of the same day, print upwards of twelve hundred Earthenware tiles of different patterns, at Liverpoole aforesaid, and which, as these deponents have heard and believe, were more in number and better and neater than one hundred skilful pot-painters could have painted in the like space of time, in the common and usual way of painting with a pencil; and these deponents say that they have been upwards of seven years in finding out the method of printing tiles, and in making tryals and experiments for that purpose, which they have now through great pains and expence brought to perfection.—JOHN SADLER, GUY GREEN. Taken and sworn at Liverpoole, in the county of Lancaster, the second day of August, one thousand seven hundred and fifty-six, before William Statham, a Master Extraordinary in Chancery." "We, Alderman Thomas Shaw and Samuel Gilbody, both of Liverpoole, in the county of Lancaster, clay potters, whose names are hereunto subscribed, do hereby humbly certifye that we are well assured that John Sadler and Guy Green did, at Liverpoole aforesaid, on Tuesday, the 27th day of July last past, within the space of six hours, print upwards of 1,200 earthenware tiles of different colours and patterns, which is upon a moderate computation more than 100 good workmen could have done of the same patterns in the same space of time by the usual painting with the pencil. That we have since burnt the above tiles, and that they are considerably neater than any we have seen pencilled, and may be sold at little more than half the price," &c. &c. "THOMAS SHAW, SAMUEL GILBODY."

In the Mayer museum are some enamels on copper bearing impressions from copper plates transferred to them, and having the name of "*J. Sadler Liverp*^l *Enam*^l," and other examples of enamels and of earthenware with the names of "*Sadler, Sculp*," or of "*Green.*" Messrs. Sadler and Green soon found their process to be as applicable to services and other descriptions of goods as to tiles, and they produced many fine examples, some of which, bearing their names as engravers or enamellers, are still in existence. Josiah Wedgwood at first opposed the introduction of this invention, as being, in his opinion, an unsatisfactory and unprofitable substitute for painting, but eventually he determined to adopt the new style of ornamentation, and arranged with the inventors to decorate such of his Queen's ware as it would be applicable to, by their process. The work was a troublesome one, and in the then state of the roads—for it must be remembered that this was before the time even of canals in the district, much less of railroads—the communication between Burslem and Liverpool was one of great difficulty. Wedgwood, however, overcame it, and having made the plain body at his works in Staffordshire, packed it in waggons and carts, and even in the panniers of pack-horses, and sent it to Liverpool, where it was printed by Sadler and Green, and returned to him by the same kind of conveyance. The works of Sadler and Green were in Harrington Street, at the back of Lord Street, Liverpool, and here they not only carried on their engraving and transfer-printing for other potters, but made their own wares, and carried on an extensive business. It was here they printed the ware for Josiah Wedgwood.

Specimens of these early printed goods, bearing Wedgwood's mark, are rare. The teapot (Fig. 907) will serve as an example. It bears on one side a well-engraved and sharply-printed representation of the quaint subject of the mill to grind old people young again—the kind of curious machine which one recollects in one's boyish days being taken about from fair to fair by strolling mountebanks—and on the other an oval border of foliage, containing the ballad belonging to the subject, called "The Miller's Maid grinding Old Men Young again." The teapot is marked WEDGWOOD. In the Museum of Practical Geology is an example of this printing, the design on one side of which is a group at tea—a lady pouring out tea for a gentleman, and on the opposite side the verse:—

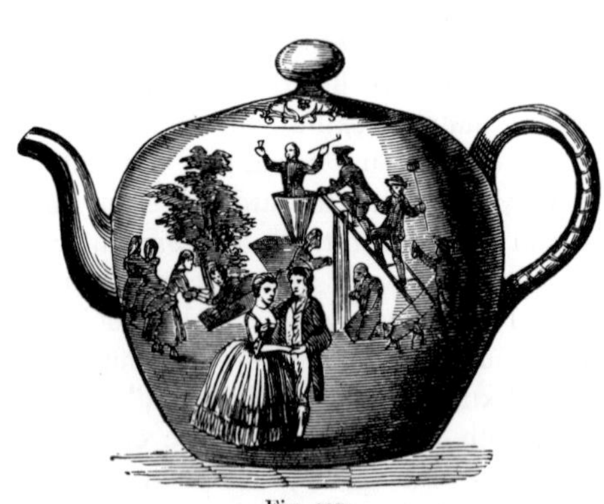
Fig. 907.

"Kindly take this gift of mine,
The gift and giver I hope is thine;
And tho' the value is but small,
A loving Heart is worth it all."

Examples of Liverpool-made pottery, printed by Sadler and Green, are in the Mayer Museum. Adam Sadler died on the 7th of October, 1788, aged eighty-three, and his son, John Sadler, on the 10th of December, 1789, aged sixty-nine, and they were buried at Sefton.

Drinkwater.—Another Delft ware pottery, at the bottom of Duke Street, in a small street which, from it, took the name of "Pot-House Lane," was conducted by Mr. George Drinkwater (born in the neighbourhood of Preston), brother to Mr. James Drinkwater, who, in the navy, acquired considerable riches and honour, and was ancestor of Sir John Drinkwater. The works were not of long continuance, and except they can be authenticated by evidence of descent, &c., the productions cannot be distinguished from those of the other potteries of the time. In the Mayer Museum, among other authenticated specimens, a large plate, 23 inches in diameter, is the most interesting.

Spencer.—Another pot-work of a similar kind was established by a Mr. Thomas Spencer, at the bottom of Richmond Row. These works were, however, carried on only for a few years, when Mr. Spencer removed to the "Moss Pottery," near Prescot, where he continued to make coarse red ware for common use.

Chaffers.—One of the most noted men connected with the ceramic art in Liverpool was Richard Chaffers, who made great advances in that art, and to whom his native town owed the introduction of the manufacture of china. He was the son of a shipwright, being born in Mersey Street, Liverpool, in 1731, and was apprenticed to Alderman Shaw, the Delft ware potter. About 1752 he took or erected some small works on the north side, and nearly at the bottom of Shaw's Brow, where he began making Delft ware on his own account, and so continued for some years. From Delft ware Chaffers passed on to the manufacture of fine white earthenware, and produced an excellent body and glaze. The rapid strides which Wedgwood was making in the art served as a strong incentive to Richard Chaffers, who determined that his productions should equal those of his great rival. In this he did not succeed, but he *did* succeed in making the pottery of Liverpool better than that of most localities. A dated, though not very early, example of his make is in the Mayer Museum (Fig. 908). It is, Mr. Mayer says, "a pepper-box of the hour-glass shape," painted in blue on a white ground, with a chequered border at top and bottom, and the name,

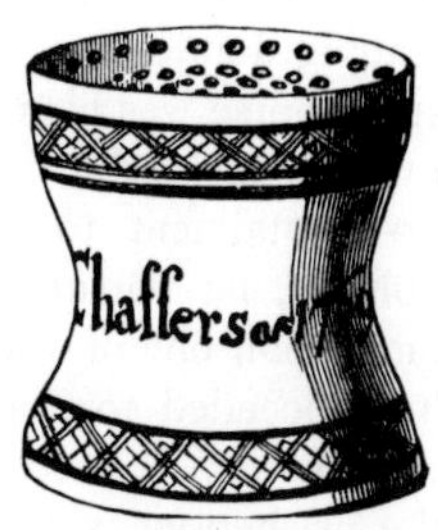

Fig. 908.

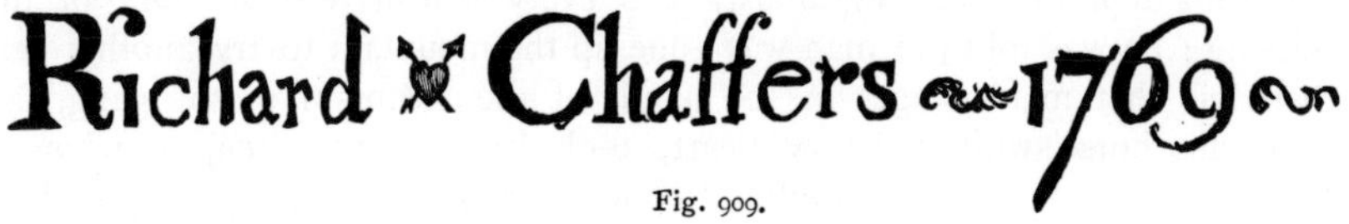

Richard Chaffers 1769

Fig. 909.

round the waist. "So well known was the ware of Mr. Chaffers in the American colonies," writes Mr. Mayer, "that it was a common saying of a person that was angry, that 'He's as hot as Dick's pepper-box,' alluding to those made by Mr. Chaffers, who exported a very large portion of his manufacture to the then English colonies." But here I think he is decidedly in error. The example is, no doubt, a pounce-box or pounce-pot of the ordinary and not at all uncommon form, and was made and prominently painted with his name and date for use on his own desk. This pounce-box remained in the family of its maker until it was presented to Mr. Mayer by John Rosson, the grandson of Richard Chaffers.

In 1754 or 1755 William Cookworthy, of Plymouth, as I have already shown in my account of those works, discovered the "moor stone, or growan stone, and growan clay"—two important materials in the manufacture of china—in Cornwall, and in 1768 he took out his patent for the manufacture of porcelain from those materials. Chaffers having determined upon prosecuting researches into the nature of china ware, and of endeavouring to produce it at Liverpool, entered into a series of experiments, but finding that the "soap-stone" was essential for his purpose, and that the district where it was found was held by lease for its production, so as to keep the monopoly of its use to Cookworthy and those whom he might supply with it, he determined to try and seek the stone in a fresh locality. About this time a Mr. Podmore, who had for some years been employed by Josiah Wedgwood, and who was a good practical potter and a man of sound judgment, left Wedgwood's employment, intending to emigrate to America and establish himself as a potter in that country. To this end he went to Liverpool, intending thence to embark for the colony. On reaching Liverpool, he called upon Chaffers, the result of their meeting being that Chaffers, finding Podmore to be a man of "so much intelligence and practical knowledge, induced him, by a most liberal offer, to forego his American project, and enter into his service." Podmore confirmed the views of his new master as to the importance of getting a supply of the Cornish materials, and the two together soon effected improvements in their manufacture, and laid plans for future operations. Chaffers accordingly set out for Cornwall upon the forlorn hope of discovering a vein of soap-rock, and to that end obtained letters of introduction from the Earl of Derby, Lord Strange, and others, to some of the leading landowners in Cornwall, then attending their duties in Parliament. A stout horse was his only means of conveyance, and having mounted, with a pair of saddle-bags under him, containing a supply of linen, &c., a thousand guineas—the first instalment to pay the wages of the miners—and a brace of pistols in his holsters, he pursued his journey to London. Having obtained permission from more than one of the principal proprietors of mountain-land to bore for soap-rock, he proceeded to Cornwall to commence operations. His first efforts for a long time were not successful, and he expended large sums of money without finding the wished-for vein. Somewhat disheartened, he determined to suspend his operations and return home. He accordingly assembled all the miners in his employ, and announced to them, to their great regret, his determination. Previously to his departure, he scrupulously paid every man his wages. One of them was missing: he was told the man was gone up the mountain to try another place. He then left that man's wages in the hands of the "captain of the gang," and, mounting his horse with a heavy heart, took leave of the men, to whom his animated and conciliatory manner had greatly endeared him. The road to the nearest town was so precipitous and rugged that a traveller on horseback made so little progress that a mountaineer on foot, by taking a short cut over the rocky crags, could easily come within ear-shot of him. After journeying for some time he thought he heard a faint cry in the distance; he dismounted, and, ascending a hill, plainly saw the signal of discovery flying from a lofty peak. It appeared that the man who had separated from his fellow-miners and pursued his researches alone had discovered a vein, and finding Chaffers had left them he hoisted the preconcerted signal, and pursued him across the mountain with the pleasing intelligence, shouting at times to attract the somewhat dispirited traveller's attention. Chaffers immediately returned, took the whole gang into permanent employment, and obtained an ample supply of the long-sought-for clay, which was conveyed to the nearest port, and shipped thence to Liverpool. On its arrival the vessel entered with its precious freight into the Old Dock, dressed in colours, amidst the cheers of the assembled spectators.

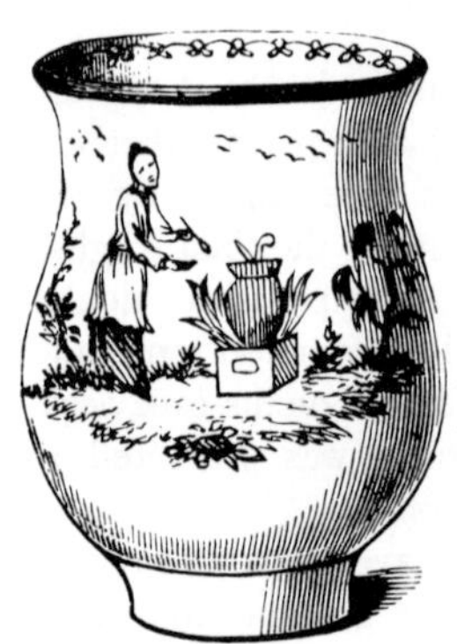

Fig. 910.

Cookworthy had discovered the Cornish stone about 1754 or 1755, and Chaffers must soon afterwards have prosecuted his researches in the same direction, for in December, 1756, it is proved by advertisement he was making "porcelain or china ware" in considerable quantities, both for home sale and for exportation. Liverpool may therefore boast of producing its china in 1756, if not in 1755, which is an early date in the annals of English porcelain manufacture. Not only, however, in this year did "Chaffers and Co." make china-ware, but another firm, that of William Reid and Co., held at the same time, as I shall presently show, the "Liverpool China Manufactory," where they produced blue and white ware in considerable quantities.

Of the china ware made by Chaffers examples are in the Mayer Museum. One of these is the cup (Fig. 910) and another is a jug, bearing in front a portrait of

Frederick the Great, with trophies of war on either side. This jug has the peculiarity of being painted inside as well as out. At the bottom, inside, is the Prussian eagle in a border; in the spout is a trophy, and all around the inside of the vessel roses and other flowers are spangled about.

Chaffers carried on his works for some years, making both earthenware and china, but was suddenly cut off in the midst of his usefulness and at an early age. Podmore, his foreman, being seized with a malignant fever, and beyond hope of recovery, sent a message to Chaffers, expressing "his wish to see his dear master once more before their final separation." Chaffers, who was a man of full and sanguine habit, at once complied, took the fever, and soon afterwards died, the master and servant being interred near to each other in St. Nicholas's churchyard. "This unfortunate event, by taking away both master and principal assistant, put an end to the prosecution of the trade, and was the commencement of the breaking up of that branch of the art which Mr. Chaffers had mainly brought to such a high state of perfection. A great number of the potters ultimately emigrated to America, whilst many of the best hands transferred themselves to the service of Mr. Wedgwood, or were hired by other Staffordshire manufacturers."

Reid & Co.—About 1753 or 1754 works were established in Liverpool by William Reid, who afterwards took a partner and conducted his business under the style of Reid & Co. These works, in 1756, were called "the Liverpool China Manufactory." In that year Messrs. Reid & Co. opened a warehouse in Castle Street, and in 1758 removed it to the top of Castle Hey, where, having largely increased their business, they occupied much more extensive premises. In the same year they were advertising for apprentices for the painters in the china manufactory. In 1760, again, the works appear to have considerably increased, and "several apprentices for the china work" were advertised for, as well as "a sober, careful man, who understands sorting and packing of ware and merchants' accounts." Messrs. Reid & Co. continued in business many years, and produced, besides their "china ware," a considerable quantity of the ordinary blue and white earthenware, most of which was exported.

Pennington.—Another of the Liverpool potters was Seth Pennington. Of the Penningtons, three brothers, James, John, and Seth, were potters, and each had separate works. James, the eldest, had his works on Copperas Hill, but produced only the commoner varieties of ware, and being dissipated and having done his youngest brother a serious injury by divulging a secret in the mixing of colour, he removed to Worcester, where he obtained employment, and where, at a later period, one of his sons painted a fine dinner service for the Duke of York. John, the second son, had his pot-works at Upper Islington, which he carried on for some time. Ultimately he sold the concern to a Mr. Wolf, "who, being a scientific man, made great improvements in the ware, but ultimately finding it did not answer, as the Staffordshire potters were making such rapid strides towards monopolising the whole trade, he gave up the manufacture, and the works were closed, never to be resumed." Seth, the youngest of the three brothers, had his works in that nest of potters, Shaw's Brow. His factories were very large, extending as far as Clayton Street, and were conducted with much spirit. At these works, Seth Pennington, besides the ordinary classes of earthenware then in use, and which he produced in large quantities both for home consumption and for exportation, made a remarkably fine kind of ware that successfully competed, for vases and beakers, with the oriental, both in its colour, its glaze, and its decoration. He also produced many remarkably large

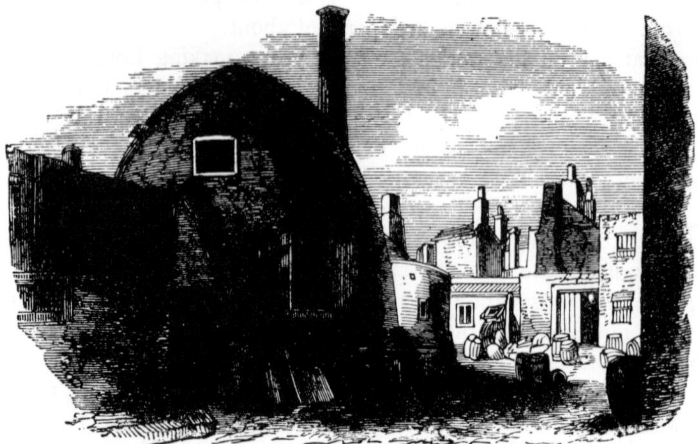

Fig. 911.—Part of Pennington's Works.

and fine punch-bowls, both in Delft ware, in fine earthenware, and, later on, in china. The largest-sized bowl I have met with was made by Pennington, at these works (Figs. 912 and 913); it is 20½ inches in diameter and 9 inches in height, and is painted in blue on the usual white ground. This bowl, which bears the words, "Success to the African Trade, George Dickinson," was painted probably about the year 1760-70, by John Robinson, who was apprenticed, and afterwards employed, at Pennington's works. Robinson subsequently removed into Staffordshire, and ultimately presented the bowl to the Potteries Mechanics' Institution at Hanley, where it is carefully preserved along with his note—"John Robinson, a pot-painter, served his time at Pennington's, in Shaw's Brow, and there painted this punch-bowl." Several other bowls of Pennington's make are in the Mayer Museum. Of these, two of the finest are dated. One bears on its outside a design of trees, birds, and butterflies, painted in yellow and green, and on its inside a ship in full sail, with the words, "Success to the Monmouth, 1760." The other has on the outside a soldier and a sailor, one of whom is seated on the stock of an anchor, and holding in one hand a sword and in the other a punch-bowl; and the other

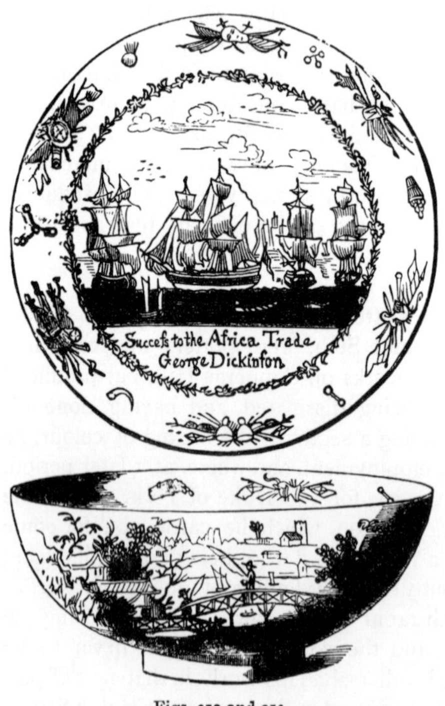

Figs. 912 and 913.

sitting, Bacchus-like, astride a barrel. Between them is a chest, bearing the words "Spanish gold;" while inside the bowl is a painting of a ship in full sail, with the words, "1779. Success to the Isabella." Of the fine earthenware vases and beakers illustrations are given on Figs. 914 to 918. They form part of a set of chimney ornaments, purchased by Mr. Mayer from the only and aged daughter of Seth Pennington, by whom they had been treasured as examples of her father's manufacture. In the making of blue colour, Pennington succeeded in beating all his competitors. Seth Pennington took into partnership a Mr. Port, but the connection was not of long duration. Having turned his attention to the manufacture

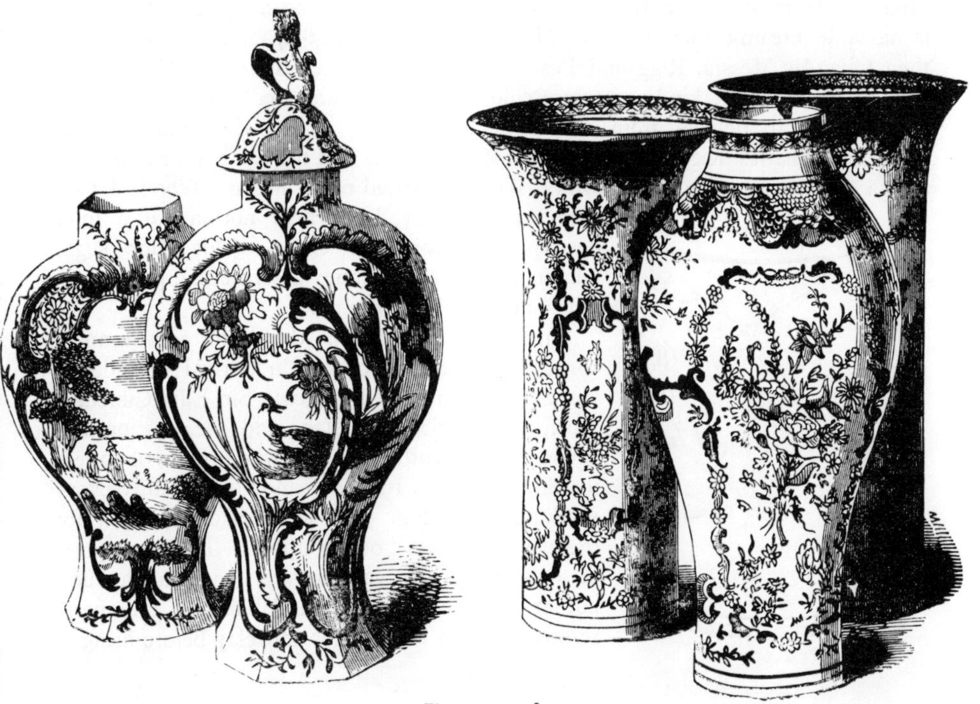

Figs. 914 to 918.

of china, he produced some excellent services, punch-bowls, and other articles in that material. He is said to have used the following marks— **P** **Ᵽ**

Figs. 919 and 920.

Christian.—Philip Christian, another of the famous Liverpool potters, had his works also on Shaw's Brow, but higher up than those of Pennington. They were on the site of what is now known as Islington Terrace. His house was at the corner of Christian Street, which was called after his name. At these works he produced octagonal and other shaped plates of tortoiseshell ware, as well as bowls and other pieces of the same material. He also made the ordinary earthenware of the time. Here, later on, he manufactured china to a considerable extent, and, after the death of Chaffers, is said to have become the leading potter in the place. Mr. Christian is said to have produced in china ware some remarkably good dinner, tea, and coffee services, as well as a number of vases and other ornaments. It is, however, impossible at present to authenticate his productions, so similar are they to those of other makers of the same time and place.

Patrick's Hill Pot-house.—In 1760 the firm of Thomas Deare & Co. took the old Delft ware pottery at Patrick's Hill, known as the "Patrick's Hill Pot-house," where they manufactured "all sorts of the best blue and white earthenware."

The Flint Pot-Works.—About the same time a Mr. Okell carried on "The Flint Pot-Works," which were situated at the upper end of Park Lane, near the Pitch House. Here he made blue and white earthenware, and afterwards the more fashionable cream-coloured ware. Mr. Okell died in 1773-74, and the works were then taken by Messrs. Rigg and Peacock, who immediately advertised their intention of "making all kinds of cream-coloured earthenware, &c." Mr. Rigg was, I have reason to believe, from Newcastle-under-Lyme, and a descendant of the celebrated Charles Rigg, the pipe-maker of that town. In the same year there was also a pot-house, called the "Mould Works," carried on by Messrs. Woods & Co., 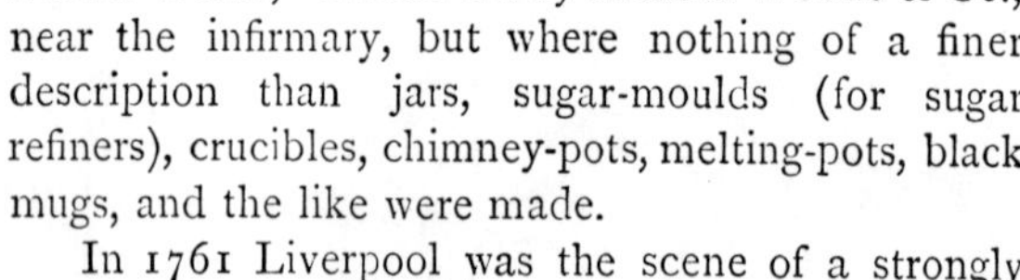 near the infirmary, but where nothing of a finer description than jars, sugar-moulds (for sugar refiners), crucibles, chimney-pots, melting-pots, black mugs, and the like were made.

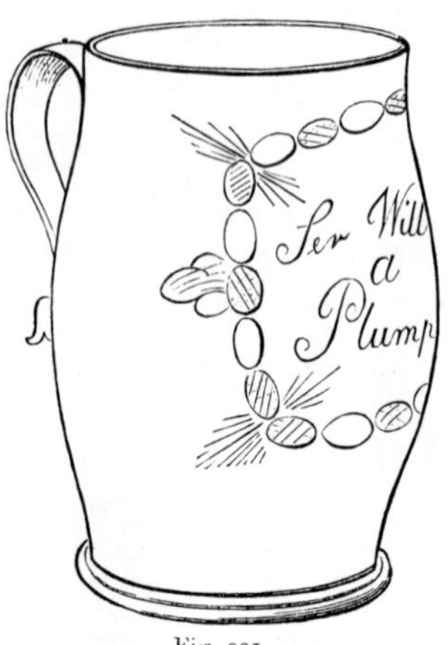

Fig. 921.

In 1761 Liverpool was the scene of a strongly contested election between three rival candidates, viz. Sir William Meredith, Bart., Sir Ellis Cuncliffe, Bart., and Charles Pole, Esq., and the election was carried by the potters, 102 of whom gave plumpers for Sir William. In commemoration of this event drinking-mugs (Fig. 921) were made specially for the "jolly potters" of Liverpool. This example is of common white earthenware, and has a rude border, with the words, "Ser William a Plumper," scratched in, in blue, in the soft clay before firing.

The Herculaneum Pottery, the largest ever established in Liverpool, was founded in 1796, on the site of some old copper-works on the south shore of the river Mersey at Toxteth Park. The pottery had originally been established about the year 1793-94, by Richard Abbey, who took into partnership a Scotchman named Graham. Abbey, who was born at Aintree, and apprenticed to John Sadler as an engraver, produced many very effective groups for mugs, jugs, tiles, &c. Of these, one of his best productions was the well-known group of the "Farmer's Arms." After leaving Sadler's employment, Abbey removed to Glasgow, where he was an engraver at the pot-works, and afterwards served in a similar capacity in France, before he began business in Liverpool. Messrs. Abbey and Graham, who had been successful in their factory at Toxteth Park, sold it to Worthington, Humble, and Holland, and Abbey retired to his native village, where he died in 1801, "at the age of 81, after breaking a blood-vessel whilst singing in Melling Church, where, being a good musician, he used to lead the choir on a Sunday." In the Mayer Museum is a teapot of cream-coloured ware, with black printing, of Richard Abbey's making.

On taking to these works, Messrs. Worthington, Humble, and Holland engaged as foreman and manager Ralph Mansfield, of Burslem, who after some years commenced a small pottery on his own account at Bevington Bush, where he made only the commoner kinds of earthenware. These works ceased at his death. Besides Mansfield, the foreman, the new company engaged about forty "hands," men, women, and children, in Staffordshire, and brought them to Liverpool. As Wedgwood had chosen to call *his* new colony "Etruria," the enterprising company determined on christening *their* colony "Herculaneum," which name they at once adopted, and stamped it on their wares. The buildings acquired from Richard Abbey were considerably enlarged, the arrangements remodelled, new ovens and workshops erected, houses for the workmen built, and then workpeople were brought from Staffordshire. The little colony was peopled in the middle of November, 1796; the works were opened on the 8th of December. The first productions of the Herculaneum works were confined to blue-printed ware, in which dinner, toilet, tea, and coffee services,

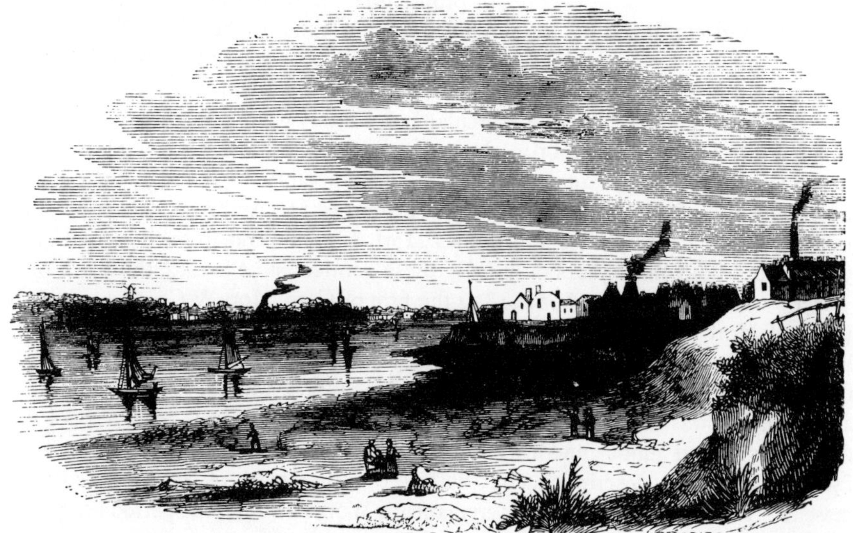

Fig. 922.—Herculaneum Pottery.

punch-bowls, mugs, and jugs were the principal articles made; and cream-coloured ware, which was then so fashionable. At a later date, terra-cotta vases and other articles were produced, as were also biscuit vases, figures, &c.

Of the cream-coloured, or Queen's ware, the examples which have come under my notice are of remarkably fine quality, and are as well and carefully potted as those of any other manufactory, scarcely even excepting Wedgwood's own. In colour they are of a somewhat darker shade than Wedgwood's and Mayer's, and not of so yellow a cast as the Leeds ware. The collector will find some good examples of this ware in the Mayer Museum at Liverpool. The Herculaneum works also produced some remarkably good jugs of a fine hard body, with bas-relief figures, foliage, &c. These pieces, which rival Turner's celebrated jugs, are marked with the name HERCULANEUM in small capitals, impressed.

In terra-cotta, vases of good design, as well as other pieces, were produced. In the possession of Mr. Beard is a remarkably fine pair of covered vases, with boldly-modelled heads of satyrs for handles and festoons on the sides. The vases are black, and the heads and festoons gilt. This fine pair is marked HERCULANEUM. In Mr. Rathbone's collection is a wine-cooler of vine leaves and grapes, of similar design, and of the same reddish colour as some of Wedgwood's terra-cotta coolers. It is marked HERCULANEUM, impressed on the bottom.

In blue printing the Herculaneum Works produced many remarkably good patterns, some services having openwork basket rims, of similar design to those produced by Davenport. One service bore views of the principal towns in England, the names of which were printed in blue on the bottoms of each piece, which mostly bear the impressed mark of HERCULANEUM in large capitals. Batt printing was also practised.

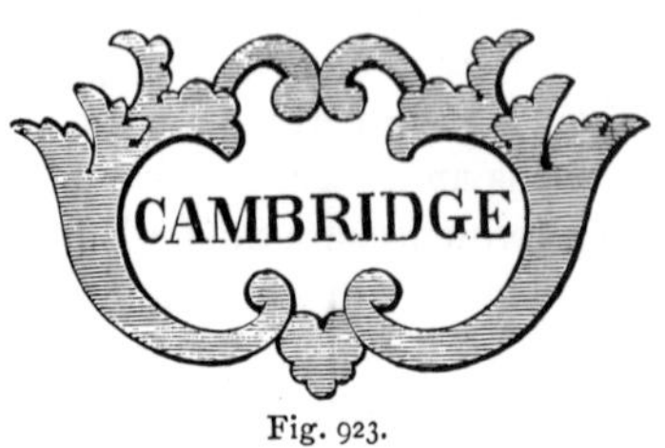

Fig. 923.

In 1800, and again in 1806, the manufactory was considerably increased, as was the number of proprietors. Early in the present century china was made, and continued to be produced to the time of the close of the works; examples are in the Mayer Museum. In 1822 it was ordered by proprietors at a meeting held in that year, that "to give publicity and identity to the china and earthenware manufactured by the Herculaneum Pottery Company, the words 'Herculaneum Pottery' be stamped or marked on some conspicuous part of all china and earthenware made and manufactured at the manufactory." In 1833 the company was dissolved, and the property sold for £25,000 to Mr. Ambrose Lace, who leased the premises to Thomas Case and James Mort, who are said to have carried on the business for about three years only. By these gentlemen, it is said, the mark of the "Liver" was introduced. About 1836 the firm of Case, Mort & Co. was succeeded by that of Mort and Simpson, who continued the manufactory until its close in 1841. During the time the works were carried on by Case, Mort & Co., a fine dinner service, of which a portion is in Mr. Mayer's museum, was made for the corporation of Liverpool. It was blue-printed, and had on each piece the arms of Liverpool carefully engraved and emblazoned. In the same collection is part of another service of somewhat similar description, but with the earlier mark of HERCULANEUM impressed. The marks used at the Herculaneum Works at different periods appear to have been the word

HERCULANEUM   HERCULANEUM

impressed in large capitals. The same in small capitals, also impressed. These have generally a number attached, which, of course, is simply the mark of the work-

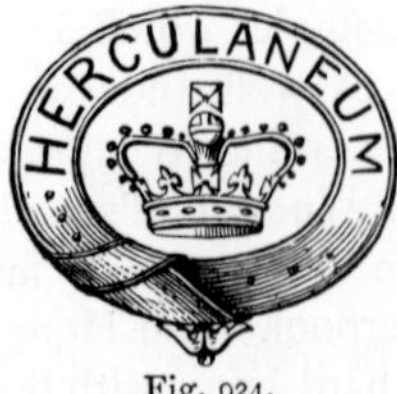

Fig. 924.

Fig. 925.

man or of the pattern. The same name also occasionally occurs in blue printing. A crown, with the word Herculaneum in a curve, above it, impressed. A crown within a garter, bearing the word Herculaneum; impressed. (Figs. 924 and 925.)

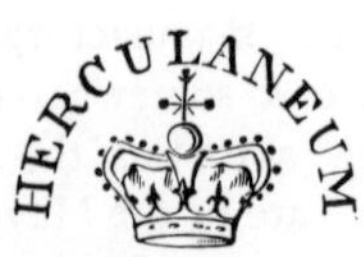

The words in capitals, impressed HERCULANEUM POTTERY.

The crest of the borough of Liverpool, a bird called the *Liver*, or *Lever*, with wings expanded, and bearing in its beak a sprig of the plant liverwort. Of this mark of the crest three varieties are shown on Figs. 926 to 928; they are all impressed in the ware. An anchor, with or without the word LIVERPOOL in a curve, above it (Fig. 929), impressed. Another, and more imposing-looking mark, has the name of the pattern ("PEKIN PALM," for instance) within a wreath of foliage, surmounted with the crest of Liverpool on an heraldic wreath.

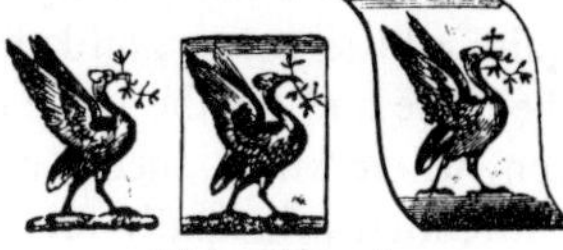

Figs. 926 to 928.

Among the men of eminence who have been connected with the potteries of Liverpool besides those named were William Roscoe, the eminent Art-critic and biographer; Peter Pever Burdett, who also worked for Wedgwood, and who introduced the process of transferring aquatints to pottery and porcelain; Paul Sandby, who assisted other manufactories; and other artists of note. It may also be well to say a word or two on those pieces which more than others are considered to be "Liverpool pottery," and which, indeed, I believe are thought by many collectors to be the only kind ever made there! I allude to the mugs, plates, &c., of cream-coloured ware which are decorated with ships or with flags of different merchants, and signals. These were principally made at the works of Guy Green, in Harrington Street. Some pieces have the engraving of the lighthouse and flags, with the name, "An east view of Liverpool Light House and Signals on Bidston Hill, 1788." The flags are all numbered, and beneath are references, with the owners' names, to forty-three different flags. Another piece with the same date has forty-four flags and owners' names, showing the addition of a new merchant in that year. Others again, without date, show fifty and seventy-five flags, and are therefore interesting as showing the rapid extension of the port. These pieces are very sharply engraved and printed in black, and the flags on some of the pieces are coloured.

LIVERPOOL

Fig. 929.

WARRINGTON.

This pottery was of but short duration, but during the time it was in operation some very good ware was produced. The works were commenced about 1797 or 1798, by James and Fletcher Bolton, who were brothers, and members of the Society of Friends. These gentlemen got their idea of starting an earthenware manufactory at Warrington from the fact that the great bulk of the raw materials from Cornwall, &c., used in the Staffordshire manufactories for the finer kind of wares, was brought by sea to Liverpool, where it was unshipped and sent on again by boats on the Trent and Mersey Canal, and thus passed within a short distance of Warrington. Messrs. Bolton, with this knowledge, and with the further fact before them that the Liverpool potters drove a very successful trade, very shrewdly argued that if the Staffordshire manufacturers could make money, with the longer freightage from Ellesmere, they, at Warrington, with the shorter freightage, might hope for equal success. Soon after the establishment of the works they associated themselves with Joseph Ellis, of Hanley, in Staffordshire, who had been apprenticed to Wedgwood as a *turner*, and was conversant with every branch of the manufacture, and he became managing partner. He is said to have directed his attention in his spare time to the discovery of new colours, glazes, and bodies, and to have been very successful in jasper and enamelled ware. To the manager of some adjoining glass-works he also gave many useful recipes for colours. A number of potters were engaged at Hanley and the other pottery towns, and they, with their wives and children, forming quite a little colony, and their household goods, tools, and everything requisite for their use and for the trade they were engaged in, were brought by canal to Warrington, where kilns, sheds, and other buildings were erected. The goods made were intended principally for the American markets, and the works continued to flourish until 1807, "when the embargo which was laid by the Americans upon all articles of British manufacture, and the subsequent war between Great Britain and America, in 1812, caused the failure, by bankruptcy, of the firm."

In 1802, Mr. Ellis appears to have fallen into a weak state, and his share in the concern was given up on condition of an annuity being granted to himself and his widow and children, so long as the pot-works were carried on. With the failure of the works of course this arrangement ceased. He died at Warrington, and was buried in the old dissenting burial-ground at Hill Cliff, near that town. The potters, with their wives and families, their household goods and tools, and all their other belongings, on the failure of the firm, returned to Staffordshire.

Of the productions of the works, my late friend Dr. Kendrick got together a number of examples, which he deposited in the Warrington Museum. The wares produced were an ordinary quality of white ware; blue and white printed goods, and common painted goods; as well as an inferior description of black-jasper ware, and both gold and silver lustre. Besides these, china is said to have been made to some extent, but of this, although the matter is generally believed, there is, perhaps, some little doubt. Among the examples in the Warrington Museum is a black teapot of a hard but somewhat inferior black ware, ornamented with raised borders and groups of figures—some of which are surface-painted in yellow, red, &c., and the lid is attached by a hinge. Another curious piece is a "tobacco-jar, comprising within itself a drinking-mug and a candlestick," and also a small upright jar, capable of holding exactly half-an-ounce of tea,—the quantity, we are told, which was served out to each visitor to the tea-gardens of that day. The china ware attributed to these works is somewhat curious. It is of a kind of creamy colour, of inferior quality and ornamented with raised borders, &c., and groups of figures in blue. In general appearance it is more like earthenware than porcelain. Among the examples stated by Dr. Kendrick to have been made at Warrington, is a lantern of Delft ware, ornamented with flowers in blue. There are, however, grave doubts as to this having been made in this locality. No mark is known.

Warrington Pottery.—These works, in a locality where older ones have long existed, were established in 1850 in Dallman Lane, by the late John Welsby, who manufactured stoneware, Rockingham and black teapots, coarse red ware, terra-cotta, chimney tops (the construction of the "Dallman Chimney Pot" being very effectual for preventing smoky chimneys), ornamental garden vases, flower-pots, pancheons, &c. On his death in 1863 the works passed into the hands of Mr. Thomas Grace, who, in 1871, removed them to the Winwick Road.

Sutton.

At Sutton, near Warrington, where some potteries for the manufacture of the commoner description of wares are still worked, Dr. Kendrick was of opinion pottery was made in mediæval times. His opinion is founded on the fact of a fragment of a vessel in form of a mounted knight (of somewhat the same character as those already described in this work) being said to be made of Sutton fire-clay. The fragment was found in Winwick churchyard, and is preserved in Warrington Museum. Fragments of similar ware are frequently dug up in the district.

Runcorn.

Old Quay Pottery.—These works were carried on in 1869 by Mr. John Cliff, who in that year removed from the Imperial Pottery, Lambeth, to this place.

Prescot.

The Moss Pottery.—Mr. Thomas Spencer, who last century established Delft ware works at the bottom of Richmond Row, Liverpool, removed them to Prescot, where he founded the "Moss Pottery," and made coarse brown ware from the native clays of the district. At his death the works passed into the hands of his son, who, in turn, was succeeded by his son, Mr. Thomas Spencer. White stoneware was afterwards manufactured to a large extent, but of late years the operations have been principally confined to ordinary stoneware and sanitary ware, one of the most notable features of which are the socket drain-pipes, for which Mr. Spencer holds a patent, dated April 10th, 1848. Sugar-moulds for sugar refiners were at one time a staple production of the Moss Pottery, but these have been superseded by the iron moulds now in general use.

St. Helen's.

Messrs. Case, Mort & Co., of the Herculaneum Works, at Liverpool, had, at one time, a manufactory at St. Helen's, where goods of common quality were produced. Messrs. Doulton, of the Lambeth Pottery, also established a branch manufactory here for drain-pipes, sanitary ware, &c.

Seacombe.

Mr. Goodwin, a potter of Lane End, in Staffordshire, in 1851 established a pottery at Seacombe, on the opposite shore of the Mersey from Liverpool. He brought his workmen from Staffordshire, and fired his first oven in June, 1852. At this pottery, now closed, blue and colour printed ware and parian was made.

Leicester.

Spinney Hill Works.—At these works, belonging to Mr. Fielding Moore, garden vases, flower-baskets, rustic ornaments, fountains, pedestals, flower-pots, and all the usual variety of terra-cotta goods are made; as are also similar articles in ordinary reds and other clays.

Wednesbury.

A pot-work existed here in the seventeenth century. Plot, who wrote in 1686, says "of these (*i.e.* clays from Horsley Heath, &c.) they make divers sorts of vessels at Wednesbury, which they paint with slip, made of a reddish sort of earth gotten at Tipton."

Winchester.

A famous manufactory of tobacco-pipes existed here in the seventeenth century. Ben Jonson notes that they were the best made in his day.

CHAPTER XVI.

DERBY.

Cock-pit Hill.—There is nothing yet known as to the time when these works were first established. It is certain that at a tolerably early period coarse brown ware was made here, of much the same general character as that made at Ticken-hall and by the Tofts, but researches have as yet failed to bring to light any particulars regarding them. There is a positive certainty that the Mayer or Mier family were potters in Derby for more than one generation. A John Mier—an ancestor, probably, of the Mayers or Meers, of Staffordshire—was a pot-maker in 1721. Some vessels bearing his name are extant. One of these, a posset-pot, bears the words IOHN MIER MADE THIS CUP 1721. Another has been described as 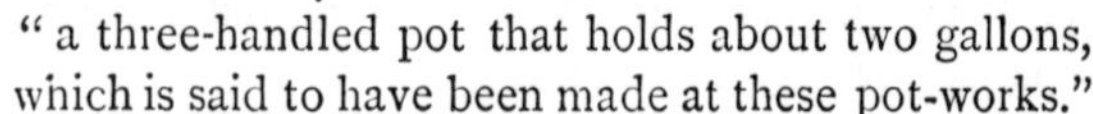 "a three-handled pot that holds about two gallons, which is said to have been made at these pot-works."

It is of coarse brown ware, glazed, and bears the words :—

" Drink be merry and mary
God Bles creae George & Queen ann
John Mier made this cup 1708."

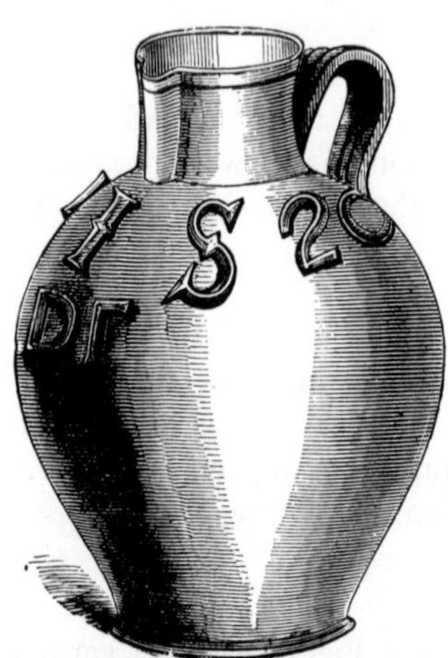

Fig. 930.

Another, a large pitcher in my own possession, traditionally said to have been made in Derby, bears the initials I S between the date 1720 (Fig. 930), and below the I S the letters D Γ, about which it is perhaps scarcely worth hazarding a conjecture. It is 16½ inches in height, and is of dark brown glazed ware. The name best known in connection with these works is that of Heath, and they were carried on by that family for a considerable number of years. How, or when, the works came into the hands of the Heaths remains to be discovered. In 1772, in some very curious and unique MS. "Lists of Gent., &c, in Derby, 1772," in my own possession, occurs in one, under "Cock-pitt Hill," "Mayer Mr. . . . . . . pott merchant," and in another, "Cock-pitt Hill," "Mr. Mayer . . . . . . pott merchant." In the same list, dealers are put down as keeping a "pott shop," while Mayer is returned as a "pott merchant." In this same list "John Heath" is entered as an "Alderman;" and "Mr. Chris. Heath" as a "Comon Council Man."

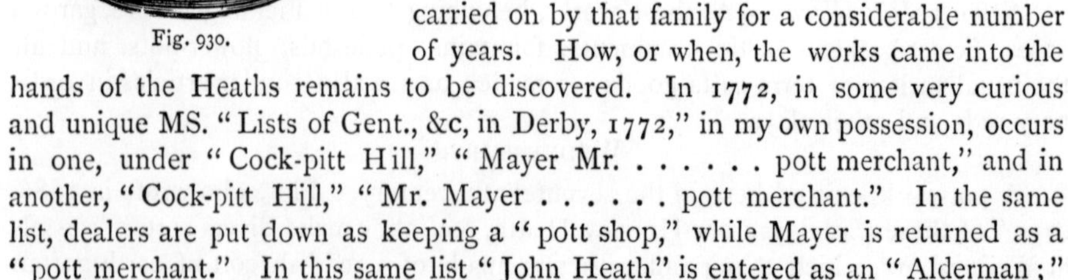

On the 1st of January, 1756, a draft of an agreement was drawn up "between John Heath, of Derby, in the County of Derby, gentleman; Andrew Planche, of ye same place, china maker; and Wm. Duesberry, of Longton, in ye County of Stafford, enameller," by which they became "co-partners together as well in ye art of making English china as also in buying and selling of all sorts of wares belonging to ye art of making china" for ten years, with power on Heath's part to extend for another ten years. In this agreement, the original MS. of which is in my possession, Heath (who, it will be seen, is described as a "gentleman," while the others are respectively described by their trades of "china maker" and "enameller") agrees to pay in £1,000 to the concern, as his share "as stock," "to be used and employ'd in common between them for ye carrying on ye said art of making china wares," for which he was to receive one-third of the profits till the principal sum of £1,000 be paid back.

One of the clauses of this agreement is as follows: "Also it is agreed between ye sd parties to these Presents that ye sd Copartners *shall not at any time hereafter use or follow ye Trade aforesaid or any other Trade whatsoever* during ye sd Term to their private Benefit and advantage." From this it would seem that John Heath could not at that time be carrying on the Cock-pit Hill Works. There is nothing to show that this deed was ever legally executed, and two years later—in 1758—I find him named as one of the proprietors of the Cock-pit Hill Works, along with two partners, "William Butts, gentleman," and "Thomas Rivett, Esquire"—Butts, I presume, being the practical man of the concern. The document in which this appears is in my own possession, and is a commitment of a man named John Lovegrove, one of the workmen "at their pottery in the said Borough of Derby," for running away from his said service.

The works were situated on Cock-pit Hill, at the commencement of Siddal's Lane. The site, still known as the "Pot Yard," is distinctly marked on some of the old maps of Derby, and appears to have stood immediately opposite the "Cock-pit" itself—an octagonal building, with a spire-roof terminated with a vane. Buildings existed on this spot as early as 1610, and at that time probably were employed for the making of the rough ware of the period. In the last century they seemed to have formed three sides of a quadrangle, and to have been of considerable extent. In 1772 it is thus spoken of in "A Short Tour in the Midland Counties." After speaking of the china works, the writer says: "Here is also a pottery, and I was showed an imitation of the Queen's ware, but it does not come up to the original, the produce of Staffordshire."

In 1780, in consequence of the failure of the Heaths (who were bankers and men of property, besides one of them being at one time the partner of Duesbury, and, later, the owners of these pot-works), the Cock-pit Hill Pottery, as proved by advertisement, sold off its stock of goods.

In the same year, 1780, a sale of a "large quantity of earthen and china ware from the Pot Works on Cock-pit Hill, in Derby, being the stock-in-trade of Messrs. John and Christopher Heath, of Derby, Bankrupts," was advertised to take place by auction at the King's Head Inn, Derby. The works were carried on for a year or two by the assignees of Messrs. Heath, but in 1782 "a lease of the Pot Works situate on Cock-pit Hill, in Derby, twelve years after which have yet to come, and unexpired, at Lady Day next, at the yearly rent of £6, and the lessee has a right by the lease to take away the buildings (except only leaving a fence wall), and except a barn that was built on the premises before the lease was granted," was advertised for sale by auction, along with other property, by the Heaths, "at the house of Mr. George Wallis (being the New Inn in Derby), on Tuesday, 12th March." The lease, however, does not seem to have found a purchaser, for in the *Derby Mercury* of March, 1785, another sale is announced "in Messrs. Heath's bankruptcy," in lots, of "the materials of some buildings at the late Pot Works on

Cock-pit Hill, in Derby, consisting of brick, tile, and timber; also some old iron, old lead, Hopton stone, a quantity of deal boards, and some lumber."

Although these works were very extensive, and produced a large quantity of goods of various kinds during the Heaths' time, but few specimens can, unfortunately, be correctly appropriated. This, of course, is owing to the fact that on mark was used by the owners of the works, and therefore, doubtless, scores of examples pass as "early Staffordshire," and as the productions of other places. Three or four well-authenticated pieces, however, may be named. The first is a jug in my own possession. It is of the "imitation of the Queen's ware," alluded to in a previous page, and bears on one side, within a border of foliage, the quaint and characteristic drinking inscription, "One Pot more and then, why what then, why another Pot." On the other side and front, within one continuous border, is a blacksmith busy at his forge, working the immense bellows with his left hand, and holding the iron in the fire with his right; while in front is a youth standing by the anvil waiting, as a "striker;" tools and other things lying about; and the inscription, "Thos. Burton, Winster, 1778." This jug was made at the Cock-pit Hill Works, for Mr. Thomas Burton, a blacksmith, of Winster, whose name it bears, and who is represented at his forge, and from his family passed into my own hands. It is engraved, Fig. 931.

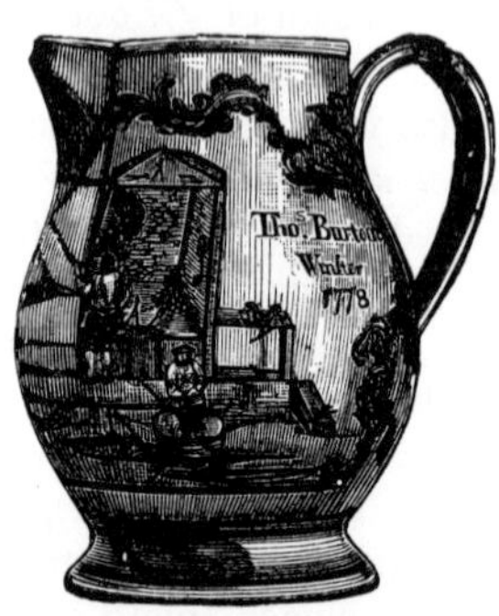

Fig. 931.

Another example belonging to my friend, the late Mr. Lucas, is a teapot, and bears on one side the words, "Harper for ever fow play and now fair dealing" —probably in commemoration of the contested election of 1768, when Sir Henry Harpur was defeated by Godfrey Clarke, Esq.

Derby China.

It is no little thing to say of Derby that the town in which the silk manufacture of England first took its rise—for here the first silk-mill ever built in this kingdom was erected by John Lombe; in which the cotton trade made its first gigantic stride —for here Arkwright and Strutt completed their invention for spinning, and within a few miles erected the first cotton-mill in England; in which the hosiery trade was first brought to perfection—for here Strutt invented his famed "Derby Ribbed Stocking Machine," and carried on his manufacture of those articles; and in which many other branches of manufacture have also had their rise—should likewise have been one of the few places and one of the *first* in which the manufacture of porcelain was matured, and in which the biscuit was first invented. But so it is, and it is no little for Derby to be proud of, that these branches of industry, which are among the most important in the kingdom, should have had their birth, and in their infancy been carefully nurtured, within its boundaries. The stories of Lombe and his silk, Arkwright and Strutt and their cotton, and Jedediah Strutt and his stockings, have been often told, and will bear telling again and again; but that of Duesbury and his china has never been fully told, and it was only by the most laborious research that I was enabled, in 1862, first to tell it, and to show to what an extent the manufacture, under the care of three generations of one family, was carried.

One of the earliest printed notices of the Derby China Works occurs in "A Short Tour in the Midland Counties of England," 1772 and 1774, as follows:—

"The manufacture of porcelain employs, in all, near a hundred men and boys; several of the painters earn a guinea and a half per week. Mr. Duesbury (who has also bought the manufactory at Chelsea) is every day bringing the art nearer to that perfection at which it has arrived in several other countries. Derby porcelain is at present by no means contemptible; figures and other ornaments are among their most capital articles. Here is also a pottery, and I was showed an imitation of the Queen's ware, but it does not come up to the original, the produce of Staffordshire."

In the "Poll Book" of 1775, when Christopher Heath was Mayor of Derby, the following names occur: "Bakewell, Thomas, Derby, Pot-man; Dewsberry, William, Derby, China-man; Hill, Joseph, Derby, China-man; Needham, Henry, Derby, Pipe-maker; Simpson, Moses, Derby, Potter; Strong, Benjamin, Derby, Pipe-maker; Wood, William, London, China-man; Withers, Robert, Rotherham, Potter; Moseley, Thomas, Derby, Potter."

Bray, in 1777, says, speaking of Derby: "The china manufactory is not less worthy of notice. Under the care of Mr. Duesberry it does honour to this country. . . . . He has brought the gold and blue to a degree of beauty never before obtained in England, and the drawing and colouring of the flowers are truly elegant." In 1777 Dr. Johnson visited the Derby China Works, and the visit is pleasantly spoken of by Boswell. Pilkington, in 1789, says: "About forty years ago the manufacture of porcelain was begun by the late Mr. Duesbury. This ingenious artist brought it to such perfection as, in some respects, to equal the best foreign china. The ornamental part of the business was at first almost solely attended to. . . . . . At this work a very rich and elegant dessert service, consisting of one hundred and twenty pieces, was lately made for his Royal Highness the Prince of Wales." William Hutton, the historian of his native town and of Birmingham, says, in 1791: "Porcelain began about the year 1750. There is only one manufactory, which employs about seventy people. The clay is not of equal fineness with the foreign, but the workmanship exceeds it. The arts of drawing and engraving have much improved within these last thirty years. The improvements of the porcelain have kept pace with these. They adhere to nature in their designs, to which the Chinese have not attained. A dessert service of one hundred and twenty pieces was recently fabricated here for the Prince of Wales. The spot upon which this elegant building stands, which is internally replete with taste and utility, was once the freehold of my family. It cost £35, but the purchaser, my grandfather's brother, being unable to raise more than £28, mortgaged it for £7. Infirmity, age, and poverty obliged him to neglect the interest, when, in 1743, it fell into the hands of my father as heir-at-law, who, being neither able nor anxious to redeem it, conveyed away his right to the mortgagee for a guinea."

The manufactory was situated on the Nottingham Road, near St. Mary's Bridge, in a locality then named Suthrick, or Southwark. On its site, in 1845-46, the Roman Catholic nunnery of St. Marie, designed by Pugin, was erected, but this has now, like the China Works, become "a thing of the past"—the nunnery having been purchased by the Midland Railway Company, and taken down in 1863. Hutton's remark as to this site being his patrimony is very curious, and adds an increased interest to the locality. The very premises he speaks of were those first occupied for the making of porcelain, and, curiously enough, they were opposite to Lombe's silk-mill, from which they were divided by the road and the broad expanse of water of the river Derwent.

It is generally believed that in 1750, perhaps a little earlier, the manufacture of china first sprang into existence in Derby—about a year or so before the works at Worcester were established; and there is a tradition that the first maker was a Frenchman, who lived in a small house in Lodge Lane, and who modelled and made small articles in china, principally animals—cats, dogs, lambs, sheep, &c.—which he fired in a pipe-maker's oven in the neighbourhood, belonging to a man named Woodward. There were, at this time, as I have shown, some pot-works on Cock-pit Hill, which afterwards belonged to Alderman Heath, a banker; and the productions of this French refugee, or rather son of a French refugee, having attracted notice, an arrangement was made between him and Heath and Duesbury, by which the manufacture of porcelain was to be carried on jointly. This man's name, to whom I take it belongs the absolute honour of commencing the Derby China Works, was Andrew Planché, and I am enabled to arrive at this conclusion by means of the original draft of a deed (alluded to on page 331) in my own possession, by which a partnership for ten years was entered into by the three already named. In this arrangement I apprehend Planché found the knowledge of mixing bodies and glazes, Heath the money (£1,000), and Duesbury the will, ability, and skill, to carry out the scheme. These articles of agreement are headed as follows:—"ARTICLES OF AGREEMENT between John Heath of Derby in the County of Derby Gentleman, Andrew Planche of ye same Place China Maker & Wm Duesberry of Longton in ye County of Stafford Enamellor. Made and enter'd into the 1st of Jany 1756." I have printed this important document in full in my first edition.

The paper is not signed, and as in no instance which has come under my notice the name of Planché again appears, and as I can only trace the firm as that of "Duesbury and Heath," I fear one is driven to the inference that the usual fate of clever men awaited Andrew Planché, and that when his knowledge was fully imparted, he was, from some cause or other, discarded by those who had taken him in hand. At all events, this is the only instance in which his name appears in any of the papers connected with the works which I have examined. Of Planché, however, whom I was first to discover and note in 1862, but who, despite all I had written, was spoken of by Mr. A. Wallis, eight years later, as "an apocryphal French refugee," I am enabled to give some additional particulars.

Andrew Planché was one of the five sons of Paul Planché, a French refugee, by his first wife, Marie Anne Fournier, also a refugee, whom he married in 1723. Andrew was born on the 14th, and baptised on the 24th, of March, 1727-28, and his youngest brother was Jacques Planché (born in 1734), who married his cousin (the only daughter of Antoine Planché by his wife Mary, daughter of Herr Abraham Thomas and his wife Catherine), and was father of my old and valued friend, the late J. R. Planché, F.S.A., Somerset Herald, the well-known dramatist and antiquary. This fact I brought to his knowledge in 1862, and again when he was writing his interesting "Recollections," in which he has embodied some of the information I supplied him with. Through the re-marriage of their father, the two boys, Andrew and Jacques, had early to shift for themselves. The latter made his way to Geneva, where he learned the business of watch-making, and the former, I believe, went into Saxony, and there learned the art of making porcelain at Dresden. How he came to Derby is at present a mystery, but that he was there, at all events as early as, if not earlier than, 1751, is proved by the birth of one of his sons. His children, by "Sarah his wife" (copies of whose registers I have given in the first edition) were Paul Edmund, baptised September 21st, 1751; James, baptised October 12th, 1754, and buried December 10th in the same year; and William, baptised July 3rd, 1756. In 1751 he would be 23 years of age, and was living in the parish of St. Alkmund, in Derby.

That Andrew Planché was not very strict in his morals is revealed by the parish register, which shows that in 1756 he had two sons baptised within four months of each other, the first March 4 (James) by a young woman named Margaret Burroughs, and the second July 3 (William) by his wife. This was in the very year, 1756, in which the articles of agreement were drawn up. What became of Planché after he left Derby is not known. He appears to have been a very erratic individual and his whereabouts uncertain. He was living at Bath at the ripe age of 76 in 1804, and died there soon afterwards. At all events, I have proof that he was in Derby eight years—how much longer I know not—and I have also, as will be seen, indisputable proof that William Duesbury had no connection with Derby till 1755-56, the date of the deed I have printed above.

When Duesbury, whether in conjunction with Planché and Heath or not, commenced business, it appears to have been in the small premises which had not long before been relinquished for a guinea by the father of William Hutton; and in them was thus commenced, in a very small way, that manufacture of porcelain which afterwards grew to so immense an extent. In 1756 the draft of agreement was drawn up, and the ware made at the manufactory must soon have found a ready sale, for in the course of a very few years Mr. Duesbury was carrying on a good trade, had a London house for the sale of his productions, and became a thriving and well-to-do man.

William Duesbury was of Longton Hall, in the county of Stafford, and was the son of William Duesbury, currier, of Cannock, in the same county, who in 1755, as evidenced by the original duly stamped and attested deed in my possession, made over to him his household furniture, leather, implements of trade, and other effects, on condition that he should find him "during the term of his natural life good and sufficient meat, drink, washing, and lodging, wearing apparel, and all other necessaries whatsoever." (See first edition for copies of this and other deeds.)

I next find William Duesbury, the enameller, of Longton, entering into partnership with Heath and Planché on the 1st January in the year following his executing this deed for the maintenance of his father; and entries in the family Bible prove that at this time he removed to Derby, to carry on his newly-acquired business "in ye art of making English china, as also in buying and selling of all sorts of wares belonging to ye art of making china." The partnership deed, bearing date the 1st of January, 1756, shows that the negotiations must have been made in the previous year, 1755, and as the deed of gift from his father is dated September 27th of that year, it is evident that the one was consequent on the other, and that the arrangement with his father was the result of his determination to come to Derby. The father lived until 1768, and died and was buried in Derby. In the parish register is the entry, "1768. Buried, Mr. Duesbrie, March 17."

William Duesbury was born on the 7th of September, 1725, and married Sarah James, of Shrewsbury (who was born on the 12th of August, 1724). In 1755 he was residing at Longton, as an enameller on china ware, &c., and in 1756 removed to Derby to carry on the porcelain works there. By his wife Sarah, who died on the 14th of September, 1780, and was buried at St. Alkmund's Church, Derby, he had several children. Mr. Duesbury himself, after a long and useful life, in the course of which he not only established the Derby China Works, but became the purchaser of those of Chelsea, Bow, Vauxhall, and Kentish Town, died at Derby, and was buried at St. Alkmund's Church, in that town, on the 2nd of November, 1786.

William Duesbury, son and successor of the last named, was born at Derby, and baptised at St. Alkmund's Church there, March 1, 1763. On the 4th of January, 1787, he married Elizabeth, daughter of William Edwards, Esq., solicitor, of Derby, the lady having three days before completed her twentieth year. By her he had issue three sons—William, who succeeded him; Nathaniel, who died in 1809, aged 19; and Frederick, who became an eminent physician in London—and two daughters, viz. Sarah, who remained unmarried, and died in 1875; and Anne Elizabeth, who became the wife of Francis Jessop, Esq., solicitor, of Derby. So far it has been necessary to summarise this bit of family genealogy, but the remainder will form a part of the thread of the history of the works.

The manufacture of china under the first William Duesbury must have rapidly risen into eminence, for in 1763, in an account of "goods sent to London," no less than forty-two large boxes appear at one time to have been dispatched to the metropolis, and the proceeds, I presume, of the sale of a part of them, on the 2nd of May, in that year, amounted to £666 17s. 6d. It is interesting to be enabled to say of what varieties of goods the consignment to London consisted, and I therefore give some of the items as follows to show the absurdity of the remark of the writer to whom I have before alluded, that "We doubt very much whether the higher sorts of fine porcelain (figures, vases, &c.) were made upon the Nottingham Road until the purchase of the Chelsea Works in 1769 and the commencement of what is called the Chelsea-Derby period, which lasted until 1785 or 1786." "Box No. 41 contained 8 Large Flower Jarrs, at 21s.; 3 Large Ink Stands, at 42s.; 1 Small ditto, at 24s.; 4 Large Britanias, at 36s.; 6 Second-sized Huzzars, at 12s.; 4 Large Pidgeons, at 7s.; 12 Small Rabbets, at 2s.; 12 Chickens, at 2s.; 16 Small Baskets, at 2s. 6d. Box No. 31—4 Large Quarters, at 40s.; 4 Shakespeares, at 42s.; 6 Miltons, at 42s.; 24 Bucks, on Pedestals, at 2s. 6d. Box No. 20—4 Large Quarters, at 40s.; 2 Jupiters, at 68s.; 2 Junos; 5 Ledas, at 36s.; 1 Europa, at 36s.; 2 Bird-catchers, at 10s. 6d.; 12 Sixth-sized Solid Baskets; 18 Second-sized Boys, at 1s. 6d. Box No. 11—24 Enammelled, round, fourth-size, open-worked Baskets; 12 blue ditto; 12 Open-worked Spectacle Baskets; 9 Second-size Sage-leaf Boats." There were also, of various sizes, blue fluted boats, Mosaic boats, sage-leaf boats, potting pots, caudle cups, blue strawberry pots, fig-leaf sauce boats, octagon fruit plates, vine-leaf plates, coffee cups, flower vases, standing sheep, feeding sheep, cats, sunflower blows, pedestals, honeycomb jars, coffee pots, blue guglets and basins to ditto; butter tubs, Chelsea jars, teapots, honeycomb pots, figures of Mars and Minerva, sets of the Four Elements, Four Seasons, Spanish shepherds, Neptune, the Muses, bucks, tumblers, roses, Jupiter, Diana, boys, garland shepherd, Spaniards, Chelsea-pattern candlesticks, Dresden ditto, jars and beakers, polyanthus pots, &c. &c.

The mark used in the earliest days of the works is not certain, but I believe, and I have reason for that belief, that it was simply the letter *D*, which would stand either for "Duesbury" or for "Derby"; probably in gold. The figures and groups, too, were numbered and registered for reproduction.

On the 17th of August, 1769, Mr. Duesbury arranged for the purchase of the Chelsea China Works, their purchase being completed on the 5th of February, 1770, when a payment of £400, in part of the purchase-money, was made by him, who thus, as the proprietor of the Derby and the Chelsea Works, became the largest manufacturer in the kingdom. Having already given the history of the Chelsea Works in the earlier part of this volume, it is only necessary here to repeat the fact I was the first to discover and make public, that Mr. Duesbury purchased "the

Chelsea Porcelain Manufactory, and its appurtenances and lease thereof," on the 5th of February, 1770, and that it was covenanted to be assigned over to him on or before the 8th of that month; the date of the arrangement to purchase being August 17th, 1769. For some few years, then, Mr. Duesbury carried on both establishments, and subsequently removed the models and some of the workmen to Derby, where also he removed models, &c., from Bow, which had likewise come into his possession. The purchase of the Chelsea Works soon entailed upon him the commencement of some heavy law proceedings, which arose from the attempt at recovery of a quantity of goods claimed by him as a part of his purchase, being goods made by Spremont, and of his material, but which were afterwards sold, it was said, wrongfully, by Francis Thomas, to a person named Burnsall. The action was commenced in 1770, and continued for several years. In 1771 Mr. Spremont, the old proprietor of the Chelsea Works, died.

Before Mr. Duesbury purchased the Chelsea works the mark of that manufactory was an anchor, (Fig. 932.) and to this Mr. Duesbury added the letter *D*; and the mark now known as distinguishing the "Derby Chelsea" ware was thus— (Fig. 933.) generally in gold. Examples of this period are of comparative rarity, and are eagerly sought after by collectors.

In June, 1773, Mr. Duesbury took the lease of premises (late the Castle Tavern) in Bedford Street, Covent Garden, for a warehouse for his Derby and Chelsea ware, and here, with William Wood as his agent (succeeded by J. Lygo), he issued a printed "List of the principal additions made this year to the new invented Groups, Jars, Vases, Urns, Beakers, Cups, Chalices, &c., of Mr. Duesbury's Derby and Chelsea Manufactory of Porcelaines, Biscuits, and China Ware, both Ornamental and Useful," in which 123 articles were enumerated. The following will show their beautiful and elaborate nature, and the amount of artistic skill they exhibited:—

"1. Their present majesties, the king and queen, and royal family, in three grouped pieces of biscuit. The centre piece represents the king in a Vandyke dress, on a blue and gold basement, supported by four lions leaning on an altar richly ornamented in blue and gold, with hanging trophies of the polite arts and sciences. The crown, *munde*, and sceptre reposing on a cushion of crimson, embroidered, fringed, and tapelled in gold. 14 inches.

"42. A large *beaker*, sky-blue ground spotted in white; two dolphins, lion-footed, standing on white goats' heads, form the two anses in crimson and white edged with gold, the mouth of the beaker and the top of the vase are furrowed with twisted crenures in white and gold; the zone of the top is adorned with golden lions, turned toward white and gold marks; the rim of the cup part is foliated and crenulated friese, white and gold, with detached patera, the pediment striped with gold in alternate triangles, the foot covered with gilt leaves; the pedestal in white and gold has four white sphinxes for angular supporters, over which runs a gold festoon fixed to the surbase; the whole, with the pedestal, 20 inches.

"105. A white *gallon cask*, with gold-edged hoops, adorned with four trophies of music, emblems of love, in chiaro-oscuro, surmounted by a young coloured Bacchus, sitting on the bung tasting a grape, of which he holds a basket full between his legs, and a cup in his left hand, the barrel is made to turn round on a pivot fixed in an *ormolu* pediment, a satyr's mask holds an *ormolu* cock in his mouth, which opens and shuts by a spring. 18 inches."

The works at Chelsea (of which the "Weekly Bills" of wages &c., are in my possession, and are printed in the first edition) were not finally discontinued until

1784, when they were destroyed by Mr. Duesbury, the kilns and every part of the works pulled down, and what was available sent down to Derby. The removal of the kilns, and the work of demolition, was entrusted to an old and faithful servant, Robert Boyer, the painter, &c.; and when his work was done he removed to Derby at twenty-five shillings per week in place of a guinea, with house-rent free, and fire as heretofore. It is also worthy of remark that Mr. Duesbury purchased the Bow business, and owned the pottery at Pedlar's Acre, at Lambeth, the rents of which he assigned in 1781.

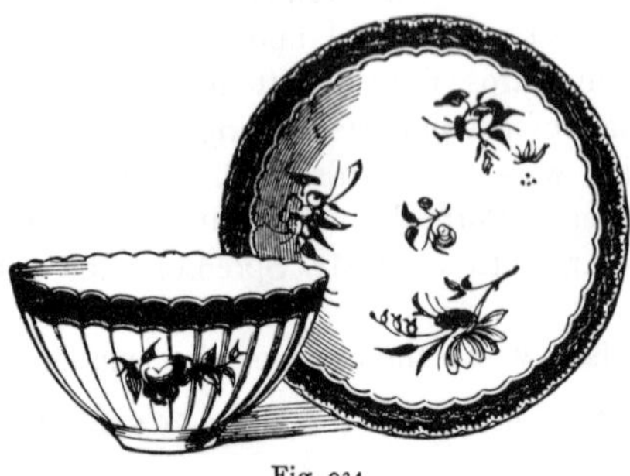

Fig. 934.

Periodical sales of stock were held in London by Mr. Duesbury, and judging by the catalogues of "Sales by Auction" by Messrs. Christie and Ansell, of Pall Mall, and "Sales by Candle," by Mr. Hunter, the articles sent up for the purpose were excellent examples of the manufacture, and just such as were likely to be sought after by the traders—the "chinamen" of London. I possess the priced catalogues of several years' sales, from which I have already printed voluminous extracts in my first edition, to which I refer collectors.

A few months before Mr. Duesbury's death—which, as I have stated, took place in November, 1786—he took his eldest son William into partnership, and the business was carried on under the style of "William Duesbury and Son." It thus appears upon the title-pages of the sale catalogue of 22nd September in that year, but is altered back to "Mr. William Duesbury" alone in that for 21st December following. For some years before the death of his father the younger William Duesbury had

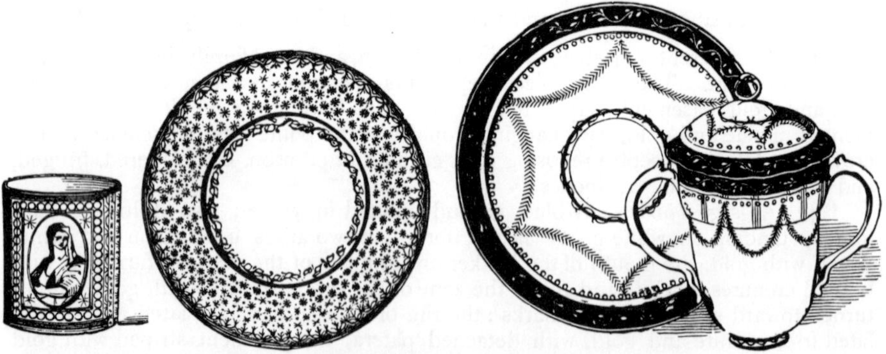

Figs. 935 to 938.—From the Museum of Practical Geology.

devoted himself untiringly to the advancement of the works. The connection which had been previously formed with the principal families, from royalty downwards, spread and increased, and among the hundreds of names of purchasers on the sale-sheets and other papers, I came across, at random, those of the King, the Queen, the Prince of Wales (afterwards George IV.), who was a large customer for dessert, tea, coffee, and other services; the Duchess of Devonshire, William Pitt, Sir Hugh Pallisser, the Margravine of Anspach, the Duke of Northumberland, Lord Howe, and indeed almost every title then in the peerage. Besides this, several ladies of distinction painted groups of flowers and other pictures on porcelain, supplied to them for the purpose by Mr. Duesbury, who afterwards fired and finished them for their own special use. Of these ladies, Lady Margaret Fordyce, Lady Plymouth, and Lady Aubrey executed some beautiful drawings, which probably still remain in their families. Lord Lonsdale also had twenty-four plates painted with landscapes in Cumberland, from his own sketches, and many other noblemen and gentlemen did the same; many sets of china being painted with views of different parts of the estates of those for whom they were manufactured. Bronze figures of horses—probably originally belonging to the famous Duke of Newcastle, whose work on Horsemanship is the finest ever produced—were lent to Mr. Duesbury from Welbeck Abbey; and Lady Spencer also sent some choice moulds for working from. Altogether the Derby works, during the latter part of the first Mr. Duesbury's time, and during the life of his son, were, as I have said, the most successful, the best conducted, and the most fashionable establishment of the kind in the kingdom.

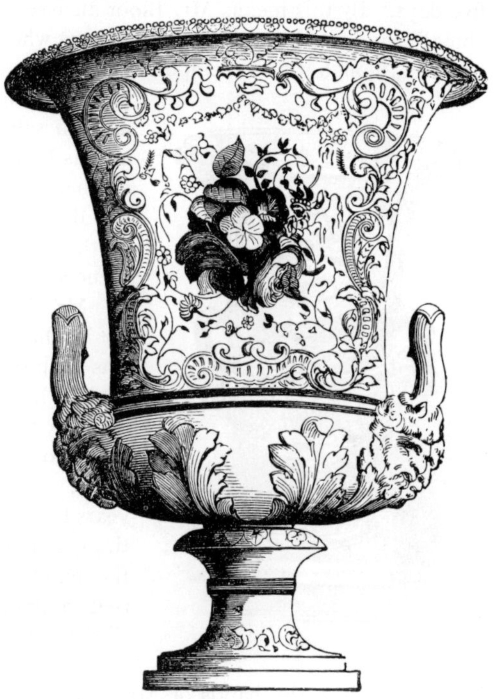

Fig. 939.—"King's Vase," Museum of Practical Geology.

Constant application to business, and the wear and tear of the brain from incessant anxieties, about 1795 made such fearful inroads on the health of Mr. Duesbury, that he was induced by his friends to take into partnership a Mr. Michael Kean, a clever miniature painter, an Irishman by birth, who brought his talents and skill in designing and drawing to bear on the works. His connection, however, became a source of still greater anxiety to Mr. Duesbury, whose mind gradually gave way under his load of care. In 1796 Mr. Duesbury died, and not long afterwards Mr. Kean (who had for a time the management of the business for the widow and her young family) married the widow, but ere long, from reasons into which it is needless to enter, withdrew hastily from the concern, and the works were then continued for, and afterwards by, the third William Duesbury. Mrs. Duesbury, by her second marriage (with Michael Kean) had a family of five children. She died in 1829, after having passed a not altogether happy life. This third William Duesbury (grandson of the founder of the works) was the eldest son of William Duesbury by his wife Elizabeth Edwards. He was born in 1787, and on the 26th September, 1808, married Annabella, daughter of William E. Sheffield, Esq., of the Polygon, Somers Town, London, and for a time the concern was carried on under the firm of "Duesbury and Sheffield." In 1815 Mr. Duesbury leased the premises to Robert Bloor, who had been a clerk to his father, and had carried on the business during his minority, and the entire concern ultimately passed into his hands, and for the first few years was carried on with judgment and skill.

Before Mr. Bloor's time it had been the constant plan of the Duesburys—so worthily tenacious were they of their reputation and of keeping up the high and unblemished character of their works—to allow none but *perfect* goods to leave their premises, and, no matter how costly the article or how trivial the fault (frequently so trivial as to be only perceptible to the most practised eye), all goods which were not perfect were stowed away in rooms in the factory, and thus accumulated to an enormous extent. When Bloor took the concern this stock of seconds goods became to him an almost exhaustless mine of wealth. Having to pay the purchase-money by instalments, he found the easiest method of doing so was to finish up these goods, take them to different large towns, and there sell them by auction, and also to have sales at the manufactory. One of these sales, in 1822, continued twenty-five days. By this means Mr. Bloor amassed large sums of money, as the "Derby china" found ready and liberal purchasers wherever it was thus offered. This system, however, though it had a temporary good, produced a lasting evil. The temptation to produce large quantities of goods specially for auction sale was so great as not to be withstood, and as by this means they were disposed of "with all their imperfections thick upon them," less care was devoted to their manufacture, and the decline of the works, principally from this cause, commenced.

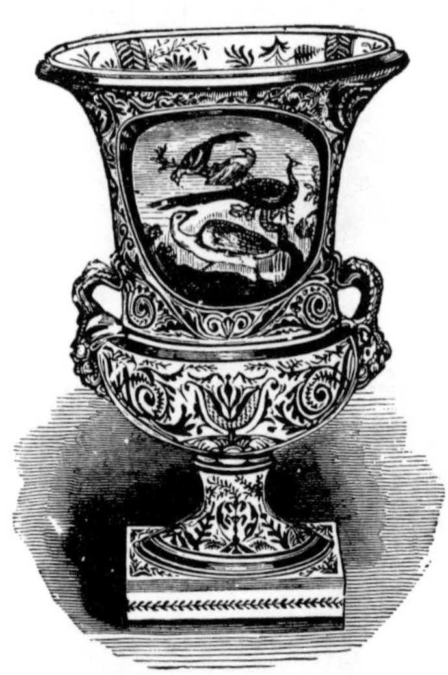

Fig. 940.

Mr. Robert Bloor was assisted in his works by his brother Joseph, by whom the "mixing" was mainly done, and from 1828, when Robert Bloor's health began to fail, they were carried on for him by a manager named Thomason. The two brothers died within a short time of each other. Robert, who had lost his mind for many years before his decease, died in 1845, and Joseph the year following. The works then passed into the hands of Mr. Thomas Clarke, who had married a grand-daughter of Robert Bloor's, who discontinued them, and sold most of the models, &c., to the Staffordshire manufacturers—the greater bulk going into the hands of Mr. Boyle, a manufacturer, of Fenton, who was son of John Boyle, and for a short time before his death a partner with the Wedgwoods. The final dissolution of the old works took place in 1848, when a number of the workmen naturally migrated into Staffordshire and Worcestershire.

At this time, however, several of the old hands—actuated by the laudable desire of securing the continuance of a business which for a century had been so successfully carried on, and of continuing it as one of the trades of their native town—"clubbed together" and commenced business on their own account. They each and all threw into the common stock what knowledge, experience, money, and tools, &c., they possessed, took premises in King Street (on the site of old St. Helen's Nunnery), and under the name of "Locker & Co." commenced making "Derby china," and adopted, very properly, a distinctive mark, which shows this epoch in the works.

Mr. Locker (who was a native of Blackfordby, and had been clerk and warehouseman at the old works in the latter part of their existence) died in 1859, and the works were next conducted under the style of "Stevenson & Co.," and "Stevenson,

Sharp, & Co.," till the death of Mr. Stevenson, when the style was changed to that of "Hancock & Co.," and the works are now continued by Mr. Samson Hancock, and although they do not rival the glory of the old works, at least do credit to the town of Derby, in which they are situated. Some of the productions are highly creditable to the taste and skill of the men, and show that "ye art of making English china," imparted to William Duesbury in 1756, is not forgotten, but remains with his successors to the present day.

One of the last large services made by Bloor was a magnificent dessert made for her present Majesty, and some large additions to that set, and pieces for replacing, have been from time to time made by the present owners of the works, which are still, therefore, as fully entitled to the name of "Royal" works as any of their predecessors.

Having now gone briefly through the HISTORY of the works, it only remains to speak of the artists employed, and of one branch of the manufacture, that of "biscuit," which requires more than a passing notice. This material was a discovery of, and quite peculiar to, the Derby Works, and to it the beautiful material "Parian" owes its origin. One of the Derby workmen having engaged himself to Mr. Copeland, was trying experiments to recover the secret of the biscuit composition, when instead of it he accidentally produced that which has been named "Parian," and in which all the exquisitely beautiful figures and groups that characterise their and other equally admirable productions have since, with modifications and improvements, been worked. It is pleasant thus to know, that although the art of making Derby biscuit figures has been discontinued, the Parian has sprung from it, and was first produced by a Derby man. Nothing could exceed the sharpness and beauty of the biscuit figures as produced in the best days of the Derby Works, and some examples, for delicacy and fineness of modelling and for sharpness of touch, have never in any ceramic material been surpassed, or scarcely equalled.

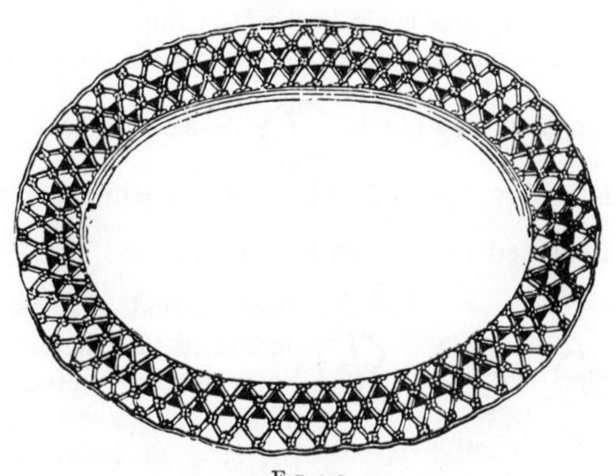
Fig. 941.

Transfer printing on china appears to have been introduced at Derby in 1764—some years before Wedgwood printed his own ware, but while he was in the habit of sending it off to Liverpool to be printed by Sadler and Green. The process, however, did not obtain much favour at Derby, and Mr. Duesbury evidently found it better and more satisfactory to adhere to hand-work in all his goods. The person who introduced the process, and whom he engaged to carry it on, was Richard Holdship, of Worcester, who by deed covenanted, for the sum of £100 paid down and a yearly sum of £30 so long as the works continued on his process, to impart in writing to Messrs. Duesbury and Heath his secret process for making china according to the proofs already made by him at the Derby Works; to supply them with all sufficient quantities of soapy rock at fair prices; and to print all the china or porcelain ware which might have occasion to be printed. The engagement with Holdship lasted, at all events, many years, but during that time the printing evidently was not much followed, as in his letters to his employers he is constantly complaining of having no work for his presses, and in having no goods made according to his process. He had an assistant named William Underwood, and in one of his letters he values his press at ten guineas in cash, and his copper-plates at a large amount, while he says, "for his process for Printing Enamell and Blew he hath been offered several Hundred Pounds." His stock of enamel colours, 151 lbs. in weight, he offers to sell for £35.

Fruit-dishes and other articles were at one time made with open-work reticulated rims or sides; a raised "Dresden" flower being placed on each intersection in much the same manner as was characteristic of one period of Worcester work (Fig. 941). These were made both in blue and white, and in enamel; they are somewhat scarce.

In 1789 Mr. Duesbury endeavoured to introduce batt-printing into his manufactory, and for that purpose prevailed on his former assistant, J. Hancock, then in Staffordshire, to inquire into and describe to him the process. I must not omit to say that earthenware, called the "Cream Ware," very closely resembling Wedgwood's celebrated "Queen's Ware," was made at Derby for a short time, and was of great beauty. Specimens of this ware are of great rarity.

In 1790 Mr. Duesbury invented a machine for exhibiting the contraction of earthen bodies when in the fire; this he had constructed by Spooner and Son.

The marks used at the Derby China Works may be thus briefly summarised. The simple writing letter 𝒟 is said to have been the first mark used by William Duesbury. The 𝒟, which stands either as the initial of Derby or of Duesbury, conjoined with the anchor of Chelsea ⚓ is the distinctive mark of the Chelsea-Derby period—the period when William Duesbury, who had purchased the Chelsea works, carried on both the manufactories, and, later, produced goods at Derby from the Chelsea moulds. Two or three varieties of this mark, according to the taste or whim of the workmen, occur (see Figs. 942, 943, and 944).

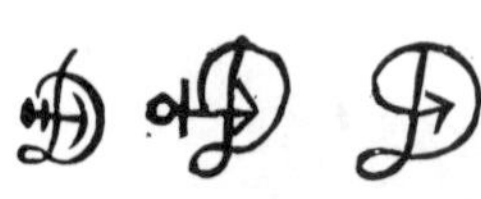

Figs. 942 to 944.

Two other marks, the one a 𝒟 surmounted by a crown, and the other an anchor, similarly surmounted, are said to have denoted respectively the articles made at this period at Derby and Chelsea (Figs. 945 to 947). Now and then the first of these is met with in connection with the anchor (Fig. 949).

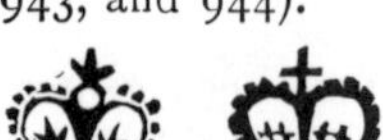

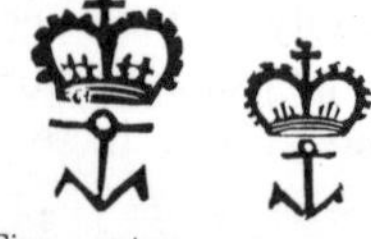

Figs. 945 to 947.

The most usual mark is that of the letter D, with crossed swords, dots, and crown, of which several varieties occur. Sometimes the initial is the writing letter

Figs. 948 to 954.

𝒟, and sometimes a Roman capital D, and the crown also varies according to the caprice of the painter. A variety of this, in which a 𝒟 and a ℋ are conjoined (Fig. 955), denotes the later period when the works were carried on by Duesbury and Kean. It was, however, only very sparsely used. For some years, at all events up to about 1825 or 1830, Mr. Bloor continued to use the old mark of the Duesburys—the crown, cross daggers with dots, and D beneath—but about that period discontinued it, and adopted a mark with his own name (Fig. 956). It is well to note, that down to the discontinuance of the old mark it had invariably been done with the pencil, *by hand*, but that those adopted by Mr. Bloor were *printed* ones. The first printed mark I believe to be

Fig. 955.

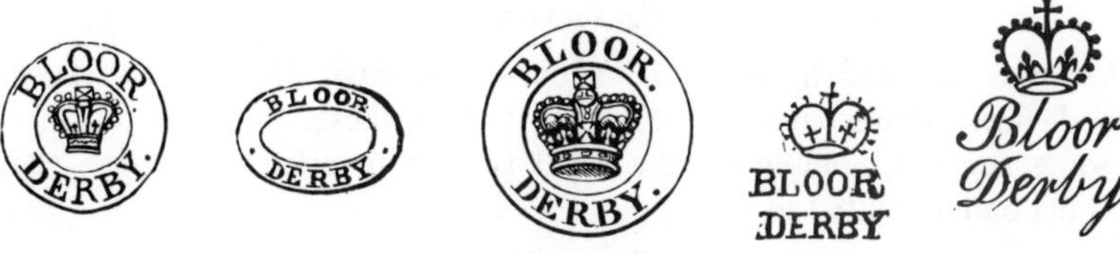

Figs. 956 to 960.

Fig. 956, and somewhat later the same was used, but slightly larger in size (Fig. 958). Other marks are shown on the engravings. Figs. 961 and 962 have an old English 𝔇

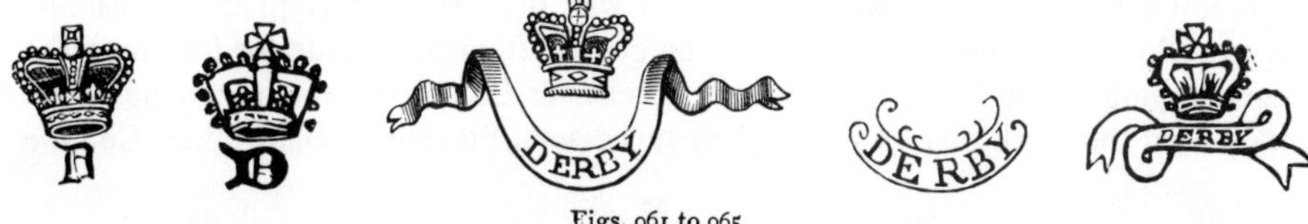

Figs. 961 to 965.

surmounted by a crown; another (Fig. 963) a crown, with a riband bearing the word DERBY in Roman capitals beneath it.

Other marks, said to have been for one purpose or other—of course as imitations—used at Derby, are the following:—

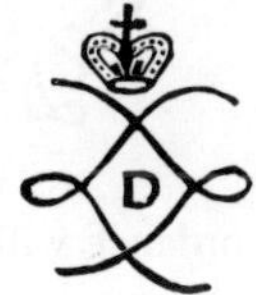

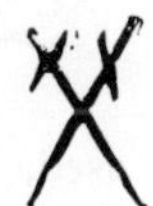
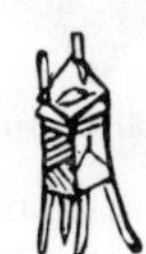
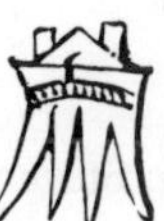
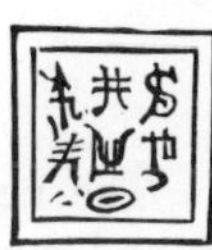

Figs. 966 to 970.

In my own possession is a design, in pencil, by Mr. Duesbury, by his own hand, for a mark, which I engrave on Fig. 970, although I believe it was never adopted. At all events I have failed in discovering a single specimen so marked. Mrs. Palliser engraves a mark of a crown between the words DUESBURY, DERBY; another has the cross daggers added, and another has the word *Derby* in writing letters. This, she states, occurs "in black on a biscuit statuette;" but I fear the mark has been added at a later date. Another mark, which has been described has the cross daggers and crown with the words "DUESBURY, DERBY," in an oval form, Fig. 975. It may be well, *en passant*, to notice a mark which appears on one of the copper-plates of the Caughley works (which see, p. 158). It is an anchor over the word "Derby." As the initials RH conjoined also appear along with the anchor and word "Wor-

DUESBURY DERBY — DUESBURY DERBY

Figs. 971 and 972.

cester," and may mean either R. Hancock or Richard Holdship, the probability is they belong to the latter (who was connected with the Derby works), and that

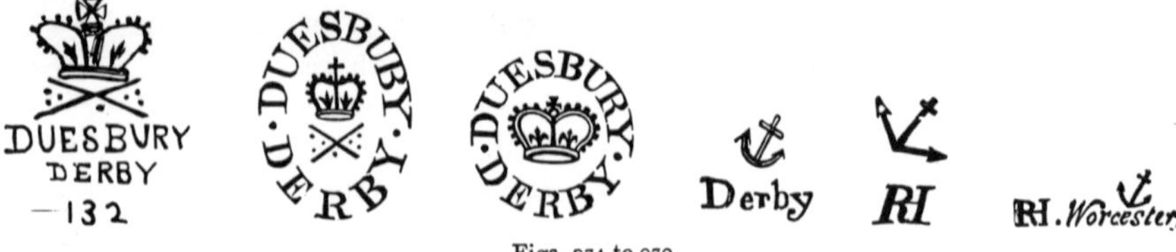

Figs. 974 to 979.

the *anchor* was adopted in allusion to his name, *hold ship*—a very clever and ingenious device. Other varieties differ slightly from these.

On some services, notably on the royal service, mentioned on page 341, Mr. Bloor has his name painted in full—

Messrs. Robert Bloor & Co.,
34, Old Bond Street,

on the back of plates, &c. The "Co." in this instance was Mr. Thomas Courteney, the London agent, through whom the order was procured. His place of business was 34, Old Bond Street, and many of the goods afterwards made for him bore the accompanying mark, Fig. 981. Messrs. Locker & Co., at the modern King Street works, used the mark, Fig. 982, and their successors, Stevenson, Sharp, and Co., the

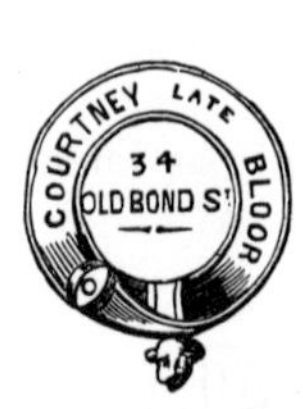

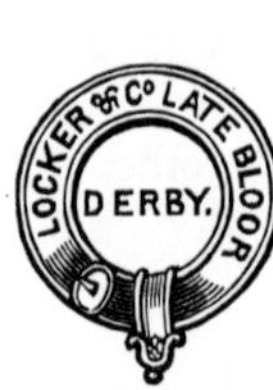

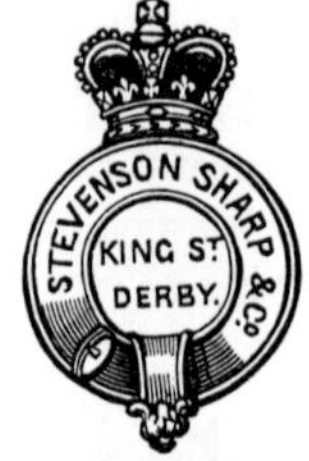

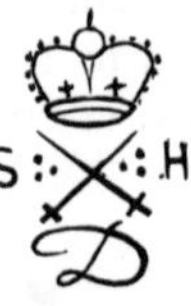

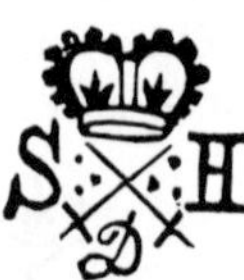

Figs. 981 to 985.

next one. The next firm, Stevenson and Hancock, used, in accordance with my suggestion, and a sketch I made for them in 1862, the old Derby mark of the crown, crossed daggers, dots, and letter *D*, with the initials of the firm S. H. (for Stevenson and Hancock); this is still continued by the proprietor, Sampson Hancock—the letters S. H. being, fortunately, his own initials, Figs. 984 and 985.

Of the artists employed at the Derby China Works, the principal modellers appear to have been Spengler, Stephan, Coffee, Complin, Hartenberg, Duvivier, Webber, and Dear; and many others, including Bacon the sculptor, were employed in London, and the models sent down to the works.

Of the painters, the principal ones were Bowman (or Boreman), who was originally of Chelsea, afterwards of Derby, and then again of London, and who was one of the best flower and landscape painters of his day; Billingsley, who received instruction from Bowman, and whose flower pieces have certainly never been surpassed; Hill, a famous painter of landscapes, who delighted in sylvan scenery; Brewer, also an excellent landscape and figure painter, and whose wife, Bernice Brewer, was also a painter; Pegg, who surpassed in faithful copying of nature, in single branches and flowers and in autumnal borders; Samuel Keys, a clever ornamentalist, who ended his days in the employ of Mintons; Steel, who excelled all others in painting fruit; John Keys, a flower painter; Cotton and Askew, two highly-gifted painters of figures; Webster, Withers, Hancock (two, uncle and nephew), Bancroft and others as flower painters; Lowton, clever at hunting and sporting subjects; and Robertson, at landscapes. But besides these, there were many other really clever artists employed, and it is pleasant, too, to know, that "Wright of Derby," the celebrated portrait painter, the contemporary and fellow-pupil of Reynolds, lent his powerful aid on some occasions in supplying drawings and giving advice, as did also De Boeuff, Bartolozzi, Sanby, Glover, and many others of eminence; and it is also interesting to add, that one of the Wedgwood family, Jonathan Wedgwood, was at one time employed at Derby. The draft of an agreement between himself and William Duesbury, dated 1772, is in my own possession, and by it he binds himself for three years to work at "the arts of repairing or throwing china or porcelaine ware," for the sum of fourteen shillings per week. Biographical notices of about a hundred of the artists, &c., of the old Derby works, the result of immense research, were given by me in the first edition of this work, to which I refer my readers.

Derby Crown Porcelain Company.

In the first edition of this work I wrote that "while this chapter is passing through the press, new china works, on a large scale, are about to be established on the Osmaston Road, Derby, by Mr. Edward Phillips, one of the proprietors of the Royal Porcelain Works at Worcester; there is, therefore, at last the pleasant prospect of one of the old staple trades of the town, that of porcelain, being brought back in all its integrity, and carried on with vigour and enlightenment;" and it is with much gratification that I chronicle, in the present edition, the fact that that prospect has been fully realised. It is a matter of congratulation not to the locality only, but to the Art-world in general, that the works have been established and are now, in that short space of time, among the most extensive, best arranged, and most satisfactory of Art-producing centres. In 1877 Mr. Phillips, having severed his connection with the Worcester works, of which he was managing director, formed the present limited liability company, and completed the purchase of the old Derby workhouse, with land and extensive premises comprising in all some fourteen or fifteen acres of ground, and converted the buildings, to which immense additions were made, into a china factory, three biscuit and three glost ovens being erected, as well as every possible requirement for the preparation of the whole of the raw materials and the turning out of a vast amount of finished goods of every class. In 1878 the first goods, undecorated, were sent away, and by 1880 the whole manufactory had, in every department, been brought into full working order. In the following year, 1881, Mr. Phillips, to whom the town and district owed the establishment of this revival of the old glory of Derby, and who had been indefatigable and unresting in every detail of its founding and development, died after a very brief illness, at the age of sixty-five. Consequent on his death Mr. Edward McInnes and Mr. Henry Litherland were appointed managing directors, and under their skilful management the works have been still further developed, the business connections much increased, and a more advanced and higher tone given to many of the productions. The works now employ some 300 hands.

The productions are china, Parian, and vitrified stoneware. In china all the usual services—dinner, tea, breakfast, toilet, trinket, and déjeuné—and a variety of other useful articles are made, as are also vases of every conceivable design, and of the most exquisite styles of decoration. In Parian, which is of fine quality in body, busts, statuettes, and groups are produced in considerable variety, and bid fair to become a marked speciality of the works.

One of the main aims of the directorate—and in this they have been eminently successful—is the revival of the old "Crown Derby" shapes, colours, and patterns, both in services and other useful classes of goods, and in vases and ornamental

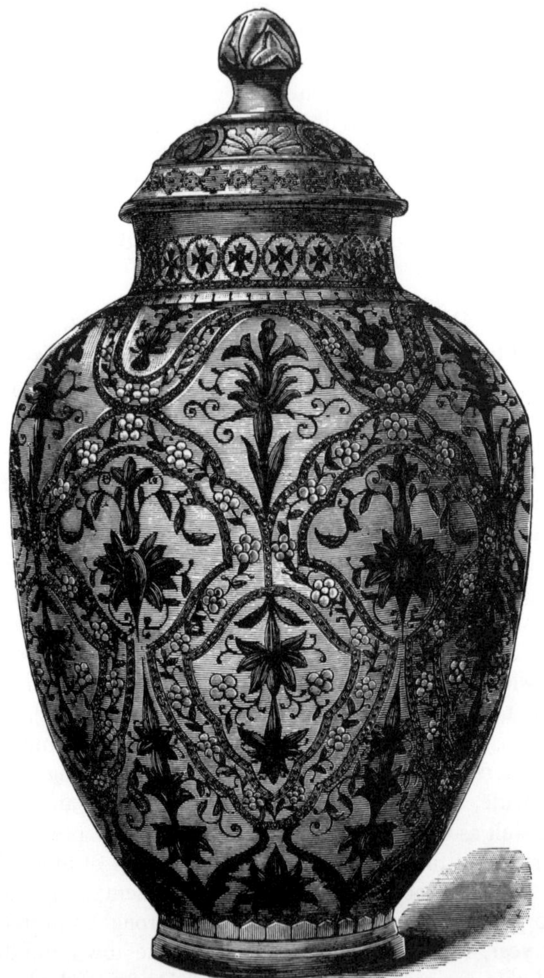

Fig. 986.—Vase. Derby Crown Porcelain Works.

articles. The famous old Derby blue, and the red, and the style of gilding, are reproduced in all their original fulness; and not only have the decorator but the thrower and modeller in all cases caught the true spirit of the old workmen, and the result is that but for a slight difference in the composition of the body and the modern mark, they might almost be taken to be genuine old examples. Most of the best-known old Derby patterns in tea-sets are thus resuscitated, as are the famous Kedleston and other vases in all their integrity.

The specialities are the vases, principally of Persian and Indianesque character, decorated in the richest of styles with a profusion of raised gilt ornament and an elaborate colouring that is eminently effective. In this raised gold species of decoration these works are markedly successful, the egg-shell china cups and saucers thus decorated being far beyond those of other houses. In these examples, which are *chefs-d'œuvre* of the plastic art, the "body" is of a high degree of transparency, of marvellous thinness, and of extreme hardness and tenacity, and on some examples the raised-gold pattern is in the finest and most delicate of lines, and yet without flaw or fault. In whatever style, indeed, the decoration of these choice cabinet specimens is done there is a studied delicacy and beauty that are in keeping with the apparently fragile body of which they are composed. An excellent example of raised gold combined with rich enamel colours is the vase Fig. 986. The ground is a delicate lavender (in which the Derby works excel), which pervades the body throughout, and on this the raised gold arabesques and other patterns and the judicious display of colours are profusely spread, and produce a pleasing and harmonious effect. While the "ornamental" is one of the main divisions of the productions, the "useful" and more commercial part is of at least equal importance, and receives the same amount of attention. The services, whether plain, printed, painted, or ornamented and gilt, are all of the better and higher class, and embrace patterns of great excellence and beauty. The productions have met with signal success in the United States and Australia, to which large quantities are regularly shipped.

The chief artists employed are, in painting, James Rowse, sen., now nearly a nonogenarian painter from the old Derby China Works, whose "right hand has forgot none of its cunning," as a flower-painter; his son, a clever landscape-painter, whose productions emulate the father's; Count Holtzendorff, a landscape-painter, whose productions have, as a rule, a soft dreaminess of colour and subdued tone that is very pleasing; W. H. Hogg, a modeller of great promise, two of whose busts found a place at the Royal Academy Exhibition of 1883; J. Platts, a painter of figures; and H. Deakin; and the principal gilders, of whom there is a considerable staff, are A. Piper and S. F. Lambert. The mark adopted by the company is the pencilled crown of the old Derby China Works surmounting the letter D (for "Derby"), repeated to form a monogram, and conveying the idea of the name "Crown Derby."

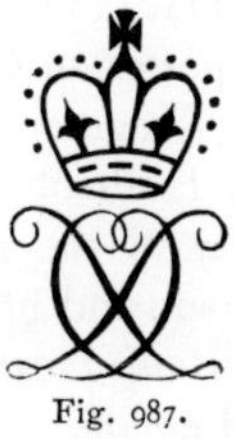

Fig. 987.

CHAPTER XVII.

Chesterfield.

The earliest potter in Chesterfield of whom there is any record is William Caskon or Kaskon, who died 8th Henry VIII. (1517), and the next is Ralph Heathcote, who was both a potter, brazier, and bell-founder. This Ralph Heathcote, who had married Elizabeth, daughter of John Tomson (or Tomason, as it is variously spelled), brazier, of Chesterfield, became by will of his father-in-law (will dated October 1, 1496) executor. Tomson lived in Saltergate, in a house previously held by William Forneday and Margaret his wife, which was surrendered to him in 1483. This house was afterwards, in 1501, "released to Ralph Heathcote, of Chesterfield, Potter." This is evidenced by two deeds, one by Thomas Moore, of Cuttethorpe, releasing the messuage in Saltergate to "Ralph Hethcote, of Chesterfield, Potter;" and the other from Thomas Moore, of Cuttethorp, and James Moore, of Syrley Grange, to "Ralph Hethecote, of Chesterfield, Potter," a bond of £20 to secure peaceable possession of the messuage in the Saltergate, Chesterfield, late in the occupation of John Tomson, deceased, and W. Forneby, deceased." It is evident, from a deed of 8th Henry VIII. (1517), that Ralph Heathcote took to the trade and goods of William Kaskon, potter, of Chesterfield, in that year. The deed is a receipt from "Isabel Kaskon, ye daughter of William Caskon, of Chesterfield, Potter, lately deceased," to "Rauff Hethcote, of ye same place, brasier, for her child's part of the goodes and money of the said William Caskon." In 1557-58 Robert Parker, of Chesterfield, gent. (son and heir of George Parker, deceased), and Mary, his wife, of the one part, and Rauf Heathcott, of Chesterfield, potter, of the other part, released a tenement in Saltergate, and lands at Tapton Lane.

The manufacture of pottery appears to have continued uninterruptedly from Heathcote's time downwards. In "A Short Tour," in 1772, it is said, "In the town is a manufacture of pots." Pilkington wrote in 1789: "A large quantity of coarse earthenware is manufactured here. In this business three potteries are worked, which afford employment to about sixty hands;" and Sir Richard Phillips, in 1828, wrote: "There are some potteries in this neighbourhood which employ about two hundred persons, at wages of from 10*s.* to 13*s.* per week, and for better workmen, from 18*s.* to 25*s.* The description of manufacture is exclusively brown ware, except in one instance, which includes black also. The number of potteries is ten, and the larger part is for home consumption, though a small proportion is sent to the Dutch market." The potteries named would include those at

Brampton.

The manufacture of brown ware at Brampton has probably been established a couple of centuries. In the early part of the present century there were here six earthenware manufactories, which were carried on by the following persons:—Mrs.

Blake (this now forms part of the works of Mr. Matthew Knowles); Mr. William Briddon (now continued by his son); Mr. Luke Knowles (now forming part of Mr. Matthew Knowles' works); Mr. Thomas Oldfield (now continued by his nephew, Mr. John Oldfield); Mr. John Wright (now discontinued; it stood on what is now

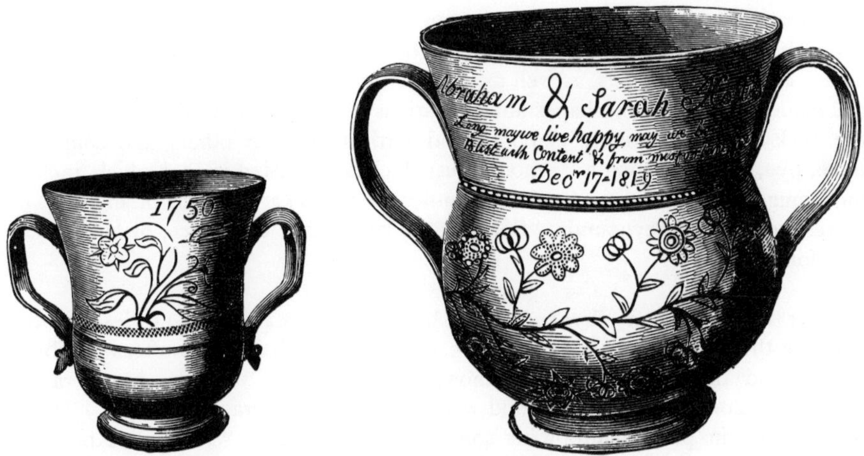

Figs. 988 and 989.—Posset Pots.

the site of the presant rectory of St. Thomas's Church); and that of Edward Wright and Son (still carried on by the family). At the present time there are eight manufactories, which will be separately spoken of presently. At these, brown ware of a remarkably hard and durable quality, and stoneware of the most imper-

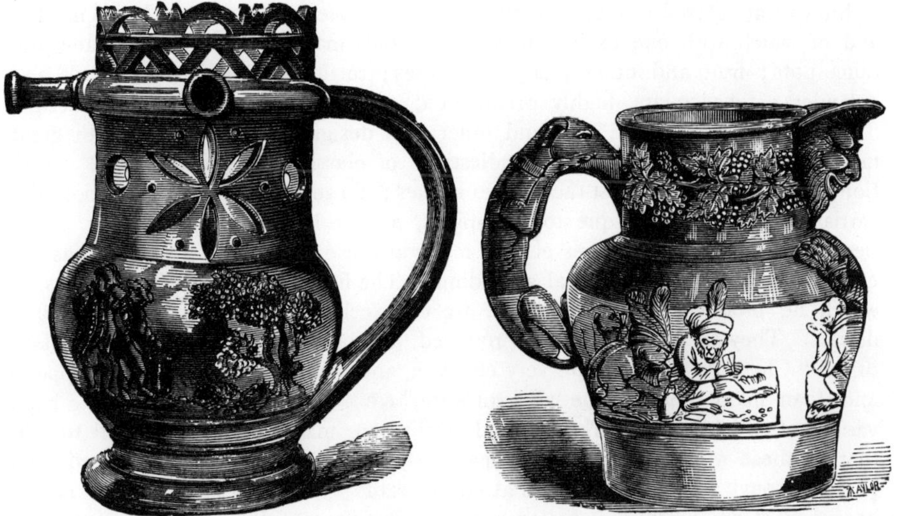

Figs. 990 and 991.—Puzzle Jug and Greyhound Jug, Brampton Ware.

vious character, are made in great perfection and in immense quantities. The clays principally used are "Stone Edge," or "Lidd clay," found at East Moor, or Wadshelf, about three miles away, and "Brampton clay," found in the immediate neighbourhood.

At Brampton, "posset-pots" have, for centuries, been, and still continue to be, made. Figs. 988 and 989 show their general form; the one is dated 1750 and the other 1819. I have myself examples as late as 1874. Usually the name of the parties for whom they are made are incised in the same manner as the pattern.

Another marked feature of Brampton, or "Chesterfield ware," has for a long period been the "puzzle jugs" (Fig. 990) there made. These, which are still produced on the old models, as well as in more modern applications of the principle, are made in a variety of shapes and of various sizes. In some the perforations in the neck and rim are more elaborate and intricate than in others, and some have three, five, or seven spouts. Another usual class of design is that which includes jugs, mugs, and other vessels whose handles (Fig. 991) are formed of more or less cleverly-modelled greyhounds. Some of the larger have two, three, or four handles thus formed.

The Welshpool and Payne Potteries, belonging to Matthew Knowles and Son, embrace the old works carried on last century by Mr. Blake, and afterwards by his widow, and those of Mr. Luke Knowles. They came into the hands of Mr. Matthew Knowles about 1835, and were by him considerably enlarged. Having been joined in partnership by his son, under the style of "Matthew Knowles & Son," the works were again in 1875 much extended. All the general descriptions of brown and stoneware goods are produced for the Australian, Russian, African, and Jamaica markets, as well as for the home trade. Among these are stoneware, spirit-bottles and spirit-kegs and barrels, which are much esteemed for their hardness, durability, and fine quality; ginger-beer bottles, both in stoneware and brown ware; jam-jars for wholesale preserve manufacturers in gallon and half-gallon sizes, in brown ware glazed inside, forming one of the staple productions of Mr. Knowles, and of which, with one exception, he is the only maker in the district; stew and sauce pots; fruit and other jars; flat dishes; turtle and beef pots; bowls and colanders; tobacco-jars, highly ornamented; "Punch" jugs of striking design, "hunting" jugs, "game" jugs, and other jugs designed and modelled with great taste; puzzle-jugs; posset-pots; candlesticks of classical design and good execution; bread-baskets; toast-racks; tea-kettles; flower-pots and vases; foot and carriage warmers; grotesque tobacco-pipes, and a large variety of other goods besides the usual domestic vessels, are made at these works, and are as good as the common nature of the material will admit. The filters made by Mr. Knowles, of which he produces a large number, are of excellent construction and of good design. They are among the best produced, and being in the fine deep rich colour of the "Chesterfield ware," are very effective, and perhaps more pleasing in appearance than many others in the "Bristol ware," &c. In china clay ware also a large variety of articles of remarkably good quality are made. It may be well to add that at these works the clay is prepared by steam. It is "blunged," and then passed through a fine sieve, driven at considerable speed on a large flat iron boiler, heated by steam, where it is boiled to a proper stiffness. It is then passed through a pug-mill, and is ready for use. Mr. Knowles's are the only works in Brampton where this process is adopted. The works have recently been considerably enlarged by the addition of "Bristol" kilns, and are now producing large quantities of every description of that class of ware, including jam-jars, 2 lbs. to 16 lbs., as used by all the leading preserve manufacturers; ginger-beer and ale bottles of all sorts; spirit-bottles, water-filters of various constructions, and, indeed. all classes of Bristol stoneware.

"*The Pottery.*"—These works were established, in 1810, by "Oldfield, Madin, Wright, Hewitt, & Co." After various changes and retirements, Mr. John Oldfield became, in 1838, sole proprietor of the works, and they continue under his name. They have from time to time been considerably extended, and are nearly the largest in the district. The goods manufactured are the usual descriptions known as "New Brampton" or "Chesterfield ware," or, as more frequently falsely called in the London and other markets, "Nottingham ware,"—a remarkably hard, compact, and durable salt-glazed brown ware; and stone-ware, which is dipped in different "slips." In "brown ware," the principal goods produced are dishes and bowls of various kinds; turtle, beef, butter, Dutch, stew, sauce, and other pots; bottles and jars of all shapes and sizes, and for all uses; pitchers and jugs in endless variety; churns; milkpans and pancheons; nappies and porringers; tea and coffee pots; Welsh trays; carriage and feet warmers; hare-pans and dog-troughs; spirit and wine barrels and kegs; figured flower pots and stands; scent-jars; "hunting," "cottage," "tulip," and other figured jugs and mugs; moulds for puddings, blanc-mange, jellies, &c., of great beauty and of excellent and even artistic design, and many other articles. In "antique ware" Mr. Oldfield makes remarkably effective and well-designed hunting, game, cottage, tulip, and other jugs; figured Stilton-cheese stands; fruit-dishes and trays; tea and coffee-pots; tobacco-pots, some of which, with goblet and candlestick, are very striking; watch-stands; "Toby Fill-pot" jugs; small figures of stags, dogs, &c.; grotesque and twisted pipes; puzzle-jugs, &c. In stoneware many articles are also produced, the great bulk being bottles and spirit-kegs of various kinds and of every size, from one pint up to ten or more gallons in capacity; and sanitary goods. Filters also form a staple branch of the manufacture, and these are fitted up on an exceedingly good principle, with vegetable charcoal, sand, &c., on the premises, and are supplied in large quantities both at home and for exportation. The manufacture of filters was here commenced in 1826. At these works spirit-bottles of a similar character to Fig. 998 were made. One was a representation of Lord Brougham, with the words, "The true Spirit of Reform." Among the marks used by this firm are—

ESTABLISHED
1826
J. OLDFIELD & CO.
CHESTERFIELD
WATER FILTER
MANUFACTURERS,
WHOLESALE AND RETAIL
AND FOR
EXPORTATION.

OLDFIELD & CO
MAKERS

OLDFIELD & CO.
CHESTERFIELD.

J. OLDFIELD.

Figs. 992 to 995.

The *Walton Pottery* was built by William Briddon in 1790, and at his death was continued by his son, William Briddon, who, dying in 1848, was succeeded by his son, William Briddon, the present proprietor. The goods made are brown ware and stoneware in all their varieties. In these are produced stew, souse, turtle, beef, and butter pots; jugs of every variety; preserve and pickle jars; pancheons, bowls, and colanders; porringers and patty-pans; bottles of every conceivable size and shape; filters; spirit barrels and kegs; foot-bottles and carriage warmers; tea and coffee pots; twisted and grotesque pipes, and many other articles. In quality they are much the same as those of other Brampton manufactories.

Wheatbridge Pottery.—These works have been in the Wright family for three generations. The staple trade of the manufactory is general brown ware for the Dutch markets.

The *Alma Pottery* was commenced by Mr. Samuel Lowe and his then partners, about 1852. After a few years Mr. Lowe's two partners withdrew from the concern, and it continued in his hands solely. The goods produced are the same general kinds, both of wares and articles, as the other Brampton potteries. In brown ware and in stoneware Mr. Lowe produces filters, bottles of every kind and size, jugs and mugs, jars of various descriptions, and all the articles usually produced in these wares, and of the same general quality as those of other works in the district.

Barker Pottery, belonging to Mr. Henry Briddon. Here all the usual articles in brown ware are made.

The Pottery of Mr. William Briddon, jun., produces the usual kinds of wares, and most of the articles, of the district.

The *London Pottery*, belonging to Messrs. F. Lipscombe & Co., of London, was established by them for the purpose of manufacturing their filters.

WHITTINGTON.

Whittington is a place of historical and antiquarian interest. The family of De Whittington, to which "Dick Whittington" belonged, took its rise and its name from this place; and at the "Cock and Pynot" (the provincial name for the magpie) ale-house here the great Revolution of 1688 was planned; the "Revolution House" and the "plotting-chair" being matters known to most historical readers. Here, too, the Rev. Samuel Pegge, the great antiquarian writer, lived, he being Rector at Whittington.

At Whittington, pot-works have existed from an early date, and are still continued. At these much good ware and many specialities of design, &c., were produced. It is only necessary to premise that the goods are commonly known by the general term of "Chesterfield ware" or "Nottingham ware," it being a fact that London houses still sell and persist in calling the products of these Derbyshire works by the latter name.

The Whittington Potteries are of very old establishment, having been in existence since about the middle or latter end of the seventeenth century, if not longer. Here the ordinary brown ware of the period was manufactured, the ware being of extreme hardness and closeness of texture, and having a rich warm reddish-brown colour. About the year 1800, and for some years later, the works, which were near the racecourse, were held by Mr. William Bromley, who, in addition to the ordinary brown ware, made also a white or cream-coloured earthenware of fine quality. In this fine body he manufactured dinner, tea, and other services, principally decorated, in the prevailing manner, with transfer-printing in blue. He also practised batt printing for some of his goods. Mr. Bromley also made some experiments in, and succeeded in producing, a very good china ware, but did not prosecute this branch of manufacture to any extent. At that time, when Mr. Bromley was making the fine earthenware and was experimenting on porcelain bodies, my late father, Mr. Arthur Jewitt, then a young man, was residing at Brampton, and was in habits of close intimacy with him. My father being a man of scientific as well as of high literary attainments, and being, moreover, a good artist, took considerable interest in his friend Mr. Bromley's manufacture, and at his own house at Brampton entered with spirit into a series of experiments in enamelling and enamel-printing, and in other processes for decorating the wares. For this purpose he caused to be erected in his own house two enamel kilns, one of which he had constructed on the ordinary simple principle of heating, and the other on the spiral principle. He also fitted up, for the purpose of these private experiments, a small printing-room, and here, being, as I have said, a good artist, he tried various processes for transferring aqua-tints and etchings (which he etched and prepared himself) by the batt-process, both on to the biscuit and on to the white glazed ware. By this process he produced many remarkably successful transfers; but, like the boy who dug up the seeds in his garden day by day to see if they were sprouting, and so killed them, he was always so impatient to see the result of his experiments that he did not wait for the fire in the kilns to die out, but opened the doors, and thus frequently spoiled all the pieces. Sufficient, however, remained each time to show that he was right in his experiments, and that his trials were all that could be desired.

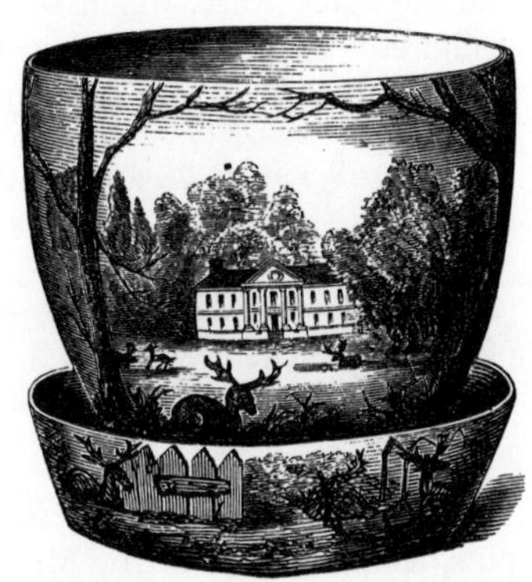

Fig. 996.

Besides transfer-printing, he tried some interesting experiments in surface-painting on the biscuit. Only one example of this ware is known to exist, and this fortunately is now in my own possession. It is here engraved (Fig. 996). It bears a view of (I believe) Renishaw Hall, and part of the park, with deer, &c. The body is extremely light, and the painting highly artistic. It is simply surface-painted on the biscuit. It is a small flower-pot, or "bow pot," and saucer, and is only $3\frac{3}{8}$ inches in height.

These experiments are highly interesting in connection with the Whittington and Brampton potteries. They were very successful, and showed that had my father devoted his time and his talents to the process, great results would have been achieved. As it was, he prosecuted his inquiries as an amateur only, and from a simple love of the art, and his name, until I made it known in the *Art Journal* a few years ago, has never been publicly associated with the fictile history of the country. I felt that it was due to the memory of one of the most talented of men and best of parents that I should place his name on record in connection with an art in which, for a short time, in the midst of a busy literary life, he took such a lively interest. Amongst many other works, Mr. Arthur Jewitt was author of "The History of Buxton," "History of Lincoln," "Lincolnshire Cabinet," "Handbook of Perspective," "Handbook of Geometry," &c., and he contributed largely to the *Penny Magazine*, Brayley's *Graphic and Historical Illustrator*, &c. &c. He was the intimate friend of Edward Wedlake Brayley, of John Britton, of Ebenezer Rhodes, and others. He was born in 1772 and died in 1852, on his 80th birthday.

Mr. Bromley continued the works for some years, when they changed hands. He was a man of great ability and of much spirit, and did more to further the standard of excellence of the works in his district than any of his contemporaries. He had three sons, Rev. Samuel Bromley, who was a poet of no ordinary stamp, and was a Baptist missionary to Jamaica and other countries; Joseph Bromley, who entered the army; and the Rev. James Bromley, whose name is well known in connection with the Wesleyan persuasion. The works afterwards belonged to Robert Bainbrigge & Co. The pot-works at Whittington, in the early part of the present century, were carried on by Mr. William Johnson and Mr. Aaron Madin. At the present time there are two manufactories at this place; viz. those of Mr. Samuel Lancaster, successor to Mr. Madin, and Mr. James Pearson.

Stone Bottle Works.—These works, at Whittington Moor, were established in 1818 by Mr. Aaron Madin, and they are continued by his son-in-law, Mr. Samuel Lancaster. The goods produced are in stoneware, brown ware, and coarse black ware. The stoneware is made of fireclay, found underneath the Tupton coal-measures at Brampton and elsewhere, and glazed with the usual compound of flint, Paris white, Cornwall stone, barytes, and ground glass. It is of good quality, and very hard and durable. The ground ware is, as is usual in the district, salt-glazed; and the black ware, which is made of the common brick-clay, is glazed chiefly with lead-ore. The goods produced are the usual domestic and other articles made in the neighbourhood, and their quality is equal to most others.

Whittington Pottery.—At these works, belonging to Mr. James Pearson, the usual classes of goods, as made at the other potteries of the district, are produced.

Whittington Moor Pottery.—Mr. S. Lancaster (late A. Madin) has a manufactory of coarse pancheon ware at this place; the body, as usual, coarse red outside, and lined with a black glaze inside.

Newbold.

There is a manufactory of coarse brown ware—pancheons, bread-pans, stein-pots, &c.,—carried on by Mr. W. Sharratt at this place. The productions are of much the same character as those of Whittington Moor, Tickenhall, &c.

Eckington.

Pilkington, in 1789, says: "A manufacture of sickles is carried on. There are also two potteries in the town."

Belper.

About the middle or towards the latter part of last century, a small manufactory of common coarse brown ware existed here, and about 1800 Mr. William Bourne took to the works carried on by Messrs. Blood, Webster, and Simpson, at Belper Pottery. Mr. William Bourne, sen., was, it appears, very much engaged in the business of the then new canal. Letters of his, and of his son, William Bourne, jun., in which reference is made to his connection with the canal, and show business transactions between them and Mr. Duesbury of the Derby China Works, are in my own possession. Mr. Bourne carried on the manufacture of salt-glazed blacking, ink, ginger-beer, and spirit bottles. The ordinary brown ware, produced from a less vitreous clay, found on the spot, consisted of bowls, pans, pancheons, dishes, pitchers, and all the commoner varieties of domestic vessels, and these were of excellent and durable quality. The stoneware bottles, &c., were made from a fine and more tenacious bed of clay, at Derby, a few miles distant. The finer or figured wares were made from clay procured from Staffordshire. By Mr. Bourne all these descriptions of goods were made, but he principally confined himself to the manufacture of stoneware bottles of various kinds. A good antique-shaped hunting jug, and other similar articles, and figures in relief, were also extensively made. In 1812, Mr. Joseph Bourne (son of William Bourne) took to the Denby Pottery then carried on by Mr. Jäger, and the two works were carried on simultaneously until 1834, when the Belper Pottery was finally closed, the workpeople, plant, and business being removed to Denby and incorporated with those works, and the premises converted into cottages. From that time no pottery has been made at Belper. The site of the works was at Belper-Gutter, and "Pot House Lane," the name of one of the streets, perpetuates the manufacture, the hamlet itself being known as "Belper Pottery."

The mark used while these works were carried on in conjunction with those at Denby was this; and it may be well to remark that a series of political bottles, bearing representations of various Reform leaders, was made. On these the head of the individual—the King, Sir Francis Burdett, Earl Grey, or whoever was intended—formed the neck of the bottle, and the arms and bust the shoulder; political references, and the name of the political leader, were impressed on the clay. One of these, Fig. 998, which represents the King (William IV.), bears in front the words "WILLIAM IV.'s REFORM CORDIAL,"—the "cordial" being the brandy or other spirit it was intended to contain. Another is a representation, in a similar form, of Lord John Russell (afterwards Earl

BELPER & DENBY

BOURNES
POTTERIES

DERBYSHIRE ✱

Fig. 997.

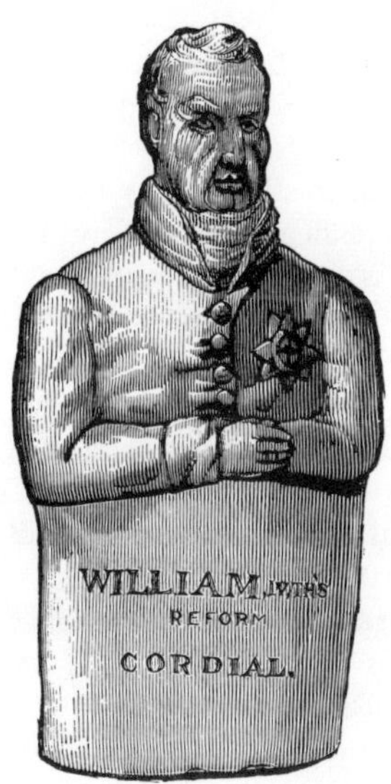

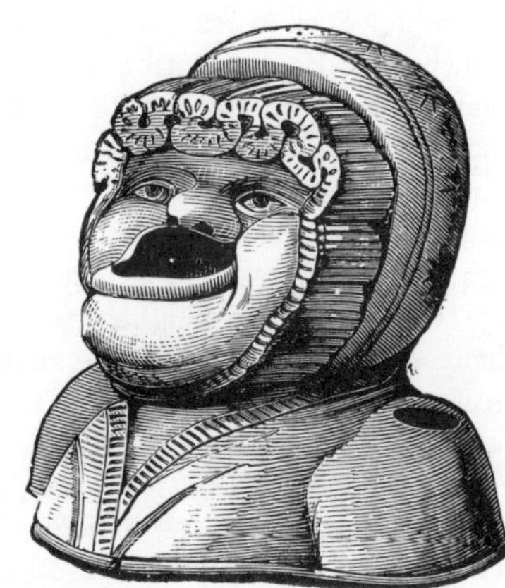

Figs. 998 and 999.

Russell); it bears, in front, the name "LORD JOHN RUSSELL," and on a scroll which he holds in his hand are inscribed the words, "THE TRUE SPIRIT OF REFORM." At the back is the mark Fig. 997. At these works too, I believe, quaintly designed vitrified stoneware inkstands, of which Fig. 999 is an example, were made. The projecting lower jaw formed the well for the ink, while holes on the shoulders served for places to put the pens in when not in use.

In 1827 a coarse-ware pottery was carried on here by Mr. Heapey.

Codnor Park.

The pottery at Codnor Park was built in 1820, by the Butterley Iron Company, the owners of the iron-works of Butterley and Codnor Park. At that time the Butterley works were under the management of the late Mr. William Jessop, son of one of the partners, and afterwards senior partner of the firm. Some years before this time the company had constructed a large cast-iron bridge for the Nabob of Oude, and on its despatch a brother of Mr. William Jessop accompanied it to India to superintend its erection, taking with him several workmen, among whom was an engine-fitter named William Burton. For some cause or other the bridge was not erected by the Nabob, and after remaining several years in India, the parties returned to England. On their return William Burton was induced to commence the pottery, and having engaged a skilled workman from the Brampton Potteries, near Chesterfield, commenced operations in 1821. The pottery was situated near the Codnor Park Iron-Works, from which it took its name, and pretty close to the Butterley Canal, and was successfully carried on for several years. Sir Richard Phillips, in his "Tour," in 1828, thus notes the pottery:—"Over near Codnor Castle I viewed a rough and ill-built manufactory, where they turn and bake those opaque bottles used for ginger-beer, soda-water, liquid blacking, &c. About 50 women and children finish 100 gross per day, and they sell the half-pints at 15*d.* and 16*d.* per doz., and all pints at 2*s.*, and quarts at 3*s.* 6*d.* They are made of the clay of the vicinity, and the agent for selling them is Kemp, in Milk Street, London. They are harder and less liable to burst than glass bottles."

In 1832, Mr. Burton having got into pecuniary difficulties, the works were closed. After remaining unworked for many months, it was, in 1833, taken by Mr. Joseph Bourne, of the Denby Pottery.

The Codnor Park Works, which gave employment to about sixty persons, were carried on by Mr. Bourne until 1861, when they were finally closed, and the workmen, plant, &c., were transferred to the Denby Works, where additional workrooms had been erected for their accommodation. The clay was of a similar kind to that used at Denby, but owing to a larger impregnation of iron the ware produced therefrom was not equal in appearance to that made at Denby, though the bottles were highly vitreous, and had an extensive sale. This clay was obtained at Cupet Green, in the immediate neighbourhood, and the coal from Birchwood Colliery. (The hard coal is the only kind adapted for burning in the salt-glazed kilns.) London was the chief market, the crates being forwarded by canal.

The goods produced at Codnor Park were the usual class of household vessels, and stoneware bottles of various kinds, and of sizes up to six gallons; and pans, bowls, jugs, pitchers and other articles. Besides these, however, a remarkably fine, compact, light, and delicate buff-coloured terra-cotta was produced. In this were made butter-coolers, vases of various kinds, flower-baskets and pots, ewers, spill-cases, and numberless other articles. Many of these were of excellent design, and beautifully decorated with foliage and other ornaments in relief. Puzzle-jugs, &c., were also made of this material, and surface-painted with a peculiar mottled effect. The mark during Mr. Burton's time was his name and "Codnor Park," or simply the name "Wm. Burton," impressed on the clay. The manafacture of ordinary household earthenware was discontinued when Mr. Bourne took to the concern, his operations being confined to the manufacture of bottles. For some of this information I am indebted to Mr. Humphrey Goodwin, who was connected with the works from their opening in 1821 until their close.

DENBY.

The "Denby Pottery" is in the parish of Denby, seven miles from Derby and two from Ripley—a village memorable as being the birthplace of Flamstead, the astronomer—in the midst of the rich ironstone and coal-fields of Derbyshire, the former of which are said to have been regularly worked from the time of the Romans. The works were commenced in 1809 by a Mr. Jäger, on the estate of W. Drury Lowe, Esq., where, some time before, a valuable and extensive bed of clay had been found to exist. This clay, previous to the establishment of the Denby Works, was used at the Belper Pottery for the manufacture of stoneware ink, blacking, and other bottles. The Denby clay was also supplied to the Derby China Works in considerable quantities, where it was used for saggers, and for a few other articles which were produced. In 1812 Joseph Bourne, son of William Bourne, of the Belper Pottery, succeeded Mr. Jäger, and the Belper and Denby works were carried on simultaneously until 1834, when the Belper Works were discontinued, and the plant and workpeople removed to Denby. The works at this time much increased, and gradually extended their operations. In 1833 the Codnor Park Works passed into the hands of Mr. Bourne, and were carried on by him, along with those of Denby, until 1861, when they were closed, and the workpeople, plant, &c., as in the case of the Belper Works, removed to Denby. In 1845 Mr. Bourne also became possessed of the Shipley Pottery, and in 1856 removed those works to Denby. With the Denby Pottery are therefore incorporated those of Belper, Codnor Park, and Shipley. Mr. Joseph Bourne having taken his son, Joseph Harvey Bourne, into partnership, the business was carried on under the style of "Joseph Bourne & Son," and has so continued until the present day. He died in 1860, and his son in 1869. In 1851 a medal was awarded to Mr. Bourne for his stone bottles.

In addition to the extensions required from time to time at Denby to provide for these continual augmentations, the business has so extended as to necessitate considerable additions and improvements. Excellent machinery has been applied to the blunging and other processes, and instead of the old system of getting rid of the water from the slip by evaporation, the clay is obtained therefrom by the patented process invented by Messrs. Needham and Kite, Vauxhall, London, ten of their presses being employed, turning out at least 25 tons per day of workable clay. The class of ware produced has not varied to any extent, though an advance in shape and quality is evident from a comparison with some of the earlier specimens extant. The great bulk of the stoneware produced by Bourne & Son is the kind known as the salt-glazed stoneware, which, on account of its peculiar vitreous and non-absorbent qualities, is in great demand not only in the home market but in all parts of the world. About the year 1836 a considerable change was made in the size and form of the salt-glazed kilns, and for these improvements Mr. Joseph Bourne obtained a patent. The old kilns were only half the height of the present ones, and had each five chimneys. To these what may be called an upper storey has been added, and, while the lower half is fired by mouths opening into the kiln and the flame passing *perpendicularly up the kiln*, the upper portion is fed by fires passing out of the kiln by means of *flues at the side*, and the modern kilns have only one chimney, thus securing a better consumption of smoke and lessening the objectionable results which would follow from such a dense volume of smoke proceeding from a low chimney. Since this patent was taken out an additional improvement has been made by the erection on the top of each kiln of a separate small oven, in which biscuit or terra-cotta fancy articles can be burnt, these being simply burnt by the heat passing up the chimney and from the top of the kiln, but no flame or salt-glaze reaching the goods. Much thought and care as well as considerable expense have been expended during the last twenty years to perfect the manufacture of telegraph insulators, and the very large business transactions in this department proves that the enterprise of the firm has not been fruitless.

The firm have for many years possessed the exclusive right to manufacture Varley's

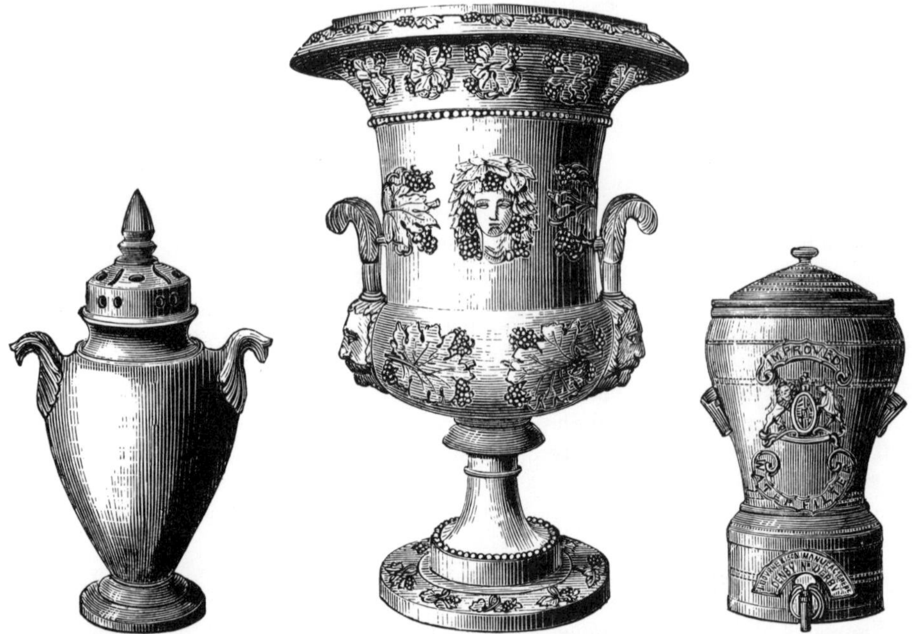

Figs. 1000 to 1002.—Denby Pottery.

Patent Double V. Insulators, and since the transfer of the telegraphs to the Government have executed immense quantities for that department of the public service. The firm also supplies large quantities of other patented insulators to the great English railway companies and private electrical engineering firms, and large orders have been recently received from the Canadian railway companies, these insulators being found much more efficient than the glass ones generally used on the North American Continent. The National Telephone Company has recently adopted insulators produced by this firm. A demand having arisen for white-glazed ink and other bottles, additional appliances have been provided on the most approved and modern principles, which have enabled the firm to produce a class of ware of this description unrivalled alike for its excellence and appearance.

Bottles are the staple production, and almost every variety both in the patented vitreous stone and white glazed, are made. Ink-bottles of every shape and size are made by thousands weekly, as are also ale, porter, ginger-beer, blacking. fruit, and every other kind. Spirit and other liquor bottles, with handles, up to a very large size, are also made. Foot-warmers, carriage-warmers, medical appliances, mortars and pestles, pipkins, feeding-bottles, candlesticks, pork-pie moulds, and every other variety of domestic and other vessels are also made, as are filters, &c.

"Hunting-Jugs"—a name by which a certain class of jugs with raised ornaments consisting of hunting subjects, are known—are made to a great extent. Some of these are made with greyhound handles, as Fig. 991. Jars for preserves, pickles, jellies, marmalades, &c., are also a staple branch of the Denby manufacture.

In terra-cotta, which is of a warm buff colour, flower vases of various designs, lotus vases, garden and other vases, wine-coolers, water-bottles, ewers with snake handles, flower-stands, Stilton-cheese stands and trays, fern-stands, fonts, Indian scent-jars, butter-coolers, mignionette-boxes, and many other articles of artistic excellence are made. A finer kind of terra-cotta vases and plaques has recently, I am informed by Mr. Walker, to whom I am indebted for much information concerning the Denby pottery, been introduced with great success to meet the large and increasing demand for such articles for painting and other artistic purposes.

The marks used by the Denby Pottery are as follows :—

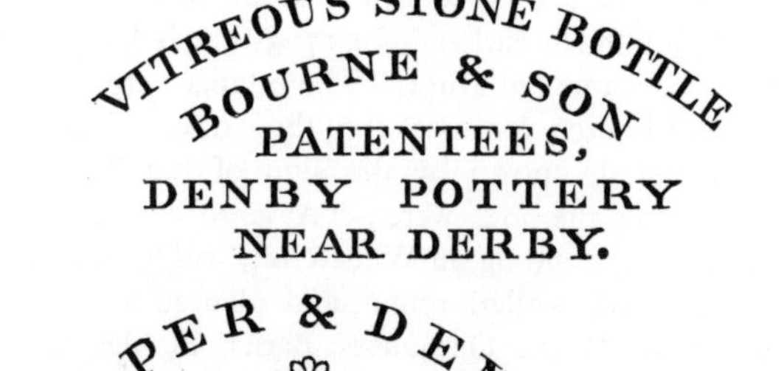

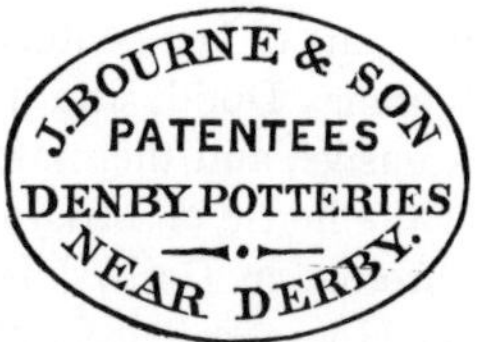

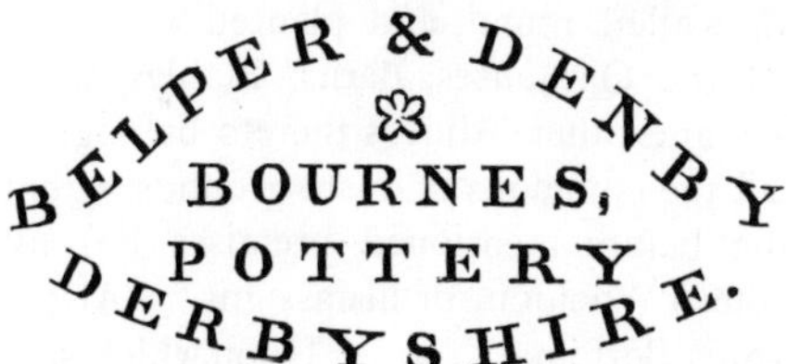

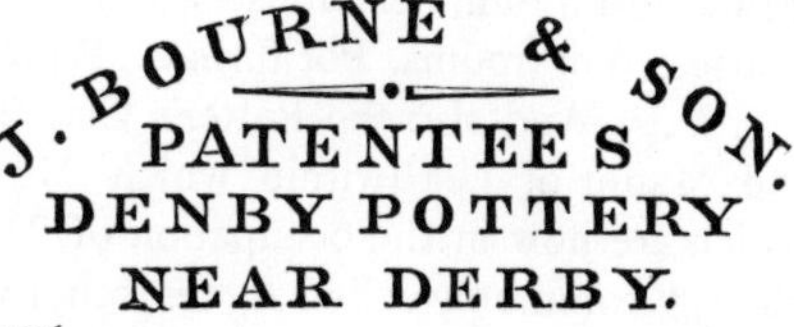

Figs. 1003 to 1006.

SHIPLEY.

These works were commenced about 1825 on the estate of Edward Miller Mundy, Esq., of Shipley Hall, by whom the buildings were erected, in consequence of the discovery of valuable beds of clay. They were first carried on by some working potters from the Staffordshire district, and the ordinary classes of goods in "cane" or "yellow" ware were produced, as were also Rockingham-ware teapots and other articles. These were made to a considerable extent, and of good quality, but the works did not answer. They were next taken by a Mr. Waite, a blacking manufacturer, from London, who commenced making stoneware bottles for his own blacking, and other articles of general use. Eventually, in 1845, the works passed into the hands of Mr. Bourne of the Denby pottery, and were carried on by him. The clay at Shipley was of two kinds—one was obtained from the hard seam coal after the coal was worked, at a depth of 250 yards. This was of a beautiful and extremely fine quality, but was of itself difficult to work owing to a want of tenacity. It was found, however, that by using in equal proportions this clay and another known as the Waterloo seam, which was about 100 yards from the surface, an excellent body was produced. At this period the coal mines on the estate furnished saline and chalybeate waters, which were much in repute, and bottles, specially designed for these waters, were made in large quantities at these works. Some of these bottles are still preserved, and are of excellent material. They bear impressed on the side a garter ribbon, on which are the words In me suprema Salus, enclosing the name SHIPLEY SALINE WATER in three lines. In 1856 the Shipley pottery was closed, the workmen, plant, &c., being removed to and incorporated with the Denby pottery.

ALFRETON.

During the last and the early part of the present century, brown ware of common quality, and red-ware pancheons, &c., were made at Alfreton, but have long been discontinued. Pilkington, who wrote in 1789, says, "There are also here six malt offices, and two potteries of the brown earthen ware." The site of the last of these pot-sheds, I am informed by Mr. Rowbottom, was purchased, in 1845, by the Gas Company, for their works, and during the progress of building, &c., only the commonest brown ware was seen.

CRICH.

Somewhat extensive pot-works existed here, on Morewood Moor, in the middle and latter part of last century, or probably much earlier. In 1763 they belonged to a Mr. Thomas Dodd, who in that year became bankrupt. The estates were somewhat extensive, and their sale—land and houses, &c.—covered three days. The sale was "at the house of Mr. Jonathan Kendall, known by the sign of the Peacock, near Alfreton, in Derbyshire," and among the lots were: "A large commodious Dwelling House, called Crich Pot House, standing in Wheatcroft, within the said parish of Crich, together with the Garden, walled round, and planted with Wall Fruit, and a Summer House within; and all the Outhouses, Barns, Stables, Cowhouses, Workrooms, Pot furnace, Warehouses, and other Edifices thereto belonging. . . . . . And also the Potter's Clay upon all the commons or waste grounds within the Manor of Lea (within which Manor the before mentioned premises lie), all which are now in the occupation of Mr. Thomas Wheldon, or his assigns." Also a close, "commonly called Agnes, otherwise Annis Bottom. . . . . . Upon which said acre of Land there is now built and standing a good new Pot House, with Workrooms, Pot furnace, Warehouses, and all other Edifices and Aparments necessary for a Pottery, now also in the posssession of the said Mr. Wheldon," and other property. The works were situated near the "Pot-House Farm," as the place is still called; the buildings which remain are known as the "Pot-House Hillocks." After the bankruptcy of Thomas Dodd the works were carried on by George Bacon, and at his death passed into the hands of his son, Edward Bacon, who gave up the earthenware manufacture and converted the place into a brickyard; this also he closed about 1810. Of the ware made here, which appears to have been brown ware, like that of Brampton, nothing reliable is known. A posset-pot, formerly belonging to the landlord of the "Horse and Groom," a public-house a mile off, is said to be an undoubted example; it bears the names of the then landlord and his wife —"John and Mary Wood, 1794." A spill-board weight, bearing on one side the date 1760, with initials, and on the other the initials G B (supposed to be George Bacon) and a fleur-de-lis, is also supposed to have been made here.

LANGLEY MILLS.

Langley Mill Pottery.—This pottery was established in 1865 by James Calvert, and was the first in the neighbourhood. The productions are vitrified stoneware of similar character and quality to that of Messrs. Bourne at Denby. In this ware a large trade is done in ginger-beer, ink, beer, and other bottles, and all the usual domestic vessels—jars, pitchers, hot-water bottles, foot-warmers, jugs, mugs, &c.—are produced from clay found in the neighbourhood. The works are extensive and well arranged, consisting of three kilns for brown ware and one for Bristol ware.

ILKESTON.

The "*Ilkeston Potteries*," established by George Evans in 1807, were carried on by him until his decease, in 1832, when they passed to his son, Mr. Richard Evans. During the lifetime of George Evans, Derbyshire stone bottles alone were made, and are still manufactured. The buildings have been considerably increased, and a general pottery added for the production of useful articles in stoneware and ornamental terra-cotta goods. The productions in stoneware are bottles, jars, pans, &c., of all sizes and of every usual form; filters of an improved construction; carriage, foot, and other warmers; sanitary pipes, and ware of every kind, &c., &c.; and in terra-cotta, vases, pedestals, flower and tree boxes and pots, garden-edgings, chimney-tops, &c., of various designs, and all the more usual productions of fire-clay goods.

PINXTON.

The village of Pinxton (a large parish in East Derbyshire, close on the borders of Nottinghamshire) is principally inhabited by colliers and other "hardy sons of toil," who work in the ironstone mines and at the furnaces of the neighbourhood. The manor belongs to the family of Coke (the same family as the Cokes of Trusley and of Melbourne), and to John Coke, Esq., the establishment of the china works is owing. Mr. John Coke was the youngest brother of D'Ewes Coke, Esq., lord of the manor; the second brother being Sir William Coke, Judge of the Supreme Court, Ceylon, who died at Trincomalee, in Ceylon. John Coke, who was born in 1775, passed several of the early years of his life at Dresden, and there, doubtless, acquired that love for porcelain ware which induced him to commence the manufactory at Pinxton on his return to this country. Having an idea that some clays found on the family estates near Pinxton might be available for the manufacture of china ware, he entered into a correspondence with Mr. Duesbury, of the Derby China Works, and sent him samples of his clays for trial and experiment. Whatever encouragement or otherwise he received from Mr. Duesbury—and I have reason to believe that encouragement was *not* given—the result of his own convictions and his own trials, &c., determined Mr. Coke on starting the works, and he ultimately made an engagement with William Billingsley, of the Derby China Works, and having built a somewhat large and very conveniently arranged factory, commenced the manufacture of china ware in 1796.

William Billingsley was the son of William and Mary Billingsley, of the parish of St. Alkmund, Derby. In 1774 he was apprenticed by his widowed mother to Mr. Duesbury, the proprietor of the Derby China Manufactory, for five years, "to learn the art of painting upon china or porcelain ware," as I have already shown in my notice of Billingsley in my first edition. In 1796 he left the Derby China Works, where he had been employed for the long period of twenty-two years, and removed to Pinxton, occupying, with his wife, his wife's mother, and two daughters, a part of the factory built by Mr. Coke. Here Billingsley succeeded in producing that beautiful granular body which he afterwards perfected at Nantgarw and at Swansea; and here, too, stimulated by Mr. Coke's good taste, he introduced faultless forms in his services and a high style of excellence in decoration. He brought with him several experienced workmen and artists from the Derby works, and took into the factory and instructed several young people of Pinxton and its neighbourhood. His own time was thus so fully occupied with the management of the works, with the arrangement of the concern, and with the " overlooking " of the persons employed that, unfortunately, his own skill and his own splendid colouring of roses and other flowers were lost to the manufacture; and thus we do not find that the expressed fear of his late Derby employers that " his going into another factory will put them in the way of doing flowers in the same way, which they were at present entirely ignorant of," was sustained. In fact, while employed by Mr. Duesbury, Billingsley was in every way master of the art he had been taught; and he had acquired a peculiar method—entirely peculiar to himself—of painting roses which, with his free and truly artistic grouping and harmonious arrangement of colours, made his pieces so much sought after that orders were constantly sent in for objects " painted with Billingsley's flowers." At this period of course his whole time was devoted to

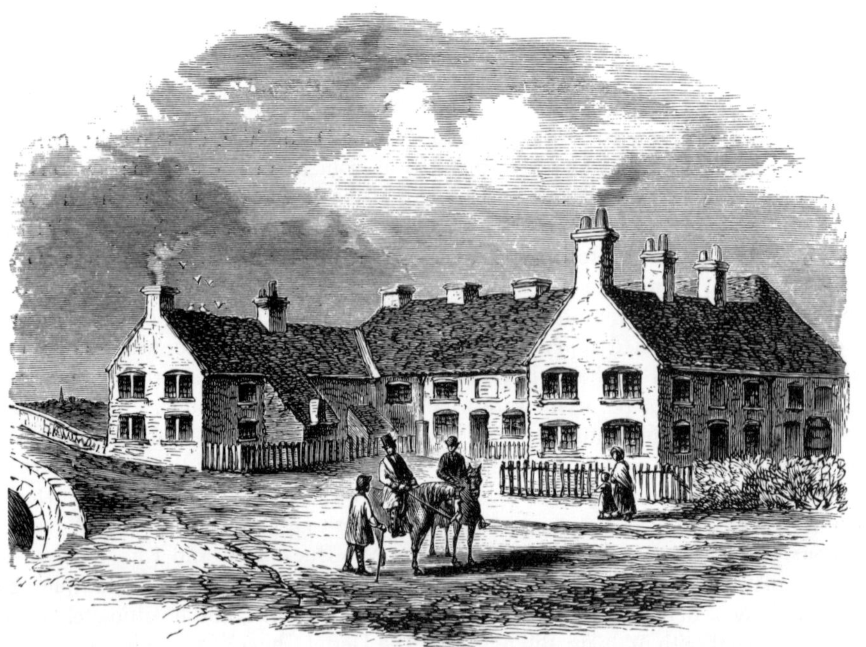

Fig. 1007.

painting, and his heart was in his work. After leaving his employer, his attention was naturally, in the new sphere in which he found himself at Pinxton, almost wholly given to the *practical* instead of the *Art* portion of the establishment, and thus none, or scarcely any, of the known examples of Pinxton china bear evidence of being his handiwork. Indeed, it is not too much to say that, from the time when he closed his connection with the Derby Works, his Art-skill declined, but his manufacturing skill became more and more apparent.

The works at Pinxton were built by the side of the canal, and the workshops formed three sides of a square. These are still in existence at the present day, and are shown in the accompanying vignette, from a sketch I made for the purpose. They are now converted into cottages occupied by colliers and others. The kilns, &c., have entirely disappeared. The place and cottages are still called " China Square," or " Factory Square."

Through some misunderstanding, the arrangement between Messrs. Coke and Billingsley was not of long duration, and in a very few years—probably about 1800 or 1802—Billingsley left the place and removed to Mansfield, where, it is said, he for some time occupied himself in decorating and finishing china ware which he bought in the white state in Staffordshire. He afterwards, as I have already shown, removed to Torksey, Worcester, Nantgarw, Swansea, and Coalport, and died about 1827 or 1828.

Mr. Coke married in 1806 and settled at Debdale Hall, where he died in 1841, in his sixty-sixth year, leaving his estates to Lieut.-Col. Coke, their present possessor. At Debdale are preserved, with religious care, some of the finest examples ever made at Pinxton. These pieces were brought there by the founder of the works, John Coke, and have remained there ever since. They consist of large semicircular spill-stands, mugs, &c., beautifully painted with views, one of which, a view of the family seat of Brookhill Hall, is remarkably fine. Some of the stands are grounded in the Dresden canary colour, and the whole are very choice and unique examples of Pinxton porcelain.

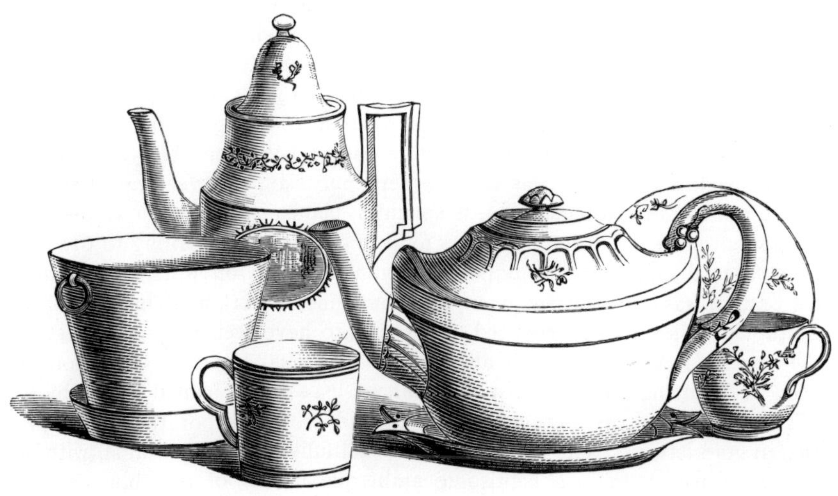

Fig. 1008 to 1014.

The group of china, Figs. 1008 to 1114, is a selection of pieces made during Billingsley's time at Pinxton. They are remarkable for the beauty of the body and of the glaze, and some of them are noticeable for the excellence of the gilding. The coffee pot is one of a set bearing views of different places either in Derbyshire or elsewhere. These landscapes are excellently painted, of a peculiar brownish effect which pervades the whole colouring, by James Hadfield, who was the best landscape-painter at the works. The views on the pieces which have come under my notice are Pinxton Church, Darley Hall, Hartington Bridge, Ashwood Dale, Buxton, Wingerworth Hall, Tong Castle, Saltram, Menai Straits, Wanstead Church, Frog Hall, Caerphilly Castle, and others. The teapot and stand are of elegant shape, unusually narrow, and carefully gilt; the stand is of peculiar form. The cup and saucer have the "Derby Sprig" (Tournay sprig), as it is frequently called. The coffee-mug and flower-pot tell their own tale.

After the close of Billingsley's connection with the Pinxton Works they were carried on by Mr. Coke with the assistance of a Mr. Banks. Afterwards Mr. Coke took

John Cutts to manage the concern, and he became a partner in the works. In the later part of the time the manufactory was carried on by Cutts alone. At the close of the Pinxton Works, which took place about 1818, Cutts removed into Staffordshire —fixing himself at Lane End—where he commenced business, at first buying ware in the white and finishing it for sale. In 1811, Davies says, "There is a considerable porcelain manufactory at Pinxton, which finds employment for several hands."

After Billingsley's removal from Pinxton the character of the ware underwent a change. The granular body of which I have spoken as produced, and afterwards brought to such perfection by him, was his own secret, and he zealously kept it. On leaving Pinxton this secret naturally went with him, and, of course, the goods produced after that time were of a different and much inferior body. The later ware approached pretty closely the ordinary china body of the time, and had a slightly bluish tint in the glaze. The decoration was also, as a rule, not equal to what it had been in the earlier days of the factory.

Among the workmen brought from Derby along with Billingsley, were Thomas Moore, a clever thrower; Ash, also a clever thrower and turner; and many others of repute. Among the painters, &c., were James Hadfield, a good landscape painter; Edward Rowland, a landscape-painter; Morrell, who painted landscapes and flowers; Richard Robins, from London; William Alvey, and others, including Slater and Marriott. Alvey left Pinxton about 1803, and became master of Edingley School, near Southwell, where he died in 1867, aged about eighty-three. He had a numerous family, some of whom re-settled at Pinxton. Alvey, who was held in high respect at Edingley, was an excellent musician, a clever draughtsman and colourist, a first-rate mathematician, a splendid penman, a very fair land-surveyor, and a poet of no mean order. He was fond of drawing and painting to the last.

No especial mark was at any period used at the Pinxton works. The number of the pattern was occasionally given, and sometimes a workman's mark was added; and although other marks *were* used, none seem to have been adopted as distinctive of the works. A writing letter 𝒫 and a Roman capital letter P have both been noticed as occurring on isolated specimens. A tea-service, named to me by Capt. G. Talbot Coke, bears, however, inside the lid of the teapot the word *Pinxton*, written in gold letters. The service is of a beautifully clear white china, with broad edges of burnished gold; a handsome arabesque border of red, blue, and gold ornamenting each piece.

One peculiarity connected with the Pinxton China Works, as with those of Wor-

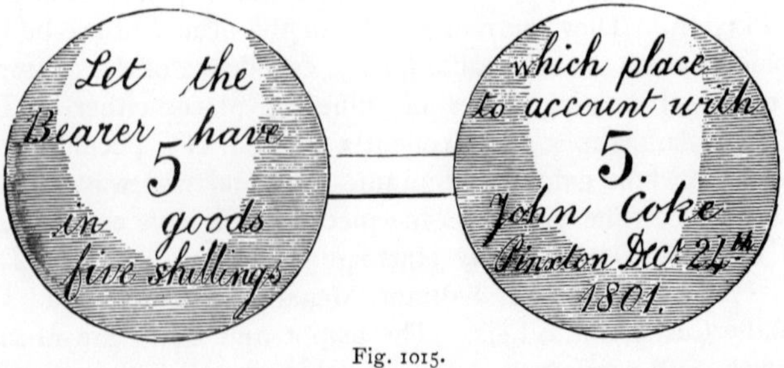

Fig. 1015.

cester, remains to be noticed: it is the issuing of china tokens, *i.e.* tokens representing different values of money, made of china, and payable as money among the workpeople and others, including shopkeepers. These were issued in a time of difficulty, so that they were only temporary conveniences, and thus they possess great interest. They were of two distinct kinds. The general form was a circular disc of white china, thicker in the middle than at the edges—in fact, exactly of the form of a common magnifying-glass—and bore on the obverse a figure of five in the centre, and the words, "*Let the Bearer have in goods five shillings*," in four lines across. On the reverse a similar figure 5 and the words, "*which place to account with John Coke, Pinxton. Decr. 24th,* 1801," in five lines across. The writing is in blue, and the tokens are well glazed. They were issued of various values, as 10*s*., 7*s*. 6*d*., 5*s*., 3*s*. 6*d*., 1*s*. 6*d*., and 1*s*. respectively. The one engraved (Fig. 1015) belongs to W. S. Coke, Esq., of Brookhill, and I am indebted for it to his nephew, Major J. Talbot Coke. Others bore simply the figure of value, gilt or painted on an oval disc. These tokens were used as promissory notes, and when returned to the works by their holders their value in money was given for them, and they were broken up and destroyed. They were payable in and around Pinxton, on one side as far as Sutton, but their payment did not extend to Mansfield. They were called "Mr. Coke's coin," or "chainé money" (china money), in the provincialism of the locality.

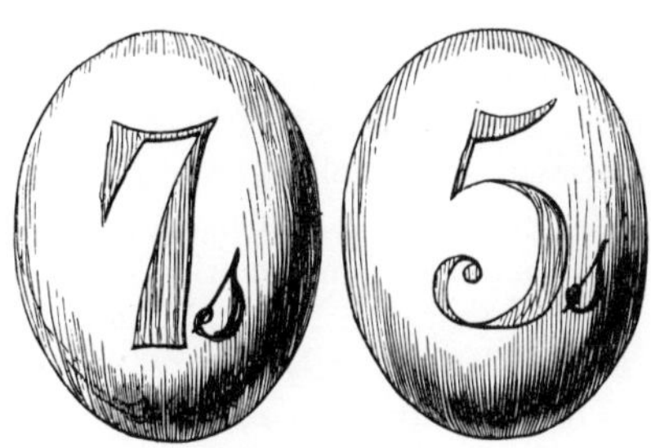

Figs. 1116 and 1117.

It is pleasant to see how the memory of the old china works at Pinxton is cherished by its inhabitants, among whom some of the people who worked there were recently, at a ripe old age, living. One of these, in her eighty-fifth year, who began to work at the factory when but a child of some eleven years of age (at that time named Elizabeth Smith), and became ultimately the chief burnisher of the works, was, when I saw her a few years back, in full possession of all her faculties, and delighted in describing, with marvellous accuracy, all the processes employed. To her wonderful memory, and to that of others, as well as to documents and long personal research, I owe the information which I, in 1868, for the first time, gave in the *Art Journal*, and now repeat, in regard to this interesting manufactory.

Wirksworth.

Wirksworth is much more intimately mixed up with the history of the Ceramic Art than is usually imagined, and yet but little is known of the works which were there carried on, or of their productions. Dugdale, in 1799, says, "About forty years ago, a manufacture of porcelain was attempted; but it proved unsuccessful. . . . . It was in the Holland Manor House that the unsuccessful manufacture of porcelain was attempted;" and Davis, in 1811, repeats the same thing: "In the Holland Manor House the manufacture of porcelain was attempted, about forty years ago, but proving unsuccessful, it was relinquished." Holland House, where this manufacture was carried on, was the Manor House of the manor of Holland, otherwise Richmonds, which was given by Thomas, Earl of Lancaster, to Sir Robert Holland, in which family it remained until the attainder of Henry Holland, Duke of Exeter, in 1461; it afterwards belonged to Margaret, Countess of Richmond and Derby, and was subsequently granted by the Crown to Ralph Gell. In 1745 Philip Gell leased the manor to "Robert Atkinson and Francis Parry, of Lincoln's Inn, gentleman," and to "Andrew Wilkinson, of Borough-bridge, com. York, Esq., and Thomas Wilkinson,

Esq., brother of the said Andrew Wilkinson." In 1777 it was "leased by Philip Gell, Esq., of Hopton, to Richard Arkwright, of Cromford, cotton merchant."

In this latter lease (dated 6th November, 1777), the china works are thus named: "All those several messuages, tenements, or dwelling-houses, and all other buildings, warehouses, workshops, and appurtenances, situate, standing, and being in Wirksworth, in the said county of Derby, heretofore used for the making and manufacturing of China Ware, and now in the tenure or occupation of the said Philip Gell, his assignee or assigns, tenant or undertenants." So that at that time the first china works had probably ceased to be in operation. In 1793, by deed dated 1st November, Richard Arkwright, Esq., assigned the remainder of the lease to Charles Hurt, Esq., of Wirksworth, in the following words: "All those several messuages, tenements, or dwelling-houses, and all other the buildings, warehouses, workshops, and appurtenances, situate, standing, and being in Wirksworth, heretofore used for ye making and manufacturing of china, but now for picking cotton."

My late friend, Mr. T. N. Ince, to whom Wirksworth is indebted for much patient research into its early history, thus wrote to me regarding the china works, having at my request turned his attention to the matter:—"I much regret that I did not extract from the original deed of co-partnership, which I once had in my hands, at least its date, parties, and the like. My opinion is that it was begun about the middle of last century, and did not continue more than a few years. I know the Hurts of Alderwasley, Gells of the Gatehouse and Hopton, Sir Thomas Burdett of Foremark, and many others were partners—nearly the same who were partners in the English and Welsh Mineral Company, of whose concerns were many papers in a bundle in my grandfather and father's office, labelled 'Tissington *v.* Burdett and others;' and amongst them, Mr. Julius Cæsar Robiglio, of Hopton, gentleman, who was said to have been present at a duel in Italy, in which the then Philip Gell of Hopton slew his antagonist and fled to England with Mr. Cæsar Robiglio, who, I have heard my mother say, was a most gentlemanlike man. He died at Hopton, and was buried at Wirksworth or Carsington. The premises called 'China House Yard' were afterwards the property of the late Charles Hurt, Esq., senr. His son, Charles Hurt, junr., died in 1834, on whose death it was sold to the late Mr. John Wilson, maltster; whose son, Mr. Daniel Wilson, wine merchant, is the present owner." Mr. Wilson, who examined his title-deeds specially for me, tells me they contain no information as to the china works. Some years ago, during excavations which were being made, portions of saggers and of china were found; some of these are in my own possession.

It is said that after leaving Pinxton and other places, Billingsley attempted to establish china works here, being probably led to do so by the fact of felspar being abundant in the neighbourhood. Of this, however, there is no proof. Earthenware is also asserted to have been made here; but of this, also, there is no proof.

Dale Abbey.

Encaustic paving-tiles were made here, within the grounds of the abbey, in the fourteenth century. The remains of the kiln in which they were fired were discovered some years back, and in and around it were several tiles and fragments of tiles. Of tiles made here a considerable number exist in the floor of Morley church.

Repton.

Encaustic tiles were made here in the fourteenth century, and the kiln in which they were fired, and a vast number of unfinished tiles and fragments of tiles, were discovered in 1866. The site of the tile-works was within the old abbey walls, and was accidentally brought to light by the boys of Repton School, who were busying themselves in levelling a piece of land for their cricket-ground. During their work they came upon patches of a stiff red clay with fragments of tiles; and, presently afterwards, found some regular layers of them, face downwards. Next they came upon masses of brickwork, which, upon careful clearing, turned out to be a kiln for the firing of the tiles. Of this, and of the tiles found within and around it, I made careful measurements and drawings, gave a fully detailed account

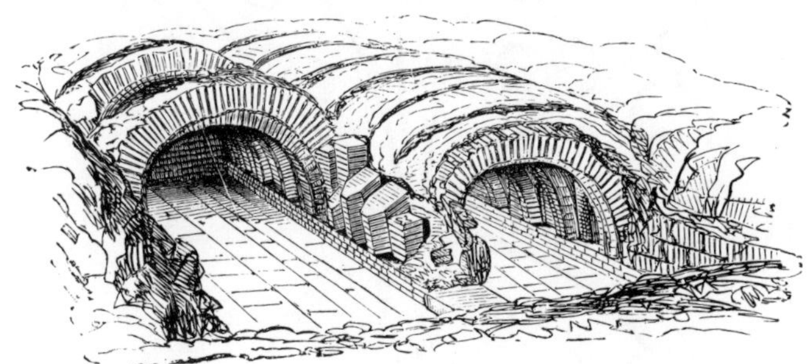

Fig. 1018.

with coloured plates, &c., in the "Reliquary," and also in the first edition of this work. The kiln, Fig. 1018, consisted of two series of arches (each series consisting of six arches alternating with the same number of openings) over what may be termed two vaults, each 7 feet 6 inches long, by 2 feet 6 inches wide, and about 1 foot 10 inches in height. The arches were formed of chamfered bricks or tiles, those composing the actual arch measuring $7\frac{1}{4}$ inches in breadth at the square or upper end; $2\frac{3}{4}$ inches in breadth at the lower end; $7\frac{1}{4}$ inches in length; $4\frac{1}{2}$ inches in length on the square sides; $3\frac{1}{2}$ on the chamfer; $1\frac{1}{4}$ inches in thickness at the upper end; and $\frac{3}{4}$ of an inch in thickness at the lower end. The basement, 4 inches in thickness, was formed of bricks or tiles. Upon this were built up, at distances of $4\frac{1}{2}$ inches apart, the chamfered bricks from which the arches sprung, these being placed broad ends together and so forming a hexagon. Between these the remainder of the wall, to a level with the top of the arches, was formed of encaustic tiles, which being $4\frac{1}{2}$ inches square exactly fill up the width. These encaustic tiles, some hundreds in number, were of various patterns, but evidently unfinished, being quite soft and pliable. The floor of the vault was paved with tiles, and at the entrance was a stone wall on either side, and against the wall-pier was placed the curious relief tile, Fig. 1019.

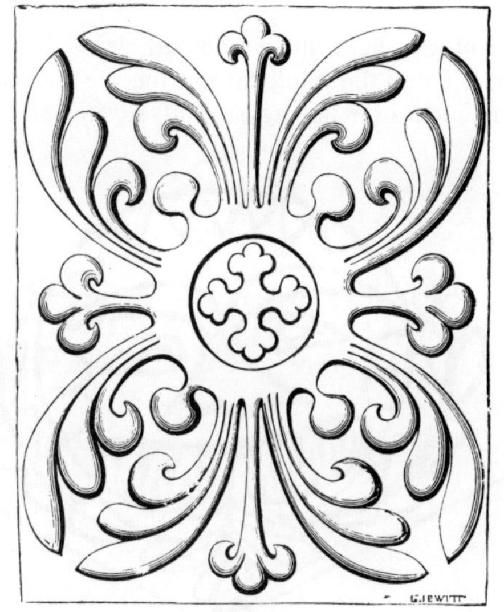

Fig. 1019.

The tiles and fragments of tiles exhibit some examples different in form, as well as in material and in design, from any others which have come under my notice, One of these, on Fig. 1020 (repeated so as to form the complete pattern in a lozenge)

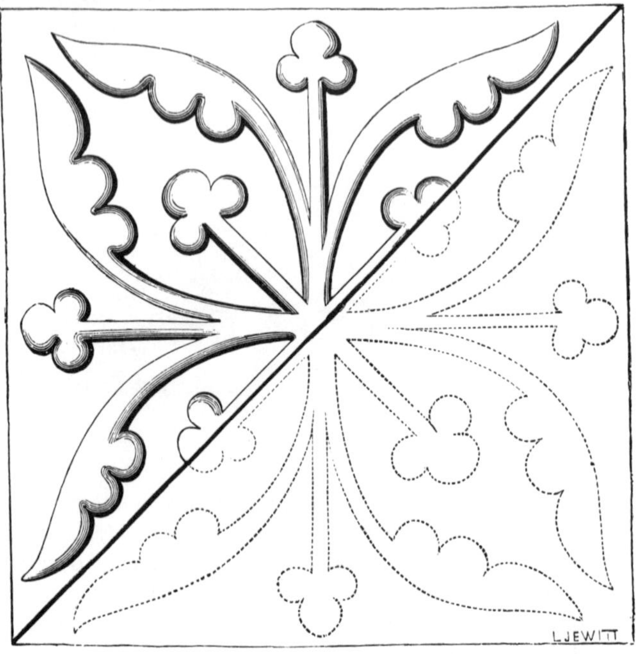

Fig. 1020.

is of very light stone-coloured clay. The foliated pattern is in very high and bold relief, and the whole face of the tile is covered with a rich green glaze. It measures 10 inches on its angles, and 14 inches from point to point on its base, and it is

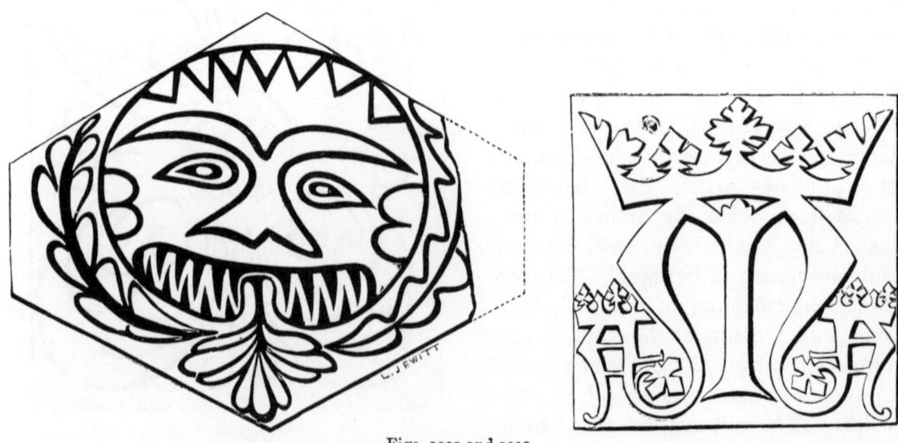

Figs. 1021 and 1022.

1¾ inches thick. Fig. 1019 is of the same material and general character; the pattern in high relief, and the face covered with green glaze. It measures 8 inches by 6½, and is 1¾ inches thick. Another green-glazed tile, also with the pattern in relief, is shown on Fig. 1022. Its design, which is extremely elegant, consists of the crowned initial of the blessed Virgin, (𝔐,) each limb of the letter M terminating in a crowned letter A and foliage. This, I take it, simply means "Ave, Maria."

Of the ordinary class of red and yellow tiles, a very large variety of patterns was found. These consisted of single, four, nine, and sixteen tile patterns of great beauty, and, in many cases, unusual intricacy; border tiles of strikingly beautiful design; heraldic tiles representing the armorial bearings of many local families of note, as well as those of the monarch, &c.; alphabet tiles, bearing the entire alphabet in Lombardic capitals; and grotesque, astronomical, and other devices. It is worthy of remark, as showing the extent to which this manufacture was carried by the monks at Repton, that tiles still existing in, or exhumed on the sites of, many of the old churches and religious houses of this and the adjoining counties are identical with those discovered in this kiln, and are therefore proved to be of Repton make.

Another description of tiles (to which the same remark will also apply) found in this kiln is very peculiar. On these, the pattern, in sharp and tolerably fine lines,

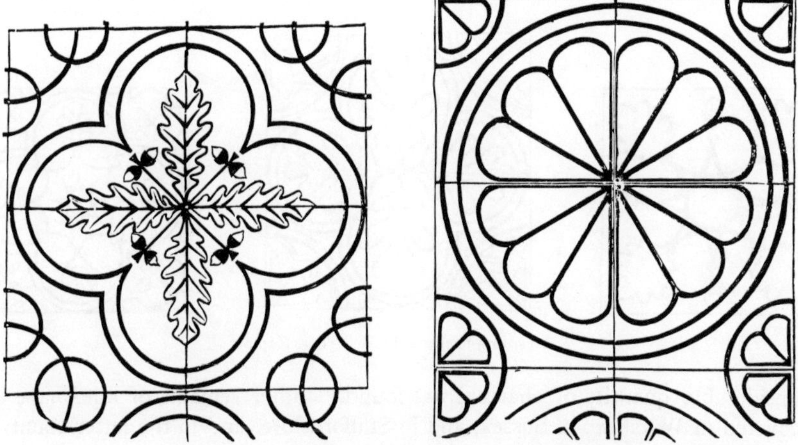

Figs. 1023 and 1024.—"Incised Tiles," made at Repton.

is simply indented or incised into the soft clay, and not filled in with "slip." These "incised tiles" are of dark blue or black colour. An unique tile of this class, given of its full size on Fig. 1021, bears a head within a wreath, and is covered with green glaze; and another, in which the simple device of four saltires within a square has been literally *cut* into the clay, not impressed, was also found.

Having described the Repton kiln, it will be well in the present chapter to give some few particulars of other remains of a like kind. In 1833 my late friend, Mr. H. Eginton, discovered a tile-kiln on land formerly belonging to the priory of Great Malvern. It consisted of two semicircular arches, strongly built, separated from each other by a thick and massive wall or pier. The length of the kiln was 35 feet, and the width of the openings 2 feet 3 inches. In each of the archways was a flooring of stone, about two feet from the ground, composed of three slabs in width; the centre one serving as a key-stone to the others, but more especially, in my opinion, so arranged as to allow the fumes of the charcoal to have proper access to the chamber where the tiles were placed. The place for the fire was on the ground, beneath this elevated flooring, and the earth, from long action of the heat, had become of extreme hardness, and had all the appearance of a thick pavement of limestone. There was no aperture for smoke, so that the process was literally that of the "*smother kiln.*" The arches were double, the outer being constructed of tiles, the inner of bricks, which from long action of the fire had become completely vitrified. The flooring on which the tiles were placed for burning was two inches in thickness, and at the time of the discovery a number of the tiles were found lying in their places as they did when the fire smouldered away beneath them four centuries before. The kiln was placed seven feet under ground—most probably to prevent injury to the structure from expansion by heat—and was firmly backed and bedded in with blocks of Malvern ragstone. The tiles found were identical with some of those now remaining in Great and Little Malvern churches. Another kiln was discovered in 1837 at St. Mary Witton, near Droitwich. It consisted of arched chambers similar to those at Malvern, and separated from each in like manner by a strong intermediate central wall or pier. The arches were 2 feet 2 inches in height, 2 feet 4 inches in width, and of several feet in length, and were partly composed of tiles, partly of brick, and highly vitrified with the heat. In them, as at Malvern,

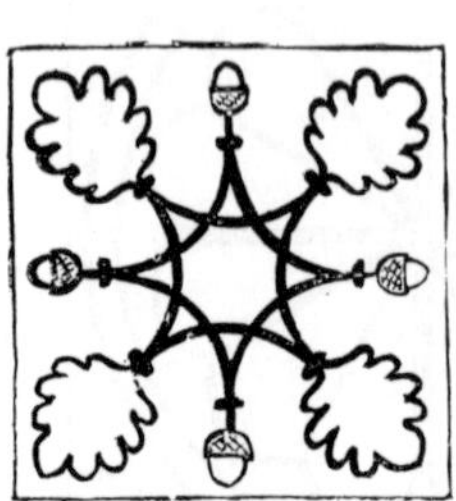

Figs. 1025 to 1027.—Incised Tiles, Repton.

a considerable quantity of charcoal was found. Other remains of kilns have been discovered in Wiltshire, in Sussex, and in Staffordshire, and in the latter county the family name of Telwright, or Tilewright, doubtless taking its origin from makers of tiles, is of great antiquity.

Another kiln was discovered in forming the Metropolitan Railway, close to the Farringdon Street Station in London. The kiln, which rests upon the natural bed of clay of the locality, was found about fourteen feet below the surface-level of Turnmill Street, on the natural bank of the Fleet River. Over it was an immense accumulation of rubbish, doubtless caused by the Great Fire of London. My friend, Mr. J. E. Price, says it was about 16 feet long and 10 feet wide, and consisted of three parallel arches, averaging 2 feet wide by 1 foot high, separated from each other by a pier of about 1 foot in width. These arches constituted the furnaces, and supported a level floor, which was pierced at equal distances with a series of openings each 2 feet long by 5 inches wide. Through these the heat would rise from below for firing the tiles. On the spaces between the apertures the tiles were probably placed for burning. There were thirty of these openings remaining, though in some instances the intervening spaces had fallen away. The entire structure is composed of plain tiles, similar to those used for roofing purposes.

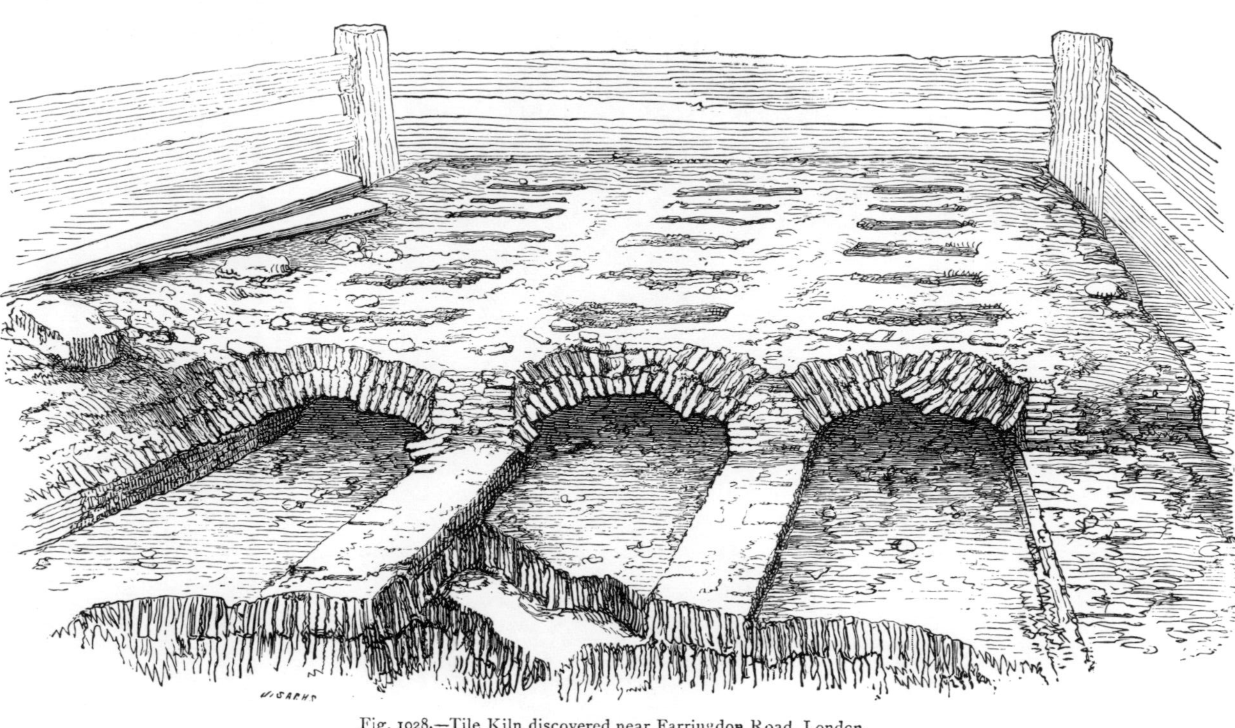

Fig. 1028.—Tile Kiln discovered near Farringdon Road, London.

LITTLE CHESTER.

A manufactory of coarse brown ware formerly existed at Little Chester, near Derby. Fragments of various fictile vessels of much the same character as the Tickenhall dishes, and also of the same kind as the Chesterfield brown ware, have from time to time been found, as well as remains of a potter's kiln. Nothing, however, is known regarding it.

TICKENHALL.

That a pottery existed at this place as early, at all events, as the reign of Queen Elizabeth is incontestably proved by remains which have from time to time been exhumed on the spot. There can, therefore, be no doubt that pottery has for more than three centuries been uninterruptedly made at this place. It 1650 Philip Kinder, in his curious MS. in the Bodleian Library, wrote:—"Numa Pompilius here might have learn't his 'Straine of Frugalities'! Here are your best Fictilias made you; earthern vessels, potts, and pancions, at Tycknall, and carried all East England through." This is the earliest mention of Tickenhall Pottery I have met

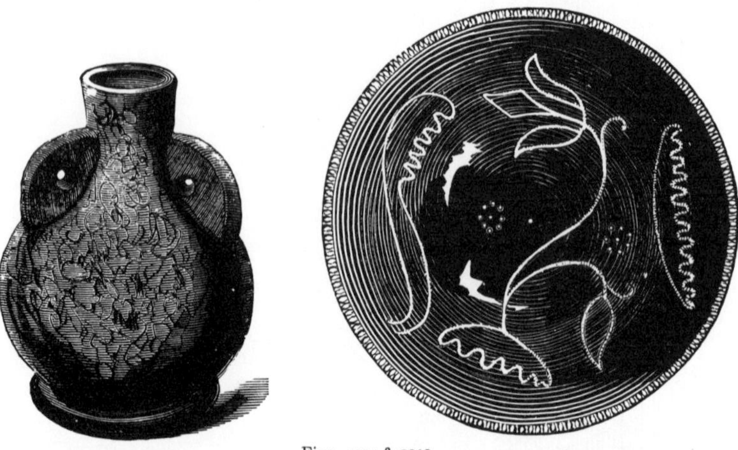

Figs. 1029 & 1030.

with. Pilkington (1789) says:—"Formerly a very large quantity of earthenware was manufactured at this place; but lately the business has very much declined. It is said that since the land in the neighbourhood has been enclosed, it has been difficult to meet with proper clay." The ordinary coarse domestic vessels—"potts and pancions," as they are called by Kinder—were made, but beyond these there were many highly-decorated ones, with human heads for handles, &c. Some fragments of these are in the possession of Sir John Harpur Crewe, Bart., of Calke Abbey, to whom Tickenhall belongs. The ware was coarse, but very hard, the colour a dull brown, nearly black, in some instances with a yellow slip. Sometimes, however, it was of the ordinary red colour. A mediæval pitcher, or jug, in my own possession, which was dug up here in the course of draining operations on the site of the old works, has the body of deep red clay, very hard and compact, and its upper part is covered with a dark glaze; it has been much blistered in firing. In Sir John Crewe's possession is a pilgrim's bottle of the ordinary shape, which was found here (Fig. 1029). He has also portions of others, the most perfect fragment being nearly black, and the other of a reddish brown colour. Two apparently well-authenticated examples of bowls (Figs. 1030 and 1031) are of the ordinary class of earthenware (like those of the Tofts, Taylors, &c.), of a dark brown or chocolate colour, well glazed, and ornamented with a white slip. The larger one bears a very rude representation of a fox-hunt—a fox and three dogs, and a tree. The smaller one, a somewhat gracefully thrown lily, and other ornaments. Another

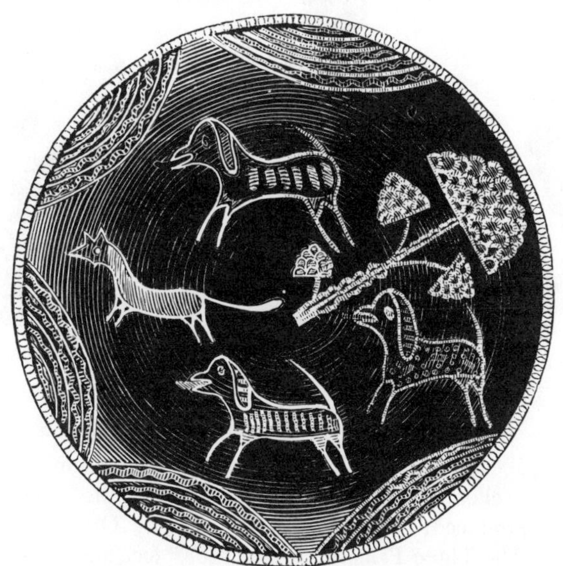

Fig. 1031.

example, in my own collection, is the candlestick (Fig. 1037). It is of precisely the same kind of ware, with white slip ornaments, and the decoration of the base bears a strong resemblance to the outer ornament of the large bowl.

Among the most interesting and undoubtedly authentic of existing examples are some fragments (Figs. 1032 to 1035) in the possession of Sir John Crewe, Bart.

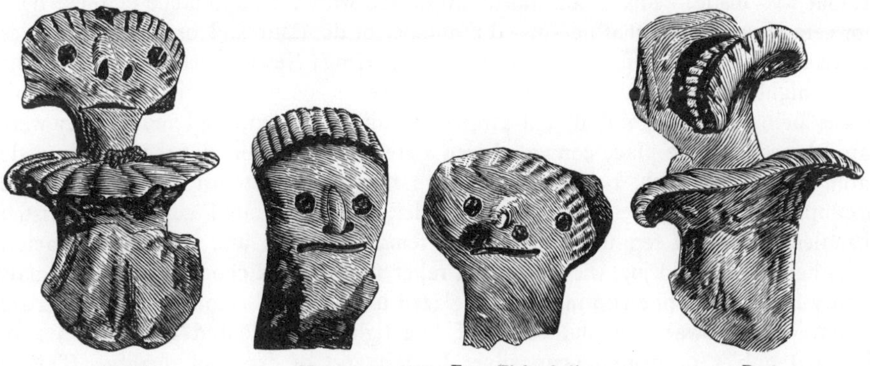

Front. Figs. 1032 to 1035.—From Tickenhall. Back.

They are heads, dug up on the spot, formed of a buff clay and "touched" with a darker slip. The head-dress and ruff of 1032 and 1035 indicate, at all events, about the reign of Mary or Elizabeth, and Fig. 1033 bears the plaited cap of the same period. They are all engraved of the full size, and in general character bear a marked resemblance to some which were found in 1854 on the site of a mediæval potwork on the North Cliff at Scarborough (Figs. 1036 and 1038). Another vessel there found is engraved on page 68, Fig. 299.

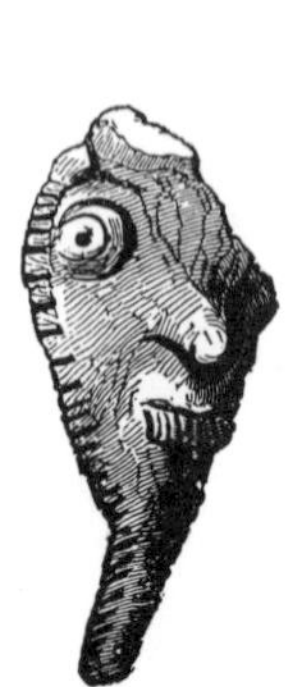

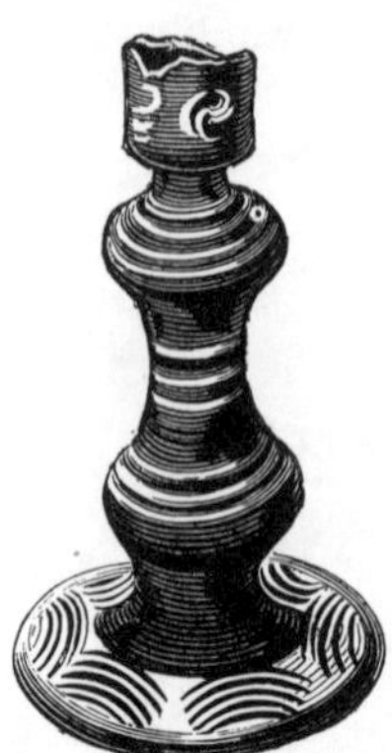

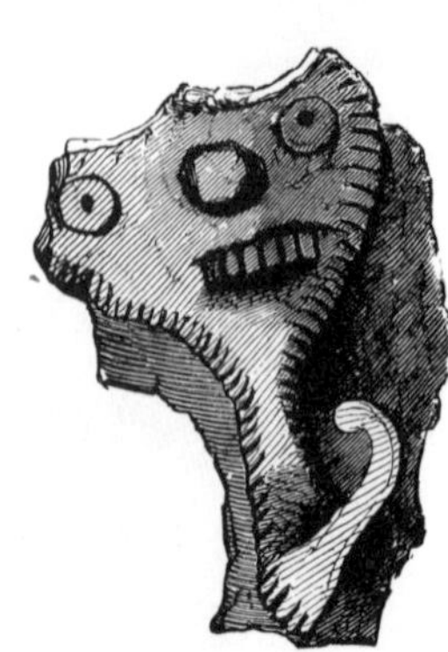

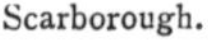

Scarborough. Figs. 1036 to 1038.—Tickenhall. Scarborough.

KINGS NEWTON.

At this village the fine assemblage of examples of Anglo-Saxon Ceramic Art spoken of upon page 58, was brought to light, and in recent times pottery of a good quality and excellent character has been made from the same bed of clay from which they were produced. About 1852 Mr. Henry Orton (brother to James Orton, author of "The Three Palaces," "Excelsior," &c., and himself a writer of no mean repute under the *nom de plume* of "Philo"), then of the Chauntry House, Kings Newton, considering the bed of clay at this place well adapted for useful and ornamental purposes, erected workshops, sheds, and kilns, and commenced the manufacture of garden-vases, chimney-tops, flower-boxes and pots, brackets, and a large variety of other articles. These he produced both in their natural colour and surface-painted and gilded, and many of them were of excellent design. From one of the beds of clay a fine red terra-cotta was produced, and from another a buff colour was made. Mr. Orton was so impressed with the importance of these beds for ceramic purposes, that he caused a number of domestic and ornamental articles to be made in the Staffordshire potteries from Kings Newton clay, and the results were highly satisfactory. Circumstances, however, occurred which prevented his plans being matured, and after a large expenditure of time and money they were abandoned, and the place converted into a steam brick-yard. Of the articles made from this clay (which, being very few, are now of the utmost rarity), I possess examples. One of these is a butter-cooler, with perforated cover and twisted handles, formed of red unglazed clay of remarkably fine and compact character. Another is a pressed jug, with groups of relief flowers, in a chocolate-coloured clay, partly lined with white slip inside, and glazed in its natural colour. The others are a terra-cotta flower-vase and stand of fine light buff-coloured clay, and a two-handled goblet or drinking-cup, silver lustred, and of excellent quality. This is made of the brown or chocolate clay. The probability is that some day these clays may yet be turned to better account than that of making bricks for railway tunnels.

BURTON-UPON-TRENT.

In 1794 a manufactory was established in this neighbourhood by Sir Nigel

Gresley, Bart., of Drakelow, and C. B. Adderley, Esq., of Hams Hall (ancestor of the present Baron Norton), who died in 1826. In June, 1795, William Coffee, one of the modellers at the Derby china manufactory, was engaged for these works, as is shown by a letter in my possession as follows:—"My being your debtor makes it my duty to inform you immediately of my arrival here, and likewise my engagement with Sir Nigel Gresley and Mr. Adderley, lest you should suppose I had forgot the obligation I lie under to you," etc. The works were situated "within fifty yards of Gresley Hall, near the village and castle of Gresley, in the county of Derby," with also a place in Burton itself. From some cause or other the project did not answer, and about 1800 the works passed into the hands of Mr. William Nadin, who carried on the manufactory for four or five years, when he discontinued it, and was succeeded by Mr. Burton, of Linton, Derbyshire, who continued the works for a few years and then closed them. By Mr. Nadin the usual classes of ordinary Staffordshire wares were made, as also was china. In the latter, one great speciality was boots, shoes, and slippers, which were extensively produced and variously ornamented. His aged son, Mr. J. Nadin, wrote me, in reference to these, "My father made a large number of china boots and shoes, and I well remember when about six years old, walking up to my ankles into a pond of water in a pair of these boots (Wellington in shape)." He also told me that when his father "had these works, he received an order for a magnificent dinner-service—the price was fixed at £700—for Queen Charlotte, through Colonel Desbrow, her Chamberlain, but he was never able to execute it, as the china always came out of the ovens cracked and crazed, though he employed the very best men he could obtain." The Duke of Kent is said to have paid the works a visit, accompanied by Colonel Desbrow. No examples of the production of these are, as far as my inquiries go, now known to be in existence.

About 1832 Mr. William Edwards, solicitor, of Derby (brother-in-law of the second Mr. William Duesbury, of the Derby china works), in conjunction with a Mr. Tunnicliffe, commenced a yellow ware manufactory at the Hay, Burton-on-Trent. Later on the manufactory of china or "artificial marble" was commenced in High Street, workmen having been brought from the Potteries and from Derby. They only continued in operation for a few years, and the productions were not marked. In ornamental ware Mr. Edwards confined himself to the production of figures, but they were complete failures. "Mr. Edwards's artificial marble gods and goddesses, made at the Burton-on-Trent works, came out of the oven with their limbs twisted into every conceivable form." On his failure the works were closed, and he removed to Butt House, near Woodville, at that time known as Wooden Box. Mr. Edwards employed some really good workmen, amongst whom was a clever modeller named Wornell, some good examples of whose work were in the possession of the late Mr. Abram Bass, by whom much of this information was supplied to me.

SWADLINCOTE.

Swadlincote Potteries.—The works of Messrs. Sharpe, Brothers, and Co. were established by Thomas Sharpe in 1821, and were carried on by him alone until his death in 1838. They were then continued by his brothers, as "Sharpe, Brothers, and Co.," under which style they are still carried on by the last surviving brother, Mr. Edmund Sharpe. The productions are the same as those of the general district—viz., the "Derbyshire Ironstone Cane (or Yellow) Ware" (a name by which this ware has for upwards of a century been known, and which is the speciality of the district); buff drab ware, fire-proof ware, Rockingham ware, mottled ware, and black lustre ware. In "Derbyshire Ironstone" every description of household vessels are made, as they are also in buff drab ware. In the Rockingham, mottled, and black lustre wares, tea and coffee-pots in an endless variety of patterns, pressed and plain jugs and mugs of good designs, and other useful articles are made. Blue printed goods are also produced. Among the specialities of these works may be named the "Toby Fillpot" jugs (Fig. 1039), which are made in both coloured and Rockingham ware, on much the same model as the older jugs of that name. Sanitary earthenware is one of the great specialities of these works, and is produced in cane-colour, white, and blue printed varieties, as well as, occasionally, of a highly decorative character. In these, plug-basins, closet-basins, with Sharpe's Patent Direct Action, requiring no fans, but acting on the principle of a hollow rim with graduated perforations; traps, cabinet wash-hand stands of excellent and convenient construction, and other articles, are extensively made.[1] Besides the home trade, Messrs. Sharpe export in large quantities to Canada, the United States, Nova Scotia, South Africa, New Zealand, India, Australia, Africa, the Sandwich Islands, Germany, Holland, Russia, Prussia, Hungary, &c.

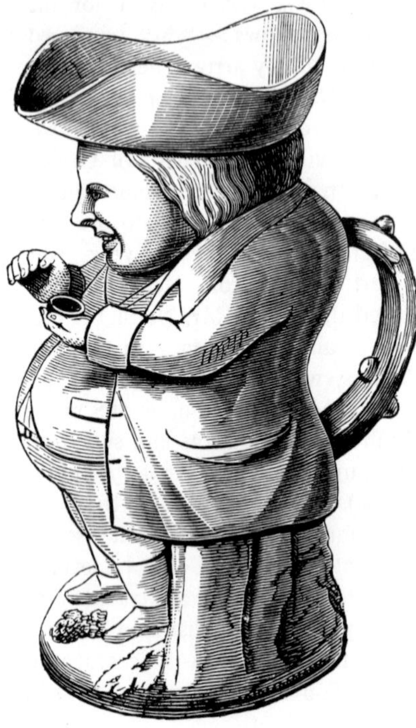
Fig. 1039.

The mark first used was simply the name THOMAS SHARPE, or T. SHARPE, impressed in the ware. That of the present firm is the monogram S. B. and Co. within a wreath of oak and ivy, and the words SHARPE'S PATENT, (Fig. 1040).

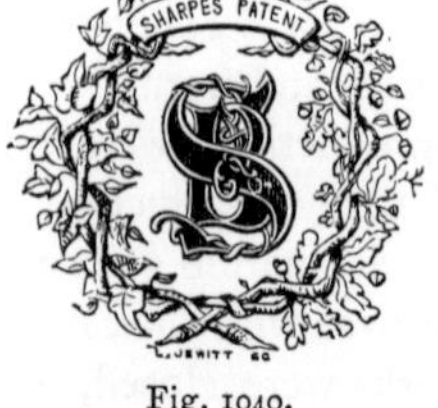

Fig. 1040.

Swadlincote Pottery.—These, established in 1790, by John Hunt, of Swadlincote, were, after his death, continued by Thomas Woodward, whose son, James Woodward, is their present proprietor; they were the first of the kind in the place. Fire-bricks, fire-clay, for Sheffield steel-works crucibles, and iron-furnaces, were the sole productions till 1859, when the manufacture of sewage-pipes, terra-cotta chimney-pots, vases, &c., was added, and since then marble, white, and cane-coloured sanitary earthenware has been introduced, the patent "Wash-out" arrangement peculiar to these works being in high repute. Majolica and Rockingham ware were also at one time made. The mark "the anchor, with a portion of cable twisted round it, forming a monogram of J. W.," Fig. 1041.

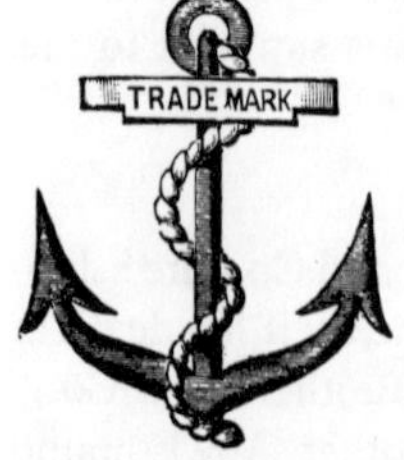

Fig. 1041.

Swadlincote Mills.—Established by Moses Cartwright, about 1837, but now carried on by Mr. Edward Grice, who produces all the usual sanitary and terra-cotta goods of the district.

The Waterloo Pottery was established in 1815 by Robinson and Rowley, and has since been worked by Mr. Robinson alone, Mr. James Staley, Staley Brothers, and Mason and Adcock. Mr. Adcock died in 1879, and in 1880 Mr. Mason removed to the Pool Pottery. Mr. R. C. Staley, one of the former proprietors, now carries on the manufactory and produces the usual descriptions of Derbyshire cane ware, yellow ironstone, and buff, Rockingham, and mottled wares.

Old Midway Pottery.—Established by a Mr. Granger, these works passed from him to Richard Staley, sen., and are carried on under the style of "Richard Staley and Sons," for the production of Derbyshire fireproof cane ware, Rockingham ware, and buff ware, in which all the usual domestic and other articles are made. The mark is the name, with "Fireproof" added upon dishes, &c.

Large sanitary pipe, fire-brick, and terra-cotta works have also been established at Swadlincote by Messrs. Wragg & Sons, who have also large works at Sheffield. Their pipes are all machine-made sockets of good quality.

Church Gresley.

The Church Gresley Pottery.—Established about 1790 by a Mr. Leedham for coarse pancheon ware, was, about 1816, bought by Mr. W. Bourne, who commenced the manufacture of Derbyshire ironstone cane ware, and was succeeded by Mr. Edwards, Messrs. Shaw and Harrison, and Mr. Henry Wileman, at whose decease, in 1864, they were taken by Mr. T. G. Green. Cane-coloured ironstone, Rockingham, mottled, black lustre, buff, and other wares are made; and at an adjoining manufactory, built by Mr. Green in 1871, the usual services and domestic articles, in painted, lined, sponged, and cream-coloured earthenware are made. Mr. Green has taken out patents for a process of moulding earthenware, and for a bat-making machine.

Commonside Pottery.—At these old-established works the commonest earthenware was first made; and, afterwards, by Mr. Edward Grice, sanitary goods and chimney-pots were made. He was succeeded, in 1873, by Mason, Gough, and Till. In 1874 Mr. Mason left the firm, which, since then, has been "Till and Gough." Yellow, Rockingham, and buff wares are made of the usual quality, and in the same general variety of articles as in the other Derbyshire potteries. No mark is used.

Commonside Works.—Mr. Edward Grice, who, after leaving the above, established these works in 1867, manufactures sanitary and terra-cotta goods of various kinds.

The Hill Top Works were established in 1810 by Mr. John Cooper, who, with partners, carried them on successively as "John Cooper," "Cooper and Massey," and "Cooper and Banks." They next belonged to Mr. Henry Ansell. The present proprietor is Mr. Nehemiah Banks. The wares produced are the ordinary "Derbyshire Ironstone Cane Ware," buff ware, Rockingham ware, and black lustre ware. Horticultural ware of superior quality is also largely made.

Hillside Works.—These are devoted to the manufacture of fire-clay goods.

BRETBY ART POTTERY.

In 1883 Mr. Henry Tooth, whose connection with the "Linthorpe Pottery" then ceased, commenced, in conjunction with a partner, some new works at Church Gresley, for the production of a similar class of goods to those produced at Linthorpe. The works, which will be carried on under the name of the "Bretby Art Pottery," are intended to produce, besides an ever-increasing variety of ornamental articles in the charming modes of decoration with which Mr. Tooth is familiar, all the usual classes of useful goods to which an art character can be imparted. The spot chosen is well calculated for their full development, coal and clays, both the ordinary red and a fine yellow, being abundant. The pieces so far produced at these works are characterised by a firmness of body, a perfectness of glaze that is not given to "craze," and a clearness of colour that is very refreshing. Simplicity—even in some instances carried to severity—of form, combined with richness, and at the same time harmony of colouring, and a softness and delicacy of blending, are indeed among the characteristics of this art pottery. The mark is a sun with the word BRETBY.

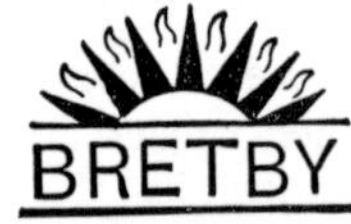

Fig 1042.

Other manufactories in the district are or were Mr. R. Quinton's brown ware and stone-bottle works; Mr. E. Jones's pancheon and flower-pot works, and the works of Mr. W. Cotterell; Mansfield & Whittaker's tile-works; and Robinson & Massey's sanitary earthenware works.

About 1846 Mr. William Edwards, formerly of Derby, and later of Burton-on-Trent, commenced a yellow-ware manufactory at Ashby Holes, Gresley Common, which he carried on for a few years.

WOODVILLE, OR WOODEN BOX, HARTSHORNE, GRESLEY, &c.

Woodville, the modern and more euphonious name given to the village of "Wooden Box," is five and a half miles from Burton-on-Trent. The original name arose from an old wooden "box" or hut which formerly stood on the site of the present toll-house, where a man used to sit to collect toll, but which was afterwards burned down. The original "box," it may be added, was an old port-wine butt, from Drakelow Hall, and in this the collector, Diogenes-like, spent his days. In 1800 only two houses existed here, the "Butt House," belonging to the then Earl Ferrars, and the residence of his son Lord Tamworth, and a farmhouse. On this farm some valuable beds of clay were found to exist, and a Mr. Peake, from the Staffordshire pottery district, established a small manufactory on the spot. From this manufactory the trade of the district has entirely taken its rise, and it is now noted for extensive manufactories of Derbyshire ironstone ware, cane-coloured, Rockingham, black, buff, and brown wares, sanitary goods, terra-cotta, &c. Its inhabitants are principally potters and colliers, and it has risen to the importance of being a parish of itself—part of the parish of Hartshorne, in Derbyshire, and of Ashby-de-la-Zouch, in Leicestershire, being taken for the purpose, the main, or High, street separating those two counties. Near Woodville is the modern hamlet of Albert village, and it has a branch line on the Midland Railway.

The Hartshorne Potteries were established in 1818 by Mr. Joseph Thompson, father of Richard and Willoughby Thompson, who succeeded him as "Thompson Brothers," and were in turn succeeded by "Holland and Thompson," who failed in 1882. Derbyshire ironstone ware, brown, cane, buff, and yellow ironstone ware (enamelled white inside), black and Rockingham wares, terra-cotta goods, and sanitary ware, etc., were made, and, by the last firm, all the usual kinds of white ware, china, and decorated goods were produced.

J THOMPSON

or

JOSEPH THOMPSON
WOODEN BOX POTTERY
DERBYSHIRE

The *Hartshorne Pottery* was established about 1790 by James Onions, who was succeeded by Luke Copeland. It was next carried on successively by Read, Malkin and Co., Read and Malkin, and G. S. Read. Mr. Read died in 1860, when the concern passed into the hands of J. B. Rowley. The goods produced are "Derbyshire Ironstone" or cane-coloured ware, Rockingham ware, mottled ware, buff ware, and black lustre ware; in these all the usual articles for domestic use are made.

Woodville Tile Works.—At these works, established by Barry & Co., sanitary goods and encaustic, mosaic, geometrical, and white-glazed tiles for baths, &c., are made, as also are terra-cotta vases, chimney-tops, and other ornamental goods.

The *Woodville Pottery* was established in 1833 by Thomas Hall and William Davenport, and in 1858 passed into the hands of Thomas Betteridge and Thomas Nadin, who in 1863 retired from the concern, which since then has been carried on by Mr. Betteridge. The goods produced are the usual classes of Derbyshire cane-coloured ironstone, Rockingham, mottled, and buff wares of the district.

Albion Works.—The Albion Fire Clay Works, established by Hosea Tugby & Co., produce all the usual fire-clay goods, bricks, tiles, &c. The firm have patented a "continuous direct-action kiln."

The *Woodville Potteries* were established about 1810 by Mr. Watts, who was joined in partnership by his relative, Mr. Cash, in whose family it has remained to the present day, and is carried on under the style of "Watts and Cash." The productions are the Derbyshire "ironstone" or "yellow" ware, buff-coloured ware, Rockingham ware, &c., of the ordinary qualities, in which all the usual varieties of domestic vessels, services, &c., are manufactured.

The *Rawdon Pottery* was built by the fourth Marquess of Hastings, on whose estate it was situate, and was first worked by John Hall, who was succeeded, on his failure, by John Brunt, who, at his death, was succeeded by his son, Thomas Brunt, who, however, did not succeed in the business, and in 1861 the works passed to Smith, Dooley & Co. The goods produced are the usual varieties of articles in "Derbyshire Ironstone," or cane-coloured ware, Rockingham ware, buff ware, and cream-coloured ware.

The "*Pool Works*" for terra-cotta fire-bricks and sanitary tubes, at Woodville, were established about 1830 by J. W. Bourne, of Church Gresley, who purchased the property from Sir Roger Gresley, Bart. After his death, in 1840, Mr. Edward Ensor, of Lyme Regis, took to the business, and the year following sent his second son, Henry Loader Ensor, at the age of fourteen, to learn, and eventually manage, the business. The clay found being suitable for making crucibles for steel refiners at Sheffield, their manufacture was introduced into that market, and has gradually grown into a very important branch of the trade of this district. In 1845 Mr. Ensor, senr., came to live at Gresley Cottage, and took the active management of the business, from which he afterwards retired. About 1850 he purchased the property, and his eldest son, Edward, having returned from South Africa, took part in the business. In 1864 Mr. Ensor purchased the right of the sole use of the Hoffman Patent in this district, and erected kilns, drying-sheds, &c., intending by it to burn all his goods, but found the Hoffman system, although good for common red bricks (which require little heat), was not adapted to fire-brick and terra-cotta, which require very great heat. This led to his inventing a process by which he retained the heat so effectively that 3 cwt. of small coal burnt more successfully 1,000 bricks than 20 cwt. of good rough coal did in the most approved old-fashioned kilns. He also adapted Carr's "Patent Disintegrator" to his process, and by improvements made it the most valuable clay-reducer ever used. About 1868 Mr. Edward Ensor, jun., having patented "a process for an improved system of burning all kinds of earthenware, salt-glazed, sanitary, and terra-cotta goods, fire, blue, and common bricks, tiles, &c., lime, and other commodities," a kiln, which has been proved a perfect success, was erected, and is still in use at these works for burning salt-glazed sanitary goods, and at several other manufactories for bricks, in each case effecting a saving of 75 per cent. in fuel and in labour. The fire-bricks made here are sent to every quarter of the globe; fireplace-backs are also extensively made. The salt-glazed sanitary goods are highly vitrified, and capable of withstanding the action of the acids in sewerage, &c. In terra-cotta vases, tazzas, pedestals, brackets, trusses, and ornamental bricks are produced. The works are now carried on by a limited liability company, under the style of "Ensor & Co., Limited," Mr. H. Loader Ensor being one of the managers.

Woodville.—Messrs. Barry & Co. manufacture all the usual varieties of glazed stoneware sewerage and drain-pipes.

Wooden Box Pottery was established by Thomas Hallam in 1817, and since then has been successively worked by Mr. Robinson, Harrison & Cash, Hallam & Co., and Watts & Cash, and its present proprietor, Thomas Nadin, who manufactures ironstone, cane, buff, and Rockingham wares of the usual kinds and qualities.

Mount Pleasant Works.—In 1847 the late Mr. John Knowles, of Matlock, established these works for the manufacture of bricks, tiles, fire-clay goods and terra-cotta. These he continued till his death in 1869, when they were carried on by his widow till 1871; since that time they have been continued by trustees, under the style of "John Knowles & Co." Besides all the usual classes of bricks, tiles, stove-backs, garden-edgings, salt-glazed sanitary and drain-pipes, &c., some highly ornate chimney-tops and garden vases of good design are made. The firm are also proprietors of crucible and cement fire-clays.

Coleorton Pottery.—Established in 1835 by Messrs. Wilson, Lount, and Proudman. The latter partners having retired, the works have since been carried on by Thomas Wilson. The productions are yellow, buff or cane, and Rockingham wares, in which all the usual domestic articles are made.

CHAPTER XVIII.

The large and commercially important as well as thickly populated district known as the "Staffordshire Potteries," or more commonly called simpiy "The Potteries," comprises a number of towns known as the "Pottery Towns," and other places adjoining them. These are Burslem, Hanley, Shelton, Tunstall, Stoke-upon-Trent, Longton, Etruria, Cobridge, Fenton, Longport, and Dresden. Of these Stoke-upon-Trent, although far from being the oldest, or largest, or busiest, is the great railway centre, and head of the parliamentary district of Stoke-upon-Trent. Some of the towns are corporate, and Newcastle-under-Lyme is both a corporate and parliamentary borough. It is estimated that in this pottery district some fifty thousand persons or more are employed in or dependent on the staple trade of the place, that of china and earthenware manufacture.

Stoke-upon-Trent.

Spode.—Copeland.—The first notice of the name of Spode that I have met with in connection with potting is the entry of the "hiring" of Josiah Spode by Thomas Whieldon, in 1749. The entry is of considerable historical interest, as being the first hiring of Josiah Spode, who, being born in 1733, would at that time be sixteen years of age, and was the founder of the family which subsequently rose to such eminence in the art. The "hiring" being for three years, and at wages ranging from 2*s.* 3*d.* to 3*s.* 3*d.* per week, while other men at the same time were being paid 5*s.* 3*d.* to 7*s.* per week, would appear to have been a kind of apprenticeship, or, at all events, a "finishing touch" to the learning of the trade. From April till Martinmas, which is the great time for all hirings in the pottery trade, the payment was to be at 2*s.* 3*d.* per week, "or 2*s.* 6*d.* if he deserves it," with the prospect of a rise of sixpence per week in successive years. He appears to have fully worked out his time, and to have been found deserving, for in 1752 his "hiring" was raised to 7*s.* a week with 5*s.* "earnest;" and in 1754 to 7*s.* 6*d.* weekly with £1 11*s.* 6*d.* "earnest." At this time he must have been married, for in the same year, 1754, it appears the second Josiah Spode was born. But little is known of the early life of this second Josiah Spode; the probability, however, is that his father, after leaving Whieldon's service, commenced a small manufactory on his own account, and that he learned the business with him. About 1770, Spode the son at that time being about sixteen years old, is stated to have taken the works at Stoke previously carried on by Turner, or Turner and Banks. He is said also to have introduced, about 1784, transfer printing into Stoke. Previous to this time Copeland, of London (a native of Stoke), who travelled in the tea trade, made the acquaintance of Spode and offered to undertake a commission to sell his tea-ware and other goods to his customers. The enterprise was successful, and a warehouse was taken in Fore Street, Cripplegate, London, for the sale of Spode's goods.

Trade increasing rapidly, Copeland, who became a partner with Spode, afterwards, in 1779, purchased the property, 37, Lincoln's Inn Fields, and, at the back, in Portugal Street, opened an immense depot for the sale of pottery goods, in the place where stood the theatre (originally built by D'Avenant in 1662, and rebuilt by Rich in 1714), famous as being the house in which Garrick first appeared, the original Joe Miller flashed out his witticisms, and where the *Recruiting Officer*, the *Beggar's Opera*, &c., were first produced. This establishment was managed by Mr. Copeland, the manufactory being conducted entirely by Mr. Spode. Mr. Spode's son, who was ultimately taken into partnership with his father, was for a time in the London house, but on the death of the latter, in 1797, he returned to Stoke, and devoted himself to the manufactory. In 1800 Mr. Spode commenced making porcelain in addition to earthenware, and was the first to introduce felspar into its composition. In 1805 he introduced an opaque porcelain, known as "ironstone china," which he manufactured to a large extent, and exported to France and other countries. In 1806 H.R.H. the Prince of Wales visited the works, and Mr. Spode was appointed potter to him. The porcelain, the ironstone china, and the ordinary earthenware manufactured at this time were of the very highest character, and rank with the best of the period.

The first partnership was "Spode and Copeland," and next, "Spode, Son, and Copeland." After the death of the elder Spode it again became "Spode and Copeland," and, next, on the son of the latter, who was afterwards alderman, being taken into partnesship, "Spode, Copeland, and Son," and was so carried on until the elder Mr. Copeland's death, in 1826. In 1827 the second Mr. Spode died, and was succeeded by his son, the third Josiah Spode, who, however, only survived his father two years, and died in 1829. The business was then carried on by the executors of the third Josiah Spode, of Hawksyard (his only son, also named Josiah, being a minor), and Alderman Copeland, until 1833, when the entire concern was purchased by Alderman William Taylor Copeland, who shortly afterwards took into partnership his principal traveller, Thomas Garrett, and the firm became "Copeland and Garrett," and so continued until dissolved in 1847, when, from that time till 1867 the style was "W. T. Copeland, late Spode." In that year Mr. Copeland took his four sons into partnership, and from that time the firm has continued under the name of "W. T. Copeland and Sons." Mr. Alderman Copeland, who was Lord Mayor of London in 1835-6, was M.P. for Coleraine from 1828 till 1832, and Stoke-upon-Trent from 1837 till 1852, and 1857 till 1865. He was grandson of William Copeland, yeoman, of the Holly Bush, in the parish of Stoke-upon-Trent, and son of the partner of the first Mr. Spode.

Of the productions of the present firm it is manifestly impossible to give even a *resumé*; the bare enumeration of the different articles in porcelain and earthenware would occupy many closely printed pages. For breakfast, dinner, dessert, tea, and toilet services the firm ranks among the very highest in order of merit. They are produced both in china and in earthenware, and in every variety of ornamentation; in the former from the simple gold or coloured lines and borders, and in the latter from the commonest sponged patterns, to the most profuse and lavish relief and painting. One of their highest efforts, and deservedly so, in the way of services, is the dessert service made especially for H.R.H. the Prince of Wales in 1866. It consists of 198 pieces, comprising a centre, eight compotiers, two cream-bowls, two ice-pails, twelve sweetmeat compotiers, seventy-two cups and saucers, and fifty plates. The commission was given shortly before the Prince's marriage, and hence, as all the decorations are floral, the orange-blossom was allowed to become a prominent object in each group; and it would be impossible to conceive flowers more exquisitely painted than they were by Mr. Hürten and others. The centre-piece is a double *assiette monté*, the principal compartment being supported by seated figures

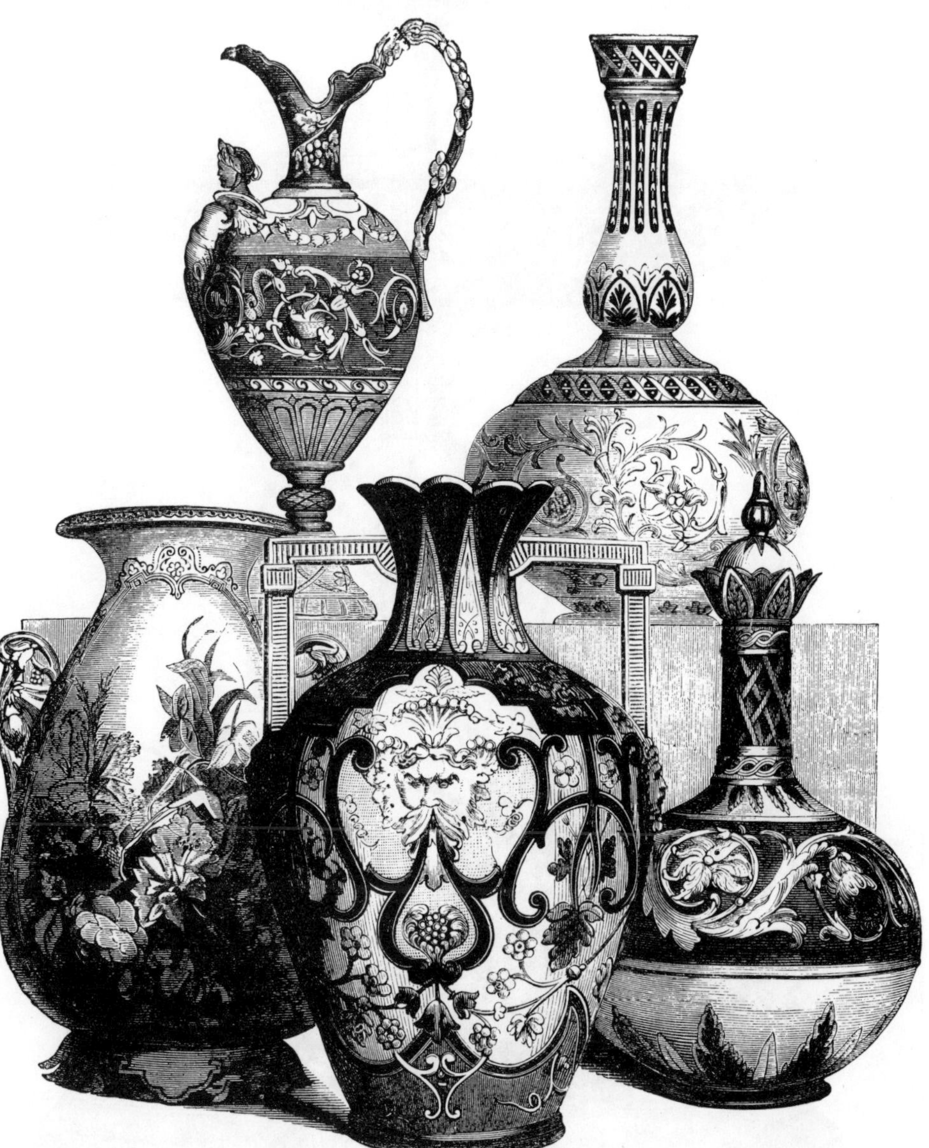

Figs. 1045 to 1049.—Copeland's Vases, &c.

representing the four quarters of the globe, and each bearing an appropriate symbol. These were the work of Joseph Durham, R.A., and are miniature reproductions of those which support the statue of "Albert the Good," in the Royal Horticultural Society's Gardens. The four raised fruit-dishes are elevated upon groups of three

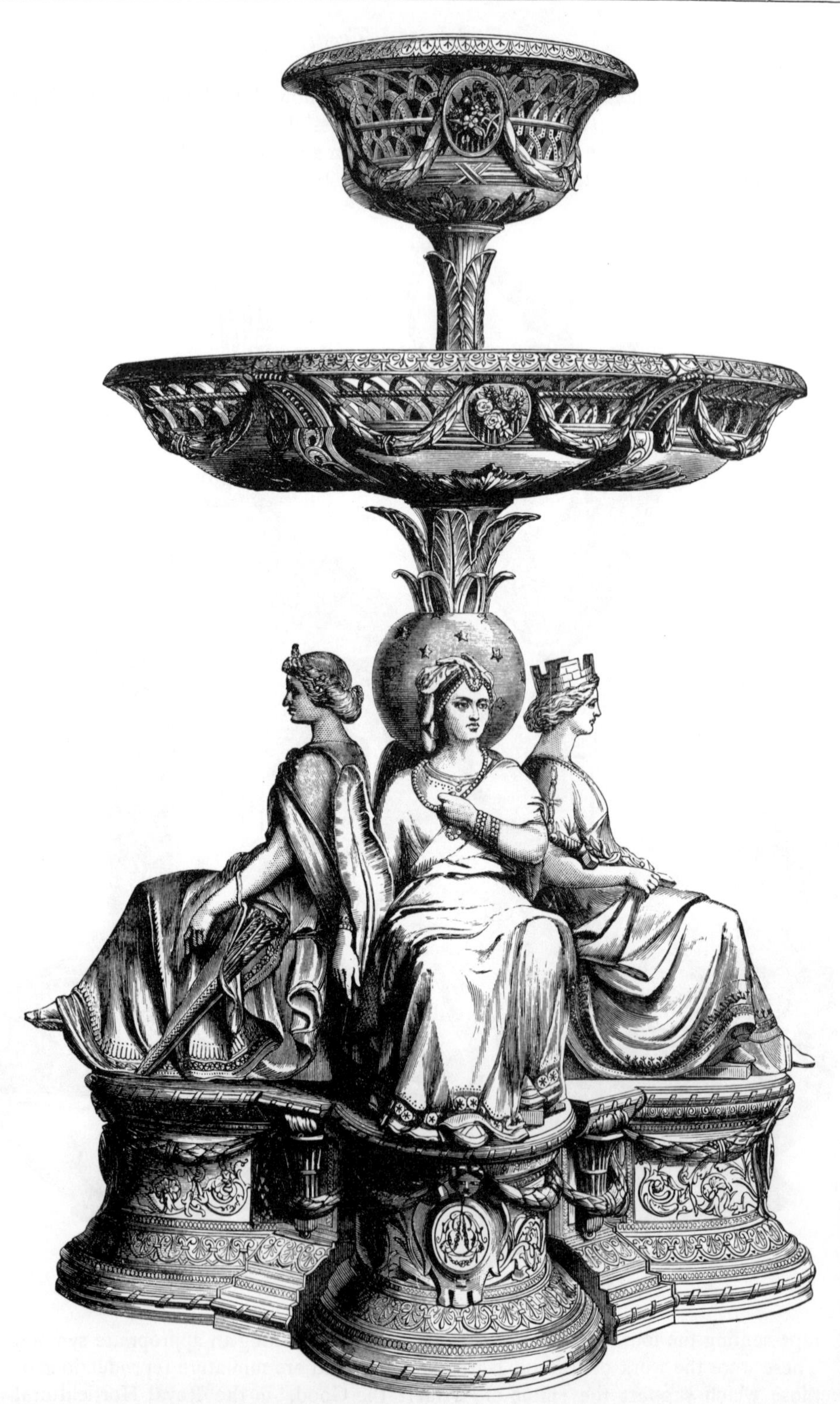

Fig. 1050.—Centre Piece, Prince of Wales's Service, made by Copeland.

figures each, typical of the twelve months of the year, admirably modelled by F. Miller. The four smaller ones, by G. Halse, equally well typify the elements, earth, air, fire, and water. The plates, as well as the pieces I have named, are of the purest porcelain, and are exquisitely and elaborately perforated. They are divided into panels of fruit and flowers, surrounded by ribbons and festoons in raised and chased gold, and in the centre of each is the monogram of the Prince and Princess of Wales. Three pieces of this beautiful royal service, of which no two pieces are alike, are engraved, Figs. 1050, 1056, and 1059.

One of the greatest improvements effected by the firm in ordinary earthenware is the production of what they appropriately term an "Ivory-tinted body." In this kind of ware they produce all the usual services of every conceivable design, and of

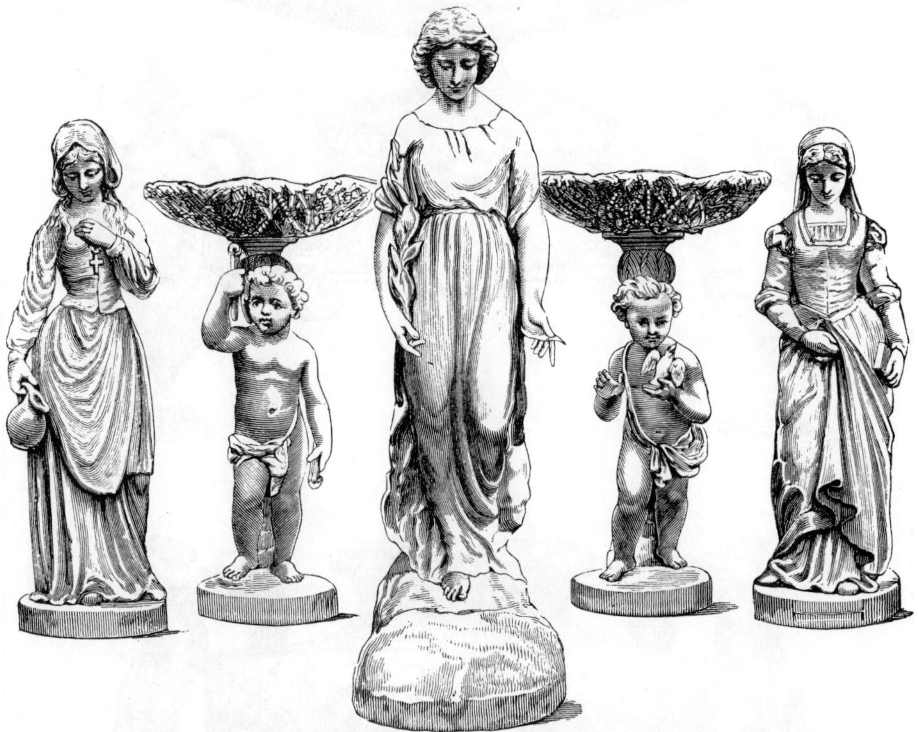

Figs. 1051 to 1055.

various degrees of decoration. In the dinner and dessert services the delicate, soft, warm tone of the ivory tint is peculiarly grateful to the eye, and has a charming effect when "set" out on the white linen cloth; it has all the softness of the finest examples of old Wedgwood cream-coloured ware, but without its somewhat harsh yellowness. In this body every variety of pattern, from the rich old Spode with its Eastern brilliant combinations of gold and rich patches of colour, down to the most ordinary printed borders, are made. One of the most striking services, the "Stork," has the pattern in relief and heightened in gold, and is peculiarly rich and good.

In porcelain, vases, tazzas, bottles, and other articles of every conceivable form, and decorated in an endless variety of ways both in painting in alto-relievo figures and flowers, and in massive jewelling, gilding, and enamelling, are produced, and

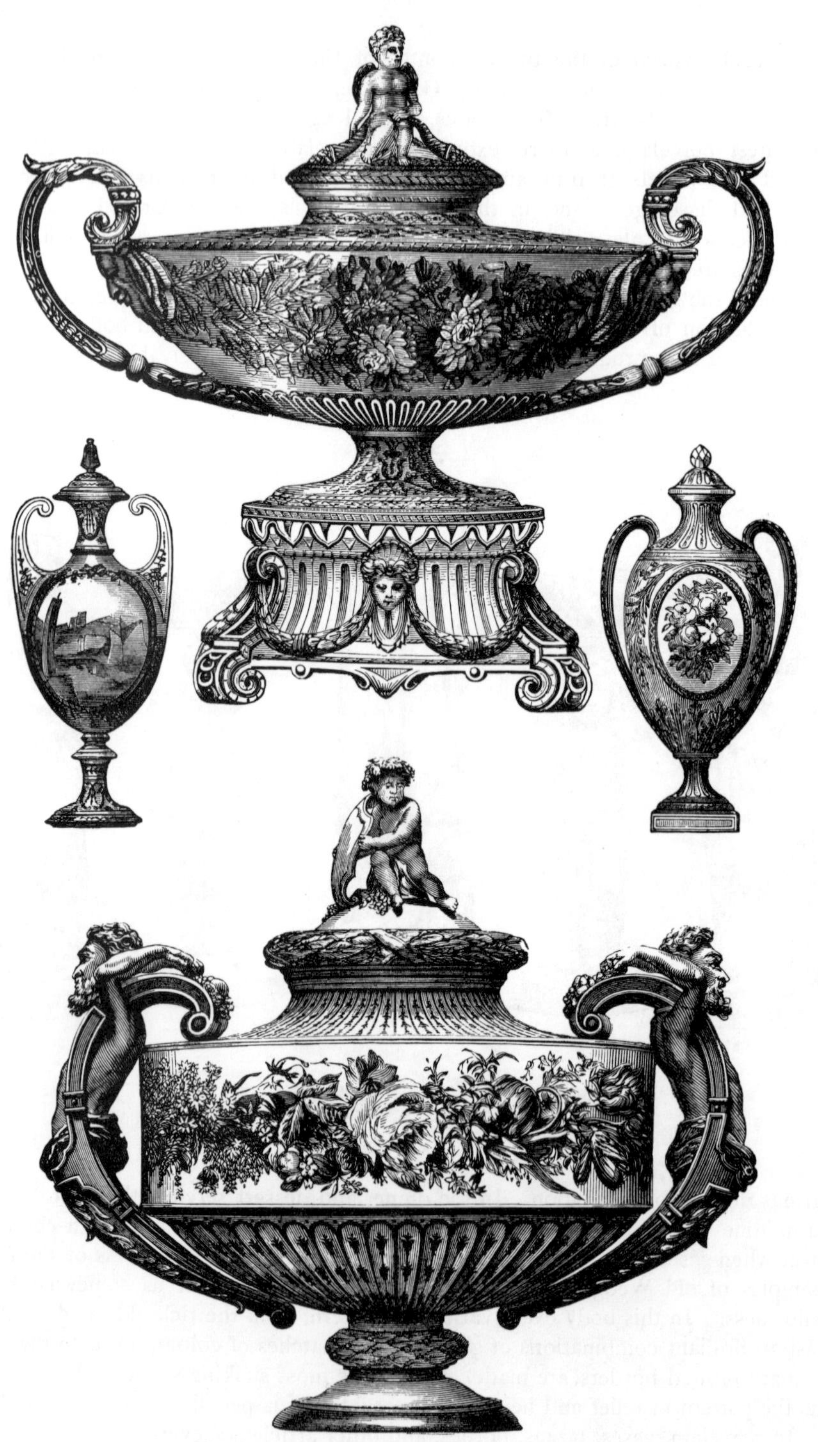

Figs. 1056 to 1059.—Messrs. Copeland's Productions.

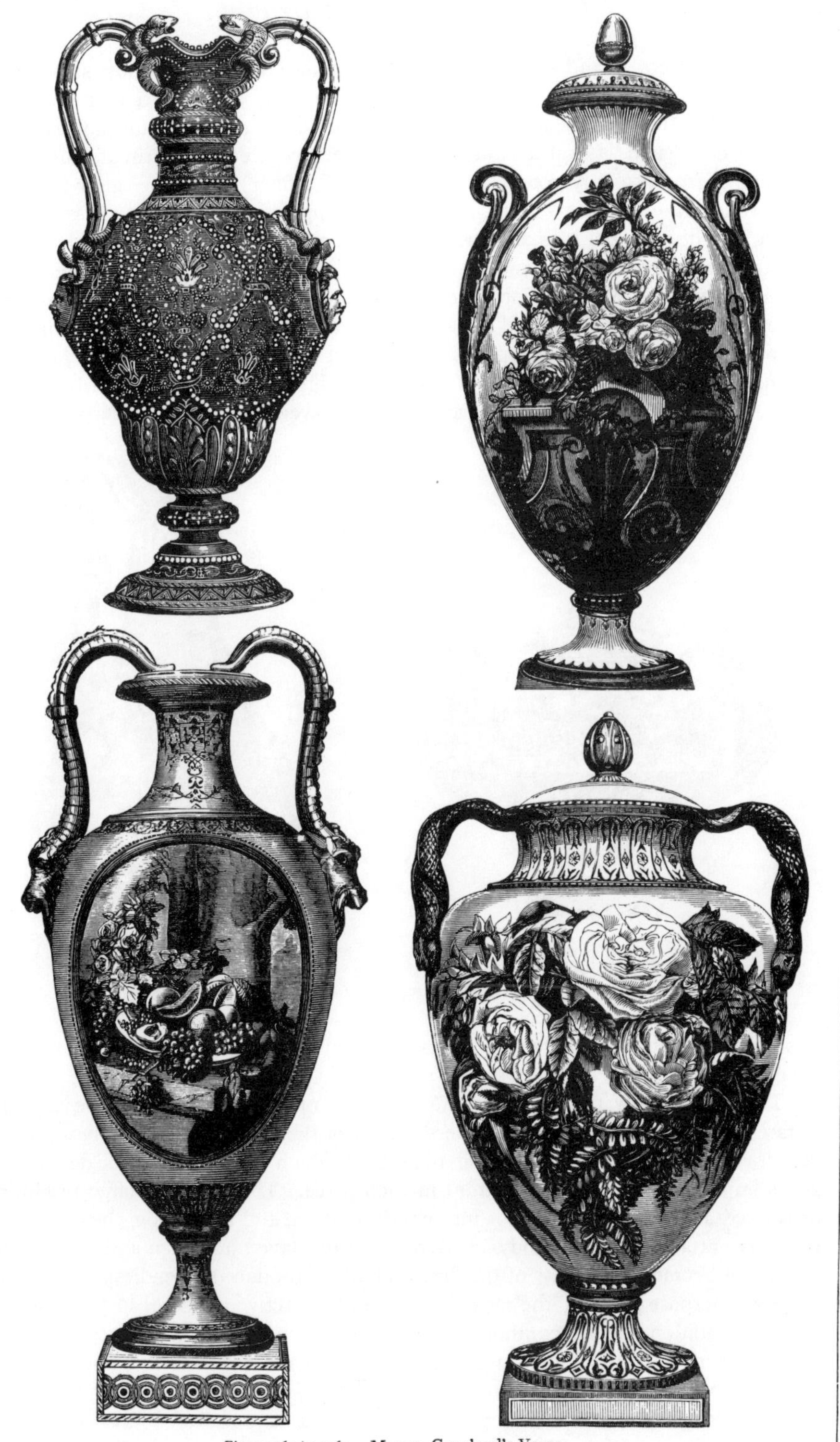

Figs. 1060 to 1063.—Messrs. Copeland's Vases.

are of the most costly and elegant character. Services, both of the most sumptuous and severely simple character, are also produced in every style of art and on every scale of cost. Among Copeland's achievements in colour are a new turquoise (which they have christened "Cerulean blue") which is remarkable for its brilliant intensity; Sardinian green, also very good; and vermilion of a finer and richer glow than has been produced elsewhere. This is especially apparent upon a Japanese dessert plate, where the decorations are upon pure enamel, requiring a very high degree of heat, and where the colours come out with exceeding brilliancy. On this plate, which is a *chef d'œuvre* of Messrs. Copeland's art, the border is purely Japanese and the centre essentially English, but all equally perfect and equally beautiful. It is, in fact, an original and brilliant conception, true to the spirit and principles of Japanese design, but in no respect a copy of any of the productions of the artists of that nation. The birds are exquisitely painted by Weaver, one of the best painters of

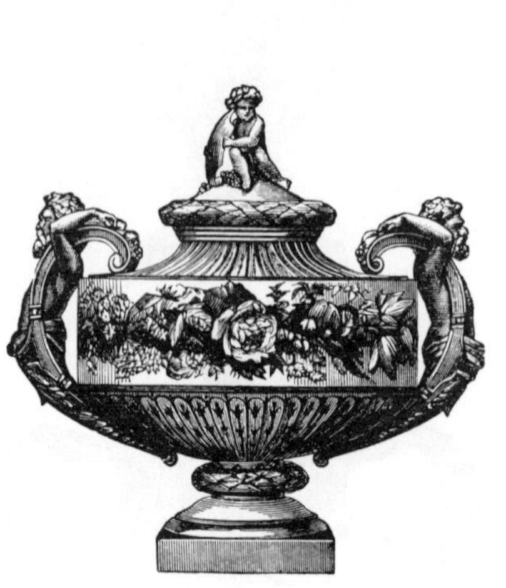

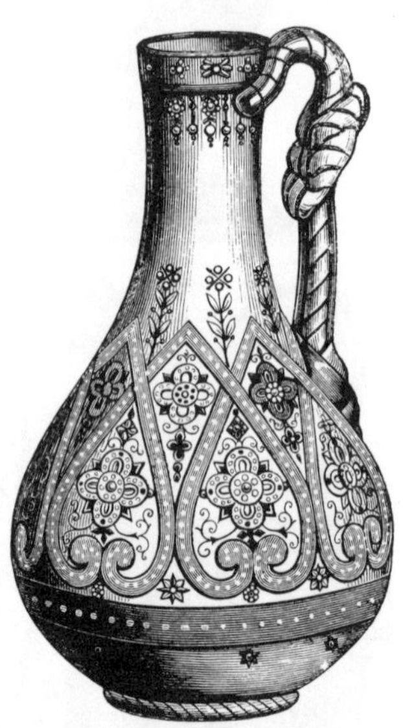

Figs. 1064 and 1065.

this class, and the remainder by artists of equal celebrity in their several walks of decoration.

The "Satsuma ware" of Messrs. Copeland is of the most exquisite beauty, and of rare excellence both in the matchless quality of the body, the peculiarly waxy and very lovely surface of the glaze, the pure taste which characterizes its decoration, and admirable manipulation apparent in each piece. They are also large producers of painted and enamelled tiles for internal decoration, and these, from the excellence they have attained in the "body" and the skill displayed in design and ornamentation, have bcome a speciality of the firm. They are produced in endless variety, and for every purpose; one of the most striking and attractive novelties in this kind of mural decoration being a continuous design for a whole room, first attempted by them for Mr. Macfarlane, of Glasgow, of which I gave an extended notice in the *Art Journal* for 1875, and also in the first edition of this work. Highly decorative tiles for flower-boxes, lily-pans, garden-seats, slabs for chimney-pieces, table-tops, fire-places, &c., and for every other purpose, are also largely produced.

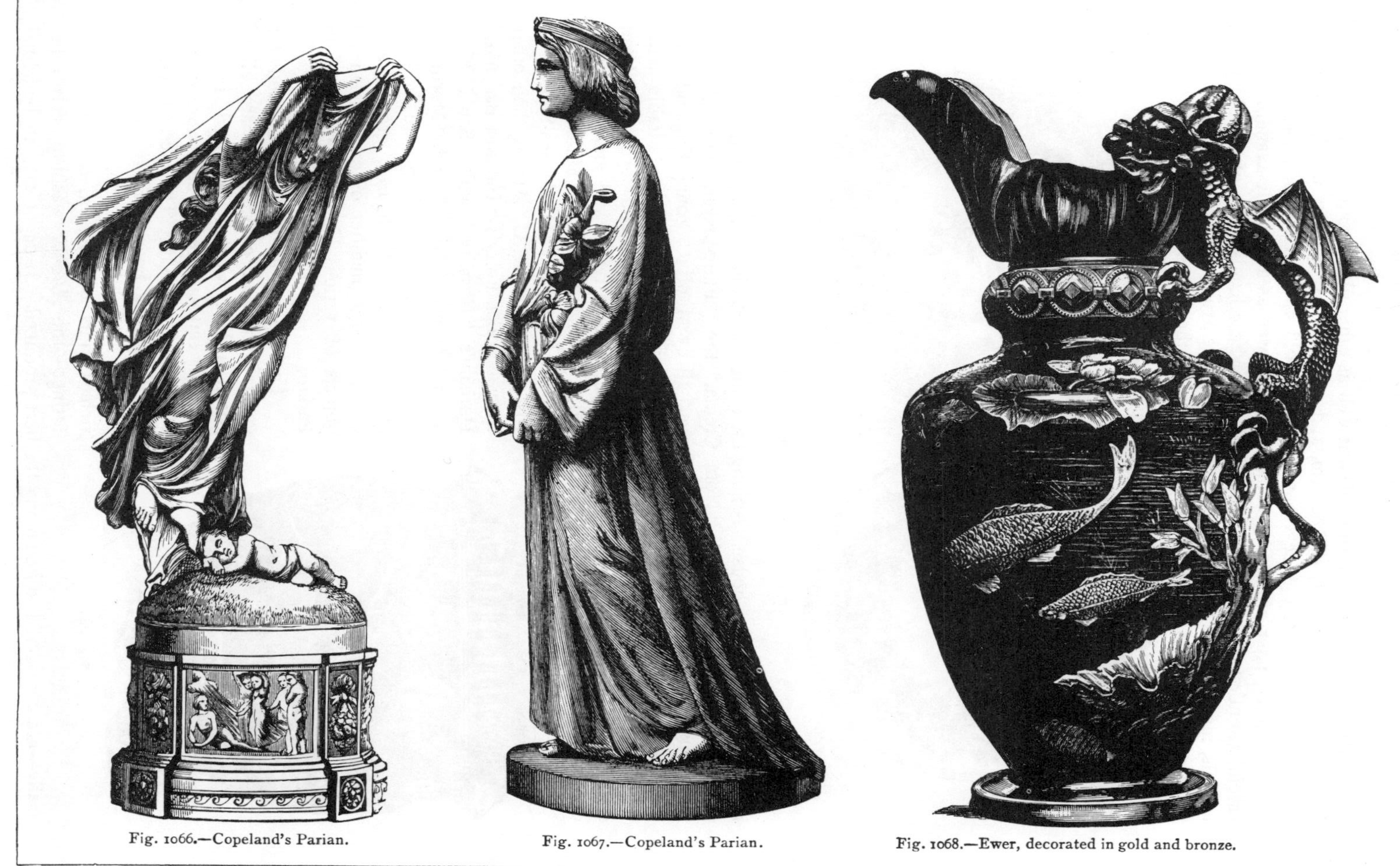

Fig. 1066.—Copeland's Parian.

Fig. 1067.—Copeland's Parian.

Fig. 1068.—Ewer, decorated in gold and bronze.

In Parian, both statuary and busts, as well as other objects, are extensively made. This is another speciality of the firm, and one the discovery of which belongs to them. It is, in fact, the development of the old and ever-famous Derby biscuit ware, rendered finer and more commercially as well as artistically available by the careful attention of the Messrs. Copeland, into whose hands many of the old Derby models, moulds, &c., passed, and have been made available. It was introduced by Copeland about 1846, and from that time to the present has been extensively manufactured by every house. Among their finest works in Parian are the "Infancy of Jupiter," "Lady Godiva," "Nora Creina," the "Flute-player," the "Reading Girl," busts of "A Mother" and of "Love," all by Monti; "Young England" and "Young England's Sister," a very charming pair by Halse; two admirable pairs, "Before the Ball" and "After the Ball," and "Prosperity" and "Adversity," and some flower-holders, by Owen Hall, a modeller of high repute and great power in design; a "Shepherd-Boy," "Spring," and "Summer," by L. A. Malampre; and "Master Tom" and "On the Sea-Shore," by Joseph Durham, R.A. Among their other special works, Foley's "Ino and Bacchus," Durham's "Chastity" and "Santa Filomena," Monti's "Night" and "Morning," and a score or two others, are brilliant examples. Besides figures, groups, and busts, a large number of other beautiful objects of various kinds are produced in Parian.

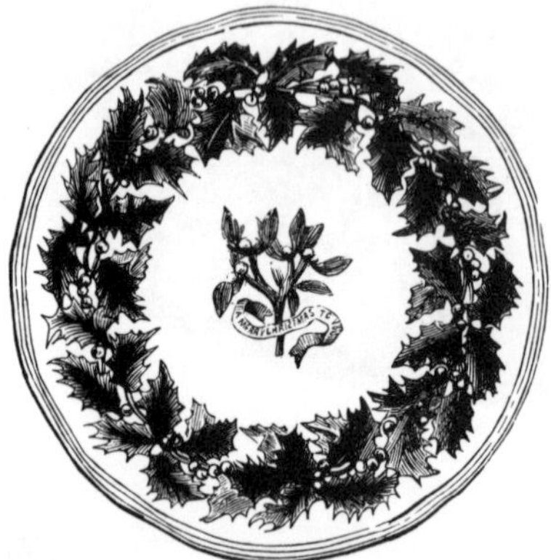

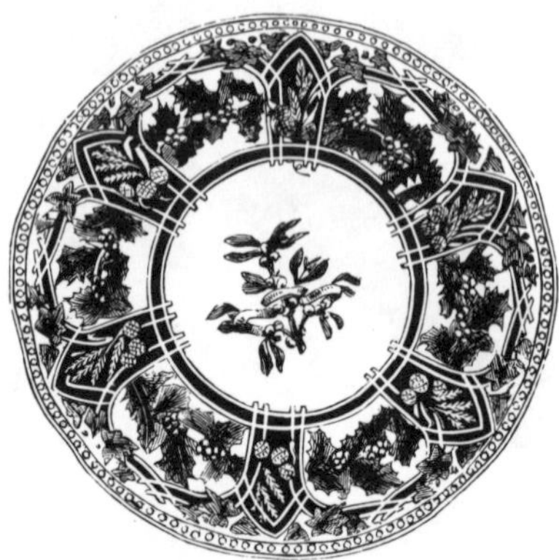

Figs. 1069 and 1070.

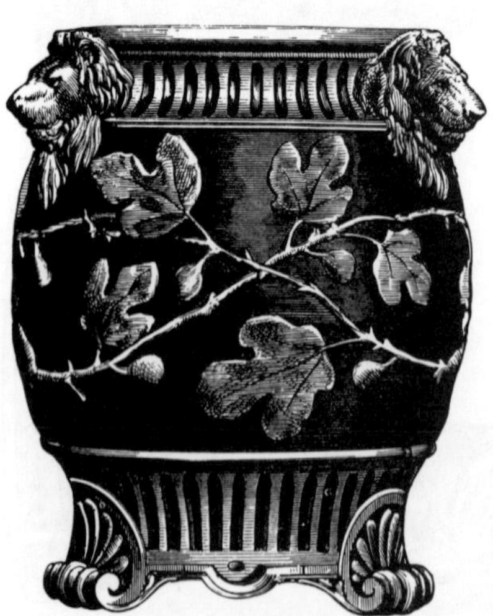

Fig. 1071.

The more ordinary classes of goods for general use and consumption are all of good quality, whether produced in the ordinary earthenware, the stoneware, or any other kind of body. The "crown ware" has so good a body as to stand the heat of the hard kiln, and thus to take the richest tints of crimson, &c. The ship-fittings—the *Atlantic* washtop slab especially—are considered to be among the best produced. It ought also to be added that Messrs. Copeland were the first to introduce those elegant and most convenient novelties, "Gordon Trays," which they produce in a variety of forms.

The principal artists employed are Hürten, who has attained, and deservedly so, the distinction of being one of the best flower-painters in Europe; Weaver, now dead (but worthily succeeded by his son), whose birds are equal to those of any other painter; Alcock, a figure-painter of great power and excellence; F. B. Abraham, a figure-painter of much promise; and Brayford, whose productions are of a high order of merit. Besides these a number of other talented artists are employed, and the staff of enamellers, ground-layers, and gilders includes some of the best obtainable in each department, Bale's speciality of jewelling being more

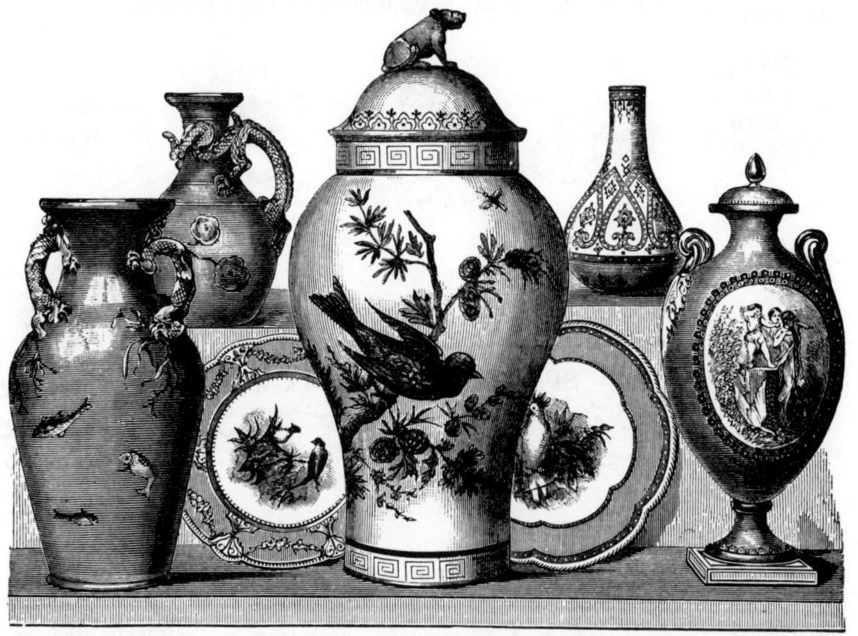

Figs. 1072 to 1078.—Copeland's Productions.

perfect and beautiful than usual. In these works, too, female talent has been highly cultivated, many of the productions of the paintresses evidencing pure feeling and cultivated taste. The Art-director of the establishment is Mr. R. F. Abraham, who was formerly at Coalport with Mr. Rose. The softness of touch, purity and delicacy of feeling, the sunny mellowness of tone, chasteness of design, and correctness of drawing produced on the best pieces of his productions, prove him a thorough artist, and render him peculiarly fitted for the post to which he has been called.

The marks successively used by this firm in its various changes are as follows:—

SPODE — Sometimes impressed in the body, and at others pencilled on the glaze; also SPODE in larger capital letters.

SPODE
Felspar Porcelain — Also impressed, or painted, or printed on the ware.

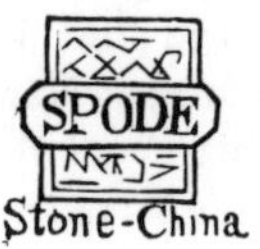

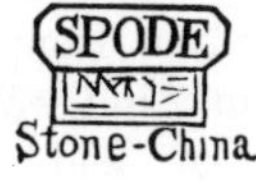

Printed in blue on the bottom of the goods of that description.

Figs. 1079 to 1082.

These, with immaterial variations in detail, were all printed on the ware.

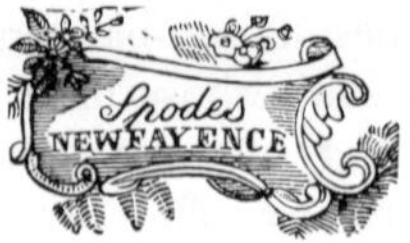

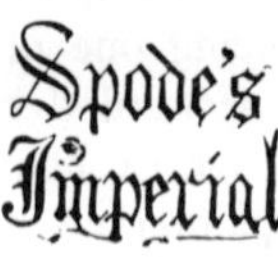

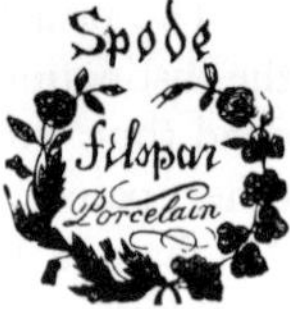

Figs. 1083 to 1086.

SPODE, SON & COPELAND or SPODE & COPELAND, both impressed and printed.

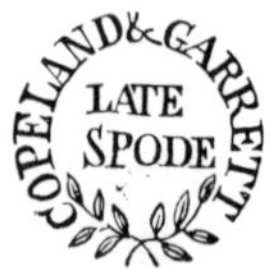

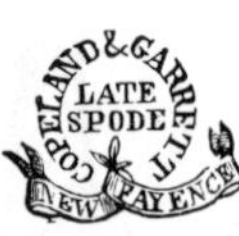

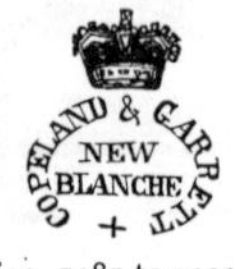

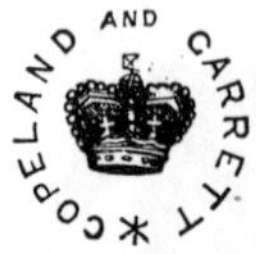

COPELAND & GARRETT

Figs. 1087 to 1093.

C & G with the name of the pattern.

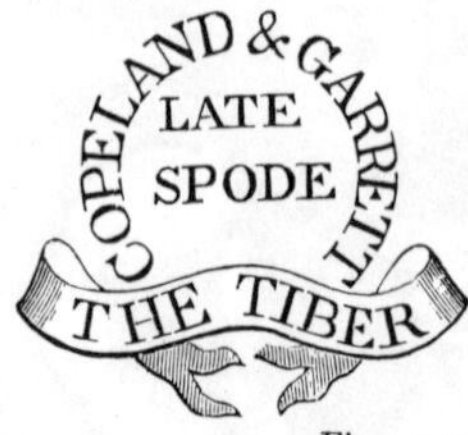

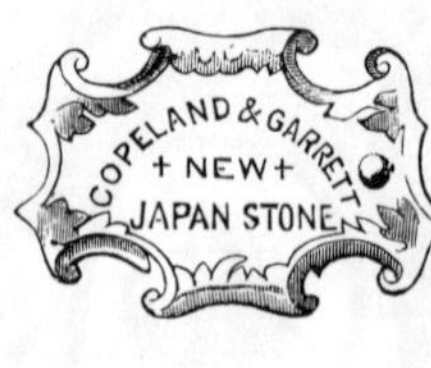

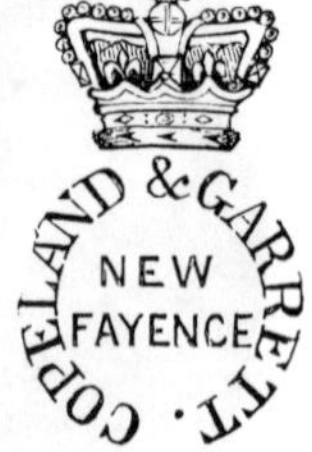

Figs. 1094 to 1097.

All the above printed on the ware.

Copeland Late Spode. Copeland Late Spode COPELAND late SPODE. COPELAND LATE SPODE.

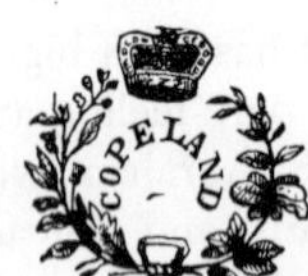

COPELAND

COPELAND PATENT JASPER

Copeland

Copeland Stone China

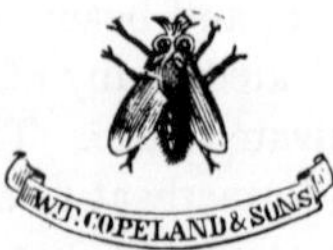

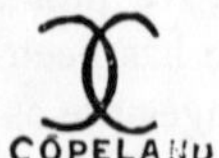

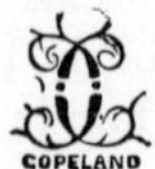

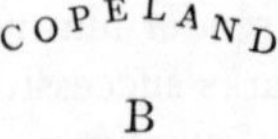

Figs. 1098 to 1110.

The following are the dates when some of the most celebrated printed patterns were first introduced:—"Castle," 1806; "Roman," 1811; "Turk," 1813; "Milkmaid," "Dagger-border," "Tower," "Peacock," and "New Temple," 1814; "New Nankin," "New Japan," and "India," 1815; "Italian" and "Woodman," 1816; "Blossom" and "Pale Broseley," 1817; "Waterloo" and "Arcade," 1818;

"Lucano" and "Ship," 1819; "Panel Japan," "Geranium," and "Oriental," 1820; "Font" and "Marble," 1821; "Bud and Flower," "Sun," "Bonpot," and

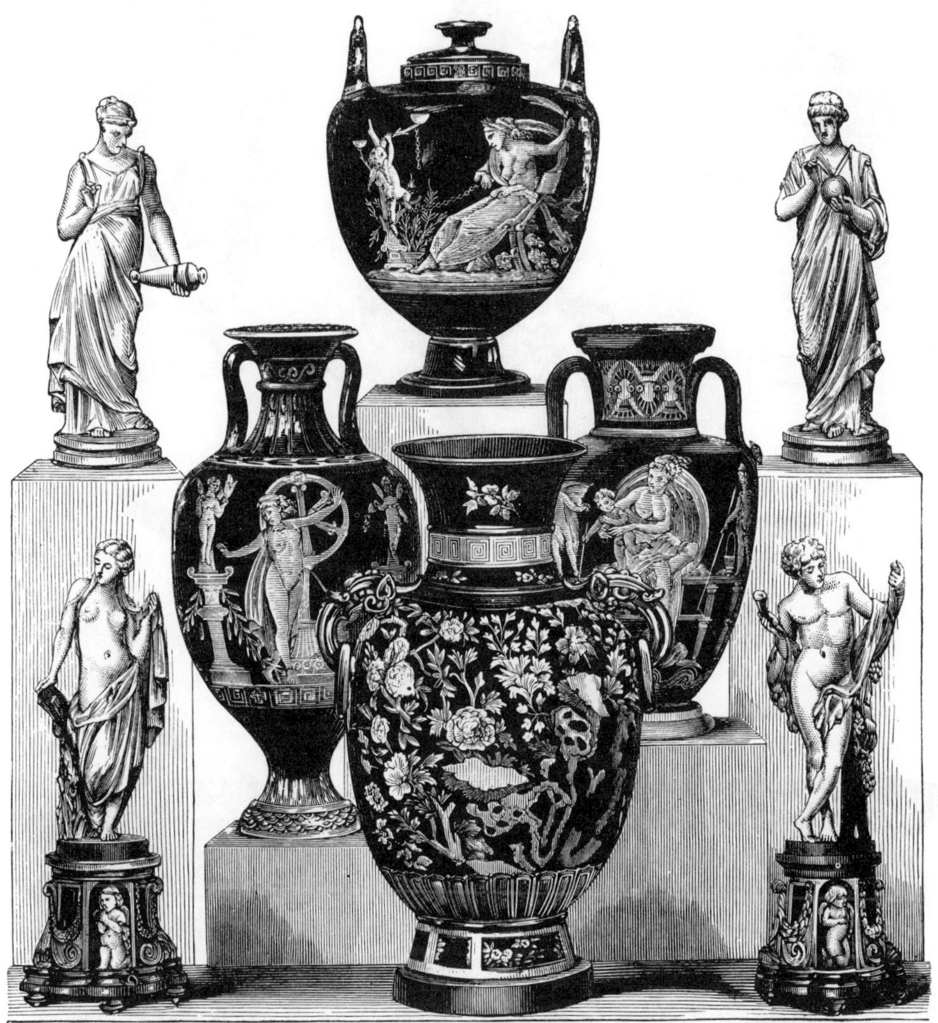

Figs. 1111 to 1118.—Copeland's Productions.

"Union," 1822; "Double Bonpot," "Blue Border," and "Filigree," 1823; "Image" and "Persian," 1824; "Etruscan" and "Bamboo," 1825; "Blue Imperial" and "Union Wreath," 1826.

MINTONS.

Mr. Thomas Minton, the founder of these works, was born in Wyle Cop, Shrewsbury, in 1765, and received his education at the Shrewsbury Grammar School. He had an only brother, Arthur Minton, and a sister, Elizabeth. On leaving school, Thomas Minton was apprenticed to an engraver (probably Hancock) at the Caughley China Works, at Broseley, one of his fellow-apprentices (also a Salopian) being Richard Hicks, who became founder of the firm of Hicks, Meigh,

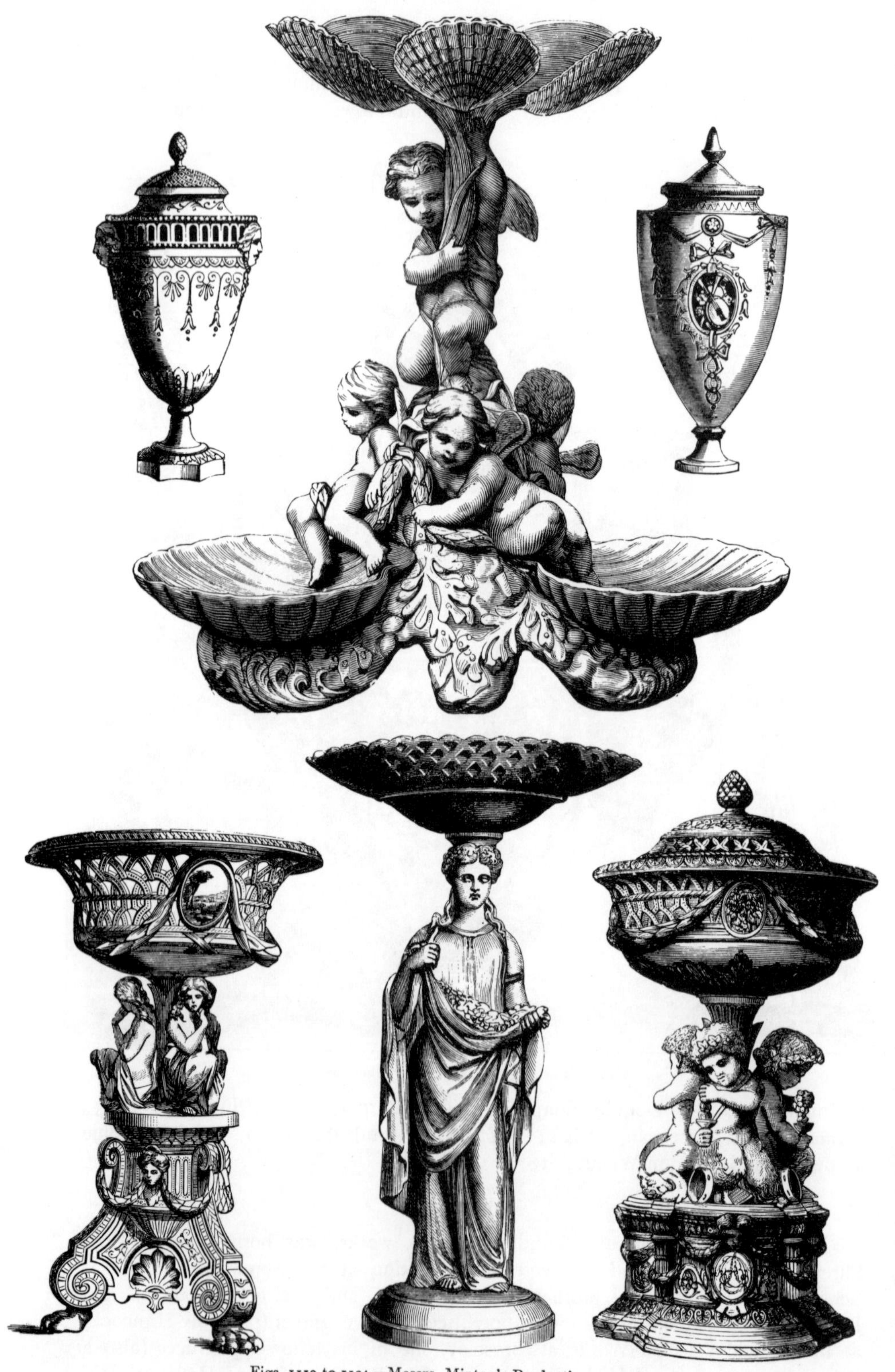

Figs. 1119 to 1124.—Messrs. Minton's Productions.

Figs. 1125 to 1128.—Messrs. Minton's Productions.

and Johnson. On the expiration of his apprenticeship, Thomas Minton continued to be employed for a time at the Caughley China Works under Mr. Turner, and then removed to London, where he engraved some patterns for Josiah Spode. From London, having married, he removed into Staffordshire, in 1788 or 1789, where the rapidly increasing demand for blue printed earthenware gave promise of a good opening for so skilful a draughtsman and engraver as he had become. On removing into Staffordshire, he set up as a master-engraver at Stoke-upon-Trent, his residence and engraving shop being one of a block of buildings then called Bridge Houses, erected by Thomas Whieldon, the first partner of Josiah Wedgwood. Here he became very successful, one of his chief employers being Josiah Spode, for whom he engraved a tea-ware pattern called the "Buffalo," which continued in demand for many years; the "Broseley," so called from being first produced at the Caughley Works, the "Willow Pattern," and many others. In the latter he was assisted by Henry Doncaster of Penkhull. The original plate from which this pattern was thus engraved passed from Mr. Doncaster into the hands of Mr. Wildblood, engraver, of Burslem, and from him into the possession of Minton & Co., where it appropriately remains, as do also some drawings and other interesting relics. Mr. Minton had two apprentices, one of whom, Greatbatch (father of the eminent artist William Greatbatch, engraver of the "Waterloo Banquet"), became chief engraver and manager of that department at Spode and Copeland's.

In 1793, having determined to commence the manufacture of earthenware, Mr. Minton purchased a plot of land, the site of the present manufactory, of Mr. John Ward Hassals, and commenced building on a very small scale. The following account of the early progress of the works has been kindly written for me by Mr. Stringer:—"To start with, there was one 'Bisque' and one 'Glost' oven, with slip house, for preparing the clay, and only such other buildings and appliances as were necessary to make good working commencement. Mr. Minton formed an engagement with the brothers Poulson, who owned the works opposite to the land he had purchased, known as the 'Stone Works,' and who were potters on a small scale, and, as was then the practice, had houses on the works, now converted into potters' workshops. They belonged to an ancient family which had been located at Boothen for several centuries. Mr. Joseph Poulson was the practical potter, and his brother Samuel was modeller, mould-maker, and useful man-of-all-work. It was not until May, 1796, that Mr. Minton's works were in operation. The next year's transactions showed a satisfactory advance in every respect, as did every subsequent year; and amongst the circumstances favouring Mr. Minton's prosperity may be named—first, that aided by Mr. Poulson's experience as a potter, and his own good taste as an engraver and designer, he produced a quality and style of ware that commanded a ready market; and in his brother, Mr. Arthur Minton, who had established himself in the trade in the metropolis, a ready and devoted agent to extend the trade; so much so that the business done by him in 1800 amounted to nearly £2,000. He was also fortunate in having the acquaintance of Mr. William Pownall, a merchant of Liverpool, who aided him with capital to extend his operations, and who was, for a few years, a sleeping partner in the business. Mr. Joseph Poulson was in a short time after the opening of the works admitted as a partner, and the firm traded as 'Minton and Poulson' for a short time, and then the style was altered to 'Minton, Poulson, and Pownall.' Mr. Poulson remained a partner until his death in 1808; and it would seem that up to this period china or soft porcelain was made at the stone-works, but was abandoned as unprofitable until Mr. Herbert Minton's experiments in after years were fully successful."

On the failure of John and William Turner, of Lane End, the first-named entered the service of Thomas Minton, and became the practical potter of the firm after the death of Poulson. He effected great improvements in the bodies and glazes, and in the general character of the productions of the works. Soon after Mr. Minton had commenced business, a scheme having been set on foot for monopolising the sale of Cornish clay, he and his partners purchased eighty-four acres of land on Hendra Common, and certain rights and a leasehold interest in Treloar Common, where there was abundance of china clay and stone, as also other valuable minerals. Having secured the property, Mr. Minton took successful steps to associate with him the leading manufacturers to work the mines; and the first meeting of "The Hendra Company" was held at the Swan Inn, Hanley, on the 8th of January, 1800, when John Brindley, of Longport, was appointed agent. The minutes of the meetings are brief in the extreme, but it appears that on July 24, 1800, stone was ordered to be sold at 50*s.* per ton at Etruria wharf, and 42*s.* at Runcorn; fifteen tons were a boat-load. A vessel, called the *Venus*, brought to Runcorn ninety-nine tons, and the freight was £72 7*s.* 9*d.* China clay was £6 per ton at Polemear.

Mr. Minton appears to have first visited Cornwall in 1798, and we are afforded an insight into the difficulty and expense of travelling at that period by the fact that the cost of each journey was nearly thirty pounds. It seems that Mr. Minton must have got the mines into something like working order during these visits, as an immediate supply of clay and stone were available at the time the company was formed. Difficulties, however, of all kinds sprung up, and as a trading concern the Hendra Company was not profitable; but it afforded the proprietors for twenty years a supply of good and pure material, and checked any attempt at monopoly. The clay mines were ultimately abandoned, but as there were good tin lodes on the property, and other minerals, the investment proved not a bad one.

From the first establishment of the pottery works at Stoke, their success was unbroken, and not only were great advances made in processes of manufacture, but they were so much enlarged that at the time of Mr. Minton's death in 1836 they were among the most important in the district. Mr. Minton married, on January 1st, 1789, Miss Sarah Webb, of Bruton Street, London, and by her had a family of four sons, two of whom were the Rev. Thomas Webb Minton and Herbert Minton, and six daughters. After his marriage, his mother-in-law, Mrs. Webb, resided with them, and was a valuable acquisition to him in his business, keeping his books and accounts, and being, in fact, the financial manager of the concern. She received and paid all money, and superintended the entire office arrangements, thus leaving Mr. Minton at liberty to devote his entire time to the manufactory and to the engraving. Mrs. Minton, also, so far as the cares of her home and family would permit, took her share in the business.

Mr. Herbert Minton, the second son, was born at the house erected at the works at Stoke-upon-Trent, in March, 1792, and when old enough, was, with his brother and sister, sent to a dame-school kept by Miss Cheadle, at the only house, beyond what is now the Queen's Inn, at that time existing on the Liverpool Road, the remainder being fields and gardens. At that time the Mintons had removed from the house at the works to one on Talbot Bank (now Hill Street, corner of Commerce Street). Later on, Herbert Minton (as was also his brother) was sent to Audlem Grammar School, under the Rev. Nicholas Breakspear, where he remained until nearly fourteen, when he was placed in his father's manufactory. In 1808, when only sixteen, he became traveller and salesman, and represented the house both in London and the provinces; and this he continued till more pressing engagements necessitated his more general attendance at the works. In 1817 Thomas and Herbert Minton were admitted into partnership with their father, the firm being "Thomas Minton and Sons." In 1821, the elder brother, Thomas Webb Minton, quitted the works, for the purpose of studying for the Church, and was ordained in 1825, taking his first curacy at Chesterfield, and afterwards at St. Cuthbert's, Darlington, and other places. He died in 1870, at Darlington, where he was incumbent of the Church of the Holy Trinity. In 1828 the partnership was dissolved, although Mr. Herbert Minton continued to devote his energies to the development of the concern. On his father's death, in 1836, he again took up the business, and shortly afterwards took into partnership John Boyle, under the style of "Minton and Boyle." In 1841 Mr. Boyle withdrew from the firm, and, about 1842, became a partner with the Wedgwoods, and in 1845, Michael Hollins, nephew to Mrs. Minton, joined the firm under the style of "Herbert Minton and Co." In

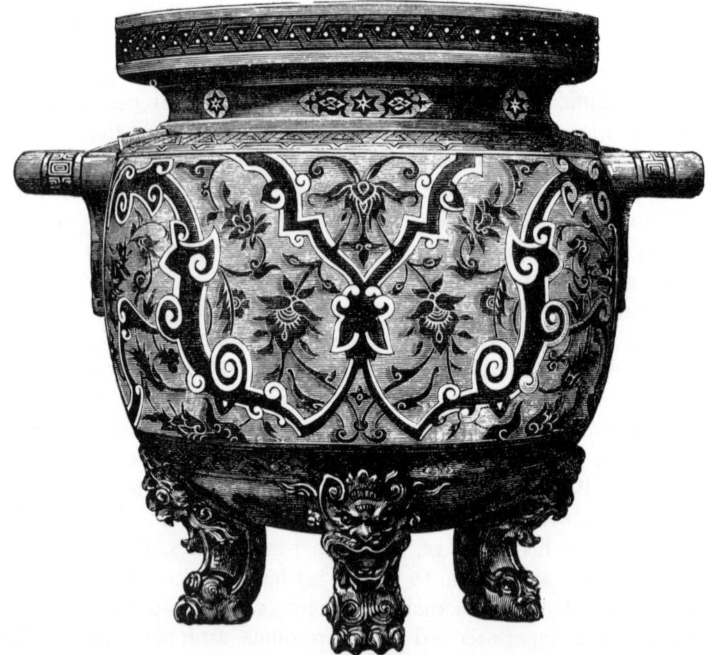

Fig. 1129.

1849 a nephew of Mr. Minton's, Mr. Colin Minton Campbell, who became M.P. for North Staffordshire, joined the firm under the same style. In 1858, Herbert Minton died, and Messrs. Hollins and Campbell continued the manufactory, which has since been formed into an extended company, the trading style being simply "Mintons."

Up to 1798 white, cream-coloured, and blue printed wares only were made at these works. In that year semi-transparent porcelain was introduced, and continued until 1811, when it was abandoned, and earthenware only again produced. In 1821 it was again made, and soon afterwards china was commenced and has been a staple branch to the present day. In 1825 some of the more skilled workmen from the Derby works found employment with Mr. Minton, and brought their skill to bear on his productions. "Among these were Steele, Bancroft, and Hancock, as painters in fruit and flowers." In 1836 Herbert Minton first conceived the idea of making encaustic paving tiles. Mr. John Simpson held the position of principal enamel-painter of figures and the highest class decorations from about 1837 to 1847, when he removed to London to take charge of the porcelain-painting at Marlborough House. Mr. Samuel Bourne, of Norton-in-the-Moors, Staffordshire, who had been apprenticed to Wood and Caldwell as an enamel-painter, entered the service of Mr. Minton in 1828 as chief designer and artist, and continued until 1863, when the infirmities of increasing years necessitated his retirement. In 1849 M. Arnoux, son of a manufacturer of hard porcelain at Toulouse, visited Stoke, bringing with him an introduction from Mr. Evans, of Birmingham; when it was

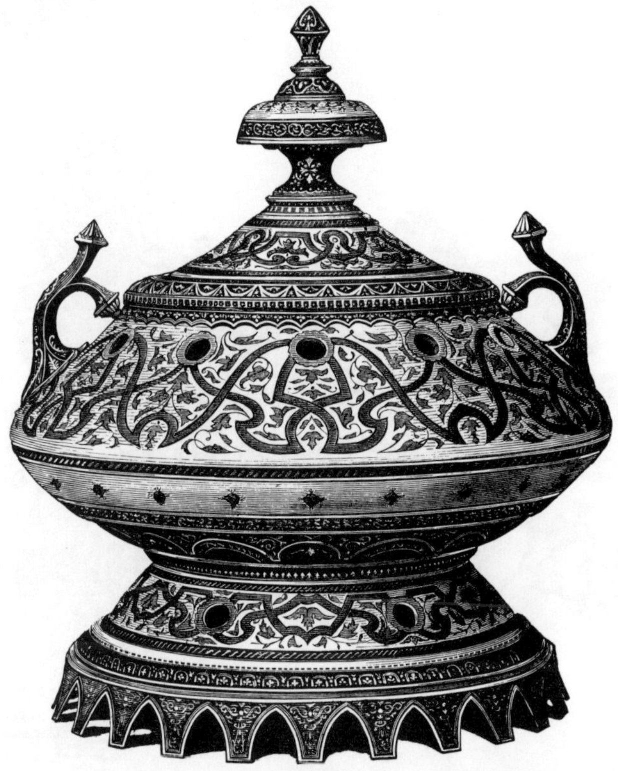

Fig. 1130.

arranged that M. Arnoux should superintend and carry out the patent which, in 1839, Mr. Minton, in conjunction with Dr. Wilton George Turner, had taken out for "an improved porcelain," "made from Kaolin or Cornish clay, made into cream and passed through sieves; Dorsetshire or similar clay treated in like manner; and pure feldspar, all in certain proportions and mixed with great care." In this the bisque was produced by submitting it to a less heat than usual before glazing, and then, when dipped, subjecting it "to a greater degree of heat than is usual for the mere purpose of glazing, and effecting the glazing at the same time." The glazes were also of peculiar composition. Beyond various experiments, this was not carried out until 1849, when this hard paste porcelain for chemical purposes was brought to

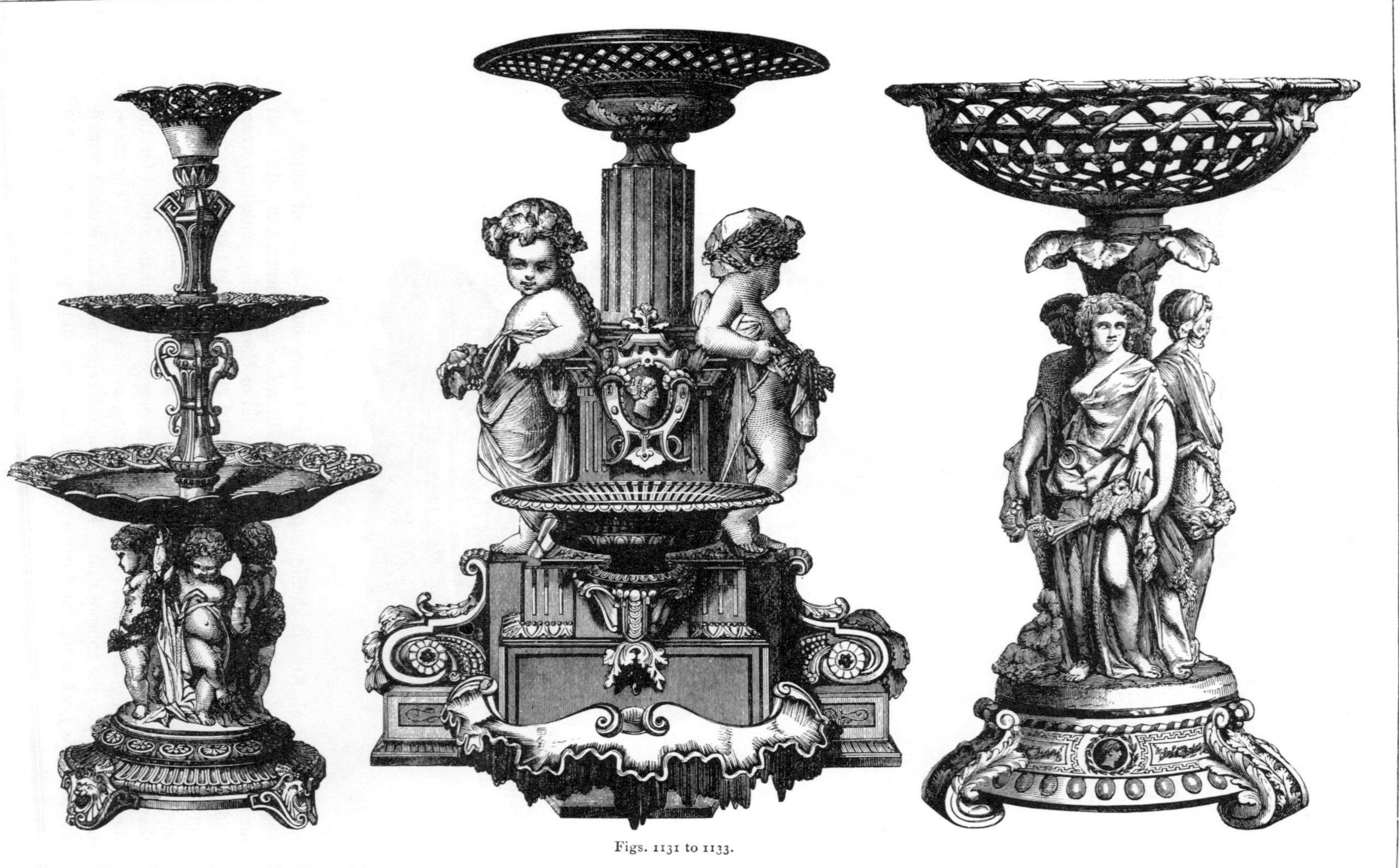

Figs. 1131 to 1133.

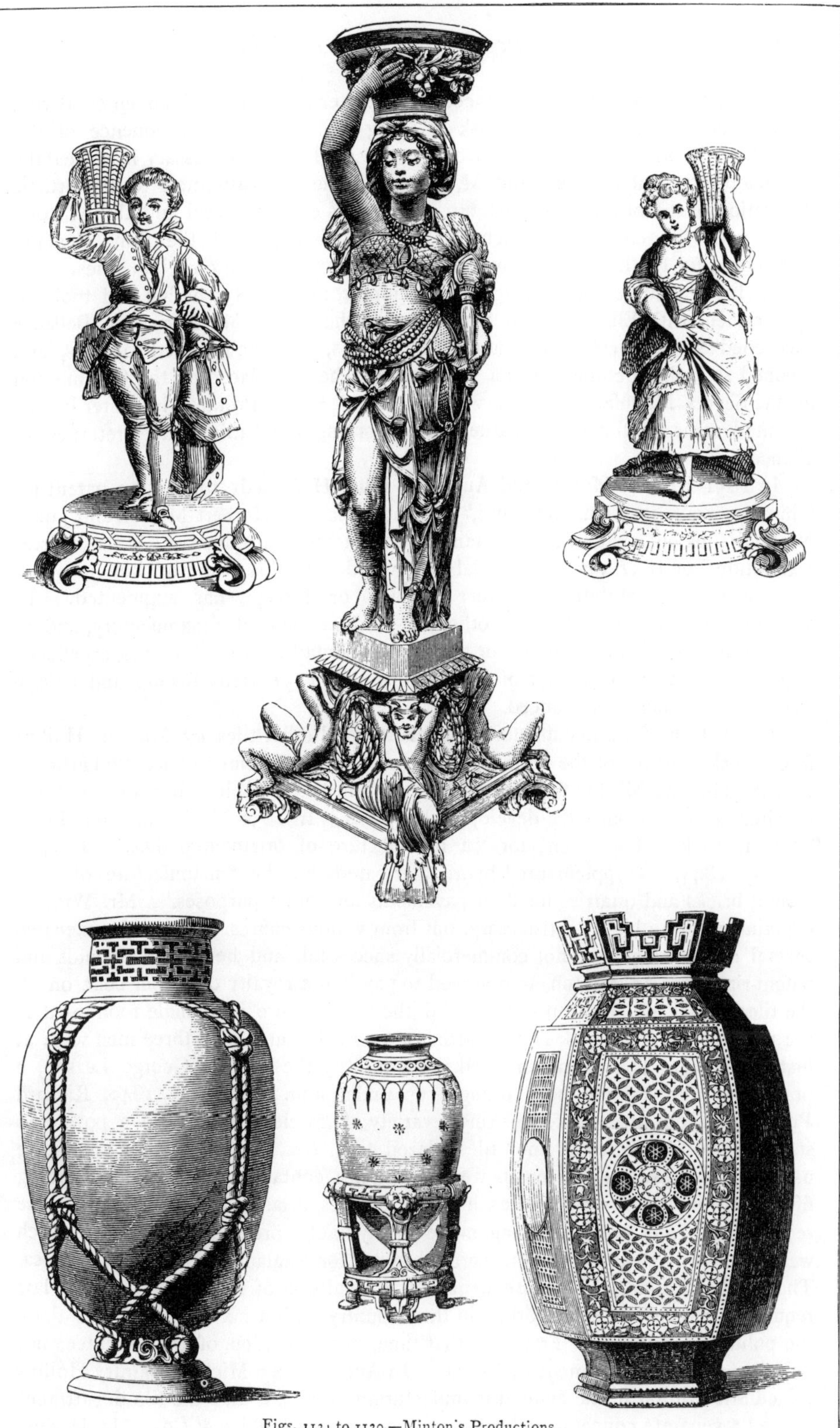

Figs. 1134 to 1139.—Minton's Productions.

such perfection that it was pronounced to be better than that of Meissen or Berlin. There was, however, so much risk in firing this ware, in consequence of the difficulty of producing a sagger capable of withstanding the necessary heat, that the manufacture was abandoned, and M. Arnoux turned his attention to the artistic decoration of the ordinary manufacture, and to his continual zeal and ability, combined with the enterprise which has always distinguished the firm, England is indebted for the highest honours in this branch of their national industries.

M. Emile Jeannest was engaged as a sculptor, and in 1854 he left and took an appointment with Elkington's, in whose service he died. M. Carrier de Belleuse succeeded M. Jeannest, and remained some years, when he returned to Paris, and attained so high an eminence as a sculptor that he was placed on the Commission for the Sèvres Manufactory. He was succeeded by M. Protât, who, after having executed some of the stone statues now adorning the India Office, returned to France.

In 1851 Herbert Minton and Augustus John Hoffstaedt took out a patent for "improvements in the manufacture," and the same year Herbert Minton and James Nasmyth took out a patent for "certain improvements in machinery." At the "Great Exhibition" of 1851 a council medal was awarded to this firm; an honour which each successive exhibition, whether English or foreign, has augmented. In 1850 majolica was added to the other Art-productions of this manufactory, and in this the firm stands pre-eminent for sharpness of details, purity of colours, excellence of glaze, and artistic character of these goods. In 1851 Della Robbia and Palissy ware were also here commenced.

The history of the manufacture of encaustic and other tiles by Minton, Hollins & Co. is the history of the entire modern trade in these useful and beautiful articles. In 1828 Herbert Minton first turned his attention to the subject, but was prevented by circumstances from fully developing his plans. In 1830 Mr. Samuel Wright, of Shelton, took out a patent for "a manufacture of ornamental tiles." This, in January, 1844, he supplemented by another patent for the "manufacture of ornamental bricks and quarries for floor pavements and other purposes." Mr. Wright's experiments were highly satisfactory, but from various causes, although he executed several orders, they were not commercially successful, and he sold his moulds and patent-rights to Mr. Minton, who agreed to pay him a royalty of 10 per cent. on all the tiles sold. Mr. Minton commenced the manufacture in a single room next to the present throwing-house at the earthenware works, and only three men were at first employed. He was much aided in his task by the late Mr. George Leason, a practical potter who had been brought up under him. In June, 1840, Richard Prosser took out a patent for making a variety of articles from clay in a powdered state, viz. buttons, tesseræ, floor tiles, glazed tiles, &c., by pressure, by preference using screw presses of different powers for articles containing up to and including fifty square inches of surface in each piece; articles of larger surface, and of course requiring a greater pressure, being made by hydraulic presses, the pumps of which were worked by steam. Patents were taken out for England, France, and America. That for France lapsed in consequence of a condition of the French patent law requiring the process being worked in that country within six months of its date, the political condition of France at that time, in the opinion of the patentee, not being safe for the investment of capital. In August, 1845, Michael Daintry Hollins joined Mr. Minton in the general manufacturing business, and the tile department formed a separate concern, under the style of Minton, Hollins & Co. Mr. Hollins

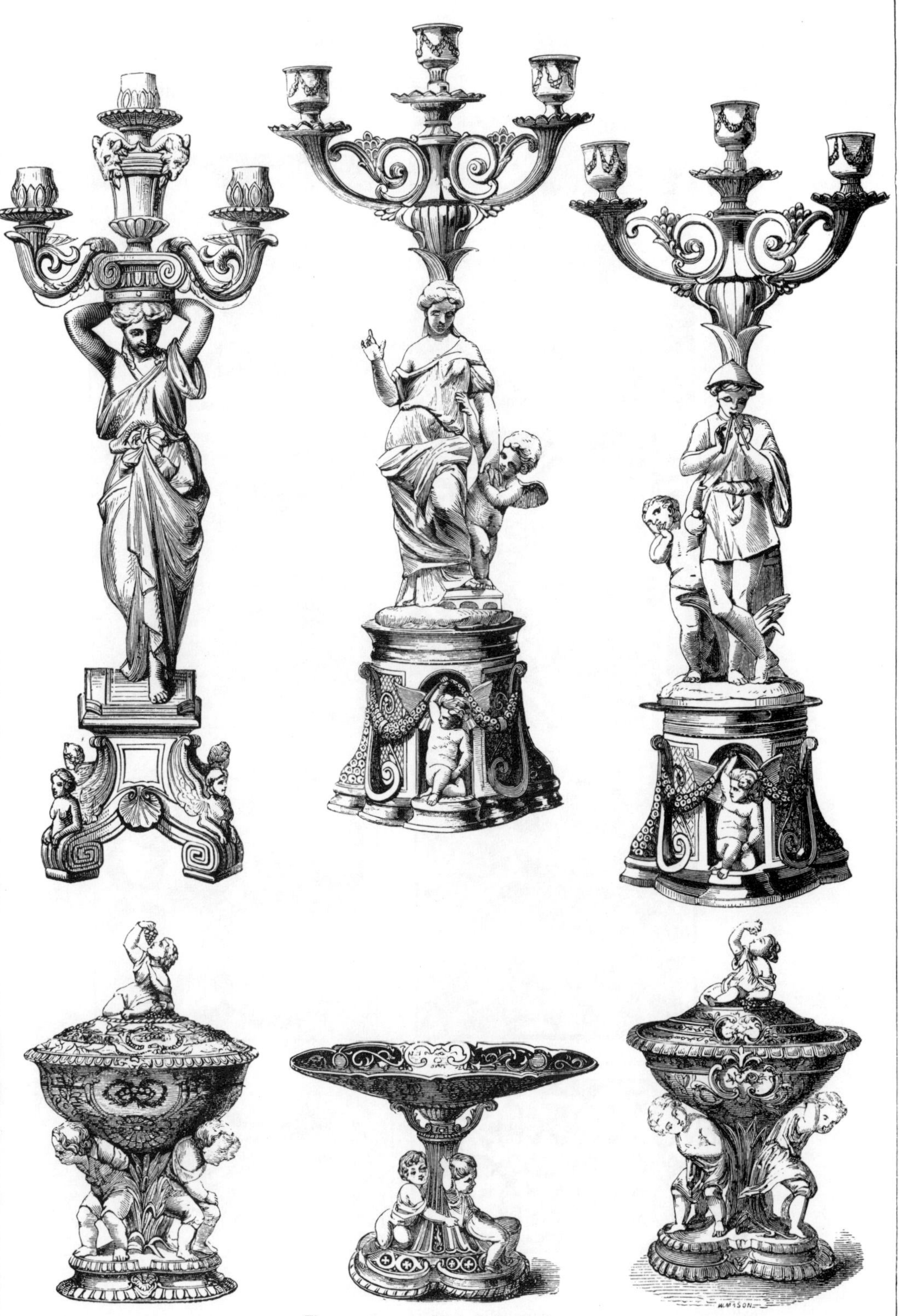

Figs. 1140 to 1145.—Minton's Productions.

was a nephew of Mr. Minton's deceased wife (who was Miss Hollins, of Shelton),

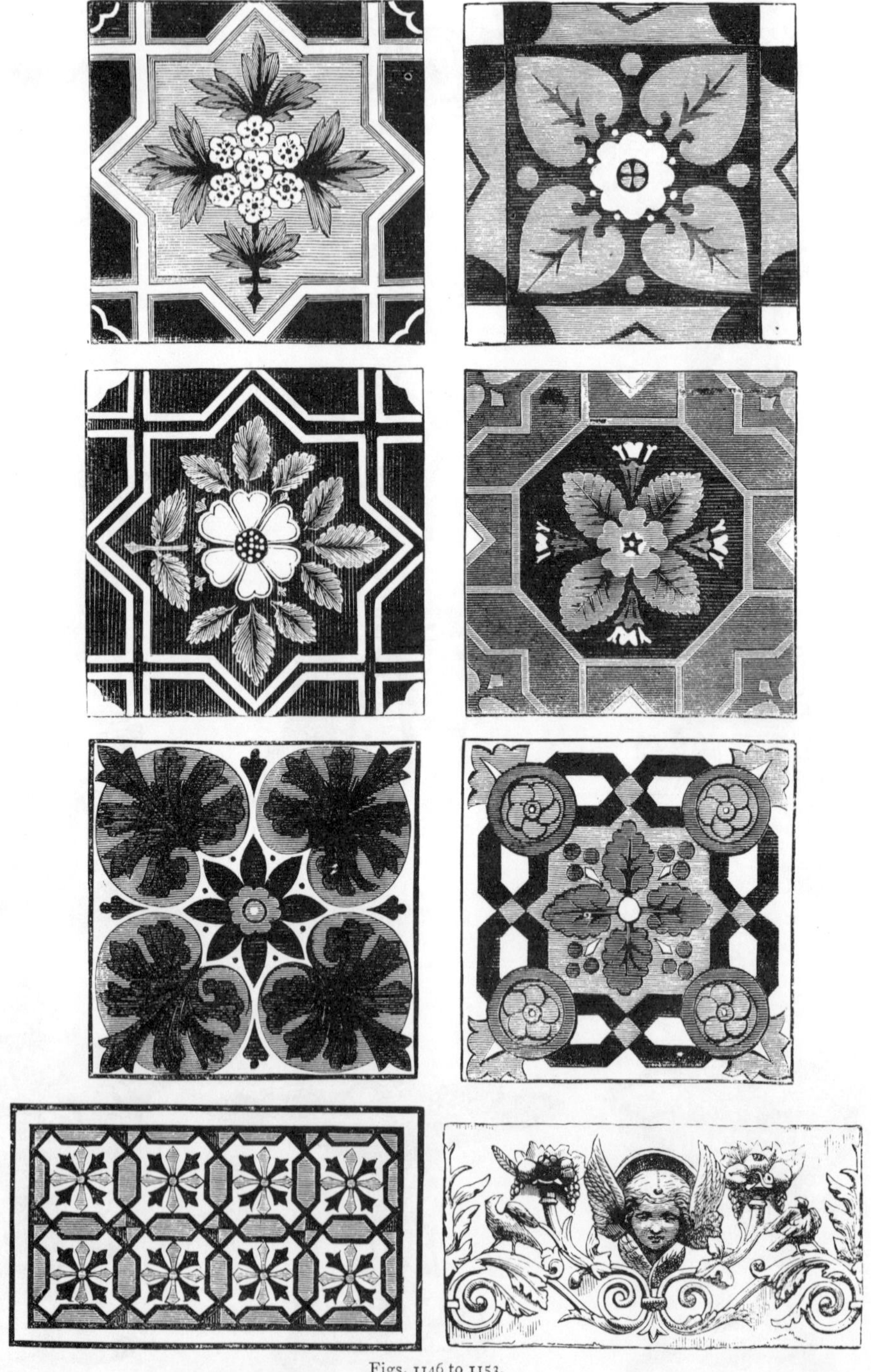

Figs. 1146 to 1153.

and had been educated for the medical profession. In 1846 Samuel Barlow

Wright, son of the original patentee, was admitted to a share of the business of the tile works, under the style of Minton, Hollins, and Wright. The patent of Mr. Wright was for fourteen years, and was renewed for seven years in 1844. At that period the works continued to be conducted at a loss, and but a small amount of business was done. It may be safely asserted that during the entire existence of the patent, so far from profit being the result, Mr. Minton had sacrificed many thousands of pounds to perfect the manufacture; to say nothing of the extraordinary liberality of his gifts of tiles. In other hands the manufacture might have proved a pecuniary success at an earlier period; but Mr. Minton was lavish in his expenditure in adopting every mechanical or other improvement — hydraulic presses under Prosser's patent, Napier's steam-hammer, &c.— that promised further success.

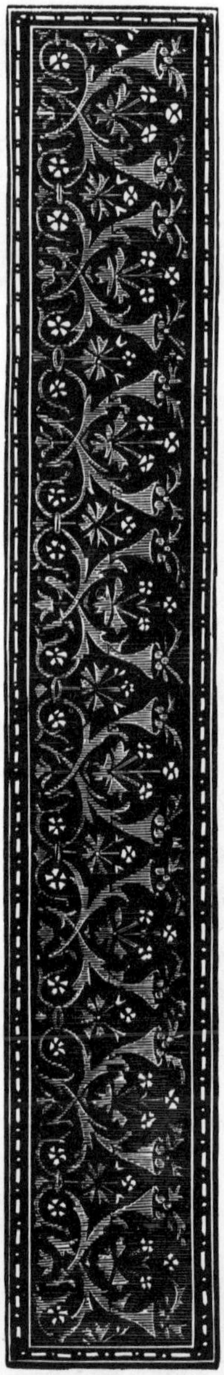

Fig. 1154.

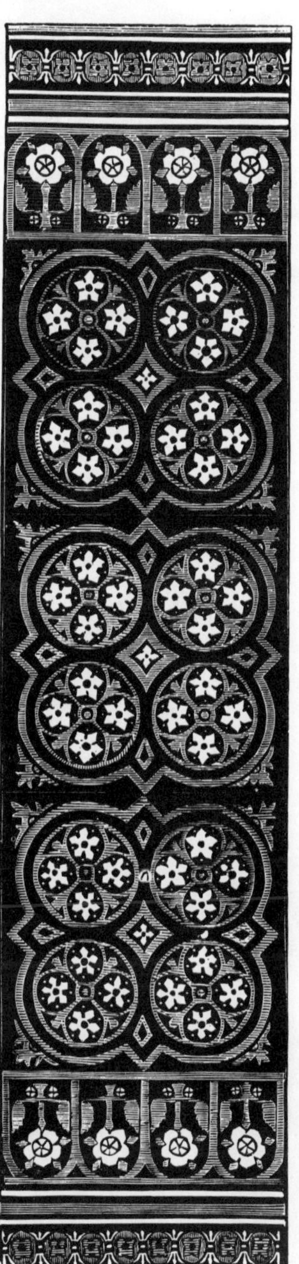

Fig. 1155.

Previous to the year 1848, the only process of printing which had succeeded for the decoration of pottery, was the one from engraved copper-plates. In this process all the lines that form the picture are cut into the metal, and these lines were filled in by the printer with the required colour, which had previously been mixed with boiled oil. The impression was then taken on tissue paper, at the ordinary copper-plate printing-press, and from the paper transferred to the ware. In that style the picture or ornament was formed by a succession of lines, so that it was almost impossible to produce an even layer of colour, so desirable in flat-surface ornamentation. In 1848 Messrs. Collins and Reynolds, who had for some years carried on in London the business of decorative and picture printers, submitted to Mr. Minton some trials they had made of transferring to pottery impressions taken on paper from the flat surface of metal or stone, instead of from the engraved

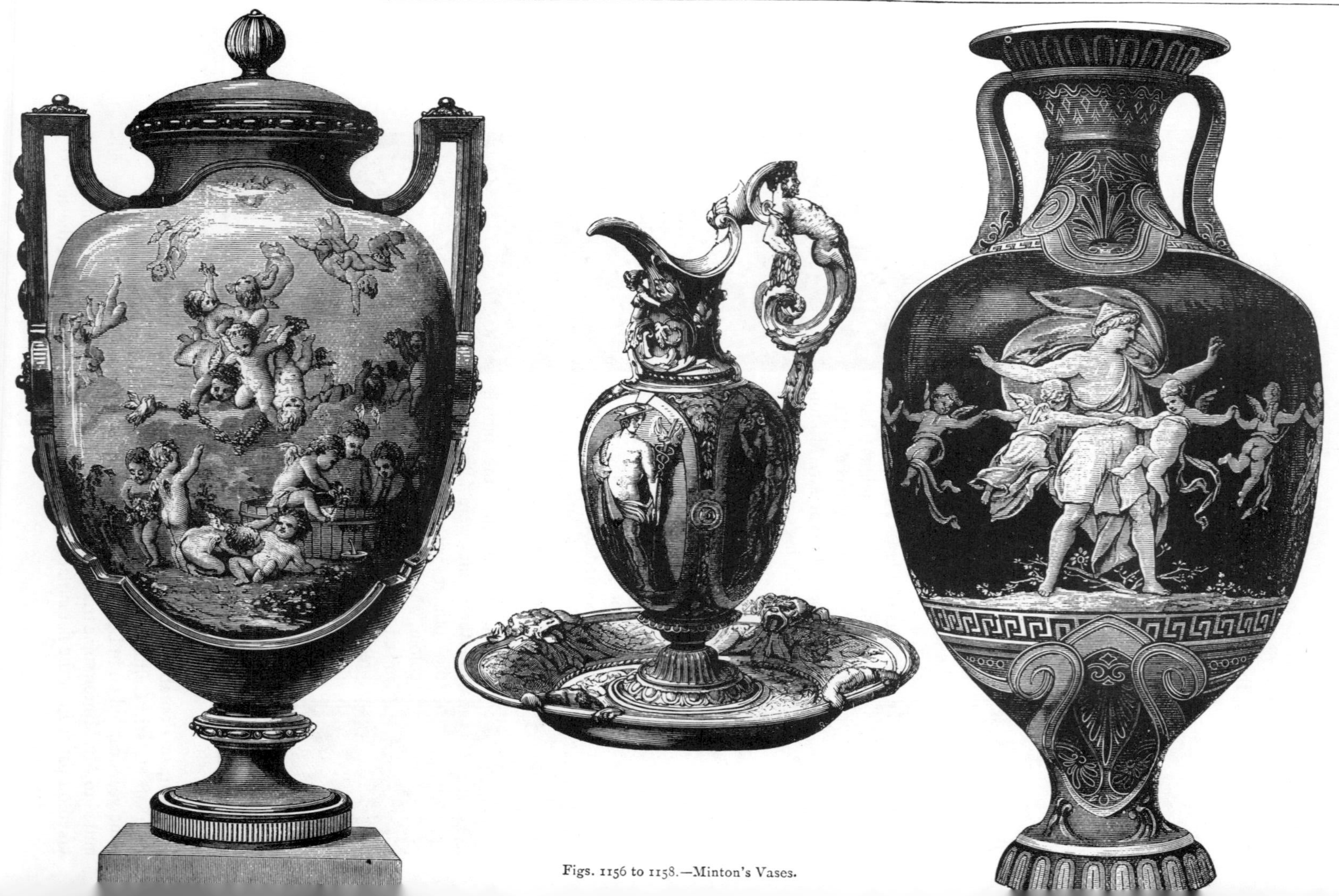

Figs. 1156 to 1158.—Minton's Vases.

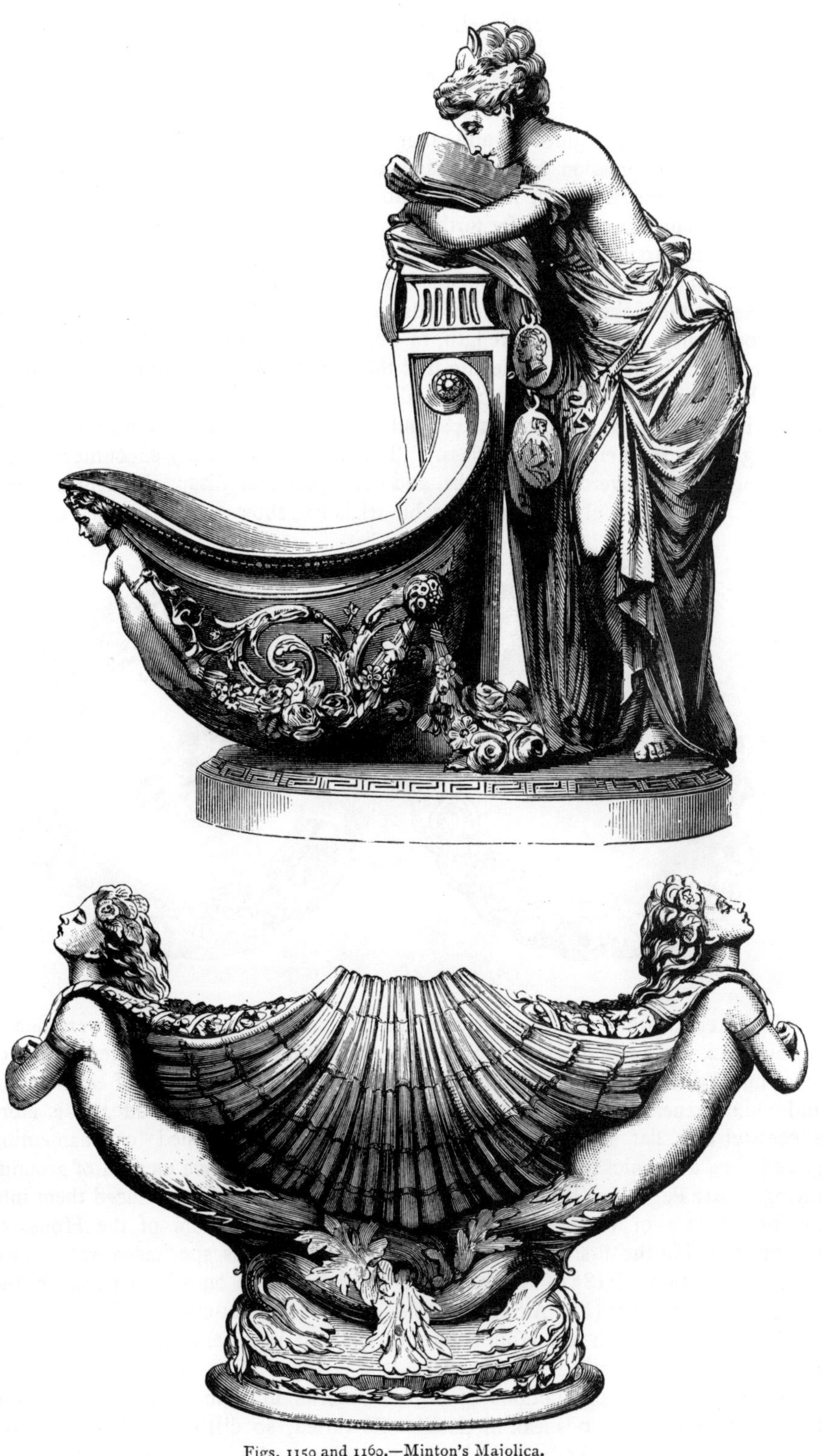

Figs. 1159 and 1160.—Minton's Majolica.

lines; and by that process broad and flat layers of colour could be produced, and several colours transferred at the same time to the ware. These first trials were made with ordinary pigments, and, therefore, only served to show the power of transferring the impression from the paper to the ware. Mr. Minton perceived at once that the process would, in all probability, prove of advantage, and supplied the proper enamelling colours for further experiments. It was now found, however, that these colours were much more difficult of management than the ordinary pigments. This arose from their being mixed with so large a proportion of glass, which necessitated the use of stronger oils to carry the colour; and this again caused the colour, when of sufficient strength, to blister in the kiln. Mr. Minton was not, however, discouraged; and, believing that the difficulties would ultimately be overcome, he joined the experimenters in taking out a patent for the process. The patent is dated the 14th March, 1848, and is entitled "for improvements in ornamenting china, earthenware, and glass." The difficulties so early encountered were very long in being overcome; months, and even years, of disappointment and loss followed, and it was only after innumerable trials had shown what particular oils and

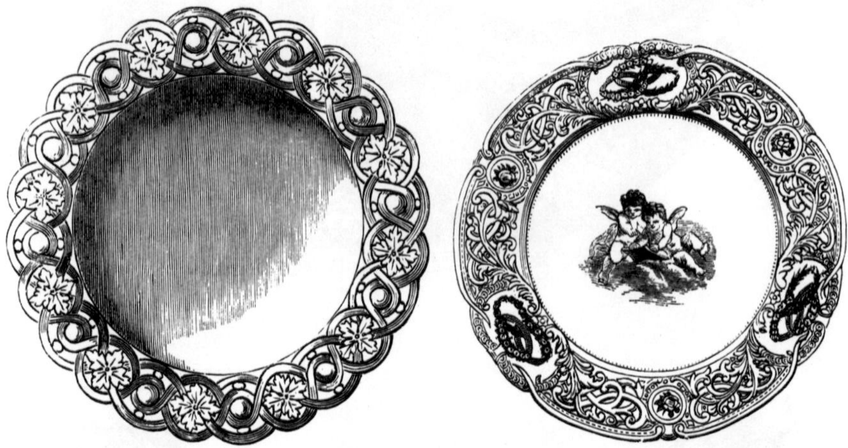

Figs. 1161 and 1162.

of what strength were required for different colours that the obstacles were finally surmounted, and the process established as an additional and improved means of mechanical decoration. The process was applied to the decoration of earthenware and china generally, both useful and ornamental, but has proved to be more successful with flat surfaces. It was at an early period applied to ornamenting glazed tiles, and quickly supplanted the old and more expensive method of ground-laying. Mr. Pugin was the earliest patron of these tiles, and introduced them into the new palace of Westminster, the walls of the smoke-room of the House of Commons being the first instance of their use. Numerous specimens were shown at the Exhibition of 1851, and again at Paris in 1855, on which occasion the inventor and manager (Mr. Alfred Reynolds) obtained a first-class certificate. Later on the partnership with Mr. Hollins terminated, and that gentleman continued the manufacture of encaustic and other tiles.

Of the variety of productions of Minton's works in former and at the present times it is impossible to speak in detail. So varied, so distinct, and so extensive are they in material, in body, in style, in decoration, and in uses, that anything like a detailed account becomes impossible. In stone-ware, all the ordinary articles—jugs, mugs, bottles, &c.—are extensively produced; and in ordinary earthenware, dinner, tea, breakfast, toilet, and other services, &c., are made in great variety, from the ordinary white and blue printed wares up to richly enamelled and gilt patterns.

One of the processes successfully adopted by Mintons is that of *pâte-sur-pâte*, a

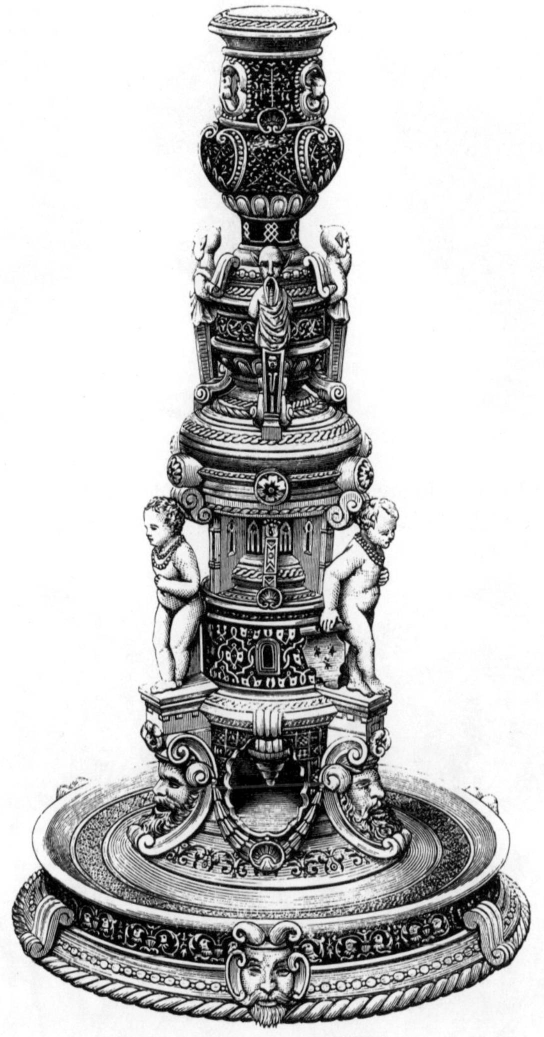

Fig. 1163.

process in which the artist, instead of using colour, employs liquid clay, in which he paints, or rather "lays on" his design; the whole being afterwards glazed. In this process M. Marc Solon, formerly of Sèvres, is particularly successful, and the trays, plaques, &c., produced by him are characterized by pure but severe taste and masterly treatment. His monogram, the combined letters M and S, distinguish his best works.

In imitation of bronze Messrs. Minton have succeeded in producing not only a perfect colour, but a thoroughly metallic appearance ; their drinking cups and other

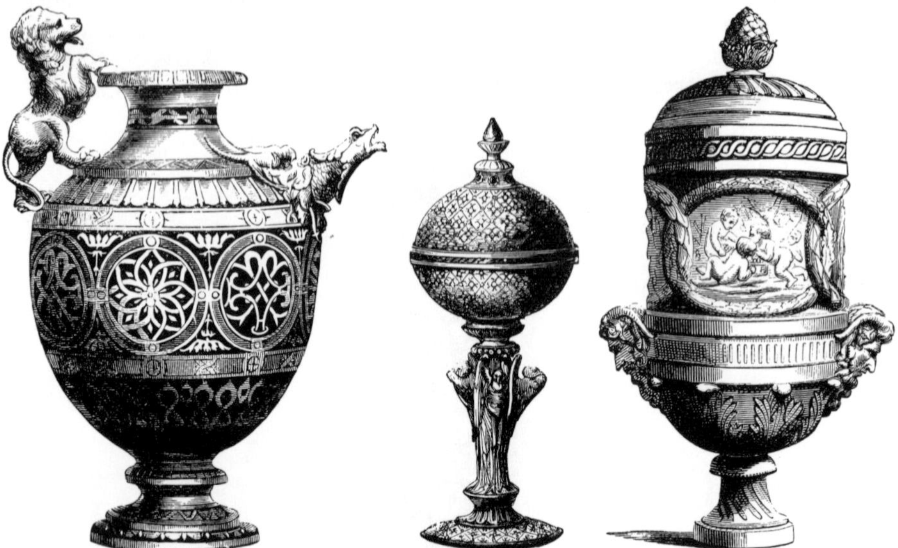

Figs. 1164 to 1166.

articles in bronzed porcelain are well designed and of high character. The Persian ware also is of the highest class, both in point of correct adaptation of design and manipulative treatment.

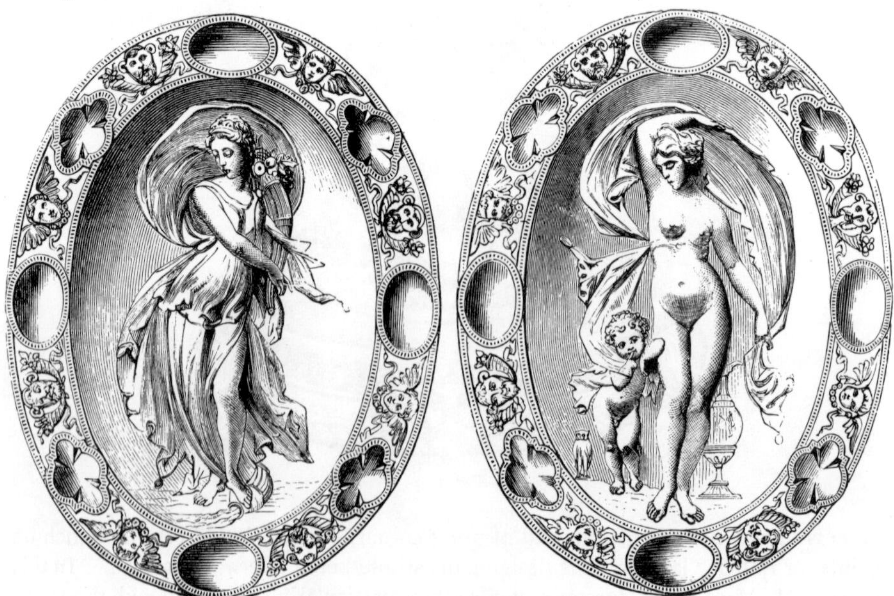

Figs. 1167 and 1168.—Minton's Productions.

The pierced or perforated articles are marvels of lightness and of skill. These, which are among the most difficult tasks for the potter, are, as emanating from

Minton's, perfect in every minute detail. In china, besides all the usual services—dinner, tea, breakfast, dessert, *déjeuner*, toilet, trinket, &c.—an endless variety of

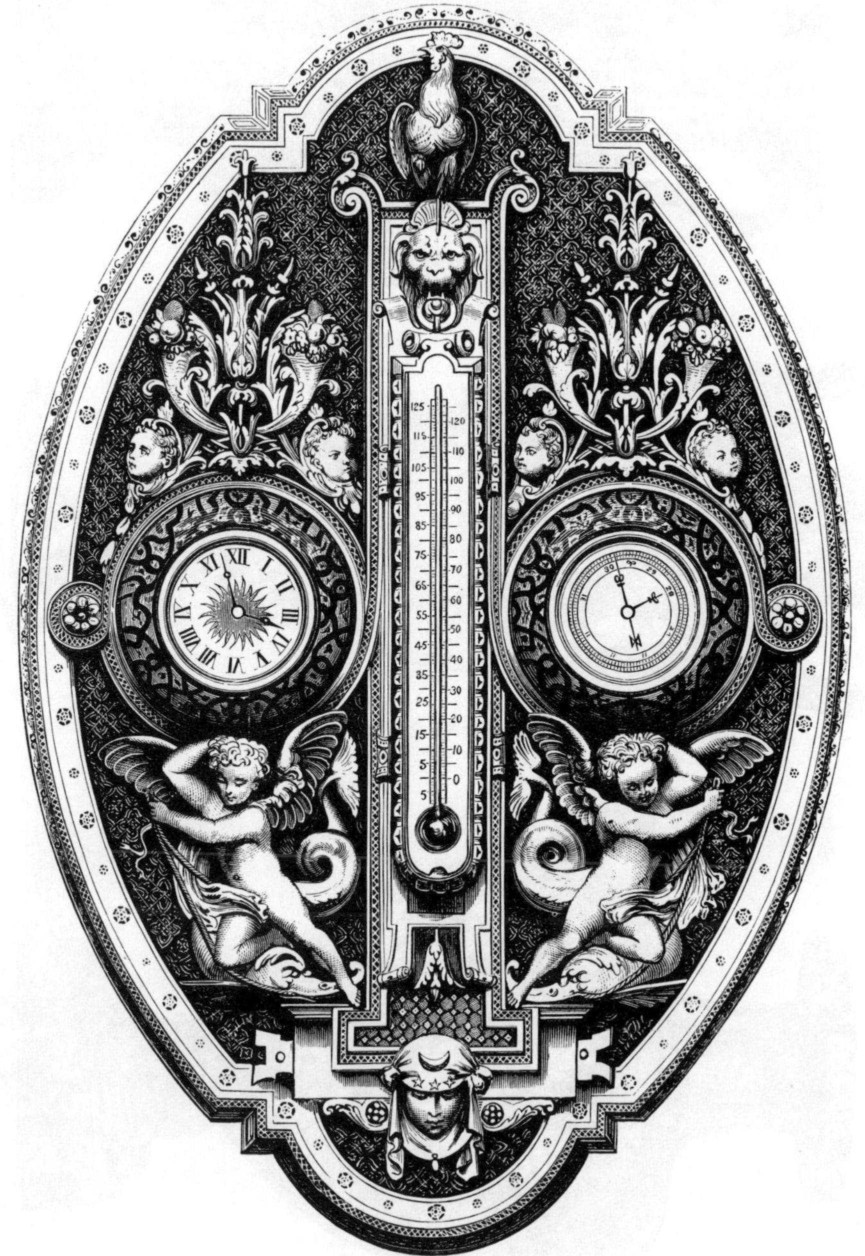

Fig. 1169.

fancy and ornamental goods are produced. Notably among these are vases, ewers, tazzæ, and other articles of extreme beauty, and of every style of decoration. A

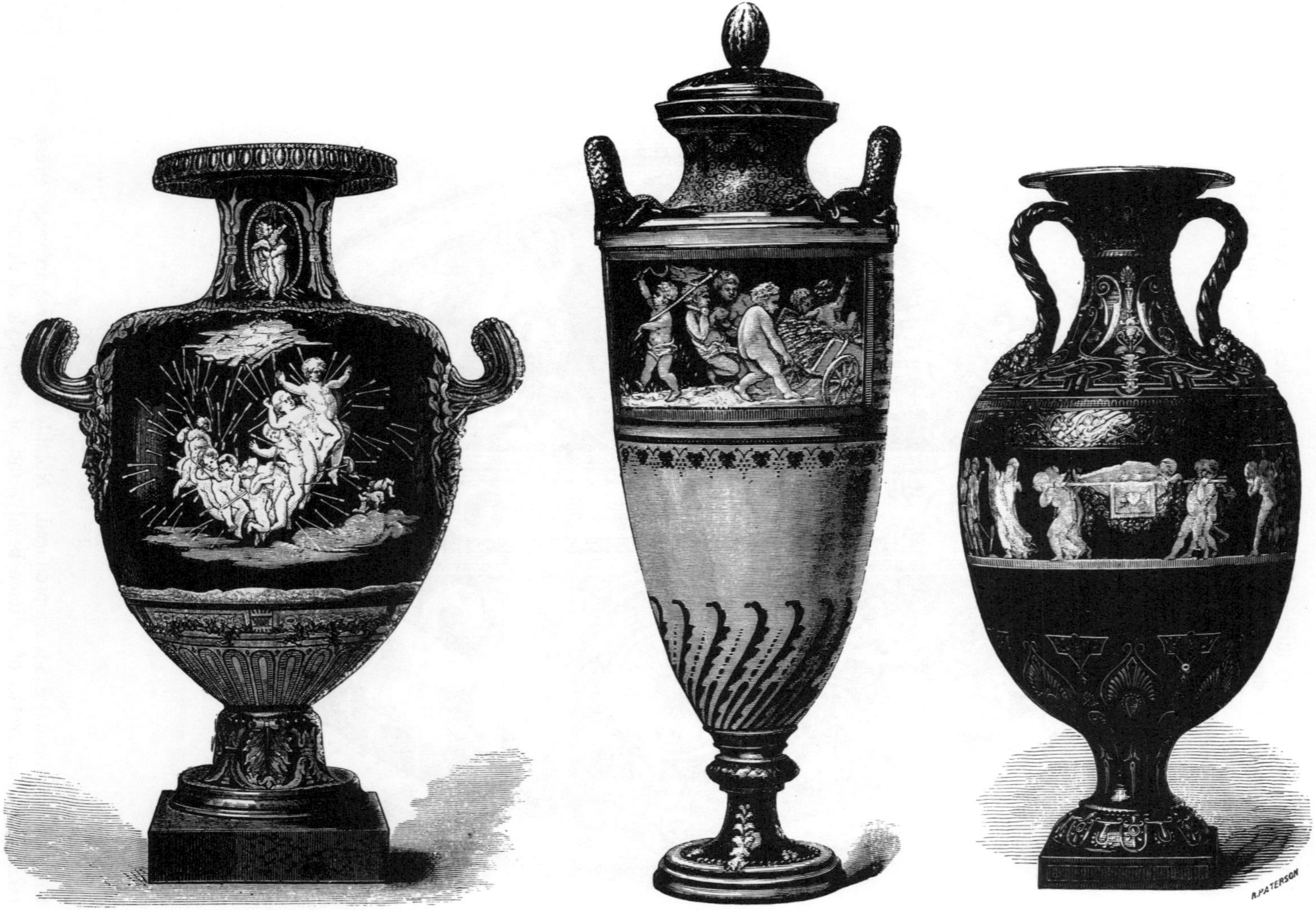

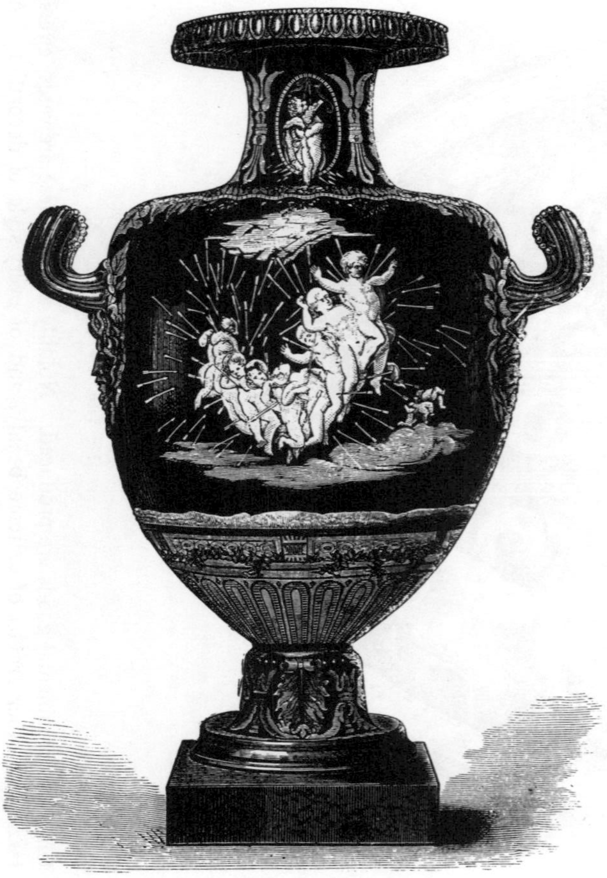

Figs. 1170 to 1172.

marked feature in these is the embossed gilding of borders, &c., by a process patented by the firm. In Parian, the statuary, busts, groups, vases, ewers, and other articles, equal those of almost any manufactory; while in majolica, Della Robbia, and other goods, the productions of this firm stand pre-eminent. The engravings, Figs. 1170 to 1172, give a fair idea of the marvellous beauty and variety of Minton's goods.

The marks used by Messrs. Minton from time to time are the name "MINTON" impressed on the body of the ware; the names "MINTON," "MINTON & BOYLE," "MINTON & CO.," etc., printed on the surface; and an imitation of the Sèvres double *L*, with the initial M added. This latter mark, of which two examples are given on Figs. 1176 and

Figs. 1173 to 1179.

Fig. 1180.

1177, is pencilled in blue on the ware; it occurs on fine porcelain tea-services, richly painted and gilt, and of remarkably good, and sometimes very elaborate, design. Sometimes also the letter M alone (Fig. 1178) occurs. Of late years, too, an ermine spot (Fig. 1179) in gold or colours has occasionally been used.

The name MINTON impressed or "stamped" in the body of the ware was not used until 1861, so that this will be a guide to possessors in appropriating examples.

Sometimes the words "FELSPAR CHINA," "NEW STONE" or "SEMI CHINA" occur.

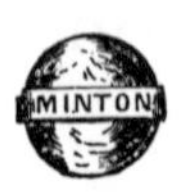

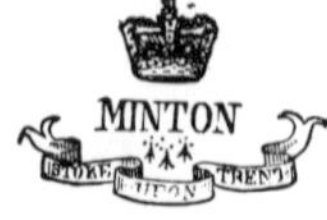

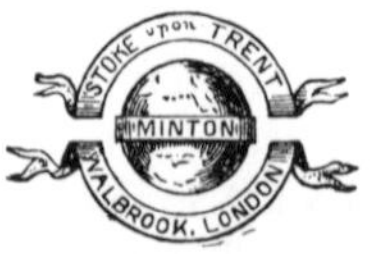

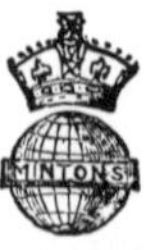

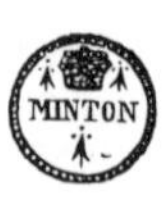

Figs. 1181 to 1189.

Other marks used by Messrs. Minton are shown on the examples here given.

Hollins.—The history of the famous works of Messrs. Minton, Hollins, & Co., and of the rise and development of their manufacture of encaustic, enamelled, majolica, and other tiles, has already been given on pages 393 to 405, and therefore need not be repeated. In 1868, as there stated, the partnership ceased, and from that time the manufacture of tiles passed into the hands of, and has been continued solely by, Mr. Michael Daintry Hollins, under the style of "Minton, Hollins & Co." The productions of the works, as of old, consist of unglazed encaustic and tesselated, or rather geometrical, tiles for pavements; glazed encaustic tiles for fire-hearths; majolica and enamelled tiles for grate-cheeks, flower-boxes, wall-linings, &c.; and plain and painted tiles for various species of decoration. These are all made from the same moulds and of precisely the same excellent quality both in body and decoration as under the old firm; the business is, indeed, in every respect the same as before the dissolution.

The engravings, Figs. 1180 to 1201, show some of the designs of Minton, Hollins & Co., and are of the highest style of art. The unglazed and the glazed encaustic tiles for pavements are made of the hardest and most durable materials that have yet been discovered—far beyond those of many other makers—and the workmanship as well as the designs are of a superior order. They are made in the simple red and buff patterns of mediæval times, as well as in various combinations of colours; among these are black, white, buff, chocolate, salmon, green, blue, red, grey, yellow, &c., and these are varied in their combinations to an almost endless variety.

In majolica tiles for flower-boxes many effective and appropriate designs, in bold relief and richly coloured, are made. Earthenware tiles, printed or painted, not in relief, are also largely produced for the same purpose. For wall decoration, fire-place cheeks and linings, and other purposes, the variety of tiles is very extensive, and embraces almost every class of design. In these are some with the patterns (notably the lily) all in very high relief, and the colouring of the richest and most effective character. Others have their patterns painted by hand on the flat surface by skilled artists; and others, again, are transfer-printed, or a combination of printing and painting. Some form a more or less rich diaper, and others are separate or continuous patterns, while others, again, form borders of more than usual elegance.

Among special patterns may be named a series of masterly designs of Morning, Noon, Evening, and Night, represented by well-conceived figures in blue on a black ground; a series of emblematic designs of the Seasons, printed in chocolate or other

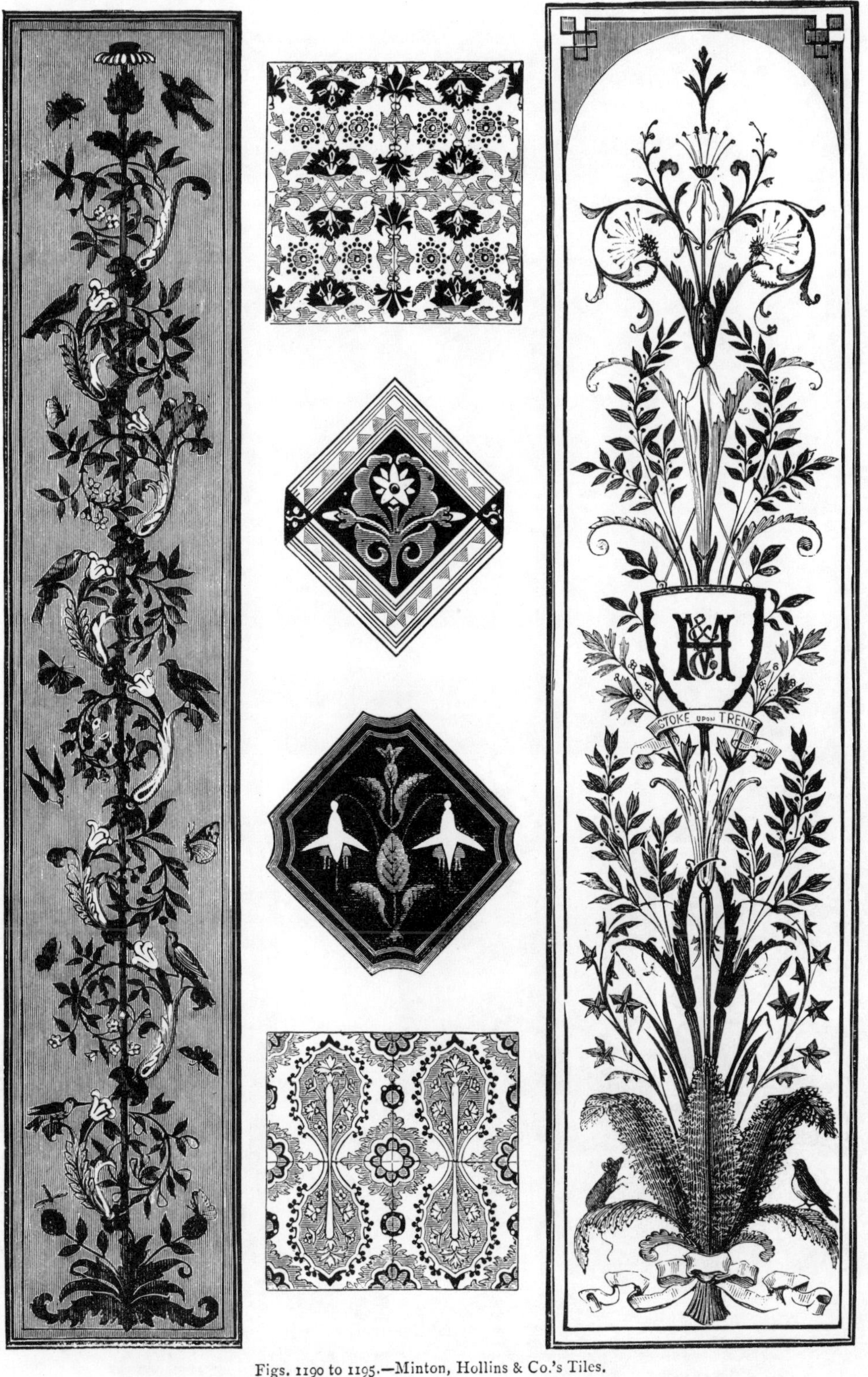

Figs. 1190 to 1195.—Minton, Hollins & Co.'s Tiles.

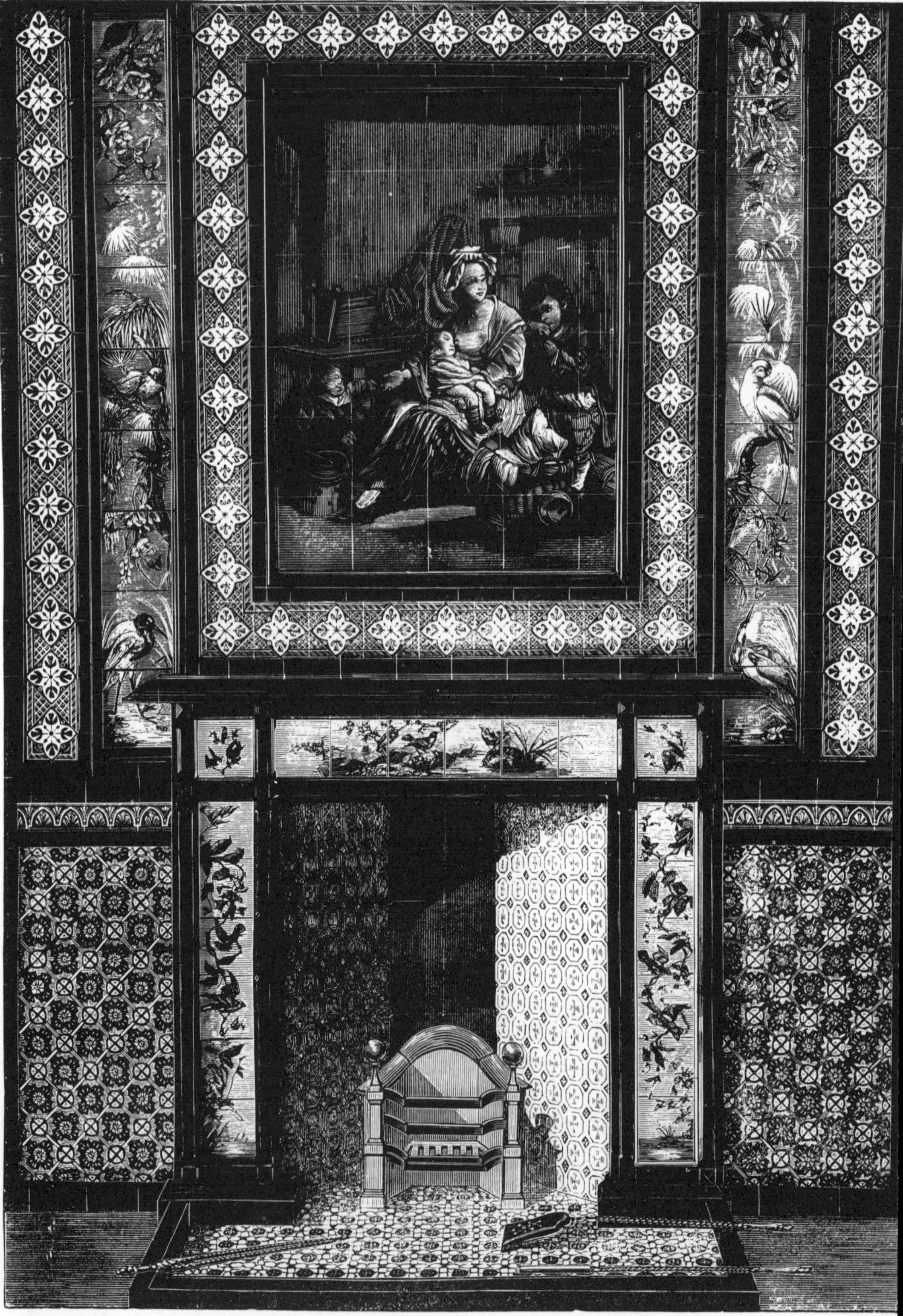

Fig. 1196.—Minton, Hollins & Co.'s Tiles, Philadelphia Exhibition.

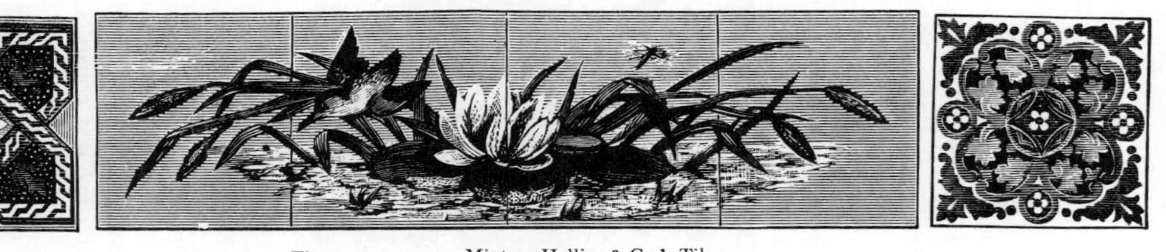

Figs. 1197 to 1199.—Minton, Hollins & Co.'s Tiles.

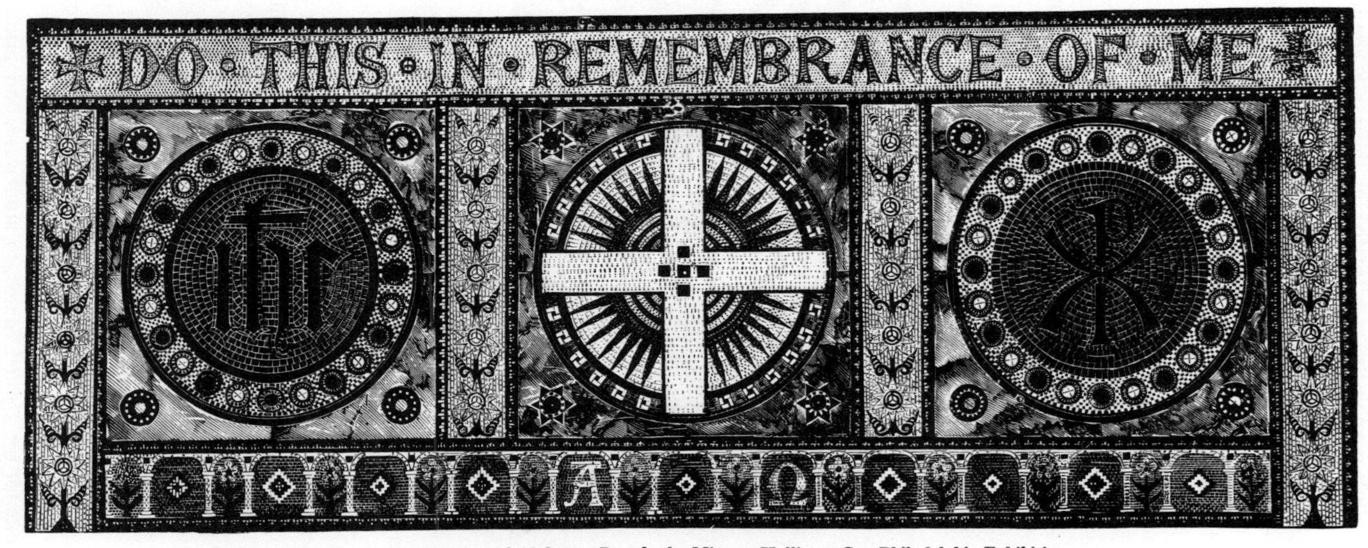

Fig. 1200.—Mosaic and Alabaster Reredos by Minton, Hollins & Co., Philadelphia Exhibition.

monochrome on the white or buff surface; and a series of allegorical, mythological, and fabulous subjects, each treated in the same admirable manner. The body of some is of fine white earthenware, very hard and durable, and others are buff, grey, or cream-coloured, and in each of these bodies the tiles are produced of many patterns and of every degree of finish.

The geometric or tesselated pavements are of every conceivable variety, of all shades of colour, and, whatever their form, are all produced with the utmost mechanical nicety, so as to "fit" in ever-changing variety. A notable feature in the tiles of this firm is the richness, the clearness, and the purity of the colours and the excellence of the glaze; these features, added to the faultless quality of body, to high-class artistic treatment of patterns, and to excellence of mechanical workmanship, place them high in estimation. Messrs. Minton, Hollins & Co. were very extensive exhibitors at the Philadelphia Exhibition, 1876, and their productions excited great interest and admiration. One of their main attractions was a lovely chimney-piece composed of tiles richly painted with humming-birds, &c., and

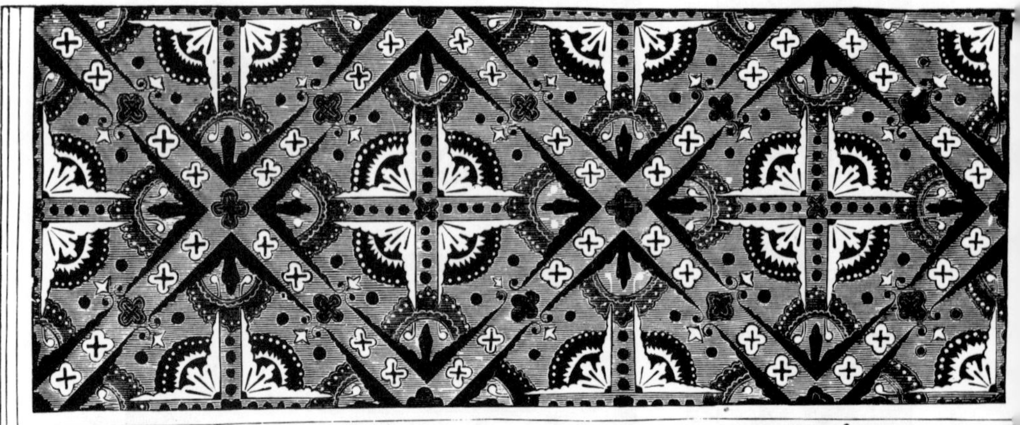

Fig. 1201.

over it an exquisite painting of a mother and her children, executed with perfect artistic taste and feeling on thirty tiles. This great achievement in ceramics is shown on Fig. 1196. Another notable exhibit was a reredos in mosaic (Fig. 1200), and in mosaic also was a fine head of Washington. The rest of their exhibits consisted of every possible variety of tiles, and all of equal excellence. The marks used are "MINTON HOLLINS & CO. PATENT TILE WORKS, STOKE ON TRENT;" MINTON & Co. Patent, STOKE ON TRENT;" "MINTON HOLLINS & CO. STOKE ON TRENT;" "M. H. & Co.," &c., at the back of the tiles. Messrs. Minton, Hollins & Co. have their London show-rooms at 50, Conduit Street, Regent Street.

The Trent Potteries, established in 1861 by the head of the present firm of "George Jones and Sons," produce all descriptions of ordinary earthenware, from the gaily-decorated articles required in Africa and in South America, and white granite for the United States, to stoneware, and printed, enamelled, and gilt wares, for home use and for the Colonies. The firm also make both useful and ornamental articles in majolica, most of which are of a high order of art. Some of the produc-

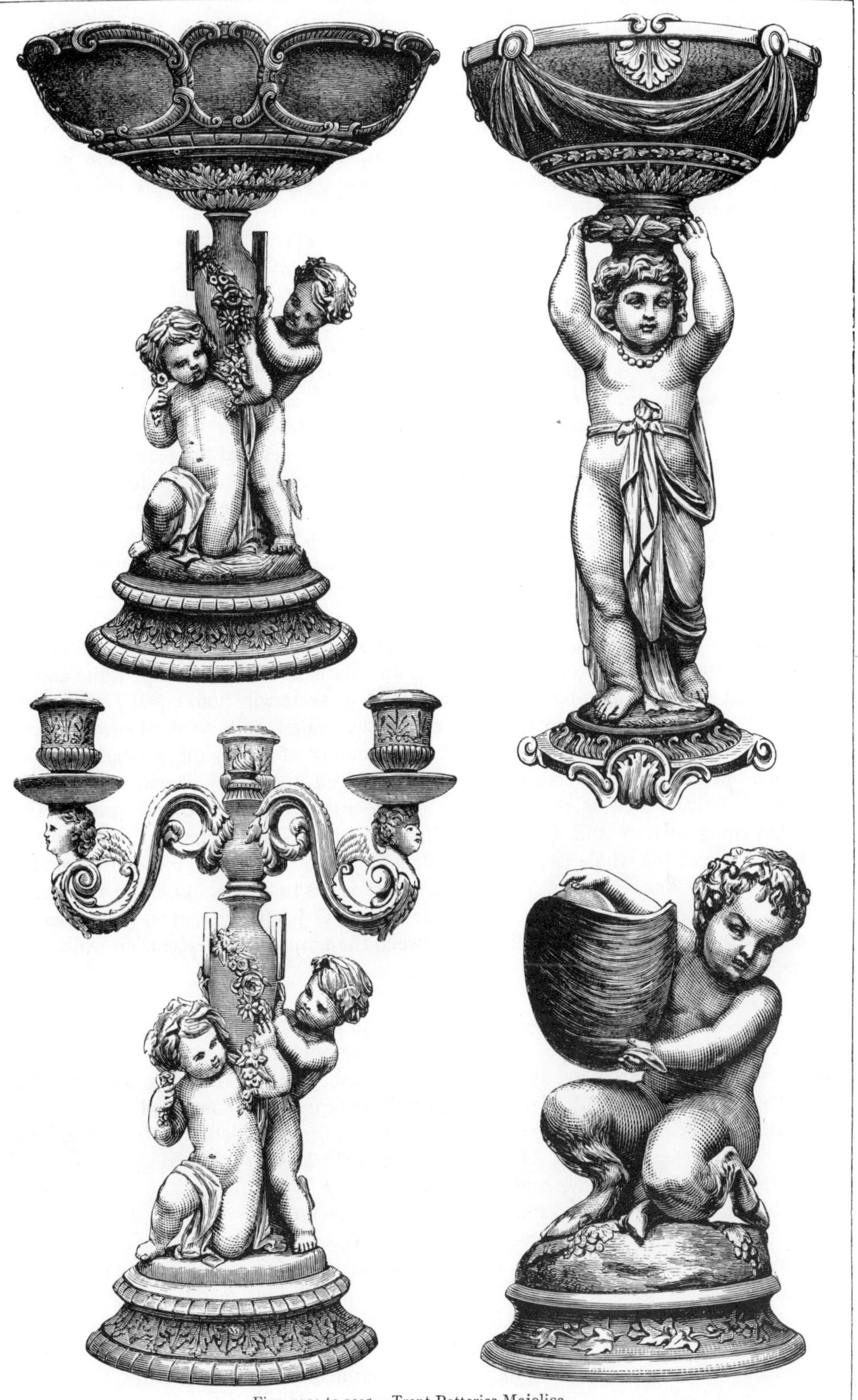

Figs. 1202 to 1205.—Trent Potteries Majolica.

tions exhibited in Paris in 1867 (when they obtained a medal), London in 1871, Vienna in 1873, and Sydney in 1876, are shown in Figs. 1202 to 1226. The imitation Palissy ware is highly successful, and in vases, candelabra, centre and side pieces, flower-shells, and other articles, many striking and good designs are produced. The manufacture of china in all its branches was added in 1876, and is produced in great variety and of a high quality, both in body, in glaze, and in artistic finish. In services some entirely new forms of cups and saucers—notably a scalloped shape—are of great merit and of particularly pleasing character. Thin in body, pleasant to the feel, the cup holds its place in the saucer with mechanical precision, and the "potting" and finish is faultless; this shape is all that can be wished for. The ornamental productions in china ware are all characterised by the purest taste both in conception of design and in finish of decoration. A flower-basket formed of the curled-up leaf of the water-lily, has its double handle, which forms a support by passing beneath the leaf, composed of the long flower-stems of the plant twisted and plaited together, with exquisitely modelled flowers and buds at the sides. It is one of the most charming of conceptions, and is just such a careless, elegant, and surpassingly beautiful object as a naïad or a water nymph, in one of her happier moments, might have improvised, as she rose from the lake, to present to some favoured mortal. Another equally charming production is a quadruple flower-basket, whose handles, crossing each other, loop up and give apparent support to the matted basket itself. These may be classed among the most elegant of novelties, and give evidence of the purest taste on the part of the firm. They are produced in celadon and white china.

What we have said about these china flower-baskets will hold equally good with regard to the *pâte colorée* in vases, which, in their finest body of earthenware, have been recently introduced. The delicate grounding of these, the masterly way in which the groups of flowers and foliage are arranged, the judicious manner in which the relief decoration is managed, the purely artistic painting of the groups, the heightening of rims and supports with gold, and the perfect harmony and unobtrusiveness of the whole is such as becomes a joy to the educated eye, and render these productions of Messrs. Jones & Son acquisitions to be sought for and cherished. The mark formerly used was simply the initials G J joined together; the present one is the same monogram of G J between the horns of a crescent, on which are the words "AND SONS."

Copeland Street Works.—(Turner & Wood.)—The business of this firm was established in 1859 in the Albert Works, Liverpool Road, by G. Turner, J. E. Hassall, and W. Bromley, as a Parian manufactory only. In 1863, Mr. Bromley having previously retired, Mr. Peake joined the firm, which continued as "Turner, Hassall, & Peake" until 1871, when the latter was succeeded by Mr. Poole, and the style became "Turner, Hassall, and Poole." In 1873 Mr. Hassall was succeeded by Mr. Stanway, and the firm became "Turner, Poole, and Stanway." Later on Mr. Turner also retired, and Mr. Josiah Wood having become a partner, the style was altered to "Poole, Stanway, and Wood," and so continued until 1880, when it changed to Turner & Wood, being now carried on by Josiah Wood and the Executors of Mr. Turner. At first Parian only was made, but after a time the decoration of china (bought in the white) was added. After about ten years the manufacture of china was commenced, and has developed into a large branch of the business. The present productions are principally Parian statuary, of a good quality in body, colour, and workmanship; china tea, breakfast, dessert, trinket, and

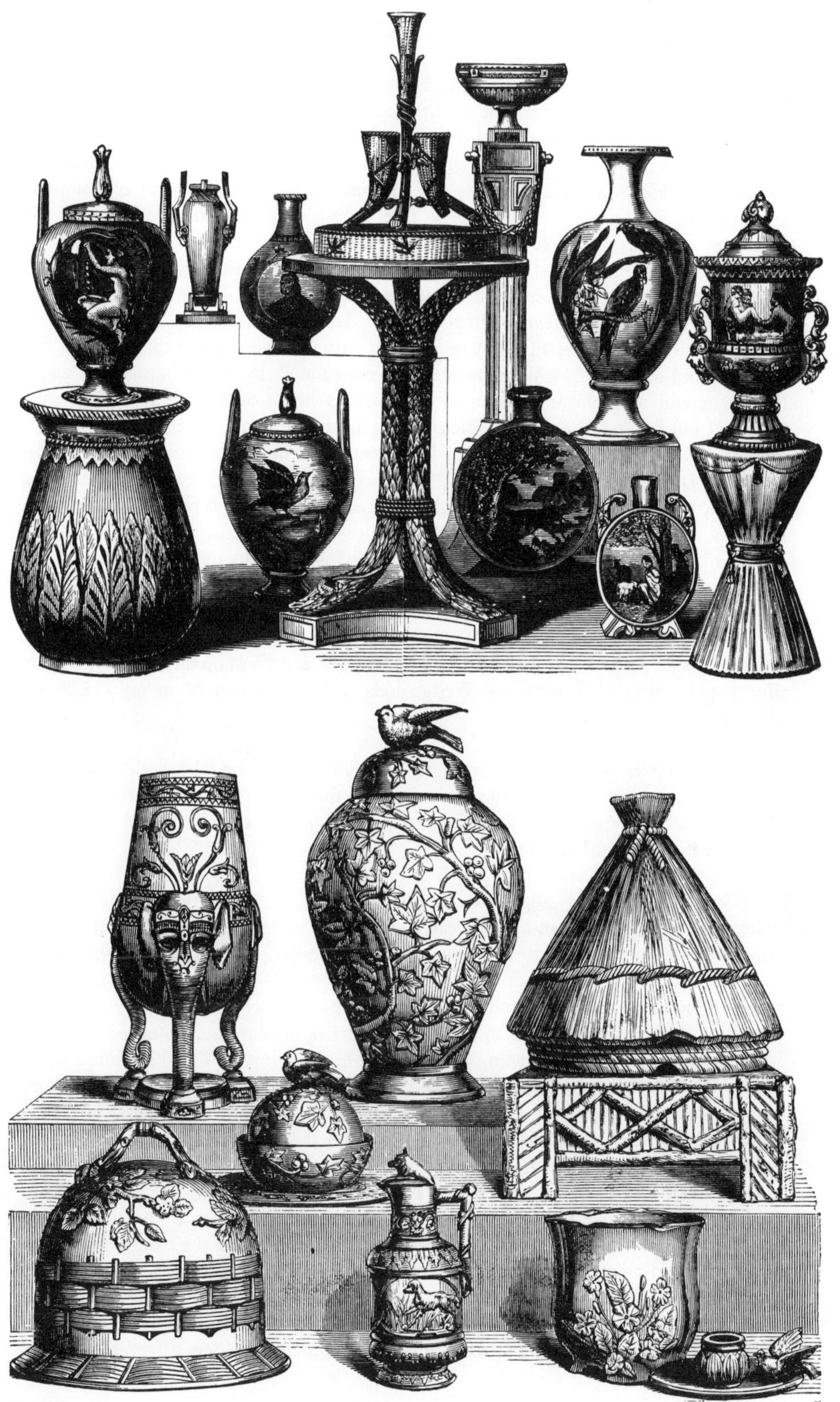

Figs. 1206 to 1226.—Trent Potteries Majolica.

other services, vases, figures, groups, &c. ; majolica, in all the usual varieties of articles ; and terra-cotta, in which are produced water-jugs, fern-stands, tobacco-jars, filters, candlesticks, flower-vases, teapots, &c. A speciality of the works, introduced by Mr. Turner, was the novelty of decorating the Parian body with majolica colours, by which means a clearness and brilliancy as well as softness of colour is attained and a pleasing effect gained. The terra-cotta goods are produced in red and cane colour, and richly enamelled. In statuary Parian, a large variety of groups, single figures, busts, animals, and ornamental pieces are produced. The groups and figures, both after the antique and original designs by celebrated modellers, are of a high degree of excellence. In centre-pieces and compotiers the firm is particularly successful. A set of four, with juvenile figures representing the Seasons, and another in which the stem is surrounded by three Cupids, are peculiarly graceful and elegant, the open-work dishes being of admirable design and faultless finish, and the tinting pleasing aud artistic, and others are of equal beauty. A very successful and powerfully conceived design is a comport in which the base is formed of three young Tritons, who, surrounding an elegant lyre standard, alternate with the same number of shells ; above them rises the open-work bowl.

It is interesting to add that Mr. Josiah Wood is a worthy descendant of a long line of potters ; his grandfather, Aaron Wood, himself a famous potter, was the son of Aaron Wood (who was apprenticed to Dr. Thomas Wedgwood), and the brother of the celebrated Enoch Wood, of whom notices are given in other parts of this volume. Mr. Stanway, a former partner, was the son of William Stanway, whose fifty years' connection with the Wedgwoods I have spoken of in my "Life of Wedgwood."

Albert Works.—The works formerly carried on by the above firm are now occupied by I. and J. Snow, who, as well as at the Pyenest Street Works, Hanley, manufacture terra-cotta, jet, majolica, and other varieties of wares, both in the useful and ornamental classes.

Glebe Street Works and *Wharf Street Works.*—These two manufactories, belonging to Robinson and Leadbeater, are confined to the production of Parian goods, of which they are among the largest producers. The *Glebe Street Works* were commenced in 1850 by a clever Italian figure-modeller named Giovanni Meli, who produced clever groups and single figures till 1865, when he sold the business, plant, moulds, and machinery to Robinson and Leadbeater, and returned to Italy with the intention of commencing a terra-cotta manufactory. This he relinquished, mainly through lack of a suitable native clay or marl for the making of his saggers, and went to Chicago, where he succeeded in his wishes, and established a manufactory of the kind he had attempted in Italy, and there he continues to the present time. The *Wharf Street Works* were commenced in 1858 by Mr. Leveson Hill, after whose death they were carried on by his executors until 1870, when they were sold to Robinson and Leadbeater, who thus became proprietors of both concerns. By them the works have been considerably enlarged, and as their business operations are rapidly extending, they bid fair to rank among the largest in the district.

They produce Parian groups, figures, and busts in large variety, classical, portrait, and imaginative ; vases of endless form and variety ; centre-pieces and comports ; flower-stands ; brackets and pedestals ; bouquet-holders ; trinket-caskets ;

cream-ewers; jugs, and other articles. By giving constant and undivided attention to this one branch of ceramic art (Parian), the firm have succeeded in so improving it both in fineness and purity of body and in tone of colour as to render their productions of far higher than average merit. They have studied excellence of body, originality of design, and cleverness of workmanship as before that of marketable cheapness, and in this they have done wisely. In material, they rank with the best productions of many competing firms, while in fineness of surface and careful manipulation they are scarcely excelled.

Among the designs produced by this firm are many of more than average merit, and they are issued, in some instances, of large size. "Clytie," a clever reproduction, is a bust of about twenty-two inches in height, "Apollo," twenty-six inches, whilst several others (Gladstone, Disraeli, Cobden, Tennyson, Dickens, and other modern celebrities) are of various heights. Among their principal groups are "Innocence Protected," "Penelope," "The Power of Love," "Cupid Betrayed," "Cupid Captive," "Golden Age," "Rock of Ages," "Guardian Angel," "The Immaculate Conception," "Christ and St. John," "The Combat," "Lion Slayer," "Dante and Beatrice," "Hubert and Arthur," and "Virgin and Child," and in single figures are many well designed and faultlessly produced. These are all good, and the same remark will apply to the remainder of the figures and busts. Among the latter, those of Abraham Lincoln, Charles Sumner, Governor Andrew, Garfield, and Longfellow, have had a very extensive sale in the United States, to which market, indeed, the greater part of their general statuary and other goods is sent. An excellent portrait statuette of Queen Victoria may also be reckoned among their successful productions. In addition to the States and the home markets, the firm export largely to Canada, the Colonies, and Germany. They use no mark.

Copeland Street.—At these works (formerly Billington & Co.), Messrs. Shorter and Boulton, who entered upon them in 1879, manufacture majolica, &c., for the American and Australian markets. Many of their designs in vases, flower-stands, jugs, trays, dejeune, and tea sets, &c., are strikingly original, and the quality is of more than average excellence.

Bridge Works.—This manufactory, formerly worked by Davenport & Co., W. Adams & Co., Minton, Hollins, & Co., Jones & Co., Grose & Son, and Hancock & Whittingham, is now carried on by S. Hancock only, for the production of the usual classes of earthenware.

Walker & Carter.—This manufactory formerly belonged to Wolf, next to his son-in-law, Hamilton, and later was worked by Z. Boyle & Co., W. Adams & Co., and Minton, Hollins, & Co. The present firm manufacture the ordinary classes of earthenware.

London Road (and Eastwood Vale).—The works of Mr. William Henry Goss were commenced in 1858 for the production of Parian, ivory porcelain, terra-cotta, &c., and their progress from that time as pure art-productions has been very marked. The most famous of the specialities of Mr. Goss's manufacture are jewelled porcelain, in which vases, scent-bottles, tazzæ, and other ornaments are produced; and vessels to be filled with perfumes, including illuminated scent-vases, pomade-boxes, rice-powder jars, pastile and scented ribbon burners, &c., the latter being made largely for the great Paris and London perfume houses. The process of modelling jewelled porcelain, just alluded to, which is of extreme richness and beauty, is the invention of Mr. Goss, who, many years ago, observing that the enamel jewels on the old Sèvres porcelain frequently dropped or were rubbed off, turned his attention to the subject. The process adopted at Sèvres was as follows:

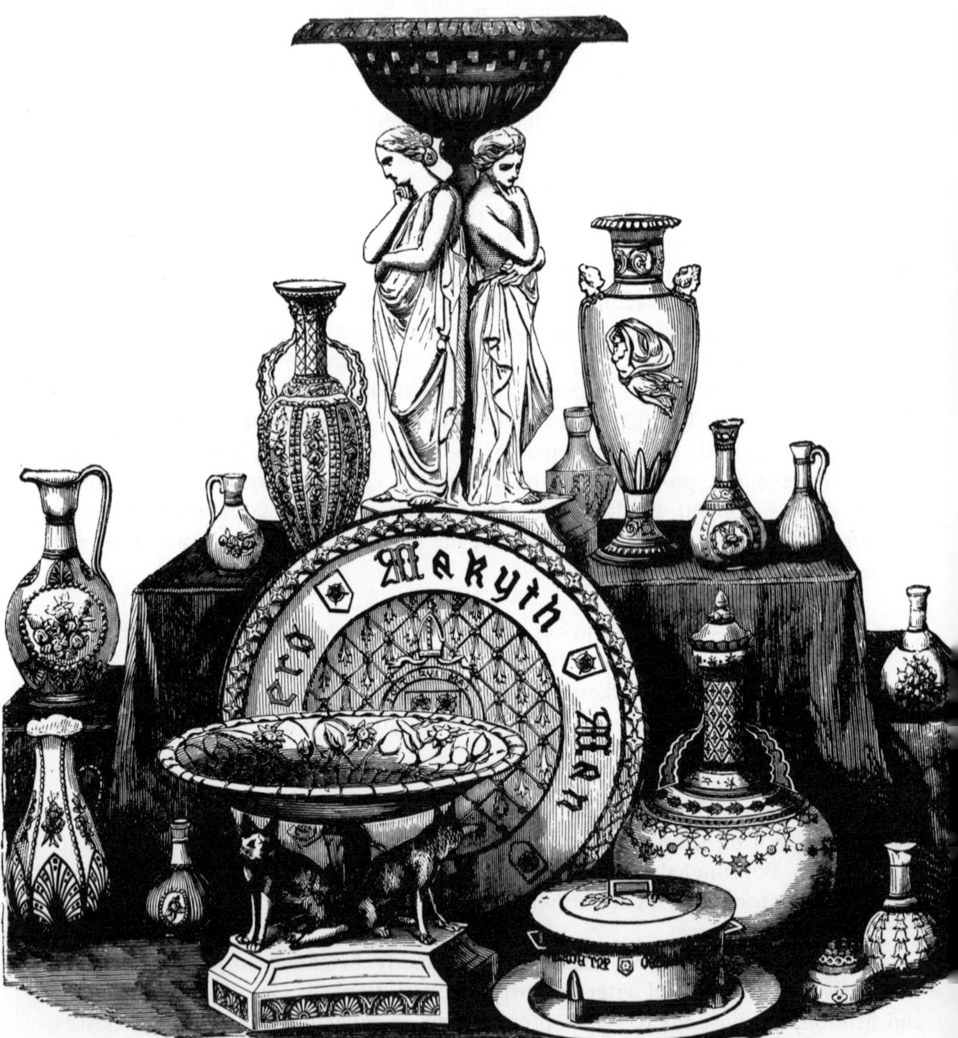

Figs. 1227 to 1242.—Mr. Goss's Productions.

a gold foil was marked into circles, ovals, and other required forms for the reception of the enamels, which were then pencilled on, and fired before applying them to the article they were intended to decorate. After being vitrified into imitations of uncut rubies, emeralds, &c., they were stuck on to the surface of the porcelain with a flux, and again fired. The adhesion was by this process often incomplete, and thus it frequently occurred that part of the design became rubbed away. The process invented by Mr. Goss for this mosaic jewellery is to indent the designs for the intended jewelled decoration in the dry or moist clay before baking, and in these to insert the jewels, which are all previously cut, and thus attain an increased brilliancy. Being inserted into the hollow or recess prepared for them, they are made secure. The process is an extremely delicate but very ingenious and beautiful one, and the effect produced is richer and finer than is attained by any other processes. Real pearls are often also introduced by Mr. Goss with good effect. For this and other purposes Mr. Goss has taken out a patent "for improvements in manufacturing articles of jewellery, dress-ornaments, dress-fastenings, smoke-shades

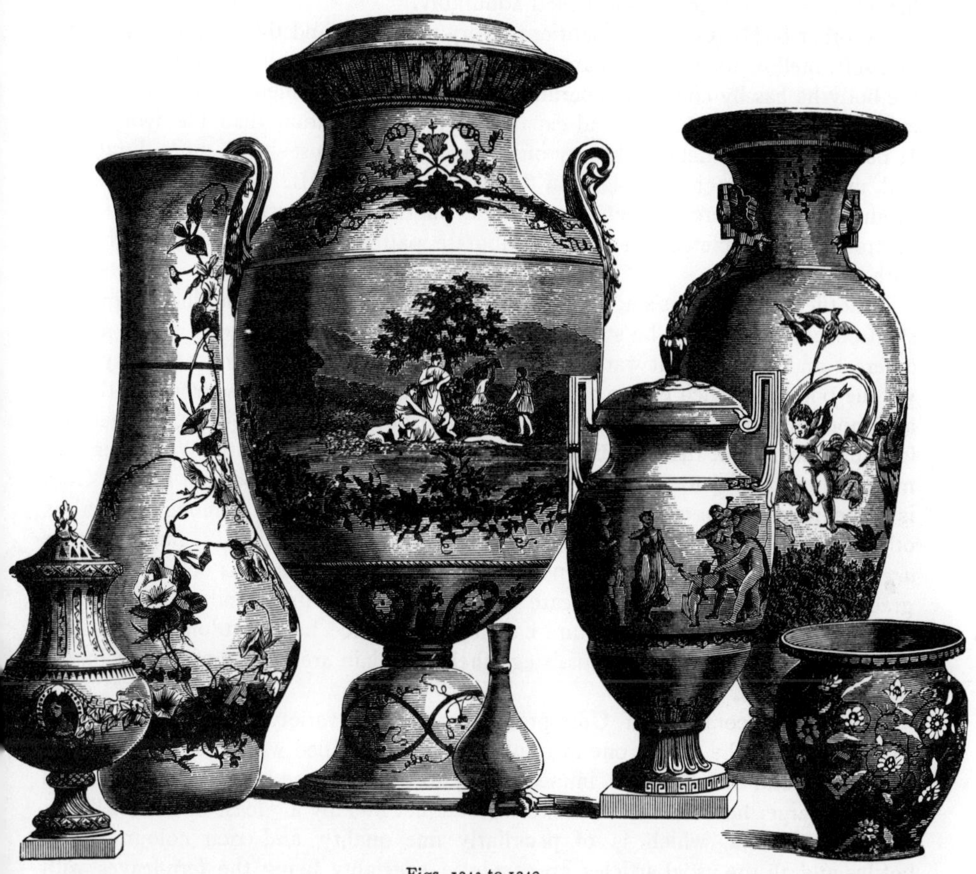

Figs. 1243 to 1249.

for lamps and gas-burners, and the handles of cups and other vessels of ceramic materials." The floral brooches, crosses, &c., are of great beauty, and in delicacy of modelling remind one of the famous Bristol and Derby floral plaques. Some are produced in pure white bisqué, others are tinted in the natural colours of the flowers represented, and others are in ivory porcelain prepared by a patented process.

In Parian, for which Mr. Goss ranks deservedly high, busts, statuary (notably an exquisite group of Lady Godiva), vases, tazzas, scent-jars, bread-platters, and many other ornamental goods, are made. Notably among these are admirable busts of our beloved Queen, of the late Earl of Beaconsfield, of Mr. Gladstone, of Lord Derby, of Mr. S. C. Hall (prepared for myself), of Charles Swain, and that of myself, an engraving from which forms the frontispiece to the first edition of this work, for which it was expressly modelled in 1875. They, as are all the busts which the pure artistic genius and manipulative skill of Mr. Goss have produced, are of the highest style of Art in point of pose and poetic treatment, and of the most careful finish in workmanship. As portrait-busts they rank far above the average, and are, indeed, perfect reproductions of the living originals. It is not often that this can be said of portrait-busts, but it has been a particular study of Mr. Goss, and in it he has succeeded admirably.

Another of Mr. Goss's specialities is ivory porcelain, and this he produces of the full, soft, mellow tone which characterizes the finest ivory, while, from the nature of the body he has by constant experiments and study succeeded in producing, it is far more lasting and durable and capable of more decoration than the ivory itself. It possesses all the delicate beauty of the ivory, with, as just stated, more durability, and, unlike it, is unchangeable. In this material one of Mr. Goss's most successful productions is a pierced scent-bottle of the pilgrim-bottle or puzzle-jug form. Its centre is double pierced in a very elaborate pattern, and judiciously heightened with lines of gold.

Another of Mr. Goss's achievements in the plastic art is the production of egg-shell porcelain, in which he stands pre-eminent. The pieces produced in this almost ethereal and very difficult ware are so light as to be almost devoid of gravity, and yet the body is of such extreme hardness and firmness as to be as strong as thicker and more massive wares. Of a finer and purer body than the Sèvres, thinner and far more translucent than the Belleek, more delicate in tone than the Worcester, and more dainty to the touch than any other, the "egg-shell" produced by Mr. Goss is an achievement in ceramics of which he may justly be proud. Among numberless other objects produced in this delicate ware the "paper nautilus"—the *argonauta argo* of naturalists, and theme of poets and prose writers alike—is one of the most graceful. Lighter and more delicate than even the shell itself, and of perfect form down to the minutest detail, nature has in this instance been outdone by imitative art. The specimens of Mr. Goss's egg-shell porcelain are worthy of places in the choicest cabinets.

For table decoration Mr. Goss produces an infinite variety of tiny baskets, which when placed by the dozen, one in front of each guest, filled with choice verbenas or other tiny floral beauties, add immeasurably to the elegance of the table, and with his other larger holders help to make the banquet literally a "feast of flowers."

In terra-cotta, which is of peculiarly fine quality and rich colour, water-bottles and all the usual articles are made, a speciality being the fern-leaves with which they are decorated. All kinds of enamel colours and lustres are made at these works. The name W. H. GOSS is generally stamped in the ware, and on the higher class goods the crest, a falcon rising, ducally gorged, is used.

London Road.—In 1856 a valuable mine of red clay having here been found, a manufactory of floor, roof, and ridge-tiles, &c., was commenced, and was purchased by Mr. W. Kirkham, who in 1862 built a manufactory for the production of terra-cotta and general earthenware for the home and foreign markets, and still continues the works. To this he has since added the making of brassfounders' fittings, chemists' goods, stoneware, &c., and a patent is also worked for the production of earthenware bottle-stoppers, &c. The terra-cotta, comprising water-bottles, ornamental flower-pots and stands, table-jugs, spill-cases, and a variety of other articles, in colour is a deep, rich, full red, and in texture is close, hard, and durable. The ornamentation consists of printed groups of Etruscan figures, borders, groups of flowers, &c., enamelling in various colours, and dead and burnished gilding. Some of the fern decorations are graceful, natural, and elegant; and those with Etruscan figures and enamelled borders are in pure taste.

London Road.—Messrs. Steel and Wood commenced the manufacture of Art-tiles in 1874, and have been very successful in producing decorated tiles of various classes for hearths, stoves, dados, pilasters, furniture, skirtings, &c.

Railway Pottery, Sutherland Street.—Established by S. Fielding & Co. in 1878 for the manufacture of majolica, terra-cotta, jet, Rockingham, and green-glaze goods, and general earthenware, in all which the usual useful, ornamental, and fancy articles are made. The mark of the firm is a game-cock.

Victoria Pottery Company.—The works of this company, in Lonsdale Street, were established in 1882 by Messrs. Robinson, Leadbeater, and Leason, for the manufacture of the higher classes of majolica and ivory or cream coloured earthenware. In these they produce all the usual varieties of useful and ornamental goods; the dessert services, game-pie dishes, and other articles being of more than average excellence.

The Campbell Brick and Tile Company.—The company was formed in 1875 for the purpose of carrying on the business of Mr. Robert Minton Taylor (nephew to

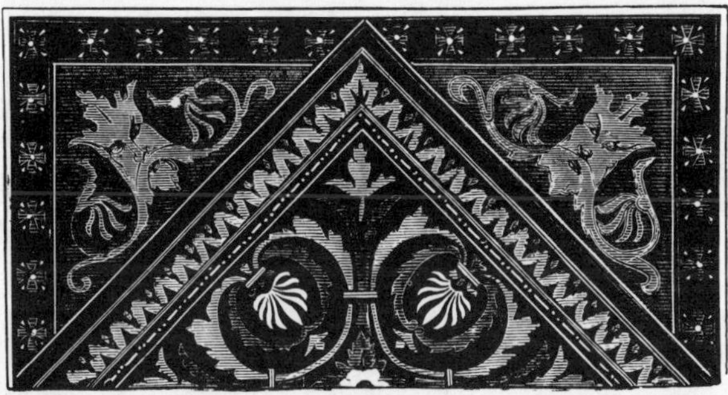

Fig. 1250.

the late Mr. Herbert Minton, and a partner in the firm of Minton, Hollins & Co., till 1868, when a dissolution, consequent on effluxion of time, took place) at Fenton. A new manufactory, to which the Fenton business was transferred, was, in 1876, erected at Stoke. The productions, as were those at Fenton, are encaustic, mosaic, geometrical, and majolica tiles. The encaustic tiles are produced not only in the usual simple red and buff colours, but in various combinations of buff, red, blue, green, yellow, white, black, brown, grey, and every shade of compound colour. The geometric tiles are prepared with mathematical nicety, and produce remarkably rich and effective pavements. The majolica and coloured tiles are of a high class of beauty and excellence, both in design and in richness of colours, and are perfect

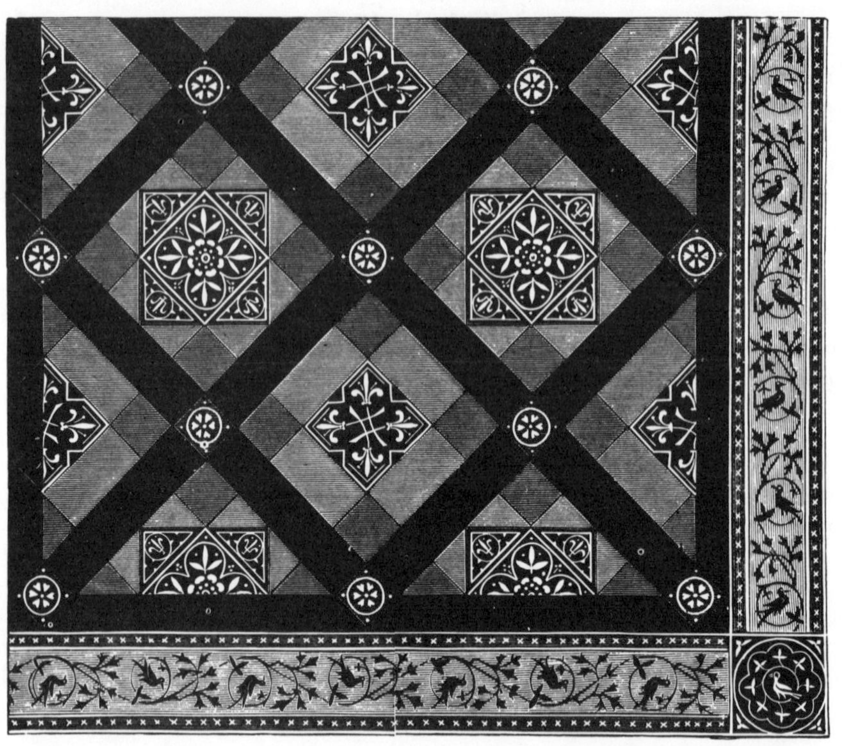

Figs. 1251 and 1252.—Campbell & Co.'s Tiles.

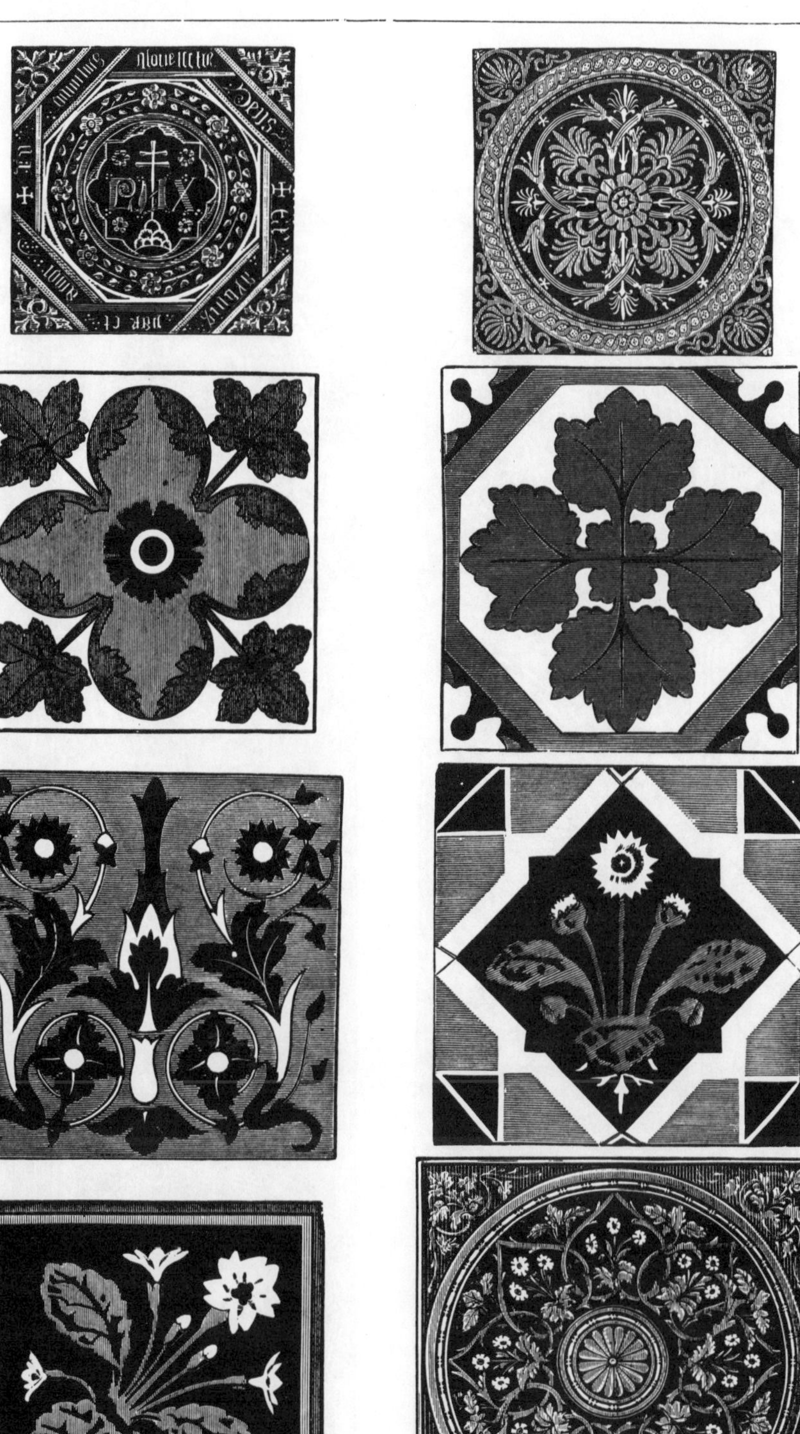

Figs. 1253 to 1260.—Campbell & Co.'s Tiles.

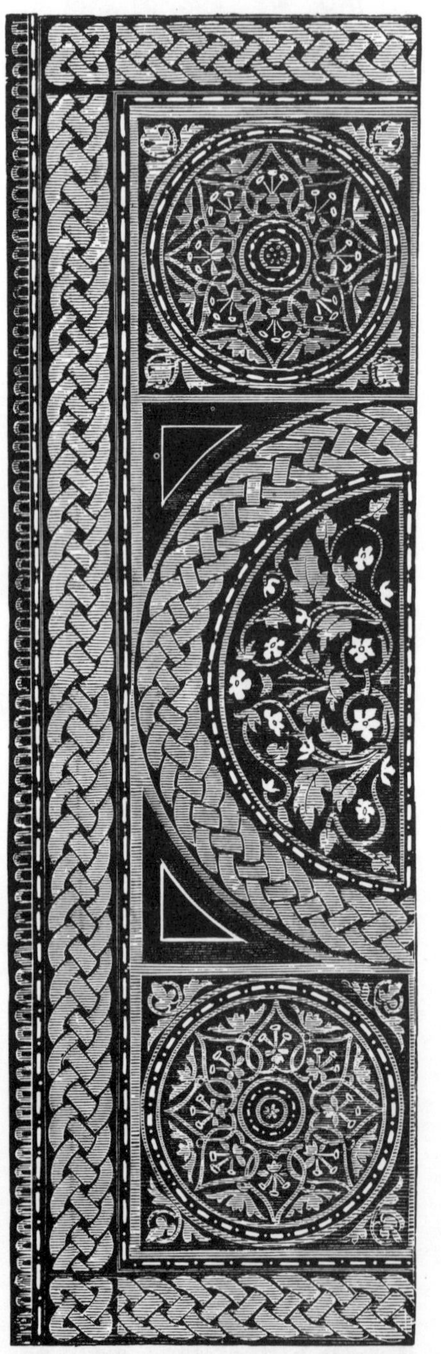

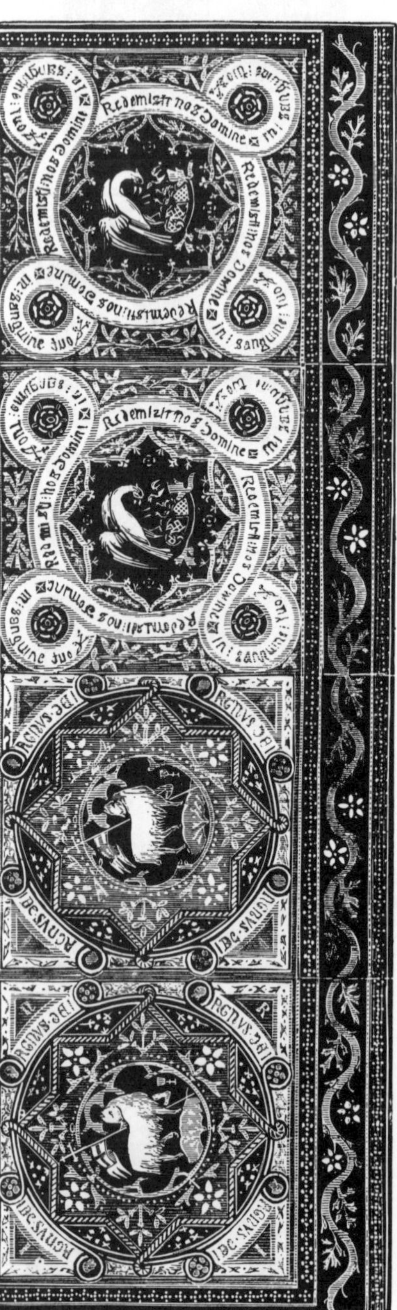

Figs. 1261 and 1262.—Campbell & Co.'s Tiles.

works of Art. Some have the ornament exquisitely modelled in relief, and in the representation of natural objects, as the hawthorn, bramble, violet, primrose, anemone, lily, or lilac, the effect is strikingly beautiful.

Another feature is the tesselated pavements, which are careful reproductions of examples of the Romano-British period. In these the antique character is well preserved, the designs copied with scrupulous accuracy, the colours kept strictly to the originals, and the effect of the rich guilloches admirably preserved. Tile-hearths, too, are produced in great variety and beauty. The mark used by Mr. Minton Taylor while at Fenton was the name "ROBERT MINTON TAYLOR, TILE

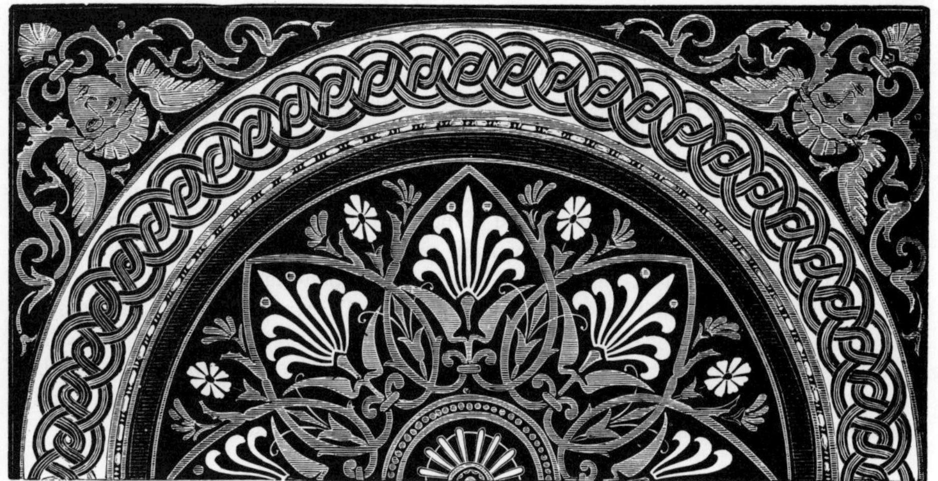

Fig. 1263.

WORKS, FENTON, NEAR STOKE-UPON-TRENT," arranged in various ways, and impressed or raised on the back; or the initials R M T / F T W used in the same way. That of the present firm (the proprietor of which is Colin Minton Campbell, Esq., and the manager, Mr. Robert Minton Taylor) is a compass N / W+E / S encircled. "CAMPBELL BRICK & TILE CO., STOKE-UPON-TRENT."

Harrison and Wedgwood.—John Harrison of Newcastle, and afterwards of Cliffe Bank, Stoke, a man possessed of some means, but little taste, entered into partnership with Josiah Wedgwood on the latter first commencing business. He was not a practical potter, but was taken into partnership by Wedgwood for the advance of capital. They carried on the business at what was Mr. Aldersea's pottery at the top of Stoke, opposite the works of Hugh Booth. Here, besides agates and other knife-hafts, they made the ordinary kinds of wares then in demand, both "scratched" and blue. In 1754 they entered into partnership with Thomas Whieldon, and later on the works were, I believe, bought and pulled down by Josiah Spode.

Bankes.—Mr. R. Bankes and Mr. John Turner, in 1756, made white stoneware on what later formed a part of Josiah Spode's premises. In 1762 Mr. Turner removed to Lane End, and about 1780 discovered a valuable vein of clay at Green Dock. This he turned to profitable and artistic use in the making of his fine and celebrated cane-coloured and other wares.

Aldersea.—John and Thomas Aldersea were makers of tortoise-shell, clouded, and other wares.

Hugh Booth, of Cliff Bank, was one of the leading manufacturers of the district. His productions were common cream-coloured, mottled, and, I believe, lustre-wares. He died, unmarried, in June, 1879, aged 57, and was succeeded by his brother, Ephraim.

Ephraim Booth (an alderman of Plymouth), took into partnership his two sons Hugh and Joseph, and carried on the business under the firm of "Ephraim Booth and Sons." Hugh, the eldest, died in 1831. The firm produced blue printed and other wares. The heading of their bills in 1792 was "Eph^m^ Booth & Sons, Potters to His Royal Highness the Duke of Clarence and St. Andrew's in the Kingdom of Great Britain, Earl of Munster in the Kingdom of Ireland." "Stoke, Stafford-shire." At that time (1792) some of their productions were "barrel-shape" and other jugs, "ewers and basons," "cups and saucers, bell-shape handled," "coffees and saucers, fluted," all "printed Dresden pattern;" "tureens and ladles, green edge, cream-coloured glaze;" sallads, baking-dishes, fish-drainers, oyster-shells, pickle leaves, egg-cups, peppers, mustards, scollop shells, sauce tureens, all stands either "green edge," "blue edge," or "blue and green;" teapots, milks, bread and butter plates, &c., "narrow flute, printed Dresden pattern," &c.

Wolfe.—Mr. Thomas Wolfe, a successful manufacturer, in the latter part of last century, died in 1818, and was, I believe, succeeded by his son-in-law, Mr. Robert Hamilton, and afterwards by W. Adams and Co.

Bird.—Daniel Bird, the "flint potter," as he was called, at Cliff Bank (afterwards Mayers), made agate-ware knife-hafts and buttons, and ordinary earthenware.

The manufacturers at Stoke, 1787, were "Sarah Bell, potter; Hugh Booth, manufacturer of china, china-glaze, and Queen's ware in all its branches; James Brindley, potter; Josiah Spode, ditto; Joseph Straphan, merchant and factor in all kinds of earthenware; and Thomas Woolfe, manufacturer of Queen's ware in general, blue, printed, and Egyptian black, cane, &c." In 1829 they were, according to Shaw, Spode; Minton; H. and R. Daniel, who here made only porcelain, their earthenware works being at Shelton; Adams, in one part of whose works the first steam-engine for grinding flints is said to have been erected; Zachary Boyle & Son, near the churchyard, who made both china and earthenware; Thomas Mayer (Clift Bank), formerly Daniel Bird's, who was called the "flint potter," through his having ascertained the exact proprotions of flints and clays required "to prevent cracking in the oven;" and Ward and Forrester. In 1843 there were Spode and Copelands; Mintons; William Adams and Co., who at one time or other had five separate manufactories, three of which had formerly been Mr. Woolfe's, the fourth the Bridge Works, and the fifth Hugh Booth's; Henry and Richard Daniel; Zachary Boyle; Samuel and George Reade; and Lowndes and Hill.

CHAPTER XIX.

Burslem.

Plot, writing in 1686, says, "The greatest pottery they have in this country is carried on at Burslem, near Newcastle-under-Lyme, where for making their different sorts of pots they have as many different sorts of clay, which they dig round about the towne, all within halfe a mile's distance, the best being found nearest the coale," &c. The town has earned for itself the name of "mother of the potteries." In the early part of the eighteenth century the potters in Burslem appear to have been as follows:—Thos. Wedgwood (two), John and Samuel Cartlich, Robt. Daniel, Thos., Isaac, and Rcd. Malkin, Dr. Thos. Wedgwood, Wm., Rcd., and Jhn. (three) Simpson, Thos. Cartwright, John Wedgwood, Robt. Bucknall, Isaac Wood, Richard Wedgwood, Thos. Taylor, Wm. Harrison, John and Robt. Adams, Moses Marsh, Aaron Shaw, Thos. Mitchell, J. Warburton, J. Bagnall, Aaron Wedgwood, H. (?) Marsh, Moses Shaw, Isaac Ball, Saml. Edge, Thos. Lockett, J. Tunstall, Moses Steel, Hugh Mayer, J. Stevenson, H. Beech, Ralph Daniel; and in 1750 the potters—*i.e.* owners of pot-works—appear to have been:—Moses Copeland, John Marsh, Ralph Allen, Moses Marsh (two), Aaron Shaw, John Daniell, Richd. Parrott, Thos. Cartlich (Olding), E. Astbury, Saml. Malkin, John Adams, Ralph Adams, Wm. Lockett, Robt. Daniell, Thos. Steel, S. Cartlich, Maria Locker, John Heath, Richd. Onions, Aaron Clowes, Ephraim Booth, John Taylor, Thos. Taylor, Joseph Simpson (two), Clark Malkin, Thos. Mitchell, John Mitchell, Josiah Simpson, Taylor (two), Wm. Burn, J. Ball, Aaron Cartlich, Timothy Lockett, &c.

In 1787 there were "Adams, William, & Co., manufacturers of cream-coloured ware and china-glazed ware painted; Bagley, William, potter; Bourne, John, manufacturer of china-glazed, blue-painted, enamelled, and cream-colour earthenware; Bourne and Malkin, manufacturers of china-glazed, blue, and cream-colour ware; Cartlidge, S. and J., potters; Daniel, Thomas, potter; Daniel, John, manufacturer of cream-colour and red earthenware; Daniel, Timothy, ditto; Daniel, Walter, ditto; Graham, John, junr., manufacturer of white stone earthenware, enamelled, white, and cream colour; Green, John, potter; Holland, Thomas, manufacturer of black and red chinaware, and gilder; Lockett, Timothy and John, white stone potters; Malkin, Burnham, potter; Robinson, John, enameller, and printer of cream-colour and china-glazed ware; Rogers, John and George, manufacturers of china-glazed blue-painted wares, and cream coloured; Smith, Ambrose, & Co., manufacturers of cream-coloured ware, and china-glazed ware painted blue; Smith, John and Joseph, potters; Stevenson, Charles and Son, manufacturers of cream-coloured wares, blue painted, &c.; Wedgwood, Thomas, manufacturer of cream-coloured ware, and china-glazed ware painted with blue, &c., Big House; Wedgwood, Thomas, manufacturer of cream-coloured ware, and china-glazed ware painted with blue, &c., Over House; Wilson, James, enameller; Wood, John, potter; Wood, Enoch and Ralph, manufacturers of all kinds of useful and ornamental earthenware, Egyptian, black, cane, and various other colours, also black figures, seals, and cyphers; and Wood, Josiah, manufacturer of fine black, glazed, variegated, and cream-coloured ware, and blue."

In 1843, according to Ward, the potteries then in work were—Enoch Wood and Sons; S. Alcock & Co.; Machin & Potts; Mellor, Venables & Co.; T. Godwin; John Wedg Wood; Barker, Sutton, and Till; Peter Hopkin; Wm. Pointon; S. Mayer & Co.; J. Hawley; Maddock & Seddon; J. Vernon & Co.; J. and T. Edwards; Cork and Condliffe; Nehemiah Massey; Ann Holland; Daniel Edge; Jones and Bell; and those not then occupied were the Churchyard Works, the Big House, the Hamill Street Works, the Knowl Works, and the Navigation Works.

Many of the names in these lists will be recognised as those of successful potters of our own day. Burslem, long the centre of the pot-making district, was the place where the Wedgwoods had their various works, and where Josiah Wedgwood was born. It has, therefore, always been, as it is now, a place of considerable importance in connection with the history of the ceramic art of our country. An interesting matter relating to the history of pottery in this locality

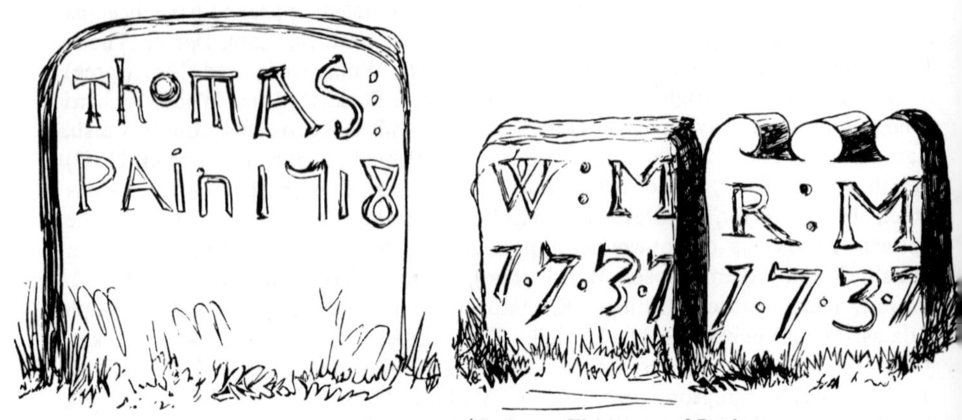

Figs. 1264 to 1266.—Earthenware Gravestones, Wolstanton and Burslem.

is the number of coarse earthenware gravestones which may be noticed in the churchyards at Burslem, Wolstanton, and elsewhere. They are formed of the common dark brown marl, or sagger clay, on which the inscriptions are generally deeply incised or pressed in. In some instances, however, they are laid on in white slip, and in others the incised letters are filled in with white clay. They are fired in the usual manner. The earliest, as regards date, which I noticed on a cursory examination of the churchyard at Wolstanton, is Fig. 1264; the latest was, "William Heath departed this life 14 February, 1828, aged 6 weeks." Figs. 1265 and 1266 are from Burslem churchyard.

Toft.—The name of Toft is intimately connected with pottery, both in Staffordshire and Derbyshire. The names of Thomas Toft and Ralph Toft occur on large coarse earthenware dishes of the middle of the seventeenth century (see pages 76 to 78), some of which are dated. The material is a coarse reddish or buff-coloured clay—common firebrick clay, and the patterns are laid on in yellow, white, or other coloured slip, and then thickly glazed over with a lead glaze. I have reason to believe that some of the Tofts were potters at Tickenhall (which see, page 373).

Talor.—Apparently contemporary with the Tofts, or at all events producing precisely the same kind of dishes, &c., was "William Talor," one of whose productions is in the Bateman collection. He was most likely of the same family as the Taylors, potters, of Burslem, in the beginning of the last century.

Sans.—Another contemporary of the Tofts was William Sans, whom Shaw states to have used manganese and pulverised galena in his processes. The name "Thomas Sans" also occurs on an example.

Turnor.—Turner is a name so long and so intimately connected with potting and Staffordshire that it is fair to presume Ralph Turnor, whose name occurs on a tyg of the same general character as Toft's dishes, belongs to that county.

RALPH TURNOR
1681

Fig. 1267.

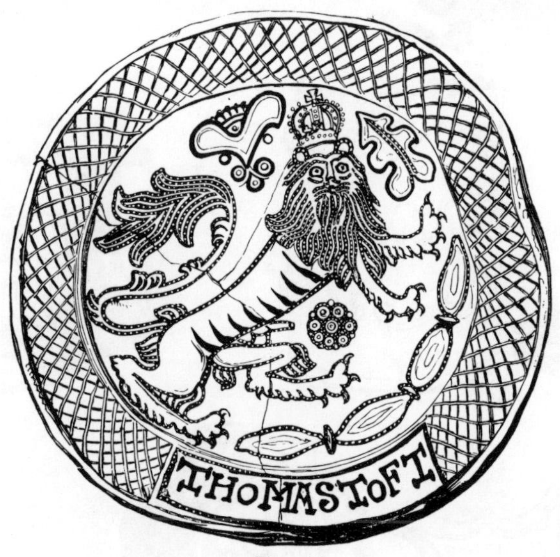

Fig. 1268.

Shawe.—Ralph Shawe, of Burslem, "earth-potter," in 1733 took out a patent for improvements in earthenware (see p. 84). In 1736 he commenced an action against John Mitchell for infringement of his rights, but was defeated. He removed with his family into France, where he carried on his trade, but his family, about 1750, returned to Burslem. About 1710 Aaron Shaw was a maker of stone and dipped wares in Burslem, with a house adjoining his works; and Moses Shaw (surely two brothers, Aaron and Moses!) made stone and freckled goods at the same place, with a house in the middle of the town.

John Mitchell.—In 1736 this potter having succeeded in producing ware very similar to that of Ralph Shawe, an action was commenced against him by Shawe for infringing his patent. This was tried at Stafford, but the defendant, being fully supported by his pottery neighbours, gained the verdict, the judge concluding with the memorable words, "Go home, potters, and make whatever kind of pots you

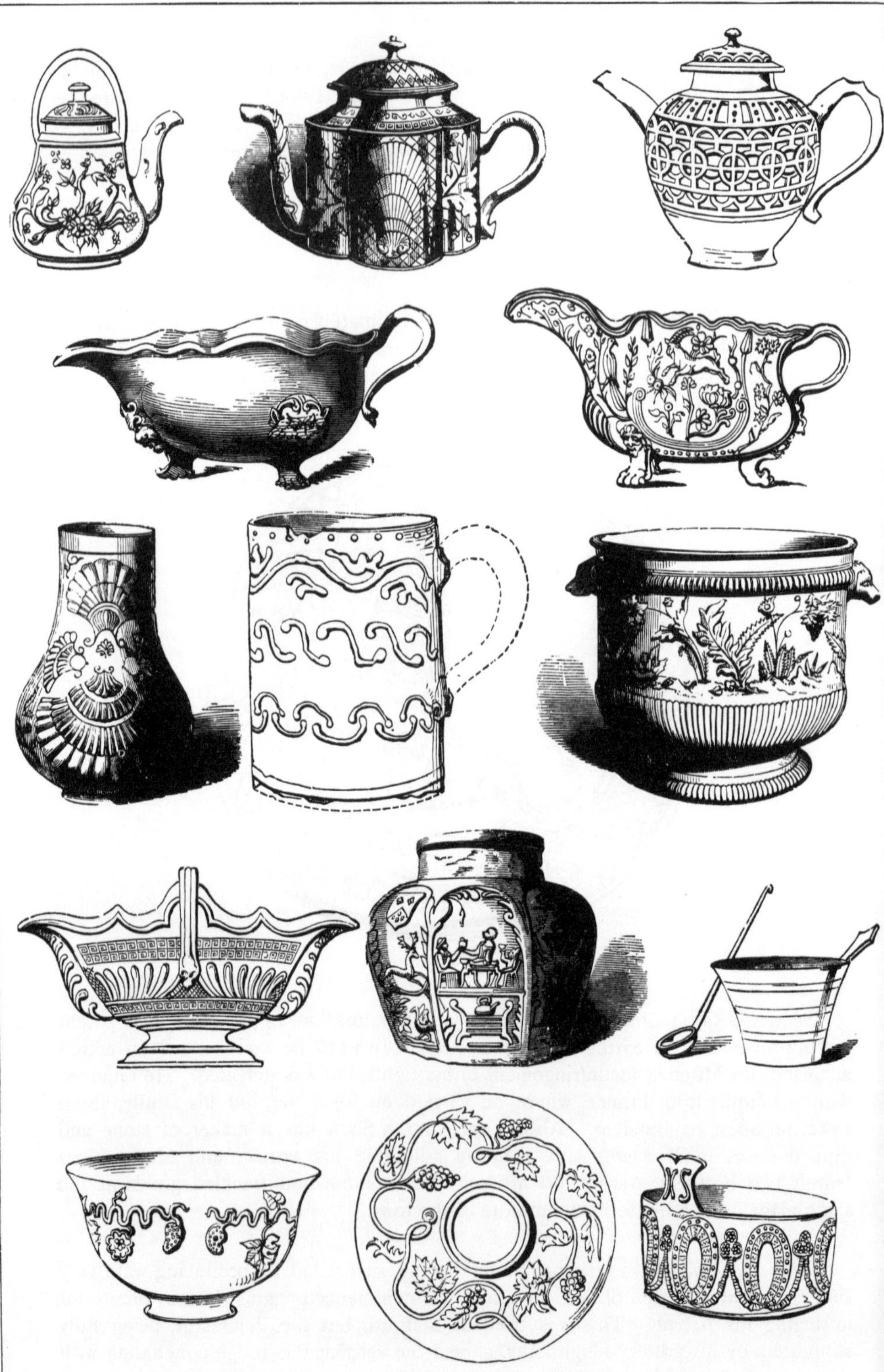

Figs. 1269 to 1282.—Examples of early Staffordshire Wares, Museum of Practical Geology.

like." Aaron Wood was at one time employed by Mitchell, whose principal productions were white stoneware and salt-glazed ware.

Cartwright.—The name "CARTWRIGHT" is stated by Shaw to occur on some butter-pots, along with the date 1640. This maker, Cartwright, at his death in 1658 gave twenty pounds yearly to the poor of Burslem for ever. Burslem, which, as I have already shown, was famed for its butter-pots (in 1670 these were ordered to be made to contain not less than 14 lbs., and to be of hard quality), was to some extent known as the "butter-pot manufactory."

Rich.—Shaw (1829) describes a crouchware dish, bearing the name, "W. RICH, 1702."

Wood.—Ralph Wood, of Burslem (probably brother of Aaron Wood, and son of Ralph Wood, miller, of Burslem), was a potter in the first half of last century.

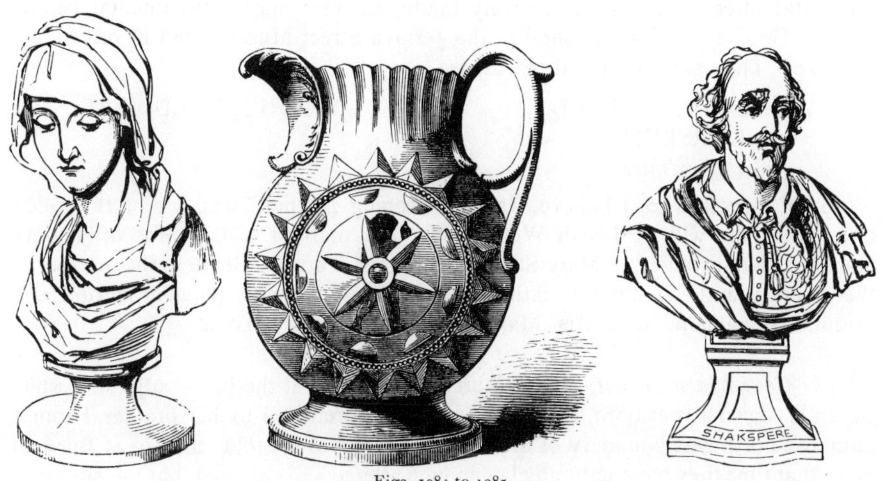

Figs. 1283 to 1285.

Specimens of his ware, which is of the same general character as Whieldon's, bear the mark Ra. Wood / Burslem and others R. WOOD, or "Ra. Wood."

Aaron Wood, son of Ralph Wood, of Burslem, in the county of Stafford, miller, was apprenticed on 23rd August, 1731, to "Dr. Thomas Wedgwood, of Burslem, potter." When out of his time Aaron Wood continued with Dr. Wedgwood for five years at 5s. per week, and afterwards worked at making moulds for the then very fashionable embossed ware erroneously known as "Elizabethan ware" (at which he was remarkably clever), for Thomas Whieldon and others. He next engaged, in 1743, with John Mitchell, of Burslem, a rival of Dr. Thos. Wedgwood, to work solely for him for seven years, at seven shillings a week, and half-a-guinea every 11th November. He afterwards became manager to Rogers & Brindley, and later on modelled for John Shrigley. Dying in 1785, he was succeeded by his youngest son Enoch Wood, "the Father of Pottery," as he is sometimes called. Enoch Wood was a good practical potter and a modeller of no little skill for the period.

In 1781 he produced a bust of John Wesley (who used to stay at his house when in the Potteries, and sat to him for the purpose) which became very popular. He was at one time joined in partnership by Mr. James Caldwell, under the style of "Wood and Caldwell." In the early part of this century Mr. Wood formed, at considerable labour, a collection of pottery, which, after his death, was dispersed; some of his specimens are in the Museum of Practical Geology, and others in the Dresden Museum and some good examples of his own work are in the possession of Mrs. Blagg, of Cheadle. The firm in 1792 was carried on as "Enoch Wood & Co.," and, after he took his sons into partnership, "Enoch Wood & Sons." The marks, so far as I am aware, are E. WOOD, or ENOCH WOOD, or ENOCH WOOD & CO., and later on, ENOCH WOOD & SONS impressed in the body of the ware. The firm was succeeded by Messrs. Pinder, Bourne, and Hope.

Wood and Caldwell.—This firm (Enoch Wood and James Caldwell) produced earthenware of superior character, both in services and ordinary articles. Some of their teapots were of admirable design and excellent workmanship. Busts and small statuettes were also extensively made, as were highly ornamental candlesticks. Good examples are found in the Jermyn Street Museum and in private collections. The usual impressed marks, are

WOOD & CALDWELL
BURSLEM
Staffordshire or WOOD & CALDWELL.

Mr. Caldwell, who, I believe, was a "sleeping partner," was one of the executors under the will of Josiah Wedgwood. He married a daughter of Thomas Stamford (half-brother to Mary Stamford, wife of Thomas Bentley, the partner of Wedgwood), and by her was father of the late gifted and popular authoress of "Emilia Wyndham," &c., Mrs. Marsh-Caldwell, of Linley Wood.

The Churchyard Works.—The Churchyard Works, at the house adjoining which Josiah Wedgwood was born, and where he was apprenticed to his brother Thomas, form the north-east boundary of the "churchyard" of the old church at Burslem. Since that time they have naturally been much altered and enlarged, but the site is the same, and some of the buildings now there are what stood and were used in his day. The house in which he was born, taken down many years ago, stood near where the present slip-house stands, but its site has since been occupied by fresh buildings. New hovels and other buildings have from time to time been added to the establishment, which is now a very complete and commodious manufactory. These works, for several generations, belonged to the Wedgwoods, and are described in 1698 as belonging to Thomas Wedgwood, "of the Churchyard House," to whom they appear to have passed on his father's death, who was also a potter. His son Thomas, eldest brother of Josiah, inherited this property on his father's death in 1739, and three years later, on his marriage with Isabel Beech, by marriage settlement dated 12th of October, 1742 (in which he is described as Thomas Wedgwood, of the Over House, Burslem, Potter), "the messuage, with the appurtenances situate and adjoining the churchyard, Burslem, and all outhouses, *work*-houses, &c., then in the occupation of the said Thomas Wedgwood, or his under tenants," were settled upon the children of this marriage. On the death of Thomas Wedgwood in 1772 this and other property descended to his son Thomas, of the Over House, subject to portions to his younger children under the settlement of 1742. The works were for some time carried on, along with the "Bell Works" and "Ivy House Works," by Josiah Wedgwood. On his removal to Etruria they were occupied by his second cousin, Joseph Wedgwood (brother of Aaron, and nephew of the Aaron Wedgwood who was partner with William Littler in the first manufacture of porcelain in the district), who lived at the house now the Mitre Hotel, near the works. This Joseph Wedgwood, who made jasper and other fine bodies under the direction of and for Josiah, occupied the works until the time of their sale to Mr. Green, when he removed to Basford Bank. About 1780 "the Churchyard premises were sold to

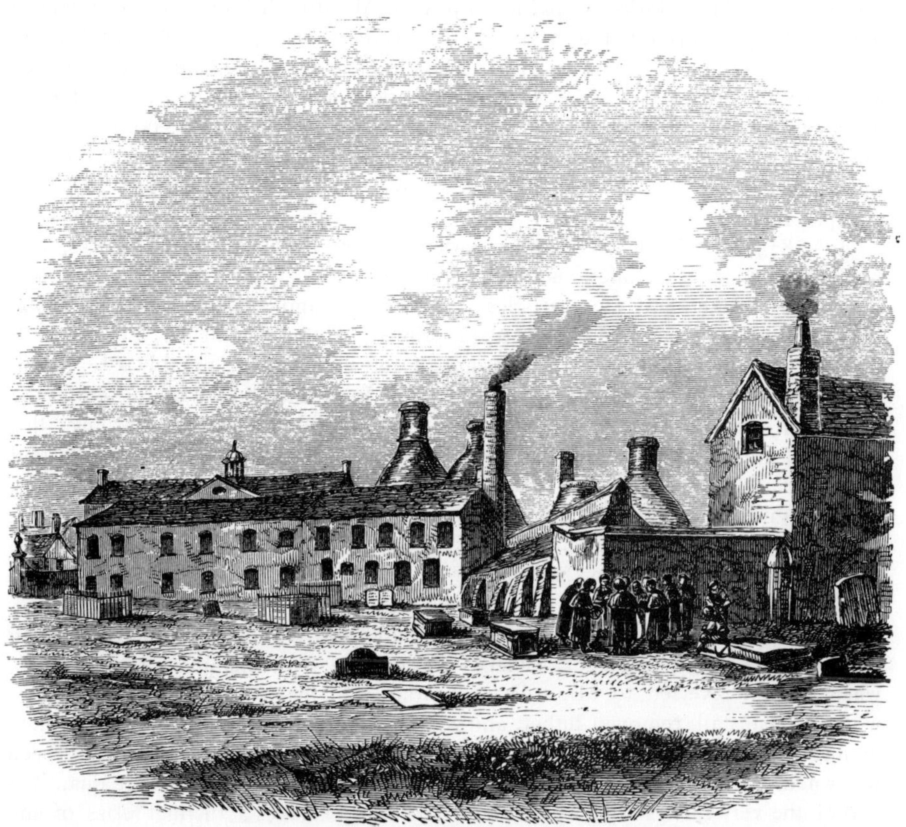

Fig. 1286.—The Churchyard Works, Burslem.

Josiah Wedgwood, then of Etruria, who in 1787 conveyed them to his brother John, also of Etruria, who in 1795 sold them to Thomas Green, at which time two newly-erected houses near the pot-work were included in the sale." Mr. Green manufactured earthenware at these works, and for some time resided at the house near the works now known as the Mitre Hotel, which had been built by one of the Wedgwood family. The property remained in Thomas Green's hands until his bankruptcy in 1811, when it appears to have been purchased by a manufacturer named Joynson, from whom it passed, some years later on, to Mr. Moseley. While in his hands, the pot-work was held by various tenants, and until about 1858 was let off in small holdings to different potters. About that period Mr. Bridgwood of Tunstall became the tenant of the premises as a general earthenware manufacturer, and was soon afterwards joined in partnership by Mr. Edward Clarke, whose large practical experience tended much to increase the reputation of the works. This firm, having taken a lease of the premises, remodelled many of the buildings, erected others, and greatly improved the whole place by bringing to bear many improvements in body unknown to, and unthought of by, their predecessors. After Mr. Bridgwood's decease in 1864 these works and the large establishment at Tunstall, were carried on by the surviving partner, Mr. Clarke, until, after a time, he ceased working them, when they passed into other hands as his tenants. The manufactory was afterwards again carried on by Mr. Clarke in partnership with Mr. Josiah Wood (a descendant of Aaron Wood, who is referred to under the head of Poole, Stanway, and Wood), under the style of Wood and Clarke. The productions of the Churchyard Works, while carried on by Mr. Clarke, were opaque porcelain or "white granite," for the American market; ordinary earthenware in the usual services; artists' goods (palettes, tiles, slabs, saucers, &c.); and door furniture. The impressed mark was "Bridgwood and Clarke," and the printed mark a royal arms, with the words "Porcelain Opaque, B & C, Burslem."

In 1874 Mr. W. E. Withinshaw entered upon the Churchyard Works, and produced dinner, tea, toilet, and other services; vases, jugs, teapots, kettles, and jug stands; trinket and fancy articles; candlesticks, and all the usual varieties of useful and ornamental goods, both plain, printed, painted, enamelled, and gilt. In toilet services he introduced many designs of novel character; notably a service in which the head of the elephant was utilised to form the handle of the ewer, the head itself forming the top of the handle and the trunk the part for grasping; this produced in mass gold had a rich and striking but at the same time simple and elegant effect. In vases also Mr. Withinshaw produced some good designs, and the decoration was judiciously managed. In jet ware all the usual articles—teapots, kettles, jugs, spill-cases, &c.—were also made. The impressed mark was W. E. WITHENSHAW; and on the dinner ware was printed the name of the pattern, with the initials W. E. W.

Mr. Withinshaw's connection with the Churchyard Works ceased in 1878, when he was succeeded by Mr. F. J. Emery, who continued the manufactory until 1880, when it again reverted to Mr. Edward Clarke, who, having relinquished his large works at Tunstall, removed hither, and still continues the production of the white granite ware for the American markets for which he has for so long a period been renowned. In addition to this white granite, which is produced in large quantities and of the very highest quality of body, Mr. Clarke makes a distinct class of fine white earthenware called "Royal Semi-Porcelain," which is specially adapted for retail trade in the United States. These goods are of a vitreous body, and in colour and richness of glazing strongly resemble French china; they have a fine and effective appearance with enamel decorations. In addition to these Mr. Clarke produces ordinary earthenware services and the usual classes of articles of various degrees of decoration in printing, under-glaze painting, and gilding. His goods are and have ever been in high repute in the United States, to which they are mostly consigned.

The Bell Works.—The Bell Works, of which, as they appeared in 1865, I give an engraving, Fig. 1287, were, at the time when the great Josiah Wedgwood entered on its occupancy, the property of John Bourne, an army contractor in the neighbouring town of Newcastle. From him the property, about 1771, passed to his grandson, John Adams, of Cobridge, and in 1847 again passed by will to the late Isaac Hitchen, of Alsager. They were occupied by Joseph Wedgwood (as tenant to John Bourne) until his removal to Etruria, after which William Bourne, an earthenware manufacturer, held them for some years, and was tenant in 1809; he afterwards entered into partnership with a potter named Cormie, and carried on the business under the style of "Bourne and Cormie." In 1836, the works having then remained for some time unoccupied, were divided. One portion was taken by Beech and Jones as an earthenware manufactory; another portion was taken away for the building of the present Independent chapel, which was erected on its site in the following year; and other parts were let off to various holders for different

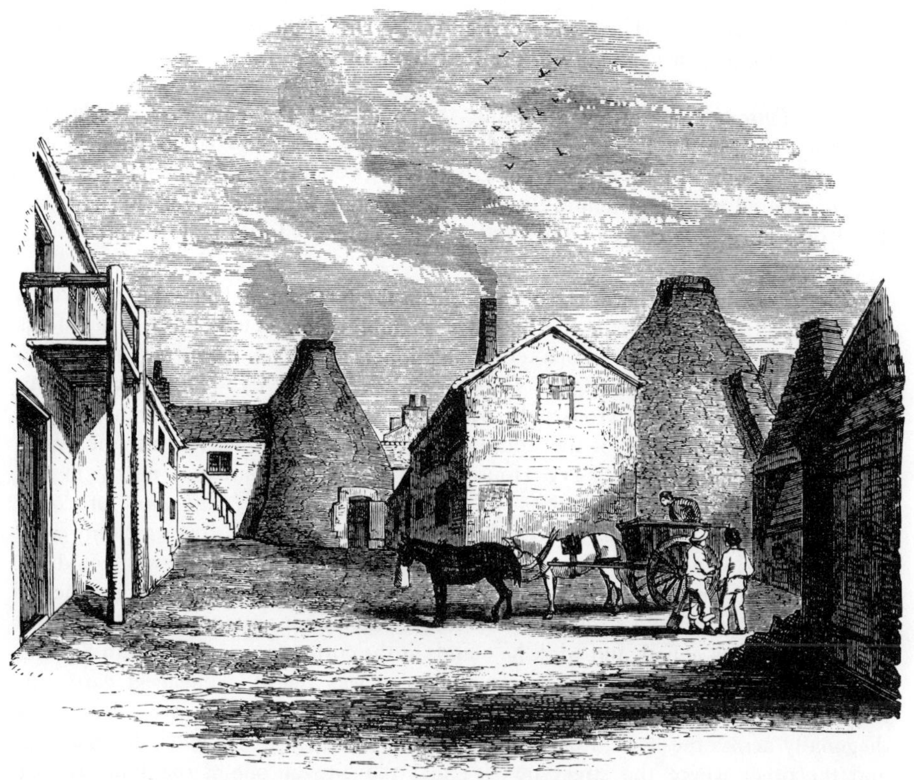

Fig. 1287.—The Bell Works, Burslem.

purposes apart from the pot trade. In 1839 Beech and Jones dissolved partnership, the former alone continuing the concern for the production of china and earthenware figures. In 1846 Mr. Beech became tenant of the whole of the remaining premises (with the exception of that part occupied by Mr. Dean's printing-office, &c.) and in 1853 took into partnership Mr. Brock, which firm, however, only lasted till 1855, from which date Mr. William Beech carried on the manufactory until his death in 1864, when he was succeeded by Beech and Podmore. In 1876 a part of the premises was purchased by the Board of Health for the purpose of building a covered market on the site, and the remainder was bought by Mr. George Beardmore of Rode Heath and taken down; thus these historically interesting works have been brought to a close.

At these "Bell Works" Josiah Wedgwood turned his attention more especially to the production of the fine and delicate descriptions of earthenware which soon earned for him the proud distinction of "Queen's Potter." The Bell Works were situated at the corner of Brick House Street and Queen Street, very near to the new Wedgwood Institution, but in the time of Josiah Wedgwood Brick House Street was not formed, but was a part of the ground belonging to the manufactory, and was, indeed, waste land, covered with "shard rucks" and other unmistakable evidence of the potter's art. Queen Street then, too, was little better than a lane, but was dignified with the name of *Queen* Street through Wedgwood being there appointed *Queen's* potter and there making his celebrated *Queen's* ware.

Red Lion Works.—These were carried on by Dr. Thomas Wedgwood, and took their name from their contiguity to the Red Lion Inn.

Big House.—The pottery adjoining this house, at the corner of Wedgwood Street and the Market Place, passing down Swan Square, belonged to Thomas and John Wedgwood. In 1787 the record is "Wedgwood, Thomas, manufacturer of cream-coloured ware, and china-glazed ware, painted with blue, &c., Big House." The works have long ceased to be used, and are converted into builder's premises.

The Ivy House and works, so called from the fact of the house being covered with ivy, was situated where the butchers' shambles now stand, the old buildings having been purchased by the market commissioners and taken down for the erection of the present market in 1835. These premises belonged to Thomas and John Wedgwood, of the "Big House," to whom Josiah became tenant, covenanting by written agreement to pay for the house and the pot-work attached to it the yearly rent of ten pounds. The "Ivy House" and works were situated nearly in the centre of Burslem, at the corner of what was then known as *Shoe Lane* or *Shore Lane*, now called *Wedgwood Street*, which at that time was a narrow way, only wide enough for a single cart to pass along, and as rough and uneven as well could be. The visitor to Burslem who desires to know exactly the site of this historically interesting house should stroll up to the fine modern-built shambles, or "butchery" as it is sometimes called, and while he stands at the corner facing down Swan Square, he may rest assured that he is standing on what was the little enclosed garden in front of Wedgwood's house; that the outer wall of the building at his back goes diagonally across the house from corner to corner, one half being under the shambles and the other where the street now is; that the site of one of the kilns is just beneath the centre of the shambles; and that another kiln was about the middle of the present street at his back; the surrounding workshops being partly where the street now is and partly where the building at present stands.

The "Ivy House" might originally have been roofed with thatch or mud, like the other buildings of the district, but it was afterwards tiled, as shown in the engraving. In front was a small garden enclosed with a low wall, and a brick pathway led from the gate to the doorway. The front faced the open space called the "Green Bank," and adjoining was a low half-timbered, thickly-thatched building, afterwards known as the "Turk's Head," and beyond this again was the Maypole, on "Maypole Bank," on the site now occupied by the Town Hall. At the opposite side of the house from the Turk's Head was a gateway leading into the yard of the works, which made up one side of Shoe Lane, the pot-works of John and Thomas

Wedgwood, with which they were connected, being on the opposite side of the lane. These works and house have the reputation of being the first roofed with tiles in the district—the usual roofing being thatch, or oftener still, mud. At the Ivy House Josiah Wedgwood carried on the manufacture of his ornamental goods, his more ordinary ware, I believe, being produced at the Churchyard. At the Ivy House works he produced many things far in advance of his day; and to the Ivy House itself he brought home his bride, and there lived happily with her for several years.

Lakin and Poole.—Messrs. Lakin and Poole were in business in Burslem and

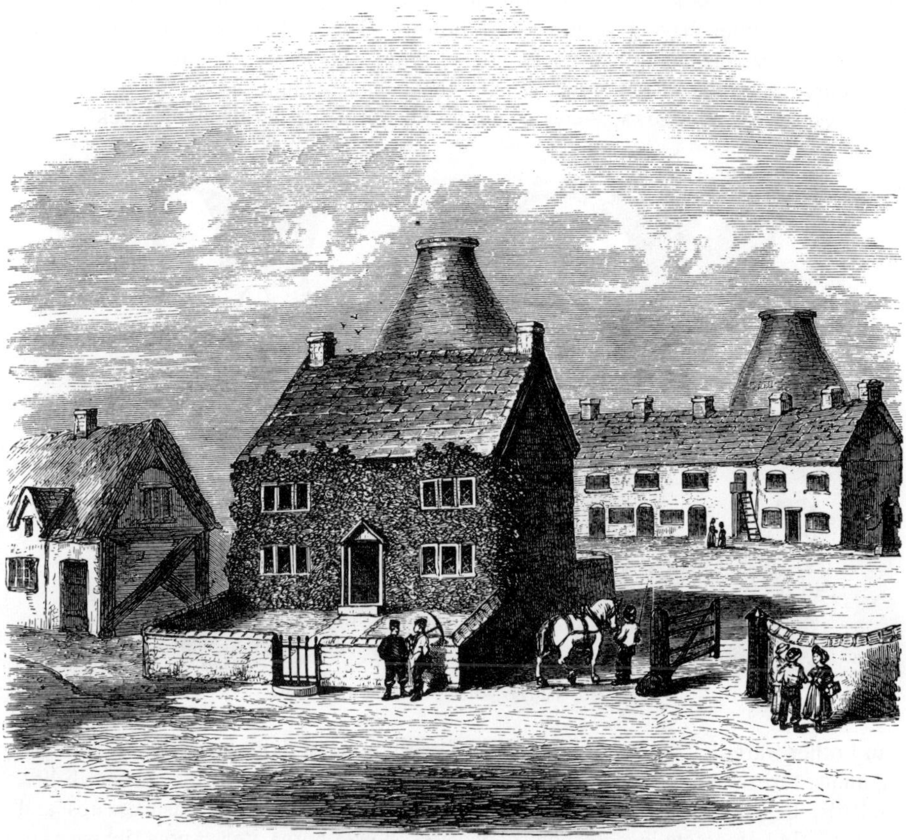

Fig. 1288.—The Ivy House, Burslem.

doing a very extensive trade at the latter end of the last century. Their bill head in October, 1792, was simply "Burslem, Staffordshire, Bought of Lakin & Poole," and in front of the heading was a garter and star, surrounding a vase, on which was "Manufacturers of Staffordshire Earthenware. Table Services Enamelled or Painted with Arms, &c., &c." On the garter "Burnished gold got up as in London." In 1793 (July) a new bill-head was used—"Burslem, Staffordshire, Bought of Lakin and Poole. Blue Painted Table Services, &c., and Coloured in all its various Branches." At the front is a standing figure of Commerce, with an anchor, against which is an oval tablet with "Table Services Enamelled with Arms, Crests, Cyphers, &c., &c.,"

to which the figure is pointing. In many of the bill-heads I have seen, the word "Painted" is altered with a pen to "Printed," and the word "Ware" is written between (over) "coloured" and "in." This heading was used till the early part of 1794. In December, 1794, they used a written bill-head. On the 14th of February, 1795, it is announced in a letter that "Mr. Thomas Shrigley has joined us in our manufactory of Earthenware, and that for the future the business will be carried on under the firm of *Poole, Lakin and Shrigley.*" In May, 1795, the bill-head (written) is "Burslem, Bought of Lakin, Poole, & Shrigley," the managing man being R. B. Swift. This firm continued until the end of 1795, but in January, 1796, another change took place, the firm now being simply "Poole and Shrigley"—Mr. Lakin either having died or withdrawn. The bill-heads were still written. T. Kempe was managing man in February, 1796. The last account I have is up to February, 1796. From 1792 to 1796 the goods manufactured appear by these invoices to be as follows:—cream-colour. blue-printed, fawn-colour, black, stone,

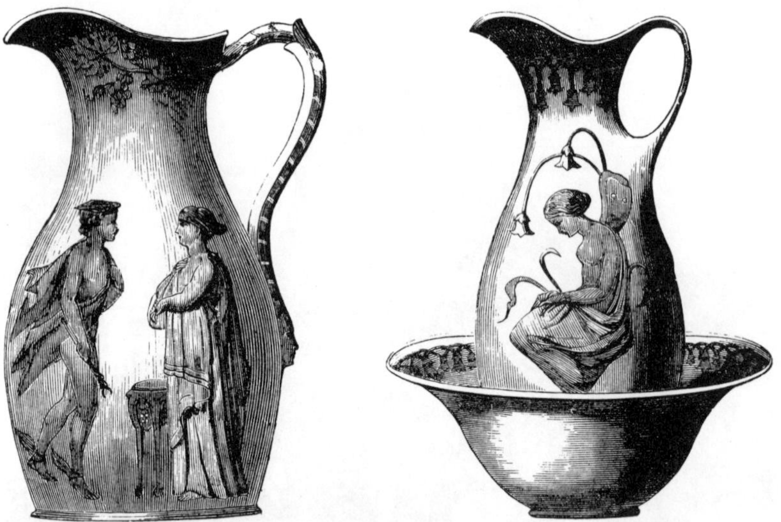

Figs. 1289 and 1290.—Messrs. Boote's Productions.

and other wares; "oval concave dishes of various sizes, flatt plates, soups, twifflers, muffins, tureen compots, sauce ditto, boats and stands, root dishes, cover dishes, sallads, bakers, dessert services of various patterns, ewers and basins, cups and saucers, bowls, cream-jugs, teapots, chocolates, flower-horns, flower-pots, jugs, sugar-boxes, double-handled coffee cups, salad dishes, sauce boats, gravy pots, candlesticks, baskets and stands, black teapots, mugs, figures in great variety, mortars, cheese-toasters, raddish dishes, paste pots, tripe pots, Mocoa tumblers, candlestick vases, bow pots, hand vases, French pies, English pies, stone jugs with and without figures, fawn-coloured porter mugs, blue printed dishes and other articles, egg-cups, custards and covers," &c. The mark was usually the words LAKIN & POOLE impressed in the body of the ware. On one or two examples the name LAKIN only occurs, and on others R. POOLE.

Waterloo Potteries.—These works were carried on in the latter part of last century by Walter Daniel, who was succeeded by Timothy and John Lockett, the manufacture at that time being principally salt-glazed ware. About 1809 the premises were purchased by Joseph Machin and Jacob Baggaley, and carried on by them for the making of china and ordinary earthenware. In 1831 Mr. Machin died and was succeeded by his son William Machin and partners. The works next passed into the hands of Richard Daniel, next to Thomas Edwards, and in 1850 were purchased by T. and R. Boote, who still occupy and work them. In 1853 Messrs. Boote took out a patent for "Certain improvements in pottery and mosaic work." These consisted in producing "coloured designs on grounds of different colours, as black on white or white on black. First, the designs are made from a mould, as in figuring, and laid on the moulds for making the ware; the ground colour is then put on. Second, the design, cut in paper, parchment, &c., is laid in the moulds and the halves fastened together, the colour to form the ground is poured in, after which the paper, &c., are removed and other colour poured in to fill its place. Third, producing different coloured raised surfaces. The figures in low relief in the inside of the moulds are filled with a composition, the halves of the moulds fastened

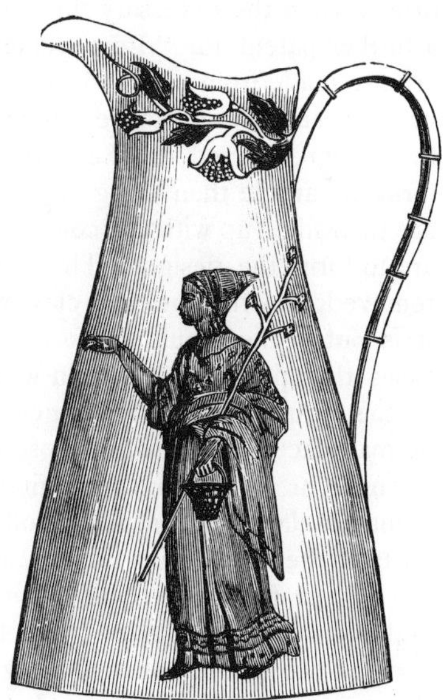

Fig. 1291.

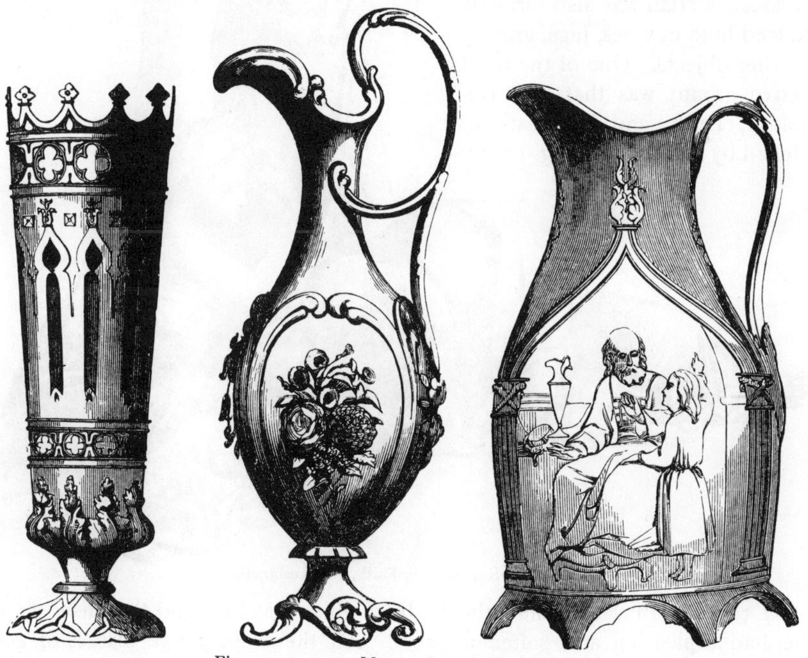

Fig. 1292 to 1294.—Messrs. Boote's Productions.

together, and the slip poured in to form a thin coating, which was then supplemented with an inner lining of a cheaper material to form a substratum, thus producing mosaic and other elaborate designs. In this process the excess of liquid is withdrawn when the necessary thickness is attained." In 1857 Messrs. Boote took out a further patent for "Improvements in the manufacture of ornamental pottery, and articles made from clay and other like plastic materials." "A thin piece of metal or other suitable substance, which forms the outline of the design, is fixed on the flattened clay intended to form the article then being made. The hollow parts are then filled up with the coloured clay or clays which are to form the design. The piece of metal is next removed, and the flattened clay with the design upon it is put in the mould to form the article. In some cases that part of the mould which is to correspond to the groundwork of the article to be manufactured is made to rise by springs or other means, suitable coloured clay is put into the hollow parts of the mould thus formed, and the clay to form the body is put in and the whole is pressed;" or the parts of the mould corresponding to the ornaments may be raised and the ground part filled in. Figs. 1289 to 1294 are examples of one of those processes. Parian was also formerly produced both in vases, jugs, groups, and other objects. One of the most effective groups was that of "Repentance, Faith, and Resignation," modelled by Mr. Gillard (Fig. 1295).

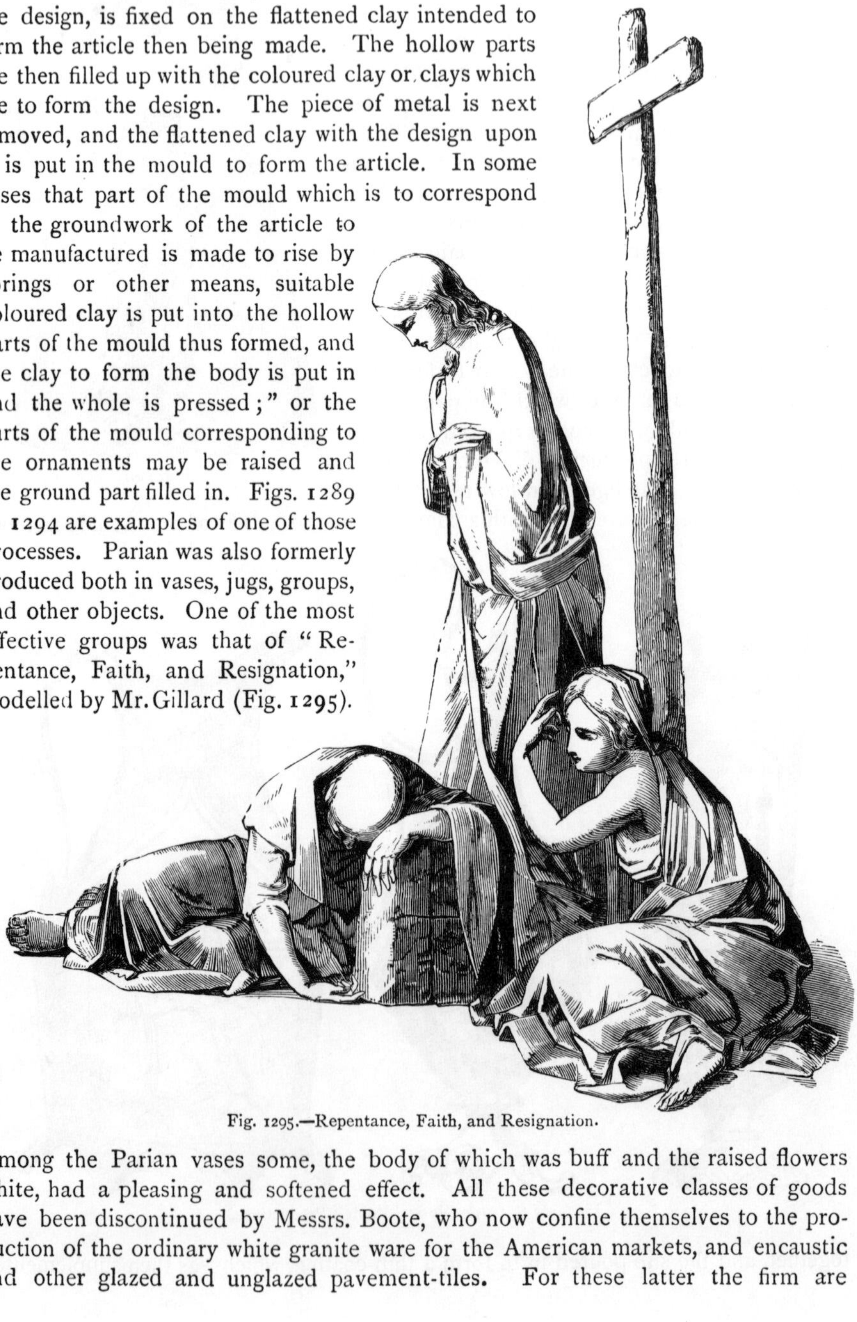

Fig. 1295.—Repentance, Faith, and Resignation.

Among the Parian vases some, the body of which was buff and the raised flowers white, had a pleasing and softened effect. All these decorative classes of goods have been discontinued by Messrs. Boote, who now confine themselves to the production of the ordinary white granite ware for the American markets, and encaustic and other glazed and unglazed pavement-tiles. For these latter the firm are patentees of a process for inlaying encaustic tiles with clay dust—a process which is also adopted for the manufacture of dishes and other articles in earthenware in what this firm called "Royal Patent Ironstone," and by which, by means of one press alone, as many as 100 dozen plates or small dishes could be made in a day. The encaustic, geometrical, majolica, and other tiles are of great variety in pattern and effective in combinations of colours.

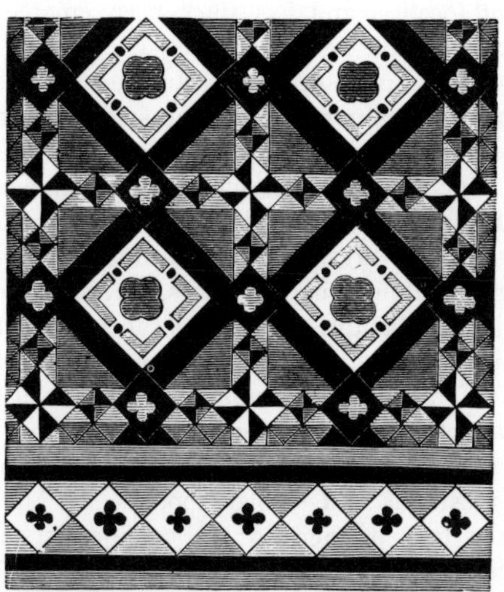

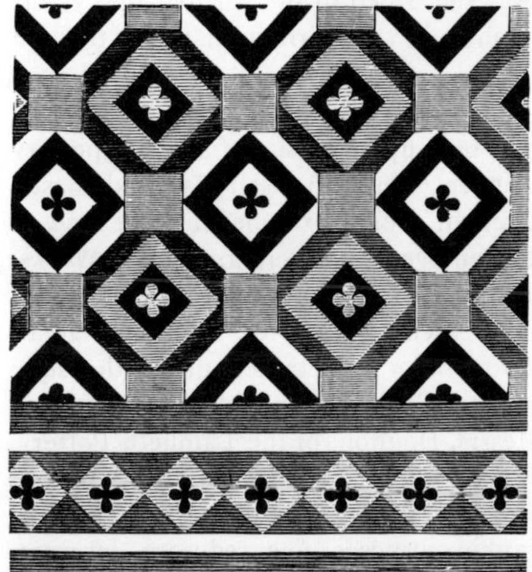

Figs. 1296 to 1298.—Messrs. Boote's Tiles.

The marks used on the white granite ware are the impressed initials T & R B.; and Fig. 1299 printed in black; and another bearing the crest, a greyhound, couchant, collared and slipped, between two laurel wreaths, with the words—

T. & R BOOTE
ROYAL PREMIUM
IRONSTONE

and above the words TRADE MARK. On the tiles the name in raised letters, T & R BOOTE / BURSLEM appears.

ROYAL PATENT
IRONSTONE
T & R BOOTE

Fig. 1299.

Washington Works.—The business now carried on at this manufactory originated experimentally in King Street, Burslem, where, about 1838, the late W. S. Kennedy commenced the production of palettes and other requisites for artists' use. Shortly afterwards, removing to a pottery in Bourne's Bank, he added the manufacture of door-furniture, letters for signs, &c., in which, in conjunction with Mr. William Maddock, great improvements were made. About 1847 the manufacture was removed to its present locality, and has since been enlarged. The marks W. S. KENNEDY and J. MACINTYRE have been very rarely used.

In 1852 Mr. Kennedy was joined in partnership by his brother-in-law, Mr. James Macintyre, who shortly afterwards became sole proprietor of the works. In 1863 Mr. Macintyre patented methods of producing oval, reeded, octagon, and other forms by the lathe, and succeeded in producing a rich cream-coloured body, which, under the name of "Ivory China," has held a high reputation. In 1867 Mr. Macintyre produced backs for hair-brushes, hand-mirrors, &c., which were patented by Mr. J. J. Hicks, and in numerous other instances, especially for France, the "body" has been used as an ivory substitute. So far as can be ascertained, the successful application to door-furniture of the earlier invention of the beautiful black, which is produced by dipping the brownish red *bisque* in a rich cobalt glaze, also originated at these works. This "jet," produced in great perfection, has been applied in plain and also with richly gilt and enamelled ornamentation, not only to door-furniture, but more recently to inkstands and similar goods. Mr. Macintyre died in 1868, having previously taken into partnership his confidential manager, Mr. Thomas Hulme, and his son-in-law, Mr. William Woodall, now M.P. for Stoke. In 1880 Mr. Hulme retired from the concern, and was succeeded in the partnership by Mr. Wiltshaw. By these two gentlemen the business is still carried on under the old style of "James Macintyre and Co."

Nile Street Works.—That these works were built upon the site of an early pottery is evidenced by fragments of pitchers, "porringers," and other salt-glazed domestic vessels "of red and yellow clay marbled together," being exhumed at one time or other during alterations. Messrs. Riley, who removed from here to the Hill Works, were succeeded by James Cormie, uncle of the late Thomas Pinder (at one time partner in the firm of Mellor, Venables, and Co.), great-uncle of Mr. Shadford Pinder, who traded under the style of "Pinder, Bourne, and Co." In 1880 the works passed into the hands of Messrs. Doulton, of the Lambeth Pottery, by whom they are successfully carried on. China was at one time made here, but latterly only printed, enamelled, and gilt earthenware, stoneware for telegraphic purposes, fine red-ware, jet-ware, and sanitary goods. The "red-ware" or terra-cotta of Pinder, Bourne, and Co. was of fine, hard, and durable quality, and the vases, spill-cases, and other articles richly enamelled and gilt in arabesque and other patterns were remarkably good. Among other specialities were flower-vases and jardinières skilfully painted in birds, flowers, &c. The firm patented improvements in ovens and in steam printing-presses; but the latter, having excited the hostility of the workmen at the time of the riots in 1842, were abandoned. The firm received medals at the London and Paris Exhibitions of 1851, 1855, and 1867. The marks were a garter, with the name of the pattern and initials "P. B. & Co." surmounted by a crown and encompassed with a wreath of laurel, and Fig. 1300.

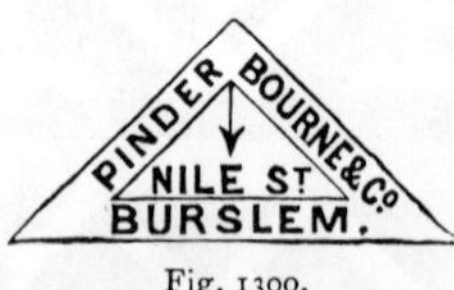

Fig. 1300.

Since the works passed into the hands of Messrs. Doulton immense strides in improvements in every department have been made, and the productions now take rank with the very best the world can show. This is especially noticeable in the body of the finest earthenware, which has now arrived at a state of pure perfection, and is in feel, in tone of colour, and in fineness and hardness of texture unsurpassed. As a rule, earthenware is, by the generality of people, looked upon as inferior in every way to china, and as unworthy of the high artistic treatment lavished upon that favoured body. This, however, is a grave mistake, and Messrs. Doulton have, as did their predecessors, wisely directed their energies not only to its improvement but its *perfection.* In this they have been successful, and the result is that their earthenware—which, from its peculiar beauty and unique excellence, really becomes entitled to be classed as another variety of " Doulton ware "—as made by them has all the fineness and beauty, the artistic treatment, and the exquisite finish of the best classes of porcelain, with, in addition, a softness of surface, a delicious creaminess of tone, a lightness, and, if I may so express it, a semi-velvety feel to the touch that can scarcely be attained in the harder china body. At the present time Messrs. Doulton employ a large number of first-class artists in the decoration of the ware, and new studios are being fitted up to meet the requirements of the increased demand that has sprung up for high-class art-productions. Among the goods produced, which embrace every article to which the plastic art is applicable, claret-jugs of varied forms are produced, and are of far greater beauty and more pleasing effect than are those of plate or glass. Of these the " Severn" (which is remarkable for the brilliancy of its under-glaze painting, which no atmospheric influence can ever affect, and for the metallic richness of neck and handle); and the "Trent" (whose vellum body, on which an accidental spray of flowers and foliage is gracefully thrown, harmonises with the various bronzes of neck, handle, and base, and presents a whole that is eminently grateful to the eye and pleasant to the feel), are among their highest achievements.

In Japanese adaptations Messrs. Doulton rank high, and their productions have the merit of being, not servile imitations and literal schoolboy-copies, but original designs imbued with the quaint ideas of the Japanese artists, rendered more graceful and acceptable by the refinement of feeling of the English mind. A remarkably good example of this style is a pitcher (A 162), whose peculiar colour, arrived at by a new glaze of extreme excellence, and decorated in gold, silver, and bronze, gives it a depth and subdued richness that is very satisfactory. Another Japanese jug, the design of which has wisely been registered, is precisely in form of a portion of an elephant's tusk, simply cut off, hollowed, and mounted with metal. The body is of pure polished ivory colour, the mountings, as imitations of metal, faultless, and the painting, gilding, and silvering of the floral designs exquisitely beautiful. In Oriental form and decoration, too, Messrs. Doulton are very sucsesful, as is evidenced by a cabinet coffee-pot (549) and other pieces. Another class of extremely effective decoration introduced by Doulton's is a ground of matt gold diapered with foliage and flowers in burnished gold, over which the floral design is painted, under glaze, with the richest and deepest cobalt. The effect is striking, and the gold ground, produced by a new method, has the advantage of increased richness at a far less cost than the ordinary metal. Of a different and in every way striking class of productions are the Tunisian-ware jardinières, vases, and other articles which in the most original and skilful manner are produced by Messrs. Doulton, and form attractive features wherever placed. In these the flowers, leaves, buds, and stems of the lotus or other plant are modelled by hand, true to nature in every minute detail, and tinted in their natural colours, and affixed loosely and gracefully to the vase, from which they stand out clear as though carelessly entwined around its form. The result is that the jardinières and the vases—some of which, of large size, have shells and seaweeds, star-fish, and other marine objects modelled from life in full relief upon them—thus produced are among the highest and best as well as most attractive and pleasing of fictile achievements. In addition to art-pottery, Messrs. Doulton produce extensively all the usual services and domestic articles in every class and variety of decoration, and suitable for every market and every household. The marks are DOULTON, impressed in and printed or painted on the ware, and a fret surrounded by the words DOULTON, BURSLEM.

The Newport Pottery, established at the close of last century by Walter Daniel, passed, about 1810, into the hands of John Davenport; afterwards to Cork and Edge,

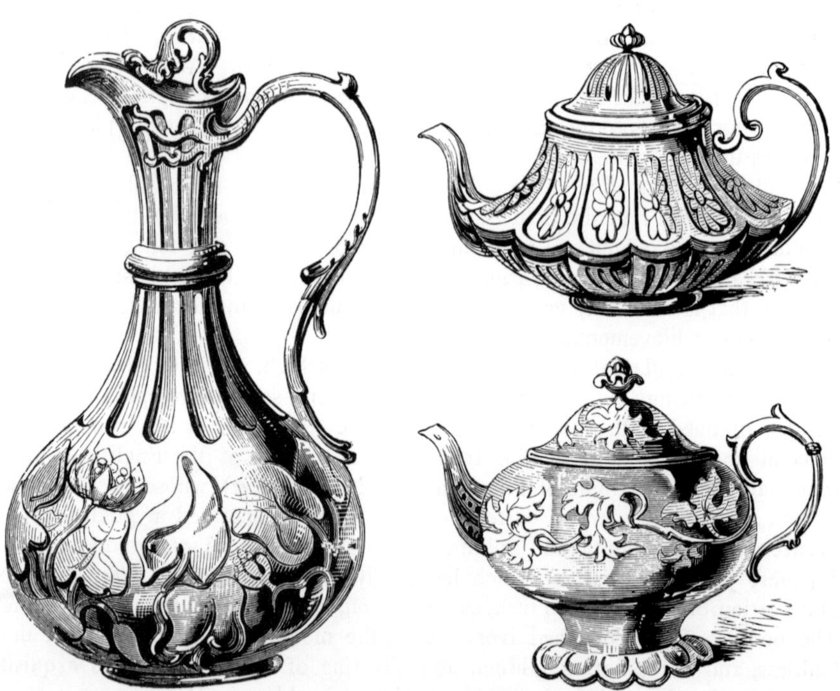

Figs. 1301 to 1303.—Newport Pottery, Burslem, 1831.

and is now continued by Edge, Malkin, & Co. Cork and Edge, in their ordinary earthenware, many years ago introduced a process of inlaying patterns in the ground-body, but of different colours. These were intended for the cheapest markets, but were produced in good taste; two teapots and a ewer, shown at the Great Exhibition in 1851, are engraved on Figs. 1301 to 1303. The productions of the firm at the present time are dinner ware; jet, enamelled, lustre, and other fancy goods; and all the ordinary wares for the home and foreign markets.

Newport Works.—Established in 1866 by Malkin, Edge, & Co. for the manufacture of encaustic and other tiles made from dust by Boulton and Worthington's process.

Dale Hall.—The extensive works at Dale Hall (or Dale Hole, as it used to be written), founded in 1790, originally belonged to Joseph Stubbs, a successful

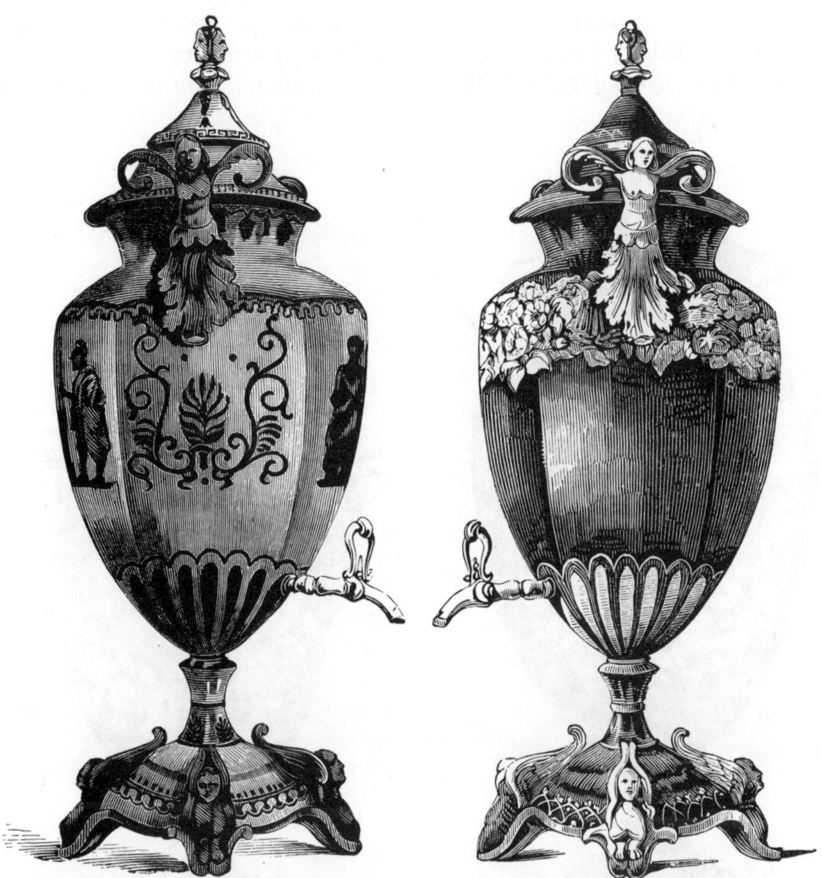

Figs. 1304 and 1305.—Mayer's Stoneware Tea Urns, Dale Hall.

manufacturer, who, having retired from business, died in 1836. He was succeeded by Messrs. Thomas, John, and Joshua Mayer, who afterwards traded as "Mayer Brothers, and Elliot," and from them, successively through the firms of "Liddle, Elliot, & Co.," "Bates, Elliot, & Co.," "Bates, Walker, & Co.," and "Bates, Gildea, and Walker," to the present firm of "Gildea and Walker." By the earlier firms ordinary earthenware was produced, but under Messrs. Mayer, who came from Stoke to Dale Hall, many important improvements were effected. Messrs. Mayer were probably from the manufactory at Cliff Bank previously worked by D. Bird. Shaw says that these works were had by T. Mayer in 1829, and continues: "We shall just notice here that Mr. T. Mayer has succeeded in a *chef-d'œuvre* of the Art of Pottery, by many considered as the best Specimen of Solid

Earthenware hitherto produced. It is an Earthenware Table, of truly elegant workmanship, thirty-two inches diameter, on an elegant pedestal of proportionate dimensions, ornamented in a very chaste style with subject from National History." Messrs. Mayer were exceedingly clever potters, especially Mr. Jos. Mayer, who died prematurely through excessive study and application to his art. They introduced many important improvements in the manufacture and decoration, especially in the beautiful polychromatic bisque printing which is continued by their successors and other firms. Besides ordinary earthenware, this firm produced stoneware of a highly vitreous quality; Parian of an improved body; a fine caneware, in which some remarkably good jugs (notably the "oak" pattern) were made; and other

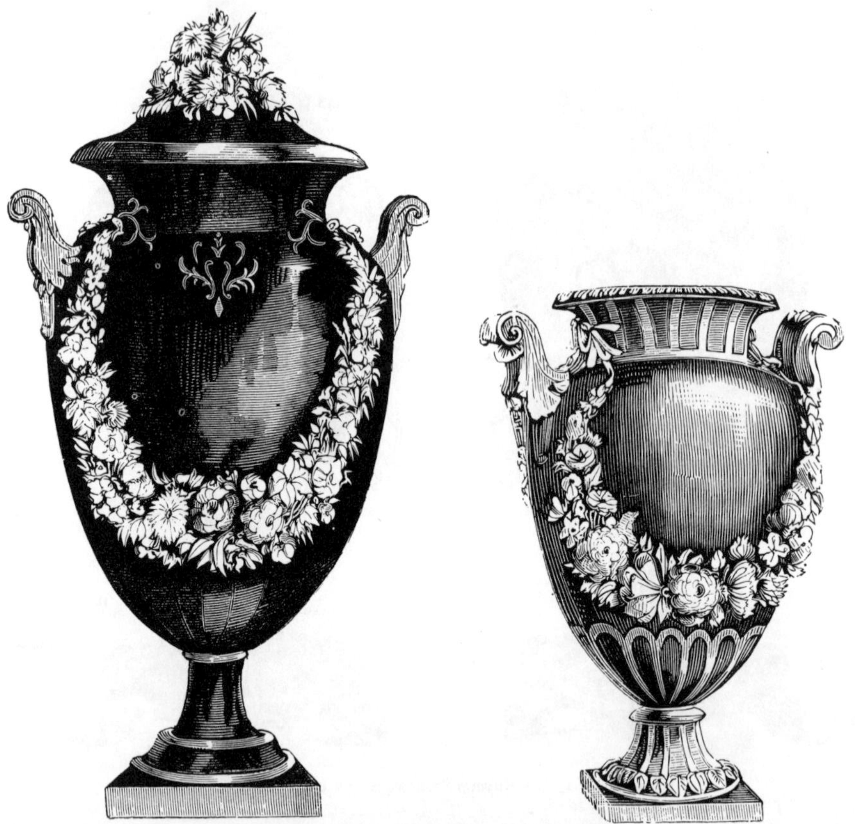

Figs. 1306 and 1307.—Mayer's Vases, Dale Hall.

wares. In the stoneware, besides many well-modelled jugs and other articles, they made tea-urns (which they were the first to introduce) of excellent design and admirable finish (Figs. 1304 and 1305). The peculiar body of the stoneware of which these were made was capable of withstanding the variations of temperature to which vessels of this kind, usually formed of metal, are liable. These were not made to any extent by Messrs. Mayer, but are now being reproduced by Gildea & Walker. Messrs. Mayer also produced some admirable designs in vases, decorated with a profusion of exquisitely modelled raised flowers. Two of these are shown on Figs. 1306 and 1307, and a jug in the following figure. The dinner-plates, dishes, &c., of Messrs. Mayer were characterised by an excellent "fit" in nesting, lightness of body, and neatness of finish. In 1851 they received a medal for their exhibits, as they again did at New York, Paris, Philadelphia, and Sydney.

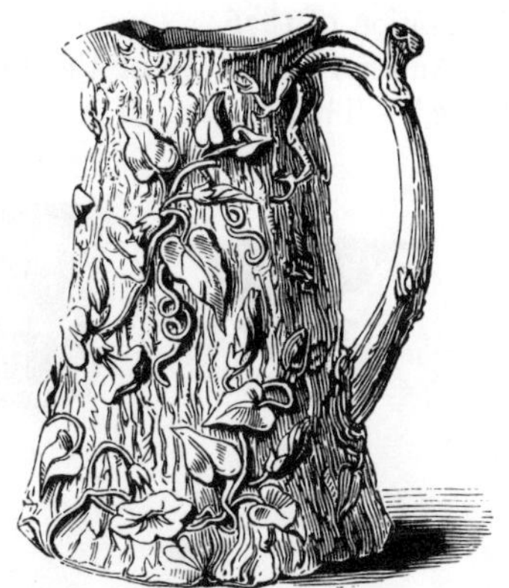

Fig. 1308.—Mayer, Dale Hall.

The present firm of Gildea & Walker produce in earthenware every variety of dinner, tea, toilet, and other services, from the plain white, ordinary printed, and flown, to the most elaborately enamelled, painted, and gilt patterns. The jugs, too, are a speciality; of these there are an immense variety of excellent shapes, and of strikingly beautiful decoration. The same remark will apply to the toilet services, which are, as a rule, characterised by good form and artistic decoration. Of these, the "Mistletoe" pattern is one of the most simply elegant yet produced. Among other articles in earthenware, the richly ornamented spirit-barrels form a distinct feature. In stoneware, of which I have spoken, well designed and sharply executed patterns in jugs, teapots, and other articles, are made in great variety.

In terra-cotta statuary groups, figures, and busts are made. The body is of

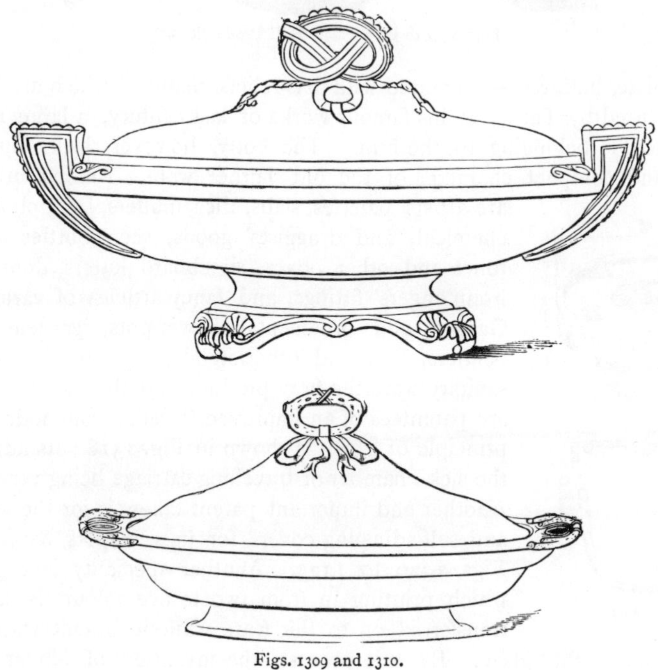

Figs. 1309 and 1310.

somewhat similar character to that of the Watcombe ware, but the process is different. The Watcombe "is fired in the enamel kiln or in an oven not subjected to greater heat, while this is fired in the biscuit oven; the one is so soft that it may be cut with a knife, while the other is quite vitreous and hard." In this material—a clay found on their own works— the firm produce a large variety of subjects, and a selection of these formed a notable figure in the Philadelphia Exhibition of 1876.

Another speciality of the firm is what they have named their "Turner Jasper Ware." This consists of a terra-cotta body with a slip of various colours—green,

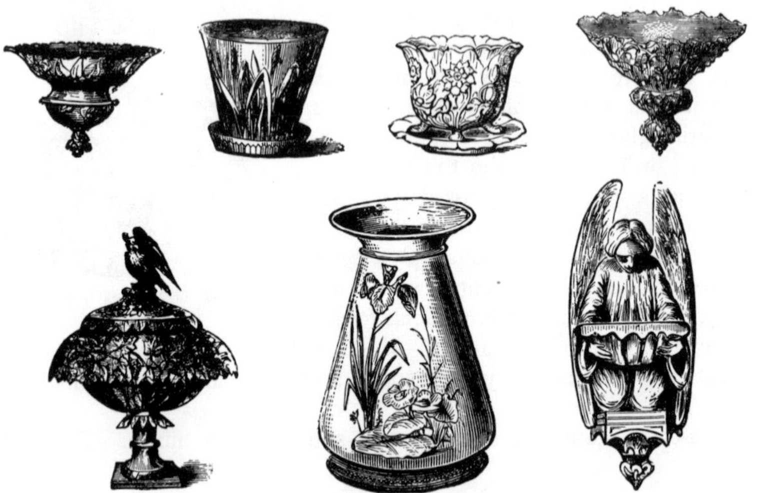

Figs. 1311 to 1317.—Dale Hall Productions.

blue, chocolate, buff, &c.—decorated with bas-reliefs, many of which are Flaxman's designs, as used by Turner at his famous works of last century, a large number of Turner's moulds belonging to the firm. The body, however, lacks the fineness, hardness, and compact character of the old Turner ware. Among other goods are artists' palettes, slabs, tiles, mullers, &c.; photographic, chemical, and druggists' goods, scent-bottles and vases, toilet and other boxes, sign-board letters, door furniture, ironmongers' fittings, and fancy articles of various kinds. Garden and ornamental flower-pots, garden-seats, suspenders, fern and other stands, &c., are also made. In sanitary ware the firm produces all the usual articles, and are patentees of an improved "wedge commode pan," the principle of which is shown in Fig. 1318; its advantage in the sick chamber or travelling carriage being very apparent. Another and important patent taken is for the self-locking and self-adjusting covers for jugs, teapots, &c., shown in Figs. 1320 to 1323. Another speciality is a process by which printing in from two to five colours is successfully transferred on to the ware while in biscuit state, and is, therefore, under the glaze. By this process, the invention of Mayer Brothers, vases, dinner and other services, and other articles are decorated in thoroughly good taste; and through there being no touching whatever by the pencil, as the entire pattern is transferred at one operation from the coloured print, they are produced at a comparatively moderate cost. By the present firm a high

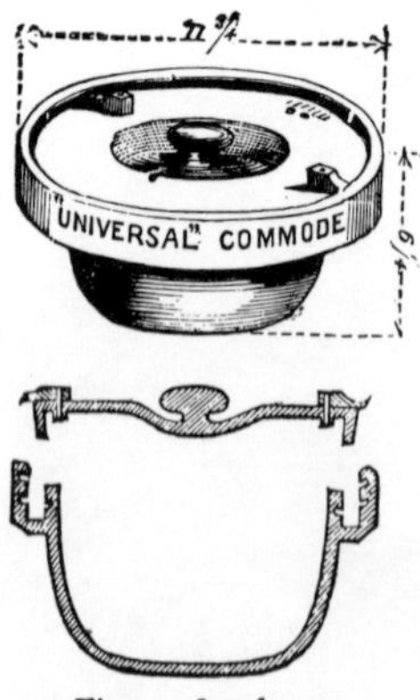

Figs. 1318 and 1319.

standard of decoration has been successfully aimed at, and many good designs have been brought out. Among others, the "Melbourne," "Satsuma," "Kioto," "Raku," and "Sunflower" patterns are notable, as are the "Leopold," "Diamond,"

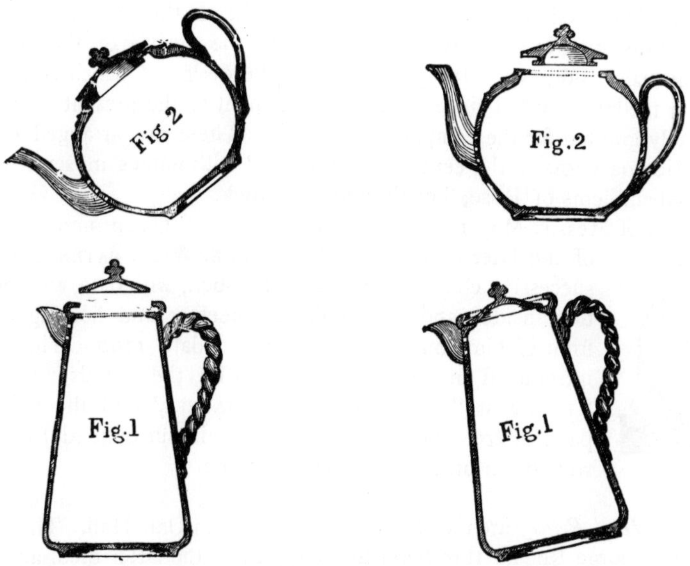

Figs. 1320 to 1323.

"Rex," "Japan," and "Paris," shapes. A special feature of Gildea & Walker's *fabrique* is their assortment of "dips" or coloured clays, embracing a great variety of shades, whose decorating adaptability is practically without limit. In using these "dips" the firm are not ignoring the traditions of their predecessors, for this

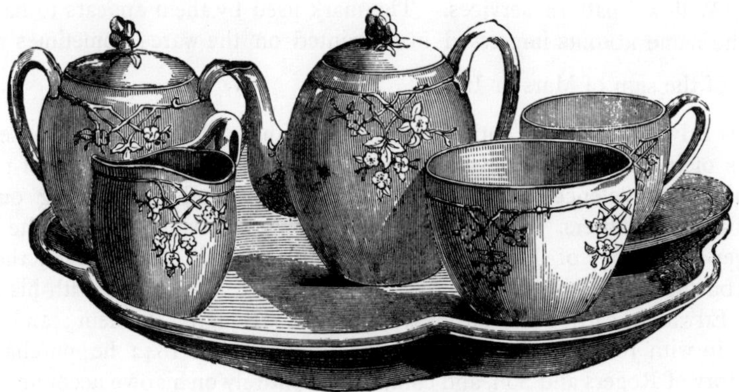

Fig. 1324.—Dejune, Dale Hall.

clay decoration is potting in its purest form. Instead of the pigments being applied to the *bisque* body, or burnt into the glaze in the form of an enamel, the colour is inseparable from the body, in fact *is* the body of the ware, and cannot be removed or affected by any chemical action, Another speciality of the firm is a process of printing in gold, which they have developed and perfected. The effect of some of the patterns printed in gold on the quiet but decorative tones of the "dips," is rich and chaste in the extreme.

A *chef d'œuvre* in engraving and gold-printing has lately been designed and produced by Major Gildea, the present senior member of the firm, who is known for his zeal and devotion in all works connected with the welfare of the families and men of the army and navy. It is a card tazza, the design of which consists of the several war medals awarded since the commencement of the present century, down to that lately granted for the campaign in Egypt. These are arranged in a circle, with the Victoria Cross in the centre, and bordered with names in scroll-work, and the national emblems of Rose, Thistle, and Shamrock.

The marks of Messrs. Mayer were T. J. & J. MAYER; MAYER BROS, &c. Those of the later firms are BATES, WALKER & CO. PATENTEES (or other successive changes), on an oval ribbon, with date, &c., of registration inside; and a nude figure kneeling and holding an ewer in front of him, on a tablet with the date 1790. This device is introduced in a variety of ways, with the initials "B. W. & CO.," "B. G. & W.," or "G. & W., LATE MAYERS," and the name of the pattern, &c. On some the device is surrounded by a circular ribbon, on others by a triangular one.

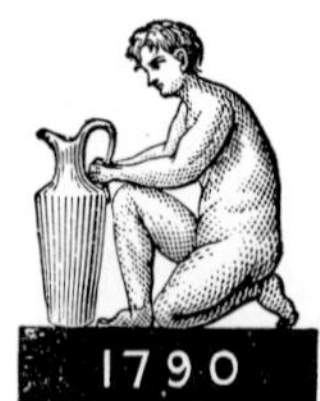

Fig. 1325

The Dale Hall Pottery are the oldest existing works in Dale Hall. They belonged to John and George Rogers (brothers) till 1815, when the latter died, and Spencer Rogers having joined his father, the business was carried on under the style of "John Rogers and Son." In 1816 John Rogers, who had erected a handsome residence, "The Watlands," near Wolstanton, died, but the firm continued as "John Rogers and Son" until 1842, when the manufactory was purchased by the late Mr. James Edwards, formerly of the firm of James and Thomas Edwards of the Kiln-Croft Works. Messrs. Rogers produced tableware of a higher and better quality than most of their contemporaries, and were especially famed for their light blue "Broseley" or "Willow" pattern services. The mark used by them appears to have been simply the name ROGERS impressed in or printed on the ware; sometimes with the addition of the sign of Mars or Iron, ♂ ROGERS

James Edwards was an entirely self-made man, and was one of those bright examples of indomitable perseverance, unflinching rectitude, steadiness of purpose, and genine benevolence which crop up every now and then among our most successful manufacturers. Commencing as a thrower at Messrs. Rogers's, he became a manager at Philips's of Longport, and at John Alcock's of Cobridge; then commenced business in partnership with John Maddock; afterwards with his brother Thomas Edwards, carried on business in Sylvester Square, Burslem; and next in partnership with John Maddock in the same town. In 1842 he purchased the manufactory of Rogers and Son, and commenced entirely on his own account. To him the white granite ware which has become so important a feature in the Pottery district mainly owes its excellence, that made by him being considered to be all that could be desired by our transatlantic brethren, and to be the standard of perfection to which the aims of other houses were directed. In 1851 a medal, with an additional certificate of merit for beauty of form and excellence of goods exhibited, was awarded to Mr. Edwards. At New York he also received honourable mention, and in 1865 a medal was awarded for his electrical, chemical, galvanic, and photographic apparatus. Mr. Edwards, who had taken his son Richard into partnership, retired from the concern in 1861 and died in 1867, one of his last acts of thoughtful benevolence being that of (only a few days before his death) sending to a number of his old workpeople at the manufactory cheques varying in amount from £20 to £100 each, according to each one's length of service. The works were continued by Richard Edwards under the style of "James Edwards and Son" until 1882, when they passed into the hands of Knapper & Blackhurst, but are now, I believe, closed.

STONE CHINA
JAMES EDWARDS & SON
DALE HALL

The marks used were the royal arms above the name, the same, with the addition, beneath, of the trade mark, a dolphin entwined round an anchor; the initials *J E & S* in writing letters, surrounded by a circular garter bearing the words IRONSTONE CHINA; the name J. EDWARDS & SON DALE HALL surrounded by an oval garter bearing the words IRONSTONE CHINA; and **Dalehall** surrounded by a similar oval garter bearing the name JAMES EDWARDS & SON. An impressed mark of EDWARDS D. H. was also used. The late firm used the name "Knapper and Blackhurst."

Dale Hall Brick and Tile Company.—These works, belonging to the Brownhills Pottery Company, produce the usual classes of plain and ornamental goods.

Dale Hall Tile Works.—These tile Works are carried on by Mr. James P. Basford, whose grandfather, above half a century ago, worked the same field of clay. His productions are all the usual classes of plain and ornamental tiles, bricks, &c.

Albert Street Works, established by John Hawthorne in 1854, were continued by him until 1869, when they were taken by Wiltshaw, Wood, & Co., and are now carried on by William Wood & Co. They were among the earliest in this branch of trade. The goods made are door-plates, lock-furniture, &c., both in white, black, gilt, and painted; drawer, shutter, and other knobs in oak, white, black, &c.; bedstead vases; caster bowls; umbrella, walking-stick, sewing-machine, closet, and other handles; ink-stands, bottles, and wells; highly-decorated jam-pots and biscuit-jars for the table; match-pots; teapot and urn stands of various degrees of decoration, painted, gilt, and enamelled; and every description of china used by brassfounders, tin-plate workers, japanners, &c. The only mark used is W W & CO.

The Mersey Pottery was established in 1850 by Anthony Shaw, and is now, since 1882, carried on as "Anthony Shaw & Sons." Goods specially adapted for the various American markets are made, the specialities being white graniteware and cream-coloured wares for the United States; the same with the addition of printed, lustred, and painted goods for South America, and printed for the colonies. In 1855 Mr. Shaw was awarded a medal at the Paris Exhibition. The mark formerly used was the royal arms, with ribbon bearing the words STONE CHINA, and beneath, in three lines, WARRANTED ANTHONY SHAW BURSLEM. That at the present time has the words WARRANTED ANTHONY SHAW & SON'S Opaque Stone China ENGLAND. The works were rebuilt on a very extensive scale in 1866.

Steel.—A manufacturer named Moses Steel had a pot-work in Burslem in 1715 and made the ordinary clouded ware of the period. Another potter of the same name, probably his descendant, carried on business in the latter part of the same century; he produced a fine earthenware and an imitation jasperware. The works are still standing by Queen Street, and are known as "Bournes Bank."

John Maddock and Son manufacture white graniteware for the American markets to a large extent.

New Wharf Pottery—(Hollinshed and Kirkham, late J. Daniel & Co.)—Printed ware of the kinds required for the home, Russian, Italian, and French markets, and all the usual kinds of painted and Paris white wares suitable for the African, Australian, and American trades.

The Over-House Works—Wedgwood Place.—The old works, now, alas! taken down, were possessed of no ordinary degree of interest from the fact of the "Over-

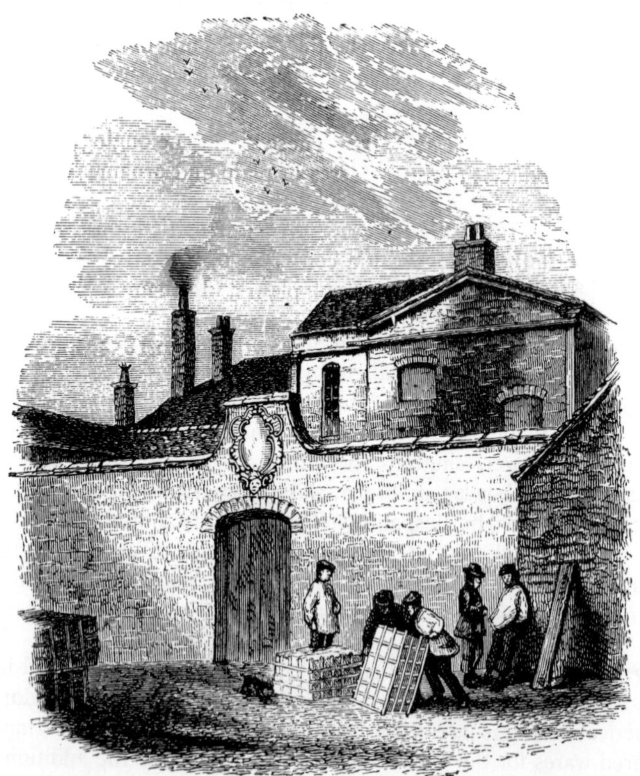

Fig. 1333.—The Over-House Works.

house," which closely adjoins them, having been the property and residence of Thomas Wedgwood, eldest brother of Josiah Wedgwood, and having been in the possession of the family for some generations. In 1787 the record runs, "Thomas Wedgwood, Manufacturer of Cream-coloured Ware and China glazed Ware, painted with blue, &c., Over-House." The old works were situated at the back and side of the "Overhouse," with entrance in Wedgwood Place, where that street joins Scotia

Road. A doorway, over which was a tablet, now no longer in existence, connected the works with the house. Of this historically interesting but now lost relic I fortunately made the sketch in 1866 from which the engraving is made.

Early in the present century the Overhouse Works were occupied by Goodfellow and Bathwell, who were succeeded in 1819 by Mr. Edward Challinor, and later by Mr. Pointon. In 1856 they passed to Morgan, Williams, & Co., afterwards to Morgan, Wood, & Co., who, in 1861, were succeeded by Allman, Broughton, & Co., and later by Robinson, Kirkham, & Co. In 1869 the old works were entirely taken down and a new and extensive manufactory erected with all the latest improvements of machinery and appliances, the jiggers all being driven by steam-power, and the drying stoves heated by exhaust steam. The rebuilding, after half a century of active occupation by one person, is thus commemorated in ornamental scroll stone-work over the entrance: "Edward Challinor commenced business here A.D. 1819, and rebuilt the premises A.D. 1869." The new manufactory was opened in 1870 by Ralph Hammersley, who removed here from the Church Bank Pottery at Tunstall, and who had previously been engaged for twenty years with Mr. Challinor. In the present year, 1883, the firm has been changed to "Ralph Hammersley and Sons."

The goods produced are the ordinary description of earthenware in services of various kinds and in the usual classes of useful articles, which, besides a good home trade, are shipped in large quantities to the United States, Canada, and Sweden. Stoneware jugs are also produced, and the firm has latterly added to the other classes a special ware for hotel, club, and ship uses. The mark is the initials "R. H. & S."

Swan Bank Pottery.—These works, after having passed successively through the hands of Thomas Edwards; Pinder, Bourne, & Co.; Beech and Hancock (now of Tunstall); and Hancock, Whittingham, and Hancock (now of Stoke); in 1873 came into the hands of Tundley, Rhodes, and Procter, and so continued till the death of Mr. Tundley, in 1883, when the style changed to "Rhodes and Procter." The goods produced are, and have been, printed, enamelled, and gilt earthenware, of the useful classes in all the usual services, &c., for the home, Russian, and South American markets. The mark is "T. R. & P." or "R. & P." beneath the name of pattern.

The Hill Top Pottery, or *Hill Pottery.*—These works, formerly belonging to Ralph Wood, were for many years carried on by Samuel Alcock & Co., by whom they were in 1839 rebuilt and enlarged; their rearranged manufactory comprising the works of Mr. Riley (formerly John Taylor), John Robinson and Sons, and William Taylor, which were all taken down for the purpose. The productions of Alcock & Co. were china and the finer descriptions of earthenware, one of their specialities being semi-porcelain of fine and durable quality. The marks were

ALCOCK AND CO.,
HILL POTTERY,
BURSLEM,

or S. ALCOCK & CO., either printed along with the name of the pattern or some device, or impressed in the ware. In 1860 the works and general estate were purchased by Sir James Duke and Nephews, and continued by them till 1865, when they sold it to Thomas Ford, who in 1866 sold it to the Earthenware and Porcelain Company, by whom (under the management of Mr. R. Daniel, once a noted china manufacturer at Stoke, Hanley, and Burslem) it was carried on under the style of the "Hill PotteryCompany, Limited, late S. Alcock & Co."

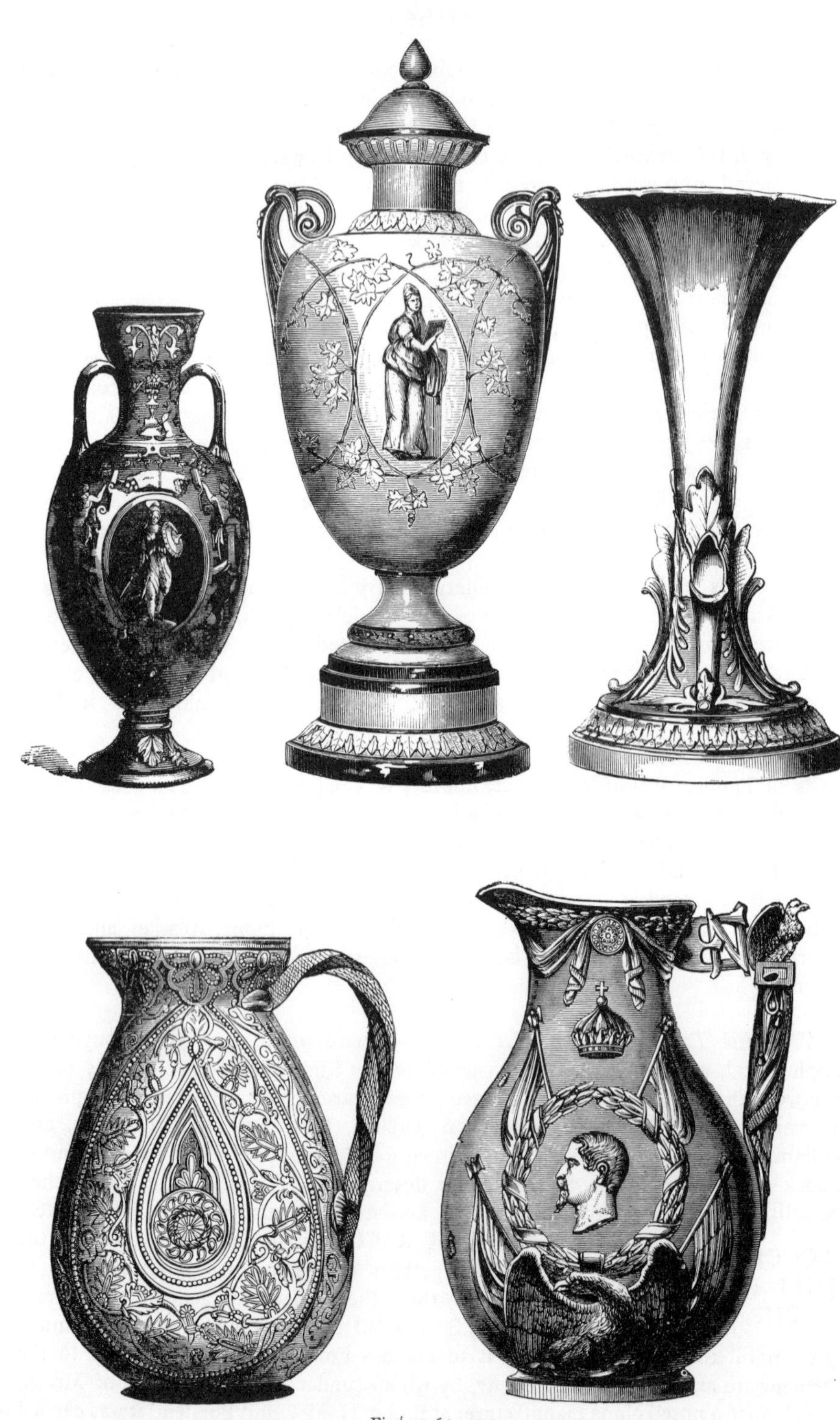

Figs. 1336 to 1340.

The productions of Sir James Duke and Nephews (Messrs. J. and C. Hill) were ordinary earthenware services, both white and cream-coloured; china and Etruscan wares some of which are shown in Figs. 1336 to 1356. The operations of the "Hill Pottery Company" were of short duration, for in 1867 it was put in liquidation

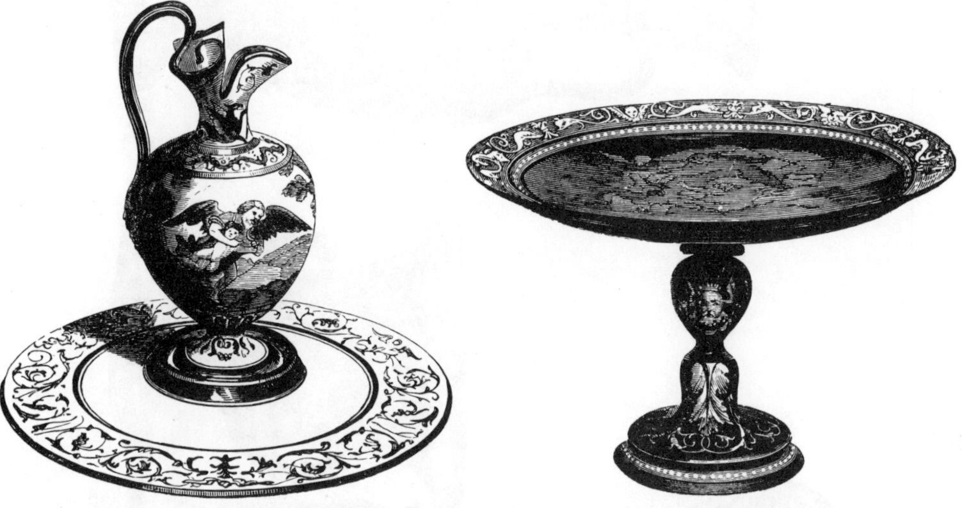

Figs. 1341 and 1342.

and sold up, when the property again came into the hands of Mr. Ford. In the same year the works were divided, the china department being taken by Alcock and Diggory, and the earthenware part by "Burgess & Leigh (late S. Alcock & Co.),"

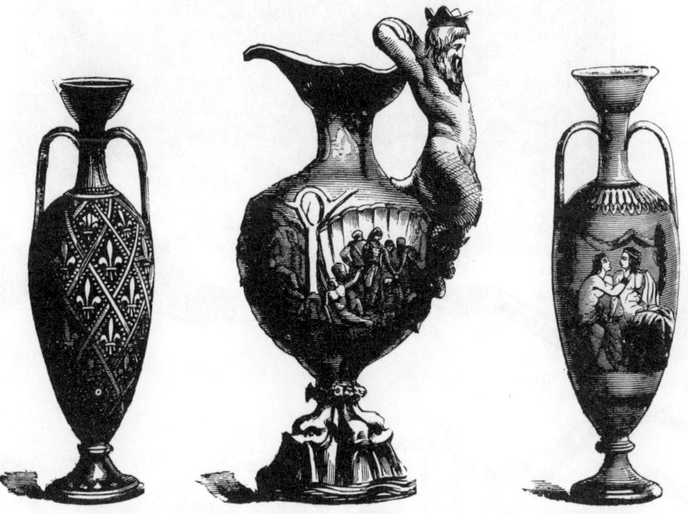

Figs. 1343 to 1345.

by whom it is still carried on under the style of "Burgess, Leigh, & Co.," who manufacture largely the commoner and ordinary as well as the higher and more artistic classes of earthenware goods, both for the home and foreign markets. The firm produce all the usual services, and useful as well as many highly ornamental

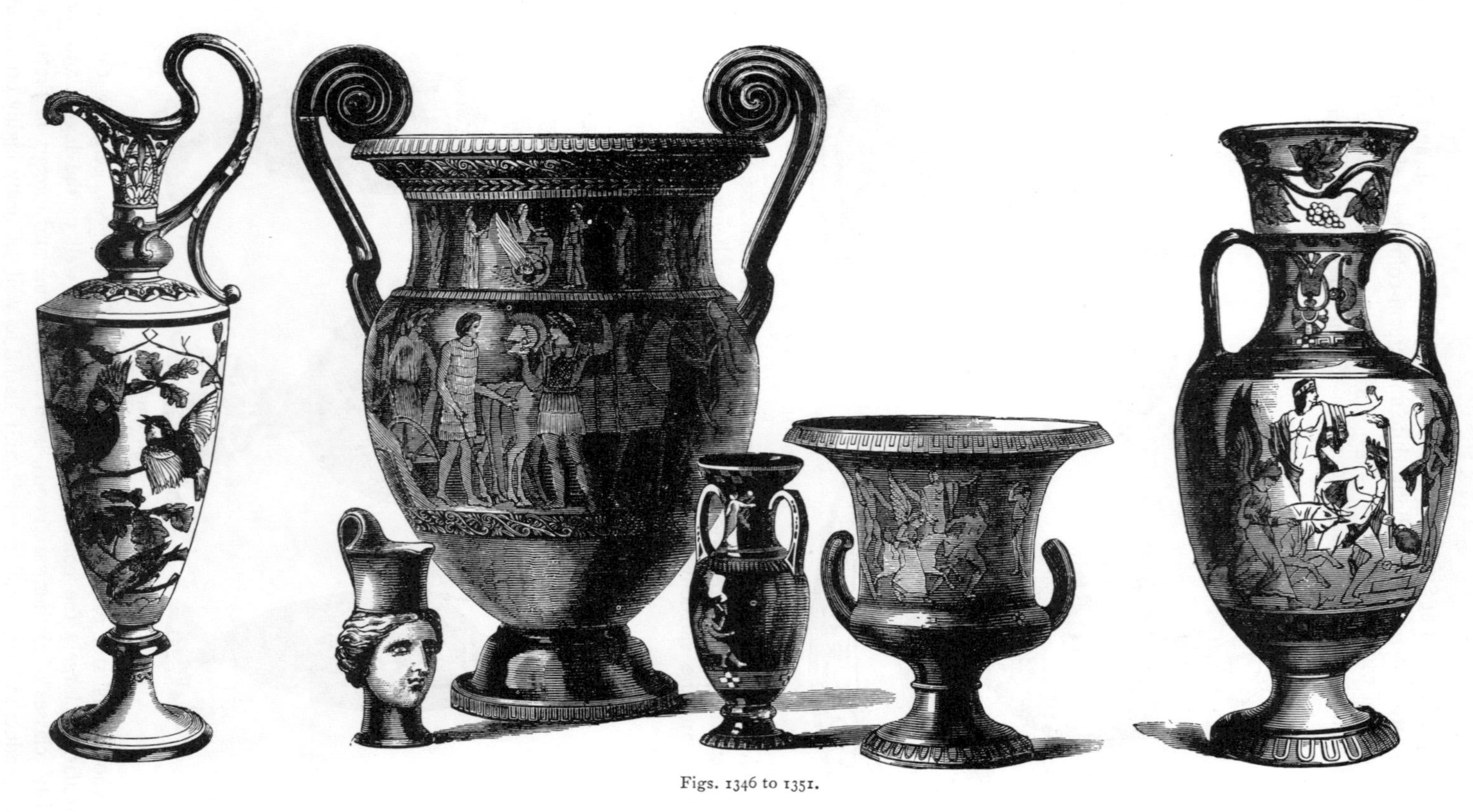

Figs. 1346 to 1351.

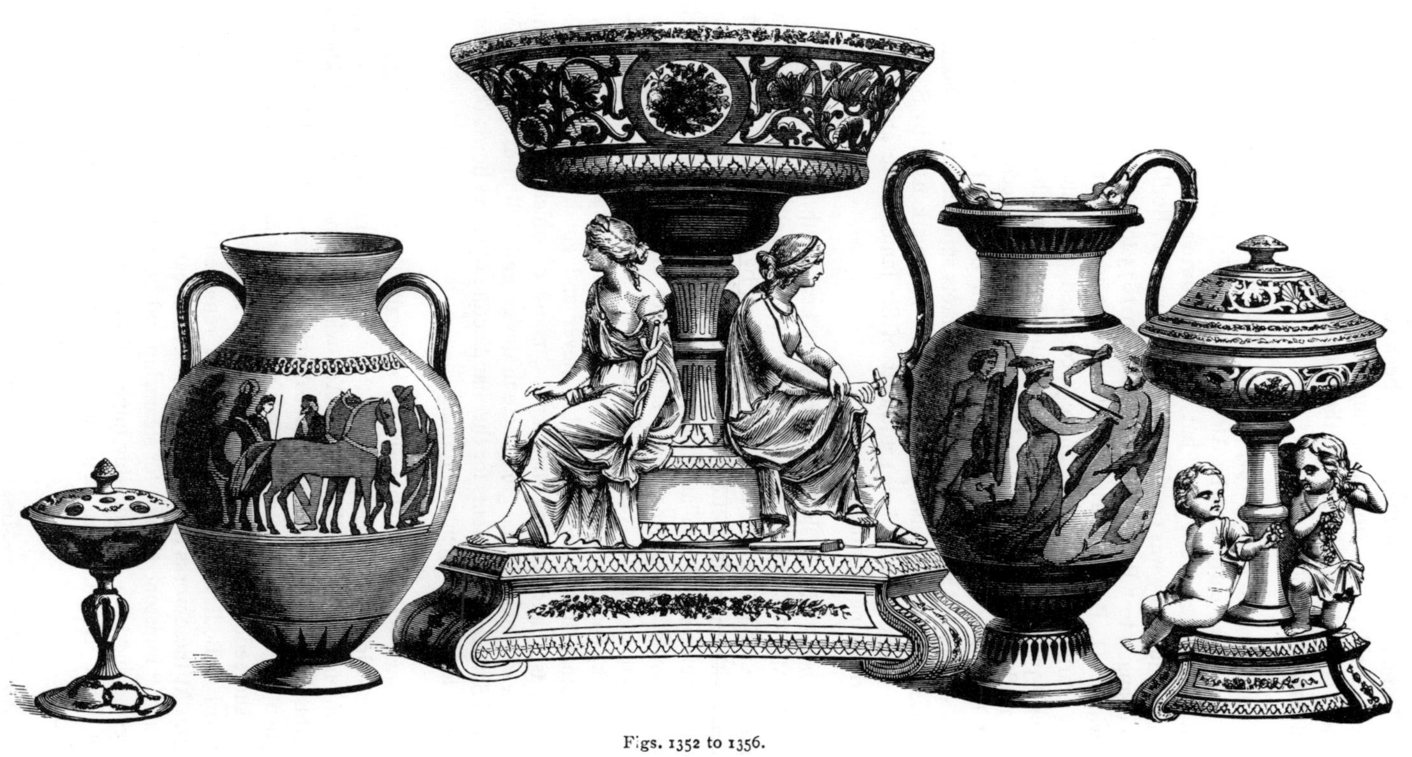

Figs. 1352 to 1356.

articles. The mark used by the firm is a beehive on a stand, with bees, with a rose-bush on either side, and a ribbon bearing the name of the pattern (" Kensington," for instance) beneath, and under this the initials of the firm, " B. L. & Co." Many of the patterns are registered.

The Hill Pottery China Works, on the division of the manufactory as already stated, in 1867 were carried on by Alcock, Diggory, & Co. In 1870 the firm was altered to " Bodley and Diggory," but in the following year, Mr. Diggory having retired, the manufactory was continued by Mr. Edward F. Bodley. In 1874 the style was again changed to " Bodley and Son," and in 1875 to that which it is at present, viz., Edwin J. D. Bodley. The productions formerly embraced china, earthenware, and Parian, but are now entirely confined to china. A speciality of Mr. Bodley's productions is that of pans and vases for chandeliers and lamps. These are made of various forms, and more or less highly decorated; they form an important branch of manufacture. Services of all the usual kinds, more or less elaborately decorated, are also made. The markets supplied are the home and the South Australian, New Zealand, and Colonial. The mark used by S. Alcock and Co. at these works was a beehive; and that of Sir James Duke and Nephews the dexter hand, denoting a baronet.

Crown Works.—Established about 1867 by Lea, Smith, and Boulton, who were succeeded by Mr. W. E. Withinshawe, and next by Gaskell, Son, and Co. In 1882 the works were rebuilt by Mr. Edwin J. D. Bodley, by whom they are carried on in conjunction with the Hill Pottery. The productions are and have always been china door-furniture and similar goods, including finger-plates, knobs, scutcheons, roses, caster bowls, and other fittings; scale plates and weights; stands and bases for lamps; and an infinite variety of articles for fittings of many kinds—white, coloured, black, enamelled, gilt, &c., &c.; while the imitations of marbles, malachites, and other stones are remarkably clever and good. Another speciality is umbrella, parasol, and walking-stick knobs, many of which, whether in imitation ivory or in dead black, evince great taste in design and skill in execution. Messrs. Gaskell and Son took out patents for the manufacture of caster bowls on an improved method, and for improvements in turning.

Scotia Works.—This manufactory was originally the parish workhouse of Burslem, and was calculated to accommodate three hundred inmates. On the establishment of unions, under the Poor Law Act, when the new union workhouse was erected, this building was occupied as barracks, and so continued for some years. It was then, in 1857, converted into a manufactory by Mr. James Vernon, who in 1862 was succeeded by the firm of " Edward F. Bodley & Co.," in 1880 changed to " Edward F. Bodley & Sons," who in 1881 removed to the New Bridge Pottery, Longport. At these works the usual descriptions of earthenware, printed, enamelled, and gilt, and " ironstone china," for steamship and hotel use, were made; the bodies and glazes having been considerably improved by the manager, Mr. Edward Beardmore, of Rode Heath. The mark was the Staffordshire knot, with the words SCOTIA WORKS.

Queen Street Pottery.—Messrs. Tinsley and Bourne entered on these works, which were formerly occupied by Mr. J. Edge and others, in 1874, and were succeeded in 1882 by Mr. W. H. Adams.

The Hill Works, on the opposite side of the road to the "Hill Pottery" already described, are of old foundation, and were, I am informed, worked by Enoch Wood (see page 459). In 1787 the business is recorded as "Wood, Enoch and Ralph, manufacturers of all kinds of useful and ornamental Earthen Ware, Egyptian Black, Cane, and various other colours, also Black Figures, Seals, and Cyphers." This Ralph Wood was a master-potter in Burslem in 1787, and a very interesting relic connected with him is now in the hands of Mr. Thos. F. Wood, of the firm of Wood & Baggaley. It is an iron tobacco-box, bearing, engraved on its lid, the words, "*Ralph Wood, Potter, Burslem, Staffordshire*, 1787." This box was given by this Ralph Wood, whose name appears upon it, to the grandfather of its present owner. About 1768 John Robinsòn, who before that time was with Sadler and Green, of Liverpool, left their employ to commence here the making of enamelled ware. In the Mayer Museum is a teapot made by him, and painted by Letitia Marsh (afterwards Mrs. Brood), who worked for him. It is of "squeezed ware," and was given to Mr. Mayer by Dr. Simeon Shaw. After Wood's time the works were carried on by Mr. Taylor, and next by John & Richard Riley (who removed to them from the Nile Street works), by whom they were rebuilt in 1814, and who produced china and earthenware and Egyptian black ware. They next passed to Alcock & Keeling; and, on the retirement of the latter, to S. Alcock & Co., who, having rebuilt and enlarged the "Hill Pottery," removed there as already detailed. About 1851 Barker & Son took the "Hill Works" for the production of goods for the home and foreign markets. On their failure they were, in 1860, succeeded by Morgan, Wood, & Co., which firm was afterwards altered to Wood & Baggaley, and, more recently, to Jacob Baggaley, the present occupier. The goods, which are mostly for the home market, comprise printed and decorated dinner, toilet, tea, and breakfast services, and green-glazed dessert ware, which, to some extent, they export. The mark used by the firm is a bee with wings expanded, beneath which is a ribbon with the initials M W & CO, or W & B, or J B.

Sylvester Pottery, Nile Street, formerly belonging to Charles G. Baker, passed by purchase, in 1876, to the present firm of Holmes, Plant, and Madew, who, in addition to ironstone china and French porcelain, produce to a large extent door-furniture and brassfounders' sundries in china. The mark is the initials "H. P. & M."

High Street Pottery.—This manufactory, usually known as "Union Bank," through its having been for some time worked by the Potters' Trades' Union, belonged at one time to a family named Marsh, and was also carried on by Whittingham, Ford, & Co., from whom it passed to the present proprietors, Buckley, Wood, & Co., who produce ordinary earthenware for the home trade. The mark used is simply the initals B W & CO.

Sneyd Pottery, Albert Street.—These works, formerly carried on for the production of ordinary earthenware, by Messrs. Bennett, came, about 1867, into the hands of Williams, Oakes, & Co., which firm was in 1876 altered to Oakes, Clare, & Chadwick. Rockingham, jet, majolica, and common earthenware of the ordinary classes are produced, as are chests of drawers' feet in large numbers and other fittings of various designs.

Hadderidge Pottery.—These works, carried on by Mr. Thomas Heath, and afterwards, successively by Mr. John Wedgwood, Mr. Phillips, and W. & G. Harding, came into the hands of Heath & Blackhurst in 1859, who were succeeded by Blackhurst and Tunnicliffe, and Blackhurst and Bourne, by whom they are still continued for middle-class quality earthenware, plain and decorated, for the home trade. In this class all the usual table, toilet, tea, and other services, and a variety of other articles, are made. The mark is a garter, encircling the initials "H & B.," "B & T.," or "B & B."

Navigation Road.—The works of Mr. Edward Corn, erected some time back on what was a timber-yard, and now carried on by W. & E. Corn, are exclusively devoted to the production of white graniteware for the United States and other foreign markets.

Bleak Hill Works.—These works formerly belonged to Moore Brothers, who produced the white graniteware for the American markets, then successively to M. Isaacs and Son, Beech and Podmore (who removed here from the *Bell Works* in 1876), and Podmore alone, who in 1880 was succeeded by Mr. F. J. Emery, of the Churchyard Works. The goods now produced are the higher and better classes of services for exportation to the United States, and in these, through the soundness of body and superior quality of glaze, Mr. Emery is able to produce a better and more artistic phase of under-glaze colouring than is attained by other firms. He has also, with marked success, introduced etching in its varied forms of "point," "aquatint," and a modification of mezzotint, as well as photographic processes for decoration. These bid fair to become highly popular not only in the States but elsewhere.

Sytch Pottery.—Of very old foundation, this was, many years ago, worked by Messrs. Keeling. The "Sytch Pottery" passed successively into the hands of Mr. R. Hall and J. Hall & Sons. About 1832 Barker, Sutton, & Till took to the works; but at subsequent periods Mr. Barker and Mr. Sutton withdrew from the partnership, and from 1850 it remained in the hands of Thomas Till, who being joined in partnership with his sons, the firm is now "Thomas Till & Sons." The wares usually produced have been good middle-class earthenware; but the present proprietors have greatly improved the ware, and added other branches to their manufacture. Besides earthenware of the usual average quality—in which services and innumerable useful articles are made by them—Messrs. Till produce coloured bodies of various kinds (cane, sage, drab, and lilac); stoneware of a hard and durable kind for jugs, &c.; jet glazed ware; terra-cotta; enamelled ware; and various coloured lustres. These are principally intended for the home trade. At the Paris Exhibition of 1855 the firm received a certificate of merit. The mark used is the name of the firm.

Kiln Croft Works.—These works are of old establishment. In or about 1800 they were carried on by a Mr. Handley, and in 1825 by James and Thomas Edwards, who were succeeded by Willett & Marsh. They were then continued by Mr. Marsh alone, and next by T. & R. Boote, who were succeeded by the present owner, Mr. Henry Burgess. The goods produced are the usual quality of white graniteware in services and various articles for the United States and Canadian markets. The mark is the Royal Arms, with the name or initials of the firm.

The Albert Pottery, built in 1860 by Mr. William Smith, of Tunstall, on whose failure in 1862 it was taken by Dix & Tundley, of Silverdale, for the production of foreign-trade goods. In 1864 the works were purchased by the late Charles Hobson (who had originally been apprenticed to Mr. Williamson, the predecessor of the Davenports at Longport), since whose death, in 1875, they have been continued by his two sons, George and John Hobson. By Mr. C. Hobson the works were considerably enlarged. New biscuit ovens were added, and flint and colour mills, steam slip-house, pug mills, and sagger-makers' mill, built. The productions are confined to the home trade, and consist of the usual services and other articles in ordinary earthenware, both white, printed, lined, enamelled, and gilt.

Waterloo Pottery.—These works were established about 1846 by Mr. James Vernon, then continued under the style of "James Vernon & Sons," and "James Vernon, jun.," and are now carried on by "J. & G. Vernon Brothers" for the manufacture of ordinary earthenware for the South American, West India, and Mediterranean markets. On this same site a manufactory was at one time carried on by Jonathan Leak, a clever potter, who, after some strange vicissitudes, went to Sydney, where, after a time, discovering a valuable bed of clay, he established the first pottery in Australia. He married a niece of Enoch Wood.

Central Pottery.—This old-established pottery was formerly worked successively by Hopkin & Vernon, Hulme & Booth, Thomas Hulme, and Burgess & Leigh, who were succeeded by Mr. Richard Alcock, by whom the works were considerably enlarged, rebuilt, and remodelled. At Mr. Alcock's death in 1881 the works passed into the hands of Mr. Arthur J. Wilkinson, by whom they are now carried on. Earthenware for the home markets was formerly made, but the operations were afterwards confined to white graniteware for the United States. In addition to this Mr. Wilkinson has introduced with considerable success gold lustres on the granite. The mark is the royal arms surmounted by the words "ROYAL PATENT IRONSTONE," and beneath, in three lines, "ARTHUR J. WILKINSON, LATE R. ALCOCK, BURSLEM, ENGLAND."

Other manufacturers in Burslem have been Joseph Machin & Co.; Thomas Heath (probably of the same family as the Heaths formerly of the Cockpit Hill Pottery, Derby); John Hall & Sons; J. R. Marsh; T. & B. Godwin; J. Cormie; Messrs. Phillips, Dale Hall.

Longport.—(Davenports, Limited.) The famous works of Davenport & Son date back more than a hundred years, the centenary of their establishment having taken place in 1873. In 1773 a manufactory was erected at Longport by John Brindley (brother of the celebrated James Brindley, the engineer, both of whom were natives of Tunstead, in Derbyshire), who also built for himself a handsome residence near at hand. This house was purchased in 1843 for a parsonage for St. Paul's, Burslem, and was again in 1858 sold to Mr. W. Davenport. Shortly after 1773 Mr. Edward Bourne built another manufactory, and this was followed by a third, erected by Mr. Robert Williamson, who in 1775 married Anne (*née* Henshall), widow of James Brindley, the engineer.

In 1793 the first-named manufactories passed into the hands of Mr. John Davenport, who in 1797 added to his other operations "the chemical preparation of litharge and white lead for the use of potters," which, however, was afterwards discontinued. In 1801 the business of glass-making was added and is still carried on. In 1803 Mr. Davenport, supported by his neighbours at Longport, offered to raise, clothe, and equip, free of expense to Government, except arms, a volunteer corps of 500 men, and his offer was accepted, the number being limited by Government to four companies of 80 rank and file each. Mr. Davenport became major of this force, and raised it to a high state of discipline. In connection with this it may be well to note that one of Mr. Davenport's workmen at that time, and a member of his volunteer corps, was William Clowes, a nephew of Aaron Wedgwood, to whom he had been apprenticed. This William Clowes was a co-founder with Hugh Bourne of the now wide-spread sect of Primitive Methodists. About 1830 Mr. Davenport retired from active business, and chiefly resided at Westwood Hall, near Leek, where he died in 1848. The business, after his retirement in 1830, was carried on by his second son, Henry Davenport, who died in 1835 (who purchased the manufactory of Robert Williamson, and added to his other works), and the youngest son, William Davenport. In 1832 Mr. John Davenport was elected M.P. for the borough of Stoke-upon-Trent, being one of the first two members for that newly enfranchised borough. After the death of Mr. Henry Davenport the manufactories were carried on by his youngest brother, Mr. William Davenport, under the style of "W. Davenport & Co." He died in 1869, and the entire business was carried on by his only son, Mr. Henry Davenport, until 1881, when he converted it into a private company.

In 1806 the Prince of Wales (afterwards George IV.) and the Duke of Clarence (afterwards William IV.) visited Davenport's works. On the accession of the latter to the throne he gave the order to this firm to manufacture for him the superb service to be used at his coronation banquet. This royal service was completed in a very satisfactory manner, and was the subject of high commendation from the King and his noble guests on that occasion. On this service the crown was first used by the firm.

In the earlier years of the Longport manufactory earthenware alone was produced, but no pieces of Brindley's make are known. Mr. Davenport at first confined his operations to the manufacture of white, cream-coloured, and blue-printed wares, and these were of good substantial quality. His blue-printed plates with open-work rim, of the same general character as those of the Herculaneum Works at Liverpool, are to be seen in most collections. Later on china was commenced, and now forms an equally extensive branch with the earthenware. In both these all the usual services and miscellaneous articles are produced, from the plain to the most elaborately decorated, both for the home and foreign markets. The china is of remarkably fine and good quality, both in body, in glaze, and in make, and in all these particulars ranks among the best produced in the district. The tea and dessert ware is of extreme excellence, and many of the patterns are unsurpassed for richness of colouring and gilding by any other house. Among their specialities are adaptations of the finest Japanese and Indian patterns; and of such designs as gave so important a character to the productions of the old Derby works in their palmiest days. The deep blues, the rich gradations of red, and the other colours employed, are in some of the patterns laid on with a lavish richness, and, being combined with the most elaborate and delicate as well as massive gilding, produce intricate patterns of great beauty and sumptuous appearance. Some of the cups (notably those with sunk panels, and others which are bowl-shaped and supported upon gilt feet) are of elegant form, and those in blue and white, whether in pencilled, ordinary transfer printing, or "flown," are highly successful. In celadon and *rose du Barry* they produce charming but simple services, as they do also in white. In the latter the "potting" of some—approaching closely to egg-shell—is remarkably delicate and clever.

Another striking speciality of design in china is the adapting of the old Willow pattern to modern déjeuner services and menu holders. The forms of the pieces composing the service are of quaint and striking elegance, and being heightened by massively gilt handles and by strictly appropriate gilding of borders, rims, feet, and raised ornaments, an effect is produced which is surpassingly "taking." The déjeuner of which I have thus briefly spoken is one of the most successful adaptations of the Willow pattern yet achieved.

In "stone china," dinner and dessert services, as well as jugs and other articles, are produced in all the best styles of decoration. The services in ordinary earthenware are also extremely varied in pattern, in decoration, and in variety of shapes.

The marks used by Davenports have been various, the anchor being the distinguishing characteristic. The crown was first used by them on the royal service

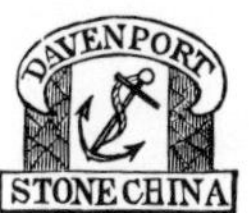

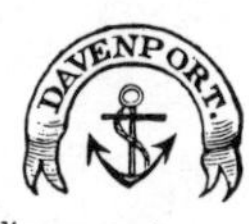

Figs. 1357 to 1359.

for William IV., and is now generally used on porcelain services. Some of these are impressed marks.

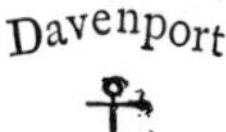

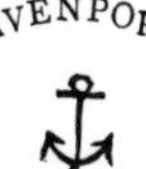

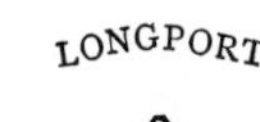

DAVENPORT
LONGPORT

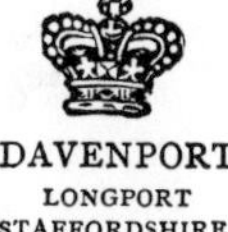

DAVENPORT
LONGPORT
STAFFORDSHIRE

Figs. 1360 to 1364.

The printed marks are a circular garter bearing the words DAVENPORT LONGPORT STAFFORDSHIRE, surrounding an anchor and the words "Stone China" in script. Another is a shield with the words 30 CANNING PLACE LIVERPOOL 32 ELY PLACE LONDON, encircled by a garter bearing the words DAVENPORT LONGPORT STAFFORD[RE] and surmounted by the crest, an anchor on an heraldic wreath. Another has a circular garter bearing the words DAVENPORTS & CO. surrounding the address, 82, FLEET STREET LONDON.

Brownhills.—About 1782 John Wood (son of Ralph Wood, of Brownhills, and Mary Wedgwood) built a manufactory, with house adjoining, on property originally belonging to the Burslem and Wedgwood families, which he had purchased of Thomas Lovatt. Here he carried on the potting business until his death in 1797, when he was succeeded by his son, John Wood, who continued it until 1830, when he took down the manufactory, enlarged the house, and extended the grounds.

Littler.—William Littler, of Brownhills, whose father had carried on a business as potter there, was the first man in Staffordshire who attempted the making of china ware. "He commenced business about 1745 when he attained his majority, and a few years afterwards removed the seat of his manufacture to Longton Hall, where he prosecuted his experiments with very good success as regarded the beauty and delicacy of his china, but with disastrous results to himself, for he soon sacrificed his patrimony in the speculation, and was obliged to abandon it. The specimens we have seen of Mr. Littler's china exhibit great lightness and beauty, and would certainly have won their way in after times. Mr. Littler had the merit of first making use of the fluid glaze which Mr. Enoch Booth afterwards improved upon."—(*Ward.*) Littler's pot-works have long disappeared. Some specimens of his porcelain are preserved in private collections, and one or two are in the Hanley Museum. To one of these is attached the following note in Enoch Wood's handwriting: "This was given to Enoch Wood by William Fletcher in January, 1809."

Longport Terra Cotta.—At the 1851 Exhibition Mr. James Marsh (modeller at Davenports'), of Longport, exhibited the wine-cooler, of bold and good design,

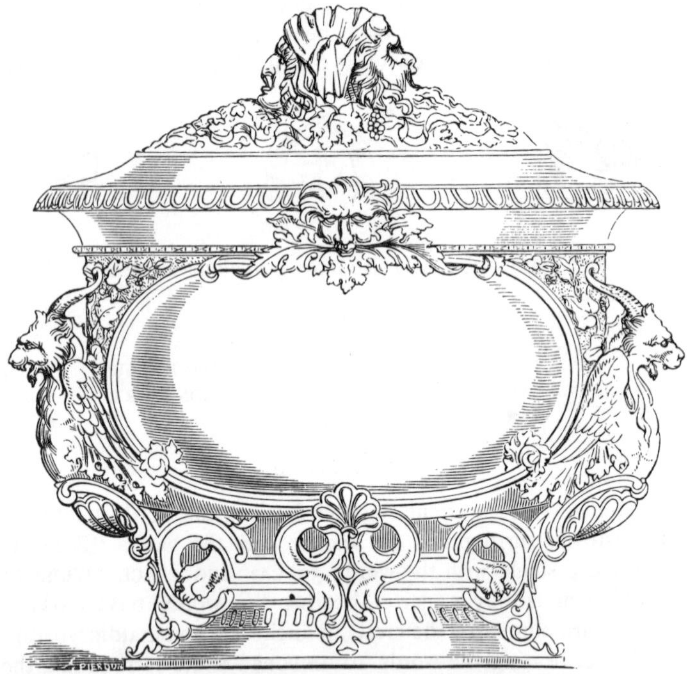

Fig. 1365.—Wine-cooler, by Marsh of Longport.

produced by him in terra-cotta (Fig. 1365). In the early part of this century Messrs. Samuel Marsh & Co. were manufacturers at Brownhills.

Marsh and Haywood.—This firm formerly carried on business here as manufacturers of general earthenware, as did also Mr. John Wood at Highgate.

Brownhills Works.—These works (formerly Marsh and Haywood's) were for many years carried on by George F. Bowers, who attained a fair reputation for china goods, and gained a medal at the Exhibition of 1851. Subsequently he commenced the manufacture of earthenware, which he continued until his death, when he was succeeded by his son, Frederick F. Bowers, at whose failure in 1871 the manufactory was purchased by James Eardley, of Alsager, and is now carried on by his son and sons-in-law, Alfred J. Eardley, Edwin Meir, William H. Bratt, Robert H. Parker, and George Hammersley, under the style of "The Brownhills Pottery Co." The goods produced are of the usual useful classes of table, tea, toilet, and other requisites, in fine earthenware, stoneware, buff, turquoise, and cream-coloured ware; and in decorations of the fine earthenware services improvements have been effected by which the printing of enamel upon the glaze and lining on the bisque are effected. The last is produced at considerably less cost than enamel lines, and while making a tolerably near approach in point of colour is more durable, because protected by the glaze. In toilet ware their "Greek" shape is remarkably good, and is made in various degrees of decoration. In stoneware some excellent designs in teapots, jugs, &c., are produced, as are also jugs and other useful articles in cream ware; the adaptations of Japanese ornamentation in the former are highly successful. In jet ware, teapots, jugs, and other articles, highly decorated in enamel and gold, are made. The firm also have a process of printing in yellow upon the glaze of their jet goods, which produces a cheap and somewhat effective class of decoration. Another speciality is a rich full deep-red terra-cotta, highly glazed, and elaborately decorated in a variety of effective patterns in enamel and gold. In this, toilet services of good design and novel appearance are largely made. In ornamental goods the company produce vases of various forms (notably among which are the "Hindoo," "Milan," "Pekin," and other designs); scent-jars, flower-tubes and stands, and other articles. The marks used, besides the name of the pattern, bear the initials "B. P. Co.," with ribbon, &c., printed on the ware.

New Bridge Works, Longport.—This manufactory, previously carried on by W. Davenport and Son (see page 467), passed, in 1877, into the hands of Mr. Edward Clarke, formerly, and again now, of the Churchyard Works at Burslem, and intermediately, of the Phœnix Works, Tunstall, who removed thither from the last-named place, and took into partnership Mr. F. J. Emery, the inventor of the process of crayon drawing and printing on the bisque surface, referred to on page 477; the mark being "EDWARD CLARKE & CO." In 1881 the manufactory was purchased by Edward F. Bodley & Son, of the Scotia Works, who removed to it in that year, Mr. Bodley dying between the time of purchase and removal. The goods produced are "Genuine Ironstone China" and earthenware in all classes of which the usual services and other domestic articles are made. The mark is the Staffordshire knot enclosing within its loops the words NEW BRIDGE POTTERY.

Waterloo Road Works, established in 1820 (on the site of a very old pottery "on Bournes Bank," afterwards worked by William Harrison) by Thomas Hughes, and carried on by him and his successors, Stephen Hughes & Co., till about 1856, from which time until 1881 they were continued by Thomas Hughes, grandson of the first named, by whom the whole place was enlarged, improved, and modernised. In 1881 Mr. Hughes removed to Top Bridge Works, Longport, and was succeeded by Mellor, Taylor & Co., who continue to produce the usual articles in hard durable "granite" or "ironstone china" for the American markets. Goods are also, to some extent, produced for the home trade. The former mark, stamped on the ware, was THOMAS HUGHES IRONSTONE CHINA. That of the present firm is the royal arms in plain shield, with crown and wreath, exactly copied from the reverse of the half-crown of Queen Victoria, surrounded by the words, MELLOR, TAYLOR & CO., ENGLAND. WARRANTED STONE CHINA.

Cobridge Works.—The manufactory of W. Brownfield & Son was erected in 1808, and worked by Bucknall & Stevenson, and afterwards by A. Stevenson alone. In 1819 the works were closed, and afterwards passed into the hands of James Clews, who continued them until 1829, when they were again closed. His mark was a crown and his name, thus—

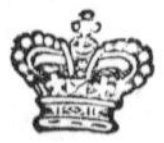

CLEWS
Warranted Staffordshire

Fig. 1366.

In 1836 the premises were opened by Robinson, Wood & Brownfield, and, after Mr. Robinson's death in the same year, were continued by Wood & Brownfield. In 1850 Mr. Wood retired, and the business was continued solely by Mr. Brownfield (who died in 1873) until 1871, when he was joined in partnership by

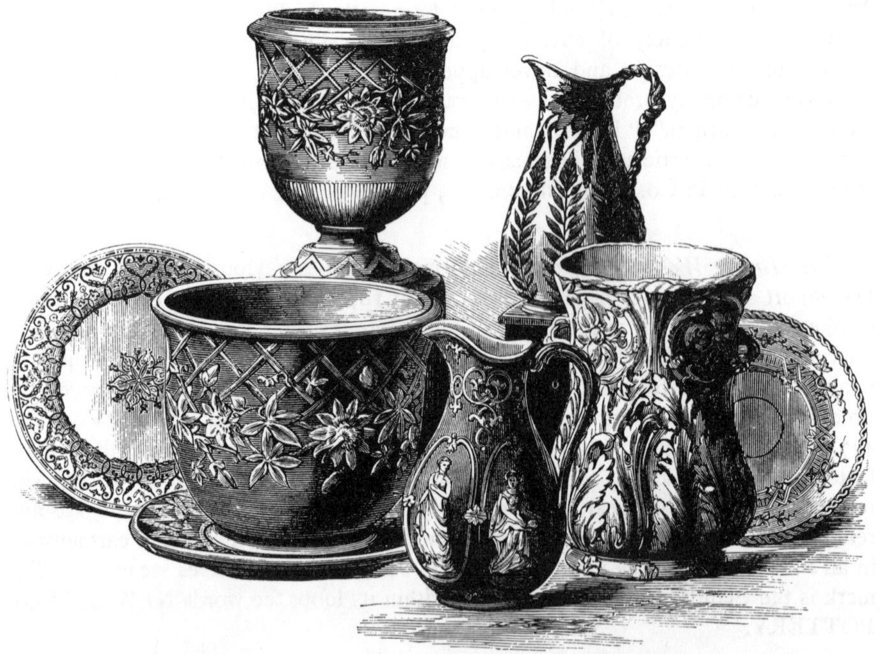

Figs. 1367 to 1373.—Brownfield's Goods at the Exhibition of 1862.

his eldest son, William Etches Brownfield, and from that time it has been carried on as "W. Brownfield & Sons." The goods produced during the earlier period of the works were the ordinary white, blue-printed, and sponged varieties of earthenware. From 1850 rapid strides were made in the improvement of the wares, and under the present firm they have become equal to any others produced. In earthenware, white, printed, enamelled, and gilt wares, from the simplest to the more elaborate and costly patterns, in table, toilet, and dessert services, and all the usual articles for household use, are made. Many of the printed patterns are well designed, and, in the better classes of goods the enamelling and gilding are very

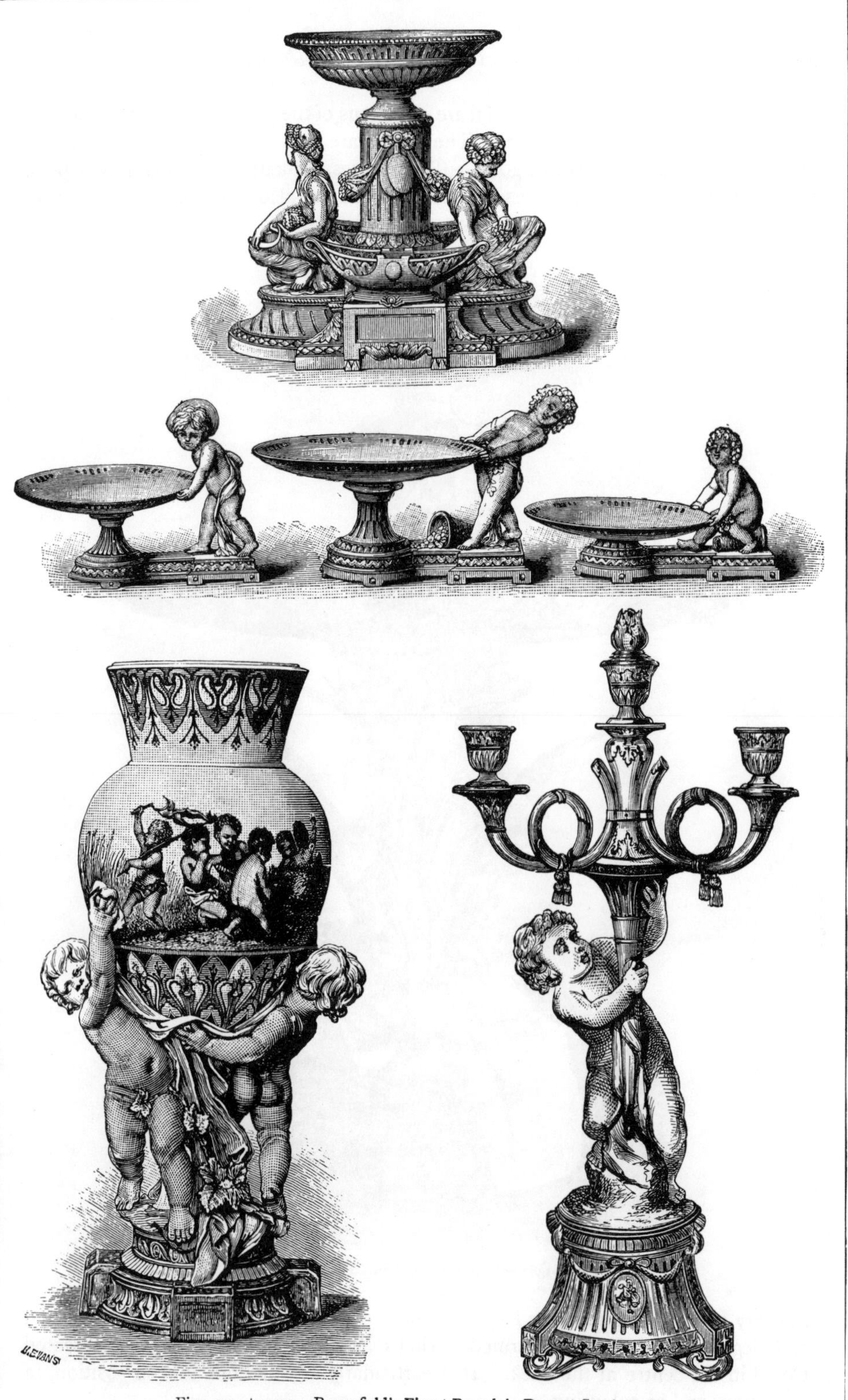

Figs. 1374 to 1379.—Brownfield's Finest Porcelain Dessert Services, &c.

effective. Some of the most successful are imitations of the grand old patterns adopted by Mason on his ironstone china. The stoneware jugs produced are a speciality of this firm, and are remarkably good. Tea services, tea-kettles, teapots, flower-pots, vases, jardinières, trinket services, and other goods, are also produced in earthenware

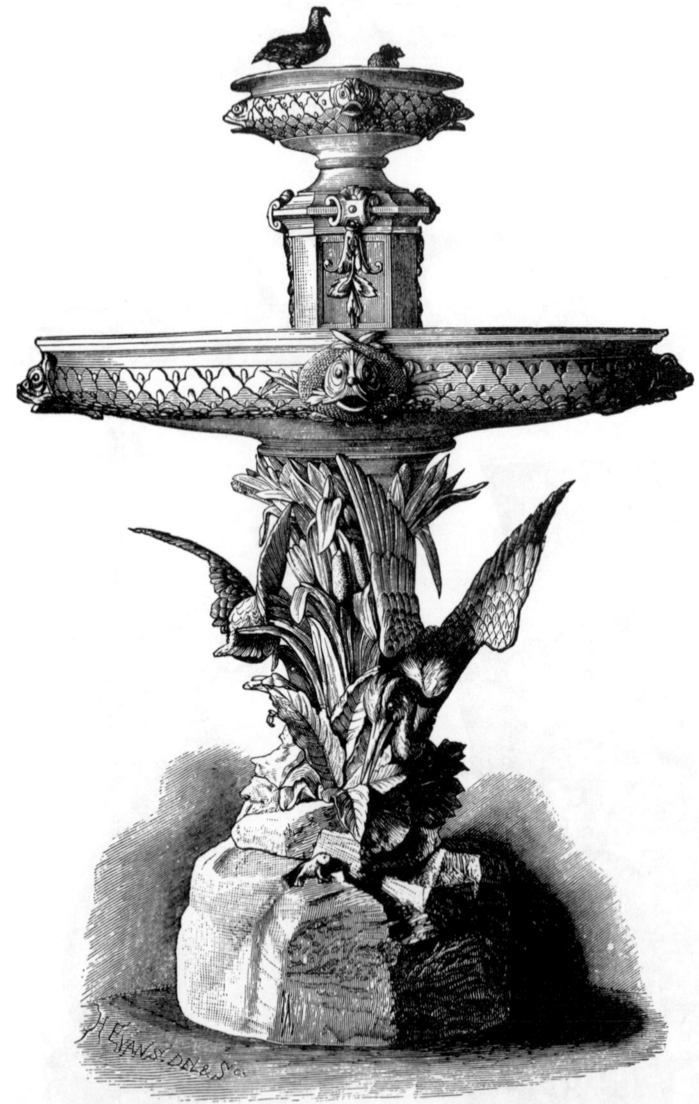

Fig. 1380.—Majolica Fountain. Brownfield's.

in every style of decoration. Notably among these is a remarkably well-designed and elegant strawberry tray, formed of shells and strawberry leaves, with a seated Cupid in the centre at the back. It is particularly artistic both in composition, in execution, and in colouring.

In 1871 the manufacture of china was added to that of earthenware (new buildings being specially erected for the purpose), and the productions in this department have made rapid strides towards perfection. In china, dinner, tea, breakfast, dessert, and other services, jugs, and a variety of useful articles, as well as vases and other fancy goods, are produced. Messrs. B. and S. have, in this branch, produced some novel and very effective designs in dessert services, centre-pieces, fern and flower-stands, &c., and some of their vases are of the highest style of excellence. Notably among these is a pair of magnificent vases, exquisitely painted, with Etty-like subjects of "Morning and Mid-day." These are among the highest achievements of modern Art. Among the minor pieces is an oviform vase representing the hatching of the egg. The body of the vase is true to nature in colour—that of a sea-bird's egg; the handles are formed of the heads, and the bird's legs and feet form the

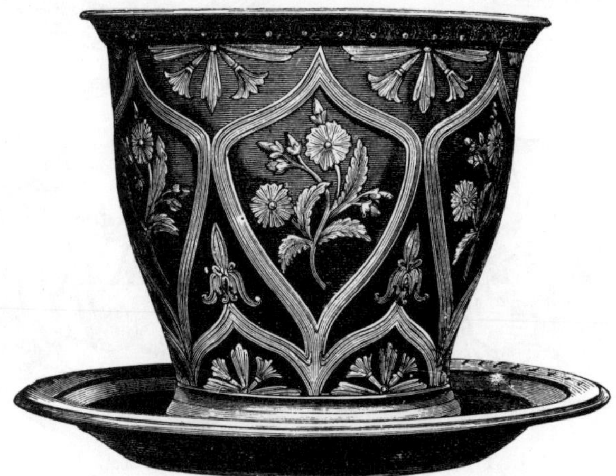

Fig. 1381.

stand. Among the more successful of these recent designs in dessert services are those of which some pieces are engraved on Figs. 1374 to 1379. These are produced in the very finest porcelain, and the figures, representing the Seasons with their attributes, are exquisitely modelled by Protat, while the colouring and gilding are all that can be wished. The candelabra, Fig. 1379, also by Protat, is a very masterly production. At the present time Messrs. Brownfield are engaged upon a fine porcelain vase, the largest ever produced, being over twelve feet in height, the numerous figures with which it is adorned, representing the Seasons and other kindred subjects, being exquisitely modelled by Carrier-Belleuse.

Majolica is another of the specialities of Brownfield's manufacture, and this they produce of the highest class of excellence both in body, in firmness of glaze, in brilliancy of colour, and in design of the various pieces they bring out. One of their latest pieces (a fountain) is engraved on Fig. 1380. It is considerably over five feet in height, and is remarkable, not only as a fine and successful piece of potting, but for the powerful and unconventional manner in which the bulrushes and other foliage, and the birds and lower forms of animal life, are modelled. In this material the firm manufactures somewhat largely all the usual ornamental and useful articles known to the trade.

In Parian, too, a large percentage of figures, groups, busts, vases, and all the usual—and many unusual—elegancies of home life are made. The body is of good quality, and the finish all that could be desired.

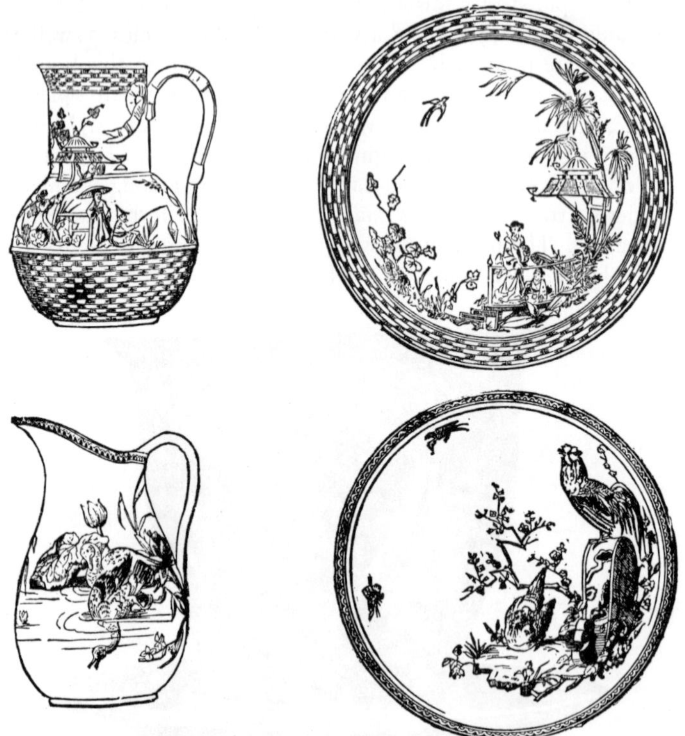

Figs. 1382 to 1385.—Brownfield's Toilet Services.

The mark of the firm upon the printed goods was formerly W & B; W B; or W B & S, in addition to the name of the pattern. The present mark on both earthenware and porcelain is Fig. 1386. The impressed marks are the Staffordshire knot (Fig. 1386), enclosing the initials W B; and the name BROWNFIELD.

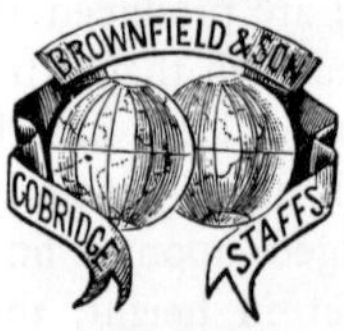

TRADE MARK
BROWNFIELD & SON
COBRIDGE STAFFS

Fig. 1386.

The firm does a large home trade, as well as an export one to Denmark, France, Germany, Holland, Russia, Italy, Spain, Portugal, United States and other parts of America, Canada, Australia, New Zealand, India, and other countries. The manufactory is very extensive, upwards of six hundred persons being employed.

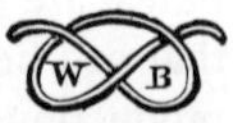

W B

Fig. 1387.

T. Furnival & Sons, who occupy two old manufactories formerly belonging to Adams and to Blackwell, is of old establishment, and rank high as manufacturers of white granite and vitrified ironstone and decorated toilet wares for the United States, Canadian, and Continental markets. For the home trade they produce "patent ironstone" dinner and other services in various styles of decoration. Among their "specialities" are dinner services, &c., of Italian design, in plain white ware, the ornamentation on which is indented from an embossed mould, the lines being as fine and delicate as if cut in by the graver, so as to have the appearance of chasing, and the lines being filled with glaze the surface is still even.

Another noticeable feature is the clever combination of transfer-printing, hand-painting, enamelling, and gilding which characterise some of the services. Figs. 1388 to 1395 show a group of Furnival's general goods, and 1396 a remarkably

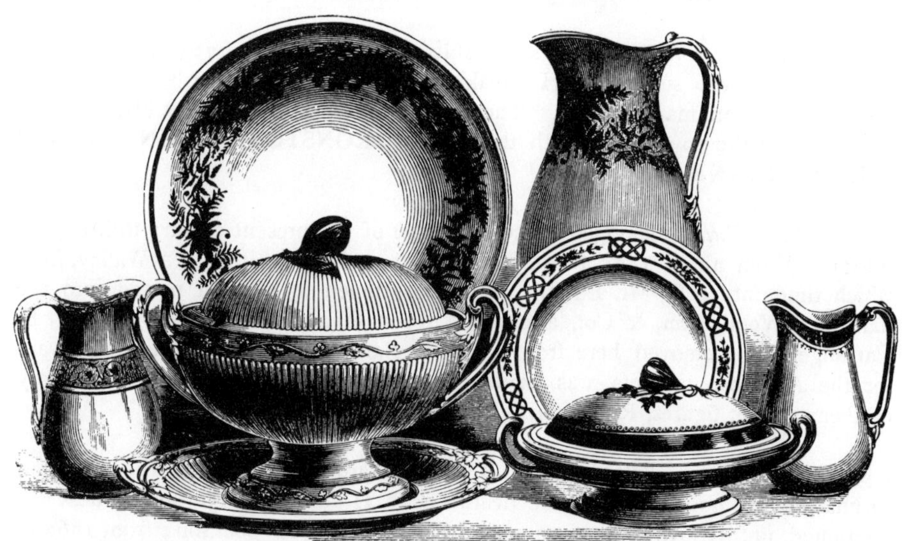

Figs. 1388 to 1395.—Furnival and Co.'s Productions.

elegant flower-pot and stand, with relief figures and other decorations. Among the more successful of their toilet services are the "Swan" and "Nautilus," which are of great beauty. The body of the former ewer is oviform, with bulrush decorations in relief, while a well-modelled swan forms the neck, mouth, and handle. These are produced in white, heightened with gold, and enamelled in colours. The "Nautilus" pattern has the mouth of the ewer formed of a nautilus shell and the handle of coral, while the decorations are sea-weeds. The mark of the firm is simply "FURNIVAL" impressed in the ware. In connection with these works Mr. F. J. Emery, now of the Bleak Hill Works, introduced, a few years ago, a method of crayon drawing and painting on the bisqué surface of earthenware and china which came much in repute, and exquisite drawings have been made in it by some of the first artists of the time, as well as by lady and other amateurs. The bisqué articles and prepared crayons and colours were supplied by Mr. Emery, who afterwards became a partner with Mr. E. Clarke at Longport, and is now proprietor of the Bleak Hill Works.

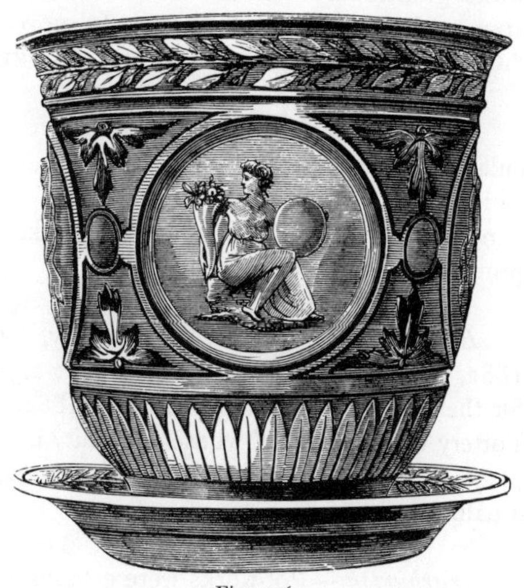

Fig. 1396.

Bates & Bennet (formerly John & Robert Godwin) are manufacturers of general earthenware of ordinary quality, the principal productions being what is called "Imperial measure ware" for the home markets, and also Egyptian black ware, and mortars and pestles.

Abbey Pottery.—At these works, established, it is said, in 1703, Messrs. Wood & Hawthorne, who succeeded H. Meakin in 1879, manufacture white graniteware for the American markets only. They were formerly carried on by Mr. Pearson. The mark is the royal arms, with the words "IRONSTONE CHINA, WOOD & HAWTHORNE, ENGLAND."

The Villa Pottery belonged at the beginning of the present century to Mr. Warburton. From about 1835 to 1850 it was carried on by Jones & Walley, from which time until 1865 Mr. Edward Walley continued it, when it passed into the hands of Wood, Son, & Co., afterwards Wood & Dunn, and in 1879 by W. E. Cartlidge, who removed here from Bourne's Bank. Formerly white graniteware for the American markets was made; Britannia-metal-mounted goods, ordinary earthenware, jet figures, Rockingham, and majolica are now made.

Cobridge Works.—Established in 1836 by Harding & Cockson, who produced ordinary china goods. From the death of Mr. Harding in 1856 the business was continued, until 1861, by his sons, in partnership with Mr. Cockson; from 1862 to 1865 by Charles Cockson alone (during the whole of which time china was produced), and from 1866, when Elijah and David Chetwynd became partners by Cockson & Chetwynd. In 1873 Mr. Cockson died, and in 1876 the firm became Cockson & Seddon, who the following year were succeeded by "Birks Brothers and Seddon." In 1866 the making of china was discontinued and the manufacture of white graniteware for the American trade substituted. The mark is the royal arms and the name "IMPERIAL IRONSTONE CHINA, COCKSON & CHETWYND," or "COCKSON & SEDDON," or "BIRKS BROTHERS & SEDDON."

Cobridge Pottery.—At these extensive works, which have recently been much enlarged (formerly carried on by John Alcock), Henry Alcock & Co. manufacture white graniteware, under the names of "Ironstone china" and "Parisian porcelain," exclusively for the American markets, and also the common descriptions of printed wares.

Elder Road Works.—This pottery, worked by Meakin & Co. from 1865 till 1882, was capable of turning out about 2,500 crates of white graniteware annually for the United States. It passed, in 1882, into the hands of the "Crystal Porcelain Pottery Co., Limited," whose speciality is the production of hard porcelain tiles and plaques, and telegraphic and chemical wares. The mark is the crest, a dove holding a palm-branch.

Warburton.—Pot-works were established here by John Warburton very early in the last century. After his death they were continued by his widow, Ann Warburton. They are stated to have made white stoneware for Holland and the Continent, and to have ultimately brought over some workmen from Delft. Jacob Warburton, the son, succeeded to the business, and died in 1826 at the ripe age of eighty-four,

His son, Peter Warburton, was one of the partners of the New Hall China Works (which see). To him is said by Shaw to belong the credit of printing in gold, and to his mother that of first using soda. In 1810 Peter Warburton took out a patent for "a new method of decorating china, porcelain, earthenware, and glass with native, pure or unadulterated, gold, silver, platina, or other metals, fluxed or lowered with lead or any other substance, which invention or new method leaves the metals after being burned in their metallic state."

Lincoln Pottery.—Messrs. Beech & Tellwright have, since 1882, at these works, manufactured ordinary earthenware, majolica, &c., for both home and foreign markets.

Daniel.—Ralph Daniel, a potter of Cobridge, employed in the early part of last century some workmen from Delft, and to keep their process secret started works at Bagnall for them. About 1743 he introduced the use of plaster of Paris moulds, such as he found were being used in France.

The potters at Cobridge in 1787 were "Joseph Blackwell, manufacturer of blue and white stoneware, cream and painted wares; John Blackwell, ditto; Robert Bucknall, manufacturer of Queen's ware, blue-painted, enamelled, printed, &c.; Thomas and Benjamin Godwin, manufacturers of Queen's ware and china glazed blue; Hales and Adams, potters; Robinson and Smith, potters; and Jacob Warburton, potter." In 1843 they were Wood and Brownfield, John and George Alcock, Francis Dillon, Elijah Jones, Stephen Hughes & Co., Benjamin Endon Godwin, John Mayer Godwin and James Godwin, John and Robert Godwin, George and Ralph Leigh, and Coxon, Harding, & Co. Potteries also, early in last century, existed at Holden Lane, at Milton, and at Sneyd Green. Other potters at one time or another at Cobridge are N. Dillon, R. Stevenson, Mansfield & Hackney, and Rathbone, Hill, & Co.

In 1770 (Feb. 4th) the following Staffordshire potters signed an agreement as to prices:—John Platt, John Lowe, John Taylor, John Cobb, Robt. Bucknall, John Daniel, Thos. Daniel, junr., Richd. Adams, (Dr.) Saml. Chatterley, Thos. Lowe, John Allen, Wm. Parrott, Jacob Warburton, Warburton and Stone, Jos. Smith, Joshua Heath, John Bourn, Jos. Stephens, Wm. Smith, Jos. Simpson, John Weatherby, J. and Rd. Mare, Nicholas Poole, John Yates, Chas. Hassells, Ann Warburton and Son (T. Warburton), Wm. Meir. Other potters were Chas. and Ephraim Chatterley, W. Mellor, and Whitehead.

CHAPTER XX.

HANLEY AND SHELTON.

Miles.—In 1685 Thomas Miles, of Shelton, was a maker of white stoneware of much the same kind as that imported from Germany and Holland. He is stated to have used the Shelton clay, such as had been used by pipe-makers, worked with other clays from Baddeley Edge.

Phillips.—Occasionally pieces are met with bearing the name of this potter, who was of Shelton.

Astbury.—The Astburys were a very old and important family, as connected with the potteries, and one of them, Samuel Astbury, was uncle to Josiah Wedgwood (having married his father's sister, Elizabeth Wedgwood), and in 1744 was one of the witnesses to the deed of his apprenticeship. The discoverer of the use of flint, it appears more than probable, was John Astbury, whose gravestone, in Stoke churchyard, is thus inscribed: "Here lieth the body of John Astbury, the Elder, of Shelton, Potter, who departed this life March 3rd, 1743, aged 55 years." The use of flint was discovered about 1720, when he was about thirty-two years old, and the brothers Elers had previously left the district, about 1710. John Astbury had a son Joshua, of the Foley, who died 1780, as recorded on the same stone. Other sons were Thomas and Samuel. "John Astbury, the elder," as recorded on his tombstone, lost a daughter Margaret, aged six, in 1828, and he had afterwards a second daughter of the same name, who married Robert Garner, potter, and was the mother of Robert Garner (father of Robert Garner, Esq., of Stoke), an eminent potter of Lane End. Twyford, who shares the credit of having wormed out the secrets of the Elers, was a fellow-workman and afterwards a partner of Astbury, and was, either himself or by his descendants, connected with the family.

Baddeley.—Another of the old potteries of this place was carried on in 1750 by R. & J. Baddeley (and in 1787 by J. & E. Baddeley), who, at a somewhat later date, were famous for their blue ware. In 1794 Ralph Baddeley was in business in Shelton, and in 1796 the firm, as appears by their bill-heads, was "John & Edward Baddeley, Shelton." The premises were afterwards used by Hicks, Meigh, & Co. (see Broad Street Works). Of another potter of this name, William Baddeley, a notice will be found on a later page.

Edwards.—Warner Edwards had, last century, works in Albion Street, where he not only manufactured various kinds of wares, but made enamel colours for other houses. He died in 1753, and the premises were afterwards occupied by J. & W. Ridgway. Thomas Daniel, an eminent potter, was his apprentice. During his last illness Warner Edwards handed his book of recipes to this Thomas Daniel, who was father of Spode's clever enameller, Henry Daniel, who afterwards, in conjunction with his son Richard, was a successful manufacturer at Stoke and Hanley. It is worthy of remark that Edwards was a maker of enamel colours full twenty years before Wedgwood took out his patent for them in 1769.

Voyez.—This clever workman, a modeller, was employed by Wedgwood about 1768, and "off and on" afterwards, but was a dishonourable and erratic character. He produced many clever imitations of Wedgwood and Bentley's wares, and is said to have even stamped them with their name, which he forged, and sold the goods as their work. Occasionally his name, J. VOYEZ, is found impressed in the body of the ware.

Palmer.—John Palmer, of Bagnall, about 1680 was a salt-glaze potter, and was the one to whom the discovery of the use of salt was first told. His son, or grandson, Henry Palmer, was also a potter at Hanley (at the Church Works, in High Street, which he probably built), and was a successful imitator of Wedgwood's productions. His Egyptian black or basalt ware, and his jasper ware, are of great excellence and beauty, and very closely resemble those of Wedgwood. He was noted for his piracy of those goods, and surreptitiously obtained Wedgwood's new designs as they came out. His piracy was, however, after a time, carried too far, and an injunction was served upon him to restrain his making Etruscan painted vases in contravention of Wedgwood's patent. This ended in a compromise, Palmer purchasing a share in the patent-right. Intaglios and seals were also, about 1772–73, closely copied by Palmer, much to the annoyance and loss of Wedgwood and Bentley. In 1778 Mr. Palmer failed. Neale, who is said to have been a partner with Palmer so far as his London business was concerned, having arranged matters, the business at Hanley was carried on under the style of "Neale & Palmer" and "Neale & Co." Palmer's mark was in the same style as that of Wedgwood & Bentley—a circle with the name in raised letters (Fig. 1331). Some examples bear the name, stamped, "H. Palmer, Hanley, Staffordshire." Palmer and Neale are said to have married two sisters, the daughters of Thomas Heath, of Lane Delph; and Mr. Pratt, of Fenton, a third daughter.

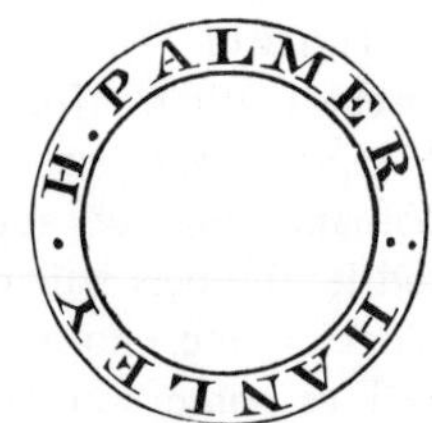

Fig. 1397.

Neale.—Neale, the successor of Palmer, continued the business at Hanley, and produced many remarkably good and artistic articles in basalt, in jasper, and in other wares, and became, if possible, even a more close and clever imitator of Wedgwood's wares than his predecessor had been. In 1780 he had partners, and carried on business as "Neale, Maidment, and Bailey," next, as "Neale & Bailey," and still later, "Neale & Wilson," or, usually, "Neale & Co." His productions are esteemed for excellence of body, cleverness of design, and sharpness of execution. He was succeeded by his partner, and for a time sole manager, Robert Wilson. The marks used by Neale, so far as I have met with them, are "Neale & Co." sometimes in large and at others in small sized letters, impressed in the ware; *NEALE & CO.* in italic capital letters, also impressed; NEALE & CO. in Roman capital letters, also impressed; and "Neale & Wilson." Another

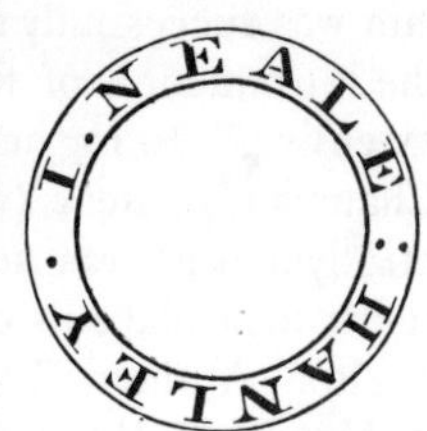

Fig. 1398.

mark, a circle with the name in raised letters, was, like Palmer's, adopted, in form, from Wedgwood & Bentley.

Wilson.—Robert Wilson, the successor to Neale & Wilson, devoted himself mainly to cream-coloured earthenware, more or less decorated. His name is occasionally met with simply as WILSON impressed in the body of the ware, and occasionally in connection with a crown and the distinctive mark C (Fig. 1333). He, and the still more celebrated potter, Elijah Mayer, whose works and residence were just opposite the Church Works, married two sisters of the name of Mayer, but of another family. After the retirement or death of Wilson, his brother David carried on the works (1802). It was afterwards D. Wilson & Sons; then Assignees of Wilson; then Phillips & Bagster. The Phillips of this firm was Jacob, brother to Jonathan Phillips of Oxford Street, London, and uncle to the present Messrs. Phillips of Oxford Street. The firm was then Bagster alone for a while, after which the manufactory and house adjoining, where Bagster had resided, came into the market and were purchased by Joseph Mayer, son and successor of Elijah Mayer. The Church Works were then (1831) rented by William Ridgway & Co., Mr. Ridgway being Joseph Mayer's cousin; and I should here mention that Job Ridgway, the father of William and John Ridgway, had married the sister of Elijah Mayer, Joseph's father. Joseph Mayer had in his employ a clever modeller, Leonard James Abington, who was also a fair chemist, and he placed him in partnership with William Ridgway, and was the "Co." About 1833 Joseph Mayer ceased potting, and let the best part of his works to W. Ridgway & Co. in addition to the Church Works. He, however, retained an oven, and other parts of the works, as well as some warehouses and stabling, &c., adjoining his residence, and had these crammed with some of the best of his stock, Egyptian black, cane, chocolate brown, and Queen's ware, some of the latter elaborately perforated and painted —an indescribable jumble of most beautiful pottery; and there it remained locked up until his death in 1860. To return to the Church Works: the next addition to the firm, as soon as he was old enough to enter it, was William Ridgway's son Edward John, the title of the firm being changed to William Ridgway, Son & Co. In course of time William Ridgway retiring, the two manufactories were carried on by his son, Edward John Ridgway, and L. J. Abington, and it was styled Ridgway & Abington. It was ultimately Edward John Ridgway alone, and is now Powell & Bishop, Mr. E. J. Ridgway having built large works in Bedford Road called the Bedford Works.

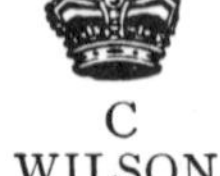

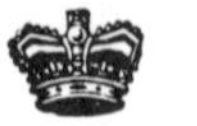

C
WILSON

Fig. 1399.

The *New Hall Works* are historically interesting as being the first in which porcelain was successfully made in Staffordshire, and to them, therefore, must be ascribed the introduction of that art into "the Potteries," since become so famous and so extensive. In my account of the Bristol china works I have shown how Richard Champion's patent (who had purchased the patent right of William Cookworthy, of Plymouth) was sold to a company of Staffordshire potters. This transfer of rights took place in or about 1777. The company consisted of Samuel Hollins, of Shelton, Anthony Keeling, of Tunstall, John Turner, of Lane End, Jacob Warburton, of Hot Lane, William Clowes, of Port Hill, and Charles Bagnall, of Shelton. Of these six persons the following are brief notices :—

Samuel Hollins, a maker of the fine red-ware teapots, &c., from the clay at

Bradwell previously worked by the brothers Elers, was of Shelton, and was the son of Mr. Hollins, of the Upper Green, Hanley. He was an excellent practical potter, and made many improvements in his art. He was afterwards one of the partners of the New Hall China Works, and his successors in the manufactory were his sons, Messrs. T. & J. Hollins.

Anthony Keeling, of Tunstall, was son-in-law of the celebrated potter, Enoch Booth, having married his daughter Ann. Keeling succeeded Enoch Booth in his business, which he carried on successfully for many years. He erected a large house near the works, but in 1810 retired on a small independence to Liverpool, where he died. He was the principal support of a small sect calling themselves "Sandemanians," who had their place of worship in his works.

John Turner, first of Stoke and then of Lane End, father of John and William Turner, was one of the most clever and successful potters Staffordshire ever produced, but one about whom little has been written. In 1762 he commenced manufacturing at Lane End, and made many improvements in the art, and by the discovery of a vein of fine clay at Green Dock was enabled successfully to compete not only with other potters, but with Wedgwood himself. Many of his productions in black and in jasper, &c., equal those of Wedgwood, and are often mistaken for them. Turner's cream-ware and stoneware (of which his jugs are best known to collectors) rank high in excellence both of design and manipulation. Mr. Turner is stated to have been deputed, with Wedgwood, by the Staffordshire potters to oppose the extension of the patent to Champion.

Jacob Warburton, of Hot, or Holt Lane, a man highly respected by every class, and who lived until the year 1826, was born in 1740, and passed his long and useful life as a potter, in which art he rose to considerable eminence. He was the "last member of the old school of potters, the early friend and contemporary of the 'father of the Potteries,' Josiah Wedgwood, with whom he was for many years in the habit of confidential intercourse and friendship. Numerous are the benefits which the public derived from the united exertions of the talents and abilities of these two venerated characters on every point connected with the local interest and prosperity of the Staffordshire Potteries." Besides being one of the most clever and energetic potters, "he was a good scholar, and a man of pure taste; he had read extensively, and his memory was tenacious in a very extraordinary degree. He was equally distinguished for his moral and convivial habits of mind, for the soundness of his intellect and the goodness of his heart. He spoke fluently the French, Dutch, and German languages, and was learning the Italian up to the very period of his death." He retained his activity of body and mind to the last, and though eighty-six years of age, set out the day preceding his death to walk to Cobridge. He died while a friend was reading to him. Mr. Warburton, who was a Roman Catholic, was twice married. For some years before his decease he had retired from business, and died at his residence, Ford Green, in the parish of Norton.

William Clowes, of Port Hill, was, it is said, only a sleeping partner in the concern. In 1787 "Clowes & Williamson" were "potters" at Fenton.

Charles Bagnall, of Shelton, who had previously been with Joshua Heath, was a potter of considerable experience in the middle of last century. He was probably a son of the potter of the same name who was a maker of butter-pots in Burslem in 1710-15. The family has been connected with Staffordshire for many generations.

The company, being thus formed, purchased the patent-right from Richard Champion, who removed into Staffordshire to superintend the establishing of the new works in that county. The first operations were conducted at the works of one of the partners, Anthony Keeling, at Tunstall, which then was a mere small street, or rather roadway, with only a few houses—probably not more than a score—scattered about it and the lanes leading to Chatterley and Red Street. To this spot, the forerunner of the present large and important town, Cookworthy's patent was brought, and here, with the experienced potters who had become its purchasers, and under the management of Champion, who had produced such exquisite specimens of art at Bristol, and who had been induced, as a part of the arrangement, to superintend the manufacture, the first pieces of china made in Staffordshire, with the exception of the trial pieces of Littler, were produced. To accommodate the new branch of manufacture at Keeling's pot-works some alterations of course became necessary, and thus it was some little time before the partners had the satisfaction of seeing anything produced under their patent-right. Disagreements also arose, which ended in Turner and Keeling withdrawing from the concern, and about 1780 Keeling is said to have removed to London. The remaining partners removed their work from Keeling's premises, and took a house in Shelton, known as "Shelton Hall," afterwards the "New Hall," in contradistinction to the "Old Hall," celebrated as being the birthplace of Elijah Fenton, the poet. At this time Shelton Hall, which had been purchased in 1773 of Alice Dalton, widow (who had inherited it from her brother, Edward Burslem Sundell), by Humphrey Palmer, was occupied by his son, Thomas Palmer, as a pot-works. In 1777 Humphrey Palmer, intending a second marriage with Hannah Ashwin, of Stratford-on-Avon, gave a rent-charge of £30 on the Hall and pot-works, and a life interest in the rest of the estate, as a dower to that lady, reserving the right for his son, Thomas Palmer, the potter, to get clay and marl from any part of the estate for his own use. In 1789 Humphrey Palmer and his wife being both dead, the estate passed to their infant and only child, Mary Palmer, of whose successor's executors, after some uninteresting changes, it was ultimately purchased by the china manufacturers. At this time the works had been considerably increased, and they grew gradually larger, till, in 1802, they are described as three messuages, three pot-works, one garden, fifty acres of land, thirty acres of meadow, and forty acres of pasture, &c. About the time of the withdrawal of Keeling and Turner from the partnership, and the removal of the works from Tunstall to Shelton, Richard Champion left.

Fairly settled at New Hall, the company (Hollins, Warburton, Clowes, and Bagnall) took as their manager John Daniel, who afterwards became a partner. A considerable quantity of china was produced under the patent, but the most extensive and profitable branch of the New Hall business was the making and vending of the glaze called "composition," made according to Champion's specification, which was supplied by the New Hall firm to the potters of the neighbourhood, and even sent to other localities, to a large extent and at a highly remunerative price. The ware made at this period was precisely similar in body and glaze to that of Bristol, to which, from the fact of some of the same artists being employed, it bears also a marked resemblance in ornamentation. In 1796 the patent, which had been enjoyed successively by Cookworthy, Champion, and the Staffordshire company for a period of twenty-eight years, expired; but the company continued to make the hard paste china, and to supply "composition" to other manufacturers. In 1810 the firm (Samuel Hollins, of Shelton, Peter Warburton, son of Jacob Warburton of Cobridge,

John Daniel, of Hanley, and William Clowes, of Port Hill) purchased the New Hall estate for £6,800. In 1815 Peter Warburton died, leaving his share in the works to his father (Jacob Warburton) and John Daniel, as trustees under his will. In 1821 John Daniel died, and two years afterwards Samuel Clowes died also. John Daniel, I presume, was a son of Ralph Daniel, to whom the potters were indebted for the discovery of making moulds in plaster of Paris instead of in brass, as previously done. Mr. Daniel is said to have visited the potteries and porcelain manufactories in France, and brought back with him a mould of cast plaster of Paris, which he showed and introduced to the English makers. The potters, however, knew so little of the process by which the mould was produced that they got blocks of the gypsum of Derbyshire and *cut* their moulds in them, until it was explained that the gypsum must be first burned and ground, and then cast.

Hard paste porcelain continued to be made at New Hall until about 1810 or 1812, when the bone paste, which had been gradually making its way in the district, finally superseded it, and the company continued their works on the newer system. In 1825 the entire stock of the concern, which had for a short time been carried on for the firm by a person named Tittensor, was sold off, and the manufacture of china entirely ceased at New Hall.

The works, after having been closed for a short time, were opened by William Ratcliffe, who for a few years made the commoner description of white and printed earthenware for ordinary home consumption. In 1842 they passed into the hands of W. Hackwood & Son, who removed from their works near Joiner Square (now called the "Eastwood Pottery"), and in 1849, Mr. Hackwood senior having died, they were continued by the son, Thomas Hackwood. The goods were the ordinary descriptions of earthenware, principally for Continental markets, and bore the name of HACKWOOD impressed. In 1856 they passed into the hands of Cockson & Harding, who manufactured the same kind of goods, using for a mark C & H, LATE HACKWOOD, impressed on the bottom. In 1862, Mr. Cockson having retired from the concern, the works were carried on by the remaining partners, W. and J. Harding (Brothers), who, besides an extensive trade with Holland and Italy in cream-coloured and printed wares, produced druggists' fittings, as well as black, Egyptian, Rockingham, and tinted wares. In 1872 Messrs. Harding gave up the business, when Mr. John Aynsley, china manufacturer, of Longton, purchased the back portion of the works and let it to Thomas Booth & Sons. The entire front of the New Hall Works was purchased by Mr. Henry Hall, metal mounter of jugs, teapots, &c., so that the manufactory became divided into two distinct properties. The portion occupied by Messrs. Booth having been burnt down has been rebuilt. Their productions were the usual classes of ordinary earthenware in printed, painted, enamelled, and gilt services; stoneware, in which a large variety of jugs and teapots were made, and jasper ware. They were succeeded in their business in 1880 by Ambrose Bevington & Co., who continue the manufacture.

Specimens of the hard paste of the New Hall Works are rare. They are almost entirely without mark, but sometimes there is an incised letter N as here shown. Fig. 1402 exhibits a beautifully painted teapot. On one side is a group of children playing at blindman's-buff. They are dressed in the characteristic costume of the latter part of last century; but what renders the group peculiarly interesting is that in the background is a view of a pot-works, with kiln, which may probably have been a representation of the works when this interesting piece was made. It was

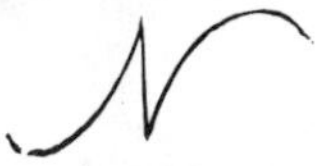

N

Fig. 1400.

painted by Duvivier, a French artist of celebrity, who, as well as Bone, was employed at these works. Fig. 1401 is a cup and saucer of excellent form and twisted fluting. Fig. 1404 is a jug bearing in front the initials S. D. of Samuel Daniel, a cousin of John Daniel, one of the partners, and is in the possession of Mr. Daniel, of Hanley.

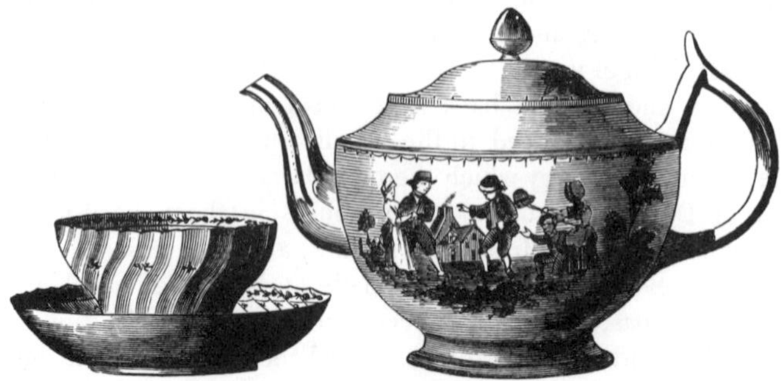

Figs. 1401 and 1402.—New Hall China.

Fig. 1340 is a coffee-cup and saucer, and Fig. 1459 is part of a dessert service belonging to Mr. Gray, which was made for Mr. Daniel, one of the partners. The porcelain made at New Hall principally consisted of tea, dinner, and dessert services of various designs; but figures and busts, as well as vases, were also to some extent produced there.

The later productions of the New Hall China Works, the soft paste, are also scarce, especially the marked pieces. The body is of good colour and clear, and the decorations, especially the flowered examples, are remarkable for the brightness of their colours. The only mark used—and this was not, it appears, adopted until after 1820—is the one here shown.

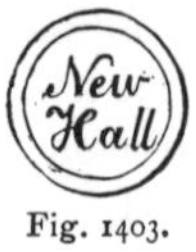

New Hall

Fig. 1403.

Batt printing was practised at New Hall, and some remarkably good examples have come under my notice. In 1810 Peter Warburton, on behalf of the company of which he was a partner, is said to have taken out a patent "for printing landscapes and other designs from copper-plates, in gold and platinum, upon porcelain and pottery." The company was also among the first to adopt the improvements in printing on ware made by William Brookes in the beginning of the present century.

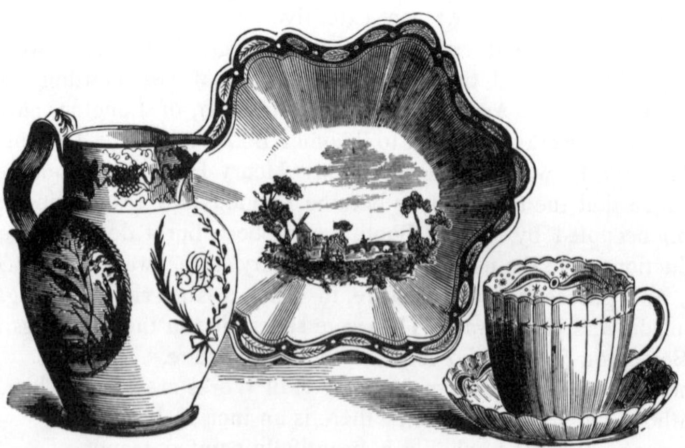

Figs. 1404 to 1406.—New Hall China.

Glass.—Joseph Glass was a potter in Hanley in the middle of the seventeenth century, and his works are stated to have been still carried on by him or his son, Joseph Glass, in the beginning of the eighteenth. "Joseph Glass . . . . clowdy, and a sort of dishes, painted with different coloured slips, and sold at 3*s.* and 3*s.* 6*d.* per dozen." A tyg bearing his name, IOSEPH GLASS S V H G X, painted round the body, is in the Staniforth collection. Later on the works were carried on by John Glass, and from him passed to Samuel Keeling & Co., then to Meakin Brothers, and lastly to Taylor Brothers. The works, situated in Market Street, have been pulled down. Samuel Keeling, who was great-nephew to James Keeling, an important manufacturer and patentee towards the close of the last century, was one of the patriarchs of the Potteries, and resided in partial retirement at Rocester.

Twyford.—Twyford, the potter already named, "commenced business near Shelton Old Hall, the seat of Elijah Fenton's family; and the only known specimen of his manufacture," says Shaw, "is a jug made for T. Fenton, Esq.," then in the possession of his descendant. He and his children and grandchildren continued as potters, and are represented by Mr. Thomas Twyford, of the Bath Street Works.

Mare, or *Maer*, or *Mayer.*—In the early part of the last century Hugh Mare and John Mare were potters at Hanley, and produced black and mottled wares. Later on were "Elijah Mayer" or "E. Mayer," then "Elijah Mayer & Son," and next "Joseph Mayer."

The potters enumerated in Hanley in 1787 were, "Sampson Bagnall, potter; Joseph Boon, ditto; C. & E. Chatterley, potters; John Glass, potter; Heath, Warburton & Co., china manufacturers; Edward Keeling, potter; John and Richard Mare, potters; Elijah Mayer, enameller; William Miller, potter; Neal & Wilson, potters; Samuel Perry, potter; George Taylor, ditto; Thomas Wright, ditto; and John Yates, ditto." In Shelton, "J. & E. Baddeley; John Hassels; Heath & Bagnell; Samuel Hollins; Anthony Keeling; Taylor & Pope; G. Twemlow; Christopher Charles Whitehead; and John Yates," all potters.

Others early last century were William Simpson, Richard Marsh, Moses Sandford, and John Ellis. Those enumerated by Ward in 1843 are the Old Hall, the New Hall, Cauldon Place, William Ridgway and partners (six manufactories), Thomas Dimmock & Co. (four manufactories—formerly James Whitehead, J. and W. Handley, Edmund John Birch, and Christopher Whitehead); Samuel Keeling & Co., formerly John Glass; William Hackwood; Samuel and John Burton, formerly James Keeling; Samuel Mayer, formerly Sarah Brown's; Thomas Furnival, junior, & Co., formerly Reuben Johnson's; George Lomas, formerly Barlow and Hammersley's; Joseph Clementson, formerly Elijah Jones's (who was a potter about 1760); Yates & May, formerly John and William Yates, successors to their father; William Dudson, formerly William Rivers & Co.; William White, formerly Poulson's; Henry Mills, then newly erected, and other smaller factories. Edward Phillips was also a manufacturer, and used his name in full, "Edward Phillips, Shelton, Staffordshire," on his goods. Other names are J. Sneyd, Toft & May, and T. Taylor.

In 1829 the manufactories named by Shaw were E. Mayer & Son; Job Meigh & Son (Old Hall); Dimmock & Co.; Toft & May; J. Keeling; W. Hackwood; T. Taylor; J. Glass; J. & W. Ridgway; Hicks, Meigh, & Johnson; H. Daniel & Sons; J. Yates; and Hollins, Warburton, Daniel, & Co. (New Hall).

John Twemlow was in business in 1797. An invoice in my possession is curious as showing some of the goods he made. These are "E Black Teapots, capt., fest^{d} and fig$^{d.}$" (Egyptian black teapots, capped, festooned, and figured); "ditto upright, fest$^{d.}$ and fig$^{d.}$"; "Oval E Black Teapots;" ditto "prest leaf," "scollop top, fest$^{d.}$ and fig$^{d.}$ and banded"; "ditto, prest leaf and fest$^{d.}$ and fig$^{d.}$ and banded a'tip;" "ditto creams" to match; "ditto fluted;" "ditto coffee-pots;" octagon teapots, with scollop top, and creams to match; oval plain teapots (all, so far, are in Egyptian black); "blue and enamelled handled cups and saucers, London size, sprig and border and vine pattern;" "bowls to match."

Old Hall Works.—The "Old Hall Works" are among the most historically interesting of any in the district, being built on the site of or quite closely adjoining

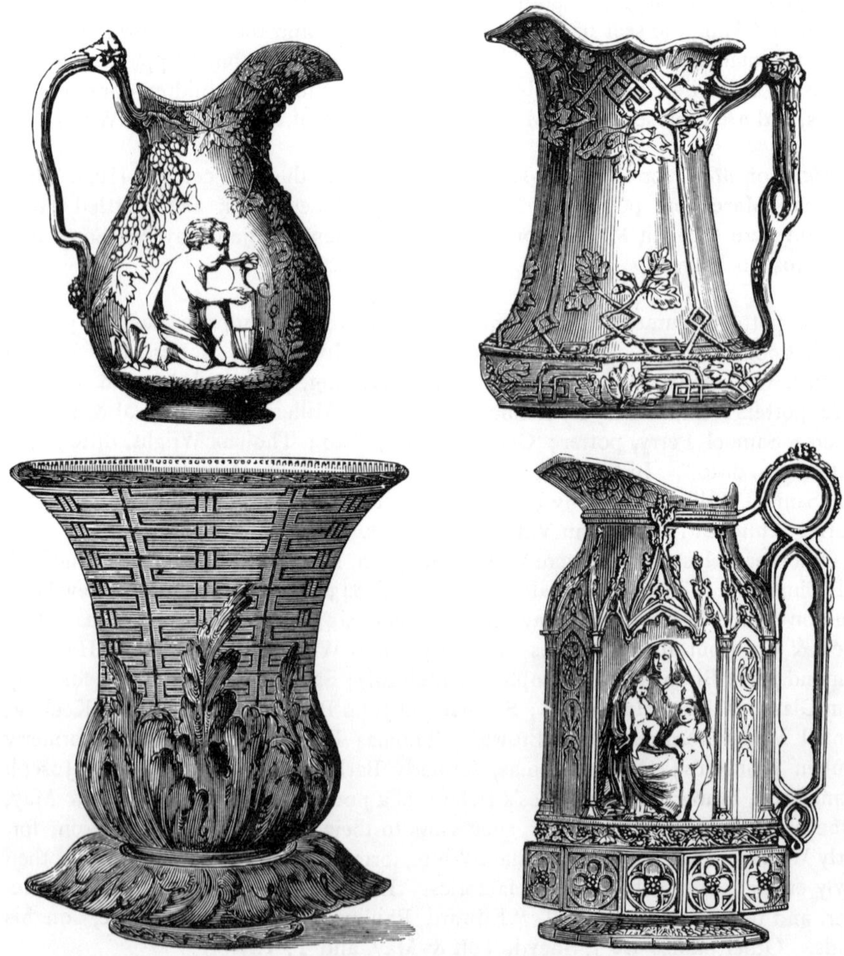

Figs. 1407 to 1410.—1851 Exhibits of Mr. Meigh, Old Hall Works.

to the "Old Hall" or Manor House of the Colclough family, who formerly held the lordship of Hanley from about the time of Edward III. until about a century and a half ago, when it passed into the family of Bagnall. The "Old Hall" or "Manor

House" has long since disappeared. The present works were built about the year 1770 by Job Meigh, on what I believe was for a time previously a salt-glaze white stoneware pottery, carried on by a Mr. Whitehead. From 1770 until 1861 the works were uninterruptedly carried on by Job Meigh, his son, and his grandson (Charles Meigh) successively. In 1861 Mr. Charles Meigh transferred the business to a limited liability company, called "The Old Hall Earthenware Company," by whom it is still carried on. The productions include every variety of earthenware, from the most highly decorated to the ordinary blue printed and plain white wares, stoneware, jet ware, and Parian. In earthenware all the usual dinner, tea, breakfast, dessert, toilet, and other services, and all other articles are made. In these the body is of the finest quality, hard, and of remarkable durability, and the glaze hard, clear, and faultless. Many of the patterns of dinner services are of great beauty and elegance. Especially among these are the "Nonpareil," the "Verona," and the "Koh-i-noor" shapes, which last is one of the most simply elegant yet produced. The form of the covered dishes is chaste and remarkably effective. They stand upon well-modelled feet, and the handles are formed of folds of ribbon held together by jewelled rings. This pattern is produced in various styles of decoration, one of the most pleasing of which is the convolvulus, exquisitely coloured after nature. The gilding is rich and substantial. Among the patterns produced by the staff of artists here employed are many others of surpassing beauty; the excellence of the painting, the gilding, the jewelling, and the enamelling being very apparent in all, and the combination of printing and hand painting carried to great perfection. Dessert services are made in every style of decoration, the richer and more costly varieties being equal to any produced by other firms, both in quality of body, in shape, in pattern, and in artistic treatment. Toilet services form a very extensive branch of the productions, and in these the firm is very successful. Among the more popular shapes are the "Buckle," "Richmond," "Perth," "Exeter," and "Mediæval," and these are produced in every style of decoration. In stoneware, jugs and other articles are produced; in black ware, water-bottles, elegant little table tea-kettles, spill-cases, vases, and other articles are made, and are effectively decorated with dead and burnished gilding, enamelling, &c.; in Parian, vases, groups, busts, figures, and other ornamental articles are produced. The body is of good quality and the modelling and finish of faultless excellence.

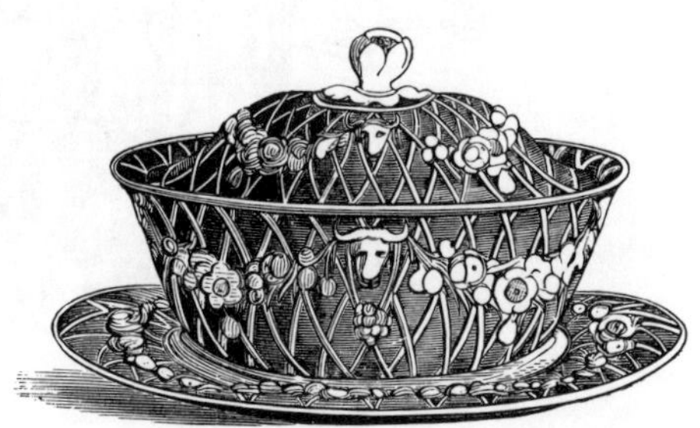

Fig. 1411.

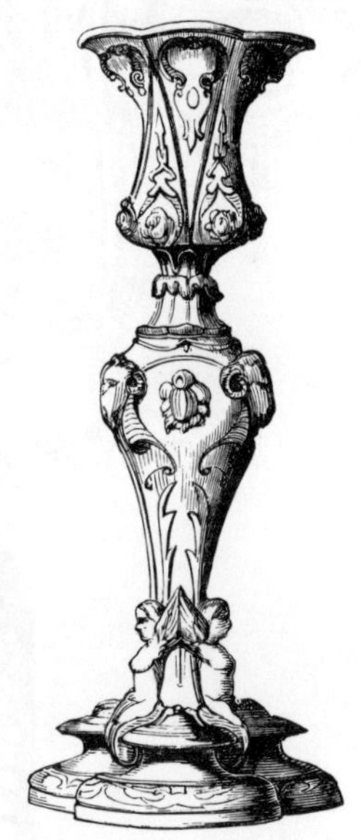

Fig. 1412.

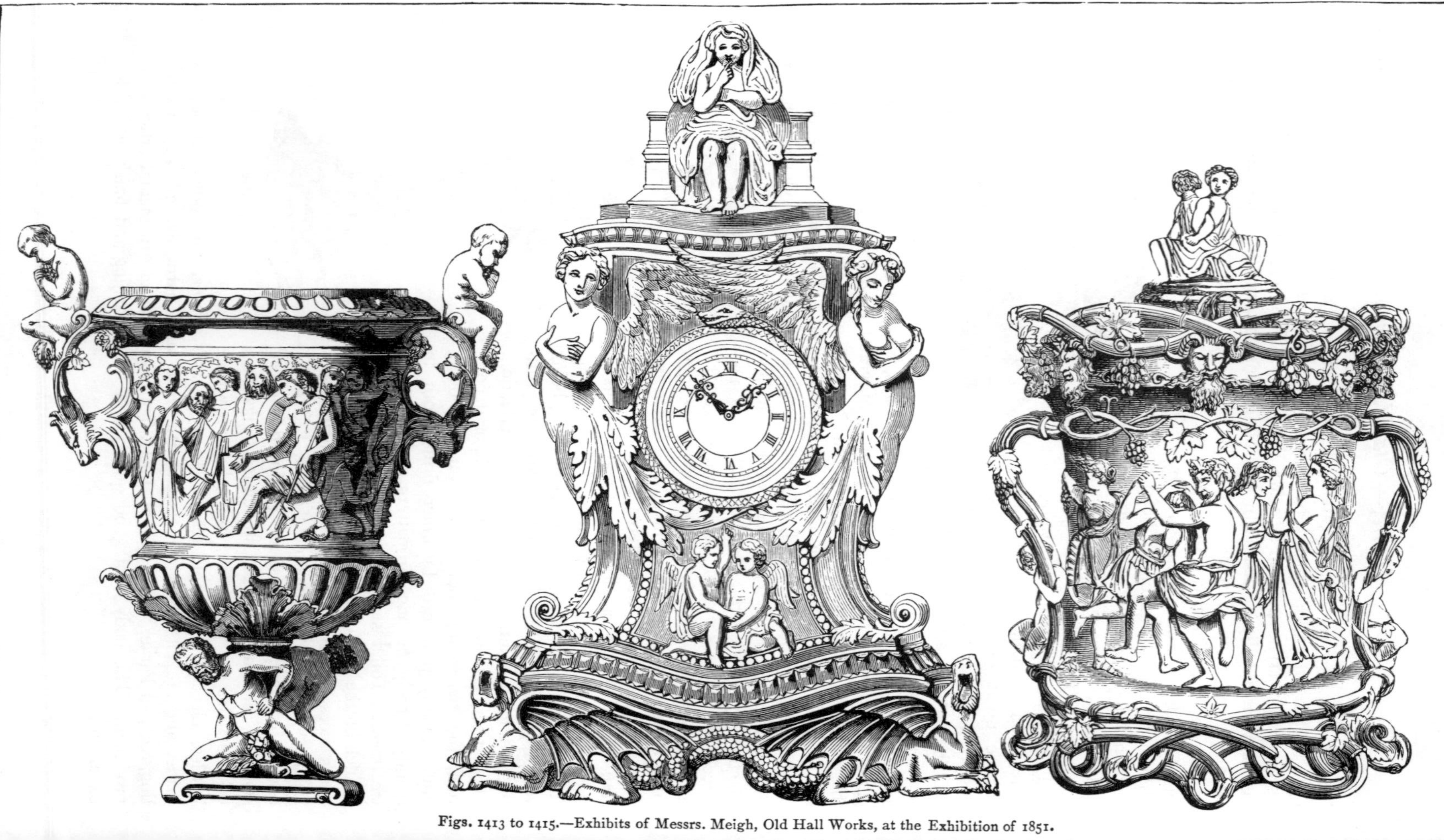

Figs. 1413 to 1415.—Exhibits of Messrs. Meigh, Old Hall Works, at the Exhibition of 1851.

The marks of these works are the following:—

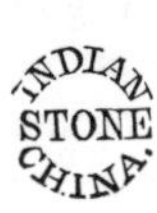

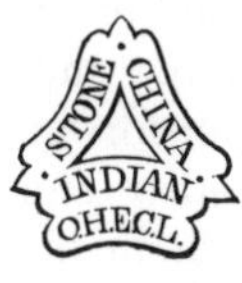

OPAQUE PORCELAIN

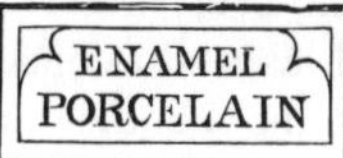

MEIGH.

Figs. 1416 to 1420.

In 1851 medals were awarded to Mr. C. Meigh, who has also received medals from the Society of Arts. Figs. 1407 to 1410 are stoneware jugs, and 1412 a candlestick adapted from a celebrated wine-cup, the work of Cellini. Figs. 1413 to 1415 exhibit a clock-case, a vase, and a drinking-cup or tankard, all in statuary porcelain and of the finest style of art. The markets principally supplied are the home, French, German, Indian, American, Australian, and colonial.

Broad Street Works.—These works are interesting as being the place where the celebrated "Mason's Patent Ironstone China," as well as the "Ironstone China" of the old firm of Hicks, Meigh, and Johnson, in addition to most varieties of useful earthenware, are made. Charles James Mason, the inventor of this famous "Mason's Ironstone China," was a potter of great taste and skill at Lane Delph (now Middle Fenton), and in 1813 took out a patent for his process. The manufacture was carried on under the styles of "G. M. and C. J. Mason" and "C. J. Mason & Co.;" the partners being Charles James Mason and his brother George Miles Mason (father of Mason the artist), who in 1832 unsuccessfully contested the borough of Stoke-upon-Trent. After a time G. M. Mason withdrew from the concern, which was then continued by the patentee alone. From want of capital and other causes it, however, gradually dwindled down, and in 1851 Mr. Francis Morley purchased the patent, moulds, copper-plates, and entire business from Mr. Mason, and removed the whole to his manufactory. Mr. Morley, who married a daughter of Mr. W. Ridgway, and was a partner in the firm of Morley, Wear, & Co., succeeded to the old-established concern of Hicks, Meigh, & Johnson, which he carried on for a time under the style of "Ridgway & Co.," and afterwards as F. Morley & Co. This manufactory was one of the oldest in the Potteries. It was in existence in the early part of the last century (probably established about 1720), and afterwards belonged to John Baddeley (in 1750 R. and J. Baddeley), an eminent potter, who died in 1772. Here, it is said, printing in oil was first practised. Hicks, Meigh, & Johnson were among the most successful of the manufacturers in the district, and produced, among other wares, a remarkably good quality of ironstone china. Besides this, they were large manufacturers of earthenware of the ordinary and finer kinds, and of china. They and Mason were the only makers of ironstone china; and when Mr. Morley became also the owner of Mason's process, moulds, plates, &c., he became the *only* manufacturer of ironstone ware, and soon established a lucrative business in "Mason's" wares. In 1856 a first-class medal for this ware was awarded at the French Exhibition. Mr. Morley retired in 1859, having sold the entire business, moulds, copper-plates, &c., to Geo. L. and Taylor Ashworth (brothers), who continued the manufacture of the "Patent Ironstone China," which they and their predecessor named the "Real Ironstone China" on their marks, and produced all Mason's best patterns in services, vases, &c., made from his original models. They also manufacture Meigh's ironstone, from his old moulds, &c. This manufacture has been very largely developed by Mr. Taylor Ashworth, to whom the art is indebted for many improvements. Messrs. Ashworth, besides these features of their trade, make table, toilet, dessert, and other services, and ornamental goods of the best quality, in every description of general earthenware; and sanitary goods are also produced, as well as insulators for our own and for foreign Governments. In vases and jugs the handles are usually dragons and other grotesque animals. The Indian vases are of perfect form, exquisite design, rich in their colours, and massive in gilding. The marks used by Mason were principally the following :—

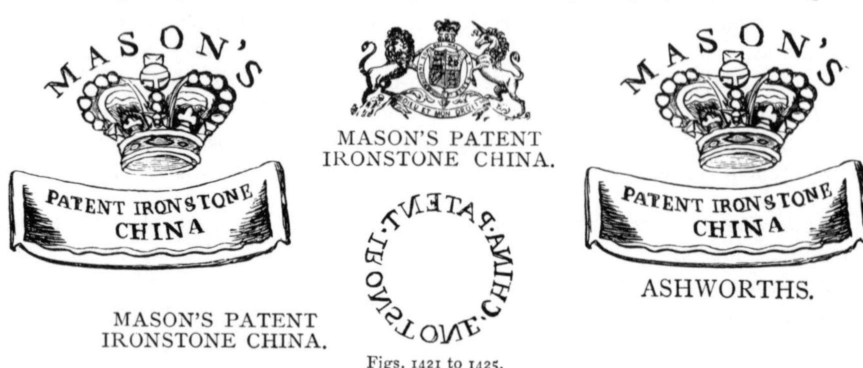

Figs. 1421 to 1425.

Figs. 1421 to 1423 are printed, usually in blue, on the bottoms of the pieces, and Figs. 1424 and 1425 impressed in the body of the ware.

After the patent passed out of Mason's hands into those of Morley and Co., the principal mark was impressed in the ware, and the royal arms, with supporters, crest, motto, &c., above the words IRONSTONE CHINA printed on the bottom of the goods. The later marks are on a garter, "Real Ironstone China," enclosing the royal arms and "G. L. Ashworth & Bros, Hanley;" Mason's mark with the addition of ASHWORTHS; a crown, with the words ASHWORTH BROS above, and a ribbon bearing the words REAL IRONSTONE CHINA beneath it; and the royal arms, with supporters, crest, motto, &c., and the words, IRONSTONE CHINA.

REAL
IRONSTONE
CHINA

ASHWORTH
REAL
IRONSTONE
CHINA.

Mason at one time produced jugs and other articles in what he called Bandana or Sandana ware, the designs of which were complicated Indian foliage and grotesque animals, printed in red and black on a buff or other ground. The mark, on a jug in my own possession, is a circular garter bearing the words, "Mason's Bandana Ware, 1851," and enclosing the words "Patentee of the Patent Ironstone China;" the whole surmounted by a crown. I have an impression of a similar mark, which for some purpose has evidently been altered to Sandana, and the date to 1801. As Mason's patent was only granted in 1813, the alteration of this mark is very palpable.

Cauldon Place.—These works were founded about 1794, and the present manufactory built in 1802, by Job Ridgway, who died in 1814, father of John and William Ridgway, and were carried on as "Ridgway & Sons." After some years, a dissolution of partnership took place, John Ridgway continuing the Cauldon Place Works, and William removing to a new manufactory which he had erected, and who, in 1843, held, with his partners—composing three or four distinct firms of which he was head—six different manufactories in Hanley and Shelton. John

Ridgway continued, with various changes of partners, under the firm of "John Ridgway & Co.," until 1855, when the Cauldon Place business passed into the hands of the present firm of "T. C. Brown-Westhead, Moore, & Co.," Mr. Ridgway continuing his connection with it until 1858. Mr. W. Moore, who had for many years been a valuable assistant of Mr. Ridgway, died in 1866, and his brother, James Moore, succeeding to the management of the potting, was admitted into partnership in 1875. Mr. James Moore died in 1881, when his nephew, Mr. F. T. Moore, took the entire management of the potting department. In 1882, Mr. T. C. Brown-Westhead died, when Mr. Wm. B. Moore, the elder son of the late Wm. Moore (unitedly with his brother Mr. Fredk. T. Moore) took the entire management of the business. Extensive additions have been made to the manufactory in a long range of new buildings, giving increased warehouse accommodation, with rooms for artists, designers, modellers, and engravers, and a new show-room 68 feet by 36 feet, 17 feet in height, with a lantern light, making the total height 23 feet (the finest in the district), fitted up at considerable cost, and approached by a noble stone staircase contiguous to the offices. The show-room contains a varied selection of patterns and goods of a costly character and of great artistic skill and beauty. The entire premises have been considerably enlarged, and the "*Royal Victoria Works*" added.

The goods produced at Cauldon Place embrace almost every description of ceramics. In earthenware all the usual table and toilet services and useful and ornamental articles of every class are made. In china, which is of high quality and especial durability, an immense variety of services and articles are produced, and all are equally good in point of artistic decoration; the ground colours are of a remarkable purity and evenness; the gilding, both dead and burnished, of unusual solidity, and the painting of the most exquisite character. The same remarks apply with equal force to the dessert ware, some of the patterns of which are of surpassing loveliness, and give evidence of the highest and most successful cultivation of decorative art. Vases of pure and severe taste in form, and displaying great skill and judgment in decoration, are also produced. Among other elegant articles are a sandwich-box of white china wicker-work, with a fern leaf laid across the lid, on which rests the butterfly which forms the handle. Another is an oblong, angular-handled square basket, with flowers, stems and foliage exquisitely modelled by the most skilful artists, and tinted true to nature; and others are vases decorated in the same charming manner, with roses and sprays of hawthorn of surpassing loveliness. In this, as in other styles of decoration, the "Cauldon Place" works is paramount above all others. In tea services several novel ideas have been introduced. One has the handle of the cup formed of a cord, doubled and passed through a loop, and either tied around the rim or formed into four knots as feet. The "egg-shell" china, white body, lined with *Rose du Barry*, is finer and of higher class than is usually produced, and the floral decorations in raised gold, silver, and colour are perfection itself, both in design and in manipulation. Another admirable contrivance, patented by Toft, is a self-acting lid or cover for hot-water jugs, &c. By this contrivance the lid is hung on a pivot or axle, which fits into a notch on each side the mouth of the vessel, so that, being lightly hung, it opens whenever the jug is sloped for pouring, and closes again when held or set down in an upright position. A novelty (registered) in tea and coffee services is the "zephyr" shape, in which the bottom rim of the cup, and the flat outer rim of the saucer, are delicately perforated and massively gilt; the pieces themselves being exquisitely painted in

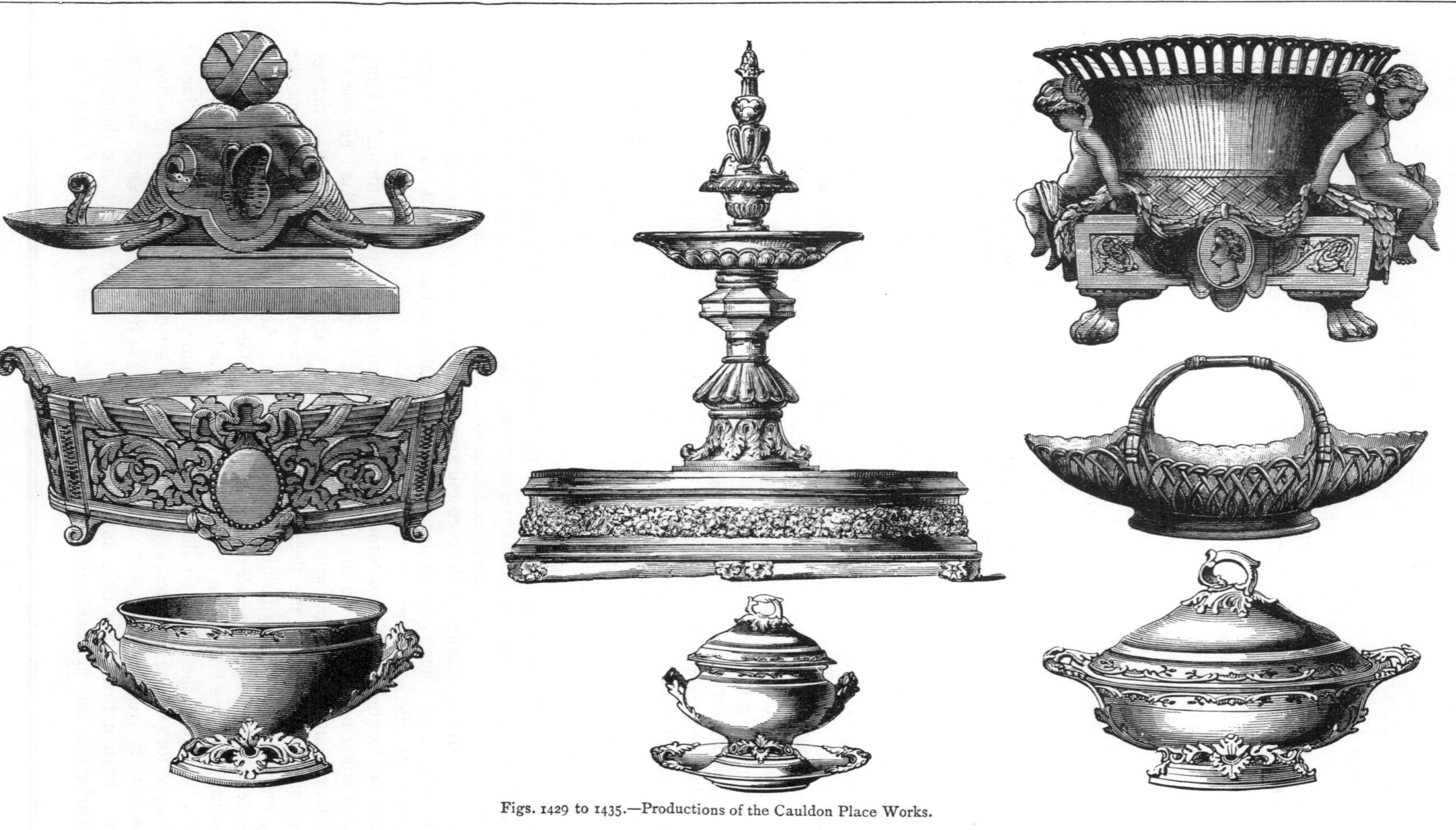

Figs. 1429 to 1435.—Productions of the Cauldon Place Works.

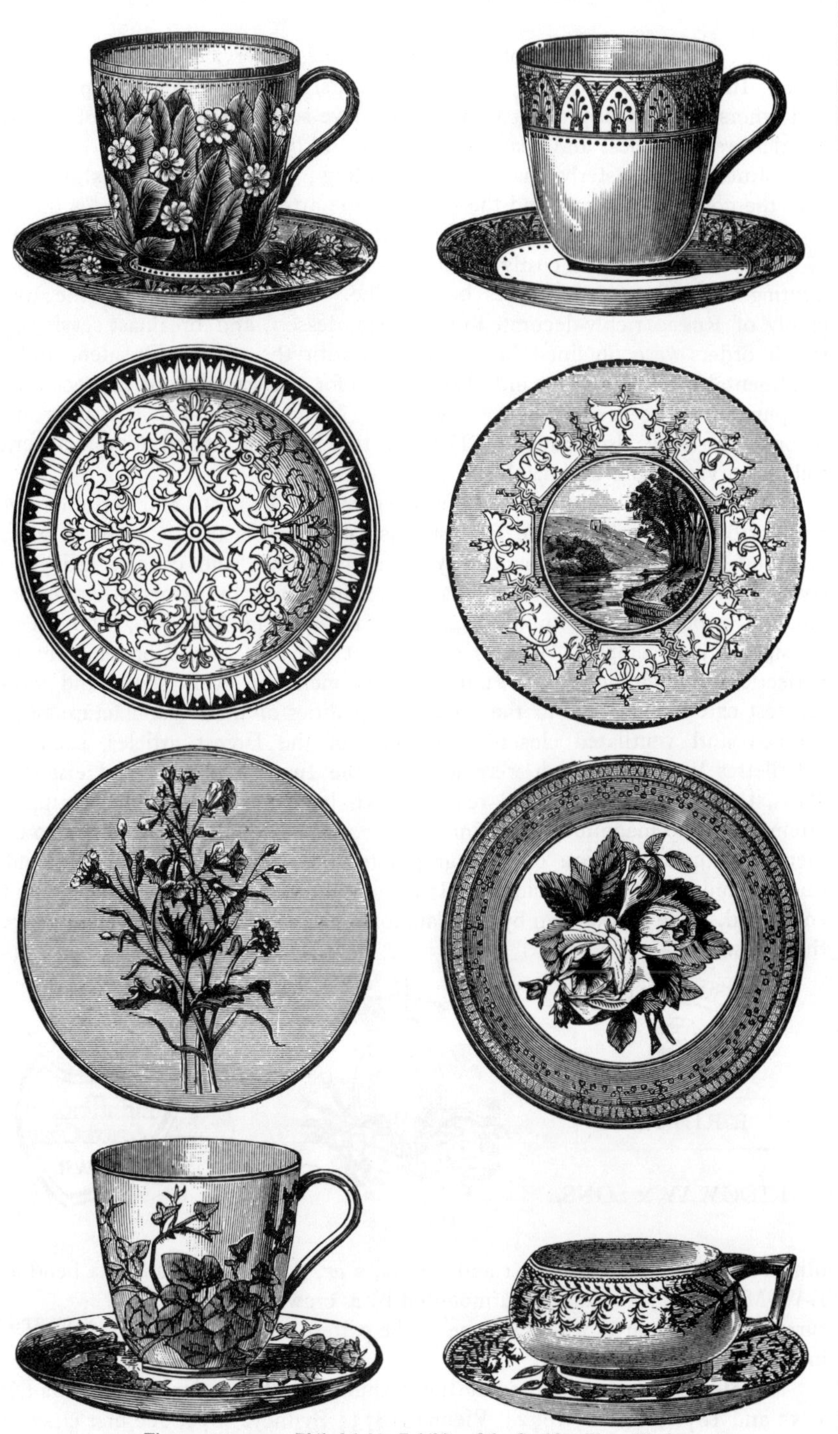

Figs. 1436 to 1443.—Philadelphia Exhibits of the Cauldon Place Works.

groups of flowers. It is one of the most charming of services and of novel appearance. In dinner services, too, the firm takes first rank; the patterns 5980 and 6245 and others being unapproached by any we have seen in the delicacy of grounding; the richness, clearness and beauty of the dead and burnished, raised and flat gilding; the softness and masterly touch of the painting; the effective admixture of silver with the gold and colours, and the purity of the art-feeling that pervades the whole.

In 1876-77 Messrs. Brown-Westhead, Moore, & Co. manufactured for the Prince of Wales a splendid and costly china dessert service, decorated with finely-painted hunting subjects, no two pieces being alike. They also made for the Imperial family of Russia richly-decorated dinner, tea, dessert, and breakfast services, all of which orders were obtained in competition with the Sèvres, Dresden, and other Continental manufactories; and also services for the Emperor of Morocco, including punch-bowls of extraordinary largeness. In addition to this it is interesting to record that they also made for H.R.H. the Duchess of Edinburgh a series of toilette services from designs drawn by herself.

The firm has also introduced improvements in druggists' and perfumery goods, anti-corrosive taps, &c. The highest class of Parian is also extensively produced. A grand feature of the manufactory is sanitary ware and cabinet fittings, plug-basins, lavatories, drinking-fountains, &c., which had the especial attention and enlarged experience and knowledge of the late Mr. Wm. Moore, by whom it was so considerably developed. In this department the firm stands pre-eminent for the perfection of their goods for sanitary requirements in every shape and form, the greatest care being given to the enduring qualities of their manufacture of Patent trapped and ventilated closets. In some of the largest articles, such as the "Toilettes Victoria," which were used by the Imperial family, and elsewhere in Paris, they have accomplished results which have never before been attained or attempted as to magnitude and finish of goods. The firm some years ago experimented in the application of photography to the decoration of porcelain, and produced some interesting specimens. It was not, however, sufficiently successful to be continued. The marks used by the Cauldon Place Works, so far as I am aware, are the following:—

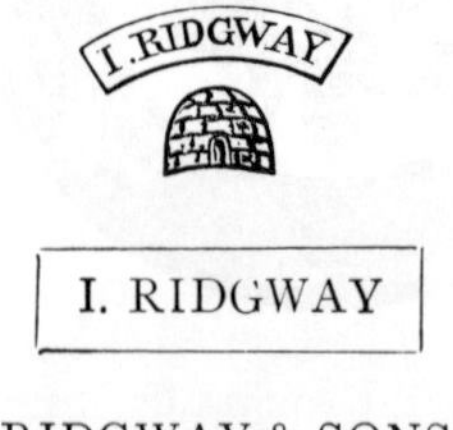

RIDGWAY & SONS.

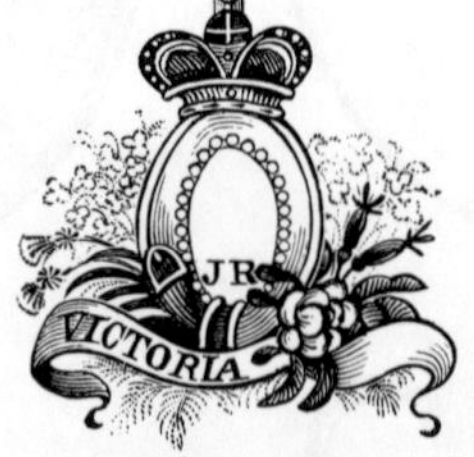

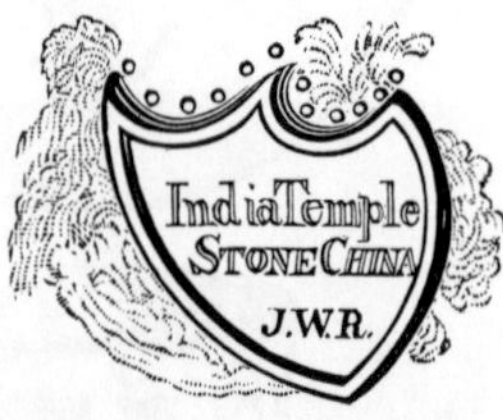

Figs. 1444 to 1448.

others are a shield, quarterly, 1 and 4 *gules*, 2 *or*, 3 *azure*, over all on a bend argent B-W. M. & Co.; the shield surmounted by a crown, and surrounded by a garter with the name of the pattern, and an impressed mark of the name,

T. C. BROWN-WESTHEAD
MOORE & CO.

Medals have been awarded at the Exhibitions of London, 1851, 1862; Paris, 1855 and 1878; Lyons, 1872; Vienna, 1873; Sydney, 1879, one first class medal and two first class awards; Melbourne, 1880, medal and diploma; and Adelaide, 1881, gold medal and first order of merit. The firm were large contributors to the

Philadelphia Exhibition of 1876; some of their exhibits are shown in Figs. 1429 to 1435.

The *Trent Works*, in Joiner Square, were built by Stanway, Horne, and Adams, in 1859, and are now carried on by the sole surviving partner, Mr. Thomas Adams. They were established for the production of ornamental goods in Parian, and useful goods of an improved design in stoneware and ordinary earthenware, and these have continued to extend themselves year by year. The great speciality is their cheap ornamental Parian, in which jugs of various kinds, vases, figures, groups, busts, and a large number of other articles are made, no less than 460,000 pieces of these alone being made and disposed of during one year. Notably among the designs for jugs and cream ewers are the Indian corn, pineapple, shell, and dolphin patterns. Of late years, classical statuettes, groups, busts, &c., in Parian, have been made a prominent feature of the works. The aim of the "Trent Works" has been the production of good average designs in Parian at a cheap rate, so as to place them within the reach of all. In this they have eminently succeeded. Stone ware, lustre ware, and terra-cotta are also produced, and of late the manufacture of pearl china has been added. The markets supplied are the home, United States, the Continent, &c. No mark is used.

Keeling.—James Keeling in 1796 patented improvements in decorative and glazing processes, and, in conjunction with Valentine Close, some improvements in ovens, kilns, and processes of firing. His ware was of remarkably good quality, and some of the services were decorated with series of scenes and views.

Booth & Co.—These potters were makers of a red ware—a kind of terra-cotta—in which they produced various articles more or less ornamented with medallions, wreaths, or other decorations, in relief, sometimes of the same colour as the body, and at others in black. The mark, of which an example occurs in the Liverpool Museum, was—

PUBLISHED BY GR. BOOTH & CO.,
HANLEY, STAFFORDSHIRE,
MAY 29, 1859.

Stafford Street Works.—This manufactory was originally occupied by Reuben Johnson & Co., who produced the ordinary classes of earthenware and stoneware. From them it passed to Thomas Furnival, jun. & Co., and "Furnival & Clark," by whom it was continued until 1851, when it was taken by Livesley, Powell & Co. In 1865 Mr. Livesley went out of the concern, when the firm changed its name to "Powell & Bishop," by which it continued till 1878, when Mr. John Stonier, of Liverpool, having joined the concern, it again changed to "Powell, Bishop, & Stonier." The firm owns two other manufactories, the "Church Works," for white granite, and the "Waterloo Works," for china (both of which see). At Stafford Street earthenware alone is produced, but this is of the finest quality and in every style of decoration, both for the home, French, Australian (principally Adelaide and Sydney), and other markets. The body is extremely hard, compact, and durable, and whether in pure white or of the rich, deep, and full creamy tint of their "Oriental Ivory" body, is clear in colour, and the glaze of faultless quality. The decoration of the dinner services, which is a speciality of these works, ranges from the plain white and printed goods up to the most elaborately and gorgeously enamelled, painted, and gilt varieties, and in each of these stages the decorations, whether simple or complicated, are characterized by the purest taste and the most artistic feeling. In toilet services a number of effective and well-conceived designs are produced in every style in transfer-printing, lustred, enamelled, painted, and gilt varieties, and the ewers are, in shape and decoration, of unusually good designs. Of these, a design on which a scarf of gold, beautifully enamelled with hawthorn blossoms, is represented in relief as threaded in and out of the neck of the ewer, and tied in a bow on the outside; and a Gordon-shaped ewer, "Gem" pattern, are the newest, and are highly successful. The first is one of the best designs yet brought out. Dinner, tea, and dessert services are also made in the finest earthenware, and of considerable variety and beauty in design. The firm has recently—besides reproducing in all its softness and delicacy of tint and evenness of surface the famous old ivory or cream-coloured ware of Josiah Wedgwood, and known as "Queen's Ware"—introduced a strikingly beautiful ware which they call "Oriental Ivory." In this, dinner, tea, dessert, and toilet services of the newest shapes and designs are made, and are among the most marked successes of the time. In this ivory ware ornamental goods—vases, beakers, &c.—of a more or less highly decorated character are also successfully produced. The firm received medals from the Exhibition in 1862; Amsterdam, 1869; Paris, 1875; "le Diplôme d'excellence" and a certificate, 1871; and were large exhibitors at Philadelphia in 1876.

The marks used by the firm have been the words BEST P & B and a triangle inclosing a circle impressed in the ware; and the initials P & B, or P B & S, in addition to the name of the pattern, printed on the surface. The trade-mark lately adopted by the firm is the Caduceus, impressed in the body or printed on the surface of the best goods; the special mark for the "Oriental Ivory" being a Chinese man seated on the ground, holding over his head an umbrella bearing the words "ORIENTAL IVORY." The "London" services have a banner bearing the words, "LONDON P B & S."

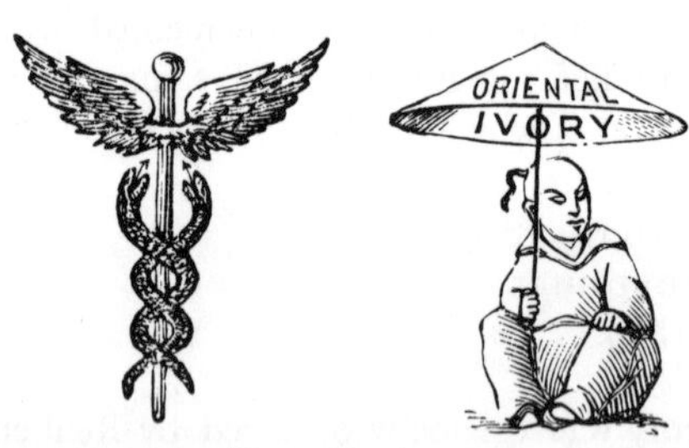

Figs. 1453 and 1454.

The *Church Works*, in High Street (see page 474, "Wilson"), passed from Mr. Ridgway to Powell & Bishop, who confine their operations at these works to "white granite" ware for the United States and Canadian markets, which they produce of excellent quality and in every variety of style, both plain, embossed, and otherwise decorated. (See "Stafford Street.")

Waterloo Works.—These works were recently erected close to their large mill on the canal side near Nelson Place, for the manufacture of china, by Powell, Bishop & Stonier, in place of one formerly occupied by them but removed for town improvements. At this manufactory china of the finest quality is made in the white, the whole of the decoration being accomplished at their principal works in Stafford Street (which see). In china the firm produces all the usual services and miscellaneous articles in every variety of decoration. In dessert services this firm ranks high, not only for the quality of the body and glaze and beauty of their designs, but for the artistic feeling and excellent finish which characterize their best productions. In these, and in tea services, they have introduced with excellent effect a species of decoration which may be said to give the appearance to the various articles of being inlaid with *ormolu*. They have also introduced a new china body of the most delicate green tint, in which they are producing a variety of articles—notably the "Dovedale" tea set and "Victoria" dessert service—which are chastely decorated and have become very popular. In services the chaste and elegant patterns produced by this house exhibit the highest phases of manipulative and artistic skill.

Kensington Works, established by Wilkinson & Rickuss, who were succeeded by Wilkinson & Sons, and next by Bailey & Bevington. Mr. Bailey having retired, the works are now carried on by Mr. John Bevington, who produces ordinary earthenware, ornamental china, Parian, and stoneware, the speciality being imitation Dresden for home, United States, and Australian markets. A monster vase, exhibited by Rickuss & Wilkinson in 1862, is in the Museum of Practical Geology.

Burton Place Works.—This manufactory is worked by Thomas Bevington, whose family have held them since 1862. The productions are china, in which all the usual useful and ornamental classes of goods are made for the home markets; fancy ivory earthenware; gold-thread ware; and a patent "Victorian Ware," in which the surface is covered with felspar crystals, decorated with veins of gold to represent gold-bearing quartz. The effect is remarkably good and eminently pleasing, and the idea is new to ceramics. The mark is the royal arms and "BY ROYAL LETTERS PATENT." The ordinary mark is the double triangle between the initials T. B., enclosing in its centre a crown. Formerly Parian statuettes and majolica goods were made, but these are discontinued. The gold-thread ware has the surface covered and matted with fine threads in the most intricate manner, and these are gilt and form a ground upon which well-modelled flowers are gracefully bestowed. In china, imitations of the old Crown Derby patterns are being produced to a considerable extent and with commendable success. The patterns, colours, and gilding are all in thoroughly good style, and the quality of the china body excellent.

Clarence Street Works.—Ambrose Bevington here produced the usual classes of earthenware and china. In 1880 he removed to the New Hall Works, and was succeeded by the "Crystal Porcelain Company," and in 1882 by C. Littler & Co., who are extensive manufacturers of high-class earthenware. In this all the usual dinner, breakfast, tea, toilet, and dessert services are made in all the most popular and saleable styles of decoration.

Nelson Place, commenced in 1850 by its present proprietor, Mr. John Bamford. These works produce ordinary stoneware and Parian.

Phœnix and Bell Works, Broad Street.—These manufactories are both worked by Clementson Brothers, who make largely the white granite and common painted ware for America and Canada. For the latter market they also produce some good decorated ware. The back part of the Phœnix Works was originally part of John and Edward Baddeley's, Broad Street Works (now Ashworth Brothers), which it adjoins. In 1832 the present business was started by Reed & Clementson, but

Joseph Clementson shortly after became sole proprietor, and in 1845 enlarged the works. In 1856 he purchased the Bell Works on the other side of the road, opposite the Phœnix, formerly William Ridgway's. In 1867 he retired from business, leaving it to his four sons, the present members of the firm. He died in 1871.

The *Bedford Works*, Bedford Road, were built by Edward John Ridgway, son of William Ridgway, in 1866, and to them he removed from the Church Works, High Street, where he had carried on business in partnership with Mr. Abington. In 1870 Mr. Ridgway took his sons into partnership, and the concern was carried on as E. J. Ridgway & Sons. In 1872 he retired in favour of his two sons, John and Edward Ackroyd Ridgway, who were joined in partnership by Joseph Sparks, and continue the business as Ridgway, Sparks & Ridgway. Their productions include all classes of fine useful earthenware, jet, stone, terra-cotta, and jasper, of very superior bodies and decoration, for the home, American, and Continental markets. One of the great specialities of the firm is their jet ware, highly decorated in raised enamel "after the Limoges ware." In these a remarkable richness, beauty, and delicacy are obtained, and the designs, as well as the treatment of the foliage and figures, are artistic and well considered for effect. Another speciality is relief decoration on various stoneware bodies, and these are faultless in taste and excellent in workmanship. The jasper (in which both tone of colour of the body and the beauty of detail in the groups and foliage and borders of the relief decoration in white remind one forcibly of the later productions of the Wedgwoods) teapots and other articles are produced and rank high as achievements of Ceramic Art. Mosaic or inlaid decoration is also successfully carried out by the firm, and their ordinary stoneware jugs and other articles are remarkable for purity of design, the high relief of their ornament, the hardness and compactness of their body, and the beauty of their workmanship. The mark is the Staffordshire knot, enclosing the letters R. S. R.

Mayer Street Works.—Mr. Samuel Lear has erected a small china works on part of the site of the old manufactory, which includes as warerooms and offices the residence of the Mayers. Mr. Lear produces common domestic china, and, in addition, decorates in the ordinary way all kinds of earthenware made by other manufacturers, a speciality being spirit-kegs. He has added to his Mayer Street works a new manufactory, built by himself in 1882 in the High Street, and there carries on a highly successful manufacture of ordinary china, etc., majolica in all its branches, and ivory body earthenware.

Mayer Street.—Mrs. Massey formerly carried on a small earthenware works on part of the site of the same old works.

Cannon Street.—These works, dating back to the beginning of the present century, were for many years carried on by Thos. Ford, who here commenced business, and has since built a larger manufactory in the same street. It is now carried on by Edward Steele, who produces earthenware of the more ordinary qualities, stoneware of good useful character, majolica, and Parian. In stoneware all the usual useful classes of goods are made, and many of the designs and workmanship are of good character. In majolica both useful and ornamental goods are made, and are of average excellence. Parian statuary, one of the specialities of the firm, is extensively made; some hundreds of different single figures, groups, busts, and animals, besides numbers of ornamental articles, being issued. Mr. Steele uses no mark.

Percy Street.—William Machin makes ordinary earthenware and common coloured figures.

Eastwood Vale.—Taylor, Tunnicliffe & Co., who used to manufacture in Broad Street very excellent door-furniture and other fittings for Birmingham houses, have here built more commodious works.

Eastwood Vale.—Buller & Co. make good door-furniture and other fittings for metal-workers.

Albion Works.—Stafford Street.—John Dimmock and Co., were large producers of earthenware of superior quality and finish. The old established firm of Thomas Dimmock & Co., when Ward's History was published, held three manufactories, viz., one "in Hanley, adjoining the New Market house, formerly James Whitehead's, afterwards J. and W. Handley's; another on the upper end of Shelton, formerly of Edmund John Birch, afterwards of Christopher Whitehead; and an enamelling and gilding establishment adjoining the King's Head at Shelton."

Eastwood Vale.—W. H. Goss (see "London Road, Stoke-upon-Trent," p. 421).

Eastwood Works.—Formerly carried on by Thomas Twyford, and afterwards by E. Hampton & Son, these works passed, in 1864, into the hands of the present proprietor, George Howson. The productions are entirely confined to sanitary ware, made of the ordinary Staffordshire fire-clay, washed inside with a white slip; sometimes blue printed.

Trent Pottery, Eastwood.—Established in 1867 by Livesley and Davis, the style was, on the retirement of Mr. Livesley, changed to J. H. & J. Davis (brothers). In 1875 J. Davis retired, and since then the concern has been carried on by J. H. Davis alone. Until latterly the productions were confined to white graniteware for the United States, but dinner, toilet, and tea services, and other articles, both for the home and foreign markets, have been added. He is also an extensive maker of sanitary wares, lavatories, plug-basins, hoppers, etc.

James Dudson, Hope Street Works, established in 1801. In 1835 Mr. James Dudson entered upon the works, and carried them on till his death in 1882, since which time they have been continued by his son. At one time ornamental china figures, vases, and services were made. The productions are white and coloured stoneware jugs, tea and coffee pots, sugar-boxes, &c., metal-mounted goods; flower-pots, candlesticks, &c. Among the registered designs for jugs, are the "Fern," "Argyle," "Barley," "Vine-border," "Pineapple," and "Wheatsheaf" patterns, which are produced in a variety of colours. In teapots the "Damascus," "Fern," and "Argyle" patterns are among the most popular. In mosaic ware Mr. Dudson makes a variety of articles in white, drab, blue, and other bodies inlaid with a variety of colours. In these are tea and coffee-pots, sugar-bowls, jugs, &c., of different shapes, the "Tanhart" and "Cambridge" being among the most successful. These goods are produced in large quantities. Mr. Dudson, who received "honourable mention" in the Exhibitions of 1851 and 1862, supplies both home and foreign markets.

Victoria Works, St. James Street.—The productions of Adams & Bromley, carried on until 1873 as John Adams & Co., are majolica and jasper wares of high

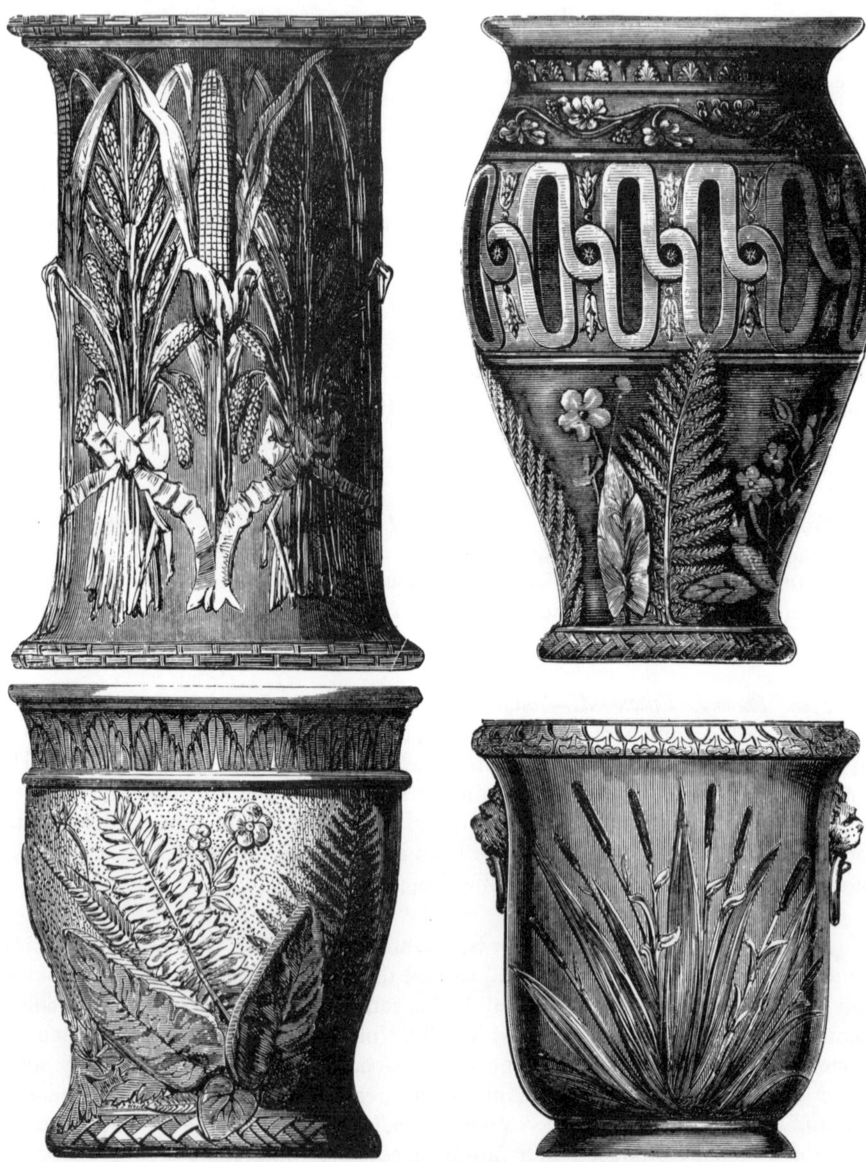

Figs. 1455 to 1458.—Adams's Productions, Exhibition of 1871.

class, both in quality and in design, and have given them an honourable name among the manufacturers of the district. Parian portrait busts (among which were those of the Poet Laureate, Lord Derby, and Mr. Gladstone) were formerly produced, and were remarkable for their truthfulness and artistic treatment. In jasper, besides vases and candlesticks, tea and other services, tea and coffee-pots, table-kettles, fruit-bowls, jugs, and a variety of other decorative and useful articles; cameos and medallions, after Wedgwood, for inlaying and other ornamental purposes, are made to a large extent and of satisfactory quality. The jasper is in quality and in general character of ornamentation, as well as in colour, a very close imitation of the more modern Wedgwood ware, and the shapes of many of the articles evince good taste in design. In majolica, bread-trays, cheese-trays, candlesticks, flower-pots, vases, garden-seats, jardinières, figures, and a very large variety of useful and ornamental goods are produced. The quality of the majolica is far above the average, and many of the designs are artistic; the workmanship in all cases is skilful and good. Notably among these are a large flower-vase, some four feet in height, with a well-modelled Cupid supporting the bowl; a masterly flower-vase on mask feet, and surrounded by a wreath of oak-leaves; another large vase in which the handles are formed of Cupids; water-lily, and other well-conceived dessert pieces, &c. Green-glazed dessert ware is also extensively made. The mark is the names ADAMS & Co., or ADAMS & BROMLEY, or A. & B.

Charles Street Works.—This manufactory, carried on by Johnson & Co., who succeeded J. W. Pankhurst & Co., is one of the oldest in Hanley. About a hundred years ago it was owned and worked by William Mellor, to whose family the property still belongs. Mr. Mellor made the Egyptian black ware for the Dutch markets, as did his successors, Toft and Keeling, who also produced other varieties of earthenware. It was next carried on by Toft & May, and then by Robert May, who was succeeded by William Ridgway, who changed the manufacture to that of white granite goods for the American markets, and was succeeded by J. W. Pankhurst & Co. The mark used by the firm is the royal arms and name, printed in black, on the ware.

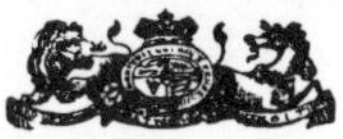

STONE CHINA.

J. W. PANKHURST & Co.

Fig. 1459.

Cobden Works, High Street.—These works form a part of those founded in the latter part of last century by Elijah Mayer, who about 1820 took his son into partnership under the style of "Elijah Mayer & Son." It was afterwards "Joseph Mayer" and "Joseph Mayer & Co." Elijah Mayer was a potter of considerable eminence, and produced an extensive variety of goods. His Egyptian black or basalt ware was, in quality of body, nearly equal to that of Wedgwood, and the ornamentation sharp and well-defined; in this he produced teapots, cream-ewers, bowls, and other articles. In cream-coloured ware services and all the usual useful articles were made, and were of unusually good style and quality; for these and his "brown-line" patterns he was noted. His cane-coloured or drab unglazed goods were another of his famous productions; specimens of these are not often obtainable. In the Museum of Practical Geology is a vase of this description, with festoons of raised flowers. Elijah Mayer produced a service commemorative of Nelson's Trafalgar and Nile victories, which became very popular. His mark was "E. Mayer" impressed in the ware, and afterwards "E. Mayer & Son." Of the later firm some examples with the name Joseph Mayer & Co. Hanley, are preserved in the

Liverpool Museum. In 1867 the premises were purchased by Gelson Brothers, who in 1876 dissolved partnership, the business being conducted by Thomas Gelson & Co., who in 1882 were succeeded by James Bevington (previously of J. & T. Bevington), who produces to a large extent and in great variety all the usual classes of decorated china and fancy goods.

Messrs. Gelson & Co., who originally made white graniteware for the American markets, abandoned that branch and confined themselves to the production of the highest classes of useful goods for the home trade. In this they made dinner, tea, breakfast, toilet, and other services in every variety of printed, enamelled, and gilt patterns. One of their specialities was the successful imitation of the old Dresden style, which had all the character, in general appearance, of the antique, and was a satisfactory reproduction of a good old pattern. Another of their happy decorative ideas was the introduction of Anglo-Saxon and early Irish interlaced ornaments in bands encircling mouth-ewers and other articles.

Eagle Works.—This business, commenced at Longton in 1845, was removed to Hanley in 1848 by Mr. James Meakin. In 1852 he retired, and was succeeded by two of his sons, James and George Meakin. In 1859 the business having considerably increased, the Eagle Works were erected, and in 1868 were considerably enlarged. The firm have also branch works at Cobridge and Burslem, and are large producers of the usual classes of earthenware, the speciality being white graniteware of ordinary quality, in imitation of French china. The mark is J. & G. MEAKIN, stamped in the ware, and printed in black.

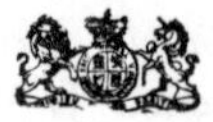

IRONSTONE CHINA.
J. & G. MEAKIN.
Fig. 1461.

Pearl Pottery, Brook Street.—These works were established by Ralph Salt, and he and his successors, Richard Booth and Williams and Willet, manufactured painted china toys. In 1860 the works passed into the hands of William Taylor, who commenced making white granite and common coloured and painted ware, but which he discontinued, and confined himself to white graniteware for the United States and Canadian markets, of both qualities—the bluish tinted for the provinces, and the purer white for the city trade. He was succeeded in 1881 by Wood, Hines, and Winkle, who produce opaque porcelain in all the usual services for dinner, tea, breakfast, and toilet; and a large number of specialities in déjune, five o'clock tea, trinket, and beer sets; vases, plaques, cruets, and other useful and ornamental articles. The works have been considerably enlarged and new machinery added.

Cannon Street.—Charles Ford (formerly Thomas and Charles Ford) manufactures the best class of china in tea, breakfast, dessert, and table services for the home markets.

William Stubbs, Eastwood Pottery, manufactures china and earthenware services of the commoner kinds, lustres, stoneware jugs, black teapots, &c., and the smaller and commoner classes of china toys and ornaments.

Norfolk Street Works, Cauldon Place.—These works, established by their present proprietors, R. G. Scrivener and Thomas Bourne ("R. G. Scrivener & Co.") in 1870, are situate about midway between Stoke and Hanley. The productions are china tea, breakfast, dessert, and other services, and fancy articles, and earthenware toilet and other services of a more than average degree of artistic decoration. They export considerably to the colonies, and also supply the home markets. The mark is the initials | R. G. S. & Co. | impressed, the registered designs having a printed mark, with the name of the pattern and initials of the firm.

Broad Street.—The old established works formerly occupied by Mr. Ash as a Parian and majolica manufactory are carried on by Grove and Cope for the production of fancy china ornaments.

Albert Works, Victoria Place.—These works were erected in 1875 by Mr. J. Buckley, who removed to them from the Vine Street Works, which he had occupied from 1861. Mr. Buckley commenced business in Hanley as a sanitary-ware potter in 1836. His productions are all the usual varieties of sanitary goods (pans, traps, tables, &c.), ship and other fittings, toilet ware, handles for various purposes, plumbers' fittings, spirit-casks, &c.

Ranelagh Works.—Established in 1846 by Mr. Stephenson, these works have been successively occupied by James Oldham, Oldham & Co., T. R. Hinde, and Hollinshead & Stonier, and since 1875 by Jones & Hopkinson, who produce all the commoner classes of earthenware and stoneware services and general articles. No mark is used.

Swan Works, Elm Street, established in 1835 by Samuel Bevington as Parian works, and afterwards carried on by his son, John Bevington, passed in 1866 into the hands of W. L. Evans & Co., and in 1871 to Neale, Harrison, & Co., who gave up the manufacturing and confined themselves to decoration only. They were succeeded by T. R. Simpson.

Brook Street Works.—Messrs. Worthington & Son produce earthenware and stoneware, both for home and foreign markets.

Dresden Works, Tinkersclough.—In 1843 Edward Raby produced at these works china ornaments with raised or "Dresden" flowers, hence the name. From 1852 until 1864 they were carried on by John Worthington and William Harrop; from that time till 1873 by Thomas Worthington and William Harrop; and from that time to the present by William Harrop alone. The productions are the cheaper classes of Parian goods, and fancy jugs in stoneware and ordinary earthenware, of good middle-class quality, all of which are supplied both to the home and American markets. No mark is used.

The works are situated at what is called "Tinkersclough,"—a place whose name is said to be "derived from the fact of its being frequented in the olden times as a place of rendezvous by gipsies and travelling tinkers."

Bath Street Works.—These works were established in 1849 by the late Thomas Twyford (father of the present proprietor), who was a lineal descendant of the famous old seventeenth century potter, Twyford, who with Ashbury wormed out the secret of the Elers, as detailed on page 77. The operations are confined to sanitary and plumbers' ware, and wine and spirit show barrels. The mark is the Staffordshire knot enclosing the letters T T (Thomas Twyford) with H (Hanley) beneath. The same firm has a manufactory of cane and white sanitary ware at Buckland.

Waterloo Works, Lower Charles Street.—These are old-established works, and have, with others, been occupied by W. Stubbs, Thomas Booth and Son, Holmes and Plant, Pugh and Glover, Beech and Morgan, and their present proprietors, G. and B. Burton. The higher and better classes of china and earthenware in toilet and other services, painted, enamelled, and grounded; stoneware jugs, teapots, &c., and jet and other wares, are largely made, and of all the usual classes of decoration, both for home and foreign markets. The "milk sets" or "beer sets" are assuredly the best in form of tray, jug, and horns, and the most artistic and "nice" of any produced; as are also their Stilton cheese-tubs, egg-frames, &c. The body is of the purest ivory, and the decoration highly artistic. Their toddy-jugs also, in ivory, maroon, and gold, are a great success.

Excelsior Works, New Street. These works were established in 1873 by Banks and Thorley, who, having removed to new premises, were succeeded by Dean, Capper, and Dean, who manufacture jet, china, and earthenware.

High Street.—Messrs. Banks and Thorley having for the purpose erected a new manufactory, removed here in 18— from their works in New Street. Their productions are majolica, terra-cotta, jet, and stonewares, and these they produce for both home and foreign markets. In terra-cotta, water-bottles of porous body, unglazed, of elegant forms and of a more or less highly decorated character, with stoppers and stands; alcorazzas, water-goblets, Malaga jars, tobacco-jars, &c., are made in great variety. These porous goods are of three distinct kinds—a clear full red, a buff, and a purplish white. They are printed, painted, enamelled, and gilt in encircling borders, wreaths, &c., in groups of flowers and ferns, or in Japanese figure subjects, and are of excellent shape and workmanship. In majolica, cheese-stands, bread-trays, dessert services, jugs, egg-holders, jardinières, flower-pots, teapots, ladies' work-baskets, water-bottles, and an infinite variety of ornamental articles are made. Many of these are of a high degree of merit in design, and their production is faultlessly good. Notably among the dessert services in majolica is one with a rich chocolate-coloured ground, which throws out, with a strikingly beautiful and rich effect, a naturally arranged group of ivy, ferns, and anemones. Another striking design in majolica is a jug. The ground of this is chocolate, and upon it are panels of rope in buff, enclosing thistle-leaves in green. The whole design, including the twisted rope handle, is novel and pleasing. Besides these, green glaze dessert services and a large variety of other articles, both useful and ornamental, are made. The firm use no mark.

New Street.—Messrs. J. & R. Hammersley (who have also works in Nelson Place) have here an establishment for decorating china of all descriptions.

Castle Field Pottery.—These works, now discontinued, were at one time carried on by Mr. Ball, who "distinguished himself as the first to bring out hollow and glazed bricks, and these he made for Prince Albert's model cottages. They were from his works at Poole, in Dorsetshire, and matured here at Etruria." In 1860 Davenport & Banks here established themselves, and manufactured fancy goods until 1873, when Mr. Banks retired, and was succeeded by Mr. Beck as "Davenport, Beck, & Co." The principal productions were fancy antique goods, majolica in all its varieties, porous goods, terra-cotta water-bottles, &c., jet ware, and the ordinary earthenware. The mark was a castle, and the letters "D. B. & CO. ETRURIA" within an oval garter, bearing the words TRADE MARK.

Henry Venables, Etruria Road, established 1860, manufactured Etruscan-red porous goods, black basalt ware, jet glazed ware, and blue and other coloured jaspers. In these he produced a large variety of vases, as well as other ornamental and useful goods.

Boothen Works.—Messrs. Dunn, Bennet, & Co. here manufacture earthenware and ironstone china in all the usual services, both for the home and American markets. Their productions are of a high quality, and having houses both in London and New York, they are in a position to cater successfully for both countries.

Pelham Street Pottery.—These works were built in 1877 by the firm of Pugh & Glover, of the Waterloo Works, from which in that year they removed. They produce all the usual services and articles in ordinary earthenware and in every style of decoration, as well as stoneware jugs and other articles for both home and foreign markets.

Pelham Street Works were built in 1881 by Alfred Bullock & Co. for the manufacture of majolica and jet wares, both of which they produce in large quantities, and of great excellence in body and decoration.

Upper Hanley Works, High Street.—In 1875 Messrs. Hollinshead & Stonier, at that time of the Ranelagh Works, were joined in partnership by Mr. Holmes, and removed to this manufactory, where they carried on the business under the style of Holmes, Stonier, and Hollinshead until 1882, when it was changed to Stonier, Hollinshead, and Oliver. Their productions are the more useful classes of earthenware and white granite for the home, American, Cape, and Australian markets.

Hall Field Pottery.—Built in 1882 by Messrs. Whittaker, Edge, & Co., who make a fair quality of general earthenware for all markets.

Havelock Works, Broad Street.—Mrs. J. Massey, formerly of Mayer Street, here makes common jugs, teapots, and general majolica.

Marlborough Works, Union Street.—Messrs. Mountford and Thomas make majolica of good quality.

Union Street Works.—H. Shenton makes common general earthenware.

Chell Street Works.—E. Rigby, jun., makes common earthenware.

Pyenest Street Works.—Messrs. J. & J. Snow (also of Albert Works, Stoke) make terra-cotta, jet, and ordinary earthenware.

Lichfield Street.—Mr. Charles Meachin has a recently-erected manufactory for American graniteware.

CHAPTER XXI.

HAVING already, many years ago, written a work (the first ever issued) devoted to the life of Josiah Wedgwood—a history of the family to which he belonged, of the works founded by him, and of his various productions—("The Wedgwoods: being a Life of Josiah Wedgwood, with Notices of his Works and their Productions," &c. By Llewellynn Jewitt, F.S.A. London: Virtue & Co., 1865), it will not be necessary here to enter at any very great length into the subject.

Josiah Wedgwood was born at Burslem in July, 1730, and was baptized on the 12th of that month, the entry in the parish register being as follows:—"1730. Josiah, son of Thomas and Mary Wedgwood, bapd. July 12th." He was the youngest, the thirteenth, child of Thomas Wedgwood (eldest son of Thomas Wedgwood and his wife, Mary Leigh, of the Churchyard House and Works, Burslem), by his wife, Mary Stringer. The Wedgwoods were an ancient family of Staffordshire, being originally, I believe, of Wedgwood in Wolstanton, where a Thomas de Weggewood "was frankpledge, or headborough, of the hamlet of Weggewood" in 1370; and a century later John Wedgwood, a descendant, then of Blackwood or Dunwood, married Mary Shawe, the heiress of Harracles. The Wedgwoods of Burslem, who belonged to this family, had for many generations before the birth of Josiah been potters there; and indeed a considerable portion of the place passed, about 1612, into the hands of Gilbert Wedgwood by marriage with Margaret Burslem, heiress of the De Burslems, the original owners of the place. The issue of this marriage was Joseph, who died without issue; Burslem, whose line became extinct in the third descent; Thomas, who married Margaret Shaw, and was ancestor of the "Church Wedgwoods," of which latter Josiah was a member, and the "Overhouse Wedgwoods;" William, Moses, and Aaron (who was ancestor of the "Big House Wedgwoods)"; Mary, married to Broad; and Sarah, married to Daniell. The eldest son of Thomas and Margaret, to whom I have alluded, was John (born 1654 and died 1705) who had by his wife, Alice, a daughter, Catherine, who married, first, her cousin, Richard Wedgwood, potter, of the "Overhouse" branch, and had by him John, an only child, who died a minor; second, Thomas Bourne; and third, Rowland Egerton, whom she survived, and died a widow in 1756. The second son of Thomas and Margaret, Thomas Wedgwood (born in 1660, and married in 1684), resided and had his pot-works close to the churchyard at Burslem, where they still exist. By his wife, Mary Leigh, he had a family of four sons and five daughters, viz., Thomas (father of Josiah), John, Abner (who died young), Aaron, and Daniel; and Catherine, married to her relative, Dr. Thomas Wedgwood, jun.; Alice, married to Thomas Moore; Elizabeth, married to Samuel Astbury; Margaret, married to Moses Marsh; and Mary, married to Richard Clifton. Thomas Wedgwood, who succeeded his father at the Churchyard Works, died in 1739, when his youngest and most famous son, Josiah, was hardly nine years old (and by his will the sum of twenty pounds, to be paid him on attaining the age of twenty, was left), and was in turn succeeded by his eldest son Thomas in the business. This Thomas Wedgwood married in 1742 Isabel Beech, and in his marriage settlement is described as "of the Over House, Burslem, potter," and probably both these and the Churchyard Works were carried on by him. To this Thomas Wedgwood, his eldest brother, Josiah Wedgwood was bound apprentice on the 11th of November, 1744, and the original indenture of apprenticeship (which, with a vast number of other documents, wills, &c., I had the pleasure to be the first to make public in my "Life of Wedgwood," and which I therein printed *in extenso*), is preserved in the Museum at Hanley. The indenture was "Between Josiah Wedgwood, son of Mary Wedgwood, of the Churchyard, in the county of Stafford, of the one part, and Thomas Wedgwood, of the Churchyard, in the county of Stafford, Potter, of the other part, Wittnesseth that the said Josiah Wedgwood, of his own free Will and Consent to and with the Consent and Direction of his said Mother, hath put and doth hereby Bind himselfe Apprentice unto the said Thomas Wedgwood, to Learn his Art, Mistery, Occupation, or Imployment of Throwing and Handleing," and is signed as follows :—

"Sealed and Delivered in the presence of

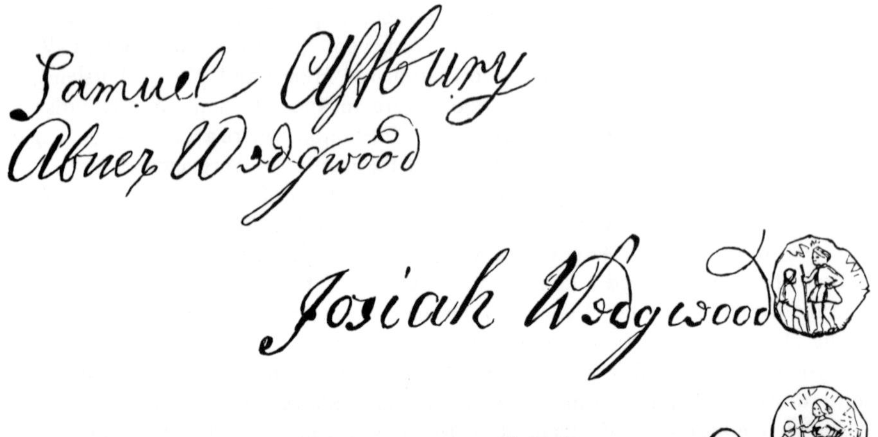

Samuel Astbury
Abner Wedgwood

Josiah Wedgwood

Mary Wedgwood

Thos. Wedgwood

Fig. 1463.—Fac-simile of Signatures to Wedgwood's Indentures.

the autograph signatures being those of Josiah Wedgwood; his mother, Mary Wedgwood; his brother, Thomas, to whom he was bound; his uncle, Samuel Astbury (husband to Elizabeth Wedgwood, his father's sister); and his brother or uncle, Abner Wedgwood. It is endorsed "Josiah Wedgwood to Thos. Wedgwood,

Indenture for 5 years. November 11th, 1744." Of the Churchyard Works a view is given on page 439.

In 1749 Josiah Wedgwood's apprenticeship expired, but he probably remained for some time in the employ of his brother. He next went to Stoke, where he lodged with a mercer, Mr. Daniel Mayer, and commenced making imitation agate and other knife-handles, and in 1752 entered into partnership with John Harrison for the manufacture of the same kind of goods. Two years later both Wedgwood and Harrison entered into partnership for a term of five years with Thomas Whieldon, at Fenton Low, at the expiration of which, in 1759, Josiah Wedgwood returned to Burslem and commenced business on his own account, first, there is reason to believe, at the "Churchyard" Works, and next at the Ivy "House" (Fig. 1288), which he rented from his relatives of the "Big House." Next he entered upon another manufactory, the "Bell Bank," or "Bell Works" (Fig. 1287), as it became

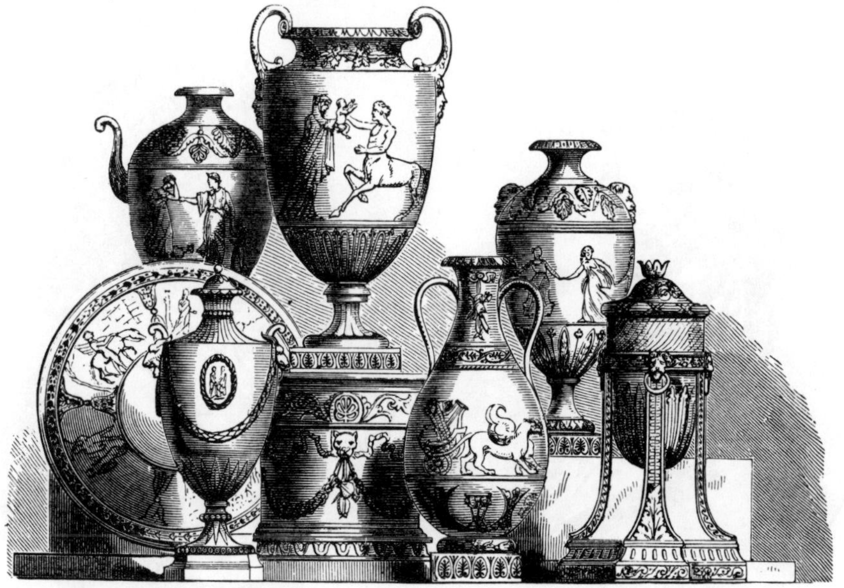

Figs. 1464 to 1470.—Wedgwood's Jasper Ware.

called, and there produced his famous "Queen's ware." In 1762, on the occasion of the accouchement of Queen Charlotte, Wedgwood, having by that time perfected the body and glaze of this fine cream-coloured ware, presented to her Majesty a caudle and breakfast service of his manufacture, which was graciously accepted This service, which was made of the finest and best cream-coloured quality which could be produced, was painted in the highest style of the day by the first artists of the works, Thomas Daniell and Daniel Steele. The ground, prepared with all the skill of which the art would then admit, was yellow, with raised sprigs of jassamine and other flowers, coloured after nature. The Queen was so pleased that she at once expressed a wish to have a complete table service of the same material. Wedgwood submitted patterns "which were approved, with the exception of the plate, which was the common barleycorn pattern then making by all the salt-glaze manufacturers. Her Majesty objected to the roughness—the 'barleycorn-work' as it is called—and therefore this part was made plain; on the edge was left only the bands, marking the compartments; and being approved by her Majesty, the pattern was called 'Queen's pattern.'" The ware was at once named by Wedgwood "Queen's ware," and he received the Queen's commands to call himself "Potter to Her Majesty." On the service being completed the King ordered a similar service for himself, but without the bands or ribs. This alteration was "effected to the entire satisfaction of his Majesty," and some little alterations being made in the forms of some of the other pieces, it was called the "Royal pattern." The patronage thus given was of incalculable benefit. Orders flowed in upon him in a regular and constantly increasing stream, and it is recorded that he received at the rate of 15s. per dozen for table plates, and for other pieces a proportionate price. The tide of fortune which thus had set in upon him was immensely increased by his subsequent inventions, and ultimately swept him from his small manufactories at Burslem to the colony he established a few miles off at Etruria. The other most usual form of

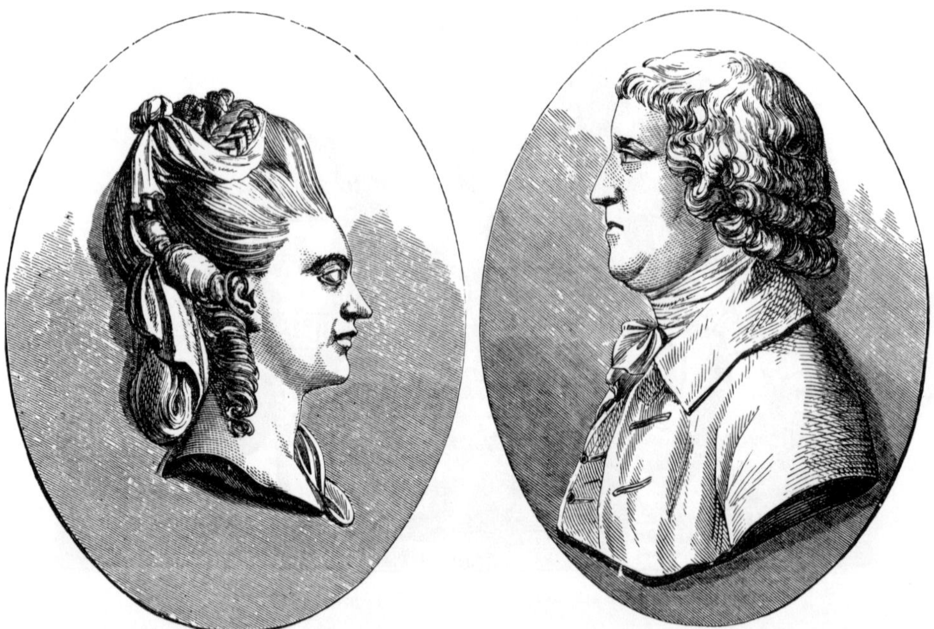

Figs. 1471 and 1472.—Flaxman's Medallions of Josiah Wedgwood and his Wife.

plate in the Queen's ware was the "Bath" or "Trencher." Some of the Queen's ware Wedgwood had decorated with transfer-printing by Sadler and Green of Liverpool, as already noted under that head.

On the 25th of January, 1764, Josiah Wedgwood married, at Astbury, in Cheshire, his distant relative—his seventh cousin—Sarah Wedgwood, daughter and eventually heiress of Richard Wedgwood, Esq., of Smallwood, in that county, and also heiress to her brother John. By this marriage Josiah Wedgwood ultimately became possessed of a fortune of some twenty thousand pounds. After his marriage he still resided at the "Ivy House;" and having failed in his proposal to purchase the "Big House" when his relatives retired from business, he set about founding an entirely new manufactory. His "Big House" relations were the brothers Thomas and John, sons of Aaron Wedgwood, by his wife Mary Hollins, who, as well as his son and his grandsons, Thomas and John, were lead-glaze potters. About 1740 it is said these two "commenced the manufacture of white stoneware upon their own account, but although very industrious and ingenious workmen (one of them being well skilled in burning or firing the ware, and the other an excellent thrower), they were unsuccessful for a long time, and had actually determined to abandon any further attempt to make the white stoneware, when an accidental circumstance encouraged them to proceed. The water with which they prepared the clay, it seems, became highly saturated with salt, owing to the shard ruck or rubbish from their ovens being placed immediately above their water-pool, and which rubbish contained much salt. The rain passing through the shard ruck dissolved the salt and carried it into the pool, whence it got into the body of the ware, and in conjunction with the flint and clay, together with the lime which generally adheres to flint stones, formed a fusible body that arrived at a state of vitrification with a lower degree of heat than was requsite

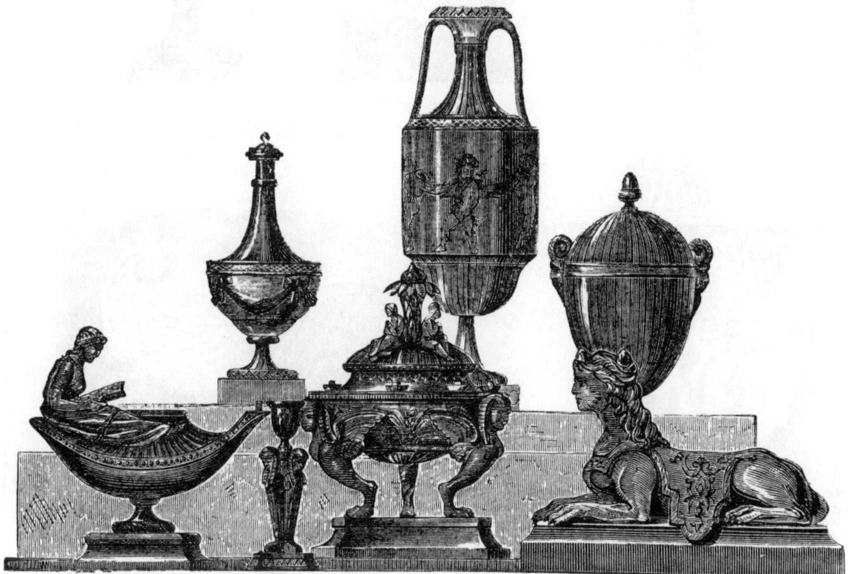

Figs. 1473 to 1479.—Wedgwood's Basaltes or Egyptian Black Ware.

to prepare this body for the salt glaze. This discovery induced them to make other and more extended trials, and in these they succeeded beyond expectation. The Wedgwoods followed up their success with unremitting diligence, and shortly afterwards built a new and commodious manufactory, where they had a supply of good water. This was near the windmill invented and erected by the celebrated Brindley for reducing flint-stones to a fine powder by grinding them in water, and thereby preventing the pernicious effects upon the health of the men employed in preparing the flint according to the old method, by pounding it by hand in a dry state in a mortar. The fine dust of the flint getting into the lungs produced coughs and consumptions which frequently proved fatal. This building, censured at the time as having been upon too extensive a scale, was the first earthenware manufactory in the Potteries *not covered with thatch*. In 1750 they erected an excellent and substantial dwelling-house adjoining their manufactory which so far exceeded the other houses in the Potteries in point of size and elegance that it then was, and now is,

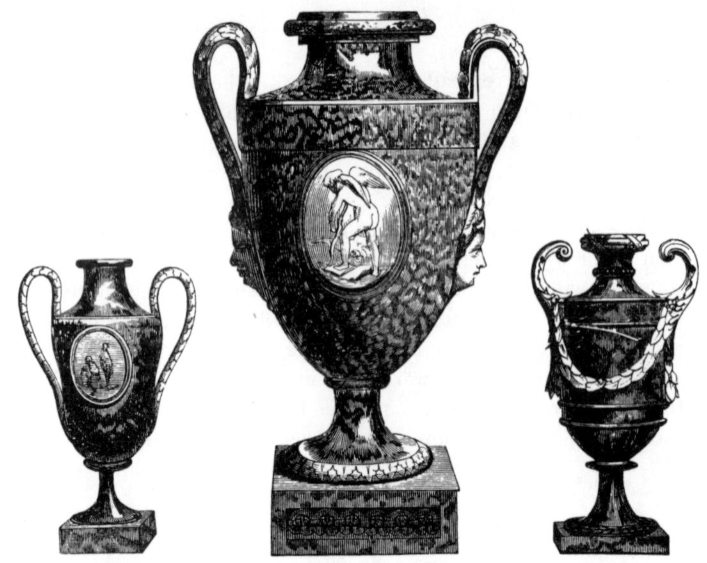

Agate and Porphyry Wares.

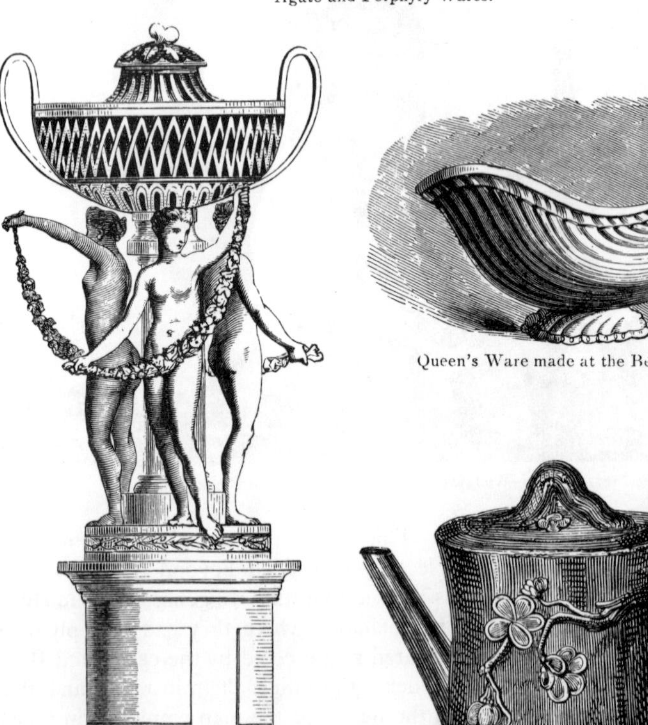

Queen's Ware made at the Bell Works.

Queen's Ware Centre.

Crabstock Red-ware Teapot.

Figs. 1480 to 1485.—Wedgwood's Productions.

distinguished by the appellation of the 'Big House;' and in the year 1763 these gentlemen retired from business in the possession of an ample fortune, the just and honourable reward of their industry and integrity."

Having taken into partnership his relative, Thomas Wedgwood, "who had been some years a faithful and industrious foreman" in the Queen's ware department, Wedgwood became more at liberty to prosecute his experiments. This Thomas married Elizabeth Taylor, of the Hill, Burslem, by whom he had issue Ralph (the head of the firm of "Wedgwood & Co." of the Hill Works, afterwards of Ferrybridge); John Taylor Wedgwood, the eminent line-engraver; Samuel, Thomas, Aaron, and Abner. He died in 1778.

In 1766 Wedgwood produced his "basaltes," or "Egyptian black" ware, which was followed by "Jasper," "White-stone," "Cane-coloured," "Mortar," and other wares. His various wares were thus described by himself:—"1. A *terra-cotta*

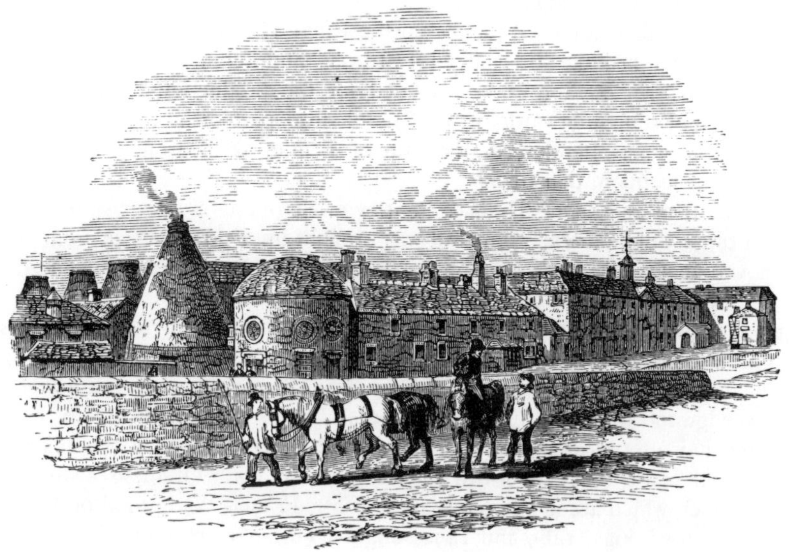

Fig. 1486.—Etruria Works.

resembling porphyry, granite, Egyptian, pebble, and other beautiful stones of the silicious or crystalline order.

"2. *Basaltes* or black ware. A black porcelain biscuit of nearly the same properties with the natural stone, striking fire with steel, receiving a high polish, serving as a touchstone for metals, resisting all the acids, and bearing without injury a strong fire—stronger indeed than the basaltes itself.

"3. *White porcelain biscuit,* of a smooth, wax-like surface, of the same properties with the preceding, except in what depends upon colour.

"4. *Jasper.* A white porcelain biscuit of exquisite beauty and delicacy, possessing the general properties of the basaltes, together with the singular one of receiving through its whole substance, from the admixture of metallic calces with the other materials, the same colours which those calces communicate to glass or enamels in fusion, a property which no other porcelain or earthenware body of ancient or modern composition has been found to possess. This renders it peculiarly fit for making cameos, portraits, and all subjects in bas-relief, as the ground may be of any particular colour, while the raised figures are of a pure white.

"5. *Bamboo* or cane-coloured biscuit porcelain, of the same nature as No. 3.

"6. A *porcelain biscuit*, remarkable for great hardness, little inferior to that of agate. This property, together with its resistance to the strongest acids and corrosives, and its impenetrability by every known liquid, adapts it for mortars and many different kinds of chemical vessels.

"These six distinct species, with the Queen's ware already mentioned, expanded by the industry and ingenuity of the different manufacturers into an infinity of forms for ornament and use, variously painted and embellished, constitute nearly the whole of the present fine English earthenwares and porcelain, which are now become the source of a very extensive trade, and which, considered as an object of national art, industry, and commerce, may be ranked amongst the most important manufactures of the kingdom."

In 1766 Josiah Wedgwood purchased the Ridge House Estate, in the township of Shelton, which he afterwards named "Etruria," and here he commenced building the "Black Works," *i.e.* the works intended for the production of his basaltes or black ware, and soon afterwards (in 1768) took into partnership, in the ornamental department, Thomas Bentley, of the firm of Bentley & Boardman of Liverpool, who were his agents in that town.

Thomas Bentley, son of Thomas Bentley of Scropton in Derbyshire, was born there on the 1st of January, 1730, and was brought up at Manchester, from whence he removed to Liverpool, and in conjunction with Mr. Boardman commenced business as Manchester warehousemen, they living together in Paradise Street. On joining Wedgwood, Bentley left Liverpool and devoted himself to the business in London. In 1769 the Etruria Works were opened, and on the 13th of June in that year its first productions were thrown; Thomas Bentley turning the wheel while Josiah Wedgwood himself "threw" the pieces. These were three vases of Etruscan form, and they afterwards passed through all the processes of the potter's art, and were painted in Etruscan style with suitable inscriptions. Of these historical and priceless vases, which are in the possession of Mr. Francis Wedgwood of Barlaston, two are shown on Figs. 1489 and 1490, engraved from careful drawings made by myself from the vases at Barlaston. They bear the words—

JUNE XIII MDCCLXIX
One of the first Day's Productions
at
Etruria in Staffordshire
by
Wedgwood and Bentley
Artes Etruriæ renascunter

and each is labelled in Wedgwood's own handwriting, "Part of Plate 129, vol i., of Hamilton's Antiq. Hercules and his Companions in the Garden of the Hesperides." In 1770 Wedgwood and Bentley established works at Chelsea for the decoration of these "encaustic vases" and for other purposes, which continued for some time, and down nearly to the close of last century painting and enamelling were done for the firm in London. In 1772 Bentley (who in 1754 had married Hannah Oates of Sheffield, who did not live long) married, at All Saints' Church, Derby, his second wife, Mary Stamford, of that town. In 1773 the partners issued their first "Catalogue of Cameos, Intaglios, Medals, and Bas-reliefs, with a general account of Vases and other ornaments after the antique; made by Wedgwood and Bentley, and sold at their rooms in Great Newport Street, London." It is of much smaller size than the later editions, and contains sixty pages, inclusive of introduction, &c.; the bodies enumerated being "terra-cotta resembling porphyry, lapis lazuli, jasper, and other beautiful stones of the vitrescent or crystalline class," such as the imitation porphyry, marble, and other vases were composed of; the "fine black porcelain, or *basaltes*," so largely used for vases, figures, medallions, and other ornamental purposes, as well as for teapots, &c.; and the "white biscuit ware, or terra-cotta," used both in combination with other materials in the production of vases, medallions, and other decorative pieces, and separately for the manufacture of stands and other ornamental goods. The combination of these two latter bodies will be called to mind by collectors perhaps more easily with regard to medallions than otherwise. In these the oval of the plaque was frequently made of the black ware, and the bust of the white terra-cotta (Fig. 1493). In the next year (1774) a fourth variety was added. This was the first appearance of what afterwards became the most beautiful of all Wedgwood's productions—the "Jasper ware." At this date (1774) it was simply spoken of as a "fine white terra-cotta," and it remained for later years to produce it with its splendid blue and other coloured grounds, with raised white figures and ornaments. In 1787 this variety, which then had attained its highest perfection, is described at greater length as "a white porcelain *bisqué* of exquisite beauty and delicacy, possessing the general properties of the basaltes, together with that of receiving colours through its whole substance in a manner which no other *body*, ancient or modern, has been known to do. This renders it peculiarly fit for cameos, portraits, and all subjects in bas-relief, as the group may be made of any colour throughout, without paint or enamel, and the raised figures of a pure white."

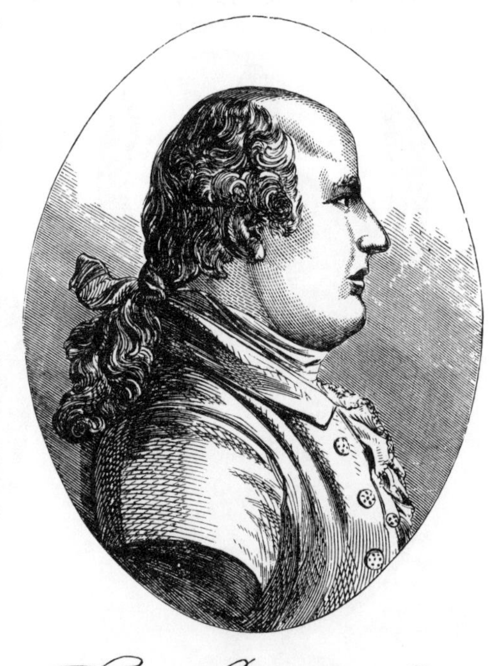

Figs. 1487 and 1488.—Medallion and Autograph of Thomas Bentley.

Of the productions of this ware Wedgwood wrote: "As these are my latest, I hope they will be found to be my most approved, works. Verbal descriptions could give but an imperfect idea of the delicacy of the materials, the execution of the artist, or the general effect, and I must therefore beg leave to refer those who wish for information in these respects to a view of the articles themselves." In 1775 a reisuse of the English catalogue, consequent on the change of the London warehouse from Great Newport Street to Greek Street, Soho, made its appearance. At the end is an addition of six pages, containing an engraving and explanation of Wedgwood's newly-invented inkstands and eye-cups. In 1775, on the occasion of Richard Champion applying to Parliament for an extension of the term of patent-right in Cookworthy's invention of porcelain (as detailed on page 198), "Josiah Wedgwood, in behalf of himself and the manufacturers of earthenware in Staffordshire," gave the scheme his most determined, but happily not successful, opposition. The printed papers connected with this matter are of the highest interest and importance, but having already been printed *in extenso* in my "Life of Wedgwood," I refrain from again introducing them.

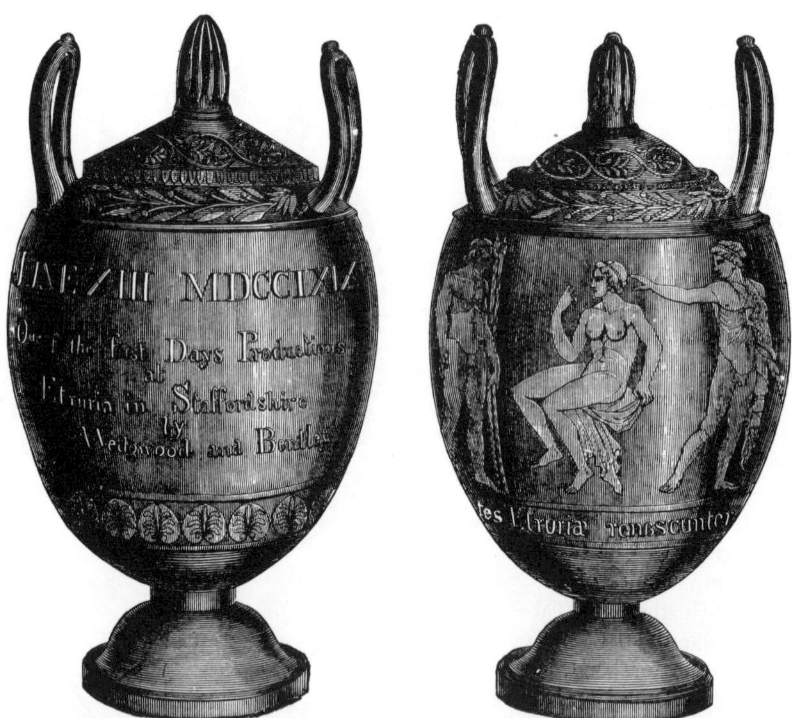

Figs. 1489 and 1490.—First Vases made at Etruria.

In 1780 Thomas Bentley died at his residence at Turnham Green, London, and was buried at Chiswick, where a tablet is erected to his memory. About this time, and probably previously as well as later, Flaxman the sculptor was much employed by Wedgwood, and I was fortunate enough to be able to print for the first time in 1864 some of the original bills for work done by Flaxman for Wedgwood, in which many well-known portrait-groups, &c., are named. Among these are "a portrait of Mr. Herschell, £2 2s.; a portrait of Dr. Buchan, £2 2s.; a portrait of C. Jenkinson, £2 2s.; a portrait of Govr. Hastings, Esq., £3 3s.; Mr. and Mrs. Meerman's portraits, £5 5s.; moulding a bust of Mr. and Mrs. Siddons, £1 11s. 6d.; a model in wax of Capt. Cook, £2 2s.; a model in wax of Dr. Johnson, £2 2s.; a figure of a Fool for Chess, £1 5s.; a drawing of Chess Men, £6 6s.;

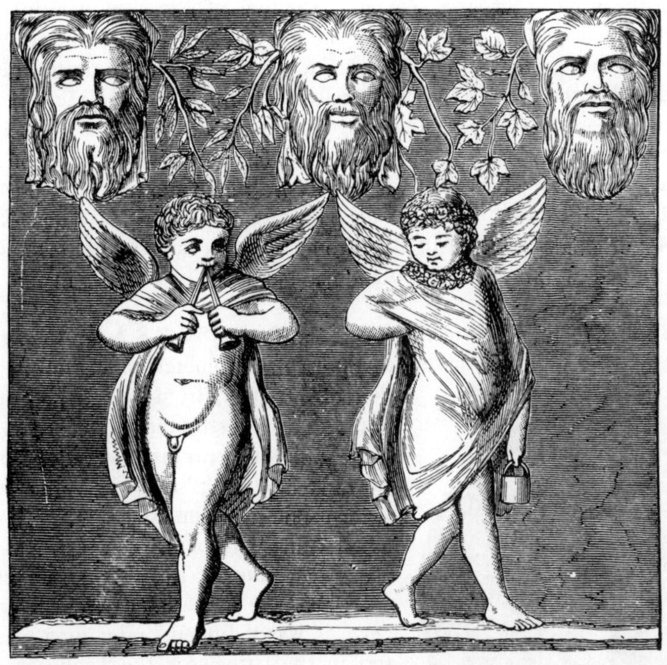

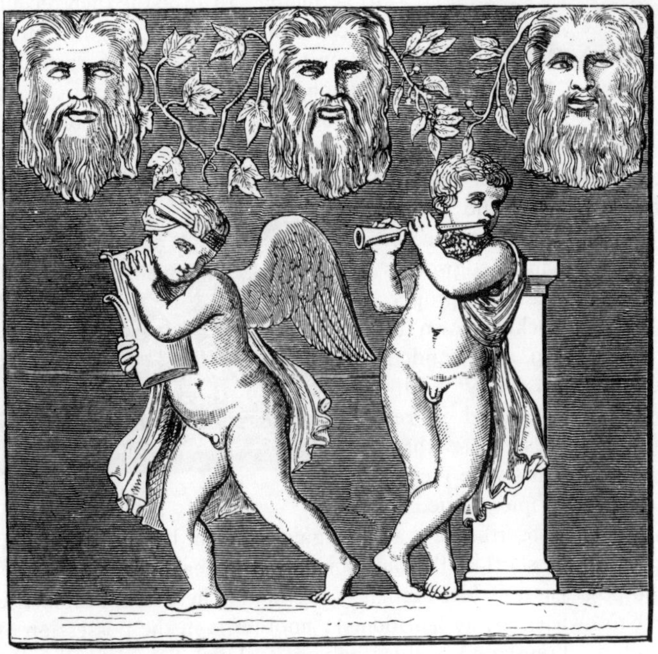

Figs. 1491 and 1492.—Flaxman's Bas-reliefs in Jasper Ware.

a model of the King of Sweden, £2 2s.; a model of Peace preventing Mars from bursting the Door of Janus's Temple, £15 15s.; a bas-relief in wax of Veturia and Volumnia entreating Coriolanus, £9 9s.; a model of Mercury uniting the hands of England and France, £13 13s.; a bas-relief of Hercules in the Hesperian Garden, £23; a model of the Queen of Portugal, £3 3s.; a bas-relief of Boys in wax, £11 0s. 6d.," and so on. Besides these he charged for drawings of crests and coats of arms; drawing bas-relief vases, &c., at a guinea a day; outlines for lamp and stand; drawings of chimney-pieces; patterns for borders for plates, &c. Many of Flaxman's originals are still in Wedgwood's hands, and the moulds are still used by them. Others, notably a series of exquisite models in wax, are in the possession of Lord Tweedmouth.

In 1782 Wedgwood was elected F.R.S., and in 1786, F.S.A., and communicated to the first learned body his invention of "a thermometer for measuring the higher degrees of heat, from a red heat up to the strongest that vessels made of clay can support;" in the following year his observations on "Derbyshire Black Wadd;" and afterwards other observations on thermometers, &c. In 1785 he invented his "Jasper Dip," which has continued in use ever since. Till 1785 the "jasper" body was the same throughout; from Nov., 1785 to 1858, it was "dipped," remaining white inside; and in the latter year the "solid jasper" body was re-introduced, and continues to some extent to be made. In 1786 the then recently deceased Duchess of Portland's magnificent collection of antiquities and objects of *virtu* were sold by auction, and among other articles of matchless interest was the Barberini or Portland Vase. This vase Wedgwood determined to possess, and having bid up to about a thousand pounds against the Duke of Portland, his grace, on learning why it was wanted, very kindly offered, if he would forego bidding and permit him to purchase, he would place it in Wedgwood's hands to copy as he thought proper. It was therefore knocked down to the Duke for £1,029, and handed to Wedgwood by him. This "inestimable jewel," as he called it, remained in his hands more than twelve months. Of this vase Wedgwood produced fifty copies (issued in 1790), which were subscribed for at fifty guineas each, but it is said that even this sum, £2,500, fell far short of the outlay incurred in making them. One of the first fifty is in the possession of Mr. Francis Wedgwood (where it will remain, it is hoped, with the first-thrown vases, as heirlooms); another is in the possession of the Duke of Sutherland, at Trentham; a third belongs to Lord Tweedmouth; a fourth is in the Mayer Museum; and others are in different collections. The body used for this vase was black jasper, and the figures, in their proper tone, were worked up

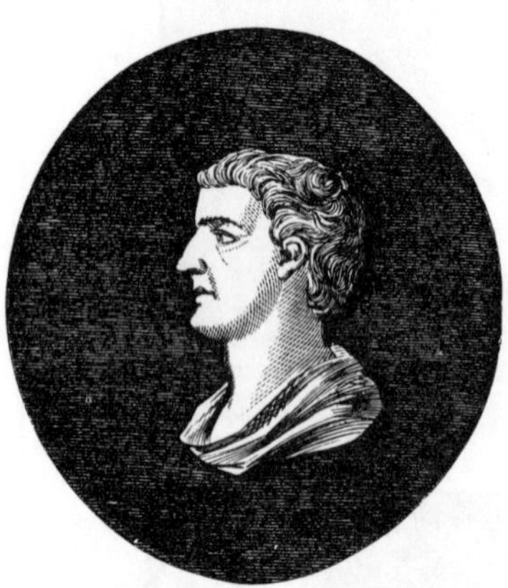

Fig. 1493.—Medallion, White on Black.

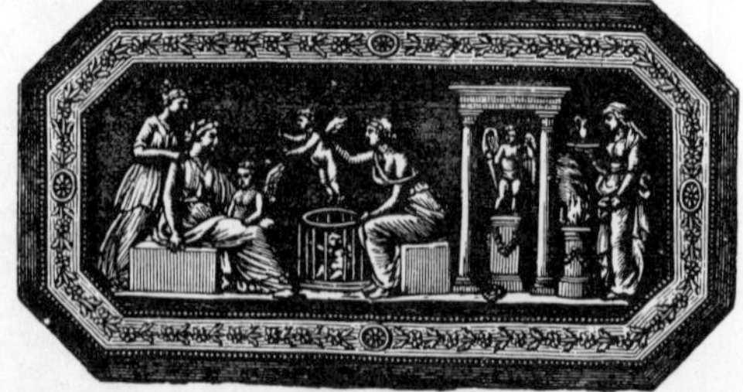

Fig. 1494.—Jasper Plaque.

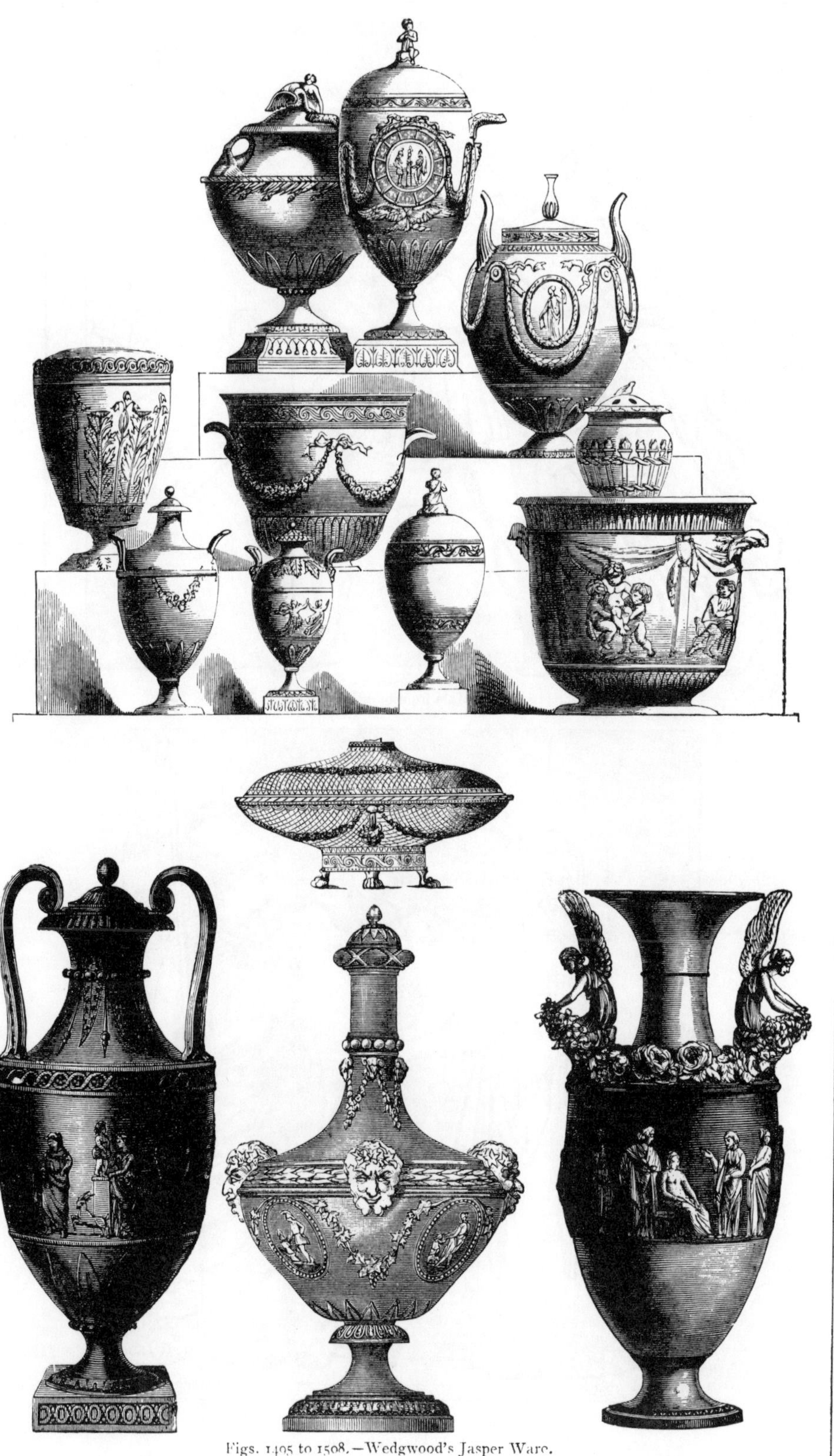

Figs. 1405 to 1508.—Wedgwood's Jasper Ware.

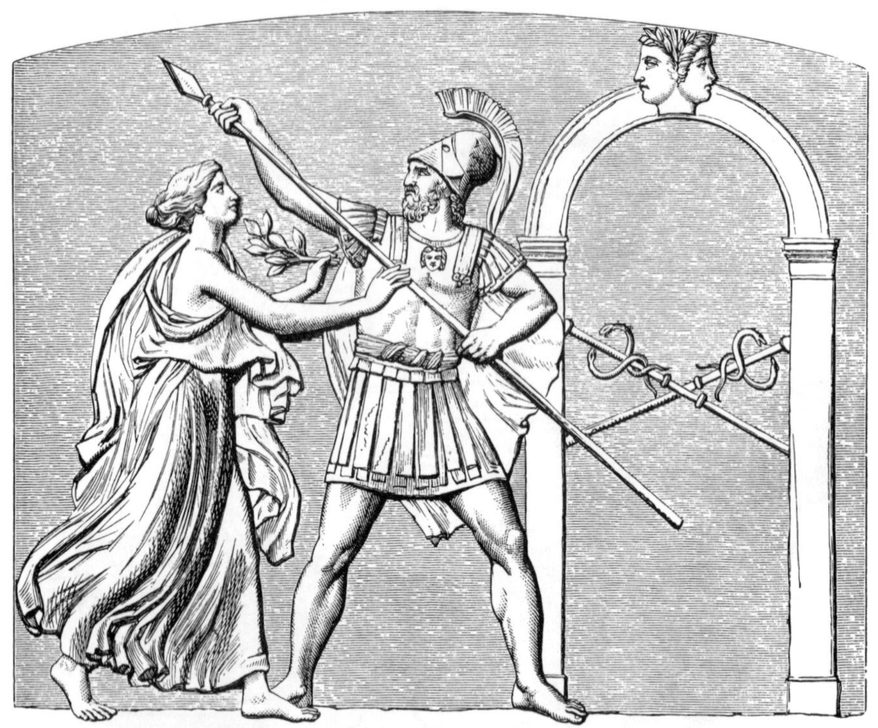

Fig. 1509.—" Peace preventing Mars from bursting the door of Janus's Temple."

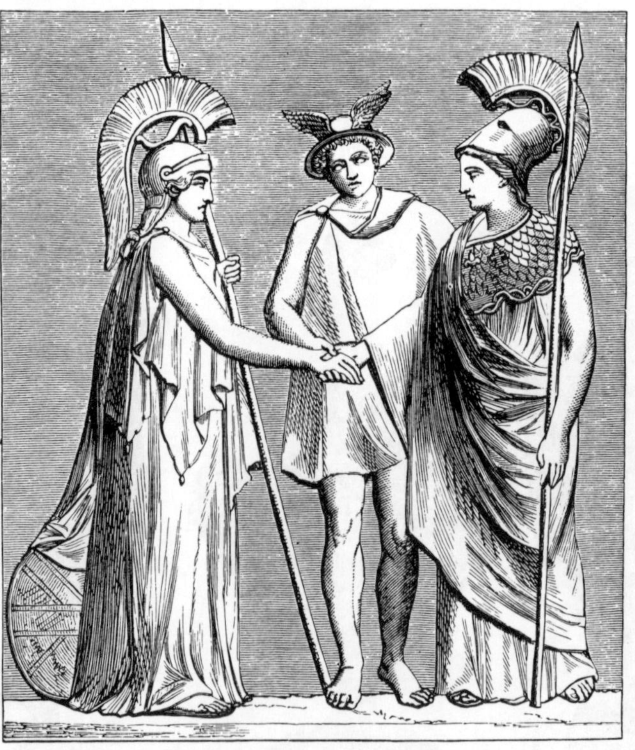

Fig. 1510.—" Mercury uniting the hands of England and France."
Bas-reliefs in Jasper by Flaxman ; charged in his bills.

and cut by the seal and gem engraver to the utmost possible degree of sharpness and finish. The original moulds are still in existence, and from them Messrs. Wedgwood still produce their Portland vase, both with a black, and with deep or light blue ground. While speaking of Wedgwood's ceramic reproduction of the Portland vase, it is interesting to add that in 1877 Mr. John Northwood and Mr. Philip Pargeter completed a unique and matchless work of art—a literal copy of the original vase in its own material, glass, and cut by exactly the same process as must have been employed by the artist who made it thousands of years back. Of this marvellous work I gave at the time a careful account in the "Reliquary." The material, glass, was, thanks to the skill and perseverance of Mr. Pargeter, produced of as nearly as possible the same rich full deep tone of blue colour, closely approaching to black when seen with the light upon it, but of vast richness in dark blue when the light passes through it. Upon this blue body Mr. Pargeter succeeded in laying a layer of fine white soft opal glass, specially made for the purpose, to a considerable thickness; and the welding of these two together was a process of exceeding difficulty. The two kinds of glass, the one being opaque and the other transparent, are usually of very different degrees of specific gravity, the usual opal being of much lighter material than ordinary glass, but for this special purpose they had to be made of the same degrees of specific gravity and of expansion and contraction. This difficult task was brought to a successful result, and the welding accomplished with the utmost thoroughness and delicacy. The body being thus entirely coated, even to half-way up the neck, with the opal, Mr. Northwood set about his herculean task and, for three years unceasingly devoted himself to it, never working less than six hours a day, and oftener more, at his gem-like material, and patiently cutting away, by hand, and by hand only, the opal coating, so as to leave the blue surface clear as a groundwork, and the figures and other parts of the design in relief. The whole of the grouping, the figures, the trees, and indeed every minute portion of the decoration was thus entirely carved and cut by hand in the opal as in the original. By the entire cutting away of the opal the amethystine glass of the vase itself was cleared and polished, while by the gradations of thickness in the carving all the most delicate shades of colour, from the finest white to the sweetest of all half-tones—produced by leaving simply a thin and fairylike film of the coating on the body—in blue, were produced. It is literally cameo engraving in its highest, most difficult, and most beautiful phase.

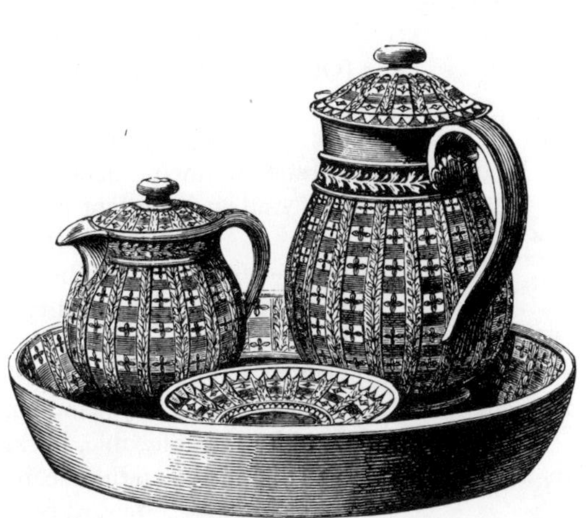

Fig. 1511.—Jasper Déjeuner.

In 1787 Wedgwood's sixth edition of his Catalogue contained for the first time the addition of the "Bamboo" and "Mortar" bodies—

"V.—*Bamboo*, or cane-coloured bisqué porcelain, of the same nature as No. 3.

"VI.—A porcelain bisqué of extreme *hardness*, little inferior to that of agate.

This property, together with its resistance to the strongest acids and corrosives, and its impenetrability by every known species of liquids, adapts it happily for mortars and different kinds of chemical vessels."

In 1789 the medallion (Fig. 1521) supposed to be made from clay brought from New South Wales, was executed. In the following year Wedgwood took into partnership his three sons, John, Josiah, and Thomas, and his nephew, Thomas Byerley (son of his sister Margaret by her husband, a descendant of the Byerleys of Byerley Hall, in Yorkshire), the style of the firm being "Josiah Wedgwood, Sons, & Byerley." In 1793 John Wedgwood retired from the concern, and the style was then altered to "Josiah Wedgwood, Son, & Byerley." In 1794 Josiah Wedgwood was seized with his last illness, and on the 3rd of January, 1795, he died, and was, on the 6th, buried in the churchyard at Stoke-upon-Trent ("Burials in 1795, Jany. 6th, Josiah Wedgwood, of Etruria"), where his tomb and a tablet erected to his memory in the chancel still remain. The tablet (Fig. 1531) bears a fine bust of Wedgwood, by Flaxman, a ewer, and a Portland vase, and the following inscription :—

Sacred to the memory of
JOSIAH WEDGWOOD, F.R.S. AND S.A.,
Of Etruria, in this County,
Born in August, 1730, died January 3rd, 1795,
Who converted a rude and inconsiderable manufacture into an elegant art
And an important part of national
Commerce.
By these services to his country he acquired an ample fortune,
Which he blamelessly and reasonably enjoyed,
And generously dispensed for the reward of merit and the relief of misfortune.
His mind was inventive and original, yet perfectly sober and well regulated;
His character was decisive and commanding, without rashness or arrogance;
His probity was inflexible, his kindness unwearied;
His manners simple and dignified, and the cheerfulness of his temper was the natural reward of
The activity of his pure and useful life.
He was most loved by those who knew him best,
And he has left indelible impressions of affection and veneration on the minds of
His family, who have erected this monument to his memory.

Josiah Wedgwood, whose wife survived him twenty years and died in 1815, had issue Susannah, married to Dr. Robert Darwin, of Shrewsbury, son of the celebrated Dr. Erasmus Darwin, of Derby (and half-brother to Sir Francis Darwin, M.D., of Breadsall Priory, and Sydnope, in the same county), and was mother of Charles Darwin, the naturalist, author of the "Origin of Species," &c., who married his cousin, Emma Wedgwood; John, who resided at Seabridge, and married Louisa Jane, daughter of Mr. Allen, of Criselly, Pembrokeshire, and by her had four sons and three daughters; Richard, born in 1767, and died in 1782; Josiah, one of the founders of the Royal Horticultural Society, first M.P. for Stoke-upon-Trent, who married Elizabeth Allen, of Criselly, Pembrokeshire, and by her had four sons and five daughters, the eldest of whom, Josiah (the third of that name), married his cousin, Caroline Elizabeth, daughter of Dr. Darwin, of Shrewsbury, and had issue Henry Allen Wedgwood, barrister-at-law, Francis Wedgwood, of Etruria and Barlaston, the late head of the Etruria firm, who married Frances, daughter of the Rev. J. P. Mosley, of Rolleston Rectory, and had issue three sons, Godfrey, Clement, and Lawrence, the present members of the firm, and four daughters.

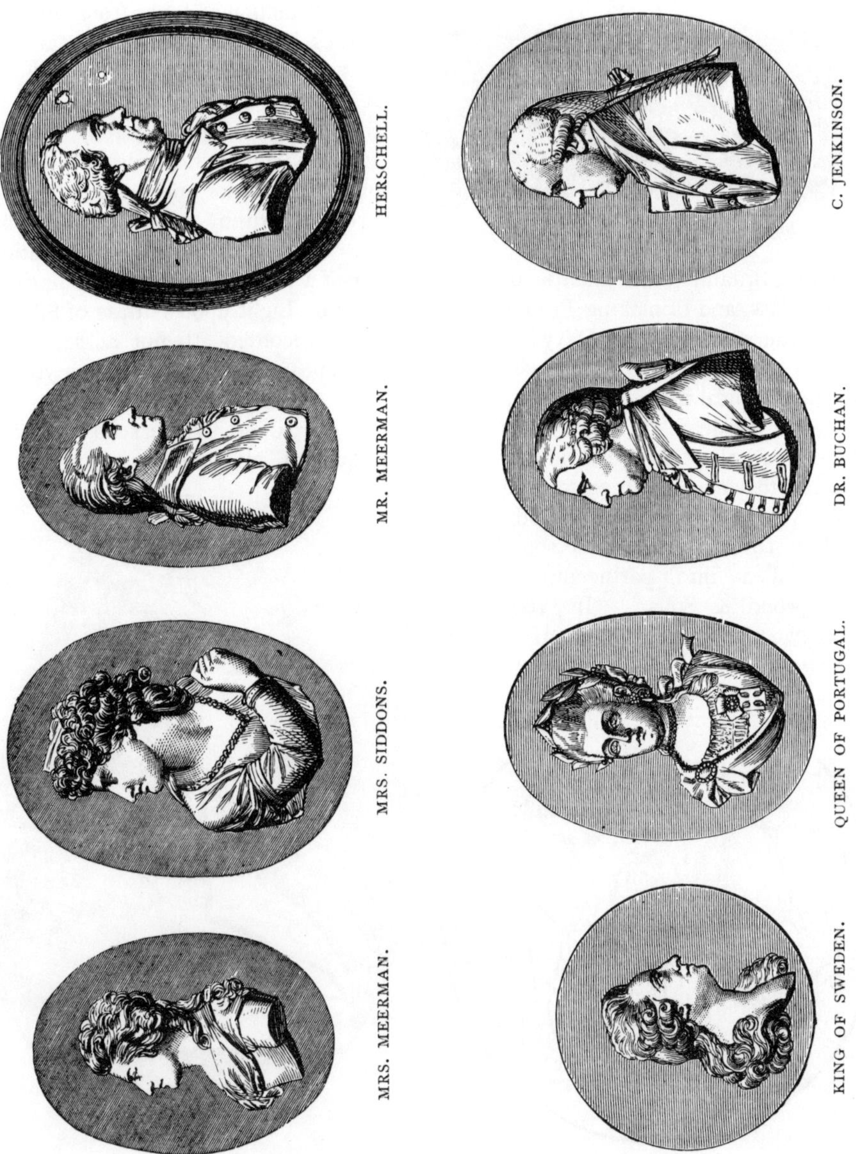

Figs. 1512 to 1519.—Wedgwood Medallion Wares.

For a time after Josiah Wedgwood's death the management of the business devolved on Mr. Byerley. In 1800 the partners were, the brothers Josiah and John Wedgwood and Thomas Byerley, and so continued until Byerley's death in 1810 Thomas Wedgwood, who suffered constant ill-health, took no part in the manage ment of the business, and died in 1805, at Gunville, Dorsetshire. He was a man of considerable scientific attainments. During his father's lifetime he prosecuted his studies with his aid and that of Alexander Chisholm, and in 1792 communicated to the Royal Society an account of his "Experiments and Observations on the Production of Light from different bodies by Heat and by Attraction." His continued experiments and researches resulted in the discovery of the process of photography, and in 1802, in conjunction with Sir Humphrey Davy, he made those discoveries known by a paper printed in the "Journal of the Royal Institution of Great Britain," under the title of "An Account of a Method of Copying Paintings upon Glass, and of making Profiles by the Agency of Light upon Nitrate of Silver; with observations by H. Davy." This is the first recorded attempt at fixing the images of the camera-obscura (which Wedgwood appears to have used from a youth) by the chemical influence of light.

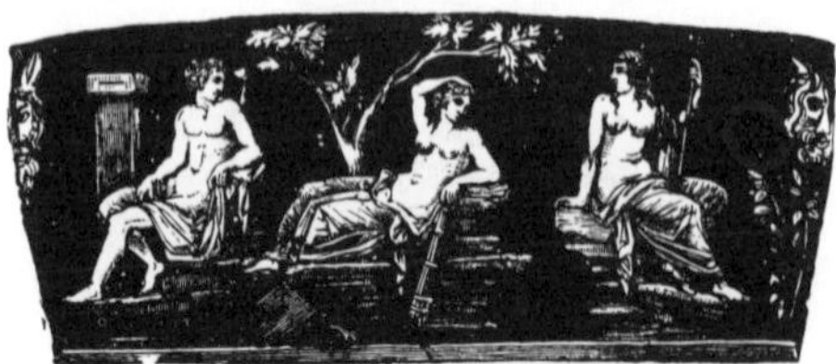

Fig. 1520.—Group from the Portland Vase.

After the death of Byerley, the business was carried on by the second Josiah Wedgwood alone until Martinmas, 1823, when he took his eldest son Josiah (the third of that name) into partnership, under the style of "Josiah Wedgwood & Son," and in 1827, when another son, Francis, was taken into partnership, "Josiah Wedgwood & Sons." In 1841 Josiah Wedgwood, senior, of Maer Hall, retired from the business, and it was carried on by his sons until the following April, when Josiah Wedgwood, junior, also retired.

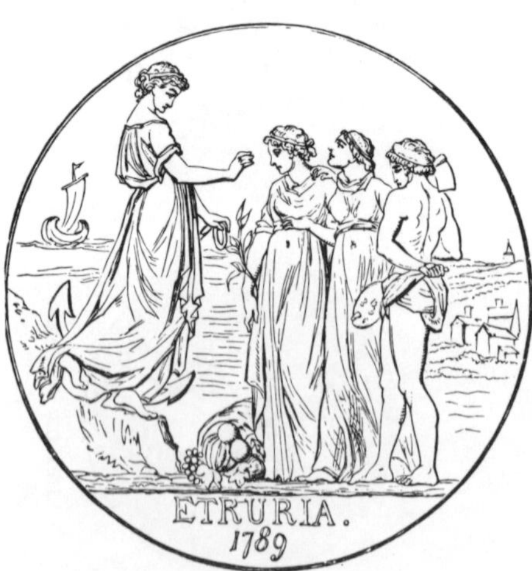

Fig. 1521.

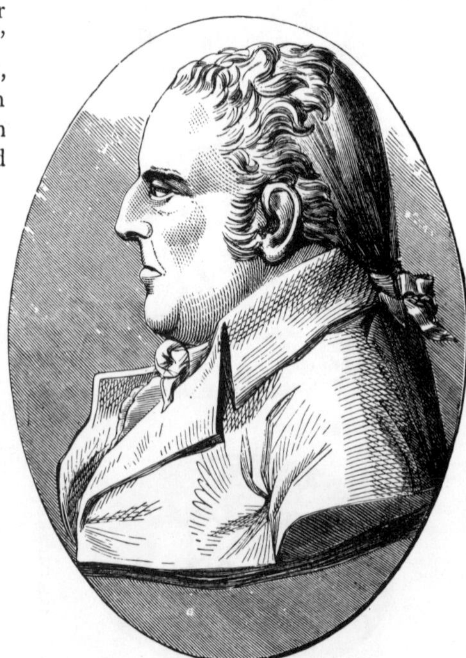

Fig. 1522.—Medallion of Thomas Byerley.

The manufacture of china, which had never been attempted by the first Josiah, was commenced at Etruria about 1808 or 1809, but was discontinued in 1815. In 1879, after a lapse of sixty-four years, the manufacture was again introduced and has

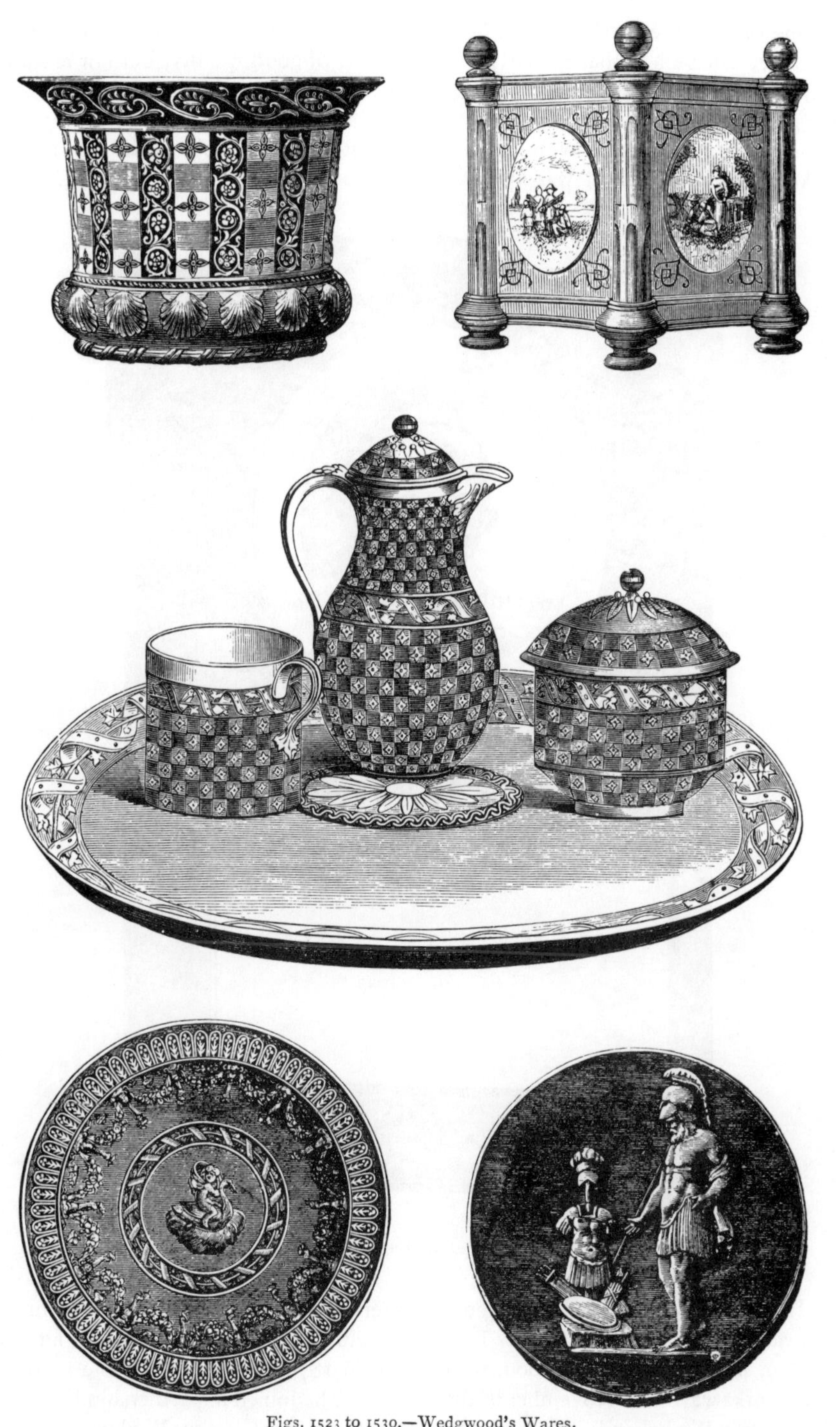

Figs. 1523 to 1530.—Wedgwood's Wares.

become one of the marked successes of the firm. The first china, none of which, of course, can be less than seventy years old, was of good quality, both in texture of body, colour, glaze, and decoration. The mark is the name WEDGWOOD, in red or blue. That of the present day ranks with the finest and best produced by any house in the trade, and is extensively made for the American and colonial as well as home markets. "Stone china" was also made at Etruria, but ceased about 1825.

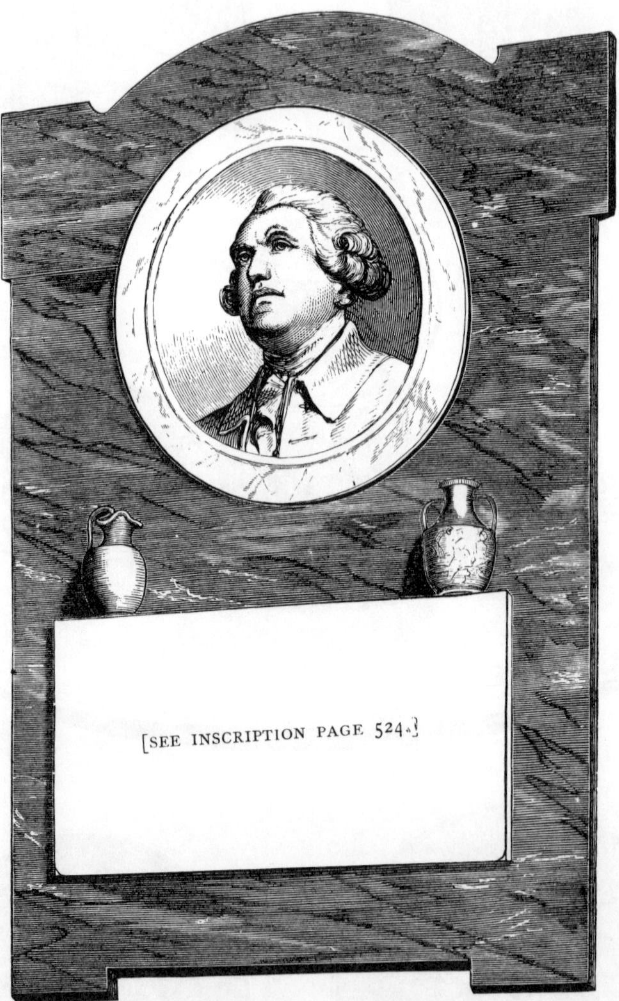

Fig. 1531.—Monument to Josiah Wedgwood in Stoke-upon-Trent Church.

In 1843 Mr. John Boyle became a partner in the firm, but died sixteen months afterwards. In 1846 Mr. Robert Brown, of Cliff Ville, became a partner, but dying in 1859, Mr. Francis Wedgwood, who retired in 1870, was again left sole proprietor of the works was. In November of the same year he joined in partnership by his son, Mr. Godfrey Wedgwood, in 1863 by his second son, Mr. Clement Wedgwood, and in 1868 by his third son, Mr. Lawrence Wedgwood, and the works are still carried on as "Josiah Wedgwood & Sons."

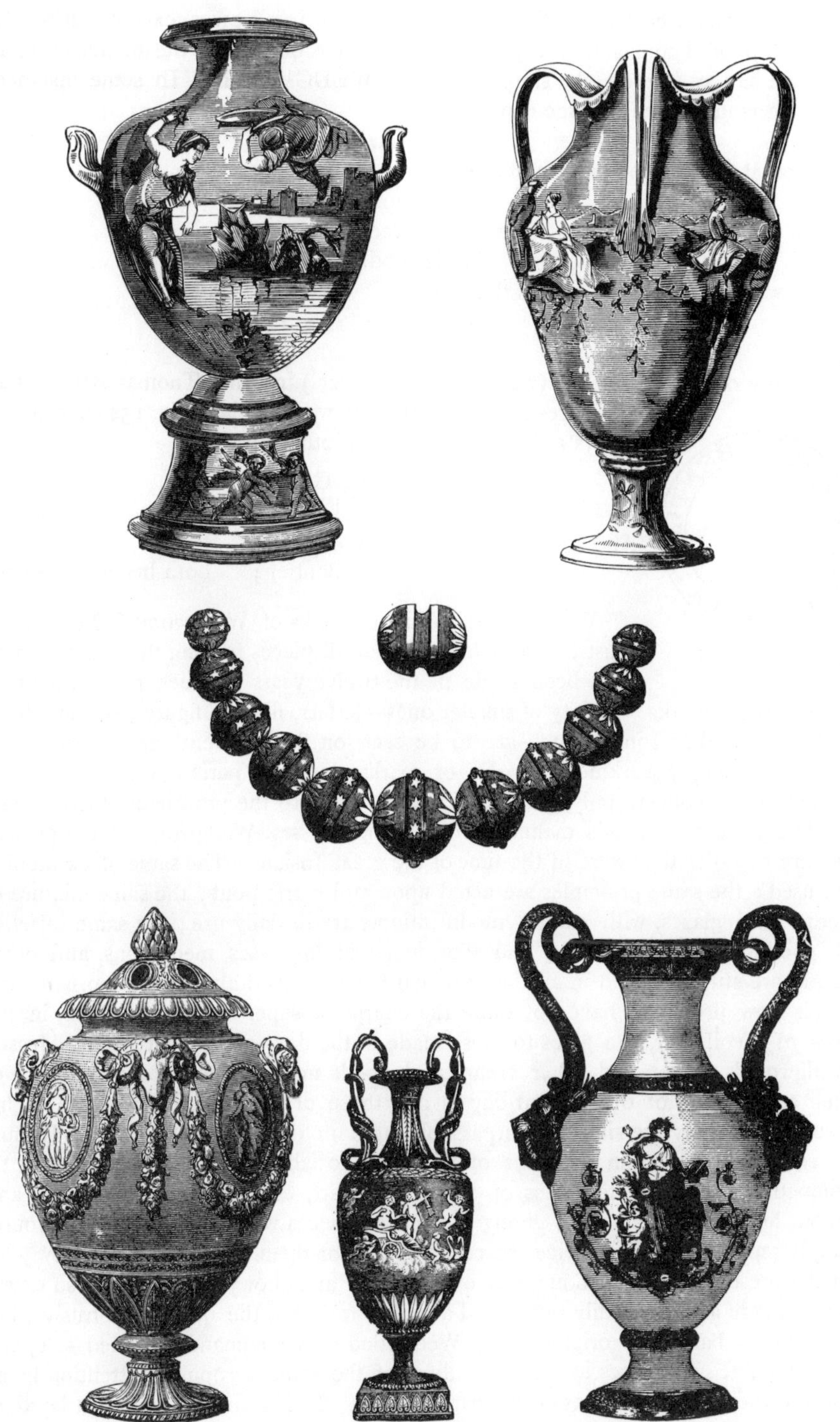

Figs. 1532 to 1538.—Perseus and Andromeda Vase by Lessore; Vase by Lessore; Jasper Beads; and three Vases.

The MARKS used by the Wedgwoods have been in all cases, except during the partnership of Thomas Bentley, on that particular branch of the manufacture in which he had an interest, the simple name of WEDGWOOD. In some instances the name is impressed in large capitals—

WEDGWOOD.

In others it appears in small capital letters—

WEDGWOOD.

And in others, though not so commonly, in the ordinary type—

Wedgwood.

On a few pieces the name occurs thus :—

WEDGWOOD
ETRURIA.

On the ornamental goods (vases, medallions, &c.) in which Thomas Bentley had an interest, the general mark was circular (Fig. 1543), with the letters *raised,* not sunk. Another was—

WEDGWOOD
& BENTLEY,

And another Wedgwood
& Bentley ; both being impressed.

WEDGWOOD & BENTLEY : ETRURIA ·

Figs. 1539 to 1545.

With regard to these marks of Wedgwood & Bentley" it must be borne in mind that all pieces bearing these names must have been made in the twelve years between 1768 and 1780. Besides these marks a variety of smaller ones—letters, flowers, figures, and numbers, both impressed and in colours—are to be seen on the different varieties of wares. These are simply workmen's marks, or marks denoting period, &c., and, being private marks, concern only, and are of interest only, to the proprietors themselves.

The classes of goods manufactured by the Messrs. Wedgwood at the present day are much as they were in the time of the great Josiah. The same block moulds are used ; the same principles are acted upon and carried out ; the same mixture of bodies and glazes, with certain modifications, are in daily use ; the same varieties of goods are manufactured ; and thus many of his vases, medallions, and other goods, are still produced in all their original beauty. And although the ornamental goods now produced have not quite the charm of super-excellence which, in the eyes of a collector, age gives to those made in the days of the first Josiah, Messrs. Wedgwood's jasper and other ornamental goods now stand as far in advance of their competitors of the present day as did those of the great Josiah those of his own time. They are simply unsurpassable both in design and execution. It must be remembered that in the days of the first Josiah Wedgwood there was little competition in other branches of the potter's art, and the great care, skill, and labour he bestowed upon his purely ornamental pieces was, there can be no doubt, amply repaid in the high prices he could obtain for them. This is not so now ; for at the present day Art productions of attractive and showy character are so extensively made and so readily purchased at a low rate that the quiet, unobtrusive, but truly lovely bas-reliefs originated by Wedgwood only command a limited sale, and even then at such prices as will not admit of the same scrupulous attention being paid to their production as in the earlier days. The unrivalled skill as a lapidary shown by Mr. Northwood in his reproduction of the Portland Vase (see page 523, by the same process of cameo-cutting as the original, led Messrs. Wedgwood to reproduce the "first fifty" black jasper Portland vases of the "great Josiah." After every care that the potters' art could lavish was expended, they were placed in the hands of the lapidary (Mr. Northwood), as was the case with at least some of the first edition, and were issued by Phillips, at whose exhibition of old Wedgwood ware, in 1880, they stood side by side with the actual original from which the first fifty were sold. The firm still produce "jasper," "basaltes," "red," "cream-coloured," and other wares. The jasper goods are still, as they have ever been since the first production of that marvellous body, the great specialty of their works. In this, since the days of Turner, although they have had many imitators, they have never even been approached, and their goods still maintain their old and high reputation. All the famous works of the olden time are still made in all their beauty, with the addition of many new and ever-varying designs and combinations. The jasper is produced in dark and in light blue of various shades (with, of course, the raised figures and ornaments in white), in sage-green, in pink, and other tints. It is also produced both in "solid jasper"—that is, the body coloured throughout—and in "jasper dip," which is a white jasper body with the colour laid on the surface. The "solid jasper" was reintroduced in 1856. The manufacture of majolica was commenced at Etruria in 1860. With regard to this it is necessary to state that the true Italian majolica, as well as Minton's reproductions, were made with a coarse cane-coloured body and decorated with opaque enamel colours; but that Wedgwoods were the first to use a white body and transparent coloured glazes. By this process much greater brilliancy of effect is produced than by the use of enamel colours. In majolica all the usual classes of goods, including umbrella-stands, vases, &c., are made.

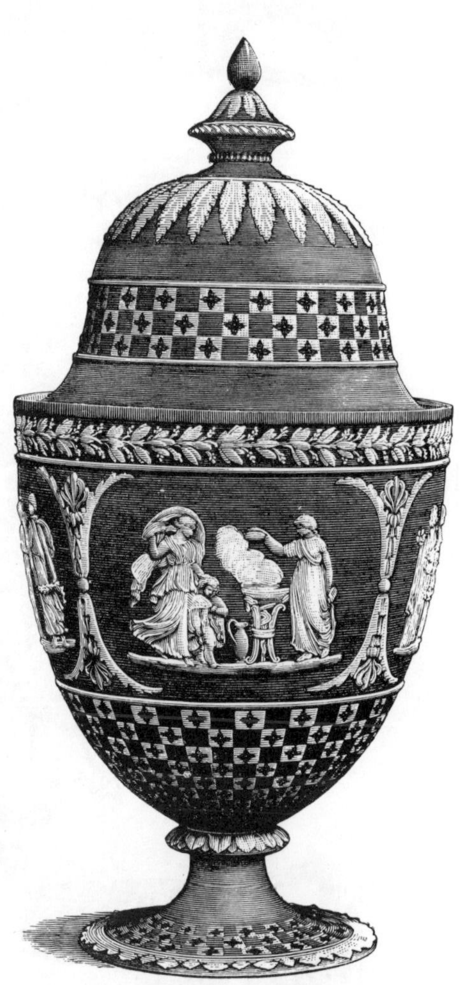

Fig. 1546.—Jasper Vase.

In "malachite," "mottled," "agate," and other wares, dessert, toilet, and trinket services, and a variety of both useful and ornamental articles are made. "Parian" busts and figures of good quality were made about 1848 or 1849. Another variety of ornamental work is the "inlaid" ware, in which the effect is much the same as the wood "Tunbridge ware." It is made by the same process as the famous "Henri Deux" wares; an impress from a metal runner being filled up with a different coloured clay, and afterwards turned or scraped level on the surface. In

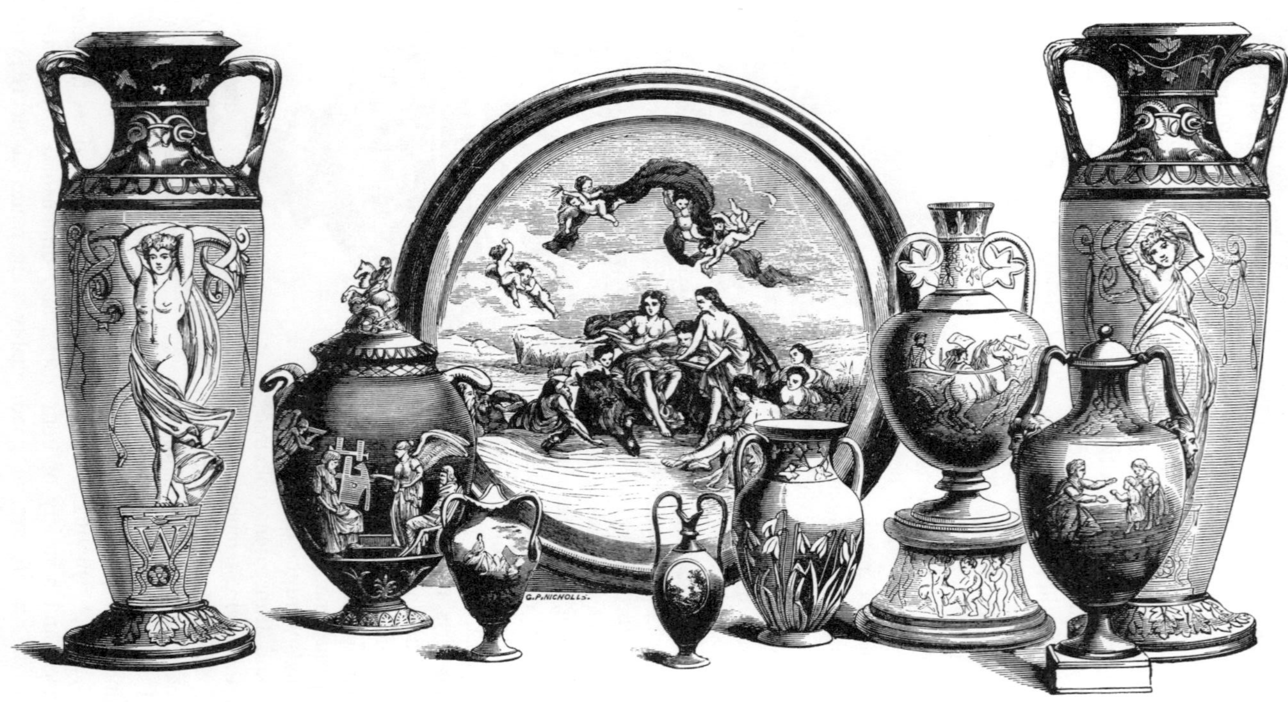

Figs. 1547 to 1555.—Messrs. Wedgwood's Productions. Lessore's Europa Plateau and other Wares.

this ware a magnificent and highly appropriate chess-table has been produced to use with the celebrated Flaxman chessmen.

"Cream-coloured" ware, the veritable "Queen's ware" of the olden time, is still extensively made. Of a delicate creamy whiteness in colour, light and pleasant to the touch, true and close-fitting in the "potting," and covered with a faultless glaze, this ware still "holds its own," and maintains its wonted supremacy. In it services and every variety of useful articles are made, and it is pleasant to add that the pieces are still made in the old moulds used in the great Josiah's time, with only such modifications as fit them for more modern notions. For instance, the "turin" modelled by Flaxman, and charged for in his bill, which I have printed, is still made, with only the addition of newly-designed handles; and hundreds of others of the "ancient forms" are still in the same way preserved and produced. In the "pearl" body, which is of great hardness and durability and of a pearly whiteness, services and useful goods are manufactured in plain white, printed, and decorated varieties. In "Rockingham ware," teapots, coffee-pots, services (the cups white inside), and other articles are made, as are also "porous ware" water-bottles, butter-coolers, &c., and "mortar ware." In the "red ware"—a rich colour and fine body—services and a large number of other articles are produced, and are frequently ornamented with raised figures, &c., in black with good and striking effect. Blue printing was introduced at Etruria at an early date, and has, with black, &c., been continued to the present day; under the third Josiah Wedgwood, from 1820 forward, it was brought to intense perfection. The firm some time ago introduced a process by which photographs of original drawings, in colours, are produced on ware by the same method as the autotype process. This forms a notable feature of progress in scientific decoration, and it is only meet that as photography itself was the undoubted discovery of a Wedgwood, its development as an aid to ceramic decoration should be left to his successors at the present day. Another feature is the revival of the old imitations of porphyry, agate, pebble, Aberdeen granite, &c., the latter being made by encrusting the pliant clay of the vase with innumerable small fragments of various coloured clays before firing. In this chaste style the "Leda Vase" is a notable example. Among the more beautiful of their recent achievements in jasper are a pair of exquisite renaissance ewers, with bas-reliefs of "Peace" and "War;" a large plaque of the "Seven Ages," modelled after a design by Walter Crane; the vase, Fig. 1546; and a series of subjects from Chaucer, Shakspere, and Milton. In porcelain are, notably, a pair of vases 2 ft. 6 in. high, painted with subjects of nymphs and amorini by J. Allen, for the Paris Exhibition, where the firm obtained a gold medal.

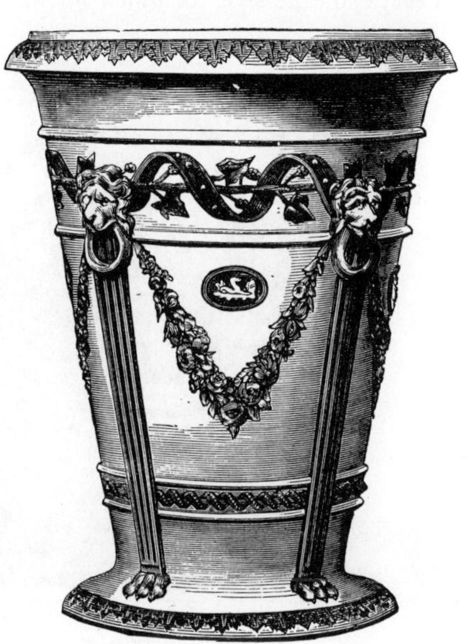

Fig. 1556.

One of the most recent additions to the productions of these works is a new method of impressed decoration of tiles, patented by Mr. Marsden, which has been adopted and perfected by Messrs. Wedgwood. The process has many advantages, foremost of which is the easy manner of exact reproduction of special designs at no additional cost over that of stock patterns. A large panel of tiles, decorated by this process, is placed in Quinta schools, Chirk, the designs for which are by Louis H. Day, under instructions from J. Raffles Davison, giving perfect satisfaction. Since this time an exhibition of these tiles has been made at the Building Exhibition in Manchester, where they received unqualified praise, and at the Sanitary Congress, held at Glasgow, in 1883, the firm received a medal in the first class. The principal charm in these tiles is the harmony of colour in conjunction with softness of tone, arrived at by the method of impressing the colours.

The principal painter at Etruria for many years was the late gifted M. Emile Lessore, an artist of more than European reputation, who took rank above all others in that exquisite style for which he was so famous. As M. Lessore (whom I had

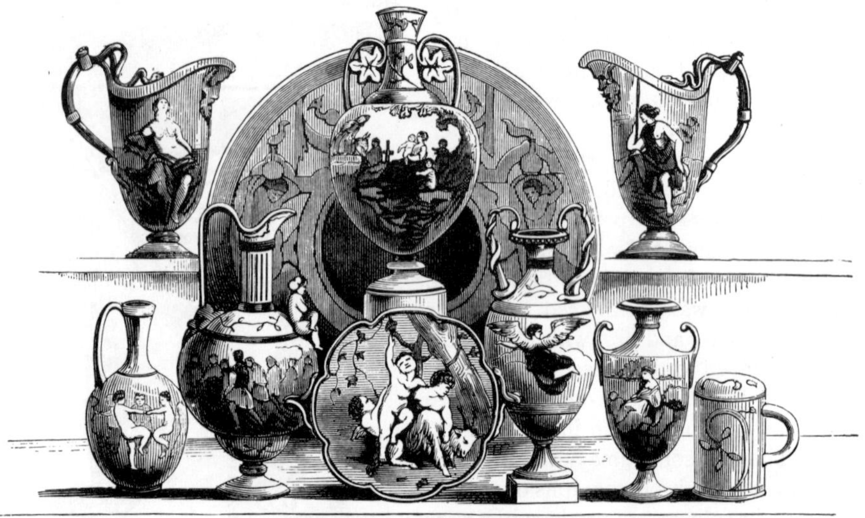

Figs. 1556 to 1566.—Painted by Lessore.

the privilege of knowing, and who pressed me more than once to visit him at Marlotte) and his works are so closely identified with Etruria, a few words on his career cannot but be interesting. He was born in 1805, his father being a notary, for which profession the son was at first intended. Giving up the law for Art, he entered for a short time the studio of Ingres. In 1831 he exhibited his first picture ("Le Frère Malade") in the Salon at Paris, and from that time until 1850 continued to exhibit both oil and water-colour pictures, which were always eagerly sought for and purchased at high prices. In 1851 Lessore was induced, through offers made to him by the Sèvres china manufactory, to turn his attention to china-painting. He attempted to introduce a more artistic feeling at Sèvres, and succeeded notably. A pair of large vases decorated by him, which were exhibited in Paris in 1853, were purchased by the Emperor of Russia for a thousand guineas. The originality of Lessore's work caused a division amongst the artists at Sèvres, and the partisans of the two camps were so virulently wearisome in their disputes that in 1858 he aban-

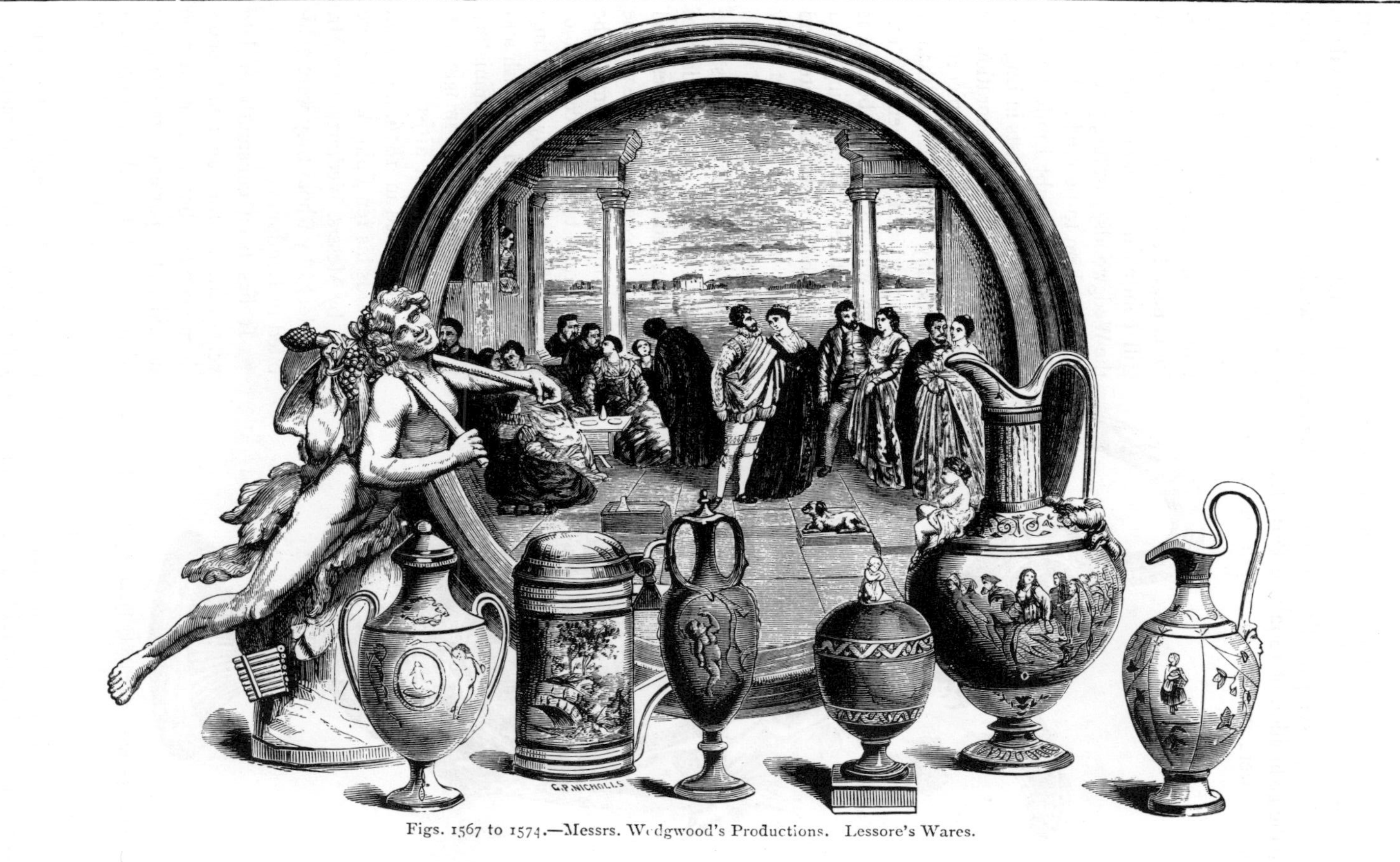

Figs. 1567 to 1574.—Messrs. Wedgwood's Productions. Lessore's Wares.

doned Sèvres and came to England, where, after being employed for a short time by Mintons, he joined Messrs. Wedgwood, who thoroughly appreciated his talents and his loyal sympathetic character. The most remarkable of his works were shown in the Exhibition of 1862, the Paris Exhibition of 1867, and at Vienna in 1873, and medals were awarded to him in all countries. The climate of England, especially Staffordshire, not suiting him, he returned to France, living at Marlotte, near Fontainebleau, where he still continued his connection with the Wedgwoods, painting pieces and sending them to be fired at Etruria. There is little doubt Emile Lessore was one of the first artists in England to revolutionise the decoration of pottery, and some of his pieces are unmistakably more artistic than is usually produced in faience. The drawing, without being laboured, is true to nature; the colouring, as a rule, is subdued and delicate, and the master hand is apparent in every touch. During the siege of Paris many of Lessore's finest works were concealed by him in the cellars of his cottage, and afterwards preserved by Messrs. Wedgwood. He was the first to employ the freedom of the artist's brush to the decoration of pottery, which previously to his time had been painted with the finish and stippled perfection of the miniature painter, but without the imagination and freshness of an artist's sketch. M. Lessore died in 1876, and soon afterwards his remaining works were sold by Messrs. Wedgwood to Mr. Mortlock, by whom they were exhibited in London.

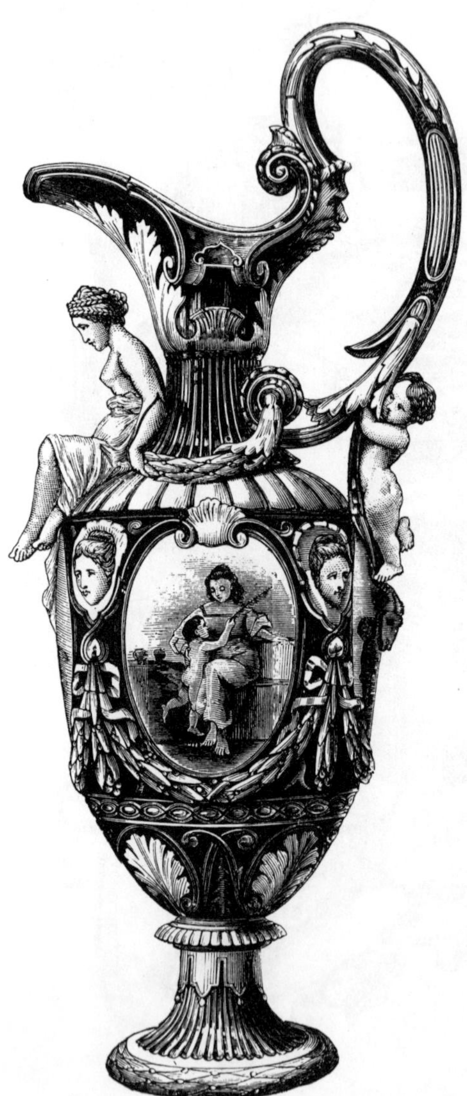

Fig. 1575.—Ewer modelled by Protat, painted by Lessore.

It has been constantly of late years said by critics, anxious to show their acumen, but to some degree devoid of the power of grasping the whole subject, that the modern productions of the Wedgwoods cannot be compared with the old. Doubtless the surface of the old examples has a peculiar polish, and a more velvetty feel than the new; but this is mainly due to the continual washing or rubbing in cleaning which for a century the old pieces have undergone. The present body, under the same circumstances, would at least equal the old in this respect, while in all others it is nowise inferior. That works of art can be, and *are*, produced now as good as formerly, where the necessity for cheapness does not stand in the way, there can be no possible doubt.

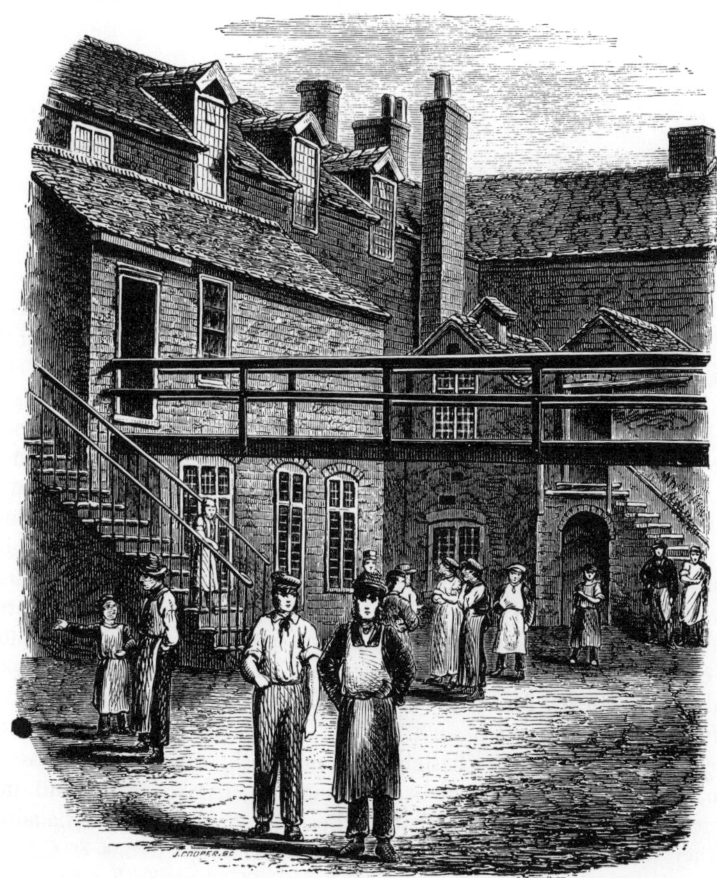

Fig. 1576.

The markets to which Messrs. Wedgwood's goods are sent are more widely spread than perhaps will be conceived by the uninitiated, and it is not too much to say that, besides the home trade, which is very extensive, the "Wedgwood ware" of the present day is dispatched, as it used to be, to every quarter of the globe.

CHAPTER XXII.

LONGTON.

Sutherland Road Works.—These works were commenced in 1862 by Messrs. Adams, Scrivener, & Co. Mr. Scrivener having a few years afterwards retired from the business, Mr. Adams was joined by Mr. Titus Hammersley, and the concern was carried on by them under the style of "Harvey Adams & Co." until the death of Mr. Hammersley in 1875, when he was succeeded by his son Mr. George Harris Hammersley, the style of the firm remaining as before. The productions comprise china, semi-china, and fine stoneware. In earthenware, toilet and all the usual table services, and numberless useful articles of the best designs and highest finish are made. In stoneware, jugs, teapots, and other articles are produced; in these many excellent shapes and designs have been introduced. In china, tea, breakfast, dinner, dessert, trinket, toilet, and other services; jugs of various kinds; vases, and an endless variety of ornamental and highly decorated goods, are made. The quality of the china is remarkably fine and good, and the glaze of more than average excellence. The decorations are remarkable for purity of conception, for admirable arrangement, for manipulative skill, and for the thorough and perfect artistic feeling which pervades each design. In tea and breakfast services many novel, but at the same time chastely beautiful, designs have been introduced by this firm, who have also the credit of being the first to make and introduce "moustache cups"—an invention that has become so popular as to be adopted by many other firms. These services are made by Harvey Adams & Co. in every style, from the simple white and gold (one variety of which, with a beaded edge, is peculiarly simple and pretty) to the most richly, even gorgeously-painted, gilt, enamelled, and jewelled varieties. In each of these their productions take rank with those of any other house. In some services, both tea and dessert, what may be called an *ormolu* decoration has been introduced with as good effect by this firm as by any other. It gives a richness and a solidity to the patterns which could not otherwise be easily obtained. The jewelling—especially the pearl borders—is admirably executed, and with marked effect. Two important features in the productions of these works—which from first being confined to the medium quality of common china have gradually progressed to the present time, when they rank among the highest and best in the district—are, the introduction of silver both as a ground and as a heightening, and of embossed leaf decoration of a peculiar and artistic character. In like manner with gold, the silver is introduced both dead and burnished, and forms a pleasing and marvellously rich combination with gold and colour. It is introduced on tea services in bands upon wreaths of flowers, and other decorations are painted with marked effect. One of the finest and most chastely beautiful of the ceramic productions of this or any other age or country is an open-work plate in which solid silver forms the ground for the centre. On this silver ground is painted, with all the skill that art is capable of, a group of flowers as true to nature as if pencilled by nature herself; the richness and delicacy of the colouring are "thrown up," and a finer and more exquisitely beautiful effect produced by this ground than could by any other means have been effected. The open-work rim, with its interlaced ribbon, and the whole of the subordinate decorations, are in excellent keeping and harmony with the central group.

In leaf-decoration Harvey Adams & Co. have, with good taste, introduced "shamrock" tea and breakfast sets, which have become deservedly popular; embossed foliage dessert services, and fern and foliage tea and dessert services and vases, and other ornamental articles, all of which they have very wisely registered. These services consist of upwards of fifty arranged groups of leaves of trees and arrangements of ferns in relief, the whole of which have been modelled from specimens obtained from the gardens of his Grace the Duke of Sutherland, at Trentham Hall. These are painted both in the spring, summer, and autumnal tints, with such scrupulous nicety, and so true to nature, that it is next to impossible to fancy it is not the leaf itself that lies on the plate. The firm has also introduced the primrose on tea, breakfast, and dessert services. The leaves and flowers of the primrose are in relief, and are beautifully painted and tinted from nature. They are also finished in various styles, but always in strict accordance with the simplicity of the original design. Messrs. Harvey Adams & Co. have also entered very largely into the work of ornamental flowering in relief *à la* Dresden, and have brought out a number of good shapes in vases, jardinières, and other articles, with flowers and plants modelled on the ware, and painted true to nature. In this and in other departments of the art-manufactory they secured the services of several well-known artists, among them Mr. Henry Mitchell, medallist of the Paris and Vienna Exhibitions, celebrated as an animal, landscape, and figure painter, and whose works are remarkable for their finish, their modelling, and their delicacy of treatment, and whose greys and flesh tints are of peculiar purity and beauty; Mr. Swan, and Mr. Longmore—the former a clever flower-painter, and the latter highly skilled in his artistic treatment of birds. The firm has also brought out in great variety a series of designs of the Chinese, Japanese, and Persian style, consisting of figure and floral decoration, and have adapted them to tea, breakfast, dessert, and ornamental goods—the cobalt blue, introduced largely in these patterns, being of a specially pure and rich colour; and while many of these are for the general buyer, a very large number are of a high-class character. In these Mr. Slater (who left the firm in 1881), happily realised the full force of the special characteristics of this ancient style of art, and produced works admirably drawn and exquisitely coloured. He was succeeded as art director by Mr. John Marshall, who has ably maintained the reputation of the firm, evincing great taste and experience in the production of new shapes and designs of the Persian, Chinese, and Japanese schools, which have commanded heavy sales both in the home and American and Australian markets. Mr. Marshall, who has for many years ranked high as a flower-painter, and some of whose works occupy a foremost place among the gems of Art at South Kensington, is at the present time engaged in bringing out a series of patterns of the Persian and Moresque schools, which for beauty of colour and finish will bear comparison with goods produced by any other firm. The A D coffees and dejuné sets, and five o'clock or kettledrum sets, recently produced are giving general satisfaction and securing fame.

Mr. Harvey Adams, to whose pure taste and artistic judgment the high state of excellence of the productions of these works is to be attributed, has, during the past few years, successively visited the United States, and having thoroughly studied the tastes and requirements of the people of that great country, is specially and to a large extent catering for the American markets, where his goods, being all of the best class, are sure to be welcome and to command ready sale.

Market Street Works.—These are said to be the oldest works in Longton—the first there established—and to be contemporaneous with those of Wedgwood at

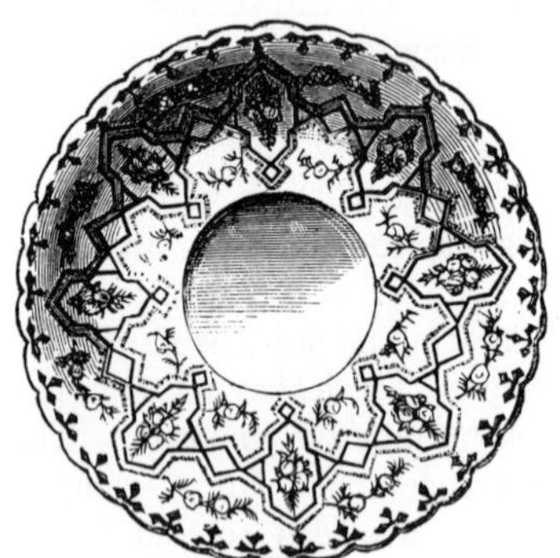

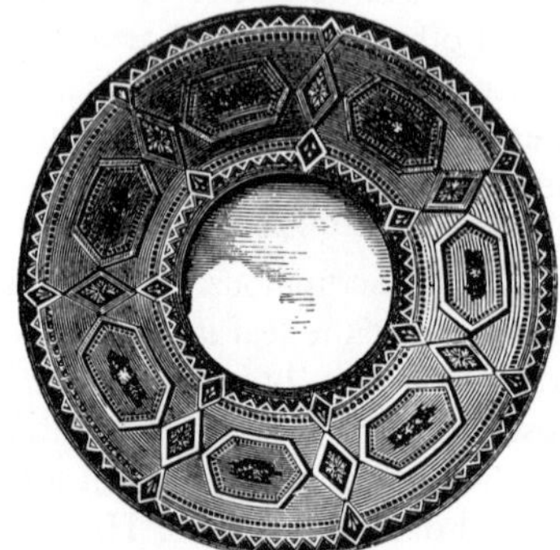

Figs. 1577 and 1578.

Etruria. They were originally carried on by Cyples, afterwards by Cyples & Barker, who were succeeded by Mr. Thomas Barlow. For many years Egyptian black and other tinted bodies only were made, but these were of a fine and very superior character. Lustre wares were also produced, and some of these were marked with

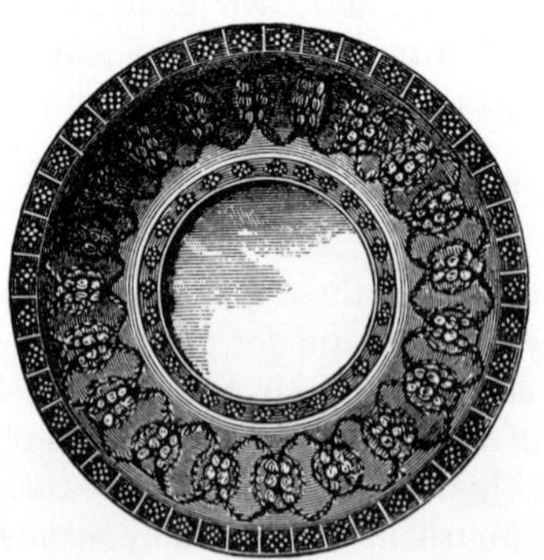

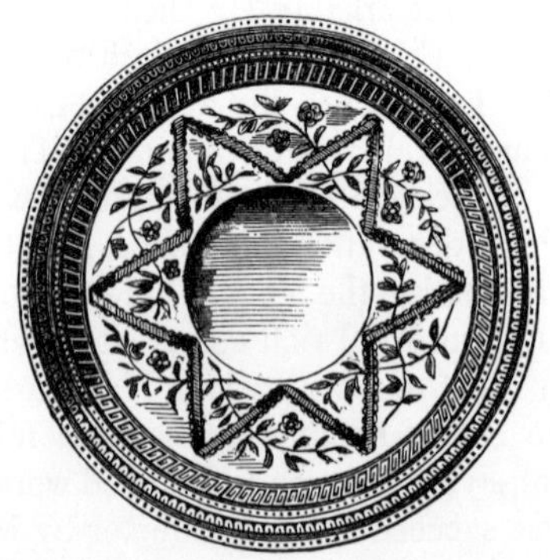

Figs. 1579 and 1580.

a large letter B impressed in the body. Later on china for foreign markets was produced of good average quality, both in body and glaze. Within the past few years the present proprietor, Mr. Thomas Barlow, has successfully turned his attention to the production of the most costly classes of decorated goods for the home markets, and in these he now vies in excellency of body and glaze, and in purity and beauty of design and decoration, with most other houses in the trade. In 1871 Mr. Barlow exhibited some of his productions, which attracted much attention; some of these are engraved on Figs. 1581 to 1588. Tea, breakfast, dessert, and

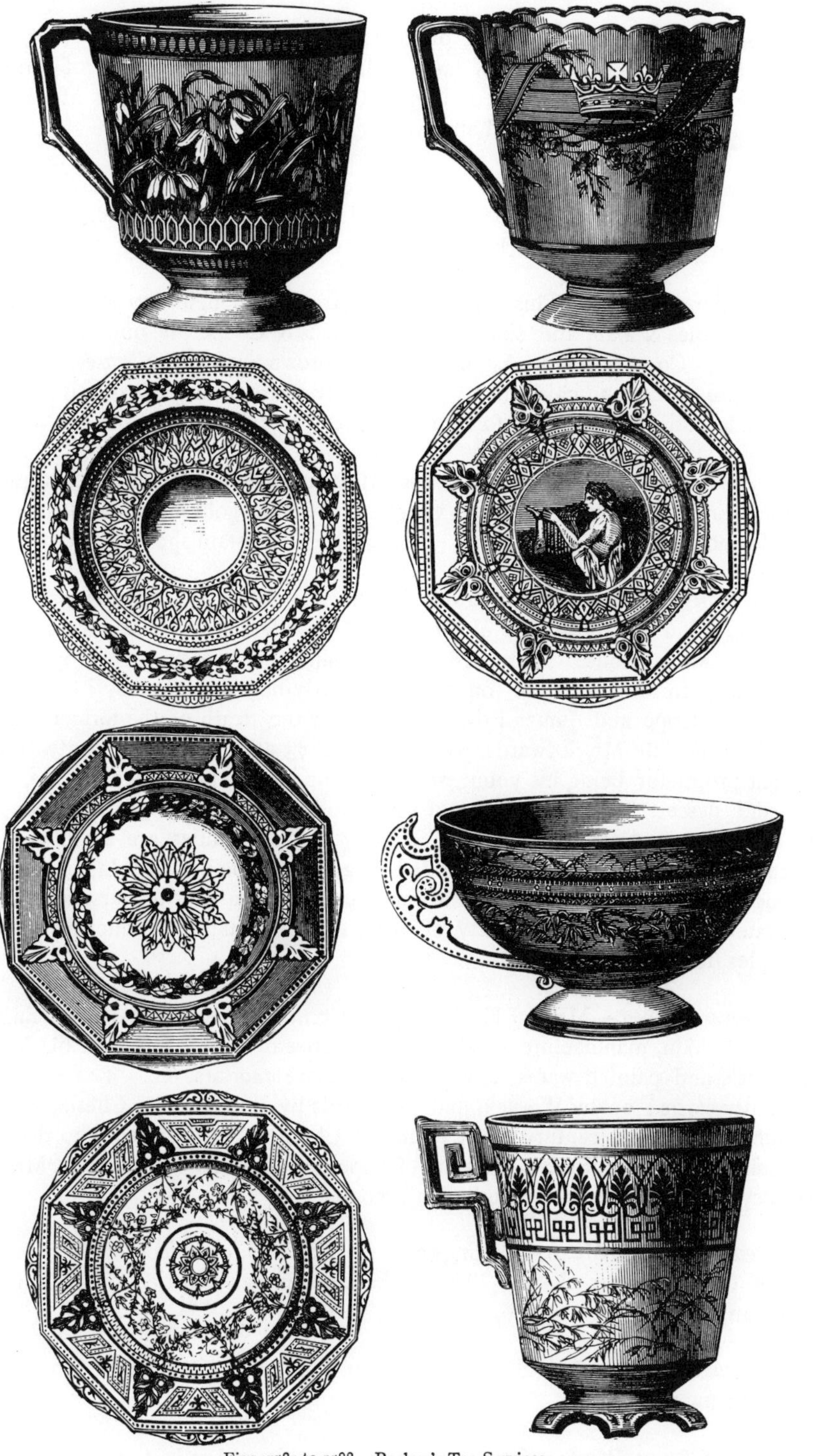

Figs. 1581 to 1588.—Barlow's Tea Services.

déjeuner services, and a number of ornamental articles in every style of decoration, are made, and evince a purity of taste, delicacy of finish, chasteness of form, and harmony of colouring highly creditable to the proprietor. Many of Mr. Barlow's designs and patterns are original and worthy of high commendation.

Coronation Works, Commerce Street.—Messrs. Thomas Waterhouse Barlow & Son produce earthenware in all the usual varieties for the South American, African, and Indian markets, with which they have an extensive connection.

High Street Works.—This manufactory, formerly belonging to the Bridgwoods, next to Cyples & Ball, and since 1842 to Adams & Cooper, is now carried on by R. Plant & Co. Formerly Egyptian black, brown and lustre wares, as well as china, were made, but china has now for many years been the exclusive product. It is made both for home and foreign markets.

Park Works, High Street.—Charles Allerton & Sons here manufacture both earthenware and china in the usual varieties, as well as gold and silver lustre wares, both for home markets and export. The works were established in 1831.

Sheridan Works.—Built in 1858 by the late Mr. John Sheridan, the works passed in 1866 into the hands of George Edwards & Co., and are now carried on by Mr. Edwards alone. About 1840 the business of the present proprietor was commenced in Market Street (on premises partly now occupied by Lloyd's bank) by Thomas Cope and James Edwards, and after the death of the former was continued by the late Mr. Edwards, who died in 1873 at the age of seventy-nine, the present proprietor being his youngest son. The productions are china tea, breakfast, and dessert services, both plain white and in every style of decoration, both for the home and foreign markets. Among the specialities are small cans and saucers richly and elaborately decorated in gold and colours, in "Japan work," for Morocco, Gibraltar, and the Turkish markets, and tea-sets, tea-jars, kettles, &c., decorated in an immense variety of patterns, in imitation of ancient Japanese examples, for the Dutch trade.

Commerce Street.—Messrs. H. Aynsley & Co., the managing partner being Mr. Oswald Deakin, manufacture all the usual varieties of lustre, Egyptian black, drab, turquoise, and painted wares, as well as stoneware mortars, &c. The works were originally carried on by Wooley, and afterwards by Robinson & Chetham. After remaining for half a century in the family of Chetham, they passed into the hands of their present proprietors. China of superior character is made at Mr. John Aynsley's manufactory in the Sutherland Road.

Crown Works.—Messrs. Collingwood & Greatbach manufacture china services, &c., of the commoner classes. The works were formerly carried on by Anderson & Bettany.

Crown Works, Stafford Street.—Mr. John Tams manufactures the usual classes of earthenware.

Stafford Street Works.—These works, amongst the oldest in Longton, were built in 1799 by John & Charles Harvey, who were succeeded by Hulme & Hawley, from whom they repassed into the hands of the former family, being carried on by Charles and W. K. Harvey, sons of Charles Harvey of the original firm. In 1841 these gentlemen worked three manufactories in Longton. In 1853 C. and W. K. Harvey were succeeded by Holland & Green. By the first two firms common and useful earthenware was made, and these were continued by C. and W. K. Harvey, who added china to the productions, and also to a large extent gold lustre ware. Later on these were discontinued, and the firm devoted themselves to printed goods and white graniteware, chiefly for the North and South American and Continental markets. The firm no longer exists, the greater portion of the buildings having been taken down for the erection on their site of a row of shops. A part of the manufactory was carried on by Green, Clay, & Co., and is still continued by Mr. Green. The mark was the name of the pattern or body, the royal arms, and the name or initials of the firm.

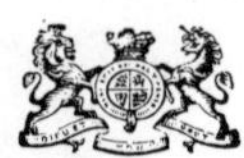

IRONSTONE
HOLLAND & GREEN.

REGINA

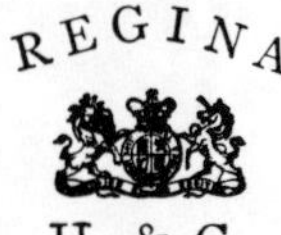

H. & G.

Figs. 1589 and 1590.

The toilet services produced by this firm are of superior quality; the ground colours, rose-du-barry, Brunswick green, &c., of great clearness and beauty, and the gilding rich and elaborate.

Peel Pottery.—These works, originally belonging to Mr. Stirrup, were continued by Bell, Deakin, & Proctor; Webb & Walters; Webb & Co.; and John Green, at whose death they passed into the hands of Mr. Thomas Hulse, and from him to Hulme & Massey. The first three firms originally produced common classes of earthenware. China was added by Webb & Walters, and is now alone made. It is of more than average excellence in body and of various styles of decoration. Many are richly gilt, and the floral and other decorations carefully painted.

King Street and Market Street.—At these works, established more than half a century, the late Mr. John Lockett manufactured the usual varieties of earthenware, china, stoneware, lustre, Egyptian black, drab, and other wares. In 1862 he pro duced the special examples for the exhibition of that year. These are shown in the group on the next page. After his death the premises, after being unoccupied for some time, were for a time held by Taylor, Waine, & Bates, Charles Glover, and Bradbury & Son, but are now vacant.

King Street.—Mr. Lockett, nephew of the John Lockett just spoken of, continues his uncle's business on premises in King Street, which he is considerably enlarging.

Chancery Lane.—Taylor, Hudson, & Middleton, who here produced all the ordinary varieties of china ware, dissolved partnership, Mr. Taylor joining his son-in-law, Mr. Rent, in new works in High Street, and the other partners removing to the Alma Works and Bagnall Street. They were succeeded by Maddox & Ridge, and are now continued by Mr. Ridge, formerly of the firm of Ridge, Meigh & Co.

High Street.—Established about 1840 by Mr. Thomas Cooper, these works were afterwards carried on by Keeling, Walker, & Cooper, and Keeling & Walker, the latter of whom, Mr. John Walker, is now the sole proprietor. He manufactures the ordinary classes of earthenware, gold and silver lustre, figures, &c.

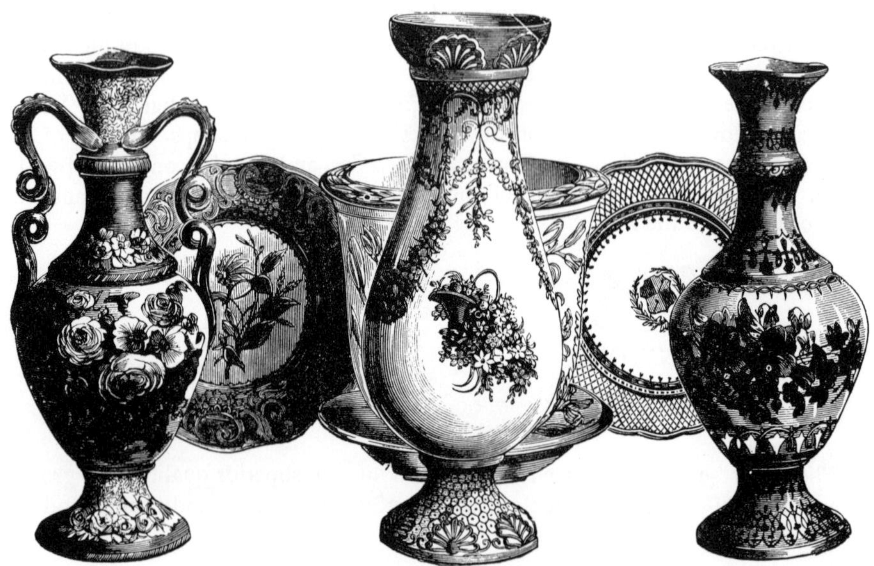

Figs. 1591 to 1597.—Mr. John Lockett's Exhibits, 1862.

St. Mary's Works, Mount Pleasant.—This manufactory was carried on from 1830 till 1832 by Moore & Hamilton, and so continued untill 1859, when Samuel Moore became sole owner. In 1862 he built the present manufactory, and in 1870 was succeeded by his two sons, Bernard and Samuel Moore, who from that time have carried on the business under the style of "Moore Brothers." The productions have from the first been china of a good marketable quality, in which all the usual breakfast, tea, dinner, dessert, déjeuner, and other services, more or less decorated, are made; but in addition to this, attention has been given with marked success to the development of the strictly ornamental departments. A camel teapot—the Arab tying on the bale forming an excellent handle, and the neck and head of the camel an admirable spout—is a well-conceived design, and is powerfully and cleverly modelled. For table decoration the firm produces many good designs. Notably among these is a group of three well-modelled Cupids (two of whom are carrying the third), the upper one of which bears a turquoise shell, massively gilt inside. It is of very artistic design, and is well executed. The Persian turquoise glaze made by the firm is remarkably clear and brilliant in colour, and not surpassed by other houses. In enamelling, Moore Brothers have made much progress, some of their designs in cloissonné enamelling being highly effective, both in form of vessel and in arrangement of colour. Notably among these are "pilgrims' bottles," the rich and massive gilding of which throws out and relieves the enamelling in a very marked and effective manner. In china, and also in majolica, Japanese reproductions are made. In these the well-known Chinese ruby glaze has been cleverly imitated; it is rich and full in colour. A turquoise majolica jardinière, the design being water-lilies, is well designed. Mirror frames of large size are also a speciality of these works. Messrs. Moore Brothers' operations are principally confined to the home markets, a large proportion of their goods bearing the name of the dealers, "T. Goode & Co., London." The mark of the makers is either the name "MOORE" or "Moore," impressed on the body of the ware; "*Moore*," incised; or "MOORE BROS." painted on the surface.

Commerce Street.—The works, now carried on by Mr. Thomas Walters (late Walters & Hulse), were, he informs me, established by Riddle & Lightfoot. The productions are china of ordinary quality for both home and export markets.

New Town Pottery.—Erected in 1845 by Mr. J. Meakin, who continued it until 1850, when it passed to Stanley & Lambert, who in 1855 were succeeded by J. & H. Procter & Co., who produced common earthenware in the usual cream-colour, printed, painted, and lustred varieties. The mark was a crown upon a ribbon, bearing the word WARRANTED; over the crown STAFFORDSHIRE. and beneath the ribbon P for Procter. In 1876 the works passed into the hands of Dale, Page, & Goodwin, of the *Church Street Works.* These were established in the latter half of last century, and in 1780 were carried on by Mr. John Forrester, who was succeeded in 1795 by Hilditch & Sons, who in their productions followed closely in the wake of Josiah Spode and Thomas Minton, at which time most of the processes here were carried out by female hands. In 1830 the firm changed to "Hilditch & Hopwood," who at the Exhibition of 1851 sent up some notable examples of their productions, one of which was a dessert service decorated in the Renaissance style in gold, with landscape and figure vignettes, mainly illustrative of Scott's "Marmion;" and they also exhibited some very successful imitations of Indian china, prepared by them from designs by Mr. Shorter, of London. The tea services exhibited at the same time were remarkable for their excellent body, the design and execution of the painted decoration, the high class of the ground colours, and the massiveness of the gilding. One example, with raised antique foliage in gold on the fine old "Derby blue" ground, was especially good; while the painting of others, with small landscapes in medallions, and wreaths of flowers, was far beyond average merit. In 1858, on the death of Mr. William Hopwood, the works were continued by the trustees till May, 1867, when the business, stock, and plant, including the moulds, copper-plates, &c., were sold to Dale, Page, & Co., who, as just stated, in 1876 removed to the larger premises called New Town Works. In 1883 Mr. Page died, and the premises are now carried on by Page & Goodwin. The productions of the firm consist of all the usual services in china, and are of a better class than those of many other houses. In tea and breakfast services the firm is particularly successful in designs where leaves, accurately copied from nature, are carelessly thrown on grounds of various tints. Others with wreaths of roses on the same ground, and others again closely diapered with burnished gold, are among their more successful patterns. Others of their productions are dessert services with fruit, flowers, and landscapes, and with richly designed festoons, borders, and gilding, dinner services, richly gilt and enamelled jet ware, &c. Majolica has of late been added to the other productions of the firm.

Church Street Majolica Works.—In 1877 Mr. Thomas Forrester commenced business at a small manufactory in High Street, and, his business rapidly increasing, took other additional premises in Church Street. These he shortly afterwards took down, and built upon their site a new manufactory, which he completed in 1879. The new premises gave him greater scope for his enterprise, and, extending his connection, they were soon found to be too small for his requirements. He, therefore, purchased the adjoining china manufactory, and completed his enterprise by joining the two works together, and thus making one factory with six large ovens and every other possible convenience and appliance. The works have grown with the business, and the business grown with the works, till now, it is believed, Mr. Forrester's manufactory may take rank among the more important pottery establishments of the locality. Certainly no other instance is on record in which, in six years only, so much has been done single-handed by any manufacturer. In the beginning of the present year Mr. Forrester took his sons into partnership, and the business is carried on under the style of "Forrester & Sons." Upwards of 400 hands are employed. The goods produced are of a varied character in both useful and ornamental classes, and include vases of unique design and of various sizes. Flowering "à la Barbotin" is carried on to a large extent, and goods are produced suitable to the cottage, while ornamental and richly-flowered vases and jardinières in every shape and size are made fit for the drawing-rooms of the noblesse. Mr. Forrester has also recently introduced various articles of cabinet ware in vases, jardinières, &c., made with Barbotin flowerwork on tortoise-shell and marble grounds; some cornucopeas, upwards of thirty-six inches high giving evidence of considerable skill. One of the most recent productions of merit is the life-size St. Bernard's dog, on a large pedestal three feet six inches in height, and which has been modelled by Gallimore from a prize dog, the property of Messrs. Bayley of Shooter's Hill. It has been modelled from actual life, and is also coloured strictly from nature. The quality of Messrs. Forrester's majolica is remarkably firm and good in body, the colouring well managed, the glaze very satisfactory, and the modelling of the floral decorations masterly in the extreme.

Borough Pottery.—These works, established in 1869 by Cartwright & Edwards, are extensive, and built as a "model factory." The ovens are on the down-draught system; the smoke is conveyed to large chimneys in which the enamel and other kilns all work. The clay—both the blunging, sifting, aud other processes—is prepared by machinery; the water is taken out by pressure. the throwing-wheels and jiggers are turned by steam-power, and the workshops are fitted with steam drying-stoves, so that no fires are used in drying the goods. The goods produced are the ordinary classes of earthenware.

High Street.—These works, formerly Thomas Birks & Co., and later Hallam & Day, but now carried on by Day & Son, formerly produced china, earthenware, and gold and silver lustre of the more ordinary qualities. China only is now made.

New Street.—Messrs. Cooper & Kent, formerly Cooper, Till, & Co. produce china goods of the more ordinary qualities.

Prince of Wales's Pottery.—These works, in Sutherland Road, were established by Mr. Benjamin Shirley, of Bangor, in Wales, on the day of the marriage of H.R.H. the Prince of Wales, March 10th, 1863, and were in honour of that event named the "Prince of Wales's Works." They were carried on for a time by Benjamin Shirley and Walter Freeman, under the style of "Shirley & Freeman," late of the Sheridan Works, and on the death of the former in 1864 Mr. Titus Hammersley became a partner with Mr. Freeman. In 1866 Edward Asbury joined the firm, which was carried on as "Hammersley, Freeman & Co." In 1870 Mr. Freeman retired from the concern, and the style at that time was "Hammersley & Asbury." Since the death of Mr. Hammersley in 1875 the works have been continued by Mr. Asbury alone, under the style of "Edward Asbury & Co." The goods produced are china tea, coffee, dessert, and trinket services—a special feature, however, being articles bearing local views in colours, for sale at watering-places—principally for the home markets, but goods are also shipped to Australia and the United States. The mark used is the Prince of Wales's feathers, with the letters H. & A. in a garter, or A. & Co.

High Street Works.—The late Mr. Walter Freeman, just spoken of as a proprietor successively of the "Sheridan" and of the "Prince of Wales" Works, withdrew from the latter in 1870, and entered on this manufactory, which he continued till his death in 1882, since which time they have been carried on by Boughey, Shire, & Martin. The productions are confined to china, in which are produced tea, breakfast, trinket, and dessert services in great variety of style, and other articles for the home, American, and Australian markets.

New Market Works, Market Street.—These are among the oldest works in Longton. Half a century or more ago they were occupied by Martin and Cope, for the manufacture of lustre ware and china. They were succeeded by Abel Booth, and after other changes the manufactory came into the hands of Messrs. Glover, Colclough, & Townsend, who were extensively engaged for the Eastern markets. From this firm the works passed to Messrs. Skelson & Plant, and from them to the late Mr. George Copestake, sen., and from him to Messrs. Radford & Co. The productions are china tea, breakfast, and dessert services, &c., chiefly for the home trade.

Alma Works, High Street.—Messrs. Hudson & Middleton (formerly Copestake & Allen) produce here the ordinary services, &c., in china.

Market Street.—These works, successively held by Knight & Rowley, Messrs. Colclough, Trubshaw, & Co., and W. Jones, are now carried on by Jones & Howson, who produce the usual classes of china goods in tea, breakfast, and dessert services, &c., for the home and foreign markets. Many of their shapes and patterns are of great beauty, and the quality of the body is good. It was here that the late Sampson Bridgwood made his first start, and after noble struggles against adversity, laid the foundation of his ultimate splendid success.

Victoria Works.—Built by the late Mr. Ralph Shaw about 1828, these works still remain the property of his executors. About 1853 they were taken by Mr. Joseph Finney, who still carries on the business. For the first fifteen years of Mr. Shaw's working earthenware was manufactured, but it was then converted into china works and has so continued to the present time. The goods produced are the usual classes of tea, breakfast, and dessert services, and fancy goods of fair average quality in body and decoration for home and foreign markets.

Stafford Street.—Mr. James Dawson occupies these works and produces ordinary earthenware of the usual classes.

Russell Street.—Mr. William Edwards manufactures ordinary earthenware.

Mount Pleasant Works.—Hallam & Co., late Wood & Co., and Hallam, Johnson, & Co., manufacture ordinary qualities of china.

High Street.—Messrs. Richard Hodson & Co., china services of the ordinary quality.

British Anchor Works, Anchor Road.—At these works, occupied by Mr. J. T. Hudden, earthenware only is made.

Royal Porcelain Works, Forrester Street, Anchor Road.—These works, belonging to Mr. Chapman, formerly Robinson & Chapman, were built as a "model factory," and much enlarged. All the throwing-wheels and jiggers are turned by steam-power, and many other operations which under the old system was done by manual labour, are here carried on by the aid of steam. China of a superior quality and style of decoration is produced.

Stafford Street.—At these works Messrs. Proctor, Wooley, & Mayer, who succeeded Hudson & Son, produce ordinary china services.

St. Gregory's Pottery, in High Street, established in 1794 by Mr. G. Barnes, and successively held by Barnes & Wood, Wood & Blood, Mr. Chesworth, Beardmore & Birks, and G. Townsend, passed in 1864 to Tams & Lowe, and now belongs to Mr. William Lowe. The goods produced comprise all the usual varieties of articles in useful ordinary earthenware, and in china of an average quality, for which new works have been specially built. In the former, dinner, tea, toilet, and other services, &c., are made in white, sponged, printed, ground-laid, and gilt varieties; in the latter only the ordinary common classes are made, principally for the home trade. The mosaic jugs and teapots, mounted and otherwise, are well formed and decorated. The usual mark is a garter, with the words STAFFORDSHIRE IMPROVED, enclosing the name of the pattern and the Staffordshire knot. The ribbon is surmounted by a crown, and beneath are the initials of the firm, T. & L., or otherwise.

Gold Street Works, near Stafford Street (Lowe, Ratcliffe, & Co., formerly Barker Brothers).—This is one of the oldest manufactories in Longton, and is historically interesting from the fact of gold lustre having been here first discovered and applied to decorative purposes. The earthenware is of the ordinary medium quality, both for home and for foreign markets, and consists of cream-coloured, white, fancy sponged, painted and printed, enamelled and other descriptions, in toilet, dinner, breakfast, and tea services, and other articles.

Wellington Works, Stafford Street, established in 1862 by G. L. Robinson & W. Cooper, and afterwards carried on by G. L. Robinson under the style of "Robinson & Son," and later, in 1871, by G. A. Robinson and others as "Robinson, Repton, & Robinson," then passed into the hands of Warriter & Co. The goods principally produced are tea, breakfast, dessert, and other services; toilet trinket-ware, vases, centrepieces, &c., and a large variety of ornamental china goblets, fruit and other baskets, open-work (or pierced) compots, moustache-cups of the same construction as those already spoken of, and the general varieties of articles which are made in this material. Majolica has also been introduced by the present firm with good artistic and commercial results.

St. Martin's Lane (Plant & Co.).—At these works, which have been established about forty years, a general assortment of plain and decorated china, in all the various services, is made both for home and foreign markets.

Heathcote Works, established in 1854 by William Brammall and John Dent, from whom it passed to William Brammall, then to Edwin Brammall and T. S. Repton, and is now carried on by W. H. Derbyshire & Co. The works are in Heathcote Road. The manufactures consist of china tea, breakfast, and other services, and all the usual useful articles in that material suitable for the home trade.

Heathcote Road.—Mr. Wilson having erected new works off Heathcote Road, has recently transferred to them his Parian works, formerly in High Street, and has added the manufacture of china to his other business.

Green Dock Works.—Mr. Bradley (formerly Hampson Brothers, and Cooper, Till, & Co.) manufactures improved stoneware, ordinary earthenwares and lustres for the home, American, Australian, and other markets. Established in 1846.

Chadwick Street.—At these works Frederick Jones & Co., and afterwards Fenton, Downes, & Co., manufactured ordinary earthenware.

High Street.—Mr. J. L. Johnson produces all the usual services, &c., in the commoner classes of china.

Baddeley.—About 1720 William Baddeley (an old name in the district) commenced making brown ware at Eastwood, Hanley. About 1740, having invented an "engine-lathe," he began to make "turned articles in cane and brown ware. He was succeeded in the pottery by his son, William Baddeley, his other son, John Baddeley, taking the business of the lathe-making, by which he acquired a competency, and died in 1841, aged eighty-five." This second William Baddeley made many improvements in the ware, and attempted, both by an imitation of body of his vitreous wares and by his mark, to palm off some of his goods as Wedgwood's. His mark was the word EASTWOOD impressed on the ware, but he contrived always to have the EAST indistinct and the WOOD clear (EASTWOOD), thus hoping to catch the unwary by the latter syllable. He died at an advanced age, and the works at Eastwood having been sold, his son, William Baddeley, commenced in Queen Street, Hanley, for the manufacture of terra-cotta articles, and a large trade was carried on in earthenware knobs for tin and japanned tea and coffee-pots. He also made fancy pipes, japanned terra-cotta, and other goods. He also, at the Market Lane Works, "was the first to make telegraph insulators in iron moulds with screw and lever pressure." The works were in 1846 removed to Longton (Wharf Street), and here the manufacture of imitation stag, buck, and buffalo-horn and bone handles for knives, forks, &c., for the Sheffield trade, was first introduced. In this branch "a very good trade was done, but the working handlers of Sheffield refused to work them up, and threats were sent to several masters that if they did not give up the terra-cotta knife-handle trade their works would be blown up." The masters, thus intimidated, gave up the use of these handles, and on Mr. Baddeley visiting Sheffield an attack was made on his life, and letters sent to him on his return threatening that if he did not give up making the handles he and his works "would be done for." The manufacture was then discontinued. Mr. Baddeley "invented the thimble-placing rack, now so extensively used. This he sold to Elias Leak, of Longton, who in 1856 took out a patent for the invention." Mr. Baddeley, who died in 1864, held the St. Martin's Lane Works, and his widow now carries on business in Commerce Street. Their son, William Baddeley, commenced manufacturing in the Normacott Road in 1862. His productions were rustic terra-cotta articles for floral, horticultural, useful, and decorative purposes, the principal articles being fern-stands, vases, flower-stands, hyacinth-pots, flower-pots, garden-seats, flower-baskets, mignonette-boxes, crocus-pots, globe-stands, brackets, inkstands, &c. The designs were all taken from nature, and appropriate to the intended use of the vessel. His imitations of bark, &c., and of various woods and plants, were remarkably good.

Waterloo Works, Stafford Street. (Brough & Blackhurst).—Built in 1815, the year of the battle of Waterloo, and in honour of that event named the "Waterloo" Works. The date 1815 occurs on the ovens. The manufactory formerly belonged to Messrs. Ratkin & Booth, who were celebrated for their gold and silver lustre wares. At these works, which are large and commodious, are produced the ordinary classes of earthenware, suitable both for the home and for foreign markets, enamelled and gilt services, &c.

Heathcote Road Pottery.—Messrs. I. and H. Procter removed here in 1876 from the New Town Pottery. The productions are common earthenware in the usual cream-colour, printed, painted, and lustred varieties. The mark is a crown upon a ribbon, bearing the words WARRANTED; over the crown is STAFFORDSHIRE, and beneath the ribbon P for Procter.

Sutherland Pottery, Daisy Bank.—Established in 1870 by Mr. Joseph Holdcroft, their present proprietor, for the manufacture of majolica, Parian, and silver lustre ware for the home, Continental, South American, and Australian markets. Mr. Holdcroft, who for eighteen years was in the employment of Minton & Co., commenced business in another manufactory in Longton, which he left on the erection of his present pottery. His majolica productions are of a high class, both in design, in quality, and in workmanship. A "Wren Vase," with well-modelled birds and flowers, is a speciality of his works. His mark is his initials impressed in the ware. The works have latterly been considerably enlarged and the business extended. His productions rank deservedly high.

Church Street.—These works, for the production of Parian, jasper, and majolica ware, belonging to Mr. G. A. Robinson, were pulled down in 1876 for town improvements, Mr. Robinson erecting new works in Sutherland Road.

Cornhill Works.—Poole & Unwin entered on these works, which had previously been carried on as general earthenware works by others, in 1871. The productions are middle-class earthenware, stoneware jugs, &c., chiefly intended for the home market. Gold and silver lustres of the ordinary kind and rustic majolica were also at one time made. The initials of the firm are P & U impressed in the body of the ware.

The Sutherland Works, Barker Street, were established by Sampson Smith, at whose death they passed into the hands of Mr. John Adderley, who continues the production of china tea and other services, silver and gold lustre, and china figures and ornaments.

Sutherland Pottery, Normacott Road.—These works were established by their present proprietors, Skelson & Plant, who were previously in the New Market Works, Chancery Lane, Longton, and the Heathcote Road Pottery. They are also proprietors of the *Heathcote Road Pottery*. These latter were established by Mr. Thomas Beardmore, and much enlarged by Stubbs & Bridgwood before they came into the hands of Skelson & Plant. At these works china is made in all the usual useful services.

St. James's Place.—The St. James's works were established by William Bradshaw, and afterwards occupied by John Gerard, Jesse Cope & Co., and Baggaley & Ball. In 1831 they were taken by Robert Gallimore, who about 1840 was joined in partnership by George Shubotham. In 1842 Gallimore retired from the concern, and the business was then continued by George Shubotham and William Webberley, under the style of "Shubotham & Webberley." In 1847 Mr. Shubotham died, and the works are now carried on by Mr. Webberley alone. In 1858 this gentleman purchased the premises, and soon afterwards pulled down the old buildings and erected the present commodious "four-oven" manufactory. Originally lustre ware only was produced, but china was added by Mr. Gallimore. In 1844 lustre was entirely abandoned, and since that time china alone has been made. This is produced in all the usual services for the home, Dutch, and Australian markets. No mark is used.

Daisy Bank.—These historically interesting works were built in the latter part of last century by a Mr. Hughes, and passed successively through the firms of Drury, Ray, & Tideswell, and Ray & Wynne, to Charles James Mason & Co., who succeeded the latter firm. It was in these works that Mr. Mason produced his famous "ironstone china," the firm at that time being "George Miles Mason and Charles James Mason," and subsequently "C. J. Mason" only. The patent taken out by C. J. Mason in 1813 was for "a process for the improvement of the manuture of English porcelain," the process, according to the specification, consisting "in using scoria or slag of ironstone pounded and ground in water in certain proportions, with flint, Cornwall stone, and clay, and blue oxide of cobalt." Doubtless, however, this was not correct so far as the first ingredients are concerned. It should also be added that the name "Ironstone" was simply a combination of "iron" and "stone," used to denote the extreme hardness of the body, as combining the strength of both. From various causes the manufactory after some years, though a great artistic and manipulative success, became a commercial failure. In 1851 the patent-right, moulds, copper-plates, &c., were sold to Mr. Morley, and in 1853 the lease (afterwards the freehold) of the premises was sold to Hulse, Nixon, and Adderley. (For an account of Mason's ironstone china, &c., see pages 491, 492.) In 1869

Mr. Nixon died, and the firm was changed to "Hulse and Adderley," and so continued until 1874, when (Mr. Hulse having died in the preceding year) it was altered to that of "William A. Adderley," who is now sole proprietor of the place. Since Mason's time the premises have been very considerably enlarged and improved. The productions are china and earthenware for the home, foreign, and Continental markets. No distinctive mark is used.

Park Hall Street.—Daniel Sutherland & Sons entered on these works in 1863, and they are now carried on by the sons under the same style. The productions are in majolica jugs, vases, tripods, flower-holders; bread, cheese, and fruit dishes; water-bottles, tea and coffee-pots, kettles, and other articles; and in Parian groups, figures, busts, jugs, brooches, crosses, and trinkets. Stoneware jugs, teapots, &c., are also made. The mark of the firm was formerly S & S, but none is now used.

Viaduct Works, Caroline Street.—Established about 1836. This manufactory in 1863 passed into the hands of Cooper, Nixon, and Co., and next to Cooper and Dethick. They produce plain and printed earthenware of the ordinary kinds, and drab and other coloured bodies, both for the home and foreign markets. The mark is the initials of the firm, C & D.

High Street and Sutherland Road.—Messrs. James Beech & Co. opened those works about 1846. Since the death of Mr. Beech and his son they have passed to Mr. Stephen Mear, by whom they are carried on. All the usual tea, breakfast, and dessert services in china of more than ordinary quality, and in various styles of decoration, are made.

King Street.—These works were established in 1875, being opened on March 25th of that year by Bridgett, Bates, & Beech, and since the death of Mr. Beech have been continued by Bridgett & Bates. They manufacture china only, but in this are produced all the usual services in every variety of style, both for the home and foreign markets. No mark is used.

Anchor Pottery.—Sampson Bridgwood & Sons, who are extensive manufacturers, first carried on business in the Market Street Works, and next for many years at a manufactory in Stafford Street, originally occupied by G. Forrester, which was purchased by the late commissioners of Longton, and pulled down for the erection of the present market buildings. They then removed to the "Anchor Pottery," where they produced both china and earthenware. Since the death of the Messrs. Bridgwood the business has been continued by the son-in-law and grandson, the Rev. J. H. Walker and George Walker. In china all the usual tea, breakfast, and dessert services are made, partly for the home, but principally for the United States and Canadian markets. In earthenware white granite is made for the United States, Australian, and Canadian trades. The speciality is what is technically called "Parisian granite" (stamped as "Limoges"), which has a fine hard durable body and excellent glaze. The marks used are, on china, an impressed stamp of the name "S. BRIDGWOOD & SON." The Parisian granite bears the impressed stamp, an oval with the word "LIMOGES," and in the centre P. G. (for Parisian granite). It also bears the printed mark of an elaborate shield of arms with mantling, sceptres, &c., and the words "PORCELAINE OPAQUE," "BRIDGWOOD & SON."

Anchor Road.—Messrs. Blair & Co. occupy the new manufactory recently erected here as china works.

Dresden Works, Normacott Road, established by Mr. John Proctor.—These works, after being worked successively by Glover & Colclough, and Goodwin & Bullock, came into the hands of the present firm of Mason, Holt & Co., in 1858, since which time they have been much enlarged. All the usual tea, breakfast, dessert, and other services, in china of excellent commercial quality, are made both for home and foreign markets.

Dresden Works, Stafford Street.—These works, established by John Ferneyhough, passed in 1858 into the hands of Shelley & Hartshorne, who were succeeded by Adams and Scrivener, who in turn were again succeeded by, in 1866, John Ferneyhough. They are now continued by Hallam & Furber, who manufacture all the usual varieties of services, &c., in china of good quality.

Pallissy Works, Chancery Lane.—These works were erected in 1862, by Mr. R. H. Grove, for the purpose of decorating, not manufacturing, china ware. In 1867 he retired, and was succeeded by his son, Mr. Fredk. Wedgwood Grove, and his partner, Mr. John Stark, who continued them for decorating purposes alone until 1867, when they commenced manufacturing, having increased the premises for the purpose, and erected the necessary kilns and machinery. They manufacture earthenware only. In this all the usual dinner, dessert, toilet, and other services and domestic articles are produced, and of all degrees of decoration, from plain and printed up to enamelled and gilt varieties. Spirit and wine show-barrels or casks are also specialities.

Minerva Works, Fenton.—In 1812 these works were held by Charles James Mason & Co., the producers of the famous "Patent Ironstone China" (which see), and from them passed to Pratt & Co., who were succeeded by Mr. Gerard (or Jerrad) and Mr. Richard Hassall. About 1833 or 1834 Mr. Hassall was joined in partnership by Thomas Green, son of Thomas Green of the Churchyard Works, Burslem, of Bank House, Fenton, who produced the common classes of china. Shortly afterwards Mr. Hassall retired, and Mr. Green was joined in partnership by Mr. W. Richards, of Great Fenton, and the business was continued by "Green & Richards" until 1847, when the latter withdrew. The business was then continued by Mr. Thomas Green alone until his decease in 1859, and since that time it has been carried on under the trading style of "M. Green & Co." The china made by the earlier firms was of the commonest kind of blue figured, white and gold, and lustre wares. During the partnership of Mr. Richards a variety of ornaments, small ewers and basins, toy mugs and jugs, &c., were extensively made. This trade, however, was checked by the introduction of a similar but cheaper class of goods from France. This had a good effect on the firm, for it induced attention to be turned to a better class of productions, and this again was more decisively done in 1851, when goods of a highly creditable character were made. The present productions are china tea, breakfast, dessert, trinket, and other services; toy sets, jugs, mugs, feeders, wheel-barrow and spade salts, and a large variety of other articles, both for home and foreign markets.

Victoria Works, for many years carried on by Mr. S. Ginders, are now held by Mr. James Reeves, who produces the more ordinary qualities of earthenware.

Fenton Potteries.—The goods produced are of the commoner class of printed, sponged, and pearl-white granite wares suitable for British North American, United States, West Indian, African, and Indian markets. None are produced for the home trade. The works are carried on by W. Baker & Co., who were awarded a medal at the Paris Exhibition.

Fenton Pottery.—This was established in 1825 by C. J. & G. M. Mason for the manufacture of their famous "Ironstone China" ware (which see). "The works of C. J. Mason & Co.," says Ward, in 1843, "standing obliquely to two turnpike-roads, and on the line of the Canal Company's railway, present an extensive front of four stories in height, inscribed in large letters 'Patent Ironstone China Manufactory.' For this article of trade, which Messrs. G. & C. J. Mason introduced some years ago, they obtained extensive public favour, and an almost exclusive sale, on account of its resemblance to porcelain, and its very superior hardness and durability." Messrs. Mason were succeeded by Mr. Samuel Boyle, from whom the works passed into the hands of E. & C. Challinor, formerly E. Challinor and Co., of Sandyford and Tunstall, who still carry them on. The goods produced are white granite, printed, sponged, and common earthenware, for the American, Australian, and other foreign and colonial markets. In these tea, coffee, breakfast, dinner, toilet, and other services, and all the usual useful articles, are largely produced. In jugs, Messrs, Challinor produce the Ceres or Wheat, Paris, Garland, Barbery, Lily, Missouri, Florence, Versailles, Lotus or Cora, and other shapes, both plain and embossed. The earthenware is of the ordinary common quality, specially designed and well adapted for the various markets to which it is sent. The marks are the Staffordshire knot 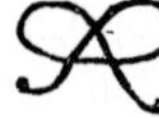 impressed in the ware—

E & C CHALLINOR
FENTON

E & C CHALLINOR

IRONSTONE
CHINA
E & C CHALLINOR

within an ornamental border, surmounted by the royal arms, &c., also impressed in the ware, and the following printed on the surface: the royal arms with crown, supporters, motto, &c., and beneath a ribbon with IRONSTONE CHINA, E & C CHALLINOR FENTON; the name of the pattern, as "Australia," "Gothic," "Portland," &c., within various borders, &c., and the name E & C CHALLINOR, or E & C C.

Old Foley Pottery.—Messrs. Moore & Co., late Samuel Bridgwood, produce white granite ware of the ordinary character, for the American markets.

Anchor Works, Market Street.—These works were carried on for some years by T. and J. Carey, until about 1845, when they came into the possession of Mr. Ashwell, who occupied them for about thirteen years. They were afterwards carried on by Mr. W. Green, from whom they passed to Copestake Brothers, and are now occupied by Mr. George Copestake, who produces china of the usual varieties for both the home and foreign markets.

Edensor Road.—Messrs. Aidney & Co. have erected new china works, and are producing all the usual classes of services, &c.

Edensor Road China Works have been erected by Johnson & Poole.

Edensor Road.—Mr. Bradley has his china manufactory next to the above.

Heathcote Road China Works have been erected by H. M. Williamson & Co.

Fenton Potteries.—These works have been in the hands of the present firm, Messrs. Pratt, ever since the commencement of this century. The style of the firm is "F. & R. Pratt & Co.," and they produce all the ordinary classes of earthenware goods in services, and the usual useful and ornamental articles. They are large makers of "druggists' sundries," and of articles in a compact, vitreous terra-cotta. Another speciality is under-glaze colour-printing, for which, and their Etruscan ware, they received a medal at the 1851 Exhibition. A silver medal was also awarded to them by the Society of Arts for a pair of the largest Etruscan-style vases up to that time produced; they were exhibited in 1851, and were purchased by the Prince Consort.

Lane Delph Pottery (Wallis & Genison, formerly John Pratt & Co., and Pratt & Simpson) produce earthenware of the ordinary class, chiefly for foreign markets.

Grosvenor Works, Foley Place, were established about 1850 by Till, Bourne, & Browne, and since their time the successive changes in the proprietorship have been Bourne & Browne, Charles Browne alone, Jackson & Browne, and Jackson & Gosling, by whom they are now carried on, and who do a large home and foreign trade. The manufactures are confined to china, in which tea, breakfast, and dessert services are produced.

Park Works, Market Street.—Messrs. Ralph Malkin & Sons, doubtless descendants of the old pottery family of Malkin, manufacture here the ordinary classes of earthenware goods.

Foley Pottery.—This is one of the oldest works in the district. It was originally occupied by Samuel Spode, who lived in a large house adjoining, which was pulled down some years ago. It was afterwards occupied by Christopher Bourne. It has been in the possession of the present occupiers (W. Hawley & Co.) since 1842. The productions are earthenware of the ordinary kind, both for home and export markets.

Lower Fenton.—A china manufactory on a large scale is in course of erection here, to which, on its completion, will be removed the business of Mrs. Natford.

Fenton.—Mr. W. Morley, of the Baltimore Works, having erected a new manufactory here, has removed to the new premises.

The Foley Potteries.—These potteries take their name from the Foley family, who own property in the neighbourhood. They were built by John Smith, of Fenton

Hall, about 1820, the first firm by whom they were worked being Elkin, Knight, & Bridgwood, who made the better classes of "Willow pattern," "Broseley pattern," and other blue printed services. On the retirement of the latter the style was changed to Knight & Elkin, and subsequently (on the retirement of Mr. Elkin) to J. K. Knight alone, till 1853, when he was joined in partnership by the late Henry Wileman, wholesale china dealer, of London, the style being Knight and Wileman. On the retirement of Mr. Knight until his death in 1856 Mr. Wileman carried on the works alone till 1864, when his two sons succeeded him as J. & C. Wileman. In 1866 the partnership was dissolved, and from that time till the present the business has belonged to James F. Wileman, the present proprietor. The goods produced are the usual granite ware, printed wares, lustres, Egyptian and shining black, and cream-coloured wares. All of these are of the ordinary classes for household use; and the great bulk of the trade is export, to the States, Panama, Australia, South Africa, Ceylon, Java, and India.

The Foley China Works were built in 1860 by the late Mr. Henry Wileman, the owner of the Foley Potteries. At his death in 1864 they were continued by his sons, J. & C. Wileman) till 1866, when the partnership was dissolved, the latter (Mr. C. J. Wileman) continuing the china and the former the earthenware works. In 1870 Mr. C. J. Wileman retired, and his brother then became proprietor of both manufactories, and shortly afterwards took into partnership Mr. J. B. Shelley, the firm being styled Wileman & Co. The china produced is of the ordinary useful class for household purposes.

The Foley.—Messrs. Robinson & Co. produce china of the usual classes both for home and export trades.

King Street Works.—These works were established in the latter part of the last century by Mr. Shelley, who was succeeded by Mr. Marsh, from whom they passed to T. & J. Carey. The productions were the ordinary Rockingham ware and common classes of earthenware, Messrs. Carey also occupying two other manufactories at Longton. They were next held by a company, and about 1850 passed into the hands of John Edwards. The goods now produced are semi-porcelain and white granite for the American markets. Until 1856 Mr. Edwards produced china in addition, but this has since then been discontinued. Mr. Edwards is patentee of a process for making thimble pins; and he also in 1859 took out a patent for "improvements in stacking or holding biscuit, earthen, china, and glossed ware for firing" by means of "a ring frame or holder, with a rim or flange projecting inwardly, so as to occupy the whole or part of the centre of the ring."

Heath.—Thomas Heath was a potter in Lane Delph in 1710, and produced a good hard grey-coloured ware. His three daughters married three potters, Palmer and Neale, of Hanley, and Pratt of Fenton. Heath was an enterprising potter, and was successful in making the coated or delft ware, same as made by Astbury.

Bacchus.—Thomas Bacchus, who, according to Shaw, married first a widow, named Astbury, manufactured cream-coloured and blue printed ware. His second wife being a skilled painter, his late productions were of a more superior character.

William Meir had pot-works at Fenton in the middle of last century, which he rented from Whieldon, as the following entry in his book shows: "Mr. Wm. Meir, of Fenton Low, for a house and pottworks & 3 small closes, March 25, 1750, a year's Rent due—£14—10—0." Whieldon at that time owned much land about Fenton, and Fenton Hall seems also to have belonged to him. This he let to Ralph Woolf at a yearly rental of £4, the "New House in Lower Lane" being at the same time let to Thos. Woolf for £2 2*s.* a year. Fenton Hall was afterwards, in 1750, let at the same rent to Wm. Marsh and Wm. Kent. It was afterwards divided.

Harrison.—George Harrison was an earthenware manufacturer in the latter part of last century. His productions, according to an invoice of August 20, 1793, consisted of "large and less tureens," "sauce tureens," "root dishes," "sallad bowls," and "tureen ladles," blue-edged, and cream-coloured "ewers."

Martin.—Anne Martin (I presume, widow of S. Martin), was a manufacturer at Lane Delph in 1793. Her productions, as appears from invoices of hers of that year in my possession, were "variegated jugs" of different sizes, "blue-gray mugs and jugs," "hand-basins," different sizes, "egg cups," "pattie pans," "cups and saucers," (these were 10*d.* a dozen!) "sauce boats," "bottles," "bowls," "cowlerd toys," "hand bowls," "dip[d] bosed jugs," "salad bowls," "flower pots," "stoole pans," "blue painted mugs and jugs," "pickel jars," "table services," &c.

Miles Mason was a manufacturer in the latter part of the last century. An invoice of his of 1797 enumerates blue dessert ware sets, each consisting of "1 centre piece, 4 shells, 2 hearts, two cucum. tureens, dishes & stands, and 24 dessert plates;" "melon shapes," "squares," oval and round baking dishes, oval and square salad dishes, "Nankeen spitting pots," basins and egg-cups. Miles Mason was the father of George Miles Mason, Charles James Mason, of "Ironstone china" celebrity (see page 554), and William Mason. The family of Mason was originally of Westmoreland, where they were tenants of Sir Michael Freeman, of Rydal Hall. One of the sons went to London and established a shop for the sale of East Indian china. He afterwards, I am informed, opened a manufactory at Liverpool. He then bought land at Fenton from the Bagnall family, on which he erected the works now occupied by Mrs. Green, and called the "Minerva Works," at Fenton. Afterwards he and his brother built the "Fenton Pottery" (which see), and after some reverses removed from it to a much smaller and less pretentious manufactory, the "Daisy Bank Works" (which also see). Miles Mason's marks were—

MILES MASON. Miles Mason. M. Mason.

M. MASON.

Whieldon.—Thomas Whieldon, whose name is more intimately mixed up with the early development of the potter's art than that of almost any other man, was a manufacturer at Little Fenton in the middle of last century. Spode, Astbury, Garner, Greatbach, Heath, Edge, Marsh, and many others were his apprentices or employés, and Josiah Wedgwood, when quite a young man, and Harrison were his partners, while his mottled and other wares were of high character. In 1740 Whieldon's works consisted of a small range of low thatched buildings. "His early productions were knife-hafts for the Sheffield cutlers, and snuff-boxes for the

Birmingham hardwaremen to finish with hoops, hinges, and springs, which himself usually carried in a basket to the tradesmen; and, being much like agate, they were greatly in request. He also made toys and chimney ornaments, coloured in either the clay state or biscuit by zaffre, manganese, copper, &c., and glazed with black, red, or white lead. He also made black glazed tea and coffee-pots, tortoise-shell and melon table plates (with ornamented edge and six scollops, as in the specimens kept by Andrew Boon, of the Honeywall, Stoke), and other useful articles. Mr. A. Wood made models and moulds of these articles; also pickle leaves, crab-stock handles, and cabbage-leave spouts for tea and coffee-pots, which utensils, with candlesticks, chocolate-cups, and tea-ware, were much improved; and his connections extended subsequently, when Mr. J. Wedgwood became Whieldon's managing partner. He was a shrewd and careful person. To prevent his productions being imitated in quality or shape, he always buried the broken articles; and a few months ago we witnessed the unexpected exposure of some of these by some miners attempting to get marl in the road at Little Fenton. The fortune he acquired by his industry enabled him to erect a very elegant mansion near Stoke, where he long enjoyed, in the bosom of his family, the fruits of his early economy. He was also sheriff of the county in the year 1786. The benevolence of his disposition and his integrity are honourable traits of character, far superior to the boast of ancestry without personal merit. Mr. Whieldon lived, I am informed by Mr. John Ward, in a large house near the lower part of Fenton, called Whieldon's Grove. The line of railway passes through the grounds, and a part of the house is used by the railway company as a store. He died in 1798 at a very old age, and in 1828 his relict was interred beside him in Stoke churchyard.

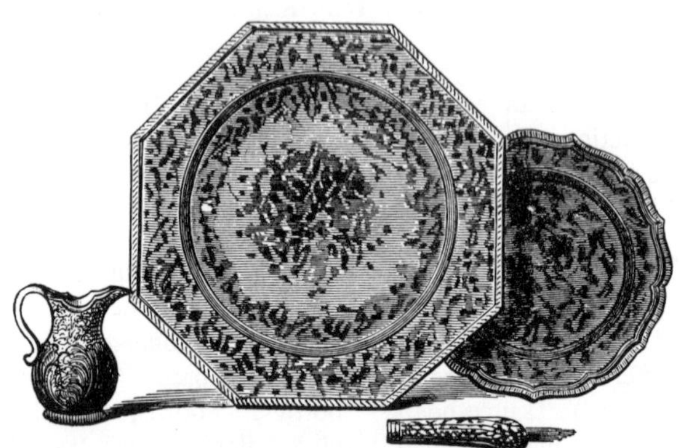

Figs. 1608 to 1611.

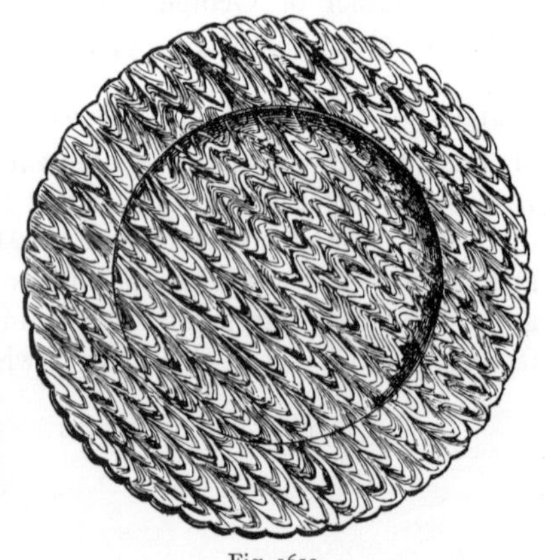

Fig. 1612.

In 1749 Thomas Whieldon built an addition to his works, and the account of the "Expenses of the new end & Seller of the Over Work-house" are in my own possession.

From this period downwards for some years the dates and terms of "hirings" of workpeople, "setting" of houses and land to different tenants, and many other matters of interest, are all entered in his own handwriting in a pocket account-book belonging to Whieldon now in my own possession, and from which I gave somewhat extensive extracts in the first edition of this work, to which I refer my readers.

The goods manufactured by Whieldon, both before, during, and after his partnership with Wedgwood, were of good quality and excellent form. They are now very scarce, and are highly and deservedly prized by collectors. Two "tortoise-shell plates," a small "cauliflower jug," a marbled, or "combed-pattern" plate, and an imitation agate knife-haft are shown by Figs. 1608 to 1612.

In 1754 Wedgwood and Harrison entered into partnership with Thomas Whieldon. The partnership with Harrison, however, continued but for a short period, and in 1754 he went out of the concern, Wedgwood and Whieldon continuing in partnership five years, and carrying on their trade at Whieldon's works at Fenton Low. In 1754 Wedgwood here produced his famous green glaze, which helped much to extend the fame of the manufactory. In 1759 the partnership expired; Wedgwood returned to Burslem, and Whieldon continued the business alone.

Turner.—Messrs. William and John Turner, whose manufactory was in the High Street, have often been referred to in this work. They were among the best and most successful potters of the end of last and early part of the present century. About 1756 Mr. John Turner and Mr. Banks made white stoneware at Stoke, but in 1762 Turner removed to Lane End, "where he manufactured every kind of pottery then in demand, and also introduced some other kinds not previously known." About 1780 he discovered a valuable vein of fine clay at Green Dock, from which he "obtained all his supplies for manufacturing his beautiful and excellent stoneware pottery of a cane colour, which he formed into very beautiful jugs, with ornamental designs, and the most tasteful articles of domestic use." Turner produced "a shining blue glazed pottery similar to that of the Japanese porcelain," as well as making many other improvements in the art. He died in 1786, and was succeeded by his sons, William and John Turner, who became, as just said, among the best potters of the day, equalling in many respects Josiah Wedgwood himself. In jasper ware, in Egyptian black, and other finer wares there is little choice between Turner and Wedgwood, although the composition of the two bodies was not the same, and had been obtained by different processes. In 1800 Messrs. Turner took out a patent for a new method of manufacturing porcelain and earthenware by the introduction of "Rafferness Mine Rock, Little Mine Rock, and New Rock." The works were closed about 1803. The mark used by the Turners was simply the name TURNER, impressed on the jasper and other fine bodies; on their blue-bordered and printed wares sometimes they used the Prince of Wales's feathers, with the name Turner beneath.

TURNER.
Fig. 1613.

Garner.—Robert Garner, or Gardner, son of Robert Gardner, was an apprentice with Thomas Whieldon, and afterwards employed by him at the same period as his fellow-workman Josiah Spode was employed.

Robert Gardner, who was hired from his father in 1751, married Margaret Astbury, daughter of Astbury the well-known potter, and at one time was in partnership with one of her brothers at Foley. He built a large house, then known as the Foley House, but latterly as the Bank House. By his wife Margaret Astbury, Mr. Garner was the father of Robert Garner, potter, of Lane End, some of whose accounts of 1797 are in my possession. He married a Miss Middlemore, by whom, with other issue, he had a son, the present Robert Garner, Esq., F.L.S., the author of the "Natural History of the County of Stafford," and other works. About 1750 it is said the elder Robert Garner, in conjunction with Messrs. Barker, "commenced the manufactory of Shining Black and White Stone Ware, salt glaze, at the Row Houses, near the Foley, Fenton, and where afterwards they made tolerable cream colour. They realised a good property here, and Mr. R. Garner rented a manufactory and the best mansion of the time in Lane End, near the old turnpike gate." Robert Garner, of Lane End, was a potter in a large way of business, and excellent in Queen's or cream-coloured ware. Some examples of his make are preserved in the Stoke Museum.

Edwards.—William Edwards, a potter at Lane Delph in 1750, made a very superior kind of earthenware. One of his productions, described by Shaw, was a plate with basket-work rim, the centre part divided into compartments of embossed work, and decorated with various devices.

Johnson.—Thomas and Joseph Johnson made white stone, crouch, and other wares. Their manufactory was afterwards held by Mayer and Newbold.

Phillips.—About 1760 a son of Mr. Phillips, of Lane Delph, commenced making white stone and other wares at Green Dock, Longton, and afterwards produced cream-coloured ware of good quality.

Sampson Bridgwood.—His manufactory was erected in 1756 by Roger Wood, of the Ash, and occupied by a Mr. Ford, for stone and brown ware.

Greatbach.—Robert Greatbach was bound apprentice with Thomas Whieldon. He afterwards carried on business at Fenton, where he produced a number of good and useful patterns in various wares. Thomas Radford was associated with him in this business, and his engravings were very popular. One of the best examples is a mug bearing "The World in Planisphere," on which occurs the name "engraved by Radford." It is very sharply and clearly engraved, and bears on an heraldic wreath the initials "E. T." Another celebrated production was the subject of the "Prodigal Son" on teapots, &c. Greatbach was afterwards engaged by Wedgwood, and was a successful modeller.

Greenwood.—A potter named Greenwood was in Fenton, in Staffordshire, about 1770—80.

Other potters in Fenton were Thomas Heath, Bourne, Baker & Bourne, Thos. Bacchus. Others, about 1760, were Phillips, Matthews, Moses Simpson, John Adams, John Prince, and William Hilditch.

Heathcote & Co.—The Heathcotes were potters in Staffordshire, I believe, at the close of last and in the early part of the present century. The wares produced were good quality blue-printed, painted, and gilt services, and ornamental goods. The mark was the Prince of Wales's feathers with the name C. HEATHCOTE & Co. above, and on a ribbon beneath the name of the pattern, as CAMBRIA, &c. Some good examples are in the Mayer Museum.

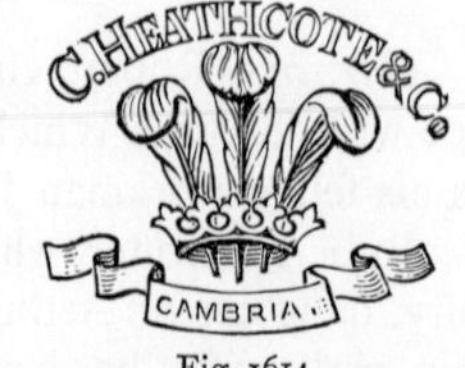

Fig. 1614.

Matthews.—William Matthews, of Lane Delph, was a maker of tortoise-shell and clouded pottery.

Myatt.—"At the southern extremity of Foley," says Shaw in 1829, "are the house and factory of the late Mr. Myatt, one of the first persons who received the Wesleyan and Methodist preachers, and in whose parlour the late Mr. J. Wesley stood, while from the window he preached to a vast congregation when last he passed through Staffordshire only a few months prior to his decease." He produced ordinary white and printed earthenware and red ware. His mark was his name, impressed : MYATT. MYATT.

Williamson.—Hugh Williamson was a potter in the latter part of last century, and principally made the ordinary blue printed ware. A plate or tray with blue flowers and border is in the Mayer collection, and is labelled as "Made at Hugh Williamson's. It was transferred by Mrs. Hancock, seventy-eight years of age, when she was an apprentice."

Harley.—Thomas Harley, a manufacturer at "Lane End," produced some good earthenware services, jugs, and other articles. He sometimes marked with his name in full in writing letters, *T. Harley, Laneend,* and at other times HARLEY.

Plant.—Benjamin Plant was a potter here at the close of last century. His name occurs sometimes as below.

B. Plant,
Lane End,

Benjamin Plant,
Lane End,

Bailey & Batkin.—This firm (see Batkin & Booth) made a fine quality of lustre wash all over outside, and often inside. In the Mayer collection is a service of it, and one large piece with "BAILEY & BATKIN, SOLE PATENTEES" running round a central band.

Mayer & Newbold.—This firm produced excellent goods in the early part of the present century. One of their marks was—*May*[r] *& Newb*[d], and another Mayer & Newbold in full.

It will be interesting to add that at Longton Hall, William Littler, of Brownhills, at one time resided, and there, according to Shaw, "continued his experiments [in the manufacture of porcelain] until his success surpassed all the expectations of his contemporaries ; but there not being much demand for this kind of ware, he sacrificed his estate at Brownhills, near Burslem, and then discontinued manufacturing porcelain. His chief workman was not only a good practical potter, but a tolerable modeller, Dr. Mills, who subsequently died at Shelton at a very advanced age." Littler's removal to Longton Hall is said to have been "about 1765." Littler is said afterwards to have been manager of Baddeley & Fletcher's works at Shelton. Ten years previously William Duesbury, the founder of the Derby China Works, was also of Longton Hall. In a deed of that year, which I have given *in extenso* in first edition, he is described as "William Duesbury, of Longton Hall, in the parish of Stoke-upon-Trent," and in another deed as "Wm. Duesbury, of Longton, in ye County of Stafford, Enamellor" (see under "Derby," *ante*).

CHAPTER XXIII.

The Tunstall potters enumerated by Shaw in 1829 are John Mear, T. Goodfellow, Ralph Hall, S. and J. Rathbone, J. Boden, Bourne, Nixon, & Co., Breeze & Co., and Burrows & Co. Ward in 1842 enumerates seventeen, viz.: china and earthenware—Hancock & Wright, Bill & Proctor, and Rathbone & Brummitt; earthenware only—Wood & Challinor, Thos. Goodfellow, John Meir & Son, Joseph Heath & Co., Hall & Holland, Wm. Adams, Jun., & Co. (Greenfield), Podmore Walker & Co. (two manufactories), James Beech (two), Thos. Bowley, and Mayer & Mawdesley; china toys and black ware—Michael Tunnicliffe and John Harrison. James Beech & Abraham Lowndes had also a manufactory here in 1829.

In the sixteenth and seventeenth centuries common coarse brown ware was made at Golden Hill, near Tunstall, and later "brown chequered and Porto Bello wares were made." In the beginning of this century there was a small manufactory of cream-colour and porcelain, but it is "now (says Shaw in 1829) discontinued, and the building converted into dwelling-houses." At Green Lane, Golden Hill, coarse black and brown ware was formerly made.

Enoch Booth established a manufactory at Cliff Bank, Tunstall, and about 1750 commenced making cream-coloured ware of a superior kind, "which was coated with a glaze of lead ore and ground flint." He married Ann, one of the daughters of Thomas Child, of Tunstall (on a part of whose property he settled and commenced his works), by whom he had, with other issue, a daughter, Ann, who married Anthony Keeling, who succeeded him in business. The works were afterwards carried on by T. Goodfellow. Keeling about 1793 built a large residence adjoining his works, and in 1810 retired from business. He died at Liverpool in 1866 (see Phœnix Works).

Child.—About 1763 Mr. Smith Child established a pottery here, which was afterwards successively carried on by Mr. Clive, Joseph Heath & Co., Anthony Shaw, and the Messrs. Adams. Some examples are known which bear the impressed name CHILD (see Newfield Works).

Winter.—"Early in the present century," says Shaw, "Captain Winter having boasted that the articles of his manufacture at Tunstall were the only true porcelain made in Staffordshire, experienced no little chagrin on ascertaining that his ware would fuse at a heat much below that usually required," &c.

Unicorn Pottery and *Pinnox Works.*—These large and important manufactories of general earthenware, situated in Amicable Street and Great Woodland Street, were, early in the present century, occupied by Mr. E. Challinor, who was succeeded in 1825 by Podmore Walker & Co. (who also occupied the Swan Bank Pottery), who were succeeded by "Wedgwood & Co.," the late head of the firm being Enoch Wedgwood, Esq., of Port Hill, J.P. for the county of Stafford, whose elder son, Edmund M. Wedgwood, is now the sole proprietor. The works, which are very extensive, and give employment to six or seven hundred persons, occupy an area of about an acre of ground, and are among the most substantially built and best arranged in the pottery district. The goods produced are the higher classes of earthenware, in which dinner, tea, breakfast, dessert, toilet and other services, and all the usual miscellaneous articles, are made to a very considerable extent, both for the home, colonial, Continental, and American markets, to which considerable quantities are regularly exported. The quality of the "Imperial Ironstone China"—the staple production of the firm—is of remarkable excellence, both in body and in glaze, and the decorations are characterized by pure taste, artistic feeling, and precision of execution; they consist of an endless variety of admirable patterns printed in various colours and on different coloured bodies, wholly or partially hand-painted, enamelled, and gilt. The aim of the firm is, and always has been, to produce the best, most artistic, and most pleasingly effective designs, and to adapt them to ordinary purposes, so that they may become the everyday surroundings of the artisan as well as of the educated man of taste. Thus they associate durability of quality in body and a perfect glaze with purity of outline in form, chasteness of decoration, and clearness and harmony of colour, adapting their designs and styles of decoration to the national tastes of the people in the various climes to which the goods are sent. One of the most successful of their original ordinary printed designs is the pattern known as "Asiatic Pheasants," which has become so popular as to be considered one of the standard patterns of this country and the colonies. Other equally effective designs have also been introduced by Messrs. Wedgwood with great success. In the higher classes of decoration—painting, jewelling, and gilding—the productions rank deservedly high, and the firm is particularly successful in services bearing monograms and armorial decorations. They also supply large quantities of ironstone china specially made for the use of ships, restaurants, hotels, &c., which is considered to be exceedingly durable. They were awarded a medal at the Paris Exhibition. The impressed marks formerly used by the firm are—

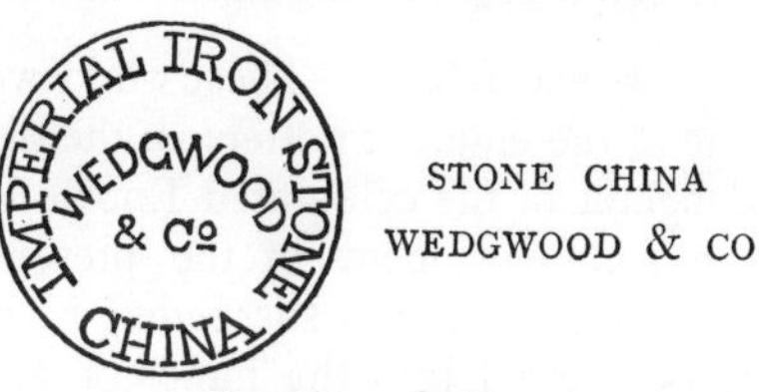

Figs. 1619 and 1620.

The present mark is the family crest, a unicorn's head, couped, ducally gorged and chained, and beneath, on a ribbon, "WEDGWOOD & CO"; it is printed on all decorated and white granitewares. The "Unicorn Works" is entirely devoted to the production of plain white graniteware for the American trade.

Greenfield Works (William & Thomas Adams).—This business was originally established at Stoke by the grandfather of the present owner, William Adams, who carried on the business in his own name until 1829, when it was changed to Wm. Adams & Sons, the second William Adams being head of the firm. In 1834 the present works at Greenfield, Tunstall, were opened, and in 1853 a dissolution took place, and the works were carried on by William Adams (the second) until 1865, when he retired in favour of his sons, William and Thomas, the present owners of the manufactory. The trade is entirely confined to foreign markets, the principal trade being with the Brazils, Cuba, Central America, Java, Manilla, Singapore, the United States, &c., the first six of which are the special trade of this firm. The earthenware is noted for the richness and variety of its coloured and sponged patterns, the bright fancy character of which is much admired in the out-markets of the world which have been named. The goods consist of tea, toilet, and table services, besides other articles. White granite (or ironstone china) is also made for the American and other markets, some of the raised patterns—as, for instance, the "Dover"—being remarkably good, and the forms of the pieces faultless. Transfer-printing is much used, and is judiciously combined with "sponged" patterns with good effect.

William Adams was an apprentice to Josiah Wedgwood, and was a great favourite with him. He commenced business for himself at Tunstall, and there produced some fine works of art in jasper and other wares. He died in the beginning of the present century, and was, I have heard, succeeded in the Tunstall business by his son Benjamin Adams. Occasionally the name ADAMS, or W. ADAMS & SON, is met with. "About 1800," according to Shaw, "Mr. Benjamin Adams, of Tunstall, was successful in the manufacture of jasper" in imitation of that of Wedgwood.

The *Newfield Works*, occupied in 1857 by the Adams's, are now carried on by Messrs. W. H. Grindley & Co., for the same classes of goods.

George Street Pottery, established 1862.—At these works Mr. W. Holdcroft (formerly Holdcroft & Wood) manufactures earthenware dinner, toilet, tea, and other services, and the usual varieties of useful articles, including jugs in great variety. The styles of ornamentation are hand-painting, transfer-printing, ground-colours, lustre-glazes, &c. The markets produced for are both home and foreign, and the general classes of goods are what may be called generally commercial. Connected with these works is the highly interesting fact that Mr. Holdcroft was the first to introduce the down-draught system of firing into the Potteries, which has effected a great saving in fuel and a freedom from smoke.

Phœnix Works.—These works were built in the last century by Anthony Keeling, one of the eminent potters of the district in the "olden days." He married Ann, daughter of the celebrated Enoch Booth, to whose business he succeeded, and at the commencement of the present century was the principal manufacturer in Tunstall. He was succeeded in 1810 by Thomas Goodfellow, from whom the works passed into the hands of Mr. Bridgwood, by whom (being later on joined in partnership by Mr. Edward Clarke) they were carried on under the style of "Bridgwood & Clarke." Mr. Bridgwood dying in 1864, Mr. Clarke became sole proprietor, and carried on the concern until 1877, when he removed to the New Bridge Works at Longport, and later to the Churchyard Works at Burslem. The manufactory has now been taken down. The marks used were EDWARD CLARKE, impressed on the body of the ware, and the royal arms, with supporters, garter, motto, &c., above a flowing ribbon on which are the words "EDWARD CLARKE, PORCELAIN OPAQUE," and beneath, TUNSTALL (see Enoch Booth).

Lion Works, Sandyford, were commenced for goods for the home trade by James Beech in 1838, and afterwards passed to Thomas Walker, who made South American goods, and in 1856 to Broughton & Mayer. In 1862 "Ford & Challinor" became proprietors, and continued the manufacture of general earthenware for the home and foreign markets.

Victoria Works.—Established in 1858, by Mr. John Tomkinson, was carried on under the style of "Turner & Tomkinson" until 1873, when Mr. Tomkinson retired, and the business was continued by Mr. Turner and his sons, under the style of "G. W. Turner & Sons." The goods produced are the ordinary printed and enamelled earthenware in dinner, toilet, and other services, &c., for the home and colonial markets. The mark used is simply the initials of the firm.

The Swan Bank Works is one of the oldest manufactories in Tunstall, and belonged, in the beginning of the present century, to Ralph Hall, and is the property of his descendant, Frederick J. Bowers, by whom (as successor to his father, George F. Bowers) the Brownhills Pottery was carried on until it was formed into a company. Ralph Hall was succeeded by Podmore, Walker & Co., from whom, about 1862, it passed into the hands of Beech & Hancock, and from them to James Beech. The productions are the ordinary classes of earthenware and stoneware for the home trade, in which all the usual services are largely made in "sponged," printed, painted, enamelled, gilt, and lustred styles. Stoneware jugs of excellent quality and other articles are also largely made, as are also black ware and other jardinières, flower vases, &c.

The Church Bank Works were built in 1842 by Robert Beswick, of Chell, by whom they were carried on until 1860, and since then by Beech & Hancock, Eardley & Hammersley, Ralph Hammersley alone, and from 1870 Thomas Booth & Son. The firm commenced business in 1864 at the Knowles Works, Burslem, as Evans & Booth, which in 1868 was altered to Thomas Booth & Co., and in 1872 to Thomas Booth & Son. The productions are earthenware of medium quality, in which all the usual services and other domestic articles are produced for the home and colonial markets.

Well Street Pottery, or the *Old Works.*—These works—of old foundation—formerly carried on by Clive & Lloyd, and after Mr. Lloyd retired by Stephen Clive, under the style of Stephen Clive & Co., are now worked by Cumberlidge & Co., whose productions are the ordinary middle classes of earthenware goods for the home and foreign markets. "About 1802 Mr. William Brookes, engraver, then of Tunstall, afterwards of Burslem, suggested to Mr. J. Clive a new method of ornamenting by blue-printing. The border of the plate was engraved from a beautiful strip of border for paper-hangings of rooms, and many of the manufacturers approved of the alteration. The New Hall Company instantly adopted it for some of their tea-services."

Black Bank and High Street Works, carried on by Mr. Ralph Hammersley, the latter for the production of ordinary earthenware, and the former for common jet, red, and Rockingham ware articles.

Woodland Pottery.—Messrs. Hollinshed & Kirkham, formerly Edmund T. Wood, is situated in Woodland Street. Earthenware for the home and foreign markets is produced in all the usual varieties.

Greengate Pottery.—Messrs. Henry Meir & Son manufacture earthenware in all the usual services of the more ordinary classes.

Sandyford Works.—Ordinary earthenware was here made by Mr. Jabez Blackhurst, but the works are now closed.

Tunstall Works.—In 1857 Messrs. Blackhurst & Dunning commenced these works for the manufacture of ordinary earthenware for the home and South American markets. In 1867 Mr. Dunning died, and the business was carried on by Richard Blackhurst alone till his death in 1877; since then by Messrs. Goode & Kenworthy.

Highgate Pottery.—Established by George Hood, who purchased the land from Mr. Randle-Wilkinson in 1831, and built the manufactory. The works were bought in 1846 by William Emberton, since whose death in 1867 they have been carried on by his sons, Thomas Isaac and James Emberton, the present owners. The goods manufactured are all the usual varieties of earthenware for the home markets, and the firm are also large producers of special goods for Ceylon, Calcutta, Bombay, and other Indian markets.

Clay Hill Pottery.—Messrs. Thomas Elsmore & Son manufacture ordinary earthenware.

Royal Albert Works.—Mr. Alfred Meakin produces the ordinary classes of earthenware goods.

Soho Works.—Mr. George Guest here manufactures common earthenware.

Marshall & Co. were manufacturers in the early part of this century, but their exact locality is unknown to me. The mark, Fig. 1621 (in the Mayer Museum), is impressed on the bottom of a shell-piece, a part of a dessert service, painted in pink waves with gilt edge.

MARSHALL & CO.
6

Fig. 1621.

Walton.—The name WALTON in a scroll, and also "Walton" alone, occur impressed in the ware of common earthenware statuettes.

Stevenson.—There was more than one firm of potters of this name in Staffordshire. Some were of Cobridge. One used a vesica-shaped mark bearing a three-masted ship with the name Stevenson above it impressed in the ware. Another used a crown within a circle, on which was A. STEVENSON, WARRANTED, STAFFORDSHIRE; and another impressed mark was the name STEVENSON.

Birch.—Mr. Birch produced Egyptian black ware articles of good quality. His mark was the name BIRCH impressed in the ware.

Eastwood.—Red ware, cane-coloured ware, with raised foliage, flowers, figures, &c., and black ware teapots, were made by Eastwood, and bear his name impressed in the body of the ware, EASTWOOD or Eastwood.

Shorthose & Co.—I have met with the marks of "SHORTHOSE & CO.," "SHORTHOSE," "Shorthose & Co.," "Shorthose," on a variety of wares, including ordinary cream-coloured services, white and printed goods, and Egyptian black and other articles.

Heath & Son.—The impressed marks, Figs. 1622 and 1623, are supposed to be those of Heath & Son. They occur on well-decorated earthenware services of average quality.

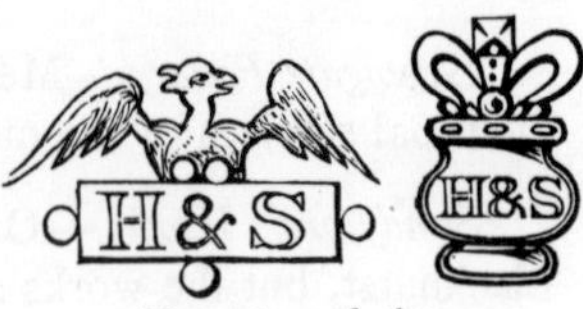

Figs. 1622 and 1623.

NEWCASTLE-UNDER-LYME.

Charles Riggs's Tobacco-pipes.—Two hundred years ago, when Plot wrote (1676), there was a famous manufactory of tobacco-pipes at this place. The maker was Charles Riggs, and he made "very good pipes of three sorts of clay." "As for *Tobacco-pipe clays* they are found all over the county, near Wrottesley House, and Stile Cop, in Cannock Wood, whereof they make pipes at Armitage and Lichfield, both which, though they are *greyish clays*, yet burn very white. There is *Tobacco-pipe clay* also found at Darlaston, near Wednesbury; but of late disused, because of better and cheaper found in Monway-field, betwixt Wednesbury and Willingsworth, which is of a *whitish* colour, and makes excellent *pipes*, as doth also another of the same colour dug near the Salt Water poole in Pensnet Chase, about a mile and a half south of Dudley. And *Charles Riggs*, of Newcastle, makes very good *pipes* of three sorts of clay—a *white* and *blew*—which he has from between Shelton and Hanley

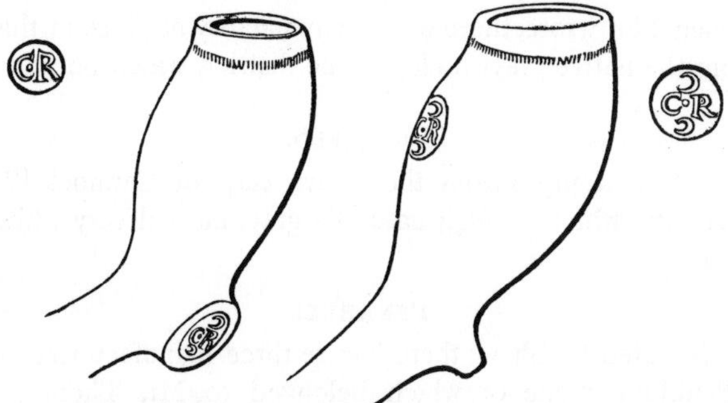

Figs. 1624 to 1627.

Green, whereof the blew clay burns the *whitest*, but not so *full* as the *white*, *i.e.* it *shrinks* more; but the best sort he has is from Grubbers Ash, being *whitish* mixt with *yellow*. It is a short brittle sort of clay, but burns full and white; yet he sometimes mixes it with the blew before mentioned."

With reference to this Charles Riggs, it is interesting to add that nearly a hundred pipes, each bearing, as a heel or other mark, the initials C R in various forms—found at Newcastle and other localities in the district—have come under my notice, and are, there can be but little doubt, examples of his workmanship. They are interesting, too, as showing the transition in the lifetime of one maker from the flat heel to the pointed spur. Fig. 1624 has a stamp on the heel bearing the initials C R between two crescents; and 1625 being a pipe with a pointed spur, has the same stamp on the front of the bowl so as to face the smoker. Another mark of Rigg's (Fig. 1626) was simply the initials C R within a circle.

Thomas Wood's Garden-Edgings.—Tiles for garden-edgings were in Plot's time made at Newcastle-under-Lyme, and must have had extensive sale, as the gardens of the better kind were in those days always laid out in "knots" of more or less elaborate design. Plot, speaking of this branch of manufacture, says: "Also at Newcastle-under-Lyme the *Tiles* burnt in a *Kill*, the usual way, being found not to last, one *Mr. Thomas Wood*, of the same Towne, first contrived to burn them (which we may look upon as an art relating to fire) in a *Potter's Oven*, wherein he made them so good and lasting that notwithstanding they have been put to the hardship of dividing the parts of *Garden Knots*, to endure not only the perpetual moisture of the earth, but frost, snow, and all sorts of weather; yet they few of them decay, scarce 5 tiles in 500 having failed in 20 yeares time; so that now he has been followed by all the countrey thereabout."

Newcastle Pottery.—Established by Harrison & Baker in 1866 for the production of red ware, ebony or jet ware, and terra-cotta, as well as ordinary horticultural goods. In red and jet wares and Rockingham ware the usual useful and ornamental classes of articles are made.

Keys and Mountford.—In the Exhibition of 1851 Messrs. Keys and Mountford exhibited, and received honourable mention for Parian statuettes.

Armitage.

In 1676, when Plot wrote, there was a manufactory of pipes at this place. They were made from the native greyish clay of the district, which burned very white.

Lichfield.

The manufactory of pipes from the native clays of Cannock Wood and other places in the county, which, though naturally grey, burned very white, is mentioned by Plot in 1676.

Penkhull.

In 1600, it is stated by Shaw, there "were three manufactories for coarse brown pottery" at Penkhull, "one of which belonged to Mr. Thomas Doody, whose descendants now reside at Tunstall."

CHAPTER XXIV.

SWANSEA.

Cambrian Pottery.—In the middle of last century a small manufactory of earthenware belonging to a Mr. Coles, who afterwards took into partnership a Mr. George Haynes, appears to have existed at Swansea. The buildings were originally copper-works, and were converted into a pottery. In February, 1783, the works were offered for sale, and were described as "a very capital Set of Works, well calculated for the Pottery, Glass, or any other Business, wherein well constructed Cones are necessary," . . . . as having "been built within these few Years, and have been employed in a very extensive Pottery and Earthenware Manufacture;" . . . . that "There are two excellent Water Mills included in the Premises for grinding the Flints," and that "Teignmouth Clay is to be had delivered at the works at 12s. per ton, and Flints for 20s." Later on, probably after the sale, Mr. Haynes became sole proprietor, and by him and his partners, under the firm of "Haynes & Co.," the works were much enlarged, and styled the "Cambrian Pottery." In 1800, according to Donovan, the works, then carried on by G. Haynes & Co., of which he gives an extended account, were extensive, and producing wares of a superior class, the buildings being said to be arranged on the same plan as those of Josiah Wedgwood at Etruria. In 1802 Haynes sold his works, moulds, models, stock, &c., to Mr. Lewis Weston Dillwyn—who was a Fellow of the Linnæan Society, was the author of "A Synopsis of British Confervæ, Coloured from Nature, with Descriptions;" "A Description of Recent Shells;" and "Catalogue of the more rare Plants found in the neighbourhood of Dover;" and, in conjunction with Dawson Turner, of "The Botanist's Guide through England and Wales"—and by him the buildings were very greatly enlarged and the business considerably extended.

At first only the ordinary descriptions of common earthenware were made, but the manufacture was gradually improved by Mr. Haynes, who produced a fine white earthenware, a cream-coloured ware, an "opaque china," and other varieties, as well as a very passable kind of biscuit ware. This "opaque china," a fine, hard, compact, and beautiful body, is doubtless the "porcelain" ware spoken of by Donovan, on which so much unnecessary stress was laid by a recent writer in attempting to prove that veritable porcelain was made at Swansea before the time when Mr. Dillwyn commenced it, the same writer forgetting to notice that in the same paragraph in which Donovan speaks of the Swansea *porcelain,* he speaks also of it and other wares bidding fair some day to vie with "Sieve *pottery.*"

In 1790 one of the "throwers" was Charles Stevens, who had been an apprentice (at the same time as William Taylor) at the Worcester China Works. In that year he applied to be employed at the Derby China Works, sending as his address "The Pot Work, Swansea," and next "at Mr. Bothwell's, engraver, in the Strand,

Swansea." In the body of the Swansea wares "the North Devon or Bideford clays seem to have been early employed, as also the Dorset or Poole clays, the last still continuing to be used. Cornish kaolin and chinastone likewise formed a portion of the porcelain body."

Upon the works passing into the hands of Mr. Dillwyn in 1802, the opaque china was much improved, and the decorations assumed a more artistic character. The principal painter was a Mr. W. W. Young, who was particularly skilful in painting flowers, but more especially natural history subjects—birds, butterflies and other insects, and shells. These he drew from nature, and was remarkably truthful and free in his delineations. He had been for some time previously employed by Mr. Dillwyn in illustrating his works on Natural History; and having been instructed in the use of enamel colours, proved a great acquisition to the manufactory. He afterwards became one of the proprietors of the Nantgarw China Works. Pieces decorated with his painting are now of rare occurrence, especially those having his name, *Young pinxit*, or *Young f.* In the Museum of Practical Geology are some interesting examples of this "opaque china," or "*opaque porcelain.*" The decorations consisted—we are told by Donovan—in 1800 of "emblematical designs, landscapes, fruit, flowers, heraldic figures, or any other species of ornamental devices," so that several artists must at that time have been employed.

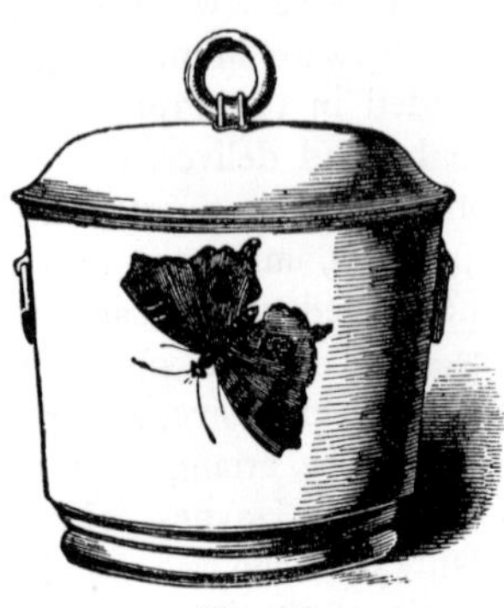

Fig. 1628.

In 1814 Mr. Dillwyn received a communication from Sir Joseph Banks that a specimen of china had been submitted to Government from Nantgarw, and he was requested to examine and report on those works. This matter is thus spoken of by Mr. Dillwyn himself: "My friend Sir Joseph Banks informed me that two persons, named Walker and Beeley, had sent to Government from a small manufactory at Nantgarw (ten or twelve miles north of Cardiff) a specimen of beautiful china, with a petition for their patronage: and that, as one of the Board of Trade, he requested me to examine and report upon the manufactory. Upon witnessing the firing of a kiln at Nantgarw, I found much reason for considering that the body used was too nearly allied to glass to bear the necessary heat, and observed that nine-tenths of the articles were either shivered or more or less injured in shape by the firing. The parties, however, succeeded in making me believe that the defects in their porcelain arose entirely from imperfections in their small trial kiln; and I agreed with them for a removal to the Cambrian Pottery, at which two new kilns, under their direction, were prepared. While endeavouring to strengthen and improve this beautiful body, I was surprised at receiving a notice from Messrs. Flight & Barr, of Worcester, charging the parties calling themselves Walker and Beeley with having clandestinely left an engagement at their works, and forbidding me to employ them."

In 1814, then, William Billingsley and George Walker commenced for Mr. Dillwyn at the Cambrian Pottery the manufacture of china of the same body and glaze as that they had produced at Nantgarw. For this purpose some new buildings, kilns, &c., were erected on a place that had previously been a bathing-place, and the utmost secrecy was observed. Mr. Dillwyn—or rather Billingsley and Walker for him—succeeded in producing a beautiful china; but the loss of time in building and altering the kilns, &c., and the losses and disappointments attending numerous experiments and trials, prevented it being made to more than a limited extent. Soon after the receipt of Flight & Barr's letter, Mr. Dillwyn dismissed Billingsley and Walker (who returned to Nantgarw), and continued the manufacture of china, but of a somewhat different body. About 1817 the manufacture was laid aside by Mr. Dillwyn, and for a time carried on by Mr. Bevington. In 1823 the moulds, &c., were purchased by Mr. Rose, of the Coalport Works, and removed to that place, and since that time no china has been made at Swansea.

The Cambrian Pottery passed successively from Mr. Lewis Weston Dillwyn (afterwards M.P. for Glamorganshire) to Mr. Bevington (at one time manager of the works), who with a partner carried them on as "Bevington & Roby," and "Bevington, Roby, & Co.," and so back again ultimately to Mr. Dillwyn, and thence to his son, Mr Lewis Lewellyn Dillwyn, M.P. for Swansea, by whom in 1840 negotiations were entered into with Mr. Brameld of the "Rockingham Works" for the letting of the "Glamorgan Pottery" to the latter firm for the purpose of manufacturing china ware. The negotiations, however, fell through, and thus Swansea was deprived of a good chance of becoming an important centre of porcelain manufacture.

About 1848 or 1850 Mr. Dillwyn commenced the manufacture of imitations of

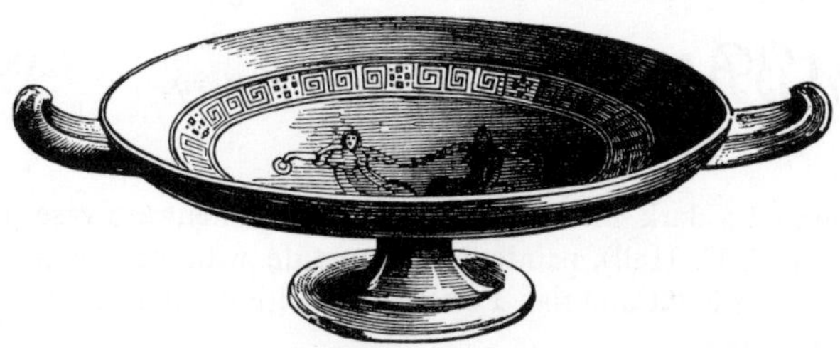

Fig. 1629.—Dillwyn's Etruscan Ware.

Etruscan vases, &c. This ware, which was called "Dillwyn's Etruscan Ware," was a fine rich red body. On this was printed, in black outline, Etruscan figures, borders, &c., and the general surface was then painted over and up to the outlines with a fine black, leaving the figures of the original red of the body. The effect was extremely good, and some remarkably fine examples, although but few pieces were made, are still preserved. Fig. 1629 is of elegant form, and the pattern, both border and figures, is in remarkably good taste. The mark (Fig. 1630) is printed in black on the bottom of the vase. The forms were all taken either from vases in the British Museum, or from Sir William Hamilton's "Antiquités Etrusques, Grecques, et Romaines." But very little was produced, as it was not a ware, unfortunately, to command a ready sale. It was made from clay found in the neighbourhood, which, when not too highly fired, burns to a good red colour.

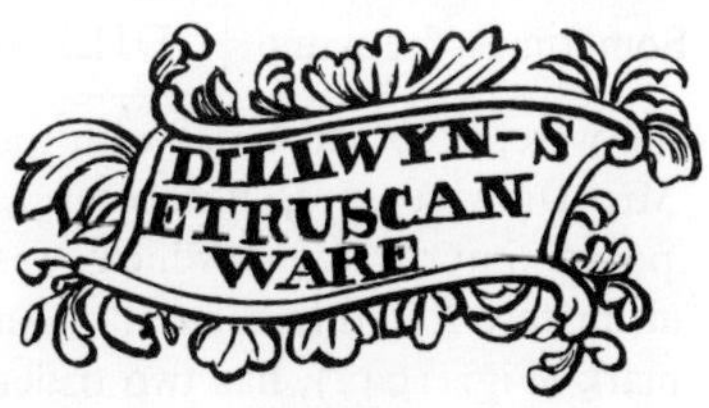

Fig. 1630.

In 1852 Mr. Dillwyn retired from the concern, and it passed into the hands of Mr. Evans, who carried it on under the firm of "Evans, Glasson, & Evans," until 1859, when, for a time, the style was altered to "Evans & Co.," and subsequently to "D. J. Evans & Co." (son of the Mr. Evans just alluded to). The manufacture consisted of the ordinary classes of white, blue and white, and agate earthenware, the markets being principally Wales, Ireland, West of England, and Chili. No trade-mark is used. About the end of 1869 earthenware was rather suddenly discontinued to be made at the Cambrian Pottery, and the bulk of the workpeople discharged. The site having become more valuable for other commercial purposes than a pottery, an arrangement was made by Mr. Dillwyn with D. J. Evans & Co., to surrender the short unexpired term of their lease, and as soon as the stock and plant had been cleared off, the buildings were taken down. The copper-plates were sold to the South Wales Pottery, Llanelly.

Among the artists at one time or other employed at Swansea, besides Young, of whom I have already spoken, were Pardoe, an excellent flower-painter (afterwards of the Nantgarw Works); Baxter, a clever figure-painter, who came to these works from Worcester, to which place he afterwards returned; Bevington, a flower-painter, also from Worcester; Reed, a modeller of considerable repute; Hood, also a clever modeller; Jenny, a tracer in gold; Morris, a fruit-painter; Colclough, who was much admired as a painter of birds; Evans, who was a talented flower-painter; and Beddoes, who was the best heraldic painter. To these, of course, must be added Billingsley, who was the best flower-painter of the day. The principal marks used at these works appear to have been the following:—

CAMBRIAN   *Cambrian Pottery.*   CAMBRIAN POTTERY.

Figs. 1631 to 1633.

1631 occurs on a dark mottled blue oviform earthenware vase (formerly in the collection of Mr. S. C. Hall), painted on one side with passion-flowers, roses, &c. Another has the words "Cambrian Pottery" in writing letters, and another the same words in capital letters.

On the porcelain made by Billingsley and Walker for Mr. Dillwyn the mark appears to have simply been the name SWANSEA printed in red; or, as on the subsequent make of china, the name sometimes occurs simply impressed—

SWANSEA.   SWANSEA,   or   SWANSEA,   or   Swansea.

Sometimes the name DILLWYN & Co. appears impressed in the body of the ware, at other times with the addition of a trident (Figs. 1640, 1641), "which," Mr. Dillwyn says, "denotes a supposed improvement which was not ultimately found to answer." Another mark (Fig. 1642), has two tridents in saltire and the name Swansea, and other marks are—

or

SWANSEA

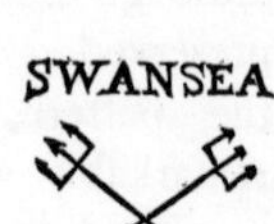

DILLWYN & COMPANY

DILLWYN & CO.

CAMBRIAN POTTERY.

OPAQUE CHINA,
SWANSEA.

HAYNES, DILLWYN & Co.
CAMBRIAN POTTERY.
SWANSEA.

Figs. 1634 to 1647.

The *Glamorgan Pottery* was situated to the west of the "Cambrian Pottery," on the opposite side of the road leading to the North Dock Bridge. In extent it was about two-thirds of the Cambrian, and produced similar wares. It was discontinued some years ago, the kilns taken down, and part of the building converted into iron warehouses. It was built about 1816 by a Mr. Baker, who was soon after joined in partnership by Mr. Bevan and Mr. Herwain, and the business carried on under the style of "Baker, Bevan, & Herwain" until 1839, when it seems to have been purchased by Mr. Dillwyn, who, in the following year, as I have shown, offered it to Messrs. Brameld, of the Rockingham China Works. Mr. Baker also at one time held another small pottery for a finer kind of earthenware, near the river Tawe, in another part of Swansea.

Rickard.—In Swansea, too, is also a small pot-work belonging to Mr. Rickard or Ricketts, who produces only the commonest kinds of black and Rockingham ware teapots, jugs, &c., and hardware jugs of mixed local clay and Dorset clay (principally for the home markets), ornamental flower-pots, garden-vases, &c.

Landore Pottery.—About 1848 Mr. John Forbes Calland, of Swansea district, built a pottery on the Swansea Canal, and near the river Tawe at Landore, about a mile from Swansea. This was worked for a few years by Mr. Calland, who produced printed and common earthenware from white clays in dinner, tea, and toilet ware for the home trade under the style and mark of—

J. K. CALLAND & CO.,
LANDORE POTTERY. and CALLAND
SWANSEA.

Not being commercially successful, Mr. Calland discontinued the manufacture about 1856, when the copper-plates were transferred to the South Wales Pottery at Llanelly, and the "Landore Pottery" ceased to exist.

LLANELLY.

South Wales Pottery.—These works, which are the only blue and white earthenware manufactory now in the Principality, were established in 1839 by Mr. W. Chambers, Jun., of Llanelly House, who carried them on up to the end of 1854. The general classes of goods manufactured were white or cream-coloured, edged, dipped, painted, and printed wares. Other descriptions of goods—viz. coloured bodies, figured, enamelled—and Parian, were tried and worked for a time, but soon discontinued. It was also intended to commence the making of china, and a kiln was built specially for that purpose, but the idea was then abandoned, and porcelain has never been made at these works. About 1850 white granite, printed, and flown printed ware was made for the United States. At the end of 1854 the business of the South Wales Pottery was transferred to Coombs and Holland, who carried them on till 1858, when the partnership was dissolved, and Mr. Holland continued the business alone till 1869, when he was joined in partnership by Mr. D. Guest, under the firm of Holland and Guest, and in 1877 the firm changed to Guest and Dewsbury. The goods produced consist of table, tea, and toilet services, and other ordinary articles in printed and flown earthenware of average quality, and the usual classes of white, cream-coloured, sponged, and painted wares. The copper-plates formerly in use at the other earthenware potteries in South Wales now discontinued working, viz. the Landore, the Ynisymudw, and the

Cambrian Pottery, Swansea, were purchased for the South Wales Pottery, and have been introduced in patterns and shapes. Mr. Holland was an exhibitor at the International Exhibition of 1862.

YNISYMUDW.

Terra-Cotta Works.—This manufactory, about ten miles from Swansea, on the Brecon road, was commenced as a fire-brick works (there having been a small common brick-works there previously) in 1840 by Mr. Williams and his brother, Mr. Williams, of Swansea, who soon afterwards introduced the "South Wales Dinas Bricks" from the Cribbath stone, obtained near the top of the Swansea Canal. These bricks are still made there, and the "Ynisymudw dinas" are equal to the best "dinas" or silica bricks made. Terra-cotta was also made in buff of good quality. About 1850 the Messrs. Williams added the manufacture of earthenware, in table, tea, toilet, and other services, &c., in common white painted and printed wares, and this was continued till about 1859, when the blue-and-white branch was discontinued (the copper-plates being purchased for the South Wales Pottery, Llanelly), and the works transferred to Charles Williams, who disposed of them to Griffith Lewis and John Morgan, of Pontardawe, who carried it on under the style of the "Ynisymudw Brick Company," "Ynisymudw Pottery Company," and "Lewis & Morgan," who also manufactured Rockingham teapots, &c., glazed stoneware bottles, and similar goods. In 1870 the works were transferred to Mr. W. T. Holland, of the South Wales Pottery, Llanelly, by whom they were continued.

NANTGARW.

These short-lived works, whose history is so mixed up with those of Swansea, Derby, Coalport, Pinxton, and other places, were commenced on a very small scale in 1813 by William Billingsley, the famous flower-painter of Derby, and his son-in-law, George Walker, the former at that time passing under the assumed name of Beeley, which was simply a contraction of his own name B'ley or B[illings]ley. Shortly afterwards, having applied to the Board of Trade for patronage and, of course, Government aid, Mr. Dillwyn, of the "Cambrian Pottery," at Swansea, went over to examine and report upon the ware; and this examination resulted in his entering into an engagement with Billingsley and Walker, by which they, with their recipes, moulds and appliances, removed to Swansea. In about two years this engagement was brought to a close, and Billingsley and Walker returned to Nantgarw, where they again commenced the manufacture of china of the same excellent and peculiar kind for which they had become so famous. The proprietors appear to have met with liberal friends to assist them in their undertaking. The Hon. William Booth Grey, of Duffryn, is said to have subscribed £1,000 towards the undertaking, and other gentlemen almost equally liberal sums. The whole of the money subscribed, understood to have been about £8,000, is said to have been expended in little more than two years. This in great measure appears to have been caused by experiments and trials and alterations in buildings, &c., and by the immense waste in "seconds" goods or "wasters," which were invariably broken up, instead of, as now at most works, being disposed of at a cheaper rate.

That Billingsley and Walker, with Mr. Young, who appears to have come from Swansea to join them, as also Mr. Pardoe, from the same works, who was formerly of Staffordshire (with Mr. Turner), and afterwards of Bristol, and who was a clever painter, were the proprietors of the renewed works, seems evident, and they were carried on with considerable success. The productions of Nantgarw were, as far as beauty of body and decoration, as well as form, are concerned, a complete success, and the works gradually, but surely, made their way in public estimation. The London houses—especially, it is said, Mortlock's—found it to their advantage to support the manufactory, and there was thus no difficulty in finding a good and profitable market. A service was made and presented to the Prince of Wales (afterwards George IV.); "the pattern was a green vase, with a single rose on every piece, and every rose different." This beautiful service was painted, I believe, partly by Billingsley and partly by Pardoe. It helped materially to make the works fashionable, and it is said that they were visited by numbers of the nobility and gentry, "as many as forty gentlemen's carriages having been known to be there in one day." A considerable quantity of the Nantgarw ware was sold in the white

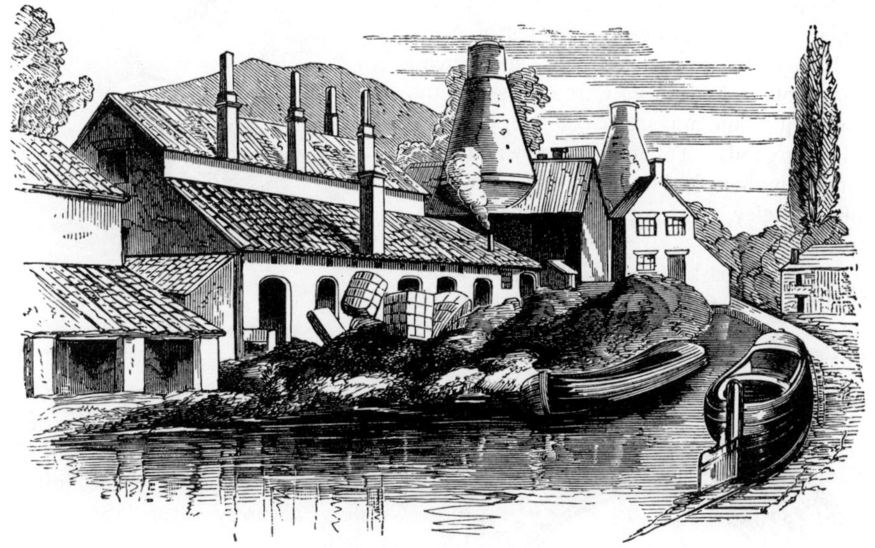

Fig. 1650.—Nantygarw Works.

to Mortlock, who had it painted in London, and fired at the enamel kiln of Robins & Randell, of Spa Fields. Webster, one of the painters of the Derby China Works, also decorated much of this ware in London. The trade, which was thus beginning to prosper, being felt to be likely to some considerable extent to affect the Coalport Works, Mr. Rose (of those works) entered into an arrangement with Billingsley and Walker by which he bought up their concern, made a permanent engagement with them, and at once removed them and their moulds, and everything else, to Coalport. The manufacture of china, therefore, closed at Nantgarw. In 1823 Mr. Pardoe died. Mr. Young removed, I am informed, to Droitwich, where he carried on a salt-work. Billingsley and Walker, as I have already stated, removed to Coalport, where Billingsley died in 1827 or 1828. Walker ultimately sailed for America, where he established a pottery, still, I believe, in operation.

In 1823 the greater portion of the china works were pulled down, the dwelling-house and some other portions alone remaining. In 1832 Mr. William Henry Pardoe of Bristol (who was a china-painter of great skill), a good practical potter of great experience in the art which had, through Richard Champion and his successors, made his city famous, entered upon the premises, and commenced a red-ware pottery, in connection with an extensive tobacco-pipe manufactory. To this he afterwards added Rockingham ware and stoneware departments, in each of which he produced goods of excellent quality. Mr. Pardoe died in 1867, and the Nantgarw works—those works around which such a halo of interest exists—were continued by his widow and family. The goods include red or brown earthenware, made from clay found in the neighbourhood—many of the pitchers being of purely mediæval form—stoneware bottles of every kind, jugs, butter-pots, cheese and bread pans, foot and carriage warmers, snuff-jars, hunting jugs and mugs, tobacco-jars, jugs, &c. and other goods. Tobacco-pipes, which experienced smokers declare to be equal to those from Broseley, garden-pots, pancheons, &c., are also made.

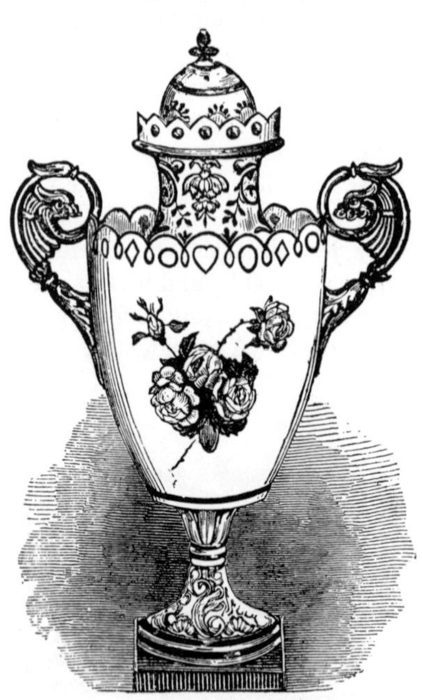

Fig. 1651.

The only marks used at Nantgarw which can be considered to be marks of the works are the following, impressed in the body of the china: NANT-GARW / G. W. the G. W. being the initials of George Walker, the son-in-law and partner of Billingsley; and the single word NANTGARW in red colours. In reference to the initials Chaffers absurdly says, "Sometimes the letters C. W. are found stamped under, which may perhaps mean 'China Works.'" Another mark supposed to belong to these works is this: ↾; with the number of the pattern as "No." added.

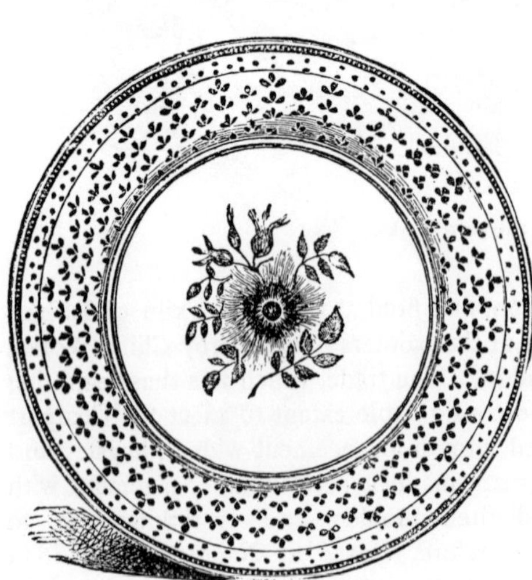

Fig. 1652.

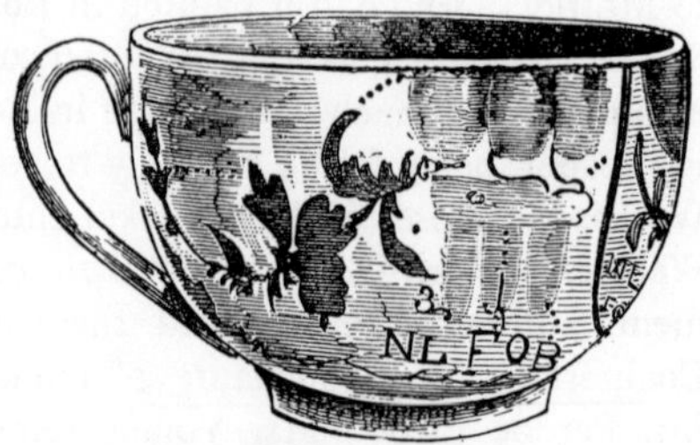

Fig. 1653.

The goods produced were tea, dinner, and dessert services, vases, match-pots, cabinet cups, pen and wafer trays, inkstands, and a large variety of other articles.

One of the most interesting relics of these works which has come under my notice is the cup here engraved (Fig. 1653), which was formerly in my own collection. It has been painted with what is technically known as the "Chantilly pattern" in blue, and then has been used as a trial piece for colours and glazes. It bears in different parts of its surface various washes of colour, with marks and contractions to show the mixture, which have been submitted to the action of the enamel kiln. In the Jermyn Street Museum the collector will find some good examples for comparison, as he will also in some private collections. Some remarkably fine examples of Nantgarw china are in the possession of Sir Ivor Bertie Guest, Bart., and others are in various collections.

The village of Nantgarw is situated in the parish of Eglw y Sillan, in Glamorganshire. It is eight miles from Cardiff, and one mile from the "Taffs Well" Station on the Taff Valley Railway, and the Rhymney Valley Railway is also equally near. The works shown in the engraving, from a sketch I made on the spot, are picturesquely situated by the side of the Glamorganshire Canal, on the road to Caerphilly, from whose glorious old ruined castle they are only a few miles distant.

Brown and Stoneware Potteries.—Among other works (besides Nantgarw) are those of Messrs. Henry James, Joseph Rogers, Evan Davies, George Sherrin, and Thomas Moore. At these only common coarse brownware pitchers and other domestic vessels are made.

Cardigan.

The Cardigan Potteries were established in 1875 by Messrs. Miles and Woodward for the production of common coarse red earthenware goods for domestic and horticultural purposes, but the clay of the district being found suitable for other classes of goods, they were added to the operations. The productions are vases, jugs, flower-stands, and other ornamental articles, and these are decorated and glazed in a manner peculiarly their own, and which gives to them a distinctive character over those of other manufactories. In some, quaint and well-designed patterns are impressed in the clay, and the whole being surface-coloured and highly glazed have a rich and peculiar appearance. The firm trade as "The Cardigan Potteries," "Woodward and Co.," and their works are called the "Patent Brick, Tile, and Pottery Works" and "Cardigan Potteries." The goods are principally for the Welsh coast and for England.

Hereford.

Lugwardine Works.—These encaustic tile-works, situated at Withington, four miles from Hereford, were established in 1861 by Mr. William Godwin, and are of considerable extent. In encaustic tiles Mr. Godwin has paid particular attention to the reproduction of mediæval patterns in all their entirety, both as to fac-simile of form and ornament and antique appearance of surface, and in these essentials to artistic effect has succeeded admirably. Many of his tiles are exact reproductions, not old designs modernised, and this it is that gives to floors laid by him that peculiar charm which they undoubtedly possess. In addition to actual copies of old tiles, Mr. Godwin has produced a large variety of new designs, in which the patterns are characterized by pure mediæval feeling and by excellent workmanship. The tiles are of extremely hard and durable quality, and the colours clear, distinct, and good. Mr. Godwin's name impressed on the back of the tile is his mark.

TORQUAY.

Terra-Cotta Works.—The terra-cotta works at Hele Cross, Torquay, were established in 1875 by Dr. Gillow, who that year discovered the bed of clay, and are worked by a limited liability company, of which he is chairman and general director. The clay, which is of remarkably fine, tenacious, and durable quality, is of a rich full red colour, and its surface is almost metallic in its hardness and fine texture. It is almost identical in quality and beauty of tone to that at Watcombe, to whose productions those of Torquay bear a marked resemblance. The company started with the aim of producing works of a high standard of excellence, and thus expressed their intention: "They (the company) believe that they have at Hele Cross the best deposit of clay yet discovered, and their one aim and object is to improve the artistic standard by persevering energy. One year's existence has given grounds for hope and encouragement; much has been done, but much more remains to be done. They trust to improve year by year, until they place terra-cotta in its old proud position as a favoured branch of Ceramic Art, and until Devonshire productions stand unrivalled throughout Europe." The success which has attended Dr. Gillow's efforts is very marked, and shows that they have been directed in a right way and in a commendable spirit. The productions of the Torquay Terra-Cotta Company are statuettes, single figures and groups, busts, groups of animals, birds, &c.; vases, ewers, bottles, jugs, and tazzæ; butter-coolers, spill-cases, and other domestic appliances; plaques of various sizes; candlesticks, toilet-trays, water-bottles, tobacco-vases, &c. Many of these are painted and enamelled in good taste, and the ornamentation, whether in colour or gilding, is characterized by clever workmanship and judicious arrangement. Many designs of vases, plaques, &c., are original and in good taste. The company supply not only the home but foreign markets, and have received high recognition, with medals, from the Royal Cornwall Polytechnic Society and from the Turners' Company. The marks used by the firm are an oval garter bearing the words TORQUAY TERRA-COTTA CO., and in the centre LIMITED, printed on the ware; the name TORQUAY impressed in the clay; the words within a single oval line; and the monogram, Fig. 1655, which is a combination of the letters T T C, for "Torquay Terra-Cotta."

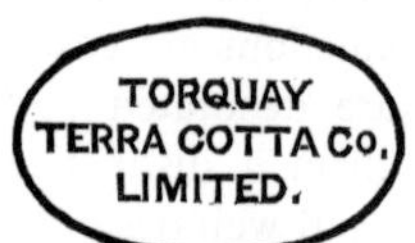

Figs. 1654 and 1655.

ALDERHOLT.

At this place, in Hampshire, potteries for common coarse ware for domestic purposes exist. The bed of clay is the same as that in the New Forest worked in early ages, as already described in this volume.

SMETHWICK.

Tile Works.—Mr. T. W. Camm commenced the business of Art decoration of tiles in 1866 in Brewery Street, and later on new buildings were erected in High Street. Having been joined in partnership by J. M. and H. C. Camm, the business was carried on under the style of "Camm Brothers," and has since been transferred to Mr. Winfield. The designs are extremely varied, and the whole being hand-painted are adapted to the tastes and requirements of their customers, and designed in strict accordance with the style of building they are intended to adorn. The figure subjects, allegorical, historical, or otherwise, of this firm are bold, firm, masterly, and effective, and the colouring rich, full, and harmonious. Some other larger works, notably historical plaques of two or three feet in length and proportionate depth, are grand in conception, and form historical pictures of considerable value. The mark is simply the name "CAMM BROTHERS, SMETHWICK."

Reading.

Coley Avenue Works.—These works were established in 1861 by Messrs. Collier and Son, and are continued under the style of "S. & E. Collier." Brown terra-cotta, glazed and unglazed brown ware, and roofing and other tiles are the products of these works.

Aylesford.

Terra-cotta Works were established here about 1850, by Mr. Edward Betts, who discovered a valuable bed of plastic clay on his estate in the neighbourhood. At the Exhibition of 1851 Mr. Betts exhibited a terra-cotta vase (Fig. 1656) made at Aylesford from this native clay, from a design furnished by Mr. John Thomas, the architect.

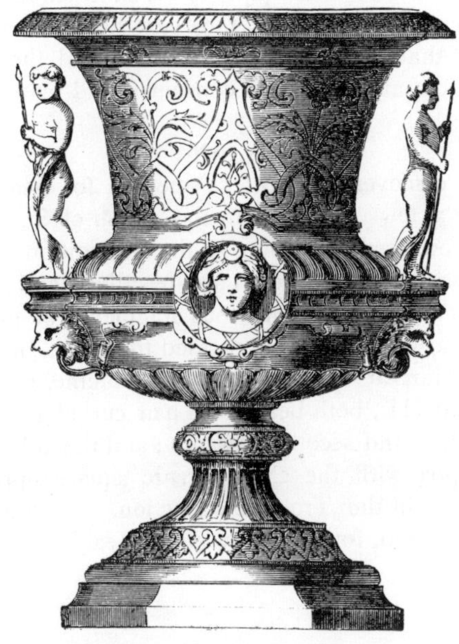

Fig. 1656.

Ditchling.

At Ditchling, in Sussex, pot-works are said to have existed for "several hundred years." Be this as it may, some old pot-works for the coarsest brown ware, and bricks and tiles, were bought in 1870 by H. Johnson & Co., in the belief that from the superior quality of the native red clay they would be able to produce architectural terra-cotta of a more than ordinarily durable quality. By them the Ditchling Works were much extended, and they succeeded in making terra-cotta of an excellent bright red colour, and a fine hard, durable, and almost metallic surface. Among public buildings where the Ditchling terra-cotta has been successfully used is the St. James's Hall, Piccadilly, and the firm received medals at the London and Philadelphia Exhibitions. In 1875 H. Johnson & Co. opened extensive works on the same vein of clay at Keymer Junction. They are the largest works in Sussex.

AMBLECOTE.

A pottery at this place is mentioned by Plot in 1686.

EXETER.

That tobacco-pipes were made in Exeter in 1654 is curiously proved by the following case of supposed witchcraft:—" 12 August, 1654. One Diana Crosse, a widow, suspected of being a witch, was ordered by the judge of Assize to be committed for trial at the city sessions. Mr. Edward Trible, a tobacco-pipe maker, one of the victims of the witch's arts, deposed that Mrs. Crosse on one occasion came to his house for fire, which was delivered to her, but for the space of one month afterwards he could not make or work his tobacco-pipes to his satisfaction—they were altogether either over or under burnt. The witch, too, cast her evil eye upon a boy in his employ, and 'affirmed' that he should never be well, and thereupon the boy 'grew into a distracted condition, and was much consumed and pyned away in body.' "

LINCOLN.

A very interesting discovery of potter's moulds for heads for impressing on earthenware was made a few years back in the parish of St. Mary-le-Wigford, Lincoln. The discovery consisted, according to the last edition of Marryat (edited by my friend Mrs. Pallisser), where the relics are described and carefully engraved, of the remains of a potter's kiln with numerous fragments of glazed pottery, among which was one piece bearing the head impressed from one of these moulds. One of them, engraved in Marryat's highly interesting volume, represents a male head, probably that of Edward III., both beard and hair curled at side as on the coins of that monarch and the first and second Edwards; and the other the head of a lady, probably Queen Philippa, with the characteristic square-topped reticulated head-dress. These moulds are in the Trollope collection. A potter's mould of a head of the Romano-British period, found by myself at Headington, is in my possession, and is engraved in Figs. 166, 167.

CHAPTER XXV.

THE early pottery of Ireland, although bearing a general resemblance in many of its characteristics to that of England and other nations, nevertheless differs from all others in some of its features, both of form and decoration. As in other countries, the great bulk of examples of early fictile art that remain to us in Ireland, and upon which we have to found our knowledge, are the cinerary urns—the clay vessels in

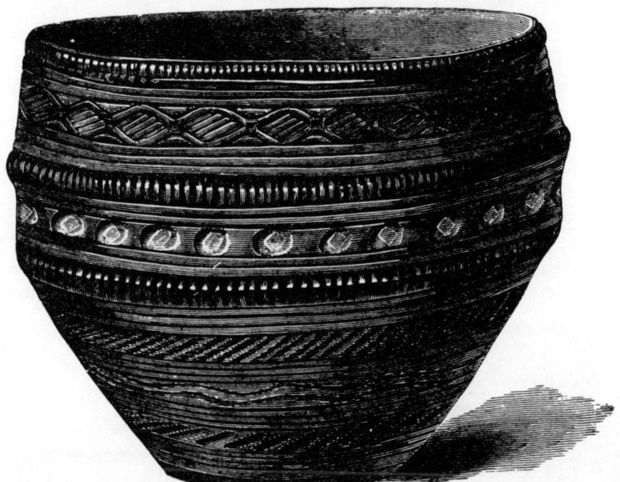

Fig. 1657.—From Altegarron, near Belfast.

which, when cremation was in vogue, the ashes and burnt bones of the dead were placed for burial in cairns or otherwise—and food and drinking-vessels found (when inhumation was observed) in the grave-mounds of the people. But in addition to this the "crannogs," or lake-dwellings of the Irish people, afford a vast fund of information upon the form and decoration of the domestic vessels in use in former ages.

In the earlier pages of this work I have written much upon early fictile art, and in other works have treated so fully upon the contents of the barrows of early ages, that it is not needful to pursue the subject here. I may, however, with special reference to Irish examples, quote the words of my late friend, Sir William Wilde —one of the most painstaking authorities upon Irish antiquities—and then pass on to a consideration of some of the examples that remain to us. "Irish cinerary urns have," Sir William says, "been found under three circumstances: in small cists, placed without any ostensible mark, at least at the present day, beneath the surface of the soil, each just sufficiently large to hold one or two vessels. The chamber is sometimes occupied with the urn and its contents alone; in other cases it also contains charcoal and portions of burned bone; and in some instances the flooring-stones have become vitrified upon the upper surface, thus leading us to believe that the funeral pyre was lighted over the grave after it was formed. Of this the charcoal

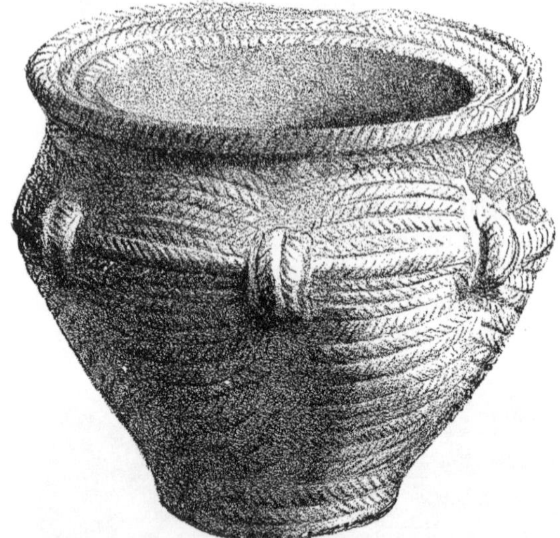

Fig. 1658.—From Ballon Hill, Co. Carlow.

and the vitrification of the stones afford presumptive proof. These small chambers are sometimes found near the surface, or on the periphery of the larger tumuli that usually cover cromlechs or surround extensive sepulchral chambers, and appear to

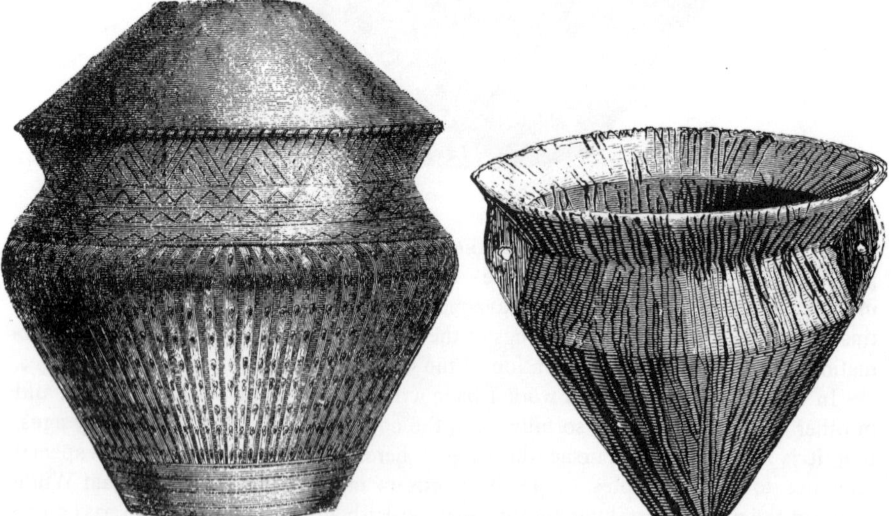

Fig. 1659.—From Cairn Thierna, Co. Cork.

Fig. 1660.—From Ballydoolough.

be of a much more recent date than the original structure of the tumulus in which they are placed. Such minor interments may have been those of the family or descendants of the persons originally interred beneath; or the place—strong in the odour of sanctity—may have been resorted to as a burial-ground long subsequent to its original foundation, from that feeling of veneration which instinctively consecrates the resting-place of the dead. These urns are also found imbedded in the earth, in which case they are generally aggregated in cemeteries upon the sides of hills." As in England, so in Ireland, interments both by cremation and inhumation were made, and with the latter vessels of clay of various forms were placed.

The material of the early Irish urns is simply coarse clay, but this varies in different localities. With some sand has evidently been more or less mixed with the clay, while "in those which show a higher degree of culture in the makers," as Sir William Wilde says, "sand and small fragments of stone, possibly broken for the purpose, were mixed through the plastic mass, and also rubbed (perhaps to assist in drying, as well as in giving them stability) upon the inner surface, especially near the bottom. A micaceous clay here appears to answer the same end; but in some of the very fine specimens minute particles of quartz and felspar may be observed coating the interior, which, from the sharpness of their fracture, would appear to have been broken specially for the purpose. These fragments of sand or stone may also be seen in the fracture, but are never observed upon the outer surface. In colour the Irish urns differ considerably upon the outer and inner surfaces. The latter is almost invariably blackish or dark brown, the result of partial torrefaction, and perhaps from the heated bones and charcoal placed within them, either when soft or after they had been sun-baked. The colouring generally passes through four-fifths of the mass. The outer surface is either a light red, grey, or brown. The first is most usual, and appears to be the result of the atmosphere, which was, however, excluded from the interior by the mass of the contents of the urn. The colour of the exterior usually passes for some distance within the lip. The drab or clay-coloured urns bear but little mark of fire, either within or without. The brown belongs only to the thinnest and hardest description of pottery. Assuming that the majority of the mortuary urns (except those for very distinguished persons) were constructed at the grave, the artist was indebted to the clay at hand in the locality for the materials with which he worked, and hence the great variety in the composition of our cinerary urns."

The ornamentation upon the earliest Irish pottery, both cinerary urns and otherwise, is extremely varied, both in character and in mode of arrangement. Sometimes simply a number of dots or punctures pretty nearly cover the surface; at others these punctures are intermixed in regular patterns with other ornaments. Sometimes again they exhibit ridges or raised bands more or less decorated, and at others the usual herringbone or zigzag patterns produced by incised or impressed lines are the most prominent feature. Again, in some examples patterns produced by pressing a twisted thong into the pliant clay are met with, while incised or impressed circular, semicircular, and other lines ornament others. "Many of these lines have a pectinated appearance, as if indicated with a traverser, or a rowel-like instrument such as that used by pastrycooks" at the present day, and sometimes the ornament is produced by simple scratches. Other urns are one mass of ornament, rich in appearance and varied in character; and others have what may not inaptly be called flat circular medallions on their sides. Others, again, present a series of "slashes" with intervening impressed ornaments.

It is a remarkable fact, as pointed out by Sir W. Wilde, that no examples, so far as his knowledge went, occurred on which "any trace of the spire, which characterizes the decorations of some of the very oldest sepulchral monuments in Ireland," is to be found; but a peculiar form of ornamentation, made by straight lines, is identical with that on some carved stones at the entrance to the most remarkable of these edifices—that of New Grange.

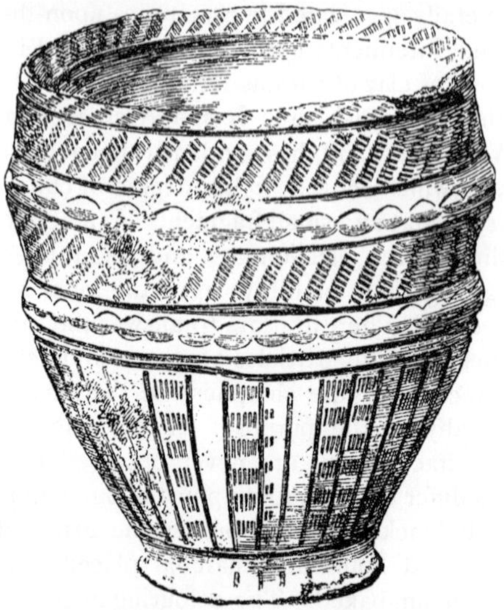

Fig. 1661.—From Trillick Barr.

Fig. 1661, found in a cairn at Trillick Barr, Tyrone, is slightly contracted towards the mouth, and has two raised encircling bands, and an extended rim at the base. The lower part is decorated with vertical lines, the spaces being filled in with

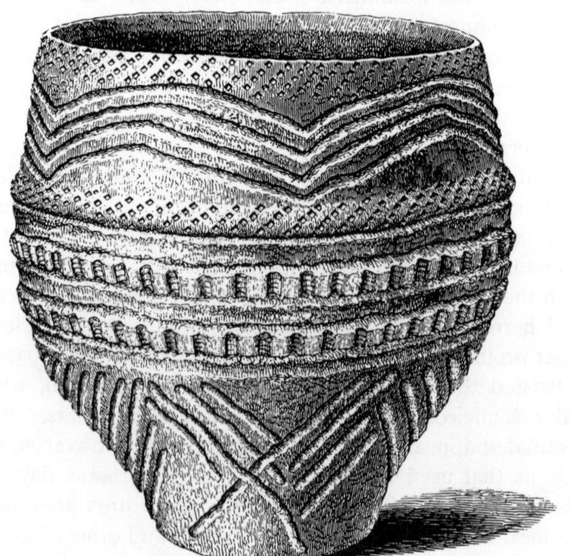

Fig. 1662.—From Ballybit, Co. Carlow.

impressed ornaments; and the portions between the encircling bands are also filled in with diagonal lines of indentations. These are also continued round the rim of the mouth, while the raised bands bear a double engrailed pattern. Fig. 1662, ound at Ballybit, Lisnevagh, county Carlow, contracts slightly towards the mouth. It has three encircling raised bands, with intervening indented ones around its centre, and these are richly ornamented. Fig. 1663, of a totally different character, both in form and ornamentation, was found in a cist, on the lands of Mackrackens, in the parish of Leckpatrick, county Tyrone. " At its greatest circumference it is surrounded by a narrow circular groove [much of the same character as some Celtic urns found in Derbyshire], and this groove is, as it were, clasped by five small pierced knobs, equidistant from each other. From their shape and closeness to the vessel," continues Mr. Geoghegan, " I cannot think they were intended for handles. There are no indentations or marks to lead us to suppose they were designed for that purpose. It appears to me their use was to retain in the groove a strong cord which twined round the urn. From this strong cord three strings could be attached, meeting in a knot, for the purpose of carrying or conveying the urn from the scene of cremation to the cist in which it was finally to be placed, or from the place

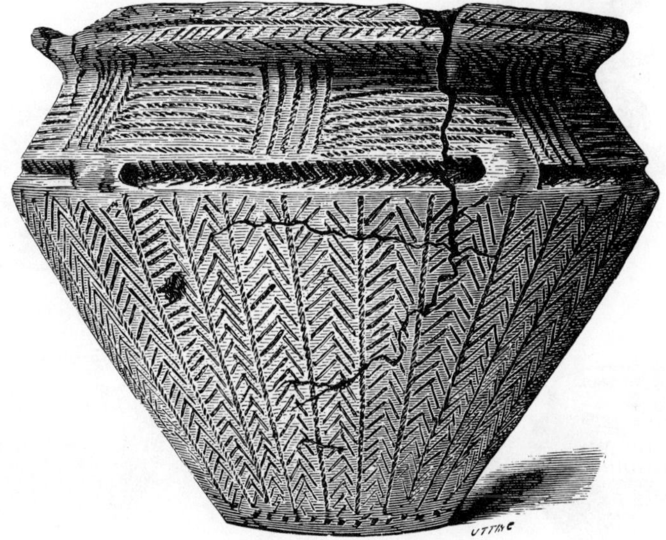

Fig. 1663.—From Mackrackens, Co. Tyrone.

where it was made." It bears a strong resemblance in outline to the wooden vessel, Fig. 1660. In the museum of the Royal Irish Academy urns of this same general form are preserved, as are also examples of almost every known variety. Figs. 1664 to 1668 are from that museum. Fig. 1680, from the "Giant's Grave," on the Loughrey demesne, in county Tyrone, is of globular form, and decorated with vertical lines of indentations and encircling lines incised in the clay. Between the encircling lines at the top, as well as those at the bottom, are rows of square indentations; and inside the mouth is also ornamented.

Urns of a different character of ornamentation were discovered some years ago at Ballon Hill, between Fenagh and Tullow, county Carlow. Among these was one more than fifteen inches in height, about fourteen inches in width at the mouth, and of "flower-pot" form, very similar to some English examples. Another was of bowl form with raised bands, and every part elaborately ornamented, the upper and lower parts bearing saltires alternating with incised lines. It was of the same general form as Fig. 1680. Others partook of the same general shapes as other examples here engraved, and were more or less ornamented with encircling lines, zigzag and other patterns, and impressed points, curves, &c.; one or two had raised knobs. One of the richest of "immolation urns," about two and three-quarter inches in height (and filled with small burnt bones when found), of the Irish series, also brought to light in this interment, is engraved on Fig. 1658. Another remarkable urn (Fig. 1659), found at Cairn Thierna, county Cork, has its outline totally different from others, and is elaborately and delicately ornamented over almost its entire surface. Fig. 1657 is an urn found at Yellow Jack's Cairn, in the townland of Altegarron, on the slopes of Divis Mountain, near Belfast. The whole surface was richly decorated with incised and impressed lines, and other ornamentation. Occasionally covers made of the same clay as the urns themselves, and ornamented in

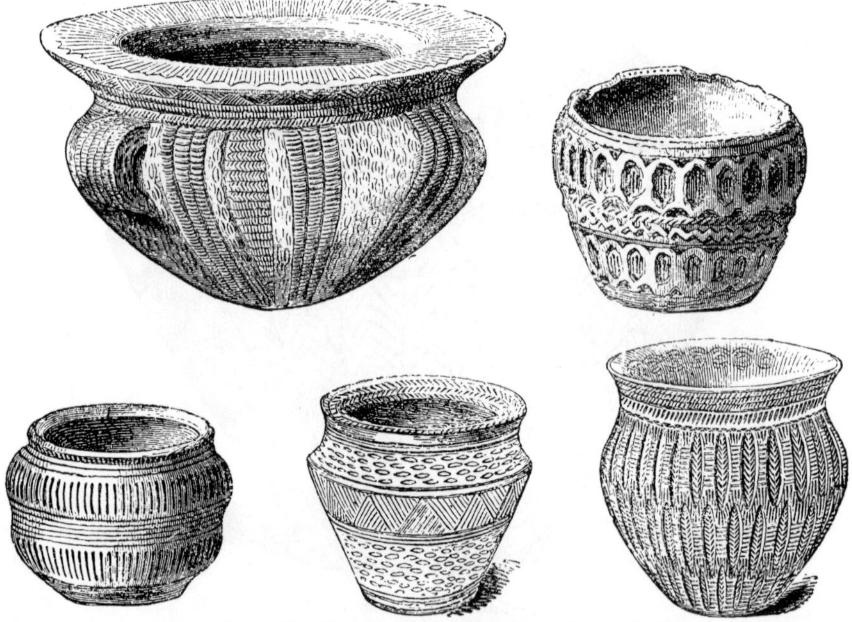

Figs. 1664 to 1668.—From the Museum of the Royal Irish Academy.

a similar manner, have been found. One remarkable example discovered at Danes Fort had a perfect cover or lid, with a handle at the top.

Some of the most curious and certainly most interesting urns which have come under my notice were found at Drumnakilly, near Omagh, county Tyrone, in 1872-3, and have been described and figured by Mr. Wakeman. The first of these (Fig. 1669) 3 feet 6 inches in circumference at the mouth, and of proportionate height, is elaborately ornamented with incised lines, "exactly of that class which we find upon the golden ornaments and other antiquities of pre-historic times preserved in our museums;" its outline bears a graceful curve from the mouth, swelling out in the middle, and gradually tapering down to the foot. Around the upper part is a series of perpendicular broad indentations with herring-bone pattern between; next follow a number of encircling lines, scoriated between; and the middle part of the urn is ornamented with zigzag and other lines. Another of

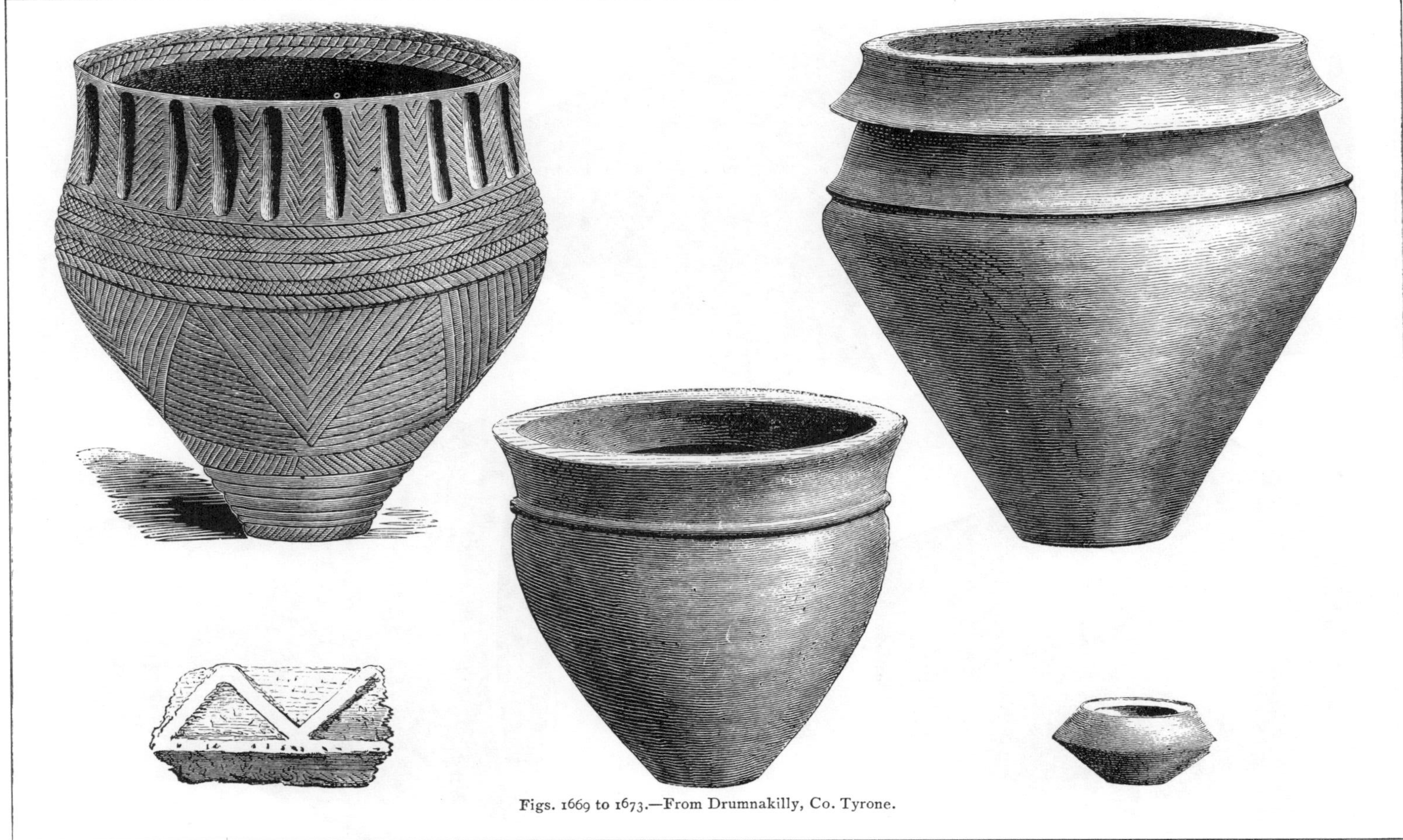

Figs. 1669 to 1673.—From Drumnakilly, Co. Tyrone.

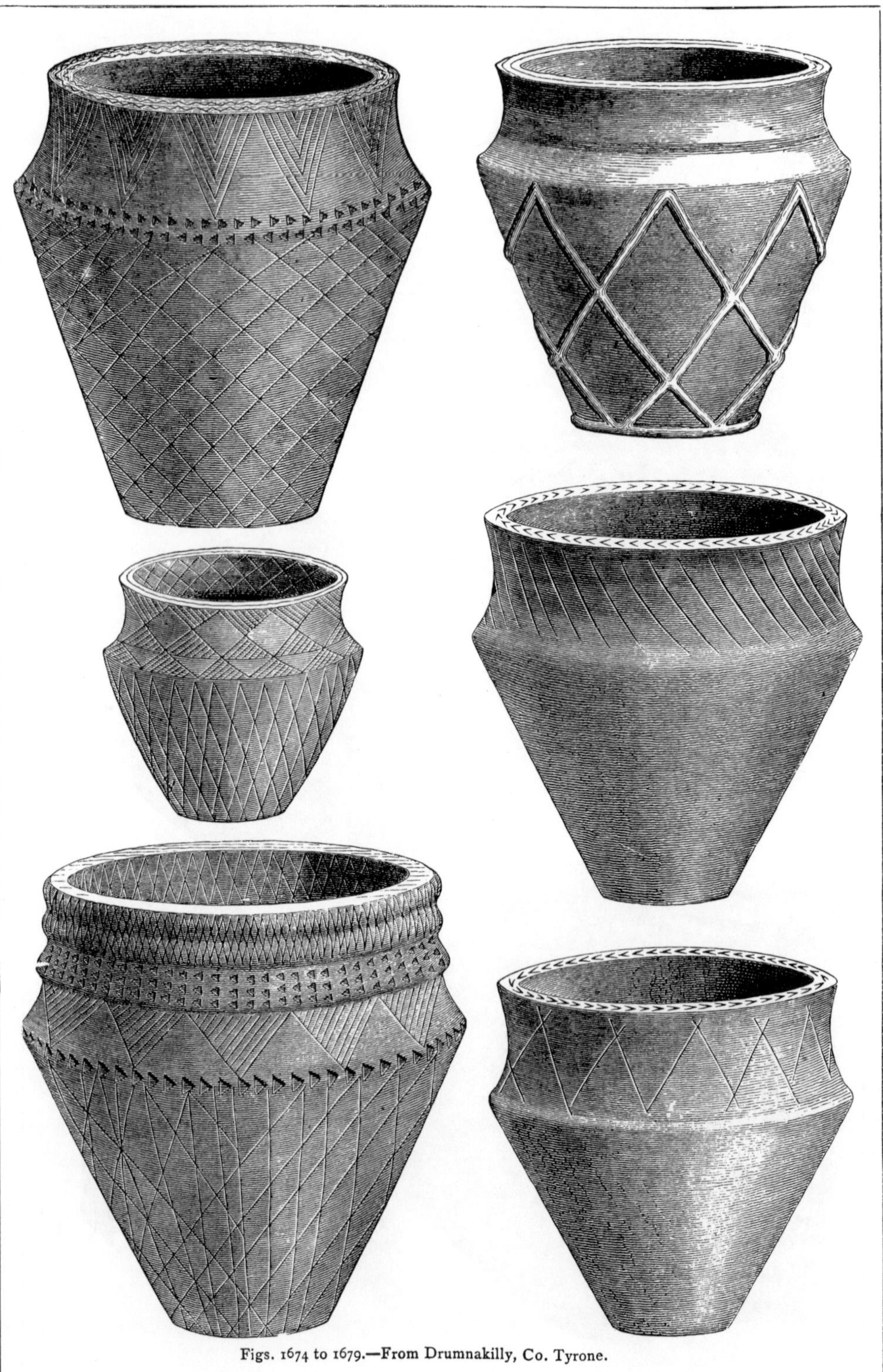

Figs. 1674 to 1679.—From Drumnakilly, Co. Tyrone.

pretty much the same general form (Fig. 1672), but devoid of ornament, contained within it an immolation urn (Fig. 1673). Another (Fig. 1675) is unique in its ornamentation; "its neck and lip, though exquisitely proportioned, are devoid of ornament, while the body of the vessel is encircled by a network pattern executed in bold relief. The substance of this pattern is different from and finer in quality than that of which the rest of the urn was composed. It is evident upon even a slight examination that this raised ornament was added after the formation and fire-hardening of the vessel, from portions of which it is easily detached." It contained a smaller urn, both being as usual filled with burned bones. Fig. 1670, 3 feet 9 inches in circumference at the neck, has an overlapping rim with a remarkably elegant outline. Figs. 1674, 1676, 1678, of much the same form as Fig. 1675, have incised lines round the neck, the body of the latter being covered with a reticulated ornament. Figs. 1674 and 1676 are of the same general form, but extremely rich in ornamentation.

Two unusually fine urns, brought to my notice by Miss Stokes, of Carrig Breac, near Dunamase, are, I believe, now in the R. I. A. Museum. The larger of the

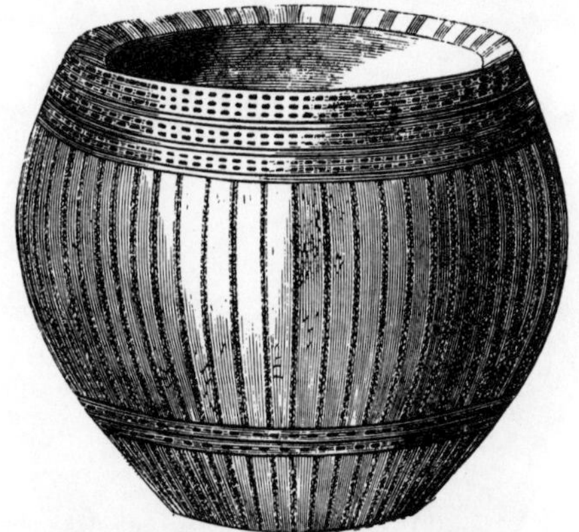

Fig. 1680.—From the Giant's Grave, Loughrey Demesne.

two, which is of the same general form as the Altegarron urn, Fig. 1657, but rather more contracted in the upper part, has two raised encircling rims around its widest part; between these the urn is ornamented with a series of diagonal lines of impressed squares. Round the upper part is a line of curves or undulations, between elaborate diagonal indented lines as before. The lower part of the urn has around its upper and lower edges a row of undulations, and around its centre an encircling border of rude lozenge-formed indentations; the whole of the rest of the surface being covered with vertical lines of square indentations, same as already described. These are of the same class as those shown in Figs. 1699 and 1711. The other urn in general form of outline resembles the one from Ballon Hill (Fig. 1658). It is richly decorated with encircling bands of herringbone lines, and three borders, one on its neck and two on the lower part, of chevron ornament.

The pottery found in the crannogs presents many peculiarities of pattern. The vessels are considered by Mr. Wakeman, to whom the antiquarian world is indebted in many cases for their discovery, to be the remains of what have been used for cooking purposes. They are mostly vessels, sometimes of very large size, wide at the mouth, contracted in the neck, and gradually, with easy flow of line, tapering downwards on the sides. Mostly they appear to have had handles at the top, which take a gradual curve from the rim down to their junction with the tapering body. They are more or less decorated with punctured, incised, impressed, or other simple ornaments.

The general form of these crannog vessels will be best understood on reference to the accompanying engraving, which is a restored example from fragments found in a crannog in Drumgay Lake, near Enniskillen, and carefully described by Mr. Wakeman in the "Journal of the Royal Historical and Archæological Association of Ireland." The lake wherein this crannog was discovered—the "Loch of Drumgay"—is a picturesque sheet of water, nearly midway between Enniskillen and the village of Bellinamallard, in the county of Fermanagh. The examination of these lake-dwellings yielded many highly interesting and important results, and brought to light several fragments of pottery, and many other objects of antiquity. Some of

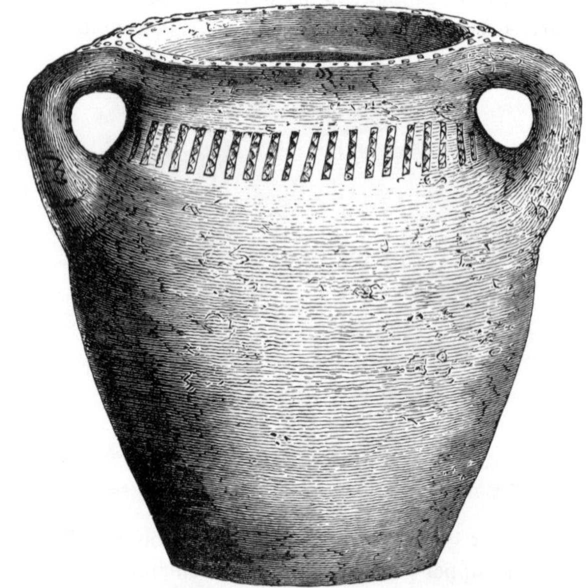

Fig. 1681.

the patterns of fictile ornamentation are shown on the Figs. 1684 to 1697, which are drawn of one half their real size. One pattern is a simple chevron; another a punched right-line ornament, very characteristic of this primitive ware; another has a series of incisions, giving the rim somewhat the effect of a cable moulding; and another is reticulated, or has what may be described as a series of saltires all round the rim.

Some other excellent examples were yielded by the examination by Mr. Wakeman of a crannog in Ballydoolough—the place or town of the dark lake—a loch of about twenty-four acres in extent, a few miles from Enniskillen, not far from the old road to Tempo. The "lake-dwelling" where these fragments were found is said to be "one of the most instructive yet discovered in Ireland." In it, "among other instructive remains, were found a very large number of fragments of pottery, along with quantities of bones of *bos longifrons*, *cervus elephas*, *sus scrofa*, *equus asinus*, and other animals, including the goat, which gave good testimony to their being portions of cooking vessels." A restoration of one of these "crocks" is given on the accompanying engraving, Fig. 1682, and its pattern is shown of a larger size on Fig. 1711. "It measures 3 feet 2 inches round the mouth, and is tastefully orna-

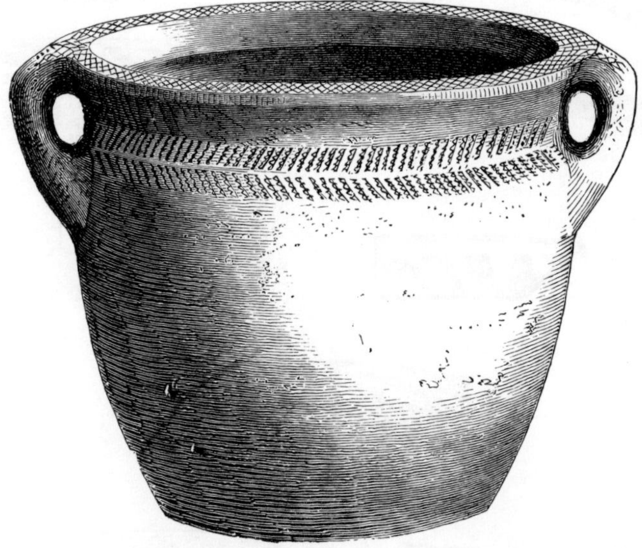

Fig. 1682.

mented on the rim and sides. The decoration, which was impressed upon the soft clay before the vessel was burnt, is extremely like that which appears upon silver bracelets preserved in the Museum of the Royal Irish Academy, and also found amongst the Cuerdale hoard." Its colour is drab, or light yellowish red, and it is

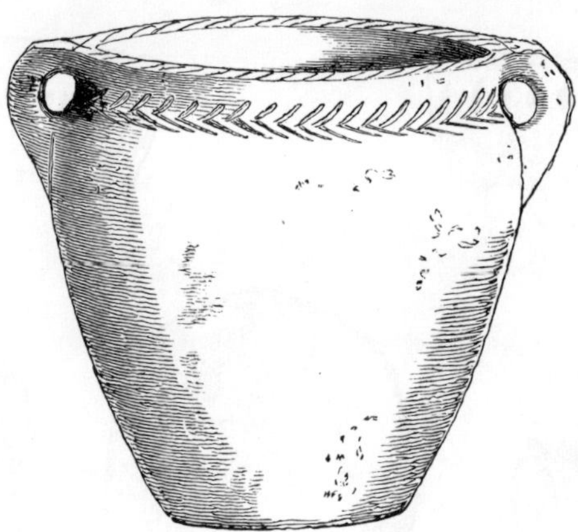

Fig 1683.

of close texture. The pattern is impressed or indented, and from its chevron character is undoubtedly early. Several varieties of this pattern occurred. The next examples exhibit simply a series of zigzag incisions of precisely the same character as is found on Celtic cinerary urns. Indeed the decoration of many of

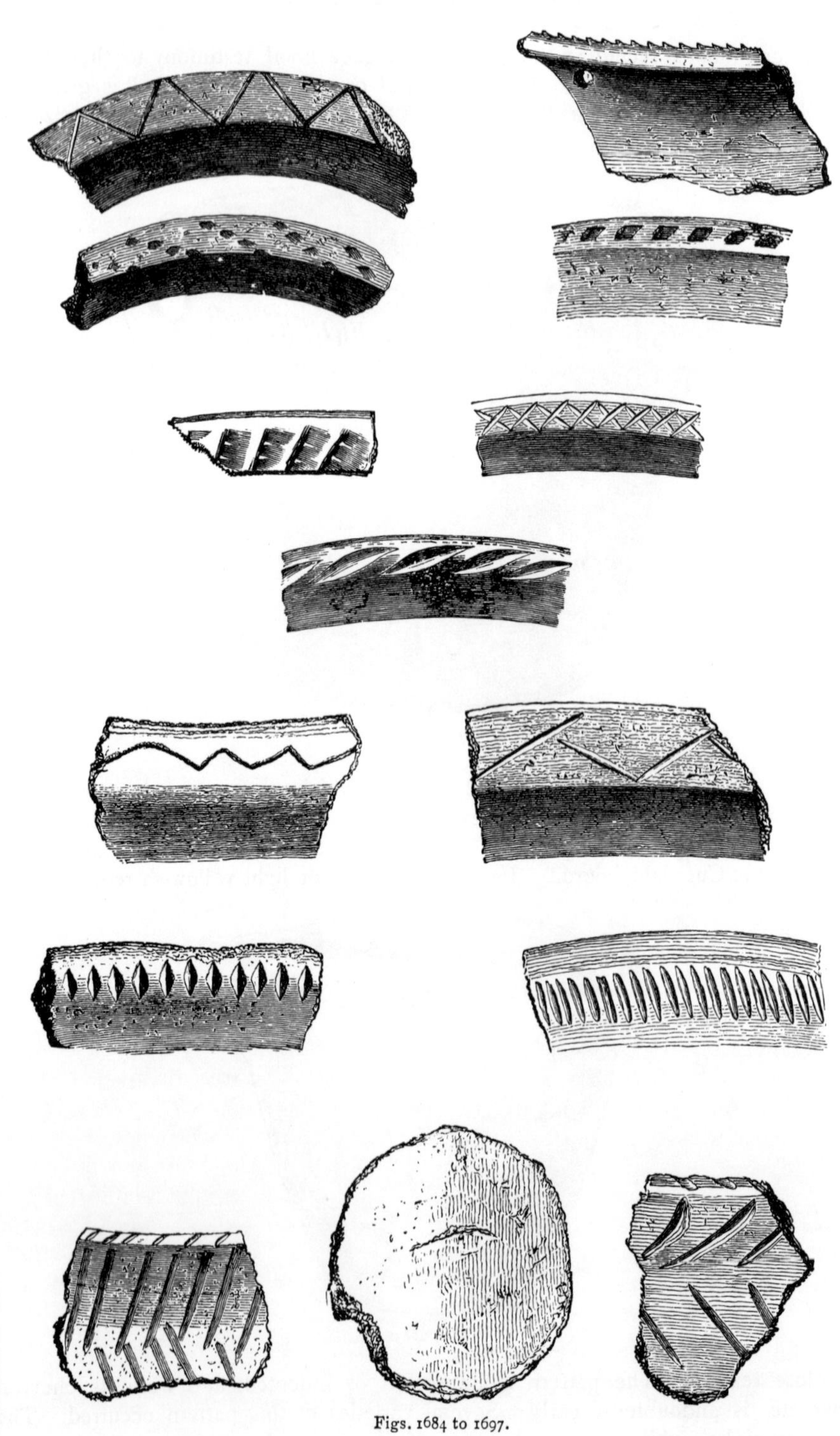

Figs. 1684 to 1697.

these domestic (?) vessels is exactly identical with that of some of the finest sepulchral urns found in that country. "It may be said further, that in the numerous designs found upon the crannog vessels there is not one that is suggestive of the work of Christian times in Ireland; on the contrary, the greater portion—chevrons and circular depressions—are expressive of pagan ideas of ornamental art. The log-house at Ballydoolough is almost precisely of the same size and of the same style of construction as the celebrated dwelling described by Captain Mudge in the 'Archæologia,' in which was found a stone hatchet." These crannog vessels must not, therefore, be assigned to a later period than pagan times.

Some other examples from this crannog are of extreme interest. The "fragment, Fig. 1712, bears upon its ear," says Mr. Wakeman, "two figures somewhat like a St. Andrew's Cross, but which here, I apprehend, need not be regarded as a Christian symbol. Such figures have been found in Ireland inscribed on rocks and upon the walls of natural or partly artificial caverns, and even within the inclosure of pagan tumuli, as at Dowth, accompanied in several instances by 'scorings'

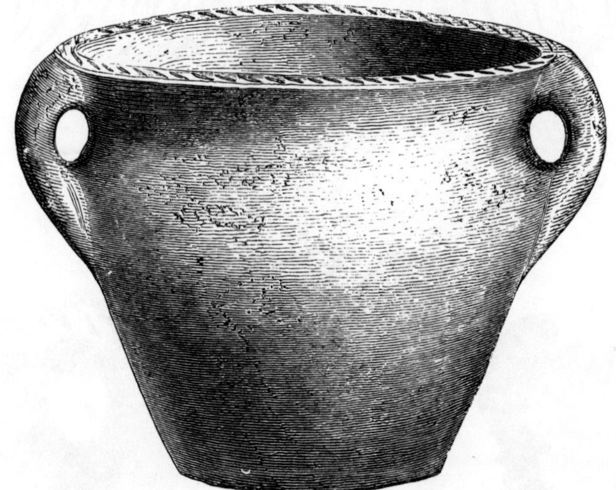

Fig. 1698.

at present unintelligible." Many appear in the cave of Lochnacloyduff (the *loch of the dark trench*, or *mound*) and in the "lettered caves" and the cliffs of Knockmore. These vessels are "of a dingy brown colour, and their 'scorings' are deeply impressed in what was a paste of unusually gritty matter. It may not be out of place to state here, once for all, that between the crannog pottery and the vases found in cairns and usually styled sepulchral, there is apparently no difference in style of manufacture. Strange to say, both classes exhibit the action of fire more strongly upon the interior than upon the external sides or base. Their colouring upon the whole is generally similar, varying from a dull red to a dark brown, nearly black; and in no instance, as far as my observation carries, has glazing been practised" (*Wakeman*).

In another lake-dwelling of Lough Eyes, not far from Lisbellaw, in the same county of Fermanagh, a variety of patterns of crocks were found. These were of the same general form as those already described, and they were more or less ornamented with indented patterns, sometimes arranged simply in lines and some-

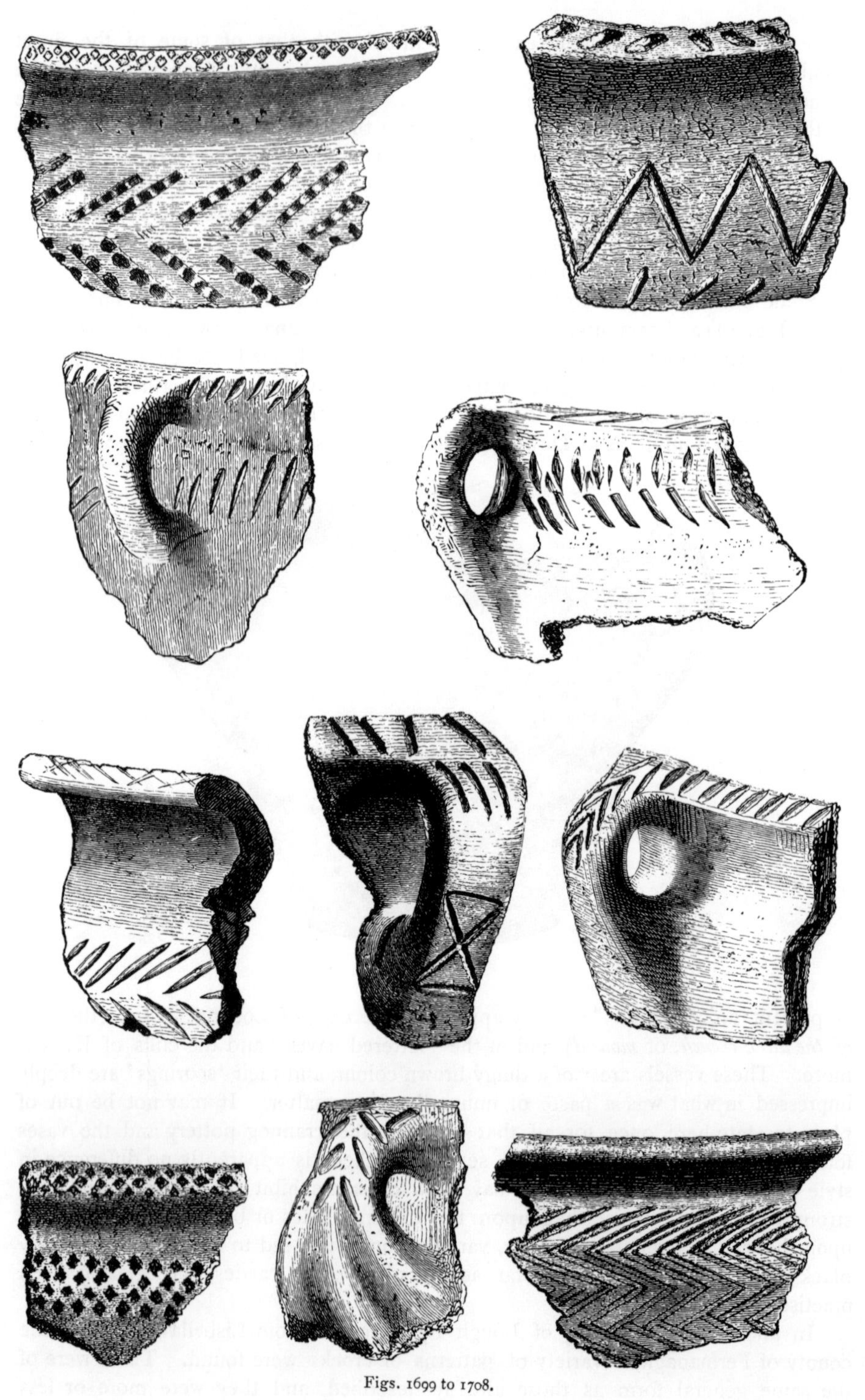

Figs. 1699 to 1708.

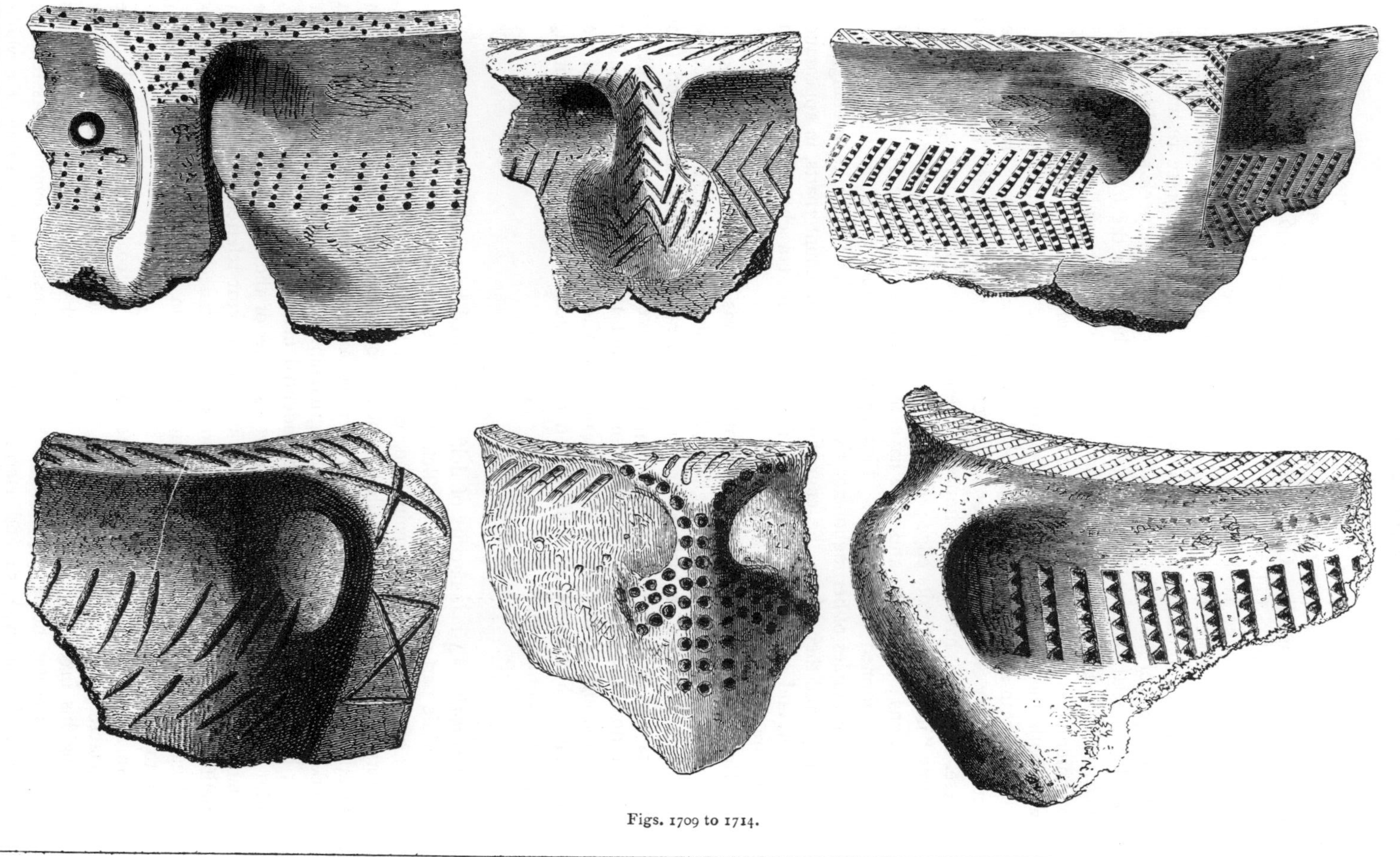

Figs. 1709 to 1714.

times in chevron or zigzag designs. It is worthy of special note, too, that several flat discs of the same material as the crocks were found with them; these were doubtless covers or lids. One of them is shown on Fig. 1696.

A very unusual and clever "provision for the escape of steam during the process of boiling or cooking is observable in several of these earthen pots. It consists of a small circular hole in the neck or upper side of the vessel, just below the point where the lid would be supported or caught;" the lid of course resting on the narrower part of the neck. Doubtless the contraction of the neck would be formed for this special purpose. The perforation is shown on the fragments engraved, Figs. 1685 and 1709. Figs. 1709 and 1713 show very carefully two examples of ornamentation on pottery from this crannog; the one with incisions only, the other with both incisions and impressed ornaments, the dotted pattern being almost identical with some found in the lake-habitations of Switzerland. The other woodcuts give very clear representations of other patterns found at Lough Eyes. One of these, Fig. 1699, has both the impressed herringbone and rim patterns; Fig. 1693 is simply "notched" on its edge; Fig. 1694 has a series of incisions or "thumb-nail" indentations; Figs. 1684 and 1692 have the zigzag pattern; and Fig. 1687 a series of lozenge-formed indentations. Figs. 1708 and 1710 are among the most pronounced examples of herringbone or zigzag patterns which these lake-dwellings have produced, and they are, as the engravings show, exact counterparts, in appearance, character, and style, with that which forms so marked a characteristic of Celtic sepulchral urns of one kind or other.

During mediæval times the pottery of Ireland was much of the same coarse kind as already described under "England;" but little, however, is known concerning either its localities of manufacture or its general characteristics. Wood (both platters and noggins) and pewter appear to have been in much more general use or domestic purposes than earthenware, and the manufacture of the latter was consequently very small. Later on, manufactories of a finer kind of ware were established in Belfast, Dublin, and other places. Of these but very meagre particulars are known.

Dublin.

Delamain.—A manufactory of delft-ware existed here in the Strand, in the early and middle part of last century. Before 1753 the manufactory had passed into the hands of Capt. Henry Delamain, who, as stated by himself, "when the Delft manufactory in this city [Dublin] failed," "being convinced that it might be carried on greatly to the advantage of this nation, took said manufactory into his hands, built workhouses and kilns, erected a mill to grind flint and metals," and so forth. In that year he appears to have had as a confidential manager Mr. William Stringfellow, who probably had either been the previous owner of the manufactory or one of the "most knowing persons" of those works. In the year referred to Capt. Delamain petitioned the Irish House of Commons for assistance in carrying out his undertaking. His case, as then stated, I printed in full in the first edition of this work, and to that I refer my readers.

In 1753 Delamain, having discovered a way to use coal instead of wood in the manufacture of earthenware, applied to the English Parliament for compensation for making his invention public. From the Journal of the House it appears his petition, wherein he is described as "Henry Delamain, gentleman," was read on the 21st of January, 1754, and referred to a committee, where, however, the whole matter seems to have ended. In it he says that "he has discovered a method of firing kilns of a particular construction," "which perfectly burn and glaze all sorts of white ware with coal in less time and in larger quantities than the method now practised by burning of wood, and at one-third of the expense." In a not very honourable letter, printed by Owen, Delamain speaks of his intention of applying to "the Parliament of England for a reward for having burnt and glazed delft-ware with coals," instead of wood or turf. In this letter Delamain writes to Stringfellow that he has seen the Liverpool potters and told them of the success of his plan, and he desires them to write how well he has succeeded with the coal; he says, even "suppose it has happened quite the reverse, do you write what I desire you, for your own advantage as well as my credit; for I have set them all on fire to burn their ware with coals, and have come to this agreement with them, that you are to come over to build their kilns, for which they will pay you handsomely." And again he says, "by all means answer to them by return of post all you can say in its favour, and more if necessary." The letter is addressed, "to Mr. Wm. Stringfellow, at the Delft Manufactory, on the Strand, Dublin," and dated 19th of December, 1753. And another letter, addressed to his wife, is to the same effect. To him, doubtless, belonged the credit of introducing the use of coal in the manufacture of earthenware, and he deserved the recognition he sought, but did not succeed in obtaining, for his invention from the English Parliament. In 1755 Capt. Delamain received from the Dublin Society a grant or "bounty" of £1,100, which he expended in furthering his manufacture. He died on the 10th of January, 1757, and his death is thus curiously recorded in the *Belfast News Letter* of that period: "Dublin, January 15th. Monday last, died, universally lamented by all true lovers of their country, Captain Henry Delamain, formerly in the Duke of Saxe-Gotha's service, Master of the Irish Delft Ware Manufactory, who, by the expense of a large fortune and unwearied application, brought that ware to such perfection as totally to prevent the enemies of our country, the French, from draining large sums yearly from this country for Burgundy and Roan ware. Mary Delamain, his widow, carries on said manufactory, and hopes for the continuance of the friendship of the nobility, gentry, and whole kingdom." On the 9th of November, 1759, Mrs. Delamain, his widow, petitioned the Irish House of Commons for further assistance to enable her to carry on and extend the business, but nothing seems to have been done for her. Mrs. Delamain, who survived her husband three years, died in March, 1760, her death being recorded in the Dublin *Public Gazetteer* of that date: "Tuesday last died Mrs. Mary Delamain, widow of the late Captain Henry Delamain, who was the first that brought the earthenware manufacture to perfection in this kingdom; and since his decease his said widow (endowed with all the virtues of a good Christian, tender parent, and sincere friend) continued it with such advantage to the purchasers as to prevent the further importation of foreign wares," &c. In 1763 the executors of Mrs. Delamain petitioned the Irish House of Commons for a further grant, and that petition, which contains many interesting particulars, I printed in full in my first edition.

A similar petition appears to have been presented by the same parties on 9th Nov. 1763, and was referred to a committee, but no votes in either case seem to have been taken.

DUBLIN.

Donovan.—Whether Mr. Donovan, of Poolbeg Street, on the Quay, Dublin, was a manufacturer or not is uncertain, but I believe not. He purchased both English and Continental wares in the white, and decorated them in his own place. He amassed a large fortune and purchased estates in Sussex. In his business he was usually known in Dublin as "The Emperor of China." "About 1790 he had a glass manufactory at Ringsend, near Dublin, and he employed a painter to decorate pottery, and placed all sorts of fancy and imitation marks on the china and earthenware." His name sometimes occurs as DONOVAN only, and at others as *Donovan* / *Dublin* or DONOVAN. / DUBLIN.

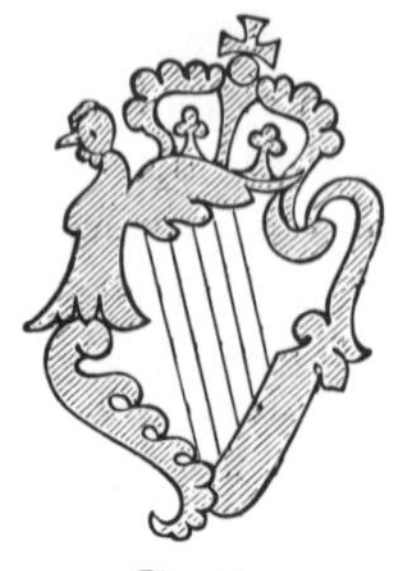

Dublin.

Figs. 1715 to 1718.

A mark on Delft ware which has come under my notice is a crowned harp with the word "Dublin." It is quite uncertain to whose make this is to be ascribed.

Two or three brown-ware manufactories also existed during last century at Dublin, and produced all the usual commoner kinds of coarse domestic vessels.

Belfast.

Leathes and Smith.—A pottery, established here in the middle of the seventeenth century by Captain Leathes and Mr. Smith, is thus alluded to by William Sacheverell, some time Governor of the Isle of Man (a descendant of the Sacheverells of Morley, in Derbyshire), who in 1688 made a voyage to I-Columb-Kill, which he printed in his "Survey of the Isle of Man." He left Liverpool on the 23rd of June, 1688, on

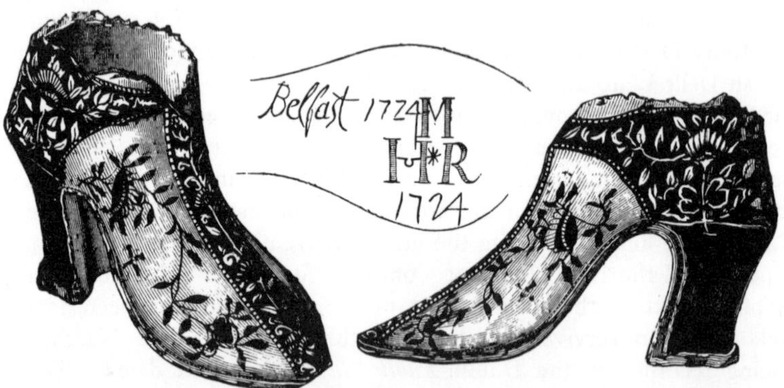

Figs. 1719 and 1720.

his way to I-Columb-Kill, and as "it blew very hard for a whole week" he "took the opportunity of visiting Carrick Fergus and Bellfast," and stayed in the latter two nights, being thither invited by "the Earl of Dunagall, whither he was going with the Earl of Orrery and the Lord Dungannon." "Belfast," he says, "is the second town in Ireland, well built, full of people, and of great trade. The quantities of butter and of beef which it sends into foreign parts are almost incredible; I have seen the barrels piled up in the very streets. The new pottery is a pretty curiosity, set up by Mr. Smith, the present sovereign, and his predecessor, Captain Leathes, a man of great ingenuity;" and, again, "Captain Leathes, who was chief magistrate of Belfast, and reputed a man of great integrity." The pottery is also spoken of at a later date, 1708, by Dr. Molyneux, in his MS. tour to the Giant's Causeway. "Here," at Belfast, he says, "we saw a very good manufacture of earthenware, which comes nearest to delft of any made in Ireland, and really is not much short of it. It is very clear and pretty, and universally used in the north; and, I think, not so much owing to any peculiar happiness in the clay, but rather to the manner of beating and mixing it up." The works were continued for very many years, and produced much useful ware of good quality. The curious example, Fig. 1719, is highly interesting as bearing the name of Belfast and the date 1724. It is a "choppine," or lady's high-heeled shoe, and is in Delft ware. It is six inches in length and the heel is two inches in height, and is decorated in blue and white, the flowers and foliage being blue on a white and white on a blue ground. On the sole are the initials M H R, M being the surname and H and R the christian-names of the husband and wife, with the name and date in writing, "Belfast, 1724," as shown on the engraving. These are painted under the glaze in blue. For the notice of this interesting example, in the possession of a lady in Belfast, to whose grandmother it formerly belonged, I am indebted to Mr. Benn, the historian of that town.

M
H * R
1724

Fig. 1721.

Coates' Pottery.—On an old map of Belfast, published in 1791, a building marked as "Coates' Pottery" occurs. This, it is recorded by Pinkerton, was "set up by Mr. Victor Coates at Lagan village, long before he established the well-known foundry at the same place. Red ware and a coarse kind of delft were made."

China Works.—On the same map of Belfast, engraved in 1791, occurs a building marked "China Manufactory," close by "Coates' Pottery." "The partners in this Belfast china manufactory," says Pinkerton, "were Thomas Gregg, Samuel Stephenson, and John Ashmore. That they carried on the manufacture of china there for some years is certain, for on January 29, 1793, the Earl of Hillsborough presented a petition from them to the Irish House of Commons. The original petition may be seen in the Journals of the House. In it the petitioners state that, recognising the great advantages arising from a manufacture of Queen's Ware, and other fine kinds of ware such as are made in Staffordshire, they united themselves into a company for producing such wares in Ireland, and by their exertions had carried this manufacture to a greater perfection in the county of Down, near Belfast, than was ever known in this kingdom; that they had been at great expenses in erecting buildings and importing machinery, and in bringing workmen from foreign places; that the difference in prices of coal between Belfast and Staffordshire had greatly exceeded their expectations, and they now prayed for pecuniary aid." A committee, consisting of the Earl of Hillsborough, Mr. Johnson, and others, was immediately appointed by the House to report on the petition, and on the 2nd of February they reported that the petitioners had fully proved their allegations. The report was then ordered to be laid on the table, but it does not appear that anything was done further in the matter.

Florence Court, County Fermanagh.

There is a manufactory at this place where common red ware is made. The products are chiefly flower-pots and the coarser kinds of domestic vessels.

Coal Island, Dungannon.

At this manufactory only the coarser kinds of fire-clay and terra-cotta goods—chimney-pots, flower-pots, vases, &c.—are produced.

Youghal.

There was a manufactory of brown ware, for pitchers and common goods, at this place. It was of old foundation.

Larne.

Larne Pottery.—Pottery works were, I am informed by Mr. Patterson, built close to the small sea-port of Larne, county of Antrim, by James Agnew, proprietor of the estate, and were worked under the management of his agent, Mr. Walker, from about 1850 to 1855, and afterwards for two or three years by the Greenock Pottery Company, since which time the works have been closed. The goods produced were white and printed earthenware, cane ware, Rockingham teapots, and brown pans, crocks, and dairy and kitchen utensils of various kinds. Some of the latter-named were made from local clays, and were very good of their kind. Their rubbish-heaps are on the borders of Larne Lough, and the beach is strewn with fragments of pottery, &c.

Castle Espie Pottery.

At Castle Espie, near Comber, county of Down, Mr. Samuel Minland, J.P., some years ago, I am informed by Mr. Patterson, established brick and tile works. Common pottery is now manufactured there from the local red clay. The brown

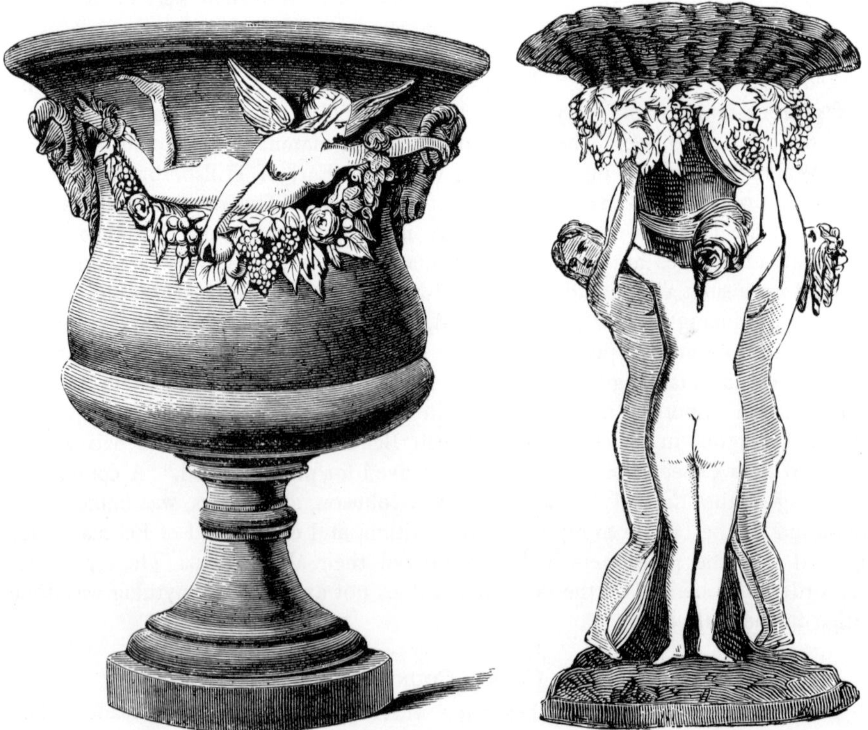

Figs. 1722 and 1723.

glazed ware consists of dairy vessels, teapots, flower-vases, and other plain household articles.

Captain Beauclerc, at the Exhibition of 1851, exhibited two terra-cotta vases, his own modelling, made in Ireland of Irish material. They were engraved in the "Art Journal Illustrated Catalogue," page 257, and are here reproduced, Figs. 1585 and 1586. They were in two tints, the body of each vase being of a deep red and the figures of a lighter and much yellower clay.

Belleek.

The village of Belleek, county Fermanagh, is situated on the banks ot the river Erne, near the borders of Donegal and Fermanagh. The manufactory—a view of which is given on Fig. 1724, stands on a small island in a bend of the river Erne,

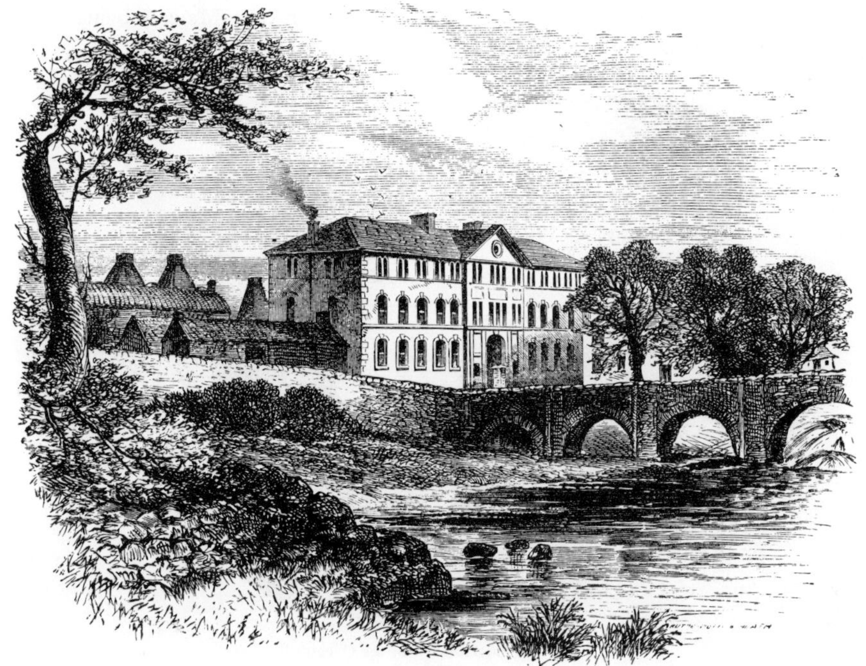

Fig. 1724.—The Belleek China Works.

and near whose bridge is a large water-wheel, over 100-horse power, which gives motion to grinding-pans, lathes, turning-plates, and all the varied and skilfully designed apparatus—was established in 1863 by Messrs. David McBirney and Robert Williams Armstrong. Before the establishment of the works, trials were made with the felspar of the Irish locality with ordinary Cornish china clay at the Royal Porcelain Works at Worcester. The results were so satisfactory that Mr. Armstrong, who at that time was architect to the proprietor, laid the project for forming a manufactory at Belleek before his friend, Mr. David McBirney, of Dublin, a gentleman well known for his energy in aiding any movement to advance the prosperity of Ireland, and he embarked with him in the attempt to produce first-class ceramic goods in Ireland. The firm, composed of these two gentlemen, traded under the style of "D. McBirney & Co." Mr. McBirney died in 1882, and Mr. Armstrong is now the sole proprietor.

The chief peculiarities of the ornamental goods are lightness of body, rich, delicate, cream-like tone of colour, and glittering iridescence of glaze. Although the principal productions hitherto are formed of this white ware—which either resembles the finest biscuit (of Buen Retiro or Dresden), or almost the ivory of the hippopotamus, or shines with a lustre like that of nacre—local clays have been found which yield jet, red, and cane-coloured wares. Fac-similes of sea-shells and of branches of coral, which might well be supposed to be natural, are among the principal features. The iridescent effect produced is somewhat similar to that of the ruby lustre of the famous Gubbio Majolica—that Italian enamelled ware which commands such fabulous prices, and of which examples are in the South Kensington Museum—but not comparable with the beauty of the Belleek ware, an idea of which can only be given by recalling the beautiful hues of a highly-polished mother-of-pearl shell. Fig. 1725 is the grounds-basin of a tea-service made for the Queen (her Majesty being one of the early patrons of the Belleek Pottery), and presented by her to the present

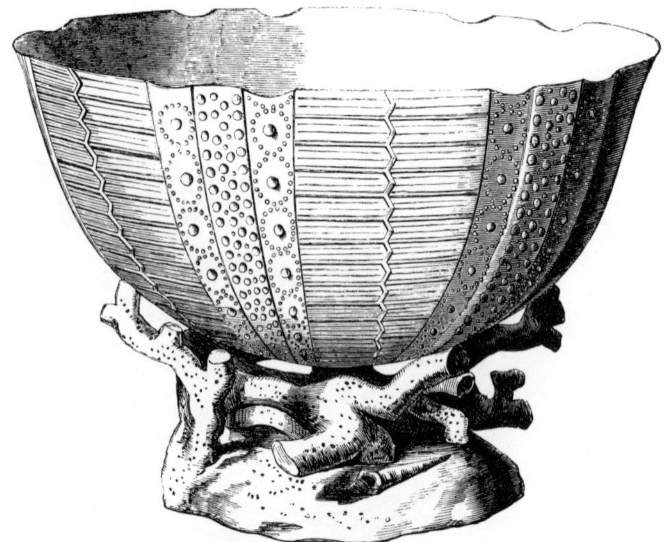

Fig. 1725.—Grounds-Basin: or the Queen's Service.

Empress of Germany. The basis of the design is the *echinus* or sea-urchin, which abounds on the coast of Donegal, and has, both the native and rarer foreign species, been utilised by the firm in many of their productions. In this instance it forms the bowl, and the supports are branches of coral. Besides the "royal" services—breakfast, dessert, and tea—made for her Majesty, other services have been made for H.R.H. the Prince of Wales and others of the royal family. From the Prince of Wales's services the engravings Figs. 1726, and 1761 to 1763, are selected. The ice-pail (Fig. 1726) has its base formed of three exquisitely-shaped mermaids, in Parian, who support the shell-formed base of the vase, around which a group of Tritons and dolphins in high relief are sporting in the water, and a wreath of coral surrounds the rim. The effect of the charming contrast between the dead and the iridescent surfaces is heightened by gilding the conches of the revellers. The cover or lid is, as it were, the boiling, surging sea, from which three sea-horses have partially risen, and in the centre is a Triton riding on a dolphin. Fig. 1761 is one of the compotiers. The centrepiece (Fig. 1762) has a triton or merman blowing a conch, a mermaid wringing and dressing her hair, and a sea-horse dashing through the spray.

Between the figures which divide the base into three compartments are placed three shells of the species *hippopus maculata*, which form convenient receptacles for bonbons, candied fruit, or other smaller delicacies of the dessert-table. A trumpet-shell is again selected to form the main stem, which is surrounded with aquatic plants, and three *paludina* shells are so introduced as to form suitable vases for sprays of flowers. The shell-dish, with its beautiful markings and projections, again forms the cap of the tazza.

Fig. 1763 is a low compotier modelled *en suite* with the others; Fig. 1764 a

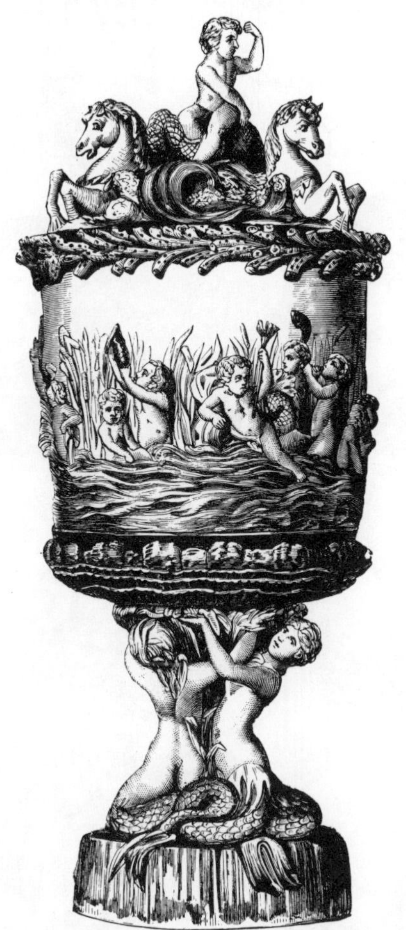

Fig. 1726.—Ice-pail: for the Prince of Wales.

tazza and pedestal; and Fig. 1765 a flower-stand composed of shells supported by dolphins.

"The reproduction of natural forms by Ceramic Art," says the *Art Journal*, "is not by any means a novelty. We are familiar with the fish, the reptiles, and the crustacea of Bernard Palissy, with the relieved and coloured foliage of Luca and of Andrea della Robbia. In England we have seen the shells reproduced by the artists of the Plymouth china, and the delicate leaves and flowers of the old Derby

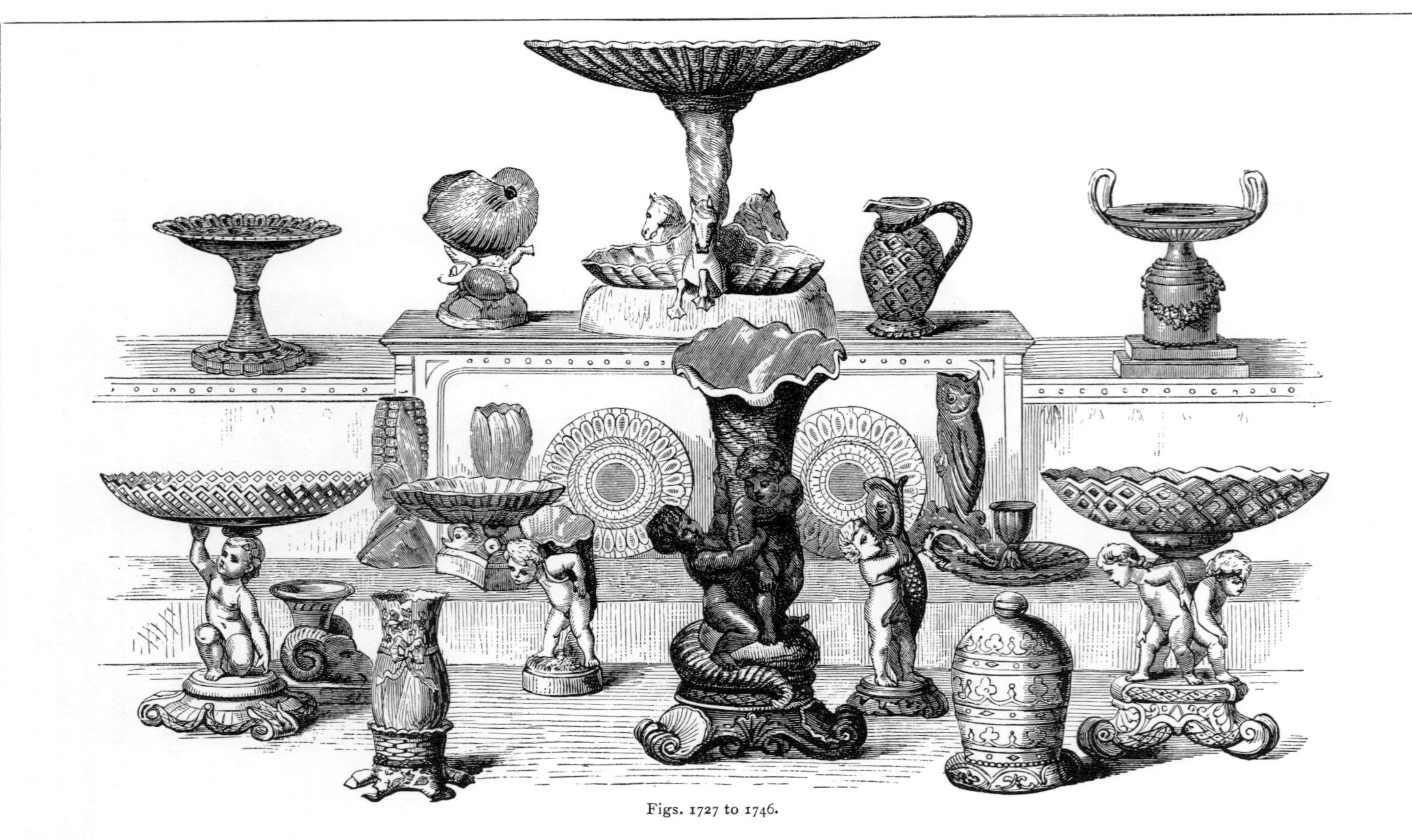

Figs. 1727 to 1746.

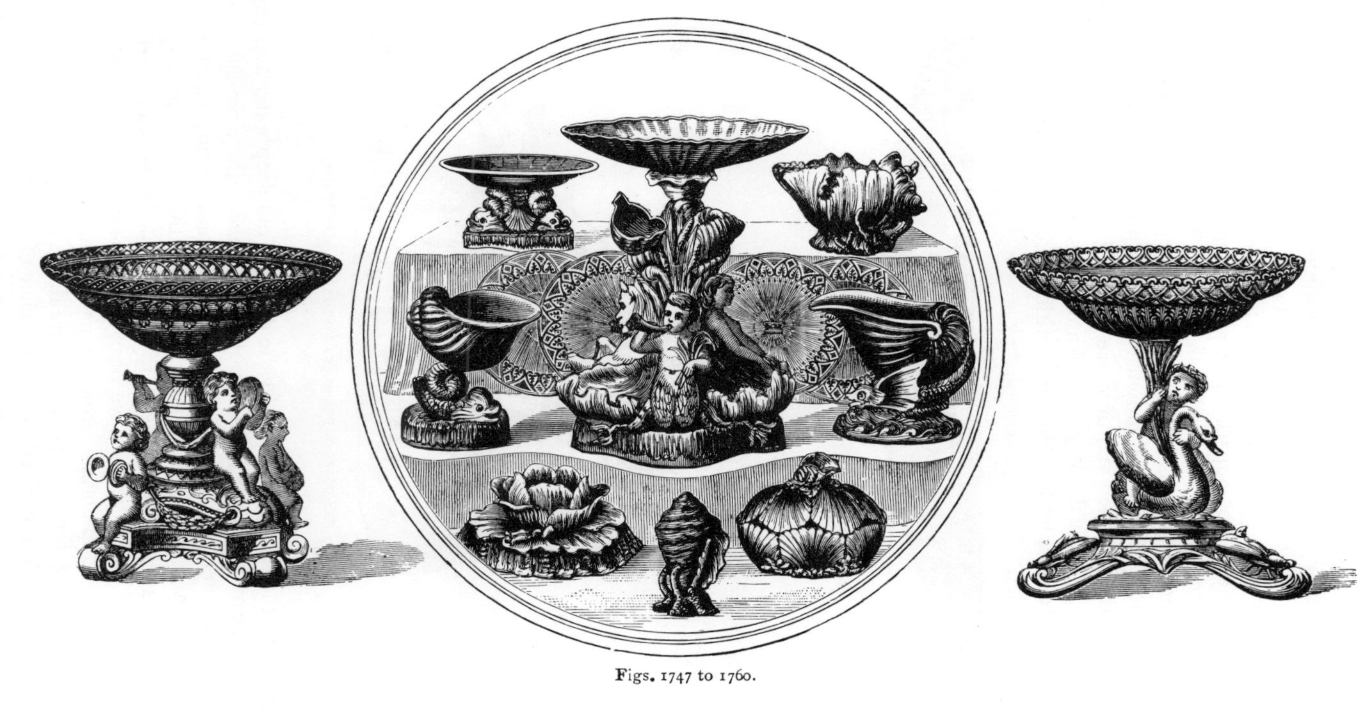

Figs. 1747 to 1760.

ware. The designer of much of the Belleek ware has the merit, so far as we are aware, of being the first artist who has had recourse to the large sub-kingdom of the *radiata* for his types. The animals that constitute this vast natural group are, for the most part, characterized by a star-shaped or wheel-shaped symmetry; and present a nearer approach to the verticillate structure of plants than to the bilateral balance of free locomotive animals. For, at all events a portion of their existence, indeed, most of the *radiata* are fixed to the earth. The five-fold radiation, which is most common among dicotyledonous plants, is the usual division assumed by these zoophytic creatures. From the globular shape of the commonest *echinus*, or sea-urchin, through the flattened and depressed form of others of the family, the transition is regular and gradual to the well-known five-fingered star-fish, and to those wonderfully branched and foliated forms which shatter themselves into a thousand

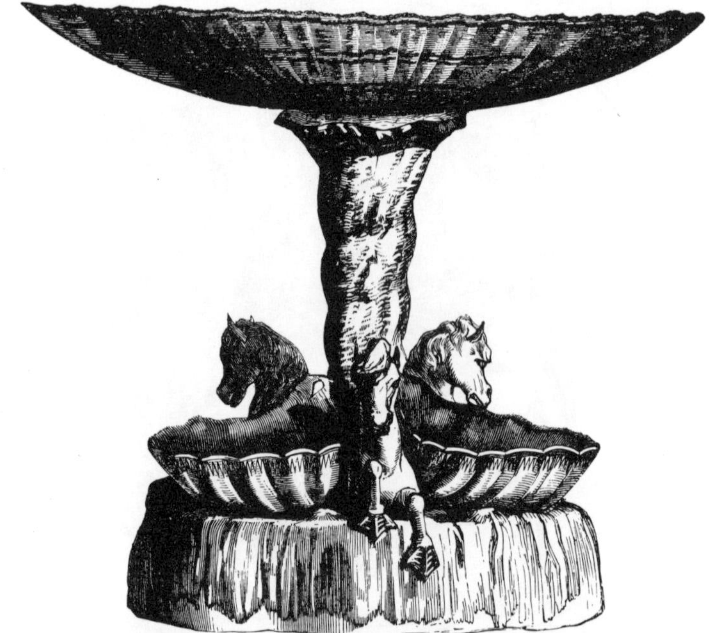

Fig. 1761.—Compotier: for the Prince of Wales.

fragments when they are brought up by the dredge from deep water and exposed for a moment to the air. Under the name of *frutti di mare*, these sea-eggs, covered as they are with innumerable pink and white spines, form a favourite portion of the diet of the southern Italians. When the spines, by which the creature moves, are stripped off, the projections and depressions of the *testa* or shell are often marked by great beauty of pattern; and it would have been hardly possible to bring into the service of plastic art a more appropriate group of natural models. Again, in the fantastic and graceful forms of the mermaid, the nereid, the dolphin, and the sea-horse, the Belleek art-designer has attained great excellence of ideality; the graceful modelling is set off with the happiest effect by the contrast between the dead Parian-like surface of the unglazed china and the sparkling iridescence of the ivory-glazed ground."

The productions of the Belleek works comprise all the usual services, and a large variety of ornamental good. Figures and groups of figures, animals, &c., are also

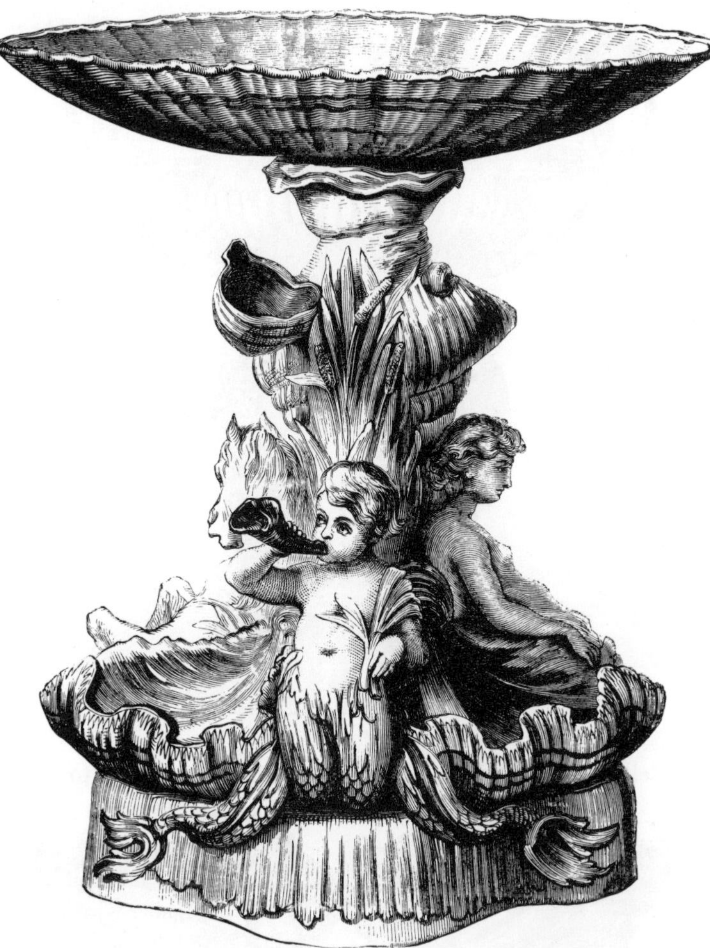

Fig. 1762.—Centrepiece: for the Prince of Wales.

made, and are characterized by excellent modelling and judicious colouring.

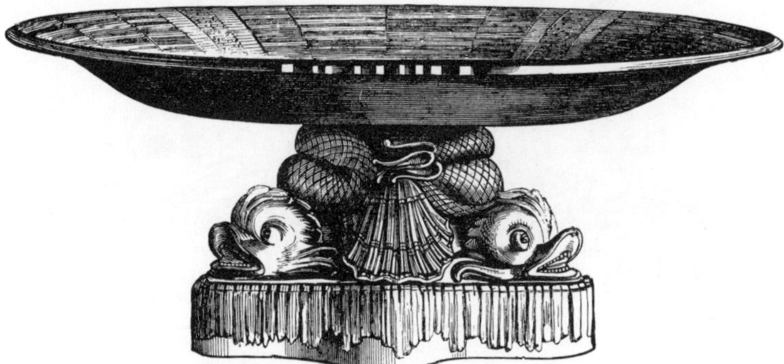

Fig. 1763.—Low Compotier: for the Prince of Wales.

Among the choice examples of manipulative skill are some cabinet cups and saucers in "egg-shell" china. The cup itself is the *echinus*, and the saucer is also

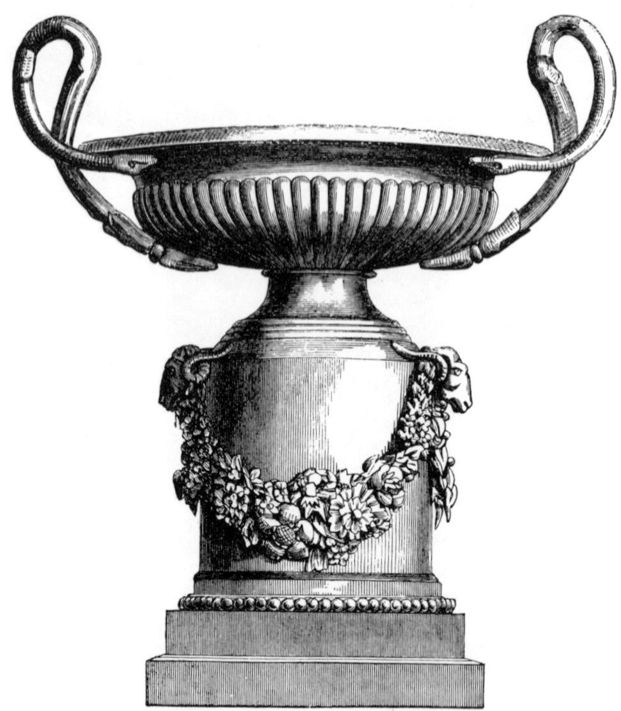

Fig. 1764.—Flower Tazza and Pedestal.

tastefully modelled from the same. The body is so thin, and worked to such a degree

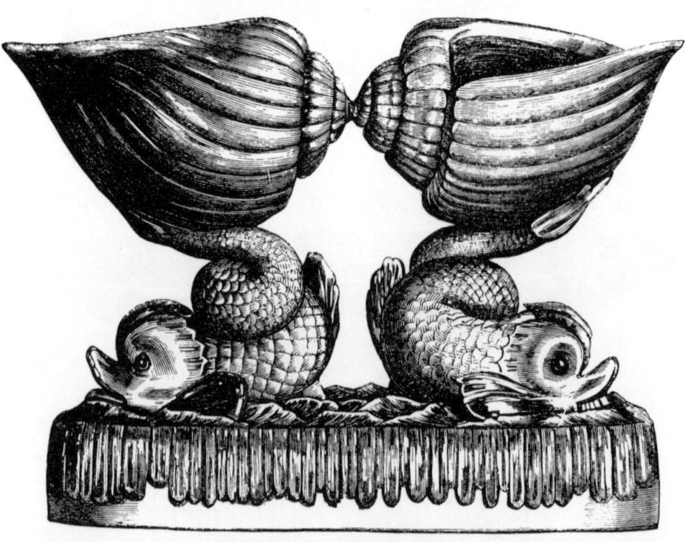

Fig. 1765.—Boudoir Flower Shells.

of nicety, as to be of little more than the thickness of common writing-paper. This delicate body, either plain or tinted and gilt, and then glazed with the iridescent glaze so characteristic of the Belleek ware, is unique in its appearance and matchless in its extreme delicacy. Of the same filmy body, exquisitely tinted, *cardium* and other shells are also produced.

Besides the speciality of these works (the "Belleek China") Mr. Armstrong manufactures white graniteware services of every variety, and of excellent quality both in body, in glaze, and in printed, painted, enamelled, and gilt decorations. Parian and ordinary white china, as well as ivory body, are also largely made in a vast variety of styles, as are porcelain insulators for telegraph-poles. Pestles and mortars, &c., and sanitary ware, form a staple part of the trade of these works.

The marks used by the Belleek Company are the following:

BELLEEK.
CO. FERMANAGH.

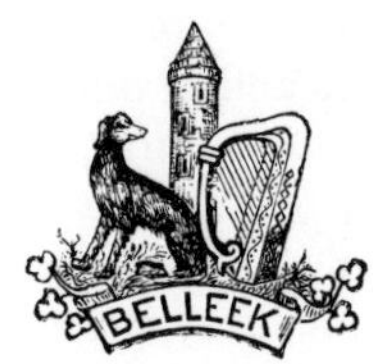

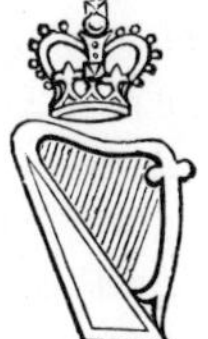

Figs. 1766 to 1768.

CHAPTER XXVI.

Scotland.

The early pottery of Scotland appears, as a general rule, to bear a close analogy to that of England both in form, in intention of use, and in ornamentation. The cinerary urns, the food and other vessels, and the immolation urns, all bear a marked resemblance to those of the sister country, and lead one to the inference that the same feelings, habits, and customs obtained in the one nation as the other. A cinerary urn found on the Hill of Tuack is of identical shape and pattern of ornament with the one engraved on Fig. 15, while others bear an equally strong resemblance to others already engraved. To Professor Wilson the antiquarian world is indebted for much valuable information concerning the early pottery of Scotland, and to his important and standard work, the "Pre-Historic Annals of Scotland," it owes most of the knowledge it possesses of this and other important branches of national history. To that work, through the courtesy of Messrs. Macmillan and Co., the publishers, I am indebted for the illustrations, Figs. 1769 to 1788, which adorn this chapter, and for which I again tender my best thanks. "It is altogether impossible," says the learned Professor, "within the limited amount of accurately observed facts with which the Scottish archæologist has to deal, to picture and classify into distinct periods the pottery found in the ancient tumuli and cairns. Many of the fictilia are so devoid of art as to furnish no other sign of advancement in their constructors from the most primitive state of barbarism than such as is indicated by the piety which provided a funeral pyre for their dead, and even so rude a vase wherein their ashes might be inurned. . . . The rudimentary form of the true cinerary urn is that of the common flower-pot, still retained as the easiest and simplest into which the plastic clay can be modelled. . . . From this simple shape was gradually developed the varying forms both of sepulchral and domestic pottery found deposited with the dead; inurning the sacred ashes and the costly tributes of affectionate reverence, or placed in the grave with offerings of food and drink designed to sustain the deceased on his final journey to the world of spirits." Fig. 1769 is of this form, and is almost identical with the English example Fig. 15. It is from the Hill of Tuack, near Kintore, in Aberdeenshire, and was found in the usual inverted position, close to one of the monoliths of the stone circle at the place. Another of the same form, Fig. 1770, ornamented with impressed dots and incised herringbone pattern, was dug up in 1855 on the farm of Belhelvie, in Fifeshire. It was 4 feet 6 inches in circumference at the mouth, and when perfect must have been about 2 feet in height. When found it was, as is commonly the case, inverted, as shown in the engraving, and was imperfect. Another fine example is engraved on Fig. 1771. It measures thirteen and a half inches in height, and was dug up at the Ha' Hill of Montblairy, in Banffshire. It bears a marked resemblance to many English examples, both in general form and in ornamentation; it bears encircling lines of herringbone or zigzag ornament.

Figs. 1772 to 1774 are of different form, the two larger being probably food-vessels, and the latter an "immolation urn." The first two were found in a cist on

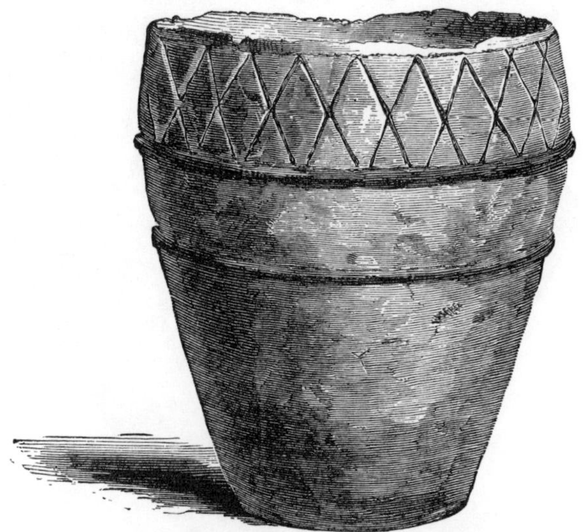

Fig. 1769.—From the Hill of Tuack, near Kintore.

a farm at Banchory, in Kincardineshire, along with an interment by inhumation, and the latter at Arthur's Seat, in Edinburgh. In the next engravings, Figs. 1775 and 1776, the larger vessel was found in a tumulus at Memsie, in Aberdeenshire, and the smaller at Ratho, near Edinburgh. Figs. 1777 to 1779 are three interesting vessels from Lesmurdie, in Banffshire, now in the Museum of the Society of Antiquaries of

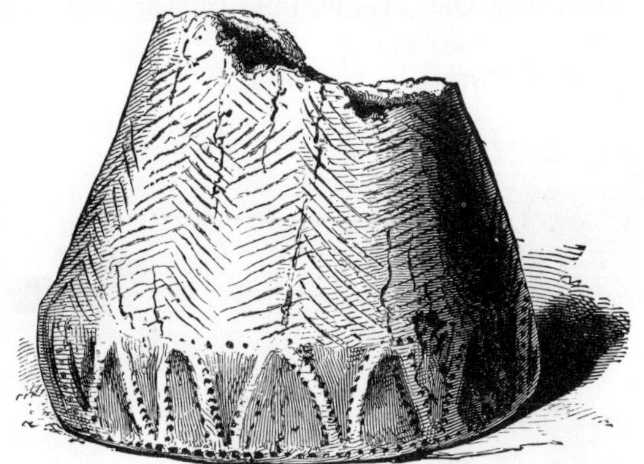

Figs. 1770.—From Belhelvie, Fifeshire.

Scotland. The largest is 8 inches in height and the smallest 5 inches. Fig. 1780 was found in one of a group of cists, under a large cairn, at Sheal Loch, in the parish of Borthwick, near Edinburgh. It is made of fine baked clay, burned to an unusually hard and durable consistency, and measures 4½ inches in height by about

6½ in diameter. Five perforated projections are disposed at nearly equal distances around it, and the interior of the vessel bears evident marks of fire. Fig. 1781 is from the Montrose Museum, and was found in that burgh some years back. The other

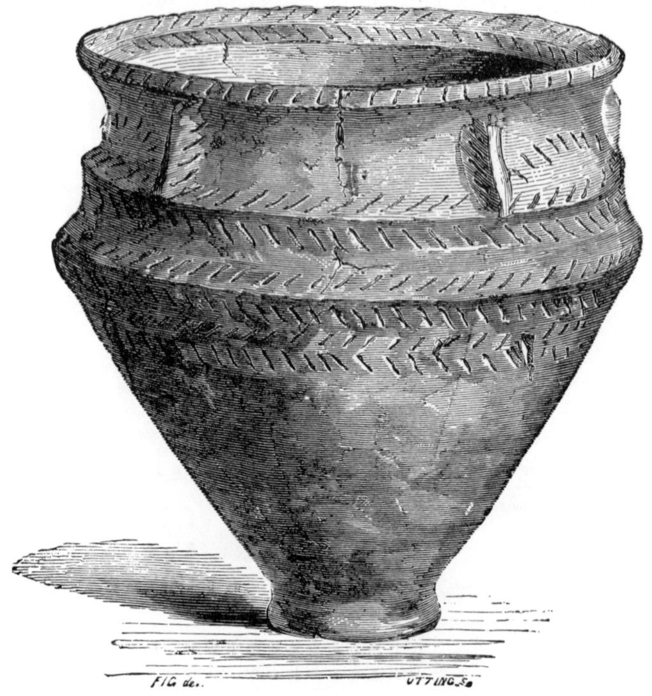

Fig. 1771.—From the Ha' Hill, Montblairy.

three, Figs. 1782 to 1784, are "immolation urns," as I have before termed them, which are respectively from Old Penrith, from Dunbar, and from Ronaldshay in Orkney.

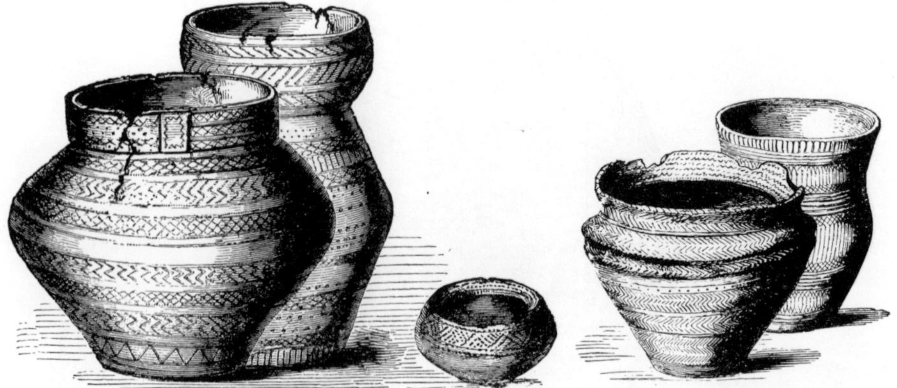

Figs. 1772 to 1774.—From Banchory, and Arthur's Seat, Edinburgh. Figs. 1775 and 1776.—From Memsie and Ratho.

During Scoto-Roman times pottery, there can be no reasonable doubt, was made in Scotland, and many examples that have been brought to light are evidently of native manufacture; there are, however, no marked peculiarities belonging to them. Of a later period, "the last pagan period in Scotland," according to Professor Wilson, some remarkable glazed urns were found, one at East Langton, the other in Aber-

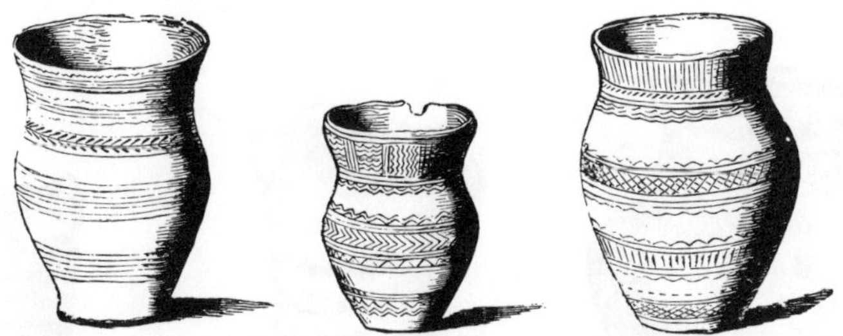

Figs. 1777 to 1779.—From Lesmurdie.

deenshire. They were found in stone cists by the side of skeletons, and were "of rough grey ware, ornamented externally with parallel grooves running round them

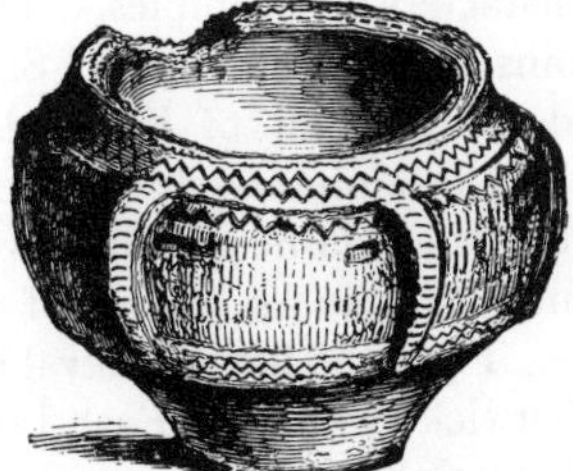

Fig. 1780.—From Sheal Loch.

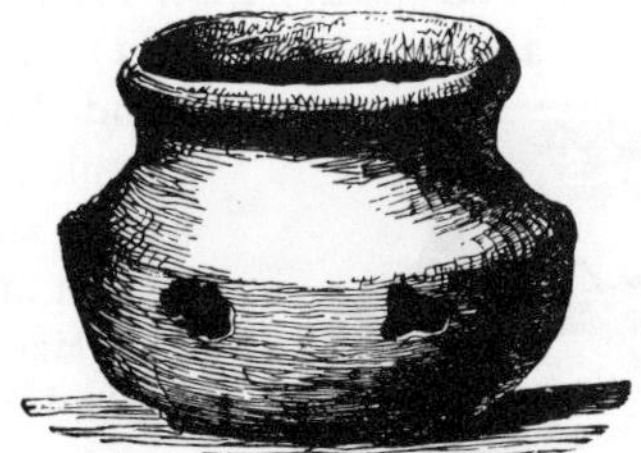

Fig. 1781.—From Montrose.

and internally covered with a green glaze." They appear originally to have had "two projecting ears opposite each other, which fitted into corresponding double

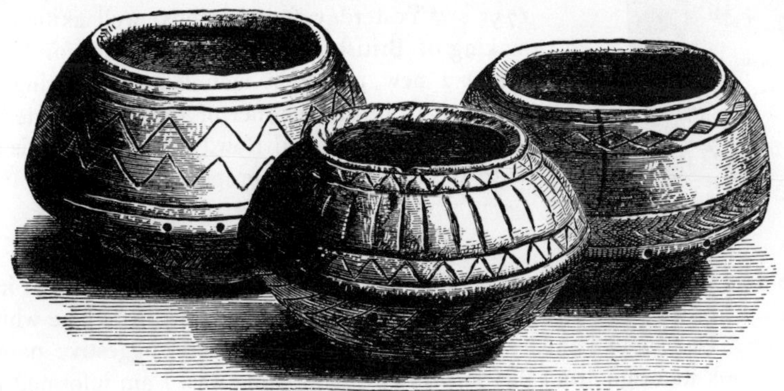

Figs. 1782 to 1784.—From Dunbar, Old Penrith, and Ronaldshay.

ones attached to a lid, by which the vessel when found was closely covered; and the whole of the projections were perforated to admit a pin which completed the fastening." (See Figs. 1786, 1787.)

As of the primitive so of the mediæval pottery of Scotland; it differs but little from that of England, and indeed, except in a few instances, cannot be distinguished from it. Pitchers of the usual form, perforated jugs, bowls, dishes, and platters—all were pretty nearly identical with those of English make, and but few seats of manufacture existed. The wares were of the commonest and coarsest kind. As in Ireland, wood was more generally used than anything else for such utensils.

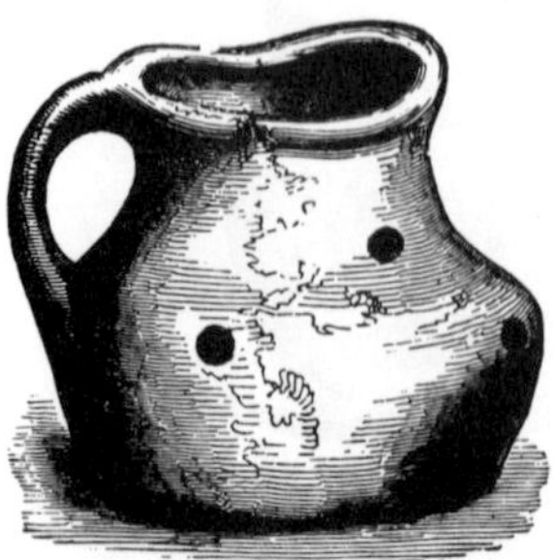

Fig. 1785.—From Penicuik.

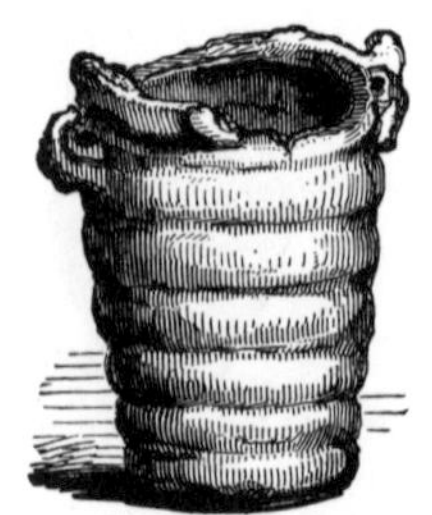

Fig. 1786.—From East Langton.

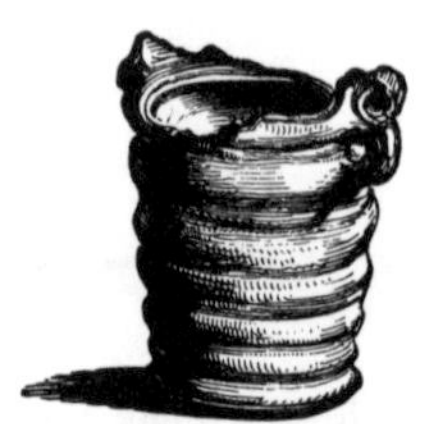

Fig. 1787.—From Aberdeenshire.

Of mediæval pottery Figs. 1785 to 1788 are characteristic examples. The first of these is a pitcher found in 1792, filled with coins of Alexander II. of Scotland and Edward I. and Edward II. of England, near Penicuick House, where it is preserved. It measures three and three-quarter inches in height, and is perforated at tolerably uniform distances. It is of coarse unglazed earthenware. Fig. 1788 is a mediæval pitcher found near North Berwick Abbey, in East Lothian; it bears a marked resemblance to some already engraved.

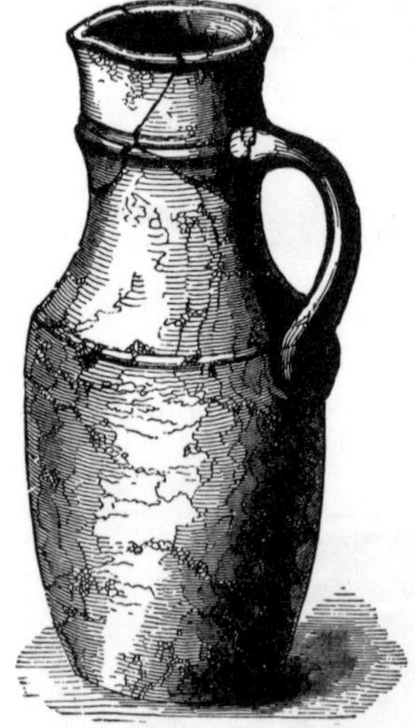

Fig. 1788.

That china was attempted to be made in Scotland in the middle of last century is evident from the following paragraph from the *London Chronicle* of 1755: "Yesterday four persons, well skilled in the making of British china, were engaged for Scotland, where a new porcelain manufacture is going to be established, in the manner of that now carried on at Chelsea, Stratford, and Bow." But nothing is known as to the locality of the proposed works.

Glasgow.

The first pottery established in Glasgow was, it would appear, founded in 1749 as a delft-ware works. It was situated near the Broomielaw, in a lane which was called the "Delft-field Lane." "Delft-field Lane" is a very suggestive name, and of course took its origin from the pot-works. The name was, I am informed by Mr. Cochran, "changed to 'James Watt Street' in later years. The celebrated inventor of the steam-engine lived in this lane, and it was in one of the rooms of the pottery that he was in the habit of working at his invention, and, it is said, perfected it. The ware manufactured at this pottery was delft ware, and was a close imitation of the old grey Dutch ware of that name; but about the year 1770 the proprietors began to make 'Queen's ware,' or white ware. They also began to make both plain and ornamented china of such excellent quality that they received the compliment of being appointed potters to the Prince of Wales. How long this pottery lasted I have not been able to ascertain, but it was working in full perfection in the beginning of the present century. The next pottery which was built in Glasgow was about the year 1801, when the "Caledonian Pottery," on the banks of the Monkland Canal, was erected. This is the oldest pottery now working in Glasgow, for although Verreville was built more than twenty years before it, yet earthenware was not made there till the year 1820."

Verreville Pottery.—In 1777, as the name implies, the Verreville Works were built for a glass-house by a Mr. Cookson, of Newcastle, and a Mr. Colquhoun, of Glasgow. In 1806 they were sold to the Dumbarton Glass Work Company, who immediately resold them to Mr. John Geddes, with this stipulation, that he was not to manufacture crown or bottle glass. Mr. Geddes carried on the manufacture of flint-glass until 1820, when he commenced making earthenware as well as glass. In 1835 the works passed into the hands of Mr. Robert Alexander Kidston, who four years afterwards added the manufacture of china to that of glass and earthenware. "He began," I am told by Mr. Cochran, "by bringing skilled workmen and artists from the principal seats of china manufacture. Figures, porcelain basket-work and flowers, were produced by workmen who had acquired their skill in the old and celebrated porcelain works of Derby, while Coalport and several of the most famous Staffordshire china works supplied a general staff of potters, together with gilders, and flower and landscape painters. Mr. Kidston carried on the business for several years and produced a beautiful porcelain, and upon his retiring from the business in 1846 was succeeded by the late Mr. Robert Cochran, who carried on the works with great vigour and success. In 1856 he ceased the manufacture of china, and devoted the whole of the works to the manufacture of earthenware. Mr. Cochran devoted great attention, and spared no expense in promoting the introduction of labour-saving machinery. He also made great improvements in the kilns or ovens in which the earthenware is fired, by which he reduced the quantity of coal used to nearly one-half. It was applied successfully in his own works of Verreville and Britannia, but was not adopted by other manufacturers. This improvement was patented in 1852, and it is only now that the same principle, with some slight alterations, has been patented and is likely to be generally adopted by potters. Mr. Cochran died in 1869, and was succeeded in the Verreville Pottery by his son, also named Robert Cochran, by whom the works were carried on. The goods manufactured consist of white, sponged, printed, and enamelled ware. No marks have ever been used except the initials of the proprietors stamped on the ware." Verreville, it is said, was the first work in Scotland where china was manufactured.

Garnkirk Works.—These works, established above half a century ago, were carried on by Messrs. Sprott, and later by Mr. Mark Sprott, and afterwards continued by trustees under the style of the "Garnkirk Fire-Clay Company." The goods produced are the ordinary classes of fire-clay and terra-cotta articles, including ornamental chimney-shafts and smoke-valves of good design and excellent mechanical construction; sanitary pipes and other appliances; architectural enrichments; garden-edgings and balustrades of more than average beauty in design, of which examples are given in Figs. 1789 to 1791; garden vases of great variety in design and of different sizes; fountains, notably an example of five tiers, supported by figures of dolphins and cranes, with basin 24 feet in height and 16 feet across, erected in the public park at Aberdeen; busts, statuary, both single figures and groups, including Baily's lovely conception of "Eve at the Fountain,"

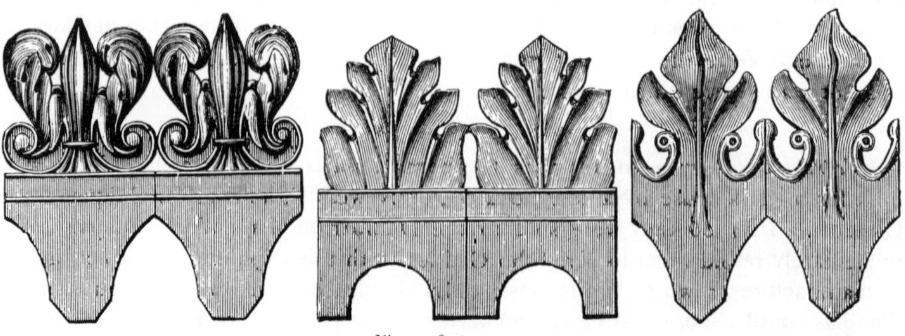

Figs. 1789 to 1791.

"Gleaner," "Minerva," "Bacchus," "Atlas," &c.; and every other variety of ornamental goods. The mark is the word *Garnkirk* impressed in the clay.

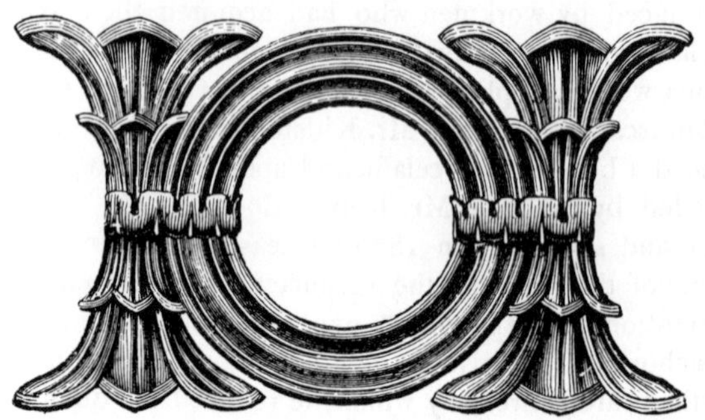

Fig 1792.

The Gartcosh Works were established by Mr. James Binnie in 1863, have been considerably extended, and produce terra-cotta vases, tazzas, pedestals, fountains, &c., of remarkably good and durable quality; ornamental and plain garden-edgings; gothic, clustered, and other chimney-tops; ridge, flooring, and roofing-tiles; cattle, horse, and dog troughs; copings; sewage and sanitary pipes of every description; glazed and unglazed fire-bricks, furnace-blocks, and all other goods for fire-resisting purposes. The clay is found about 50 fathoms below the surface at Gartcosh, the strata being from 18 to 25 feet in thickness, and underlying large beds of sandstone in what is called the limestone series, which lies between the upper and lower coal series of this district.

Heathfield Pottery.—At these works Messrs. Ferguson, Miller, & Co. produced the admirable terra-cotta vases shown at the 1851 Exhibition, and here engraved. One of these (Fig. 1793), a vase of large size and excellent modelling, bore a frieze of figures typical of the great gathering in 1851. Fig. 1794 shows among its other ornaments a nuptial procession, designed in the style of the antique. These figures were modelled with great accuracy, and are arranged in an artistic manner. The works passed in 1862 into the hands of Messrs. Young, the moulds, &c., including those of these vases, becoming the property of the Garnkirk Company.

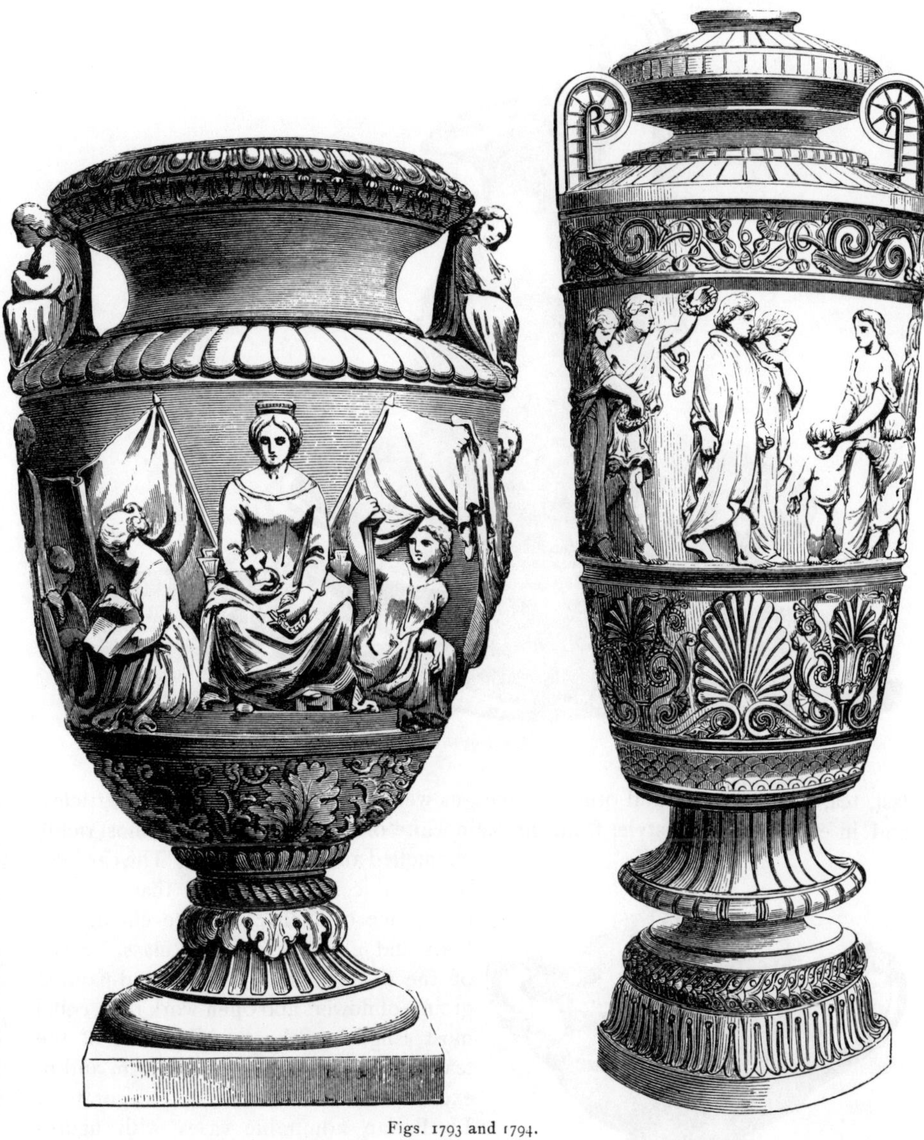

Figs. 1793 and 1794.

Glasgow Pottery.—These works, established in 1842, by J. & M. P. Bell & Co., in Stafford Street, Glasgow, for the manufacture of white and printed earthenware, soon rose to the first rank among the potteries of Scotland. Particular attention was from the first paid not only to the excellence of body of the ware, but to improvement in form and in style of decoration. In these particulars they were eminently successful, and in 1851 received honourable mention at the Great Exhibition. Later on the manufacture of china was commenced, and later still the fine white and pearl granite wares, and white and decorated sanitary wares. The works are of great extent, and produce all the usual varieties of goods in dinner, break-

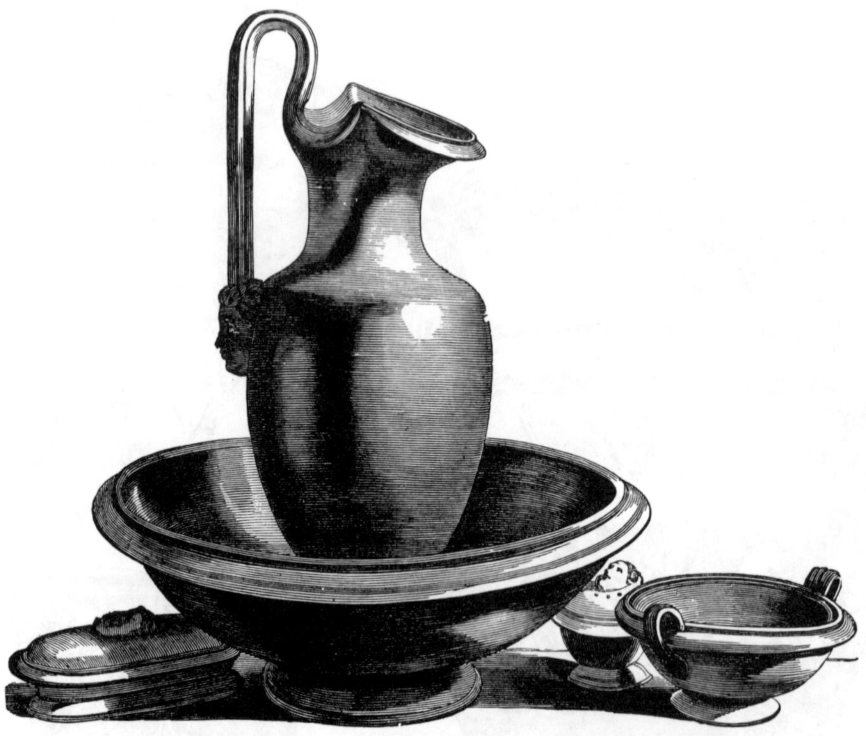

Figs. 1795 to 1799.

fast, tea, toilet, dessert, and other services, as well as all the usual classes of articles, and in every variety of style, from the plain white or cream colour to the most richly enamelled and gilt patterns. The earthenware services are of more than average excellence of quality, and the china, both body and glaze, of superior class. Some of the dessert plates, with hand-painted groups of flowers and open-work rims, equal most English makes; while some of the tea services are of tall classic form and of excellent taste in colour and decoration. In Parian admirable vases with figures in relief, and other ornamental goods, are produced. The old marks used by the Glasgow Pottery are Fig. 1812, an eagle holding a roll, on which is inscribed the name of the pattern, and, underneath, the initials of the firm, J. & M. P. B. & Co.; Fig. 1813, the Warwick vase and the name, J. & M. P. BELL & Co. The latter marks are (Fig. 1814) a garter bearing the initials of the firm, J. & M. P. B. & Co.,

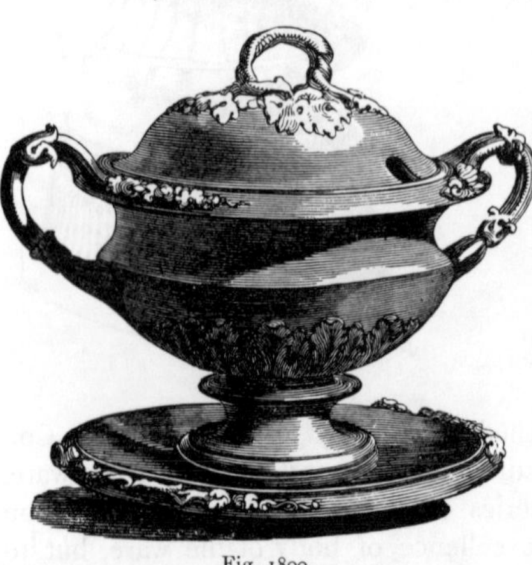

Fig. 1800.

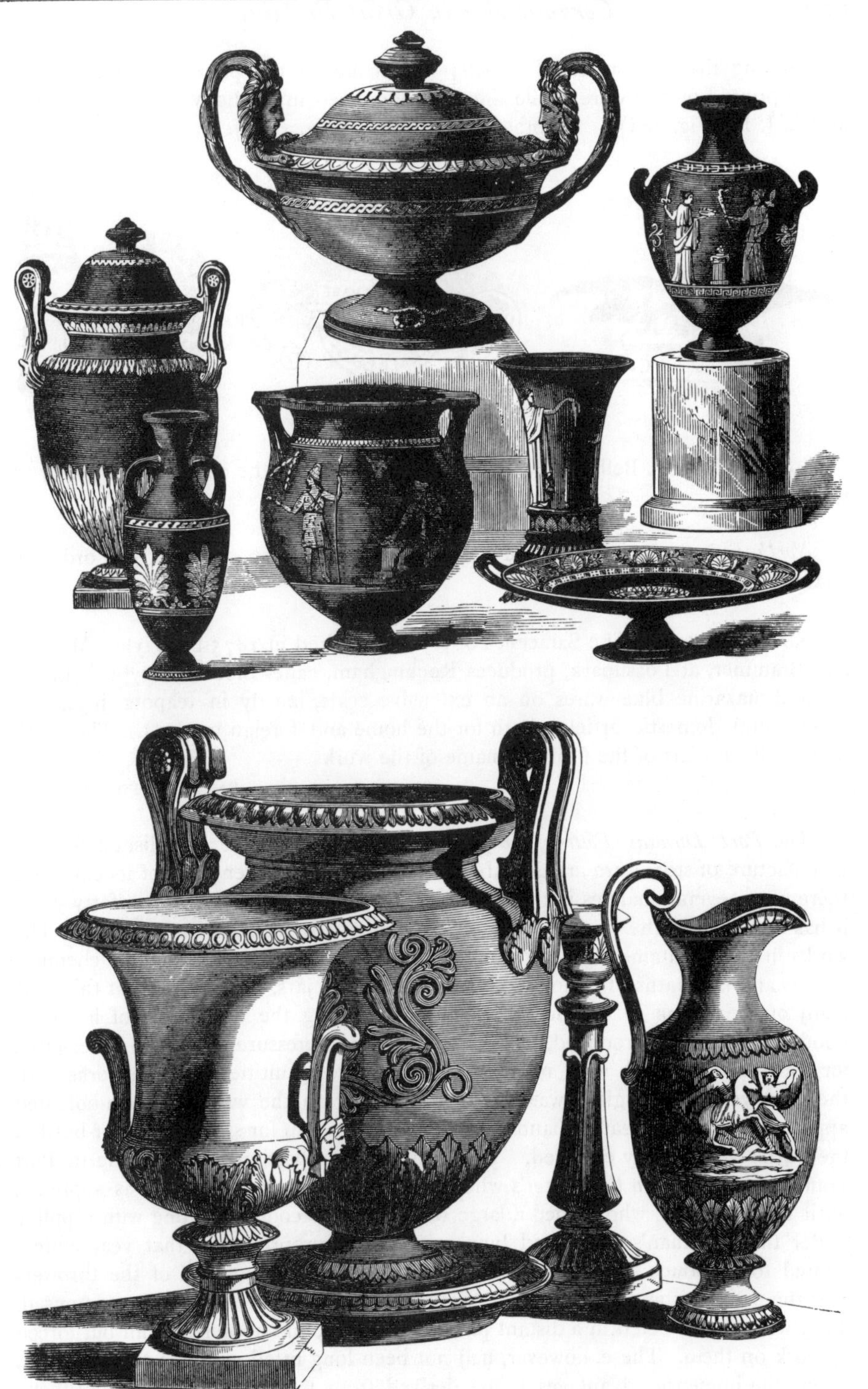

Figs. 1801 to 1811.—Messrs. Bell and Co.'s 1851 Exhibits.

surrounding the trade-mark of a bell; the name of the pattern below. These are all printed on the ware, while another, impressed in the body, is a bell with the initials J. B. (Fig. 1815). Another is a bell only (Fig. 1816).

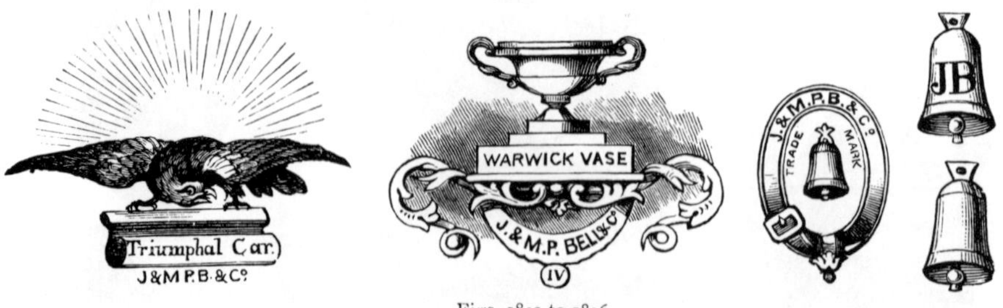

Figs. 1812 to 1816.

Some of Messrs. Bell & Co.'s exhibits are shown in the engravings Figs. 1795 to 1811.

North British Pottery.—These works, on Dobbies Loan, produce the ordinary qualities of earthenware goods.

Saracen Pottery.—The Saracen Pottery, established in 1875 by Bayley, Murray, and Brammer, at Possilpark, produces Rockingham, cane-coloured, Egyptian black, jet, and mazarine blue wares on an extensive scale, mostly in teapots, jugs, and other useful domestic articles, both for the home and foreign markets. The mark used is the initials of the firm and name of the works— B M & Co

SARACEN POTTERY.

The *Port Dundas Pottery Company.*—These works were established for the manufacture of stoneware articles about 1819. In the earlier years of its existence there were several changes in the proprietorship, but for the last thirty or forty years it has remained in the hands of and been carried on by Mr. James Miller. The works in 1856 contained three salt-glaze ovens, in which were manufactured chemical vessels and apparatus of various kinds, spirit-bottles, jars, &c.; and about this time many of the towns in the north of Scotland, finding the desirability of having a good water-supply introduced, had recourse to high-pressure stoneware water-pipes for that purpose, which were manufactured in large quantities at these works. In the same year a new glaze was introduced, giving to the ware a cream-coloured appearance, and a great demand having thus sprung up for stoneware beer-bottles, the works were greatly enlarged. By far the greatest portion of ware made in Port Dundas is thrown on the potter's wheel, the motive power for which was supplied, until 1866, by girls, who turned a large driving-wheel communicating with a pulley under the workman's wheelhead by a rope. The proprietor in that year endeavoured to introduce steam-power, but so strong was the opposition of the throwers that the machines and accompanying shafting, &c., lay aside for three years unused. They were then erected in a distant part of the works, and apprentices all but forced to work on them. These, however, had not been long fitted up when the workmen, seeing the immense advantages to be derived from their use, gladly availed themselves of the offer of the proprietor to substitute steam machinery for hand-power throughout the whole factory, the immediate result of which was to raise the piece-work earnings of the workmen from 30 to 49 per cent. They had one attendant less to pay, a part of whose wages the workman kept to himself, while a proportion of it was paid to the company for the use of the steam-power and up-keep of the machinery. The speed of the wheel requiring to be varied according to the different operations performed upon it, is now under the complete control of the workman's foot, and not, as formerly, at the will or according to the strength of the assistant wheel-turner. In this way a complete revolution was quietly effected in the stoneware potting of Scotland, and the incentive having been given, orders came from many potteries in England to the Scotch machine-maker for similar steam-machines.

With the introduction of the cream-coloured stoneware glaze the ovens had to undergo extensive alterations, the old salt-glaze cupboard-kilns giving place to much larger sagger-ovens, in which the ware is now burned. The improvement in the appearance of the ware having brought it into much greater demand, the works rapidly extended, until at the present time, in the Port Dundas Pottery, with its branch work the Crown Pottery, there are fifteen ovens in regular operation.

The wares produced are beer, ink, and spirit bottles; preserve, acid, butter, and druggists' jars; chemical vessels and apparatus, and every kind of article made in stoneware; water-filters, Rockingham and caneware. All the goods made are stamped with the name of the firm in an oval stamp. A few years ago a process of printing on the unfired stoneware body was perfected and patented by this firm, who exhibited their manufactures at the Chilian Exhibition at Santiago in 1875, and there received the first prize gold medal for the general excellence of their ware.

Hyde Park Potteries.—This manufactory of ordinary stoneware bottles, jars, spirit-casks, feet and carriage warmers, pans of various kinds, and all the ordinary classes of stoneware goods, was established about 1837 by Mr. John McAdam.

Britannia Pottery.—These large works at St. Rollox, Glasgow, were established in 1855 by Mr. Robert Cochran, the senior partner of the Verreville Pottery Company, the succeeding partners being Mr. Alexander Cochran (son of the above) and Mr. James Fleming. The works contain six biscuit and seven glost ovens, and produce all the usual varieties of ordinary earthenware goods in granite and cream-coloured ware for South America, and printed, enamelled, painted, and gilt wares for the home markets.

Annfield Pottery.—Messrs. John Thomson & Co., at the Annfield Pottery, Gallowgate, formerly manufactured both china and earthenware goods for the home and foreign markets. The works have been closed some time.

Bridgeton Pottery.—The "Bridgeton Pottery" was built in 1869 by Mr. F. Grosvenor (who for some years previously had been a partner in the "Caledonian Pottery" at Glasgow) for making the usual articles in stoneware, including chemical wares, bottles for various uses, spirit-jars, bottles, &c., and Rockingham ware teapots. In 1870 he took out a patent for the manufacture of bottles and jars by machinery, and has also invented an improved bottle-stopper.

Barrowfield Pottery.—Established by Mr. Henry Kennedy in 1866, these works produce all the usual classes of articles of "glass-lined stoneware," including "glass-lined bottles and jars" for domestic and other purposes, both for home and foreign markets. The mark used is three bottles side by side beneath a ribbon bearing the words "Established 1866."

COATBRIDGE.

Glenboig Star Works.—The Glenboig Star Fire-Brick Works produce bricks, retorts, furnace-blocks, and similar goods.

Glenboig Fire-Clay Works.—These works belong to the Glenboig Fire-Clay Company, and produce sewage and sanitary pipes, &c.; retorts, fire-bricks, &c.

Cardowan and Heathfield Works.—The first of these works, belonging to John Young and Son, was built in 1852 by Messrs. John Hurll and John Young, previous to that time of the Garnkirk Company. The clay is the Garnkirk seam, and is of much the same character as the Stourbridge clay. The Heathfield Works were acquired about 1860 from Miller and Ferguson, and were extended and altered. The clay was won at 350 feet, passing through a solid bed of freestone of 120 feet, giving off much water. The seam itself is known as the Glenboig seam of clay, as it was first wrought at the "Glenboig Works," with which Mr. Young was also a partner. At the "Cardowan Works" the firm manufacture fire-bricks, blast-furnace blocks, gas retorts and fittings, vases, garden-edgings, and plain and ornamental chimney-shafts. At the "Heathfield Works" they produce fire-bricks, vitrified salt-glazed pipes and blocks for sewerage and water purposes, and all the usual salt-glazed articles. In 1874 Hurll and Young dissolved partnership, Mr. Young, along with his sons John and Robert, continuing the works.

PAISLEY.

Ferguslie Fire-Clay Works.—These works, established in 1839, are carried on by Robert Brown and Son. The productions are mainly chimney-shafts, sewage pipes and sanitary goods of all kinds, garden-vases and tazzæ, flower-boxes, suspenders, fern and flower stands, &c., of various designs; statuary, both single figures and groups, architectural enrichments, pedestals, brackets, garden-edgings, fire and other bricks and tiles, copings, finials, &c.

Shortroods and Caledonia Works.—These are brick and tile works connected with the Ferguslie Works of Messrs. Robert Brown & Co.

Paisley Earthenware Works.—Messrs. Robert Brown & Co. established these works in 1876, and produce white enamelled earthenware goods of a similar quality to those of Staffordshire. Their principal productions are cabinet stands and lavatories, plug-basins, pans, and other sanitary appliances, baths of every kind (a speciality being the larger baths, five feet six inches in length, a size rarely attempted in earthenware), &c., plumbers' fittings, washhand-table tops, plain and coloured pavement and wall tiles, &c.

Crown Works.—At the Crown Crucible Works, belonging to Messrs. Robert

Brown and Son, plumbago crucibles and kindred goods are manufactured. The marks are a crown and name, BROWN PAISLEY, and a crucible within an oval border surmounted by a crown.

GRANGEMOUTH.

Fire-Brick Works.—These works, belonging to the Grangemouth Coal Company, were established in 1842. The clay, which is of good quality, is got at a depth of about forty-eight fathoms, under lease from the Earl of Zetland. The productions of the works consist of ornamental vases and tazzæ of various patterns; statuary, both single figures and groups; fountains, vases, and plinths; flower-stands and pots; chimney-shafts, some of which are highly decorated in relief; pedestals, brackets, &c.; and salt-glazed pipes, grate-backs, bricks, tiles, &c. The company received honourable mention for their goods at the Exhibition of 1851, and at the Hamburg Exhibition of 1866 had a medal awarded to them for their vases and ornamental figures.

GREENOCK.

The Clyde Pottery.—The "Clyde Pottery" works were established by James and Andrew Muir and others in 1815, the business being then carried on under the style of the "Clyde Pottery Company," with Mr. James Stevenson as manager. He was succeeded by Thomas Shirley, to whom the business was transferred, and who altered the style to Thomas Shirley & Co. In 1857 the Messrs. Shirley were succeeded by the "Clyde Pottery Company (Limited)," with James Brownlie as manager, which, having existed for five years, was succeeded by John Donald, Robert Gibson Brown, and John McLauchlan, under the old style of the "Clyde Pottery Company." The goods produced are the ordinary qualities of cream-coloured, sponged, painted, printed, pearl-white, enamelled, and gilt, suitable for home trade, and various kinds of ware also to suit particular foreign markets. The mark is "C. P. Co." (Clyde Pottery Company).

DUMBARTON.

There were pot-works at Dumbarton in the latter part of last and the beginning of the present century. About 1800 or thereabout Anthony Amatt, originally of Derby, and afterwards with Champion, of Bristol, worked at Dumbarton. He afterwards returned to Bristol, and died there in 1851, aged ninety-two.

RUTHERGLEN.

Caledonian Pottery.—The "Caledonian Pottery" at Rutherglen, near Glasgow, was established at Glasgow about 1780 by a joint-stock company, and from the company was acquired, about 1825, by Messrs. Murray & Co. In 1870 the works were removed from Glasgow to Rutherglen, about a couple of miles from that city. At first fine porcelain and china were made; then cream-coloured printed ware, with Rockingham and salt-glazed wares. In 1851 the demand sprang up for stoneware ale and other bottles, and this has become one of the staple trades of Glasgow and the surrounding district. The goods now produced are the usual classes of "Bristol" glazed stoneware, salt-glazed stoneware, cane ware, and Rockingham and Egyptian black wares. A speciality of Murray & Co. is their patent "spongy iron filter," which has been officially recommended by Royal Commission, and has been awarded a medal. It is one of the most perfect and useful of filters, and its principle of construction is thoroughly good. The mark used is a lion rampant.

Portobello, near Edinburgh.

Midlothian Potteries.—The Midlothian Stoneware Potteries at Portobello and Musselburgh, near Edinburgh, were established about 1857 by Mr. W. A. Gray, for the manufacture of general stoneware goods, but they had, I am informed by him, been in existence as earthenware works for upwards of a century before that time. They are carried on under the style of "W. A. Gray & Sons." The goods produced are all kinds of stoneware and the more ordinary descriptions of earthenware.

Portobello Pottery.—These works were established in 1770, and are now carried on by A. W. Buchan & Co. For a number of years they turned out ordinary white earthenware and Rockingham ware, but since 1842 the manufacture has been entirely confined to stoneware bottles, jars, jugs, feet and carriage warmers, spirit-bottles, and the usual classes of such goods. The mark of the firm is a star.

Kirkcaldy.

Sinclairtown Pottery.—Messrs. George McLachlan & Son were manufacturers of ordinary earthenware at this place. The works are now closed.

Other manufactories are the *Kirkcaldy Pottery*, belonging to David Methven & Son, and the *Gallatown Pottery*, belonging to Robert Heron & Sons.

Boness.

The Boness Pottery, as it is now called, dates from 1766. It was originally planned and partly constructed by a Mr. Roebuck, an enterprising Englishman, who having left for England sold the pottery to a Mr. Cowen. Afterwards, in 1799, it was continued by Mr. Alexander Cumming, who was succeeded by his nephew, James Cumming, and it became one of the largest potteries in Scotland. Earthenware and brown ware were manufactured in all their branches. The firm had another manufactory, called the "South Pottery," where brown ware was made for the home markets. At the death of James Cumming the works passed into the hands of his nephew, William Cumming, and were sold in 1836 to James Jamieson, and carried on for a number of years under the firm of James Jamieson & Co., the later proprietors being John Marshall and James Jamieson. After Mr. Jamieson's death his part of the works was, in 1854, bought by John Marshall, who in 1867 took as a partner Mr. William McNay, and continued under the style of John Marshall & Co. These works were the first in Scotland to adopt Needham's patent for manufacturing clay. The ordinary useful classes of earthenware dinner, tea, toilet, and other services, and all the usual domestic articles, are produced in white, sponged, printed, painted, enamelled, and gilt styles, and are supplied both to home and foreign markets.

Prestonpans.

Prestonpans Pottery.—There were until 1838 two old pot-works, each more than a century old, in Prestonpans. In that year they were both closed. In 1836 Belfield & Co. established the "Prestonpans Pottery," where Rockingham teapots, cane jugs, &c., are produced.

Alloa.

Alloa Pottery.—These works were established in 1790 by James Anderson, and were afterwards carried on by William Gardner, and in 1855 passed by purchase into the hands of W. & J. Bailey. At first the works, under Mr. Anderson, produced common brownware pans and crocks, and by Mr. Gardner the addition was made of Rockingham ware teapots, and later this branch of manufacture has been considerably improved, and so greatly extended that, at the time I write, I am informed no less than twenty-six thousand teapots can be produced by them per week. Majolica and jet ware goods are also largely made, and a speciality of the firm is its artistic engraving of ferns and other decorations of the finer qualities of teapots, jugs, &c. The excellent quality of the Alloa goods "arises from the nature of the clay got in the neighbourhood," and the density of colour and softness to touch of the glaze are highly commendable.

The Hebrides.

Hand-made pottery is still made and used in all its primitive simplicity. The following letter, which I am permitted to print, is so full of interesting matter concerning this curious phase of fictile art that I give it entire. It was addressed by W. Morrison, Esq., M.P., to my friend Mr. W. H. Goss, and dated from the House of Commons. It runs as follows: "The circumstances under which I came upon the hand-made pottery were as follows. In conversation with a Scotch friend on archæological matters, he happened to mention that *hand-made pottery* is still used in the Hebrides. Taken in connection with the fact that the inhabitants of some of the islands still, I believe, live in the same circular dry stone huts, with their cattle under the same roof, of which so many traces remain on Dartmoor, Ingleborough in Yorkshire, the Yr Eifel Hills in Carnarvonshire, and with the curious speculations contained in the introduction to the popular tales of the West Highlands, by Mr. Campbell, the fact seemed to be of some archæological interest. Mr. Tyler, in his 'Early History of Mankind,' gives many instances of the old savage instruments having lasted to our times, *e.g.* the flint knife used to cut cabbages by some old woman in Orkney, the bone 'barker' from Cornwall, in Christy and Blackmore Museums, the stone hammer for breaking the shells of the whelks in Brittany, and so on.

"My friend gave me an introduction to Mr. D. Munro, the chamberlain of Sir James Matherson, Bart., at Stornoway, in the Lewes, and Mr. Munro promptly sent me a complete tea-service consisting of teapot, milk-jug, sugar-basin, slop-basin, egg-cups (or probably dram-cups), cups and saucers, and marmalade pot! which he had purchased for the magnificent sum of 10s. from an old woman at Stornoway, who was actually using them in the year of grace 1868 at her tea-table. The pottery is evidently hand-made, and is of a very rough quality and form, baked, but not turned on the wheel. I gave half the set to the Blackmore Museum at Salisbury, and half to the Christy Museum, at 103, Victoria Street (visible on Fridays between 10 and 4 P.M. by ticket obtained at the British Museum. No doubt a letter enclosing stamped envelope would save the trouble of an application to the British Museum.) The pottery is in a case in the secretary's room. I am not sure if this room is shown to the public, but of course it would be shown to any one having an object in view.

"The remarkable thing is that the pottery is distinctly copied, rudely enough, from modern pottery. The forms are ordinary Tottenham Court Road forms, and their continued use in an island with a regular steamboat service from Glasgow strikes me as very curious.

"Of course the view of the pottery is open to you, and all the information contained in this letter. I should prefer, however, not having my name published, unless to substantiate any statements I have made."

Manufactories of brown ware, of delft, of common earthenware, and fire-clay goods have also existed, or exist, in other parts of Scotland.

Railway Pottery, Stoke.—Messrs. S. Fielding & Co. (alluded to on page 427) have introduced a new feature in majolica goods, which they have named "Majolica argenta," in which they are producing a vast variety of articles of a remarkably "taking," pleasing, and useful character. This, as its name implies, consists of a white body and glaze, with the proper majolica colouring liberally and judiciously used either on the body or the embossed decorations. The effect is extremely pleasing. Some of the more popular and artistic patterns are the "Shell and Net," the "Ribbon and Leaf," the "Daisy," and the "Fan," and in each of these the idea of the pattern is fully carried out in an infinite variety of articles, ranging from large ice-dishes and bread-trays down to cups and saucers and all the minutiæ of the table. One of the distinctive artistic features of the majolica produced by Messrs. Fielding & Co. is the masterly and effective way in which they introduce, on some of their best pieces, hand-modelled flowers and foliage. Modelled and coloured true to nature in every minute detail, and thrown in graceful negligence around the bodies of the vases, they become such perfect reproductions that it is difficult to divest the mind of the idea that the roses are not fresh gathered from the tree and temporarily twined around the vase for its adornment. One of these vases, some two feet or more in height, is one of the highest achievements in this phase of the plastic art. Its double handles on either side are formed of branches of the rose-tree cut off from the parent stem and elegantly arched into form, the leaves, the buds, and the full-blown roses—every petal of which is exquisitely modelled by hand—being gracefully and naturally arranged on the sides. The cover, in keeping with the general idea of the design, is a robin (which serves as a handle) in a "bed of roses." In addition to majolica, which until recently has been their staple trade, Messrs. Fielding & Co. have extended their works by adding the manufacture of a good quality of earthenware, in which they produce all the usual services and other articles. Among the latest novelties in toilet sets are the "Spring" and "Fruit" patterns, the under-glaze decoration of which is of an highly satisfactory character; and another in which the handle of the ewer is formed of a riding-whip, the thong of which is brought round the sides, which are further decorated by a horseshoe in relief suspended from a ribbon. Messrs. Fielding also produce terra-cotta, Rockingham, green glaze, and jet, as well as other wares. The mark is FIELDING impressed, or the name of the pattern on a ribbon, with the initials S. F. & Co., printed.

GENERAL INDEX.

INDEX OF NAMES OF PLACES.

INDEX OF NAMES OF PERSONS.

THE END.

GW01606067

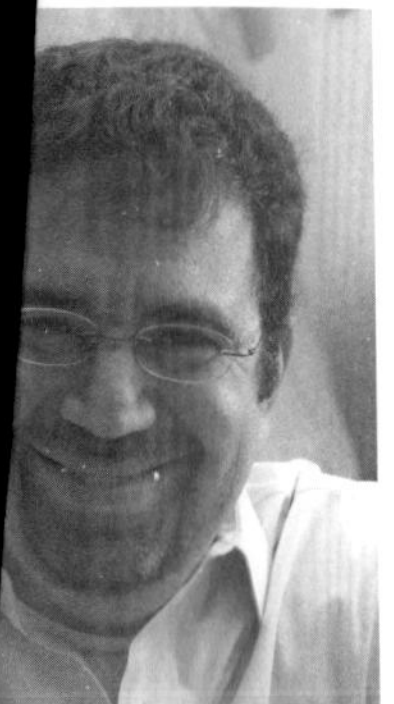
t

Daron Acemoglu ist Institutsprofessor für Wirtschaftswissenschaften am MIT. Seit fünfundzwanzig Jahren erforscht er die historischen Ursprünge von Wohlstand und Armut sowie die Auswirkungen neuer Technologien auf Wirtschaftswachstum, Beschäftigung und Ungleichheit. Er ist Autor (mit James Robinson) des internationalen Bestsellers *Warum Nationen scheitern* (dt. 2014).

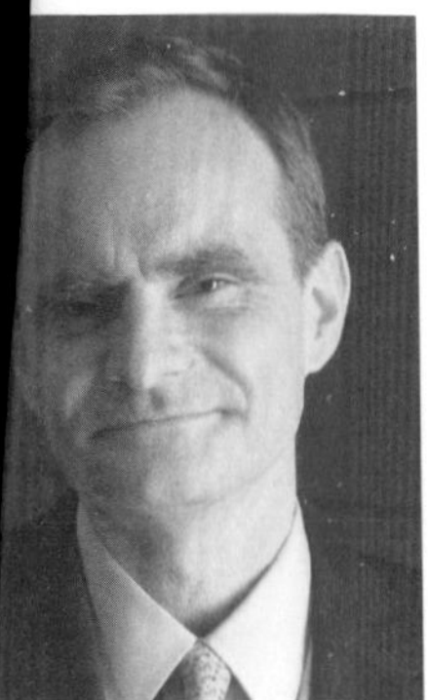
ichelle Fiorenza

Simon Johnson ist Ronald-A.-Kurtz-Professor für Unternehmertum an der Sloan School des MIT, wo er auch Leiter der Gruppe für globale Wirtschaft und Management ist. Als ehemaliger Chefvolkswirt des Internationalen Währungsfonds beschäftigt er sich seit dreißig Jahren mit globalen Wirtschaftskrisen.

Macht und Fc

© priva

© M